Contemporary
Literary Criticism

Guide to Gale Literary Criticism Series

For criticism on	Consult these Gale series
Authors now living or who died after December 31, 1999	*CONTEMPORARY LITERARY CRITICISM (CLC)*
Authors who died between 1900 and 1999	*TWENTIETH-CENTURY LITERARY CRITICISM (TCLC)*
Authors who died between 1800 and 1899	*NINETEENTH-CENTURY LITERATURE CRITICISM (NCLC)*
Authors who died between 1400 and 1799	*LITERATURE CRITICISM FROM 1400 TO 1800 (LC)* *SHAKESPEAREAN CRITICISM (SC)*
Authors who died before 1400	*CLASSICAL AND MEDIEVAL LITERATURE CRITICISM (CMLC)*
Authors of books for children and young adults	*CHILDREN'S LITERATURE REVIEW (CLR)*
Dramatists	*DRAMA CRITICISM (DC)*
Poets	*POETRY CRITICISM (PC)*
Short story writers	*SHORT STORY CRITICISM (SSC)*
Black writers of the past two hundred years	*BLACK LITERATURE CRITICISM (BLC)* *BLACK LITERATURE CRITICISM SUPPLEMENT (BLCS)*
Hispanic writers of the late nineteenth and twentieth centuries	*HISPANIC LITERATURE CRITICISM (HLC)* *HISPANIC LITERATURE CRITICISM SUPPLEMENT (HLCS)*
Native North American writers and orators of the eighteenth, nineteenth, and twentieth centuries	*NATIVE NORTH AMERICAN LITERATURE (NNAL)*
Major authors from the Renaissance to the present	*WORLD LITERATURE CRITICISM, 1500 TO THE PRESENT (WLC)* *WORLD LITERATURE CRITICISM SUPPLEMENT (WLCS)*

ISSN 0091-3421

Volume 130

Contemporary Literary Criticism

Criticism of the Works
of Today's Novelists, Poets, Playwrights,
Short Story Writers, Scriptwriters, and
Other Creative Writers

Jeffrey W. Hunter
EDITOR

Jenny Cromie
Justin Karr
Linda Pavlovski
ASSOCIATE EDITORS

Rebecca J. Blanchard
Vince Cousino
ASSISTANT EDITORS

Detroit
New York
San Francisco
London
Boston
Woodbridge, CT

STAFF

Lynn M. Spampinato, Janet Witalec, *Managing Editors, Literature Product*
Kathy D. Darrow, *Product Liaison*
Jeffrey W. Hunter, *Editor*
Mark W. Scott, *Publisher, Literature Product*

Jenny Cromie, Justin Karr, Linda Pavlovski, *Associate Editors*
Rebecca J. Blanchard, Vince Cousino, *Assistant Editors*

Patti A. Tippett, Timothy J. White, *Technical Training Specialists*
Deborah J. Morad, Kathleen Lopez Nolan, *Managing Editors*
Susan M. Trosky, *Director, Literature Content*

Maria L. Franklin, *Permissions Manager*
Margaret Chamberlian, *Permissions Specialist*

Victoria B. Cariappa, *Research Manager*
Tracie A. Richardson, *Project Coordinator*
Tamara C. Nott, *Research Associate*
Scott Floyd, Timothy Lehnerer, Ron Morelli, *Research Assistants*

Dorothy Maki, *Manufacturing Manager*
Stacy L. Melson, *Buyer*

Mary Beth Trimper, *Manager, Composition and Electronic Prepress*
Gary Leach, *Composition Specialist*

Michael Logusz, *Graphic Artist*
Randy Bassett, *Image Database Supervisor*
Robert Duncan, Dan Newell, *Imaging Specialists*
Pamela A. Reed, *Imaging Coordinator*
Kelly A. Quin, *Editor, Image Content*

Library of Congress Catalog Card Number 76-46132
ISBN 0-7876-3205-8
ISSN 0091-3421
Printed in the United States of America

10 9 8 7 6 5 4 3 2 1

Contents

Preface vii

Acknowledgments xi

Preface

Named "one of the twenty-five most distinguished reference titles published during the past twenty-five years" by *Reference Quarterly,* the *Contemporary Literary Criticism* (*CLC*) series provides readers with critical commentary and general information on more than 2,000 authors now living or who died after December 31, 1999. Volumes published from 1973 through 1999 include authors who died after December 31, 1959. Previous to the publication of the first volume of *CLC* in 1973, there was no ongoing digest monitoring scholarly and popular sources of critical opinion and explication of modern literature. *CLC,* therefore, has fulfilled an essential need, particularly since the complexity and variety of contemporary literature makes the function of criticism especially important to today's reader.

Scope of the Series

CLC provides significant passages from published criticism of works by creative writers. Since many of the authors covered in *CLC* inspire continual critical commentary, writers are often represented in more than one volume. There is, of course, no duplication of reprinted criticism.

Authors are selected for inclusion for a variety of reasons, among them the publication or dramatic production of a critically acclaimed new work, the reception of a major literary award, revival of interest in past writings, or the adaptation of a literary work to film or television.

Attention is also given to several other groups of writers—authors of considerable public interest—about whose work criticism is often difficult to locate. These include mystery and science fiction writers, literary and social critics, foreign authors, and authors who represent particular ethnic groups.

Each *CLC* volume contains individual essays and reviews taken from hundreds of book review periodicals, general magazines, scholarly journals, monographs, and books. Entries include critical evaluations spanning from the beginning of an author's career to the most current commentary. Interviews, feature articles, and other published writings that offer insight into the author's works are also presented. Students, teachers, librarians, and researchers will find that the general critical and biographical material in *CLC* provides them with vital information required to write a term paper, analyze a poem, or lead a book discussion group. In addition, complete biographical citations note the original source and all of the information necessary for a term paper footnote or bibliography.

Organization of the Book

A *CLC* entry consists of the following elements:

- The **Author Heading** cites the name under which the author most commonly wrote, followed by birth and death dates. Also located here are any name variations under which an author wrote, including transliterated forms for authors whose native languages use nonroman alphabets. If the author wrote consistently under a pseudonym, the pseudonym will be listed in the author heading and the author's actual name given in parenthesis on the first line of the biographical and critical information. Uncertain birth or death dates are indicated by question marks. Single-work entries are preceded by a heading that consists of the most common form of the title in English translation (if applicable) and the original date of composition.

- A **Portrait of the Author** is included when available.

- The **Introduction** contains background information that introduces the reader to the author, work, or topic that is the subject of the entry.

- The list of **Principal Works** is ordered chronologically· by date of first publication and lists the most important works by the author. The genre and publication date of each work is given. In the case of foreign authors whose works have been translated into English, the English-language version of the title follows in brackets. Unless otherwise indicated, dramas are dated by first performance, not first publication.

- Reprinted **Criticism** is arranged chronologically in each entry to provide a useful perspective on changes in critical evaluation over time. The critic's name and the date of composition or publication of the critical work are given at the beginning of each piece of criticism. Unsigned criticism is preceded by the title of the source in which it appeared. All titles by the author featured in the text are printed in boldface type. Footnotes are reprinted at the end of each essay or excerpt. In the case of excerpted criticism, only those footnotes that pertain to the excerpted texts are included.

- A complete **Bibliographical Citation** of the original essay or book precedes each piece of criticism.

- Critical essays are prefaced by brief **Annotations** explicating each piece.

- Whenever possible, a recent **Author Interview** accompanies each entry.

- An annotated bibliography of **Further Reading** appears at the end of each entry and suggests resources for additional study. In some cases, significant essays for which the editors could not obtain reprint rights are included here. Boxed material following the further reading list provides references to other biographical and critical sources on the author in series published by Gale.

Indexes

A **Cumulative Author Index** lists all of the authors that appear in a wide variety of reference sources published by the Gale Group, including *CLC*. A complete list of these sources is found facing the first page of the Author Index. The index also includes birth and death dates and cross references between pseudonyms and actual names.

A **Cumulative Nationality Index** lists all authors featured in *CLC* by nationality, followed by the number of the *CLC* volume in which their entry appears.

A **Cumulative Topic Index** lists the literary themes and topics treated in the series as well as in *Literature Criticism from 1400 to 1800, Nineteenth-Century Literature Criticism, Twentieth-Century Literary Criticism,* and the *Contemporary Literary Criticism* Yearbook, which was discontinued in 1998.

An alphabetical **Title Index** accompanies each volume of *CLC*. Listings of titles by authors covered in the given volume are followed by the author's name and the corresponding page numbers where the titles are discussed. English translations of foreign titles and variations of titles are cross-referenced to the title under which a work was originally published. Titles of novels, dramas, nonfiction books, and poetry, short story, or essay collections are printed in italics, while individual poems, short stories, and essays are printed in roman type within quotation marks.

In response to numerous suggestions from librarians, Gale also produces an annual paperbound edition of the *CLC* cumulative title index. This annual cumulation, which alphabetically lists all titles reviewed in the series, is available to all customers. Additional copies of this index are available upon request. Librarians and patrons will welcome this separate index; it saves shelf space, is easy to use, and is recyclable upon receipt of the next edition.

Citing *Contemporary Literary Criticism*

When writing papers, students who quote directly from any volume in the Literary Criticism Series may use the following general format to footnote reprinted criticism. The first example pertains to material drawn from periodicals, the second to material reprinted from books.

Alfred Cismaru, "Making the Best of It," *The New Republic* 207, no. 24 (December 7, 1992): 30, 32; excerpted and reprinted in *Contemporary Literary Criticism,* vol. 85, ed. Christopher Giroux (Detroit: The Gale Group, 1995), 73-4.

Yvor Winters, *The Post-Symbolist Methods* (Allen Swallow, 1967), 211-51; excerpted and reprinted in *Contemporary Literary Criticism,* vol. 85, ed. Christopher Giroux (Detroit: The Gale Group, 1995), 223-26.

Suggestions are Welcome

Readers who wish to suggest new features, topics, or authors to appear in future volumes, or who have other suggestions or comments are cordially invited to call, write, or fax the Managing Editor:

Managing Editor, Literary Criticism Series

The Gale Group

27500 Drake Road

Farmington Hills, MI 48331-3535

1-800-347-4253 (GALE)

Fax: 248-699-8054

Acknowledgments

The editors wish to thank the copyright holders of the excerpted criticism included in this volume and the permissions managers of many book and magazine publishing companies for assisting us in securing reproduction rights. We are also grateful to the staffs of the Detroit Public Library, the Library of Congress, the University of Detroit Mercy Library, Wayne State University Purdy/Kresge Library Complex, and the University of Michigan Libraries for making their resources available to us. Following is a list of the copyright holders who have granted us permission to reproduce material in this volume of *CLC*. Every effort has been made to trace copyright, but if omissions have been made, please let us know.

COPYRIGHTED EXCERPTS IN *CLC*, VOLUME 130, WERE REPRODUCED FROM THE FOLLOWING PERIODICALS:

America, Vol. 167, No. 13, October 31, 1992, v. 173, October 21, 1995 . Reproduced by permission of America Press, Inc., 106 56th Street, New York, NY 10019.— *Belles Lettres,* v. 5, Summer, 1990, v. 7, Fall, 1991, v. 9, Fall, 1993. Reproduced by permission.—*The Bloomsbury Review,* v. 13, November/December, 1993 for "Hotel Insomnia" and "Dime-Store Alchemy," by Scott Edward Anderson. Copyright © by Owaissa Communications Company, Inc. 1993. Reproduced by permission of the author.—*Book Week-New York Herald Tribune,* September 13, 1964. Copyright © 1964 by The New York Times Company. Reproduced by permission.— *Book World-Washington Post,* v. xvi, April 13, 1986 for "Poets of Exile and Isolation" by Peter Davison. © 1986, Washington Post Book World Service/Washington Post Writers Group. Reproduced by permission of the author.—*The Centennial Review,* v. xxxvi, Spring, 1992 for "The Poet on a Roll: Charles Simic's The Tomb of Stephane Mallarme" by Ileana A. Orlich. © 1992 by The Centennial Review. Reproduced by permission of the publisher and the author.— *Chicago Tribune Books*, May 18, 1988, June 23, 1989, July 11, 1993, September 16, 1993, June 9, 1994, November 22, 1996, October 11, 1998, December 7, 1998. © 1988, 1989, 1993, 1994, 1996, 1998 Tribune Media Services, Inc. All rights reserved. Reproduced by permission.— *The Christian Century,* v. xcv, September 13, 1978, v. 106, March 15, 1989, v. 170, February 7-14, 1990, v. 110, March 17, 1993, v. 111, March 2, 1994, v. 111, May 18-25, 1994, v. 112, December 20-27, 1995. Reproduced by permission.—*Christianity Today*, v. 39, no. 11, October 2, 1995. Reproduced by permission.— *Commonweal,* v. xcvi, August 25, 1972, v. cxiii, November 24, 1978, March 28, 1986, v. cxiv, January 30, 1987, v. cxiv, March 13, 1987, v. cxx, January 29, 1993, November 6, 1998. Copyright © 1972, 1978, 1986, 1987, 1993, 1998 Commonweal Publishing Co., Inc. Reproduced by permission of Commonweal Foundation.— *Contemporary Literature*, v. 21, Winter, 1980, v. 23, Fall, 1982. Copyright © 1980, 1982 The Board of Regents of the University of Wisconsin System. All rights reserved. Reproduced by permission.—*Contemporary Sociology*, v. 20, March, 1991 for a review of *Holding the Line: Women in the Great Arizon Mine Strike of 1983* by Marc W. Steinberg. Reproduced by permission.—*Critique,* v. xxxiii, Winter, 1992. Copyright © 1992 Helen Dwight Reid Educational Foundation. Reproduced with permission of the Helen Dwight Reid Educational Foundation, published by Heldref Publications, 1319 18th Street, NW, Washington, DC 20036-1802.—*English Journal*, Vol. 86, December, 1997. Copyright © 1997 by the National Council of Teachers of English. Reproduced by permission of the publisher.—*The Explicator,* v. 51, Summer, 1993. Copyright © 1993 Helen Dwight Reid Educational Foundation. Reproduced with permission of the Helen Dwight Reid Educational Foundation, published by Heldref Publications, 1319 18th Street, NW, Washington DC 20036-1802.— *FIELD: Contemporary Poetry and Poetics,* n. 44, Spring, 1991. Reproduced by permission.—*The French Review,* v. liii, no. 5, April, 1980. Copyright 1980 by the American Association of Teachers of French. Reproduced by permission.—*The Georgia Review*, v. xli, Spring, 1987, v. xlix, Winter, 1995. Copyright, 1987, 1995 by the University of Georgia. Reproduced by permission.—*The Hudson Review,* v. xxiv, no 2 (Summer, 1971). Copyright © 1982 by Hayden Carruth, v. L, Winter, 1998. Copyright © 1998 by The Hudson Review, Inc. Reproduced by permission.—*Industrial and Labor Relations Review*, v. 44, April, 1991. Reproduced by permission.—*Journal of American Culture*, v. 18, Winter, 1995. Reproduced by permission.—*Journal of Ecumenical Studies*, v. xxx, Summer-Fall, 1993. Reproduced by permission.— *Los Angeles Times Book Review,* January 12, 1986, March 16, 1986, September 9, 1990, July 4, 1993, August 4, 1994, March 19, 1995, November 24, 1996. Copyright, 1986, 1990, 1993, 1994, 1995, 1996 Los Angeles Times. Reproduced by permission.— *Maclean's,* v. 98, November 18, 1985. © 1985 by Maclean's Magazine. Reproduced by permission.—*The Massachusetts Review,* v. XXXII, Spring, 1991. © 1991. Reproduced from The Massachusetts Review, The Massachusetts Review, Inc. by permission.—*Meanjin,* v. 44, March, 1985 for "Keri Hulme: Sparalling To Success" by Eliabeth Webby. Reproduced by permission of the author.—*The Missouri Review,* v. vii, 1984. Reproduced by permission.—*Modern Age,* v. 33, Summer, 1990. Reproduced by permission.—*The Nation,* April 20, 1946, v. 236, March 12, 1983, November 26, 1990, January 11-18, 1999. © 1946, 1983, 1990, 1999 The Nation magazine/The Nation Company, Inc. Reproduced by permission.—*New Perspectives Quarterly,* v. 8, Spring, 1991. Reproduced by permission.—*The New Republic*, March 22,

COPYRIGHTED EXCERPTS IN *CLC*, VOLUME 130, WERE REPRODUCED FROM THE FOLLOWING BOOKS:

Beryl Bainbridge
1933-

(Full name Beryl Margaret Bainbridge) English novelist, short story writer, nonfiction writer, and screenplay writer.

The following entry presents an overview of Bainbridge's career through 1999. For further information on her life and works, see *CLC*, Volumes 4, 5, 8, 10, 14, 18, 22, and 62.

INTRODUCTION

English author Beryl Bainbridge is best known for creating spare, morbidly humorous fiction that examines the bizarre, often violent, turns of events that reflect the tenuous, menacing quality of modern life. Drawing upon her stormy upbringing in working-class Liverpool, Bainbridge was initially known as a writer of thrillers that chronicled ordinary lives in postwar England, as in *Harriet Said* (1972) and *The Bottle Factory Outing* (1974). In subsequent novels, however, she has reenacted historical events—the Polar expedition of Robert Falcon Scott in *The Birthday Boys* (1991) and the sinking of the *Titanic* in *Every Man for Himself* (1996)—to great effect and critical acclaim.

BIOGRAPHICAL INFORMATION

Bainbridge was born in Liverpool in 1933, the daughter of Winifred Baines and Richard Bainbridge, a salesman. Her childhood was decidedly unhappy; her class-conscious mother was discontented with her working-class husband, who was moody, dictatorial, and bad-tempered, and the couple often clashed. Bainbridge began dancing at age six and worked steadily as a child performer. When at age 14 she was expelled from school for drawing a rude picture, her parents sent her to ballet school. However, she ran away to London the next year. After several years of acting, including appearances on stage, television, and radio, she returned to Liverpool and married artist Austin Davies in 1954. While pregnant with the first of her three children, Bainbridge began work on her first novel, *Harriet Said.* This book was completed in 1958, but editors were so appalled by its gruesome plot and amoral child characters that Bainbridge could not find a publisher for it until more than a decade later. Bainbridge put the book aside and continued to write, publishing *A Weekend with Claud* (1967) and *Another Part of the Wood* (1968). After her divorce from Davies in 1959, Bainbridge held various jobs, including a stint in a wine bottling company, which

inspired *The Bottle Factory Outing.* In 1970 Bainbridge began working as clerk for publishers Duckworth & Company, where fiction editor Anna Haycraft befriended her and published *Harriet Said* in 1972. The following year, Bainbridge received a Booker Prize nomination for *The Dressmaker* (1973; published in America as *The Secret Glass,* 1974), based on the paternal aunts she knew as a child in Liverpool. Bainbridge subsequently earned Booker Prize nominations for three additional works: *The Bottle Factory Outing, An Awfully Big Adventure* (1989), and *Every Man for Himself* (1996). Bainbridge has also written several television scripts, among them adaptations of her novels *Sweet William* (1975) and *A Quiet Life* (1976). In 1983 she traveled with a television crew throughout industrial England, recording her observations in the nonfiction work *English Journey* (1984). In 1986 Bainbridge began writing a quirky weekly column for the London newspaper *Evening Standard;* these columns were subsequently collected in *Something Happened Yesterday* (1993). Bainbridge continues to live and write in London.

MAJOR WORKS

Bainbridge draws upon her maladjusted family and working-class upbringing as inspiration for much of her work. Portraits of disappointed, temperamental, manipulative men based on her father recur in her stories. Elaborate plotting, alternating points of view, and bizarre humor also characterize her fiction, in which the central dramatic device almost always involves a death or violent act. Bainbridge based *Harriet Said* on a news story about two Australian girls who murdered the mother of one of them. The unnamed thirteen-year-old narrator, in league with her manipulative friend Harriet, chronicles how the two girls ensnare their married neighbor Mr. Biggs in a carefully planned seduction and proceed to frame him for the murder of his wife. The book's complex narrative structure begins with the aftermath of the central crime. The narrator then recounts the events leading to the climax and neatly ends the story where it started. Bainbridge experimented with stream-of-consciousness techniques in *A Weekend with Claud,* a departure from her usual spare style. A photograph serves as the unifying motif of the novel, prompting Claud—the first of Bainbridge's manipulative, predatory male characters—to recall his relationship with a woman named Maggie. The book recounts Maggie's disappointing interactions with Claud and three other men in her life. *Another Part of the Wood* concerns Joseph, a selfish, insensitive man who brings his mistress, his son Roland, and some friends to a cabin for a weekend, setting off events that lead to Roland's death. Bainbridge considered both *A Weekend with Claud* and *Another Part of the Wood* artistic failures. As a result she revised and re-issued them in 1981 and 1979, respectively. In *The Dressmaker,* Bainbridge fully realized the minimalist writing style for which she is known. As in *Harriet Said,* the book begins and ends with the cover-up of the same murder. Seventeen-year-old Rita lives with her aunts Margo and Nellie, who are inspired by Bainbridge's own Liverpool relatives. Bainbridge creates an unnerving portrait of Rita, Margo, and Nellie's lonely, colorless lives during World War II. Rita falls in love with an American G.I. named Ira, with whom Margo also becomes involved. When Nellie finds Margo and Ira together, she stabs Ira, causing him to fall down the stairs to his death. In *The Bottle Factory Outing,* central characters Brenda and her friend Rita experience misadventures while planning an outing with their co-workers at the bottle factory. Bainbridge explores their desperate self-deceptions in a grotesque comedy of errors resulting in Freda's death and Brenda's discovery of her body. A typical bizarre Bainbridge plot twist has Brenda pickling Freda's body and sending it to sea in a barrel in order to minimize trouble for everyone. In *A Quiet Life,* Bainbridge's most autobiographical novel, the central characters Alan and his sister Madge are reunited as adults. Bainbridge uses Alan and Madge to explore the alternate reality that people create which enables them to endure their lives; Alan and Madge revisit events of their childhood, but Alan has reconstructed his story in order to cope with his past. *Young Adolf* (1978) was Bainbridge's first work of historical fiction. Based on an unproven account that Adolf Hitler traveled to England in his youth to visit his brother and sister-in-law, who actually lived in Liverpool around 1910, the novel chronicles a series of comic incidents that influence Hitler's later life.

An Awfully Big Adventure follows the experiences of a teenager named Stella, who serves as an apprentice at a Liverpool theater during the production of *Peter Pan*. In her innocence, paralleling that of Peter Pan, Stella triggers comic misunderstandings and misalliances in the theater company. Bainbridge's based her next novel, *The Birthday Boys,* on Sir Robert Falcon Scott's failed attempt to be the first man to reach the South Pole in 1910. In a framework constructed from alternating journal entries by each of the expedition's five members, Bainbridge explores Scott's delusional self-confidence during the ill-conceived trek and the crew's relationships among each other and with Scott. The title derives from the crew members' childish insistence on holding birthday celebrations in the middle of the Antarctic. Bainbridge presents each man as a representative of different facets of British society and of human personality, as they begin the expedition with high expectations and gradually freeze to death in the bleak Antarctic landscape. *Every Man for Himself* takes place on the *Titanic* as Morgan, a wealthy young American, travels on the doomed ship with several friends. Morgan interacts with characters such as the sinister Scurra; the beautiful and unattainable Wallis; and the earnest Adele. The rich on the *Titanic* show their true colors when the ship begins to go down, coinciding with Morgan's learning the truth about his life and parentage. *Master Georgie* (1998), another novel based on historical events, begins in England in 1846 and ends during the Crimean War in 1854. The story revolves around young George Hardy, described in alternating narratives by Myrtle, a Liverpool orphan rescued by and taken to live with the upper-class Hardy family; Dr. Potter, a geologist married to George's sister; and Pompey Jones, a street child who is befriended by Myrtle and George. Bainbridge once again uses the motif of a photograph to structure the novel, presenting each chapter as a photographic scene that relates to George and Pompey's interest in photography. Each character is inexorably linked to the selfish, careless George, and each relates a facet of George's character and his impact on themselves and the world as they journey toward disaster in the war.

CRITICAL RECEPTION

Bainbridge is recognized as an accomplished raconteur of middle- and lower-middle class postwar English life and death. More recently she has won distinction for her reinterpretations of historical events, particularly in *The Birthday Boys* and *Every Man for Himself,* both of which received critical approbation. Her talent for intricate plotting, true-to-life dialogue, convincing characters, and ability to convey volumes of meaning in a single sentence has earned her strong praise from critics, inspiring comparisons to Franz Kafka, Harold Pinter, and Iris Murdock. Many reviewers consider her macabre humor and startling, violent plot twists refreshingly original. However, for other readers such devices render her books implausible and predictable, as her predilection for shocking endings has become a regular feature of her work. Some commentators have also expressed dissatisfaction with Bainbridge's overly lifelike characters, considered realistically flawed to the point of being wholly unlikable and unattractive. In addition, Bainbridge's extreme detachment from the implications of her narrative has been cited as problematic. Her tendency to refrain from judging characters that commit repugnant criminal acts, or showing the consequences of their actions, is often felt to detract from the impact of her novels. Yet, despite such criticism, Bainbridge is well regarded as an innovative and gifted writer whose explorations of the dark side of the human psyche represent an important contribution to contemporary literature. Though Bainbridge is still more popular in Britain than in the United States, some critics have begun to lobby for greater recognition and serious reevaluation of her work.

PRINCIPAL WORKS

A Weekend with Claud [revised edition, 1981] (novel) 1967

Another Part of the Wood [revised edition, 1979] (novel) 1968

Harriet Said (novel) 1972

The Dressmaker [also published as *The Secret Glass*, 1974] (novel) 1973

The Bottle Factory Outing (novel) 1974

Sweet William (novel) 1975

A Quiet Life (novel) 1976

Injury Time (novel) 1977

Young Adolf (novel) 1978

Winter Garden (novel) 1980

English Journey, or the Road to Milton Keynes (nonfiction) 1984

Watson's Apology (novel) 1984

Mum and Mr. Armitage (short stories) 1985

Filthy Lucre, or The Tragedy of Andrew Ledwhistle and Richard Soleway (novel) 1986

Forever England: North and South [reprinted in 1999] (nonfiction) 1987

An Awfully Big Adventure (novel) 1989

The Birthday Boys (novel) 1991

Something Happened Yesterday (nonfiction) 1993

Collected Stories (short stories) 1994

Every Man for Himself (novel) 1996

Master Georgie (novel) 1998

CRITICISM

Colin Thubron (review date 23 September 1984)

SOURCE: "An Unsentimental Journey," in *Washington Post Book World,* September 23, 1984, pp. 11, 13.

[*In the following excerpted review, Thubron contrasts Bainbridge's* English Journey *with J. B. Priestley's 1933 book of the same title.*]

In the autumn of 1933 the British novelist and playwright J. B. Priestley undertook a celebrated expedition through his own country, which resulted in his *English Journey.* At a time when most literary travelers were wandering the Mediterranean or were still describing an England of hedgerow land and cathedral close, Priestley confronted the country head-on. With no more than a glance at Salisbury and the Cotswolds, he plunged into the Midlands and the North: Birmingham, the Black Country, his childhood home of Bradford, the Potteries, Liverpool, Tyneside. Here was the demoralized heart of an England still locked in the Depression. At worst its sordidness and decline were unrelieved—a wilderness of derelict factories and rotting suburbia. At best it achieved, in Priestley's prose, the somber majesty of an industrial Gehenna.

Priestley's strength is that he himself belonged to this world. "If I declare that Coketown is a horrible hole," he wrote, "I do not merely mean that it cannot be fitted into some private fairy-tale Merrie England of my own: I mean that it is a damned horrible hole. And I hope you will take my word for it." He recorded what he found without condescension or maudlin pity. His tone is robustly independent, worldly, anti-Puritan, commonsensical. His compassion is grounded in reality, and leavened by a North-country humor and business sense. His familiarity with urban drabness makes him sensitive to differences which would elude a writer from another background. He is never facile: he does not always equate people with place. Viewing from a tram the fly-blown anonymity of Birmingham, he wonders "if this really represented the level reached by all those people down there on the pavements. I am too near them myself, not being one of the sensitive plants of contemporary authorship, to believe that it does represent their level. They have passed it. . . . They have gone and it is not catching up.". . .

Not all the questions roused by Priestley are answered in Beryl Bainbridge's own ***English Journey,*** published half a century later. She is too much her own woman—which is nothing at all like Priestley's man. Whereas he wrote with a magisterial fullness, generalized, pontificated, indulged a masculine kindliness and an earthy poetry, Bainbridge is wry, introverted, idiosyncratic. She writes a clipped, impressionistic diary. She is eccentrically funny. Where Priestley presents himself as a down-to-earth man of the world, Bainbridge makes much of her female scattiness, and from behind this camouflage peers out with offbeat wit and shrewdness.

But she has not Priestley's attachment to place, to social issues, to people at large. To her, things often appear more ridiculous than important. Salisbury Cathedral she describes as "too big, too separate"—and the reaction typifies her. She relates best to the intimate. She is not a natural traveler at all. Priestley meets hazards in the grand Victorian manner (in other words, he scarcely mentions them), but exertion makes Bainbridge ill. She gets in traffic jams; she has too much luggage; there are never any porters at the stations.

Is Priestley's expansiveness a symptom of his time—and Bainbridge's enclosedness of hers? Partly, perhaps. Certainly Bainbridge's desire to share her problems and ineptitudes is typical of the modern traveler, while Priestley's book belongs to an age where travel writing was still about the places traveled through, not about the author traveling through them. But there is also a powerful contrast in individual temperament. Bainbridge loves the untypical. Her narrative is laced with zany conversations. Even her memories are quirky (there's a lovely description of a demented stagedoor Johnny who courted her when she was in repertory theater). Her efforts to summarize places—to assess the wholeness of things—are no more than hesitant genuflections to Priestley. She avoids both his pedagogy and his breadth.

At heart she dislikes all modernity. ("There should be a rule against change. Memories have to live somewhere.") She even feels a sentimental nostalgia for Priestley's England, which he deplored. Certainly the 1980s England she discloses is no lovelier than his. At best it is orderly, vulgar and a bit absurd. At worst it is a demoralizing slum. The crowded factory staff of Priestley's time have been shredded thin by automation (robots mesmerize and appall her) and the familiar specter of unemployment now hovers over a landscape of black and Asian minorities.

Yet Bainbridge's chief loathing is reserved for motorways and modern shopping precincts; for all sameness. And perhaps it is in this, at last, that the two authors concur—condemning a world where (in Priestley's words) "everything and everybody is being rushed down and swept into one dusty arterial road of cheap mass production and standardized living." Priestley looked forward to a brighter future while Bainbridge stares back at a romanticized past. The present, as usual, goes unloved.

David Punter (essay date 1985)

SOURCE: "Beryl Bainbridge: The New Psychopathia," in *The Hidden Script: Writing and the Unconscious*, Routledge & Kegan Paul, 1985, pp. 59-77.

[*In the following essay, Punter examines the presentation of psychological trauma in Bainbridge's novels and the struggles among her characters, particularly those who are female, to deal with both familial and cultural forces of alienation, deprivation, abuse, and rejection.*]

Beryl Bainbridge has acted Krafft-Ebing in response to the self-aware Freudianism of many of her fellow-writers; where Lessing, Carter, Barth, have paraded analysis, she has presented herself during the 1970s as a meticulous chronicler of 'everyday' events, who would raise an innocent eyebrow at any mention of psychosis, whether attached to writer, character, reader or text.[1] The calamities she depicts are, so the surrounding authorial fiction goes, conventionally implicit in our lives: they are a mechanical consequence of our upbringing, and either they will spring out, fully armed, at a later date; or, indeed, they have happened already, and only a thin skin of self-protection prevents us from remembering the terror of adolescence or of poverty. We do not need psychological sophistication to see through to the depths: events are hideously transparent, naturally manifesting the results of age-old cultural trauma. Yet of course in her descriptive and guileless way she forces us back to the schoolroom, back to early occupational experience: did we not then, she asks, experience the fear of being alone, of being unversed in the ways of our parents/employers? Were we too not brought on to a scene where everybody else understood the conventions, and then victimised for not possessing that unobtainable knowledge?

The question below that runs again in terms of gender, and has a curiously symmetrical relation to the question Nabokov poses to his audience. Where he asks whether we too shared, long ago, his experience of dividing the world (of young girls) into the 'knowing' and the 'unknowing' (and he is not so unsubtle as to be referring merely to carnal knowledge), Bainbridge asks whether we shared in the more dire experience of *being known* (as inferior, as junior, as incomplete); and whether, if as readers and particularly as male readers we claim not to remember such a time,[2] we are thereby collaborating in a great refusal, a refusal of understanding which perpetuates hegemony and the transmission of fear between the sexes. The central characters in Bainbridge's fables of psychosis are mostly small, by nature or by nurture:[3] they experience, indeed, the undeniable fact that, through murder, rape or anger, they produce large effects in the world, but there is a gap between cause and effect, between desire and achievement; and is this not, runs the apparently supplementary but really more important question, something which has been specifically done to women? Are not these acts of moral and carnal outrage precisely the inverted reflection of what a masculine culture has visited upon women, and are not male desires in the end fulfillable only through violence, of one kind or another?

None of this is to deny that Bainbridge writes about victims; but when her victims turn, there is a gleefulness in the outcome, even with the young Hitler. All of this, all this grotesquerie and bloodshed, is after all only to be expected while you (the reader?) capitulate in subjecting others to inhumanity. Thus there is in Bainbridge a wish for rebellion, but no special interest in the rebel: the excitement is more pure than that, more focused on downfall and the upturning of a deadly world. The time for the Other, the inversion, to emerge is, of course, the traditional moment:[4] it is the moment of celebration, the bottle factory outing, the particular exemption granted in the form of injury time. It is at these moments, when we most hopefully imagine that some form of ritual is going to crown our efforts and achievements, that the voices of those whom we have suppressed in our facile forms of organisation, of those whom we have never prepared to understand the pleasures of our parties, will be raised; in a scream which, at first, we may mistake for participation, but which is eventually revealed as a cry of anguish and fury, the inarticulate sign for all that has been swept under the carpet in order to prepare the (primal) scene for a confirming ritual.[5]

During the 1970s, the furrow Bainbridge has ploughed has appeared a lonely one, in that she has consistently refused the displacements which have become conventional in the 'new fiction', the construction of a mythicised future or the return to a putatively explanatory past; she has also refused to parenthesise her fiction, to frame it within a satisfyingly self-conscious exploration of the writerly task. Her stories stand on their own, largely unweighted by a tacit compact between writer and reader: the signifier remains uncompromisingly rooted in the signified, resisting that increasingly convenient tendency towards play which could convince us that these traumas and psychoses are merely 'effects of the text'. If anything, they are the effects of Liverpool, as a sign for the anti-metropolitan, as the standing rebuff to the existing modes of economic and social organisation, as the continuous 'harbour' of a freer interplay between the material and the aesthetic, as, implicitly, the place where art is determined by the mere resources available and the imagination which seeks to soar over the Mersey is more or less severely punished. For every success which emerges from the North-West, Bainbridge suggests to us, there are a hundred enactments, not of failure, but of simply not breaking through: a hundred endeavours hurled against the wall of deprivation, which receive only the answer, 'Not here, dear', or, at least, 'Not *now*'. Bainbridge country is a land where the most bizarre of denizens may be found, but only on sufferance: anything can be entertained, but only a few transplants 'take', in either direction. Mostly, we will be condemned to tread the same gravelly roads, only as time goes on they will be all the more bitterly sprinkled with the detritus of hope.

The volumes are therefore slim, and motionless: they stack, like the early recordings of forgotten pop groups, redolent of spent sweetness, of untasted deadly nightshade, of ambitions carried through in thought only. The fact that, so often, the narrator comprehends a larger portion of the story than any one character does not serve as a guarantee of readerly wisdom, real or to be attained, but as a reminder of interpretations unmade, of understandings un-

reached, of all the moments we *could* have seized to construct patterns which might have continued to inform us. It is thus that childhood and adolescence are the essential terrain: for it is only back there, in the painful re-memoration of the fear of parental absence, that we can be brought to admit to the continual defeat of expectation. If, Bainbridge says, these fables appear to resonate with present experience, that is by chance: it is too late to learn those lessons, and when the lessons were on offer we were usually looking out of the window. All that remains is a 'quiet life', a life in which those peremptory voices are content to remain silent, having weighed up their chances of audibility; yet it is also within those quiet lives that our secrets are held, every moment of collapse held sequestered in the continuing story of a locked family, an individual reduced to silence by the pressures of conflict. Each family, each place of work, stands as a silent monument to our past; each gesture we made is replicated at large in the frozen posture of some group locked into fear, incomprehension, worst of all guilt. Behind the net curtains, our own past survives; we can be brought, by the narrator, to see it, but the possibility of learning has probably been eclipsed, many years ago. These situations survive as hieroglyphs, encapsulated signs in the language of the unconscious, visible warnings on the road; but we give them little credit, and cannot predict the future moment when we too will see ourselves in the waxworks, will realise that our movement, our escape to the bright lights, has been illusory, that we too are being observed in our role as monitory sculptures, turned to permanent stone in the very moment of indignity.

In *Harriet Said* (1972), the narrative plays delicately around the problem of signification: that is to say, the central characters are clearly enacting a script, but we are never certain whose, and thus the meaning of events remains in doubt. At a fairly obvious level, Harriet is the succubus, the ever-present whispering self who eggs the narrator on (harries her) to mate with her father (the Tsar) and kill her mother (Mrs Biggs—who is, just before her death, 'huge and menacing',[6] the frozen statue of adulthood before whom the narrator initially quails, but who has to be reduced to dust.)[7] Yet at every turn Harriet's plans are in fact undercut by the narrator's; this blank and terrible 'I' takes Harriet's words and injunctions and twists them to an unconscious but preformed plan of her own. Thus there is an inversion: Harriet becomes the blank slate on which the narrator inscribes the record of her own desires, the ambiguous authority who can be invoked to justify any practice. If the unconscious is indeed structured like a language, the narrator's ritual progress through puberty is depicted as a dramatised encounter with that language, and as a subjugation of it: Harriet ends up baffled and threatened by the power of the narrator (who is, of course, structurally the only agent who can confer meaning) to distort her comparatively puny imaginary crimes into a realised tale of sex and murder. Thus the narrator acts as a pure 'embodiment': she exists to give carnal form (and the form of carnage) to the promptings of the unconscious. She is thus herself empty (nameless); and the fear we experience as readers springs from our uncomfortable proximity to a superior shaping power (Bainbridge incarnated) before whose unseen plans we can manifest only a shudder. What *Harriet* says is significant only insofar as it provides the pretext for the narrator's interpretation: Harriet offers, for instance, the category of humiliation (the Tsar/father must be 'humbled'),[8] but it is the narrator who connects this empty signifier with the available contents of the unconscious, and carries the desire through to a dreadful completion before which the prompter can only stand aghast—for a moment, before she begins again to act her role and fabricate cover stories after the event. Yet for the narrator, it is vital to maintain the claim that Harriet is the true 'agent':

> How could I not understand her? I would have given all the power of my too imaginative mind and all the beauty of the fields and woods, not to understand her. And at last I gave in to Harriet, finally and without reservation. I wanted the Tsar to be humiliated, to cower sideways with his bird's head held stiffly in pain and fear, so that I might finish what I had begun, return to school forgetting the summer, and think only of the next holidays that might be as they had always been.[9]

What is thus enacted is the story of the girl-child's revenge against the father (the real father is constructed as a caricature, compounded of practical ineffectuality and swearing, absurdly laying claim to a power which is actually wasted beyond recall), in its full duplicity: the narrator constructs a false Other (the script of Harriet) in the name of which (in the name of the sister) she is then freed to humble and mutilate the masculine.[10] As well as an absent father, the text also presents us with an actual absent sister (Frances); we are invited to suppose that the narrator acts under an imperative to fill in those blanks in the familial text, even though violence is the only sign under which they can come to have meaning: only through death can life be affirmed.

The narrator is stout and imaginative, body-full and fantasy-full: Harriet's dry and slender presence provides only a frame within which this over-present femininity can perform a drama, *the* drama. And yet there is no fullness in the narrator's response: the subjugation of the male and mother-murder contain a meaning to which she (so we are invited to suppose) has no conscious access. It is only by reference to the mythical authority of Harriet that she can convey to us the significance of her actions. Before this mirror (and filling the empty reflection with her own wishes), she can experience fullness, but in so doing she renounces the claim to interpretation: thus we are drawn into a circle of shared naivety, and invited to examine the Others we erect as justifications, as objective correlatives, for our crimes.[11]

> How often had Harriet recoiled from me, telling me I was ugly, that I must modify and govern the muscles of my face. It was not that my feelings illuminated and transformed me, as Harriet became transformed in diabolical anger or joy, it was more a dreadful eagerness and vulnerability that made my face like an open wound, with all the nerves exposed and raw.[12]

Thus Harriet provides the pretext on which the 'wound', the assumed castration, can be made manifest, and the Tsar can be 'un-manned'; we suspect that this 'ugliness' is the outward sign of something quite different, of the unmanageability of female trauma, something before which Harriet, like the Tsar, cowers. We are thus presented with a drama of female omnipotence: if, as Cixous claims, the feminine consciousness is plural, in part a defensive linking of many in the face of the demanding, phallic 'one',[13] then we should not be surprised if this plurality begins to act like a team of bent detectives, endlessly covering for each other in an unscripted spiral so that the excuses for crime are themselves multiplied as the alibi becomes totally secure. Like Macavity, the narrator was never there, and so the story of her own burgeoning sexuality and its links with violence is again buried. There is no growth possible in the text, only an increasing complexity of cover stories:

> At last I was allowed to go to bed. I lay in the dark wide-eyed. I had avoided real displeasure, I had been kissed, I had explained the broken window. They would never trace it to me, the more so as Harriet had been home early. I had lied very well and cried effortlessly; I would look white and ill in the morning. I thought of the beautiful night and my god-like strength in the church and I began to smile when I remembered the Tsar's banged nose under the lamp. Harriet could not have managed better.[14]

It is thus, Bainbridge suggests, that the girl-child grows to maturity: fragmenting, developing a spurious self-management, endlessly referring desire to a hypothesised Other (Harriet is the spurious plural, 'Woman'), and thus becoming, paradoxically, the means for enacting the necessary vengeance for the thousands of years of male domination.

The construction of the female superego, and its purposes (which are quite different from those of the male equivalent), are again the ground against which *The Dressmaker* (1973) takes its form, and here again we are given a story which we are invited to see through: coupled with female vengeance, we are invited to a view of female 'transparency', as the writer's own revenge for generations of pornographic scopophilia. The tiniest of devices is significant:

> Afterwards she went through into the little front room, the tape measure still dangling about her neck, and allowed herself a glass of port.[15]

In the 'allowance' to her self, a severance of the female subject already suggests that one part is going to be capable of anything; there is a ridding of scruple, a preparing for the feast, and this premonition is confirmed by the description of the fleshy young male American:

> A great healthy face, with two enquiring eyes, bright blue, and a mouth which when he spoke showed a long row of teeth, white and protruding. It was one of those Yanks. Jack was shocked. Till now he had never been that close. They were so privileged, so foreign; he had never dreamt to see one at close quarters in Nellie's

kitchen, taking Rita and Marge, one on each arm and bouncing them out of the house.[16]

The masculinity evidenced here is expressed in consumerist metaphors: yet also this manifestation of flesh is to be consumed and discarded, the developed but useless teeth finally helpless against the deprivation which breeds a truer violence. For the overall sign of *The Dressmaker* is deprivation: as in *Harriet Said,* it is as though Bainbridge is chronicling the grotesque shapes which the passage to maturity may take if the main channel (and the coastal setting makes the metaphor apt) is no longer negotiable; the difficulty of transit through dried tributaries and across unmeasured sandbanks, which always carry the threat of permanent beaching, of a sudden and premature halt after which we can never again progress. Nellie and Marge between them, riven and full of friction as they are, incarnate a solid maturity before which Ira (the ambiguous name, anger with a feminine ending) cannot even begin. In any case, he is simply a refraction of 'Rita', but thus, of course, derives the complexity of the story: for the vengeance the aunts wreak is displaced, does not fall on the phallic (Chuck, the drill-bit) but on a junior manifestation of masculinity, and similarly Rita fades from the narrative as the aunts reassert a complementary hegemony.

This displacement is crucial, because Bainbridge is not trying to offer a simple reversal of norms, or to claim that the force of the feminine can somehow rejuvenate society: on the contrary, she is showing the destruction which has been visited on the female in order to convert it into a force for conservatism, and therefore the insurrection performed is not a real insurrection but rather one which re-enacts the dominance of the phallic. The dressmaker 'wins' her battle through her employment, by sticking pins in wax effigies, but also through a fake penetration in a more general sense, a penetration of the potential links between the other characters. Partly she is enabled to achieve this by the fact that the forces of masculinity are already really dead: in the triumvirate of Nellie, Marge and Rita the entire force of the family is contained, with Marge (a name-changer; she is also Margo, but she cannot 'go', she is stuck, familially and sexually, within rememoration)[17] as the substitute father, especially since she alone is presumed to have had previous sexual experience. Within that drama, what is predicted is that the line of communication which carries the sexual charge (father/daughter, but here Margo/Rita) falls within the control of the mother as the transmitter of inhibition: Nellie can sever that relationship at will, and thus reaffirm the future Rita-as-mother as the only possible shape for progression. It thus falls to Nellie, as the reincarnation of an unchangeable and frozen past, to lay down the tracks into the future; thus Rita is herself symbolically killed when Ira meets his (masculine) fate, but more significantly thus is depicted the fate of an entire culture, starved of meaning (in the shape of products for consumption, but also of the affections, sexual relations, feelings presented in the world) and thus trapped into a murderous resentment of change. The phallic sign which Ira represents, in however weakened and limp a form, cannot penetrate the tensed surface of

this constructed and well-defended world, in which men have been reduced to Jack's role as absent provider; but meanwhile, within that hygienic bubble from which the male is excluded, significance has drained away and been replaced by a discourse of ritual.

It is in ways like this that Bainbridge, for all her surface naturalism, nonetheless provides us with a map of unconscious process: for her narratives are situated at those points where the covering operations are ceasing to be effective and the barbarous shapes of desire are poking through the torn fabric. The doubling of roles which lies at the root of *Harriet Said* reappears in Brenda and Freda in *The Bottle Factory Outing* (1974), and accompanied, as in *The Dressmaker,* by a diminution of the phallic. Here the men are almost all Italians, illegal immigrant workers, hidden and cowering, often described as a group of children and largely unable to speak the language of power: Rossi's sexual desires extend only as far as rumpling Brenda's clothing to the accompaniment of a meaningless and evasive patter. In this world of masculine midgets, the abundant Freda draws into herself all the power of conveying signification: it is only through her suggestions, her ideas, her interpretation that the world has any meaning at all, and it is only she who retains a potential for change, although this potential becomes increasingly unreal. Not surprisingly, this gigantism is the prelude to humiliation and death: and when Freda dies, she too has to be hidden away, in a barrel, to show that the forces of weary containment have won another battle. Yet, in a sense, it is Brenda, thin and anxious, who has won a Pyrrhic victory: it is her emaciated version of femininity which proves the only one able to survive in a run-down and barely moving world. It is as though she projects all the hope and desire into Freda, thus pumping her up into an unstable shape which causes her death: symbolically, Brenda wonders whether it was Freda's horse-ride which caused the bruises found later on her body, speculating really on whether any manifestation of sexuality might be irrevocably linked with Thanatos. Thus Freda's death acts, for Brenda, as a redemption of an awful kind: she is confirmed in her knowledge that there is nothing to be done about fate. After the death, she has a dream, and when she wakes 'she didn't feel ill any more or cross':

> She had been in a cinema with Freda: Freda was wearing a trouser suit and one of those floppy hats with cloth flowers on the brim. She complained bitterly that she couldn't see the bloody screen. The men in the row behind said 'Sssh!' loudly and kicked the back of the seat. Brenda whispered she should take her hat off. 'Why should I?' said Freda; and Brenda remembered a little doggerel her mother had taught her, something about a little woman with a great big hat . . . went to the pictures and there she sat, Freda shrieked and recited rapidly . . . man behind couldn't see a bit . . . finally got tired of it. Somehow it made Brenda very happy that Freda too knew the little rhyme. She beamed in the darkness. She turned and kissed Freda on the cheek and woke instantly.[18]

What appears to cheer Brenda up is her recognition that Freda too, despite her ambitions, knows that underneath it all women are merely laughable, that the big hat is only a sham and below it lies fear and withdrawal. In this dream, Freda is an honorary man, trouser-suited and swearing, but this does not make her acceptable, it only renders her a target because she has dared to put her head above the parapet. She confuses the men, who cannot see past her; but this does her no good, for she herself cannot see either. By transgressing the stereotypes to which Brenda rigidly adheres, she turns into a kind of chimera and hence cannot survive. Brenda finds comfort in her mother's 'doggerel', as Rita is reduced to belief in the defeatist wisdom of Nellie: in Freda's trajectory through power to death, Brenda watches an enactment of what might happen if femininity were to cut itself loose from these apron-strings, and learns the lesson that it is better, in the end, not to have emerged into the world at all than to risk the violence visited on the admired.

What is appalling in *The Bottle Factory Outing* is the portrayal of low expectations: that nothing can be hoped for except the shoddy and the inappropriate, and thus the outing itself, hilarious though it is, is also sinister. Throughout it there is the fear that, really, even if we get the chance we shall not remember how to enjoy ourselves; and the concomitant fear that, in our flailing efforts to remember the nature of pleasure, we shall go too far and the 'games' will turn into mayhem and inarticulate rage. It is as though, for Brenda, all experience is bracketed: as though she is waiting, exhausted by past attempts to participate (her defunct marriage), for her mother to call her in for tea. At the end, she calls herself in, and regresses: the entire process of the story comes to seem as though it has itself been only an outing, an excursion into activity; the 'real life' which will be resumed by those who survive will be a life devoid of incident, in which Brenda can subside into a role of pure observer, those parts of herself which she has invested in Freda safely cut out, buried, forgotten.

Sweet William (1975) describes a similar trajectory: Ann is presented, in the shape of the ambiguous William, with a text which she makes a continuous series of attempts to read, in that she involves herself in an effort to bring her own life into an intelligible relation with the life of another. But as she reads this text, she becomes increasingly aware that such completeness of comprehension is not possible: that there are always further corners which cannot be explored, always unexplained absences and erasures.[19] As the book moves on, Bainbridge signifies the way in which understanding eludes Ann by talking increasingly over her head to the reader; thus we sense Ann slipping away, as only we, for example, divine the probable secret of William's relationship with Mrs Kershaw, or the reasons for his reported fight with Roddy. No matter how close Ann seeks to draw to this reincarnation of the father, there is always something in the way, some surviving element of his earlier life, some continuing manifestation of his previous wife or wives. Ann, of course, goes through a period of strong ambivalence towards Edna, the principal incarnation of William's past, sensing the appropriateness of Ed-

na's 'theatrical' manner to William's way of life: it is only by considering action as though it were bracketed on a stage (William is a playwright) that we can bring ourselves to refrain from asking illicit questions. Where do the actors go at night? Do they even continue to exist? Or are they, in fact, merely two-dimensional, and must we settle for a version of living in which facts are reduced to whatever William wants to present as his current fiction?

The splitting of the female self which is a habitual theme in Bainbridge is present here too, in the relation between Ann and Pamela; and its contours are becoming clearer.[20] The nameless 'I' of *Harriet Said,* Brenda in *The Bottle Factory Outing* and now Ann experience an impossibility of role: they cannot hold on to their ability to observe the world if they simultaneously have to be themselves observed objects, and so they slide into invisibility and project the contours which they seek to shed into their Others, Harriet, Freda, Pamela. It is as though the body itself is too much of a burden to bear, and must be exiled so that its shapes will not give away anything of the self's identity or gender; but whereas in *Harriet Said,* this process still permits of a terrible victory, and thus the disguise enables a real crime, by the time of *Sweet William* there is less to achieve, and disguise has become an unconscious device for its own sake. Where *Sweet William,* however, diverges more radically from the previous fictions is in its insistence on the role of the male in producing this projective self-mutilation: it is William's capacity for generating self-justifying fictions which reduces women to the actants of roles in a predetermined script. Thus also, by a reticulative process, it is male writers who have laid down the terms of female 'character'.[21] and Bainbridge's response is to move towards dispensing with this concept of 'character' altogether, rendering her women progressively more emptied, so that, paradoxically, they shall not fall victim to the domineering habits of masculine interpretation. What is rejected is the familiar recourse to the portrayal of a 'rich inner life' as a substitute for thwarted action: these women do not have rich inner lives, or if they do they salvage them only at the expense of articulacy, because their words are not valued. William, we are invited to suppose, is at best a pretty poor playwright, a second-rate Pinter, yet even as that he is in a position to transmit within the social body: to the extent that he is given credibility, as playwright, director and philanderer, there is a concomitant societal refusal to credit the different accounts of women, and at the same time a blocking of the paths for communication within the feminine. William's need to separate his life into compartments is itself a reflection of fear, fear that for women to talk *about* him rather than *through* him would be to produce him too as an object, and that this would sap his agential status in the world.

But for Alan, in *A Quiet Life* (1976), the choices available for the male are themselves limited by the ineradicable record of parental defeats and disasters.

> Most of the time he thought about Janet Leyland—the
> way she looked at him, what she said, a certain man-

nerism she had, of touching the lobe of her ear when she was unsure. He wasn't lovesick or anything like that. He wasn't off his food. It was more that he was engrossed in her acceptance of him—his ideas, his cleverness. She thought he knew a lot. He came from a household that regarded men as inferior; they were fed first and deferred to in matters of business, but they weren't respected.[22]

Yet this experience of subjugation does not lead to rebellion: for Alan, ingrained habit is far too deeply laid.

> He knew, somewhere at the back of his mind, that he could only hope to be an extension of his parents—he'd step a few paces further on, but not far. His progression was limited, as theirs had been. . . . He'd always be polite and watch his manners. Most likely he'd vote Conservative, in rebellion against his father.[23]

Thus rebellion is converted into political regression, and the lesson Alan learns has also to do with not taking risks, with adopting a discretion which will ensure that he does not, indeed, end up despised like his father; but there is a terrible price to be paid. His life is to be led in the same way as, in childhood, he moves nervously about the cluttered living-room stuffed with reminders of richer and better days. The wish is to vanish, to become part of the pattern in the over-ornate wallpaper; and now it is he who, in his 'wild' sister Madge, watches warily as adolescence shudders its emergence from the chrysalis. Claustrophobia can itself become a habit: Alan experiences no desire for the wide open spaces, but wants instead to turn himself into the ideal and non-frictive inhabitant of a space seen as inevitably closed.

The inversion of the oppressive interior and its burden of partially visible trauma is in the pinewoods, where Madge not only encounters more real experiences, but simultaneously covers them under a patina of lies. Seen like this, the question posed by the text is symmetrical with that posed in *Sweet William:* in a world where knowledge can never be complete because the story (the play) began before we arrived, how are we to make the necessary adjustment to an acceptable level of incomprehension? And worse than that, in a real or projected sibling situation, where the Other has somehow already adopted or grown into the admired role, the role of freedom, how are we to find another space to occupy without falling prey to the sneaking suspicion that all we have done, every shape with which we have wrestled in the process of self-formation, is not simply itself an inversion, a fitting into a space already unconsciously designed by our elders? This, certainly, is Alan's fear, and it recurs to him when he meets Madge again years later: 'immediately he felt disturbed. He hated reviving the past, the small details of time long since spent. Seeing her, he was powerless to push back the memories that came crowding into his mind.'[24] What, of course, he is also scared of is the possibility which was ever present to him as a child: that Madge, from her position across the boundary of the family, from her magical haven in the pinewoods, might in fact also have a story to tell, a story about *him,* which would invalidate the years of patient and painful self-

suppression; the possibility that, in fact, the neurosis now so carefully grown over might have been there and evident all along and that Madge might have seen it more clearly than he had cared to see himself.

Thus to be watched, indeed to be seen at all, is to be humiliated: the net curtains, the unused parlours do not seem strange to Alan, because he shares with his parents a despairing assumption that what might otherwise be seen would not bear the light of day. His own watchfulness, initially of his parents and later of himself, can survive and continue to operate as a protective mechanism if he is himself out of the reach of harm or affect. At the end, coming back to his wife from the brief meeting with Madge which frames the earlier narrative of memory, 'turning his back on the house, in case his wife watched from the window, he let the flowers spill from his folded newspaper on to the pavement. Then', freed from any incriminating evidence and thus restored to his conception of untrammelled masculine strength, 'squaring his shoulders, he walked up the path'.[25]

In many ways, Edward in *Injury Time* (1977) shares Alan's situation, as a conformist whose tissue of habits papers over early cracks: but here there is something softer in the writing, some flicker of hope as Edward, forced towards a change of behaviour by his bizarre encounter with a gang of bank-robbers, has to attend again, if only momentarily, to voices he believed he had silenced. Here, for the first time, there is a fair match between the major subtexts: Edward and Binny, telling fragments of their own stories, have perceptions which at least connect with each other's, even if, time after time, the possibility for an actual sharing of these perceptions is lost, and shafts of light cross the gloom to no avail. This is structurally Bainbridge's most conventional narrative: a complex set of marital secrets, already on the point of blowing themselves apart, are thrown into full relief by the chance appearance of the criminals, and we are led to believe that, as usual, some kind of growth, if only into a deepened realisation of inadequacy, will occur—as indeed, to an extent, it does. But what is foregrounded is the essentially regressive content of this narrative structure. Edward's obsession is, like Alan's, with childhood events, with a difficult matrix of public-school betrayal and paternal excommunication: what the eruption of violence achieves is a return to that world. Edward, Binny and the others are themselves plunged back into a realm where callow bids for leadership and adolescent resentments replace previous emotions; and in this they enter into a curiously mirrored relationship with the invading gang. Where the dramatic interest of previous Bainbridge texts, and the apparent interest of the first part of *Injury Time,* lay in a splitting and redoubling of individuals, here the interest shifts to the redoubled interaction between the two separate groups.[26] At some points where the various representatives of the bohemian and respectable middle classes are being held hostage by the workers, the two groups crosscut and intermingle; elsewhere, they hold themselves rigidly apart, fastidiously drinking their breakfast tea in the separate halves of Binny's kitchen/diner. The criminals, on the whole, are shocked: by Edward's infidelity, by the squalor of Binny's house. There is no change at stake for them; it is only the unstable syntheses of the initial appalling dinner party which might get remade, but in the end there is little felt impact across the groups, except perhaps for Edward himself: forced at one point to 'stand in' for Ginger, and purged by his repetition of an early cricketing incident, he becomes able to seize a moment of potential heroism, with—as we might by now predict—the proviso that it almost certainly entails his death.

But behind this drama lies another one, more marginalised, and more to do with youth and age than with gender relations. In the face of the toughness of their children, women like Binny and Alma are reduced to meditating on their own softness, and the relationship between Binny and Edward becomes a mutual consolation for ageing. Binny's elder daughter has acquired masculine disguise, army boots and overalls, although this is curiously parodied by the female disguise of one of the criminals, a disguise to which Edward proves completely unable to accommodate, continuing to treat him as a woman despite full evidence to the contrary. It is, indeed, as the title suggests, as though the time given to Edward and Binny for their faltering relationship does not really count: as though it is extra time, snatched from death, in which boundaries become unimportant, and the yearning is for the state of undifferentiation which age might bring. And this, in fact, is what is enacted, as under pressure the characters start to swap roles at regular intervals, and become immersed in a common predicament. The reader is soothed by suggestions of collectivity: but the price to be paid is a desexualising, as though we are supposed to share in a welcome abandonment of real concerns to the young, and to approximate ourselves to the image of Mrs Montague, over sixty yet still looking for a suitable hedge behind which to take her pleasures. Binny is made to feel young and old in dizzying succession, ending up in a grey area where nothing much matters any more, but where also, consequently, there is no need to accept the damaging descriptions offered by her children, by the criminals, by Mrs Montague: once again, there is a kind of invisibility to be achieved, and thus it is Binny, by virtue of her lack of determinate outline, who is the one chosen by the robbers to serve as a continuing hostage. Edward, with his suspect high profile and his suddenly found new reserves of energy, cannot survive: his final inducement of himself to take a risk is fatal, as, symbolically, the entire risk of the affair with Binny has been bracketed within the sign of an imminent heart attack. Bainbridge presents us, for once, with images of at least partial success in the acquiring of self-knowledge, but only by suggesting that the boundaries of the self are in any case pointless, that we may as well resign ourselves to the unpreventable invasion signified in the hostage process and in Binny's ambiguous rape.

Thus in *Injury Time,* the body is frail, softened by careless living and weakened by corrosive memories; we are in the constant whispering presence of imminent paralysis, shadowed for Binny by imminent menopause. There is a sense in which the main characters are already ghosts, although the arrival of the gang does not increase their reality: rather, it is as if two species of half-beings seek to inhabit the same space in the unconscious hope that, somewhere among the tangle of crossed wires, a spark might jump and a whole might be formed. It is mostly around Binny that these hopes are encouraged to coalesce, as though, perhaps because of her extensive motherhood, she might possess the alchemical skill necessary to convert waste material into gold, but her experiences with Edward and Ginger demonstrate bitterly for us that the hope of resurrection is a foolish one, and that nothing is about to be born of these sterile and furtive unions. The doubling of relationships passes down the line: from the public and ceremonial life of Edward and Helen (whom we never see, who is, perhaps, herself already an emptied shell), through the apparently more broadminded marriage of George and Muriel Simpson, which turns out to be a vicious fiction barely covering hatred and envy, through the relationship between Edward and Binny, which is finally forced to 'go public' by the intrusion, and on to the brief and 'ineffectual'[27] encounter between Binny and Ginger: at each point of intersection, we are invited to share a moment's hope that *here* at last there may be some form of life which has both shape and content, but it is never the case. The symbol with which we are left is the one offered to us in despair by Muriel: of the house prepared for union, where one partner never arrives.

If the secret of *Injury Time* is sterility (a lack of the materials for birth, but also a multiple sealing-off of incompatible areas of life), then *Young Adolf* (1978) offers us a monstrous birth which provides an ironic exit from the dilemma. Adolf Hitler, we know, at least went on to make a mark on the world; but equally, that 'mark' was to be a gigantic magnification of the marks inflicted on Adolf himself by his environment and upbringing. The text is riddled with the signs of displaced violence and birth trauma: most significantly in the extraordinary sequences which feature the appearance and disappearance of the hole in the wall of the third-floor room.[28] Time after time, the apparently solid surface of that wall shatters ('Old Shatterhand' is Adolf's 'alter ego') and Adolf, among others, is flung violently through it in a parody of birth, to find his account unbelieved. His trajectory, then, becomes bound up with the attempt to discern the secret of the appearing and vanishing point of entry into the world; and that act of continuing displacement underpins his sexual hatred. The problems of accounting for his origins are further symbolised in his role at the hotel where his brother Alois finds him a job: although here is a luxurious sign of the kind of world for which Adolf longs, he is condemned never to enter or leave it by the front entrance, his complicated circuits through side and rear doors becoming ever more bizarre as he becomes increasingly involved with criminal designs. Through these symbols, a world is established where all the principal doors and windows are blocked up, and Adolf—and the reader—has to creep furtively around the edges, often occupying spaces apparently actually within the walls: the wider implication is of a world twisted so far out of true by divisions of birth and class that we have to make our passage through it in secret and by night, and where the questions we might need to ask, in order to explain how we got to our present point, are always thwarted.

As with many of Bainbridge's previous fictions, there is a tissue of interlocking texts and plans, half-revealed, constantly conspiring to prevent achievement. It is not, indeed, that we are drawn to feel much sympathy with Adolf; but it is suggested that, after all, from this tangle of errors and deprivation nothing much better can be expected, unless it be the passivity of Bridget, who acquiesces, half helplessly and half resentfully, in manipulation and inarticulacy. Kephalus and Meyer try to 'save a few',[29] prevent one or two of the most deprived from falling directly victim to the presumed cruelty of the authorities, but not much real hope is attached to their activities: indeed, it may even be that their efforts are misplaced, a romantic charade which does not touch upon the roots of evil. Whatever location we seek to establish for ourselves as subjects, the very word 'subject' carries a fatal duplicity of meaning: our subjectivity involves also our continuing subjection, and we are left perennially listening through the wall for intimations of the real agency of the story in which we are acting a minor and subjugated part. It is this inevitable subjugation, Bainbridge suggests, which produces the hideous fantasies of domination which Adolf will go on to act out; this sense of rootlessness which will engender the fantasies of 'roots' which emerge into the world as racism and sexual violence; this knowledge of being battered which will make us in turn find people to batter. Alois and Bridget act as substitute parents for Adolf, but we know that this is merely a displacement: the real father exists only as a portrait on the wall, and as a nameless sign around which contradictory narratives are constructed; there is no path back to the truth.[30]

Taking the fictions as a series, we find ourselves in the presence of a detailed investigation of familial conditioning and of the baroque shapes for the self generated in a world where wholeness is not possible. The key process of splitting, from which later shapes derive, is between the acceptable and the rebellious, between the self as defined by an already present pattern and the self as a point of divergence from the familial norm. The problem is that neither choice actually leads away or forward: both enter us into an endless circuit where the only possible dialogue is with father or mother, the only reaction to the possibility of other relationships a terrified probing to see whether this stranger has the quasi-parental gift of seeing through the fictions we wish to present as our life story. The most feared figure is thus the sibling: because at the moment when we settled for an option, or claimed to have done so, he or she was there, observing, and might have a different account to give which would undo all the decades of self-suppressive work. And even if there was no real sibling, or not a significant one, the problem still remains: there is

still the fear that our disguise is inadequate, that we have not sufficiently approximated ourselves to the shape we want, and that this will be glaringly obvious to the Other.

Thus, at all costs, we must not be *seen:* and it is, of course, at this point that the account of familial development (or lack of it) interlocks most importantly with the account of gender differentiation. For observation is also objectification, freezing the Other and turning it to stone; and principally, says Bainbridge, this is what men do to women, partly by regarding them as sexual objects and founding an entire culture on a violent pornography, but also by in a thousand other ways using the 'gaze' as an instrument of control.[31] Not, of course, that this does the men much good: by replacing real women with moving statues, they in fact create a world of monsters before which they can only cower. Thus the ambition towards control is shown as fundamentally circular; and while we are embedded in these self-defeating ways of dealing with the outer world, we also stand no chance of achieving control over ourselves.

Bainbridge's characters can rarely interpret each other's behaviour: they are too preoccupied with trying to fight clear of acknowledging the constraints on their own. And, certainly, there is no freer, better, less ritualised life available at those levels of society where we might expect to find the regulations less rigorously observed; on the contrary, 'down there' is where deprivation makes itself most clingingly felt, and where there is barely enough substance available to flesh out the form of the individual. The experience is of an overwhelming scarcity, either actual or imagined: and that scarcity is itself a reflection of a deprivation of love, of an endless competition to achieve the security of having at least one parent, for a time, all to ourselves. By splitting, perhaps we hope that we might double our chances: that we might become, on the one hand, the competent agent in the world who might expect to attract a father's approval, and on the other the figure of pathos who might hope for a reincarnation of a mother's love. In fact, the trick results in a locked solipsism, in which the only object on view is our self-as-agent; meanwhile we, as subjects with an inner life, are further starved of the resources for survival.

And thus, in the end, this fiction which apparently makes little concession to the modernist habit of self-consciousness produces a highly self-conscious reader: because we are made increasingly aware that, in gazing at the squirmings of these Others, we too are looking only at parts of ourselves, that all these enactments are ones in which we too have shared or will share, objective correlatives for the dilemmas of maturation. And further, we become uncomfortably aware that the readerly position is itself voyeuristic: that we are being treated to a banquet of secrets which we would rather not have known, are being beckoned into the empty and sheeted front parlour where every framed photograph tells a story of defeat. And thus of course, if this is possible, if we can be beckoned through the net curtains and shown the skeletons, what of our own secrets? Is it that we too in time will find ourselves listening dumbfounded to the *other* story, to the narrative about our self which we have refused to acknowledge, but which nonetheless remains, somewhere, to haunt us with the possibility that our self-development has been a massive artifice built on willed ignorance, and that our power of relating is built on half-subdued hatred and half-known fear?

Notes

1. Richard von Krafft-Ebing was 'the great clinician of sexual inversion, rather than . . . its psychologist' according to Havelock Ellis, *Studies in the Psychology of Sex* (2 vols, London, 1897-1900), vol. I, p.30; see, of course, Krafft-Ebing, *Psychopathia Sexualis,* trans. F. S. Klaf (London, 1965).

2. It seems to me that Bainbridge's fictions are in fact directed towards the male reader, and that the tacitness of the text thus becomes a silence and a reserve in the presence of the masculine: as a male reader, I am forced to enact my own responsibility for this silence, and to experience, as an object, the grimace of contempt.

3. Cf. Freud, *Notes upon a Case of Obsessional Neurosis* (1909) (the Rat Man case history), in *Standard Edition,* vol. X, pp.241, 244. The most relevant development in Freudian discourse, and one which is, naturally, radically undermining is Juliet Mitchell, *Psychoanalysis and Feminism* (London, 1974).

4. I use the term 'Other' throughout in the strong sense, often thought of now as the property of psychoanalysis but in fact reaching back into older Hegelian traditions. The depiction of historical and interpersonal process in Alexandre Kojève, *Introduction to the Reading of Hegel,* ed. A. Bloom (New York, 1969), at, e.g., pp.45-60 and elsewhere still remains a relevant model for dialectical interpretation.

5. Cf. Freud, *The Claims of Psycho-analysis to Scientific Interest* (1913), in *Standard Edition,* vol. XIII, p.173; *Introductory Lectures on Psycho-analysis* (1916-1917), in *Standard Edition,* vol. XVI, pp.264-70; and the continuing discussion of the 'primal scene' in *From the History of an Infantile Neurosis* (1918) (the Wolf Man case history), in *Standard Edition,* vol. XVII, pp.7-122.

6. Bainbridge, *Harriet Said* (London, 1972), p.154.

7. Freud's arguments in this area, as in, for instance, *An Outline of Psychoanalysis* (1940), in *Standard Edition,* vol. XXIII, pp. 193-4, are of course problematically phallocentric. See, for instance, 'Women's Exile: Interview with Luce Irigaray', *Ideology and Consciousness,* No. 1, (May 1977), pp.62-76.

8. Bainbridge, *Harriet Said,* p. 134.

9. Bainbridge, *Harriet Said,* p. 135.

10. Cf. Freud, 'Some Psychical Consequences of the Anatomical Distinction between the Sexes' (1925), in *Standard Edition,* vol. XIX, pp. 243-58; clearly what is suppressed in this brief text has to do with the power of women *together.* There is no entry under 'sister' in the Index volume to the *Standard Edition.*

11. I have in mind, of course, Lacan's comments on mirroring:

    The *mirror stage* is a drama whose internal thrust is precipitated from insufficiency to anticipation—and which manufactures for the subject, caught up in the lure of spatial identification, the succession of phantasies that extends from a fragmented body-image to a form of its totality . . . and, lastly to the assumption of the armour of an alienating identity, which will mark with its rigid structure the subject's entire mental development.

    ('The mirror stage as formative of the function of the I', p.4). But the relation between 'armouring' and the substitution of an Other for the evacuated self remains unclear.

12. Bainbridge, *Harriet Said,* p.105.

13. See Hélène Cixous, 'The Character of "Character"', *New Literary History,* V (1973-4), 383-414.

14. Bainbridge, *Harriet Said,* p.99.

15. Bainbridge, *The Dressmaker* (London, 1973), p.5.

16. Bainbridge, *The Dressmaker,* p.28.

17. Cf. the parapraxes concerning names cited by Freud in *The Psychopathology of Everyday Life,* pp. 224-5 (also pp. 83-4, 240-2).

18. Bainbridge, *The Bottle Factory Outing* (London, 1974), p. 146.

19. I mean 'erasures' in the sense used by Derrida in *Of Grammatology* and elsewhere; but there is also a connexion here with the Freudian erasure of women's specificity (and its frequent historical return in the ghostly).

20. Cf. Breuer and Freud, *Studies on Hysteria* (1893-5), in *Standard Edition,* vol. II; and particularly Breuer's case history of Fräulein Anna O. (21-47). For instance, the characteristics of her illness are said to have comprised:

    the existence of a second state of consciousness which first emerged as a temporary *absence* and later became organised into a '*double conscience*'; an inhibition of speech, determined by the affect of anxiety, which found a chance discharge in . . . English verses; later on, paraphrasia and loss of her mother-tongue, which was replaced by excellent English; and lastly the accidental paralysis of her right arm. (42)

    Each of these symptoms appears imagistically in Bainbridge's writing.

21. See again Cixous, 'The Character of "Character"', where this history is connected with Freud on the primal horde.

22. Bainbridge, *A Quiet Life* (London, 1976), p. 41.

23. Bainbridge, *A Quiet Life,* p. 42.

24. Bainbridge, *A Quiet Life,* pp. 7-8.

25. Bainbridge, *A Quiet Life,* p. 156.

26. There is a complex further mirroring going on here, because each of the groups is searching symbolically for a way of (sexual) relating which will give birth to the future: the pram which is present throughout contains only money and a doll. Binny is pulled out of her group to occupy a space in the middle, between two groups of four: whereupon much of the puzzling seems to be around the question of whether the group symbol, or totem, into which she is thus fashioned represents hope or despair.

27. Bainbridge, *Injury Time* (London, 1977), p.134.

28. It is only when the hysteric renounces being what men fight over—we will have to precede her there—that she will be ready to conquer the truth. . . . It is then that we learn from her, from this mother in sufferance, that there is only one pertinent trauma: that of birth.

    (Moustapha Safouan, 'In Praise of Hysteria', in *Returning to Freud: Clinical Psychoanalysis in the School of Lacan,* ed. S. Schneiderman (New Haven and London, 1980), p. 59.) The paternalistic tone matches precisely the Bainbridge response, in the discursive hall of mirrors: thus the frozenness of trauma is re-enacted, not only within the unconscious but also in the conflicts of discourse *around* the unconscious.

29. Bainbridge, *Young Adolf* (London, 1978), p.134.

30. In any case, man cannot aim at being whole . . . , while ever the play of displacement and condensation to which he is doomed in the exercise of his functions marks his relation as a subject to the signifier.

    (Lacan, 'The signification of the phallus', in *Écrits,* p.287.) *Cf.* also Lacan on the *'Name-of-the-Father'* in, e.g., 'On a question preliminary to any possible treatment of psychosis'.

31. See, for instance, Colin MacCabe, 'Theory and Film: Principles of Realism and Pleasure', *Screen,* XVII, 3 (Autumn 1976), 7-27, as one introduction to the politics of 'the point of view and the look'; and, in more detail, Lacan, *The Four Fundamental Concepts,* pp.67-119.

Suzon Forscey (review date 12 January 1986)

SOURCE: A review of *Watson's Apology,* in *Los Angeles Times Book Review,* January 12, 1986, p. 3.

[*In the following review, Forscey offers favorable assessment of* Watson's Apology.]

Beryl Bainbridge's 11th novel is a grim pleasure, but then so is life, and it is from life (and its documentation) that **Watson's Apology** is lifted.

On a Sunday afternoon in October, 1871, an elderly and respected clergyman scholar, the Rev. J. S. Watson, brutally murdered his wife Anne by cracking open her skull with a horse pistol. What British writer wouldn't find tempting material in the trial proceedings, newspaper accounts and an untidy packet of old love letters? Bainbridge, one imagines, pounced.

And succeeded brilliantly in bringing murderer and victims alive, in spite of some maddening tricks of organization.

John Selby Watson, after courting the impoverished, 30-ish Anne Armstrong at a remove and wedding her at almost first sight, immediately wants only to be undisturbed, to be left to the classical scholar's life. The activities of the wedding night, spent in a wallowing boat on the Irish Sea, dictate there will be no chance.

How fatal the bride's post-coital reverie: "My dear, my dear, she said to herself . . . They would never be parted. Soon her arm ached and he smelled like an invalid, but she would have died rather than shift him."

And Watson? "He was afraid he should see . . . some vestige of that expression of pure delight, of impure joy which had ravaged her face the night before."

So, through the decades of marriage, there was Anne's obsessive love in response to her husband's withdrawal and sexual revulsion, and there was Watson's corked-up fury. Such a wife (kin to both Alice James, the unemployed woman of intelligence, and Hedda Gabler, the untamed, powerful sadist) and such a husband (today he would be a doctor or politician) are agonizingly real.

But what frustration to have in hand an excellent novel that only the hardiest will tackle. There are lives that sensible people don't want to experience. To be so convincingly trapped inside the heads of two excruciatingly tormented people is not much fun.

Though Bainbridge has never been sentimental, her best-known novel, **The Bottle Factory Outing,** is a rather lively place where bad things happen only because of an unfortunate juxtaposition of events. "Nothing personal!" is the typical attitude of the usual English murderer. "Watson's Revenge" is a much bleaker black.

This is not to say that the book is without humor. Perhaps, one even suspects, the sly Bainbridge has put over one huge joke. Maybe the line "I should have bought her a piano" is the wickedly glittering solitaire in a massive Victorian setting.

The final pages, describing the dreariness of Watson's enfeebled prison life and his undignified death, deprive the reader even of the grandeur of tragedy—though with the uneasy feeling that our own griefs can be so pragmatically resolved by divorce or therapy.

How sad it is, though, that at the finish of **Watson's Apology**—as at the termination of most miserable marriages—one cannot remember any earlier admiration or happiness.

Richard Ingrams (review date 22 August 1987)

SOURCE: "England, Our England," in *Spectator,* August 22, 1987, pp. 28-9.

[In the following excerpted review, Ingrams offers positive assessment of Forever England.]

Last year I took on the task of compiling an anthology about England, since when I have been delving around among my books looking for bits and pieces that might merit inclusion. There are basically two categories. One is the writing of foreign observers like Henry James who see the country from the point of view of a tourist to whom everything is fresh and strange. The other is that of the English themselves—more rewarding from the anthologist's point of view because in writing about England they reveal, if they are any good, the character of the English people.

One conclusion I have reached is that the hallmark of the authentic English writer, to be found on a whole range of authors from Dr Johnson to Philip Larkin, is the assumption that England has gone to the dogs. True patriotism is not to be found in the outpourings of men like Rupert Brooke, whose famous sonnet would be just as effective if one substituted, say, Finland for England throughout. The most English book about England is probably Cobbett's *Rural Rides,* which is inspired by the true patriotism of a man convinced that the country is done for. This general attitude of indignation is actually what has preserved England (what is left of it). It is because a small but significant band of people have always been confident of imminent collapse that something at least has survived.

In a lesser role are those writers, especially prevalent today, who feel that a way of life, thought to be particularly English, has vanished for ever beneath a flood of motorways, tower blocks and television aerials. Northerners, like Beryl Bainbridge, are especially aware of the drastic changes. The Liverpool that she grew up in, with its docks, its tramlines and cobblestones, has been obliterated. More important, the institution of the family, which dominated her childhood, has been undermined in all kinds of ways.

Her new book, which is commendably short, is devoted to the theme of North and South and much of it is taken up with a series of portraits, based on television interviews, of young couples who illustrate the national differences. However, as in her previous *English Journey,* the real meat of the book is Miss Bainbridge's own memories which keep breaking in to interrupt the more humdrum accounts of day-to-day life in Mrs Thatcher's Britain. I assume that her own humility is what prevents her from writing a proper autobiography, for there is more than enough in both her books to provide the material for an excellent one. All she needs, I suspect, is a bit of encouragement. It is easy to see why she might be regarded as an unfashionable writer. A lapsed Catholic, a lapsed socialist, she can write about herself with humour and detachment and without any of the feminist self-consciousness which mars so much of the writing of those modern women who are preoccupied with 'sexual politics'.

Nicci Gerrard (review date 5 January 1990)

SOURCE: "The Death of Tinkerbell," in *New Statesman and Society,* January 5, 1990, pp. 38-9.

[In the following review, Gerrard offers tempered assessment of An Awfully Big Adventure.]

This is Beryl Bainbridge's first adult novel for five years, and initially it seems as if a sweet whiff of her writing for children curls round the edges of its chilly humour. The title harks back to jolly yarns and to Peter Pan's brave hopes; the setting is the raffish fifties society of weekly rep in Liverpool, where everyone is smeared with greasepaint and called "ducky"; the central character Stella—no star but assistant stage manager—is an aspiring actress who extracts drama out of the dustiest situations. The novel that Beryl Bainbridge evokes and rewrites is, inevitably, Priestley's *Good Companions*—a novel that has always struck me as more suitable for children than adults; and the play they rehearse is *Peter Pan.*

But in *An Awfully Big Adventure* Tinkerbell dies when Stella fails to re-illuminate the torch that represents her: "For a moment the clapping continued, rose in volume, then died raggedly away, replaced by a tumult of weeping." And Stella herself might be innocent, but she is also conniving. Nor does she achieve stardom or the admiration of her hero, the camp and ageing director, Meredith Potter. Instead the novel, with its ear for provincial manners, its undercurrents of violence, unlovely sexual encounters and increasingly brittle theatrical dialogues, tells a sinister story of emotional abuse. Beneath the saccharine surface lies a bitter subtext of deserted children and neglected mothers.

Beryl Bainbridge has always been a mistress of mordant humour and cruel insights. Puffed-up whimsy collides with reality's pricks, becoming absurd: when Stella is kissed by callow Geoffrey (she thinks of it as a rehearsal for Meredith), she is simply "glad her ears were clean. Every fortnight, on bath night. Lily probed them with a kirby grip." When she loses her virginity to Captain Hook ("it had to happen sometime and now was as good time as any"), she shrugs off the experience: "I expect there's a knack to it. It's very intimate, isn't it?"

But in spite of its sharp set pieces, self-conscious theatricality and hilarious one-liners, *An Awfully Big Adventure* is wistful rather than edgy. The Liverpool that Bainbridge describes manages to be both Gothic and sepia-tinted. Behind the gilt and bright light is a colourless and seedy world.

Death, as Peter Pan says, might be an awfully big adventure—but life seems an awfully joyless business.

Francine Prose (review date July 1991)

SOURCE: "With Poison Pen in Hand," in *Women's Review of Books,* Vol. VIII, Nos. 10-11, July, 1991, p. 37.

[*In the following review, Prose defends Bainbridge's work against demeaning critics and offers praise for* An Awfully Big Adventure.]

Traditionally, the back of the book jacket is the venue for quotes from past reviews and blurbs conveying fevered, near-hysterical praise. Yet some of the praise accompanying the British novelist Beryl Bainbridge's new book, ***An Awfully Big Adventure,*** strikes one as curiously diminutive and puzzlingly restrained. *New York Times Book Review* calls Bainbridge "a dazzling miniaturist" while the *Times Literary Supplement* rather poignantly expresses its regret that "we cannot, on Oriental lines, designate Miss Bainbridge a Minor [sic] National Treasure."

Given the considerable virtues of ***An Awfully Big Adventure,*** and of Bainbridge's thirteen previous books of fiction, it does make one wonder, if not exactly for the first time: Who precisely *is* that signifying angel of literary judgment, perusing the hopeful little books as they come along and winnowing wheat from the chaff? Who separates elect from damned? Who tags Bainbridge's novels as minor (domestic or kitchen dramas) while Saul Bellow and John Updike (also writers of domestic and kitchen dramas, though much less precisely observed) are ushered, with considerable fanfare, into the Major Leagues, where no one, to my knowledge, ever refers to them as miniaturists or minor treasures?

The question, of course, is not whether Bainbridge is in fact a major writer (whatever *that* is). The question is why this extraordinarily good writer is, despite having published so many fine novels, not better known on this continent; why her reputation should lag so far behind that of her less accomplished compatriots—for example, Martin Amis.

Readers who go to Amis and Ian MacEwan for a certain sort of sinister, deliciously creepy (and somehow particularly British) nastiness will find plenty of that in Bainbridge, who is a master of the quick, sharp, poisonous barb that can make character description indistinguishable from character assassination. (A man in the new novel describes a woman as having nothing wrong with her "apart from her love of beauty, an affliction which she was ill-equipped to fight. He put it in a nutshell when he said she was the sort of girl who, if there had been a meadow handy, would have been out there in a flash picking cowslips.")

Bainbridge is as good as anyone on the subject of social class and at the way people, hoping against any reasonable hope to make themselves more upwardly mobile, transform themselves in the most inappropriate fashion and for all the wrong reasons. Moreover, the themes that recur almost obsessively in many of her novels—the ways that power

gets tossed back and forth as people manipulate one another, mostly through unsatisfied desire and unrequited affection—are as important (and subtly handled) as any that one might hope to find in the work of writers whom the *TLS* might wish to designate "on Oriental lines" as Major National Treasures.

At the risk of sounding like the sort of whiner who blames every last little thing on gender discrimination, one can't help wondering if Bainbridge's relegation to the minors may not have something to do with the fact of her sex. That is, despite the considerable gains that (as they say) women have made, in literature and elsewhere, certain sorts of women writers still appear to have a rather difficult time gaining acceptance in this country: writers who see "too much" (that is to say, the most unsettling and inglorious small human flaws), hear too much and too sharply, and who write about it with wit, humor, irony and—perhaps most damningly—without any desire to seem at all times forgiving and redemptive.

More disturbingly, this sort of writer is frequently also less than beloved among female readers, many of whom still, depressingly, expect a sort of "niceness" and "nurturance" from writers of their own sex (the rather cozy maternal sense that some appear to find—mistakenly—in Doris Lessing). Even women seem to feel more comfortable when, if anger is expressed, it is directed at politically correct targets.

The bookish, sharp tongued, dismayingly observant little girl is never the most popular child in the schoolyard (with other little boys *or* girls), and there is some of her in Bainbridge, who maintains a very careful and particular distance from her characters (even her main characters)—a cool remove from which she watches, records, but refuses to psychologize, justify, emote, or explain. She's less interested in making you like her characters than in showing you who they are, how they behave, how they push and pull each other as they try for (and miss by a mile) something remotely resembling what might be called human connection.

What's most striking about ***An Awfully Big Adventure*** (aside from the most immediately obvious thing—how amazingly funny it is) is how sympathetic its characters are without being, exactly, likeable. At the center of the book (set in Liverpool, circa 1950) is a teenage girl named Stella, a theatrical, ambitious, theatrically ambitious high school drop-out whose mother runs a boardinghouse that seems to specialize in war-damaged traveling salesmen.

> Several regulars, including the soap man with one arm and the cork salesman with the glass eye, were seen lugging suitcases of samples into Ma Tang's next door . . . the commercial travellers pushed back sleeves and rolled up trouser legs to point at scars; they tapped their skulls to show where the shrapnel still lodged.

In the world of the novel, everyone is damaged, every time a character looks out of a window, it's to see some mindless cruelty or awful grotesquerie (a boy with ringworm throwing stones at a cat, a malicious looking tramp sucking on a chicken bone). And the members of the repertory theater company Stella joins are, at least in this respect, thoroughly unexceptional. Each of these actors is troubled, in pain, ineffective, or incomplete, and inconveniently enamored of entirely the wrong person; none of them are what the helping professions might call "high functioning"—artistically or emotionally. Putting them together for a performance of (of all things) J. M. Barrie's *Peter Pan* is rather like shaking a mixture of incompatible chemicals in a beaker; the effect is dangerous, volatile and (as in many Bainbridge novels) ultimately explosive.

The book is a joy to read; the narrative jogs along swiftly, turning and circling back on itself, pushed forward by the momentum of the characters' separate ambitions, quirks, desires and frustrated imbroglios. One might have wished that Bainbridge had tempered the slightly melodramatic ending, resisted the urge to tie things up with a series of rather predictable plot twists and revelations. But these minor reservations hardly spoil our pleasure in her immense (and not in any sense "minor") gifts—her terse wit, her precision, her economy of style and, above all, the absolutely unique sensibility with which she observes and records the unjust, upsetting, clumsy and terribly moving comedy of errors that we call human relations.

Nancy Engbretsen Schaumburger (review date Fall 1991)

SOURCE: "Briefly Noted," in *Belles Lettres,* Vol. 7, No. 1, Fall, 1991, p. 54.

[*In the following review, Schaumburger offers praise for An Awfully Big Adventure.*]

If you can imagine a coming-of-age novel set in post-war Liverpool that trespasses on the macabre and metaphysical terrain of Penelope Fitzgerald and Muriel Spark, with a bow to Alfred Hitchcock and Graham Greene, then you will have some notion of Beryl Bainbridge's latest novel *An Awfully Big Adventure.* Despite these influences, it is still a unique work, wry and disturbing in its own way. The plot centers around the experiences of an insecure, unflinching young woman who never fails to give the world a hard stare as she bumps into some complex aspects of life, such as love and death, during her apprenticeship to a seedy theater company. The twists and turns of backstage intrigue are juxtaposed to the equally odd rooming-house milieu of Stella's uncle and aunt, who worry that she will turn out like her long-absent mother, "bloody Renée." Ironically, the play that Stella assists with is *Peter Pan,* a work that has a lot to say about eluding love, time, death, parents, and normal life. (You will recall, for example, that Peter regards confrontation with death as "an awfully big adventure.") Stella has a similar attitude

toward learning about life, but one steeped in the hard-boiled realism of the Liverpool slums. She knows a grim joke when she sees one.

Meredith, the director with whom she falls hopelessly in love, and O'Hara, the star from London who is cast as Captain Hook and who falls hopelessly in love with her, are only two of the mysteries abounding behind the curtains: they both have a painful past, as everyone deduces, but the facts are obscure. *All* of the troupe members are star-crossed in some area of life, Stella discovers. Complicating the romantic subplot is the material of Greek tragedy that Stella unknowingly revives. Other mysteries emanate from the strange telephone conversations that Uncle Vernon holds with his supplier, a man named Harcourt whom he barely knows, on the subject of Stella's troubling behavior; Harcourt delivers Delphic pronouncements on the problems of childrearing. There's also the puzzle of Stella's frequent phone calls to "Mother," which Bainbridge deftly defers clarifying to the very last, sad, funny, chilling paragraph.

The finest feature of this quirky novel consists in the background details. It's not just the bombed-out buildings and the population of the maimed and corrupt who seem to drag out their lives in these ruins—one is reminded of the film *The Third Man*—but the frequent snapshots of casual cruelty, to children most of all, which Stella notes in passing down the street. One unforgettable instance of the principle of savage mischance operating in this novel is the sight of a boy carrying a pane of glass down the steps, stumbling, and winding up a pool of blood and shards. Nobody much notices these sidewalk catastrophes or comments upon them, which is perhaps the point. It resembles the appalling background detail of the drowning Icarus in Breughel's beautiful, otherwise serene painting that Auden rendered even more famous in his poem *Musée des Beaux Arts.* Despite the footlights and the greasepaint, Stella's world is still full of suffering. Like Uncle Vernon's roomer, the badly burned salesman with no eyelids to close, Stella perceives it all and goes about her business.

Francis Spufford (review date 20 December 1991)

SOURCE: "In Scott's Footsteps," in *Times Literary Supplement,* December 20, 1991, p. 24.

[*In the following review, Spufford offers favorable evaluation of The Birthday Boys.*]

My grandmother was born in March 1911, the month in which this novel starts. Its famous events, then, are still in one sense within the reach of living memory. While Beryl Bainbridge's "birthday boys"—"Taff" Evans, "Bill" Wilson, "Con" Scott, "Birdie" Bowers and "Titus" Oates— were ragging each other in the polar snows, and stepping out the stately dance of class divisions, and dying, my grandmother's parents ran a small Turkish Delight factory in the West Country. But at the weekends, a world away from ice and darkness, and at least one social level beneath the officer corps, they too were devotes of the Edwardian style of fun. They went on country jaunts, they japed, played Wellsian practical jokes and called each other by nicknames as silly as the explorers': "Pebby" and "Japonica" were two; I forget the others. The vanished manners that make up a prize part of Bainbridge's interest in Scott's expedition lived in these vanished relatives of mine as well. They are still, just, accessible to recall.

And yet to see the five dead men as they appeared to themselves requires a journey back through layers and layers of time that cannot quite be managed. Between now and then stand, not only the enormous differences of the century's history, but the many screening versions of the story with which different decades have beguiled themselves. Before the present debunked picture of Scott's fatal expedition to the South Pole, there was the secure (if shrunken) place it had as a children's story, a Ladybird book on a tragic theme. Before that, the film (with John Mills as Scott) had shaped it as a post-war fable of class integration, apt for the austerity era. Before that, the 1930s had fashioned its concern with natural history into something congruent with *Tarka the Otter* and rambling in shorts. In the 1920s, when the nervously wonderful *Worst Journey in the World* appeared, the sense of *anomie* that followed the Great War had separated even participants in the expedition from their former selves, and already filled the gap with matter alien to 1911. And even if we could draw all these later meanings aside, like stage scenery on painted flats, one after another parting to reveal the boards going back and back and back, the chances are that all we would arrive at, in the end, would be a tableau from a toy theatre of the time, the birthday boys as Duty's cardboard cut-outs, against a final backdrop inked in lurid red and blue and white (a lot of white). Imagination has a difficult journey to go to reach them, one complicated by the busy work imagination has been doing on them for eighty years.

Bainbridge divides the three-year story of the expedition, from Cardiff Docks to the tent on the Great Ice Barrier, into five monologues, one for each of the five who died on the return from the Pole. Their birthdays—something not remarked till now—index the downward fortunes of the party beautifully, and also, though these are days without festivities, provide a chink into the private minds that weren't disclosed as the explorers rubbed along together. How I wish these documents were real. They are exactly what curiosity looks to find, and fails to find, in the true accounts, official and otherwise. They dip beneath the social frictions and the expedient silences; they test for cheese to the bottom of the honey. They can do this because they enact the stoic gruffness of the time without adhering to it. A lovely directness, instead, fills the mock-Edwardian musing. Petty Officer Evans's monologue makes a beeline for the drinking sprees that shamed the man ashore, and gave Scott's choice of him its permanent question-mark; Wilson's, for the pious death-wish that

makes the doctor's goodness seem, in retrospect, more than a little sinister (His last letter to his wife ends, "All is well."); Bowers's, for the muscular simplicity that dares the future to find him stupid; Scott's for the tortured attitude to commanding others, and for his endlessly intriguing marriage to a New Woman; Oates's, the last in the novel, for the motives behind his horsiness.

Not that Bainbridge goes after secrets, exactly. She exercises the right to spring surprises, and certainly does her share at peeling off her boys' veneer, but she is wise enough to know that no secret—no hitherto unsuspected revelation—could be sufficiently explosive to re-shape the story wholesale, without also shattering the interest of it. It is, implicitly, a narrative of inhibition, in which death comes to silence the characters' half-understanding of themselves, not to complete it. The interesting thing is *how* they handled what they guessed about themselves; how far they let truths filter into awareness. It matters far more that (one of Bainbridge's best invented details) Birdie Bowers cherished an empty jam jar, his sole souvenir of female affection, than that, ugly and virgin till he died, his polar feats were obvious sublimations.

The polar past, so other and elusive, is also vulnerable to the present. It can be trampled on, and the acuteness of the explorers in their own mode be drowned out if present perceptions are condescendingly applied. Their ideas of cowardice and "nerve" and providential guidance allowed remarkable articulations of themselves. It was not, after all, a vocabulary that constricted Conrad. The polar story, Apsley Cherry-Garard knew, "involved all kinds of questions"; and Beryl Bainbridge, though her brush is broad and comic, treats the fragile parts of polar narrative with delicacy. From the ventriloquistic point of view, she isn't entirely successful. I cannot quite credit her Taff Evans, for in the extant letters the "other ranks" who use the officers' registers of voice do so more individually, without the jerks that signal a literary amalgamation. Nor does her Oates escape sounding stiff and expository when ("this somewhat embarrassing outburst") he tells a story about a picture of Queen Victoria which prepares for Bainbridge's ultimate special effect; the gallant man's conviction, as he stumbles away to die, that the Queen's gillie, John Brown, is holding a pony waiting for him. But she succeeds wonderfully in navigating the story, with laughter and grief, as if it were happening fresh, for the first time, in all its brave absurdity, thus grasping intact the hope of every reader of the original accounts that, this once, somehow, the idiots may get through.

And here there is something important to be observed, for Bainbridge has incorporated the debunking research done by Roland Huntford, and yet the story persists. It survives, in imagination, the evidence of incompetence. It still manages to be present, for the reader; though so foolish, and all so long ago.

Andro Linklater (review date 4 January 1992)

SOURCE: "No Longer Hero or Villain," in *Spectator,* January 4, 1992, pp. 25-26.

[In the following review Linklater offers praise for The Birthday Boys.]

The fall of a hero produces a curiously intense sensation—a surge of libertarian delight pitted against pangs of filial anguish until both are swamped by cynicism. Those at least were the emotions I remember from reading Roland Huntford's admirable demolition job on Scott of the Antarctic, *Scott and Amundsen,* about ten years ago.

It brought down a figure epitomising the gentlemanly virtues of courage, generosity and a masculine resolution which endured without self-pity to the end. In its place stood a vain, impractical creature, racked by feminine ir-resolution, whose short-comings in preparation and equipment were exposed, cruelly by the hard-headed Amundsen in the race to the South Pole, and fatally by the Antarctic cold on their journey back.

Years of hero-worshipping made it impossible to wipe from one's mind the last photograph of Scott in his huge fur gloves and outsize boots, surrounded by the other members of the expedition, or to forget the poignancy of the final entry in his log. 'For God's sake look after our people'. Yet now it was equally impossible to ignore the fact that the photograph showed the party on foot because of Scott's reckless antipathy to skis and dog-drawn sledges, while 'our people' needed looking after due to his failure to finance the expedition properly. In the end, each cancelled the other out, leaving nothing but contempt for someone who might have had the triumph he yearned for had he been a little more the professional and a little less the gentleman.

Beryl Bainbridge has taken Scott's expedition as the theme of her latest novel, **The Birthday Boys,** and not the least of its virtues is that it allows another more charitable conclusion. Her story runs from the last desperate fund-raising dinner in Cardiff, through the *Terra Nova's* long voyage south, to Oates's despairing walk into the snow. It is told through the thoughts of each of the five members of the group who made the assault on the Pole: the boozy, powerful petty officer, Taff Evans; Scott's right hand man, Dr Bill Wilson; Scott himself; the immature but iron-willed naval officer, Birdie Bowers; and the wealthy regular soldier, Captain Titus Oates.

At first sight, the story of five men struggling through the Antarctic and doomed to die in the attempt is a long way, both in scale and subject matter from Beryl Bainbridge's usual turf. In the past her characters have struggled simply to survive urban life with their dignity, if not their sanity, intact, and some of her sharpest comedy has been centred on women who had to face this struggle handicapped by impossible children and all too possible lovers. For such an author, it might be thought that the scale of the Antarctic, with its epic spaces and tragic ends, would simply be too great.

In fact it is precisely her understanding of the intensity of small-scale drama which brings Scott and his companions

into focus. No longer either heroic or contemptible, they are restored to human dimensions.

As drawn by Bainbridge, each of them is aware of their leader's shortcomings, but each quietens his doubts out of a kind of protective love for Scott. Both Evans and Wilson acknowledge his touchiness and lack of foresight, but confess that he was a man they would die for, while Oates, the least starry-eyed, goes further.

'I've never known such a man for making mistakes and shifting the blame onto others', he exclaims, and then, knowing that Scott's faults have killed him, admits that:

> I had none the less come to recognise his other, more important, qualities, not least his ability to put himself in another's shoes. One could see in his eyes, even when he wasn't blubbing, that his heart was too big for his boots.

She builds up the complexities of this passionate loyalty with considerable skill, slipping easily from Evans's self-confident, lower-deck voice, to Wilson's reserve, Bowers's eagerness and Oates's well-bred irritation. At the centre is Scott's feminine presence, his very perversity and impulsiveness inciting them to achieve impossible tasks as intoxicatingly as the foibles of a troubadour's lady.

It is a beautiful piece of story-telling. Far more accurately than any biography could do, it catches what must have been Scott's hold on his followers, and I do not know of any other woman writer who could have conveyed the curious tenderness of male companionship so deftly. Finally, and perhaps most valuably, it teaches compassion for fallen heroes.

Michael Cross (review date 11 April 1992)

SOURCE: A review of *The Birthday Boys,* in *New Scientist,* April 11, 1992, p. 43.

[In the following review, Cross offers tempered assessment of The Birthday Boys.]

Well into the 1960s, my schoolmasters solemnly taught that Amundsen—he merited neither rank nor Christian name—beat Captain Robert Falcon Scott to the South Pole only by the most dastardly trickery.

Luckily, no era set itself up for debunking quite as much as the final decades of the British Empire. By the 1970s, the line "I am just going outside and may be some time," had launched a thousand comic sketches. In 1979, Roland Huntford's *Scott and Amundsen* (later republished as *The Last Place On Earth*) completed the job by portraying Scott as a self-deluding romantic whose incompetence cost lives.

Beryl Bainbridge leans heavily on Huntford and the more veiled criticism of Apsley Cherry-Garrard's *The Worst*

Journey in the World for her fictional first-person portraits of the five men who died returning from the South Pole in the autumn of 1912. Scott's companions are the boozy and loyal Evans, saintly Wilson, cheerful Bowers—and Oates, stoic and aloof to the end. The theme of birthdays celebrated in extraordinary circumstances casts a suitably juvenile light on their characters.

However, Bainbridge keeps her novelist's licence oddly in check by shying away from issues that Polar historians still debate: the sudden choice to take five men to the Pole, for example, and the exact circumstances of the deaths of Evans and Oates. Probably only one episode, an instant of unrequited homosexual attraction, will raise real hackles among the old guard of the British Antarctic Survey. My great disappointment was that Bainbridge did not work harder at the character of Edward Wilson, doctor, ornithologist, artist and Christian, the "Uncle Bill" upon whose shoulder the other birthday boys lean.

Bainbridge is not the first person to borrow Scott's story. Whether to ridicule or imitate, we still enlist the spirit of Scott's men on our own winter journeys, 80 years after their blood congealed into black ice.

Elisabeth Wennö (essay date 1993)

SOURCE: "Introduction: Background," in *Ironic Formula in the Novels of Beryl Bainbridge,* Acta Universitatis Gothoburgensis, 1993, pp. 1-8.

[*In the following excerpt, Wennö discusses Bainbridge's critical underestimation and argues that her novels, though regarded as conventional narratives, actually embody sophisticated distancing techniques that call into question the illusions and constructions of literary realism.*]

Background

Little scholarly work has been done on the novels of Beryl Bainbridge despite their wide publication and readership. Apart from a few articles in literary journals[1] and a discerning interpretative chapter, dealing with six of her novels in David Punter's *The Hidden Script,*[2] there is, to my knowledge, only one book-length study. This is a textual study which provides a detailed comparison of the original and revised editions of two of Bainbridge's novels, and discusses the stylistic changes made in the second versions of these novels.[3]

Despite the fact, then, that Beryl Bainbridge has written a number of TV scripts and documentaries, published a collection of short stories, a short novel written in her teens, a documentary, and thirteen novels, the main body of critical commentary to date consists of reviews, interviews, and brief references in bibliographies and literary history surveys.[4] The present thesis is an attempt to redress in part this lack of academic attention. The reason for the academic neglect is perhaps displayed in the assessment

that "Beryl Bainbridge is hardly a writer who will be the object of scholarly interest or given a place in literary history—for that she is probably too 'simple'."[5] The motivation for my interest in Bainbridge's writing is a wish to explore the workings of simplicity in her novels. In this way, I also hope to contribute to the current contesting of the hierarchical order of study objects implied above, and of the criterion of unexamined simplicity as grounds for relegating texts to the academic periphery.[6] For, the apparent simplicity of Bainbridge's fiction contains a degree of subtlety that warrants attention. In this respect, a study of her fiction might serve to contribute to the ongoing discussion of textual significance and the validity of the canon, to which the growing interest in non-canonical forms of discourse, not least feminist re-evaluation, bears witness.

Bainbridge's fiction represents a narrative form that is based on 'life as experienced', and rooted in the mimetic tradition which is characterized by "chronological time as the medium of a plotted narrative, an irreducible individual psyche as the subject of its characterization, and above all, the ultimate concrete reality of things as the object and rationale of its description."[7] Asked to comment on her writing, Bainbridge explains:

> As a novelist I am committing to paper, for my own satisfaction, episodes that I have lived through. If I had had a camera forever ready with a film I might not have needed to write. I am not very good at fiction . . . it is always me and the experiences I have had. . . .
>
> I think writing is a very indulgent pastime and I would probably do it even if nobody ever read anything.
>
> I write about the sort of childhood I had, my parents, the landscape I grew up in: my writing is an attempt to record the past.[8]

In this mimetic sense, Bainbridge's fiction may be seen as a traditional and straightforward form of novel writing. And in comparison with the notable influx of avant-garde writing in the same period, which demonstrates the impossibility of recording 'lived experience' adequately, it may seem even more so.

Against the background of the emergence of postmodernism in literature as a reaction to and development of both realism and modernism, and in the context of the theoretical challenges to humanist notions of subjectivity, history and language, it is not surprising, therefore, that Beryl Bainbridge's fiction might be considered academically peripheral. It does not draw attention to itself as an artefact with frame-breaks, exposure of fictional conventions or comments on the writing process; it does not openly parody other texts; it does not flaunt the instability of language by playful practice; subjective consciousness is not demonstrably at stake, and there are no challenging typographical experiments or strikingly innovatory features. It is, in other words, not an example of the self-reflexive fiction that covertly or overtly demonstrates the linguistic and ideological foundation and fictive status of any representation.

However, it is my contention that, simultaneously with their apparent mimetic simplicity and their allegiance to the referentiality of language, her novels display gestures and properties in their modes of construction, presentation and representation that not only produce a recognizable style or characteristic formula, but also emphasize the transforming potential of narrative fiction. In addition, they can also, to some extent, be read as sharing the post-modern characteristic function of increasing reader awareness of reality as a social construct. In other words, although the novels simply seem to mimetically reflect reality as dramatized expressions of the author's personal outlook and experiences, thus inviting a literal reading in terms of verisimilitude, their gestures and properties work to transform the material in such a way that the biographical context of the author and the horizon of literal reference become of subordinated interest.

These concerns are superseded by a consciousness-raising effect that provokes the reader to reflect on the function of construction, narration and interpretation in fiction and in life. Instead of simply serving as the mirrors of reality before which the reader may test whether or not these reflect or correspond to his/her own views and experiences, her novels lead the reader to examine his/her own modes of 'constructing', 'narrating' and 'interpreting' life. Compared with the more demonstrably provocative contemporary writings, Bainbridge's novels achieve a similar effect. But it is achieved by a different route and with a different implication. The Bainbridge provocation serves to recentre rather than decentre the contradictory humanist notion that both asserts the autonomy of the individual and relates the individual to the "social whole" in terms of a "universalized human nature."[9] This recentring takes the form of asserting the inviolable autonomy of individuality but also its inevitable dependence on the social whole for its development and fulfilment.

The consciousness-raising quality of her writing and its humanistically normative stance have largely been overlooked in the critical reception, which instead focuses on characteristic features of style and content, and the moral or immoral quality of her novels. While the features of style have generally attracted appreciative comments, the evaluation of the novels in terms of moral significance has varied. Indeed, the latter aspect proved an initial stumbling-block in her writing career. Beryl Bainbridge's first novel *Harriet Said* (written in 1958; first published in 1972) was, for instance, rejected on moral grounds by several publishers, one of whom commented that the characters were "repulsive beyond belief" and that one scene in the book was "too indecent even for these lax days."[10] The manuscript was then misplaced by a publisher and only resurfaced after *A Weekend with Claud* and *Another Part of the Wood,* which were written in a different style from *Harriet Said,* had been published without attracting much attention. The rediscovered manuscript was shown to the Haycrafts at Duckworth, where Beryl Bainbridge at the time was employed. They immediately recognized her talent, and not only published the novel,

but encouraged her to abandon the rambling and elaborate style of the two previous novels in favour of the tauter and simpler style of *Harriet Said.* The publication of *Harriet Said* (1972) was therefore the beginning of "a series of original and idiosyncratic works,"[11] which has been called the Duckworth Bainbridge line: *Harriet Said* (1972), *The Dressmaker* (1973), *The Bottle Factory Outing* (1974), *Sweet William* (1975), *A Quiet Life* (1976), *Injury Time* (1977), *Young Adolf* (1978), *Winter Garden* (1980), *Watson's Apology* (1984), *An Awfully Big Adventure* (1989), *The Birthday Boys* (1991),[12] and the rewritten versions of *Another Part of the Wood* (1979) and *Weekend with Claude* (1981).

Although described as a "family of gifted eccentrics"[13] and no longer dismissed on moral grounds, this body of texts somehow defies description and understanding beyond the similarities in content and in the style which was heralded in *Harriet Said.* Gloria Valverde's comparative study of the original and the rewritten versions of the first published novels shows that the difference between them is primarily the result of deletions. Cuts were made in narrative descriptions, explanations, critical commentary, and in analysis of and delving into character action and behaviour. Also numerous didactic passages were omitted. As a consequence of these alterations, the revised editions constitute a reversion to what Valverde defines as Bainbridge's original and personal style, which is now generally seen by critics as characteristic of her production, that is, "that of being objective and detached," and with an ability to "select details and discard peripheral material." These features also make "the wry humour, an important element of her style, more pronounced."[14] Although she does not analyse its implications, Valverde also recognizes that, despite the deletion of the many didactic passages in the original versions, there is still a moralizing tendency although "it is more subtle."[15]

The combination of the laconic, detached style and the pervading bleakness of the world depicted tends to obscure the reader's recognition of the consciousness-raising quality as well as the kind of moral aspect that Valverde discerns. Valentina Yakovleva, for instance, declares her growing discontentment with Bainbridge's works:

> The more I read Bainbridge novels the more disappointed I grew in her attitude to the surrounding reality and in her choice of characters. She deliberately strives to remain 'outside the story', an impartial observer. Yet the personality of the author cannot be hidden—the very striving after complete objectivity, the abstaining from judgements, from taking sides, from any commitment is in itself a 'position', a revelation of the writer's world outlook and of her moral principles.[16]

In contrast to Valverde, Yakovleva sees the detached style and the depiction of the world as signs of lack of morality. These positions are partly balanced by Krystyna Stamirowska who draws attention to the "complex responses that Beryl Bainbridge's fiction generates" in the way it elicits the reader's sympathy for the situation of the characters despite their unpleasantness and the detached narration.[17] "Complex responses" do, in fact, characterize the reviews on Bainbridge's novels, and this *per se* suggests a degree of ambiguity and subtlety in her works.[18]

Thus, the characteristic features that Yakovleva sees as examples of an apparent lack of commitment, Valverde sees as implying a subtle moralizing quality, and Stamirowska as forming a deterministic framework that evokes sympathy. David Punter, however, recognizes the consciousness-raising quality as he convincingly shows in his Lacanian approach that the characteristic features are the result of unconscious structures of signification that speak of gender differentiation, deprivation of love, and continual defeat of expectation and knowledge. The effect of this, he concludes, is that

> this fiction which apparently makes little concession to the modernist habit of self-consciousness produces a highly self-conscious reader: because we are made increasingly aware that, in gazing at the squirmings of these Others, we too are looking only at parts of ourselves, that all these enactments are ones in which we too have shared or will share, objective correlatives for the dilemma of maturation.[19]

What Bainbridge's critics in their various focuses—on text as expression of the author, on text as linguistic style, on text as narrative display, and on text as structures of signification—have failed to emphasize is that the intriguing effect of Bainbridge's fiction is *the tension between the firm allegiance to realism and the implicit challenge of the premises that underpin it.* In the context of this tension, it is useful to remember, as Elizabeth Deeds Ermarth reminds us, that realistic fiction does not necessarily suggest a naive acceptance of referentiality, but that both "referential and reflexive functions [are] at work in realism."[20] In other words, realistic fiction, in the descriptive sense of the term, as a mode of writing that through its conventions creates the illusion of 'truthful' imitation of commonsensical reality, like other modes of writing, also serves to contribute to our understanding of how the world is constituted by its texts and by conventions. Consequently, the realistic illusion in Bainbridge's novels not only displays the myth of realism as the objective representation of reality in their artistic transformation of 'lived experience', but it also emphasizes the functions of myth as both illusory conception and as narrated interpretation of life. In doing this, the novels achieve the twin effect of increasing awareness of the formative function of conceptualizing reality, and reasserting the reality of the mundane and the sublime.

Notes

1. For instance, Valentina Yakovleva, "On Reading Beryl Bainbridge: A Voice from the Public," *Soviet Literature* 11. 440 (1984): 141-149; Karl Miller, "A Novelist Worth Knowing," *New York Review of Books* 16 May 1974: 25-28; Krystyna Stamirowska, "The Bustle and the Crudity of Life: The Novels of Beryl Bainbridge," *Kwartalnik Neofilologiczny* 35. 4 (1988): 445-456.

2. David Punter, *The Hidden Script: Writing and the Unconscious* (London: Routledge & Kegan Paul,

1985). This study deals with J. G. Ballard, Angela Carter, Doris Lessing, Kurt Vonnegut and Beryl Bainbridge. Although Punter sees Bainbridge as set apart from this group through her naturalistic mode and contemporary settings, he argues that her novels contain similar materials of deprivation and entrapment.

3. Gloria Valverde, "A Textual Study of Beryl Bainbridge's *Another Part of the Wood* and *A Weekend with Claude,*" 2 vols., diss., Texas Tech U, 1985.

4. See, for instance Lorna Sage, "Female Fictions: The Women Novelists," *The Contemporary English Novel,* ed. Malcolm Bradbury and David Palmer, Stratford-upon-Avon Studies 18 (London: Arnold, 1979) 85; Robert Barnard, *A Short History of English Literature* (Oxford: Blackwell, 1984) 206; Mary Cadogan and Patricia Craig, *Women and Children First: The Fiction of Two World Wars* (London: Gollancz, 1978) 279-281.

5. Inger Hullberg, rev. of *Sweet William,* by Beryl Bainbridge, *Nerikes Allehanda* 7 Sep. 1983: 4 (my translation). As the Bibliography and other references to reviews will show, page references will not always be given. The reason for this is that the major part of my review material is copies made from various clipping files and this information was not always available.

6. In *A Theory of Literary Production,* trans. Geoffrey Wall (London: Routledge & Kegan Paul, 1978) 3-4, Pierre Macherey divides "criticism-as-explanation" into the two categories of "criticism as appreciation (the education of taste) and criticism as knowledge (the 'science of literary production')." This thesis attempts to apply the latter focus by asking how Bainbridge's fiction works in terms of its formative principles rather than in terms of success and failure.

7. Ronald Sukenick, "The Death of the Novel," *The Death of the Novel and Other Stories* (New York: Dial, 1969) 41.

8. As quoted by Val Warner in *Contemporary Novelists,* ed. James Vinson and D. L. Kirkpatrick (London: St. Martin's 1976) 79-80.

9. Linda Hutcheon, *The Politics of Postmodernism,* New Accents Series (1989; London: Methuen, 1990) 13. For further accounts of the poetics and politics of postmodern fiction, see, for instance, Linda Hutcheon, *A Poetics of Postmodernism: History, Theory, Fiction* (New York: Routledge, 1988); Patricia Waugh, *Metafiction: The Theory and Practice of Self-Conscious Fiction.* New Accents Series (London: Methuen, 1984); Postmodern Fiction: A Bio-Bibliographical Guide, ed. Larry McCaffery, Movements in the Arts 2 (New York: Greenwood, 1986), and Brian McHale, *Postmodernist Fiction* (New York: Methuen, 1987).

10. As quoted in *World Authors 1970-1975,* ed. John Wakeman, The Wilson Authors Series (New York: Wilson, 1980) 49.

11. *The Oxford Companion to English Literature,* ed. Margaret Drabble, (London: Guild, 1987) 60.

12. This thesis will not include a consideration of *The Birthday Boys,* not because it deviates from the claims I make about Bainbridge's fiction, but because it appeared too late for inclusion.

13. Diane Johnson, rev. of *Young Adolf,* by Beryl Bainbridge, *Times Literary Supplement* 1 Dec. 1978: 1385.

14. Valverde 91, 183-184.

15. Valverde 93.

16. Yakovleva 143.

17. Stamirowska 456.

18. Reviewers frequently comment on the mixed feelings that reading Bainbridge occasions and characterize her novels in oppositional terms: they are described as neither wholly comic, nor wholly tragic; they are both real and surreal, macabre and authentic, simple and complex, subversive and cheering, entertaining and instructive, convincing and unimaginable, comic and sinister, witty and depressing, funny and appalling, farcical and menacing, very odd and totally relevant, thought-provoking and unnerving, grotesque and pitiful.

19. Punter 77.

20. Elizabeth Deeds Ermarth, *Realism and Consensus in the English Novel*

   (Princeton: Princeton UP, 1983) xiii. A similar point is made by David Lodge in "The Novel Now: Theories and Practices," *Novel: A Forum on Fiction* 21. 2-3 (1988): 133, where he suggests that "it would be false to oppose metafiction to realism; rather, metafiction makes explicit the implicit problematic of realism."

Dennis Drabelle (review date 10 April 1994)

SOURCE: "In a Cold Climate," in *Washington Post Book World,* April 10, 1994, p. 7.

[*In the following review, Drabelle offers favorable assessment of* The Birthday Boys.]

Fifteen years ago an iconoclast struck what may be the most telling blow to an English reputation since Lytton Strachey took aim at his *Eminent Victorians.* The aggressor was journalist Roland Huntford. The target was Robert Falcon Scott, Scott of the Antarctic, the very incarnation of English heroism in a lost cause, whose last written words—scribbled feebly in 1912 as he and his two surviving comrades lay tentbound and starving after coming in second to the South Pole expedition led by the Norwegian Roald Amundsen—included this self-serving tribute: "I do not think human beings ever came through such a month as we have come through."

In his book *Scott and Amundsen,* Huntford demonstrated that the inept Scott had only himself to blame. In contrast to Amundsen, who through years of study and preparation

had made himself a professional Polesman, Scott had learned little from his own previous Antarctic experiences and nothing from anyone else's. The methodically prepared Amundsen met with comparably harsh conditions on his trek but actually gained weight while coping with them. Afterwards he could boast on behalf of his team, "We haven't got much to tell in the way of privation or great struggle. The whole thing went like a dream." Scott's legend, Huntford argued, owed much to the British love of "heroic disaster," especially when committed by dash-it-all amateurs.

The paradox is that, even after being thoroughly debunked, the Scott expedition still holds up as an engrossing story—at least as told by Englishwoman Beryl Bainbridge. Examining the historical record with a fiction-writer's eye (she is also the author of *The Bottle Factory Outing, Young Adolf, An Awfully Big Adventure* and other novels), she credits Scott with a virtue that Huntford overlooked: empathy for his men. "One could see in his eyes . . . that his heart was too big for his boots. God knows how, but he's managed to surmount his naval training and retain his essential humanity." Bainbridge gives these lines to Titus Oates, whose grudging praise gains credibility from his being Scott's chief detractor among his four subordinates on the Polar trek.

Otherwise, her Scott looks very like Huntford's: whiny, "nervy," bull-headed, short on self-confidence, intent on attributing his own errors to poor performance by colleagues or plain bad luck—altogether a captivating fool. Here he is, taking his turn as one of the novel's five first-person narrators, weaving a series of miscues into a farrago of destiny: "Everything fitted into place—the decline of the ponies, the death of Wearie Willie [the weakest of those ponies], the calamitous fall of the dogs into the crevasse. Let those who believe in random happenings, Caesar among them, carry on believing the fault lies in ourselves; nobody will ever convince me that the stars don't play a part in it."

The counterpoint to this sense of impending doom is the fey optimism of "Birdie" Bowers, the expedition's navigator. One night (or was it day?—and who's to say which is which during the austral winter?) the moon comes out from behind clouds, lighting up "a gigantic crevasse lidded with a shiny covering of thin ice."

"At the time," Bowers recalls, "we were running downhill, the sledges at our heels and, but for that sudden pale illumination, we would most certainly have perished. I understood then that providence was on our side; it was unthinkable to believe God would save us simply to prolong the agony." It turned out, though, that providence was indeed a sadist.

In case you're still scratching your head about those ponies, there was a precedent for importing them as Antarctic beasts of burden. Ernest Shackleton, Scott's chief British polar rival, had done so. But what Scott didn't bother to find out was how and why they had failed Shackleton. For Scott, they performed much as any schoolchild might predict, breaking through soft snow and sinking up to their rumps. Some died; the others had to be put down. Similarly, he brought motor cars south for transport without properly testing them; they seized up in the cold almost immediately. He and his men were reduced to serving as their own draft animals, hauling sledges loaded with food and fuel and gear. Amundsen and some of his men skied alongside while dogs pulled their sledges.

Bainbridge is known for mixing comedy and dread. We get a glimpse of Scott's wife, Kathleen, accidentally squirting him while eating grapefruit at a testimonial breakfast before departure. Then, as the expedition blunders toward catastrophe, the humor takes on a gallows tinge: One man's dream of a tap-dancer performing onstage gives way to the real-life sound of his tentmate's teeth chattering. There is nothing funny, however, about the novel's climactic scene: the crew's discovery, near the Pole, of a flag in their path—crushing proof that Amundsen has beaten them.

Frequently the narrators pause to evoke their sensations en route. Bowers again: "We ran into a series of blizzards of such icy ferocity that our minds threatened to become as numbed as our bodies. We were almost worse off in the tent than out of it, for our breath and the steam from the cooker deposited a rim of boar frost on the inner lining which, if we left the cooker burning long enough, gradually melted and dropped mercilessly down upon us. Our sleeping bags were daily turned into frozen boards, and in trying to prise them open one had to be careful lest the leather [break] like glass."

The Birthday Boys (the title comes from the trekkers' placement of inordinate value on birthday celebrations so far from home) is something of a departure for the author, whose novels typically depict half-baked characters in prosaic settings—e.g., the young Hitler repeatedly spooking himself on his 1912 visit to his emigre-brother in Liverpool. Here, rather commonplace characters (perhaps too much so for their own good) flail about in a milieu whose peculiarity knows no bounds. Either way, the author provides her customary sculpted prose, throwaway dark jokes and keen-eyed scrutiny of human flaws. If not all of Beryl Bainbridge's previous novels have traveled well beyond England, perhaps the lasting appeal of the Scott saga will bring her the wide readership she deserves.

Gary Krist (review date 17 April 1994)

SOURCE: "Antarctic Antics," in *New York Times Book Review,* April 17, 1994, p. 15.

[*In the following review, Krist offers favorable assessment of* The Birthday Boys.]

"All Englishmen are virtuous," wrote George Orwell in his novel *Burmese Days*—"when they are dead." And certainly death does seem to have a remarkable effect on the moral character, regardless of the corpse's nationality. No sooner is a body cold in the ground than the eulogies begin, obscuring the psychological complexities of the living person beneath a layer of sonorous pieties. This kind of posthumous revisionism is especially pronounced in the case of soldiers, politicians, explorers and others who have fallen in service to God and country in remote latitudes. Whatever these people may have been in life, in death they are transformed.

It is, I feel, partly to debunk such sentimentalized views of the figures of our past that some writers are drawn to the historical novel. And few have risen to the task more ingeniously than Beryl Bainbridge in her extraordinary new novel, *The Birthday Boys.* Ms. Bainbridge, the British writer responsible for such refreshingly eccentric books as *The Bottle Factory Outing* and *An Awfully Big Adventure,* takes as her subject Robert Falcon Scott, a dead Englishman, but one whose most famous act in the service of his country is naggingly difficult to sanctify.

Scott, of course, was the British naval officer and explorer who led two celebrated expeditions to Antarctica in the early decades of this century. The second culminated in an all-out race to the South Pole, with Scott's team reaching the objective in January 1912, only to find that Roald Amundsen, a Norwegian, had already come and gone a month earlier. Disheartened, Scott and his four companions planted a Union Jack on the spot, photographed themselves around it and then headed back home. On the way, pummeled by blizzards and debilitated by dwindling supplies, they all died—gradually, agonizingly and (some would say) futilely.

The rehabilitation of this tragic fiasco has presented a challenge for the official spin doctors. Most early accounts seemed to find little ambiguity in the heroism and worth of Scott's achievement. But later historians sensed troubling dissonances: hints that the tragedy may have been attributable more to Scott's organizational weaknesses than to unusual weather; suspicions that Scott's resolve may have been diluted by uncertainty and petty jealousies; suggestions that the whole idea of dashing to the Pole was a folly to begin with. The debate has been colored by the fact that the only detailed, firsthand source of information about the group's final days is Scott himself, through his diaries and letters, which contain a few too many self-justifications and *pro forma* paeans to the courage of his fellow English gentlemen to be entirely reliable. Interestingly enough, the diary of Capt. Lawrence Edward (Titus) Oates, Scott's colleague and principal critic on the march, was never published, destroyed, by order of his mother, after her death.

And that's where Ms. Bainbridge comes in. Bringing her subversive and ever-mischievous imagination to bear on the subject, she fills in the details neglected by Scott's diary, deepening the portrait of stiff-upper-lip heroism by adding the sometimes ugly shadows that suggest real life.

She accomplishes this by creating a separate monologue for each of the five men who died on the return from the Pole—Petty Officer Edgar (Taff) Evans, Dr. Edward (Uncle Bill) Wilson, Lieut. Henry Robertson (Birdie) Bowers, Titus Oates and Scott himself, who comes off here as the complex man he must really have been: insecure yet determined; insightful but often unfairly critical; strong in his leadership but all too ready to blame others and poor luck for his own mistakes.

These five monologues, which contain some of the most convincing and slyly revealing first-person narrative I've ever read, span a remarkable range of voices and dispositions, but what they share is a mesmerizing readability. Taken in tandem, they relate a story far more interesting than that of five virtuous Englishmen rising nobly to the occasion in extreme circumstances; instead, they present us with a microcosmic society of flawed individuals, pushed and pulled even in a frozen wilderness by the subtle dictates of class, personality and ambition.

Hovering above these five distinctive sensibilities, moreover, is a sixth—that of Kathleen Scott, the explorer's irreverent, unconventional wife, whom we see only through the prism of the other narratives. Kathleen, I feel, is Ms. Bainbridge's own representative in the novel, gazing down on the entire polar endeavor with a mixture of emotions—a compassionate respect for the obvious courage of these men, on the one hand, but also a critical, somewhat ironic detachment, the judging eye of one whose penetrating intelligence cannot be switched off, even by the sentimental requirements of familial or patriotic duty.

There is, in fact, an amused, almost maternal indulgence in Ms. Bainbridge's stance toward these "birthday boys," who seem noticeably, even abnormally, preoccupied with horseplay, their mothers and their birthday celebrations. The author seems to regard their embarrassed need to be the center of attention on their own special days as not entirely unrelated to their motives in being first to reach the South Pole. "Is it nothing more than a game?" one expedition member asks while preparing a foray into the Antarctic wasteland. This is a question that hangs suggestively over the entire book. Ms. Bainbridge is too subtle a writer to engage in blatant polemics, but her novel does imply a critique of something more than just the so-called "Heroic Age of Polar Exploration." It seems to pass judgment on the whole ethos of action, conquest and empire upon which so much of European history has been based.

Of course, I may be reading too much into the book, and fortunately it succeeds on many levels besides the political, most notably the visceral level of the adventure story. Much of the action is related with a brutal directness that can set the bones to aching in sympathy: "On the 12th day the temperature registered -69 degrees. Cherry crawled out of the tent and turned his head to the right, and instantly his balaclava froze to his windjacket. For four hours he had to pull with his head stuck in that position." When reading of such exertions, my amazement that a person

could endure such hardship was exceeded only by my astonishment that anyone would actually *choose* to do so.

But there is another endurance tale associated with *The Birthday Boys*—that of the book's prepublication history in this country. First released in Britain in 1991, the novel apparently did not please Ms. Bainbridge's previous American publishers and did not readily find another home. The reason for the delay is perhaps understandable. Ms. Bainbridge's exhilarating refusal to produce a homogeneous, easy-to-categorize body of work has prevented her from achieving a wide audience on this side of the Atlantic, and the sheer unexpectedness of this brilliant novel might prove even more confusing to potential readers. Certainly the editors at Carroll & Graf deserve credit for taking a chance on it. But the fact that a work of this caliber should have any trouble at all reaching readers is disheartening, another ominous sign that American publishing may be entering a long, cold, Antarctic winter of its own.

Michael D. Schaffer (review date 9 June 1994)

SOURCE: "Sculpture of Courage," in *Chicago Tribune*, June 9, 1994, p. 5.

[*In the following review, Schaffer offers positive assessment of* The Birthday Boys.]

Nothing punishes like the cold. If you doubt this, remember how miserable you felt just a few months ago when winter seemed endless.

Not surprisingly, some modern fiction writers have found that they can map the terrain of the human soul more accurately at horribly low temperatures, when body and mind move in slow motion.

English author Beryl Bainbridge does this skillfully in *The Birthday Boys,* a fictional account of Robert Falcon Scott's disastrous expedition to the South Pole in 1912.

Scott and each of the four men who will die with him tell part of the story of their doomed project. Despite differences of personality and background, they share the naive bravery of overgrown boys on a great adventure-boyish enough to remember their birthdays even under the most desperate conditions. Hence, *The Birthday Boys.*

Imbued with all the robust self-confidence of pre-World War I England, they are men who live by a code of sportsmanship. Winning is not the most important thing; honor is. And they would politely brush aside a helping hand, certain that success counts only if achieved under the most formidable odds.

"The world is changing, and soon the machine will be of more importance than the body," observes the most boyish of the birthday boys, Lt. Henry Robertson "Birdie" Bowers. He marvels that "it's tremendous luck to have been born into the last few seconds of an epoch in which a man is still required to stand up and be counted."

Bainbridge explores friendship, loyalty, leadership, class differences and the love that grows from sharing hardships.

She uses Petty Officer Edgar "Taff" Evans, a blustering drinker and spinner of tales, to tell us what real cold is all about:

"To be cold is when . . . the mercury freezes in the thermometer. Petrol won't burn . . . and even an Eskimo dog can't work, because its lungs will stop functioning," Evans says, recalling an earlier trip to Antarctica.

To survive under those conditions, the members of the expedition must rely on the leadership of Scott. And Scott, though brave and conscientious, is unequal to the task.

Scott's worst decision is to disregard the conventional wisdom on Antarctic travel and use ponies rather than sled dogs to haul the expedition's supplies. The dogs—snarling, vicious and always ready to fight—offend Scott's sense of propriety. The ponies flounder in the deep snow and their failure cripples the expedition.

Whatever his deficiencies as a leader, Scott is a relentless competitor. "For Scott, there was no such word as impossible, or if there was, it was listed in a dictionary for fools," observes another member of the expedition, the stiff-necked Capt. Lawrence Edward "Titus" Oates.

When the English explorers arrive at the South Pole, they find that the Norwegian Roald Amundsen has beaten them by about a month.

"We took a photograph of ourselves," Oates tells us. "I don't think any of us had the heart to smile. Then we started for home."

Bainbridge creates images that are startling, beautiful, haunting. Evans, who has fallen into a crevasse and is dangling by the traces of the sledge he has been pulling, tells us: "I was scared for my life, but at the same time I couldn't help noticing how bright everything was, the ice not really blue at all but shot through with spangled points of rosy light so dazzling that it made me crinkle up my eyes as though I had something to smile about."

While the principal characters are skillfully drawn, Bainbridge doesn't quite pull off the five different voices. Each narrator sounds like the same person affecting five different accents.

But that's a small flaw, and it doesn't detract from Bainbridge's accomplishment. She has created an elegant ice sculpture of courage, loyalty and brotherly love.

Amy Gamerman (review date 13 July 1994)

SOURCE: "A Writer's Dreams of Darkest Antarctica," in *Wall Street Journal*, July 13, 1994, p. A12.

[*In the following review, Gamerman offers praise for* The Birthday Boys.]

The Antarctica of Beryl Bainbridge's novel ***The Birthday Boys*** is a land of "ice not really blue at all but shot through with spangled points of rosy light," a land of cold so intense it can shatter a man's teeth into crumbs.

In fact, Ms. Bainbridge's novel about Robert Falcon Scott's doomed 1910 expedition to the South Pole is so convincingly icy, you might think she packed her parka and went there herself. But she confined her polar explorations to London.

"I did think of spending one night in Regent's Park, but I never got around to it," the 59-year-old British novelist confides in her low, scratchy voice on a recent visit here. "I don't like the cold."

So she just imagined it. ***The Birthday Boys*** weaves fiction around the facts of Scott's expedition, doomed almost from the start: The motorized sledges Scott lugged to Antarctica broke down, his ponies collapsed, and he didn't bring enough dogs. Scott and his four-man party did make it to the South Pole—only to freeze to death after discovering that they had been beaten there by the Norwegian explorer Roald Amundsen.

Drawing on her reading of their letters and journals, Ms. Bainbridge delves into the minds of those five men: from Scott, a driven and emotional leader who writes off his blunders as bad luck, to the heroically chipper Birdie Bowers, who risks death for a ludicrous mission to collect penguin eggs, because "there was something splendid, sublime even, in pitting oneself against the odds." In the process, she captures the doomed idealism of a British empire on the verge of dissolution, whistling in the dark of an antarctic blizzard.

It's one of Ms. Bainbridge's best novels yet. Curiously, ***The Birthday Boys*** is also the one that has taken her farthest from her factual and fictional home turf: Liverpool, where many of her 13 novels are set. She was born there in 1934, the daughter of a traveling salesman and his slightly better-born wife. Her early childhood was shaped by World War II and the hail of bombs that fell on Liverpool.

"One went into shelters every night," recalls Ms. Bainbridge, a birdlike woman in a brown suit who smokes cigarette after cigarette from her mother's old monogrammed case. "Then I got double pneumonia and my parents put me under the dining-room table instead."

The blitz from above was echoed in the turmoil in the Bainbridge house. Her father went bankrupt, a secret so shameful it was kept from young Beryl and her brother. That secret poisoned an already turbulent family life. Her parents "loathed each other," she says. Her father alternated between explosive fits of rage and periods of moody withdrawal. (After one blowup, 15-year-old Beryl tried to rent rooms for her mother and herself at a local hotel—not knowing it doubled as the local brothel.) It was to make sense of her home life that she began writing at the age of eight or nine.

"I had a huge book on the travels of Dr. Livingston and Stanley in the jungle, beautifully cut like a huge old Bible," she remembers. "I used to get an exercise page from my schoolbooks and make paste from flour and water and stick that over the marvelous prints, and write about my mother and father. The only thing is that in time the flour and water swelled, so the book wouldn't close. There was no privacy in that house, and I was terrified of them ever seeing it. So I burnt it."

From then on, she only wrote "sub-*Treasure Island* and Dickens." Such literary aspirations notwithstanding, she was expelled from her upscale grammar school at the age of 14 for illustrating a naughty rhyme by one of her classmates. "Since I was quite good at showing off," her parents sent her to ballet school instead.

She had proven her talent at showing off by the age of 11, when in answer to a newspaper ad she began acting in BBC radio plays. But after nine months at the ballet school, Ms. Bainbridge left—never to return to school of any kind again. Instead, at 15 she got a job at a local playhouse as stage manager, bit player and general dogsbody: an experience she drew on for her 1989 novel, *An Awfully Big Adventure.* Her acting career continued until her first marriage, and included small parts in a few London productions and in the popular British TV series *Coronation Street.*

Although Ms. Bainbridge had written a few children's stories for radio, her writing career didn't begin in earnest until her marriage ended (she has three children). She moved to London and has remained there ever since. But the novels she began to write were all set in Liverpool of her youth, their characters figures from her past. In some cases, she didn't even bother to change the names: Nellie and Margo, the eccentric aunts of her 1973 novel, *The Dressmaker* (published here as *The Secret Glass*)—a darkly funny story about a young girl's ill-fated crush on an American soldier—are based on her own very real aunts.

"The first six or seven books were based on my childhood," she says. "After a while, I used it all up and had to go elsewhere."

But "elsewhere" often took her back to her own doorstep. Ms. Bainbridge's 1978 novel, *Young Adolf,* is based on Hitler's actual stay of several months in Liverpool with his half-brother in 1912. "Adolf was my father," she declares. Both men were born in 1889, and for a brief time lived in the same city. Young Hitler—like her father—"had no friends, no money and no future." Her 1984 novel, *Watson's Apology,* was inspired by the story of a real-life Victorian schoolteacher who bludgeoned his wife to death. Ms. Bainbridge drew on Watson's actual letters, but the character she created "was half my dad and half Dr. Johnson"—the curmudgeonly 18th-century literary critic.

Like those novels, *The Birthday Boys* is closer to home than one might think. Asked how she went about creating the British navy Capt. Scott, the writer answers: "I tried to imagine my father as upper class and naval."

She also hung expedition members' photographs on her study walls, and even did paintings of them. Chance phrases gleaned from their letters and diaries helped bring them to life, such as the comment by one party member that "Scott was a dreadful man for blubbing" (Britspeak for crying).

"You act them in your head," she says. "I mean, I'd walk around going, 'Put up the mainsail,' that sort of thing."

Those men are still in her mind. Even now, she is haunted by the thought of them, lying in the shroud of their collapsed tent somewhere beneath the snow in that land of luminous ice.

"They're still there . . . perfectly preserved. They're on an ice shelf that moves terribly slowly. They won't tip into the sea for a long while yet," she murmurs. "They're the lost boys."

Judith Freeman (review date 7 August 1994)

SOURCE: "Polar Adventure," in *Los Angeles Times Book Review,* August 7, 1994, pp. 10, 15.

[*In the following review, Freeman offers favorable assessment of* The Birthday Boys.]

The Birthday Boys, a new novel by the English author Beryl Bainbridge, is an imagined account of Capt. Robert Falcon Scott's expedition to the South Pole in 1912, told in the voices of Scott and four men who followed him to their deaths. In each account a birthday is celebrated, or mentioned—thus the title. It's an ironic touch by a novelist noted for her droll humor. A darker, more tragic story couldn't be masquerading under a more jovial veneer.

I read *The Birthday Boys* in one sitting, in a state of complete absorption, stunned by its beauty, by the depth of its accomplishment, but perhaps most of all by the audacious choice of historical subject matter which Bainbridge has appropriated and so flawlessly rendered into fiction.

The facts of Capt. Scott's adventure are known. His second expedition (the first failed) was mounted shortly after hearing that Shackleton, in 1911, had been forced to turn back only half a dozen marches short of the South Pole. Scott's subsequent race for the prize was thwarted by Amundsen, who set out around the same time and beat him to the pole by a matter of days—some argue because Scott had chosen to experiment with motorized vehicles and the ill-fated ponies for transport rather than relying on the sled dogs Amundsen had favored.

But these are only the facts, and what seems less explored, and the perfect provenance for a novelist, is the deeper story of who these men really were. Each had a mother or a wife, a life he left behind, and these relationships are so subtly and economically evoked they become as much a part of the story as the physical privations that are endured.

It was a brilliant decision to chose to tell this story from five different perspectives, for it allows the complexities and contradictions to emerge. For instance, Petty Officer Taff Evans, a working-class Welshman valued for his brute strength and mechanical prowess, has a dogged devotion to Scott, who treats him with deep respect in spite of their class differences; the upper-crust Capt. Oates, sensing Scott's weakness for making mistakes and shifting the blame to others, mutters behind his back and offers quite a different portrait of their leader.

The actual march to the pole takes up the smallest portion of the story. It's the preparations, the long journey to Antarctica by sea, the months spent acclimating, waiting for the weather to break, Scott's mistrust of dogs, the motors that fail or are lost, that provide the bulk of the drama.

The little recollections of the lives they've left behind weight the story emotionally. Scott misses his wife, whose absence feels like an "amputation." Birdie Bowers, still a virginal young man, swears his mother appears at the edge of a crevasse and weeps frozen tears before the apparition.

To the very end, the men behave with consummate kindness toward each other. They seem to increase in humanity as their chances for survival dwindle. "One just has to believe that it's within one's spiritual domain to conquer difficulties," Scott says. "That is not to say that I don't recognize there has to be a time to submit, possibly a time to die, merely that I've never yet been taken to the brink."

But he is soon taken to the brink, and beyond. Weak and starving, dispirited beyond words at finding Amundsen's tracks at the pole when they arrive, the men turn back, huddle in their tent, their frostbitten flesh red and purple, "shining with that same sort of sweet glaze one sees on rotten meat."

For Scott, who in his ruthlessness of purpose resembled Napoleon, there was no such word as *impossible,* or if there was, as one character says, it was listed in a dictionary for fools. Bravery was a conscious act of discipline. "Is it true that adversity brings out the best in men?" Dr. Wilson is asked at one point. "Yes," is the answer, "good men, that is."

In a sense, Bainbridge has made all five characters "good men," by simply giving them such full and rich human

dimensions. "It's to be regretted that the best of me, the part that recognizes both the horror and beauty of destiny, remains submerged," Scott writes. But it is exactly those submerged parts that Bainbridge excavates.

Scott always claimed that he meant his journey to be as much a scientific expedition as a quest for the pole (he derided Amundsen for being interested only in glory). In one of the most moving sections of **The Birthday Boys,** Lt. Bowers, a scientist, leads a small party to retrieve some emperor penguin eggs and endures a nightmarish ordeal. Later, musing on the horrors of that experience and the affection he feels for his companions, he comments: "It may be that the purpose of the worst journey in the world had been to collect eggs which might prove a scientific theory, but we'd unraveled a far greater mystery on the way—the missing link between God and man is brotherly love."

Alex Clark (review date 6 January 1995)

SOURCE: "Awfully Small Adventures," in *Times Literary Supplement,* January 6, 1995, p. 20.

[*In the following review, Clark offers tempered evaluation of Bainbridge's* Collected Stories.]

Beryl Bainbridge is a prolific and highly accomplished writer, not simply in terms of the volume of her output—she has fourteen novels and five television plays to her credit—but also because of the range of ideas it displays. She seems capable of pressing her distinctive style into the service of the most inspired of plot structures, but is not entirely keen on the short story as a vehicle for her ingenuity. We know this because in a piece in this collection, entitled **"How I Began,"** she reflects on how she embarked, at the age of thirteen, on her novella *Filthy Lucre:* "It seemed to me, even then, that a short story was a waste of a good idea." She remains unconvinced, explaining that this lack of faith lies behind the recycling of many of the stories, restricted here by the format, into television plays or full-length novels. *Filthy Lucre* itself, which was published separately in 1986, forms part of this volume, as if to reassert the author's commitment to the grand scale. It is a Dickensian saga of precocious complexity and extravagance, spanning several generations and peopled by fantastically named characters. The rest of the book consists of a previously published collection of twelve stories, *Mum and Mr Armitage,* and six uncollected stories, four of which have already appeared elsewhere.

The pieces from *Mum and Mr Armitage* are by far the most successful, although they definitely derive something from the cumulative effect of being written for a specific collection. Despite her misgivings, Bainbridge's style, and in particular her talent for deadpan dialogue, survives the constraints of the shortened form and, in some places, even seems to thrive. The quirky situations and casts of eccentrics are enhanced by the elliptical and immediate qualities that further elaboration might destroy. Bainbridge is at her best when giving full rein to her characters, often awkward and lonely people who feel that the plot is getting the better of them.

In the story **"Mum and Mr Armitage,"** a group of regulars at a country hotel await the arrival of the inappropriately nicknamed "Mum" and her shadowy companion with a near-hysterical devotion that prevents them from seeing the reality of their own situations or the true nature of what they admire. Mum is a practical joker driven by spite and an unerring sense of other people's weaknesses; but by the time we find out that she herself has suffered injury and pain, our sympathy is all but spent. This is a neat piece of equivocation that reinforces the sense, present throughout the story, that there is a complicity between victim and oppressor, and that it is closely related to the fictions we employ to protect ourselves from the truth. It is a theme reiterated in **"The Worst Policy,"** a tale of marital infidelity, and **"Through a Glass Brightly,"** the story of a lonely divorcee who dabbles with a crystal ball and consequently learns the dangers of setting oneself up as a truth-teller.

Some of the pieces scarcely seem to be stories at all, but are more like vivid fragments of writing attached to rather slight ideas. It may be true that you can squander a good idea in a short story; it is also true that good short-story writing can be blighted by an ill-conceived or semi-digested idea. This problem is particularly prevalent where Bainbridge mixes the supernatural with her original style of comic realism. **"Beggars Would Ride,"** an amusing exploration of male rivalry and pretension, is somewhat scuppered by the italicized paragraph at the beginning tenuously relating the action to a mysterious happening in 1605. Similarly, the almost identical stories **"Poles Apart"** and **"Kiss Me, Hardy,"** which rely on liars being caught out when their make-believe comes true, start from an interesting premiss but peter out in a welter of brilliantly realized details of little substance. At these times, Bainbridge does appear to be rehearsing for the main act; and although these stories contain good writing, they only occasionally achieve any depth. One feels that she is holding back, and this denies her short stories the resonance that they seem to promise.

Judy Cooke (review date 13 September 1996)

SOURCE: "Before the Deluge," in *New Statesman*, September 13, 1996, p. 46.

[*In the following review, Cooke offers favorable assessment of* Every Man for Himself.]

"Though not vain, I'm aware that my outward appearance raises expectations." Thus 22-year-old Morgan, narrator of Beryl Bainbridge's novel: a gilded youth aspiring to

significance, a romantic, hopeless with girls, a Wooster looking for a Jeeves. His uncle owns the shipping line shortly to launch the miracle of the age, the unsinkable *Titanic*.

On 8 August 1912 Morgan travels to Southampton to join his chums for the maiden voyage. Melchett and Van Hopper complain they wasted three hours waiting for him to turn up at the Café Royal. A baronet's daughter flirts with him. Wallis Ellery, "clever and absolutely unobtainable", begins to obsess him. His range of acquaintances broadens to include Rosenfelder, a Liverpool tailor; a deserted *chanteuse,* Adele, intent on rebuilding her career in the States; the mysterious Scurra, dapper and well-informed; and a host of American and European types, from the aristocrats travelling incognito to a devoted old couple, Mr and Mrs Straus—whose role is reminiscent of Mr and Mrs Smiths' in Greene's *The Comedians,* a novel comparable to Bainbridge's in scope and tone.

Having assembled this varied and doomed cast, the author describes their inner journeys on the road to oblivion. The *Titanic* was afloat only five days before she struck the iceberg; within that tight dramatic framework the novel creates, then subverts Edwardian glamour. The coming war, as much as the immediate tragedy, is a brooding presence.

Right from the start, when a stranger dies in Morgan's arms on a London street, the omens are bad. A fire rages unchecked in the stokehold. The *Titanic*, pushed to beat her estimated arrival time in New York, is going too fast. Why does Scurra, before the catastrophe, insist that "it's every man for himself"?

Morgan is an engaging narrator, increasing in moral stature as the certainties of his life begin to crumble. His parentage has always been in doubt: at last, he learns the nightmarish truth. Scurra, who enlightens him, teaches him about self-interest, never more effectively than when making noisy love to Wallis within earshot of his aroused and anguished young rival. There are no nice gels, and no reliable father figures.

Bainbridge hits a tremendous pace as her story reaches its climax. In a remarkably concise book, shot through with laconic wit, she establishes complex characters who engage first the reader's curiosity, then affection. The elegiac theme extends far beyond the historical event. There are some choice farcical scenes in the swimming pool and on the dance floor. Then shots are heard as resolution dissolves into panic; the orchestra plays hymns on deck and "the water, first slithering, then tumbling", reveals the identities of those who will survive.

Jane Gardam (review date 14 September 1996)

SOURCE: "It Was Sad When That Great Ship Went Down," in *Spectator,* September 14, 1996, p. 35.

[In the following review, Gardam offers positive assessment of Every Man for Himself.*]*

Beryl Bainbridge's first novel in five years is a short, taut piece of historical fiction, an account of the classic tragedy of the sinking in 1912 of the 'unsinkable' *Titanic* on her maiden voyage to America.

Every novel, of course, unless it is pure fable or allegory, is a historical novel. There is no present moment. Describe a current fashion or event—the gold ring in the navel, the heart-disease of Mr Yeltsin—and at once it is in the past. We need the sense of history in fiction, the light catching the provincial tea-service of Maggie Tulliver's aunt, Anna Karenina's black velvet ballgown heavy with lace. When it comes to a story like the *Titanic,* however, researched, physical, homely detail is not only poignant but essential. The vanishing of the *Titanic* was symbol of the end of an age and ghastly omen of what was coming next, when the Great War was to sweep first-class and steerage away again, but this time in larger numbers.

It is quite brave to retell a story so well known. *Titanic* means hubris. It is almost hackneyed, but it will not go away. This summer, nearly a century on, two million pounds have been spent unsuccessfully trying to raise her bones. The story can hold no surprises. There is no surprise even about Bainbridge's hero, Morgan, for being the narrator he must have survived.

Bainbridge places him and his set of bright young things, the hugely wealthy, aimless, idle, American and English glitterati, shadowed by familial madness and dissipation, inside the wonderful structure of the ship. A visit to her engine rooms suggests to them that man is catching up with God. For their last four days on earth they move about the eight towering decks, each 800 feet long, gymnasia, Turkish baths, concert hall, ballrooms, church. The reflection off the mahogany panels in the saloons makes their expensive complexions glow. The corridors are inlaid with mother-of-pearl. The restaurants are indistinguishable from the Ritz. On the upper decks the women are hung with sapphires, in steerage with shawls and crying babies. We know that everything is eggshell-fragile and soon will plunge the two black miles to the bed of the ocean.

When the iceberg strikes it rips the ship's great flank like a surgeon's scalpel and on the lower deck they begin to lark and play with snowballs. Detail gathers, begins to take on significance, great vividness. A long, terrifying chronicle ends with Morgan's noticing, just before the final great wave, the excellent polish on the shoes he has changed into from his evening dancing pumps.

There are some revelations and I'd like to know which are imagined, which researched. I believe her, but how does Bainbridge know that iceberg tastes of rancid fish? Was there really a container in the hold labelled 'Hairnets'? Why does she avoid the folklore we were all brought up

on—such as the Egyptian mummy travelling incognito on account of a curse? The description of the orchestra's playing to the last moment *Nearer My God to Thee* is heart-breaking and wonderful, though she has the players trembling into silence before the end.

And she put me right. I'd always imagined that the *Titanic* sailed from Liverpool and that this accounts for the creepy atmosphere of the Adelphi Hotel to this day, for it was where passengers spent their last night ashore. It seems that the rows of the doomed stood at the rails looking cheerfully back on Hampshire hills, the woods 'nudging the town' and the spire of a church.

But facts, real or imagined, don't make a novel on their own and I'd guess that the spur of this one was the character of Morgan. Who was this bemused, erratic, hard-drinking, lecherous young virgin, heir to great wealth? He has had a dark childhood and believes himself to be cast as an observer of tragedy. Perhaps to cause tragedy. He has an animal awareness of evil and sees it as infectious. On board there is a terrible man called Scurra, a purveyor of poison. Hypnotically attractive, hopeless of the human condition, he spreads the gospel of the impossibility of selfless love. 'Love is a woman's word.' It is every man for himself.

As the crowds gather on deck in their top hats ('useful for baling') and their rags, at first joking, then scuffling, at last screaming and fighting for the inadequate lifeboats, Scurra lies back in the saloon discussing the Peloponnesian War with a drunk. Morgan, fascinated to the end, can't help sending him a signal as he is swilled away, 'a fluttering of the fingers as if we were both guests at a social function'.

The novel is overloaded somewhat by Morgan's melodramatic personal history. It lists a bit. But it asks good questions. Can personality affect the physical world? What is fate? Are there people who can engender disaster? And beyond the immediate subject Bainbridge spreads a sense of the darkness outside the ring of temporal light. The ineffectual stars. The last part of the book, and particularly the last scene where dawn comes up over an ocean 'dotted with islands and fields of ice . . . a pale fleet on which the little life-boats rocked', is superb.

John Updike (review date 14 October 1996)

SOURCE: "It Was Sad," in *New Yorker,* October 14, 1996, pp. 94-98.

[In the following excerpted review, Updike discusses the Titanic *disaster and Bainbridge's fictional recreation of the tragedy in* Every Man for Himself.*]*

The R.M.S. (Royal Mail Steamer) *Titanic*, whose sinking, more than eighty-four years ago, made the biggest news splash of the new century, still generates headlines. The discovery of the wreck, in 1985, three hundred and seventy miles southeast of Newfoundland and two and a half miles below the surface of the Atlantic, by a team of scientists from the Woods Hole Oceanographic Institution and the Institut Français de Recherche pour l'Exploitation de la Mer, revivified a fascination that had never quite died. Though the leader of the expedition, Robert Ballard, denounced salvage of the wreck, and placed a plaque on the *Titanic*'s stern declaring it "a sacred resting place," his French partners in *l'exploitation de la mer* did not share his qualms. More submersible vessels rather than fewer will likely visit the watery grave and bring sacred relics to the surface. Lumps of coal from the *Titanic*'s bins can be bought for twenty-five dollars each, and nine bottles of Bass Ale (of twelve thousand on board) have been recovered, along with plates, chamber pots, toilet articles, a camera, a gilded chandelier, and a wallet stuffed with money and receipts. The debris is scattered over a square mile; the ship lies in two big pieces, the stern badly damaged but the bow still grand. Touted as "unsinkable," the *Titanic* at its launching became the largest movable object ever made by man—eight hundred and eighty-two feet (nearly three football fields) in length, forty-six thousand tons in weight. Her rudder weighed a hundred and one tons, and her hull contained three million rivets. This August, an eleven-ton, twenty-by-twenty-four-foot section of the hull slipped away from the diesel-fuel-filled lifting balloons, giving rise to another headline. A more modest retrieval, a small piece of inch-thick hull steel holding three rivet holes, led to a scientific test in Canada demonstrating that the *Titanic* steel was sulfur-rich and brittle; modern steel might simply have bent upon contact with the iceberg. So our sense of the *Titanic* undergoes yet another modification: it was made of bad steel. . . .

The cries are heard, though, by the twenty-two-year-old hero of Beryl Bainbridge's new novel, ***Every Man for Himself,*** when he surfaces out of the undertow of the plunging ship:

> I had thought I was entering paradise, for I was alive and about to breathe again, and then I heard the cries of souls in torment and believed myself in hell. Dear God! Those voices! *Father . . . Father . . . For the love of Christ . . . Help me, for pity's sake! . . . Where is my son.* Some called for their mothers, some on the Lord, some to die quickly, a few to be saved. The lamentations rang through the frosty air and touched the stars; my own mouth opened in a silent howl of grief. The cries went on and on, trembling, lingering— and God forgive me, but I wanted them to end.

Bainbridge is attracted to disasters and male perspectives; her previous novel, ***The Birthday Boys,*** brilliantly renders the Scott expedition to the South Pole, another casualty of 1912, in the voices of the five participants who perished. She boils British heroism down to a boyish camaraderie that makes light of hideous hardships. In ***Every Man for Himself*** Bainbridge writes with a kind of betranced confidence, seeming to lose all track of her story only to pop awake for a stunning image or an intense exchange; as postmodern a fictionist as [Steven] Biel is a historian, she only intermittently gives us the *ding an sich*. Her sud-

den details make a surreal effect. The hero, Morgan (called nothing else, as if in blunt token of his condition as an adopted son of his uncle J. P. Morgan, the owner of the *Titanic*'s White Star Line), remembers from his childhood a housemaid interrupting her scrubbing to comfort him: "A bubble of soap burst in her hair as she took me on her knee." When a friend on the *Titanic* displays a fragment of the iceberg that has brushed the ship, "he thrust it under my nose and it smelt rank, a bit like a sliver of rotten mackerel." And when the famous band on the doomed vessel goes on deck to play, Morgan, heading down into the lounge, notes, "I could see the score in the carpet where the cellist had dragged up his instrument." These precisionist visions loom out of a fog of obscure motivation and vague portentousness: "In Scurra's company it was necessary to contemplate the exquisite darkness of the world"; "Pity welled up in me, and envy too, for I might never know the sort of love that gripped her by the throat."

Hard-drinking Morgan, returning from England to New York in a crowd of chummy nobs, is in love with the "absolutely unobtainable" Wallis Ellery. "Dancing with her was like holding cut glass; Hopper [a chum] got it about right when he complained she made him feel he left finger marks." Relations between the young in 1912 were sexually constrained:

> Most of our time was spent thinking what we might do with women if only we had the chance. There were houses we could go to, of course, but with girls of our own set there was never the slightest opportunity of trying out even a little of what we'd learnt.

Morgan gets a distinct shock, then, when at close quarters he overhears Wallis making kinky love (she likes being tied) with their sinister fellow-passenger Scurra, whose grotesquely split lip is never satisfactorily explained. Scurra is ready to share, however, any number of aperçus. "One must distinguish," he says, in refutation of Morgan's idealistic Marxism, "between use-value and exchange-value. . . . Philosophically speaking, life may be said to have use-value, but only for the individual. Its exchange is death, which has no value whatsoever unless one is in severe torment." Asked by his slowly illumined acolyte if he is in love with Wallis, Scurra replies, "Love? Good heavens! Love is what women feel."

Wallis is so enamored of Scurra that she has to be dragooned into a lifeboat. In historical actuality, many of the women did at first resist exchanging the vast deck of the luxurious *Titanic* for a lifeboat swaying in its davits above the black midnight ocean. Captain Smith gave few clear orders; no safety drills had been rehearsed. The confusion of the ship's last two and a half hours could have been worse; crew members, knowing in the pit of their stomachs that these were most likely the last hours of their lives, by and large performed dutifully, and the second- and third-class passengers tended to observe the proprieties, sticking to their sections even as the decks perilously tilted. The band played on. The class system held, though it failed of its basic promise to its lesser orders: Know your place, and you will be taken care of.

In the progress of Morgan's coming of age via glimpses of sex and death, fictional and real characters mingle: he brushes against Mrs. Straus on the ship's Grand Stairway, and observes the Astors looking "as if they'd barely finished a thundering row . . . he nearing fifty, his long gloomy nose nudging his moustaches, she barely nineteen, her flower head drooping on the stalk of her neck." He happens to overhear that there are no binoculars in the crow's nest—a detail dear to *Titanic* scholars. Morgan's knowledge of the ship is above average, since, in obedience to his uncle, he worked for eleven months as an apprentice draftsman to Thomas Andrews, the designer of the great ship and himself on board, attentive to such minute details as the number of screws in the rooms' coat hooks. Amid the novel's somewhat bizarre and ghostly swarm of characters, the phlegmatic Andrews stands out in deserving pity. He was, of the foundering's fifteen hundred victims, the quickest to understand the fatal damage, and the one who knew best the love and labor lost when this nautical masterpiece was carelessly condemned to the bottom of the sea. . . .

The sinking of the *Titanic* seems, like the world war that commenced twenty-seven months later, tragically avoidable; it was a disaster that men coasted into, confident of their invulnerability and righteousness. Its awful majesty is not easily assimilated, however, into invented narratives. Reading novels that take place on board is like sitting through the warmup acts of a rock concert, waiting for the star—the crash—to appear. The *Titanic*'s story can't be topped, though it is being extended and reversed by the ship's piecemeal raising. The story's august moral remains: Nothing human is unsinkable.

Karen Heller (review date 22 November 1996)

SOURCE: "*Titanic* Resurfaces in Yet Another Novel," in *Chicago Tribune,* November 22, 1996, p. 3.

[*In the following review, Heller offers positive assessment of* Every Man for Himself.]

The most famous shipwreck of our century has launched its own literary genre. Walter Lord, who penned the 1955 best seller *A Night to Remember,* "recently remarked, without much exaggeration, that a new book about the *Titanic* disaster is published every week," writes Steven Biel in *Down With the Old Canoe,* a cultural history of the disaster published a few weeks ago.

Sure enough, this week's *Titanic* volume is British novelist Beryl Bainbridge's lyrical *Every Man for Himself,* which follows Norwegian author Erik Fosnes Hansen's *Psalm at Journey's End.* These books all arrive on the heels of the failed attempt in August to dredge a 21-ton section of the *Titanic* from the North Atlantic floor.

The narrator of *Every Man* is young Morgan, named for his relative J. Pierpont Morgan, owner of the *Titanic*'s

White Star Line. Morgan is confused about his heritage and uneasy with the great wealth it brings—though not the swells he attracts.

On board the *Titanic,* Morgan makes friends with a fashion designer, an opera singer and a mysterious, almost mystical man named Scurra. Morgan pines for a beautiful, unobtainable woman. "No one even dared flirt with Wallis. Dancing with her was like holding cut glass. . . ." But Wallis, like almost everyone else in Morgan's circle, is not who she appears.

Bainbridge intermingles her own characters with the *Titanic*'s real passengers: Macy's owner Isidor Straus (whose wife, Ida, chose to stay on board and die with her husband), Benjamin Guggenheim, British journalist W. T. Stead and Broadway producer Henry B. Harris.

Like many *Titanic* books, ***Every Man for Himself*** concerns itself with the microcosm of the upper deck. Most of the characters, including Morgan, are hardly admirable. The best of the lot are the wealthy who actually work for a living, including the sage clothing designer Rosenfelder, who observes that Morgan's friends "were not living in the proper world. Their wealth, their poorly nurtured childhoods, their narrow education, their lack of morals separated them from reality."

While the ship begins to sink slowly, the band plays on and the robber-baron society continues its social swirl.

"Scurra sat below in the Palm Court, sprawled at a table with his legs stretched out. He was discussing the Peloponnesian War with Stead, the journalist. Neither of them took any notice of me. Mr. Stead was neatly dressed for a windy morning on Wall Street. His life-preserver lay draped across his knee."

Several paragraphs later, the discussion ends politely. Presently, the journalist stood and shook us both by the hand.

'It's been an interesting trip,' he observed. 'I doubt we'll see another one like it.'

"'Quite,' said Scurra."

As the *Titanic* ruptures, so do conventions. Time seems to slow to a halt even as death laps at the passengers' heels. In luminous and often witty prose, Bainbridge constructs a prism of an era prattling on even as it drowns in the icy deep.

Susan Heeger (review date 24 November 1996)

SOURCE: "Ship of Fools," in *Los Angeles Times Book Review,* November 24, 1996, p. 6.

[*In the following review, Heeger posts a positive assessment of* Every Man for Himself.]

Its very name described its lordliness on the sea. So vast its passengers got lost on it, so strong it was thought invincible, the *Titanic* remains one of the most compelling images of prideful folly in modern maritime history. Who doesn't know the story of its maiden voyage and midnight meeting with an iceberg, chandeliers blazing, orchestra tootling out ragtime? Two hours later, mortally wounded, the great double-hulled wonder heeled over and sank, sucking 1,500 people to watery graves.

Ever since, the facts have been hashed and rehashed, the 1912 voyage re-created in articles, books, documentaries and feature and television films. We can't seem to get enough: how many millions of rivets went into that hull and how much oak paneling and inlaid mother of pearl were used to decorate the Palm Court, the Grand Staircase and the first-class writing room? Why weren't they carrying more lifeboats? And, of course, how did it feel to be a passenger—to spend five days downing champagne with the glitterati till the jolt came, the lights blinked and ice showered across the decks?

Joining the throng of Titania is a fast-paced novel that blends known facts with fiction into a coming-of-age tale that also captures a social moment. For acclaimed British novelist Beryl Bainbridge, tragic death is only part of it. What interests her are the thorny moral questions—of fate versus human intervention, of compassionate acts versus an individual's responsibility for himself. Twenty-two hundred people—all with dreams, stories, families, futures—came together on the ship and eventually faced the same nightmare. Many were poor and traveled in steerage, never glimpsing the fabled Palm Court. Others labored below deck, hauling coal and stoking the engines. At the top of the heap, oblivious to dirt and danger, a couple of Astors, a Guggenheim and a Lord and Lady Duff Gordon dined formally and lolled in furs, observing the good form that went with their set. But when all hell broke loose and the upper-crust made for the lifeboats, there were heroes and cowards from every class, those who saved themselves and those whose first thought was for others.

One of the book's heroes, much to his own surprise, turns out to be Morgan, the narrator, a 21-year-old adopted nephew of J. P. Morgan, who owns the *Titanic* and its shipping line. A bit of a ne'er-do-well, Morgan drinks too much and hangs around with other moneyed wastrels while considering what to make of himself. In search of direction, he listens to just about anyone. Riley, the low-life seaman; Willis, the icy girl he wants; his cronies, who inadvertently show him the ugliness of his own kind. His true mentor is Scurra, a mysterious, charismatic fellow passenger familiar with Morgan's past as an abused and abandoned orphan. Scurra understands that Morgan's beginnings have set him apart from his ilk and made him complicated and kind in ways his friends will never be. Though Morgan's view of himself keeps shifting, Scurra awakens him to something solid at his core.

Bainbridge, author of 14 short, witty books (the most recent, the 1994 ***Birthday Boys***), tells, as usual, a deceptively simple story. It opens with the thunderous moment before the ship sinks and then cuts away to a book-length flashback of the events leading up to it. Throughout Morgan's day-to-day account of social lunches, shipboard intrigues and musicales (all full of perfect-pitch details about manners, clothes, food and slangy chit-chat), the air of doom drifts like a deadly gas. People joke about accidents and bet on the boat's arrival time in New York. There's talk of thickening ice and nearby ships changing course for warmer waters. Meanwhile, the *Titanic*'s designer is busy fussing over bathroom taps and passengers are having affairs and scrambling to make social and business connections.

All of which considering what we know is coming, adds up to an ongoing meditation on fate—the fate that puts some people on a sinking ship and moves others to change their plans or miss the boat; the fate that hooks up an aspiring *couturier* with the perfect model and then drowns them both. "We are like lambs in the field," Scurra muses, "cropping the grass under the eye of the butcher who chooses first one then another to meet his requirements."

Yet, as Morgan discovers, something inside us has a say in things too, and through adversity we come face to face with what we're made of. No theoretical discussions of character can prepare him for his own courage on the night of every-man-for-himself. In fact, the chief pleasure of the book—apart from the thrill of sailing the *Titanic* with Bainbridge—lies in watching this likable goof-up emerge from his shell of privilege and become a person to be reckoned with.

F.Y.I. *Titanic* buffs: W. W. Norton has just released two new nonfiction books on the legendary boat: In *Titanic: Destination Disaster. The Legends and the Reality*, John P. Eaton and Charles A. Haas update their 1987 book, which attempted to make sense of the tragedy. Steven Biel's *Down With the Old Canoe: A Cultural History of the Titanic Disaster* examines America's complicated reactions to the sinking and what this says about America.

Kate Saunders (review date 1 May 1998)

SOURCE: "History As You Have Never Seen It Before," in *New Statesman,* May 1, 1998, p. 59.

[*In the following review, Saunders offers praise for* Master Georgie.]

Some well-established novelists, garlanded with praise and blunted by success, become tired or lazy, or allow their once zeitgeisty voices to date. Not Beryl Bainbridge, who gets better and better. ***Master Georgie*** completes a trilogy of remarkable historical novels, following ***The Birthday Boys*** and ***Every Man For Himself***.

The novels themselves have no links, except that they revisit events overburdened with legend—Scott's last expedition, the sinking of the *Titanic*—and cut away all received notions. This is history as you have never seen it. Heaven help you if you like your Great Moments softened and sentimentalised. Like a latter-day Lytton Strachey, Bainbridge knocks down monuments merely by highlighting all the little things that did not fit in to the accepted versions. Her heroes are reduced to their proper human size, and magnified to represent much more than their own experiences.

Master Georgie is narrated by three characters, all being swept towards the carnage of the Crimean War. Myrtle is rescued from a Liverpool cellar and taken into the home of the wealthy Hardy family. She is probably the illegitimate child of dissolute Mr Hardy. Pompey Jones is a hard-headed urchin with a talent for survival. Dr Potter is a failed geologist, with a fatal and comical inability to see beneath the surface of things.

Georgie, seen through these three pairs of eyes, is the eldest Hardy son. Myrtle is his slave. She is at his heels when he discovers the dead body of his father, in the bed of a whore. Both Pompey and Myrtle help him to avoid disgrace by getting the corpse home in a *Punch-and-Judy* wagon—a bizarre hearse, destined to appear again at the novel's end as a symbol of the indignity and casual brutality of death.

Years later we find Myrtle transformed from a grubby slave to a young lady, accepted and loved by the whole Hardy family. She appears to be a devoted, spinsterish, quasi-aunt, but appearances were never more deceptive. "If ever there was a woman with fairy dust in her eyes," comments Potter, married to George's sister, "it was she." Myrtle has made an idol of George. When she follows him to Scutari (he is a doctor working in hideous conditions), she gladly becomes like Sweet Polly Oliver in the old ballad, dressed in dead men's clothes to follow her love to battle.

Pompey, whose fortune was also made by helping at old Hardy's embarrassing death, knows another side of George, which stirs him into a stunted approximation of sympathy for the sacrifices Myrtle has made for him. He is in the Crimea as a photographer's assistant. The Crimean War was the first to be photographed, and the camera is presented here as a great liar and manipulator of history.

As for Dr Potter, he muddles along, reducing history to absurd personal detail: for instance, when "over 200 cavalry horses of the Light Brigade stampeded into the camp, their riders having perished in a charge," he notes his transport problems are solved. History, before the history-makers have set to work, is an untidy and pathetic business. Bainbridge uses her supremely ironic hindsight to convey the fragility of life, the chaos and squalor of war, and the human craving for idols.

Master Georgie is a teeming epic, reduced to fit into a nutshell. Beryl Bainbridge is at her most brilliantly original

in the dangerous and undignified area between high tragedy and low farce. Her triumphant novel deserves to be read at least twice, to milk every inference from sentences laden with meaning.

Daniel M. Murtaugh (review date 6 November 1998)

SOURCE: "Worth Reading Twice," in *Commonweal*, November 6, 1998, p. 26.

[*In the following review, Murtaugh offers favorable evaluation of* Master Georgie.]

Beryl Bainbridge's *Master Georgie* pursues the interests and, to some extent, the methods of her two previous historical novels, *The Birthday Boys* (1995) and *Every Man for Himself* (1996). Those two novels dealt with memorable events of 1912: the fatal expedition to the South Pole led by Robert Falcon Scott and the sinking of the *Titanic*. These disasters were celebrated in England for their displays of chivalry *in extremis,* the attractive, manly imprudence and amateurism which, to the disenchanted and postimperial eye, were largely responsible for bringing them about. Scott's expedition failed, after all, because it lacked the prosaic professionalism of the Norwegian team that reached the Pole with no casualties. And nearly half of the capacity of the *Titanic*'s lifeboats went unused because there were no precautionary boat drills. But this incompetence was the *felix culpa* that gave a premise to heroism and models for England's young men. *Master Georgie* takes us back some six decades to the Crimean War, a scandalously mismanaged campaign which squandered troops to disease and mud and had its most conspicuous folly, the charge of the Light Brigade, burnished into another chivalric myth by Lord Tennyson.

The charge impinges obliquely on the action of *Master Georgie.* On the miserable periphery of battle, one of its three narrators takes some comfort in being "at least better off as far as transport is concerned; three days ago over two hundred cavalry horses of the Light Brigade stampeded into the camp, their riders having perished in a charge along the north valley." He buys at auction a "mare so shocked by its recent subjection to bombardment as to have passed beyond nervousness into a state bordering on imbecility, and therefore manageable."

That obliqueness characterizes the whole novel. The central character, George Hardy, is visible to us only in the cracked mirror of the accounts of three dependents. He is a restless, attractive bisexual, heir to a Liverpool fortune, a surgeon and amateur photographer who feels "that the war would at last provide him with the prop he needed." He is, in different ways, a beloved central concern of Myrtle, a foundling servant girl who bears his children; Pompey Jones, a child of the streets who learns photography from him; and Dr. Potter, a pompous and touchingly uxorious amateur scholar who is married to George's sister Beatrice. Each of these tells two of the novel's six chapters, starting in Liverpool in 1846 and ending outside Sebastopol in 1854.

George's interest in photography informs the structure of these chapters. Each is called a "Plate," dated, and given a title which is actually a caption: "Girl in the Presence of Death," "A Veil Lifted," "Funeral Procession Shadowed by Beatrice," and so on. Each chapter moves toward the exposure of one of these plates and the production of the captioned picture. So the narrative action resolves itself into a pictorial summary, which, as it turns out, falsifies what we have been told. The medium that gives its very name to an ideal of verisimilitude conspires with Victorian sentimentality. In plate 1, the twelve-year-old Myrtle acts the part of a pious mourner over the corpse of George's father after joining with George and Pompey Jones in a cover-up of the disgraceful circumstances of his death. In plate 6, George's own corpse is propped among the living to round out "a group of survivors to send to the folks back home" and urged, with them, to "Smile, boys, smile."

The most affecting use of photography involves a bit of magic realism. The debilitated Dr. Potter, attending a funeral for a cartload of naked soldiers, resorts to hallucination and conjures up the image of his longed-for wife Beatrice, smiling and beckoning him with a maternal sweetness that suggests her namesake in Dante. Just then Pompey Jones has set up his tripod and taken a picture of the funeral party. In the following chapter, Pompey examines his print and sees a blur in the corner resolve itself into the figure of Beatrice. The longing that created Potter's hallucination has burned itself into the plate.

The three characters are bound to one another in their orbits around George by fated linkages of coincidence which I do not need to detail here, and which are the subject of reflection by Potter. The three are also linked erotically: Potter through his relationship to Beatrice, Myrtle and Pompey through their separate liaisons with George. In the end, tipped out of their wagon into the mud as they barely escape death in battle, Myrtle and Pompey grope toward, then back away from, a sexual union. Pompey then dismisses the episode as "not being a matter of great importance. All I'd ever wanted, as regards Myrtle, was the recognition that she and I were of a kind, seeing that fate had tumbled the two of us into Master Georgie's path." That erotic dimension of social class is expressed more tellingly by Myrtle earlier in the novel in a conversation with the mistress of a colonel of the Guards. Her colonel and she "talk for hours at a stretch," her friend tells Myrtle. "That's unusual, isn't it?" Myrtle agrees politely but thinks to herself: "Georgie's not one for talking, at least, not to me. Nor would I wish to be his equal, for then I might find him wanting."

In the novel's first chapter, in Liverpool, that self-protective deference shows itself as she walks quickly behind George, wishing but not expecting that he will turn back to look at her. In its final pages, outside Sebastopol,

rashly, she calls to him from behind because she has hurt her foot. He turns to her and away from a rifle raised against him, and, in a variation on Orpheus and Eurydice, he meets his death.

I hope I have conveyed that this is a very rich novel. It is not an ingratiating one on the first reading. It is ironic. It works very quickly in its 192 pages, demanding close attention and not yielding the pleasures of uncomplicated identification with its characters. But go back and read it again, and it will astonish you.

Francine Prose (review date 29 November 1998)

SOURCE: "Expiration Dates," in *New York Times Book Review,* November 29, 1998, p. 5.

[*In the following review, Prose gives positive evaluation of Master Georgie.*]

Beryl Bainbridge's novels are like elegant teacups that contain a strong dark, possibly sinister but remarkable brew. Models of compression, they show us how much (character, plot, subplot, psychology, wit and depth) can be poured into a thin, deceptively delicate vessel. For over 30 years, her best books—from *Harriet Said* and *The Bottle Factory Outing* to *An Awfully Big Adventure*—have resisted the tide that has caused so much modern fiction to bobble, inflated and bloated, in increasingly murky waters. Indeed, Bainbridge's writing is so unlike anyone else's that it may be more instructive to find analogues in the visual arts. Her fiction is reminiscent of medieval woodcuts—their spare, authoritative line deployed to render some grisly scene (martyrs burning at the stake, victims felled by a plague) with antic, animated high spirits. Or perhaps the art it most nearly evokes is Hogarth's engravings, those richly detailed snapshots of mass depravity and mayhem.

A number of her books are set in the past. *Young Adolf* deals, nervily, with an imaginary sojourn in England by the youthful Hitler. *The Birthday Boys* considers the ill-fated Scott expedition to Antarctica; *Watson's Apology* exhumes a Victorian murder. Yet these are not the sort of historical fictions that serve up warmed-over *Masterpiece Theater* plots, larded with period costumes, periwigs and bared bosoms. Rather, Bainbridge's concerns—the heartbreaking, nuanced transactions between the strong and the weak, the perceptual differences dividing men and women, the roles of chance and character in determining our fates, the eager glee with which Nemesis undoes our careful plans, the influence that social class exerts on sexual morality—remind us of how much about human behavior and destiny is timeless and universal.

Bainbridge's new novel, *Master Georgie,* is organized, thematically and structurally, around a succession of upsetting photographs; several of them, as was not uncommon in the 19th century, picture the newly deceased. At the novel's center is George Hardy, an amateur photographer and (more or less) professional physician, whom we first glimpse (as always, from a distance) in 1846, racing through the streets of Liverpool toward the brothel in which his father has suddenly and inconveniently died. By the time the elder Mr. Hardy has been brought home and his body arranged to create the impression that he has expired in his own bed, a large and varied cast of characters has been efficiently assembled. In addition to the bisexual, seductive and mysterious George, there are (among others) Dr. Potter, the libidinous geologist who marries George's sister, Beatrice; Pompey Jones, the wily street urchin who becomes George's assistant and lover; and, most important, Myrtle, a foundling whose blindly obsessive passion for the man she calls Master Georgie is the luminous thread that holds the novel together. Narrated by the simultaneously starry-eyed and down-to-earth orphan, the vertiginous first chapter begins and ends with George photographing her beside his dead father, a grimly comic event that the enamored Myrtle experiences as an occasion of romantic transcendence:

> I fixed my gaze on the dead man and told myself God would strike me blind if my eyelids quivered. So intense was my concentration, it was only Master Georgie who breathed in that sun-dappled room. Outside, the birds continued to twitter. All my life. I thought, I will stand at your side; and then I did blink, for the grandness of such a notion welled up tears in my eyes.

Much of the novel's drama—marriages, births, miscarriages and deaths—takes place during such blinks, in the months or years that elapse between chapters. The book has a rare, rather flattering faith in the reader's ability to extrapolate crucial information from what is—or, more frequently, what is not—said. This characteristic spareness, dryness and pared-down intensity can, I suppose, be confused with a certain surface chill and may explain why Bainbridge's novels have failed to achieve in this country the popularity earned by some of her windier countrymen.

When George volunteers to serve as an army medical officer and the others follow to be near him, the action moves to Constantinople and on to the cholera-infested camps and gory battlefields of the Crimean War. Throughout, the characters take turns telling their harrowing stories and offering their conflicting versions of reality—interpretations shaped by how much they can (or can bear to) comprehend about their situation and one another.

Everything is refracted and refocused, as if by a series of lenses, as Myrtle, Pompey Jones and Dr. Potter alternately assume the task of advancing the plot. Myrtle's adoring view of Georgie ("Of average height, stout of build, he walked with his feet turned out and back straight as a ramrod. I watched the way he swung his arms. How strange it is that even a mode of walking can inspire love") refuses to recognize his polymorphous sexuality and so bears little resemblance to that of Pompey Jones, who sees his master and lover as a privileged, petulant drunk. Likewise, our sense of the minor characters is subject to

major revision. Mr. Hardy, whose embarrassing death has set events in motion, is remembered by Myrtle as "cheerful and lacking in malice," fond of entertaining party guests with bellowed renditions of maudlin ditties; in contrast. Dr. Potter recalls him as "a bully and a fraud."

Perhaps what's most striking about the book—and about Beryl Bainbridge's work as a whole—is its companionable alliance between wry, dead-pan humor and nightmarish horror. Everywhere the characters look, there's something grotesque to see—if only they're willing or able to see it. Meanwhile, the cumulative effect of such an abundance of disconcerting incidents, described so dispassionately and flatly and with such understatement, is that they begin to seem at once awful and oddly funny.

Myrtle's life has got off to an unpromising start ("I'd been found . . . in a cellar in Seel Street, sat beside the body of a woman whose throat had been nibbled by rats"), and though the plucky, unshockable and sympathetic girl is educated and "made into a lady," she never sheds her intimacy with hideous misadventure. In the Crimea, a brief pleasure excursion with an officer's garrulous mistress involves an ominous encounter with a three-legged black dog, an invitation to accept a farmer's hospitality that ends with a goat messily giving birth in the middle of a table and, finally, the sight of a dead soldier, propped against a tree: "The pink had quite gone from his cheeks and his skin was mottled, like meat lain too long on the slab. . . . Flies crawled along his fingers and buzzed at his mouth."

Scattered throughout the novel are many similarly horrific moments, so that the narrative comes to resemble a cord stretched tightly, connecting these glittery dark jewels. One of Pompey Jones's photographic assignments is to assist Georgie in documenting cataract surgery on a captive ape. An evening of opera erupts in an outburst of jealousy and aggression. A child's puppy is torn apart by feral dogs. When a Punch-and-Judy show is interrupted by a collision between a horse and a van, the accident is explained with Bainbridge's typically dry, ironic, goofy logic:

> A vegetable cart had spilled cabbages on the road, all of which, save one, had been recovered or run off with. The gentleman's horse, who had seen service with a cavalry regiment, mistaking it for a puff adder, had reared up and crashed down sideways, striking the van with its flank. The animal had recently returned from Africa, where puff adders were quite common. They hadn't any teeth but if they bit you their tongues imparted a poison that could turn your blood to treacle.

Of course, the level of violence and chaos escalates as the book nears its conclusion, and the sort of disaster that we anticipate and dread in all of Bainbridge's fiction inevitably occurs. A final photograph is taken, and the book ends with a searing image of grief and loss.

Beryl Bainbridge's novels are not exactly testaments to their author's faith in redemption; she places little stock in the ability of good intentions and common sense to dampen our natural appetite for duplicity, cruelty and violence, or to defeat the threatening, "disruptive force of haphazard actions." For these reasons, *Master Georgie* is hardly a feel-good book—unless you're a reader whose spirits are lifted by the prospect of a writer so original and so firmly in control of her art.

John Gallagher (review date 7 December 1998)

SOURCE: "A Unique and Haunting Vision of Wartime Chaos and Death," in *Chicago Tribune,* December 7, 1998, p. 3.

[*In the following review, Gallagher offers favorable assessment of* Master Georgie.]

In this short, melancholy tale, British novelist Beryl Bainbridge all but reinvents the historical genre. Gone are moments of derring-do; gone, too, any notions of simple, linear plot. In their place, Bainbridge delivers a fitful, episodic story of death, disease and unfulfilled longing.

The Master Georgie of her title is George Hardy, a surgeon and amateur photographer in England during the 1840s and '50s. He is assigned to the British army during its disastrous adventure in the Crimea in Britain's mid-19th Century war against Russia.

Like American writer Charles Frazier in *Cold Mountain,* Bainbridge is more interested in war as background than in war itself. Battles are mere eruptions of violence in a landscape already strewn with victims of cholera, tainted food and other maladies.

A conventional narrative form would be too orderly, too forward-moving, for what Bainbridge wants to accomplish. Her tale unfurls in the voices of three people close to George. One is Myrtle, an orphan girl who adores George and bears him the children his wife cannot. Another is Pompey Jones, a vagabond photographer's assistant. The third is Potter, George's brother-in-law and a would-be naturalist in the mold of Darwin.

Through their eyes, we see George struggling to make sense of a world that begins and ends with a photographer's view of death. The photographer's art here stands in for the long view of history. But that view is flawed.

So, too, the medical arts that George practices. His army assigns him to the front but denies him proper supplies. He learns there is no rhyme or reason to a wounded man's fate. Soldiers hideously hurt in battle survive, while those with hardly a scratch die. Fever and bloated corpses are everywhere, but the greatest malady is the delusory belief in the army's mission.

Much of George's world seems enigmatic, as unresolved as a half-developed photograph. Bainbridge, for example,

dismisses the famous charge of the Light Brigade in a single oblique paragraph. The troopers' horses stampede into camp, and Potter and others auction off the mounts with no thought for their dead riders.

This is neither an adventure yarn nor a bitter anti-war novel. Instead, with deadpan precision, Bainbridge sketches in fleeting vignettes of horror and madness.

Her prose is as sharp and cold as one of George's surgical instruments. Yet she manages to illuminate an entire world in this slim novel. That world haunts us with images of chaos and death. But no reader can deny the force of Bainbridge's vision.

Gail Pool (review date January 1999)

SOURCE: "Pictures From an Expedition," in *Women's Review of Books,* Vol. XVI, No. 4, January, 1999, pp. 5-6.

[*In the following review, Pool offers tempered praise for* Master Georgie, *citing shortcomings in the novel's contrived events and characterizations.*]

In her two previous novels, *The Birthday Boys* and *Every Man for Himself,* Beryl Bainbridge took her fiction in a new direction, creating a distinctive kind of historical novel. Like all of her books, these were slender works, not so much small as concentrated: it has always seemed to me that a Bainbridge sentence carries twice the information of the ordinary variety, and she practices a ruthless selectivity. But unlike her earlier novels, which focused mainly on individuals grappling with their lives, these gave her characters a wider stage: casting them as participants in a man-made tragedy symbolic of its time— Robert Falcon Scott's ill-fated Polar expedition in one case and the sinking of the *Titanic* in the other—enabled Bainbridge to interweave societal issues with the individuals' own. Although I didn't find these novels equally successful. Bainbridge's method in both seemed to me ingenious: the contrast between spareness and scope gave a sense of viewing events through a zoom lens that somehow had a wide-angle capability as well.

The photographic analogy seems particularly apt for Bainbridge's latest work, *Master Georgie,* another slim novel set against the backdrop of a man-made tragedy: the Crimean War. Notorious for senseless carnage and the abominable treatment of troops, this conflagration was also known for the war photography it produced: technological innovations achieved not long before the war enabled correspondents to send home pictures from the front for the first time.

Fittingly, Bainbridge gives photography a central role in her novel, not only by making two of her main characters photographers, by centering each of the book's sections around a photograph and by rendering the prose highly descriptive, almost photographic, but also by using the subject of photography to express ideas about perception and reality that are crucial to the novel. If these themes threaten heavy-handed reading, quite the opposite is the case. *Master Georgie* jostles along so easily, so much of it seems trivial or playful, that while one is reading it is difficult to know what if anything really matters, what the story is actually about and whether, adding up *Master Georgie*'s vivid scenes, a meaningful Big Picture will emerge. This effect seems to me part of Bainbridge's intention—and there is nothing in this consciously written book that is not intentional.

Master Georgie opens in Liverpool, in 1846 and takes us by a sequence of disjointed episodes to the Crimean battlefield in 1854. The book's six sections are narrated in rotation by three of the central characters, each of whom is linked in some way to the fourth, George Hardy, a young doctor interested in the newly developing art and technology of photography. The narrators, a bizarre trio, include Myrtle, a foundling raised by the Hardy family and obsessively devoted to George, whom she calls Master Georgie; Pompey Jones, a street-smart boy whom George takes under his wing; and Dr. Potter, a philosophizing geologist who marries George's sister. All four will end up in the Crimea, though the moves that carry the story forward can be hard to discern.

This narrative indirection is striking from the first. In the opening section, Myrtle describes how, at the age of twelve, already so devoted to Georgie that she followed him like a shadow, she was present when he accidentally discovered his father dead in a brothel bed. With the help of Pompey, who got hold of a Punch and Judy van, the three carted the corpse home to his own bed, thus concealing the truth of his scandalous demise.

There is such a strong element of farce in this scene that it is easy to dismiss it as insignificant. Only later can we trace how the death and shared cover-up are pivotal in all three of the lives concerned and help lead each to the Crimea. First, the affair so affects George—Potter tells us—that he falls apart, turns to drink, never entirely recovers and in regret for "wasted opportunities, lack of application, etc." offers his services in the Crimea, believing the war will be a "prop." "A man like me needs something to hold him upright," he says, a remark that will turn out to be grotesquely funny.

Second, the event appears to intensify Myrtle's already intense devotion to Georgie into such an obsession that she eventually chooses—almost incredibly—to bear his children when his wife proves unable, and to follow him to the Crimea when he seeks to offer his medical services because "she is unable to let George out of her sight." Third, the episode wins young Pompey the patronage of George, who trains him as a photographer, an occupation that takes him to the Crimea on an assignment for a newspaper. Actually, it might be said that the circumstances of Mr. Hardy's death lead even Potter to the Crimea, since the decision to make the "ill-advised excursion" is

George's more than his own, and he accompanies his brother-in-law in the belief that he might be of use as an observer.

Reading back, it is possible to trace all of these effects to the first grimly farcical scene, but it requires effort; nothing is made plain. By forcing us to piece it together in hindsight. Bainbridge suggests how difficult it is in life to read forward, to see ahead of time what will ultimately matter in part because so much is accidental: had George not wandered down a particular street he would not have come upon that brothel; if Pompey had not been nearby, he would never have met George; both lives might have been entirely different.

And by forcing us to piece it out, Bainbridge also provokes us to ask ourselves what "the story" here really is, what the whole that we are putting together amounts to. Is the novel, as its title suggests, the story of George Hardy? But he is the one we know least about; his, after all, is the voice that is missing. We are never inside his head, we never hear his view of his father's death, his mother's manipulation, Myrtle and those children. We perceive him only through the eyes of his companions, each of whom sees him differently. We gradually learn about his drinking, his homosexuality. But viewing him externally, we hear only what people choose to tell, which may not even be true, and which does not add up to a portrait.

This question of how much we can really perceive of the truth, the entire picture, by what we see from the outside seems to me central to the book. The inability to gain an accurate overview of what is happening is evident in Bainbridge's depiction of the war: witnessed from the ground, by our narrators, the battles appear as vivid individual frames of mud and slaughter that do not coalesce into any meaningful whole. "I didn't know what cause I was promoting, or why it was imperative to kill," says Pompey, as he makes his way, with Myrtle, through the bloodshed.

The question of what can be perceived—and whether there is any truth to perceive—is underscored by the use of photography in the book. Each section bears the title of a plate that refers to a photograph, taken in that section, which, as the accompanying narrative makes clear, in some way distorts reality. In the first section, for example, the described photograph of Myrtle with the corpse of Mr. Hardy in his bed makes it look as if he'd died in bed which is true, as Myrtle observes, if "one didn't dwell on which particular bed." Still more distorting, the final photograph, "Smile, Boys, Smile," taken by a war photographer to show folks back home a group of survivors, includes a corpse, propped up to appear to be among the living. These are posed photos, of course, artfully arranged. But then, narratives are artfully arranged as well.

Master Georgie is a meticulously constructed novel and, as always, Bainbridge's controlled prose is a pleasure to read, even when she is describing terrible carnage. It may come as a surprise, then, when I say that I didn't really find it worked all that well as a novel. To me, it felt too conspicuously constructed, the story too contrived and the characters too artificial.

To believe that life is as accidental as Bainbridge suggests. I need to believe that the accidents she depicts could occur: here, I felt they were contrived to achieve their effect—to connect people who would not otherwise have been connected, to transport characters to the Crimea who would not otherwise have been there. To believe in the bizarreness of people. I need to believe in the people; but for me these characters were never more than an arrangement of the characteristics Bainbridge gave them. As they wander through the Crimea, each may bring a different viewpoint—Myrtle drawing strength from the proximity of Georgie, Pompey surviving as he did in the streets of Liverpool, Potter so overwhelmed by the horror of his situation that he loses his bearings and mentally retreats. But they all tend to sound like Bainbridge herself. Here, for example, is Pompey on the battlefield:

> The carnage was horrid. Men died posed like the statues in Mr. Blundell's glass-house. I saw a horse crumpled on its chest, its rider with his arm held up as though he breasted a river. I saw two men on their knees, facing one another, propped up by the pat-a-cake thrust of their hands. On the wall, stuck to the steps of a ladder, a grenadier clutched at the steel that pinned him like a butterfly.

This is wonderful writing. But is it really a young man from the streets of Liverpool speaking? I felt so detached from the characters that while Potter was reflecting on what had brought him to the Crimea, whether it was fate or chance. I found myself offering up a third possibility: the author. This isn't really what a reader should be thinking. *Master Georgie* seems to me a novel to appreciate rather than to love—for its prose, its observations, and its clear-eyed view of our imperfect vision.

Christopher Lehmann-Haupt (review date 5 August 1999)

SOURCE: "Yes, There'll Always Be An England, or Two," in *New York Times*, August 5, 1999, p. E10.

[*In the following review of* Forever England, *Lehmann-Haupt finds weakness in Bainbridge's generalizations, though interest in her autobiographic reminiscences.*]

Considering the differences between the North and the South in the United States, one might find it hard to believe that in relatively compact England similar disparities are thought to hold true. Yet that is the subject of Beryl Bainbridge's quirky new book, *Forever England.* As the author explains in her preface, the book is based on a television series "which, in an attempt to examine the roots of that evergreen assumption, the notion that England is two nations, focused on the expectations and attitudes of six

families, three in the North and three in the South." Much of the perceived difference is based on myth. Ms. Bainbridge, who grew up in Liverpool and is best known as a novelist, writes in her introduction. "In the South they rode to hounds and went to Ascot; in the North we kept pigeons and raced greyhounds. When we had our tea, people in London sat down to their dinner dressed up as if they were off out to a Masonic hot-pot supper."

"All the same," she continues, "these simplistic myths, matters of manners and money and location never for one moment obscured the real differences that separated us, hid the severing wound that well-nigh cut us in half and could never be healed, for hadn't we been plundered by the South, laid waste, bled white? It was not just industrial. They had drained away our talent and our brains; who had ever heard of anyone once they got on in the world, from William Gladstone to Thomas Handley, who had been content to stay in the North? We learned this from our parents."

To test both myth and parental lore, Ms. Bainbridge interviewed people on the dole in Liverpool. Fishermen in Hastings, descendants of coal miners in Barnsley, the extended family of a financier in Bentley, sheep farmers in Northumberland and a multiracial family in Birmingham.

A few arresting generalizations emerge. "Up here in the hills we have crisis after crisis," says the wife of a tenant farmer who keeps 2,000 sheep. "There's no time to consult with anyone else. It could make you very self-opinioned, this sort of life. If you were in the South, you wouldn't need to be so determined, so dogged."

"It is a softer life down here in the South," Ms. Bainbridge concludes after visiting with the fishing family in Hastings. "They're not given to self-analysis, and perhaps the so-called southern reserve is not so much a matter of unfriendliness as a detached complacency born of comparative affluence."

But since the people she visited with seem selected to illustrate her various points, one finds it hard to put much stock in them as a sampling. Their main value is to fix in our minds the geographical distinctions of various regions in England.

Far more diverting are the autobiographical tangents on which the interviews inspire Ms. Bainbridge to take off. Her return to Liverpool triggers memories of her parents, of her father's contradictory ways—he lamented the loss of the empire yet always voted for Labor—and of her mother, whose hands were always full "painting the furniture and rearranging the ornaments."

Her visit to Hastings reminds her of a novel she once wrote in which she had to send her protagonist on vacation somewhere. "I didn't think he should go to Brighton—Brighton was too flashy for him. So I chose Hastings. The name came out of my head like a number out of a hat. I say that, but then nothing is ever as random as it appears. In my opinion there's no such thing as imagination—in the sense that we have the power to form images of our own making—for unless we've already acquired images in the first place, from somewhere, how can we possibly summon them into existence, reformed or not?"

A discussion of politics reminds her of the Cuban missile crisis, when she was chosen to go and protest to the American consul but was "struck dumb with admiration" because he looked like "a cross between Gregory Peck and Rasputin."

What emerges from these musings besides the portrait of an amusing, original, opinionated individual? Because Ms. Bainbridge rarely wastes a word in her fiction—the most recent of her novels are *Master Georgie, Every Man for Himself* and *The Birthday Boys*—you look for a hidden pattern here, some subterranean message that helps you to see beyond easy generalizations.

But in vain. Instead what you get is the story of one unusual individual. "If you come from the North as I do," she writes, "and you left it, as I did, you have ambivalent feelings towards the old working communities. It's an uneasy mixture of pride and irritation, sentimentality and mistrust, for you broke away from a narrowness of outlook and a lack of expectation which well-nigh crushed you. And yet—the heart lies back there in the past, and everyone longs to return and find things just as they were, the arguments in full spate and the home fires still burning."

In *Forever England,* Ms. Bainbridge doesn't find the home fires still burning. But she manages to set a few on her own.

FURTHER READING

Criticism

Wennö, Elisabeth. *Ironic Formula in the Novels of Beryl Bainbridge.* Göteborg, Sweden: Acta Universitatis Gothoburgensis, 1993.
   The only book-length study of Bainbridge's novels.

Additional coverage of Bainbridge's life and career is contained in the following sources published by the Gale Group: *Contemporary Authors,* **Vols. 21-24R;** *Contemporary Authors New Revision Series,* **Vols. 24, 55, 75;** *Dictionary of Literary Biography,* **Vol. 14;** *DISCovering Authors Modules: Novelists;* **and** *Major 20th-Century Writers,* **Eds. 1-2.**

Keri Hulme
1947-

New Zealand novelist, poet, and short story writer.

The following entry presents an overview of Hulme's career through 1993. For further information on her life and works, see *CLC*, Volume 39.

INTRODUCTION

Hulme came to international fame in 1984 when her novel *The Bone People* (1983) won the New Zealand Book of the Year Award, the Mobil Corporation Pegasus Award, and the 1985 Booker McConnell Prize. Set in Hulme's native New Zealand, the novel explores gender, ethnicity, and estrangement, particularly between native Maori beliefs and Western culture. Hulme, who is one-eighth Maori, explores similar themes in her short story collection *Te Kaihau/The Windeater* (1986) and her poetry collections *The Silences Between* (1982) and *Strands* (1991).

BIOGRAPHICAL INFORMATION

Hulme was born in Christchurch, New Zealand, on 9 March 1947. Her maternal grandfather was Maori, the Polynesian racial group indigenous to New Zealand. Hulme credits the time she spent with her Maori relatives, which she recalls fondly, with her close identification with the Maori ethnicity as an adult. The importance of family, the primacy of traditional Maori teachings, and the need to find balance are common themes in her poetry, short stories, and novel and can be traced to her youthful experiences in a close-knit family. When she was eighteen Hulme wrote a story about the three characters whom she resurrected over a decade later, creating the four hundred plus page manuscript *The Bone People* in the late 1970s. She attended Canterbury University, Christchurch, and pursued various occupations while concurrently writing. Although she successfully published her first collection of poetry in 1982, she was unable to find a publisher for her novel because of the unusual subject matter and her unwillingness to alter or edit the manuscript. A New Zealand feminist collective, Spiral, provided the funding for four thousand copies of *The Bone People* to be published. The novel achieved popular success in New Zealand before winning audiences in the United States and England. In 1986 she published her first collection of short stories, many of which expound upon the themes raised in *The Bone People*. Hulme lives in isolation in rural New Zealand and continues to write.

MAJOR WORKS

Similar themes recur in Hulme's work despite the fact that she has published in many genres. Her poetry, short stories, novel, and novella all center on issues of Maori culture and identity, the importance of family, and the conflict between identities. Hulme is known for merging genres; her poetry is prose-like while her novel and stories feature poem excerpts. In fact, critics called her novel *The Bone People* a prose-poem. She infuses her writing with Maori words and her English prose is influenced by Maori cadence and structure. In addition, the theme of violence features in her work prominently, most notably in *The Bone People* and in short stories such as "While My Guitar Gently Sings" and "Hooks and Feelers." In her poetry and fiction Hulme does not advocate feminist ideology as much as she features strong women's voices. Her novel *The Bone People* centers around such a voice, the character Kerewin Holmes, based loosely upon Hulme. Holmes is a one-eighth Maori artist living in a spiral house that she built for herself in an isolated region of New Zealand. A gender neutral character, Holmes befriends Goe Gillaylay, a Maori laborer, and his ward Simon, a mute boy of unknown parentage. Each character must overcome obstacles to restore harmony in their lives before they can unite as an unusual, but functional, family.

CRITICAL RECEPTION

When Hulme published *The Bone People* she was met by almost universal praise in New Zealand. Although she had earned attention for her poetry collection and short stories printed in periodicals, she had not established herself as a major writer until the publication of her novel. Reviewers praise Hulme for her imaginative and powerful style that blends reality and myth in a simple, yet serious, narrative; her fine ear for New Zealand vernacular and dialogue; and her unusual yet compelling structure. Elizabeth Ward describes the novel as "a work of immense literary and intellectual ambition, that rare thing, a novel of ideas which is also dramatically very strong." However, some critics, such as C. K. Stead and Michiko Kakutani, took issue with Hulme for refusing to edit *The Bone People*. They argue that she is too verbose, unfocused, and self-indulgent. Other critics bemoan the lack of development in the characters Joe and Simon. The issues of child-abuse and questions about the authenticity of Hulme's description of the Maori bother other reviewers. Stead foreshadows critics of Hulme's short story collection *Te Kaihau/ The Windeater*, published in1986, by criticizing the violence and bitterness in her writing. Many critics were silent or gave negative reviews of her short stories. However, both Tim Armstrong and Robert Ross argue that in these stories Hulme addresses many of the weaknesses found in her novel. Susan Ash writes, "I believe that Hulme's ambiguous attitude to individualism and to violence accounts for both the critical dissent regarding *The Bone People* and the relative silence regarding *Te Kaihau*." Hulme has continued to gain attention as a New Zealand poet; reviewers cite *Strands* as an example of work emerging from an up-and-coming voice of New Zealand.

PRINCIPAL WORKS

The Silences Between: Moeraki Conversations (poetry) 1982
The Bone People (novel) 1984
Lost Possessions (novella) 1985
Te Kaihau/The Windeater (short stories) 1986
Strands (poetry) 1991

CRITICISM

Elizabeth Webby (essay date March 1985)

SOURCE: "Spiralling to Success," in *Meanjin*, Vol. 44, No. 1, March, 1985, pp. 14-23.

[*Webby is an associate professor at Sydney University. In the following essay, she traces the themes in Hulme's writing, focusing in particular on Hulme's novel* The Bone People.]

    Aue, te aroha me te mamae

The title of one of Keri Hulme's poems seemed an appropriate epigraph for this introductory account of her work. 'Ah, the love and the pain' is one's immediate response to her poems, stories and, in particular, her major novel, *The Bone People*. Pain and love are also abundant in the story of how the novel eventually came to be published.

I first read Keri Hulme's work in 1982 when Heinemann sent me a copy of an excellent new anthology of Maori writing, *Into the World of Light*, edited by Witi Ihimaera and D. S. Long. This confirmed what I had suspected from reading stories by Ihimaera, Patricia Grace and Rowley Habib in other anthologies. In a country famous for its short fiction, the best was now coming from Maori writers. I was particularly impressed by stories by two writers new to me: Bruce Stewart and Keri Hulme. Since it was then impossible to buy copies of New Zealand books in Australia, I wrote to a friend in Auckland asking if any titles by them were available. In return I received Hulme's first collection of poems, ***The Silences Between (Moeraki Conversations)***, recently published by Auckland University Press, and the news that her novel, ***The Bone People***, was

having trouble finding a publisher because of its length and unconventionality. A small but striking extract from this work had appeared in *Into The World of Light*. I was very keen to read more of it.

About a year later I was excited to hear that Keri Hulme had been invited to the 1984 Adelaide Festival. As always, teaching commitments kept me in Sydney, where I attentively scanned the media for news of her. 1984 was one of those rare years when there were no international dropouts from Writers' Week; an unknown New Zealander attracted little attention. There was a brief report of consternation in the audience when she began her talk in Maori and then the news that Keri Hulme would give one reading in Sydney before returning home. Disappointingly few turned up to hear her; she had a heavy cold as a legacy of Adelaide; the good news was that ***The Bone People*** had at last been published by Spiral.

A few weeks later I had a ring from Marian Evans, one of the three women who had produced the novel. From her, and from the copy of ***The Bone People*** she brought me, I learnt of the novel's long gestation, its rejection by commercial publishers, the support given by Hulme's family, friends and, finally and successfully, the Spiral Collective. In her preface, 'Standards in a non-standard Book', Hulme tells how the work, begun as a short story, gradually warped into a novel:

> The characters wouldn't go away. They took 12 years to reach this shape. To me, it's a finished shape, so finished that I don't want to have anything to do with any alteration of it. Which is why I was going to embalm the whole thing in a block of perspex when the first three publishers turned it down on the grounds, among others, that it was too large, to unwieldy, too *different* when compared with the normal shape of novel.
>
> Enter, to sound of trumpets and cowrieshell rattles, the Spiral Collective.

Spiral, actually not one but a series of non-profitmaking feminist publishing collectives, had begun in 1976 when a Christchurch group produced the first issue of *Spiral*, a magazine for women's art, writing and criticism. Marian Evans was one of the Wellington collective producing *Spiral 5*. She had met Keri Hulme at the opening of Wellington's Women's Gallery in 1980 and read the manuscript of ***The Bone People*** the following year. Deeply moved by it, she made a further fruitless search for a publisher. Again the book's length and, one suspects, its feminism as well as its Maoriness, went against it. So a Spiral Collective was formed—Marian, Miriama Evans, Irihapeti Ramsden and another search, for funds, began. Ironically, one of the first groups approached, the Advisory Committee on Women, thought the novel did not give a positive enough image of women, especially Maori women, and turned it down. But, as one sees from the acknowledgments at the front of the novel, help did come from some Maori organisations, from women writers, both Maori and Pakeha, from a Catholic Church Commission and from the New Zealand Literary Fund. The latter offered two thousand dollars, higher than any previous subsidy for a novel, but the novel had first to be in print. The collective now searched for the cheapest quotes on typesetting, printing and binding. Typesetting was done by the Victoria University Students Association; proofreading and pasting-up by the members of the collective, often at night when their other commitments were over. While obvious misprints are surprisingly rare, the book that resulted has an engaging or annoying, depending on one's perspective, lack of uniformity. Inking and margins are uneven; page numbers go in and out of italics; occasionally the type goes up or down a point for a few pages. I was reminded of early issues of the *Sydney Gazette* and it's likely that first editions of **The Bone People** will become collector's pieces. (My two copies also have variant bindings.) But the eager buyers of the four thousand copies printed were clearly not all bibliomaniacs. The novel was very favourably reviewed and rapidly sold out. It has since won the three thousand dollar New Zealand Book Award for fiction and the Pegasus Prize for Maori Literature. Hodder and Stoughton have joined with Spiral to produce a reset second edition; Louisiana State University Press are to be the American publishers.

If the story that I've just told was fiction, it would probably be dismissed as too romantic, too Hollywoody. The happy coincidences between the novel's themes and structure and its eventual publishers might seem beyond even Hollywood. Three women, Maori and Pakeha, publish a novel which argues that biculturalism is fundamental to the future of New Zealand. The novel, rejected by monocultural publishers, is a huge success. For the reasons outlined above, the women call themselves Spiral. And, as Peter Simpson noted in an excellent review of **The Bone People** in the *Australian Book Review* for August 1984, 'the spiral form is central to the novel's meaning and design; it is in effect the code of the work informing every aspect from innumerable local details to the overall structure'.

Though **The Bone People** has a fairly simple plot—three characters meet, separate and are reunited—its structure is, indeed, that of the double spiral, where beginning and ending are in perpetual interchange. The first section, entitled 'The End at the Beginning', offers brief glimpses of three unnamed characters, two male, one female, before concluding

> They were nothing more than people, by themselves. Even paired, any pairing, they would have been nothing more than people by themselves. But all together, they have become the heart and muscles and mind of something perilous and new, something strange and growling and great.
>
> Together, all together, they are the instruments of change.

Next come three brief flashback sections, one for each of the still unnamed central characters. The first two, beginning 'In the beginning', and focusing on the male characters, are filled with images of terror and shipwreck, death and despair. The third opens with a marked change of tone:

> She had debated, in the frivolity of the beginning, whether to build a hole or a tower; a hole, because she was fond of hobbits, or a tower—well, a tower for many reasons, but chiefly because she liked spiral stairways.
>
> As time went on, and she thought over the pros and cons of each, the idea of a tower became increasingly exciting; a star-gazing platform on top; a quiet library, book-lined, with a ring of swords on the nether wall; a bedroom, mediaeval style, with massive roof-beams and a plain hewn bed; there'd be a living room with a huge fireplace, and rows of spicejars on one wall, and underneath, on the ground level, an entrance hall hung with tapestries, and the beginnings of the spiral stairway, handrails dolphin-headed, saluting the air.
>
> There'd be a cellar, naturally, well stocked with wines, homebrewed and imported vintage; lined with Chinese ginger jars, and wooden boxes of dates. Barrels round the walls, and shadowed chests in corners.
>
> All through the summer sun she laboured, alone with the paid, bemused, professional help. The dust obscured and flayed, thirst parched, and tempers frayed, but the Tower grew. A concrete skeleton, wooden ribs and girdle, skin of stone, grey and slateblue and heavy honey-coloured. Until late one February it stood gaunt and strange and embattled, built on an almost island in the shallows of an inlet, tall in Taiaroa.

This woman, artist, connoisseur, builder, is obviously anything but the traditional damsel in distress, locked in a tower by the sea. Yet, at the end of this section, the tone darkens. She is, after all, imprisoned. Having built the ideal artist's retreat, she finds herself no longer able to create.

The narrative proper opens in mid-sentence, in a pub. As the woman, now finally named as Kerewin Holmes, sits drinking alone, her thoughts are counterpointed with the pub conversation:

> Somebody's in the middle of a rambling drunken anecdote. A Maori, thickset, a working bloke with steel-toed boots, and black hair down to his shoulders. He's got his fingers stuck in his belt, and the heavy brass buckle of it glints and twinkles as he teeters back and forwards.
>
> '. . . and then fucking hell would you believe he takes the candle . . .'
> I'd believe the poor effing fella's short of words. Or thought.
> Or maybe just intellectual energy.
> The word is used monotonously, a sad counterbalance for every phrase.

This passage shows how surely Hulme handles her narrative, weaving together inner and outer events, in a seemingly effortless flow of realistic dialogue, interior monologue, and just the right amount of detailed description.

As we will shortly learn, the drunken Maori is Joe Gillayley, the male figure of the central trio, who has much more in common with Kerewin than appears at first sight. Like her, he has become trapped in a false role, self-adopted but essentially the creation of others. Hers is the Romantic ideal of the artist as a person apart; his the Pakeha view of the typical Maori: 'made to work on the chain, or be a factory hand, not try for high places.' Yet he is neither inarticulate nor unintelligent, has spent two years as a seminarian and trained as a teacher. If this were a conventional novel one might expect a variation of the ever-popular sexual comedy/romance: tough male and sophisticated female, initially antagonistic but irresistibly attracted to each other. But, though in many ways a romance and, given its happy ending/beginning, a comedy, *The Bone People*, perhaps uniquely among 470 page contemporary novels, has not a single sex scene. If it had, it may not have suffered so many rejections.

Kerewin and Joe are brought together by the third character, Joe's foster son, Simon. In another literary echo, Kerewin is made aware of Simon's intrusion on her solitude via discovering his sandal in the dust. Her meeting with its owner is initially as unpromising as her first sight of Joe. Simon is a weird little boy of seven, who cannot speak. 'She doesn't like looking at the child. One of the maimed, the contaminating'. As with Joe, Kerewin's first reaction to Simon is the typical one. People avoid him, assuming he is an idiot. In fact, he is highly intelligent and has many other special abilities. His false role is very much one imposed from outside.

Besides its brief opening sections, *The Bone People* has four parts, with three chapters in each, and an epilogue. It would be simplistic to equate these four parts with the four seasons, yet there are certain links. In Part I the relationship between Kerewin, Joe and Simon is gradually built up; in Part II Kerewin takes the others to Moerangi, her 'real home', for a holiday; the relationship breaks up, with great violence and suffering, in Part III. In Part IV, each character is given a separate chapter as, in different parts of the country, they each encounter death and undergo different forms of rebirth, in preparation for their reunion in the Epilogue to form 'something perilous and new'.

Fairly early in *The Bone People* we are told, through Kerewin, that the double spiral is 'an old symbol of rebirth, and the outward-inward nature of things'. Both these features are strongly reflected in the novel's structure and shifting narrative perspectives. The double spiral is also a traditional Maori symbol, and fundamental to the novel is the idea that change and renewal do not mean a total rejection of the past. The title derives from a pun on the Maori word 'iwi' which means both 'bones' and 'people'. So 'the bone people' are both the ancestors—the old people—and also the beginning people—the three central characters. Both Joe and Kerewin initially feel cut off from their cultural heritage: 'the Maoritanga has got lost in the way I live'. Kerewin has broken all ties with her family and almost, as the tower image suggests, with humanity generally. Joe's wife and baby son have died and he is becoming increasingly alienated from his other relatives because of his mistreatment of Simon. Both recover their Maoritanga during their suffering in Part IV. Joe becomes custodian of a mauri, a very special one that contains the vital spirit of the whole country. Kerewin rebuilds the marae at Moerangi and is reunited with her family.

As Witi Ihimaera and D. S. Long note in the introduction to *Into the World of Light*, the need to recover and preserve Maoritanga has been a strong theme in Maori literature and one of the reasons for the remarkable recent growth in Maori writing in English. Hulme goes one stage further in demonstrating that Maori and Pakeha cultural heritages not only must coexist but can, together, produce 'something strange and growing and great'. The third member of *The Bone People*'s trio, the child Simon, has no Maori blood. Thrown from the sea at the beginning of the novel, he also has no name or family; his only inheritance seems to be the terror which his conscious mind represses. Kerewin, well aware of the literary associations of her surname, attempts to recover Simon's past. Appropriately, the trail leads her to an ancient Irish family, whose crest is the phoenix. It is Simon, with his Celtic love of music and uncanny perceptiveness, who first realises that the three 'only make sense together' and who makes the greatest sacrifice to bring this about. The horror of Keri Hulme's portrait of the child as victim, of well-meaning even more than not so well-meaning adults, would be unbearable if she had not created in Simon such a tough little nut of a character.

It is possible to read *The Bone People* allegorically, with Kerewin, Joe and Simon respectively representing the mind, body and spirit which, according to the doctrines of Aikido, once studied by Kerewin in Japan, must be unified if humankind is ever to achieve perfection. But these characters are far from being bloodless abstractions. As the similarity in names suggests, Kerewin Holmes is something of a self-portrait, though a very unflattering one. Yet the two male characters are portrayed with equal understanding and sympathy; the reader becomes totally involved with all three of them. Despite its literary allusions and host of abstruse lore, *The Bone People* offers much more than the cerebral game-playing of much recent fiction—it engages the heart and spirit as well as the mind. While truly deserving the title 'novel', its strong narrative drive and mixing of the fantastic with the all too grimly real has something in common with the 'magic realism' of Gabriel Garcia Marquez and Salman Rushdie. Unlike the male novelists, however, Hulme does not deal with national politics, wars and revolutions. Instead, she concentrates on the, no less bloody and violent, politics of everyday life: relations between the sexes, between races, between parent and child. Though her novel has particular relevance to New Zealanders, it is bound to make a strong and lasting impact on anyone who reads it.

Reading Keri Hulme's previously published works after *The Bone People*, one becomes aware of many links and continuing preoccupations. Her collection of poems, *The Silences Between (Moeraki Conversations)* includes one song which reappears in the novel and another which might well have, as it tells of Simon dancing. As in the novel, there is much subverting of conventions and breaking of boundaries, including those between literary genres. The collection can best be described as a discontinuous narrative or, if one wishes to be grander, a *livre composé*. As in some of Frank Moorhouse's collections and in Brennan's *Poems 1913*, different type faces are used to link and separate individual pieces. There are six 'Moeraki Conversations' set at the beach which, there named Moerangi, is the setting for Part II of **The Bone People**. Moeraki was also the place where one of the ancestral Maori canoes was wrecked, so the poems in these sections are particularly concerned with Maoritanga and interconnections between the past and the present, the natural, and human and the supernatural.

The five interspersed 'Silences' each has a different setting: the city, overseas, other places in New Zealand. Here the emphasis falls on isolation and alienation, the *mamae* rather than the *aroha* of life. One of the most moving and powerful of these sections describes a visit to Hawaii, to a poetry conference. It consists of a sequence of twenty-one brief poems, **'Leaving My Bones Behind'**, and a longer poem, **'Spotlight'**. **'Spotlight'** is a very striking piece, intercutting scenes at a poetry reading with scenes of a pornographic floorshow in a Honolulu nightclub:

> 'I think people are the only interesting
> people,' says Kim-Lee, the Korean.
> 'No people are interesting,' says Nosun, the
> Filipino.
>
> They are poets in a conference of poets: I am
> a pair of stark eyes on the fringes.
>
> 'This time this younga lady she gonna blow
> your mind!'
>
> A flaming cannister-like torch, like a distress
> flare or a small stick of napalm.
> 'Shove it in' yells some sick thick in the
> crowd 'shove it right in'
>
> but with a huff of her trained vagina
> she blows it right out.
>
> 'O we can't compete with that,' says Kim-Lee sorrowfully.
> 'Do we try?' asks Nosun, grinning.

This brief extract can only hint at the impact of the whole poem, particularly when read as the conclusion of 'Silence . . . overseas', and within the context of the whole interrelated collection.

Into the World of Light includes some poems not collected in **The Silences Between**. Among them is my personal favourite, **'He Hoho'**, a marvellous celebration of

> this hoha, this buzz and fright,
> this wave and sweat and flood,
> this life.

Again, it's a long poem and one which needs to be read in its entirety but, as celebrations of menstruation are still pretty rare, I can't resist quoting

> It is cliché that once a month, the moon stalks through
> my body,
> rendering me frail and still more susceptible to brain
> spin;
> it is truth that cramp and clot and tender breast beset—
> but then
> it is the tide of potency, another chance to walk the
> crack
> between worlds.

The anthology also includes a less characteristic piece, a protest song, **'Whakatu'**. The title roughly translates as 'set speech'—this is a send-up of the Pakeha view of the Maori, the sort of stereotype Joe becomes trapped in **The Bone People**.[1]

> Eh man!
> They like us on the chains
> we do a good killing job
> and we look so happy
>
>> Hei tama tu tama
>> tamma go away
>
> They like us in the factories
> cleaning floors and shifting loads
>
>> hei tama tu tama
>
> they like us driving trucks and dozers
> and working on the roads
>
>> hei tama tu tama
>
> Hey boy!
> They like us in the pubs
> we drink up large
> and we look so happy
>
>> Hei tama tu tama
>> tama go away
>
> E tama!
> they like us
> they like us
> drinking & shouting & singing
> when it's someone else's party
> or swinging plastic pois
> in a piupiu from Woolworths
> and thumping hell outa an old guitar
> Because we look so happy
>
>> Hei tama tu tama
>> tama go away
>> Aue, tama go away.

'Hooks and Feelers', the only story by Keri Hulme I've so far been able to read, though a collection is soon to appear from Victoria University Press, has a male narrator with some resemblances to Joe. There are further echoes in the other central characters, a woman artist and a maimed, unchildlike, boy. Here, however, they are a family—husband, wife, child—which is destroyed through accident and disease. This is a story of *mamae* rather than *aroha*, compelling and disturbing. Also a very accomplished one, opening 'On the morning before it happened' and gradually, through hints, nuances and recurring images, revealing the full horror of 'it'. First published in 1976, *'Hooks and Feelers'* has rapidly achieved classic status and has appeared in at least four anthologies. At present, it's the only work by Keri Hulme easily obtainable in Australia, in both *New Zealand Writing Since 1945* (eds. Jackson and O'Sullivan, O.U.P.) and *Some Other Country, New Zealand's Best Short Stories* (eds. McLeod and Manhire, Unwin Paperbacks).

That Oxford, Allen and Unwin and also Penguin are now distributing some of their New Zealand titles in Australia is a hopeful sign that the Tasman literary gulf may be narrowing. I understand, however, that at least one major Australian publisher has turned down local rights for ***The Bone People***. So it seems you'll have to wait until the novel takes the final turn on its spiral path to success. Then it, too, will reach us, via London and New York.

Notes

1. After reading this article, Keri Hulme wrote '"Whakatu" is indeed a formal set speech. It is also "making a stand", "being vehement", and the name of a major North Island freezing works, and God knows which one was uppermost in my mind when I said it.'

Walter M. Miller, Jr. (review date 28 March 1986)

SOURCE: "Roots and Sinew," in *Commonweal*, Vol. CXIII, No. 6, 28 March 28, 1986, pp. 186-88.

[In the following review, Miller praises The Bone People.*]*

Once upon a time a female Maori tobacco field worker who owned a portable typewriter started writing a story about a magic child washed up on a New Zealand beach. The tobacco field worker spent twelve years writing the story in her spare time. Now that she is done with it, she takes it to three major publishers down under. They all hate it. So she bundles up the manuscript, mixes a bucket of quick-setting resin, and prepares to embed twelve years of work in a commemorative block of solid plastic, when—ta-ra! ta-ra!—three angels swing down from the skies on god-hoisting tackle. These lovely *deae ex machina* start a feminist collective which publishes the fieldhand's book.

And lo, it comes to pass that Keri Hulme wins the prize for Maori Literature and the Pegasus prize as well, the latter bringing with it publication in the United States. That's not the plot of ***The Bone People,*** that's the plot of how it came to exist. But there's not a happy ending yet. The happy ending is when all you who wish a taste of Maori fiction turn out to buy a copy of her book so that she will have a chance to write another one for us. Buy it now. Hollywood will never show it to you—it has no sex scenes, and the wrong kind of violence.

And yet it is a love story among three highly explosive characters, one of them the seminal magic child. The heroine is Kerewin, an alienated ex-artist; she has money, a bad conscience, an intact hymen at thirty-five, the hands and feet of an aikido fighter, and she weighs in at a chubby twelve stone. She smokes cigars, has built herself a phallic tower on the beach to live in, and half-heartedly tries to paint again. She has no interest in men *or* women. The child, the mute sea-waif Simon, appears in Kerewin's tower window one day after breaking and entering. Kerewin has no interest in children either, but the boy has a wounded heel and she can't throw him out in the rain. The other adult is Joe Gillaley, decently educated, but a Maori and a factory worker. Joe and his wife Hana had taken in the sea-foundling, but soon afterwards Hana and their baby died, leaving Joe with a beautiful, brutalized Simon to look after alone.

Simon can't talk, but he can understand, and even write. He can also steal, get drunk, start fights, throw tantrums, play hooky, break windows, accept money from the town pederast, and set off fire alarms. Joe gets drunk and batters him repeatedly, but they continue to love and cling to each other. Kerewin, against her will, becomes involved. Joe is grateful. She learns of the beatings and is sickened. When she catches him in the act, *HAI!*—she cuts him down with martially trained hands and feet; but as he lies bleeding in the sand (with Simon by his side crying for him), Kerewin is stricken with a spasm of abdominal pain which will become her nemesis and lead her as a willing, guilty follower toward the grave. For the moment, the pain passes. Joe forgives her the beating; they are temporarily reunited in friendship.

But the child's behavior arouses even Kerewin's wrath, and this time Joe's beating sends the boy to the hospital with severe and permanent injuries. Arrested, Joe loses custody and goes to jail. Kerewin, after a self-diagnosis of the swelling in her belly packs her bag with opiates and hallucinogens and goes away to die.

Everything seems hopeless, but—ta-ra! ta-ra!—out come the Bone People from the god-hoisting tackle. Believable gods they are, though, as believable to us, probably, as the gods that came to the rescue in Greek theater were to the audiences of that day. The Bone People belong to the landscape, to the life force (*maoriora*) of the Earth, to the culture (*Maoritonga*) and kinship of a people. They are those from whom Kerewin, Joe, and Simon, have been ultimately alienated, cut off from divine roots. They are the old ones, the relatives, the ancestors who Aeneas-like sailed their gods to New Zealand in the great outriggers long before the coming of the *Pakeha* (white settlers). Their power of binding and healing and uniting will pass to the new and future Bone People: Kerewin, Joe, Simon, the magic trinity (the author's word), reunited and healed by a mysterious fourth. They form a quaternity now, rooted in the Earth of kinship, and representing the future of a nation-people, part Maori, part Pakeha. These "gods" may be seen as the inner graces of the characters themselves, but these graces transcend any human individual; they are the secret inner power drawn from one's ancient roots in the Earth of origin and of redemption. "O the bones of the people, O the people of the bones." (*E nga iwi o nga iwi*.)

Knowing the ending spoils nothing, Keri Hulme begins this timeless novel with the End, and ends it with the Beginning. In between is the dance, in which all of humanity is revealed in three of the dancers, and the universal Earth in a particular island on which they dance. My appraisal: A-plus. Why not buy two copies? When an author has as much promise as Keri Hulme, a first edition of a first novel kept in mint condition can be a good investment.

Bruce King (review date Spring 1986)

SOURCE: "Fiction from the World's Edge," in *Sewanee Review,* Vol. 94, No. 2, Spring, 1986, pp. xlv-xlvii.

[*In the following review of* The Bone People, *King examines the feminist aspects of the novel, praising Hulme for her skill and innovations.*]

That Keri Hulme's only previous book is a good volume of poems published in New Zealand may explain why the reviewer in the *Times Literary Supplement* complained about the nomination of *The Bone People* for the Booker Prize—or why the *Sunday Times* claimed that the nomination was reward enough. The award of England's prestigious literary prize is only the latest episode in the unusual history of this unusual novel. Rejected by New Zealand commercial and small presses, it was eventually published by Spiral, a feminist collective; and it became a local sensation, winning the New Zealand Book Award for Fiction and, later, the Mobil Corporation Pegasus Prize for Literature, "to introduce American readers to distinguished works of fiction" from abroad. Penguin plans a paperback edition.

A strange powerful novel in subject, form, and style, *The Bone People* focuses intensely and obsessively on the relations among three characters. The woman has rejected her family and has withdrawn from society to become an artist, but, living alone in a tower she has built for herself on the sea-coast, she no longer creates. One-eighth Maori, she claims to be spiritually and culturally Maori rather than European, but she belongs to no community. Her self-enclosed world is breached by a mute, blue-eyed, blond-haired seven-year-old boy of unknown parentage, who is the only survivor from a wrecked boat and is cared for by the man who found him. The man, a pure-blooded Maori who has dropped out from a seminary and teachers' college, works in a factory and, since the death of his wife, lives alone except for the child. Probably a victim of polio at a time when vaccines were unknown, he was beaten by his mother to force him to walk, and he doles out savage punishment to the child, since he is unable to conceive of any other form of inducement or communication.

Although the perspective is mainly the woman's, Hulme continually shifts the narrative voice between the narrator and the three main characters and between what is said and felt, so that the text consists of a mosaic of short, clipped, economical paragraphs of interior monologue, dialogue, and description, in which oblique understatement controls intense feelings. Through dialogue and with little direct description she swiftly sets the scene, catching, for example, the overcrowded matesmanship of New Zealand's pubs—or noting the bare windy New Zealand beaches with their dangerous tides. A sentence or two establishes the dislike many New Zealanders have for Australians, the closeness to the surface of Maori-white racial tensions, and such feelings as isolation, aimless drift, and unfocused alienation. Hulme has an excellent ear for the flat dry characteristics of New Zealand speech, including the implicit aggression in the laconic, and the rich language of the novel ranges from Maori expressions, colloquialisms, personal coinages, and humorous curses to the highly poetic.

Organized around the structural motif of a double spiral, a Maori symbol of life as interwoven continuity and of rebirth, *The Bone People* begins with poems and short cryptic paragraphs alluding to the conclusion; besides the circularity of the end being implied at the beginning, the spiral symbol is found in the staircase in the woman's tower, in a strange sandcastle the child builds, in Maori greenstone carvings, in seashells and other natural objects, and in the house built at the end so that the three can live in "Commensalism." The relations and oppositions between men and women, New Zealanders of Maori and European descent, individuals and communities, mothers and children, the artist and society, medical science and the soul, past and present are among the many pertinent if fashionable themes in the novel.

The Bone People is one of the more impressive works of fiction written from a distinctly feminist position: it reflects a change in New Zealand society, a shift from a provincial, colonial, imitation British culture, in which sports and male values dominated, to a post-sixties culture, open to new ideas, cosmopolitan, and with an increasingly prominent role for women and Maoris. The isolation of the woman, her unwillingness to be involved, her instinctual liking for the child and distrust of him as taking from her energies are the fictional representation of ideas, as are the ways in which the woman's actions quietly imitate Robinson Crusoe, James Bond, and other male heroes of fiction. Hulme attempts to revise the novel tradition to include a woman who invents, controls, fights, who is a connoisseur of fine wines and tobacco, and who stands aloof. Such values are, however, criticized when the woman learns she needs others, family, and tradition, although in new forms of sharing. The source of the novel's themes and narrative in feminism can also be seen in such techniques as the intense probing focus on the inner world of the characters as relations develop and change and in the contrasts delineated between what is felt and what is said. Hulme is excellent in the nuanced way she shows evolving feelings and the subtleties of relationships: in balancing the subjective with the exterior, she has moved the novel form closer to an extended narrative lyric poem in several voices.

The novel also involves the renewal of Maori culture: the bones of the title are those of the ancestors who must be regained as sources of life and creativity. The ending, with its mysterious intervention of a tribal elder and a strange healer, might be explained by the way novels by women often resolve conflict through transformation of character, by Maori myth, or by the magic realism currently found in Third World literature. This is an impressive novel that lends itself to endless critical discussion.

Robert L. Ross (review date Spring 1986)

SOURCE: A review of *The Bone People*, in *World Literature Today*, Vol. 60, No. 2, Spring, 1986, p. 363.

[*In the following review, Ross, who teaches at Southern Methodist University, argues that* The Bone People *is too long and overwritten, but finds that it has merits despite its weaknesses.*]

Much honored by literary prizes, **The Bone People** supposedly challenges the conventions that govern the novel. Keri Hulme in a preface announces to prospective readers that her book, like exotic food, will offer satisfaction once such taste develops. Modern literature, however, has produced any number of pretentious, tedious, overwritten, and undisciplined works posing as forerunners of strikingly original forms. So, in truth, **The Bone People** fails to contain much that startles anew, only familiar excesses that too often hide the abundant talent lurking within. Hulme's writing at its self-conscious worst emerges as thoroughly unpleasant, but when natural and unforced, it is altogether brilliant.

For one thing, the book records vividly a side of life largely ignored in New Zealand literature. The courage and tenacity of early white settlers any number of novels has documented; and Janet Frame and Joy Cowley have denuded the smug descendants of those pioneers. Sylvia Ashton-Warner provided some insight into Maori culture, but only from a white perspective. Hulme, a Maori herself, chronicles the day-to-day life of her people, recording with apparent honesty and accuracy their frustrations, devotion and loyalty to family, distrust of those who govern them, their bouts of cruelty and inherent kindness, and their love of food and drink. In so doing, she establishes the fluidity which plagues those people whose traditions the Europeans' supposedly superior ways have eroded. Long a theme in African literature, for instance, this displacement has just begun to come to the forefront in many of the new literatures. Hulme has introduced the conflict dramatically into the New Zealand tradition.

This first novel, in spite of its excesses, shows abundant promise. The dialogue captures the rhythms of everyday speech, in part through effective use of Maori words and phrases. The descriptive passages do justice to the often cold and bleak but forever beautiful New Zealand landscape. The conflict and suspense depend not so much on a record of actual events but on the characters' emotional upheavals and reactions. Such strength throughout makes forgivable those passages that try the reader's patience. In writing her next novel, Hulme should remember that exotic food, when eaten too often, turns ordinary.

Virginia Quarterly Review (review date Summer 1986)

SOURCE: A review of *The Bone People*, in *Virginia Quarterly Review*, Vol. 62, No. 3, Summer, 1986, p. 91.

[*In the following review, the critic contends that aspects of* The Bone People's *unique New Zealand cultural setting are sacrificed for a more universal tale.*]

This startling first novel [**The Bone People**] by a 38-year-old Maori woman from New Zealand has already won the New Zealand Book Award, England's Booker Prize for fiction, and Mobil Corporation's Pegasus Prize for foreign literature—plus extravagant praise from the critics. Hulme's story is simple, perhaps shockingly plain, yet almost bottomless in its emotional depth. A reclusive Maori woman (a somewhat autobiographical figure), bitter at the world yet ironically made wealthy by a lottery, has her steely exterior pierced by an orphaned, psychologically-disturbed boy who, though of normal intelligence, refuses to speak for some mysterious reason in his past. The boy's foster father, a rough-hewn Maori widower, is alternately protective and physically abusive of the boy. These three characters, and the way their love for each other develops, describe the limits of the story; but the author's concern for the characters' emotional life, as shown through the use of multiple point-of-view and stream-of-consciousness, is so obsessive in its purity that the reader doesn't miss the lack of a depiction of a real social context in this admittedly long (440 pages) novel. Where Hulme is less successful is in her attempt to use the story as a metaphor for the current fate of New Zealand and the Maori people. Maori myth, culture, and language are constant themes in **The Bone People**, but Hulme is done in by her success; her tale is so universal in its beauty that it passes by the uniqueness of New Zealand on its way to higher literary heights.

Robert Ross (review date Summer 1987)

SOURCE: A review of *Te Kaihau/The Windeater*, in *World Literature Today*, Vol. 61, No. 3, Summer, 1987, p. 494.

[*In the following review, Ross claims that Hulme has created honest, evocative images of the human condition in*

Te Kaihau/The Windeater *and predicts important writing from her in the future.*]

That the author of the much-praised novel *The Bone People* should make violence, despair, maiming, drunkenness, and such other human weakness and misfortune subjects for a volume of short stories should not be surprising. After all, *The Bone People* must have been the first international best seller to chronicle child-beating.

In *Te Kaihau/The Windeater,* as in the novel, Hulme sidesteps the pitfalls of sensationalism and constructs instead a compelling image of humankind's state, first on the level of the Maoris in New Zealand, then on a universal scale. **"While My Guitar Gently Sings,"** for example, re-creates a Maori family and follows its dissolution, the narrator mourning her mother's death while sitting amid the aftermath of a drunken brawl. She cries too over the loss of the old ways and the vacuum created. Attempts at recovery fail, however, as illustrated in another of the stories, **"He Tauware Kawa, He Kawa Tauware,"** which records a pathetic attempt to rediscover and revive Maori tradition.

The vision bleak, the landscape dark and lonely, the characters maimed both physically and spiritually—such is the world Hulme brings into being through a style imbued with those same qualities. At times, unfortunately, the writing calls attention to itself, the eclectic and imitative nature, the penchant for obscurity, and the self-conscious experimentation marring the narrator's intention. When the vision and the language blend, however—and they most often do—the stories open to view the human condition, naked, brutal, alone.

Whether written before or after *The Bone People*, the fiction collected in *Te Kaihau/The Windeater* displays a greater sense of discipline, with most of the excesses that scarred the novel trimmed away. Much more will be expected from so inventive a prophet, disguising herself as a maker of fiction.

Susan Ash (essay date 1989)

SOURCE: *"The Bone People* after *Te Kaihau,"* in *World Literature Written in English*, Vol. 29, No. 1, 1989, pp. 123-35.

[*In the essay below, Ash reinterprets* The Bone People *after reading Hulme's short story collection* Te Kaihau, *arguing that neither work emerges favorably.*]

Does a Booker Prize ensure wide and critical attention for the winner's subsequent publication? Expecting to satisfy a "pent-up demand," retailers in New Zealand "ordered up heavily" when 1985 recipient Keri Hulme smartly released a volume of short fiction, *Te Kaihau/The Windeater*, in 1986. However, as one area book manager has said, her company "took a big punt" with *Te Kaihau* and "just did a

nose dive" (Parker 70), *Te Kaihau* has been a publishing non-event; the book has not sold well and no one has much to say about the stories. The fiction elicits only brief and oblique mention in Ian Wedde's review which focuses on the prefatory poetry.[1] Was Wedde off on a linguistic tangent close to his own heart, or did he consciously avoid engaging with the actual fiction? Much of *Te Kaihau* was written contemporaneously with *The Bone People*; stylistically and thematically the two books have much in common. Why then has one book attracted wide acclaim while the second has received relatively little attention despite the propitious circumstances of its publication?

The tensions in *The Bone People* inspire diametrically opposed readings. One critic praises Hulme's skill in rendering the protagonist a "living, realistic woman" (Smith, "Breaking Ground" 49), while another argues conversely that Kerewin is "too omnicompetent to be believable in fiction" (Jones 203). Similarly, *The Bone People* divides readers on the symbolic as well as the realistic level. The novel succeeds as a model for post-colonial harmony because Kerewin's "sexual neutrality" suggests that "bonds need not be biological," a point which relates "overtly to individuals" but could be seen as an "optimistic blueprint for future race relations" (Prentice 72). This same model fails, however, because the "last quarter of the novel" extends itself "too far," and the "characters cannot stand up under the mythic burden placed on them" (Jones 204). If the model does not work for individuals, it cannot work for the community.

Judith Dale's reading may account for the critical opposition. She suggests that the novel's ideas and structures "work against each other" (414) and "unsettle" the "stability of one another" (414). Patterns which appear settled in one direction are "disturbed in another" (426). Hulme's "primary accomplishment" in devising Kerewin is the protagonist's "self-sufficiency and tough independence, united as they are with intelligence, competence, knowledge and insight." Dale asserts that this image would be "lost" in the very notion of an idealized "people-family, tribe, tangata whenua" (415). The dissonance between the new, communal Kerewin offering the "gift" of her name while remaining independent, "the cold-forged lady" (460), is not resolved. The strength of individualism in the novel undermines the commensal resolution. Dale, it seems, prefers Kerewin alienated.

In my reading of the novel, the strength of Hulme's characterization does not subvert the vision of commensalism and the possibility of harmonious, post-colonial race relations. *The Bone People* is explicitly patterned by the quest motif; Kerewin works as a female hero who undertakes an archetypal quest journey which culminates with the return to society.[2] A novel like Frame's *Living in the Maniototo* ends with the hero-artist pursuing a life free from "human entanglements." *The Bone People* reverses the process. The hero-artist aspires for human isolation, *denying* her "connection with all living things." However, she undergoes a literal and symbolic journey and acquires the strength to return to society with the gift of her new knowledge: the paramount importance of bridging human alienation and establishing community. I disagree that the ending, the vision of commensal co-existence, is "an act of will" rather than something emerging "naturally from the rest of the story" (Jones 204). Within the framework of the novel, the heroic quest is convincing.

C. K. Stead has written that there is "something black and negative deeply ingrained" in *The Bone People*'s "imaginative fabric" (107). Reluctant to explain this "negative element" even to himself, Stead implies that Hulme feels an "imaginative complicity" with the novel's violence. Because I found the novel convincing, I was able to dismiss Stead's ominous conclusion. However, rereading the novel after reading *Te Kaihau* has unsettled my response. The novel's ending intends to reconcile tensions; *Te Kaihau* lays these tensions wide open. This is not necessarily a criticism. However, where the "negative element" is apparently resolved in *The Bone People,* the short fiction is unrelentingly "black and negative". Viciousness is rarely mitigated with *aroha* in *Te Kaihau*. Reading the short fiction in one volume becomes a painful undertaking. This article, then, mirrors the process of my reading Keri Hulme and reflects two positions: first, reading the novel on its own terms and secondly, reconsidering my response in light of the short fiction. Aware that the structures of my own argument unsettle each other, I discuss the success of the individual's quest for commensalism and its positive implications for the post-colonial society in *The Bone People*, only to argue subsequently that *Te Kaihau* shows a fundamental lack of authorial belief in those very models. I believe that Hulme's ambiguous attitude to individualism and to violence accounts for both the critical dissent regarding *The Bone People* and the relative silence regarding *Te Kaihau*.

The Bone People, like *Living in the Maniototo*, considers the artist's "place to be." At first glance Kerewin Holmes appears to have secured for herself the physical requirements for the female artist: she has a reliable income independent from her art and a "room" of her own. Kerewin has achieved the circumstance which Mavis possesses in *Living in the Maniototo*: the complete absence of oppressive human relationships with family, friends, or lovers. But, like Anna Wolf in Doris Lessing's *The Golden Notebook*, Kerewin is an artist with an artist's block, and the block is related to her choice to live in a place of human isolation. Kerewin protects herself by creating a "stasis" (261) for herself within her artist's place. She denies entrance to the Tower to all other people because:

> she was self-fulfilling, delighted with the pre-eminence of her art, and the future of her knowing hands. (7)

She insists that her rejection of people signifies her superior intellect: "The smarter you are, the more you know, the less reason you have to trust or love . . ." (128). However, she comes to recognize stasis as "a hell in itself" (261). Her intention in building the tower was to create a "hermitage" or "retreat" on "almost an island" (7). But the "sanctuary" becomes a "prison" (7) which she can not tear down. Deceiving herself that her self-imposed exile is in fact the condition of self-knowledge, she follows systems of knowledge with intense self-consciousness and monitors the condition of her self or "soul":

> Futureprobe, Tarot and I Ching . . . A broad general knowledge, encompassing bits of history, psychology, ethology, religious theory and practices of many kinds. Her charts of self-knowledge. . . . (90)

All are "tools" which help her to "make sense of living," but she is honest enough to admit that "none of them helped" (90).

To refer to Kerewin as a "heroine" would be a contradiction in terms. "Heroine" connotes a passive position where a female is rescued by or at least subordinate to a male. Feminist critics[3] refer to a "conceptual difficulty" when speaking of female heroes as "heroines" because women do set out actively on paths to self discovery in which they demonstrate individual relationships to the world. The conventional female, fulfilling conventional female roles, accepts these (self-) destructive conventions and exists as "heroine." To do so, she represses her "essential" self and presents a mask to the world. Rather than act herself, the "heroine" waits passively for a male rescuer to change her circumstance. Kerewin may repress her "essential" self (the self who can lead), and present a mask of self-satisfied isolation to society, but at no time does she adopt conventional female roles. While she waits passively for change, she does not wait for a male rescuer. As Hulme says, Kerewin has "got herself into that slough of despond" and she's "waiting for *something* to change it" ("Constructing the Author", emphasis added).

Thus, although Kerewin has rejected conventional female (heroine) roles, she is, nonetheless, in flight away from her quest. At this point it is typical for supernatural intervention to lead the reluctant hero away from frequented paths. That Simon fulfills this role is implied by his similarity with the Maori mythical hero, Maui. Both Simon and Maui are abandoned to the sea as infants and raised by adoptive parents. Simon is mischievous and his mates reject him just as Maui's own brothers reject his companionship. Undaunted, Maui makes a magic bone hook and stows away in a fishing boat intending to catch the greatest fish. He strikes his own nose and, using the clotted blood for bait, lands the whole North Island of New Zealand, an act which frightens his more timid brothers. This "story" occurs literally in the section, "The Sea Round," when Simon overcomes his aversion to the sea and lands his fish at the expense of his thumb's flesh. Symbolically, Simon's fish represents his idea of human community, a concept which Kerewin has resisted. Literally, Simon intervenes when he enters Kerewin's enclosed domain. His presence forces her to accept some human responsibility. He uses his own blood to bait Joe and Kerewin into a confrontation which he hopes will help them acknowledge the importance of their family bond.

Simon also evokes association with Rehua, the long-haired, sacred child of Rangi and Papa. Rehua is variously significant in Maori myth.[4] He is the god who released the bellbird from his long hair as a gift to mortals. He is known as the sun-god, which the novel directly reflects as Kerewin thinks of Simon as the "sunchild". Furthermore, he is the god who disperses sadness, a role Simon enacts in the novel as he ultimately disperses Kerewin's "unjoy" and alienation. That Hulme had Rehua in mind is suggested by several references in the text.[5] In addition Rehua is discussed "in A. W. Reed's retellings" of Maori legend which Hulme has been reading since her school days (Ricketts 19).

Although Kerewin tentatively accepts a degree of responsibility, eventually she rejects Simon. Thus, as hero, Kerewin "refuses" the quest throughout most of the novel. She is protagonist, but not heroic. However, at the point of catastrophe, two crises initiate her literal and archetypal quest journey. The brutal events in the relationship with Simon and Joe, and the apparent threat to her life from a tumour send her away from the frequent paths of home, into the darkness. After Simon is hospitalized Kerewin is in full flight away not only from human community, but from life itself. Always identifying with *te kaihau*, she "travelled for weeks in an aimless way" (411). The identification with *te kaihau* is appropriate in that the Maori may mean either "wanderer" or "loafer" (12). For most of the novel, Kerewin is "loafer." Kerewin's "intrinsic nature" (essential self) according to Hulme, is that of a "very active person who's reneged on her responsibilities." Thus, Kerewin is a "very passive kind of person" who "sort of sits and sulks in her tower and does virtually nothing" ("Constructing the Author" 26).

After Kerewin flees her tower, she becomes the "wanderer". This section, "The Woman at the Wellspring of Death," is the quest journey proper. She has given up her "base" or home, symbolized by the burning of her Tower, entered the world of darkness when she walks "away into the night" (331). She moves in the fluid dreamscape which characterizes this phase of the quest. She undergoes trials of pain with the tumour and eczema, and listlessly watches the ruin of her body. The trial is "atonement" for her past life which she endures with new-found humility:

> You have given up your home. Because the burden of uselessness became too much. Because the loneliness of being a stranger to everyone grows. Because knowledge of your selfishness has grown to be unendurable. (412)

Kerewin chastizes herself for her lack of charity and faith: "you do not have the gracemeet of faith, faith in anything" (412). She is not entirely despondent as she knows the "meaning and signpost for the journey is Hope Obscure" (330). Despite her certain death, "spiritually" she "still hopes" (412) and she gives herself over to the darkness. Kerewin does not resist self-annihilation, the prerequisite to rebirth. She willingly relaxes to whatever may come to pass. In doing so she is divested of her humanity. She experiences the ruin of her body—symbolically the ruin of her old ego. Paradoxically, the hero dies to be reborn; so

Kerewin understands, "I went away. Now, I am come." She experiences a "new strength" after deciding to come to "the high barren hills, the anchored remote land" (419).

At the point when Kerewin experiences the total disintegration of her human self, (suggested when she thinks, "I haven't got bones now. They're fired, dissolved, earth to earth again" [423]), she encounters the "goddess." The figure is androgynous, of "indeterminate age" with a marled, scarred face. The quester having reached the Chapel Perilous must ask the correct question; Kerewin, however, must answer correctly the question posed by the supernatural figure: "What do you love" (423)? The answer, which gives her the "ultimate treasure" or the gift of life, is:

> not me alone. [Simon's] the bright sun in the eastern sky, and [Joe's] the moon's bridegroom at night, and me, I'm the link and the life between them. (424)

The significance of the symbolism may be found in a proverb from Tane, "tenei nga tokorua, te ra, te marama." ("There are two, the sun, the moon," from which came the perfection of light.) According to some legends, this union resulted in the birth of Nga Whetu, the stars (Reed 31). Another legend has Te Ra, Te Marama and Nga Whetu all children of Rangi and Papa, three different, but necessary forms of light (Reed 411). Both legends are reflected in the novel as the presence of Joe and Simon leads to Kerewin's rebirth; at the same time Kerewin considers herself the "moon's sister" (89).

Kerewin's "return" from darkness to the human world is marked by a purging of her body, and by the sound of supernatural voices (in a karanga) which welcome and call her to come, "Haere mai! Nau mai! Haere mai!" The voice from "no-one living" "floods" through her with a "tide of wellbeing . . . a fierce joy at being alive" (426-27). She recognizes:

> Art and family by blood; home and family by love . . . [sic] regaining any one was worth this fiery journey to the heart of the sun. (428)

Kerewin has become the "sun door"[6] through which others may pass. She dreams of a "wrecked rusting building" which when "she touched the threshold, . . . sprang straight and rebuilt, and other buildings flowed out of it in a bewildering colonization" (428). And "new marae from old marae" (3) initiates her return.

Kerewin's new sense of responsibility takes several forms: she rebuilds the marae; she shelters a cat which she names Li, a Buddhist term and "part of the doctrine which affirms that the harmony of the universe is realized when each thing is allowed to be itself without interference" ("Breaking Ground" 49); she investigates Simon's true origins, arranging legal and binding responsibility for him; finally, she rebuilds her home, not in the narrow, vertical spiral of the Tower's staircase which accommodates only one, but in a wide, horizontal spiral which accommodates many, offering "privacy, apartness, but all connected and all part of the whole" (434). The act fulfills the dream vision in which she restores one building and "other buildings flowed out of it" (428). Just as her act of rebuilding the marae leads to "other building," the restoration of her self will lead to the restoration of Simon and Joe.

Symbolically, Kerewin's final break with the past is marked by her attitude and actions towards "The Book of the Soul," in which she records the significant events of her life. This "logbook," so precious she keeps it under lock and key, accompanies her when she flees the Tower. However, upon completing her quest, the "Book of the Soul" elicits her contempt, "Pretentious bugger, Holmes, taking yourself that seriously . . ." (430). After recording the final events of her "journey" Kerewin follows, "the Chinese: on the funeral pyre" of dead selves, she places a "paper replica of what is real" (437). The book had been her "last resort, a soul-hold beyond even the bottle" (430), but now, having "come a way since" (431), she places the book in "the heart of the fire and closes the range door upon it" (437). In early drafts, Hulme had Kerewin pack the book away, however, to show how significantly Kerewin had moved beyond her "whimper book," Hulme decided to "get rid of it altogether" (Hall 21). The action signifies the final death of her old self. Kerewin has won the freedom to live, redefining human love and anchoring it in work and community.

Whether the novel "succeeds" depends largely upon the reader's response to Kerewin as a character and her successful completion of the quest. Joe's quest to recover his Maori spirituality is essential to the mythic structure, but the potential to create a new future lies with Kerewin. It is Kerewin in whom Hulme is most interested. Whether one accepts the character as "hero" is finally personal and largely dependent upon one's own polemical preferences. If the reader is threatened by the concept of "androgyny/ neuter-ality", and concerned that in the "real world" a male ego could not endure a beating from a female,[7] the novel is restricted to a personal, limited perception of reality and probability. However, if in receiving the events of the novel, we allow that a female may search for identity in creative, rather than procreative means "we are presented with an image of a woman with the power to surprise, disturb, and even rearrange ideas" ("Breaking Ground" 49). It is possible that Hulme fulfills one feminist critic's challenge to print stories with "images of women" that can provide "new visions of individual and shared power that can inspire the transformation of a culture and society." (Christ 131). Hulme says she wanted to suggest that everyone in New Zealand has "lost out by Maori people not being spiritually fully alive" (Hall 17). With Kerewin leading, the three characters become the bone people, that is, the model for the "people who make another people" (469), the model for bicultural community.

Does the novel extend itself too far? Do the characters stand up under the symbolic burden placed on them as redemptive figures? These are questions which *pakeha* academics ask themselves. Although some contemporary,

theoretical positions will not privilege the author's reading above any other, I think it is worth noting that Hulme herself resists affiliation with the *pakeha* literary world in New Zealand:

> I haven't much liked it—not from any idea that I'm special, just simply because it doesn't nourish or seem good to get involved with. (Ricketts 29)

By choice, Hulme is outside the *pakeha* academic world. Thus, it is the response from within the Maori community which she values:

> The bloody nice thing about *The Bone People* was the way it circulated round Maoridom. That to me was the best thing of all. (Ricketts 24)

The Pegasus Award for Maori Literature meant to Hulme that "regardless of how mongrel you are" the work was "accepted as a Maori thing" (Ricketts 24). *Pakeha* critics, however, deny the novel's Maori elements. C. K. Stead argues that Joe's quest to recover his Maori spirituality, "read as Maori lore or fiction," is "almost totally spurious" (107). Prentice sees the novel as the "balancing of positions within the post-colonial society" and agrees with Stead; reading the novel as Maori is "inherent ludicrousness" (69). However, the commensal vision depends upon accepting Maori spirituality in *The Bone People*. If Joe's quest is "spurious," the novel collapses. Perhaps it is opting for the easy response, but as a *pakeha* inevitably outside Maori spirituality, I cannot criticize the novel as mythicized self-projection. A Maori critic, writing from inside, may justify such a response,[8] but imposing *pakeha* value judgements on the novel feels too much like racism.

I have, however, become uneasy with the commensal vision. By whatever means Kerewin may "win a home" in *The Bone People,* she is the exception rather than the rule in Hulme's work. Questers abound in Hulme's short fiction. The characters are similar to Kerewin in ways I shall suggest, but no other character, as yet, completes the heroic journey to return to a new-found community. These endings in *Te Kaihau* may be more "believable" in the light of the real world in which we think we live and, therefore, more convincing to readers like Stead; they also point to Hulme's resistance against the possibility of commensalism or community. Simply, images of alienation dominate over community in Hulme's oeuvre.

Hulme subverts gender roles as consciously in the short fiction as in *The Bone People*. Females do not seek selfhood in conventional roles of wife and mother. Although Hulme insists that there is "no way [her] actions are those of somebody who has a commitment to a feminist cause," she reacts against being forced into the socially constructed "female role" ("Constructing the Author" 31). Thus, several characters are of indeterminate gender.[9] We are never certain whether the narrators in **"Unnamed Islands in the Unknown Sea,"** or in **"King Bait"** are male or female. For example the narrator in **"King Bait"** says:

> I shot out of bed, into my denims and t-shirt faster than it's said, grabbed my boots . . . (*Te Kaihau* 39)

Written in first person, Hulme effectively uses the pronoun "I" to hide the narrator's gender. The text gives no conclusive evidence in either direction. The clothing is sufficiently uni-sexed; the narrator is never addressed or referred to in dialogue.

Other characters are approximations of Hulme's "neuter" concept. A "neuter" person has "no sexual loyalties" and, therefore, is "free to adopt whatever blend of qualities society deems to be specifically male or female" ("Constructing the Author" 31). The narrator in **"A Nightsong for the Shining Cuckoo"** is female ("Aunt Frances") but gender boundaries are crossed until she becomes effectively "neuter." The name, for example, is both male and female, differentiated only by spelling. The physiotherapist refers to her as, "you old bush-ahh-person, you" (119). The taxi driver addresses her with the typically male, "Where to, *mate*?" (120, emphasis added). She associates herself with the male when she thinks, "I'm one of the maimed . . . Like tired old men wed to alcohol" (132-33). Like Kerewin, she has lived alone in the country, built her own house, and is "strong in the shoulders and arms" to prove it (120). Furthermore, she has done male associated work—contracting to cut "white pine posts" (127). As with Kerewin's relationship with Joe, Frances is identified with male associated work, while the male, Charlie, cooks for them both, "cleans most of the place" (129), and doesn't "know a shovel from a spade" (128). As in *The Bone People*, it is not a matter of simple role reversal. Frances is also the conventional nurturer, concerned for Bird, earning Charlie's contempt, "You haven't gone soft. You've gone bloody soppy" (126).[10]

Te Kaihau contains several trinities of male, female, and child relationships. Unlike *The Bone People*, none endure. In **"Nightsong For the Shining Cuckoo,"** the bonds are not the conventional blood bonds of family. The maimed woman, her nephew, and a Maori orphan interact but circumstance and the nephew's cruelty defeat any possibility of community. **"Hooks and Feelers"** shows three members of a conventional marriage alienated by sickness and physical mutilation. In **"One Whale Singing,"** the female and her unborn child are oppressed by her jargon-spouting, academic partner from whom she longs to escape. The story leaves her swimming alone in the warm, nurturing sea, but implicitly too far from the shore to survive the swim.

As in *The Bone People*, characters are alienated from family. Despite the "rare times" in the community of "guests" when she woke to hear her mother's "thin perfect soprano" and the father's "velvet baritone," the young girl in **"The Knife and the Stone"** flees from her family and the incestuous abuse from an alcoholic father who "would come lurching and whispering God I love you girl love you girl, fumbling, delving" (100). The woman in **"While My Guitar Gently Sings"** also feels alienated: "all the time I wanted to be alone and quiet down by the creek" (107). She rejects the Maori community which her family represents, but like Kerewin, she has found nothing to replace it:

> I still hate all that shit, men being tapu, and women being noa. Don't eat here; don't put your head there. Don't hang your clothes higher than the men's: never get up and talk on the marae. (114)

The bleakness of her life-style contrasts the generosity of her mother presenting her first guitar. The image of the mother "six feet tall and nearly sixteen stone" standing "ebulliently," contrasts the "shuddering" narrator (115-6). Thus, as in so much of Hulme's short fiction, images of human warmth give way to alienation to the point of psychosis; the story ends typically with the woman "alone in the dark" (116).

The short fiction also shows Hulme's preoccupation with supernatural encounters, as in **"Planetesimal"** and **"Te Kaihau/The Windeater."** Unlike the supernatural figures in *The Bone People*, neither encounter rejuvenates the protagonist, rather they initiate the characters' final destruction. Like Kerewin, the narrator in **"Te Kaihau/ The Windeater"** is both "wanderer" and "loafer." She lives on the Cook Strait Ferry, sleeping alternately in Wellington and Picton. Later, she isolates herself in a house where, again like Kerewin, she "grows things;" "pet slime moulds" and "umbrella toadstools on a dishcloth" that she recalls "fondly." She drinks and would have "kept on that way" until her "liver gave out except for a series of accidents" (225). Similarly to Kerewin, she is a quester, but she "always asked the wrong questions" (212). She is obsessed with knowledge, distrusts what she sees (214), and privileges intuitive knowledge above intellectual. She "lays" before the reader "the unusual and irrational bits" from her life because they are "the only bits that make sense" to her "right now" (211). However, in contrast to Kerewin's encounter with Simon/Maui, the "young Rasta" who is the Maui figure in this story initiates the narrator's death and, presumably, the end of the world. Maui was raised by his aunts, the Winds, but in this story the wind is ambiguously both mythic and realistic. The narrator's final vision of the "sinker" is like a bomb; "just before the fish [Aotearoa] shatters . . . the incandescent cloud will roar" (236).[11]

As suggested above, the Maori myths which fuel *The Bone People* also fuel **"Te Kaihau/The Windeater."** Where Hulme "made a hook" with *The Bone People* to raise the characters to face the "bright broad daylight" of "home" (445), she has "made a sinker" with the "Windeater" persona who, "in another second," will "be gone" (237). Where Kerewin is the spider and ultimately sees herself "weaving webs" of future events (431), the windeater's life is "an old spiderweb" with the remains of "past feasts." What is missing, however, "what is needed to make sense of it all, is the spider" (235). Kerewin, as "spider," makes "sense" of her world; the "windeater" cannot find the spider and comments on the impossibility of making "sense":

> a woman trying to make sense of her self and her living and her world. Which all goes to show the charming naivety of us humans. Sense of a world indeed! (237)

The passage exemplifies what Wedde calls Hulme's "bleak vision with the garrulous humour" (35).

Te Kaihau may reveal Hulme's anxiety about "the authenticity of transferring experience to paper" (Wedde 35). Certainly the stories do exhibit an anxiety about language and experience. The fragments in **"Lost Possessions"** and **"Unnamed Islands in Unknown Seas"** show that words do not prove existence. On the contrary, the "authorities" in **"Unnamed Islands"** decide that the words are "an obscure joke." The "Department's" reader doubts the authenticity of the fragment examined because as [s]he says, "Nobody has explained satisfactorily to *me* why . . ." (170, emphasis added). Thus, the "Department's" reader becomes narrator and creates the problem of deciding which, if either, narrator to believe. In **"Kite Flying at Doctor's Point,"** the narrator wonders if words have the capacity to represent experience:

> Have I told you anything? Or is it all just writing? All just words?

Hulme knows from her reading of the Maui cycle, that words are potentially lethal. Several versions of the myth explain Maui's death by the inaccurate use of language. A particularly *tapu* word was omitted from the *karakia* in his baptismal blessing, a mistake which Maui's father knew would cause Maui's death (Reed 123). Hulme confirms her anxiety about the elusiveness of language: "You've . . . got all the words there but sometimes it's the spaces between that are conveying the full impact of emotions" (Smith 28). This gap seems out of the writer's control, but Hulme recognizes it is in this gap where the power she desires exists. As the narrator in **"Te Kaihau"** says "if you split" the word [windeater] a "power leaks out" (237).

Te Kaihau, then, exhibits an anxiety about language and experience. At the same time the short fiction is working out problems the novel raised for the writer. Hulme's tendency to write multiple endings is evident in **"A Tally of the Souls of Sheep"** in which the narrator, as scriptwriter, considers a series of six, possible endings for the characters. Like the multiple versions behind any Maori myth, the outcome:

> . . . depends
> on what story
> you hear. (240)

Pluralism results from the fact that "someone else sees the same thing very differently" (215), and, thus, "there are many stories/told" (239). Every event has infinite tellings. Every tribe has a variation on the myth. One "story" tells the survival of Maui, rescued by his aunt, the "Wind." However, if we pursue the myth, we know that ultimately Maui is destroyed ("crushed between the thighs of Hinenui-te-po" 240). *The Bone People* is one narrative, and must be considered as separate; nevertheless, the possibility of community is undermined by the destructive vision of *Te Kaihau* where one after another, the characters are inevitably "crushed." In *The Bone People*, Hulme glosses

over the literal definition for *te kaihau* to emphasize the comparatively innocuous associations with loafer and wanderer. However, by including the word "Windeater" in the title to her volume of short fiction, she foregrounds the literal (that is, in English), "windeating" makes simply breathing a potentially voracious, threatening activity. Thus, if *The Bone People* represents Hulme's ascendant spiral, *Te Kaihau/The Windeater* is the descendant spiral. The Maui, who ties the sun to the moon in order that they might pull each other up into the sky and benefit humankind, is reflected in *The Bone People*. The vengeful Maui, who turns his brother-in-law into a dog because his crops were more bountiful than Maui's own, belongs to *Te Kaihau*.

Perhaps it is to Hulme's poetry we must turn for a synthesis. The final poem in *The Silences Between*, **"Moeraki Conversations 6,"** seems to incorporate the simultaneous ascent and descent of the double spiral. The poet says, "we are full of talk and singing, sprawled / in a ring round the fire." In the course of the night, "one, by one, two by two, *we* drift away to bed." The poet says, "there is only *us*" (54-55). The reader is drawn into the poem because the poet, writing as "we," includes the reader as the subject and object, implicating the reader in the writing. At the same time, the plural pronouns seem to integrate the poet into the group which the now familiar image of the solitary poet "waiting in the dark" contradicts. "We" may drift away, but the poet remains. Just as Hulme can hide gender with the pronoun "I," she can hide an essentially isolationist vision with the pronoun "we." What Hulme gives the reader is the "self" constantly on the move, shifting ground to prevent the reader from latching onto the poet. The poet is both visible and invisible.[12] Thus, I find that the poem's ideas and structures "work against each other" and "unsettle" the "stability of one another." The use of "we" obscures the fundamental separateness of the "I" speaker.

Hulme says that her "intention" in writing *The Bone People* reflects Jung's idea of individuation: "You cannot be, obviously, a total isolate and you have a responsibility as a communal person to be a constructive force rather than a destructive force" ("Breaking Ground" 27). Traditionally, the Maori individual just doesn't "make sense" apart from "whenua, your hapu." It is the reason, Hulme notes, that other Maori writers "tend to work from a 'we' perspective. It's thoroughly Maori and thoroughly proper." However, "people are now taught to be individuals and to see themselves apart . . . from the community." Traditional, Maori, collective identity, Hulme says, "can no longer work" in the eighties ("Breaking Ground" 27). Hulme seems to regret the impossibility of the Maori "we," but elsewhere she validates the *pakeha* "I":

> We're taught to have regard for other people and to put ourselves down. I do that. We all know what happens if you don't. (Wichtel 21)

Hulme demonstrates for the interviewer exactly "what happens" as she "delivers herself a karate chop to the neck, lethal variety" (Wichtel 21). "We" then becomes a pretense, a "commensal" camouflage behind which the "I" pursues the self. It is Hulme's way of avoiding society's "lethal karate chop." Hulme's writing reflects her ambivalence between the "learned response," the socially acceptable vision of community, and a more fundamental belief in the isolate self—a belief which I believe goes beyond Hulme's desire to subvert gender roles. ("There is no way my actions are those of somebody who has a commitment to a feminist cause. . . .") While **The Bone People** may attempt a synthesis between the Maori "we" and *pakeha* "I" (see Peter Simpson), **Te Kaihau** demonstrates the defeat of "we" with the holocaust sinking of "o so many islands" (240) in the title story. Ultimately, because Hulme believes the Maori "we" can no longer work, it is the **Te Kaihau** vision which dominates. I am more terrified by the violence, menace, and doom in **Te Kaihau** than I am heartened by the vision of the "bone people" as instruments of future change. And so, I believe, is Keri Hulme.

Notes

1. This preface in *Te Kaihau* might be considered "poetic fiction," a duality reflected in the title word "*tara*," meaning half and half. However, I call it poetry because it was published separately in a recent anthology of poetry, *The New Poets*.

2. To describe Kerewin's quest as a female hero, I use a model which feminist critics Pearson, Pope, and Pratt have amended from Joseph Campbell. The hero's journey is divided into three stages: the Departure which includes the call to adventure, the refusal, and the intervention of supernatural aid; the Initiation, which includes the meeting with the goddess, atonement, and reconciliation; and the Return where the hero returns to society.

3. Pearson, Pope, and Pratt.

4. Reed's *Treasury of Maori Folklore* reflects the variations in myth.

5. Shona Smith notes the association with Rehua in "Breaking Ground" (45).

6. Campbell's term.

7. See C. K. Stead, "When an argument between [Joe] and Kerewin turns into a fight, Kerewin . . . beats him effortlessly, a beating which he accepts with great good humour and with no apparent damage to his ego. This is not the only point at which the reader is likely to feel the novel has taken a dive from reality into wishful day-dream" (106-07).

8. See Merata Mita, for example, who writes that "an elusive realm of embryonic dreamtime and unformed imagination tends to mystify Maori spirituality to the point of regression, especially in the case of Kerewin."

9. Prentice accurately notes that "some of Hulme's stories . . . present characters of indeterminate gender." The point is valid, but she misreads "Stations on the Way to Avalon." The narrator is not "indeterminate" as Prentice claims; he is clearly addressed as Robert.

10. See Smith and Prentice. Both discuss behaviourally ambiguous characters.

11. Wedde implies this reading in his review.

12. We have seen this protection of the "self" in the short fiction with the double narrator, "Lost Possessions" and "Unnamed Islands," or the narrator/script-writer whose consciousness controls the characters in "Tally." The narrative layers form a barrier between the implied or external narrator (self) and reader.

Works Cited

Campbell, Joseph. *The Hero With A Thousand Faces*. 2nd Ed. Princeton: Princeton U. P., 1968.

Christ, Carol. *Deep Diving and Surfacing*. Boston: Beacon Press, 1980.

Dale, Judith. "*The Bone People* (Not) Having It Both Ways." *Landfall* 39. 4 (1985).

Hall, Sandi. "Sandi Hall and Keri Hulme talk about *The Bone People*." Broadsheet 121 (1984).

Hulme, Keri. *Lost Possessions*. Wellington: Victoria University Press, 1985.

———. *Te Kaihau/The Windeater*. Wellington: Victoria U.P., 1986.

———. *The Bone People*. Auckland: Spiral in association with Hodder and Stoughton, 1985.

———. *The Silences Between (Moeraki Conversations)*. Auckland: Auckland U. P., 1982.

Jones, Lawrence. *Barbed Wire and Mirrors*. Dunedin: Otago U. P., 1987.

Mita, Merate. "Indigenous Literature in a Colonial Society: rev. of *The Bone People*." *The Republican* 52 (1984).

Parker, Selwyn. "Bankable Authors." *North and South* Nov. 1987.

Pearson, Carol, and Katherine Pope. *The Female Hero in American and British Literature*. New York and London: R. R. Bowker Company, 1981.

Pratt, Annis. *Archetypal Patterns in Women's Fiction*. Brighton: The Harvestor Press, 1982.

Prentice, Chris. "Re-writing their Stories, Renaming Themselves: Post-colonialism and Feminism in the Fictions of Keri Hulme and Audrey Thomas." *SPAN* No. 23 (1987).

Reed, A. W. *Treasury of Maori Folklore*. Wellington and Auckland: A. H. & A. W. Reed, 1963.

Ricketts, Harry. *Talking About Ourselves*. Wellington: Mallinson Rendel, 1986.

Simpson, Peter. *Press* 1 Sept. 1984.

Smith, Shona. "Constructing the Author." *Untold* 4 (Spring 1985).

———. "Keri Hulme: Breaking Ground." *Untold* 2 (Spring 1984).

Stead, C. K. "Keri Hulme's *The Bone People* and the Pegasus Award for Maori Literature." *Ariel* 16. 4 (1985).

Wedde, Ian. "Trying to Make Sense." *Listener* 31 May 1986.

Wichtel, Diana. "Taking Off." *Listener* 16 Nov. 1985.

Thomas E. Benediktsson (essay date Winter 1992)

SOURCE: "The Reawakening of the Gods: Realism and the Supernatural in Silko and Hulme," in *Critique*, Vol. XXXIII, No. 2, Winter, 1992, pp. 121-31.

[*In the essay below, Benediktsson compares the treatment of realism and indigenous myth in Leslie Silko's* Ceremony *and Hulme's* The Bone People.]

Realism in the contemporary novel depends on two contradictory claims. The first one is that the narrative is not literally true. The familiar statement in the frontispiece that "the characters and incidents portrayed herein are entirely imaginary and bear no resemblance to real persons, living or dead" is not only a protection against lawsuit but also a statement of the conscious fictionality of realistic narrative. Of course, that statement is duplicitous if viewed in the light of realism's second claim, that the work bears a resemblance to social and psychological reality, that in important ways it tells us the truth about "the effect of experience on individuals" if not about "the nature of experience itself." The distinction is Edward Eigner's, who argues that the attempt in the nineteenth-century novel to reconcile scientific truth with metaphysical truth was initiated to discredit the empirical, not to validate it. In this paper I am taking a similar position: attempts to reconcile realism with the supernatural in the contemporary postcolonial novel are undertaken in an effort to undermine the ideological base that supports realism.

The act of reading a realist text, then, is based on the reader's conscious or unconscious assimilations of the text's incorporated contradictions: fictionality and mimesis. Like Chief Broom in *One Flew Over the Cuckoo's Nest,* readers (I should say readers innocent of literary theory) say to themselves "It's the truth, even if it didn't happen."

Increasingly, however, theory has focused our attention on realism's first claim by attacking the second. Defining mimesis as a set of conventions, structuralism analyzed its arbitrary, elaborated codes. Terry Eagleton discusses S/Z, Roland Barthes's classic structuralist study of mimesis as the "work of the break," which points the way toward poststructuralism by emphasizing the "irreducibly plural" nature of texts (138). Poststructuralism, asserting that language does not so much reflect reality as create the reality we know, had led in the 1970s and early 1980s to many discussions of the way realistic texts construct and deconstruct their own claims to representations.

The poststructuralist "death of the author" (Barthes) has led us in two directions: on the one hand into an emphasis on textuality and intertextuality, on the other to an explora-tion of the social and material conditions that generate literary texts. In this latter respect the text is "always charged by ideology—those unspoken collective understandings, conventions, stories and cultural practices that uphold systems of social power" (Kaplan 6). For some, then, realism engages in an active dialogue with a changing culture, creating and critiquing its meanings. In that sense realism is "one of the crucial symbolic forms through which collective sense is forged" (Pendergast 217). For other poststructuralist critics, the realist novel, born in the late eighteenth century and persisting in a conservative literary tradition into the present, is part of the vast project of bourgeois capitalism; its emphases on totalization and closure, in fact on the mimetic correspondence between narrative form and social reality, are hegemonic, or as Derrida puts it, "a matter for the police" (102). Ruptures in realism—violations of its codes—can be construed as acts of rebellion against this tyranny.

In this essay I would like to examine some "ruptures" in the realism of two postcolonial novels, each of which attempts to find alternatives to the Western rationalism, pragmatism, and linearity that support realism's codes. In the first, Leslie Silko's *Ceremony,* Tayo, half white and half Pueblo Indian, is a young World War II veteran who, as a prisoner of war, cursed the jungle monsoon that he felt was causing his step-brother's death. Having returned to the reservation after a time in a veteran's hospital, Tayo is convinced that his curse caused the drought that is now afflicting his reservation. Suffering from this guilt and from other forms of distress, Tayo learns that his illness is part of a larger pattern of evil—the "witchery" brought about by those who seek the world's destruction. Tayo is healed by a series of Pueblo and Navaho purificaton ceremonies and by a personal ceremony he performs for himself. During his quest he has an encounter with a mysterious young woman named Ts'eh, later identified as Spider Woman, a supernatural figure from Pueblo legend.

The second work I will discuss is Keri Hulme's ***The Bone People***, a novel first published in 1984, by the Spiral Collective, an independent press formed in New Zealand to bring out the book after it had been rejected by the major publishers in that country. Kerewin Holmes, part white and part Maori, is a failed artist who lives alone in a stone tower by the ocean. Her alcoholic solitude is broken by the wayward mute orphan child Simon and by his step-father Joe, a nearly full-blooded Maori. Kerewin's growing love for Joe is blighted by her discovery that he brutally beats Simon, and she decides tragically to intervene. When she gives Joe permission to beat Simon, and he beats the child nearly to death, he is imprisoned and Simon institutionalized. Kerewin, afflicted by stomach cancer, withdraws to a distant place to die; she is cured by the miraculous intervention of a supernatural figure. Joe, released from prison, is cured of his violence and guilt by the discovery of a sacred place, the landing-site of one of the original Great Canoes. Simon, escaping from his foster home, is reunited with Kerewin and Joe at the end, as his character blends with Maui, the Trickster figure of Maori myth.

These two novels share a plot that has become common in the postcolonial novel. In labelling novels by an American Indian and a New Zealand Maori "postcolonial," I am using the term in a fairly broad sense. My point is that the plot pattern I have identified here, common in postcolonial novelists as diverse as Achebe, Narayan, and Ousmene, is a literary representation of a deep cultural conflict among formerly colonized people. A member of an oppressed and marginalized people is suffering from a grave illness, a malady that seems simultaneously to be psychological, physical, and spiritual. Eventually this character is healed through traditional ritual and through a literal encounter with the supernatural, whose reawakening accompanies the main character's rebirth. At the end of the novel this powerless person has appropriated a source of transcendent power, and there is hope for a new society based on the values of the reborn traditional culture: as Silko puts it at the end of *Ceremony,* the witchery "is dead for now" (261).

The form of both novels involves breaking the codes of realism, not only introducing romance elements and evoking the supernatural, but also disrupting the linearity of the narrative and altering its spatial and psychological geography. The stream-of-consciousness technique, used in both novels, alters rationalism through the nonrational flow of sensation, perception, and intuition. The introduction of myth layers the text further by juxtaposing the temporal with the timeless, the diachronic with the synchronic. These textual strategies not only force the Western reader to abandon empiricism, but they also create a fictive realm of possibility and power—the possibility of the awakening of the traditional gods, and the power of those reawakened gods to cure the postcolonial malaise.

From the beginning of *Ceremony,* Silko introduces textual elements that disrupt the linearity of her narrative. By far the greater part of the novel is told from the point of view of Tayo. At first, the narrative moves freely and confusingly, juxtaposing incidents in Tayo's life which are separated widely in time:

> . . . he got no rest as long as the memories were tangled with the present, tangled up like colored threads from old Grandma's wicker sewing basket when he was a child. . . . He could feel it inside his skull—the tension of little threads being pulled and how it was with tangled things, things tied together, and as he tried to pull them apart and rewind them into their places, they snagged and tangled even more. (7)

The reader's task to "untangle" these threads of experience is rather difficult in the opening fifty pages of the novel. Before long, however, through iteration a temporal pattern emerges, and the reader can reconstruct the linear narrative of Tayo's life. What seems at first to be ruptures in realism are actually representations of the flow of consciousness of a disturbed man. As Tayo begins to heal, the narrative attains more linearity until the last eighty pages are told in straightforward chronological order. Thus realism, understood as the mimetic representation of linear experience, is not threatened.

A second disruptive element, however, is not so easily reconciled. From the beginning the "realistic" prose narra-

tive—the novel—is interrupted by free-verse texts of Pueblo myths and stories. Thematically and tropologically, the stories bear complex intertextual relations to the novel, which by the end is understood as a part of a much greater web of meaning, encompassing all Pueblo cultural experience. Edith Swan has discussed the intricate structural relationships between Silko's novel and Pueblo and Navaho ceremonies.

The stories construct their own hermeneutic. From the opening creation myth, Silko establishes the Pueblo storyteller's claim to an art in which language is directly related to the physical world:

> Thought-Woman, the spider,
> named things and
> as she named them
> they appeared.
>
> She is sitting in her room
> thinking of a story now
>
> I'm telling you the story
> she is thinking. (1)

Stories are corporeal, as real as the five worlds of Pueblo cosmology. Stories keep the people alive:

> I will tell you something about stories,
> [he said]
> They aren't just entertainment.
> Don't be fooled.
> They are all we have, you see,
> all we have to fight off
> illness and death. . . .
>
> He rubbed his belly.
> I keep them here
> [he said]
> Here, put your hand on it
> See, it is moving.
> There is life here
> for the people. (2)

The text of the novel enfolds and incorporates the texts of the stories. By the end, however, in a kind of chiasmus, the stories have incorporated the novel. The stories inscribe and circumscribe Tayo's own story, until the ceremonies by which he is healed serve a kind of hermeneutic: he can read his own life as a Pueblo story. Just as the limited claims of realism have become subsumed into the much greater claims of Pueblo storytelling tradition, Silko's role as novelist has been subsumed into the role of the Pueblo story-teller—naming the world, defending the people, helping fight off illness and death. In the process, the linear flow of meaning that dominates mimetic representation has been supplanted by a kind of "spider web" of meaning in which the interrelationships among the stories revise time and space, just as Thought Woman tells her stories in a timeless realm.

The key moment in *Ceremony* that proclaims the storyteller's victory is the moment when the world of Pueblo myth enters the text of the novel itself, not as an intertextual referent but as a third and irrevocable disruption of realism. In his relationship with Ts'eh, Tayo has an encounter with divinity. Ts'eh's love restores him to health, and she warns him of the plot against his life by the veteran Emo, agent of the witchery that now no longer seems merely figurative. The last stage of Tayo's ceremony occurs when, at the site of the uranium mine that supplied the ore for the Manhattan Project, he successfully resists the urge to kill Emo. In his victory over the witchery, Tayo has been healed with the help of incarnate divinity. In the process the realist novel, itself a manifestation of the hegemony of the white world over the Pueblo and therefore a symptom of the malaise from which Tayo has suffered, has been transformed.

Unlike *Ceremony*, **The Bone People** does not include traditional myths and stories that challenge realism's codes. Rich in physical and psychological detail, the novel's dialogue and indirect discourse employ a pungent New Zealand vernacular interspersed with Maori phrases, which are translated in an appendix. With considerable vividness and plenitude of detail, there is a strong impression of verisimilitude. The ruptures in realism occur in other ways.

The first is an issue that should in some ways reinforce rather than subvert the novel's claim of mimesis. The name "Kerewin Holmes" bears obvious similarity to that of the author Keri Hulme. We suspect that Joe, Simon, and other characters have living counterparts as well, and we are thus encouraged to read the text both as novel and as autobiography. Thus the novel may contain traces of an implied autobiographical text or texts. Tempted to deconstruct the text as we read it, we search for autobiographical clues that may or may not be present in a narrative that in other ways proclaims its fictionality. This double reading does subvert realism.

Traces of still other texts abound in **The Bone People**. The lonely woman living in a stone tower by the sea, visited by a mute child, a changeling who himself came from the sea—the plot is redolent of fairy tale, of Celtic romance. Further, since Kerewin is both eclectically well-read and verbally histrionic, her voice, which dominates the text, is filled with allusions and echoes. And finally, the technical influence of James Joyce is ubiquitous.

These intertextual elements, leading the reader to an encounter with the materiality of the text itself, comprise ruptures in realism. As in *Ceremony*, the linear flow of the narrative is altered through the introduction of a controlling metaphor or hermenuetic trope—not the spider web of Thought Woman's design, but the spiral, a design element in Maori art that has special meaning to Kerewin and ultimately to the narrative itself, which will move not only linearly but in a spiralling, concentric pattern, as Kerewin and Joe confront their innermost fears and desires. Like *Ceremony*, realism here is ruptured irrevocably by the introduction of the supernatural that accompanies the re-awakening of the traditional gods.

Late in the novel, when Joe meets the kaumatua (old man) who has been guarding the sacred site of the landfall of one of the Great Canoes, he learns that he, Kerewin, and Simon are the foretold new guardians. He also learns that the spiritual power of the place emanates not from the site but from a stone that came on the canoe, a stone holding a mauriora (life-power) that has not yet departed from the world. After the kaumatua's death, when Joe takes the stone with him, there is hope that Kerewin, Joe, and Simon—reunited and cured of madness, illness, and violence—will create a new "marae" or site of community, inspired by the presence of the awakened mauriora. Like Tayo, they represent hope for a new world.

Both *Ceremony* and **The Bone People** portray characters who are at first trapped in narratives of victimization and oppression, narratives inscribed and supported by the codes of realism. It is the ideological task of realism to make its structures seem "natural" and "inevitable"—"natural" in the conviction that language offers a clear and undistorted view of social reality, and "inevitable" in the conviction that the social reality portrayed exercises a determining influence on the life of an individual. Tayo's plight is the *necessary* outcome of the oppression of the American Indian. Joe's abuse of Simon is the necessary behavior of a Maori who, brutally beaten himself as a child and deeply thwarted in his life, cannot cure himself of violence. For Tayo and Joe to evade their "fates" is for the novels in which those lives are inscribed to evade the structures of realism.

In that sense, we could argue that Silko and Hulme, in providing their characters with an escape from their narratives, may have devised sentimental evasions, fantasy solutions for problems that cannot be solved in "real life," but which can be solved literarily by disrupting mimesis, the correspondence of "fiction" to "life." Violating the reader's sense of verisimilitude and probability, attaching magical "happy endings" to otherwise tragically determined narratives, Silko and Hulme may be evading responsibility for their own plots; as one cynical student put it when my class finished **The Bone People**, "Well, roll the credits!"

The evasion might be not only sentimental but also political. *Ceremony* was written toward the end of a time of activism when American Indians, in an effort to call attention to their historic oppression, demonstrated at Wounded Knee Battlefield, occupied Alcatraz Island, and called for the restoration of traditional salmon fishing rights in the Columbia River. Hulme's novel, written a few years later, coincided with a Maori nationalist movement that led to some parliamentary reforms but has otherwise polarized New Zealand society. Both novels, by dramatizing the awakening of a traditional spirituality and by portraying characters who heal themselves by rejecting conflict, may be advocating quietism and avoiding the threatening but potentially more effective arena of political action, an arena avoided by both authors.

In his study of Black nationalism in American literature, Larry Neal gives ethnic nationalism and the recovery of traditional culture a classic formulation: "A group withdraws into itself and labels the historically oppressive culture as the enemy. . . . The nation or group feels that its social oppression is inextricably tied with the destruction of its traditional culture" (782). To recover an aspect of the suppressed culture—even as fantasy—can be an act not only of revival but of subversion, a way of reifying the oppressed group's sense of separateness and entitlement.

It is not easy, even in fantasy (or perhaps we should say especially in fantasy), to escape from the ideological pitfalls inherent in the postcolonial situation. In *Manichean Aesthetics,* his study of the literature of African colonialism, Abdul JanMohammed has written of the double binds of assimilation: for the native to choose the traditional culture is to doom himself to remain in "a calcified society whose momentum has been checked by colonization." On the other hand, to choose assimilation is to be "trapped in a form of historical catalepsy" in which his own culture has been replaced by the colonizers (5). The literature of postcolonialism is a literature of marginality and liminality, portraying characters caught between one culture and another.

JanMohammed's title is taken from a passage in Frantz Fanon's *The Wretched of the Earth,* in which the double binds are moral, almost metaphysical. Fanon argues that the colonizer, in order to justify his conquest of an indigenous people, constructs a Manichean world-view in which the native is perceived as "a sort of quintessence of evil. . . . The native is declared insensible to ethics; he represents not only the absence of values, but also the negation of values." For Fanon, then, the recovery of a traditional spiritual culture is a way of defeating that Manichean polarization. In the process, however, there is the risk of a counter-Manicheanism in which "to the theory of the absolute evil of the native the theory of the absolute evil of the settler replies" (41 and 93; cited by JanMohammed 4). Both Silko and Hulme, in their equivocations and evasions, may be trying to slip the double binds of assimilation and to avoid a counter-Manicheanism that could be the unhappy effect of the theme of the recovery of the traditional culture. To forestall this counter-Manicheanism, both authors invent protagonists of mixed racial origin; and significantly, both construct alternative versions of the traditional myths.

Tayo's illegitimacy is shameful to his aunt, who sees in his hazel eyes the sign not only of miscegenation but also of her sister's promiscuity. Taunted by his reservation schoolmates and continuously held inferior to his full-blooded cousin Rocky, Tayo ironically has a clearer appreciation of the importance of native ritual than his contemporaries. For Aunty, who has become a middle-class Christian, Rocky the college-bound football hero represents a dream to escape from reservation life into mainstream America. When Tayo returns alive from the war that has claimed Rocky, he has the terrible feeling that "It was him, Tayo, who had died, but somehow there had been a mistake with the corpses, and somehow his was

still unburied" (28). In spite of his illegitimacy the half-breed Tayo, tutored by the part-Mexican Betonie, represents the true hope of his people.

Betonie becomes the spokesman for Silko's critique of both assimilation and of separatism. The traditional ceremonies of the Pueblo healer Ku'oosh will not cure the sickness Tayo carries. Only when he encounters Betonie can a healing ceremony be devised. For Betonie, the old ceremonies must change: ". . . after the white people came, elements in this world began to shift; and it became necessary to create new ceremonies. I have made changes in the rituals. The people mistrust this greatly, but only this growth keeps our ceremonies strong" (126).

In Betonie's hogan a litter of calendars and telephone books suggests the multiplicity of lives that must be incorporated into a unified vision to combat "the witchery," which Betonie specifically defines as Fanon's "counter-Manicheanism":

> They want us to believe all evil resides with white people. Then we will look no further to see what is really happening. They want us to separate ourselves from white people, to be ignorant and helpless as we watch our own destruction. But white people are only tools that the witchery manipulates; and I tell you, we can deal with white people, with their machines and their beliefs. We can because we invented white people; it was Indian witchery that invented white people in the first place. (132)

To Betonie, the world brought by the white people is profoundly evil. Whites hated the land, hated life; in their effort to master it they destroyed it. And their technology threatens to destroy the world:

> Caves across the ocean
> in caves of dark hills
> white skin people
> like the belly of a fish
> covered with hair.
>
> Then they grow away from the earth
> then they grow away from the sun
> then they grow away from the plants and animals
> They see no life
> When they look
> they see only objects.
> The world is a dead thing for them. (135)

The evil of the white people is powerful; the responsibility for combatting it is an Indian responsibility, but to combat evil through violence is to succumb to it and be lost. The key moment for Tayo—the conclusion of his ceremony—is when he refuses to use violence.

In *The Bone People*, as in *Ceremony,* the mixed ancestry of the protagonist is emphasized. Kerewin is only part Maori by blood, but like Tayo, the native part of her is the deepest:

> "It's very strange, but whereas by blood, flesh and inheritance, I am but an eighth Maori, by heart, spirit,

and inclination, I feel all Maori." She looked down into the drink, "I used to. Now it feels like the best part of me has got lost in the way I live." (61-62)

Though many New Zealanders can claim mixed ancestry, Hulme stresses Kerewin's marginality in other ways—her solitude, the tragic break with her family that has led to the failure of her art. Kerewin's sexuality is also marginal:

> ". . . I've never been attracted to men. Or women. Or anything else. It's difficult to explain, and nobody has ever believed it when I have tried to explain, but while I have an apparently normal female body, I don't have any sexual urge or appetite. I think I am a neuter." (266)

Hulme stresses Kerewin's androgyny. Physically powerful, she smokes cigars, performs hard physical labor when the occasion warrants it, and dominates the few relationships she enters. Trained in the combat skills if not the spiritual discipline of aikido, she intervenes in Joe's violence toward Simon violently. She beats Joe to insensibility; and having thereby established her dominance over him, she makes him promise never to beat Simon again without her permission, a permission which, tragically, she gives.

At a public reading of her work at Montclair State College in May 1987, Hulme remarked that violence against children is a pervasive social problem in New Zealand, among Maoris and Pakeha (white New Zealanders) alike, and that she had written **The Bone People** in part to draw attention to it. In this culture of violence, the key to personal redemption for both Joe and Kerewin is the renunciation of violence. The Maori society discovered by the Europeans who colonized New Zealand was itself exceptionally violent, with ritual cannibalism and continual bloody warfare among rival clans and kingdoms. To heal her characters through a recovery of Maori spirituality, Hulme, like Silko, must create an alternative narrative of Maori culture.

The kaumatua, an old man with facial tattoos inscribed in a pattern not seen for hundreds of years, is, like Betonie in *Ceremony,* the key to Joe's healing and to the recovery of a lost spirituality. Known in his neighborhood as "the last of the cannibals," he tells Joe of his relationship with his grandmother, who urged him to eat of her flesh when she died. Unable to do that, he took over her life's work, the guardianship of the sacred stone. In describing to Joe the nature of the spirit he guards, he, like Betonie, is the spokesman for the author's revision of traditional history:

> I was taught that it was the old people's belief that this country, and our people, are different and special. That something very great had allied itself with some of us, had given itself to us. But we changed. We ceased to nurture the land. We fought among ourselves. We were overcome by those white people in their hordes. We were broken and diminished. We forgot what we could have been, that Aotearoa was the shining land. Maybe it will be again . . . be that as it will, that thing that allied itself to us is still here. I take care of it, because it sleeps now. It retired into itself when the world changed, when the people changed. (364)

The "sleeping god" to whom the kaumatua has dedicated his life is the spirit of a powerful, nonviolent spirituality that was debased, not only by the Europeans but also by the original Polynesian settlers who became the Maoris. If this "mauriora" were to awaken, an entirely new society, constructed on principles even more ancient than those of the Maoris, would be formed.

When, after the kaumatua's death, Joe brings the stone that holds the mauriora to Kerewin's property in Whangaroa, it sinks deep into the earth. The spiral house Kerewin builds there, and the family relationship that is established among the white child and the two Maoris, represent not only their triumph over their own personal demons but also the germ of a new society, neither Pakeha nor Maori, whose spirituality is based on the mauriora life-energy, now grounded in the land and in its people. The power has awakened:

> They were nothing more than people, by themselves. Even paired, any pairing, they would have been nothing more than people by themselves. But all together, they have become the heart and muscles and mind of something perilous and new, something strange and growing and great.
>
> Together, all together, they are the instruments of change. (4)

In both novels the central characters will become leaders of a revitalized society, one that embraces traditional spirituality but that does not seek the counter-Manicheanism of nationalism. The ideological project of the novels is not to overturn the white culture but to transform it. In the process, realism as a literary mode of representation has been transformed.

These speculations have led us from a consideration of the technical disruptions of realism into a discussion of the political stance of the novels. Yet we have not really digressed; realism is intrinsically ideological. Barthes argues that realism is "unhealthy" because it denies that language is socially constructed (Eagleton 135). Its claim that it is natural and that it offers the only way to view the world is totalitarian and hegemonic, an esthetic equivalent of colonialism. The gods reawaken: Silko and Hulme disrupt "unhealthy" realism in order to heal their characters, just as they challenge the narrative of colonial oppression in order to offer an alternative narrative of entitlement.

Works Cited

Barthes, Roland. "The Death of the Author." *Image-Music-Text: Roland Barthes.* Ed. Stephen Heath. New York: Hill, 1977.

———. *S/Z.* Paris: Editions du Seuil, 1970.

Derrida, Jacques. "Living on: Border Lines." *Deconstruction and Criticism.* Ed. Harold Bloom, et al. New York: Seabury, 1979.

Eagleton, Terry. *Literary Theory: An Introduction.* Oxford: Oxford UP, 1983.

Eigner, Edward. *The Metaphysical Novel in England and America*. Berkeley: U of California P, 1978.

Fanon, Frantz. *The Wretched of the Earth*. New York: Seabury, 1979.

Hulme, Keri. *The Bone People*. 1984. New York: Viking/Penguin, 1986.

JanMohammed, Abdul. *Manichean Aesthetics*. Amherst: U of Massachusetts P, 1983.

Kaplan, Amy. *The Social Construction of American Realism*. Chicago: U of Chicago P, 1986.

Neal, Larry. "The Black Contribution to American Letters." *The Black American Reference Book*. Ed. Mabel Smythe. Englewood Cliffs: Prentice, 1976.

Prendergrast, Christopher. *The Order of Mimesis: Balzac, Stendahl, Nerval, Flaubert*. Cambridge: Cambridge UP, 1986.

Silko, Leslie. *Ceremony*. New York: Viking, 1977.

Swan, Edith. "Healing via the Sunwise Cycle in Silko's *Ceremony*." *American Indian Quarterly* 12.4 (1988), 313-28.

———. "Laguna Symbolic Geography and Silko's *Ceremony*." *American Indian Quarterly* 12.3 (1988), 229-49.

Giovanna Covi (essay date 1993)

SOURCE: "Keri Hulme's *The Bone People:* A Critique of Gender," in *Imagination and the Creative Impulse in the New Literatures in English,* edited by M.-T. Bindella and G. V. Davis, Rodopi, 1993, pp. 219-31.

[*Covi is a PhD. candidate at the State University of New York at Binghamton. In the following essay, she discusses Hulme's unconventional treatment of gender and ethnicity in* The Bone People.]

When Keri Hulme's first novel, **The Bone People,** was finally published in 1984, it quickly attracted both passionate fans and hostile detractors. This polarized response focused almost entirely on extra-textual considerations.

The novel was initially rejected by three established New Zealand publishers before Spiral, a small feminist collective formed specifically for the purpose, published it. Promoted as a feminist text by a Maori writer, the book enjoyed surprising commercial success. It was first reprinted and then issued in a second edition, this time with the cooperation of a mainstream publisher; it was subsequently published in the United States and Great Britain.[1] Along the way, Hulme's novel was honored with several literary prizes.[2]

However, this attention was short-lived, and six years after its publication, the responses to **The Bone People** still amount to little more than a handful of reviews. In order to understand the scarce interest of literary critics, I think it is helpful to reconsider the circumstances which shaped its initial success.

First, it must be pointed out that of the three publishers who turned down the novel, one was a feminist who thought it was insufficiently feminist for her list and another was a woman publisher who thought it needed more work.[3] Evidently, there was something else at stake other than traditional patriarchal bias against a feminist text. It seems that a certain institutionalized feminism was also in the position to dictate its own "correct line." In fact, even those critics favorable to **The Bone People** have shown an uneasiness with the characters' indeterminate or irrelevant gender; Susan Ash, for example, concludes her appraisal of the novel by observing that a "belief in the isolate self . . . goes beyond Hulme's desire to subvert gender roles."[4]

Another important point is that **The Bone People** appeared at a time when there were great expectations for the consummate New Zealand novel. But although the author emphasizes her one-eighth Maori ancestry, the book turned out to be no vindication of a lost, idealized *Maoritanga*. Neither is it the glorification of a dominant *Pakeha* culture that is at last distinct from the European tradition. Rather, the novel addresses the issue of New Zealand's mixed culture, which has led C. K. Stead to complain that it is "a novel by a Pakeha which has won an award intended for a Maori."[5] This cultural complexity is disturbing, "disconcerting the reader's expectations"—as Susan Braidy has remarked—because the work shows "the difficulty of expressing or achieving a national voice," and the artist's "national identity . . . is confused, diffused and derivative." This reviewer goes on to lament the presence of an "uneasy blend of two cultures": a "paradox," in her view, that "produces a lack of focus" and "a lame ending," and she shows—by way of acrobatically jumping out of the novel and into the nation for which the former should allegedly stand—that, "New Zealand still has some spiritual growing-up to do."[6]

Under these conditions, **The Bone People** initially appealed to critics that were likely to become either frustrated (traditional feminists) or infuriated (kiwi chauvinists) by it, thereby demonstrating the validity of the Vietnamese American critic Trinh T. Minh-ha's trenchant observation that: "Imputing race or sex to the creative act has long been a means by which the literary establishment cheapens and discredits the achievements of non-mainstream women writers."[7] No doubt these remarks apply to nationality as well.

I first became intrigued by **The Bone People** while searching for contemporary texts that challenged both the specification of the writer as historical subject and the effacement of race and gender in the name of textual technicalities. I am interested in interrogating the new canons—"postmodern," "ethnic" and "feminist"—and assessing them in relation to their theoretical precepts. My expectations are thus quite different—seeking to establish correspondences rather than lines of separation—and my fascination with *The Bone People* persists.

I wish to stress that I approach Hulme's work from a comparative angle, as part of a project which focuses on experimental women writers and aims to show, on the one hand, that postmodernist fiction must not necessarily be academic, white and male, and on the other that feminist and minority literature should not be confined to a mimetic realm, respectful of phenomenal facts and of the principles of non-contradiction and coherence of the self. I insist on the political significance that the questioning of the binary logic of rational speculation acquires under the various historical, cultural and social circumstances.

I privilege the critique of the opposition form-content as instrumental in bridging the gap between a purely technical, academic textual deconstruction and a militantly substantive, feminist analysis of content. I agree with Edward Said's proposal that critics should move along the "contrapuntal lines of a global analysis," observing that it is indeed "texts" that "are protean things; they are tied to circumstances and to politics both large and small" and that no single theory can account for them. Therefore, "just as it is true that we cannot read literature by men without also reading literature by women . . . it is also true that we cannot deal with the literature of the peripheries without also attending to the literature of the metropolitan centres."[8] For instance, I have found it fruitful to read Keri Hulme while listening to the voice of Kathy Acker, a punk writer of Lower East-Side New York.

Postmodernist feminism provides a useful starting point for rethinking the contemporary world of literature without renouncing either the radical politics of culturalism or the experimental playfulness of formalism. I think that "the excluded middle" which Thomas Pynchon's works call for can be retrieved by foregrounding the logical meaning of the discourses of the margins within a context of postmodern linguistic games. Minh-ha insists on the focus on language in these terms:

> As focal point of cultural consciousness and social change, writing weaves into language the complex relations of a subject caught between the problems of race and gender and the practice of literature as the very place where social alienation is thwarted differently according to each specific context.[9]

That *The Bone People* "weaves into language . . . complex relations" is precisely the point of my paper. Keri Hulme displays her acute sensitivity for the influence of words on one another in **"Tara Diptych"**: "I know there are at least 21 meanings for *tara* . . . one marvellous 21-joined word, full of diversities—and because I am merely weaver, making senses for sounds—I shall weave anew."[10] But it is equally important to keep in mind Kathy Acker's warning against subsuming everything within language. In her novel *The Empire of the Senseless* she puts it this way:

> Ten years ago it seemed possible to destroy language through language: to destroy language which normal-

izes and controls by cutting that language. Nonsense would attack the empire-making (empirical) empire of language, the prisons of meaning.

> But this nonsense, since it depended on sense, simply pointed back to the normalizing institutions.[11]

Wordplay alone is no more than a carnivalesque transgression, just a ruse of the Law, contained within the dominant culture. As Gayatri Spivak has observed, it is for "their *substantive* revision of, rather than their apparent *formal* allegiance to, the European avant-grade" that women's texts should draw our attention.[12] I would specify that it is the intersection of a critique of patriarchy and a critique of representation that adds significance to the works of such seemingly diverse writers as, for example, Keri Hulme, Angela Carter, Jamaica Kincaid, Maxine Hong Kingston, and Kathy Acker.

The last, for example, has opened up crucial space for discussing the importance of body language. Acker, whose shoulders are covered with a huge tattoo and who has dedicated one of her novels to her tattooist, has unquestionably given "substance" to the French slogan "body language," by insisting on the semiotic function of the tattoo, which is "both material and not material and it's also a sign of the outcast," of outcasts as "people who are beginning to take their own sign-making into their own hands."[13] This deep form of body language is the middle ground in the opposition words-world. It is the language of the subject aware of its being thrown between words and things.

Keri Hulme's novel is a tattoo, a text that, as Nancy Miller would put it, "speaks in tropes and walks in sensible shoes."[14] It shifts continuously from a Realist to a Symbolic mode, from language that is meant to be taken at face value to language that calls for interpretation. The story is minimal—"the smallest smidge of story" according to one unsatisfied reviewer[15]—deriving from the triangle woman-man-child, where the three characters are first slowly drawn together, then catastrophically thrown apart, only to be united again in their final physical and spiritual rebirth. The plot is neatly organized around a Prologue, four parts of three chapters each, and an Epilogue. With love as its main theme and its miraculous happy ending, it invites a Harlequin Romance-like reading. However, the interaction of the symbolic and realistic plane shows that a splendid degree of complexity is woven into this seemingly simple pattern.

The love story is complicated by the fact that there are no family relations among the three characters, nor any sexual bond between the two adults. And yet there is genuine love, so fundamental as to make it impossible for them to live apart. Moreover, the tragedy that hurtles them towards the brink of destruction is determined apparently by the same love that propels the story to its sentimental happy solution: the brutal violence that Joe persistently perpetrates against the child, with the complicitous non-intervention of Kerewin, does not cancel the fact that they are the only people who truly love and understand, and are in turn loved and understood by Simon. To add social depth, Kerewin is the artist isolated in the Tower and is of mixed Maori-European heritage; Joe is an educated man forced to work in a factory because he is a Maori; Simon is a misfit: the only survivor of a wreck, mute and too young to know his age and parentage, he will turn out to be the son of an Irish hippie. Indeed, *The Bone People* is structured by identities which are multi-faceted.

Overall the novel is so multi-layered that it might well be cited as exemplary of the postmodernist canon, and not only because it is written in a mode that draws on both the Realist and Modernist traditions, or because it problematizes the unity of the self. If the model of popular romance is certainly there, so are the repeated intertextual references to the production of high culture—from Joycean language games (one example must suffice: Kerewin saying, "o my serendipitous elf, serendipitous self" p. 395), to Surrealist puns (such as the bone people, which means both the bones of the people and the people of the bones—i.e., both ancestors and progenitors) to the circular structure of the book ending with the words "The End—or the Beginning" and opening with a Prologue entitled "The End at the Beginning."

A closer reading, however, shows that the circular frame is only superficial and functions rather as one of many citations: *The Bone People*'s structure is actually that of the double spiral. As the mythological symbol of the outward-inward, of endless repetition, the spiral could be taken again as a most appropriate postmodernist figure. It represents a moment of extremely tragic or extremely playful self-consciousness of the present, which is understood as a problem of repetition with respect both to the past and to the future. Moreover, this dynamic symbol questions a single reading of an ending that is necessarily open.

Other features situate Hulme's novel among the ranks of postmodernism. Certainly no critic sympathetic to the encyclopedic works of Robert Coover, Thomas Pynchon, John Barth or Vladimir Nabokov would subscribe to the complaint that *The Bone People* "unsuccessfully . . . stretch[es] over the length of nearly 500 pages, hoping . . . [to] become a plot," or that it is a "simple tale . . . inflated."[16] In addition, the writing proceeds by fragments of prose woven into poetry (Prologue, pp. 4-5; p. 219), of philosophical speculations (p. 196) interlaced with ejaculatory remarks (p. 12, and note Kerewin's relentless passion for the expression "berloody"), of scientific descriptions (the passage on sea life; p. 125), which echoes the opening chapter of *Moby Dick*, "Cetology") beaded into scripted dialogue (the rendering of Kerewin and Simon playing cards; pp. 181-2) and the careful pacing of Simon's thoughts (pp. 236-7)). This collage of styles and genres is augmented by numerous metafictional interventions like, two pages from the end of the last chapter, "we're nearing the end now, soul of the book" (p. 435), or the passage where the artist abandons "the old discipline of mirror and

candle . . . to use image and living light as pointers to the self beyond self" (p. 275), providing a definition of the novel as postmodernist. In addition, there are clear instances of *mise en abime* provided by her journal in which the narrative is fully explained and by her own "Book of Godhead" containing "an eclectic range" of writing (p. 329). In other words, the text defies symbolic interpretation because it inevitably provides an explanation of its figurative discourse. If in Manuel Puig's *Kiss of the Spider Woman* the footnotes progressively invade the text, in *The Bone People* they are all incorporated in the narrative.

As one might expect in this context, the narrative voice is absolutely non-authorial. Judith Dale has observed that most readers incorrectly remember the novel as written by an autobiographical speaking-I.[17] Chris Prentice has pointedly examined a number of passages in which the narrative moves almost imperceptibly from third to first person, or in which the third person narrative is unmistakeably Kerewin's voice, a voice which often pervades also the consciousness of Joe and Simon.[18] This fluctuation in narrative voice effectively questions the subject 'Author'.

Moreover, the superwoman-like qualities of Kerewin, who "has it all," are meant to leave her "dissatisfied, because 'all' in the Pakeha sense is not enough."[19] In this way *The Bone People* deconstructs one of the "most powerful fantasies of Western culture"—"the self-sufficient individual," modelled on Robinson Crusoe.[20] Fee recalls the words of the *kaumatua* (elder)—"It is horrifyingly easy to make people perform as you wish, if they think they are in control all the time" (p. 356)—as evidence that Holmes' powerful individualism is eventually undermined, together with the narrator's control over her material.

Finally, since the anti-detective is a featured character in many postmodernist fictions, it is not surprising that we find a narrator-protagonist named "Holmes" engaged in a search which results only in more mystery and questions; in the process of her investigation, Kerewin ironically addresses herself, commenting on her last name: "what clues do we have, Sherlock? (Hey, that's good! why haven't I thought of it before?)" (p. 95).

Almost a textbook of postmodernist fictional strategies, the novel is also a striking example of the foregrounding of language. The title, a Maori pun meaning both ancestors and progenitors, calls attention to the unreliable nature of words. In addition, there are many Maori words and expressions in the text, which—as Dieter Riemenschneider has observed in his paper in this collection—show that English cannot absorb all the difference of ethnic minorities; the Maori words emphasize their own untranslatability. Maryanne Dever has argued that this double-voiced text "challenges the dominant Eurocentric version of reality" and "offers an alternative voice, one that enfranchises multiplicity and undermines the authority of imperialism's homogenising linguistic imperative."[21] This is apparent in the final scene of "commensalism," which recovers the marginalized selves "through tolerance"—an acceptance underlined "by a noticeable shift in viewpoint from the 'I' of Pakeha discourse to the 'we' of Maori discourse, as the three prepare for their reunion and the possibility of some shared future."[22]

But most pertinent to my argument, *The Bone People* also displays a metalinguistic treatment of the deeper signifi- cance of language. This is precisely the site where a the- matization of sexual difference shows the limitations of the concept gender—one of the "critical terms for literary study" in Frank Lentricchia and Thomas McLaughlin's recent book of that title, as well as the increasingly official referent of American feminist theory. I am convinced, along with Teresa de Lauretis, Judith Butler and Susan Suleiman among others, that a working tool resting on two exclusionary categories is inevitably totalizing. Like other binary oppositions, the concept of gender perpetuates a symmetrical order which sees male and female as op- positional and complementary, trapping them within the obligatory choice between nature and culture.

Etymologically linked to a rigid biological dualism by way of its kinship with the word "generate," gender invari- ably reduces and essentializes sexuality—complex, contradictory, changing and unlimited like desire—to a biological relationship between the two sexes. It has also polarized criticism into two ideologically opposed camps, with the proponents of the term denying that it depends upon anatomy, as does Myra Jehlen when she claims that "a good definition of gender" is "'the business facts' of sexual identity."[23] In order to escape the risk of anatomical determinism, the body seemingly has to be denied altogether. Certainly the inclusion of grammar in its semantic field—i.e., of the possibility of an arbitrary free play within a purely linguistic context—shows that the other side of the coin of sexual dichotomy is the erasure of the body in an idealized, androgynous levelling of dif- ference. The opponents of the term, on the other hand, reject the intrinsic dualism of gender as indicative of bi- ologism and essentialism. A new journal is entitled *Genders* and proposes to "get beyond the number two" and move toward a "dizzy accumulation of narratives."[24]

I think that it is the neo-feminist concept of sexual differ- ence that should be proposed in the plural instead. Etymologically "sex" means "to be divided;" thus a study of sexual differences focuses on the plurality of differences which, according to the socio-political evaluation of sexuality in a specific context, concur to separate, to divide, to make a difference. This way the polarization is not predetermined by biology and does not risk formulat- ing masculine and feminine as pure essences. According to circumstances, "sexual differences" may allow for the pertinence of the hetero-homosexual over the male-female opposition, letting difference shift to create new differ- ences—differences that are not necessarily opposite and complementary—rather than pinning it down to the fixed identity of the gendered subject.

In relation to literature, gender is a useful analytical category only for those texts that deconstruct the traditional division of sexual roles, such as Robert Coover's *Spanking the Maid,* in which male and female roles are continuously and parodically inverted. But when a text, like the works of Kathy Acker and Keri Hulme, forces the boundaries of language and reality beyond the deconstruction of logo- centrism and towards the rethinking of a new episteme, it metamorphoses gender into sexual differences. When the recurrent question is "who am I in relation to others?" rather than the fixed identity's obsessive "who am I?," then language strives to include both the nameable and the unnameable, to enunciate multiplicity and contradiction simultaneously, to say the sign and the body, like a tattoo.

The Bone People is a tattoo. It has a certain association with criminality for its transgressive subject matter—the violence against a child. This theme has certainly disturbed Stead, among others, who concludes his article declaring that "the line between charity and imaginative complicity is very fine indeed."[25] Dever is more tolerant; she interprets the violence within the text "as a further frustrated effort to communicate," and calls it "an extreme or perverse form of *lingua franca*."[26] The primitive, rudimentary com- munication of a *lingua franca*, however, cannot account for the spiritual and emotional complexity of human relationships: Kerewin Holmes would say that it is like reducing Aikido—"the way to reconcile the world, to make human beings one family"—to "a technique to fight with" (p. 199). Margery Fee states that by having Simon's body brutally mutilated, Keri Hulme critiques "Western society's smug faith in technique and prowess as a solution to problems."[27]

But *The Bone People* is a tattoo also because it thematizes language in its strict relationship to the body. The characters are first encountered in three short sections written in the present. They are nameless "people" referred to as "instruments of change" (p. 4): a he-"singer" for whom "silence is music," and who is "holding a hand out to [the people]" (p. 3); a second "he" whose "mind is full of change and curve and hope," and who is also holding out his hand which "is gently taken" (p. 3); and a "she" who "knows a lot . . . is eager to know more," and "sings as she takes their hands" (p. 3). This introduction is fol- lowed by three longer sections, each of which begins in the past and moves into the present. These illustrate the characters' "beginnings": the first lived in "darkness" and "fear," and has "in the memory . . . words, different words" (p. 5); the second inhabited "tension" and "despair," and is gnawed by the words of his dead wife, who foretold his destiny (p. 6); the third was imprisoned in the "frivolity" of her self-isolation, a Tower in which she was initially "delighted with the pre-eminence of her art" but which "became an abyss . . . encompassed by a wall . . . with only [her] brainy nails to tear it down," and she "cannot do it" (p. 7). In different ways, they have all been prisoners of language.

Kerewin is the artist who inhabits the Symbolic. Precisely because she believes in the subordination of the Symbolic to the Real, she has reduced the latter to the former: the

Tower of her art is literally and literally a tower; she *is* the letter: not accidentally when the crisis precipitates, she packs the *Concise Oxford Dictionary* for her journey away from the Tower; and even her alter-ego, Snark, is a literary creature, invented by the master of nonsense Lewis Carroll. Her unitary self can be addressed in the mirror as she does throughout the first chapter of the third part. Moreover, she is a "neuter," sexually an androgyne. "She knows a lot," but she knows by analogy—her awareness is representational and her cognitive value is that of a figure of speech.

Simon and Joe belong to the Real and the Imaginary spheres, respectively. The child is uncanny and mysterious and the man is the expression of free sexuality and sexual orientation. The union of the three characters—a union they keep striving for—is what I have called "tattoo": a language which is neither body (the Real) nor sign (the Symbolic), and not even dream (the Imaginary); rather, it is a weaving of all three, "the heart and muscles and mind of something perilous and new, something strange and growing and great. Together, all together, they are the instruments of change" (p. 4).

This point is fundamental for understanding my critique of gender in relation to language. In fact, the crisis of representation has precipitated a reconsideration of the relationship between time and space, which in turn has entailed a re-thinking of sexual difference.[28] Within the temporality of being, Kerewin's knowledge shows its limitations. So if Kerewin "knows a lot," she is also "eager to know more"—to learn a new type of knowledge, one that does not depend on a hierarchical relationship between language and the world as well as one that does not erase the difference between the two. Such fundamental knowledge Kathy Acker calls "sympathy." In her "Introduction" to *Boxcar Bertha,* the autobiography of a hobo who "felt for other humans to the extent that she had to know them, become them, a whore, homeless, willing to suffer, to learn," Acker states: "Such knowledge, such *human* knowledge is complex."[29]

Kerewin's development of "human knowledge" is triggered by Simon's invasion of her tower. He appears in the library—where else? one might ask—and she promptly reduces him to "a weird saint in a stained gold window" (p. 16), while she is fascinated by the pendant with address, name and the words "cannot speak" that he wears around his neck (p. 17). In her library, the boy becomes an icon—not accidentally referred to as "it"—and this section of Chapter One ends with her journal entry: just "today" without a date, above a drawing of the boy's sandal done "with careful realism" (p. 36). Simon—the uncanny Real—has been allegorically fixed and metonymically reduced to a dead letter by the artist.

Kerewin is fascinated by Simon: she is eager to "read," to interpret, to comprehend him. On the contrary, she denies any interest in Joe; when she first sees him in a bar, she disregards him as "a poor effing fella . . . short of words"

(p. 12); only after receiving *a letter* from him, she decides to meet him, and here is her reaction: "the pink paper plus the stream of fucks becomes a roaring ribald laugh in her mind" (p. 46). But Kerewin's symbolic order in which words metaphorically substitute for things—the Tower for the world—and Joe's imaginary metonymical displacement of things for words—a blow on the child's body for an explanation—are two sides of the same coin of the unconscious which, according to Lacan, is structured like a language. So Kerewin's tower is real because it imposes its symbolic order upon the world, in the same way that Joe's blows upon Simon's body are identical to the words he should rather use to explain his point. He is the signifier of desire and it shouldn't surprise us that "his mother named him true"—his Maori name means "the bitter-hearted man" (p. 323). It shouldn't surprise us also that he is the only person who truly loves Simon, despite the fact that he nearly kills him. His love, together with Kerewin's fascination for the boy, show the dependence of the unconscious from the tangible but ungraspable world of the signifieds.

Simon is the Real, which the Symbolic and Imaginary depend upon and which eludes their comprehension. Not accidentally he points out the arbitrariness between signifiers and signifieds. Like Ishmael he never "is" his name: "Hana called him Simon Peter" (p. 87) but Joe's parents use another name, Haimona/Himi. Moreover, "he has called himself . . . Clare, Claro. . . . He doesn't know if that's his name, and he's never told it to anyone. He has a feeling if he does, he'll die" (p. 112)—he'll die indeed if he allows the symbolic reduction of himself to a rhetorical figure. So when Kerewin teaches him the names of the various sea creatures, he thinks: "knowing names is nice, but it don't mean much. . . . Names aren't much. The things are," and with an air of ironic superiority he laughs "secretly at himself" because he knows he "can't say names." But he also tries to expose Kerewin's power when he "blows into her ear" to show that "it was just air." To this "just air" that language is, he opposes the factuality of his hands—the hands of sign language and the hands of touching, of reaching for other people communicating with them without objectifying them: "my hand was more real, see?" (p. 126). But Kerewin "hates touching" (p. 174) and Joe, who doesn't, who kisses and hugs him, also brutally beats him with his hands, adding new scars on a body already marked by past abuse (p. 328).

Kerewin hurts Simon with her words in a similar way: "She can't touch him physically so she is beating him with her voice" (p. 307), and Joe later "recalls the wordless choking of pain the child had made . . . while Kerewin hit him with words" (p. 326). Simon's violated body and mind have a counterpart in the broken message he leaves on the beach—"CLARE WAS HE" (p. 435)—, because he doesn't have enough stones to finish the letters of the third word (p. 256). This episode marks the point in the novel at which the tragedy approaches its climax and Simon's rebirth entails moving from his initial scepticism towards language (p. 238), then through a protest in which he rejects language altogether (p. 395), and finally to an acceptance of its inevitability.

In the hospital, Simon decides to stop communicating, to let his pad "gather dust," when he desperately becomes aware of his separation from Joe and Kerewin (p. 395). He realizes the interdependence that unites the three of them, and although "he doesn't know the words for what they are," he knows that "they only make sense together" (p. 395). All three characters experience rebirth with the assistance of a special healer. Simon's helper is significantly called Dr. Sinclair, a combination of the child's two names (p. 397). This serves to teach Simon that language is inevitable—inadequate but inevitable. At this point, also his chance name "Simon Peter" can acquire some significance, when Joe recovers the photo of the child's father and discovers that he was Timon Padraic (p. 378). After his re-birth, words start meaning a lot more (p. 408) and he begins to enjoy puns and double entendres (p. 408). He has made his move towards the other two characters.

Joe's helper is an elder Maori covered by a tattoo that is "a complicated maze of spirals" (p. 346). He will die in order to save Joe, leaving only a symbol of his tattoo on the paper of his will. Joe's encounter with his healer forces him to understand the meaning of figures and signs and consequently their relationship to and difference from the body. In fact, it is only after he has jumped off the rock thinking of suicide as "a sign" (p. 341), that Joe is finally capable of taking language as something serious and meaningful. He shows his newly-acquired awareness by carving boundary markers representing the people he cares for and putting them on the land received from his healer (p. 383).

Kerewin is assisted by a nameless person of indeterminate age, sex, race and accent (p. 424). Her rebirth entails a temporary abandoning of language and immersion in the body. This is clear when she gives Joe one of her jades, pointing out it has no name (p. 313); when she sends her guitar to her family without any letter to accompany it (p. 419); and when she packs the bunch of things that Simon had "stolen" from her house and sends them to him "care of the public hospital," but doesn't send a letter with them (p. 323). Moreover, after 400 pages of fancy language games, this is what we read:

> An odd little set of thesaurisms kept running verse-wise through her head:
> geegaw
> knicknack
> kicksure
> bric-a-brac
> That's all the whole thing matters eh, as this snowflake world splinters and glistens. Gimcrack trumpery in gold and azure and scarlet and glory silver . . . be-casually nerthing is . . . (pp. 417-18)

A "because" turned into "becasually" puts under discussion the whole logic of cause and effect upon which the symmetry of a complementary opposition between the sexes also depends. It follows unsurprisingly, then, that "rebuilding the Maori hall . . . in spiral fashion [seemed] the straight-forward thing to do" (p. 431).

Thus, weaving becomes naturally the final image in *The Bone People*. Kerewin says of herself that she is now "weaving webs" (p. 431) and the vocabulary describing the scene in which the three characters come together repeats such words as weaving, reeling, spinning, braiding (p. 445). To reinforce this feminine image is Kerewin's "wordless embrace" with her mother (p. 434). This is no triumph of a feminine language over the superiority of a phallic order, however: no victory of a fluid, silent mother tongue such as that theorized by the feminist thinking engaged in defining the essence of "woman." In fact, at the same time that Kerewin is "throwing away sparks of words" (p. 445), she is also announcing her decision to finally take responsibility and give her name to Simon, "as umbrella, as shelter, not as binding. No sentiment about it . . . just good legal sense" (p. 444).

"On the funeral pyre of our dead selves," saying: "I place a paper replica of what is real. Ghost, follow the other ghosts . . . and if we ever meet in a dimension where dreams are real, I shall embrace you and we shall laugh, at last" (p. 437). This is a clear critique of patriarchal logocentrism that widens the boundaries of Lacanian theory. And Kerewin's is certainly a *new* name of the father—the feminine father of a child adopted together with his own adoptive father (and mother too, since he was widowed). There is no space for the closed family unit in the double spiral hall weaving new human relationships at the end of the novel. Just as *The Bone People* exposes the fiction of the supremacy of the Phallus by dismantling Kerewin's Tower, it also shows the devastating consequences of an imaginary identity between words and acts by making Joe the main culprit. Moreover, the novel emphasizes the independence of cultural roles from anatomical difference by assigning a woman to the Symbolic sphere and a man to the Imaginary. But most importantly, Hulme's text moves beyond the simple reversal of gender roles. By inserting the complex and ungraspable element of sexual orientation and by adding the figure of the child to a difficult relationship between a man and a woman, *The Bone People* exposes the limitations of absolutist categories such as gender.

To borrow once again from Acker, *The Bone People* does not address the question, "why do women whore?" but the more interesting question, "why do they give their money to pimps?" The interesting question that this novel poses is not whether Hulme is "really" a Maori or a feminist writer, but rather how established categories of critical interpretation are disrupted by experimental writers from the periphery.

Notes

1. The novel was published and reprinted in 1984 by Spiral, and a second edition was published in New Zealand and London the following year in

conjunction with Hodder & Stoughton. Louisiana State University Press published the first U.S. edition in 1985; Pan published a paperback edition in 1986. Page references of the U.K. and U.S. editions are identical.

2. These included the New Zealand Book Award (1984), the Pegasus Prize for Literature (1984) and the Booker-McConnel Prize for Fiction (1985).

3. C. K. Stead, "Keri Hulme's *The Bone People*, and the Pegasus Award for Literature," *Ariel*, 16.4 (1985), 102.

4. Susan Ash, "*The Bone People* after *Te Kaihau*," *World Literature Written in English*, 29.1 (1989), 134.

5. C. K. Stead, *op. cit.*, p. 104.

6. Susan Braidy, letter, *London Review of Books*, 19 December 1985, 5.

7. Trinh T. Minh-ha, *Woman, Native Other: Writing Postcoloniality and Feminism* (Bloomington: Indiana University Press, 1989), p. 6.

8. Edward Said, "Figures, Configurations, Transfigurations," *Race and Class*, 32.1 (1990), 15.

9. Trinh T. Minh-ha, *op. cit.*, p. 6.

10. Keri Hulme, *The Bone People*, 1984. (Baton Rouge: Louisiana State University Press, 1985. London: Spiral in association with Hodder and Soughton, 1985. Rprt. London: Picador, 1986), p. 11, Further references in the text.

11. Kathy Acker, *Empire of the Senseless* (New York: Grove, 1988), p. 134.

12. Gayatri C. Spivak, "French Feminism in an International Frame," *Yale French Studies*, 62(1981), 167.

13. Ellen G. Friedman, "A Conversation with Kathy Acker," *The Review of Contemporary Fiction*, 9.3 (1989), 18.

14. Nancy K. Miller, "The Text's Heroine: A Feminist Critic and Her Fictions," *Diacritics*, 12.2 (1982), 53.

15. Rev. of *The Bone People*, by Keri Hulme, *Kirkus Reviews* September, 1985, 967.

16. See *ibid.*, p.967 and Angela Huth, "The Booker Club," *The Listener*, 25 October 1985, p. 33.

17. See Judith Dale, "*The Bone People*: (Not) Having It Both Ways," *Landfall: New Zealand Quarterly*, 156 (December 1985), 413-28.

18. See Chris Prentice, "Re-Writing their Stories, Renaming Themselves: Post-colonialism and Feminism in the Fictions of Keri Hulme and Audrey Thomas." *Span: Newsletter of the South Pacific Association for Commonwealth Literature and Language Studies*, 23 (September 1986), pp. 68-80.

19. Margery Fee, "Why C. K. Stead Didn't Like Keri Hulme's *The Bone People*: Who Can Write as Other?" *Australian and New Zealand Studies in Canada*, 1 (Spring 1989), 20.

20. Margery Fee, *ibid.*, p.21.

21. Maryanne Dever, "Violence as *Lingua Franca*: Keri Hulme's *The Bone People*," *World Literature Written in English*, 29.2 (1989), 25.

22. Maryanne Dever, *ibid.*, p.34.

23. Myra Jehlen, "Gender," in Frank Lentricchia and Thomas McLaughlin, eds., *Critical Terms for Literary Study* (Chicago: University of Chicago Press, 1990), p. 272.

24. Susan Bordo, "Feminism, Postmodernism, and Gender/Skepticism," in: Linda J. Nicholson, ed., *Feminism! Postmodernism* (New York: Routledge, 1990), p.134.

25. C. K. Stead, *op. cit.*, p. 108.

26. Maryanne Dever, *op. cit.*, p. 31.

27. Margery Fee, *op. cit.*, p. 25.

28. The crisis of spatial representation has affected the category "woman," which in our culture has existed only as a text (Lacan). But now that the subject has been thrown into temporality (Heidegger), knowledge and language are no longer interdependent (Foucault), sexual difference is subject to the same revision that the relationship time-space is undergoing (Irigaray). Beyond the realistic conception of representation, sexuality might find a new expression, as Toril Moi contends. Certainly a novel that opens with a woman artist suffering this kind of crisis and moving beyond it, promises a re-thinking of sexual difference within the temporality of being.

29. Kathy Acker, Introduction, *Boxcar Bertha: An Autobiography* (New York: Amok Press, 1988), p. xii.

Bernard Gadd (review date Spring 1993)

SOURCE: A review of *Strands*, in *World Literature Today*, Vol. 67, No. 2, Spring, 1993, p. 452.

[*In the following review, Gadd praises the poems in* Strands.]

Keri Hulme is internationally better known for her Booker Prize-winning novel ***The Bone People*** (1983) and for her short stories than for her poetry. ***Strands,*** a collection of work of the past decade, seems intended to present her also as a poet worth noting—and it succeeds.

The sustained major work in the volume is **"Fishing the Olearia Tree,"** followed by a group of substantial poems, **"Against the Small Evil Voices."** (The title **"Deity Considered as Mother Death"** captures some of her concerns here.) The collection ends with **"Some Wine Songs,"** considerably lighter and indeed so far out of kilter with the major poetry as to suggest that the publishers wanted to bulk up the collection.

Hulme employs an array of familiar contemporary techniques of impressionistic linguistic collage: the swift glides from place to place, time to time, register to register, language to language (Maori to English), focus to focus, source to source of imagery, allusion, and symbolism. She says in a prologue note: "Words mean / precisely what you want to hear them say / exactly / what you see in them." Nevertheless, this is not poststructural, postmodernist, and certainly not "language" poetry. Hulme's work is too much grounded in a specific place, New Zealand's remote Okarito Lagoon territory (whose image is suggested by the author's cover design), and in a particular people, the Maori. Her purpose too is very different. In the main poems a sustained voice meditates on death, life, their interactions—predatory or otherwise—in renewal, and on a sense both of belonging to nature and of the otherness of nature learned through life in this place and through belonging to this people. The poetry expresses her sense of the discovery, or perhaps the fashioning of, herself, and the overall tone is more earnest, more zestful than witty or verbally gaming.

For those interested to hunt them, there are interconnections with *The Bone People,* even an apparent direct reference to a reader's response; but I think these are more the result of the similarities of the source materials than of a deliberate literary playfulness. Occasionally the use of Maori strikes the ear as no more than a verbal flourish. Sometimes abrupt register switches jar pointlessly. Sometimes Hulme falls into cliché, platitude, or truism. Sometimes the language is a little self-conscious, striving to make its effects. Sometimes the adjectives seem to crowd in. Sometimes the use of Maori cultural allusions may puzzle the uninitiated reader. Still, the voice encourages us to accept all these on our literary voyage with her across a persistent groundswell of romanticism, past wry reflection, the jokey, the intriguing, the beautiful, the bitter, the reminiscent, and a score of other moods and days. In the major poem the olearia tree itself is sighted again and again, affirming each time its central role as potent natural symbol.

The end of the entire collection is celebration: "Ah, sweet life, We share it / with cancers and tapeworms / with bread moulds and string beans / and great white sharks." With this work Keri Hulme at last emerges as a notable New Zealand poet.

Additional coverage of Hulme's life and career is contained in the following sources published by the Gale Group: *Contemporary Authors*, **Vol. 125 and** *Contemporary Authors New Revision Series*, **Vol. 69.**

Barbara Kingsolver
1955-

American novelist, short story writer, essayist, nonfiction writer, and poet.

The following entry presents an overview of Kingsolver's career through 1999. For further information on her life and works, see *CLC*, Volumes 55 and 81.

INTRODUCTION

Barbara Kingsolver has attracted a large readership and critical appreciation for creating highly entertaining stories that feature strong, appealing female characters. These stories typically address contemporary social and political evils, from poverty and child abuse to environmental pollution and human rights violations. Her best-selling novels *The Bean Trees* (1988), *Animal Dreams* (1990), *Pigs in Heaven* (1993), and *The Poisonwood Bible* (1998) revolve around women from rural, working-class backgrounds who struggle to form connections and find their place in society. Through idiomatic prose and compelling storytelling, Kingsolver creates popular fiction that presents strong opinions on contemporary America and its problems.

BIOGRAPHICAL INFORMATION

The daughter of a country doctor and a homemaker, Kingsolver was born in Annapolis, Maryland, in 1955 and grew up in the rural and impoverished town of Carlisle, Kentucky. When she was in second grade her parents moved the family to the Belgian Congo, where her father worked as a physician for a year before returning to Kentucky. In high school the shy and cerebral Kingsolver shared little in common with her rural classmates, few of whom went to college or moved away from Kentucky. She was a talented pianist and won a music scholarship to De-Pauw University in Indiana, later changing her major to earn a bachelor's degree in biology when she realized career opportunities in music were limited. Kingsolver earned a M.S. in Ecology and Evolutionary Biology from the University of Arizona in 1981. She began a doctoral program at Arizona but left to take a job as a technical writer for the Office of Arid Land Studies. Later, she worked as a freelance writer and journalist. Much of her writing focused on social issues, including protest against nuclear power plants and drawing attention to human rights abuses in Latin America. Kingsolver married chemist Joseph Hoffman in 1985. While pregnant with her first child, Kingsolver began work on *The Bean Trees,* which won a 1988 American Library Association Award. Its suc-

cess helped her to complete and publish *Holding the Line* (1989), a nonfiction work that she began prior to writing *The Bean Trees*. She continued to write and publish short stories, many of which appeared in *Homeland and Other Stories* (1989). She published *Animal Dreams* the following year, winning the PEN fiction prize and the Edward Abbey Ecofiction Award. Kingsolver later wrote *Pigs in Heaven,* a sequel to *The Bean Trees,* published a collection of essays, *High Tide in Tucson* (1995), and produced her best-selling work to date, *The Poisonwood Bible.* Kingsolver divorced her first in husband in the early 1990s and married ornithologist Steven Hopp in 1995. She lives with her husband and two daughters, Camille and Lily, in Arizona.

MAJOR WORKS

Kingsolver uses her writing to address social and political issues that are important to her. Her working-class characters generally suffer from sociopolitical ills and discover they cannot succeed alone—they must unite with others to triumph over the obstacles they face. Kingsolver's intricate plots unfold quickly, and she alternates points of view between characters, employing humor and witty colloquial dialogue to engage the reader. Kingsolver frequently draws on her biology background to create parallels between the interconnections of the natural world and human society. *The Bean Trees* traces the journey of Taylor Greer as she travels west from her small Kentucky hometown. Taylor wants to escape the limited opportunities in her rural town and to establish a new life on her own terms. However, she soon becomes the reluctant caretaker of Turtle, a Cherokee toddler who has been molested and abused by her family. When Taylor and Turtle arrive in Tucson, Arizona, they meet Mattie, who owns Jesus is Lord Used Tired Company and shelters Latin American political refugees, and Lou Ann Ruiz, a single mother whose husband has left her and her child. Taylor takes a job at Mattie's tire store and she and Turtle room with Lou Ann and her son. Taylor's political consciousness is raised when she meets Estevan and Esperanza, Guatemalan refugees who were tortured in their native country. As she becomes aware of persecution in the world and gains affection for her new makeshift family in Tucson, Taylor learns to embrace human connections and engineers an unorthodox plan to adopt Turtle.

Holding the Line began when Kingsolver covered the Phelps Dodge Copper Company strike in Arizona in the early 1980s as a freelance journalist. She became intrigued by the stories of the families involved in the strike and used her interviews to tell the story through the eyes of the women family members. When the workers were forbidden to picket through a court injunction, the wives and daughters of the strikers organized and continued a female picket line. Though the copper mines eventually closed down, Kingsolver recounts how a group of working-class women, most of whom were scarcely educated homemakers with little political awareness, united to change their circumstances and became empowered community activists with a new sense of self-worth. *Homeland and Other Stories* features a title story about Great Mam, an aged Indian woman whose family takes her on a trip to see her birthplace. Great Mam arrives to find that the area has turned into a vulgar tourist trap and refuses to get out of the car. The protagonists of the other stories include a paroled kleptomaniac struggling to stay out of jail, a strike organizer who is jailed for her activism, and a young pregnant woman who reconciles with her pregnant mother. In *Animal Dreams,* Codi Noline returns from a lonely life in the city to her hometown of Grace, Arizona, to care for her father. The story's point of view alternates between Codi, her Alzheimer's-stricken father Homer, and letters from Codi's sister, a human rights activist in Nicaragua. Codi forms an attachment with Loyd, an Indian man she dated in high school, and when she learns a nearby factory is polluting Grace, she becomes involved in the crusade to save the town's orchards. Codi is accustomed to thinking of her sister as a hero, but by becoming involved in the community she becomes a local hero herself.

Pigs in Heaven, the sequel to *The Bean Trees,* revisits Taylor and Turtle. Six-year-old Turtle is brought to the attention of the Cherokee nation when she and Taylor help rescue a man who falls into the spillway at the Hoover Dam. As a result they appear on the Oprah Winfrey show, where Cherokee lawyer Annawake Fourkiller hears about Taylor's questionable adoption of the Cherokee Turtle and attempts to reunite her with her forebears. Taylor flees with Turtle but finally realizes she owes Turtle a connection with her heritage. They return and work out a compromise with the Cherokees that allows Turtle a connection to her adoptive mother and the Cherokee culture. *The Poisonwood Bible* was inspired by the Kingsolver family's sojourn in the Congo in the early 1960s. Kingsolver uses the six members of the fictional Price family to represent the different ways white people have viewed and affected the Congo. Nathan Price, a missionary, brings his wife and four daughters from Georgia to the Congo in order to bring God to the natives. He arrives determined to mold the village natives in his own image, remaining completely oblivious to the values and nuances of the native culture. Nathan represents the most reprehensible forces the West has brought to bear on the Congo. As Belgium and the United States drove the Congo into political and social chaos, so Nathan breaks apart and destroys his family. Kingsolver shows Nathan entirely through the eyes of his wife and daughters, who narrate the story in alternating chapters. Nathan's wife sees that he is headed toward disaster but is powerless to stop him. Rachel, a self-absorbed princess, observes her father's errors but never moves beyond concern for her own problems. The silent, partially paralyzed Adah recognizes Nathan for what he is and silently records his journey into madness. Adah's twin sister Leah worships her father at the beginning of the story, though later falls in love with a native man and stays in Africa to build a life and attempt to pay the psychic debts her country owes to the Congolese. The youngest child, Ruth May, is the innocent who ultimately pays the highest price for Nathan's madness.

CRITICAL RECEPTION

Kingsolver is praised for her strong humor, vivid characterization, absorbing plots, and ability to combine colorful dialogue reminiscent of her native Kentucky with evocative imagery of the Southwest. Kingsolver's sociopolitical messages, however, are a point of contention among critics. Her books draw attention to issues including political torture in Latin America, industrial pollution in the United States, and the damage caused by American imperialism in Africa. Some view her messages as a strength that gives her work greater weight, while others consider them heavy-handed and obvious. Though critics admire her strong storytelling abilities, some consider her symbolism clumsy and her plots contrived in order to bring home her moral points. Because her stories usually support popular liberal social causes, some critics note that they present minimal conflict and rarely risk challenging the reader's point of view. Critics applaud Kingsolver's ability to create convincing, strong female characters, but some point out that her few male characters tend to be one-dimensional. While the merit of her sociopolitical commentary is much debated, Kingsolver's witty style, engaging plots, and vibrant characters are regarded by many as a notable contribution to popular literature.

PRINCIPAL WORKS

The Bean Trees (novel) 1988
Holding the Line: Women in the Great Arizona Mine Strike of 1983 (nonfiction) 1989
Homeland and Other Stories (short stories) 1989
Animal Dreams (novel) 1990
Another America/Otra America (poetry) 1992
Pigs in Heaven (novel) 1993
High Tide in Tucson: Essays from Now or Never (essays) 1995
The Poisonwood Bible (novel) 1998

CRITICISM

Margaret Randall (review date May 1988)

SOURCE: "Human Comedy," in *Women's Review of Books,* Vol. V, No. 8, May, 1988, pp. 1, 3.

[*In the following review, Randall offers praise for* The Bean Trees.]

Here's a first novel that's fast reading but long-staying. It starts off with the narrator's first-person childhood memories. You think this is great: something for light consumption on the daily commuter train or to be absorbed in the pleasure of a steaming tub. And this is certainly a book that can be read in just those places. But it's not simply another trashy (read: delicious) piece of fiction. You are thoroughly hooked by the time you realize Barbara Kingsolver is addressing and connecting two of our most important issues.

The Bean Trees is about invasion. Invasion, not as it is probed and theorized about by political thinkers, psychologists, or academics. Invasion as it is experienced by middle America. And not middle-*class* America, but real middle America, the unemployed and underemployed, the people working in fast-food joints or patching tires, Oklahoma Indians, young mothers left by wandering husbands or mothers who never had husbands. In this novel you travel from Kentucky to Arizona and never even have to consider the sophisticated complexities of New York, San Francisco, or Chicago.

The Bean Trees is hilariously funny. You laugh out loud. I literally fell off my chair. You turn the pages and wheeze, empathetically amazed and delighted by the characters who people these pages; by their perceptions of themselves and the world and by the decisions they make for their moral as well as physical survival.

Our heroine, Taylor, makes it through high school with the support of a brave and truly loving mother. She remembers one special teacher, whose chief claim to local fame is that his nails are clean; he becomes her key to a first real job: analyzing blood, urine and feces at the small town hospital. This enables her to save $300 for an old VW: her ticket to the world. She leaves her provincial destiny behind, and hits America's roads.

Pace-wise, or in some of its rhythms, *The Bean Trees* has something in common with Jack Kerouac's classic *On the Road.* But its meaning is exactly the opposite. Kingsolver's characters don't opt for dropping out of society; they are desperately trying to survive within its confines. For unexpected yet believable humor, made from the more painful observations of our culture, it takes me back to William Eastlake's *Portrait of the Artist with Twenty-Four Horses.*

But it would be misleading to compare Kingsolver with either of these male authors. In style and vision, she has written a book all her own, and with a deep female consciousness that feels like bedrock when put up against some of the preachier, more explicitly feminist works. Attempting to define this published-yet-new author, Georgia Cotrell's name comes to mind; Kingsolver's prose style has something in common with Cotrell's use of language in *Shoulders.* She also shares Cotrell's curiosity about a given (although different) social group, her integrity in shying away from surface judgments when looking at complexities and contradictions, and her explorations of non-traditional families.

Two lines of narrative eventually converge in Kingsolver's novel. There is our heroine, telling her story with the quiet unsophisticated irony of a tough and travelin' Kentucky woman. She leaves home bent on getting herself a new name and decides she'll take the cue from wherever she runs out of gas. "I came pretty close to being named after Homer, Illinois, but kept pushing it. I kept my fingers crossed through Sidney, Sadorus, Cerro Gordo, Decatur, and Blue Mound, and coasted into Taylorville on the fumes. And so I am Taylor Greer," she announces early in the story.

And there is an alternating-chapter third-person narrative: Lou Ann, also from Kentucky but already a sometime Tucson resident, whose rodeo-riding husband Angel Ruiz loses what sense of self he may once have had when an accident takes one of his legs below the knee. Irritable and dissatisfied, he leaves Lou Ann before their child is born.

Taylor's VW breaks down the first time in Oklahoma where, along with repairs enough to get her on the road again, she acquires a child of her own. An Indian woman presses a silent baby of indeterminate age and origin into her arms. The woman retreats, leaving Taylor no choice but to continue on her way, now the adopted mother of this mystery bundle. The child seems slow in her responses; Taylor dubs her Turtle.

Her VW breaks down definitively in Tucson. From then on, it's Taylor as a sudden mother, trying to make it for two, and Lou Ann with her little Dwayne Ray. *The Bean Trees,* on one well-fashioned plane, is the story of how these two poverty-level women find one another through want ads and mutual need, how they aid one another by pooling their meager resources and sharing a house, how they help one another go on learning about life and what it means.

The end of the scene in which Taylor and Lou Ann join fortunes is worth repeating. The former has answered a house-to-share ad placed by the latter. "Lou Ann hid her mouth with her hand. 'What?' I said. 'Nothing.' I could see perfectly well that she was smiling. 'Come on, what is it?' 'It's been so long,' she said, 'You talk just like me.'"

These two apparently different women are immensely compatible:

> Within ten minutes Lou Ann and I were in the kitchen drinking diet Pepsi and splitting our gussets laughing about homeostasis and bean turds. We had already established that our hometowns in Kentucky were separated by only two counties, and that we had both been to the exact same Bob Seger concert at the Kentucky State Fair my senior year.

Lou Ann has been carefully programmed to ask permission for breathing. Many of us will recognize in her that part of ourselves that has trouble believing we do anything well enough, are ever good enough, belong anywhere— even inside our own skins. Taylor offers Lou Ann a piece of her life-earned philosophy, this one about men:

> one time when I was working in this motel one of the toilets leaked and I had to replace the flapper ball. Here's what it said on the package; I kept it till I knew it by heart: "Please Note. Parts are included for all installations, but no installation requires all of the parts." That's kind of my philosophy about men. I don't think there's an installation out there that could use all of my parts.

This is also the story of Mattie, Mattie of Jesus Is Lord Used Tires, and the occupants of her labyrinth second floor; people like the nervous young priest on the motorcycle, and Estevan and Esperanza, who come and go in the night. After a short stint frying up fast food at Burger Derby, Taylor rebels and goes to work for Mattie, a knowledgeable woman who drinks coffee from a white mug on which hundreds of tiny rabbits are having sex in hundreds of different positions.

Mattie can tell right away that Turtle is a girl. And Taylor begins to learn about Mattie's world:

> Mattie's place was always hopping. She was right about people always passing through, and not just customers, either. There was another whole set of people who spoke Spanish and lived with her upstairs for various lengths of time. I asked her about them once, and she asked me something like had I ever heard of a sanctuary. I remembered my gas-station travel brochures. "Sure," I said. "It's a place they set aside for birds, where nobody's allowed to shoot them." "That's right. They've got them for people too." This was all she was inclined to say on the subject.

Nothing more is said at that point. But if we didn't get it when we experienced Taylor's shock at discovering the damage suffered by Turtle's victimized body, by this time we are sure that this is a tale about something more complex than two uniquely ordinary women making their way in the world.

There are endless delightful moments in this book. A typical Kingsolver scene happens when Taylor is introduced to Lou Ann's cat:

> "You wouldn't believe what your cat is doing," I said. "Oh yes, I would," Lou Ann said. "He's acting like he just went potty, right?" "Right. But he didn't as far as I can see." "Oh no, he never does. I think he has a split personality. The good cat wakes up and thinks the bad cat has just pooped on the rug."

As is necessary to any decent novel about ordinary America, fundamentalism as a *leitmotif* surfaces every once in a while. Taylor hits Oral Roberts country on her trip West, and the knowledge that she can always call 1-800-THE LORD keeps her going through many a near-desperate time. Towards the end of the story, a fully confident Taylor decides more out of nostalgia than anything else to dial the "help" line:

> The line rang twice, three times, and then a recording came on. It told me that the Lord helps those that help themselves. Then it said that this was my golden opportunity to help myself and the entire Spiritual Body by making my generous contribution today to the Fountain of Faith missionary fund. If I would please hold the line an operator would be available momentarily to take my pledge. I held the line.
>
> "Thank you for calling," she said. "Would you like to state your name and address and the amount of your pledge?" "No pledge," I said. "I just wanted to let you know you've gotten me through some rough times. I always thought, If I really get desperate I can call 1-800-THE LORD. I just wanted to tell you, you have been a Fountain of Faith."
>
> She didn't know what to make of this. "So you don't wish to make a pledge at this time?" "No," I said. "Do you want to make a pledge to me at this time? Would you like to send me a hundred dollars, or a hot meal?"
>
> She sounded irritated. "I can't do that ma'am," she said. "Okay, no problem," I said. "I don't need it anyway. Especially now. I've got a whole trunkful of pickles and baloney . . ."

Taylor doesn't read about the brutal sexual abuse of children in a book. She discovers it the first time she bathes Turtle. Her knowledge is confirmed months later when she takes the child to a pediatrician and listens to him tell her the terrified little girl she has imagined is perhaps a year and a half is probably closer to three. Sometimes they just stop growing, he says.

Taylor knows nothing about the wars in Central America, and how the US government promotes those wars and then rejects their victims, until she becomes friends with Estevan and Esperanza and accepts the fact that some people work fast-food or assemble lines, others have used tire shops and sanctuaries.

Two related versions of invasion, the sexual invasion of a child's body and the political invasion of a nation's sovereignty, come together and unfold in this story of ordinary people who understand both realities as they touch their own lives. This is also a story about racism, sexism and dignity. It's a story propelled by a marvelous ear, a fast-moving humor and the powerful undercurrent of human struggle.

Something happens in **The Bean Trees.** It's one of those old-fashioned stories, thankfully coming back onto our literary scene, in which there are heroines and anti-heroines, heroes and anti-heroes, ordinary humans all. They go places and do things and where they go and what they do makes sense for them . . . and for us. There are surprises in this book. There is adventure. And there is resolution, as believable as it is gratifying.

Barbara Kingsolver, herself a Kentuckian living in Arizona, clearly knows whereof she writes. Her prose is effortless and lovely, her structure easy, her evolutions warm and deeply satisfying. Invasion as metaphor is not new with this novel. It has surfaced over the past several years in poetry and prose by some of our most important women writers. Here it occupies a new territory, that of the commonplace, mostly undramatic, story, told and lived by commonplace people, most of them women.

Trite as it may sound, reading **The Bean Trees** bolsters my belief in an isolated but essentially generous American people. The system will continue to hype us with words and images that systematically distort our sense of world and self. But as long as we retain the capacity to see and feel, as long as the connections are made in our lives and as long as books like this one are written to help us recreate our common memory, we will be able to leave worthy lives to those coming along behind us.

Carol Kleiman (review date 18 May 1988)

SOURCE: "Loving, Nourishing as a Way of Life," in *Chicago Tribune,* May 18, 1988, p. 3.

[*In the following review, Kleiman offers positive assessment of* The Bean Trees.]

Barbara Kingsolver's first novel is a quietly building, powerfully moving story about a mother's fierce love for her daughter, even if she isn't legally the mother and the child literally was dumped in her car, and even if the mother pretends for the longest time that the little girl isn't of paramount importance.

Taylor Greer, out to conquer the world, leaves her own mother in rural Kentucky, happy to get away and proud that she was one of the few girls in her class who "stayed out of trouble" and finished high school.

"This is not to say that I was unfamiliar with the back seat of a Chevrolet, . . . but Mamma always said barefoot and pregnant was not my style. . . . Believe me, in those days the girls were dropping by the wayside like seeds off a poppyseed bun, and you learned to look at every day as a prize." So Taylor, who avoided pregnancy so adroitly, becomes a mother at 18 to the 2-year-old she names Turtle, a Cherokee Indian. The transaction occurs in Oklahoma while Taylor is en route to her destination and, she hopes, destiny in Tucson.

The instant mother keeps the child fed and cared for, but Taylor is so intent on her own survival—on finding a job, on finding a place in the world—that at first Turtle is just there, silent, unresponsive. Taylor seems no more than her custodian, a senior Girl Scout doing a good deed.

Taylor, who has a phobia about tires exploding, gets a job at, of all places, Jesus Is Lord Used Tires, owned by Mattie, a warm, wonderful woman who gives sanctuary both to tires and to Guatemalan refugees.

The young mother also becomes friendly with another Kentuckian, Lou Ann, and rents a room in her house. All the women become friends, and their circle of warmth is augmented by two more female neighbors, one of whom is blind.

One of the nicest qualities about this absorbing story is that even though it deals with traumatic issues such as child abuse, the sanctuary movement, growing up and growing old, Kingsolver is always entertaining. Her mountain style is reminiscent of the humor of Southern novelist Rita Mae Brown.

Surrounded by love, Turtle begins to speak. But her vocabulary is limited to vegetables. Kingsolver, a biologist, uses her background as the theme of the book and to make a point about Mattie's purple bean vines drying in the sun, which broke Taylor's heart to see but did not faze Mattie.

"That's the cycle of life, Taylor," Mattie said. "The old has to pass on before the new can come around."

And so it is with Taylor, who becomes energized after her long metamorphosis and is determined to adopt Turtle. She uses means not quite legal but certainly acceptable to the reader, who is cheering all the way.

She explains the adoption papers to Turtle: "That means you're my kid, and I'm your mother, and nobody can say it isn't so."

Taylor is now "the main ingredient" in Turtle's life, she says, and vice versa.

Bill Mahin (review date 23 June 1989)

SOURCE: "Brilliant Stories Test Values, Truth," in *Chicago Tribune,* June 23, 1989, p. 3.

[*In the following review, Mahin offers positive assessment of* Homeland and Other Stories.]

Barbara Kingsolver's **Homeland and Other Stories** is about community and generations and families and relationships and the passing on of wisdom.

Each story tests values; each is a search for meaning.

In the title story, the father—"a soft-spoken man who sometimes drank but was never mean"—works in the mines; the mother raises the family and sets the standards. "If I have to go out myself and throw a rock at a songbird," she says at one point, "nobody is going to say this family goes without meat!" They sustain the family, but it is the great-grandmother who is wise. "My great-grandmother belonged to the Bird clan," the story begins.

"Hers was one of the fugitive bands of Cherokee who resisted capture in the year that Gen. Winfield Scott was in charge of prodding the forest people from beds and removing them westward."

Her values—"Sometimes a person has got to take a life, like a chicken's or a hog's when you need it. If you're hungry, then they're happy to give their flesh up to you because they're your relatives"—contrast harshly with those in **"Rose-Johnny."** "My daddy was white," the woman in that story confides:

"After he died my mama loved another man and he was brown. . . . People will tell you there's never been no lynchings north of where the rivers don't freeze over. But they done it. . . . They lynched him up there, and drowned her baby Johnny in Jackson Crick, and it was as froze as you're ever going to see it. They had to break a hole in the ice to do it. . . . Poor little baby in that cold river. Poor Mama, what they did to Mama. And said they would do to me, when I got old enough."

The stories are frequently about mothers and daughters. (An abused infant is central to Kingsolver's highly praised earlier novel, **The Bean Trees.**) In **"Stone Dreams,"** a woman having an affair with the man who built their cabinetry finds a note from her daughter acknowledging the affair yet refusing to admit the possibility that it might interfere with their own relationship. The mother in **"Qual-ity Time"** watches the hands of her 5-year-old and discovers how parents "find the courage to believe in the resilience of their children's lives." A woman in **"Bereaved Apartments"** shoplifts an expensive sweater, the way her aunt taught her when she was little.

There are telling images as well as vivid characters. In **"Jump-Up Day,"** a young girl finds herself enmeshed in a battle between the science of her father and the sorcery of his enemy:

"It was dark before she reached the convent. The stars shone in patches between the clouds rolling up from the ocean. On the deserted banana plantation the long drainage ditches, channels of infected water, shone like an army of luminous snakes marching towards the sea."

There are flaws. Men play minor roles, are absent entirely, or are too perfect. The overall goodness of her characters—though never cloying—sometimes tests credibility. And sometimes the imagery weakens the narrative: "Lena was a mother waiting to happen."

Such lapses hardly matter, because Kingsolver is such an extraordinary storyteller. The little girl in **"Homeland"** slips out her window after going to bed to sit beside her great-grandmother, watching the glow from her pipe in the darkness, waiting for her next story. So do we.

Eleanor J. Bader (review date Summer 1990)

SOURCE: "They Would Not Be Moved," in *Belles Lettres,* Vol. 5, No. 4, Summer, 1990, p. 16.

[*In the following review, Bader offers positive assessment of* Holding the Line.]

> When the company began bringing in workers to replace them, striking miners lined up at the mine gates in protest. A few days later, when Phelps Dodge won a court injunction barring the miners from assembling at the gates, women strike supporters began holding mass pickets of their own. When the National Guard and riot troops from Arizona's Department of Public Safety (DPS) were summoned to occupy Clifton and Morenci, no one expected the strike to last much longer. The women organized rallies, pickets and more rallies. They were tear-gassed and arrested. They swore and screamed and sometimes threw rocks, and always they showed up for the picket. Thirteen months later, when they were still on the line, a DPS officer remarked, in what was to become the most famous summation of the strike, "If we could just get rid of those broads, we'd have it made."

But intrepid they were. For eighteen months, between June 1983 and December 1985, women from the tiny mining towns of Ajo, Clifton, Douglas, and Morenci, Arizona, defied propriety and cultural norms to demand justice, fairness, and decency from the company that ran their lives, Phelps Dodge (PD).

Predominately Mexican-American, these feisty women— many of whom had never before been to a meeting, spoken publicly, or questioned authority—took to the streets and union halls to defend their way of life and clamor for adequate wages and benefits. In the face of Phelps Dodge's intransigence, they railed against the company's demands and exhorted the bosses to recognize their need for equitable recompense. Resistance to their efforts was fierce. The National Guard invaded the four towns, families were evicted from company-owned housing, and individuals were threatened by PD-hired thugs. Soila Bom was jailed for "harassment" after she called a former friend a scab. Although the charges against her were eventually dropped, "being legally in the right did [strikers] no more good than if they had been pedestrians run down in a crosswalk," writes Barbara Kingsolver in her eloquent, inspiring history of the strike, *Holding the Line.*

Arizona, Kingsolver reminds us, is one of twenty right-to-work states, giving employees in unionized industries the right to refuse to join the bargaining unit and allowing employers to ignore picket lines, union jurisdiction, or the sanctity of a striker's job. And, given the climate of the early 1980s—the air traffic controllers union, PATCO, had been broken and Greyhound strikers had been forced to concede major contractual losses—the women, and the miners themselves, knew they were facing an uphill battle.

There was a lot at stake. By attempting to bust the union, said Carmina, a member of the Women's Auxiliary, Phelps Dodge was trying to turn back the clock to the days of rampant discrimination. For evidence she brought out a newspaper article describing a brand new PD policy forbidding employees of the company store from speaking Spanish (the preferred tongue of most Clifton residents) either to customers or to one another. "Do you see what I'm saying?" she asked Kingsolver. "The union is the only thing we have that's our own. PD likes to tell us what to do, where to live. But I don't think they're going to run us out of Clifton. This is our home and we are staying, regardless."

Which is not to say that the thirteen unions on strike against Phelps Dodge always welcomed the women's fire-and-brimstone brand of organizing. When the Women's Auxiliary invited United Steelworkers of America insurgent Ron Wiesen to Arizona, many male unionists felt the Auxiliary had overstepped its bounds and a rift developed, pushing both groups to address questions about female autonomy and sexism before things were patched up.

"These were women," writes Kingsolver, "raised under the dictum of 'speak when spoken to,' and it had taken months for some of them to gather the nerve to express their opinions in their own Auxiliary meetings. Some were still uncomfortable expressing their opinions at the family dinner table. Now they were venturing into the great wide world and standing up before the multitudes." Harnessing their fears, the women began speaking publicly about their strike and PD's despicable anti-union tactics. Before

church groups and labor federations in other cities, at college campuses and on street corners, the women told the truth as they saw it. "Some had the full support of their families, while others were fighting in several war zones at once, but they all kept going," writes Kingsolver. Many were divorced in the process; for having taken steps toward self-actualization and assertion, there could be no return to prior domestic arrangements.

And in the end individual growth is what mattered. For although the strikers and their supporters won many a moral victory, they lost the war. By the end of 1985, the company's mining and smelting interest in Arizona—once the youthful, healthy giant among the state's industries—was an ailing skeleton. Phelps Dodge had sold a part interest in the Morenci operation to the Sumitomo Company of Japan and had more or less turned its back on the rest of the Arizona mines. The Ajo plant was closed, and the town of Ajo may as well have rolled up its sidewalks. The countdown had begun for closing down operations in Douglas within the year. . . . Most of the retirees had stayed in Clifton, and some of the younger families kept up the difficult life of divided households, with one spouse driving to a job in some faraway city.

Tragic? Enraging? A callous and preventable outcome? Of course. But somehow, Kingsolver's portrait of these indomitable women, changed forever by standing their ground and demanding to be treated as serious, intelligent thinkers and doers, makes the book uplifting and heartening.

"Just look at us," laughs Diane as she tells Kingsolver about her new self-image. "At the beginning of this strike, we were just a bunch of ladies." Anna concurs. "Before, I don't know what we talked about. Who got married, did you go to the last wedding, who's messing around with who. Now we talk about Nicaragua, about apartheid. This is a change for everybody, but especially for us."

"Before the strike," adds Cleo, "I did nothing. I just didn't know there could be anything like this. Before, I was just a housewife, now I'm a partner."

By linking arms with women strike supporters in Arizona, Kingsolver has presented us with a unique, important look at a history often ignored. Feminism's sweep—in subtle ways changing how women across race, class, and ethnic lines see themselves as shapers of destiny—is, she implies, an undeniable reality.

Barbara Kingsolver with Lisa See (interview date 31 August 1990)

SOURCE: "Barbara Kingsolver: Her Fiction Features Ordinary People Heroically Committed to Political Issues," in *Publishers Weekly,* August 31, 1990, pp. 46-7.

[*In the following interview, Kingsolver comments on her life, work, and sociopolitical preoccupations.*]

Across the scorched desert toward the lower Tucson Mountains, up a gravel-covered dirt road identifiable only by two weather-bleached yellow pillars, lies a house almost hidden by native cacti and scrub. Here Barbara Kingsolver, author of **The Bean Trees, Homeland and Other Stories** and Harper Collins's soon-to-be released **Animal Dreams,** weaves her stories of plucky, sometimes downtrodden, characters "ecologically" placed in a world of issues—the U.S. involvement in Central America, Native American traditions, feminism, the environment. Her office is reached through a courtyard draped with grapevines and flourishing with squash. The window looks out across a terrain that to many seems inhospitable but to Kingsolver brings inspiration and solace. On the bulletin board above her computer are several fliers announcing speakers on the underground railroad for South American refugees. On her desk is a paint brush. When the writing gets tough she takes the brush out to the courtyard, where she hand-pollinates her squash blossoms.

Kingsolver and her husband, a chemist at the University of Arizona, have been remodeling this cabin for five years, incorporating original beams into a practical and beautiful modern design. The couple did all the work themselves, consulting how-to's from the local library. Complimented on the extensive tile work, much of which she laid herself, Kingsolver quips, "It represents about 12 nervous breakdowns."

Raised in rural Kentucky, she grew up among farmers. "Our county didn't have a swimming pool and I didn't see a tennis court until I went to Depauw," says Kingsolver, 35. "I didn't grow up among the suburban middle-class. If I wrote a novel with that background, I'd have to do research. It's not that I try to write about poor people or rural people, I am one myself. It's important to illuminate the lives of people who haven't been considered glorious or noteworthy."

Some critics contend that Kingsolver's characters live on the margins of society. "That's a shock to me," she bristles. "I write about people who are living in the dead center of life. The people who are actually living on the margins of society are those you see on *Lifestyles of the Rich and Famous.* I like to remind people that there's nothing wrong with living where we are. We're not living 'lives of quiet desperation,' but living in the joyful noise of trying to get through life."

Kingsolver claims she was always a writer. "Eudora Welty, Carson McCullers and Flannery O'Connor were the stars in my sky as a child," she says. Later she was influenced by Doris Lessing and Ursula LeGuin, with Faulkner as the one male admitted into her personal constellation. "But I couldn't figure out how you could manage to get paid for being a writer or that you could do it for a living," she says. Beginning in college and through two years traveling in Europe, she took a number of jobs: typesetter, X-ray technician, copy editor, biological researcher and translator of medical documents. After graduate school at the University of Arizona, she became a science writer. Armed with a single creative writing course at Depauw and later a class with author Francine Prose in Arizona, Kingsolver "sneaked" slowly into freelance journalism, selling pieces to the *Progressive,* the *Sonoran Review, Smithsonian,* and gradually into short story writing for *Mademoiselle* and *Redbook.*

In 1983, Kingsolver began a book on the long, bitter copper strike against the Phelps Dodge Corporation in Arizona, focusing on the women—mostly union wives—in the isolated company town of Clifton. "People's internal landscapes turned out to be so interesting. The women earned a sense of themselves and their own value and personal power. When I first interviewed them, they'd say things like they didn't go out of the house without their husband's permission. By the end of the strike, these same women were going on national speaking tours." A year later, she'd written half of the book, but her agent was having a hard time placing it.

Kingsolver went back to freelance work. In 1985, she found herself pregnant and suffering from terrible insomnia. Her doctor recommended that she scrub the bathroom tiles with a toothbrush. Instead she sat in a closet and began to write **The Bean Trees**—about a woman who leaves a rural life in Kentucky for the urban world of Tucson, where she encounters the sanctuary movement. "I saw that book as a catalogue of all the things I believe in, and not in any way commercial." If baby Camille hadn't been three weeks late, Kingsolver observes, she might not have finished the novel. Her agent, Frances Goldin, read the book overnight and called in the morning to say she wanted to auction it. "I look back on that time as a never-never land," says Kingsolver. "To be able to write with no one looking over your shoulder! Now I try to pretend I'm back in that closet."

She took her advance from **The Bean Trees,** finished **Holding the Line** (published by ILR Press of Cornell University in 1989) and began a book of short stories that she was determined would be different from her first novel. "People always say that a first novel sounds so much like the author," says Kingsolver. "I think that's certainly true of **The Bean Trees.** The voice of Taylor, the main character, was very strong, and she wanted to tell all of my stories. I've had to lock her away." In **Homeland and Other Stories,** Kingsolver again dealt with many of the same political themes, but seen through the eyes of a menopausal woman, a male biology teacher, an old Native American woman and other so-called "marginal" characters. "In **Homeland,** I was really stretching my voice and trying to break into the land of real fiction," she says.

In **Animal Dreams,** the author has taken all of her previous themes—Native Americans, U.S. involvement in Nicaragua, environmental issues, parental relationships, women's taking charge of their own lives—tossed them into a literary pot and created a perfectly constructed novel. In the book, Codi Noline—bereft of her sister, who's left for Nicaragua to fight for social justice—returns to her hometown where she confronts her painful past, a father afflicted with Alzheimer's, family tragedy and an environmental disaster. "*Animal Dreams* is about five novels," concedes Kingsolver. "About two-thirds of the way through I realized I wasn't just a fool; I had jumped out of a plane and the parachute wouldn't open. I wanted to go back to bed, but Harper had already designed the book jacket." She turned on the answering machine, yelled at her family, pollinated the squash and set about answering the questions she had asked.

While Kingsolver has, in fact, answered all of them admirably, her subjects and themes won't disappear. "Those issues will keep turning up in everything I write. They're central to my reason for living. The only authentic and moving fiction you can write is about the things that are the most urgent to you and worth disturbing the universe over. If you're willing to get up and face a blank page every day for a year or more, then it has to be an idea you're willing to be married to."

"The issues are fundamentally related, fundamentally the same. I wasn't really trying to drive five horses, but one horse. I don't want to be reductionist, but all of the issues can be reduced to a certain central idea—seeing ourselves as part of something larger. The individual issues are all aberrations that stem from a central disease of failing to respect the world and our place in it."

In *Animal Dreams,* Codi learns to place herself within her family, then the community, then the political world. The Stitch and Bitch Club, a group of women who have spent years making hand towels and gossiping, harnesses its talents to save the fictional town of Grace, so much like the real-life strike-stricken community of Clifton. "The women knew how to fight to save their town. They knew how to do ordinary things to maintain life. I like stories about ordinary people doing heroic things that are heroic only if you look close enough."

Can a novelist truly educate and change the world about man's basic inhumanity to man? "I have to believe that, don't I?" she answers. "What keeps me going is the hope that I might be able to leave the world a little more reasonable and just. I grew up in the '60s when convictions were fashionable. We believed we could end the war just by raising a ruckus. I've been raising a ruckus ever since." Ten years ago, Kingsolver was writing mimeographed leaflets on the "outright villainy" of what was happening in El Salvador or on the building of the Palo Verde Nuclear Power Plant; she believes that her job description hasn't changed much. But with fiction, Kingsolver maintains, the author must both refrain from diatribe and respect the reader.

That balance may have its origins in Kingsolver's own choice of physical environment and habitat. After years of what she terms a "rolling stone existence," Kingsolver—liking the sound of Tucson but knowing absolutely noth-

ing about it—went there for what she thought would be a few weeks. "The Southwest appealed to me on hearsay," she says. "I thought it would be a wide open place that would allow for some eccentricity." That was 14 years ago.

"I probably would have become a writer no matter where I was, but the Southwest has informed my subjects. Culturally, the Southwest is so rich. I can drive from here to Albuquerque and pass through a half-dozen nations." The Central American issues which infuse her work come from living in an area that derives its cultural plurality both from the people who've been there for hundreds of years and from the refugees who come from the south. "A lot of my friends are refugees and they got here because our government dropped phosphorous bombs on their villages. How can you not do something about that?"

Kingsolver's "anthropologist's heart" has compelled her to seek out different world views. "For research, I look for open doors, read what there is, depend on friends." For *Animal Dreams,* that meant poring over doctoral dissertations on kinship relations, as well as visiting a pueblo. Kingsolver believes that Americans have a lot to learn from cultures like the Navaho and Pueblo, whose cultural myths have less to do with conquest and more to do with cooperation. "I don't even like to use a word like 'religion,' because all Pueblo life is religious. It's about keeping this appointment with humility which reminds us of our kinship with the natural world. I was trained as a biologist, so I know intellectually that human beings are one of a number in the animal and plant family. We are only as healthy as our food chain and the environment. The Pueblo corn dances say the same things, only spiritually. Whereas in our culture, we think we're it. The Earth was put here as a garden for us to conquer and use. That way of thought was productive for years, but it's beginning to do us in now."

In her new novel, backed by a 45,000-copy first printing, first serial rights to Confetti, and a 15-city tour, Kingsolver isn't about to lose the casual reader over ideas, ideals or philosophy. "If people are provided with information, then they can draw their own conclusions," she says. "A novel can educate to some extent. But first, a novel has to entertain—that's the contract with the reader: you give me 10 hours and I'll give you a reason to turn the page. I have a commitment to accessibility. I believe in plot. I want an English professor to understand the symbolism while at the same time I want one of my relatives—who's never read anything but the Sears catalogue—to read my books."

Ursula K. Le Guin (review date 2 September 1990)

SOURCE: "The Fabric of Grace," in *Washington Post Book World,* September 2, 1990, pp. 1, 8.

[*In the following review, Le Guin offers positive assessment of* Animal Dreams.]

The "search for the father" is so common a theme in American fiction that one might be tempted to wonder why so many sons seem to mislay Pa somewhere, and then have epiphanies when they find him. When it's a daughter that seeks the father lost or disguised, however, we are on less familiar ground.

Cosima/Codi Noline/Nolina (seeking identity, she seeks her true name) comes back home to Grace, Ariz., a canyon mining town, hoping to keep an eye on Dad, who though still the town doctor is in the early stages of Alzheimer's, and to get a handle on herself. The father's voice and memories alternate with Codi's in the narration to create a haunting interplay of revelation, concealment and confusion.

The terms of the daughter's search for selfhood widen gradually and vastly out from the paternal ego-center. In the father-son story, the mother is often dead or negligible. In this story she is dead but vitally present, not a non-quantity but an aching absence. And the central person in Codi's life, the second self, is her sister Hallie—but Hallie too is absent, having gone to Nicaragua. Her voice and presence weave through the book in memories and letters. Then there are the friends in Grace: Emelina who gives Codi a house to live in, Emelina's brood of kids, Loyd the Apache-Navajo-Pueblo friend who never knew Codi had miscarried his baby way back in high school. And there's Emelina's mama Viola, and all the mamas in town, the members of the Stitch and Bitch Club—"the fifty mothers," Codi begins to call them. It is through the mothers and the grandmothers that she finds her way finally to the father, and so to the mother, and to the truth—a very relative truth.

The story is about relatives, relatedness, relationships. Perhaps all novels are. But I think **Animal Dreams** belongs to a new fiction of relationship, aesthetically rich and of great political and spiritual significance and power. The writers have been predominantly women of color—African-American, Latina, Native American. In Leslie Marmon Silko's *Ceremony,* Louise Erdrich's novels, Toni Morrison's *Beloved,* Paula Gunn Allen's collection *Spider Woman's Granddaughters,* one can see relationship as the central and motive force of the work. There are relatives, often in large numbers, family all over the place, family that may include coyotes, pecan trees, the dead and other people's children. The imagery underlying the narrative is of networks, bonds, patterns, connections, bodies, the body politic, the web, the weft.

When the weaving is broken the pattern is lost. Things don't make sense. Work defeats itself. The orchards of Gracela Canyon are poisoned by mercury from the mine tailings, the old croplands are salt-white from irrigation and the Black Mountain Mine Company plans a dam that will finish killing the canyon by stopping its river at the source. The men are worn out, defeated. The members of the Stitch and Bitch Club want to act, to try to darn the holes in the fabric of things. How do a bunch of small-town middle-aged housewives stop a dam? By organizing. By getting woven together. Kingsolver's last book was nonfiction: **Holding the Line: Women in the Great Arizona Mine Strike of 1983.** Her insight into this form of relationship, organizing industrial or environmental action, is keen, and her description of this particular example (which involves artificial peacocks) is vivid and very funny.

The stories in Kingsolver's **Homeland** are so extraordinary, and her stunning first novel, **The Bean Trees,** is already so widely loved, that her readers may come with very high expectations. In **The Bean Trees** the narrator's voice is like Emmylou Harris's, so true it makes your throat ache. Told in that young voice, the terrible has happened before you even recognize it. The main voice in **Animal Dreams** is that of a grown woman, a loner, highly educated, self-doubting, savvy, scared. She knows the terrible will happen, and it does. The story is slower, weightier. The language is rich, complex, witty. Codi's confusions impede simplicity, and Doc Homer's voice speaks from ever further in the fog of dementia.

Sometimes the patterning seems over-explicit. Doc Homer confuses times and persons, takes Codi for Hallie or her mother or herself 20 years ago, but he never *loses* her. He always has an emotional thread to follow. My idea of Alzheimer's as a clueless labyrinth struggled with this less dreadful vision of it, half-convinced.

Again, Loyd is a lovely man, a dream-man, with his dream-pueblo—too good to be true? Wishful thinking? Maybe, maybe not. We are too used to novelists who play safe. The celebration of goodness in this book is incredibly, irresistibly courageous. It rises to unforgettable intensity in passages such as the chapter called "Bleeding Hearts." And the longing for closure, for the "happy ending," is fulfilled in an absolutely legitimate fictional way: happiness for these particular people, in this particular place and moment. There is no faking, no cheating. The small comedy is seen in the great, tragic perspective of the despoiled West. The web is not mended. And always the wound to the south, the unacknowledged war of the great power against the weak, bleeds and drains and gangrenes. The beloved sister's murdered body is buried in that ground. What then is the home ground, the homeland?

"So you think we all just have animal dreams," Codi says. "We can't think of anything to dream about except our ordinary lives." And Loyd answers her: "Only if you have an ordinary life. If you want sweet dreams, you've got to live a sweet life."

This is a sweet book, full of bitter pain; a beautiful weaving of the light and the dark. This one will be with us for a long time.

Margaret Randall (review date 9 September 1990)

SOURCE: "Time, Space, and Heartbeats," in *Los Angeles Times Book Review,* September 9, 1990, pp. 1, 15.

[*In the following review, Randall offers praise for* Animal Dreams.]

When Barbara Kingsolver's first novel, *The Bean Trees,* appeared in 1988, it was deeply moving and also highly successful: a book that addressed a difficult subject matter with delicious humor, yet never trivialized the issues. Readers laughed out loud through page after page, then realized they had just acquired a new understanding of childhood sexual abuse and the grass-roots movement providing sanctuary to those who flee the war zones in Central America.

That book gained an immediate audience for this new writer from Kentucky by way of Arizona. Kingsolver didn't keep her fans waiting long for the next book. She promptly followed *The Bean Trees* with the well-received *Homeland and Other Stories* and a piece of nonfiction. *Holding the Line: Women in the Great Arizona Mine Strike of 1983.*

Animal Dreams, her second novel, solidly establishes Kingsolver as someone who will give her public more than one great book. It is more ambitious than *The Bean Trees* and the writing achieves a greater intensity, without ever losing the ease and familiarity that made the first novel so appealing. She also has emerged as an important regional writer.

Animal Dreams evokes the powerful cultural mix of the American Southwest, where Native American, Anglo and Hispanic people inhabit a dramatic landscape that has taken on mythic connotations. The spiritual (and power-plant-invaded) Four Corners area comes to mind.

Kingsolver sets the stage when she warns: "Grace, Arizona, and its railroad depot are imaginary, as is Santa Rosalia Pueblo, although it resembles the Keresan pueblos of northern New Mexico. Other places, and crises, in the book are actual."

Animal Dreams is a story of two sisters, Cosima (Codi) and Halimeda (Hallie), and their father, a small-town doctor. Kingsolver uses two first-person narratives. The main voice we follow is that of Cosima. Her storytelling is interspersed with brief, disturbing commentary by Doc Homer, who develops Alzheimers as the book unfolds. One of the most extraordinary aspects of the novel is the way Kingsolver allows us into the labyrinthine fog of Doc Homer's stumbling, shifting mind. The deepest counterpoint is that which builds between Cosima's frank narrative and Doc Homer's darker mind travels.

Codi, the book's protagonist, is a medical student in her 30s who has worked at a 7-Eleven as well as the usual internships common to her future profession. In this book, she travels from medical school and an uncomfortable relationship with a fellow doctor back home to the remote western town of her childhood. Hallie, who feels vibrantly present despite the fact that she is always offstage, has gone to offer her agricultural engineering skills to the struggling revolution in Nicaragua.

There also is Cosima's ex-lover, Carlo, left behind in an acceptable but meaningless future in the city, and there is Loyd, part Apache, Navajo and Pueblo, who spells his name "wrong" but understands both living and Cosima in ways that help her change how she will walk in the world.

There are the other women of this story: young Emelina, whose husband is mostly off somewhere working the trains; the elders of the Stitch and Bitch Club, Uda Ruth Dell and Dona Althea.

A common story—going home again. A warm and energizing story. But *Animal Dreams* is much more. It is a story of female vision and courage, of what can happen when a daughter loses her mother and believes she remembers her death. It is a tale of racial and cultural differences as well as commonality, of death and life and what they mean to one another. It is also a book about time and its overlaps, about memory's use of time and our human use of memory. It is a story about the pain of love:

> "His two girls are curled together like animals whose habit is to sleep underground, in the smallest space possible. Cosima knows she's the older, even when she's unconscious: One of her arms lies over Halimeda's shoulder as if she intends to protect them both from their bad dreams. Dr. Homer Noline holds his breath, trying to see movement there in the darkness, the way he's watched pregnant women close their eyes and listen inside themselves trying to feel life."

> "He feels a constriction in his heart that isn't disease but pure simple pain, and he knows he would weep if he could. Not for the river he can't cross to reach his children, not for distance, but the opposite. For how close together these two are, and how much they have to lose. How much they've already lost in their lives to come."

Everyone fully inhabits his or her character: "Loyd and I shared one chair; apparently we were the official lovebirds of this fiesta. He spent a lot of time telling me what I was eating. There were, just to begin with, five different kinds of *posole,* a hominy soup, with duck or pork and chilis and coriander. Of the twenty or so different dishes I recognized only lime Jell-o, cut into cubes. I gave up trying to classify things by species and just ate. To everyone's polite amusement, my favorite was the bread, which was cooked in enormous, nearly spherical loaves, two dozen at a time, in the adobe ovens outside. It had a hard brown crust and a heavenly, steaming interior, and tasted like love. I ate half a loaf by myself, believing no one would notice. Later, in bed, Loyd told me they were all calling me the Bread Girl."

And the landscape itself comes alive: "Eventually we stopped in a protected alcove of rock, where no snow had fallen. The walls sloped inward over our heads, and long dark marks like rust stains ran parallel down the cliff face at crazy angles. When I looked straight up I lost my sense of gravity. The ground under my boots was dry red sand, soft and fine, weathered down from the stone. . . ."

Kingsolver brings to our literary panorama a social consciousness that is bedrock to her rich prose style. In this respect, her work reminds us of some of the important Latin American writers, novelists like Mexico's Juan Rulfo, Colombia's Gabriel Garcia Marquez or Chilean Isabel Allende. Yet her concerns are rooted in 20th-Century North America: the problems of rampant, ecological destruction, sexual and other abuse issues, our responsibility toward the victims of U.S. foreign and domestic policies, and the grass-roots response to the terror rising about us as society comes apart at the seams. These concerns, evident in her first novel and further developed as well in her second, make Kingsolver a writer who is as profoundly regional as uniquely global.

As I read the last few pages of **Animal Dreams,** I felt a brief moment of panic. Would this book really end as it seemed it was going to? Suddenly the outcome I had hoped for unwound before my grateful eyes. Things happened as I wanted them to, as I breathed a sigh of relief. This neat wrap up may be the single flaw in an otherwise exceptionally crafted narrative.

Most important for me, however, is my conviction that Kingsolver is giving a new voice to our literature, one that fulfills its promise even as it begins its journey: four books in as many years.

Animal Dreams is one of those rare novels I could not put down. It demanded a single span of my attention, and left me wondering whether to go back to the beginning or simply anticipate the next product from this woman's pen.

Paul Gray (review date 24 September 1990)

SOURCE: "Call of the Eco-Feminist," in *Time,* September 24, 1990, p. 87.

[*In the following review, Gray offers positive assessment of* Animal Dreams.]

Though routinely maligned as a decade of swinish greed, the 1980s also produced a kinder, gentler brand of storytelling, one that might be described as "eco-feminist" fiction. The central plot of this evolving subgenre has become reasonably clear. Women, relying on intuition and one another, mobilize to save the planet, or their immediate neighborhoods, from the ravages—war, pollution, racism, etc.—wrought by white males. This reformation of human nature usually entails the adoption of older, often Native American, ways. Ursula K. Le Guin's *Always Coming Home* (1985), an immense novel disguised as an anthropological treatise, contains nearly all the quintessential elements, but significant contributions to the new form have also been made by, among others, Louise Erdrich and Alice Walker.

Now comes Barbara Kingsolver, whose second novel, **Animal Dreams,** is an entertaining distillation of eco-feminist materials. There is the fragile landscape—the fictional town of Grace, Ariz., whose river and Edenic orchards face extinction by the Black Mountain Mining Co. And there is the doughty heroine—Codi Noline, who grew up in Grace and returns home after 14 years of wanderings to teach at the high school and look after her father, the town doctor, who seems to be losing his mind.

Codi certainly does not imagine herself a heroine when she arrives in Grace. "I felt emptied-out and singing with echoes, unrecognizable to myself: that particular feeling like your own house on the day you move out." Codi believes that the brave one in the family is her sister Hallie, three years younger, who has gone to Nicaragua to help peasant farmers. "I'd spent a long time circling above the clouds, looking for life, while Hallie was living it."

But Codi also finds herself busier than she expected. She meets Loyd Peregrina, half Pueblo, half Apache, whom she had dated briefly in high school; she never told him of the pregnancy and miscarriage that followed. Now she and Loyd fall into an affair that threatens to turn serious, not to say somber. He drives her about neighboring reservations and takes her to some ancient Pueblo villages. She begins to see a difference between inhabiting the land and trying to conquer it: "To people who think of themselves as God's houseguest, American enterprise must seem arrogant beyond belief. Or stupid. A nation of amnesiacs, proceeding as if there were no other day but today."

Yes, Codi does have her preachy side, not that it seems to bother Loyd. After she lectures him, he agrees to get rid of his birds and give up cockfighting. There is enough fun in this novel, though, to balance its rather hectoring tone. Codi has a deft way of observing her small, remote hometown, caught uneasily between past and future. When Halloween arrives, she notes, "Grace was at an interesting sociological moment: the teenagers inhaled MTV and all wanted to look like convicted felons, but at the same time, nobody here was worried yet about razor blades in apples." And the matriarchs who make up the town sewing circle, called the Stitch and Bitch Club, are both amusing and formidable.

It is these women, with Codi's help, who set out to save the town from the mining company. Kingsolver introduces other complications, particularly the fate of Hallie, who has been captured by the U.S.-supported *contras.* To say everything is resolved happily would be misleading, but one hint may be allowed. Anyone who thinks a giant mining concern is any match for the Grace Stitch and Bitch Club has a lot to learn about eco-feminist novels.

Carolyn Cooke (review date 26 November 1990)

SOURCE: "Arizona Dreaming," in *The Nation,* November 26, 1990, pp. 653-4.

[In the following review, Cooke offers favorable evaluation of Animal Dreams.]

Mark a route from Bobbie Ann Mason's Kentucky through Willa Cather's grainy plains to Georgia O'Keeffe's Southwest, and you will have followed Barbara Kingsolver to the spot on the map where she stakes her literary claim. Kingsolver the Kentuckian has been seduced by the high contrasts of Arizona, by the mythic scale of the landscape: the surreal pinks and red dust, canyons and arroyos, prickly pear and acacia trees, petroglyphs written in the walls of rock, the chalky skulls of buffaloes immortal in the dirt.

Arizona is exotic as the Amazon in *Animal Dreams,* Kingsolver's second novel and third work of fiction. Just as Cather's hard-baked plains reflect images of corn bent like the backs of so many yellow-haired Norwegians, so is *Animal Dreams* an elaborate equation between the vibrant landscape and its peoples, the Native Americans whose gentle hands have shaped and lent a rhythm to the land and the later immigrants whose Spanish names Kingsolver slathers on her prose like guacamole on a taco—Emelina and Viola Domingos, Homero, Halimeda and Cosima, Pocha and Juan Teobaldo, Cristobal. Transcending regionalism, Kingsolver makes the Southwest the Garden of Eden, Eldorado and Xanadu rolled into one. It is a state of, well, grace, and she examines the possibilities the town of Grace, Arizona, might imply: being born into Grace, leaving it and returning changed.

Animal Dreams comprises an intelligent, moving chronicle of three lives at different points on a shifting timeline: Cosima (Codi) Noline, the central character, who returns to her hometown of Grace in *dis*grace, having dropped out of medicine in her first year of residency; her eccentric father, Homero (Doc Homer), who serves Grace both as obstetrician and coroner but suffers from Alzheimer's disease; and Halimeda (Hallie) Noline, Codi's sister, an activist who appears in the novel only in her letters home from Nicaragua. At its best, *Animal Dreams* resists summary: It aspires to the gluey, webby, inexplicable condition of life. At its weakest, and like Kingsolver's first novel, *The Bean Trees* (1988), this one flirts with the condition of heartwarming-ness; in celebrating ordinary life, it looks blindly over the occasional meanness or venality that give texture and contrast to our experience of goodness. There are no bad guys in Kingsolver's Graceful universe. Codi's Pueblo-Apache-Navajo lover gives up his brilliant career in cockfighting because Codi—and his mother—ask him to.

The short story is this: Codi Noline has fallen from Grace. She has gone from med school resident to 7-Eleven clerk in one freefall; she has felt the blue pall of the great world, lost her innocence and her empathy in the mountains of Crete, birthplace of Zeus. Sister Hallie, meantime, has become a hero in the classical mode and is off to Nicaragua to save the very soil. Codi, postmodern down to the Billy Idol haircut, tries to save herself. She leaves Carlo, the boyfriend she met back in parasitology, and catches a Greyhound home to Grace, where she spends a year teaching general biology to a gaggle of high school students and chasing down the shadows of her past.

Grace is a town where people roast a goat to make you feel welcome. Everywhere are the brilliant colors of poverty in a warm climate—the reds, oranges and livid purples of the vegetation and women's dresses, the graves meticulously studded with white stones and tequila bottles, "the simplest thing done with the greatest care." Silver loafers pass as *haute couture* in the airless windows of the Hollywood Shop; the Baptist Grocery survives to recall a time of more serious spiritual divisiveness; and the *semilla besada* trees are bedecked hopefully with baby socks and the envelopes of pension checks. When Codi returns to Grace after her years in the great world, everyone remembers how tall she was in seventh grade and her orthopedic shoes.

Those who know Kingsolver from *The Bean Trees* and her 1989 story collection *Homeland and Other Stories* will recognize a few familiar riffs. Her characters have a strong sense of science at work in the world and use the plant and animal kingdoms to explain each other. (In a short story called **"Covered Bridges,"** a young woman who lost a sister to a bee sting devotes herself to saving others via a poison hotline; in *Animal Dreams,* Hallie Noline grows restless dispensing agricultural advice on the Tucson house-plant hotline and makes a beeline south to help peasant farmers reclaim soil denatured by poverty and politics.)

The symbolism of Grace (the town) is almost hopelessly heavy-handed, but she redeems herself with her clear and original voice, her smart, plucky women, her eye for the nuances of personality and the depth of her social and moral concerns. Kingsolver can help you learn how to live.

Her previous fiction shows her mind migrating westward from Bobbie Ann Mason country (Kingsolver grew up in eastern Kentucky, the setting of her stories and starting point of her first novel). Like Mason's characters, Kingsolver's are sometimes funnier than they mean to be. But although the spunky voice from her earlier fiction remains in characters like Emelina Domingos ("Shoot, you look like a fifty-dollar bill. Where'd you get that haircut, Paris, France?") and the woman Codi meets on a bus ("'I'm Alice Kimball,' the woman explained. 'I get the worst slugs'"), Kingsolver has here traded some of the raw, hurtling energy of *The Bean Trees* for a spiraling narrative that interweaves Codi's point of view with her father's in a complex investigation of the relationship between memory and truth.

In Doc Homer, Kingsolver brilliantly delineates the quality of a dissolving but wholly practical mind. Lost in time, Doc Homer lives in an overflowing, eternal present. Seeing his 15-year-old daughter pregnant, Doc Homer does not confront her with what he knows, but suffers alone and lets her suffer.

> He feels a sharp pain in his spleen when he looks across the breakfast table each morning and sees this: his wife's face. The ghost of their happiest time returned to inhabit the miserable body of their child. He can't help feeling he has damaged them all, just by linking them together. His family is a web of women, dead and alive, with himself at the center like a spider, driven by different instincts. He lies mute, hearing only in the tactile way a spider hears, touching the threads of the web with long extended fingertips and listening. Listening for trapped life.

Doc Homer has not lost his memory to Alzheimer's, he is drowning in its waves and crosscurrents. Even Codi isn't sure where her father ends and disease begins. Seeing his forceps on the kitchen drain-board, she admits: "This didn't signify any new eccentricity on his part. He'd always had a bizarre sense of utility. I could picture him using the forceps to deliver a head of cabbage from a pot of boiling water. Holding it up. Not in a showoff way, but proud he'd thought of it, as if he were part of a very small club of people who had the brains to put obstetrical instruments to use in the kitchen."

Word gets around that Codi is a doctor bent on amazing Grace—come to save Doc Homer with a miracle cure she learned in Paris, France; come to save the river, which is contaminated by the Black Mountain Mining Company's excretions of sulfuric acid and copper sulfate. Codi demurs. It's her sister Hallie who is the hero, she insists. Hallie is the one who is saving what's worthwhile—rain forests, farmers, the earth itself.

But in Grace heroes are made, not born. They are driven by exigency, by being needed. Even the housewives in the infamous Stitch and Bitch club get serious about saving Grace when events prove dire. (It isn't giving away too much to say that the town, plagued by a toxic river, is saved by a few hundred peacock-feather *piñatas*.)

What impels us to right action? Kingsolver seems to be asking. How do we know what to do? Codi suffers from chronic insomnia and occasional, lurid dreams. Her Native American lover, Lloyd Peregrina, articulate in the high language of legend, tells her, "Animals dream about the things they do in the daytime, just like people do. If you want sweet dreams you've got to live a sweet life."

Like all good novels, *Animal Dreams* is a web of interlacing news. It is dense and vivid, and makes ever tighter circles around the question of what it means to be alive, how to live rightly and sweetly even as we feel the confining boundaries of the skin, the closing walls of past and present, with memory like a badly wired lamp, spitting sparks and shorting out.

The Arizona pueblo of Malpais is the last refuge of free life in Aldous Huxley's *Brave New World*—a little nation of outsiders, savages so backward they still believe in his-

tory and take their morality from Shakespeare. Grace, Arizona, is Codi Noline's refuge from anonymity and empty life. In Grace she discovers the comforts of tradition and obligation, and migrates from the shapeless melancholia of youth to a deeper humanity—living, as Huxley's savage hopes to, painfully and richly and well.

Marc W. Steinberg (review date March 1991)

SOURCE: A review of *Holding the Line: Women in the Great Arizona Mine Strike of 1983,* in *Contemporary Sociology,* Vol. 20, No. 2, March, 1991, pp. 236-8.

[*In the following review, Steinberg offers positive evaluation of* Holding the Line.]

Occasionally we look beyond the myopic confines of academic writing, and find a book that enriches our understanding of the phenomena we study. ***Holding the Line*** is just such a volume.

Ostensibly this is a chronicle of the role of miners' wives (and female miners) in the eighteen-month strike against the Phelps Dodge mining company. Foremost, however, it is a story of women's empowerment and of the struggles and triumphs of a collective transformation. The strike, conducted from June 1983 to December 1984, was waged by copper miners and smelter operators in several mining communities in southern Arizona in reaction to Phelps Dodge's insistence on wage and benefit reductions and the dissolution of pattern bargaining in the copper industry.

Barbara Kingsolver's recounting of this struggle centers on the Morenci mine in the southeast and its neighboring community of Clifton, a "company town" in the classic sense. Her artful narrative is anchored in her observations of the strike over a year-and-a-half period, and seventy-five in-depth interviews with participants, most of whom are women. To provide context she also frames this story with an introductory chapter on mine work and mining communities of Arizona, with much material being drawn from other anthropological and historical investigations.

The heart of the volume, however, is the narrative of the tenacious struggle between Phelps Dodge with its state allies and the mining families of Clifton. Kingsolver documents in captivating detail how the women of the community were able to construct and maintain an effective strike organization and a militant class consciousness in the face of Phelps Dodge's continued operation and protracted scrutiny and harassment by the state Department of Public Safety. With the largely male work force legally restrained from protest, perpetuation of the strike fell into the hands of their wives at an early point. Initially their participation was conducted through the union's women's auxiliary. However, the women rapidly learned that their prosaic knowledge of domestic maintenance was fertile material for organizing the strike community. With their consciousness and organizational acumen expanded, they moved beyond the supporting role of the auxiliary, becoming quintessential actors, frequently to the consternation of union officials and their husbands. The emigration of the men in the search for work cemented the control the women exercised over the strike through their vigilance.

A product of these women's evolving control was a widening consciousness of their collective empowerment. Their participation arose out of an abiding belief in the union, nurtured in the struggles of earlier generations. Through their increasingly expansive efforts they experienced a feminist transformation. Concepts of rights and justice—the fount of their initial resolve—were revamped in challenging an intransigent company and resistant husbands. Traditional domestic and community roles were cast aside in their commitment to continue the strike, for themselves and their children as well as their husbands. As one of the main combatants recounts, "the strike has completely remolded my mind." Indeed it has. Radiating from their feminist rebirth of self and collectivity are re-evaluations of politics and government, the dynamics of industry in an international economy, and the meaning of their ethnic, mostly Mexican, heritage. Parochial visions of life are gradually shed, left behind in the desert dust as so much ore scrap.

Kingsolver's extensive field research and meticulous exposition make this book as rich an ethnography as the discipline can offer. This is not a volume designed to test the mettle of a theory via a case study. However, those interested in gender dynamics, labor relations, collective action, and community studies will find a wealth of empirical material to put to such a use. The superb writing makes it excellent material for courses in any of the above fields.

Several reservations can be expressed about Kingsolver's account. My principal concern is the waning attention to ethnicity as the story unfolds. As Kingsolver prominently notes at the start, these copper mines were built and operated through the exploitation of Mexican and Native American labor. The history of the union and the community shows an attempt by these workers to break ethnic barriers. The strike itself transparently divided Clifton along ethnic lines, with white workers serving as strike breakers who kept Phelps Dodge in operation. Yet the role of this ethnic cleavage in rending the community and perpetuating the strike on both sides receives insufficient attention in the greater part of the narrative. Additionally, readers may question whether the large strike community shared the leaders' view of the strike as a great moral victory, given its ultimate dissolution. Some may also wonder about the strike's lasting effects on the women's lives, but that is largely beyond the author's scope.

Kingsolver makes no secret of her support for the strikers in her account. To be sure, this is a partisan account of the best kind, and the pathos she exhibits for the women and their families is part of what keeps her account tightly focused and engaging. In *Holding the Line* Kingsolver has tapped a mother lode on gender, class, and collective action, and many should delight in mining its contents.

Rosellen Brown (review date Spring 1991)

SOURCE: "The Year in Fiction: 1990," in *Massachusetts Review,* Vol. XXXII, No. 1, Spring, 1991, pp. 123-46.

[*In the following excerpted review, Brown offers qualified praise for* Animal Dreams, *finding fault in the novel's idealized characters and resolution.*]

Barbara Kingsolver's ***Animal Dreams,*** on the other hand, is a book almost too perfectly made. This is a wonderfully capacious novel that was easy to enter and to stay in, and I was delighted with its gemmy treasures of insight and phrase. And yet when I'd finished it I felt the ingratitude that wishes artfulness to be roughed up into art, wants intelligence and moral earnestness to be shaken a little bit more by uncertainty: wants, I suppose, at least a little of the willful improvisatory quality I have just found in excess in [John Edgar] Wideman's book [*Philadelphia Fire*]. John Gardner called it "raggedness."

Animal Dreams asks its questions as straightforwardly as a child: *How should one live? Of what shall our souls be made? In pursuit of our own fortunes or for the liberation of the oppressed? For the sake of the earth that is being ransacked by the greedy? By the hard light of "modern" intelligence or in the profound shadows of an ancient wisdom?* The characters and situations that embody these clear-voiced challenges have a good deal more charm than this litany lends them, but the questions don't turn out to be quite as open as they seem; their answers feel, in the end, predetermined. If this were painting, what we'd have on the canvas is something decorative and symmetrical, rather than agonized, torn from the depths, free to find its own shape.

Codi (Cosima) Noline, a young woman so depressed by the mysteries and deprivations of her motherless childhood that it never occurs to her that she's depressed, comes home from an aimless life to her small half-Indian town in Arizona where her father, the local doctor, is disappearing into an Alzheimer's fog. As she's reclaiming this territory, old and new, her younger sister Hallie (Halimeda) is travelling hard in the opposite direction, from self to selflessness, to work as an insect specialist-cum-liberator in Nicaragua. Codi has led such an adventurous life, geographically speaking, that she complains "people took me for an adventurer," but she knows she is only lost. Her sister, grounded, knowledgeable and passionate about social justice, does what she's convinced she must and regrets none of her losses. The story is entirely Codi's—by the end it's clear that Hallie is only her other half; for all her detailed reality she is almost a projection. (Whether Kingsolver intends that or not, it's the effect she achieves; I suspect she could animate a stone.)

Along the way Codi (with some intervening chapters in her father's voice) encounters neighbors, a perfect Apache boyfriend who drives a train, a save-this-poisoned-river movement which she accidentally originates, and an intense attachment to the lore of the Indian pueblo, from which the novel's title is derived: "Animals dream about the things they do in the daytime, just like people do. If you want sweet dreams, you've got to live a sweet life." With one large exception—a necessary sacrifice—everything in the novel works out for the best, except for the past, which can only be redeemed by taking it into oneself.

There is real sadness, there are comings-to-terms with unpleasant realities, and through all of it, thick and thin, Codi has the most appealing narrative voice I've run into in a long time, amused and amusing, capable of intricate and engaging detail. This is a rich book, generous in its perceptions and judgments. But its single failing is a serious one in spite of the satisfactions Kingsolver provides: the characters are so good and bad (mostly good) that you can hear the celebratory music even as they approach. You know Codi's lover will be without flaw, and so, in spite of her initial suspicion—hers, not ours—he turns out to be. Just about every "native" is without stain, and a few of the scenes in which everyone pulls together to save the dying river feel like Hollywood: Unanimous Effort music (flutes, bassoons) followed by Triumphant (trumpets).

I don't want to condescend to **Animal Dreams** because it gave me ample pleasure. But I wish Barbara Kingsolver would unlearn a little of her admirable professionalism and next time let her book take her out into an uncharted place where she can discover, rather than lead us surefootedly, to her truths. Worse than her tendency to idealize her characters is the feeling that (in spite of some truly painful acknowledgements) the existential pain that dooms us is not larger than we are, and more persistent, that it can be neatened up at the end—that the perfect-circle form that resolves the novel is a fair reflection of the resolution of sorrow in the world. This is what happy endings are, even those that are achieved through tears. Kingsolver seems to me both smart and wise. For her next book I wish for her some salutory surprises, and even a few untied loose ends.

Dorothy Sue Cobble (review date April 1991)

SOURCE: A review of *Holding the Line: Women in the Great Arizona Mine Strike of 1983*, in *Industrial and Labor Relations Review*, Vol. 44, No. 3, April, 1991, pp. 585-6.

[*In the following review, Cobble offers favorable evaluation of* Holding the Line.]

"Used to be a confrontation and I'd want to cry. Now I can fight back. I'm not going to make any excuses for who I am or what I think." These spirited words of a female strike-supporter, reflecting a new sense of entitlement and self-knowledge, came in the wake of a disastrous two-year battle between the predominantly Mexican-American copper miners of Southern Arizona and Phelps Dodge Copper Corporation. Barbara Kingsolver's new

book offers an absorbing blow-by-blow account of the "great Arizona mine strike of 1983," raising disturbing questions about corporate power and the neutrality of the state in labor-management affairs. Yet, paradoxically, against a backdrop of economic decline, family dissolution, and the downward-spiraling fortunes of the local union, Kingsolver also provides a compelling, even inspiring, portrait of female activists—women for whom the strike was "an opportunity" for profound transformation and personal growth. "A new bunch of confident women came rolling hell-for-leather out of the strike, for the norms of Arizona's old, stagnant mining camps had been turned upside-down and dumped like a laundry basket."

In 1983, Phelps Dodge balked at the pattern settlement agreed to by the other major copper producers, provoking a confrontation not only with the miners and their union, the United Steelworkers of America, but with their families and communities. As Kingsolver vividly portrays, the striking unionists bit back again and again "like fleas," but they were no match for the combined force of the employer and the state. After an initial 10-day cooling off period—called by Arizona's Governor Bruce Babbitt following the successful shutdown of the Morenci mine by a massive picket line—Phelps Dodge reopened with the help of four hundred state troopers, armored personnel carriers, Huey helicopters, and seven units of National Guard.

The mining communities reeled under marshal law, the wholesale violation of their civil liberties—hundreds of strikers were arrested but few were ever convicted or even prosecuted—and the unrelenting surveillance of strikers, their children, and anyone living in the mining towns. Yet, the small local and its supporters hung on for eighteen months, bolstered by meager strike benefits and a fiercely union heritage. Grandparents had survived the infamous 1917 assault on the IWW in nearby Bisbee. Parents boasted of their militant days in the red-baited Mine, Mill, and Smelter Workers Union of the 1930s and 1940s or their union-supported efforts to end job and housing discrimination against Mexicans in the late 1960s.

For the female activists, "what began as an extension of domestic servility"—slapping out tortillas for the picketing male strikers, organizing clothing exchanges and other barter networks to save household expenses, helping their husbands in the union office—"became a contradiction of it in the end." When court injunctions prohibited striking miners from picketing, the women set up their own mile-long, all-female picket line. Soon they were going to the local bar with other women, traveling to California and New York on speaking tours, corresponding with union activists in Latin America and Europe, and having opinions of their own concerning strike strategy, politics, and the proper role of Hispanic women. Kingsolver argues that this strike permanently altered women's perceptions of "what was important, worthwhile, and within their power to do." They had "crossed the Rubicon" and would never go back.

Although Kingsolver never quite acknowledges fully the bittersweet nature of her story—a story of the rise of women set against the receding fortunes of their class (and to some extent their male compatriots)—her book is nonetheless an impressive achievement. She has produced a stirring, densely documented narrative that works both as drama and as social history. Rich ethnographic passages detailing work life in the mines for the female pioneers of the 1970s and the culture of Mexican-American workers alternate with evocative descriptions of clashes between miners and police or analyses of union-management strategy. Her book deserves a wide audience among scholars as well as the general public. In particular, it would be an exceptionally fine book to use in undergraduate classes on collective bargaining, work and work organization, or labor and women's history—or in any other course concerned with the fate of minorities, women, and workers in 1990s America.

Lorraine Elena Roses (review date July 1992)

SOURCE: "Language and Other Barriers," in *Women's Review of Books,* Vol. IX, Nos. 10-11, July, 1992, p. 42.

[*In the following review, Roses offers qualified praise for* Another America.]

This is the first volume of poetry for Barbara Kingsolver, whose previous books include *The Bean Trees* (1988), *Animal Dreams* (1990) and the short-story collection *Homeland and Other Stories* (1989). The first thing one notices about this collection is that each poem comes with a Spanish translation by the Chilean writer Rebeca Cartes. There's no preface to tell us how the bilingual arrangement came about or for which audience it was designed, but it's clear from the outset that Kingsolver feels a deep connection to the Spanish-speaking lands that begin before the Rio Grande and stretch all the way to the windswept limits of Tierra del Fuego.

Kingsolver knows that a political gulf much wider than the river separates North from South. Often there is no welcome for those who flee northward, seeking sanctuary. Ironically, the regimes that force them into exile enjoy aid from the US. Over the last century our policymakers have seldom understood populist or revolutionary leaders, but have chosen to support the authoritarian "stability" of military regimes and their protection against "subversion." This disquieting knowledge gives rise to many of the poems of *Another America/Otra America.*

These are, for the most part, highly political poems by a committed human rights activist who seeks to stir our consciences and enlist us in the cause of social justice and pacifism. Taking the high moral ground, she draws inspiration from two Latin American beacons: José Martí, the Cuban patriot-poet, and Ernesto Cardenal, the Nicaraguan poet-priest and Minister of Culture. A particular closeness binds Kingsolver, born in rural Kentucky, to Father Cardenal, who as a novice in 1957 entered the Trappist

monastery at Gethsemane, Kentucky. In **"The Monster's Belly"** Kingsolver wishes she could have shared the comfort of knowing Cardenal and his nurturing God:

> Now, Father Ernesto, I find you were there all along
> with the monks at Gethsemane, Kentucky.
> I could have walked there
> in my blunt shoes, could have visited you
> and your laughing Lord who made the best rain fall
> on beans and rice.

Though aspiring to Cardenal's quiet joy and theology of love and liberation, she feels caught "in the belly of the monster," a phrase coined by Martí at the turn of the century to describe the United States ("Conozco al monstruo / He vivido en sus entraflas: I know the monster. I have lived in its belly.") Kingsolver contrasts Cardenal's "laughing Lord" with the forbidding, apocalyptic one of her own religious training:

> . . . What a difference
> to have known this Lord,
> or at least to know
> he shared the same small sky with mine, who promised only
> that the horned and headed monster
> would come out of the sea
> for the purpose of ending the world.

Leaping from a spirituality that she envies to Cardenal's unsympathetic view of America, Kingsolver arrives at a picture of herself, too, as a victim of her country's aggression:

> You and I were no closer than the living and the dead
> who share a cemetery on a Sunday afternoon.
> Father Ernesto, you were a citizen of the domain
> of your profound desire to kill the monster,
> and I was already in its belly.

How does she construct this image of a poetic self devoured by her own country? Her experiences are surely not commensurate with those of Martí, who witnessed US annexationist fever, nor of Cardenal, whose country was invaded and occupied by the US. For Kingsolver the issue is a psychological one. Born in 1955, she recalls a childhood when mock air-raids and civil defense drills instilled fear of the supposed Soviet peril, implanting an enduring xenophobia that she detects everywhere, especially in the anti-Communist rhetoric still alive in the 1980s:

> The television says McAllen, Texas
> is closer to Managua than to Washington, D.C.
> and housewives in McAllen check their own
> possibly Bolshevik eyes in the mirror
> and lock the windows.

(**"Justicia"**)

Fear of "the other" is what Kingsolver seeks to denounce. The allusion to intimidated Texas housewives (from whom the poet distances herself as much as she can) also furnishes us with a key to Kingsolver's perspective on

Latin American victimization as paralleling that of women. Time and again she imagines the female body as a house invaded, robbed and sullied, a magnet for violence. In **"Refuge,"** dedicated "to Juana, raped by immigration officers and deported," the Latin American female is a metaphor for double oppression. The poem's narrator speaks to a woman wetback just as she arrives at the border:

> *Give me your hand,*
> he will tell you. *Reach*
> *across seasons of barbed wire*
> *and desert. Use the last*
> *of your hunger*
> *to reach me. I will*
> *take your hand.*
> *Take it.*
> First he will spread it
>
> fingers from palm
> to look inside
> see it offers nothing.
> Then
> with a sharp blade
> sever it.
> The rest he throws back
> to the sea of your
> blood brothers.
> But he will keep your hand,
> clean, preserved in a glass case
> under lights:
> *Proof*
> he will say
> *of the great*
> *desirability*
> *of my country.*

That amputated hand, the officer's trophy becomes a searing and memorable emblem of cruelty, a symbol intended to arouse our indignation at official callousness. It also signifies suffering, sacrifice, the desperate bravery of a woman rejected at the threshold of redemption.

But can lyrical poetry bear the weight of politics? Can the leap from spiritual identification to militancy bridge the gap between the Latin American experience and our own? Not, I think, when the poet demonizes US history. My sense, reading these poems, is that Kingsolver believes that if the US didn't conjure up enemies there would be none. Perhaps it is an illusion that a progressive, pacifist American can join ranks with militant Martí and priest Ernesto Cardenal, two Latin American male patriarchs dedicated to their countries' sovereignty and self determination who have given little thought to machismo, sexual oppressions and gender in equalities. Mixing poetry and politics is a volatile business, and given the demonological assumptions that run through these poems, I suspect they will appeal primarily to those who seek to commemorate and mark political occasions.

The last two sections of ***Another America/Otra America*** transcend both hemispheric differences and programmatic politics. Here, Kingsolver's tone becomes celebratory, as she wrests serenity from personal and collective suffering, and embraces trust as an acceptable substitute after love has failed. In haunting and telling natural images, she memorializes people she has known (**"Poem for a Dead Neighbor," "Your Mother's Eyes"**), moments of grace (**"Bridges"**) and witness to survival (**"Remember the Moon Survives"**). She excels particularly in poems about the female condition and our spiritual connection to animal life, either wild or free. **"Apotheosis,"** for example, is on the order of a Pablo Neruda ode, but, unlike Neruda's, hers is female-centered, affirming daily life, creativity and personal autonomy:

> There are days when I am envious of my hens:
> when I hunger for a purpose as perfect and sure.
> as a single daily egg.
> If I could only stand in the sun,
> scratch the gravel and blink and wait
> for the elements within me to assemble,
> asking only grain I would
> surrender myself to the miracle
> of everyday incarnation: a day of my soul
> captured in yolk and shell . . .
> . . . .
> And yet I am never seduced,
> for I have seen what a hen knows of omnipotence:
> nothing of the miracles in twelves,
> only of the hand that feeds
> and,
> daily, robs the nest.
>
>   (**"Apotheosis"**)

The North-South gap—political, economic, and cultural—is as unbridgeable as ever, but in these poems Kingsolver creates room for coexistence through her bilingual format and fruitful collaboration with a Latin American woman. Cartes' graceful translations often enhance the originals. This arrangement encourages Anglos to cross over and discover the pleasures of the Spanish text; Latin American readers, regularly ignored by mainstream publishers, are addressed at the same time. If Spanish and English can be made to coexist on the facing pages of an open book, Kingsolver seems to say, then a cultural dialogue between North and South can be brought into being as well. That is something to look forward to, even if only in the sanctuaried space of more literary texts like this one.

Antonya Nelson (review date 4 July 1993)

SOURCE: "Heaven in Oklahoma," in *Los Angeles Times Book Review,* July 4, 1993, p. 2.

[*In the following review, Nelson offers tempered assessment of* Pigs in Heaven, *praising Kingsolver's prose and intelligence though finding fault in the novel's "cheery" tone and unrealistic plot.*]

Barbara Kingsolver's new novel, ***Pigs in Heaven,*** takes up where her first novel, ***The Bean Trees,*** left off, with the abandoned Cherokee girl, Turtle, and her adopted white mother, Taylor Greer, living in Tucson. Turtle is 6 years old now, still vaguely damaged from the abuse she suffered as an infant and toddler, but getting along fine in the world.

Turtle and Taylor wind up on the Oprah Winfrey show, which is where tribal lawyer Annawake Fourkiller sees them; he decides to reclaim the obviously Cherokee Turtle for the Nation.

The premise of this novel is wonderfully timely, drawing on two issues that have recently compelled America: the rights of adoptive parents as opposed to biological ones, and the rights of jurisprudence in tribal matters—especially those concerning children adopted off the reservation. The book painstakingly details these issues by making them personal and familial: These are two mothers battling for the best interest of the child. The two women are complex, their passions persuasive. And the stakes are high. The reader is quietly educated on the benefits of tribal life and, by extension, the loss all America has suffered of its own extended families. The writing is lovely, especially in the first half of the book, where images and observations are breathtaking; the author's intelligence and great care show in nearly every line.

Kingsolver has tossed into this novel several other topical concerns for us to look at: the scourge of eating disorders, as illustrated by the minor character Barbie, a life-size fashion doll, complete with wardrobe and pathologies; the danger of television; the difficulties of single motherhood; and the inevitable breakdown of the American family. I think many of us would agree with Kingsolver's observations concerning white America: We are driven by image rather than substance, we consume rather than give back. We have lost our sense of community and family. We watch too much television. We underestimate and under-value women. We do not know how to care properly for our children, how to make them feel connected to the world and, therefore, engaged in it. We are not good parents.

But the book's tone is perhaps too cheery, its characters perhaps too good-natured and forgiving, too plucky and wise. A few coincidences fuel the plot, pushing the focus away from the tremendous moral quandary, finally making the novel a bit frustrating. The persecution Taylor feels, as a mother whose child can be taken from her without her permission, is diluted by two implausible decisions she makes early on. The first is her agreeing to appear on Oprah (and unwisely reporting on how she came by her child). The second is her illogical road trip.

True, the road trip allows Taylor to be physically separated from her own world and thereby receptive to understanding the separation Turtle might feel later concerning her culture, but it is a trip her character takes unconvincingly. Taylor is smarter than both missteps; had the writer pulled her aside and consulted her, Taylor might have explained

that she would never make her life public on national television, and, once threatened, would sit tight until there was real menace—then move. Once on the road, Taylor must meet Barbie, a larcenous bimbo whose aspiration is to purge herself into the proportions of her namesake: 36-18-33. A victim of the sexist marketing campaigns of our body-obsessed culture, Barbie is shallow, self-absorbed, stupid and heartless. What role does she play? She is the nightmare white girl. Why does Taylor need to pick her up and carry her around in this already character-heavy novel? It's difficult to say. She appears to fill space in the story the way a marshmallow does in the food chain: empty calories.

Taylor's mother, Alice, a woman separating from her long-time husband because he won't turn off the TV, also joins Taylor on the road. Alice is a civilized Southern woman, part Cherokee herself, and her husband is pushed aside in order to make room for the romance that later emerges. The convenience of these event suggests that this is not meant to be read as a realistic novel. This would not be disappointing if the reader weren't fascinated by the issues the book hints at but then refuses to debate.

The book wishes us to condemn the vicarious experience television provides in favor of the real experience of our lives. But the lives the book presents are idealized ones. True, there's darkness in the past: Turtle was abused, her mother killed. But there's no darkness in the present, not in the events of the novel, not in the minds of the characters. The "mothers" involved are the principals in the legend of King Solomon, who had to determine which mother most loved a disputed child. In this telling, however, the mothers decide they all like each other enough to just settle in as one big happy family, brown and white, old and young, "Cowboys and Indians." The dispute dissolves; the complex issue of tribal jurisdiction over the lives of its members can be put aside as a distressing one; we can stop weighing the arguments in favor of adoptive family over biological family. Because the reader is invited to believe that the world is inhabited by moral, ethical folks who get along socially, the genuine controversy of community versus individual rights is trivialized.

Barbara Kingsolver is a gifted stylist with a keen eye toward America's political preoccupations. However, in **Pigs in Heaven,** the United States she offers up contains a benevolent corner for all her characters' various trajectories to intersect and come to rest, an ideal place that looks and feels like, and is even named, Heaven—a place that, unfortunately, Kingsolver can't make us believe in.

Hilma Wolitzer (review date 11 July 1993)

SOURCE: "Child of Two Cultures," in *Chicago Tribune Books,* July 11, 1993, p. 4.

[*In the following review, Wolitzer offers positive assessment of* Pigs in Heaven.]

Fictional characters can continue to live inside a writer's head long after a novel is written, sometimes for so long it seems they ought to pay rent. And sometimes the only way to evict them is to imagine where fortune might have taken them since last encountered on the page and write about them again.

Barbara Kingsolver's charming first novel, **The Bean Trees** (1988), contained a bunch of such memorable squatters, including Taylor Greer, a spunky young single woman; her adopted daughter, Turtle; Taylor's hilariously wry mother, Alice; and her hypochondriacal friend, Lou Ann Ruiz. In **The Bean Trees,** these women without men (for the most part), struggled against poverty and other adversities with valor and wit. Now, in that novel's sequel, **Pigs in Heaven,** the characters, with a few inspired additions, are the same, the Southwestern milieu is similar, but the writing and the story's reach are far greater.

In **The Bean Trees,** Taylor is heading west alone from Kentucky to Tucson in search of the future when she finds herself in sudden possession of an abandoned child. The child's age is indeterminate—she doesn't speak or walk or respond in any way except to cling tenaciously to Taylor, reminding her of a snapping turtle and thereby earning her that unconventional name.

What is soon discovered, during a medical examination, is that Turtle is an approximately 3-year-old Cherokee Indian who has been severely abused. Under Taylor's patient mothering, the little girl gradually learns to relate to others and to speak; her first words are the names of vegetables, as if the world is a kind of soup in which she's been immersed. Most importantly, the bond between Taylor and Turtle is firmly forged. As Taylor observes at the end of **The Bean Trees,** she is her new daughter's "main ingredient."

At the beginning of **Pigs in Heaven,** Turtle is 6 years old, and she and Taylor are tourists at the Hoover Dam, when the girl witnesses a freak accident. This brings her into modest celebrity; she and Taylor wind up as guests on Oprah Winfrey's talk show, and there they come to the attention of Annawake Fourkiller, a lawyer representing the Cherokee Nation.

The white mother/Cherokee child image alerts and disturbs Annawake. Her own family disintegrated during her childhood, and her twin brother, Gabriel, was adopted-"stolen"—by a white family. Their good intentions were overcome by ignorance of Gabriel's unique needs, and he's grown up to become an habitual criminal.

Annawake questions both Taylor's moral and legal claims to Turtle. As we've learned in **The Bean Trees,** the adoption was carried out, by necessity, with fabricated information. Still, by virtue of her fierce love, Taylor considers herself Turtle's true and irrevocable parent. Annawake, however, worries about Turtle's forfeited heritage, her rights of access to her tribe, as well as the tribe's rights to her.

It is the author's particular achievement that both sides of the issue are wholly sympathetic, and that in the midst of this compelling story we're given a undidactic, historical overview of the oppression and deconstruction of the Native American family. As a bonus, there are thought-provoking riffs on aging, pop culture, art and the ego, tribal vs. individual instincts, and the nature of sexual fidelity.

Kingsolver crosscuts nimbly among her considerable cast of players, entering everyone's heart and mind with curiosity and courage. Annawake, propelled into the pursuit of Taylor by her ongoing grief about her lost brother, observes that she "has spent years becoming schooled in injustices and knows every one by name, but is still afraid she could forget the face." Taylor doesn't hesitate to flee with Turtle as soon as she feels threatened by Annawake's interest in them. Yet even in flight, her racial consciousness is raised, and she begins to notice images of Indians everywhere: "the Indian-chief profile on a Pontiac, the innocent-looking girl on the corn-oil margarine, the hook-nosed cartoon mascot of the Cleveland Indians."

Taylor's mother, Alice, who joins her in exile, is escaping, too, from a husband whose "idea of marriage is to spray WD-40 on anything that squeaks." Taylor's boyfriend, Jax, a musician with a band called the Irascible Babies, is left on his own after her sudden departure. His response to her absence—a mixture of comical, philosophical acceptance and pure yearning—makes him one of the most appealing characters in recent fiction. And Barbie, a waitress obsessed with the doll for whom she's named herself (including the trademark symbol), is one of the funniest.

Even quiet Turtle is indelibly rendered, especially by those buried memories of abuse that begin to surface whenever her current security is threatened: "Somewhere else in the old place was that shine of angels or stars too close, the underwater, shoes on the floor and no light and a man's voice across your mouth and you can't get air."

Things are resolved rather neatly at the end of **Pigs in Heaven,** but that seems less a literary copout than a model for diplomatic negotiations. One feels that the characters of **Pigs in Heaven** are lucky to be living inside Barbara Kingsolver's head and that her readers are lucky to be able to visit there for a while, too.

Christopher Lehmann-Haupt (review date 12 July 1993)

SOURCE: "Community vs. Family and Writer vs. Subject," in *New York Times,* July 12, 1993, p. C16.

[*In the following review, Lehmann-Haupt offers tempered assessment of* Pigs in Heaven, *praising Kingsolver's prose and humor though finding fault in the novel's lack of moral tension.*]

"Women on their own run in Alice's family. This dawns on her with the unkindness of a heart attack and she sits up in bed to get a closer look at her thoughts, which have collected above her in the dark." So begins the appealing homespun poetry of Barbara Kingsolver's new novel, *Pigs in Heaven,* about a moral conflict between the claims of mother love and the needs of a community.

What Alice Greer sees above her in the dark are the thoughts that her latest marriage has gone dead and that she longs for the company of her daughter, Taylor, who lives in Tucson, Ariz., with Turtle, her adopted 6-year-old Cherokee girl, and Jax, the charming leader of a band called the Irascible Babies. The trouble is that when Taylor and Turtle were visiting the Hoover Dam, Turtle happened to notice a man falling into a spillway.

After Turtle convinces the authorities that she didn't imagine what she saw, the successful rescue of the man brings her national celebrity. This catches the attention of Annawake Fourkiller, an idealistic young lawyer for the Cherokee Nation who lives in Heaven, Okla.

Annawake insists that Cherokee children can only survive if they are reared in a community of their people. She illustrates this by explaining that to Cherokees the Pleiades are known as the Six Pigs in Heaven, after six bad boys who were turned into pigs by their mothers for not being civic-minded.

In response, Taylor Greer points out that she didn't seek out Turtle for adoption; the child was abandoned in Taylor's car after suffering abuse that left her traumatized. The three-year healing process has left Taylor and Turtle deeply attached to each other. When Annawake gently warns Taylor that she may press her community's claim, Taylor runs away with Turtle.

The author of *The Bean Trees,* to which this is a sequel; other works of fiction and *Holding the Line: Women in the Great Arizona Mine Strike of 1983,* Ms. Kingsolver writes with down-home humor that never patronizes her characters but rather underlines their generosity and spiritedness. Unfortunately, there isn't much conflict or tension in her story. On the one hand, Taylor and Turtle have a terrible time trying to survive the American rat race by themselves. On the other hand, even adolescent boys are polite and considerate in the Cherokee community. There are in fact no pigs in Heaven, Okla.

The case for community is so one-sided and the outcome so predictable that the reader begins to suffocate in all the sweetness. You begin to cringe at treacly lines like "Heaven's on down the trail a little bit" and "I oftentimes have communication problems with my heart." Ms. Kingsolver is oftentimes a talented, funny writer in *Pigs in Heaven,* but after a while you begin to wish she would invent a Hell, Okla., and make a case for living there, too.

Barbara Kingsolver with Sarah Lyall (interview date 16 September 1993)

SOURCE: "Novel Beginning," in *Chicago Tribune,* September 16, 1993, p. D13.

[*In the following interview, Kingsolver discusses her life, literary beginnings, and* Pigs in Heaven.]

Barbara Kingsolver arrived for lunch so promptly as to be early, a refreshing gesture from someone who was soon casually confessing that her writing career began with an enormous white lie.

The lie occurred some years ago, before Kingsolver had published her three novels and one book of short stories, and before her latest book, *Pigs in Heaven,* made its gently opinionated author a bona fide literary success. Back then, Kingsolver was a graduate student at the University of Arizona, studying the social life of termites.

"It's a very interesting question if you're in this special filed of population biology," Kingsolver said. "But if you're not, and most people aren't, it's very difficult to understand what it has to do with the state of the union."

Her thesis was to have been called "Kin Selection Among Heterotermes Aureus," but the whole thing was making her increasingly dispirited, she said.

She was growing tired of the grinding lab work, the academic back-stabbing, the struggles to keep her subjects alive (termites are very sensitive to temperature changes). So she decided to quit and take her first writing job, as a science writer for the university. Fine for her, dismaying for her academic advisers.

"My thesis committee was really mad at me—they all thought I had great potential—so I felt under great pressure to come up with a legitimate excuse," said Kingsolver, 38.

"I can't say what it was—I'm too with a family member who is still embarrassed—but it had to do alive. I made up a terrible lie involving a car accident and a permanent disability, and said I needed to take another job to support my unnamed, maimed relative."

Until now, Kingsolver's career has been quietly successful, gaining momentum with each book. Independent booksellers have nominated her three times for their Abby Award, which they give to the book they most enjoyed recommending and selling to their customers.

Pigs in Heaven is her first book on the New York Times best-seller list. The novel tackles so many personal and public issues that it defies easy description. But at the heart it is an account of a custody battle between a white woman who adopted an abused, terrified little Indian girl left behind at a roadside rest stop, and the Cherokee nation, whose members identify the girl as one of their own and fight to get her back.

It ends with a Solomonic compromise that is either fatally contrived or wonderfully creative, depending on how you see it.

Women are undeniably Kingsolver's biggest fans. Some men seem puzzled by her appeal, pigeonholing her as a touchy-feely women's author even as their sisters, mothers, girlfriends and wives read, reread, borrow, lend and discuss her books.

Kingsolver, who lives in Tucson, writes books with strong idealistic messages, about the environment, the working poor, Central American refugees, single motherhood, and Indian rights.

Her books show a droll wit and an intricate understanding of the almost imperceptible subtleties of relationships. They feature exceptionally strong women who act unexpectedly, if emphatically, and who aren't so sure they need men around. This seems, in part, to be wishful thinking on Kingsolver's part: she has just undergone a wrenching divorce from her husband, a chemistry professor.

"I don't much enjoy being single," she said, her voice cracking a little and becoming even more measured. "I hear it's supposed to be fun, but what it means is that you fix dinner and you do the dishes and you bring in the groceries and you balance the checkbook, and you do it all while you're on a book tour."

Being a novelist seems to have been the remotest of career possibilities for Kingsolver when she was growing up, gawky and string-bean thin and different from everyone else, in rural Kentucky.

"I wanted to read *Anna Karenina* and everybody else wanted to do stuff in the back of cars," she said. School was decidedly unchallenging. She recalled that the only math and science courses offered were called "Math" and "Science" and so, rather than stay home and become a tobacco farmer's wife, she fled to DePauw University in Greencastle, Ind., winning a music scholarship.

"I was trained in classical piano, but it dawned on me that classical pianists compete for six job openings a year, and the rest of us get to play 'Blue Moon' in a hotel lobby," she said. So she switched to biology.

After arriving in Arizona, embracing and then abandoning her termite studies, Kingsolver took the science-writing job, addressing such topics as the potential of gopher weed as a fuel crop for the university. All the while, she wrote poetry and short stories, showing them to no one.

About a decade ago she entered a short-story contest held by a Phoenix newspaper, *The New Times,* which she described as "one of those free weekly alternative papers that's arts oriented and does investigative pieces like uncovering the dirt on the city council."

Months passed by and nothing came of it, until more than a year later, when a friend congratulated her—she had won and nobody had told her.

More short stories were published (a compilation is called *Homeland*); then in 1988 came *The Bean Trees,* which she wrote during the chronic insomnia of pregnancy, and *Animal Dreams.*

She says that she writes easily and fluidly, as if writing a screenplay for a movie in her head, and that she thinks of her characters as house guests who have come to stay for a spell. Her daughter, Camille, 6, was a big help with *Pigs in Heaven,* providing her mother with useful child's-eye-view observations.

Kingsolver said that she had expected some questioning of the adoption issues in her *Pigs in Heaven,* but she seemed taken aback later on in the day when two enraged women got up at a mostly cozy reading at Shakespeare & Company on the Upper West Side to noisily condemn her book for, they said, endorsing the notion that adoption is bad for children.

But she says she is used to taking criticism, even from the most unexpected sources. Early in the summer, for instance, she appeared on a television call-in show to discuss her book and her work. "One guy in New Mexico was listening in his pickup truck," Kingsolver said.

"He pulled over to the side of the road to call and tell me that I was all wrong." He didn't say exactly what he meant.

"What could I say? 'Get back in your pickup truck, sir, and have a nice day.'"

Travis Silcox (review date Fall 1993)

SOURCE: "Welcome to Heaven," in *Belles Lettres,* Vol. 9, No. 1, Fall, 1993, pp. 4, 42.

[*In the following review, Silcox offers positive assessment of* Pigs in Heaven, *though notes that "the novel suffers from a midpoint flatness."*]

Barbara Kingsolver, in the acknowledgments to her new novel, *Pigs in Heaven,* writes: "Other people would tell this story differently, and none of them would be wrong." The same generosity of spirit and down-to-earth wisdom that we have come to expect from a work by Kingsolver is evident in *Pigs in Heaven,* a novel confronting some of the thorniest of contemporary issues.

A sequel to her much-loved and much-loaned *The Bean Trees, Pigs in Heaven* picks up the story of single mom Taylor and her adopted Cherokee daughter, Turtle, three years after we left them in Tucson, Arizona. A no-frills, self-confident wordsmith from a working-class Kentucky background, Taylor has settled into her life with Jax, her new boyfriend, and Turtle. Her loving, seat-of-the-pants mothering has helped the formerly abused Turtle to open up and begin expressing her six-year-old's view of the world.

While on a trip to Hoover Dam, Turtle is the only witness to a man's fall into the dangerous waterworks. Taylor's belief in Turtle and her perseverance (the local paper calls it "perseverance") bring about his rescue. As a result, Turtle appears on the Oprah Winfrey show, and her adoption story comes partly to light. Watching the program is Annawake Fourkiller, a recent law school graduate and attorney for the Cherokee Nation, who, citing the Indian Child Welfare Act of 1978, begins proceedings to remand Turtle to the Nation. Kingsolver directly confronts this situation, making the focus of *Pigs in Heaven* the dilemma facing King Solomon: Whose claim to the child is greater? Thus, the novel places itself at the center of contemporary debates about identity politics, cultural heritage, nationalism and multiculturalism, and individualism.

The title is derived from the Cherokee story of Anitsutsa, "The Six Bad Boys." Where Euro-Western eyes see the seven sisters of the Pleiades, Cherokee eyes see the six boys turned into pigs and cast into the firmament for lacking respect and not being "civic-minded." This guiding myth comes to represent a Cherokee way of seeing the world, one with which the white characters clash as surely as they "see" the constellation differently.

The novel is the same blend of sharp political engagement and old-fashioned storytelling that Kingsolver delivered in *The Bean Trees* and *Animal Dreams*. She bridges what has been seen as the gap between politics and fiction by spinning committed stories that hinge on family relationships, making the connections between our civic and personal lives. What is "politics" after all, but a series of complex social relationships?

With painful family stories at the root of this novel, only family resolutions are possible. *Pigs in Heaven* comes to be as much the story of Alice, Taylor's mother, as it is the story of Taylor, Turtle, or Annawake. Through shifts in narrative point of view, many of the possible stories are told, creating a meditative work. Kingsolver's prose bathes us warmly, with characters who remind us that the United States is not populated solely by middle-class white suburban and urbanites.

Despite its action, the novel suffers from a midpoint flatness. Taylor and Turtle are on the lam, and the consumerism and related bulimia of the waitress Barbie (named after the doll) feel like filler, a *Thelma and Louise* road chase with a grandma and a child in tow.

Kingsolver's other supporting characters enrich the story. Jax, Taylor's anarcho-punk musician boyfriend, threatens

to steal the show whenever he is on stage and is a vehicle for Kingsolver's irrepressible humor. We also meet Gundi, the European painter who forms an open-minded commune in the desert, and Cash Stillwater, who quietly returns to the Cherokee reservation to face his losses.

With a cast to rival any Shakespearean comedy, the novel's romantic resolution and plot coincidences tie *Pigs in Heaven* to the tradition of 19th-century romance novels, which also expressly addressed rapid social change and the imperatives of race, class, and national tensions. Noisy, full of life and chaos, open to change and revelation, even improbable, *Pigs in Heaven* reminds us that this is what the lives of real people are like: dynamic, a bit crazy, and certainly—crucially—interdependent.

Mary Scott (review date 10 December 1993)

SOURCE: "Solomon's Wisdom," in *New Statesman and Society,* December 10, 1993, p. 40.

[*In the following review, Scott offers favorable assessment of* Pigs in Heaven.]

The pigs in question are stars. Six of them were bad Cherokee boys to whom their parents, to teach them a lesson, fed pig food. The children became pigs, then stars. The spirits anchored them in the sky, "to remind parents to love their kids, no matter what". The seventh star in the cluster is the mother who wouldn't let go.

It's a neat central image for a novel that reworks Solomon's judgment on two women who claim the same child.

Turtle is Cherokee. She has been abused by her uncle and is wont, when distressed, to lie speechless in a dry bathtub with a blanket over her. Taylor, her fiercely loving adoptive mother, is white. Taylor is fortunate in her own mother, the redoubtable Alice, raised on a hog farm and ex-wife of a man who is wedded to his TV. They are a family without men: a man, pronounces Alice, is "somebody who won't go out of his way for you".

Taylor's lover, gangly musician Jax, is not of this breed. The entire weight of his edgy intelligence is bent on Taylor. Dialogue between the two of them is shot through with the self-irony of a man who knows his woman is her *own* woman; and that his only sensible course is patience and restraint. It is also elliptical, wry, smart and very funny.

Turtle's quick eyesight leads to nationwide celebrity. She is spotted on TV and identified as Cherokee by chip-on-her-shoulder Indian lawyer Annawake Fourkiller. Annawake's efforts to return the child to the Nation prompt Taylor into flight; mother and child's odyssey across middle America in the company of a real-life bulimic Barbie doll is by turns glorious farce and—as Taylor loses both money and job—a tragedy of despair.

On the way, she learns the realities of mixed-race adoption; and her return to negotiate with Annawake becomes inevitable. Rather less inevitable is Alice's involvement with the Cherokees and the final, utterly whacky resolution of Turtle's custody by the Nation's council.

There are many small delights from a cast of alternately dippy and super smart people. Taylor plays rock music in her peach tree to frighten the birds; Jax dallies with a landlady who talks like a 19th-century romance; the town lunatic sticks empty bottles over the branches of a tree. The minor characters are as vivid and as numerous as the family of which everyone—Alice, Taylor, Turtle and Jax—eventually find themselves to be part.

In other hands, the heartwarmingly happy ending could have become sentimental tosh. But Kingsolver maintains throughout the delicate balance between irony and tenderness that makes this novel a real treat.

Maureen Ryan (essay date Winter 1995)

SOURCE: "Barbara Kingsolver's Lowfat Fiction," in *Journal of Popular Culture,* Vol. 18, No. 4, Winter, 1995, pp. 77-82.

[*In the following essay, Ryan provides an overview of the major themes and critical reception of Kingsolver's novels. According to Ryan, Kingsolver's "aggressively politically correct" fiction is undermined by elements of sentimentality and implicit reversions to traditional values.*]

The world of contemporary American fiction must be a bewildering circus for many readers, though sales figures indicate that we're buying tickets at a record rate. Venues range from the intimate neighborhood bookshop where the owner knows your tastes and puts aside a choice new morsel that she's sure you'll love, to the new discount book megamarkets that always stock 5,000 copies of Danielle Steel's latest, at 25

off. The reading choices—just in contemporary American fiction—are staggering: mysteries—hundreds of mysteries; Stephen King and the other scary guys; sexy vampires; countless romances; as well as the latest from Robertson Davies and William Gass, and (always) Joyce Carol Oates. Serious; popular; experimental; postmodern. It's an exciting time to be a reader. But how does one know what to buy?

Somehow a great many readers have learned to choose the fiction of Barbara Kingsolver. Kingsolver's novels and short stories—*The Bean Trees,* 1988; *Homeland and Other Stories,* 1989; *Animal Dreams,* 1990; and *Pigs in Heaven,* 1993—are commercial and critical successes, books that enjoy numerous, almost invariably glowing reviews that attest to their status as serious literature, even as they sell impressively at all those bookstores.

Kingsolver's work (and here I will concentrate on her three novels) consistently floats among the verbiage that vies for our dwindling reading time. Her novels and stories are seductively appealing, offering, as they do, sympathetic, interesting characters; well-paced plots with clear resolutions; and a breezy, colloquial, eminently readable style. That is to say, they give us all the comforting conventions of old-time realistic fiction, flavored with the cool contemporary lingo favored by so many of the truly hip young guns. In short, Barbara Kingsolver's novels and stories are a good read. But I would argue that more importantly—and distressingly—Kingsolver's fiction is so very popular because it is the exemplary fiction for our age: aggressively politically correct, yet fundamentally conservative.

Kingsolver knows what she's about. In the battle that rages in literary magazines for the elusive soul of contemporary American fiction, she unabashedly proclaims herself to be "old-fashioned." It's a popular position: on the attack against so-called minimalist writing and in defense of his very popular behemoth, *The Bonfire of the Vanities,* Tom Wolfe in 1989 bemoaned what he perceived to be the sterility and social irresponsibility of contemporary American fiction and called for a return to the "big, rich" social novel of Dickens and Steinbeck.

Reviewers of Barbara Kingsolver's work perhaps inadvertently betray their sympathies with the call for a return to traditional realistic fiction, generally welcoming her mobilization of political themes and her dissimilarity to the ostensibly clever, narrow, MFA-burdened writers—the Absurdists and Neo-Fabulists and Minimalists—that Wolfe and so many others decry. Karen FitzGerald, for instance, finds *The Bean Trees* to be "refreshingly free of cant and the self-absorption of . . . overrated urbane young novelists" (28). Diane Manuel applauds *The Bean Trees* for giving readers "something that's increasingly hard to find today—a character to believe in and laugh with and admire" (20). Margaret Randall likes the novel because "it is one of those old-fashioned stories, thankfully coming back onto our literary scene, in which there are heroines and anti-heroines . . . ordinary humans [who] go places and do things and where they go and what they do makes sense for them . . . and for us" (3). Russell Banks detects in the characters of *Homeland* "a moral toughness . . . a determination to find value and make meaning in a world where value and meaning have all but disappeared" (16). Karen Karbo, in her *New York Times Book Review* review of *Pigs in Heaven,* maintains that Kingsolver's "resounding achievement" is that "she somehow manages to maintain her political views without sacrificing the complexity of her characters' predicaments" (9).

Kingsolver herself makes clear that her commitment to tackle the social issues of our day is conscious—and central to her undertaking. "I only feel it's worth writing a book if I have something important to say," she asserted in a 1989 interview. And she, like Wolfe, dismisses the fashions of contemporary fiction, claiming that she sees "a lot of beautifully written work that's about—it seems to me—nothing" (*Contemporary Authors* 287). One of the generation that came of age in the 1960s, and consequently believes that "we can make a difference in the world," Kingsolver too laments the "divorce" between "politics and art" in our culture. (Farrell 29). "I am horribly out of fashion," she boasts. "I want to change the world. . . . I believe fiction is an extraordinary tool for creating empathy and compassion" (*Contemporary Literary Criticism* 68). Kingsolver wrestles the beasts of contemporary society: child abuse, labor unrest, political repression, feminism, the disintegration of Native American culture, and environmentalism. But she proffers her medicine sprinkled with Nutrasweet. This is fiction for everyone. "I have a commitment to accessibility," she asserts. "I believe in plot. I want an English professor to understand the symbolism while at the same time I want one of my relatives— who's never read anything but the Sears catalogue—to read my books" (*Publishers Weekly* 47). In fact, Barbara Kingsolver's books do appeal to both the literary scholar and the Sears shopper. And why not? The problem is that for all their apparent attention to the pressing social problems of our time, Kingsolver's light and lively books—which purport to give us food that's both nourishing and appetizing—leave all of us feeling just a bit too fine.

Kingsolver's critically acclaimed first novel, *The Bean Trees,* introduced the elements of her fictional world, which she develops in the recent sequel, *Pigs in Heaven.* When plucky, ingenuous Taylor Greer leaves Kentucky and "lights out for the territory" at the beginning of *The Bean Trees,* she sets out on a physical and spiritual journey that thrusts her into a world fraught with danger, evil, and the unexpected. In Oklahoma, enroute to Tucson, Taylor has found herself entrusted with the care of a silent, abused three-year-old Native American child who clings to Taylor with such ferocity that she christens the girl "Turtle." Like it or not, Taylor becomes an instant mother, a "bewildered Madonna," with a new understanding of the hazards of contemporary life (*The Bean Trees* 75). An afternoon at the zoo promises "stories of elephants going berzerk and trampling their keepers; of children's little hands snapped off and swallowed whole by who knows what seemingly innocent animal" (*The Bean Trees* 124). Taylor wonders "how many . . . things were lurking around waiting to take a child's life when you weren't paying attention" (*The Bean Trees* 45).

Of course, the trip to the zoo is a pleasant afternoon in the park, but there are real dangers in the world that Taylor encounters in her new life. When she first bathes Turtle and discovers the child's "bruises and worse," Taylor acknowledges that "I thought I knew about every ugly thing that one person does to another, but I had never even thought about such things being done to a baby girl" (*The Bean Trees* 23).

The Bean Trees and *Pigs in Heaven* are Taylor's story, and they present Taylor's education into the perplexities of contemporary society, as she ventures out of her small, rural Kentucky hometown into a heterogeneous, confusing world. But Taylor's lessons are finally less of the hazards and atrocities of the world than they are about its consolations and strategies for survival. For despite the peril and attendant vulnerability that pervade these characters' lives, real danger is displaced and diffused by the characters' resilience and the inherent goodness of the world. The indifferent aunt who abused, then abandoned Turtle is, for example, only a fleeting, fading presence in *The Bean Trees* (just as Barbie, the amoral waitress in *Pigs in Heaven,* is written out of the novel before she can do much damage). And Taylor, whose commitment to and competence at motherhood develops throughout both novels, puts her worried friend Lou Ann's anxieties into proper perspective: "The flip side of worrying too much is just not caring. . . . If anything, Lou Ann, you're just too good of a mother" (*The Bean Trees* 156).

The threats of everyday life are less obvious in *Pigs in Heaven,* but here, two years later, Taylor confronts her most threatening crisis when Annawake Fourkiller, an earnest young attorney who works for the Cherokee Nation Headquarters, learns of Turtle and her bogus adoption and resolves to return Turtle to her family and her heritage. Years earlier, Annawake lost a twin brother to the racist social system that allowed Native American children to be removed from their reservations and placed in the care of white families, and she intends to see to it that Turtle is returned to her home.

The plot of *Pigs in Heaven* discloses Taylor's attempts to flee with Turtle, then finally her compromise with Annawake and the Cherokee nation that will allow her to remain Turtle's mother while immersing the child in the culture that claims her. Annawake, for all her righteous insistence that Turtle belongs with her nuclear and Indian families, since only they can "tell that little girl who she is," is feminized by the force of Taylor's love for Turtle (*Pigs in Heaven* 68). As her short, spiky hair grows into a "glossy, earlobe-length bob," Annawake, who experiences a "crisis of faith" about her determination to take Turtle away from Taylor, develops into a caring woman and a skilled negotiator, who proposes an unbelievable plan that will let everyone live happily ever after.

The Cherokee community that welcomes Turtle, Taylor, and her mother Alice in *Pigs in Heaven* adores and nurtures its children, values its culture, and preserves its myths, all of which "add up more or less to 'Do right by your people'" (*Pigs in Heaven* 88). The extended Indian family of Heaven, Oklahoma, is incapable of producing the indifferent aunt and her abusive boyfriend who have abandoned Turtle in the earlier novel; here, they have been replaced by Turtle's grandfather, Cash Stillwater, a sexy, sensitive, communicative man who deserves—and gets—a second chance at happiness.

Taylor and Turtle begin the novel essentially alone, but by the denouement, they have been embraced by an extended family including the perfect grandfather; Taylor's newly-enlivened mother, Alice; and all of Heaven, Oklahoma. In her review of *Pigs in Heaven,* Sybil Steinberg notes, correctly, that one of the strengths of the novel is Kingsolver's ability to "mak[e] the reader understand and sympathize with" both claimants on Turtle's life—the Cherokee Nation and Taylor (652). It is, therefore, all the more unrealistic—and dishonest—that this disquieting dilemma is resolved so neatly. For once again, hazards and unpleasantness are neatly vanquished by the end of the novel. Over and over, Kingsolver has her characters recognize, grapple with, and finally overcome hazards large and small. Her keen awareness of the tenuousness of contemporary society, its vulnerability to everything from MTV to failing farms, is a theme that runs throughout her fiction. In *Pigs in Heaven* Alice discards a husband who watches television with "perfect vigilance" because she believes that TV "promises whatever you want, even before you knew you wanted it" (*Pigs in Heaven* 4, 116).

In Kingsolver's most recent novel, Taylor teaches her daughter how to choose the fastest line in the grocery store: "As a general rule I say go for the oldest. Somebody that went to school in the days when you still learned arithmetic" (*Pigs in Heaven* 99). Modern life is fragile, changeable, and uncertain. And for Kingsolver, the only antidote for the perilous fragility of our world is the preservation of traditional values and time-honored customs.

In *Pigs in Heaven,* it's the Native American community that maintains old-fashioned values—polite teenagers, tribal ceremonies, and extended families. When Cash decides to return home from his injudicious journey to Wyoming, he envisions a home "where relatives will always move over to give you a place at the table" (*Pigs in Heaven* 112). Kingsolver's second novel, *Animal Dreams,* interjects a Latin American influence into her contraposition of the old world and the new. In her mid-thirties, Codi Noline returns to her childhood home of Grace, Arizona (as pointedly and heavy-handedly named as Heaven, Oklahoma) to come to terms with her ailing, distant father; her miscarried child; her sense of isolation from the community that nurtured her as a motherless child. Codi's sister Hallie is a distant yet compelling presence in the novel, whose letters from Nicaragua, where she is an agricultural adviser to the peasants who resist the U.S.-backed Contras, offer guidance to the aimless Codi.

Grace is a dangerous world, too. The local mining company is poisoning the water and soil and threatening to dam the river altogether, thus cutting off the town from its water supply. A baby chokes on a pinto bean. And Hallie is kidnapped, then murdered, in Nicaragua. But the consolations in the life of old-world Grace are considerable. The women and children still tend the graves of their dead relatives and, on all Souls' Day, festoon the cemetery with chrysanthemums and picnic food. "The unifying principle was that the simplest thing was done with the greatest care," Codi marvels. "It was a comfort to see this attention lavished on the dead. In these families you would never stop being loved" (*Animal Dreams* 163).

Each of the protagonists in Kingsolver's novels must come to acknowledge the authority of seasoned customs, which is variously embodied in an appreciation for continuity, a sense of place, and family—values that prevail over danger and instability in their fictional world. Of course, aware as she is of the exigencies of modern life, Kingsolver defines family in the broadest possible terms.

In *The Bean Trees,* after she hears political refugee Estevan's horrid story of life in Guatemala, Taylor remembers the paper dolls that she played with as a child. She knew then that the "Family of Dolls," which consisted of Mom, Dad, Sis, and Junior, was an unrealistic dream, and she knows that now; but she can't help thinking that in "a different world" she and Turtle, Estevan and his wife Esperanza, "could have been the Family of Dolls" (*The Bean Trees* 138). Instead, in this mercurial world, families are composed of any people who come together to care for each other. Taylor and Lou Ann recognize that they and their children are a family; so are their neighbors, blind Edna Poppy and cantankerous Virgie Mae Valentine Parsons. In *Pigs in Heaven* the Cherokee community of Heaven offers the model for non-traditional families. Identifying her numerous grandchildren to Alice, Cousin Sugar explains that her young grandson is raised by her son Junior though he was born to her daughter Quatie. "She already had six or seven when he was born, so Junior adopted him. You know how people do. Share the kids around" (*Pigs in Heaven* 223). Annawake challenges Alice's insistence that Taylor has a right to keep Turtle because no one in her family wanted the child. The entire Cherokee nation is Turtle's family, according to Annawake: "We don't think of ourselves as having extended families. We look at you guys and think you have *contracted* families" (*Pigs in Heaven* 284).

Perhaps Taylor has always known that a father and mother and 2.3 children don't necessarily make a family, but she has an important lesson to learn about families nonetheless. When the much-loved Turtle innocently tells a social worker that she has no family, Taylor is astonished and hurt, until she figures out that feeling like a family isn't enough; she tells Alice,

> She's confused, because I'm confused. I *think* of Jax and Lou Ann and . . . of course you, . . . all those people as my family. But when you never put a name on things, you're accepting that it's okay for people to leave when they feel like it.
>
> They leave anyway, Alice says. My husbands went like houses on fire.
>
> But you don't have to *accept* it, Taylor insists. That's what your family is, the people you won't let go of for anything. (*Pigs in Heaven* 328)

Taylor learns what Codi must discover, too; that family—blood or found—must be claimed.

Taylor is right, but so is Alice. Men do leave in Kingsolver's world; and in fact, her protagonists are nearly always women, women confronting the vicissitudes of *being* women in late twentieth-century America. Kingsolver's feminism is unassailable. Writing about her failure to appreciate the current men's movement, she notes that "women are fighting for their lives, and men are looking for some peace of mind. . . . The men's movement and the women's movement aren't salt and pepper; they are hangnail and hand grenade" (**"His-and-Hers Politics"** 70). Kingsolver's novels are set in an unpredictable, baffling, imperfect world that is always a women's world.

It's not that men are cruel or boorish in *The Bean Trees;* they're simply irrelevant. Taylor's father is "long gone," and Taylor suspects that she's all the better for his absence (*The Bean Trees* 2). Lou Ann's husband slides quietly out of her life, and the novel, as Taylor pulls into Tucson. His absence doesn't matter much either; Lou Ann listens to him packing up his belongings and notices that "his presence was different from the feeling of women filling up the house. He could be there, or not, and it hardly made any difference" (*The Bean Trees* 63).

Taylor has spent her life avoiding the likely prospect for a girl like her in Kentucky, getting "hogtied to a future as a tobacco farmer's wife." She knows that "barefoot and pregnant" is not her style (*The Bean Trees* 3). And her (and the novel's) attitude toward men is best articulated by the Valentine's card she sends her mother: "On the cover there were hearts and it said, 'Here's hoping you'll soon have something big and strong around the house to open those tight jar lids.' Inside was a picture of a pipe wrench" (*The Bean Trees* 82).

The perspective on men changes in *Pigs in Heaven.* Alice, who on the first page of the novel walks out on her taciturn second husband because "his idea of marriage is to spray WD-40 on anything that squeaks," discovers life, when she ventures to Heaven to help her daughter, and love, when she meets Cash Stillwater, a Robert James Waller dream of the perfect aging man (*Pigs in Heaven* 3). And Taylor, who throughout the novel is unable to commit to her quirky, rock-n-roll boyfriend, Jax, decides (rather inexplicably) by the end that she wants "to start thinking of me and Jax as kind of more permanent" (*Pigs in Heaven* 327).

There is a place for men in the family-driven world of *Pigs in Heaven,* but here, too, it is women who can be counted on, women who endure, "Isn't that the dumbest thing, how the wife ends up getting filed under the husband?" Alice asks, as she struggles to contact her long-lost cousin in Oklahoma. She knows that "the husband is not the most reliable thing for your friends to try and keep track of" (*Pigs in Heaven* 182).

Grace, Arizona, the setting of Kingsolver's second novel, *Animal Dreams,* is a matriarchal community dominated, and finally preserved, by the elderly Mexican-American women of the Stitch and Bitch Club. When the community's very survival is threatened by the mining company that has long controlled the town, as the men squabble about lawsuits and get sidetracked by football games on television, the women mobilize a clever, and successful, campaign against big business. And Kingsolver's protagonist, Codi Noline, who has just returned after fourteen years to the community in which she always felt like an outsider, gradually comes to understand that those same women, twenty years before, were "fifty mothers who'd been standing at the edges of my childhood, ready to make whatever contribution was needed at the time" (*Animal Dreams* 328).

Kingsolver's is a world, not simply of women, but, significantly, of women and children, *mothers* and children. When Taylor steers her '55 Volkswagen west at the beginning of *The Bean Trees,* she leaves behind her beloved Mama (the Alice who discovers her independence, acquires her own name, and becomes an important character in *Pigs in Heaven*). Mama has struggled to raise Taylor alone, and has always let her daughter know that "trading Foster [Taylor's father] for [her] was the best deal this side of the Jackson Purchase" (*The Bean Trees* 5). All of the women in *The Bean Trees* raise children alone; in fact, child-rearing and marriage seem mutually exclusive.

Apparently, the newly domesticated men, Jax and Cash, will help to raise Turtle in her life after *Pigs in Heaven,* but this novel, too, is adamant about the sanctity of motherhood. Annawake's male law partner is less certain than she that Turtle should be wrested away from Taylor; and Annawake accepts his suspicion that she cannot understand Taylor's feelings about her daughter because "she isn't a mother" (*Pigs in Heaven* 67). Alice, reunited with Taylor, notices that her daughter is wearing pink, a color that the exuberant Taylor has always disliked. And Alice knows then that Taylor is truly Turtle's mother, since "she has changed in this way that motherhood changes you, so that you forget you ever had time for small things like despising the color pink" (*Pigs in Heaven* 138).

Motherhood—and its concomitant values: family, community, sacrifice, caring—are sacrosanct in Kingsolver's world. In the "different world" that she envisions throughout her fiction, we'd all care for everyone's child; in our world, exhausted, selfless mothers get the nod—and the approbation. Indeed, Kingsolver's apparent appreciation for non-traditional families is compromised by her unrelenting admiration for mothers. And though undoubtedly she means to suggest a vision for improving society; in fact, her privileging of family values works to compromise her message about the injustices of our society, which finally just don't seem all that ominous.

Barbara Kingsolver wants to say something important in her fiction about contemporary society and our responsibility to try to make the world a better place. She wants to challenge us to confront and do something about child abuse, the Native American Trail of Tears, and the

American-backed crimes in Central America. Finally, she wants to tell us (through Hallie) that though "wars and elections are both too big and too small to matter in the long run[,] [t]he daily work . . . goes on, it adds up. . . . Good things don't get lost" (**Animal Dreams** 299). Hers is a considerable and admirable undertaking. As Jack Butler writes in his review of **The Bean Trees,** "who can be against the things this book is against? Who can help admiring the things this book is for?" (15). "But," Butler continues, "reality suffers. . . . At one point late in the book, Turtle experiences a frightening reminder of her early horrors, and much is made of the damage this sort of recurrence can do—but then the subject is dismissed" (15). The problem with Barbara Kingsolver's fiction is that the big subjects, the looming dangers, are always dismissed. Everyone in her books turns out to be inherently good and well-meaning; the men sensitive and sexy, the women intrepid and resilient (and *always* perfect mothers). Karen Karbo raves about **Pigs in Heaven** in her review, but she unconsciously articulates the unease that Kingsolver's books inspire. "Her medicine is meant for the head, the heart, and the soul—and it goes down dangerously, blissfully, easily" (9). The dangers in Kingsolver's novels are not the challenges and perils that her characters all too easily overcome; they are the soothing strains of that old-time religion, lulling us into oblivion with her deceptive insistence that if we love our children and our mothers, and hang in there with hearth and home, the big bad world will simply go away.

It's a seductive, seditious message. We get to feel good about ourselves for crying over Turtle's scars and Hallie's murder, and we end up like Annawake, who settles herself sentimentally under her three quilts, "remembering from her childhood the noisy aunts who made [them]; they lived in one house, and could never agree on anything in this world except that love is eternal" (**Pigs in Heaven** 179).

The conventions of traditional realistic fiction that Wolfe and Kingsolver's reviewers miss in so much contemporary writing are the meat of Barbara Kingsolver's writing, which she serves with a soupçon of sentimentality for seasoning; and for dessert, the funny, slick patois of so much of that very hip recent fiction. She even gives us a healthily helping of vegetables: we may not like learning of Nicaraguan Contras and child abuse, but we know it's good for us. Finally, however, Kingsolver's work is contemporary American fiction *lite.* It's what we're supposed to eat these days, and it's even fairly tasty, but it's not very nourishing—and we go away hungry.

Works Cited

Banks, Russell. "Distant as a Cherokee Childhood." Rev. of *Homeland and Other Stories.* Barbara Kingsolver. *New York Times Book Review.* 11 Jun 1989: 16.

"Barbara Kingsolver." *Contemporary Literary Criticism.* Vol. 55: 64-68.

Butler, Jack. "She Hung the Moon and Plugged In All the Stars." Rev. of *The Bean Trees.* Barbara Kingsolver. *New York Times Book Review.* 10 Apr. 1988: 15.

Farrell, Michael J. "In Life, Art, Writer Plumbs Politics of Hope." *National Catholic Reporter.* 22 May 1992: 21, 29-30.

FitzGerald, Karen. "A Major New Talent." Rev. of *The Bean Trees.* Barbara Kingsolver. *Ms.* Apr. 1988: 28.

Karbo, Karen. "And Baby Makes Two." *Pigs in Heaven.* Barbara Kingsolver. *New York Times Book Review.* 27 June 1993: 9.

Kingsolver, Barbara. *Animal Dreams.* NY: HarperCollins, 1990.

———. *The Bean Trees.* 1988 NY: HarperPerennial-Harper & Row, 1992.

———. *Homeland and Other Stories.* 1989 London: Virago, 1990.

———. "His-and-Hers Politics." *Utne Reader* Jan.-Feb. 1993: 70-71.

———. Interview. *Contemporary Authors.* Vol. 134: 284-89.

———. Interview. *Publishers Weekly.* Lisa Lee. 31 Aug. 1990: 46-47.

———. *Pigs in Heaven.* NY: HarperCollins, 1993.

Manuel, Diane. "A Roundup of First Novels about Coming of Age." Rev. of *The Bean Trees.* Barbara Kingsolver. *Christian Science Monitor.* 22 Apr. 1988: 20.

Randall, Margaret. "Human Comedy." Rev. of *The Bean Trees.* Barbara Kingsolver. *Women's Review of Books.* May 1988: 1, 3.

Steinberg, Sybil S. Rev. of *Pigs in Heaven.* Barbara Kingsolver. *Publishers Weekly.* 5 Apr. 1993: 62.

Wolfe, Tom. "Stalking the Billion-Footed Beast." *Harper's* Nov. 1989: 45-56.

Barbara Kingsolver with Robin Epstein (interview date February 1996)

SOURCE: "Barbara Kingsolver," in *The Progressive,* Vol. 60, No. 2, February, 1996, pp. 33-7.

[*In the following interview, originally conducted in December of 1995, Kingsolver discusses* High Tide in Tucson, *her literary and social preoccupations, and critical reception.*]

In a chapter in her new book of wide-ranging essays, **High Tide in Tucson,** Barbara Kingsolver describes a trip to Phoenix's Heard Museum with her daughter, Camille, who was five years old at the time. One of her hopes for the visit, she writes, is that Camille will shed the notion that Native Americans are "people that lived a long time ago," an idea she picked up from the dominant culture even though it contradicted her own experience with Tohono O'odham and Yaqui playmates. Thanks to the museum's mission of appreciation for modern Native American life as well as history, Camille gleans some understanding of

Native American reality outside spaghetti westerns. Indians, she tells her mother as they leave the museum, are "people who love the Earth, and like to sing and dance and make a lot of pretty stuff to use." Then she adds, "And I think they like soda pop. Those guys selling the fry bread were drinking a lot of Cokes."

Barbara Kingsolver's work takes readers on a similar journey. It makes real the daily lives lived by people who are seldom presented with all their smarts and sorrows. Among the people we meet in Kingsolver's novels (all published by HarperCollins) are, in **The Bean Trees,** working-class white women from Appalachia and Central Americans fleeing death squads; in **Animal Dreams,** Mexican-American grandmothers fighting to save the river that nourishes their town's orchards, a garden-pest hotline worker who joins the Sandinistas' agricultural efforts in Nicaragua, and a part-Apache train engineer with a penchant for cockfighting; and in **Pigs in Heaven,** a Cherokee lawyer who tries to resolve a conflict over a child adopted out of the tribe.

Thanks to her gift for creating characters we care about, for giving them voices that situate them firmly in time and place, and for taking them through plots that unfold inside their hearts and minds as well as out in the world, Kingsolver has been nominated three times for the ABBY award, a booksellers' prize that goes to the author they most love to recommend to customers.

She is also the author of **Homeland,** a collection of short stories (HarperCollins again); **Another America/Otra America,** a book of poems in English and Spanish (Seal Press); and **Holding the Line: Women in the Great Arizona Mine Strike of 1983** (ILR Press), an oral history of the women in three small towns who for eighteen months sustained a picket against the Phelps Dodge Copper Corporation despite arrests, evictions, and excoriation from some union bosses and some men in their communities who thought they should stick to making tortillas.

In early December, I spent a day with Barbara Kingsolver in Sabino Canyon on the outskirts of Tucson. Though I had only been in Arizona all of two days, I thought I had figured out the weather—hot during the day and cold at night. It was daytime, so I didn't wear many layers. Well, I didn't know from canyons. I shivered as we rode the Forest Service tram that takes you in. Though she had hoped we would stay in the "v" of the mountains, near the running water that reminds her a tiny bit of the landscape of her childhood in Kentucky, Barbara agreed right away to hike a short distance up the slope to where the sun would reach us faster. We found a suitable rock just off the trail and plopped ourselves down to talk. Nourished by good conversation and Barbara's homemade raisin bread, I warmed up in no time.

[Epstein:]Some of the essays in your new book read like a kind of Feminine Mystique for a new generation. Were you especially trying to reach women with the information in those essays? I wonder whether they've prompted some heated dining table conversations between women and the men in their lives.

[Kingsolver:] I think so. I've heard about a few. I've heard from women who said, "I gave this to my husband with underlines." But when I'm writing I don't really think, "Who's going to read this?" I don't feel my books are mainly for women. When students ask, "Is this a chick book?" I say, "*Moby Dick* is a whale book, but I don't think only whales should read it."

You know, John Updike writes about penises and lusting after women, and he's really one of the most male writers that I read. His point of view is so deeply male. And when he's writing, does he think, "Oh, women aren't going to be able to relate to this?" I don't think it crosses his mind. So there's a role model for me, right?

I do think we can learn so much from reading the perspectives of people we are not. I can learn a lot from John Updike. I'm never going to have a penis in my whole life, so I can read John Updike and I can get some clue. I mean, that's sort of reductionist, but that male ego that's his focus, that's the eye of his storm, is very interesting. It's kind of heady to read it and get a glimpse of what it would be like to live in the eye of that storm instead of dancing around it all the time saying, "Are you OK? Are you OK?"

I grew up learning about women by reading men and becoming convinced at a pretty early age that they were getting a lot of it wrong. I felt usurped by *Lady Chatterley's Lover*. But a lot of people did it right, too. Look at *Anna Karenina;* look at Emma Bovary. So I will never say men have no right to represent women. That would be absurd. What I will say is I think our first responsibility, and also our first treasure as writers, is to represent ourselves. So women are always dead center in my novels. And my novels are about the things women most think about, like keeping our children fed, and how to manage on not very much income. I think it's important to do that, because it's not traditionally been the main stuff of literature. And it needs to be.

A lot of what I also do is tell people, "Look, you're noble. The things you do in your life, from day to day to day, which you have probably never thought of as the stuff of literature, are heroic. And if it's not you, it's your mother, or your neighbor, or your sister. And think about that. Think how wondrous that is." I think it really might be the main thing I do. And that's crossing a new street. It's looking at yourself and looking at heroism in a new way. Forget about Power Rangers, Power Mongers, Power Bombs, Power Suits, for just one minute of your life. All those icons we associate with power are hard to leave behind. It's hard to build a new iconography of heroism, but that's kind of my bailiwick. I owe that to the people I grew up with.

Do you mean your family or your community?

Both. Just to see people survive. Survival itself, in certain circumstances, is heroic. To live through mean times without becoming mean-spirited is heroic. I saw a lot of that.

In the new book, you explore our anti-child policies on the political level, and imply we also have some anti-child practices on the family level.

The "terrible twos" is an excellent example. I asked all my Latino friends, "How do you translate terrible twos?" "What?" they said. "There's no terrible twos." They didn't even know what I was talking about. Not only is it not in their language, it's not in their thinking. To define individuation from the parent as terrible is an anti-child mindset. Now, I'm not saying it's not difficult to have a two-year-old, but it's a cultural difficulty. We expect our two-year-olds to fit smoothly into adult schedules.

I think the reason that my friend Carmen was baffled when I said "terrible twos" is that the children in her household don't have to punch a clock. They're with her or there's other people in the household. There's this troupe of kids coming in and out, and always adults to take care of them. They don't have to get up, get dressed, eat breakfast, and get strapped into the car seat by 7 o'clock, which is a schedule that would make any two-year-old cranky. Think about if you had to crawl around and play with blocks all day. You'd be cranky; you'd be a terrible whatever-you-are.

And that's not the fault of the parents. Obviously many, many mothers have no choice but to bundle their kids off to daycare, so I'm not blaming them. What I'm saying is our culture doesn't make allowances for kids; it doesn't give parental leave. Children are an aberration in late capitalism. They're also a liability, because they're not productive. So that's why capitalism treats them like toxic waste.

Where did you get the desire to learn about different cultures?

I went to school with African Americans and whites. It was a segregated town. When I went to first grade, it was an all-white school. Second grade, the kids who had gone to school in the CME church came down to our school. I remember thinking, "They must be so scared," and wanting to ask, but being afraid. Marilyn and Karen were the two African-American kids in my class. I wanted to be friends with them and I didn't know how. I was a little bit scared, not because my parents said, "Stay away," nothing like that. Just that I knew that they came from a different world, and I knew that they were outnumbered.

It impressed me, because I was also an outcast. I think one of the great pluses is that I grew up as a social outsider. And that had to do with being really skinny and really tall, and physically not blending in, which is so important in pre-adolescence and adolescence—it's sort of the main thing.

But also my family was different. My parents just expected me to do things like read books—big, good books—and one day go to college. Nobody else I knew had that sort of expectation. Nobody in my class was going to college. Everybody kind of had the plan. They'd get married and they'd have kids and they'd stay right there. There was something in my training that was telling me, "You're going to go away."

And then you lived for a while in Africa as a kid?

Yes, my dad was a physician, and he wanted to go where he could be extremely useful. So we ended up living in St. Lucia for a while in a convent hospital, and we lived in Central Africa. The people in our village had not seen white kids. I had really long hair that I could sit on, and people didn't think it was hair, because hair doesn't look like that, and they'd try to pull it off. My mom would explain to me, "They're not trying to hurt you. They just think you're wearing something weird on your head and they're trying to get you to quit showing off."

So you were an outsider?

Very much. I got a real extreme look at what it's like to be a minority. It was an enormous adventure that let me know at the age of seven that there's a great big old world out there that I don't know anything about, that I'm going to see, and that I'm going to know if I can.

*Was your connection to small-town life one of the things that led you to write **Holding the Line: Women in the Great Arizona Mine Strike of 1983,** about the small towns of Morenci, Ajo, and Clifton?*

Yes, even though I didn't grow up in a mining county. Nicholas County is not mining, it's agricultural. It's a tobacco town, so it's deeply depressed. Times have been tough there for as long as I've known about, and I think they're tougher still now that tobacco doesn't have the economic base it did. So, there are all these divisions. There was black and white. There was merchant and farmer. That was a very clear distinction in my school. The popular kids—the ones with new clothes every year—were the merchants' kids, the ones whose parents owned the dime store or the men's clothing store, or were the county attorney. And then all the other kids were farm kids, and they didn't get to wash their hair every night because they didn't necessarily have hot water. They had to walk through mud to get to the school bus, so they had mud on their shoes.

I was in that group, not because we were farmers but because we lived in the country, and my parents didn't believe in new clothes. They didn't value spending lots of money on superficial things, which of course really irritated me when I was fourteen. But I somehow lived through that and learned to appreciate it.

So in high school I learned about class, and I didn't even know the words. I never read Marx until I was about eighteen, but the first time I read *Grundrisse* and *Capital* I said, "I know this stuff. I grew up with this stuff." Kentucky is such a laboratory of class consciousness because you have really oppressed workers shoulder to shoulder with big capital, which is not something you see necessarily in other parts of the country. Maybe the rust belt, maybe the auto belt, though I still don't know if it's as clear as mining bosses and the way they sort of own their workers wholesale. So it's very clear whose side everyone's on. And add to that, Nicholas County is right in between, it's sandwiched.

You see the wealth of Lexington?

It's just one county away. Nicholas County holds a really interesting geographic position between the wealth of Lexington and the poverty of Appalachia, and people define themselves depending on which way they're facing. In our county we didn't have a swimming pool, not in the whole county. And we would go to Lexington once in a while, and pass through these horse farms. And there was a horse farm where—I swear this was true—the horses had a swimming pool. It was for therapy or something. I remember driving by that every time and smashing our faces against the glass of the window and hating those horses for being so rich. It was so unfair.

One thing that comes through so much in your writing is that people, like those you grew up with in Nicholas County, can understand power. I guess some liberal people would say they know that, but they don't really believe it at a gut level.

That's really wrong. That's a huge underestimation. I think certainly in Kentucky people understand class and power relations. And that's why Kentucky—and Arizona, too—has a history of radical class action, and radical labor organizing. And that's of course what drew me to the strike.

My first national publication was in *The Progressive* and it was about the strike. I started going down there with a friend of mine, Jill Fein. We were activists and organizers and we went there in solidarity with the strikers. I figured I'd write about it, but I didn't at first have an assignment. I loved *The Progressive,* so I wrote a query. We wrote the article together and they published it and it was an enormous thrill when it arrived. Seeing it in print was even more important than the check. There it was, with the photograph we'd taken of the women on the picket line. I remember just standing by the mailbox holding it in my hand and thinking, "All over the country people are reading about this." That's the power of being able to get the word out. After bonegrinding years as an activist, a door opened. I got some sense of the possibilities and of the power of this kind of writing. It was really a turning point for me.

Some people criticize your work as being too political. They try to erect a huge wall between art and politics.

There's this idea that political art is bad, and that a divider between the two can actually exist. Where does this idea come from?

I'm not sure. My personal theory is it has a lot to do with McCarthyism. Because if you go back before the 1950s you find great political writers like Steinbeck, Walt Whitman, Carl Sandburg, Henry Thoreau. And then that stopped; things just sort of ground to a halt in the 1950s.

I don't know whether it's cause or effect. I don't know whether it was because of McCarthyism, or whether there was some evil humus in this country from which sprang Joe McCarthy and people who supported him and this idea that art and politics should separate themselves. For whatever reason, it's with us now and we haven't recovered from that time.

What can we do about it?

It's being done to us. Artists are losing the minuscule amount of support that we had. The NEA, I heard Christopher Reeve say when he was in town years ago, gives out each year less money than the money for military band uniforms. So, there wasn't an enormous amount of public or federal support for artists to begin with, and it's dwindling. And there's a hue and cry, and artists are looking around and saying, "Why doesn't the public support us?"

Well, I have a clue about that. Look to some of the poorest countries in Latin America. They revere their poets. Their poets do not starve. They elect their poets to public office. Their poets are talking about important stuff. Their poets have their finger on the pulse of the human-rights situation, the core of economic oppression, where it's going and where it's coming from. They write about power relations and the common good. They write about all of this stuff that in the United States many artists avert their faces from as being too political. Well, if we write and paint and film things that people understand to be vital to their lives, we'll get public support. Any artistic commission that has Jesse Helms on it is scary. Censorship of any kind is scary. But I don't think we're really talking about censorship here. I think we're talking about a responsiveness of artists to their public that's sort of waning.

It's waning, but it has the potential to come back?

I think if artists can speak of things that matter, then they will be supported. I feel like I say stuff that people really don't want to hear. I write about child abuse, and about sexism and racism and illegal immigration laws, and I think, "Nobody's going to read about this," and yet, they do. I think that you can say difficult things, but do it artfully, and you'll be heard.

And the critics may say, "Oh, this is too political," but people are reading the books.

The gatekeepers of art are the ones who are saying this is too political. I don't hear that from many people. One letter in 100, or even less, will say, "I don't think you should be writing about this stuff."

I think we also have in this country a rare phenomenon in which people are very uneducated about art. I think the average African in Africa, let's say the average citizen of Cameroon, understands more about the art of Cameroon than the average Tucsonian understands about the art of Tucson. Understanding and appreciating art is something you learn from other people who do it, and historically it's been part of oral tradition. You appreciate stories because you sit around in groups where people tell them. You appreciate dance because you participate. You grow up seeing other people moved to tears by the events, and you learn what that's about.

Do you think the people who criticize your work are people who already know about the issues and have decided they're on the other side? Or are they people who have so much of their personal and professional identities invested in the idea that they don't take stands that they feel threatened by the fact that your characters do?

Usually when people say, "You're too political," what they mean is, "I don't agree with you." In **High Tide in Tucson,** I wrote about that anecdote at the mall, where the managers decided that the people passing out yellow ribbons and WE KICK BUTT bumper stickers were not political, and the people who were passing out anti-war propaganda were political. That's come to be a significant definition of the word political in this country, and it's something I don't agree with. The people who have panned my work as being political are people who are not on my side, so I feel kind of proud of that.

Do you think the popularity of your fiction speaks to people's hunger for the acknowledgement of the political in their lives, in addition to the fact that they're drawn in by the great stories and great characters?

Yes, I don't think it's necessarily things people would define as political, although sometimes it is, explicitly. I hear from activists who say, "We've been trying and trying to tell people about Nicaragua and finally what a relief to pick up a book that does it, a real book that people are reading."

You've said a novel can move people in a way a newspaper article can't, because it gets in their heart and because they can't switch to the sports pages. But your new book is nonfiction. Did you want to speak in your own voice instead of through your characters?

I've been writing essays all along, but to write a book of them that all added up to something was really wonderful. This is a really scary thing to say, but it has worried me at times that my work is so popular. Sometimes I think, "Are they just reading the love story and didn't notice the part

about Guatemala?" I think people do, on some level, understand the politics of my fiction. Even if only to be awakened to the possibility that the government is doing something not right in Central America and maybe they'll be more open to reading stuff that's more explicitly about that subject. Or sort of an attitude about the environment, or an attitude about women that comes through. You can hear on the left sometimes an elitism of unpopularity. I don't know how many times I've heard people say, "Well, I write, but my work will never be popular because it's so political," and I think, "Well, am I chopped liver? Are you saying that I sold out, or what?"

I felt that I did at this point in my life have a chance to be more direct. Everything in **High Tide in Tucson** I think I've said before behind the mask of fiction, but this time I stepped out from behind the mask and said, "I, Barbara Kingsolver, believe this." And it sold more in the first four months than all six of my other books combined in their first four months.

So you're probably reaching people who haven't heard about these issues from your perspective before.

I have to think so. I can't get over that I get to do this. It also comes with a certain responsibility. You know you get handed in your life this chance to go all over the country and talk and talk and talk, and answer and answer and answer questions, and go on *McNeil/Lehrer* and national shows. I would much rather not do that. I would much rather stay home and bake bread and write another book. That's what I do. That's what I love. And I do have my limits. I'll do it for a few months after a book comes out, and try to make the most of that time.

The reason that I do it at all is that I can still remember how recently it was that I was cranking out leaflets about the Palo Verde Nuclear Generating Plant, or whatever was the crisis of the week in Tucson, Arizona. And I don't mean to demean these crises; they are all very real.

It's very hard to criticize this country, our domestic or our foreign policy, or our attitude, or our Americanism. And so, given the chance to do that, given this strange moment that I have, little old socialist me, to go talk to David Gergen and be in everybody's living room, I have to do it. And I have to do it right. I have to say the important stuff, not just smile and nod and say, "Oh, yes, I have written another book."

I don't imagine you have time to crank the mimeographs anymore.

No, and it wouldn't be a good use of my time. But I'm still involved locally. It used to be I was the one who would organize the events. Now I go to them. Or I'll go and read a poem. They put my name on the list to draw a different crowd. I find that I can be an effective activist in very different ways, but I feel like I still believe exactly the same things I did when I was twenty.

It seems to me that as disparate as they are, all the essays in the new book fit together. What's the unifying theme?

I didn't title the book, *Barbara the Marxist Takes on Life,* but that's what it is. Let's face it. I steered clear of the M word, because people are so ignorant. Even though we're a secular state, we're deeply religious about the religion of America. We rely on so many things on faith, without having to have any evidence. Like this belief about how anyone can make it in America if you're smart and you work hard. Well, for how many generations now has that been untrue? In some families, a lot. And in almost all families, my generation is not as well off as our parents, even though we worked just as hard, and more of us got more of an education than they did. It's staggering to me to read statistics of how many people in this country live in poverty: 20 percent of kids, right? Yet turn on the television and you still see rich people idolized. Popular culture reflects a population that still identifies with the ruling class.

You weave your scientific training into your writing, which is pretty unusual.

There's this whole realm of natural history metaphors and symbols you can use if you know about them that gives a kind of freshness to your writing, because most writers haven't studied science. People think it's sort of funny that I went to graduate school as a biologist and then became a novelist, but the process is so similar. What I learned is how to formulate or identify a new question that hasn't been asked before, and then to set about solving it, to do original research to find the way to an answer. And that's what I do when I write a book. It's very similar. I think I might be a lot more process-oriented than a lot of writers are. I've never talked with another writer about process who does it exactly the same way I do it. It used to make me certain I was doing it wrong. Now I just figure it's as good as any way. It works for me.

In the essays you let on that there have been days when you didn't think you could keep going, when you questioned your abilities as a writer.

I still have them. Beginning a book is really hard. I'm trying to begin one now and I just keep throwing stuff away and thinking, "Can I do this? I don't think I'm smart enough." But it has to be hard. You have to have a reverence for the undertaking. And I think reverence implies a certain lack of self-esteem, doesn't it?

If you're reverent towards something, you feel . . .

Lowly. You feel daunted and unworthy. But in this age of glorifying the individual and self-esteem, I think there's something healthy about being daunted. Cockiness doesn't lend itself to good writing. It really doesn't.

How was your recent book tour?

This book tour just took me from city to city to city, into hotel rooms out of whose windows I would look and see the same skyline. One of the things that was psychologically and emotionally tiring was that it was all city, and I was surrounded continually by people who took their city so seriously. I don't mean just their city, like. "Oh, this is Pittsburgh." But people who look around at the city and say, "This is what's real." For me, *this* is what's real. [*As she said this, she gestured emphatically to the saguaro-studded canyon rising all around us.*] We're just a blink in the eye of this. We haven't been around very long, and we're probably not going to persist. And it's sort of laughable that we take all of our stuff so seriously. We've had two hundred-year floods here in the last ten years, and both times the city was completely cut off, for days and days. You couldn't go anywhere. It was roaring water. And some things happened that were deeply reinforcing on the human level. For the first day you're still trying to get to work, or get to your appointments, and then slowly you give it up, and you realize that this whole schedule—all these things in our date book—are just little scratches on the surface of this old Earth, and she doesn't much care.

How do we build more awareness of that?

I think urban life is a big part of the problem. If people could just get out and look. And to just sit still and be. Ed Abbey, who was my neighbor, said something that continues to impress me in new ways. I told him I'd been to Zion, and I said, "It's enough to make you religious." And he said, "Those mountains don't inspire religion. They are religion."

In your new book, **High Tide in Tucson,** *in the essay, "The Spaces Between", you write, "I'm drawn like a kid to mud into the sticky terrain of cultural difference." You say, "I want to know, and to write, about the places where disparate points of view rub together—the spaces between. Not just between man and woman but also North and South; white and not-white; communal and individual; spiritual and carnal."*

The reason I'm attracted so much to those places and those moments is you can learn so much. You go through the world on some kind of search, and you take so much for granted. And when you run up against somebody else who's moving right beside you but looking for completely different stuff, it can stop you in your tracks, and you can start thinking. "Why am I looking for this?"

So few of us examine our motives and our mythology, the things that we believe in without question. Like humans are more important than any other species. Most people with your background and mine go through their whole lives without questioning that. I am more important than a Kirtland's warbler. Don't even think about it. And, so when you run up against somebody who says, "Of course the Kirtland's warbler is just as important as I am," that can throw you for a loop.

In *Pigs in Heaven* I wanted to choose a high-profile event in which a Native American has been adopted out of the tribe and in which that adoption is questioned and challenged. Because it brings into conflict two completely different ways of defining good, of defining value. The one is that the good is whatever is in the best interest of the child; the other is that the good is whatever is in the best interest of the tribe, the group, the community. What I really wanted to do in that book was not necessarily write about Indians. I wanted to introduce my readers to this completely different unit of good and have them believe in it by the end, have them accept in their hearts that that could be just as true as the other.

Your fiction, you've made clear, is not autobiographical, but the essays . . .

Are. It used to be people thought they knew all about me because they thought I was my characters. Now they do. I didn't really reveal anything that intimate in that book. I included a lot of details about where I live and so forth, only as kind of a springboard to issues or ideas. For example, I wrote about divorce. I didn't really write about my divorce. It seems like I did, but I didn't.

That it happened, yes.

That was sort of part of the public record already, anyway. Also, we moved right before the book came out, so people think they know all about my house, but they don't.

Including details about your life made the book more accessible?

That's the idea. It was so much like writing fiction. You use the same techniques. You create characters and you have a plot. All of the essays really are little stories that mean something, and what they end up being about is not the events but some larger ideas. It just happens that I used real people or real events or incidents in my life as the starting points. You can't just put the ideas there. You have to put clothes on them and make them walk around. I keep coming back to the term creative nonfiction to describe this book, because it really was more creative writing than journalism. You can look at the same event fifty different ways, so the story I chose to tell from a particular event was the creative part.

The choosing how to tell it?

And, I suppose before that, deciding what it means. What can you make of someone telling you, "Love it or leave it, bitch?" That can be at the starting point of a lot of different stories.

In that same essay you came back and said that guy could think critically.

I speculate that if I asked him, "Do you think patriotism means turning your back on evidence that your country has done immoral acts?" I think he would say, "No." Then he'd say, "Prove it." I think "my country right or wrong" is not such a common slogan as "my country always right,"

and "by God I want to believe that, and so don't mess with me, don't confuse me with the facts."

But it's suspect to be a writer whose purpose in part is to change the world.

Oh, yeah. And it's funny that I still shock people when they say, "Why do you write?" and I say, "Well, to change the world." It's like heresy. It's like absolute heresy for an artist to say that. That's why I say it. Seven or eight years ago I couldn't.

You couldn't?

I thought it, but I couldn't admit it because I was afraid of not being taken seriously. Now I'm pretty confident of being taken seriously. Shocking but true. And so I feel I have an obligation to tell truths like that. You like what I write? Well, get this: I'm a pinko and I want to change the world.

Karen M. Kelly and Philip H. Kelly (essay date December 1997)

SOURCE: "Barbara Kingsolver's *The Bean Trees:* A New Classroom Classic," in *English Journal,* Vol. 86, No. 8, December, 1997, pp. 61-3.

[*In the following essay, the Kellys discuss the major themes, symbolism, and literary style of* The Bean Trees, *arguing that the novel holds excellent instructional value for high school students.*]

Barbara Kingsolver, author of **The Bean Trees,** has produced three national bestsellers, and we realize that using bestselling writers in the high school classroom carries some potential hazards. Nonetheless, we, secondary school teachers with some experience, think **The Bean Trees** has the earmarks of becoming a new classroom classic.

BARBARA KINGSOLVER

Barbara Kingsolver is an award-winning writer whose works have been published in more than 65 countries around the world. Her works are available in a range of media: she has recorded her novels and personal essays on audio tape, and she has at least one story on the World Wide Web (**"Fault Lines"** at http://buzzmag.com/issue28/faultlines28.html). It sometimes seems that she is everywhere.

Kingsolver is multidimensional. To her credit so far she has two books of nonfiction: the gripping neo-journalism of **Holding the Line: Women in the Great Arizona Mine Strike of 1983** (1989), a story of the role that women played in the Phelps Dodge Copper Company labor dispute, and **High Tide in Tucson** (1995), a collection of personal essays that made the *New York Times* Bestseller list. She has a volume of poetry, **Another America/Otra**

America (1992), featuring Kingsolver's English poems interleaved with translations by Rebeca Cartes, a volume of short stories, and three novels, two of which have been national bestsellers.

Barbara Kingsolver is obviously not an unknown, undiscovered writer. Nonetheless, she is one of the fresh new American voices whose work could find a comfortable niche in the curriculum canon for high school literature classes.

THE BEAN TREES

The Bean Trees is a "teachable" text, a meaningful novel that wrestles with significant personal and social issues while at the same time avoiding the pitfalls that frequently incur the wrath of censors. These characteristics may sound like a prescription for blandness, but the bright vision and loving wisdom of Barbara Kingsolver coupled with the wit and absolute audacity of the central character combine to make *The Bean Trees* an eminently usable text for faculty and an engaging novel for students.

The story begins with Taylor Greer's determination not to become pregnant in high school and thus face a premature marriage that would likely result in her being stuck in Pittman County, Kentucky, the rest of her life. The story is positive, uplifting, never depressing or even sad, yet the subject matter is substantial and varied, ranging from the long-term effects of child abuse to the plight of Guatemalan political refugees and the struggles of Native Americans. All of this subject matter is presented amidst a general atmosphere of care and concern for others.

The characters are admirable and engaging, and almost all are women. Yet, though this is basically a woman's novel, it is not a story bereft of men; both Taylor and Lou Ann exhibit interests in the opposite sex. Furthermore, the character of Taylor is tough enough to elicit admiration from even the most macho males in the class. And Taylor's independent, adventuresome spirit appeals to their yearning to go into the world. This is an engaging novel for many high school students.

To fit the needs of the classroom setting, *The Bean Trees* also lends itself to chapter-by-chapter teaching. The first two chapters may be treated almost as short stories. In fact, in a *Contemporary Authors* interview (1984, Detroit, MI: Gale Research, Vol. 134, 287), Kingsolver points out that she originally wrote the first chapter of *The Bean Trees* as a short story but was encouraged to reconceptualize it as a novel. Approaching the first two chapters as short stories may be an effective strategy for engaging more reluctant students.

THEMES IN THE BEAN TREES

While *The Bean Trees* features family values, these values work themselves out in a nontraditional setting. Taylor's mother raises her alone, Taylor's father having cleared out long ago. Taylor's mother supports and encourages Taylor

in all that she does—not heroically but clearly and consistently—so that Taylor's recollections are of a mother who felt all the positive things Taylor did were grand achievements. The result is that Taylor apparently regards herself as capable of grand achievements, some of which we see in the course of the novel. The support from her mother probably contributes to Taylor's determination to avoid an out-of-wedlock pregnancy, a plight that seems all-too-common among her high school classmates. Clearly, the support from her mother sustains Taylor throughout the novel: it serves her when she seeks a job at the Pittman County Hospital; it sustains her in her cross-country travel; and it strengthens her in her decision to adopt Turtle, an abused and abandoned Cherokee baby.

But maybe the most impressive expression of nurturing values comes from the nontraditional extended family in Taylor's Tucson neighborhood. Taylor becomes an integral part of that neighborhood community. In fact, Taylor seems to crystallize that community's bonding. It is a community of mutual support and interdependence consisting of two single mothers, Taylor and Lou Ann, living together each with an infant; two older neighbor women (one of whom is blind); Mattie with her tire store and residence which doubles as a safe-house for Central American refugees; and two of the refugees themselves, Estevan and Esperanza.

The novel pictures an underside of life: independent women with children scratching out a meager existence. They are able to do so because of their mutual interdependence, and that's a lesson in living.

Among other things, *The Bean Trees* is a lesson in the maturing process. As Taylor's confidence waxes and wanes, students may come to understand maturing as a process, not as an on/off proposition.

There are no depictions of sexuality. There are some urgings toward adultery (between Estevan and Taylor), but Taylor resists them, albeit for practical rather than for any inherently moral reasons. It is important to note that we see Taylor's interest in or at least infatuation for Estevan, but we do not have any substantial, positive indicators from Estevan regarding his inclinations.

A central element in the novel is the sexual and physical abuse that Turtle has experienced. We see none of the abuse itself, but do see the consequences, both physical and psychological. Taylor discovers bruises on Turtle the first time she changes her. Later in the novel, a doctor checks Turtle and discovers her now-healed broken bones and detects her "failure to thrive." In addition, we witness her clinging behavior; in fact, that's how Turtle got her name: her tenacious grip reminded Taylor of the myth that once a turtle locks its jaws onto something it supposedly holds on until the next thunder. It seemed as if Turtle's grip was that tenacious. We also witness Turtle's reticence about talking and later her seemingly compulsive talk about seeds, plants, and vegetables.

In teaching the novel, we can effectively encourage students to become aware of alternate perspective on an issue by asking them to rethink the adoption of Turtle. When we finish *The Bean Trees,* we feel relieved that Taylor has in fact secured adoption papers for Turtle. As readers, the adoption feels right to us and brings a satisfying closure to the novel.

But a letter in *Pigs in Heaven* (1993, New York: Harper-Collins, 148-150), the sequel to *The Bean Trees,* invites us to rethink that ending. The letter is from Annawake Fourkiller, a Native American who becomes aware of Taylor's adoption of Turtle and recognizes its irregularities. Annawake's letter comes three years after the close of *The Bean Trees* with Turtle now six years old. In it, Annawake asks Taylor to consider the plight of the Native American child raised in white society. Sharing that letter with students a week or so after having completed *The Bean Trees* is an excellent tool for encouraging both reflection and an alternate way of viewing what happens in the novel. The letter admits to the charm of raising a cute little Cherokee infant and appreciates the advantages of that upbringing, but it also articulates the grim reality of the racial discrimination that Turtle is likely to face in adolescence, and the fact that she will have to face that discrimination without any of the cultural supports or reinforcements that she might otherwise have if she were living among her people on a reservation. In addition, this letter on discrimination might be an excellent opening for a lesson on prejudice.

LITERARY TECHNIQUE IN *THE BEAN TREES*

From the perspective of literary techniques, this novel is, again, eminently teachable. Lessons on character come easily, especially in the case of Taylor because she is an inherently engaging persona. Lou Ann, Angel, and Turtle are also strong character studies.

Lessons on plot profit from the inherently engaging nature of the story. The classic plot construction builds the story effectively as it combines basic conflicts, both external and internal, in a model of plot development.

In addition to plot and character, lessons on symbol and irony are readily available and accessible for most students. For example, *The Bean Trees* features strong instances of irony. Two things that Taylor was intent on escaping by leaving Kentucky were tires and babies. When she was about twelve years old, she witnessed Newt Hardbine's father being hurled through the air when an overinflated tire he was working on exploded. That experience impressed on Taylor an inordinate fear of tires. Ironically, by the time Taylor gets to Tucson she has a baby, Turtle, and in a matter of weeks, she finds herself working around tires daily in Mattie's used tire store.

Some standard symbols are also readily apparent. To symbolize embarking on a new life, Taylor changes her name as she starts her journey westward. The fact that she journeys westward, the direction of new frontiers in the U.S., makes use of another standard symbol. Finally, for name symbolism, the Hardbines seemed continually on hard times.

The symbol with the best potential for development is rhizobia, the microbe that lives on the roots of the wisteria and provides a direct infusion of nitrogen to the plants, allowing them to grow in the most hostile of environments. In addition to an opportunity to teach a little lesson in biology, the rhizobia is a fitting symbol for systems of mutual support that constitute the thematic life blood of the novel.

OTHER CONNECTIONS

The Bean Trees offers the opportunity to teach a range of lessons in geography (by tracking Taylor's travels during the novel), biology (through the study of rhizobia), sociology (the sociology of single-parent families), psychology (the effects of child abuse as borne out in Turtle), and world politics (in terms of the story of Estevan and Esperanza as political refugees from Guatemala). All of that is in addition to the opportunity to teach *The Bean Trees* simply as good literature.

Jeanne Ewert (review date 11 October 1998)

SOURCE: "Shadows of 'Darkness,'" in *Chicago Tribune Books,* October 11, 1998, p. 6.

[*In the following review, Ewert offers tempered assessment of* The Poisonwood Bible, *citing weaknesses in Kingsolver's "heavy-handed" interpretation of events.*]

In 1890 Joseph Conrad traveled to the Congo in the employ of a Belgian trading company, under contract as a steamboat pilot. He made only one trip upriver before returning to England, desperately ill with dysentery and sick also of what he'd seen in the Congo. What he'd seen—gross cruelty inflicted by European colonists on the Congolese—became the subject of his novel *Heart of Darkness.* But Conrad's own conflicted position on race makes his novel notoriously resistant to interpretation. Do its most famous words, "The horror, the horror," refer to the hypocrisy of the Belgians who preached Christian enlightenment while profiting from the enforced slavery of millions, or to "unspeakable rites" Conrad thought were practiced by the Congolese?

Shadows of Conrad's book run through Barbara Kingsolver's newest novel, *The Poisonwood Bible.* Based on Kingsolver's childhood experience in the Congo, the novel takes the reader to a 20th Century Congolese village to show precisely where the horror lies—in the act of colonizing: white men taking over the Congo, husbands taking over their wives' minds and lives, one culture taking over another. Her novel floods light on the darkest consequences of those acts, although Kingsolver's outrage sometimes overpowers her narrative.

The Poisonwood Bible recounts the misfortunes of Nathan Price and his family. Price is an American missionary on a holy crusade who arrives in the Congo in 1959 without knowledge of the country's language or the least understanding of its culture. He sets out to evangelize his village by insulting its leaders, tries to baptize children in a river he fails to realize is full of crocodiles, and mangles the language so badly that he refers to Jesus as "poisonwood," a local plant that causes hives and intense itching. The novel is not a wholesale indictment of Western missionary efforts in the Congo, although it's merciless in its critique of the sort of missionary who lacked interest in the distinctive culture and history of the region, or was even able to admit that it had a culture and a history separate from his own egotistical efforts.

Kingsolver is careful to present another kind of missionary also, those who "organize hospitals under thatched roofs, or stoop alongside village Mamas to plant soybeans, or rig up electrical generators for a school." And Nathan himself is only one culprit. Behind him stand the hundreds of other white men who made decisions about the Congo without consulting any Congolese (American and Belgian trading companies, the CIA and an American president); who conspired to murder its first democratically elected president and keep it enslaved to the International Monetary Fund through costly, pointless projects it couldn't afford; and who maintain a greedy and utterly amoral leader who helped them rob his country of its extraordinary natural resources.

The story, however, is not told by any of these, but by the five women that Nathan enslaves in his own household. His wife, Orleanna, has been carefully taught by her husband that God rewards virtue, and that their lifelong poverty and misery were God's punishments for a failure of virtue—a failure that could only be hers, as Nathan himself is perfectly righteous. "Lodged in the heart of darkness," is how Orleanna describes her marriage.

Out of that darkness come four daughters: Rachel is a budding Barbie, who looks disdainfully at the Congo's sacrificial victims and thinks, "I refuse to feel the slightest responsibility. I really do." The twins, Leah and Adah, are in many ways the moral center of the novel. Leah worships her father until her innate sense of justice forces her to reject him, and to spend her life saving a Congo he never even observed. Adah is the novel's most complex character. Born with a damaged brain and a crippled right side, she reads backwards and forwards and prefers her name spelled Ada to accommodate that. (Readers of Nabokov will appreciate the reference to his masterpiece of linguistic legerdemain, *Ada*.) Her isolation in a crippled body leads Adah to sympathize with the plight of the Congolese under Nathan's gospel: Would God condemn children to eternal suffering merely for having been born out of earshot of the gospel, she asks her American Sunday

school teacher before the family departs. She is sent to the corner and forced to pray while kneeling on grains of rice for an hour for daring to even question God's plan. The baby in the family, Ruth May, is too young to know how to judge the Congo, and merely accepts it as it is. She is the only one mourned in the Congolese village when the missionary effort goes awry.

These women's narratives—especially in the first half of the novel, as they anticipate the tragedy that marks the end of the mission—are compelling, lyrical and utterly believable. As Congolese independence approaches, however, Kingsolver's writing becomes more heavy-handed, insisting on interpreting the meaning of the events for us in ways that the most sympathetic reader may find intrusive.

The parrot Methuselah, for example, is a potent symbol of the Congo, pre- and post-independence. Captured from the wild and kept in a tiny cage, Methuselah learns too well the discourse of his white masters, mechanically repeating their prayers, but also their secret curses. Nathan throws him back into the jungle for this crime, but the bird's wings are too stunted to fly far, and he hangs around the compound, begging for scraps. The analogy is clear enough, more so when he is slaughtered by a rapacious civet cat on the very morning of independence. Yet Kingsolver insists on also providing the obvious interpretation, as though her readers could not quite be trusted to get it right: "At last it is Independence day, for Methuselah and the Congo. . . . After a lifetime caged away from flight and truth, comes freedom. . . . This is what he leaves to the world: gray and scarlet feathers strewn over the damp grass. . . . Only feathers, without the ball of Hope inside."

The second half of the novel, which traces the adult lives of Nathan's daughters, is too often characterized by this sort of heavy-handed exposition and plot summary, and we begin to lose track of the women's daily experience. Kingsolver's outrage over what happened "the day a committee of men decided to murder the fledgling Congo" is historically justified, but her novel is weakest when she begins to use her protagonists to merely vent that anger, rather than letting them speak (as they do in the first half) to the rich complexities of their personal experience.

Verlyn Klinkenborg (review date 18 October 1998)

SOURCE: "Going Native," in *New York Times Book Review,* October 18, 1998, p. 7.

[*In the following review, Klinkenborg offers positive evaluation of* The Poisonwood Bible.]

The phrase "heart of darkness" occurs only once, as far as I can tell, in Barbara Kingsolver's haunting new novel, ***The Poisonwood Bible.*** When it does, it falls from the mouth of Orleanna Price, a Baptist missionary's wife who uses it to describe not the Belgian Congo, where she, her husband and their four daughters were posted in 1959, but the state of her marriage in those days and the condition of what she calls "the country once known as Orleanna Wharton," wholly occupied back then by Nathan Price, aforesaid husband and man of God. Joseph Conrad's great novella flickers behind her use of that phrase, and yet it doesn't. Orleanna is not a quoting woman, and for the quoting man in the family, her strident husband, there can be only one source—the Bible, unambiguous and entire, even in a land that demonstrates daily the suppleness of language. "Tata Jesus is *bangala!*" he shouts during his African sermons. It never occurs to him that in Kikongo, a language in which meaning hangs on intonation, *bangala* may mean "precious and dear," but it also means the poisonwood tree—a virulent local plant—when spoken in the flat accent of an American zealot.

The Prices are Nathan and Orleanna and their daughters: Ruth May, the youngest; Rachel, the oldest, a pale blond Mrs. Malaprop of a teen-ager; and the twins, Leah and Adah. Both twins are gifted, but Adah suffers from hemiplegia, which leaves her limping and nearly speechless. The female members of the family narrate *The Poisonwood Bible* in turn. Orleanna does so in retrospect, from her later years on Sanderling Island, off the coast of Georgia. The girls, however, tell their story from the Congo as it happens, on the precipice of events, like an epistolary novel written from a place with no postal service and no hope of pen pals.

Nathan Price narrates nothing. And yet his certitude—and the literal-minded ferocity with which he expresses it—is the altar around which these women arrange themselves. We already know his story, Kingsolver implies. Most of what we have always heard, she suggests, are stories told by men like him. *The Poisonwood Bible* thus belongs to the women, and it is a story about the loss of one faith and the discovery of another, for each woman according to her kind. As Adah, so bright, so willing to torque the mother tongue, puts it, "One god draws in the breath of life and rises; another god expires."

The Prices travel from Bethlehem, Ga., to a village called Kilanga on the Kwilu River in the summer of 1959, just a few months before Patrice Lumumba becomes Prime Minister of the newly independent Republic of the Congo—not long, therefore, before he is arrested and murdered with the complicity of the United States and its President, Dwight D. Eisenhower, whose photograph Orleanna hangs in the kitchen hut behind their mud house: "I'd cut it out of a magazine and nailed it over the plank counter where I kneaded the bread. . . . I remember every detail of him; the clear-rimmed glasses and spotted tie, the broad smile, the grandfatherly bald head like a warm, bright light bulb. He looked so trustworthy and kind. A beacon from home, reminding me of our purpose." The irony in Orleanna's words is the same irony she uses to describe the early days of her marriage, when there was still room for laughter in her husband's evangelical calling, before her pregnancies embarrassed him, before he returned from World War II a different man—a man who

planned "to save more souls than had perished on the road from Bataan." Nathan Price escaped that road by sheer luck, and knowing it curled his heart "like a piece of hard shoe leather."

In Conrad's novella, the heart of darkness is both Kurtz's despoiled purpose and the terrain in which that purpose is worked in Kingsolver's novel, the heart of darkness belongs only to men like Nathan Price and a local pilot named Eeben Axelroot, a figure from Graham Greene who shuttles spooklike in and out of Kilanga. The Congo is a hard place for the Price women, and its people are unfathomable at first, but Kilanga contains no Conradian darkness. Army ants, drought, hookworm, hunger, pestilential rain, diseases and still more diseases and green mamba snakes, yes, but no darkness. What all the Price women discover—all except Rachel, "whose only hopes for the year were a sweet-16 party and a pink mohair twin set"—is the near-perfect adaptation of the Congolese to the harsh conditions of their existence, a fittedness that is beautiful in itself. With that knowledge comes the discovery of the Prices' own profound ignorance. Once the comedy of colliding cultures ends, the tragedy begins. As Leah says: "Everything you're sure is right can be wrong in another place. Especially *here.*"

The Congo permeates *The Poisonwood Bible,* and yet this is a novel that is just as much about America, a portrait, in absentia, of the nation that sent the Prices to save the souls of a people for whom it felt only contempt, people who already, in the words of a more experienced missionary, "have a world of God's grace in their lives, along with a dose of hardship that can kill a person entirely." The Congolese are not savages who need saving, the Price women find, and there is nothing passive in their tolerance of missionaries. They take the Americans' message literally—elections are good, Jesus too—and expose its contradictions by holding an election in church to decide whether or not Jesus shall be the personal god of Kilanga. Jesus loses.

And yet, for all its portraiture of place, its reflexive political vitriol, its passionate condemnation of Nathan Price, *The Poisonwood Bible* is ultimately a novel of character, a narrative shaped by keen-eyed women contemplating themselves and one another and a village whose familiarity it takes a tragedy to discover. Rachel is the epitome of America's material culture, a cunning, brainless girl who parodies television commercials and says of Eeben Axelroot, "I'm willing to be a philanderist for peace, but a lady can only go so far where perspiration odor is concerned." Ruth May, the baby, is the innocent whose words betray the guilty; she is the catalyst that splits the Price family apart. When Orleanna speaks of the Congo, many years later, she does so by addressing Ruth May, whose questioning eyes watch over Orleanna's life with more compassion than ever fell from the burning gaze of her husband's God.

These are precious creatures, but none are as precious to the reader as Leah and Adah, the twin and the *niwt,* as

Adah calls herself, referring to her backward condition. Limping, nearly silent, Adah is a verbal gymnast, a dedicated diarist, a profound skeptic. Her father, she reports, probably interpreted her twisted newborn state "as God's Christmas bonus to one of His worthier employees." Adah's wit bristles throughout this novel; it is wit of a kind that Leah, a tomboy who eagerly seeks her father's approval, would never use. Leah's, instead, is an entirely ethical understanding.

The Poisonwood Bible turns on several axes, and one of them is Leah's struggle to rebalance herself morally when she finally realizes exactly who her father is. Once she had said, "My father wears his faith like the bronze breastplate of God's foot soldiers, while our mother's is more like a good cloth coat with a secondhand fit." But when the armor fell, she saw that Nathan Price's "blue eyes with their left-sided squint, weakened by the war, had a vacant look. His large reddish ears repelled me. My father was a simple, ugly man."

All the Prices adapt to the Congo, in their way, but Adah and Leah are carried farthest in their adaptation. Rachel accomplishes this by not adapting at all. "The way I see Africa," she says, "you don't have to like it but you sure have to admit it's out there. You have your way of thinking and it has its, and never the train ye shall meet!" For Adah, adaptation comes in the form of unforgiving self-discovery, the realization that "even the crooked girl believed her own life was precious."

Leah, the conscience of this striking novel, is forever measuring the distance she must travel before her adaptation is made perfect. It was so when her father owned her, in her mother's words, "like a plot of land," and it is still so in her maturity—wed, so to speak, to the continent. In the end, she explains: "I am the un-missionary, as Adah would say, beginning each day on my knees, asking to be converted. *Forgive me, Africa, according to the multitudes of thy mercies.*"

John Skow (review date 9 November 1998)

SOURCE: "Hearts of Darkness," in *Time,* November 9, 1998, p. 113.

[In the following review, Skow offers positive assessment of The Poisonwood Bible.*]*

A forest: monkeys, army ants, poisonous frogs. Below, on a path, a woman and four girls, all in shirtwaist dresses. "Seen from above this way," writes novelist Barbara Kingsolver at the outset of *The Poisonwood Bible,* "they are pale, doomed blossoms, bound to appeal to your sympathies. Be careful. Later on you'll have to decide what sympathy they deserve." Fair warning, though what the reader must decide before finishing this turbulent, argumentative narrative goes beyond judging four white

American daughters and their mother, set down deep in the Congo in the precarious year 1959.

What follows would shame the gods, if any were paying attention. Here's the mother, back in the U.S., in old age: "Now that every turn in the weather whistles an ache through my bones, I stir in bed and the memories rise out of me like a buzz of flies from a carcass." The memories, eloquently relived and regretted, are of grotesque cultural arrogance, unraveling in a very small place. Rumblings of the Congo's struggle for independence from Belgium—and U.S. plotting to assassinate Patrice Lumumba, the new nation's first Prime Minister—are distant thunder in Kingsolver's tale. Her story, a symbolic parallel to the national upheaval, takes place in an isolated village. Nathan Price, an evangelical Baptist preacher, fanaticism in bitter parody, lugs his wife, daughters and rigid preconceptions to Kilanga, a small jungle settlement, where faith plays out as farce. To the hospitable but puzzled tribesmen, he rails against nakedness and multiple wives, and he insists on river baptisms though crocodiles lurk in the river. Fittingly, though he does not understand this, the Congolese word *batiza* means both baptism and, pronounced differently, terrify. Worse, "Tata Jesus is *bangala,*" as Price mispronounces it, means not Father Jesus is precious but Father Jesus is a poisonwood tree.

The preacher is an engine driving the novel toward chaos, a man who obstinately and relentlessly refuses to change ideas that do not suit the time or place. But in terms of portraiture, he is a stick figure, dismissed by his older daughters as "Our Father." Mother and daughters, on the other hand, are fully drawn. As the months go by, they come to understand what Price cannot, and they tell their stories in sharply distinct voices. Orleanna, the mother, at first an obedient 1950s wife who does not question bringing salvation to the heathens, struggles with remorse in her musings years later: "You'll say I walked across Africa with my wrists unshackled, and now I am one more soul walking free in a white skin." Sixteen-year-old Rachel, a teen queen who yearns for pop music and beauty aids, squawks, "Jeez oh man, wake me up when it's over." Ruth May, who is six and fearless, plays mother-may-I? with the village kids.

But a pair of 14-year-old identical twins, Leah and Adah, are the author's most vivid characters. Leah is a thoughtful, idealistic beauty who at first idolizes her father, then sees through his pious bluster. Adah, crippled at birth, is a wry, inward-turning genius who refuses to speak but silently reshapes the world in bitter palindromes: "amen enema," and "evil, all; its sin is still alive."

A writer who casts a preacher as a fool and a villain had best not be preachy. Kingsolver manages not to be, in part because she is a gifted magician of words—her sleight-of-phrase easily distracting a reader who might be on the point of rebellion. Her novel is both powerful and quite simple. It is also angrier and more direct than her earlier books, *Animal Dreams* and *Pigs in Heaven,* in which social issues involving Native Americans remained mostly in the background. The clear intent of *The Poisonwood Bible* is to offer Nathan Price's patriarchal troublemaking as an example in miniature of historical white exploitation of black Africa. Kingsolver, 43, lived in the Congo in the early '60s, and fondly remembers the people and the terrain. But this is a novel, not travel writing salted with guilt. The author's strong female characterizations carry a story that moves through its first half like a river in flood.

It must be said that Kingsolver's men are less interesting. One male African teacher, in particular, is so patient and virtuous that he seems—cultural bias alert here—almost Christ-like. Perhaps that is because unlike the women, whose thoughts we hear, the men are observed only from the outside. It is also true that the novel's second half is subdued in tone. The author has made her point, and the rest is told almost as afterword. The rapacious Mobutu Sese Seko is in power, thanks to U.S. influence. And the Price women, their calamitous adventure mostly behind them, do what people do: get married, or not; follow a profession, or not; grow older.

John Leonard (review date 11-18 January 1999)

SOURCE: "Kingsolver in the Jungle, Catullus and Wolfe at the Door," in *Nation,* January 11-18, 1999, pp. 28-30.

[*In the following review, Leonard offers favorable evaluation of* The Poisonwood Bible.]

Out of a child's game of Mother May I, looked down upon by a green snake in an alligator-pear tree, Barbara Kingsolver has dreamed a magnificent fiction and a ferocious bill of indictment. The mothers so solicited are white American and black Congolese and matriarchal Africa herself. In their turn, on their knees, keening like birds in a rain of blood, these mothers beseech some principle of naming and knowing, some macrohistorical scale of justice and some mechanism of metamorphosis to console them for their lost children. As in the keyed chords of a Baroque sonata, movements of the personal, the political, the historical and even the biological contrast and correspond. As in a Bach cantata, the choral stanza, the recitatives and the da capo arias harmonize. And a magical-realist forest sings itself to live forever.

To be less lofty about it, Kingsolver, whose own public-health-worker parents took her to the Congo when she was a child, who has been thinking about that season for thirty years while she wrote other, quieter, less ambitious books like *Animal Dreams* and *The Bean Trees,* has gone back to Africa and somehow transfigured it. *The Poisonwood Bible* is *not* a Safari Novel. Her village, her river, her forest and her snake aren't symbol dumps or Rorschach tests or manhood rites or local-color souvenirs—nor a pilgrim's gasbag progress past Pygmies to afflatus. An intelligence in transit will invest itself in and be exacerbated by

particulars of place; the North American is unmoored, unmasked, astigmatic and complicit; the woman is de-coupled, unchosen, rewound; a shadow world of the geopolitical and the clandestine rolls over domestic scruple. Not Conrad's heart-of-darkness lapel pin, Graham Greene's crucifix, Hemingway's penis fetish or Evelyn Waugh's slice of Hamlet on wry toast is powerful enough to protect these tourists from the mamba eye of Kingsolver up an alligator-pear tree, all-seeing, all-knowing . . .

From the peanut plains of Bethlehem, Georgia, in the peach-blossom summer of 1959, on a twelve-month mission to baptize and civilize the animistic heathen, the Rev. Nathan Price, his wife, Orleanna, and their four daughters arrive in a Congo still Belgian (though not for long)—to be greeted by bare breasts and goat stew. Before they can extricate themselves from Kilanga, they will have endured a year and a half of hunger and disease, ants and snakes, wars and witchcraft, Lumumba and Mobutu, Ike and the CIA. For their incomprehension, a Price will be paid: a portion of their sanity, all their arrogance and one of their girls. On the day the child dies, so does Lumumba.

The Price women, all remarkable, take contrapuntal turns telling the story:

Orleanna, whose dreams are full of eyes in the trees, of rivers of wishes, of animal teeth, blames herself for failing to protect her children from Africa and their father: "No wonder they hardly seemed to love me half the time—I couldn't step in front of my husband to shelter them from his scorching light. They were expected to look straight at him and go blind." And: "I wonder what you'll name my sin: Complicity? Loyalty? Stupefaction? . . . Is my sin a failure of virtue, or of competence?" And: "Poor Congo, barefoot bride of men who took her jewels and promised the Kingdom." And: "Maybe I'll even confess the truth, that I rode in with the horsemen and beheld the apocalypse, but still I'll insist I was only a captive witness. What is the conqueror's wife, if not a conquest herself?" Finally: "And now I am one more soul walking free in a white skin, wearing some thread of the stolen goods: cotton or diamonds, freedom at the very least, prosperity. Some of us know how we came by our fortune, and some of us don't, but we wear it all the same. There's only one question worth asking now: How do we aim to live with it?"

Rachel, the oldest daughter at sweet 16, "the most extreme blonde imaginable," a Queen of Sheba in her green linen Easter suit, batting her white-rabbit eyelashes, painting her fingernails bubblegum pink to match her headband, is shocked to be anywhere with "no new record album by the Platters" but capable of entertaining her sisters with imitation radio commercials: "Medically tested Odo-ro-no, stops underarm odor and moisture at the source!" She's also the mistress of the delicious malaprop: "feminine wilds," "sheer tapestry of justice" and, best of all, "Who is the real Rachel Price? . . . I prefer to remain anomalous." Tata Ndu, the village chief, asks for her hand in marriage, and Eeben Axelroot, the Afrikaner bush pilot, diamond smuggler and CIA mercenary, bargains for the rest of her. If Rachel never imagined the Congo to be more than a story she'd someday tell "when Africa was faraway and make-believe like the people in history books," she still knows how to bounce: "Honestly, there is no sense spending too much time alone in the dark." And so she won't.

Ruth May, the youngest—"my little beast, my eyes, my favorite stolen egg," her mother calls her—populates the village with the "Lone Ranger, Cinderella, Briar Rose, and the Tribes of Ham"; teaches Tumba, Bangwa, Mazuzi and Nsimba to play Mother May I; refuses to take her quinine tablets; is so thin-skinned that she suffers Africa like a bruise; and carries around a magic matchbox with a picture of a lion on it and a chicken bone inside and a tiny hole with a tiny peg, in order to disappear herself. One of her sisters, pushing Ruth May in a swing, thinks this:

> She flew forward and back and I watched her shadow in the white dust under the swing. Each time she reached the top of her arc beneath the sun, her shadow legs were transformed into the thin, curved legs of an antelope, with small rounded hooves at the bottom instead of feet. I was transfixed and horrified by the image of my sister with antelope legs. I knew it was only shadow and the angle of the sun, but still it's frightening when things you love appear suddenly changed from what you have always known.

Leah, "the tonier twin," the tomboy Goddess of the Hunt, only ceases to be desperate for the approval of her father when she decides he's insane. And keeps a pet owl even though owls are known to devour souls. And is called "Leba" by the villagers, which means "fig tree" in Kikongo, instead of "Léa," which means "nothing much." And is called "béene-béene" by the schoolteacher/revolutionary Anatole, which means "as true as the truth can be." And will be taught by Anatole to shoot arrows from a bow he carves for her from greenheart wood. And has read enough Jane Eyre and Brenda Starr to realize she's fallen in love with this Anatole who "moves through the dappled shade at the edges of my vision, wearing the silky pelt of a panther." This is how Leah will end up:

> I rock back and forth on my chair like a baby, craving so many impossible things: justice, forgiveness, redemption. I crave to stop bearing all the wounds of this place on my own narrow body. But I also want to be a person who stays, who goes on feeling anguish where anguish is due. I want to belong somewhere. . . . To scrub the hundred years' war off this white skin till there's nothing left and I can walk out among my neighbors wearing raw sinew and bone, like they do.
>
> Most of all, my white skin craves to be touched and held by the one man on earth I know has forgiven me for it.

And finally Adah, the damaged Quasimodo twin: speechless and limping, she is always left behind, even by her mother in the plague of ants; "I have long relied on the comforts of martyrdom." She was born "with half my brain dried up like a prune, deprived of blood by an unfortunate fetal mishap. My twin sister, Leah, and I are identical in theory, just as in theory we are all made in God's image. . . . But I am a lame gallimaufry and she remains perfect." In the Congo, though, nobody stares at her misshapenness; most of *them* have something missing, too. In Katanga she is called "white little crooked girl." And in her crooked mind, from phrases she's found in Edgar Allan Poe, Emily Dickinson, William Carlos Williams and *Dr. Jekyll and Mr. Hyde,* she will make wicked palindromes: "Amen enema," "eros, eyesore," and "Evil, all its sin is still alive!"

There is nothing Adah doesn't notice, bringing up the rear: the bodies of dead children wrapped in layers of cloth "like a large goat cheese," under a funeral arch of palm fronds, with the howling sweet scent of frangipani; her father's First Evangelical Church of the Lost of Cause, full of lepers and outcasts, who try Jesus on for size because nothing else has fit; the fact that "bangala" pronounced one way means "precious," but pronounced as her father does ("Jesus is *bangala!*") means "poisonwood": The Lord will make you itch. It is Adah who learns in Africa that "the transition from spirit to body and back to spirit again" is a "ride on the power of *nommo,* the force of a name to call oneself." *Nommo* rains from a cloud, or rises in the vapor from a human mouth: "a song, a scream, a prayer." And it's Adah who echoes her mother: "All human odes are essentially one. 'My life: what I stole from history, and how to live with it.'"

The history they steal from belongs to their family (an abusive and cowardly father, gone mad for the second time in a Third World jungle: the missionary position as a form of rape); the village (which refuses baptism because the river is full of crocodiles, although Mother May I is another matter); the Congo of the Belgians (where white occupiers cut off the hands of black workers who failed to meet their rubber-plantation quota); a Congo briefly free to elect its own future (independent for just fifty-one days in 1960, before Eisenhower authorized the murder of Lumumba for the greater glory of rubber, copper, Katanga's diamonds and the cold war); all of Africa; and all of empire. As Orleanna understands in retrospect:

> We aimed for no more than to have dominion over every creature that moved upon the earth. And so it came to pass that we stepped down there on a place we believed unformed, where only darkness moved on the face of the waters. Now you laugh, day and night, while you gnaw on my bones. But what else could we have thought? Only that it began and ended with *us.* What do we know, even now? Ask the children. Look at what they grew up to be. We can only speak of the things we carried with us, and the things we took away.

How they live with what they stole involves frogs, monkeys, thatch, mud, a parrot named Methuselah and a chameleon named Leon. It includes mosquito netting and malaria pills, breadfruit and manioc, bushbuck and gecko, elephant grass and bougainvillea, tarantulas in the bananas and hookworms in the shoes. It engages a six-toed *nanga,* Tata Kuvudundu, who leaves bones in a calabash bowl in a puddle of rain and his guilty footprints in the white dust around the chicken house, where "a basket of death" waits in ambush. It will take us up a colonial watchtower, into a circle of fire, as far away as Angola, Jo'burg and the Great Rift Valley, all the way back to Atlanta, for graduate work in viruses and whiteness. It will seek some sort of balance—"between loss and salvation," damage and transgression—and settle for . . . what, precisely? A forgiving song instead of a punishing Verse? Some "miracle of dread or reverence"? An okapi like a unicorn? As once upon a time there had been the four American daughters of Nathan and Orleanna Price, "pale, doomed blossoms . . . bodies as tight as bowstrings," so in the future there will be the four African sons of Leah and Anatole, "the colors of silt, loam, dust, and clay, an infinite palette for children of their own"—suggesting to their mother "that time erases whiteness altogether."

In case I haven't made myself clear, what we have here—with this new, mature, angry, heartbroken, expansive out-of-Africa Kingsolver—is at last our very own Lessing and our very own Gordimer, and she is, as one of her characters said of another in an earlier novel, "beautiful beyond the speed of light."

Aamer Hussein (review date 5 February 1999)

SOURCE: "Daughters of Africa," in *Times Literary Supplement,* February 5, 1999, p. 21.

[*In the following review, Hussein offers favorable assessment of* The Poisonwood Bible.]

The Poisonwood Bible, the fourth and the most ambitious novel by Barbara Kingsolver, begins in 1959 and proceeds to cover three decades of the turbulent and tragic history of Zaire: before, during and after independence. History, to many contemporary writers, has meant the nostalgic reworking of canonical texts; others, like Margaret Atwood and Timothy Mo, have renamed countries and personages in the Caribbean or in South-East Asia, claiming fictional licence to unveil true stories. Kingsolver takes the risk of locating her book in the real terrain of documented events; she includes at its end an impressive bibliography. Though the offstage rise and betrayal of Patrice Lumumba adds a crucial moral element to the construction of the novel, the author nevertheless succeeds in making the human dimension of her story its most compelling feature.

The wife and four daughters of Nathan Price take turns to narrate. Fired by missionary zeal, Price, an American Baptist, moves with his family to Kilanga in the Belgian Congo. He thinks the word of Christ will transcend all barriers of culture and race, while Orleanna, his wife, gets on with the job of living and feeding her offspring in a strange and often hostile land. Kingsolver draws on their beliefs to present contrasting visions: the intransigence of

evangelical Christianity pitted against a gentler humanitarian faith that embraces difference. For each of the daughters—Rachel, the twins Leah and Adah, and the baby of the family Ruth May—the experience of Africa is far removed from the Christian duties they are exhorted to propagate. Ruth May is absorbed into Africa with a child's innocent fervour. For Rachel, terrified by the disasters around them, the Congo is hell on earth; she longs for the comforts of her lost American girlhood. Adah, handicapped at birth and locked in wilful silence, creates for herself a world of subversive palindromes.

Leah, driven, passionate, oddly influenced by her father's doctrinaire spirit which in her case translates into political commitment, is the novel's central presence. Her growing consciousness absorbs decades of African history. She also inherits the burden of American guilt which she feels her white skin proclaims. She delivers the novel's poignant and at times polemical critique of her country's neocolonialist interventions in the destinies of "backward" nations; she articulates Kingsolver's concern for ancient cultures threatened by capitalist trajectories and Western hegemonies. But Leah's is primarily a story of abiding love, and her idealism born of this love—for the revolutionary Anatole, for the continent she adopts as her own, and for her part-African children. Her righteous anger finally gives way to compassion; she learns that "time erases whiteness all together".

Kingsolver uses other perspectives as an ironical counterpoint to Leah's ideological passions. The framework of the family's life collapses when the country is decolonized; the structure of the novel, too, becomes fragmentary about halfway through, exchanging chronological sequence for an elliptical view of time and a frenzied interweaving of voices. Orleanna sounds a distant echo; yet it is she who succinctly chronicles America's hideous role in the defeat of Lumumba. Rachel, with her malapropisms and retrograde notions, represents prejudice and clichéd Western fears of the Third World's oppressive poverty; but she, like Leah, stays on in Africa, exemplifying the eternal expatriate, exploitative and upwardly mobile, unable to identify but always fearful of return. Ruth May dies young. Adah's eventual release from her mute and crippled state of being reveals, in retrospect, a tracery of symbolism—almost allegory—woven delicately into this naturalistic novel. The damaged twin finds a destiny of her own in America as a scientist, linking her life to Leah's and to Africa. "To live", she learns, "is to be marked. To live is to change, to die one hundred deaths."

Then, distanced by the third person but not peripheral, there are the men. Nathan is, for all his flaws, an oddly heroic figure, whose foolhardy desire to divert the Congolese from their age-old beliefs by appropriating and misusing their language gives the novel its title. Anatole is the democratic conscience of post-colonial Africa; his constant conflicts with oppressive regimes force Leah into exile, but his love continues to give her a reason to live and believe.

Barbara Kingsolver's prose is both precise and lyrical, soaring at times like the sermons she parodies or inverts, at others immediate and sensuous—particularly in the descriptions of African village life. Her art is proof of the way today's fiction is traversing new boundaries in its ability to engage with conflicting realities. She can be didactic, and occasionally risks idealizing and mythologizing Africa's precolonial past (as she has done with Native American culture in *Animal Dreams*). But this is in keeping with the impassioned sensibilities of her protagonists. She finds in Africa an ultimate message of survival and reconciliation. For the Price women, the weight of memory, too, will in time become a gift. "You are afraid you might forget, but you never will. You will forgive and remember. . . . Move on. Walk forward into the light."

Lee Siegel (review date 22 March 1999)

SOURCE: "Sweet and Low," in *New Republic,* March 22, 1999, pp. 30-37.

[*In the following review, Siegel criticizes the exploitation of personal suffering in contemporary literature and offers negative evaluation of Kingsolver's fiction, including* The Poisonwood Bible. *Siegel condemns Kingsolver's popular and uncritically received style of "Nice Writing" as disingenuous and self-righteous.*]

I.

Barbara Kingsolver is the most successful practitioner of a style in contemporary fiction that might be called Nice Writing. Nice Writing is a violent affability, a deadly sweetness, a fatal gentle touch. But before I start in on Kingsolver's work, I feel I must explain why I feel that I must start in on it.

I do so for a younger version of myself, for the image that I carry inside me of a boy who was the son of a sadistic, alcoholic father, and of a mother who was hurt but also hurtful, and abusive. And I do not feel the need to make a pretense of sweetness or gentleness as I confess this.

"She told me that maybe one out of every four little girls is sexually abused by a family member. Maybe more," says Taylor, the protagonist of Kingsolver's first novel, *The Bean Trees,* reporting her conversation with a social worker; but in her "Author's Note" to *The Poisonwood Bible,* Kingsolver writes that she herself was "the fortunate child of medical and public-health workers, whose compassion and curiosity led them to the Congo. They . . . set me early on a path of exploring the great, shifting terrain between righteousness and what's right." It is easy for Kingsolver, then, to spin such tragic conceits. But I remember my father's heavy hand on my face and the door slamming behind him, as if the slap were a firecracker and the slamming door its echo in some grotesque celebration of violence.

The flesh has its own memory, and sometimes my skin heats up before the flashback lays its heavy hand across my consciousness. It is the opposite of when you touch something hot and it takes a second to feel the pain. I cannot really talk about all the ways my father hurt me. Later, when the door slammed for the last time, and my father left for good, I lay in the dark with my older brother and younger sister and listened to my mother and her boyfriends. Sometimes the men she brought home stayed the night, and sometimes they didn't. I can remember my little sister, Mandy—my brother and I called her "Ostrich" because of the way she buried her head in the bedclothes when she heard the strangers' voices—crying herself to sleep.

I also remember my mother storming into the bedroom that we shared, and screaming at Mandy to shut up. Sometimes my mother kissed me very hard on the mouth, a kiss that no mother should ever give to a son. Then she returned to the bedroom where her boyfriend of the hour, or her crazy solitude, waited for her. Those nights are like sudden breaks in a film at a dingy porn-house. They are desolate lapses in a desolate movie that no one should ever have to see.

Since she was born with Gibson's syndrome and was mentally impaired, Mandy might have had in her unlucky brain an avenue of escape from all the pain. I don't really know. She went to live in a special place when I was fifteen. As Gibson's got worse and worse, she lost all recollection of me. I remember a strange girl-woman sitting in a big chair, wearing a white blouse, a pleated navy-blue skirt, and a plaid bow tie. She would stare for hours at art books that she held upside down in her lap. Her small bare legs hung motionless off the chair and looked like skittles. They made me wince.

The plaid bow tie had belonged to my maternal grandmother. It was the only one of her husband's things that she was able to bring to this country. David Schnorr, my grandfather, died in a concentration camp. So when I read the portrait of a Native American woman named Annawake in Kingsolver's *Pigs in Heaven,* I think of my mother's father, because Kingsolver approvingly has Annawake make a historical analogy: "That's us. Our tribe. We've been through a holocaust as devastating as what happened to the Jews. . . ." (David Schnorr had been a minor literary figure in Odessa. He was not as lucky as Barbara Kingsolver.) And when I read no less than two novels by Kingsolver centered on a cringingly cute little girl named Turtle—*The Bean Trees* and *Pigs in Heaven*—I think of the real little girl we called Ostrich.

This hurts me. I really don't want to use my family to make a point. But when Kingsolver writes so facilely about lost people, I think of my brother's drug addiction, and the hand that he lost in Nicaragua to the machete of a contra, and his psychotic breakdown in the offices of *The New Yorker,* where he was a frequent contributor. And I think of my father coming back to live with us after a car accident left his entire right side paralyzed. Once I cried from rage and shame after he hit me; now, whenever I saw him in his wheelchair, I cried from rage and guilt.

That was during my first year of college. In my third year, my mother became gravely ill. Fortunately, my brother had straightened his life out, and he returned home with Luisha, his black wife, who had been his nurse in the psychiatric hospital. Together they tended to my mother. It was Luisha, having grown up hearing stories about the lynching of her great-grandfather, who taught my reckless brother lessons about dignity in adversity. She had seen her own teenage daughter shot dead before her eyes by drug dealers in her neighborhood. We were all very proud of Luisha.

After a while, my uncle Jeremiah came to help out with Tobey, who had been his lover and was now his friend and companion. Jer had been in jail in the '60s and had the soles of his feet beaten so badly by prison guards that he could barely walk. Tobey was HIV-positive and too depressed to work. I admired Jer, and I loved Tobey's spirit. Eventually I took a couple of years off from school and came back home to look after people who had so injured my young life. At night, my mother cried out, my father whimpered, my brother banged his fist against the wall, Luisha screamed in her sleep, Jeremiah sobbed, and Tobey wept. Sometimes I could not make sense of what I was doing there. But somehow I stayed.

I have a pretty good life now, but I cannot forget those nights. They, and all the history behind them, are why I write criticism. I write for the little boy that I was, the little boy crushed by untruth. He was surrounded by facts, but they were inaccurate facts. They did not correlate with the reality of human freedom. They were not true, or beautiful, or good. So these facts might just as well have been fiction; and any fiction that preserved their raw unreality would be an emaciated lie. It would not be true fiction at all.

Thus whenever I see the promulgation of such illusions by two fraudulent Russian artists, or by sanctimonious academic theorists, or by icily virtuous novelists, I sit down and I write for the little boy who craved the truth. I write for all the young boys and young girls who crave the truth. I strike for the children, and for their children's children. And I hope that anyone who takes exception to the ferocity of my tone will think of my father's hand across my face, and of my cruel mother, and of my dying mother, and of poor Ostrich, and of what the Nazis did to David Schnorr. And I hope, cherished reader, that you will not be angry about what I have to confess to you next.

II.

By now you will have realized, I hope, that nothing that I have written here is true, except for the quotations from Kingsolver and the references to her work. I made everything up; I meant it to be satire. I have passed beyond the boundary of good taste, and I apologize to anyone I have offended, since I know that the situations I described happen, and I know how much pain and sadness they bring. And though I have my own portion of pain and sadness, I also know that there are degrees of suffering. But the actuality and the complexity of suffering: that is precisely my point.

For at least the past decade, American writers have been pouring forth a cascade of horror stories about their condition or the condition of their characters. The Holocaust, ethnic genocide, murder, rape, incest, child abuse, cancer, paralysis, AIDS, fatal car accidents, Alzheimer's, chronic anorexia: calamities drop from the printer like pearls. These are elemental events of radically different proportions, and the urge to make imaginative sense of them is also elemental. Some contemporary writers treat these subjects strongly and humbly and insightfully, but too many writers engaged in this line of production turn out shallow and distorted work. They seem merely to be responding to a set of opportunities created by a set of social circumstances. In their hands, human suffering goes unimagined, and the imagination goes hungry and deprived.

There are a handful of reasons behind this trend. For a start, we live at a uniquely prosperous time in a uniquely prosperous society, a moment in which tragedy and catastrophe seem all the more confusing and inexplicable, and so their depiction is all the more gripping. Also, we are fortunate to inhabit a culture in which practical techniques for mastering life's hardships have become so successful that it is perhaps natural for writers to develop a technique—a Calamity Style—for the conceptual mastery of life's inevitabilities.

Maybe we also feel, in our increasingly freewheeling culture, less protected as the forms of gratification multiply. The more gratification you seek, after all, the less stable and constant you are, whether you consciously feel yourself shifting or not. In this sense, these catastrophic tales are the emblems of a faintly enveloping anxiety. Then, too, since we live in such flush and tranquil times, more and more people have the privilege of shunning conventional work-routines and taking up creative labors. Writing, which requires no special training, holds out the promise of the freest kind of life. The problem is that not everyone who takes up the occupation of writer has the writer's gift. Thus extremity becomes an aid to straining imaginations.

But I think there is one reason for Calamity Writing that looms much larger than the others: it advances the amoral pursuit of a virtuous appearance. This is where Calamity Writing blossoms into the plastic flower of Nice Writing. The portrait of people doing evil things to each other, or of someone sick and dying, or of a person psychologically hurt, flatters the portraitist. It can enfold the writer in a mantle of invincible goodness. The artistic worth of the portrait fades away as an issue. What remains is the invaluable appearance of goodness.

I am not talking about hypocrisy. I am talking about the mere appearance of goodness as a substitute for honest art. The trend is everywhere. It is to be found, for example, in Lorrie Moore's short stories, especially "People Like That Are the Only People Here," the longest tale in *Birds of America,* her acclaimed new collection. The story is about a newborn baby dying of cancer. That is, the story's emotional register begins, from the very first paragraph, far beyond the reader's capacity to develop his or her own response to it. The effect is to place the supremely empathetic author in a protected niche, far beyond the reader's capacity to criticize. In this way Nice Writing fosters Nice Criticism. Anyone who writes nice writes with impunity.

Barbara Kingsolver can be a very funny writer; her infrequent outbursts of humor make up her best quality. And those plots: when they do not hit patches of dense cuteness and saccharine emotion, they unfurl swiftly and engagingly, as the newspaper reviewers like to say. Still, if it were not for professional purposes, I would never read her. The loveliness becomes unbearable. From *The Bean Trees:*

> But it didn't seem to matter to Turtle, she was happy where she was. . . . She watched the dark highway and entertained me with her vegetable-soup song, except that now there were people mixed in with the beans and potatoes: Dwayne Ray, Mattie, Esperanza, Lou Ann and all the rest.
>
> And me. I was the main ingredient.

From *Animal Dreams:*

> Sure I remember when we almost drowned in a flood. Plain as day. God, Codi, don't you? We found those abandoned coyote pups, and the river was flooding, and you wanted to save them. You said we *had* to.

From *Pigs in Heaven:*

> Taylor puts up her hand, knowing what's coming. "Mama, I know I wasn't nice, but she's a kook." She glances at Turtle, who is using Alice's ballpoint carefully to blacken the entire state of Nevada.
>
> "A kook in need of kindness."

From **"Paradise Lost,"** an essay in the collection *High Tide in Tucson:*

> I went to the Canaries for nearly a year, to find new stories to tell, and to grow comfortable thinking in Spanish. Or so I said; the truth is closer to the bone. It was 1991, and in the U.S. a clamor of war worship had sprung like a vitriolic genie from the riveted bottles we launched on Baghdad. Yellow ribbons swelled from suburban front doors, so puffy and ubiquitous as to seem folkloric. But this folklore, a prayer of god-speed to the killers, allowed no possibility that the vanquished might also be human. I grew hopeless, then voiceless. What words could I offer a place like this? Five hundred years after colonialism arrived in the New World, I booked a return passage.

"An easy book to enjoy," *The New Yorker* said about Kingsolver's first novel, *The Bean Trees;* "rich fodder," said the *Denver Post,* meaning well, about her second novel, **Animal Dreams;** full of "issues that are serious, debatable and painful," said the *Los Angeles Times Book Review* about **Pigs in Heaven,** her third novel; "delightful, challenging, and wonderfully informative" wrote the *San Francisco Chronicle* about **High Tide in Tucson.** The standard congratulations are especially appropriate for Kingsolver's work, for they echo her work's self-congratulatory quality. Still, if these smug and trivial books do any violence to clarity or to reality, it is a minor aesthetic crime. It is a matter for the local authorities. Let *Elle* or *Allure* handle it. When they are praised for their seriousness, well, that is another matter.

III.

Kingsolver does not exactly outrage me, because she is so damn nice; but she is becoming outrageous. With the publication of **The Poisonwood Bible,** this easy, humorous, competent, syrupy writer has been elevated to the ranks of the greatest political novelists of our time. The *New York Times Book Review* praised **The Poisonwood Bible** as a "profound work of political, psychological, and historical understanding." An obtuse profile of the writer in *The New York Times Magazine* declared that "perhaps only Kingsolver, of all contemporary novelists, has the expertise to pull off' **The Poisonwood Bible**'s portrayal of white Europeans and Americans confronting black Africans in the 1950s and 1960s. In *The Nation,* John Leonard anointed Kingsolver as "our very own Lessing and our very own Gordimer."

Nearly all the reviews that I have read of **The Poisonwood Bible** have praised it in approximately the same lofty terms. Those who found something to criticize in the bestselling novel couched their criticism in the most anguished idiom, as if they were forced by circumstance to leave litter in a National Park. Writing in *The Washington Post,* Jane Smiley rightly observed that Kingsolver's portrait of Nathan Price, an abusive father and fanatical Baptist missionary, is so flat and one-dimensional as to be totally implausible as a fictional construction. But this is not, Smiley adds, Kingsolver's fault. No, Kingsolver's admitted "failure" is the fault of American culture.

> And yet. Nathan's enigmatic one-sidedness reflects our culture's failure to understand the humanity of those who seem to be the source of evil. . . . The author loses interest in Nathan, tries to compensate by giving him a dramatic death that seems pale in the telling. This failure goes right to the heart of who we are as a culture and how we look at ourselves: Yes, there are those who hurt others and show no remorse, who do not acknowledge the damage they have done. But they, in the end, are us. They should be acknowledged, allowed to say who they are, recognized. Loved, even, if not by readers and citizens, then at least by their own creators.

Smiley's peroration on self-abnegating goodness is the bonus of virtuous appearance that Nice Critics instantly reap when they nicely review Nice Writing. Since Kingsolver is the queen of Nice Writing, she has been the constant beneficiary of this kind of criticism. You can find a representative example of her niceness in a talk that she gave in 1993 called **"Careful What You Let in the Door."** It appears in *High Tide in Tucson,* which came out that same year.

Three years earlier, Kingsolver had published *Animal Dreams,* a novel that was partly about American involvement in the Nicaraguan civil war during the 1980s. Its dedication reads "in memory of Ben Linder," a reference to Benjamin Linder, a young American engineer working in Nicaragua whom the contras killed in an ambush. In her essay, Kingsolver writes:

> It matters to me . . . that we citizens of the U.S. bought guns and dressed up an army that killed plain, earnest people in Nicaragua who were trying only to find peace and a kinder way of life. I wanted to bring that evil piece of history into a story, in a way that would make a reader feel sadness and dread but still keep reading, becoming convinced it was necessary to care.

There is something characteristically fishy about Kingsolver's language here. Why are all the good, murdered Nicaraguan people "plain" and "earnest"? If some of them had been complicated and ironic, then would caring readers have regarded killing them as a public service? And if the Nicaraguan peasantry really had been behind the Sandinista revolution, would it have been because they were trying to find "a kinder way of life," and not because the revolution offered peasants ownership of their land and the freedom to decide for themselves whether to be kind or unkind? The surfeit of sentiment rings with an absence of true conviction.

This does not bode well for fiction. You can fault Kingsolver for not knowing—or refusing to know, or not caring—that the mass of impoverished Nicaraguans astutely saw the Sandinistas as elites trying to steal their land and impose their will; or for not acknowledging that the Sandinistas were displacing and murdering Nicaragua's Miskito Indians; or for not knowing—or not caring, or not being convinced of the fact—that "Ben" Linder, whom Kingsolver never met, was carrying a rifle when he was cut down. But the writer has her politics, and she is entitled to believe that her advertisement of virtue is sufficient for her politics. In politics, certainly, rhetoric can be very effective. Yet the political novelist is *not* entitled to think that her politics are sufficient for her art.

Gordimer or Lessing—for all their differences—would have so complicated a novel about Nicaragua that the truth about the revolution, when it finally unfolded, would have been already embedded in the novel's multilayered psychic and social world. And they would have retained, as they do, their political values. Yet *Animal Dreams* is not about character or society. It is about "serious, debatable, and painful issues": a father with Alzheimer's; a corporation's health-threatening exploitation of a small town; class prejudice; ethnic prejudice; cruelty to animals.

Its sub-subplot of a young woman agriculturist from America named Hallie—whom we never meet—doing volunteer work in Nicaragua—where we never go—is just one heart-tugging flourish among all the others. It clinches the novel's principal plot, which is the not-terribly-gripping saga of Hallie's sister, a thirty-two-year-old woman named Codi, who goes back to her hometown to figure out who she is and what she should do with her life. (Kingsolver's books are self-help books disguised as novels.) When Codi learns that the contras murdered Hallie, she suddenly matures. Hallie's murder, she tells us, is like a "flower in the soil of another country." One woman's political assassination is another woman's step toward personal growth.

There was once an American president whose cloying promise to Americans of a "kinder, gentler nation" was a gift to anyone who wanted to prove his or her principles without acting on them. The simple derisive repetition of the phrase guaranteed the right adversarial status. Kingsolver may be a favorite figure on the left, but in truth her "kinder way of life" rhetoric spans the ideological spectrum. Who, really, is for evil corporate interests or for class or ethnic prejudice? Is there anyone who would like to go to bat for cruelty to animals, or for Alzheimer's? Kingsolver's novels are filled with indictments of people and forces that make children suffer. They are bursting with tender affirmations of motherhood. In the acknowledgments to *Pigs in Heaven,* she thanks Nancy Raincrow Pigeon and Carol Locust, among others, "who helped me understand the letter and spirit of the Indian Child Welfare Act." I dare you to give that novel a negative review.

Such a guaranteed universal appeal is why, Kingsolver might be surprised to know, she has been referred to enthusiastically in places such as the *Federal Reserve Bank of New York Economic Policy Review* and *Management Review.* According to the *ABA Journal,* a judge ordered women offenders to read *Animal Dreams.* They love Kingsolver even in *The Washington Times,* and they like her fiction even in *The Weekly Standard* ("a gentle allegorist . . . easy, flowing prose, engaging characters, and a biting wit"). And there is no reason why they shouldn't. Under the guise of a strong political stance, Kingsolver purveys a potpourri of tried-and-true soppy attitudes that are attached, with demographic precision, to an array of popular causes. She is something new: a political novelist who is careful not to step on anyone's toes. There is not a single sentiment expressed in her fiction that you could not express in an exchange with a stranger at a convention, or during a job interview, or on a first date.

But this seamlessness with the superficial rhetorical conventions of everyday life is actually a terrible disjunction from life. It is why Kingsolver's working-class characters look and sound like the idea of working-class people held by a professional couple's privileged daughter who studied music and languages at DePauw. (I mean Kingsolver.) Her working-class characters are dumb or saintly, and her young working-class women—except for her brilliant, confident, heroic fictional personae—are almost always stupid and selfish and reckless with the nail polish and mascara. They are literary tautologies: they are so much like themselves that they bear no relation to who they really are.

Kingsolver is so committed to keeping up the appearance of conventional morality that she sometimes mixes up her molasses-sweet descriptions of animals with her molasses-sweet condescension to the downtrodden. Seeing some pigs wander into her yard, the elderly Alice in *Pigs in Heaven* thinks: "The poor things are just looking for a home, like the Boat People." Underneath all the whispering of sweet nothings into the reader's ear, Kingsolver doesn't really seem to like human beings. She is sweetly lethal. It is the obverse side of her unremitting Niceness; perhaps it is the source of her Niceness. She describes her characters with an air of haughty repulsion, the way adolescents will stand in a corner at a party and quietly annihilate the other people there, until the other people come over and reveal that they do not have the power to hurt.

> He was bald and red-faced and kind of bossy.

> Otis is very old and bald with bad posture and big splay feet in white sneakers.

> Her eyelashes were stuck together with blue mascara and sprung out all around her eyes like flower petals.

> The woman has colorless flippy hair molded together with hairspray so that it all comes along when she turns her head.

> Her doughy breasts in a stretched T-shirt tremble.

> The manager has fat, pale hands decorated with long black hairs.

> They look strange: one is shrunken-looking with overblown masses of curly hair; another is hulky and bald, the head too big for the body.

> The cousin she's just met is a thin, humpbacked woman in canvas shoes and a blue cotton dress that hangs empty in the bosom.

> The woman has swollen knuckles and a stained red blouse.

This is perhaps the same icy indifference to humanity that is behind Kingsolver's portrayal of a retarded character who speaks perfect English. It is a safety measure for the preservation of the Nice Appearance of respecting retarded people: "Mom, I accidentally walked on the railroad tracks to Havasu." (The retarded character is named Buster; and Buster happens to be, Kingsolver tells us in her essay **"High Tide in Tucson,"** the name of a real-life hermit crab she keeps as a pet.)

It is the same polar numbness, this time to social reality, that lets Kingsolver depict the evil corporation in *Animal Dreams* as leaving its lucrative position in the small town without a legal challenge. And a cognate authorial glacialness has the lower-class Native American man in that novel, Loyd Peregrina, immediately decide to abandon his decades-old business enterprise of investing in fighting cocks. Why? Because the heroic Codi, his new girlfriend from a higher social stratum—and Kingsolver's fictional

persona in this novel—thinks that the spectacle of battling birds is mean and icky. Even if the income from training the birds helps Loyd to survive. This is the sort of cruelty of which the saintly-in-their-own-eyes are especially capable.

And what cold-heartedness lies behind *The Bean Trees*'s subplot of a Mayan couple from Guatemala, with connections to the left-wing guerrillas, escaping from the death squads to the United States. The Guatemalan soldiers, the narrator tells us, wanted information from the couple. So the army abducted their infant child—for Kingsolver, political violence is not political violence unless it affects the adorable Turtles of the world—and threatened to give her to a presumably upper-class family unless the couple told the army what it demanded to know about their rebel comrades. This, miraculously, gave the couple the time and the opportunity to flee.

In the real Guatemala, however, during the army's onslaught against the Indians in the 80s, the army simply tortured people from whom they wanted information. They raped the wives in front of their husbands, they beat the husbands to death in front of their wives, they killed the children in front of their parents. In *The Bean Trees,* Kingsolver introduces us to a relatively Nice death squad. For Nice Readers must not get the idea that politics has other features besides Nice Attitudes. Otherwise they might stop singing the vegetable-soup song, and get real.

IV.

From the terror in Guatemala in *The Bean Trees,* to the revolution and the counter-revolution in Nicaragua in *Animal Dreams,* to the plight of Native Americans in *Pigs in Heaven,* Kingsolver has, as she would say, "booked a return passage" to Africa and produced *The Poisonwood Bible.* Of all her books, though, her new book most closely resembles *Animal Dreams.* They both embody the full flowering of the Quindlen Effect.

I date the Quindlen Effect from December 13, 1992, though other readers might have their own favorite moments from the newspaper career of Anna Quindlen, the former *New York Times* columnist and one of the original Nice Queens. On that December day, Quindlen published a scathingly indignant editorial comment on the Glen Ridge sex assault trial, in which four male high school students were accused of sexually assaulting a twenty-one-year-old retarded woman.

True to her niche, Quindlen attacked with scathing indignation actions that no sane *Times* reader would ever defend. No neutral observer would defend four boys who manipulated a retarded girl into performing oral sex on them and inserted a broomstick and then a bat into her vagina; no more than any neutral observer would defend death squads or evil corporations. But Quindlen went on. She displayed a surfeit of sentiment ringing with an absence of true feeling that was downright Kingsolverian: "Most neighborhoods are divided into three kinds of children: those who torture the slow kid, those very few who defend her, and the great majority, who stand silent." But the great majority of teenagers in Glen Ridge, New Jersey did not stand silent as the assault took place. The assault took place in a basement, and the great majority knew nothing about it. And most neighborhoods are really not like that.

During that time, though, there was a place where the neighborhoods really had deteriorated. Right next to Quindlen's commentary, the *Times* published an essay by the Croatian writer Slavenka Drakulic exposing the mass rapes of Bosnian Muslim women by Bosnian Serb men. Drakulic was not attacking actions that everyone already despised; she was exposing actions that few Americans knew were happening. Her essay included chilling first-person descriptions of rape and mutilation and murder in Bosnia. The last account, given by a sixteen-year-old girl, ended with a paragraph that was also the final paragraph of Drakulic's piece: "I would like to be a mother some day. But how? In my world, men represent terrible violence and pain. I cannot control that feeling."

Looking at the Op-Ed page that morning, it was hard to avoid the implication that it had a theme. With Drakulic's article right there alongside Quindlen's article, the point was made that the male violence in Bosnia and the male violence in that suburban basement were phases of the same moral phenomenon. The analogy was appalling, and not only owing to its childish moral equivalence. It was appalling also because the moral equivalence promoted the idea that condemning the male violence at home would suffice as a response to the male violence abroad. (And of course we never did fight the violence in Bosnia, not until it was too late.) In the hands of monsters of empathy such as Anna Quindlen, the immediate preoccupations of the American self subjugate and domesticate and assimilate every distant tragedy.

Lenin famously declared that imperialism was the final stage of capitalism. He was wrong. A narcissistic capitalism, in fact, is the final stage of imperialism. Kingsolver is the bold anti-imperialist who fled to sunny Spain in order to escape government repression in Arizona during the Gulf war. And she is also the narcissist-imperialist par excellence. For the conclusion of *Animal Dreams* depicts an inversion based on a Quindlen-like connection. Kingsolver transforms the contra helicopters that mow down plain, earnest people in Nicaragua into the helicopter in which Codi's mother died after giving birth to Hallie. If it had not been for Hallie's letters describing those helicopters, we learn, Codi would never have remembered seeing her mother taken up in the helicopter. This was a memory that she needed to recover so that she suddenly could become an adult. Thus Hallie's death is redeemed by Codi's finally getting a life. Black night in Nicaragua; morning in America.

Kingsolver has perfected the Quindlen Effect in *The Poisonwood Bible.* The novel's cartoonish mainspring is a tyrannical Baptist missionary named Nathan Price, who takes up residence in the Congo in the late 1950s with his wife, Orleanna, and their four daughters. Told by Orleanna and each of her daughters in turn, *The Poisonwood Bible* portrays Nathan's fanatical insensitivity to the Congolese, which alienates his small congregation, resulting in the death of his youngest daughter Ruth May (the children again), and in his own madness, and in the disintegration of the family.

The novel has a silver lining, though. The silver lining is the indignant Kingsolver's most characteristic device. The other daughters—the bigoted right-wing Rachel; the sensitive and conscientious Leah; Leah's twin, the hemiplegic clairvoyant genius and verbal prodigy Adah—all come into their own by novel's end. In the course of all this, we also enjoy saintly glimpses of Patrice Lumumba, Congo's first democratically elected prime minister, whose probable murder by Mobutu's men got an enthusiastic green light and support from an Eisenhower worried about Lumumba's alliance with the Soviet Union.

"There is wisdom in every sentence," wrote the editors of the *New York Times Book Review* about *The Poisonwood Bible.* I hope they are not referring to the analogy that Kingsolver makes between Nathan's harshness toward the women in his family, and Belgium, whose King Leopold annexed the Congo in 1901, and cold-war America. As Orleanna puts it, again and again:

> And where was I, the girl or woman called Orleanna, as we traveled those roads. . . . Swallowed by Nathan's mission, body and soul. Occupied as if by a foreign power. . . . This is how conquest occurs. . . .

> Nathan was something that happened to us, as devastating in its way as the burning roof that fell on the family Mwanza; with our faces scarred by hell and brimstone we still had to track our course. . . . But his kind will always lose in the end. I know this, and now I know why. Whether it's wife or nation they occupy, their mistake is the same: they stand still, and their stake moves underneath them. . . . A territory is only possessed for a moment in time. . . . What does Okinawa remember of its fall? Forbidden to make engines of war, Japan made automobiles instead, and won the world. It all moves on. The great Delaware moves on, while Mr. Washington himself is no longer even what you'd call good compost. The Congo River, being of a different temperament, drowned most of its conquerors outright. . . . Call it oppression, complicity, stupefaction, call it what you like, it doesn't matter. Africa swallowed the conqueror's music and sang a new song of her own.

Wisdom in every sentence. And here is Leah on the same theme:

> Anatole explained it this way: Like a princess in a story, Congo was born too rich for her own good, and attracted attention far and wide from men who desire to rob her blind. The United States has now become the husband of Zaire's economy, and not a very nice one. Exploitive and condescending. . . .

> "Oh, I understand that kind of marriage all right," I said. "I grew up witnessing one just like it."

The reduction of history to an afternoon with Oprah is bad enough. But it is really extraordinary, is it not, that our very own Gordimer has written a "political novel" about Africa that does not refer to the present-day shattering events in Africa. In *The Poisonwood Bible,* we hear a lot about how American men, especially bad American Baptist missionary men, physically abuse their wives and daughters (though, as ever, Kingsolver is too nice to portray the abuse). Yet we do not get the slightest reference, or the most veiled allusion, to the Rwandan genocide and its ongoing blood-drenched aftermath, one of the least nice events in modern history, in which even the children were killed. For Kingsolver, Africa is happily singing "a new song of her own." Something like the vegetable-soup song.

In *The Poisonwood Bible,* instead of the momentous present, Kingsolver scavenges for heart-rending bulletins from the past. It is all so easy, this sentimental carpetbagging of a far-away history. We hear about how Belgian overseers on the rubber plantations disciplined their Congolese workers by cutting off their hands. About how the Belgians jailed Lumumba at one point, and how he miraculously "got out" in time for the elections. What Kingsolver doesn't tell her readers is that by 1959, when her novel begins, such cruelty had been defunct for over fifty years. (For the amputation of hands as a widespread instrument of torture, it is contemporary Sierra Leone to which one must look.)

In 1908, the Belgian parliament bought the Congo from King Leopold as a response to the international outcry against the atrocities that Belgian companies had been committing on the Congolese. By 1959, the Belgian Congo had the highest literacy rate and the most widespread health care of any European colony. Almost all of those improvements had to do with the work of missionaries. Most of the missionaries were Catholic, but some were Protestant like Nathan Price. And Lumumba did not magically "get out" of jail in time to get elected prime minister. The Belgians let him out, knowing full well that he was going to win.

This is not to say, this is really not to say, that the Europeans did not do atrocious things in Africa right up to decolonization, or that Belgium did not display calamitous self-interest in rushing Congo's independence when the colony was completely unprepared for it. (The Belgians had prohibited the Congolese from obtaining a university education, and when independence came there was not a single trained administrator or military officer.) It is also not to say that Europe and the United States do not have to answer for some portion of Africa's ordeal. But it is Kingsolver who is not playing fair with her readers.

For again she substitutes the image of goodness for honest representations. Almost every reviewer has rightly praised her beautiful evocation of the African landscape and her vivid treatment of African life; but not a single reviewer I read mentioned the twenty-eight-book bibliography that Kingsolver obviously felt obligated to include at the end

of her novel, a list with books such as *The Accidental Anthropologist, Congo Trails, Congo Cauldron, The River Congo, Back to the Congo, Travels in West Africa, Swimming in the Congo, On the Edge of the Primeval Forest.* Many of these books are travel books containing beautiful evocations of the African landscape and exhilarated treatments of African life. They lift the spirit with their vividness, the way Putamayo's compact discs do. The influence of this apolitical, upbeat ethnography accounts for the difference in the style of Kingsolver's new novel. And it is why the *The Poisonwood Bible* is so distant from its subject.

Still, the Nice Writing has not disappeared, and it extends its usual protections. You would not know from any of the reviews also that all the women in the family express the same tough ironic contempt for Nathan. Here is Ruth May: "'Africa has a million souls,' is what Father told him. And Father ought to know, for he's out to save them all." This is presented as the thought of a five-year-old girl, who is supposed to be brutally suppressed by her authoritarian father.

"Ultimately," the *Times* editors wrote, "this is a novel of character; the women discover themselves as they lose faith in Price." But the women in *The Poisonwood Bible* are on to their father's hypocrisy from the very beginning of the novel. They express their skepticism in the same jaunty sarcastic tone, which is the identical tone Kingsolver used for her earlier fictional personae, Taylor and Codi. This is the fifteen-year-old Rachel: "[Father] was getting that look he gets, oh boy, like Here comes Moses tromping down off of Mount Syanide with ten fresh ways to wreck your life." This is the fourteen-year-old Leah, supposedly in her father's thrall more than her sisters: "'Heavenly Father, deliver us,' I said, although I didn't care for this new angle . . . what was this business of being delivered through hardships?" This is the fourteen-year-old Adah, who refers sardonically to Nathan as "Our Father" and "Reverend": "When the Spirit passed through him he groaned, throwing body and soul into this weekly purge. The 'Amen enema,' as I call it. My palindrome for the Reverend." If this is the story of women struggling for psychic autonomy, they do not have terribly much work to do.

V.

Barbara Kingsolver does not finally give a hoot about Africa. She does not care about Africa (I mean, intelligently and respectfully care, with a sense of its alterity and its complexity) any more than she cared about the simple folk of Nicaragua. That is why the penultimate climax of *The Poisonwood Bible* is not about Africa. It is about our very own Gordimer's favorite domestic themes: cruelty to children and cruelty to animals. Thus her novel begins its climax in a scene depicting the Congolese villagers engaged in a hunt. They set the brush on fire and herd the animals inside the flames.

> For every animal struck down, there rose an equal and
> opposite cry of human jubilation. . . . Of the large

animals who came through the fire—bushbuck, warthog, antelope—few escaped. Others would not come out and so they burned: small flame-feathered birds, the churning insects, and a few female baboons who had managed against all odds to carry their pregnancies through the drought. With their bellies underslung with precious clinging babies, they loped behind the heavy-maned males, who would try to save themselves, but on reaching the curtain of flame where the others passed through, they drew up short. Crouched low. Understanding no choice but to burn with their children.

This breaks new ground in monster empathy. Abusive husbands are like conquering countries; mothers and children are the same whether human or animal. Killing is killing. And although, as Kingsolver herself tells us, the villagers are starving, she goes on to explain that this massacre was so cruel that it brought down upon the village a streak of terrible luck.

It is an icy marvel, this spectacle of a writer who can manipulatively wax so emotional and with such impressive virtue over the killing of animals by starving villagers in a place where, in reality, hundreds of thousands of people had just been exterminated. In a place where, perhaps at the very moment Kingsolver was writing her book, men were raping and murdering wives in front of their husbands (those selfish "heavy-maned males"), and beating the fathers to death in front of the mothers, and killing the children in front of their parents.

But Kingsolver has too much respect for other cultures to refer to the bad things that happen in them. Other cultures have different attitudes toward life and death. Through Adah, who later becomes a medical researcher—she works on the AIDS virus *and* the Ebola virus!—Kingsolver guides us through African values:

> People are *bantu;* the singular is *muntu. Muntu* does not mean exactly the same as *person,* though, because it describes a living person, a dead one, or someone not yet born. *Muntu* persists through all those conditions unchanged. . . . The transition from spirit to body and back again is merely a venture.

> In the world, the carrying capacity of humans is limited. History holds all things in the balance, including large hopes and short lives. . . . Africa has a thousand ways of cleansing itself. Driver ants, Ebola virus, acquired immune deficiency syndrome: all these are brooms devised by nature to sweep a small clearing very well . . . the race between predator and prey remains exquisitely neck and neck.

In Africa, then, death is a state of mind. There they are used to dying, and dying is so exquisitely good for them. The *Times* editors enthusiastically took this up: "perhaps [*The Poisonwood Bible*'s] greatest character is collective, the Congolese, whose perfect adaptation to the harshness of their lives amid drought, hunger, pests and diseases is simply beautiful." What a ravishing, talented, instinctive, unself-conscious race of people. And how beautiful is their extinction!

In Kingsolver's Africa, only her intrepid heroines, not the Africans themselves, get the burdensome dignity of moral struggle, confusion, and anguish. Here is Leah, who has chosen to live in Africa with her Congolese husband:

> I rock back and forth on my chair like a baby, craving so many impossible things: justice, forgiveness, redemption. I crave to stop bearing all the wounds of this place on my own narrow body. But I also want to be a person who stays, who goes on feeling anguish where anguish is due. I want to belong to somewhere, damn it. To scrub the hundred years' war off this white skin till there's nothing left and I can walk out among my neighbors wearing raw sinew and bone, like they do.

But enough of this frigid treacle. Let me tell you a story about my family, and this time I am writing the truth. My grandfather, Saul Siegel, who died a few months ago at the age of ninety-two, was with UNICEF in the Belgian Congo in 1960, when Congo got its independence. He was there during the riots and the strife and the civil war, and he stayed for some time after the United States installed Mobutu. I could not even begin to describe the lives that he saved and the good that he did. He knew that true goodness is the virtue that dare not speak its name. He knew all about the cold, calculating phonies who spray their virtue into your eyes like mace, and also about the cowards and the fools who abet them to aid themselves. I loved him very much. I sat next to his bed and watched him die as he struggled to keep breathing. I saw the light start to fade from his beautiful green eyes, and I let him pull me toward him by my shirt with his trembling hands so that he could whisper to me his farewell. With my heart full of love and grief and terror, I leaned toward him, and he pulled himself up a little and he rasped softly, and then he screamed: "Get Kingsolver!"

I did it again. I lied. I am sorry, but I cannot resist the temptation. The rewards are so great. And the words are so cheap.

Gayle Greene (review date April 1999)

SOURCE: "Independence Struggle," in *Women's Review of Books,* Vol. XVI, No. 7, April, 1999, pp. 8-9.

[*In the following review, Greene offers favorable evaluation of* The Poisonwood Bible.]

The Poisonwood Bible begins with a mysterious command: "Imagine a ruin so strange it must never have happened." The opening lines invite us in—"First, picture the forest. I want you to be its conscience, the eyes in the trees." We are summoned to see, through these eyes, a woman and four girls on a path below, "pale doomed blossoms, bound to appeal to your sympathies. Be careful. Later on you'll have to decide what sympathy they deserve." We cannot at this point know what this means, this injunction to imagine, decide, to be the eyes in the trees; by the end of the novel, we can.

The "I" is Orleanna Price, wife of Baptist missionary Nathan Price. She and her four daughters are here in this jungle because Nathan, in his zeal to convert the heathens, has landed them in a remote village in the Congo. The time is 1960, when the Congo's struggle for independence from Belgium gets ensnared in Cold War maneuvering for Africa. Orleanna is looking back on events, arguing with an unknown accuser, hounded by guilt, by questions of complicity: "but still I'll insist I was only a captive witness. What is the conqueror's wife, if not a conquest herself? . . . That's what we yell back at history, always, always. It wasn't just me; there were crimes strewn six ways to Sunday, and I had my own mouths to feed. I didn't know."

The story is told from her point of view and her daughters'. We begin from where they do, these Baptist girls growing up in Georgia in the 1950s—a narrative technique that, like the opening, draws us in, enlists us as participants. Rachel, the eldest, with a mane of blond hair and a head full of advertising jingles, is disconsolate at leaving behind her Breck Special Formula and five-day deodorant pads and the other things she has taken "for granite": "Jeez oh man, wake me up when it's over." Ruth May, the youngest, has a little-kid perspective that similarly illuminates this family's background: wondering why the village children have big bellies even though they're hungry, she reckons it's because they're the Tribes of Ham, "they're different from us"—"Jimmy Crow says that, and he makes the laws. . . . Their day for the zoo is Thursday. That's in the Bible."

Between these two are the twins, Leah as upright and perky as Adah is halting, limping. Adah is hemiplagic, born with "half a brain dried up like a prune," cannibalized in the womb (or so she imagines), grown weak as Leah grew strong. Whereas Leah strives for heaven and her father's approval, Adah has no such aspirations, having lost her faith when she realized her father's God condemned the unbaptized to hell "for the accident of a heathen birth." Adah, who has spent more time than most pondering "unfortunate accidents of birth," well sees the ironies: "May Africa talk back? Might those pagan babies send *us* to hell for living too far from a jungle? Because we have not tasted the sacrament of palm nuts?" Adah does not speak, but she writes, makes puns and palindromes, loves word play and Emily Dickinson and—unlike Rachel, whose words get the better of her—has a dazzling verbal facility. And she sees: low to the ground and slow of movement, her slant gives her special perspective. In the time-honored tradition of the soothsayer who is blind but sees better for it, her infirmity confers vision.

Much of the novel's meaning is in what these characters see, fail to see, learn to see; in what is seen by the eyes in the trees.

Even Rachel can see that, from day one, they're in trouble: "We are supposed to be calling the shots here, but it doesn't look to me like we're in charge of a thing, not even our own selves." Though the congregation is initially well disposed to them, it does not remain so. Nathan wields the Word like a rod, invoking the wrath of God upon the bare-breasted women, trying to drag the children to the river to baptize them (the river is full of crocodiles). His rigid reading of the Word ill prepares him for the nuances of Kikongo, the language of the region, which has a disconcerting tendency to use the same word, intoned differently, to say antithetical things. "Jesus is *bängala*," Nathan announces week after week, meaning Jesus is precious, unaware that the word, as he pronounces it, refers to the deadly poisonwood tree.

Orleanna sees the problems early on, but she can do nothing, caught as she is in the daily struggle to protect her daughters from snakes, killer ants, dysentery, disease, starvation—and their father. "What did I have? No money, that's for sure. No influence, no friends I could call upon in that place, no way to overrule the powers that governed our lives. This is not a new story: I was an inferior force." She has no way to resist her husband, let alone take a role in the Congolese resistance, the struggle for independence that's happening all around them—the election of Patrice Lumumba, the ousting of Lumumba, the murder of Lumumba in a village a mere forty miles away. How could she know that the coup that destroyed him was backed by the CIA, or that President Eisenhower, whose bald head and grandfatherly smile beams down from a photo on her kitchen wall, authorized his killing and replacement by Mobutu, the ruthless dictator who ruled, with US support, until 1997? She could barely, as she says, get her shoes on the right feet.

We get glimmers of these events from a newspaper article that finds its way to their village: "Soviet Plan Moves Forward in Congo." US media vindicate US intervention by portraying a Khrushchev ambitious for world domination, caricatured in sinister collusion: "big, fat, bald-headed Nikita Khrushchev . . . holding hands and dancing with a skinny cannibal native with big lips and a bone in his hair. Khrushchev was singing, 'Bingo Bango Bongo, I don't want to leave the Congo!'" Who better than Adah to understand the scapegoating here: "That is the story of Congo they are telling now in America: a tale of cannibals. I know about this kind of story—the lonely look down upon the hungry; the hungry look down upon the starving. The guilty blame the damaged. . . . It makes everyone feel much better." Who better than she to imagine what Africa might say back: "So sorry, but Ike should perhaps be killed now with a poisoned arrow. . . . What sort of man would wish to murder the president of another land? None but a barbarian. A man with a bone in his hair."

As the snatch and grab of power politics plays itself out, so finally does Orleanna Price, herself an occupied territory, move toward independence. What jolts her into action is personal rather than political tragedy—"Lumumba paid with a life and so did I." Only gradually is she dragged into an understanding of history, as she hears, a decade and a half later, a radio broadcast of the Congressional investigation of CIA involvement in Lumumba's unseating: "History didn't cross my mind. Now it does." She sees that to be ignorant is not to be innocent, and she begs, implores, the very earth for forgiveness. She seeks—as she recognizes all the sisters do—a way "to live with our history."

Adah must piece together a new account of her past and relinquish the categories that have disempowered her, which means letting go of her view of her twin Leah as having victimized her. She takes a degree in medicine, but rather than become a doctor, she becomes (as she says) a sort of witchdoctor—not one who lives among her congregation, but one who studies it from her lab at the university. She is surprisingly successful in her research because she has a kind of intuitive understanding of viruses as partners rather than enemies, a sense that derives from what she's learned in the Congo of the interrelationship of life and death—an awareness that makes her appreciate voodoo, which honors the balance between the living and dead and "embraces death as its company, not its enemy."

Leah, too, must let go of her categories, relinquishing her father's simplistic scheme wherein righteousness is rewarded and evil punished. Just as Adah, assuming voice and agency, becomes more like Leah, so does Leah, learning to question appearances, become more like Adah; and as the twins become closer, they come to see how each distorted the other and that their antipathy was based on a misunderstanding—an insight that resonates beyond the family drama to the political tragedy.

As these characters let go of old beliefs and construct new visions, Barbara Kingsolver leads us to see the limits of our own. There are ways besides ours of organizing social systems. Having experienced the droughts and the floods and the jungle, we understand that Congolese social practices and systems of exchange evolve from an affinity with the environment. There are ways besides ours of conceptualizing and describing reality; the language of the region, with its rich tonal ambiguities, is more adequate than English to the complex intertwining of antitheses so stark in the Congo. We balance Western against African values. Christianity against voodoo, and come to see through the eyes in the trees—a perspective which shows, among other things, the colossal arrogance of the West in imagining its language and culture as the measure of all things.

Not since *Beloved* have I been so engaged by a new work of fiction. **The Poisonwood Bible** is a good read, offering a point of entry anyone can start from, a story and characters that are gripping, a family saga that assumes epic and Biblical proportions. It addresses questions of history, the weight of the past, of memory, of narration. It has a strong political message, offering a scathing indictment of America's part in carving up Africa, yet it is also very funny, playful for all its seriousness, with the down-home humor familiar from Kingsolver's other novels though it has you laughing one moment and gasping with horror the next.

This is a complex, textured work, its imagery patterns resonating across levels of meaning. The idea of feeding, for example, plays out on ecological, biological, psychological and political levels: ants eat their way across Africa, the forest eats itself yet lives forever, crocodiles devour children; there is famine, hunting, poison, a snake in the belly, a dog-eat-dog world, a consumer society, a stewpot we're all in together. It is multivocal and multiphonic, its meaning not in a single voice but in the play of voices against one another, the mother and four daughters who tell this tale making five tones like those of the ancient pentatonic scale.

The Poisonwood Bible gives a way of thinking about cultures, a way of imagining otherwise. By the end, we—unlike the European explorers who first approached the shores of Africa to conquer, plunder, ruin—might imagine differently.

Roberta Rubenstein (review date April 1999)

SOURCE: "The Mark of Africa," in *World and I,* Vol. 14, No. 4, April, 1999, p. 254.

[*In the following review, Rubenstein offers favorable evaluation of* The Poisonwood Bible.]

When novelist Barbara Kingsolver was asked by a reader whether her fiction is based on her own life, she replied that her narratives are not drawn directly from her immediate experience; rather, they emerge from her struggle to give literary form to ideas. As she explained,

> I devise a very big question whose answer I believe will be amazing, and maybe shift the world a little bit on its axis. Then I figure out how to create a world in which that question can be asked, and answered. . . . I populate my setting with characters who'll act out my theme, scratching their heads in wonderment all along the way until their interactions with the world and each other have finally caused them to cry Aha! and my question is answered at last. (http:www.kingsolver.com/dialogue/11_question.htm)

Kingsolver's fascination with such large questions arose from rather unlikely sources. The daughter of a physician, she was born in 1955 and grew up in a poor rural farming area of eastern Kentucky. She reached high school "at the close of the sixties, in the Commonwealth of Kentucky, whose ranking on educational spending was I think around fifty-first" (**High Tide in Tucson,** 46-7).

As a bookworm who enjoyed writing poetry and short stories, Kingsolver was an outsider among her high school peers, whose expectations upon graduation were to become either farmers or farmers' wives. She was rescued by a high school librarian, who, in giving her a cataloging job, placed her in an environment of books that ultimately led her to her vocation. Browsing as she cataloged books, Kingsolver "caught the scent of a world. I started to dream up intoxicating lives for myself that I could not have conceived without the books" (**High Tide in Tucson,** 49).

Kingsolver attended DePauw University in Indiana, where she studied biology, graduating magna cum laude in 1977; subsequently, she earned a master of science in biology and ecology at the University of Arizona. A position as a science writer enabled her to combine her scientific training with her interest in writing. Following several years of writing feature stories for such journals as the *Nation,* the *New York Times,* and *Smithsonian,* she published her first book, **Holding the Line: Women in the Great Arizona Mine Strike of 1983.** The nonfiction narrative focuses on the stories of women in small Arizona mining towns whose lives were radically transformed by an eighteen-month strike against the Phelps Dodge Copper Corporation.

Kingsolver, who still lives in Arizona, has married (twice) and has two young daughters. Her other publications include a volume of poetry, **Another America** (1992); a volume of essays, **High Tide in Tucson: Essays From Now or Never** (1995); a collection of short stories, **Homeland and Other Stories** (1989); and, including **The Poisonwood Bible,** four novels.

Each of Kingsolver's novels demonstrates her deeper preoccupation with ideas as they achieve expression through the interactions of fully realized characters and events. For example, her training as a biologist is artfully demonstrated in **The Bean Trees** (1988), as organic metaphors of growth and nurturance in the natural world reflect her characters' progress. Taylor Greer, a young woman from Kentucky on her way west, finds herself the custodian of an utterly endearing 3-year-old Cherokee girl who is left in her car one night. The relationship evolves from Taylor's early attitude toward Turtle—so-named because of her extraordinary grip—as "not really mine . . . just somebody I got stuck with" to her decision to become the child's legal mother. Along the way, Kingsolver movingly explores issues of moral responsibility and community.

In **Pigs in Heaven** (1993), Kingsolver extends Taylor and Turtle's story, elaborating on ideas of family, community, ethnicity, and different belief systems as they shape identity. The question animating the latter novel is how to act in a child's best interest when two cultures disagree fundamentally on the matter.

Between these two novels, Kingsolver published **Animal Dreams** (1990), an absorbing fictional exploration of notions of identity, home, and people's greater relationship to the earth. For Cosima (Codi) Noline, the possibility of reclamation assumes both emotional and political meanings. Returning to her childhood home in Arizona after years away, the disaffected Codi eventually renews her relationship with her father and discovers her affinity with Native American values concerning people and the land.

She is also politically awakened, discovering by accident that the nearby river and land are being poisoned by unchecked chemical pollution from a mining operation. Galvanizing people in her community to rally against the mining company's irresponsibility, Codi explains, "People can forget, and forget, and forget, but the land has a memory. The lakes and the rivers are still hanging on the DDT and every other insult we ever gave them."

PINNING THE WATER TO ITS BANKS

Although one might term Kingsolver a "political" novelist on the basis of such preoccupations, those matters are always persuasively rendered through character and event. Thus, although **The Poisonwood Bible** tackles a complicated political question—what happened in and to the Congo during the crucial transition from colonial protectionism to national independence?—Kingsolver avoids didacticism by approaching her subject through multiple perspectives; large issues are filtered through the seemingly small daily challenges and discoveries of particular individuals as they live their lives.

One might ask first, why the Congo, given the southwestern American setting of Kingsolver's previous novels? Though **The Poisonwood Bible** is not autobiographical, it is based on a personal experience: Kingsolver spent a life-changing year in the Belgian Congo when her father served there as a physician. Considering Africa as a 7-year-old child, she later wrote, "I couldn't begin to imagine the life that was rolling out ahead of me. But I did understand it would pass over me with the force of a river, and that I needed to pin the water to its banks and hold it still, somehow, to give myself time to know it" (**High Tide,** 119).

In a comment made during a reading in Washington in November 1998, Kingsolver acknowledged that the story that ultimately became **The Poisonwood Bible** grew from a subject she has been pondering for twenty years, hoping to acquire the wisdom and skill to give it written form. She needn't have worried: She has achieved a narrative of enormous moral depth and aesthetic mastery.

The story centers on the Prices of Bethlehem, Georgia, a Baptist missionary family headed by the fundamentalist Nathan, who intends to bring salvation to the "heathen" of Kilanga, Belgian Congo. Nathan's rigidity and evangelical conviction are so immoderate, however, that he ultimately alienates himself not only from the Kikongo people whom he wishes to convert but from his wife and four young daughters as well. Nathan's story subtly comes to represent the intertwined moral and political failures of colonialism and Western exploitation in West Africa.

When Orleanna Price later reflects on her husband's actions both before and while in the Congo, she concludes that her family was "swallowed by Nathan's mission, body and soul. Occupied as if by a foreign power." Similarly, various outside interests, blind to the customs and wishes of the indigenous peoples, pursued their own self-serving missions in Africa, with repercussions that continue to affect the region to this day.

When the Prices first arrive in the village near the Kwilu River in 1959, they are all innocents, imperiously believing that Nathan's mission to "bring salvation into the darkness" is ordained by God. Only much later does Orleanna understand that Nathan's error was in trying not only to deliver the word of God but to assume His place.

> We aimed for no more than to have dominion over every creature that moved upon the earth. And so it came to pass that we stepped down there on a place we believed unformed, where only darkness moved on the face of the waters. . . .What do we know, even now? Ask the children. Look at what they grew up to be. We can only speak of the things we carried with us, and the things we took away.

The last comment effectively frames *The Poisonwood Bible:* The Price family arrives in Africa literally weighted down with objects carried from America that they believe will be needed for survival in the Congo, from Betty Crocker cake mixes to pinking shears. What they slowly discover is that they "brought all the wrong things"—they are burdened not simply by irrelevant objects and supplies but their beliefs—and that what they carry away when they leave is not their possessions but the distinct and ineradicable mark that Africa has left on each of them.

During their seventeen months in Kilanga, Nathan stubbornly persists in his mission to convert and baptize the natives, oblivious to the fact that they already have a perfectly satisfactory religion. Kingsolver is especially adept at embodying in human terms the collisions between worldviews, both spiritual and secular. While Nathan's daughters come to recognize the undertones that "shimmer under the surface of the words right and wrong," Nathan, deaf to such subtleties, finds his task further complicated by the richly tonal language of the Kikongo people.

Indeed, language functions not only as a linguistic code but as the source of the deepest possibility for communication or, more often, misunderstanding between people. (One might add that it is Kingsolver's own accomplished language that makes this novel so richly absorbing.) The Kikongo word bangala, for example—which Nathan employs in his frequently repeated evangelical exhortation, "Tata Jesus is bangala!"—carries meanings as contradictory as "most precious," "most insufferable," and "poisonwood." No wonder the villagers are puzzled by the missionary's garbled message.

The Kikongo chief expresses his concern about the moral decline and spiritual corruption of the villagers if they abandon their faith in their traditional spirit-protectors and convert to Christianity; Nathan insensitively retorts that the tribe's spiritual leader is a witch doctor who leads his people in the worship of false idols. The reader, privy to both sides, ponders which idols are the false ones.

WHAT THEY CARRIED WITH THEM

The Poisonwood Bible, Kingsolver's most structurally ambitious novel to date, unfolds through five distinct narrative perspectives. Interestingly, although the author omits Nathan Price's point of view by disclosing the family's sojourn in Africa exclusively through the accounts of his wife and daughters, we know Nathan as well as we know those who speak. Given his monomaniacal vision, his perspective is quite clear, even without the benefit of entry into his thoughts.

Because the Price girls are naive observers, abundant ironies emerge between their limited comprehension and the reader's understanding of events. For example, 14-year-old Adah contemplates the arbitrary injustice revealed by her father's Baptist religion, wondering how a child could be "denied entrance to heaven merely for being born in the Congo rather than, say, north Georgia, where she could attend church regularly. . . . Would Our Lord be such a hit-or-miss kind of Savior as that? Would he really condemn some children to eternal suffering just for the accident of a heathen birth, and reward others for a privilege they did nothing to earn?"

The early sections narrated by the oldest daughter, going-on-16 Rachel, reveal an utterly conventional adolescent who, because of her pale skin, white eyelashes, and platinum-blond hair, stands out like an albino in Africa and who is far more concerned with the social life she is missing back home in Georgia than with the social customs of the Kikongo people. She is also (unintentionally) comic; her accounts are punctuated by such malapropisms as "I prefer to remain anomalous" and "I was feeling at loose odds and ends."

The youngest daughter, 5-year-old Ruth May, offers the most naive perspective, that of a child who can scarcely comprehend the magnitude of the challenges that confront her family struggling for survival in the inhospitable African bush, let alone the deeper ramifications of their mission. The least encumbered, she is the first member of the family to connect with the people of Kilanga, teaching her eager peers how to play "Mother-May-I?" Yet even that innocent children's game mimics her father's attitudes, with Ruth May benevolently reigning over the village children as they obediently ask, "Mad-da-meh-yi?"

Between Rachel and Ruth May are the twins, Leah and Adah. Fourteen when they arrive in Kilanga, both girls are intellectually gifted; however, Adah's physical circumstances disguise her exceptional intelligence. Born with hemiplegia, a condition that renders her mute and severely lame, she is, for most of the narrative, a silent observer whose words only the reader hears. Yet those words are often composed of marvelous poetry, wordplay, and a "slant vision" that uniquely melds her accommodation to her physical handicap and her fascination with Emily Dickinson: "tell the truth but tell it slant."

As a result of her ability to read not only forwards but backwards, Adah enjoys creating palindromes.

> "Walk to learn. I and Path. Long one is Congo."

"Congo is one long path and I learn to walk."

"That is the name of my story, forward and backward."

"Manene is the word for path: Manene enenam, amen. On the Congo's one long manene Ada learns to walk, amen. One day she nearly does not come back. Like Daniel she enters the lions' den, but lacking Daniel's pure and unblemished soul, Ada is spiced with the flavors of vice that make for a tasty meal. Pure and unblemished souls must taste very bland, with an aftertaste of bitterness."

As this passage suggests, Kingsolver is especially successful at creating a distinctively nuanced idiom, perspective, and voice for each of her characters; one can quite clearly hear them speak. Moreover, drawing on the fact that the Price family is steeped in Nathan's Bible-thumping evangelism, Kingsolver effectively plays the girls' emerging insights against scriptural parallels.

Adah's twin, Leah, emerges as the wise child and moral consciousness of the Price family. Her concern with social justice first develops within their own village circumstances and later expands to encompass the history and future of the Congo itself. Like Adah, she is fascinated with language:

In the beginning we were just about in the same boat as Adam and Eve. We had to learn the names of everything. Nkoko, mongo, zulu—river, mountain, sky—everything must be called out from the void by the word we use to claim it. All God's creatures have names, whether they slither across our path or show up for sale at our front stoop. . . . Our very own backyard resembles the Garden of Eden. I copy down each new word in my school notebook and vow to remember it always, when I am a grown-up American lady with a backyard garden of my own. I shall tell all the world the lessons I learned in Africa.

What They Took Away

The voices and perspectives of the four Price daughters are counterpointed by that of their mother, whose commentaries begin all but one of the novel's seven major sections. Unlike her daughters' accounts of daily life in Kilanga, Orleanna's are narrated years later, after she has returned to Georgia to ponder what happened to her family in Africa. Her reflections are colored by the moral perspective not of innocents in paradise but, as it were, after the fall; Orleanna struggles to comprehend her own complicity in tragic events and—with difficulty—to forgive herself.

Each member of the Price family is marked in a different way by the experience in the Congo. In addition to learning to surrender ideas they had taken for granted about such matters as how to raise crops (Nathan brings Kentucky Wonder bean seeds from Georgia but disdains valuable advice from a village elder on how to plant them and watches his potential crop wash away in a rainstorm) or how to protect themselves from other encroachments of the environment, the children are daily exposed to events that test their American assumptions.

During their ill-fated sojourn, they contend with aggravations and dangers large and small: sunburn, boredom, mosquitoes, malaria, poisonous snakes and poisonwood trees, parasites, worms, driver ants, crocodiles, and lions—to say nothing of the extremes of drought and torrential rain and the shocks of famine, illness, and death. As Leah wryly observes, "Africa has a thousand ways to get under your skin."

Nonetheless, far more than their parents, the four girls endeavor (to different degrees) to adapt: to learn the local language and customs, to befriend their Kikongo peers, and to understand cultural differences as the complicated politics of the country's transition to political independence swirl above their heads. Still, as Adah phrases it, "the things we do not know, independently and in unison as a family, would fill two separate baskets, each with a large hole in the bottom."

While Orleanna struggles simply to keep her family alive in a hostile environment (even cooking is a thrice-daily struggle), Leah—guided by Anatole, a Congolese schoolteacher—slowly comes to understand the meaning of colonialism. As Belgium siphons off the country's natural riches—diamonds and rubber—America and Russia compete for a stake in the Congo's postindependence future by manipulating political events. The hasty death of the country's first democratically elected leader, Patrice Lumumba, following the election of 1960, is presumably orchestrated by the CIA to thwart the Soviet Union, the perceived challenger to American interests in the region. Leah, in the light of her increasing political awareness, weighs her loyalty to her father against her growing disillusionment with his mission.

The Poisonwood Bible is chock-full of interesting, vividly drawn characters and surprising turns of plot, far too many to summarize here. Two-thirds of the novel encompasses the seventeen months that the Price family lives in Kilanga, concluding with terrible losses both in their family and in the country; the remaining third of the narrative follows each of the surviving Prices over nearly thirty succeeding years. Without revealing crucial details that readers are better rewarded by discovering on their own, I will simply note that it is the Congo that exacts its price on the Prices and not the other way around.

Following different paths out of Kilanga according to their distinct perspectives, each Price daughter ultimately makes peace with Africa and gives something back to it. As Leah phrases it, "we've all ended up giving up body and soul to Africa, one way or another." Each comes to appreciate the "balance between loss and salvation"; however, what each gives back is as different as are Nathan's daughters themselves. As Rachel comes to realize, "You can't just sashay into the jungle aiming to change it all over to the Christian style, without expecting the jungle to change you right back. . . . Some fellow thinks he's going to be the master of Africa and winds up with his nice European-tailored suit rumpled in a corner and his wits half cracked from the filaires [parasites] itching under his skin. If it was as easy as they thought it was going to be, why, they'd be done by now, and Africa would be just like America with more palm trees. Instead, most of it still looks exactly how it did a zillion years ago."

From a different perspective, Ruth May, the daughter who is granted the narrative's final commentary, concludes that "every life is different because you passed this way and touched history. . . . Everyone is complicit."

The satisfaction for readers of **The Poisonwood Bible** are many, including Kingsolver's brilliant braiding of fictional invention, historical fact, and emotional truth as she distills a complex moral and political vision. Drawing her readers into the contingencies of a fully imagined time and place, the author invites us to reconsider American notions of family and faith as they intersect—or, rather, collide—with culture, history, and destiny in West Africa in the 1960s and afterward. Magisterially, Kingsolver lets us see, hear, and feel how each of her characters has "touched history."

FURTHER READING

Criticism

Campbell, Kim. "Novelist's Wry Wit Inhabits Latest Essays." *Christian Science Monitor* (20 December 1995): 14.

A positive review of *High Tide in Tucson.*

Clinton, Kate. "The Best Books of 1998." *Progressive* 62, No. 12 (December 1998): 38-41.

A positive review of *The Poisonwood Bible.*

Neuhaus, Denise. "On Dependable Ground." *Times Literary Supplement* (7 September 1990): 956.

A positive review of *Homeland and Other Stories.*

Norman, Liane Ellison. "Ignorance and Grace." *Sojourners* 28, No. 2 (March 1999): 59

A positive review of *The Poisonwood Bible.*

Spaid, Elizabeth Levitan. "Saga of an Adopted Indian Continues." *Christian Science Monitor* (9 August 1993): 13.

A positive review of *Pigs in Heaven.*

Trachtman, Paul. Review of *High Tide in Tucson,* by Barbara Kingsolver. *Smithsonian* 27, No. 3 (June 1996): 24.

A positive review of *High Tide in Tucson.*

Additional coverage of Kingsolver's life and career is contained in the following sources published by the Gale Group: *Authors and Artists for Young Adults,* **Vol. 15;** *Contemporary Authors,* **Vols. 129, 134;** *Contemporary Authors New Revision Series,* **Vol. 60; and** *DISCovering Authors Modules: Popular Fiction and Genre Authors.*

Hans Küng
1928-

(Hans Kueng) Swiss theologian.

The following entry presents an overview of Küng's career through 1998.

INTRODUCTION

Hans Küng is one of the world's most celebrated and controversial Christian theologians. A Roman Catholic priest, his criticism of Pope John Paul II and his questioning of some of the major tenets of the Catholic religion have caused him to be censured by the Church. Despite the controversial nature of his ideas, critics have praised him for his scholarly, well-researched, and ecumenical approach to questions of theology.

BIOGRAPHICAL INFORMATION

Hans Küng was born on March 19, 1928, in Sursee, Lucerne, Switzerland, to Hans and Emma Küng. He was ordained a Roman Catholic priest in 1954. In the 1960s, Küng was an up-and-coming member of the hierarchy of the Catholic Church. During the reign of Pope John XXIII, Küng was appointed the official theologian to the Second Vatican Council and is recognized as its architect. Küng's relationship with Rome changed during the reign of subsequent popes whom he felt were reversing the important reforms set in motion by Vatican II. In 1979, in response to Küng's controversial examination of Catholic beliefs, the Vatican forbade Küng to call himself a "Catholic theologian" or to examine candidates for the priesthood. Küng was personally devastated by the Church's disciplinary measures, but his commitment to his faith and his career as a theologian continued to flourish. Küng is a professor of theology at the University of Tubingen in West Germany. He has also been a visiting professor at several universities throughout the world.

MAJOR WORKS

Küng has been particularly critical of Pope John Paul II and what he considers the pontiff's repressive policies. He has written several articles on the subject. *Wozu Priester?* (1971; *Why Priests?*) delineates Küng's conception of the leadership of the Church. As with many of Küng's works, this book raised eyebrows among conservative theologians by espousing that a lifelong, celibate, male priesthood is unnecessary according to the New Testament. In *Christ sein* (1974; *On Being a Christian*), Küng described what is

common among the various Christian religions and discussed the reasons a person would choose to believe in Christianity. The book focuses on the life and teaching of Jesus Christ and the nature of his divinity. *Signposts for the Future* (1978) is a collection of essays that reiterates the uniqueness of Christianity explained in *On Being a Christian*. It further goes on to discuss Christians' relationship with larger society and their relationship with the Church. Beginning with *Christentum und Weltreligionen* (1984; *Christianity and the World Religions*), Küng began to focus on the relationship between Christianity and the other major world religions. He collaborated with Julia Ching on *Christentum und Chinesische Religion* (1989; *Christianity and Chinese Religions*) in which they analyze the place of Confucianism, Taoism, Buddhism, and Christianity in modern China. Kung's *Theologie im Aufbruch* (1988; *Theology for the Third Millennium*) asserts that the postmodern Church lacks direction and proposes a course that will cause it to flourish and bring it to a closer relationship with the other world religions. *Projekt Welthethos* (1993; *Global Responsibility* is a continuation of the

ideas set forth in *Christianity and the World Religions.*
Kung asserted three points in this volume: our survival is
dependent on the development of a world ethic; we can
have no world peace without peace between the religions;
and there will be no peace between the religions without a
dialogue between the religions. In his attempt to foster a
greater understanding between people of different faiths,
Kung has begun a trilogy tracing the foundations of the
major religions, including volumes entitled *Judentum*
(1992; *Judaism*), *Christentum* (1995; *Christianity*), and a
proposed volume on Islam.

CRITICAL RECEPTION

Even when critics disagree with Küng's assertions, they
praise him for his intellectual courage and honesty. Andrew
M. Greeley called Küng "a priest and scholar who is doing his best to live that life no matter what the cost in
professional envy and institutional isolation." Reviewers
credit his work as scholarly and rooted in the Bible. Carl
J. Armbruster asserted that "one of Küng's special merits
as a theologian is that he takes the Bible very seriously."
Many reviewers note how Küng's work puts him at odds
with liberal theologians and the Roman Catholic Church
alike. The former because of his assertion that the typical
responses to the evils of capitalism have failed, and the
latter for his questioning of the basis of papal authority.
Some critics have accused the theologian of going
overboard in his criticism of Pope John Paul II, marring
some of his otherwise laudable work. While most critics
agree that Küng's goal of creating a greater understanding
between the religions is a commendable one, there is some
disagreement about the effectiveness of his approach. Some
reviewers complain that in Küng's attempts to foster
understanding and ecumenism, he does not put sufficient
focus on the uniqueness of individual faiths and has lost
the true meaning of his own religion. Specifically, some
critics found Küng's *Judaism* to be dismissive and patron-
izing to Jews. Eugene Fisher and Jack Bemporad state,
"At some risk of being insufficiently respectful of Küng's
well-established reputation, we must report that Jewish
readers—with good cause—are likely to find this volume,
which purports after all to present *their* faith and *their*
traditions, to be insensitive and inaccurate." Robert P. Imbelli summed up Küng's virtues in his review of Küng's
Christianity, stating that the book "bears all the marks of
Küng's virtues: stunning erudition, moral passion, provocative honesty and sometimes unrelenting polemics."

PRINCIPAL WORKS

*Rechtfertigung: Die Lehre Karl Barths und eine katholische
besinnung* [*Justification: The Doctrine of Karl Barth
and a Catholic Reflection*] (nonfiction) 1957
*Konzil und Wiedervereinigung: Erneuerung als Ruf in die
Einheit* [*The Coucil and Reunion*] (nonfiction) 1960

Kirche im Konzil [*The Council in Action: Theological
Reflections on the Second Vatican Council*] (nonfiction)
1963
Wozu Priester? Ein Hilfe [*Why Priests? A Proposal for a
New Church Ministry*] (nonfiction) 1971
Christ sein [*On Being a Christian*] (nonfiction) 1974; also
published as *Die christliche Herausforderung,* 1980
Existiert Gott? Antwort auf die Gottesfrage der Neuzeit
[*Does God Exist? An Answer for Today*] (nonfiction)
1978
*Signposts for the Future: Contemporary Issues Facing
the Church* (articles) 1978
Ewiges Leben? [*Eternal Life? Life After Death as a Medi-
cal, Philosophical, and Theological Problem*]
(nonfiction) 1982
*Christentum und Weltreligionen: Hinfuehrung zum Dialog
mit Islam, Hinduismus und Buddhismus* [*Christianity
and the World Religions: Paths of Dialogue with Islam,
Hinduism, and Buddhism*] [with others] (nonfiction)
1984
*The Church in Anguish: Has the Vatican Betrayed Vatican
II?* [editor; with Leonard Swidler] (essays) 1987
Theologie im Aufbruch [*Theology for the Third Millen-
nium: An Ecumenical View*] (nonfiction) 1988
Christentum und Chinesische Religion [*Christianity and
Chinese Religions*] [with Julia Ching] (nonfiction) 1989
Theologie—Wohin? and *Das Neue Paradigma von Theolo-
gie* [*Paradigm Change in Theology*] [editor; with David
Tracy] 2 vols. (essays) 1989
Judentum [*Judaism: Between Yesterday and Tomorrow*]
(nonfiction) 1992
Credo: The Apostles' Creed Explained for Today
(nonfiction) 1993
Projekt Welthethos [*Global Responsibility: In Search of a
New World Ethic*] (nonfiction) 1993
Christentum [*Christianity: Essence, History, and Future*]
(nonfiction) 1995

*Includes translations of *Zwanzig Thesen zum Christsein, Was ist Fir-
mung?* and *Jesus im Widerstreit: Ein juedisch-christlicher Dialog.*

CRITICISM

Carl J. Armbruster (review date 25 August 1972)

SOURCE: A review of *Why Priests?* in *Commonweal,* Vol.
XCVI, No. 19, August 25, 1972, pp. 458-60.

[*In the following review, Armbruster analyzes Küng's
discussion of the priesthood in* Why Priests?]

This latest book by Hans Küng is a fine piece of popular-
ization. Not that it is unscholarly, for Küng's scholarly
credentials in the area of ecclesiology have been established elsewhere. But he dispenses with footnotes and
references in order to develop in broad strokes his
"proposal for a new church ministry" (the subtitle). To
those who are well-informed about current trends in the
theology of the priesthood, the book offers no startling

surprises. However, both for the specialist and for the general public it summarizes and locates the cutting edge of theological thought on the priesthood. It also pushes to the foreground questions which are ripe for discussion and argument.

What does Küng say about the priesthood? First he situates the crisis of the ministry within an ecclesiological context, namely, "a nuanced democratization of the church" (p. 24). The word "nuanced" is important here, for Küng stresses that it is an analogous, even ambiguous political concept that must be critically adapted in the light of the N. T. when applied to the church. Theologically, it means "an increasing co-responsibility of all members of the ecclesial community," which should produce a community of "liberty, equality, and fraternity." This choice of the slogan of the French Revolution to describe what the new church should be strikes me as somewhat strained and even "old hat," though the ecclesial realities behind these political terms are well described.

As Raymond Brown has noted (*America,* May 20, 1972), one of Küng's special merits as a theologian is that he takes the Bible very seriously. His treatment of the N. T. ministry underscores its functional as opposed to its "official" nature, the model of flexibility it presents, the underlying concept of leadership as more basic than that of cultic priesthood, the centrality of charism, the functional rather than the historical understanding of apostolic succession, and the norm of service which Jesus proposes.

On one point, however, Küng seems too touchy, if not inconsistent, and that is his aversion to the term "office," for he states that "church 'office' is not a biblical concept." (p. 39) He prefers "function" or "service." Yet he repeatedly refers to the ministry of leadership as a "permanent public responsibility" or uses phrases which are the equivalent (cf. pp. 43, 83, 92, 103-106, 113). If a "permanent public responsibility" is not an "office," not necessarily in the authoritarian or bureaucratic sense that Küng fears, then I do not know what it is. As for the fact that "office" is not a biblical word, neither is the term "Trinity," but the absence of terminology does not imply the absence of the reality designated. Just as "democratization" is an analogous term, so too is "office," and I believe it to be sociologically and theologically apt to express the ecclesial fact of "permanent public responsibility."

In a provocative chapter on the historical development of the theology of priesthood, Küng describes the sacralization of the ministry from the fifth and sixth centuries on, the sacramentalistic conception that developed during the Middle Ages, and the relativity of Trent's dogmatic declarations on the indelible character of Holy Orders, its institution by Christ, and the concept of Eucharistic sacrifice. This is the chapter that doubtless will raise the hackles of conservative theologians, for here Küng attacks the dogmatic bastions that defend the conservative view of pastoral renewal. For instance, in rejecting the heretofore

traditional interpretation of the Tridentine doctrine of the indelible character of Orders, Küng undercuts a static ontological view and makes room for his functionalism, while at the same time he sets up the possibility of a temporary ordained ministry by a new idea of the permanency of the sacramental character. In these matters Küng tantalizes more than he expounds, for he holds unrepeatability and permanency, but does not plunge too deeply into this theological thicket. More could have been said about the peculiar nature of Holy Orders which is unrepeatable but often "received" three times by one who is successively ordained deacon, priest, and bishop. At least Küng stimulates a long overdue reconsideration of such anomalies.

His final chapter on the form of the church's ministry of leadership distinguishes between the variables and the constants in that ministry. The variables actually constitute a program for radically restructuring the priesthood. According to Küng, the church's ministry of leadership does *not* have to be full-time, for life, associated with social status, set aside in a sacral sphere, trained academically, celibate, or male. His point, based on the N. T. and history, is that "even today we are still too little aware of the extent to which the ecclesial community has the freedom . . . to shape the concrete forms of the church's ministry and leadership and too little aware of how great the possibilities are to satisfy modern man's diverse requirements in today's society." (pp. 75-76)

The constants in the church's ministry are that it is a nondomineering service of spiritual leadership by stimulating, coordinating, and integrating the charisms of the congregation. It is flexible and pluriform in order to respond to pluriform communities. It is rooted in a personal charism, a call for the Spirit of Jesus Christ which is tested by the community. It is apostolic in its continuity with the original faith and mission of the apostles. The charism is recognized and its bearer mandated by the ritual imposition of hands in the sacrament of ordination. In short, the minister is permanently and publicly responsible for building up the congregation by means of the Word and the sacraments in an exercise of committed love.

In a final section, Küng states: "The image of the church leader today will continue to be determined essentially by the apostolic model, which in turn looks to Jesus himself." (p. 111) Without realizing it, this appeal by Küng to the imitation of Jesus—which he makes in a passing way in several places (pp. 18, 27, 50, 115)—poses the most overlooked question in theology and spirituality today. What does it mean for a Christian and for an ordained minister to imitate Jesus? Which Jesus—the historical Jesus, the corporate Jesus, the risen Jesus? What criteria are used to validate genuine imitation and to distinguish it from superficial aping? To what extent do culture and time affect our imitation of Jesus?

John B. Breslin (review date 28 November 1976)

SOURCE: "God and Küng," in *Washington Post Book World,* November 28, 1976, pp. H1-H2.

[*In the following review, Breslin praises Kung's* On Being a Christian, *stating that "Kung provides a skillfully argued, theologically nuanced and personally appropriated set of arguments for the liberating power of Christianity."*]

Religious bestsellers in this country usually mean inspirational books by Billy Graham or slightly kooky tracts like Hal Lindsey's *Late Great Planet Earth*. And even when they sell zillions of copies, they don't make the standard bestseller lists because they're sold in bookstores that are not surveyed. They do things differently in Germany, to judge by the startling success of the original edition of this theological work by Hans Kung. For months, it hovered near the top of *Der Spiegel's* chart, just behind Alexander Solzhenitsyn's *Gulag*.

That's not likely to happen here, unfortunately, but it's just possible that the combination of Kung's reputation (both as premier theologian and as ecclesiastical maverick) and the current interest in religious questions may save this book from the fate of most theology: professional wrangling followed by popular oblivion.

On Being a Christian is most certainly theology, aimed at the head, not just at the heart, and Kung offers no excuses for raising difficult questions or for providing 80 pages of footnotes, heavily Teutonic in flavor. But it is theology of a special kind, what used to be called apologetics—a defense of, or argument for Christian belief. If that smells a bit musty to you, reminiscent of ugly black textbooks, don't be put off. Kung knows that the most serious challenge Christianity faces today, at least in the Western hemisphere, is indifference: why bother to be a Christian? And he knows, too, that other challenges, from secular humanism and the world religions, have to be faced squarely and argued with in earnest. In short, he knows his audience—university educated, religiously interested but often ecclesiastically disenchanted—what he calls, in the generalizing way of theologians, "modern man."

For those who fit the description—and they include a large number of nominal and once-upon-a-time Christians across this country—Kung provides a skillfully argued, theologically nuanced and personally appropriated set of arguments for the liberating power of Christianity. His twin lodestars are human experience and human reason and he insists that separating them leads inevitably to a mindless subjectivism or a desiccated reactionalism. His discussion of theism turns, then, not on series of "proofs" but on a reflection about human trust. To move from such trust to Christian faith still requires a leap, but Kung's approach—in opposition, say, to Barth's—emphasizes a fundamental continuity between the two experiences.

After a brief, and necessarily superficial, excursus on the genius and flaws of the great world religions, Kung turns to the book's principal question—what is it that makes Christianity different? The answer he gives is surprising only in its simplicity: Jesus the Christ, experienced as the central figure in human history and as the decisive religious event in a person's life, alone guarantees the uniqueness of the Christian gospel. Without "an explicit, positive reference to Jesus Christ," Kung refuses to baptize good will or good deeds as Christian, and he scorns any facile use of the term "anonymous Christian" to solve the problem of salvation outside the church. Almost two-thirds of his 600 pages of text is devoted to explicating the meaning of this central affirmation about Jesus Christ, and this core forms the most successful part of Kung's book.

As in the introductory section, objectivity remains a prime apologetic tool. Without discounting the importance of myth and legend, symbol and metaphor, Kung insists on the history that undergirds a faith commitment to Jesus Christ. To get at that historical foundation he employs all the implements of New Testament criticism, most neatly summed up in the phrase, "historical-critical method." What that means is a systematic attempt to identify the various layers that make up the New Testament, from the particular theological visions that shaped the final written texts, back through the interpretations that were given to the oral tradition by the various early Christian communities, to the most primitive strata of all where we can perceive the outlines of Jesus's own preaching. It is not a process to cheer the hearts of fundamentalists, but it represents the majority view of contemporary Scripture scholarship. Many experts will disagree (some already have disagreed) with specific uses to which Kung puts this method, but few would quarrel with his basic approach.

What the process yields, while hardly a "Life of Christ" in the old-fashioned sense, is a fascinating portrait of Jesus of Nazareth, an itinerant preacher who appeared only briefly on the Palestinian scene but who managed to throw into question most of the accepted religious, social and even political beliefs of his day. He joined no party, whether of the Establishment or of the revolutionaries, and he embraced neither the legal compromises of the Pharisees nor the world-shunning asceticism of the Essenes. He had only one overriding interest, the coming reign of God, and he believed passionately that every other human concern must be interpreted in light of that impending reality—whether it was the Mosaic Law or the structure of the family or the way individuals dealt with one another. God's kingdom, God's cause came first, but on closer analysis, Kung argues, we find that God's cause, as understood by Jesus, meant man's cause as well. "God wills nothing but man's advantage, man's true greatness and his ultimate dignity. This then is God's will: man's well-being."

Unfortunately, the men of Jesus's time were no better than ourselves in recognizing what constituted their "true greatness and . . . ultimate dignity." And when Jesus made it clear that forgiveness, service of others and renunciation of self-interest were integral parts of that well-being and that, moreover, God's special concern was for the despised and the outcasts rather than for the conventionally law-abiding, then God's reign became a threat to man's self-sufficiency and His messenger an expendable rabble-rouser.

Kung insists that Jesus went to his death precisely because of his religious messages; because the freedom and the intimacy with God that he claimed both for himself and for all who accepted his preaching were rightly perceived as undermining the elaborate religious structure of the Jewish leaders. He died like those whose cause he championed—the disinherited—and if we are to believe the most primitive Passion accounts, with a fear of being abandoned by his Father as well.

And then something extraordinary happened, so extraordinary in fact that suddenly the frightened and scattered disciples became bold heralds, the preacher now the subject of their preaching. Kung's handling of the Resurrection accounts and of their subsequent interpretations reveals in brief compass his method of dealing with complex questions. First of all, he argues convincingly from the New Testament evidence that something more than a psychic quirk or an historical ruse is at issue. Jesus died and then was experienced by his followers as being alive, but not in the manner of a resuscitated corpse. God, the Creator and Conserver of life, had bestowed on him a wholly new existence, which was quickly associated, especially in light of Jesus's own preaching, with the Jewish expectation of the resurrection of the dead at the end of time. But it was emphatically the same Jesus, and so as long as we don't become too materialistic about it, we can speak of his "bodily resurrection." In classical homiletic style (a recurrent feature of the book), Kung returns to this basic point several times, attempting to separate the essential message from legendary and other accretions. He perhaps overplays his dismissal of the importance of the "empty tomb" or the "appearances" as evidence of the Resurrection, but he seizes the main point and presents it clearly: "The living Christ and through him the living God, who called him from death to life, are the object of the Easter faith."

This passion for getting at essentials is, not surprisingly, the strength and weakness of this book as an introduction to Christianity. Better than any other theologian I can readily think of, Kung can read the "signs of the times," especially when it comes to gauging the skeptical temper of his contemporaries; he also combines a wide knowledge of Scripture scholarship with a sure grasp of more philosophical theology. But in his eagerness to get back to the basic New Testament message, he often gives the impression that theological and doctrinal development over the past two millenia has largely meant distortion. One example: He is right, I think, in insisting that many of the Hellenistic distinctions (for example, person and nature, consubstantiality) used in Trinitarian and Christological formulas no longer speak to the modern mind, indeed, often confuse it. But the question remains whether a theology that remains satisfied with describing what Jesus does without asking what and who he is does sufficient justice to the mystery of Jesus and his Father as revealed in the whole New Testament. Similar questions could be raised about his dismissive treatment of the Marian doctrines and of the priestly significance of Christian ministry.

It is in specifically ecclesiastical matters, however, that Kung's cherished objectivity fails him most, to be replaced by an unpleasant haranguing tone. In an example of rhetorical overkill, he attributes the lack of a section on "prayer, meditation and Christian worship," no doubt accurately but not very gracefully, to his time-consuming battles with "the Roman Inquisition." Did the already enormous size of the book have something to do with that decision as well? One wonders at the buck-passing.

But Kung's achievement rises above such quibbles, if not above serious theological disagreement. He recently described himself as a "centrist," and though more conservative Christians may scoff at such a designation, it rings true for most of this book. He reminds proponents of "political theology" that others traveled that same road, from the right, in pre-Nazi Germany, and he warns church leaders that a primacy built on privilege is neither consistent with the New Testament nor convincing to 20th-century believers.

Beyond this balancing act, however, Kung has done something much more significant. He has captured some of the liberating power of the earliest Christian preaching and translated it into contemporary terms. Belief in the Crucifixion is not very hard to come by these days (or any days): one only has to look around. But to believe that it was precisely the Crucified One whom God raised from the dead as a sign of His free and complete commitment to human kind is a staggering thought—almost too good to be true. Such faith, Hans Kung reassures us once again, is what being a Christian is all about.

Andrew M. Greeley (review date 19 December 1976)

SOURCE: "Hans Küng: Embattled Teacher and Priest," in *New York Times Book Review,* December 19, 1976, pp. 5, 16.

[*In the following review, Greeley praises Küng's* On Being a Christian *for the author's scholarly and truthful approach.*]

The controversial Swiss theologian Hans Küng has written the best defense of traditional Catholic Christianity to appear in this century. *Christ Sein* sold several hundred thousand copies in its German edition and was on the best seller lists in Germany for several months. It is unlikely, however, that so many American Catholics have the intellectual discipline to plow through a 720-page book on their faith, and more's the pity. They will miss what may well become a religious and spiritual classic.

Küng has earned himself the reputation of being a "radical" by being severely critical of the way authority has been exercised in Rome and by questioning some of the doctrinal foundations of that exercise of authority. In fact, however, he has always been a profoundly conservative person; his concern about the style of papal leadership and the theory behind it has been based on a conviction about the importance of the papacy—a conviction that many other less controversial Catholic theologians have long since given up.

Küng divides his large volume[, *On Being Christian,*] into four major sections, "The Horizon," "The Distinction," "The Program" and "The Practice." The "horizon" is that dimension of human life that opens us to the uncertainty, the obscurity, but also the possibility of human life:

> *What can we know? Why is there anything at all? Why not nothing? Where does man come from and where does he go to? Why is the world as it is? What is the ultimate reason and meaning of all reality?*
>
> *What ought we to do? Why do what we do? Why and to whom are we finally responsible? What deserves forthright contempt and what love? What is the point of loyalty and friendship, but also what is the point of suffering and sin? What really matters for man?*
>
> *What may we hope? Why are we here? What is it all about? What is there left for us: death, making everything pointless at the end? What will give us courage for life and what courage for death?* (author's italics)

To assert in the face of those questions that one "believes in God" is to assert that the possibility of life is more real than its uncertainties, and the openness of life a better indicator of its meaning than its ultimate closing in death. It is not a totally rational decision made by the intellect; it is rather a leap—not altogether unreasonable but surely not forced by reason—of the whole human personality in the direction of goodness and possibility.

The special "distinction" added by Christianity to this commitment is to claim that in Jesus that to which we are asked to commit ourselves has been most adequately revealed.

The "program" follows from the vision of reality to be observed in Jesus: a vision in which good and evil are inextricably mixed, with good finally edging out evil by suffering all that evil can do to it and still surviving and living again in God's power.

> The cross then is not only example and model, but ground, strength and norm of the Christian faith: the great distinctive reality which distinguishes this faith and its Lord in the world market from the religious and irreligious ideologies, from other competing religions and utopias and their lords, and plunges its roots at the same time into the reality of concrete life with its conflicts. The cross separates the Christian faith from unbelief and superstition. The cross certainly in the light of the resurrection, but also the resurrection in the shadow of the cross.

If one accepts such a "program," then one is committed to a "practice" of loving service to other human beings. The Christian will minister to others in *"unconditional trust, goodness, giving, loving good will, in advance and without any compelling reasons. And in all this he will refuse to let anything deter him."* (author's italics)

It is not a new idea, but one that has not been much honored in practice, despite its antiquity. The genius of **Christ Sein** is not so much the new things Küng says but his way of saying old things in such new ways, so that one is struck again with the perennial novelty of their challenge. You mean we are *really* supposed to live that way? You gotta be kidding.

Hans Küng is anything but a romantic. He is as severe in his critique of the religions of the third world and of the currently fashionable liberation theology as he is of the exercise of power in the Roman curia. One begins to see why Küng gets into trouble: His careful integrity does not permit him unreserved enthusiasm for any human institution or any "movement." Thus to write in the face of the current theological enthusiasm for Karl Marx that a "Christian may be a socialist but need not be one" is to strike a balance that the romantics of the day find unacceptable. And to insist that no substitute for capitalism has been able thus far to avoid making things worse is an intolerable affront to the fashionable theological left. But Küng's integrity is such that he will risk their ire as much as he risks the ire of the Vatican bureaucrats.

For all its command of the scholarly literature and all its rigorous intellectual honesty, **On Being a Christian** is neither a dull nor a lifeless book. Küng made the decision to let his own personality show through, to let the reader share in the excitement of his quest and the passion of his faith. One comes away from the book knowing a lot more about the challenge of the Christian life, and also with a clear picture of a priest and scholar who is doing his best to live that life no matter what the cost in professional envy and institutional isolation.

James C. Logan (review date 13 September 1978)

SOURCE: "A Passionate Participant," in *Christian Century,* Vol. XCV, No. 28, September 13, 1978, pp. 832-33.

[*In the following review, Logan asserts that Küng's* Signposts for the Future *shows the personal side of the author's Christianity.*]

Usually a collection of essays such as [*Signposts for the Future*] (by a leading theologian covering a wide range of topics) is a disappointment. Either the essays were written prior to the publication of a major work which says the same thing better, or the essays are dribblings left over from a major work and simply offer the publisher an opportunity to cash in. In either case, the net result is redundancy.

While there is nothing startlingly new in Küng's volume of essays it does something which his previous works do only indirectly. These essays allow the reader to see Küng—the man and the Christian—in a way which earlier books only hint at. *Signposts* provides a clear picture of a theologian who is intellectually candid while being a passionate participant in the church of Christ.

Part one ("On Being a Christian: Twenty Theses") is a propositional outline of Küng's recent major work. The theses will be of considerable help for those studying the larger volume; the theological questions which arise from the earlier work persist. Küng is clearer in what he rejects than in what he affirms regarding the uniqueness and absoluteness of Jesus Christ. That Christ enables the Christian to be "truly human" is still maintained with the same ambiguity surrounding that phrase. Küng summarizes the doctrine of the redemptive death of Christ as "the fulfillment of the curse of the law" whereby "Jesus becomes the representative of lawbreakers, of sinners." Accompanying this summary is a strong emphasis on Jesus as "a basic model of a view of life and practice of life to be realized in many ways." To be sure, Küng is no Abelardian in his doctrine of the atonement, but neither is he Anselmian. He doesn't have to be either! But it is not clear how Jesus the "representative" and Jesus the "model" are ever brought together in a coherent interpretation of his passion and death. Nevertheless, Küng has attempted a Christology "from below" which deals honestly with many questions being asked today by thoughtful Christians. It is unclear, however, whether the task ahead is one of theological tidying up or of significant modification.

Part two really should be divided into two sections; the material has two definite foci. The first is on the Christian in society, the second on the Christian in the internal life of the church. In part two we gain real insight into the personal ecumenism of the author and his passionate commitment to the church. Küng's ecumenism has at least three dimensions. First is a human ecumenism which embraces the whole human family as well as the church. Küng rejects any ideas that Jesus was a "revolutionary" or an "enthusiast." What Jesus called for was the strict requirement of inner freedom from possessions—a "poverty of spirit" which renounces "something for the other person, so that we do not prove to be slaves of our possessions but try to use them to serve others."

Here is also a transreligious ecumenism. Küng demonstrates his ecumenical spirit in a most insightful dialogue with Jewish scholar Pinchas Lapide about the meaning of Jesus. Third is a transconfessional ecumenism. Across the historic Protestant/Catholic divide Küng again shows his ecumenical spirit with an "ecumenical inventory," the conclusion of which is that "being truly Christian today means being an *ecumenical Christian.*" Probably nowhere in the book does the irenic spirit of the man ring clearer than in the tribute which Küng presented at the funeral of his old professor, Karl Barth. No one is better prepared than Küng to appreciate the genius of Barth's formulation of the doctrine of justification by grace through faith. After all, he wrote his doctoral dissertation on this very subject. Küng returns to the centrality of grace in the funeral tribute with a masterful pastoral statement sensitive to both the spirit and faith of Barth.

The internal focus upon the church deals with such matters as parties within the church, lay participation in leadership (including elections), women in the church (a short but carefully reasoned statement on their ordination), contemporary worship and finally confirmation. These are weighty theological issues with direct implications for the concrete church. Typically, Küng does not dodge the concrete by escaping into the abstract. Whatever else one may say about his theology, Küng writes to be understood and keeps a steady eye on matters of church praxis.

There are no great surprises in this book. What does greet us is the character of the theologian—a person rendered thoroughly human by his Christianity.

Gerard S. Sloyan (review date 24 November 1978)

SOURCE: A review of *Signposts for the Future,* in *Commonweal,* November 24, 1978, p. 767.

[*In the following review, Sloyan lauds Küng's* Signposts for the Future.]

[*Signposts for the Future*] is a collection of essays, interviews, and one radio dialogue (with Pinchas Lapide) done by the priest of the diocese of Luzern who is professor of dogmatic and ecumenical studies at the state university of Tübingen in Germany. Like anything the embattled Swiss theologian writes, it is well worth examining. Primarily it shows a Catholic reminding fellow-members of his church in whatever station that their fidelity to the person and teaching of Jesus is their best fidelity to God and his Holy Sprit. A church made up of faithful such as these is worth adhering to. Its teaching is their teaching and conversely. The call Jesus of Nazareth issued was to perfect trust in God and to doing his will, which is nothing other than humanity's total well-being. The ethics or behavior of the Christian is the proof of discipleship.

The author is on the firmest ground in discussing the intra-confessional Christian questions that are his specialty. He acknowledges in a preface that the ecumenical dialogue with Jews is comparatively new to him and proves it discussing the church's origins from Israel and the gospel narratives of Jesus's trial in a spirit bordering on New Testament fundamentalism. Balancing this naïveté is a quite splendid discussion of the psychological and sociological problems attending participation in the Sunday worship currently available in Catholic and Protestant churches. Scattered through the book are certain insights of the highest quality—not least of them one by Orthodox Rabbi Lapide, on the resurrection of Jesus, who opts for a biblical and humble "I do not know" in preference to defining *a priori* God's saving action. A similar humility of Professor Küng on other topics marks his many withheld judgments in these thoughtful essays. Other, forceful judgments are not withheld.

Philip E. Devenish (review date June 1985)

SOURCE: A review of *Eternal Life? Life After Death as a*

Medical, Philosophical, and Theological Problem, in *Theological Studies,* Vol. 46, No. 2, June, 1985, pp. 361-62.

[*In the following review, Devenish complains that Küng's* Eternal Life? *fails in comparison to the first two works of the trilogy.*]

In this series of nine public lectures given in Tübingen and Ann Arbor, we have the final installment, [*Eternal Life?*] along with **On Being a Christian** and **Does God Exist?,** of K[üng]'s "trilogy" (xvi). His basic approach parallels that taken in **On Being a Christian.** In the first section, "The Horizon," K[üng] sets the "background" of his question and poses it from the point of view of medicine, contemporary philosophy, and the history of religions. He confronts the reader with a "decision" between "alternatives": "a definitive extinguishing in nothingness or an eternal permanence in being" (68). In the second section, "Hope," he sets out what he takes to be the Christian answer to the question of eternal life. After treating the development of the concept of resurrection in Jewish thought, he sets forth his answer of eternal life as "a new future, wholly different," based on resurrection as "assumption into the absolutely final and absolutely first reality" of God through a consideration of the "difficulties with the resurrection of Jesus" and then discusses attendant issues concerning ascension, descent, and hell (114, 113). In section 3, "The Consequences," K[üng] explores the individual, social, and cosmic dimensions of eternal life for people today. He closes with a brief epilogue, comprising a personal confession.

As always, K[üng] is at his best here in two respects. He can tell you clearly and even movingly what practical difference his subject makes: "A dying in gratitude—this would seem to me to be dying, not only with human dignity, but with Christian dignity" (175). He also conducts a wide-ranging and insightful dialogue with representatives of contemporary culture.

The book is disappointing at several key points. K[üng] bases his Christian answer to the question of eternal life on "the resurrection of Jesus." It is not clear, to me at least, how, if at all, the events of the emergence of Easter faith imply an event of resurrection as their basis. Jesus' followers did, in fact, infer his resurrection from their encounter with the Jesus who had died. But this inference does not show that there ever was such an event. Nor does K[üng] treat this problem elsewhere.

When he discusses the character of eternal life, K[üng] can say that it is a "wholly different, unparalleled, definitive state . . . totally otherwise" (105). Yet he can also hold that "the *consummation* can be described in a dialectical movement of thought: as life, justice, freedom, love, salvation" (220). One runs across the same problem in reading **Does God Exist?:** K[üng] has not developed a theory of theological language that permits one to judge claims such as that eternity, "understood dialectically," is "the temporality which is 'dissolved' (*aufgehoben*) into finality" (221).

Finally, K[üng] at one point places "'faith' in God, in an eternal life" in apposition (78). I am not sure K[üng] is sufficiently aware of the temptation to idolatry here or, for that matter, in making the topic of eternal life a third part of his trilogy. The first two books hang together. This one is the odd man out.

John Bierman (essay date 18 November 1985)

SOURCE: "Rome's Blunt Renegade," in *Maclean's,* Vol. 98, No. 46. November 18, 1985, pp. 5, 8.

[*In the following essay, Bierman discusses Küng's contentious relationship with Pope John Paul II and the Catholic Church.*]

To many conservative Roman Catholics the action appeared treasonous. For many reformists, on the other hand, it seemed courageous. On Oct. 4 and 5, newspapers in Toronto, London, Madrid, Zurich, Hamburg and Rome carried the latest polemic of Dr. Hans Küng, Pope John Paul II's most celebrated and persistent Catholic critic. The two-part article was a 6,000-word onslaught on what Küng says is the reactionary and repressive policies of the pontiff and his church bureaucracy, the Curia. "The old Inquisition is dead; long live the new one," wrote Küng. "'Persistent doubt' about a truth of the faith is punishable with excommunication. No one is burned at the stake any more, but careers and psyches are destroyed as required."

Küng, 57, a professor of theology at West Germany's secular University of Tübingen and currently a visiting professor at the University of Toronto, is one of the world's most celebrated Christian theologians. But even to many of his supporters his latest attack seemed excessive. After all, Küng himself has not even been expelled from the priesthood, despite his own persistent doubts, freely expressed over the years, about such central Catholic beliefs as the Virgin birth and papal infallibility. Still, since 1979 the Vatican has forbidden him to call himself a "Catholic theologian" or to examine candidates for the priesthood. His biographer, Karl-Josef Kuschel, says it was "the blow of his life."

The prohibition might have ended the careers of many Catholic theologians. But, said Urs Baumann, Küng's teaching assistant at the University of Tübingen, which has kept him on despite the censure, "the ban, far from detracting from his following, has greatly increased his stature." Before the Vatican disciplined Küng, his lectures at Tübingen drew an average of 200 students; lately they have attracted as many as 1,000. As well, his widely acknowledged brilliance and his provocative books, **Infallible?—An Inquiry** and **Does God Exist?** have also guaranteed his professional survival.

Despite his fame, Küng recently told *Maclean's* that he was brought "to the brink of breakdown" by the Vatican's lengthy disciplinary procedures, which began in the early

1970s. Said Küng: "These are really authoritarian—even totalitarian—methods. They burn you psychologically." Indeed, in an apparently coincidental action, the week after Küng's articles appeared in *The Globe and Mail* Emmett Cardinal Carter, archbishop of Toronto, issued a lengthy pastoral letter. Carter said that if the "false and exaggerated" ideas of free dissent are allowed to proliferate, "the very unity of the church is in danger."

Küng's current status is a sharp contrast to the 1960s reformist reign of Pope John XXIII. At that time it seemed that the Swiss-born, multilingual Küng—he speaks Greek, Latin, Hebrew, English, French, Spanish, Italian and Dutch as well as his native German—was destined to become one of the towering figures of the church establishment, rather than a rebel. In fact, at 34, he was appointed official theologian to the epochal Second Vatican Council, which was convened in October, 1962, by John XXIII to "let some fresh air into the church." But, in Küng's opinion, subsequent popes reversed the progressive tide of Vatican II on such issues as the woman's role in the church and ecumenical dialogue with other faiths. Said the Swiss theologian bitterly: "John XXIII was seen by most as the living symbol of the new papacy. Now we have again the old papacy. The difference is only that he [John Paul] has a jet."

To laymen Küng would seem to live in a rarefied spiritual and intellectual atmosphere. His personal life is simple and rigorous. Regular jogging, swimming and skiing and a spartan diet keep the 57-year-old thinker fit. Aside from work his passion is music, from Gregorian plainsong to Stravinsky. He also has a gift for down-to-earth communication. Said Kuschel, author of *Hans Küng: His Work & His Way,* published in 1980 by Doubleday: "His teaching style is lively, uncomplicated and contemporary. He reaches people whom no orthodox theologian could hope to approach."

That ability adds to his power as a critic of Rome. Although he describes himself as "the Pope's loyal opposition," Küng makes little attempt to be diplomatic in his criticism of the pontiff. "You must remember," he said, "that John Paul grew up first under the Nazis [in wartime Poland] and then the Communists. He does not understand democracy. Democracy for him means pornography, drugs, consumerism—all very real problems, of course, but only part of the picture. He is now busy proclaiming human rights but he does not see that we have no human rights in the Catholic church."

Still, the acerbic nature of Küng's attacks sets him apart from other dissident Catholic theologians. Holland's Edward Schillebeeckx, whose criticisms have also caused him to be disciplined by the Vatican, argues that Küng's split with Rome is partly his own fault. Said Schillebeeckx: "Had he been more open to compromise and dialogue, it would not have happened." Canadian Catholic theologian Gregory Baum, who described Küng as "enormously gifted, cheerful and warm," added, "Father Küng is very

angry with what is wrong in the church; I am much more angry with what is wrong in the world." But for all Küng's anger, Baum said, "he is essentially a reformer, not a radical."

Many Catholic traditionalists disagree. Father Alphonse de Valk, a teaching father in Toronto, for one, commented in an Oct. 10 letter to *The Globe and Mail:* "If I were him, I would get out [of the church]. Anything else seems dishonest."

But Küng says he will pursue his campaign. "You know," he said, "I would like to work quietly, to listen to music, to live without fuss. But if I gave up, people would say, 'It really *is* a lost cause.'"

Hans Küng with David Toolan (interview date 30 January 1987)

SOURCE: "The Way Forward: Talking with Hans Küng," in *Commonweal,* Vol. CXIV, No. 2, January 30, 1987, pp. 44-5.

[*In the following interview, Küng discusses the current and possible future path of the Catholic Church in terms of reform and tradition.*]

Last November *Commonweal*'s David Toolan spoke with Hans Küng in New York City. Among other topics covered were issues of authority and dissent in the Catholic church today.

[*Toolan:*] *What do you think of the Vatican's current actions?*

[Küng:] If you want an explication of the context of Rome's present attitude, you have to see that the Catholic church in the Second Vatican Council achieved an integration of the two great paradigm changes after the Middle Ages. We integrated the paradigm change of the Reformation: vernacular language, participation of the people in the liturgy and the church, collegiality, people of God. . . . We used the arguments for the vernacular that Martin Luther employed four hundred years ago. But we were not absolutely consistent. Had we been, we would have had to introduce the marriage of priests or optional celibacy. Pushed by the American bishops especially, we also achieved the integration of the modern paradigm: freedom of conscience, freedom of religion, and a new attitude toward Judaism and world religions.

The principal compromise here was that, practically, the bishops were not able to integrate democracy in Rome. It is said that the church is not a democracy, but it's also not a medieval, hierocratic, pre-modern system of the *ancien régime* type either. The whole question today is who will ultimately come through. Will the pope and the curia be able to reimpose on the Catholic community the medieval, Counter-Reformation, anti-modernist paradigm? Or will we finally, despite this setback, move again under a new pope? I am sure that under the present pope nothing will basically move to what I would call the post-modern paradigm—which implies another attitude in most fields.

What would you say, however, if you were trying to find common ground with sensible, critical conservatives? I think of a recent book by Robert Bellah and his colleagues on American culture where the argument is made that our individualism destroys any sense of public good. Sensible conservatives—not reactionaries—are concerned about some very real weaknesses in the Enlightenment paradigm.

I think we progressive theologians could agree to a great extent with conservative thinkers on such a criticism of the modern paradigm. I am also a critic of the Protestant paradigm as divisive and destructive of the unity of believers. It has the consequence of continually dividing people into smaller and smaller churches. So yes, I think we could agree with much conservative criticism of both the Reformation and modern paradigms. I agree with the pope on many of his criticisms of modern society. But the real way is not to go back to Catholic Poland as he believes. The way is to go forward on the line traveled by those people who showed in recent decades that religion can be, at one and the same time, preserving of the old values certainly, but also liberating. I do not see a contradiction in these two functions.

But if the proposal is to go back to an authoritarian religion, then we will only succeed in alienating people within the church and also Protestant churches. I cannot imagine that the Catholic clergy, sisters, intellectuals, and even ordinary people would be willing to go back to the medieval paradigm which prescribes everything in the bedroom. Restoration is the great illusion.

Of course conservatives would claim that they are merely being faithful to the spirit of Vatican II, or to the tradition. The tension I see here seems to lie between the spirit of Vatican II and the Code of Canon Law.

The new code is precisely an expression of the medieval paradigm. For instance, the code puts women in the same state of dependency and inferiority that they suffered in the Middle Ages and before modern times. I mean it is a medieval code. The words are Vatican II but the spirit remains that of medieval clericalism, authoritarianism, and a passive laity.

Hans Küng with David Toolan (interview date 13 March 1987)

SOURCE: "Religions of the One God," in *Commonweal*, Vol. CXIV, No. 5, March 13, 1987, pp. 143, 146-47.

[In the following interview, Küng discusses the similarities and differences between the major world religions and his

attempt to create an understanding among different religions with his book Christianity and the World Religions.]

World religions was the major topic of conversation last fall when *Commonweal*'s David Toolan spoke with Hans Küng in New York City. Küng's comments on authority and dissent within the Catholic church [appear above].

[Toolan:] How did you come to write your current book, **Christianity and the World Religions: Paths of Dialogue with Islam, Hinduism, and Buddhism***? It represents a new direction for you, does it not?*

[Küng:] My interest in world religions goes back to my student days in Rome when I first visited North African Muslim countries. I realized that relating Christianity to world religions is an extremely difficult job to do theologically. You may recall that Chapter Three of *On Being a Christian* contained a big section on world religions as a horizon of Christianity. I indicated there that this relation had to be studied, well aware that I needed many years for that.

Now, after the Roman intervention—which I still find unjust, theologically unfounded, and politically counterproductive—I find myself relieved of a lot of administrative work, faculty meetings, examinations of students, and the responsibility for teaching dogmatics. It has freed me to travel, and given me the opportunity to concentrate on the subject of non-Christian religions and to write this book.

So there have been positive results from Rome's action?

(Laughter) Yes.

This may be one of the ironies of church repression. I seem to recall that Henri de Lubac wrote some of his best books—about Buddhism and atheism—when he was silenced.

Of course I'm still very much involved in the critique of the present reactionary course of Rome. But I did not want to get fixed on those problems. The issues raised by my new book are the problems of the future, the ones Christianity will have to face in its third millennium. To quarrel about birth control, admitting divorced people to the sacraments—these are really problems of the pre-conciliar church.

What do you think the central issues for the post-conciliar third millennium are?

Seen from the outside, it is obvious that many of the world's current conflicts—in Northern Ireland, in the Near East, between Iran and Iraq, between Pakistan and India, in India between Hindus and Sikhs, and previously in Vietnam between Buddhists and a Catholic regime—are heavily influenced by religious motives. I do not want to reduce the military, economic, and political conflicts to religious ones. But my thesis is that these conflicts become bloody and without pity if they are done in the name of God. And so my conclusion is that without peace among the *religions* there will be no peace among the nations.

If we had been able to initiate dialogues between Christians and Moslems twenty years ago when I was in Lebanon with Cardinal Willebrands and Dr. Visser T'Hooft, talking one week with Muslims and the next week with Christians, we could have avoided a great deal of bloodshed. But at that time we were not allowed to meet.

I think we see President Carter more positively today because in the Camp David Accord he really achieved something in this domain, which was possible because both he and Anwar Sadat were religiously motivated to a high degree. To a certain extent Begin was, too. This was a sign that you could have religious peace on religious grounds.

Some time ago, Chancellor Helmut Schmidt told me that when he and Sadat were alone one evening going down the Nile, Sadat said he wanted to have a sanctuary in the Sinai for the three Abrahamic religions. Because, Sadat said, we will never have peace in the Near East without mutual understanding between the three religions. This is not only what is called political theology but a *world political theology*. It will involve all the other questions which are treated in my current book: the problems of whether Islam is a way of salvation, whether Mohammed is an authentic prophet, whether the Koran can be considered the Word of God, and so on. From these high theological positions stem more ordinary problems: the secularization of Islam and Christianity, what the law means in Islam and Judaism and Christianity. In fact, one of the difficulties with the original lectures, from which my current book is drawn, was how to bring all these complex questions into the space of an hour.

Were there any surprises in this interreligious dialogue? Agreements or understandings that hadn't been there for you before?

The whole process was a great adventure. My Tubingen colleagues (van Ess, Stietencron, and Bechert) are highly competent in the fields of Islam, Hinduism, and Buddhism, and I thought my own background in Christian theology would enable me to respond each week to their presentations. The greatest discovery in the process was that you can see Christianity in the mirror of the other religions. This became fascinating. Despite all the divergences, I saw that there were many parallels and convergences—some not at all positive. For instance, it is obvious that Roman Catholicism at present has the same problems as Islam does with religious reformation and with the Enlightenment of modern times. The current Roman regime can be compared to that of the ayatollahs of Iran who are trying to go back to medieval Islam. For both Teheran and Rome, the paradigm of authentic faith is drawn from the Middle Ages, in opposition to nearly everything that came afterward. Both try to go back to a medieval paradigm with various modern adaptations—television, helicopters, jets, and so on.

The use of modern communications means that authorities can make the organization even more centralized than things ever were in the Middle Ages.

Certainly. I found that conservative Judaism, conservative Islam, and conservative Roman Catholicism have very similar attitudes and patterns of behavior. I had a long discussion in Teheran about the case of Galileo. The Muslims defended the pope, and I defended Galileo.

In earlier periods we had Christian specialists in Islam, but Muslims never carefully studied Christianity. The Muslims I have been speaking with on my travels knew next to nothing about the application of historico-critical exegesis to Christianity. Their understanding of Christianity predates the critical approach. But when I was confronted with questions regarding the Incarnation, I was able—because of the basis I had developed in books like *On Being a Christian*—to explain how you can understand the title, Son of God, from a monotheistic Hebrew perspective. If the title is so understood, as it was applied to the kings of Israel and then transferred to Jesus, it does not contradict monotheism. Muslims, I found, were very interested to learn of this common Semitic background to divine sonship. It made for mutual understanding, whereas the Hellenistic background (to the definitions of the councils of Nicaea and Chalcedon) made for misunderstanding.

The same was true in explicating the doctrine of the Trinity. If taken within a Hebrew context, this too could be affirmed without contradicting monotheism. In this way, two hundred years of historical-critical research affords us the possibility of giving very different answers to the old, divisive questions.

I assume that Iranian Muslims would be very reluctant to adopt a historical-critical approach to their own traditions, would they not?

Well, every religion has its neuralgic, non-negotiable points. For Judaism, it's the Land of God; for Christianity, it's the Son of God; and for Islam, it's the Word of God, the Koran. In Teheran, Pakistan, and elsewhere, I would always ask how we can understand the Koran without having to follow it literally—say by cutting off hands and so forth. How were we to understand the revelation of the Koran? Was it possible to understand the Koran as the Word of God and at the same time the word of the prophet? And what does that distinction mean? Is it possible to adapt the great message of the one God, all merciful and compassionate, to the modern situation without taking everything literally?

What was the response to that?

I think it was new for them, and presupposed that you were very positive about Islam as a way to eternal salvation, about Mohammed as an authentic prophet of God, and the Koran as a Word of God. When you had said this quite clearly, they were ready to discuss some other things.

I would say that in the world religions discussion, we are where we were fifty years ago between Protestants and Catholics: I remember that in 1957 when I wrote my dissertation on the doctrine of justification, it was commonly said that justification is the main difference between Protestants and Catholics and there's no common ground there. It was a great surprise, then, when Karl Barth wrote his famous preface to my book on justification, saying that he agreed with my interpretation. After having had so many positive experiences over the last twenty-five years, I am very hopeful that even on these difficult topics—the Son of God, the Land of God, and the Word of God in the three Abrahamic religions—we may yet arrive at mutual understanding.

I do not believe in the unity of all the religions—that is an eschatological problem—as I believe in the unity of Christianity, the unity of Judaism, or the unity of Islam. But I do believe in what I call not the unity but the *peace among different religions*—that we could understand each other as brothers and sisters and not as opponents and enemies. It happened before. Pope John XXIII took up what had been a matter of small, elite groups working in dialogue over several decades. The pope said let us have peace, and somehow it happened: Were the current pope to take up the interreligious dialogue, something momentous might happen again, as rapidly as it did in John XXIII's time.

Brian A. Haggerty (review date 15 March 1989)

SOURCE: A review of *Theology for the Third Millennium: An Ecumenical View*, in *Christian Century,* Vol. 106, No. 9, March 15, 1989, pp. 290-91.

[*In the following review, Haggerty discusses Küng's retrospective look at Christian theology and the development of his own theology in* Theology for the Third Millennium.]

We live life forward but understand it backward, Soren Kierkegaard observed. For Hans Küng, professor of dogmatic and ecumenical theology at the University of Tübingen and theological thorn in the papacy's side, the observation may apply equally well to theology. In fact, it may help explain why Küng has been at odds with Rome for so long.

In the foreward to [*Theology for the Third Millennium*], Küng acknowledges that he has never approached theology by doing a detailed analysis of how theology ought to be done. Rather, he says, challenged by ever-changing human experience, he has dealt directly with the substance of theology, trusting that his work would prove itself by eliciting both Catholic and ecumenical consensus. It is hardly

surprising then that his work has not won acceptance from the Vatican, which has long been attached to doing theology a priori—shunning experiment and downgrading contrary experience.

Looking back on his theological endeavors of the past 30 years and the opposition he has encountered, Küng concludes that there has been a paradigm change in theology, a change in the basic model of explanation—one that has certainly escaped the attention of Roman Catholicism's theological gatekeepers. The author attempts to sketch what that change has involved and to "help religion perform a new critical and liberating function of both the individual and society."

Küng begins by trying to clear up a number of classical theological conflicts left over from the Enlightenment and Reformation: conflicts between theology and magisterium, Scripture and tradition, Scripture and the church, and scriptural exegesis and dogma. He concludes in each case that it is not a matter of accepting one or the other, or of assigning priority to one, but of recognizing that none of these sources of Christian understanding is unconditionally reliable. Only God, who spoke to believers through Jesus Christ, is worthy of unreserved trust. However, Küng gives Scripture primacy as the source and measure of faith and theology in the church. His emphasis, though hardly startling, still leaves unanswered questions of how Scripture is to be understood and what emphasis church authority, tradition and theology should be given in interpreting it.

Küng devotes the core of the book to defining and discussing the implications of the apparent paradigm change in theology. He borrows the term from science and uses the work of American physicist and historian of science Thomas S. Kuhn to explain how knowledge emerges, progresses and evolves. A paradigm, he says, is "an entire constellation of beliefs, values, techniques, and so on shared by members of a given community." Just as Kuhn finds a connection between conceptual changes in science and the replacement of one paradigm, or model of interpretation, with another, so Küng finds a similar progress and transition of knowledge in theology. When a new paradigm arises in Christian theology, however, unlike in science, it cannot completely replace or suppress the old paradigm because Christian testimony, found in the gospel, is permanent. It is common to those who accept the old paradigm and to those who advance the new, and it calls both to judgment.

After tracing the paradigm changes in the history of Christian theology and the church, Küng sketches the characteristics of the postmodern paradigm that he believes has emerged as a guide for theological understanding. From it, he says, emerges a theology that offers a thoughtful account of faith; one that is free to profess and publish its reasonable convictions; one that honors methodological discipline and church supervision; and one that is oriented toward understanding not only other Christian theologies but other cultures, religions, ideologies and sciences. Indeed, for Küng, the world of experience provides the horizon against which contemporary theology must be done. Doing theology is no longer a matter of merely applying a timeless doctrine but of translating a historical message "from the world of past experience into our present-day world of experience."

Theology for the Third Millennium is not a book for the casual reader. Küng is not a prose stylist; his complex treatment of the subject demands careful reading and rereading. This task is made more difficult by the way most of the chapters seem to have been forged out of pieces that have appeared elsewhere. And the book is riddled with more typographical errors and copy-editing oversights than one would expect from Doubleday. Nonetheless, diligent readers will be rewarded for their efforts. In seeking to understand his own theology in retrospect, Küng also sheds light on the work of many of his colleagues, both those who agree with him and those who do not.

Clyde F. Crews (review date 7-14 February 1990)

SOURCE: A review of *Paradigm Change in Theology*, in *Christian Century*, Vol. 107, No. 5, February 7-14, 1990, pp. 254, 256.

[*In the following review, Crews discusses the exploration of pardigmatic studies by major theologians in* Paradigm Change in Theology, *edited by Küng and David Tracy.*]

"Take my hand," began a song in the 1953 musical *Kismet*, "I'm a stranger in paradise." Those who have been off the theological planet for the past few years could substitute the word "paradigm" at the end of that phrase. Paradigmatic studies became coin of the realm in the '80s. To round out the decade, Hans Küng and David Tracy directed an international symposium of some 70 thinkers to explore the topic in occasionally exhausting detail. A gathering at the University of Tübingen brought together both Protestant and Catholic theologians, including Baum, Boff, Cobb, Gilkey, Marty, Metz, Moltmann, Ogden, Ricoeur and Schillebeeckx. The resulting text[, ***Paradigm Change in Theology,***] provides some wonderful summations of postwar developments in science (Matthew Lamb and Stephen Toulmin) and in theology (Anne Carr and Leonardo Boff). But this book calls for intensive reading and is far from being a primer on the subject. Strangers in paradigm need not apply.

The study is divided into preparatory papers—three in systematics and four in historical analysis—and the symposium presentations themselves, covering such areas as scientific theory, biblical theology, philosophy, history and political and global issues. The symposium responded to Thomas Kuhn's nearly classic definition of paradigm as "an entire constellation of beliefs, values, techniques and

so on shared by the members of a given community," alongside the postmodern awareness that theology and science both go about their business paradigmatically. In addition, Küng provided a leitmotif for the proceedings with his insistent question: "Where do we stand, those of us who have to do theology with Auschwitz, Hiroshima and the Gulag Archipelago at our backs?" Küng's preparatory paper is especially useful in its delineation of a series of macromodels in theology: Greek Alexandrine, Latin Augustinian, medieval Thomist, Reformation, Protestant orthodox and contemporary interpretive.

In a text as complex as this one, there are some surprisingly epigrammatic moments: "Theology," writes Gregory Baum, "unlike the sciences, may and must learn from the unlearned." And Tracy suggests, "We belong to history far more than history belongs to us." While the participants became a bit recondite at times, there are dashes of reality: Norbert Geinacher points to nuclear missiles and devastated forests near the conference site, while Martin Marty notes that traditional bases of the theological enterprise— the printed text and the exclusive academic setting—are themselves undergoing rapid transformation.

Küng himself provides the best review of the symposium, masterfully assessing the differences between and commonalities among the participants. In the process he provides a catalog of the crises facing both theology and science, including the end of Western hegemony, the social antagonism of repressive structures, the undermining of solidifying symbols of a culture, and historical catastrophe.

One final and minimal irony of this book: some of the foremost theological historians met, yet in 488 pages no one thought to provide the reader with the date of the convocation—May 23-26, 1983. A slight and forgivable fact surely, but for an enterprise so deeply concerned with gestalt and contextualization, perhaps just a trifle embarrassing.

Byron C. Lambert (essay date Summer 1990)

SOURCE: "Reflections on Hans Küng's *Theology for the Third Millennium*," in *Modern Age,* Vol. 33, No. 2, Summer, 1990, pp. 157-64.

[*In the following essay, Lambert outlines Küng's vision for the Church in the twenty-first century as expressed in his* Theology for the Third Millennium.]

If Erasmus returned to the earth today would he be a Catholic or a Protestant? There is one who believes he would be a Küngian.

Hans Küng, Catholic theologian at Germany's University of Tübingen, whose books, ***On Being a Christian*** and ***Does God Exist?,*** provoked broad discussion in the seventies among both Catholics and Protestants, has brought his thinking of the past thirty years into focus with another book, *Theology for the Third Millennium: An Ecumenical View.*[1] Küng believes the Church is drifting into the postmodern age without any sense of where it is going and so offers a proposal to set it on a true course, one which will not only guarantee the Church's survival but also help it find common ground with other great world religions.

Küng's program calls for more than casual review, since he is regarded by many Protestants to be the Catholic of the future and a prophet of Christian restoration and unity.[2] He is certainly not unrepresentative of certain Catholic thinking I have run into despite his conflict with the Curia, and so is not ignorable by Catholics either. I do not know what the Eastern Orthodox think of him, but he includes them too in his wide-sweeping trimillennial vision.

Küng's project is complex. I propose to examine only his notion of managing theology in the postmodern age, what he means by the Gospel and truth, and where he thinks Christianity is going in the next millennium.[3]

THE POSTMODERN PARADIGM

Küng holds the division of Christendom in the sixteenth century was a disaster from which the Church has never recovered. What was needed at the time was an Erasmus without the historical Erasmus's flight from commitment, a weakness which allowed the Church to be torn between Luther's fanatical excesses and Rome's blind intransigence.[4] Küng, perhaps, thinks of himself as the Erasmus of today, as he calls for a revival of biblical thinking without biblicism, a renewal of tradition without traditionalism, and a restoration of Christian authority without authoritarianism.[5]

Küng puts it simply: the Church has lost the world. The modern age is dead; the new age, the "postmodern," is here; and the Church has no credible relation to either. He does not want Christians to give up the triumphs of the Enlightenment—scientific method and the democratic process, but does want them to move beyond "the superstitious faith in reason and progress." A new religiousness has taken off on its own outside the Church, he maintains, and its energies must be engaged in reconstructing the Christianity of the future.[6]

Küng finds Thomas S. Kuhn's *The Structure of Scientific Revolutions* suggestive for what he would like to see done in Christian theology.[7] Kuhn, in that now famous book, argues that new hypotheses in science arise through what he calls "paradigm changes" in scientific thought, those global shifts in theory, like Newton's and Einstein's physics, which turn science in fundamentally new directions. Although the new theoretical models build on the methodology accepted in their time, they push those systems into breakdown by creating questions beyond their power to answer. The result is that, partly through rational and partly through irrational gropings, a novel scientific insight, adequate to the questions, arises. Meeting resistance at first, it weaves a pattern of credible data

around itself and becomes the only thing thinkable. Kuhn holds that no old model can be replaced until a new one is ready; and that the new model can even get shelved briefly, while the necessary psychological and institutional changes necessary to receive it get moved into place. Witness the resistance to the work of Galileo. Kuhn believes that science is now entering a new "third" phase, in which the positivist falsification method will yield to a more holistic inductive approach.[8]

Küng says the theological epochs through which Christian thinking has passed can be understood in terms of Kuhn's paradigm analysis.[9] "Macro-paradigms" in theology can be illustrated by the Augustinian and Thomistic revolutions; "meso-paradigms" by the intermediate shifts in thinking like those surrounding the idea of grace or those in sacramental theology; and "micro-paradigms" by the debates over the hypostatic union in Christology.[10] Küng acknowledges that Kuhn's theory constitutes a problem for theology, for while science can treat every paradigm as "provisory," theology must hold to a continuing truth that doesn't so much need *dis*covering as *re*covering.

Distinguishing between theological and scientific paradigm upheavals, Küng states that Christian theology is "essentially defined by its relation to history," especially to its origins. The primal testimony, the New Testament, remains "its continual reflexive point." All the historic creeds and theologies take as a presupposition that the Gospel as presented in Scripture is the norm of Christian thought.[11] Changes in theology take place on the *basis* of the Gospel, but never *against* the Gospel, he asserts. The "norming norm" (*norma normans*) of the living Word always corrects all historic "normed norms" (*norma normata*), those creedal standards by which the Church has met the challenges to its teaching. Changes in theological history, however, in contrast to shifts in scientific history, tend to come about regrettably through defiance and condemnation, shelving new ideas by suppressing their discussion, then transforming accepted new models into iron dogma.[12]

What theological model is right for the postmodern era? Küng answers that it must be "true" (neither conformist nor opportunistic), "free" (non-authoritarian), "critical" (non-traditionalistic), and "ecumenical" (non-denominational). The two constants for this theology are (1) the ever-changing world and (2) the never-changing Gospel.[13]

In 1983, an International Ecumenical Symposium took place in Tübingen, in which Küng was a participant along with theological notables like Langdon Gilkey (Chicago), Jürgen Moltmann (Tübingen), J. B. Metz (Münster), Jean-Pierre Jossua (Paris), Edward Shillebeeckx (Nijmegen), Mariasussi Dhavamony (Rome), to name a few. The symposium took up the paradigm approach as a means of piloting Christian theology through the postmodern crisis. Kuhn was invited, but could not be present; Stephen Toulmin, of Chicago, a student of developing scientific concepts and critic of Kuhn, was present and helped shape the discussions.[14] It was concluded by all present that while no one theologian or theology can create a paradigm change, every theologian must face the question of whether his thinking meets the paradigm expectations of his time.[15] The symposium believed there were some matters that "we don't have to argue about anymore": the polycentrism of the political world, the ambiguous powers of technology for good or ill, persisting social antagonisms, the weakening of the belief in progress, the threat to the university world and "book" culture by the spread of specialization, the jolt to Christianity as the one, true religion, and the awakening of suffering minorities, especially women.[16] From the distance of just six years one can see the costive leftward tilt of such ecumenism.

Further illustrative of the quite un-Erasmus-like extremes to which the conferees gave utterance was the outline of the four dimensions which are to be translated into theological reality: (1) the *biblical,* in which theology must remain true to the "one constant" of the Gospel while subjecting Scripture to historico-critical exegesis and demasculinizing biblical terminology; (2) the *historical,* in which the universal relativism of liberal humanism is replaced with "the relativism of a universal network of connections" (time reconceived as a "web" instead of a "line") and in which there will be created a viable symbiosis (!) between history and the environment with a view to world peace; (3) the *ecumenical,* in which Christian thought moves from a denominational-controversial style to an inclusive, "relatively absolute" (!) style, reading the Scripture in the "Indian" (Far Eastern) manner and paving the way through an "inner Christian ecumene" for a future ecumene of all religions; (4) the *political,* in which is born a new whole-world political consciousness. The symposium couldn't decide whether European or Latin American liberation theology would prevail in the struggle against fringe colonialism, but agreed that there had to be theological diversity in the postmodern paradigm. Küng summarizes the ethos of this new "critical ecumenical" theology as *both* Catholic and Protestant, traditional and contemporary, Christocentric and ecumenical, scholarly and practical.[17] No Christian point of view, whatever its origin, is to be left out of the communal process.

MANAGING THE PARADIGM SHIFTS

Putting aside Küng's summary of the ethos of critical ecumenical theology, from which it would be difficult to demure, given its limitless inclusiveness, if one takes up the "no longer debatable" assumptions that the International Ecumenical Symposium accepted as operative for postmodernism and the four dimensions which the conferees said must be translated into theological reality, one is puzzled about the shape of the paradigm under discussion. Is there a clue as to which of the postmodern leitmotifs is fundamental to the rest? Most models of understanding which alter history seem, in retrospect, to have been determined by seminal work in a single arena of thought, or even by a single figure: the apostolic age,

the work of Augustine, or Aquinas's recovery of Aristotelianism. We deal here with what Jacob Burckhardt aptly called "the theory of storms."[18] Paradigm changes are immensely complex, this the symposium confessed.[19] Yet in the tabulation of "musts" the symposium asks postmodern theology to take up some issues which seem less than paradigmatic; in fact one might ask whether the whole set together constitute a credible paradigm. What mysterious mustering of ontic shocks does "the relationism of a universal network of connections" point to? What epistemic metamorphosis is a "relatively absolute" style of ecumenical conversation coming to grips with? Does the advocacy of an "Indian" way of reading the Bible or demasculinizing biblical terminology amount to anything more than surrender to current politico-expository rages? How permanent is the concussion of specialization on the life of high culture? Isn't the damage to intellectual life more in the way of a "capitulation of the clerks"? Isn't what Küng and the symposium ask theology to do, despite their objections to the domestication of Christianity by Western culture, really a step toward the assimilation of Christianity to a vague, even Eastern religionism?

What *is* postmodernism? Used first as an appellative for changes in architecture . . . àla Mies van der Rohe and Frank Lloyd Wright, it then invaded the other arts to denote anything anti-traditional, even nihilistic. Küng uses the term simply as a heuristic device, although preferring the term "ecumenical" to describe the presuppositional changes through which the world is moving.[20] Modernity's confidence in enlightened reason, science, and progress is giving way, he says, to something not yet nameable. Central to this change, however, is a world religious crisis. The duty of theologians, thus, is to "sublate" the repressed dimensions of modernity, especially those of religion, "to produce a new, liberating, enriching effect."[21]

Postmodernism, thus, is little more than a tag for something ambivalent, even indeterminate.

Are immediately visible alterations in scientific theory, social arrangements, or political enthusiasm portents of global shifts in human consciousness? If they are, can they be programmed for? It is vital to recognize the challenges to faith that arise, but can one build a *heilsgeschichtliche* technique which will enable the Church to meet religious assaults for the next one thousand years? Even the next one hundred? One can be pardoned for being skeptical when programs like those of Küng are put before the Christian public.

What "world" is Küng talking about? We cannot blame Küng for missing the recent tidal shifts in the communist world, but were there not signs of a boom in the world market economy during the eighties? Surely, it was not unknown in 1983 that technology was changing the character of labor. The symposium drops not one tear over family disintegration in the West. How were these issues missed?

What "theologians" is Küng talking about? Küng is no stick-in-the-mud. He confesses that theological subjects and locales can change: "[N]ot only the university, but the case community can be a place for theology."[22] Non-academic types can participate—industrialists, engineers, seamen—anyone who has a serious theological interest. Yet he appears to set aside as of no consequence the thinking of rapidly growing fundamentalists, evangelicals, and traditional Catholics. Shouldn't the Church in its entirety be represented at ecumenical paradigm conferences? "Ideological opponents are neither to be ignored nor labeled as heretics," he asserts.[23] Where, then, are the exegetical scholars like F. F. Bruce and George Eldon Ladd, the theologians like Bernard Lonergan and Carl F. H. Henry, the historians of thought like Russell Kirk and Thomas Molnar, journalists like William F. Buckley and George Will, scientists like Stanley Jaki?

What "theologies" get included? Where do the humble sects come in—the Mennonites, the holiness alliances, the charismatics? Do fringe groups like Jehovah's Witnesses, Christian Scientists, and Mormons have a word of faith for the ecumene? Küng's proposals seem addressed to a very exclusive circle whose thinking is congruent with the outer limits of mainline Protestantism. Küng has even less longitudinal sympathy, the kind that embraces the triumphant dead. Augustine, Aquinas, yea even Peter and Paul, are all to be brought under the corrective ordination of the new paradigm.[24]

Most conservatives would share Küng's belief that the death of religion expected in late modernity (Marx, Nietzsche) has not taken place and that what is at issue is not "forgetfulness of being" (Heidegger) but forgetfulness of God (Buber).[25] This presupposition, however, is hardly enough to warm one up to Küng's ecumenism.

KÜNG AND THE TRUTH

"There can be no true Church without a true theology," he announces. Christianity needs "a thinking account of faith that seeks and says Christian truth in truthfulness."[26] These statements present Küng's first criterion for the new theological paradigm.

All theological truth is to be measured, he writes, by "the Gospel." Even the New Testament must be measured by the Gospel, since the New Testament is a collection of apostolic and sub-apostolic responses to the original oral *kerygma* concerning Christ. In fact, according to Küng, the New Testament is the first instance of adapting the Gospel to a thought-world receiving it and thus provides a model of how Christians of every age are to rethink the Word of God in terms of the ever-changing paradigms controlling their discourse.[27] Küng couldn't be more specific:

> The common key experience of salvation in Israel and Jesus as coming from God is never given "pure," but always through varying modes of interpretation, through varying sorts of concepts and images, schemata and models of understanding. These can be concepts such as "Son of Man" and "Son of God," images such as the descent into hell and the ascent into heaven, individual schemata such as bloody sacrifice of atone-

ment and ransoming of slaves in the doctrine of redemption, whole models of understanding such as the apocalyptic vision of the end of time. . ..: they all derive from a *past* world of experience and language, which for the most part no longer speaks directly to us.[28]

What needs to be done?

> . . . [T]he crucial point is that . . . the Gospel . . . once again be heard afresh *and* understood. . . . Theology, then, is interested not just in a simple "application" of a supposedly eternal doctrine, but rather in the "trans-lation" of a historical message . . . into our present-day world of experience.[29]

He asks,

> What then should decide the issue in the crucial first-and-last questions affecting man and humanity? The biblical experiences, the Christian message, the Gospel, Jesus Christ himself. For this Christ Jesus is in person the "essence of Christianity," the "Christian message," the "Gospel" itself, indeed God's "Word," "made flesh."[30]

The test of all theological truth, then, is the Gospel. But what is the Gospel? Scanning Küng's language at this point is a test in reading. In one statement above the Good News has a threefold character: (1) "biblical experiences," (2) "the Christian message" ("Gospel" is in apposition to this?), and (3) "Jesus Christ himself." The phrases in the series, by no means identical, move as if by subliminal direction from experience through speech to personal reality as if one were doing the most obvious thing in the world. Küng teases logic while weaving a spell in order to say that Christian truth is a non-propositional Person: "for this Christ Jesus is in person the 'essence of Christianity' . . . the 'Gospel' itself."

What is gained by metamorphizing the *kerygma* into a numinous presence, even if the presence is that of the living Christ? Well, it removes the embarrassment of propositional revelation for one thing. God can thus reveal himself immanently within human experience; and since, on Küng's terms, human experience is already saturated with pre-understandings which shape revelation as it arrives, the Gospel is always relative to its time. If the New Testament writers use the only apparatus available to them—the legendary-miraculous, their schematic cannot be binding on us. To be faithful to Saints John and Paul we must use non-supernaturalistic keys to unlock the Word for our day.

Küng's principle, however, undermines his assertion that the Gospel brings all theologies under judgment. The nominalism of his formative notion does just the reverse of what he affirms: it focuses the weight of interest on the interpreting instead of on the thing to be interpreted. If this is the case, are age-old narratives and concepts ever disposable? Does not continuity in Christian belief, on its nearer, more accessible human side, mean we have to focus on *all* interpretive models, not just our own, as a way to discovering the *aletheia* of Scripture? Surely, if the older models were so potent a source of discovery in their time, shouldn't something of rare perspicacity be left over in them by which we can be enriched? If the Church includes the mighty dead in glory, would not churchly continuity suggest we are in interpretive communion with Christian experience in all its catholicity?

More directly, one can raise the epistemological question of how we can "experience" Jesus apart from all authoritative criteria of faith, such as are found in the canonical texts. Abandoning these, how does one know, in publicly persuasive terms, that he is in touch with the "Living Word"? When is a "presence" *the* Presence?

Küng protests that he does not want to break with tradition, only decalcify it.[31] The Gospel will take care that old paradigms are not wholly repressed.[32] The antique modalities, however, must never get in the way of the living Christ nor be equated with his truth.[33] The criterion has to be "understood in and through the *experiences* that believers have had, in very different ways, in this history with their God."[34] The truth of Scripture can only be revealed to faith. We must bring faith *to* the testimony, we cannot get it from the testimony.[35] One asks what kind of credulity is here being demanded of the seeker that couldn't with equal justification be demanded were he confronted with the *Zend-Avesta*?

Most orthodox Christians could accept Küng's position that the Bible is a gathering into one the many experiences believers have had in history with their God; but if "experience" is taken as something nonverifiable either historically or rationally, even the most sympathetic reader must fall into bewilderment.

It is clear that Küng is using the word *truth* axiologically. He treats truth sheerly as a value.[36] His program is addressed not to the intellect but to the will. He has no criterion of truth to offer but that of being reasonable and open. When is one's faith a "true" faith? Why, when it is trusting. The fundamental *a priori* of all knowing, he argues, is *trust*.

> . . . [T]he very act of having this basic trust reveals an original rationality, an inner reasonableness: a basic trust that in this so broken world can be experienced as a gift.[37]

Has Küng happened on a new Cartesian certainty? I reason as if I could, therefore I can! If he has, he vitiates his discovery by adding that this rationality is "original" (does he mean a founding act of consciousness or something simply unique?); or further, when he describes this trust as "inner reasonableness" (is reasonableness ever anything but "inner," or does he mean "innate"?); and still further, when he states that this basic trust is a "gift." Does he mean a "given"? But Küng ranges from the discursive to the devotional with mystifying agility.

Küng's implicit usage contradicts his explicit teaching. The truth in Christianity, he is declaring, is its ethical adaptability to the changing paradigms of discourse

through the Christian's ineffable relationship to Christ. It is on the basis of this judgment that we are to go on agreeing with all the rest he says. But to say this is to be propositional not numinous. Dare we then go on to believe that there are only propositional truths *about* Christianity, but none *in* Christianity?

CHRISTIANITY AND OTHER RELIGIONS

In the third, climactic section of his book, "A New Departure Toward a Theology of the World Religions," the true *telos* of Küng's critical ecumenism comes into view. He asks the question, "Is there one true religion?"

His answer? From the outside (*i.e.,* objectively) there are many true religions; from the inside (subjectively) there is only one—*mine*.[38] There is no neutral position from which one can see which religion is the true one.[39] What then can one do? Confess his "historically conditioned position" and say, "Since I cannot possibly take all the paths at the same time, I'll take the one I know."[40] We must realize, Küng argues, that real Christians, after all, have never believed in Christianity, but in Christ. The *living* Word is their regulative theological principle.[41] Forgetting this, Christians over the centuries have fallen into *untrue* religion. Prophets have had to arise in the Church and "enlightened ones" outside the Church to call the faithful back to this truth, "among whom the prophet Muhammed and the Buddha should no doubt be included *par excellence*."[42]

There is no Christianity-in-itself, no Buddhism-in-itself, he advises. No given configuration of a religion should be considered its one holy form.[43] During its history a religion wears many faces. Is the real for religion, then, the apparent? Once again Küng's theology hovers on suicide, for if a religion is whatever it happens to be at a certain time and place, then there are no untrue versions into which that faith can fall, nor need any prophets arise to correct them.

The *intentio* of his theology is consistent when he winds up by saying that Christianity, like all religions, is *in via* ("on the way"). In the end, he pronounces, no religion will be left standing, only "the one Inexpressible, to whom all religions are oriented."[44]

But wait. There *is* a test for true religion, one to which every religion must submit. A religion is true, he tergiversates, *when it promotes human flourishing*—when it creates social solidarity and tolerance, when it replaces ecclesiocentrism with philanthropy, when it relativizes religious constitutions for human good:

> This means that the more humane (in the spirit of the Sermon on the Mount) Christianity is, the more it appears to the outside as a true religion.[45]

And so the pragmatist, not the existentialist, test prevails.

I have not seen the German edition of Küng's book, so I cannot be certain what word is being translated by Heinegg to give *humane* in English. Judging from Küng's approach, I am sure that the sentimental-humanitarian reading is accurate. It is clear Küng cannot understand at least one strand of New Testament theology if he thinks the Sermon on the Mount is humane. It is true that in the opening beatitudes certain qualities of life, like poverty of spirit, meekness, and purity of heart are praised, but thereafter the severest burdens of discipleship are imposed on the believer, even to the climactic, "Be ye perfect, even as your Father in Heaven is perfect."[46] "Humane" for whom?

Küng shows only a conventional knowledge of Hinduism and Buddhism, both of which are based on the profoundest pessimism about the nature of existence and hold that deliverance from the horrors of karma is achieved by the nihilation of consciousness (*moksha*). The Buddha's originality consisted in offering a way of meditation which made the vigors of yoga sutra and the tortures of Jain asceticism unnecessary. What Christianity, with its assumptions about the goodness of creation and the meaningfulness of history, can have to do with such acosmic religions is difficult to understand. One would have expected Küng to begin his "synthesis" by an approach to the theistic faiths of the East, like Parseeism and Sikhism.

Is Küng's critical ecumenical theology Christian, or Christianistic—something imitative of Christianity, an attempt to restore the appearance of apostolicity, yet alien to apostolicity at the core?[47]

Küng may think of himself as an Erasmus at heart, but he is no Erasmus in style. Learned, prodigiously energetic, he writes repetitiously and cumbrously. What he needs are the opposite virtues of restraint and elegance to approach the Erasmian ideal.

If Erasmus were alive today would he be a Catholic or a Protestant? Who knows? I think he would not be a Küngian.

Notes

1. Translated by Peter Heinegg (New York, 1988). Hereafter to be cited as "Küng."

2. I belong to a religious movement originating largely in nineteenth-century rural America, the broad aims of which were a plea for Christian unity on the basis of the New Testament alone. Some present-day adherents of the movement believe Küng is speaking their language.

3. To be fair to Küng it might be more accurate to say, "where Christianity should go in the future," since Küng, in spite of the book's title, makes no claim to be spelling out a thousand year program. Yet if his dream of a single world religion comes to pass, it will take at least another thousand years, and then some, to bring about, if the past two thousand years tell us anything about religious progress.

4. Küng, pp. 20-46.

5. *Ibid.,* pp. 2-8.

6. *Ibid.,* pp. 3-10.

7. Chicago, 1962.

8. Küng, pp. 129-131, 147.

9. Küng prefers "models of interpretation" for "paradigm," but rarely uses his preferred expression.

10. Küng, p. 134. I am not prepared within the limits of this paper to debate the appropriateness of Küng's taxonomic illustrations, but suspect they could be vigorously challenged.

11. Vatican II calls Scripture "the soul" of Christian theology, Küng points out. *Ibid.,* p. 17.

12. *Ibid.,* pp. 155-160.

13. *Ibid.,* pp. 164-168.

14. Stephen Toulmin, *Human Understanding: The Collective Use and Evaluation of Concepts* (Princeton, 1972).

15. Küng, p. 173.

16. *Ibid.,* pp. 175-177.

17. *Ibid.,* p. 206.

18. Jacob Burckhardt, *Force and Freedom: Reflections on History,* edited by James Hastings Nichols (New York, 1943), p. 79.

19. Küng, p. 173.

20. *Ibid.,* p. 2.

21. *Ibid.,* p. 9. Religion in the modern period has, Küng states, "for thoroughly understandable reasons, been ignored, tolerated, repressed, and persecuted," but will rise in the postmodern paradigm to "play an important, though more diffuse role." Ibid., p. 10.

22. *Ibid.,* p. 174.

23. *Ibid.,* p. 205.

24. Küng says traditional theology is to be included in the postmodern ecumene, yet he pans the Thomistic metaphysics in which he was schooled.

25. Küng, p. 7.

26. *Ibid.,* p. 161.

27. *Ibid.,* p. 167.

28. *Ibid.,* pp. 167-168.

29. *Ibid.,* p. 168.

30. *Ibid.*

31. *Ibid.,* pp. 154-60.

32. *Ibid.,* p. 158.

33. *Ibid.,* p. 159.

34. *Ibid.,* p. 167. ". . . God writes straight even in crooked lines and can reach his goals *by way of our humanity and historicity* without doing any violence to human beings." *Ibid.,* p. 55.

35. "Anyone who experiences Scripture this way, as the Gospel in faith, becomes certain that the Bible is interpenetrated and filled with the Spirit, that it is truly 'inspired.'" *Ibid.,* p. 63.

36. *Emeth* in the Hebrew and *aletheia* in the Greek, he points out, mean fidelity, constancy, reliability. *Ibid.* The question of truth, he says, aims at more than

pure theory; the truth is never only established in systems of true propositions, "as opposed to which all others are false," truth is at the same time a *praxis,* a way of experience. If religion promises an ultimate unity of meanings for living, then "the *True (verum)* and the *Good (bonum)* . . . overflow into one another in religion; and the question of the truth . . . is at the same time the question of . . . valuableness." *Ibid.,* pp. 238-39.

37. *Ibid.,* p. 202.

38. *Ibid.,* p. 248.

39. *Ibid.,* p. 250.

40. *Ibid.,* p. 254.

41. *Ibid.,* p. 251.

42. *Ibid.*

43. *Ibid.,* p. 223.

44. *Ibid.,* p. 255.

45. *Ibid.,* p. 253.

46. Matthew 5:48 (KJV).

47. Is Küng's theology a revival of the modernism of Alfred Loisy and George Tyrrell? A number of the old marks are there: the desire to bring Catholic thought into line with Protestant higher criticism, the demand for a wholly naturalistic/immanentist account of the origins of Christianity, the notion of revelation as man's interpretation of his religious experience, opposition to propositional revelation, the test of truth as fruitfulness for life and society, and so on. Frederick Copleston finds the clue to modernism in the assumption that the human mind cannot transcend the sphere of consciousness. Loisy, Copleston says, held that Christianity promoted the ideal of humanity and was passing into the religion of humanity. See Frederick Copleston, S. J., *A History of Philosophy,* Vol. IX. *Maine de Biran to Sartre* (Garden City, 1985, c1974), p. 247.

Hans Küng with Nathan Gardels (interview date Spring 1991)

SOURCE: "The New Ethics: Global Responsibility," in *New Perspectives Quarterly,* Vol. 8, No. 2, Spring, 1991, pp. 44-9.

[*In the following interview, Küng details his ideas for the future of religious understanding and a common world ethic.*]

[*Gardels:*] *Is this the last modern century?*

[Kung:] I would be more radical than that. Strictly speaking, modernity ended in 1918. World War I shattered the belief in inevitable progress toward peace and prosperity, "the end of history," as Hegel put it. And the hegemony of Europe—cradle of the Enlightenment and the secular ideology of Reason—began splintering with the breakdown of the colonial system and the devolution of power to several centers including America, the Soviet Union and China.

And, already by 1918, the bad faith of nihilism, the moral detritus of modernity, had become the key concern of writers and intellectuals . . .

Yes, after all, Nietzsche, who died in 1900, had already pronounced that once the supreme value of God was discarded, other values would also disintegrate, leaving only unbounded power to fill the void.

At the end of the 20th century, mass consciousness has caught up with the historical facts and the cutting-edge, turn-of-the-century intellectuals. Now, the malaise of spiritual homelessness and moral arbitrariness afflicts the whole civilization. Fragmented and morally confused, we are enmeshed in an epochal paradigm shift—from the modernity we have found wanting to a new "post-modern" constellation.

Especially with the ecological imperative, the entire world now realizes that modern progress threatens our survival. In our interdependent world, everyone senses that we need "global standards" and "universally binding ethical norms." Yet, modernity itself is incapable of generating a new, unifying world ethic to save us from ourselves. From the beginning, modern scientific and technological thought has proved incapable of providing the foundation for universal values, human rights and ethical criteria.

The response of some to this age of devolution and what you call bad faith has been to seek a return to the certitudes and centers of pre-modernity. The Ayatollah Khomeini is an example of the Islamic quest for a return to premodernity. Another example is Pope John Paul II, who, it seems, wants the whole world to resemble Polish medieval Catholicism.

But the church's strategy of re-evangelizing postcommunist Europe through a program that denounces western democracy as nothing more than consumerism, hedonism and materialism—instead of unambiguously affirming freedom, pluralism and tolerance—will not work. It is the clerical delusion of a prudish pope that appeals to the youth of Eastern Europe about as much as communism.

How, one asks, can the purveyor of such a repressive religious attitude criticize Islam's xenophobia, its theocratic conception of politics, its rigorous sexual morality and the exclusion of women from public life?

Yet the other response to pre-modern orthodoxy is hardly more attractive. For the most part, the alternative has been to float uncommitted amidst an ultra-modern potpourri of beliefs, content with radical pluralism or relativism, the anarchy of trends, the methodological "anything goes" and the indifferent attitude that "all is permissible." This has been called "post-modernity" by social critics like Jean François Lyotard, but is, in fact, characteristic of the disintegration of late-modernity.

Such an apologetic modernism, with its fixation on the fleeting present, offers no contribution to a new set of ethics that transcends the morally confused paradigm of modernity.

The mechanisms of modernity can displace a past ethic, but they cannot themselves produce a new ethic or, in an age "beyond good and evil" as Nietzsche properly called our modern times, even provide a justification for ethical behavior. Reason cannot rehabilitate what it has destroyed; more science and technology cannot correct the defects and repair the damage done by science and technology.

What we need now, above all, is to strive for a new basic consensus of integrative human convictions that are commonly accepted and applied across all situations and in all contexts of this fragmented world.

As the secular age runs out of steam because its unity has splintered, would you say that we are now in a pre-religious moment much the same as Rome was in its decadent twilight? Having hit bottom in the void, are we perhaps prepped for the birth of a great, unifying religion rooted, for instance, in an ecological imperative?

Well, I would say that the passing of the modern paradigm gives religion a new chance. In an age beyond good and evil that is also an age of unprecedented technological capacity that can destroy the environment and disrupt genetic integrity, it seems doubtful that we can survive without a set of absolute moral limits on human freedom.

Only a dimension of judgement that is transcendent, that provides accountability to a higher authority—in short, a responsibility to God—can provide the basis for the absoluteness and universality of ethical demands.

To be sure, a non-believer can be a moral person. He may decide not to kill others or destroy the natural environment, but that is a hypothetical imperative conditional to his interests; it is not "categorical," as in "thou shalt not" under any circumstances.

After the 20th century—with its world wars, mass exterminations, mass-destruction weapons and ecological catastrophes—who can believe in a naive humanism that trusts the Kantian "ought"—the innate imperative to do good in each of our hearts?

Never before has mankind had the technological capacity to end life on earth. In such an age, the metaphysical question raised by Albert Camus—"why not commit suicide"—is now faced by humanity collectively. Why should we respect the genetic heritage of humankind? Why not destroy the rainforests or deplete the ozone layer? Why should there be life at all?

Only religion can answer that question. The unconditional moral imperatives that will preserve life can only come from an Absolute that provides over-arching meaning and that embraces and permeates individual and human nature. Religions can present their ethical demands with an authority man does not have.

I'm not calling for the naive God of Sunday school "who sees you." I'm speaking of a higher authority to which we are accountable and responsible for our actions. An authority that is not the Pope, not the President, not the Party, not professional success, not Science and not the Market.

However, I do not believe that a new unifying religion will emerge. Rather, I see a new set of universal ethics, based in the humane convictions of great world religions. In the post-modern era of communications, economic complexity and interdependence, ethics must again become public instead of merely personal.

What would be the moral substance, so to speak, of this world ethic?

The ethical goal for the third millennium is "planetary responsibility." That is the slogan for the future.

Such an ethic is, above all, the opposite of the reigning ethic of success whereby any means of behavior is justified by the end result of profit, power, enjoyment or the good life.

Such an ethic also cannot be what is called a mere "dispositional" ethic, where absolute, abstract values such as justice or love are concerned only with purely inner motivation of the person without regard to concrete consequences in the real world. This kind of ethic is ahistorical and apolitical. It can be a kind of moral isolationism.

When I say an "ethic of responsibility," I mean it in the sense that Max Weber did. Such an ethic asks realistically about the foreseeable "consequences" of our actions and takes responsibility for them.

To be sure, without a personal ethic, the ethic of planetary responsibility could easily collapse into an ethic in which the ends justify the means. And without an ethics of responsibility, personal ethics would decline into self-righteous inwardness. A situation without norms is morally blind; norms without a situation are empty.

Relating this to the post-Modern Age, I would agree with the philosopher Hans Jonas, who argues that the threat of economic and population growth to Earth's biosphere requires the human species to adopt an ethic that reveres nature and limits freedom in the present for the sake of long-term survival.

How does this view differ from eco-theology, pre-Christian Pantheism, or even Japanese Shintoism where, in effect, the sacred is the equilibrium of a whole natural world that would fall into destructive imbalance if limits are transgressed?

There is much with which I agree concerning the notion of ecological equilibrium.

The monotheistic, prophetic religions—Judaism, Christianity and Islam—have much to learn from Shinto and some

Indian religions that emphasize the cycle of cosmic birth and death over the reality of the person.

The prophetic religions should take nature more seriously and not concentrate so much on the person. In the Hebrew Bible, the New Testament and the Koran nature is background. There were six days of creation, then everything else is about the human being.

Yet, for me, it is not enough to believe only in nature. I think there is a great neglect of the individual in some of the Far Eastern religions.

If one believes, as many adherents to polytheistic Eastern religions do, in a cosmic equilibrium as the ultimate reality, an equilibrium without a core or an accountable center, it is not clear where the notion of personal responsibility comes from.

This seems clearer in the Abrahamic religions, where there is one source of authority, one God who judges our actions.

True, there are different ways to see ultimate reality that imply different imperatives for individual and collective behavior. But many Indians would say that they are just as monotheistic as the Judeo-Christian culture and Islam. They believe in one ultimate reality that stands behind all their gods; who can be compared, though they have more natural gods, to saints or prophets. In the Chinese Confucian tradition, heaven is the center. The will of heaven is decisive for the behavior of the human being.

In Japan, where religions are not exclusive, there are very strong social ethics from the Confucian tradition and from Buddhism, with its ethics of compassion.

Yet, despite these differences, it is my argument that all the world's major religions share a *humanum*—a humane ethical code that, while rooted in the *divinum,* or absolute, of a particular concrete religion, is common to all and the minimum requirement of any faith.

Whether Bahai, Buddhist, Confucian, Christian, Hindu, Jew, Moslem, Shintoist, Sikh or Zoroastrian, all share in their basic beliefs a conviction of the fundamental unity of the human family and the equality and dignity of all human beings; a sense of the sacredness of the individual person; a sense of the value of human community; a recognition that might is not right, that human power is not self-sufficient and absolute; a belief that the force of inner truthfulness and of the spirit ultimately has greater power than hate, enmity and self-interest; a sense of obligation to stand by the poor and oppressed; a profound hope that good will prevail in the end. All world religions place a distance between man and his bestial drives.

The task of theology today, as in the past, is to place this *humanum* in the post-modern historical context so that it is ethically meaningful.

During modernity, a process of reflection and self-criticism moved all religions toward the direction of this common *humanum*. For example, the inquisitorial practices with fire and torture were removed from Catholicism, which then embraced the notion of human rights born in the French Revolution; human sacrifices were eliminated in Indian religious practices and, in several Moslem countries—though obviously not in those that remain two paradigms (the Reformation and the Enlightenment) behind—the doctrine of *jihad,* or Holy War, was moderated, penal codes reformed and respect for the rights of women and non-Moslems enhanced.

In the post-modern millennium, I am convinced the preservation of human rights, the emancipation of women, the realization of social justice and the acknowledgement of the immorality of war will become leading convictions of all major religions.

How is what you propose any different than syncretism, the facile synthesis of religions, or the indifferent pluralism of tolerance—relativism really—that accepts all things equally?

I am not proposing mere tolerance, religious coexistence or indifference, but a truly ecumenical approach in which the new global ethic can be supported by all religions from within their own tradition.

Ecumenicism is based in a critical attitude toward one's own religious traditions, but also a steadfastness of belief that one's own religion is the true religion.

My belief that Christianity is the one true religion in no way excludes truth in other religions. Indeed, it allows their validity insofar as their message does not directly contradict the Christian message.

The *humanum* I respect as unconditional I respect because of my belief in the Christian God. On this solid foundation of faith, I am able to look at my own religion critically and engage in dialogue with other believers about the establishment of a new moral order, an ecumenical world order that embraces the ethic of responsibility.

In such an order, the motivation to conform to moral norms, the degree of compulsion and, indeed, the meaning of one's participation in a common moral order must come from within a specific religious tradition.

What might the rules of the new moral order be as mankind heads toward the next century with our Promethean ambitions intact?

I think there are several general ethical rules.

First, there must be no scientific or technological progress that, when realized, creates greater problems than solutions; for example, the eradication of hereditary illness by genetic manipulation.

Second, the burden of proof that a new technology won't cause social or ecological damage must rest upon the authority—government or corporate—that approves the innovation.

Third, the common good should have priority over individual interest, as long as human rights and personal dignity are protected.

Fourth, the more urgent value of survival must have priority over a less equal value such as self-fulfillment.

Fifth, the ecosystem must have priority over the social system.

Finally, mankind must abide by the rule of reversibility. In technological innovation, irreversible development should occur only when absolutely necessary. For example, operations involving gene surgery could irreversibly alter the genetic information system in a person, and germ-line engineering could have fateful effects on countless generations to come.

You've called for an ecumenical world in the first post-modern century. Yet, the world is embroiled in war and conflict involving Islam, Judaism and Christianity in the Middle East.

What can the ecumenical approach bring to the intractable moral dilemmas of the Middle East?

The nations involved in the Middle East conflict, and here I include the US as well as Israel and the Arab nations, represent the great world religions: Christianity, Judaism and Islam.

As prophetic religions they have much in common. All three are of Eastern Semitic origin; all are prophetic in character (a belief in creation and in an ultimate redemption), and all claim Abraham as their ancestor.

If they were to reflect on this origin, they could make an extremely important contribution to world peace.

Of course, there are essential differences between these three prophetic religions. Judaism focuses on God's people and land, Christianity on God's Son and Messiah, Islam on God's word and book. These differences cannot and should not be concealed.

A union of these great world religions is not necessary for peace. In any case, a single world religion is an illusion.

What we need, though, more than ever after the crisis of the Gulf War, is peace between the religions. I cannot repeat often enough that there can be no world peace without religious peace; no peace among the nations without peace among the religions, no peace among the religions without dialogue between the religions.

All prophetic religions—Islam, Judaism and Christianity—believe in one and the same God, the God of Abraham.

These three religions believe in the one God who tolerates no other gods, powers, rulers and figures, but who is not just the God of one people but of all peoples, who is not a national God but Lord of the world, who wants the well-being of all peoples.

Jews, Christians and Moslems hold fast to a basic prophetic ethic: humane demands for justice, truth, faithfulness, peace and love—which are claimed as requirements of God himself.

Judaism, Christianity and Islam have been shaped by the prophetic criticism of the unjust and inhuman circumstances under which humiliated, enslaved and exploited people must live—there can be no worship of God without respect of human beings and human rights.

We can see that there is a very real foundation for an ecumenicism of the three religions which together form a monotheistic world movement with an ethical focus. This relationship could be called an Abrahamic ecumenical movement. I am convinced that there will be no peace in the Near East, and no resolution of the Palestinian question, unless this Abrahamic ecumenical movement can be made an effective factor in world politics. How else can anyone guard against the religious fanatics in all camps?

But the most difficult question of all is: How will a solution be found for the city of Jerusalem, which in the course of its three-thousand-year-old history has known so many overlords; a city that is holy to Jews, Moslems and Christians and that even secular Jews and Moslems do not regard with indifference?

The destiny of Jerusalem in world history is to be holy to all three Abrahamic religions at the same time. And to all three because of Abraham. In addition, there are also "holy" ties to Jerusalem that are specific to all religions: for Jews it is the city of David, for Christians the city of Jesus Christ and for Moslems the city of the prophet Mohammed.

Jerusalem is not just a piece of land; it is a religious symbol. But religious symbols need not necessarily be politically exclusive. Some people have called for an internationalizing of Jerusalem; Tel Aviv could be Israel's capital, Ramallah that of the Palestinian state. But perhaps there is yet another solution. The Palestinians are seeking a political identity, are claiming self-esteem, and want their own flag. Why, in a new age, shouldn't peaceful coexistence be possible so that two flags can wave over Jerusalem: the Jewish flag with the star of David and the Palestinian flag with the crescent?

This could be the first element of an overall political and religious solution for Jerusalem; why shouldn't the symbolic Old City become the capital for the state of Israel and the state of Palestine—since a new division would be nonsense in economic, political, social and religious terms?

Jerusalem could be a capital that, for the well-being of all, is not divided. Would that be so unheard of in history? A city with two flags? Don't the standards of Italy and of the Vatican now fly over Rome, which was similarly disputed?

A second element in the future status of Jerusalem could be provided by a differentiation between the capital and the seat of government, which need not necessarily go together. As with Bonn and Berlin in Germany, why couldn't the Old City of Jerusalem, which is the symbolic section, be the neutral capital for Israel and Palestine? The Israeli center of government would remain in Jewish New Jerusalem and the Palestinian center of government could be formed in Arab New (East) Jerusalem—each center of government on its own territory, not separated from the Old City. Specific conditions could be negotiated. Where there is an ethical will to make peace, there is usually a political way.

But how, in the center of Israel, can the question of the old Temple site, the Haram el-Sherif, be incorporated into a peaceful solution? Let me venture a constructive suggestion—a third element in an overall political and religious solution for Jerusalem. The three Abrahamic religions need a religious symbol, a common holy place, as a great sign that all three worship the one God of Abraham and therefore have something fundamental in common that could overcome all divisions and all enmity.

Peace, founded on common faith, could be symbolized in a common holy place. The fact is that there already is a sanctuary for the one God of Abraham: the "Dome of the Rock," a unique holy place on the old Temple site of Jerusalem that is often wrongly called the Omar Mosque, although it is not in fact a mosque. According to Jewish and Moslem tradition, the Dome of the Rock commemorates not only the blinding of Abraham's son Isaac but also the creation of Adam. And, too, these religions believe the Dome will be the scene of world judgement.

Is it so utterly absurd to believe that after a religious and political settlement between Israelis and Palestinians, Jews, Moslems and Christians could pray to the one God of Abraham at this holy place? In this way the Dome of the Rock would be a Dome of Reconciliation for the three religions that derive from Abraham.

Is all this an illusion? After the war the cards are being reshuffled, and it will be even more difficult to win the peace than to win the war. Violent aggressive emotions have been let loose—almost as in the Second World War. But a more sober mood will follow on all sides—just as after that war. Humanity as a whole, like individuals, seems to learn only from bitter experiences. Will we all become mature enough to arrive at a new peaceful order in the Near East after this catastrophic Gulf War, just as a new peaceful order arose in Europe after the Second World War?

Alan Race (review date 16 August 1991)

SOURCE: "Credo in Unum Humanum," in *Times Literary Supplement,* August 16, 1991, p. 27.

[*In the following review, Race asserts, "Hans Küng's* Global Responsibility *aims to provide a rationale for overcoming the tragic fissure between peace and truth, both within and between the world religions."*]

While the moral summons to peace ought to instil friendship between the religions, their neurotic desire for the absolute truth, as the respective traditions have symbolized and defended it, has driven them to war. If religions have historically placed a premium on truth over peace, then the declining state of the globe now cries out for a reversal of priorities. Hans Küng's **Global Responsibility** aims to provide a rationale for overcoming the tragic fissure between peace and truth, both within and between the world religions. It is an extension of his earlier **Christianity and the World Religions** (1984), where the author was in dialogue with Islam, Hinduism and Buddhism. Since then, Küng has engaged more seriously with Judaism and the Chinese religions. His resulting aspiration has become a threefold slogan: "No survival without a world ethic. No world peace without peace between the religions. No peace between the religions without dialogue between the religions." Given the world's radical plurality, the conceptual difficulties of a "world ethic" seem virtually insurmountable. But Küng's boldness lies in the belief that, among all human systems, the world religions still represent the best *loci* for discovering the foundational values needed for our survival. As the abysmal record of the religions and the modern critique of religious belief tell against such boldness, each strand of this triple chord begs further examination.

First, Küng repudiates the Nietzschean prediction that humankind is moving "beyond good and evil." We are now post-moderns, he believes, in the sense that global survival demands a "new, differentiated, pluralistic and holistic synthesis," beyond the confrontational ethics and politics endemic within modernity. If the limitations of the modern technological experiment have become abundantly self-evident in the degradation of human and ecological life, Küng believes that only through the religions' grounding the finite human conscience in the sense of the divine unconditional can the impasse be transcended. While this move is not a return to religious orthodoxy (for it is religion purged of exclusive prejudice in truth, and of inhumaneness in morality, that Küng is advocating), it nevertheless allows religious ethics a serious place in the painful transition from autonomous ethics to shared ethics. The point is not unreasonable, in spite of the secular philosopher's claim that religion has only ever sanctified existing ethics *post hoc*. But Küng overstates his case by claiming that the religions provide an unambiguous ground for morality. Most characterizations of postmodernity assume that there is no unambiguous anything; and this is surely right. Even the religious belief in the world's essential contingency points in the same direction.

The second strand of Küng's chord is an expansion of a lecture he gave at Unesco in Paris in 1989. He specified the shared ethical goal between the religions as the *humanum,* an ecumenical criterion of basic human dignity shared by all the religions. Yet as the religions define what is truly human differently within their respective traditions, the question of their relationship at the theological level cannot be lightly abandoned. Küng knows this and therefore embarks on the difficult road of combining what he calls "steadfastness" to one's own tradition with "maximal openness" to others. So he eschews exclusivism, because it indicates a fortress mentality; inclusivism, because it spells death by another's embrace; and the pluralist view that all religions are the same underneath, because it leads to indifference. His view that the religions might correct and complement each other nevertheless jars with his Christian retention of Christ's finality. It is not wholly clear whether Küng's theological desire to uphold even a mild form of the finality of Christ is methodologically compatible with the "rough parity" between the religions that genuine dialogue demands. There is no reason for thinking that the assumption of parity leads inexorably to the forgetting of truth.

The first two strands of the chord present a flow of argument as punchy as any that this troubling Swiss Catholic has ever produced. By comparison, the third strand is rather disappointing. It amounts to a research plan for writing world history from a new religious perspective. In the circumstances of post-modernity, where the religions are assuming a continuing importance, the necessity for a new historical perspective cannot be gainsaid. The religions are going to need information of the patterns of continuity and discontinuity that historical study yields. Former examples, which Küng discusses, are too aprioristic (Hegel), or pessimistic (Spengler), or fail in the face of the evidence (Toynbee). Distinguishing the Near Eastern Semitic religions and the Far Eastern Chinese and Indian religions, Küng believes the future lies in understanding their differences and commonalities. If the purpose of religion is salvation/liberation, rather than simply arriving at the correct mental picture of the Godhead, then the analysis would unearth the achievements that could be harnessed as experiential data for a world ethic. It may be that, as John Hick believes, the religions have probably produced good and bad in about equal measure. Even so, such a new historical analysis would provide a semi-empirical backing for any proposed world ethic.

Global Responsibility, as the title implies, is Utopian. HRH the Duke of Edinburgh, who has written the preface, hopes that it will "stimulate a more determined search for a shared belief in the beauty and value of this planet Earth as our common and unique home in the vastness of the universe". Küng's vision is not yet so green as that. But endeavouring to unite peace and truth in the service of the *humanum* prises open a new way of being religious fully compatible with that greater green awareness. It would add to history's tragedy not to take up the invitation.

Raymond Carr (review date 12 September 1992)

SOURCE: "Paradigms Lost and Found," in *Spectator,* September 12, 1992, pp. 36-7.

[In the following review, Carr outlines Küng's investigation of Judaism in his book by the same name.]

Hans Küng is Professor of Ecumenical Theology and Director of the Institute for Ecumenical Research in Tübingen. The thesis of his long and learned book (90 pages of dense footnotes) is that religion, rightly conceived, offers humanity its last chance for peace and justice in what he terms the post-modern world. There can be

> no peace among the nations without peace among the religions; no peace among the religions without dialogue between the religions; no dialogue without investigation of the foundations of the religions.

The present book[, *Judaism,*] is the first volume of a trilogy that will investigate the foundations of the three great monotheistic world religions which share a common founding father in Abraham: Islam, Judaism and Christianity. It is their shared belief in one God, the 'Abrahamic ecumene' that can be the basis of a new world order.

For his investigation of Judaism Küng takes from the philosopher of science, Thomas Kuhn, the notion of 'paradigm shifts'. Paradigms are those 'entire constellations of beliefs, values etc' which are shared by a 'given community'. Just as in the exact sciences hypotheses are discredited in the light of new discoveries and replaced by new hypotheses which fit the facts, so religions suffer great sea changes. In Küng's hands the history of Judaism becomes a drama as each paradigm is replaced by a new constellation, a new world outlook.

Thus the paradigm of the kingdom of the priest kings, David and Solomon—that Jewish, golden age which was revived in the state of Israel with the star of David on its flag—collapses to be replaced, after the Babylonian exile (586-538 BC), by a new paradigm: the theocracy of the Jerusalem Temple. The prophets who have thundered against the worship of false gods and called for repentance are domesticated and subordinated to the teachers of the law. The strict observance of the law (circumcision, ritual slaughter, prohibition of mixed marriages, etc) becomes the core of Judaism with cultic life centred on the Temple of Jerusalem. Judaism persists as a religious community within a Roman province. It no longer needs a state. Rebellion against Rome to re-establish the lost independent state brought the destruction of the Temple (70 AD) and the prohibition of entry into Jerusalem for circumcised Jews. With the religious capital gone, cultic life is decentralised. The local synagogue replaces the Temple. The local rabbi the Temple Priest. This is the 'mediaeval paradigm' of the diaspora based on Torah piety (the Torah contains the revealed will of God) and the ritualisation of everyday life according to the instructions of the Mishnah and the Talmud. Judaism has become a closed circle, a society co-

cooned in its ritual practices, alien to the Christian world. And Jews are persecuted by Christians as the murderers of Christ. The collective guilt of the Jewish people was not formally rejected as slander until the Second Vatican Council.

How can Jews, Küng asks, escape from the segregation they sought for themselves, which was then forced on them by the anti-Semitism of the Catholic church in the Middle Ages? Assimilation is the last paradigm. Jews can escape from the ghetto as citizens of the modern state. Moses Mendelsohn's (1729-86) escape, as both a Jew and a card-carrying member of the European Enlightenment, served only to reveal the dangers of assimilation. Jews like the poet Heine converted to Christianity as the 'entrance ticket to European culture'. The Holocaust was to prove that there was no such entrance ticket.

Professor Küng's chapters on a possible Jewish-Christian dialogue is heavy going, as the excellent translation struggles with the opacity of the German original. All enlightened scholars of both faiths have long acknowledged that Jesus is inconceivable outside the Jewish world of his time. The Jewish theologian, Martin Buber, called Jesus his great brother. But for less enlightened minds difficulties persist. Jewish strict monotheism finds it difficult to accept Christ as consubstantial with God and a member of the Trinity. But for Küng there is no need for the doctrine of the trinity and the incarnation; all that matters is belief in the one and only God and acceptance of the 'liberal' message of Jesus Christ.

Fundamentalism, with its refusal to face up to the common problems of the post-modern world, precludes dialogue. Far from facing up to these problems, Orthodox Judaism turned its back on the modern world and remained stuck in the 'mediaeval paradigm'. A Jew who substitutes for Torah piety and the strict observance of the law a fixation on the Holocaust and commitment to the state of Israel is a lost soul. For the resilient reader there is an informative account of the attempts to reform and modernise Judaism, particularly in the United States where more Jews live than in the state of Israel. The Orthodox negate modernity: Liberal Reform Jews seek 'assimilation to modernity'. But reformers have a hard time, as the eminent Jewish rabbi, Louis Jacobs, found out to his cost in London when he dared to treat the Torah as an historical document.

If Orthodox Judaism is a stumbling block to dialogue, on the Christian side there is the Catholic church. It is not merely that mediaeval Catholics invented modern anti-Semitism. Popes have, and still do, inhabit a mediaeval world. Pius XII's pontificate, with his concern to preserve his church as an institution by concordats with dictators whose human rights record was deplorable and his silence on the Holocaust, constitutes a 'Christian tragedy'. The present Pope, from the 'provincial city of Krakow' has 'no understanding of modern life'. He uses 'the practices of the Inquisitors' to muzzle liberation theology. His blind opposition to contraception condemns the Third World to starvation, and, according to Küng, endows Catholic Poland with the highest rate of abortion in Europe as the main method of birth control. The process of self-criticism that is the premise of dialogue is 'hardly to be found at present on the part of official Roman Catholicism'.

No wonder Professor Küng warms to the great Jewish prophets. Much of his own message will be rejected or misunderstood, and not only by Rome. Jews must not harp on the Holocaust but exercise forgiveness; Christians, particularly Germans, must not forget or 'relativise' their guilt, but assimilate it. Only then is reconciliation possible. As for the Middle East, only the dovest of doves can accept his message: a 'sovereign Palestine state' and the acknowledgement that Israel has no sovereign rights over Jerusalem. There can be no peace in the Middle East 'unless the Abrahamic ecumene can be made an effective force in world politics'.

This demands the abandonment of the exclusive fundamentalisms that have set—and still set—nations at each others' throats. For Küng there must be an act of repentance for the past record of Christians as crusaders and persecutors. Only by concentrating our minds on the common message of the Hebrew Bible, the Gospels, and the Qu'ran may we discover what Mr Curdle in *Nicholas Nickleby* called 'a kind of universal dovetailedness'. As our economies, so our faiths must converge if the 'Abrahamic ecumene' is to serve the ethic of the post-modern world.

I sense in my ecumenical friends a certain animus against the Enlightenment. For Küng the 'substitute Gods' of the Enlightenment—reason and faith in humanity—have nothing to offer the post-modern world, having made a hash of the modern one. Ecumenicism is not only a message of hope; it can be seen as one of the defensive responses to the post-Enlightenment erosion of the simple certainties of traditional faith: belief in the resurrection of the body which makes the loss of loved ones tolerable; fear of hell fire which encourages right conduct, in this world. Küng would have us believe that on death we will be admitted 'into God's incomprehensible, all-embracing reality'. The old faiths may have been simple to the point of absurdity. But at least they were comprehensible.

Ronald Modras (review date 31 October 1992)

SOURCE: A review of *Judaism: Between Yesterday and Tomorrow,* in *America,* Vol. 167, No. 13, October 31, 1992, pp. 332-34.

[*In the following review, Modras asserts that Küng's Judaism will not change the course of Judaism or Mid-East politics, "But here is a book that religious leaders and theologians in all three Abrahamic communities can read with profit, a book that all interested laity can understand."*]

Publishers are known for hyperbole. When the dust jacket claims this is the "most important book written by a

Christian about Judaism in this century," it sounds exactly like that mix of audacity and gall known in Yiddish as *chutzpa*. But when one skims the notes, the subject index and the page upon page of authors cited, even so bold a claim suddenly appears quite plausible.

For any other scholar this encyclopedic tome[, *Judaism: Between Yesterday and Today,*] would be the work of a lifetime. For the Rev. Hans Küng, it is but the first part of a trilogy, with books to follow on Christianity and Islam in the same programmatic scheme of creating a foundation for what he calls "Abrahamic ecumenism." His productivity long ago warranted Küng the reputation of being a one-man cottage industry, but there is a passion behind this particular effort whose reasons may not be immediately apparent.

A clue, I believe, is to be found in the 1990 prologue to this trilogy, *Global Responsibility: In Search of a New World Ethic.* There Küng recounts lecturing in Beirut, when Lebanon was still the Switzerland of the Middle East. When he asked why there were no Muslim scholars on the program with him, he was told that it was "too soon" for such dialogue. Now that it is too late, Küng looks with apprehension to Jerusalem, as he insists repeatedly that there will be no world peace without religious peace, and there will be no religious peace without religious dialogue.

The method Küng honed in his years of inter-Christian dialogue, he now employs on behalf of the Abrahamic *ecumene*. He outlines in detail what Judaism, Christianity and Islam hold in common and where they differ, not only with respect to monotheism but to Abraham, Moses, David, the prophets and basic ethics. Here with the Hebrew Scriptures as with the New Testament, Küng espouses and elucidates the consensus of critical-historical exegetes. He espouses as well, however, Thomas Kuhn's concepts of paradigms and paradigm shifts and translates them from the sphere of the natural sciences to religion and theology.

Kuhn described a paradigm as the constellation of beliefs and values shared by a given community. The passage of time and new circumstances create crises that generate new epoch-making constellations. Holding that this is the case not only in societies but in communities of faith, Küng divides Jewish history into five major paradigms: tribal (Moses); monarchic (David); the second-temple priests (Ezra): the rabbis of the Talmud and Middle Ages, and the modern paradigm of assimilation. He sees the Holocaust as the end of the modern paradigm and the creation of the State of Israel as the entrance into a new epoch, a postmodern paradigm yet to be developed let alone named.

Amid all these paradigm shifts, Küng asserts that the abiding substance of Judaism resides in the conviction that Israel is God's chosen people who have been given a promised land. The operative words here are Israel, people and land. Most notably not law, or at least not law in the sense of the 613 commandments the rabbis have drawn from Mosaic (written and oral) tradition. Here Küng will surely be attacked for presuming to define what is and is not essential to Judaism. Even the Vatican has accepted the principle that Jews should be allowed to define themselves. Küng is consistent, however, in his arguments from biblical history, Enlightenment values and modern praxis. He is willing to confront the champions of rabbinic orthodoxy the same way he does their Roman Catholic counterparts, both of whom he sees as locked in analogous medieval paradigms.

After a survey and interpretation of history, Küng takes up, in equal parts, questions and challenges of the present and future. He looks at issues like the Holocaust, Zionism, disputes between Jews and Christians today (Jesus, Paul, the meaning of messiah, divine sonship, Trinity) and, above all, the Israeli-Palestinian conflict. Here Küng demonstrates that interreligious dialogue and overcoming historic hostilities are not equivocal concepts.

On the issue of the Holocaust he is anything but vague in reproaching Pope Pius XII for his silence and the German bishops for their capitulation to the Nazis. Although a Swiss earning a living at a German university, he pulls no punches in laying the primary blame for the Holocaust not only on Germany's ruling elite but on the masses as well. "Adolf Hitler," he writes, "was neither an 'accident' in German history nor a 'decree of fate.' Adolf Hitler came to power with the broad assent of the German people, and for all the hidden criticism was supported to the bitter end by the majority of the population with a loyalty that is still terrifying even today."

Protestant churches fare no better in Küng's analysis, and he charges both the United States and his own Switzerland with an effective indifference to the Holocaust. No nation or church, he concludes, can claim innocence. Acknowledging the need for remembrance, he goes on, however, to make a plea for forgiveness that is not altogether clear. (Forgiveness of whom? Of the perpetrators? Their children? Do Germans born after 1945 need to forgive?) He then criticizes those Jews for whom the Holocaust has become a fixation, a substitute for religion and, even worse, an excuse to deny Palestinians their own autonomy and human rights.

Küng appeals for a "critical solidarity" with the State of Israel. He insists on its right to exist and upbraids the Vatican for refusing to grant it diplomatic relations. But he is unstinting, too, in criticizing the leadership of the Likud block that until recently ruled Israel, particularly Menachem Begin (whom he labels a "former terrorist"), Ariel Sharon (a "warmonger") and Yitzhak Shamir, whom he indicts for obstructing the peace process for the sake of a "greater Israel."

The positions he advocates are those of the Israeli left (the Mapai Party), Abba Eban and the so-called "Jews of Conscience" who are ready to trade land for peace. Küng faults Yasser Arafat and the P. L. O. as sharing in the responsibility for making Jerusalem a powder keg. He sees Israel since 1967 as the armed Goliath, guilty of disproportionate use of deadly weapons against stone-slinging (like David) Palestinian boys. In Küng's view, the aftermath of the Gulf War offers an unprecedented opportunity for solving the Palestinian issue; but, as matters stand now at least, it is primarily up to Israel.

In what unfortunately appears almost like an afterthought, Küng concludes his book with a discussion of how to justify and understand God after the Holocaust. In it he repents of his earlier flirtation with a Hegelian God of process and distances himself from the Rev. David Tracy (a "suffering God") and Jurgen Moltmann (a "crucified God"). The classical view of God as omnipotent is just as indispensable as divine justice and compassion. Meaningless suffering cannot be understood theoretically, he concludes, only endured with trust.

In a book of such monumental proportions, it would be niggling to cavil at the occasional typographical errors in the English translation (the millions of other victims of the Nazis were Slavs, not slaves) or to suggest other areas for development. It is unfortunate, however, that Küng did not treat of the supposed Jewish-Masonic conspiracy against the church, which so exercised European Catholics in the 1930's. There is no denying the need to differentiate, but the efforts in those years to create a Catholic Poland, for example, are evocative of efforts by contemporary Jewish fundamentalists to create a Jewish state along pre-modern lines.

It is fundamentalists of every stripe whom Küng takes out after in this book, whether Jewish, Christian or Muslim. It is doubtful that he will convince any orthodox Jews of the ambiguity of law. It is doubtful, too, that many political figures involved in the mid-East conflict will take kindly to proposals offered by a theologian. But here is a book that religious leaders and theologians in all three Abrahamic communities can read with profit, a book that all interested laity can understand.

It just may foster the cause of dialogue within the Abrahamic *ecumene.* That would certainly argue for its being the most important book on Judaism any Christian has written in this century. It would certainly make it Küng's most important book to date.

Eugene Fisher and Jack Bemporad (review date 29 January 1993)

SOURCE: "Opportunities Missed," in *Commonweal,* Vol. CXX, No. 2, January 29, 1993, pp. 29-30.

[*In the following review of* Judaism, *Fisher and Bemporad complain that "Jewish readers—with good cause—are likely to find [the work] insensitive and inaccurate."*]

When a scholar of great stature enters a new, albeit related field of endeavor to his own, it is an event of significance for both his usual followers and those in the field itself. For the potential for creative insights is great. So it is with anticipation that one approaches Küng's monumental volume on Judaism and Jewish-Christian relations. Küng attempts here a critical survey of all of Jewish history and thought, as well as an analysis of and major contribution to the present historic dialogue between Christians and Jews.

As he notes in his introduction, Küng utilizes "paradigm theory" as a means of organizing the enormous body of literature and history with which he deals. Similarly, he states in the same context, "for the first time in my books of this length I have taken care to make use of additional *teaching aids* (such as charts and graphs) . . . to make it easier to grasp the composition and conception of this long and multi-level book." There are, then, methodological innovations in the text that will be of interest to scholars.

The volume is divided into three general sections. The first, the "Past," describes Jewish history and literature from its ancient "Tribal" and "Kingdom" paradigms to what Küng surprisingly believes is Judaism's "modern paradigm"—"assimilation," symbolized for Küng by Moses Mendelssohn, whose descendants converted to Christianity. The second major section, the "Present," deals with such matters as Christian guilt for the Holocaust; Zionism; Jewish-Christian "disputes" (e.g., Jesus as historical figure and as Messiah; what caused the split between Jews and Christians; "self-criticism" of each tradition in the light of the other); and the ways in which selected modern Jewish thinkers have sought to confront modernity (Abraham Heschel, Joseph Soloveitchik, Abraham Geiger, Louis Jacobs, Zacharias Frankel, and Mordecai Kaplan).

In the third section, Küng offers future "possibilities," beginning with "postmodern" Judaism and what he feels is its unresolved "conflict" between "life" and "law." Here, he invokes especially Martin Buber, Yeshayahu Leibowitz, Judith Plaskow, and Eugene Borowitz, leading up to a discussion of "Paul against the Law?" and "The Future of the People of God."

After a lengthy political excursus on the Middle East conflict, a discussion already dated by the defeat of the Likud in the 1992 Israeli elections, Küng briefly ponders Holocaust theology and Jewish and Christian theology "after Auschwitz," using a single lecture given by Hans Jonas in Tubingen as a virtual foil over against which to show his own theories of creation and theodicy. Both the subject and Professor Jonas deserve more thorough treatment than Küng here allows.

The volume concludes with an epilogue titled, "No New World Order without a New World Ethic." While the lesson offered here is potentially important, its presentation is again dated, this time by the author's reliance on the 1991

Gulf War as its guiding paradigm. In retrospect, the Gulf War has assumed less awesome significance than Küng accorded it at the time.

As the reader is doubtlessly beginning to suspect by this point, the present reviewers came away from this volume with a feeling of being let down by its eminent author. While the volume's heft and voluminous academic apparatus give it the appearance of a major work, we cannot recommend it even as a popular introduction to the several fields that it undertakes to survey, much less a useful scholarly one for professionals in those fields. Pondering why this is so has led us to the following reflections.

First, Küng's aim may simply have exceeded his reach. A clue to this can be seen in the schema we outlined above. In the first section, for example, he attempts in a bare two hundred pages to summarize virtually *all* of Jewish history since Abraham, adjudicating in the process innumerable highly complex textual and historical questions that have consumed generations of scholarly endeavors. While one may impute the failure of the resulting presentation to limitations inherent in the "paradigm theory," his "Notes," for all their length, reveal a critical thinness of research.

On numerous topics where entire literatures exist in creative tension and debate, Küng tends to rely on one or two volumes, seldom explaining why he has chosen one particular school over another, or, in some cases, even indicating the existence of multiple alternative views. One example: the contention that "the" synagogue formally "excommunicated" Jewish Christians. Küng represents this alleged expulsion as a historical given, going on to editorialize that "the excommunication of Christians by Jews preceded the persecution of Jews by Christians." In fact, however, the excommunication claim is highly controversial in current scholarship. And, ironically, the sole article cited by Küng to support his claim was actually written to *refute* it.

Second, the amount of attention Küng is able to give to many of the complex issues he raises is simply not adequate to enable him, even with the creative use of charts and lists, to do justice to them. Twenty-five pages, for example, is not sufficient to present (and sit in judgment upon) the entire history of the Zionist movement. One hundred pages provide minimal scope in which to treat the intricacies of Hebrew biblical history. Three pages are not adequate to define the issue of Paul and the Law. And, certainly, three sentences are not sufficient discussion to preclude the Jewish people from using their own Hebrew term, *Shoah,* for what happened to them in World War II.

This last example brings us to our third and most delicate reflection. It is the tone of the volume. We have talked now with several Jewish scholars who have read the volume and all have had a similar reaction. First comes a sense of puzzlement. Why does the author appear so negative toward Judaism? So judgmental? Examples abound.

Modern Jewish Orthodoxy is written off as "Pharisaic-Talmudic . . . faithfulness to the letter," while Reform is reduced to "the assimilation paradigm." Jews are accused of a lack of "readiness for forgiveness" after the Holocaust, the latter in direct contrast with Christian forgiveness in the Sermon on the Mount. And what is one to say of Küng's affirmation that "contrasts between Jesus and Pharisaism . . . led to Jesus' arrest and death" or his reduction of Rabbinic Judaism to "casuistic trivialization" and the "purely formal aspect of the practice of the law," in which there was "no freedom for open criticism of the Torah" (presumably oral as well as written)?

Such examples of needlessly harsh rhetoric sadly are not rare in this volume. At some risk of being considered insufficiently respectful of Küng's well-established reputation, we must report that Jewish readers—with good cause—are likely to find this volume, which purports after all to present *their* faith and *their* traditions, to be insensitive and inaccurate. However well-intentioned the author was in taking up this study and however excellent some individual sections may be, the final product as a whole does not live up to its promise.

Robert H. Bryant (review date 17 March 1993)

SOURCE: A review of *Judaism: Between Yesterday and Tomorrow,* in *Christian Century,* Vol. 110, No. 9, March 17, 1993, pp. 299-301.

[*Bryant is professor emeritus of constructive theology at United Theological Seminary of the Twin Cities in New Brighton, Minnesota. In the following review, he praises Küng's* Judaism *for its scholarly merit and its accessibility to the general reader.*]

Hans Küng, director of the Institute for Ecumenical Research at the University of Tübingen, is internationally recognized as a foremost participant in ecumenical dialogue. He wrote his doctoral dissertation on Karl Barth at a time when that topic was still unusual for a Roman Catholic scholar. Since then he has continued to foster friendly Catholic-Protestant exchanges around the world. By his critical-historical and systematic studies on the church, the dogma of infallibility and other traditional teachings, he has continued to embody the progressive spirit of Pope John XXIII and Vatican II. He has thus inspired those who would follow in that way but provoked the ire of more cautious Catholic hierarchs.

This book[, *Judaism: Between Yesterday and Tomorrow,*] is the first volume in an ambitious trilogy titled *The Religious Situation of Our Time.* The second volume will be on Christianity and the third on Islam. Küng describes the conviction motivating the trilogy: "No peace among the nations without peace among religions. No peace among the religions without dialogue between the religions. No dialogue between the religions without investigation of the foundations of the religions."

Küng challenges not only Christians and Muslims but also others to "see how the basic conflict between tradition and innovation is dealt with and resolved in Judaism." He invites Christians who view Judaism as only "a past Old Testament" to understand the text as an "independent entity with amazing continuity, vitality and dynamism." He painstakingly surveys "the transitory and the abiding" in that religious-cultural movement from its beginnings to the present. "The one passion which drives this book on," notes the foreword, "is a concern to understand the foundations, the development and the future opportunities of Judaism in the transition to a new world era." He seeks to describe Judaism as a "comprehensive living unity," thereby not only challenging existing preconceptions but also encouraging "growing mutual understanding."

Just as Küng has previously used paradigm theory as a key to interpreting the history of religions, so in this volume he identifies the cultural and religious constellations or paradigms that have shaped Judaism throughout its 3,000-year history: the tribal (in premonarchical time), the kingdom, the theocratic (in the postexilic period), the medieval (associated with the rabbis and the synagogue), and the modern assimilation paradigms. Küng demonstrates a broad knowledge of past and contemporary scholarship as he moves through this expansive tapestry. His extensive endnotes add a fine stimulus to those who wish to explore his many original and secondary sources.

This book is valuable both to scholars and to those interested in learning more about Judaism's past or present. With the help of numerous assistants thanked in the preface, Küng made the lengthy text more accessible by including bold-face headings and subheadings as well as numerous graphs and summaries.

I found part two ("The Challenges of the Present") and part three ("Possibilities for the Future") particularly interesting. In these Küng deals empathetically but also forthrightly with many of the most critical issues for those engaging in post-Holocaust dialogue, including the Israeli-Palestinian land dispute, the danger of the Holocaust's becoming a fixation, and understanding God and suffering after Auschwitz. He is also quite critical of the Persian Gulf war and its aftermath. Finally, he presents "presuppositions for peace in the Middle East." His hope is that every synagogue, church and mosque will contribute to religious understanding. "For that we all need a vision, . . . imagination, courage and indefatigable, creative commitment." He amply demonstrates these attributes.

Clark M. Williamson (essay date Summer-Fall 1993)

SOURCE: "The Christology of Hans Küng: A Critical Analysis," in *Journal of Ecumenical Studies,* Vol. XXX, Nos. 3-4, Summer-Fall, 1993, pp. 372-88.

[*In the following essay, Williamson traces Küng's Christology and explains the difficulty of using such a Christology to further a Jewish-Christian dialogue.*]

PRECIS

The purpose of this essay is to criticize Hans Küng's Christology in light of his intention to develop a Christology that will support a theological conversation with Jews and contribute to mutual understanding and cooperation. Upon analysis, Küng's is a historical-Jesus Christology, in which Jesus' identity is formed by locating him at the center of a quadrilateral conflict with four ideal types of Judaism. This historical Jesus is the criterion and base for Christian truth. The conclusion is that such a Jesus does not serve the development of mutual understanding with Jews and that a different christological model is required for that purpose, as well as for the task of formulating a Christology appropriate to the gospel. A Jesus who "shatters" and "overcomes" Judaism will not serve Küng's stated purpose. What is required is a Christology that locates Jesus firmly within the context of the covenant between the God of Israel and the Israel of God. Jesus Christ must be understood in terms of the graciousness of the God of Israel and as a gift to the church from the God of Israel and the Israel of God.

Among contemporary theologians who have given serious and sustained attention to the issue of Christology, Hans Küng is among the few who are clearly aware of the history of the church's teaching and practice of contempt for Jews and Judaism. The purpose of this essay is to question the adequacy of Küng's Christology to his stated awareness of the problem of Christian anti-Judaism. The question is put to Küng's Christology, rather than to other aspects of his theological work, because how theologians understand the church's confession of Jesus Christ will disclose their theological stance on Jews and Judaism.

When we turn our attention to Küng, our initial expectation is that here we will find some reflection on Christology that is both aware of the problem of Christian anti-Judaism and addresses it. Unquestionably, Küng *knows* there is an issue. He not only claims that "[t]he sufferings of the Jewish people begin with Jesus himself."[1] He also realizes that Jesus was a Jew who was active among Jews, that his name "Yeshua" ("Yahweh is salvation") was Jewish, and that his prayers were Jewish. "His message was for the Jewish people: but for the entire Jewish people, without any exception."[2]

Küng also makes it clear that the history of relations between Christians and Jews has been "largely a history of blood and tears."[3] He recites the history of massacre and pogrom, of the annihilation of 300 Jewish communities in German-speaking lands in the years 1348-1349, of the expulsion of Jews from all major Western European countries during the Middle Ages. He notes, to the church's chagrin, that neither the Protestant nor the Catholic Reformation effected any change in this regard but, rather, humanism, pietism, and the Enlightenment did. He does not devote explicit attention to the ambiguities of these movements in this regard. He deplores the continuing efficacy of "a recalcitrant anti-Judaism in Rome and

Moscow" as well as in New York and argues that Christian anti-Judaism was a *necessary,* if not sufficient, cause of the Nazi program of *Judenvernichtung:* ". . . without the almost two-thousand-year-long pre-history of 'Christian' anti-Judaism which also prevented Christians in Germany from a convinced and energetic resistance on a broad front, it would not have been possible!"[4]

With regard to how relations between Christians and Jews might change, Küng contends that the time has come for Christians "to 'convert' themselves: to an encounter . . . , to a theological dialogue with the Jews, which could serve not 'mission' and capitulation but understanding, mutual help and cooperation, and—indirectly perhaps—even a growing understanding between Jews, Christians, *and* Muslims."[5] Küng sees evidence of the possibility of this theological dialogue in heightened appreciation of the First Testament on the part of the church and of the Second Testament on the part of the rabbis. Judaism, too, has changed, says Küng, in the "decreasing influence of casuistic and legalistic piety, . . . and an increasing importance of the Old Testament in contradistinction to the earlier universal emphasis on the Talmud."[6]

Küng's apparent lack of awareness of the role of Christian anti-Judaism in renaming as "Old and New Testaments" what had previously been known as "the scriptures" seems odd in one committed to transforming relations between Jews and Christians after the Holocaust.[7] His view of Judaism as having been overly concerned with "casuistic and legalistic piety" betrays unfortunate and inaccurate conceptions, conceptions that seem to remain unchanged in his most recent work, *Judaism: Between Yesterday and Tomorrow,* where Second Temple Judaism is described as a "constriction of religion" characterized by legalism, ritualism, and clericalism.[8]

Yet, the theological dialogue is most likely to founder on the point of the significance of Jesus. Küng hopes that, in response to a "Christian readiness to reach understanding," Jews might be willing to "extend an historically objective judgment, genuine understanding and perhaps even a valuation of the person of Jesus."[9] Citing several instances of the Jewish rediscovery of Jesus, beginning in the nineteenth century, he hopes that Jews and Christians can engage in dialogue about Jesus not "from above," but "from below," based on the *historical* Jesus. This would entail seeing Jesus from the viewpoint of his Jewish contemporaries.

The importance of this proposal to Küng's theology cannot be overestimated. In stating what he has in common with Edward Schillebeeckx, Küng asserts: *"The source, standard and criterion of Christian faith is the living Jesus of history."*[10] Lest there be confusion as to what he means by the "living Jesus of history," Küng makes it clear that Christianity "is based primarily on the historical personality of Jesus of Nazareth who was seen as the Christ of God."[11] The kerygmatic character of the Gospels does not allow a reconstruction of his biographical or psychological development, nor can critical historical research prove that

the man Jesus is the Christ. Nonetheless, asking the hard historical questions is essential in order for theology to establish what it can know "about the Jesus of history with scientific certainty or great probability."[12] It was, after all, this historical Jesus who was experienced and proclaimed as Lord and Christ.[13] Fortunately, agreement among those who conduct research into his life is "quite extensive."[14]

In his *The Church—Maintained in Truth,* Küng persists in insisting that the historical Jesus *is* Christian truth. Christian confidence in God and in God's future "is based on the promise given with Jesus of Nazareth: he himself is the promise in which God's fidelity to his people can be read."[15] In Jesus of Nazareth, God's "ultimate, decisive call, God's definite truth about himself and man, found expression."[16] Hence, the church is maintained in truth "whenever *Jesus himself* and not some other secular, political, or clerical figure *remains the truth* for the individual or the community."[17] Jesus "personifies, he is the truth that leads to life."[18] Unlike the prophets whose words were freshly inspired each time they spoke, Jesus "speaks and acts *continually* in virtue of his unity with God."[19]

Küng does not explain how he can move from not being able to provide a biography of Jesus to being able to comment on how he acted "continually." Nor does he clarify how he acquires critical-historical confidence with regard to Jesus' "unity with God." Nonetheless, he affirms that the criterion for what is true in the church can be nothing but Jesus Christ himself, in the sense of the critically reconstructed Jesus of history.[20] Christian truth is essentially historical truth.[21] The church is maintained in truth whenever "Jesus himself is and remains the way, the truth, and the life for the individual or for a community" and when and where discipleship to him and his way is present.[22] *Jesus himself* is the criterion and basis of Christian truth; he *is* Christian truth.[23]

Küng has asked this question in essentially the same way over the course of his career: "Is the Church we have really backed up—in its essentials, not in its inessentials—by the message of Christ?"[24] As later, he professes that, in spite of the kerygmatic nature of the sources, they produce remarkably clear and consistent answers that "speak to us with the original words of Jesus."[25]

What we learn from our historical-critical inquiry, says Küng, is that the nuclear, pivotal idea controlling all of Jesus' preaching is that of God's *basileia,* God's reign.[26] What Jesus meant by God's *basileia* is distinguished by contrasting it with what was meant by other groups at the time. Unlike the rabbis, Jesus had in mind "a powerful *sovereign act of God himself,*" not something achievable by faithful adherence to the law.[27] Unlike the Zealots, Jesus viewed the reign of God as "a *purely religious kingdom,*" not an earthly, national theocracy.[28] Unlike the monks of Qumran, the *basileia* of Jesus is "a *saving event for sinners,*" not a vengeful judgment on them.[29] Nor did Jesus' proclamation offer a new, improved moral code for people to follow; instead, it demanded "*a radical decision for God.*"[30] In his life and works, Jesus is both the great sign of his times and the sign that the old aeon has passed away with his coming.[31] Küng quotes Kasemann approvingly on the authority with which Jesus taught:

> To this there are no Jewish parallels, nor indeed can there be. For the Jew who does what is done here has cut himself off from the community of Judaism—or else he brings the Messianic Torah and is therefore the Messiah. . . . The unheard-of implication of the saying testifies to its genuineness. It proves, secondly, that while Jesus may have made his appearance in the first place in the character of a rabbi or a prophet, nevertheless, his claim far surpasses that of any rabbi or prophet; and thirdly, that he cannot be integrated into the background of the Jewish piety of his time. Certainly he was a Jew and made the assumptions of Jewish piety, but at the same time he shatters this framework in his claim.[32]

In spite of the promise with which we began this study of Küng, so far we have found nothing that deviates from the structure of thought of, for example, Harnack's Christology. He asks the same questions that Harnack did and receives the same answers to them. To this point, Küng's is not, in any sense of the word, a post-Holocaust reflection on the question of Christology. At the same time, it is remarkably innocent of recent scholarship on the Judaisms of the first century. Since the time of the earliest *adversus Judaeos* literature, the doctrine of the church has been the pay-off doctrine of Christian anti-Judaism, the point at which the cash value of the anti-Judaism of all the other doctrines, particularly Christology, is redeemed. This remains true for Küng's doctrine of the church.

Since *Jesus himself* is the basis and criterion of Christian truth and apparently did not found a church, Küng is at some pains to "back up" his claims for the church in the life and teachings of Jesus himself. He admits that Jesus did not call a church or separate his disciples from the rest of Israel, nor did he contrast them as a new people of God with the ancient people of God.[33] "The Church . . . is therefore a post-Easter phenomenon."[34] Is it, therefore, an illegitimate development, something that should not have happened? No! In spite of the difficult nature of the sources, nonetheless, the Gospels are concerned with Jesus' pre-Easter preaching and teaching "down to the last detail" and therefore show us how Jesus himself really laid the groundwork for the emergence of the church. Particularly, since Jesus foresaw that Jerusalem would reject him and his message "and that instead the heathen would be called to the eschatological feast, he proclaimed a new people of God, one not based simply on ethnic origins."[35] The origins of the church rest not only in the message of the pre-Easter Jesus but also in the whole history of his life and ministry. This, plus God's act of resurrecting him, "turned the group of those who believed communally in the risen Jesus into a community of those who, in contrast to the unbelieving ancient people of God, could claim to be the new eschatological people of God."[36]

Küng's claims that Jesus foresaw his rejection and the coming of gentiles into the church call seriously into question his protestations to be engaging in historical-critical inquiry. His contrast of the new, *believing* community with the old, *unbelieving* community is inherently works-righteous: We can claim to be the new people of God because we do the good work of believing. His old/new contrast is also inherently supersessionist in its implications—but more on this later. The question raised here by this aspect of his work is whether the identity of the church is bought at the price paid by the Jewish people of no longer being God's eschatological people.

Küng's answer to this question is a highly dialectical "yes-and-no," but he proves unable to sustain the dialectic. Whether a dialectical response to this question is even appropriate is a good question. Why not a plain affirmation of the covenant between God and Israel? Since a major plank of traditional Christian anti-Judaism held that the Jews (they) were rejected when the gentiles (we) were elected—hence, that Jews are religiously out of business and have no business continuing to exist *as Jews*—one would think that a serious post-Holocaust theological enterprise would avoid reinforcing this position. Instead, such a theology could formulate a new christological rule, to the effect that every proper christological statement will make it clear that the covenant between God and Israel is affirmed.[37]

Küng's first question in his discussion of the church as the people of God is this: "Beyond Judaism?"[38] Was the church really more than the Zealots or the Pharisees? Yes. The disciples of Jesus saw themselves not only as the *true* but equally as the *new* Israel.[39] Küng overlooks the fact that in the Second Testament neither "true" nor "new" ever modifies "Israel." Many things therein are so described, but Israel is *never* one of them. Despite a total lack of supporting evidence, Küng concludes from the "fact" that the disciples saw themselves as the true and new Israel that they were.

"They *were* already the new Israel, even if externally little different from the old."[40] The earliest disciples retained Jewish forms while giving them entirely new content, which "new content was bound, sooner or later, to burst the bounds of the old forms."[41] The seeds of separation from Judaism lay in baptism, in the communal service of prayer, in the eschatological meal, in the leaders of the community, and in its living fellowship of love.[42] Hence, the development of a gentile Christianity freed from Judaic laws was made possible.[43] In this historical process "the ways of Israel and the Church totally diverged. Yet the two remain, whether they like it and know it or not, undissolubly bound together. This is inevitable, since the Church claims to be the new *Israel*, the new *people of God.*"[44]

The clear import of Küng's answer is: Yes! Beyond Judaism! He does not specify that the opposite of true is false, that if the church is the true Israel, Israel must be the false Israel. One might interpret Küng as meaning just that. Alternatively, one could argue that a simple affirmative statement carries no negative implications, that to say that the church is the true Israel is not to say that Israel is the false Israel. If so, however, in what sense is the church "beyond Judaism"? Nonetheless, according to Küng, this development of the new people of God in contradistinction from the old one is the fault of the old people of God, specifically of the majority's rejection of the message of the disciples. Thus did the Jews make it inevitable that the church would describe itself as the true and new Israel.[45] Confusingly, however, Küng goes on to say that the ancient people of God still keeps its name, "even after Christ," and the church remains linked to Israel: "Gentiles are only the grafts on to the old stem."[46] The spirit is inclusive, the logic exclusive.

Further, Küng retains some of the hoary themes of the *adversus Judaeos* ideology. He asserts that Israel's history "is a story of repeated failures and betrayals, backslidings and loss of faith: a story of sin."[47] This sin resulted in total crisis and destruction of the state, interpreted by the prophets as God's judgment on and rejection of a faithless people, as well as of God's mercy and renewed election of them. What is wrong with Küng's view here is more the emphasis on what is said than in what is said itself. Israel gets credit once again for having a history that is a "trail of crimes," not for continually producing a remarkable record of prophetic self-criticism.[48] If Christian religious history is any clue, we might contend that every such history is a history of failure. Whatever else be the case, Christian history *vis-à-vis* Jews, women, colonized-now-third-world people, and racial and ethnic minorities in Christian cultures is, beyond doubt, a failure.

We find the second classic theme of anti-Judaism in Küng's description of the so-called "late Judaism." In this "nationalistic, rabbinistic, hellenistic, and apocalyptic" Judaism we have nothing but "misinterpretations" and "misunderstandings of the idea of the people of God."[49] Doubtless this, which is clearly *Judaism* for Küng if anything is, needed to be superseded by the "correct" understandings.

Third, Küng accords to the covenant between God and Israel only a provisional validity. Israel's function is to prefigure the church; it "provides a contrast with the people of the new covenant."[50] The difference of the new people from the old one is that its word of revelation "is no longer a provisional one, but the final and definitive word."[51] The promise given to the new people of God is eschatological; it "cannot be reversed." Küng does not discuss Paul's claim that the promise and call of God to Israel are "irrevocable" (Rom. 11:29). He simply declares of the new promise that it is "definitely guaranteed by a better covenant between God and his people . . ."[52] "Thus," concludes Küng, "the old covenant, image and parable of the coming covenant, is confirmed and at the same time dissolved and exceeded."[53] In Hegelian fashion, it is *aufgehoben* in Jesus Christ. This is a historical-developmental version of traditional supersessionism, not new to the late twentieth century, and long subjected to searching critique.[54]

There is no point in leaving a misimpression. Küng seriously wants to overcome the anti-Jewish legacy of the Christian tradition. He unquestionably affirms that all that will suffice from Christians in this regard is "a radical metanoia, repentance and re-thinking."[55] He *wants* things to be different. However, it does not occur to him that the place to start doing the rethinking is at the beginning, with the structure and method of his Christology and the manner of his appeal to the historical Jesus. He still pictures a Jesus at odds with and overcoming all kinds of Judaism and *on this basis* expects to be able to criticize anti-Judaism. This is a well-intended but self-defeating effort. It leaves him contradictorily claiming that Israel did *not* lose its special position as the people of God after Jesus' death and that "*solely* faith in Jesus Christ . . . decides who belongs to the people of God."[56] He cannot have it both ways.

In his later work, **On Being a Christian,** and in its shortened version, **The Christian Challenge,** Küng takes up the christological task again in a way that differs in detail, but not in method and structure, from what we have already seen. After dealing with the challenge of modern humanism and of the other religions, Küng turns his attention to Christianity, asking what about it is special. His answer is: "this *Jesus himself,* who is known even today by the ancient name of *Christ.*"[57] He is "ultimately decisive, definitive and archetypal for man in all his dimensions."[58]

By "Christ," Küng is still at pains to show that he means not the Christ of piety or of dogma or of the enthusiasts or of literature, but the "real" Christ, the Jesus of Nazareth whose "history can be *dated.*"[59] Despite uncertainties as to exactly when he was born, when he died, and where he came from—"not particularly relevant" matters[60]—and despite the fact that we cannot write a biography because we know how the Gospels arose and that they are "*committed testimonies of faith meant to commit their readers,*"[61] nonetheless, we can ask and answer questions about the historical Jesus. Using all the pertinent methods of biblical study, including the criterion of dissimilarity,[62] we can reconstruct "*the typical basic features and outlines of Jesus' proclamation, behavior and fate.*"[63] Such a historical-critical research into Jesus can neither provide reasons for faith nor destroy faith, says Küng; it does enable us "*to give an account of our faith.*"[64] Apparently, Küng means here, as was noted previously, that such critical inquiry can "back up" faith or show that certain strongly held views can be warranted. That seems quite like giving reasons for faith.

Before moving into his attempt at describing the historical Jesus in **On Being a Christian,** however, Küng discusses the relation between Christianity and Judaism. He says nothing here that he has not said before. He describes the "history of blood and tears," asserts the Jewishness of Jesus, claims that Christians who are anti-Jewish are anti-Jesus, and asks about future possibilities for relations between Jews and Christians, specifically suggesting that

Jews and Christians should discuss Jesus and that, "if . . . we start out from Jesus of Nazareth as man and Jew, we shall be able to go *a good part of the way together* with an unbiased Jew."[65] The description of Jesus that follows, however, differs from the ones we have already seen by being more finely tuned. Jesus' identity now is located not only by the method of dissimilarity but, as a result of it, by placing Jesus in a "simultaneous quadrilateral conflict" with all kinds of Jews of his time.

Jesus was (1) not a member of the establishment, ecclesiastical or social. He was not a high priest, not an elder, not a scribe, not a Sadducee.[66] He rejected their Hellenistic lifestyle, their conservative view of the law, and their conservative theology, and he did not care about the religiopolitical *status quo*.[67] Unlike the conservative-liberal establishment, he was sustained by an intense expectation of the eschaton.

Although he expected radical change, Jesus was (2) not a revolutionary, one of the Zealots; "we cannot make Jesus a guerrilla fighter, a rebel, a political agitator and revolutionary or turn his message of God's kingdom into a program of politico-social action."[68] Instead, Jesus "waits for God to bring about the cataclysm and proclaims as already decisive the *unrestricted, direct world dominion of God himself, to be awaited without violence*."[69] A political, social revolution is not, for Jesus, the alternative to the system. Jesus condoned neither the goals of the Zealots nor their path to these goals.[70]

Yet he also rejected (3) the equally radical if extremely different alternative offered by the monks of Qumran: emigration, the great refusal, repudiation of the world. Jesus was not an Essene. In spite of some similarities to them and perhaps some connections between Qumran and the beginnings of Christianity, Jesus was not "a religious."[71] He rejected altogether their isolation from the world, their bifurcation of reality, their legal fanaticism, their asceticism, their hierarchical order, their monastic rule, their elitism.[72]

Jesus would not identify with the establishment in his society or revolt against it or leave it. Would he, then, (4) compromise with it? No. He was not a Pharisee. Pharisees followed the way of moral compromise, says Küng.[73] Küng recognizes that the reason that the Pharisees are the chief opponents of Jesus in the Gospels is because they were the sole party to survive the great revolution against Rome in the years 66-70 C.E. and were, therefore, the foundation of the subsequent development of Judaism.[74] Nevertheless, he insists on viewing the strife between Jesus and the Pharisees in the Gospels as historical: "The conflict with the Pharisees was bound to come to a head, since there was so much in common between the two sides."[75] In spite of what they had in common, "Jesus was not a pious legalistic moralist."[76] He acted against the law when he thought it important to do so, placed himself above it, recognized no ritual taboos, was no ascetic, was not scrupulous about observing the Sabbath, and opposed self-

righteousness.[77] The Pharisees "look for honors, titles, adulation, and put themselves in God's place. They build monuments to the former prophets and kill those of the present time."[78] Finally, it is their piety and morality itself that stands between God and the people and for which they become Jesus' worst enemies.[79] In all of this, it is obvious that Küng takes the picture of the Pharisees in the Gospels at face value, regarding it as a historically reliable account. That precisely this is what we may *not* do has been ably argued by several scholars.[80]

Fitting into none of the categories of his society, culture, and religion, "*Jesus is different*."[81] "Despite all parallels in detail, the historical Jesus in his wholeness turns out to be completely unique—in his own time and ours."[82] This view of Jesus as "completely unique" by virtue of standing at the crossroads of a four-way conflict with Sadducees, Essenes, Pharisees, and Zealots is repeated unchanged in Küng's most recent work.[83] Consequently everything about him was improper, libelous, scandalous to any devout Jew.[84] He relativized the law and the temple. Despite his total alienation from his society, "love of one's fellow man is present everywhere in Jesus' proclamation."[85] Interestingly, Küng has to introduce that last remark with a "nevertheless." Jesus advocated not merely love of the neighbor but, even more, of the enemy, and it is this that is typical of him.[86] This and his openness to such non-Jews as Samaritans differentiates him from the Pharisees. He was also a partisan for the handicapped and the poor. Indeed, the God of Jesus was unlike the one whom Küng calls "the God of Judaism." This latter God, according to Küng, could only forgive the sinner who had already become righteous.[87] Jesus' God forgives sinners as such, "loves sinners more than the *righteous*."[88] Jesus is here pictured as preparing the way for Marcion. Is this a Jesus with whom an unbiased Jew is supposed to be sympathetic? Küng's Jesus hardly differs from the Jesus of the anti-Jewish tradition; this Jesus lived, died, and taught in conscious and consistent opposition to Judaism. So does Küng's.

Jesus, unique and thoroughly alienated from all kinds of Jews and Judaism except those looked down upon by all the official representatives of the community, both was aggressive toward all sides of the religious world and, in turn, was attacked by all of them.[89] He was brought to trial for having "offended against almost everything that was sacred to this people, this society and its representatives."[90] He called into question the law, the society, the cult, and the identity of the people in his love for the stranger. Inconveniently, for Küng's point of view, love for the stranger is commanded in the Torah (Lev. 19:34). How could love for the stranger overthrow the law that commanded it? In any case, Küng contends that Jesus "shattered the foundations, the whole theology and ideology of the hierarchy."[91] As a result, he incurred the hostility of virtually everybody, "of rulers and rebels, the silent majority and the loud minority."[92] He proclaimed the ancient God of the patriarchs, not the God of late Judaism.[93] Yet, he spoke of this God differently, as a God of redeeming love, "a new God: a God who has set himself free from his own law, . . . not a God of God-fearers, but a *God of the godless*."[94] This is a different God, one not of law but of grace.[95] Jesus "constantly addressed God as *abba*."[96]

This explains why Jesus' whole career is marked from the beginning by a foreboding of death.[97] He was "murdered" on the true religious charge that he assumed a sovereign liberty with regard to law and temple, questioned the religious system, and proclaimed God's mercy.[98] It is needless to ask whether the Jews or the Romans murdered him, says Küng, without explaining why the Romans would have cared about a figure so totally at odds with other Jews theologically. In any case, "It was the law which sought his death,"[99] says Küng, blaming it on a reification. Yet, the one whom the Jews rejected was raised from the dead and warranted by God. God "approved of his proclamation, his behavior, his fate."[100] In his total alienation from all the Judaisms of his time, he was "confirmed" by God, "justified" by God, "put in the right" by God, acknowledged by God to the world.[101]

In the most extensive study yet done in English of Küng, the point is clearly and repeatedly made that in his understanding of and relation to God Jesus was brought into direct opposition to Judaism: "[I]n the last analysis the whole battle between Jesus and Judaism would come down to the question of God."[102] His understanding of God "forged the battle between Jesus and Judaism,"[103] setting the stage "for the final struggle between Jesus and Judaism."[104]

What can we say of Hans Küng's Christology in light of his concern for the reconstruction of Christology after the Holocaust in a way that is appropriate to the gospel of Jesus Christ and no longer anti-Jewish? Is Küng's Christ not precisely the superseder of Judaism, Christ the supplanter who creates a "new" Israel in place of the old, and, at the same time, the champion of the new against the old? Surely, in spite of Küng's commitment to overcome anti-Judaism, we cannot but answer this question in the affirmative. Just as with the classical tradition and its liberal revisionists, so with Küng, Jesus "shatters" Judaism and warrants its displacement by the creation of another people of God that is the new and the true Israel.

Is Jesus' significance for Christians tied up with his having done this "good work" of delivering us from Judaism? It is precisely because Jesus was "different" that the Jews rejected him and God "justified" him—certainly God justified him (according to Küng) in his difference.

Do Küng's claims about the historical Jesus go beyond what we can responsibly claim to know? Obviously, Küng knows full well the problem with the Gospels as sources of historical knowledge, yet on the basis of them he regularly contends that Jesus experienced God in a certain, immediate way, that he always did so, that he experienced himself as God's son and advocate, as God's final and unsurpassable prophet, that Jesus' whole life was totally dedicated to God, that he lived entirely in virtue of the One whom he called "abba," that he was always faithful to God's will, and that he "foresaw" the temple's destruction and his own death. Küng never tells us how he knows these things, because he cannot. He merely asserts them and, on that basis, attempts to "back up" his Christology.

Are the claims that Küng makes about Jesus appropriate to the Christian faith? It would seem not. The gospel is the promise of God's love graciously offered to each and all and the command of God that justice be done to each and all of those whom God loves. Küng's Christology fails to do justice to Judaism in Jesus' time or in the present. It merely repeats the images of Judaism that have long been known to be merely pejorative and lacking in historical authenticity.[105] The commandment against bearing false witness applies also to theologians. Also, by stressing as he does Jesus' immediate relation to God, like Schleiermacher and Harnack, he makes of Jesus the "perfect believer," the one *with* whom we believe, not the one *in* whom we believe.

Is Küng's Christology intelligible? Not unless a "completely unique" historical figure is intelligible. One cannot think the idea, if it is one, of a totally unique historical person, at least not in the empirical-historical sense in which Küng speaks of Jesus' uniqueness. Indeed, no one would ever know how in any way to hold such a figure as significant. There would literally be no analogies in terms of which to appropriate the meaning of a totally unique figure; one is dealing here, rather, with a total anomaly, someone so strange that nothing could be made of him. Nor, by the way, should anything be made of the claim that the Jews "rejected" this "completely unique" person. Nothing else could be done with the "completely unique," except that even "reject" is too strong here; the "completely unique" would necessarily be completely puzzling to everyone. Such a unique figure is docetic, a shadow of a concrete human being.

Two further intelligibility questions arise. First, how can a "completely unique" Jesus serve as the "source, standard, and criterion" of Christian faith? How can he be "the truth"? How can he be both definitive and totally undefinable? Functioning as the criterion and being completely unique are incompatible, with the possible exception that the outcome could be that nothing could possibly be true. Second, Küng appeals to Jesus in differing ways, depending on what he needs to acquire from his "source." He sometimes invokes Jesus' message, sometimes his person (his awareness of God), sometimes his whole history. Finally, that which is the "source, standard, and criterion" is itself in turn warranted by the resurrection, in which God "backs up, acknowledges" the historical Jesus' message, person, and history, and particularly his conflict with all kinds of Jews and Judaisms. God vindicates Jesus against all his opponents in the simultaneous quadrilateral conflict that was his life. As a warrant-structure, this is simply confusing. Also, it raises the question whether Jesus Christ is not more than any mere norm to Christian faith.

What clues toward reconstruction do we find in Küng? In his desire to overcome anti-Judaism and in his conviction that a complete rethinking and a radical *metanoia* are necessary, he is certainly correct. In his case, continuing as he does the methodology and warrant-structure of, for example, Harnack, and making the same assumptions as to the question that Christology must answer, such a rethinking is not forthcoming. That we need precisely such a rethinking is the point of which Küng makes us keenly aware.

This rethinking must begin on two fronts. The first has to do with historical scholarship on the Judaisms of the early first century. The scholarship on which Küng relies presents a now largely discredited and highly pejorative view of what he continues to call "late Judaism." The new scholarship, which sets forth a more balanced and nuanced picture, needs to be consulted by theologians interested in the "most likely story" that can be told of the historical Jesus.[106] Küng's disparaging remarks about the God of "late Judaism," for example, must now be resolutely set aside as false and inaccurate.[107] In this context, another question has to do with what one thinks one is doing when one is trying to reconstruct critically the figure of the historical Jesus. Küng is typical of modern, liberal theologians in his effort to "back up" Christology by reference to putative empirical statements about Jesus; the purpose of historical-critical inquiry for him is to warrant Christology by establishing the "picture" of Jesus that will serve as the "norm" for theology and ecclesiology. It is a very different thing to engage in what James H. Charlesworth terms "Jesus research," the purpose of which is *not* to warrant any Christology but to develop the most reliable historical picture we can of the Jesus whom we *already* confess to be the Christ. This effort, motivated by no need to set Jesus over against Jews and Judaism, situates him within the context of Judaism and within the covenant of the God of Israel with the Israel of God. It frees historical criticism from coming up with the "right" results and "frees" the historical Jesus to be himself, a first-century Jew. It also allows Jesus to correct the anti-Judaism of our Christologies, a correction that pointedly does not happen in Küng's "historical-Jesus Christology." Whether such a correction is allowable within a typical "historical-Jesus Christology" is trenchantly, if unintentionally, raised by Küng.

Although it moves ahead into the next point, a word about what can serve to "warrant" Christology must be said. If Christology is, as I contend below, an attempt to ask and answer one complex set of interrelated questions, questions about *who* God is, how we are to understand ourselves, and what role Jesus Christ plays in these two questions, then any attempt to warrant Christology would have to ask and answer the questions whether the one whom we say is God really is, whether the way we are given to understand ourselves is indeed true, and whether Jesus Christ, in fact, is the savior who confronts us with the truth about ourselves. Appeal to the Jesus of critical-historical reconstruction cannot warrant christological

claims, although appeal to the Jew *Yeshua ha Notsri* can contradict anti-Jewish claims made on his behalf, if Jesus is seen within the covenant between the God of Israel and the Israel of God. Whatever Jesus was, he was that Jewishly. No Christology appropriate to him could possibly be anti-Jewish.

The second point has to do with more strictly methodological and theological issues; it raises the question of what we are doing when we are doing Christology. Küng apparently takes the christological question to be a question about the Jesus of historical reconstruction, and he is at pains to produce a Christology that answers this question, telling us who Jesus *was* (it is to be noted that the christological confession is always in the *present* tense), how he was related to God, how he was in an empirical-historical way "unique," and what he did, which was to overcome Judaism and create in its place a "new Israel," the church. I take my own bearings from a set of fairly diverse theologians (Paul Tillich, Schubert M. Ogden, and Paul M. van Buren) who disagree on much but agree that the question that Christology seeks to answer is not "who was Jesus?" but a complex question having to do with how we understand ourselves in relation to God, the neighbor, and the Israel of God. That is, the questions Christology answers are: Who is God? Who are we? What is the meaning of Jesus Christ to us? The answers are: God is the God of Israel, who justifies the ungodly (including gentiles). We are those who, through the church's witness to Jesus Christ, learn that the only appropriate way in which we can understand ourselves in any ultimate sense is in terms of the unfathomably free love and total claim of the God of Israel. Jesus Christ is the risen Jew from Nazareth who, through the witness of the church, continues to confront us with the promise and command of the God of Israel.

Tillich gives us the insight that any Christology that is merely a "Jesusology," that makes claims of perfection (such as being the "perfect believer") for a finite and relative historical figure, always ends up being another oppressive heteronomy to be imposed on other faiths—and particularly on Judaism.[108]

Ogden powerfully argues that any appropriately Christian Christology must be understood as a "re-presentative" Christology, in which what it means to have Christ as our Lord is existentially the same as having the God of Israel as God. Paul's intent, says Ogden, is to affirm that the disclosure of God in Jesus Christ "is the decisive re-presentation to all mankind of the same promise and demand re-presented by the Old Testament revelation (cf. Rom. 3:21)."[109] The word addressed to us in Jesus Christ "is precisely the *same* word" that had been previously "re-presented through 'the law and the prophets.'"[110] Along with this goes the insistence that the significance of Jesus Christ be understood utterly in terms of the graciousness of the God of Israel. God saves us by grace alone in total freedom "from any saving 'work' of the kind traditionally portrayed in the doctrines of the . . . work of Christ."[111] Although Ogden does not make the application explicit, this includes the good work of overcoming Judaism and saving us from it.

From van Buren, a post-Holocaust Christology with any hope of being adequate learns that the only context in which our language about Jesus Christ makes any sense is that of the covenant between the God of Israel and the Israel of God and that the one whom we call Christ is the Jew Jesus of Nazareth through whom God calls into existence the church.[112]

As far as I can see, to encounter Jesus Christ in the witness of the church is to encounter the God of Israel, maker and redeemer of heaven and earth. This Jesus, whose very name proclaims that "Yahweh is salvation," is the one through whom, by the witness of the church, we are laid bare before the maker and redeemer of heaven and earth, the God of Jesus Christ, of Paul the apostle, and of the people Israel. More specifically, the role of Jesus Christ in relation to gentile Christians, whether of Teutonic derivation (as Küng) or Celtic (as Williamson), is fundamentally different from his role in relation to the Jewish people. What Jesus of Nazareth *did* for his followers was to call them *back* to the God of Israel whose *basileia* had been promised to them. What Jesus Christ through the church has done and continues to do for the Küngs and Williamsons of this world has been to call us away from Wotan and Thor, Maeve and Fergus, *to* the God of Israel and *to* the Israel of God. Paul, for example, spoke little of the typical Jewish notion of "returning" (*shuv*) to God because he was trying to persuade his gentile followers to "turn" to God in the first place. That is, rather than being the one who drove a wedge between the gentile church and the Jewish people, the proper role of Jesus Christ is that attested by Ephesians: to bring gentiles in out of the cold of being "without God in the world," aliens to God's grace and promise, and to bring gentiles *into* the family and household of God (Eph. 2:11-22).

Therefore, Jesus Christ is never properly attested, either in the witness of the church or in the critical christological reflection of theologians, unless it is made quite clear that, when we say that "Jesus Christ is Lord," we can never do so without saying that this is so "to the glory of God the Father" (Phil. 2:11). Nor may we ever forget that the One whom Paul calls "God the Father" is the "God of Israel," who is theologically unthinkable without the "Israel of God." That is, if Jesus Christ is a *gift* to the church from the God of Israel, an entirely correct theological proposition, then he is also by the same token a gift to the church from the Israel of God. Jesus Christ took form in the people Israel and is inseparable from the covenant between the God of Israel and the Israel of God. If God is not faithful to that covenant, a faithfulness that supersessionist teaching denies, then there is no ground for Christian hope in God's faithfulness. If God's grace does not continue to be extended to Jews as Jews after the time of Jesus Christ, then the gospel of God's gracious justification of the ungodly is untrue for gentiles. If this God rejects Jews because their history is a history of sin, what can we expect of God after a Holocaust in which all the killers were Christian? Christology must in each of its statements give voice to the grace of God, never to the works-righteousness implicit in anti-Judaism.

That there is much more to be worked out in a Christology is a point of which I am keenly aware. What I have tried to indicate (and merely that) in this last section is a suggestion of a starting point and direction for a post-Holocaust Christology.

Notes

1. Hans Küng, "Introduction: From Anti-Semitism to Theological Dialogue," in Hans Küng and Walter Kasper, eds., *Christians and Jews,* Concilium, vol. 8, no. 10 (New York: Seabury Press, 1974/5), p. 9.

2. Ibid.

3. Ibid., p. 10.

4. Ibid., p. 11.

5. Ibid., p. 13, his emphasis.

6. Ibid.

7. "The very concept of a New Testament as distinct from the Old may well go back to Marcion's repudiation of the Jewish scriptures" (Norman Perrin, *New Testament: An Introduction* [New York: Harcourt Brace Jovanovich, 1974], p. 331).

8. Hans Küng, *Judaism: Between Yesterday and Tomorrow,* tr. John Bowden (New York: Crossroad, 1992), pp. 109-111.

9. Küng, "Introduction," p. 14.

10. Hans Küng, "Toward a New Consensus in Catholic (and Ecumenical) Theology," in Leonard Swidler, ed., *Consensus in Theology?* (Philadelphia: Westminster Press, 1980 [co-published as *J. E. S.* 17 (Winter, 1980)]), p. 6, his emphasis.

11. Ibid., p. 7.

12. Ibid.

13. Ibid., p. 8.

14. Ibid., p. 11.

15. Hans Küng, *The Church—Maintained in Truth: A Theological Meditation,* tr. Edward Quinn (New York: Seabury Press, 1980), p. 11.

16. Ibid., p. 12.

17. Ibid., p. 20, his emphasis.

18. Ibid.

19. Ibid., p. 28, his emphasis.

20. Ibid., p. 40.

21. Ibid., p. 41.

22. Ibid., p. 65.

23. Küng seems to be foundering here, as do many theologians, on his collapse of the distinction between the *meaning* of truth and its *criteria.* What he is saying might be put as: "Jesus is a necessary condition of truth," whereas I would want to say that "Jesus Christ is a sufficient condition for the criteria of truth." The two statements are very

different. Jesus Christ is the ultimate source of the church's criteria but certainly more than any mere criterion.

24. Hans Küng, *The Church,* tr. Ray and Rosaleen Ockenden (New York: Sheed and Ward, 1967), p. 43.

25. Ibid., p. 44.

26. Ibid., p. 45.

27. Ibid., p. 48, his emphasis.

28. Ibid., p. 49, his emphasis.

29. Ibid., p. 51, his emphasis.

30. Ibid., p. 52, his emphasis.

31. Ibid., p. 57.

32. Ibid., p. 58, quoting Ernst Kasemann, *Essays on New Testament Themes, Studies in Biblical Theology* 41 (London and Naperville, IL: SCM, 1964), pp. 37-38.

33. Ibid., p. 73.

34. Ibid.

35. Ibid., p. 75.

36. Ibid., p. 76.

37. Paul M. van Buren formulates precisely such a rule in his *A Theology of the Jewish-Christian Reality—Part 3: Christ in Context* (San Francisco, CA: Harper & Row, 1988), p. xix.

38. Küng, *The Church,* p. 107.

39. Ibid., p. 108.

40. Ibid., p. 109, his emphasis.

41. Ibid.

42. Ibid., pp. 109-110.

43. Ibid., p. 111.

44. Ibid., p. 113, his emphasis.

45. Ibid., p. 114.

46. Ibid., p. 115.

47. Ibid., p. 118.

48. Of course, those alert to issues of sensitivity might find it callous of any Christian theologian, after the attempted *Endlösung der Judenfrage,"* to say of the Jewish people that theirs is a history of sin.

49. Küng, *The Church,* p. 119.

50. Ibid., p. 123.

51. Ibid.

52. Ibid.

53. Ibid.

54. See, e.g., Ernst Troeltsch, *Die Absolutheit des Christentum und die Religionsgeschichte* (Tübingen: J. C. B. Mohr, 1929), pp. 1-20.

55. Küng, *The Church,* p. 138.

56. Ibid., p. 145, his emphasis.

57. Hans Küng, *On Being a Christian,* tr. Edward Quinn (Garden City, NY: Doubleday & Co., 1976), p. 123, his emphasis.

58. Ibid.

59. Ibid., p. 148, his emphasis.

60. Ibid., p. 149.

61. Ibid., p. 153, his emphasis.

62. Ibid., p. 159.

63. Ibid, his emphasis.

64. Ibid., p. 161, his emphasis.

65. Ibid., p. 174, his emphasis.

66. Ibid., pp. 178-179.

67. Ibid., p. 180.

68. Ibid., p. 187.

69. Ibid, his emphasis.

70. Ibid., p. 190.

71. Ibid., p. 195.

72. Ibid., pp. 196-201.

73. Ibid., p. 202.

74. Ibid.

75. Ibid., p. 206.

76. Ibid., p. 207.

77. Ibid., p. 252.

78. Ibid., p. 209.

79. Ibid., p. 211.

80. See, e.g., E. P. Sanders, *Paul and Palestinian Judaism* (Philadelphia: Fortress Press, 1987); and Jacob Neusner, *From Politics to Piety* (Englewood Cliffs, NJ: Prentice-Hall, Inc., 1973).

81. Küng, *On Being a Christian,* p. 212, his emphasis.

82. Ibid. Needless to say, the expression "completely unique" is redundant.

83. Küng, *Judaism,* pp. 319-336.

84. Küng, *On Being a Christian,* p. 252.

85. Ibid., p. 255.

86. Ibid., p. 258.

87. Ibid., p. 273.

88. Ibid., p. 274, his emphasis.

89. Ibid., p. 278.

90. Ibid., p. 291.

91. Ibid., p. 293.

92. Ibid., p. 292.

93. Ibid., p. 296.

94. Ibid., p. 313, his emphasis.

95. Ibid., p. 314.

96. Ibid, his emphasis.

97. Ibid., p. 319.

98. Ibid., pp. 336-337.

99. Ibid., p. 339.

100. Ibid., p. 382.

101. Ibid.

102. William F. Buggert, "The Christologies of Hans Küng and Karl Rahner—A Comparison and Evaluation of Their Mutual Compatibility" (unpublished Ph.D. dissertation, The Catholic University of America, 1978), p. 109.

103. Ibid., pp. 109-110.

104. Ibid., p. 110.

105. George Foot Moore, *Judaism in the First Three Centuries of the Common Era: The Age of the Tannaim,* 3 vols. (Cambridge, MA: Harvard University Press, 1927-30).

106. A representative, but far from exhaustive, list of relevant titles includes: James H. Charlesworth, *Jesus within Judaism* (New York: Doubleday, 1988); James D. G. Dunn, *Jesus, Paul, and the Law* (Louisville, KY: Westminster/John Knox Press, 1990); Paula Fredriksen, *From Jesus to Christ* (New Haven, CT: Yale University Press, 1988); John G. Gager, *The Origins of Anti- Semitism* (New York: Oxford University Press, 1983); Lloyd Gaston, *Paul and the Torah* (Vancouver, BC: University of British Columbia Press, 1987); Howard Clark Kee, *Jesus in History* (San Diego, CA: Harcourt Brace Jovanovich, 1977); Bernard J. Lee, *The Galilean Jewishness of Jesus* (New York: Paulist Press, 1988); and E. P. Sanders, *Jesus and Judaism* (Philadelphia: Fortress Press, 1985).

107. See, e.g., Fredriksen, *From Jesus to Christ,* p. 108.

108. This is one of the crucial points in Tillich's discussion of "final revelation": Paul Tillich, *Systematic Theology,* vol. 1 (Chicago: University of Chicago Press, 1951), pp. 135-137.

109. Schubert M. Ogden, *The Reality of God and Other Essays* (New York: Harper & Row, 1963, 1965, 1966), p. 202.

110. Ibid., p. 203, his emphasis.

111. Schubert M. Ogden, *Christ without Myth* (New York: Harper & Brothers, 1961), p. 145.

112. van Buren, *Christ in Context,* p. 5.

Larry A. Green (review date 2 March 1994)

SOURCE: A review of *Credo: The Apostles' Creed Explained for Today,* in *Christian Century,* Vol. 111, No. 7, March 2, 1994, pp. 231-32.

[*In the following review, Green calls Küng's* Credo *"worth the effort."*]

If Hans Küng's 21st book[, **Credo: The Apostles' Creed Explained for Today,**] were listed on a computer disk, its file name might be Küng.sea, indicating that this is a compressed file in the form of a "self-expanding archive." Compression shrinks computer files to use less space on the disk. To make the files usable again, they must be expanded. One of contemporary Roman Catholicism's best-known theologians, Küng has created a compact reader with far more content than its 190 pages would suggest.

Küng introduces each of his six chapters with an example of Christian iconography. He then draws on his admirable mastery of biblical, scientific, psychological and artistic arguments to compare that traditional image of faith with a contemporary conception. Küng writes for people who want to believe, but cannot do so in the manner of earlier times. "Too much has changed in the overall constellation of our time. Too much in Christian faith seems alien, seems to contradict the natural sciences and the humanities and indeed the humane impulses of our time. This book is meant to help here." Each article of the creed, therefore, is explored both from the perspective of contemporary concerns and in its historical context. The reader is confronted by Küng's thoroughly modern hermeneutic. For example, in his treatment of the resurrection, Küng observes, "The Easter event is not determined by the empty tomb but at best illustrated by it."

Küng also examines the creed in relationship to ethical issues. Woven into the discussion of eternal life is a provocative treatment of the meaning of dying. Referring to the artificial prolongation of life, he notes that "the end of life is also, more than hitherto, made a human responsibility (not a whim!) by the same God who does not want us to foist on him a responsibility which we ourselves can and should bear."

Credo is an important resource for theologians, students and any Christians who would like to revisit the creed with an eye toward revitalizing their faith through understanding. This is a book that seeks to bring a solid biblical interpretation to the creed while avoiding "an esoteric or sterile dogmatic interpretation." It is meant for those "who already believe," but to be understandable, "as far as possible, also for those who do not believe." Declares Küng: "Despite all my sorry experiences with my church, I believe that critical loyalty is worthwhile, that resistance is meaningful and renewal possible, and that another positive turn in church history cannot be ruled out." Read Küng.sea. Expanding its compressed ideas will be worth the effort.

William P. George (review date 18-25 May 1994)

SOURCE: "The Promise of a Global Ethic," in *Christian Century,* Vol. 111, No. 17, May 18-25, 1994, pp. 530-33.

[*In the following review, George briefly outlines* A Global Ethic, *developed by the Parliament of the World's Religions and edited by Küng and Karl-Josef Kuschel, and briefly compares it to John Paul II's encyclical on Roman Catholic moral theology,* Veritatis Splendor.]

"Come together in unity. Speak in profound agreements. May your minds converge (in deep consensus). May your deliberations be uniform and united in your hearts. May you be firmly bound and united in your intentions and resolves." In this way a Hindu sacred text (*Rig Veda*

X-191, 2-4) encourages and blesses its hearers. Despite its complexity, politics and even pratfalls, one could argue that the Parliament of the World's Religions in Chicago last summer was vivid testament that exhortations believed to be divinely inspired sometimes find their mark.

The full significance of the parliament, which drew 6,500 participants from virtually every religious community, is not easily assessed. But one tangible result was a 20-page consensus statement on a global ethic. Given the fact of religious diversity, which too often degenerates into bloodshed, one can hardly imagine a greater challenge. Even with this achievement, one is left to ask just what has been accomplished and what it all means.

Whatever the merit of debating the existence of a genuinely universal moral order and the possibility of articulating a global ethic, the fact of immense human suffering, endemic poverty for hundreds of millions, deep and protracted violent conflicts, oppression and exploitation of several kinds and ecological devastation ought to be its context. If multiculturalism, antifoundationalism, deconstructionism, postmodernism, etc., are to be the formal terms of scholarly ethical debate, then its matter ought to be such things as child prostitution in Thailand, domestic violence in the U.S., the destruction of the world's great rainforests, racial and tribal violence in South Africa, the present horror in Rwanda, and religious and ethnic warfare in Bosnia.

And things may be getting worse. Perhaps it is the onset of end-of-the-millennium fever, but writers like Paul Kennedy, in *Preparing for the Twenty-First Century,* and Robert Kaplan, in a recent *Atlantic* article, have painted the global future with Hobbesian and Malthusian brushes. For all but a more or less insulated elite, the world will not, they fear, be a pleasant place to live.

The framers and the first signatories of the Global Ethic are acutely aware of such foreboding, as well as of present horrors. The ethic is introduced by a jeremiad against the evils of the age—poverty, women and men estranged from each other, massive injustice, and especially aggression and hatred in the name of religion. Those who gathered in Chicago have experienced many of these first hand. The repression of the parliament's most illustrious participant, Tibet's Dalai Lama, may stand for all the rest.

In the face of these global problems, what is the Global Ethic about? What does it try to do? Most important, why ought anyone take it seriously? Given its brevity, the declaration may not answer such questions satisfactorily. For that reason the commentaries [included in *A Global Ethic: The Declaration of the Parliament of the World's Religions*] by Hans Küng, who drafted a major part of the document, and his Tübingen colleague, Karl-Josef Kuschel, are helpful. Küng recounts the genesis of and the process leading up to the finished document and discusses its key points. Kuschel places the parliament and declaration in historical context by reminding the reader of

advances in interreligious dialogue since the first parliament a century ago. He also discusses the collapse of Eurocentric Christian modernity and the polyreligious situation of our time. Taken together with the declaration, these two essays explain the intent of the Global Ethic, its limitations and its promise.

Küng's commentary helps clarify what the declaration is not: it is neither an ethical system nor a philosophical treatise. It is neither a sermon nor a political declaration. It is not the Universal Declaration of Human Rights dressed up in religious garb, not "a global ideology or a single unified religion beyond all existing religions, and certainly not the domination of one religion over all others."

Rather, this global ethic is "a fundamental consensus on binding values, irrevocable standards, and personal attitudes." As Küng explains in the preface, the consensus "does not reduce the religions to an ethical minimalism but represents the minimum of what the religions of the world already have in common now in the ethical sphere." Even the declaration title—"ethic" rather than "ethics"—is crucial. "Ethics" connotes a philosophical or theological theory that the declaration does not purport to present.

The declaration consists of two texts, a short "Introduction," drafted by an editorial committee of the "council" for the parliament, and "The Principles of a Global Ethic," drafted by Küng in Tübingen. The fact that there are two texts is a story in itself, having to do with the history of the declaration and its purpose (the Chicago-based committee wanted a short statement; Küng insisted on a longer text). This is a story that, unfortunately, I must bypass. As presented in this Continuum edition, the two texts together make up the Global Ethic.

The longer text, dealing with principles, is simply structured (although Küng points out that how he arrived at this structure was no simple matter). After noting the crises we collectively face, the declaration states that there can be "no new global order without a new global ethic." A new phase in our history requires a new vision; laws, prescriptions and conventions alone will not do. Joint responsibility for the new ethic issues in "a fundamental demand: every human being must be treated humanely."

This demand—the linchpin of the ethic—is then articulated as "a principle which is found and has persisted in many religious and ethical traditions of humankind for thousands of years," namely, "What you do not wish done to yourself, do not do to others! Or in positive terms: What you wish done to yourself, do to others." The Golden Rule is then expressed through four "irrevocable directives": commitment to a culture of nonviolence and respect for life; commitment to a culture of solidarity and a just economic order; commitment to a culture of tolerance and a life of truthfulness; commitment to a culture of equal rights and partnership between men and women.

These directives, each of which can be stated negatively ("You shall not kill!") or positively ("Have respect for life!"), are then given further, but by no means complete, specification. For instance, the commitment to truthfulness enjoins the media to respect and stand up for human rights. The fourth directive urges men and women "to resist wherever the domination of one sex over the other is preached—even in the name of religious conviction." Of special note in the section on nonviolence (the first directive) is the opening left for self-defense. Küng explains that this was of concern especially to Muslim representatives at the parliament.

The closing section of the declaration, titled "A Transformation of Consciousness," urges further consensus on specific issues such as those arising in the biomedical sphere. This search for further agreement is to build upon the declaration's principles. This final section also urges "the various communities of faith to formulate their very specific ethic"—something that Küng calls, perhaps tongue slightly in cheek, an "enjoyable task." Finally, the declaration calls upon all women and men of good will to undergo a conversion of heart.

Readers of all traditions may quite legitimately quibble over or contest any number of points, or note lacunae in the text as it stands. But as both the text and the commentaries make perfectly clear, the declaration is only a first step on the road to a full global ethic. Indeed, for some strange reason, the parliament's own official title, "Declaration *Toward* a Global Ethic" (emphasis added) appears in the table of contents of the Continuum edition, but not on the title page or cover. Its openendedness may be its most significant feature, and in many respects its most problematic. The declaration left at least two tasks unfinished: one is clearly stated, the other implied. The stated task is for various religious communities to work out their own specific ethic, one that builds upon the consensus statement. Besides carrying on dialogue among themselves in order to resolve their differences, religious communities should also, one can infer, engage and learn from institutions and communities not explicitly religious or those wishing to distance themselves from religion.

An example of greater specification of the ethic within a particular tradition is John Paul II's encyclical on Roman Catholic moral theology, *Veritatis Splendor,* which arrived on the scene five weeks after the parliament. Some argue that this long-awaited document was prompted by the same concerns that occupied those responsible for the emergence of the Global Ethic, namely, concerns for a perceived loss of moral bearings on a global scale. A careful comparative study of the two documents would be revealing; some brief observations must do.

While the papal document lacks specifics, Roman Catholicism's well-known proscriptions of artificial means of contraception, direct abortion and other "intrinsically evil acts" are amply and forcefully reaffirmed. With this "hard line" in view, juxtaposition with the Global Ethic is instructive. It exposes the large gap that can loom between the Global Ethic and the developed ethic of a particular

tradition, a gap of both content and degree of consensus. It is safe to say that not everyone who signed the Global Ethic would fully ascribe to the substantive views of *Veritatis Splendor;* the encyclical has failed to meet with unanimous approval even within Roman Catholic ranks.

To get a further sense of the extreme and in some respects strange tension that can exist between the minimal consensus of the declaration and the maximal ethic explicated by a particular tradition, I encourage the reader to puzzle over this fact: the Vatican's representative to the parliament, along with Chicago's Cardinal Joseph Bernardin and other Catholic leaders, signed their names to a document drafted by Hans Küng, whom the Vatican declared some years ago to be no longer a Catholic theologian; it is highly doubtful that Küng could return the favor and sign his name to *Veritatis Splendor.*

The nature of the tension between the Global Ethic and further intracommunity explication is even more visible in John Paul II's recent remarks. In keeping with *Veritatis Splendor,* he recently criticized a draft document of the upcoming International Conference on Population and Development, set for Cairo, because of its view of abortion and sexuality in general. "There is a tendency," the pope has said, "to promote an internationally recognized right to access to abortion on demand, without any restriction, with no regard to the rights of the unborn."

Although the core of the Global Ethic is the formal norm "treat human beings humanely," the declaration never ventures to say whether fetuses count as human beings or what humane treatment of prenatal life ought to entail. One hardly wonders at this silence; after all, as Küng explains in his commentary, a key operative principle guiding his drafting of the Global Ethic was a capacity to secure consensus. One can easily imagine why neither abortion nor prenatal life is mentioned anywhere in the text.

Silence about entailments of the Golden Rule might be golden: the lack of specificity in the Global Ethic may be its strength. While the principles enunciated by the ethic do not directly affirm John Paul II's stance on abortion, neither do they close it off. As a result, the pope and in principle other traditions can have it both ways: they can affirm a moral consensus with other religious communities on vague, formal, visionary principles while retaining their own distinctive moral stance. Unity and distinctiveness all at once—the very thing the parliament wanted to affirm.

But herein lies an enormous task as well. If greater explication is not to end in the total fracture of moral consensus, the various communities will have to stay connected through mutual exchange—in order both to challenge and to be challenged. John Paul II's explication of directives concerning respect for life and sexual ethics may challenge other religious traditions, but Roman Catholicism needs to listen to these traditions as well.

All consensual partners to the Global Ethic must stay in touch with those organizations, institutions and patterns of life that are less explicitly religious or even intentionally removed from religion. This is the second of the declaration's unfinished tasks. Insofar as the declaration calls upon all women and men of good will to join in the realization of a global ethic, a connection is clearly envisioned between those who gathered in Chicago last summer, those who will gather in Cairo in September, and those who gathered for the Rio de Janeiro Earth Summit two years ago. What does not emerge clearly from the declaration is the sense that religious traditions can learn a great deal from those whose moral viewpoints are not explicitly grounded in claims of transcendence.

To an extent, this apparent lack of receptiveness is understandable. As Küng points out, the declaration is a self-critical document. Religiously minded people and communities need first to reflect upon and repent of their own instigation of and participation in the violence, social disruptions and ecological destruction that mark our age. Second, the declaration's ethic should not be confused with either politics or law. "An ethic," Küng explains, "is primarily concerned with the inner realm of a person, the sphere of the conscience, of the 'heart,' which is not directly exposed to sanctions that can be imposed by political power."

But neither should a religiously grounded ethic be separated from politics and law. And this is not simply because, as Küng points out, "a global ethic should . . . have relevance at the economic and political level and support efforts towards a just ordering of the economy and of society." Rather, I suggest that politics and law can, in their inner dynamics, illuminate the very nature of the Global Ethic—even with its religious grounding.

Particularly striking is the mutually illuminating relationship between religion and law. As the eminent legal historian Harold J. Berman has argued in *Faith and Order: The Reconciliation of Law and Religion* and elsewhere, law in various cultures is infused with a moral underpinning more or less equivalent to the Decalogue of Judaism and Christianity. This underpinning, as Berman describes it, is strikingly similar to the parliament's ethic. In other words, law and explicitly religious claims may provide distinct avenues that converge and arrive at roughly the same global ethic.

One clear example of law's intersection with religion in search of an ethic is in human rights law, a new and rapidly developing area of international legal doctrine and practice. As Küng points out, the Global Ethic is meant to affirm the International Declaration of Human Rights without simply repeating it. But perhaps an equally notable example is the Law of the Sea. The result of the most complex and extensive negotiations in history (1970s and early 1980s), this multilateral treaty is due to take legal effect in November 1994.

The Law of the Sea is instructive for several reasons. Like the Global Ethic, formulation of a new sea law was based on consensus—a novel procedure in international negotiations. Furthermore, its content clearly converges with that of the Global Ethic. The movement toward a new sea law in the 1970s was intimately linked to demands, especially from the world's poorer nations, for a new and more just international economic order. The Law of the Sea might thus be construed as a "secular" attempt to explicate the Global Ethic's religiously grounded second directive: "commitment to a culture of solidarity and a just economic order."

The philosophical crux of the negotiations was the "common heritage of humankind" ("mankind" during the negotiations), a novel legal concept applied to the riches of the ocean floor beyond national jurisdiction. This concept clearly implies a culture of solidarity and a just economic order.

But the relevance of this concept to the Global Ethic runs deeper still. As Küng explains, and as the declaration makes clear, the Global Ethic is to be explicitly religious in its grounding—though the absence of God-talk, primarily out of deference to Buddhists, will be noteworthy for many. By contrast, the ethic captured by the Law of the Sea is explicitly nonreligious. Indeed, international law has long been suspicious of religious discourse for the same reason as the parliament: religious belief has been, and continues to be, a scandalously frequent ingredient of violent conflict.

Nevertheless, the Law of the Sea—especially the common-heritage concept—is arguably religious despite itself. It is difficult to explain what it means to say that the earth is humankind's heritage without any sense of a transcendent source of that great gift. Thus, while the Global Ethic is religious but makes a sidelong bow to politics, economics and law, the Law of the Sea is explicitly political, economic and legal but with an implicit religious core.

The Law of the Sea is instructive for another reason. While the common-heritage concept gained clear consensus as a negotiating principle at the Law of the Sea Conference, the move toward practical explication of the concept brought sharp and sometimes acrimonious division as individual states and ideologically committed blocs pursued their own versions of the truth about who owns—or ought to own—the earth. As a vision of a world where sharing triumphs over greed, ecological devastation and massive disparities of wealth, the common-heritage concept was fine; realization of that vision is another matter. As the Law of the Sea moves toward implementation, its detractors (primarily in the U.S., which during the early Reagan years pulled back from the negotiations and refused to sign the final text) have renewed their attack (like one in a recent William Safire column). Thus we see in the world of law the same sort of tension, sometimes to the breaking point, that we well might find in the movement from consensus on the Global Ethic to greater intra-ommunity and intercommunity explication of its principles.

But failure to realize a vision—fully or even in part—does not falsify the vision itself. In a world in which fragile ecosystems and ozone shields heed no political boundaries, the vision of a unified global community sharing and caring for one earth rings true. Continued exploitation of the earth and its denizens, human and nonhuman alike, render the vision truer still. In a similar way, the Global Ethic's vision of a world in which human beings are treated humanely and the earth is treated with respect is made no less true when children starve, when dissident voices are silenced by the torturer's tools, when poison fills our waterways and the air.

The fullest significance of the Global Ethic resides, then, in the journey from vision to realization, from aspiration to implementation. One might say that the ethic is the journey. The Global Ethic, Küng points out, is rooted in the existing commitments of the various religious communities. But moral failure on a massive scale—a failure of vision and a failure to realize that vision—is real as well. If an ethic rooted in religious conviction is also to be rooted in reality, then it ought to say something about moral failure—not just its fact, but how, or at least whether, redemption precisely from a transcendent source (which, Küng argues, is not foreign to Buddhism) might be sought. The Global Ethic might have said more about this, for religious traditions have spoken on the theme for a long time. Put in Christian terms, what I find lacking in the Global Ethic is a vigorous doctrine of grace. Without such emphasis one in fact wonders just how deep the ethic's desired religious grounding can go.

Still, as an ethic primarily of aspiration the declaration is both remarkable and necessary. Its real story is found, however, not in the commentaries by Küng and Kuschel but before us, in continual divinely aided efforts to specify and clarify and especially to act.

The story is told of a French general returning from his last Middle East campaign with the seedling of a wonderful olive tree. The first morning back, he delighted in presenting his gardener with the seedling and telling of the joy that ripe olives had brought to him when he was far from home. The gardener was dismayed. "But sir," he said. "I have heard of these trees. This seedling will not bear fruit for 75 years!" "In that case," the elderly general replied, "do not wait until after lunch to plant it."

The seedling of a new Global Ethic with its vision of a new world order requires transplanting. With so many climates and soils, and so much harsh weather ahead, it must be replanted and tended with care. We may not live to see it bear fruit, but with our world in such pain and agony, we ought not wait until after lunch to begin planting.

Thomas W. Currie III (review date January 1995)

SOURCE: A review of *Credo: The Apostles' Creed Explained for Today,* in *Theology Today,* Vol. 51, No. 4, January, 1995, pp. 618-24.

[*In the following excerpt, Currie states, "Earnest, eager to resolve doubt, anxious not to give offence,* Credo *is remarkable in its breadth of learning, yet is strangely non-threatening, hardly disturbing to either the faithful or the unbelieving."*]

[Daniel L. Migliore's *The Lord's Prayer: Perspectives for Reclaiming Christian Prayer*] delights in no small part because it invites us more deeply into the gospel and enables us to see connections there that cast new light on the world. Unfortunately, Hans Küng's book, **Credo,** has neither this intent nor this effect. As the sub-title indicates, Küng seeks not so much to understand what faith believes as to "explain" the faith. In so doing, his "explanations" aim at a world in which the "Christian faith seems alien, seems to contradict the natural sciences and the humanities and indeed the humane impulses of our time." By employing the insights of depth psychology, recent findings in cosmology, biology, and chaos theory, and in conversation with other great traditions (for example, Protestantism and Greek Orthodoxy), as well as other great religions, (for example, Hinduism, Buddhism, Islam, and Judaism), Küng hopes to translate the insights of the Apostles' Creed into the language of a post-Kantian, post-Darwinian, even post-Einsteinian world.

In undertaking this project, Küng enlists in the honorable ranks of those who would make use of new insights to unfold the gospel's story. The question, however, is whether Küng, in so earnestly seeking to be understood by present-day culture, has not made its approval the criterion for what is permissible to be heard in that story. Earnest, eager to resolve doubt, anxious not to give offence, **Credo** is remarkable in its breadth of learning, yet is strangely non-threatening, hardly disturbing to either the faithful or the unbelieving. Küng's finding that the virgin birth does not lie at the center of the gospel he calls a "momentous decision." The resurrection appearances are for him "probably . . . inward visionary events and not external reality." Who is God? "God is the all-embracing and all-permeating ground of meaning of the world process, who can of course only be accepted in faith," a definition, one might note, which is unencumbered by reference to Abraham, Isaac, and Jacob, much less the disturbing singularity of the Word made flesh.

Although Küng seeks to answer the concerns of a remarkably diverse number of conversation-partners, his primary audience appears to be those same "cultured despisers" who, having gone to school in the Enlightenment, can pick apart the church's failings and contradictions without breaking into much of a sweat. These folk, he thinks, are embarrassed by talk of miracles, saints, and human sinfulness and need reassurance that committing to the faith will not implicate them in something foolish. *Credo* is happy to oblige on almost every count, finding in Jesus Christ that "guide for Christians" in whose company "it should be possible to achieve a psychological identity for oneself in the face of all imprisonment in anxiety, and also social solidarity against all resignation in face of compulsive pressure." So it is that the gospel makes sense in the world and proves its usefulness in its ability to help people lead satisfying, fulfilling lives.

And just so fails to wound or to heal.

Credo is a nice book written by a nice man. His gifts of interpretation, especially in art history and philosophy, are striking, just as his diligence is everywhere apparent. If the faith could prove itself by the breadth or depth of its range of knowledge and culture, this little book would be a masterpiece. But the gospel does not give itself to us in that way, but, as Küng himself knows, in the not very nice form of a man dying on the cross, a man who was put there, after all, by nice people who were, for some reason, terribly offended with him. His story has embarrassed more sophisticated cultures than our own, and it may well be that our own culture's salvation will be found not in the "explanations" that render that story harmless but in the offense and contradictions that story exposes.

Donald G. Bloesch (review date 2 October 1995)

SOURCE: "A Jesus for Everyone, A Christ for None," in *Christianity Today,* Vol. 39, No. 11, October 2, 1995, pp. 40, 42.

[*In the following review, Bloesch calls into question Küng's historical focus on the life and teaching of Jesus, instead of Jesus's preexistence as a member of the Trinity, in* Christianity, *although he praises the book's comprehensiveness.*]

In [*Christianity: Essence, History, and Future*], which the author presents as the culmination of a lifetime of study and reflection, noted Catholic theologian Hans Küng undertakes a comprehensive theological history of Christianity, showing its biblical roots and global implications. Küng differentiates the ceremonial and doctrinal embellishments of the Christian faith from its essence— the historical person of Jesus Christ. Küng seeks to get beyond a "Eurocentric" understanding of the Christian religion to a "universal historical view" that nevertheless maintains continuity with the original New Testament message. He sees Christianity not as an outmoded traditionalism but as a "radical humanism"—"being human to the full."

He calls for a Christology from below—beginning with the historical life and teachings of Jesus rather than the creedal interpretation of the early church, where he discerns a shift from the New Testament paradigm to the Hellenistic paradigm in which the faith was articulated and in some instances drastically altered by Greek ontological categories. He believes that a Christology from below also has ecumenical promise, for it would facilitate dialogue with Judaism and Islam, both of which could never accept Hellenistic Christianity and the Trinity.

According to Küng, the process of Hellenization created a church burdened by hierarchy, ritualism, and creedalism. The call to discipleship, which characterized the ministry of Jesus, was overshadowed in the patristic church by a mounting concern for right doctrine. He expresses unhappiness with the medieval paradigm of the church, which tightened the grip of hierarchy with its emphasis on papal supremacy. He is grateful to the Protestant Reformation for rediscovering the gospel of justification by faith and recovering prophetic spirituality as opposed to mysticism and ritualism. He believes, however, that the present age necessitates a global spirituality and a global ethic that will still focus on Jesus but now in relationship to other world teachers and prophets.

While appreciating the comprehensiveness of Küng's vision and the lucidity of his proposals, I have real difficulties with his analysis and interpretation. First, Küng shows himself at odds with the apostolic church by making the Jesus of history the final criterion for faith. Whereas the apostles and theologians of the early church proclaimed the preexistent Christ incarnate in human flesh, Küng's emphasis is on the life, death, and teachings of Jesus as determined by historical research. He disputes both the preexistence of Jesus Christ and the dogma of the Trinity on the grounds that they represent deformations of New Testament faith. While it is certainly true that the fathers of the church resorted to philosophical terminology in elucidating the mysteries of the Incarnation and the Trinity, a powerful case can be made that both Nicaea and Chalcedon resisted and countered the Hellenization of the faith. Küng sees Jesus as "God's eschatological prophet and emissary" rather than God himself in the garb of humanity.

Küng proposes that we move from the Enlightenment paradigm focused on the historical-critical study of Scripture and the moral teachings of Jesus to a postmodern paradigm focused on universal religious experience and global values. He believes a binding ethical consensus can be reached through interreligious dialogue. While maintaining that Christianity is the "*one* true religion," he also is ready to acknowledge that there are "*many* true religions" in the sense that salvific truth can be found in all the world religions, though it is supremely embodied in Jesus Christ—at least for Christians. Küng calls for a postconfessional, ecumenical paradigm in which Christianity breaks out of its cultural insularity and enters into fruitful conversation with the other great world religions. Our goal should be a "pluralistic holistic synthesis." Küng can be faulted for subverting the uniqueness of Jesus Christ in the interest of cultivating interreligious peace and saving the planet from ecological destruction.

I can appreciate Küng for his appeal to the New Testament over church tradition, his penetrating critique of papalism and Marianism, and his warnings against sacramentalism and ritualism. I must take exception, however, to his reduction of the faith to the original teachings of Jesus and the facts of his life and death (though these certainly belong to the fuller perspective of faith).

The author's Christology from below fails to do justice to the church's teachings of the Incarnation and the Trinity, both of which are solidly anchored, though not precisely elucidated, in the New Testament. Küng urges sensitive Christians to create an ecumenical global paradigm if the church is to maintain its relevance and avoid the risk of becoming insular and sectarian. But is not our task as biblical Christians to develop the ecumenical implications of the Reformation or evangelical paradigm, which Küng acknowledges to be basically faithful to the New Testament? Christians need to enter into dialogue with fellow Christians in order to advance the truth of the gospel and the cause of church unity, and here we would do well to listen to Küng. Yet we must insist that unity will come only when we identify with the apostolic interpretation of the gospel already given in the New Testament and amplified and clarified in the confessions of the early church and the Protestant Reformation.

Robert P. Imbelli (review date 21 October 1995)

SOURCE: A review of *Christianity: Essence, History, Future,* in *America,* Vol. 173, No. 12, October 21, 1995, pp. 23-4.

[*In the following review, Imbelli calls Küng's* Christianity *"a monumental, if flawed, achievement," and goes on to delineate the book's problems.*]

In the course of a theological career of almost 40 years, Hans Küng has performed singular service to Christian theology and ecumenical understanding. His early works of the 1960's on the church helped prepare and promote the reform movement of Vatican II. His major works of the 1970's, *On Being a Christian* and *Does God Exist?,* attempted to set forth the meaning of Christian faith in God and his Christ and to engage in sympathetic but critical dialogue with believers and non-believers alike.

Most recently Küng and his Institute for Ecumenical Research in Tübingen have embarked upon an extraordinary undertaking. Under the rubric of "No World Peace Without Religious Peace," Küng is seeking to further religious dialogue through a writing project that will comprise a trilogy of volumes on each of the "Abrahamic faiths": Judaism, Christianity and Islam. This is *not* a "least common denominator" ecumenism. Küng wants to identify the distinctive parts of the different faiths, precisely in order to further understanding and draw upon deep commonalities of these religions, even in the midst of difference.

The first volume of this project, *Judaism,* appeared in 1992, and now the volume on Christianity has just been translated into English. With its 800 pages of text, 115 of endnotes and 20 of indices, *Christianity* bears all the marks of Küng's virtues: stunning erudition, moral passion, provocative honesty and sometimes unrelenting polemics. In sum, the work is a monumental, if flawed, achievement.

As its title indicates and its insertion into the wider project dictates, we have here no detached academic study of Christian origins and history. This review of 2,000 years of Christian history, whose pace is frenetic even for its length, serves a further purpose: "To understand the present more deeply," indeed, to show "how and why Christianity became what it is today—with a view to how it could be." A reformist and ecumenical agenda, animated by the dichotomy between Christianity and the modern world, underlies the analysis and structures the "Questions for the Future" with which Küng peppers his text. These "Questions," variously framed and often posed to challenge each of the three Abrahamic religions, propel the exposition forward and recapitulate its almost prophetic passion.

Küng has two strategies. He first seeks to identify the distinctive "essence" of Christianity. As he had done at greater length in *On Being a Christian,* Küng holds that this essence lies in the commitment to Jesus Christ as Messiah and Son of God and the confession that in his life, death and resurrection we have the abiding center and norm of Christian faith. He then traces the manifestations of this essence in history by employing the concepts of "paradigm analysis" and "paradigm shift," which he borrows from Thomas Kuhn, the American philosopher of science. Küng postulates that five paradigms of beliefs, values and techniques have structured Christian consciousness to the present. He designates them as Early Christian Apocalyptic, Early Church Hellenistic, Medieval Roman Catholic, Reformation Protestant and Enlightenment Modern.

Each of these paradigms, which continue to be influential, has succeeded in conserving the abiding substance of faith and transmitting it to new ages and cultures. On the other hand, each has also hardened and hindered the expression of that faith. On the threshold of the third millennium, now a new ecumenical, postmodern paradigm is called for. And Küng, with the considerable resources of the Tübingen Institute at his command, is its prophet!

The entire enterprise appears at once daring, perceptive and problematic. As Küng's book on *Judaism* has been severely critiqued by Jewish scholars, so his book on *Christianity* will be by Catholic theologians. For example, the transference of the tool of "paradigm analysis" from the scientific to the religious sphere runs the risk of superficiality. Küng is not content to speak merely of theological paradigms, but rather of paradigms of Christianity that embrace dauntingly disparate cultural, political and economic factors. Küng's extension is so wide that the schema becomes progressively less illuminating, until "paradigm" finally loses any explanatory suggestiveness and becomes merely an umbrella term for designating a particular era, like modernity.

Regarding theology, Küng is excessively wary of ecclesiastical institutionalization, even as he concedes its inevitability, and is too distrustful of dogma. He is very uneasy, for instance, about the doctrine of the Trinity, which he finds unintelligible to Christians and an ecumenical obstacle to the other Abrahamic religions. Like the great 19th-century Protestant theologian, Friedrich Schleiermacher, to whom he devotes a masterful essay, Küng seems to see the doctrine of the Trinity as no more than an appendix to the substance of the Christian faith.

It is not surprising, then, that Bernard Lonergan, S. J., the foremost analyst of doctrinal development in Catholic theology, merits no mention in the more than 900 pages of the book. Also not mentioned is the work of Küng's former Tübingen colleague, the Catholic theologian and bishop, Walter Kasper, who has written significant studies of the doctrine of the Trinity as the distinctively Christian understanding of God. Moreover, Küng's presentation is so thoroughly laced with anti-Roman polemic, maximizing the failures and infidelities of the hierarchy and downplaying anti-Catholic prejudice and persecution, that even the historical exposition becomes skewed. One sad consequence of this, and indeed of the vitriolic dismissals of the present pope as simply a "restorationist," is that the postmodern elements of John Paul II's program are not even acknowledged. Küng fails to draw upon them to support his own criticisms of modernity and his hopes for an emerging global ethic of responsibility.

The English translation of the book, though generally fluent, is marred by too many typographical errors, including even mistakes in referring to the paradigm designations themselves. In addition, the word "future" has been added to the English title. This latter term is not just publisher's exaggeration, since Küng does discuss questions and orientations for the future, but it does camouflage Küng's announced intention to devote a second volume to the issue of Christianity's present and future. In the meantime, no matter the astringency of the current volume, *Christianity* remains vintage Küng and will enliven the theological debate as we approach the coming millennium in the never dull company of Tübingen's Professor Maximus.

Theodore C. Ross, S. J. (review date 20-27 December 1995)

SOURCE: "Küng's Synthesis," in *Christian Century,* Vol. 112, No. 37, December 20-27, 1995, pp. 1250-51.

[*Ross is a lecturer in historical theology at the Catholic Theological Union of Chicago and Mundelein Seminary of the University of St. Mary of the Lake in Mundelein, Illinois. In the following review, he asserts that Küng's Christology in* Christianity *derives from his desire to reconcile Christianity with Judaism and Islam.*]

Hans Küng is both predictable and unpredictable. He is scholarly yet populist, fascinating yet shocking, hopeful yet desperate. And his latest book[, *Christianity: Essence, History, and Future,*] gives every indication of being one more Küng battlefield. Cardinal Joseph Ratzinger and his

Congregation for the Doctrine of the Faith will be neither pleased nor amused. The very first page sets the book's tone and direction: "Don't many people even in our 'Christian' countries and especially Catholic countries associate Christianity with an institutional church greedy for power and lacking in insight, with authoritarianism and doctrinaire dictatorship, which so often breeds anxiety, has complexes about sex, discriminates against women, refuses to engage in dialogue and treats with contempt those who think differently?"

Though all the Christian traditions are Küng's target, he saves his most destructive and loudest salvos for his own, the Church of Rome—as he has for more than 25 years. Many things he writes here repeat what he has said in previous books and articles.

Küng sees massive crises in the whole of Christianity, and where there is no real crisis he does his best to create one. The solution for all these problems must be radical: unshakable faith in the person of Christ. But the churches, Küng contends, have replaced Christ with the Roman system, Orthodox traditionalism and Protestant fundamentalism—indeed, with ecclesiasticism in general.

For Küng the churches have made a cat's breakfast of Christianity, and only the sacred scriptures can give us the essence of Christ's vision. He is hardly the first to claim the Bible for the renewal of Christianity. The Friars of the 13th century, Luther in the 16th and the Second Vatican Council in the 20th all went back to a biblical base. But the rub, as any historian knows, is the interpretation of these scriptures. What is the correct interpretation?

Küng gives the impression that he and many in the Tübingen school have seen the light. Theirs is the true biblical eye-opener. Much of the first quarter of the book involves conclusions drawn from scriptural interpretation. But these conclusions are very much influenced by Küng's goal in writing the book: he aims to create a synthesis of the three great monotheistic religious systems—Judaism, Christianity and Islam. He has written a volume titled *Judaism.* After this book, he plans to complete the trilogy with *Islam.* Küng wants all three faiths under one umbrella. Locating paradigm shifts is the essence of his method, and his interpretation of scripture is crucial to give his synthesis credibility.

The person and nature of Christ is the key to Küng's theory. He goes to great pains to ground Christology in the Christ of the Jewish Christians. In Küng's low Christology, Christ was not pre-existent with the Father in the act of creation or in anything else. This view of Christ is key to reconciling Christianity with Judaism and Islam. Though Küng's theory is exciting, he railroads any authorities whose positions contradict his own, even if these are inspired writings accepted as canonical by the faith community.

His three whipping boys are the papacy (as would be expected), the idea of a pre-existent Jesus, and the Gospel of John, whose prologue comes under special fire. He gives the creeds a very low priority because they oppose his interpretation of certain passages of the New Testament. He would go so far as to say that the Koran's Christology is more accurate than that of the Greek councils.

As usual, Küng is brilliant and exciting, but many of his positions, such as his defense of Gnosticism, reflect his hang-ups and *bêtes noires.* He sees Gnosticism as a healthy reaction to the privileged and dominating hierarchy of bishop, priest and deacon.

Using paradigm shifts, Küng unfolds the whole story of Christianity. Many of his observations are fascinating and challenging, especially his contrast of Luther and Erasmus, his accusations against Luther for replacing argument with ardor and wrath, and his criticism of Luther for expecting too much from the church (does Küng recognize himself in that observation?). Calvinism and Anglicanism are among the other traditions that come under his scrutiny.

Küng's insights on the contest between faith and reason that marked the Enlightenment are excellent. In analyzing the trauma of the French Revolution, as well as the Restoration, he shows a church struggling with modernity. Science and scientists, philosophy and philosophers are studied for the most part in the context of the church's weakness. He sees the church as judge, but not as victim.

Despite Küng's many virtues, the reader is constantly tempted to tell him what Riviere told Claudel: "Show me that the church and not just you holds this. What am I to make of a church misunderstood by all except one?"

John P. Galvin (review date June 1996)

SOURCE: A review of *Christianity: Essence, History, and Future,* in *Theological Studies,* Vol. 57, No. 2, June, 1996, pp. 363-65.

[*In the following review, Galvin criticizes Küng's* Christianity *for "the thin description of the essence of Christianity, the general aversion to high Christology (even in John) and to trinitarian theology, the reticence in speaking of soteriology, and the frequent glossing over of complex issues through rhetorical questions and appeal to simplistic alternatives [which] prevent the work from achieving its objective of fostering deeper understanding of the Christian faith."*]

This massive volume[, ***Christianity,***] is but the second of a planned trilogy. Preceded by ***Judaism*** and soon to be followed by *Islam,* it is part of a grand project, supported by the Bosch Jubilee Foundation and the Daimler-Benz Fund, for promoting world peace by fostering peace among religions through an interreligious dialogue rooted in investigation of each religion's foundation. Yet even the trilogy will not complete the project, for Küng reserves for a future work a treatment of the Church in non-European

areas and a full presentation of his proposals for Christianity's future. Accordingly, apart from a systematically important but brief account of the essence of Christianity, the present volume is largely devoted to an analysis of Christianity's history.

K[üng]'s basic thesis is relatively simple. Freely adapting Thomas Kuhn's conception of paradigm shifts to the exigencies of his historical material, he argues that Christianity's essence, which can never exist in pure form, has been embodied over the course of Christian history in five distinct paradigms, each of which originated in a particular historical-cultural context, and most of which have survived to the present, despite having been superseded in later situations by a new paradigm. Since the specifics of a given paradigm do not pertain to the essence of Christianity, such elements ought not to be sources of division among Christians or of conflict with other monotheistic religions.

As K[üng] understands it, the essence of Christianity lies in its concentration on the person of Jesus Christ, crucified but raised to eternal life with God. Though always in danger of compromising monotheism, obscuring openness to the activity of God's Spirit outside the Church, and degenerating into sterile preoccupation with dogmatic formulas, concrete and practical orientation on Christ constitutes Christianity's specific identity amid the vicissitudes of its history.

The bulk of the book presents the five paradigms which K[üng] detects in the history of Christianity. K[üng] does not seek to be exhaustive, but to locate the emergence of each paradigm, provide information about its major exponents, and diagnose its chief strengths and weaknesses. This approach allows him to range widely and yet be selective in choosing historical topics for examination.

At the origin, closest in time and apparently also in spirit to Jesus, stands the apocalyptic paradigm of early Jewish Christianity, which combined faith in Jesus as the Messiah with continued observance of Mosaic ritual law. Enmeshed in conflict with other tendencies within Christianity even in the New Testament period, Jewish Christianity survived the destruction of Jerusalem but receded from clear historical view in the centuries which followed. The only paradigm unable to maintain its existence to the present, it nonetheless offers resources for interreligious dialogue with Jews and Muslims because of its uncompromising fidelity to monotheism.

The rival and immediate successor to Jewish Christianity, the ecumenical Hellenistic paradigm of Christian antiquity, also originates in the New Testament period. Inaugurated by Paul, it reaches its theological heights in Origen and continues to exist to this day in the Christian East. Responsible for developing a fixed rule of faith, a New Testament canon, and a monarchical episcopate, it tends to shift emphasis from concrete orientation on Christ to speculative theological questions and is inclined to identify its embodiment of Christianity with the essence of the faith.

Even greater problems in this regard are detected in the third paradigm, that of medieval Roman Catholicism. Developing theologically from Augustine through its peak in Aquinas to contemporary Roman theology, and marked from Leo I through the Gregorian Reform to Vatican I by increasing claims on behalf of the papacy, this form of Christianity has also lasted to the present, though not without compromise of the basic message of the gospel. The fourth paradigm, that of the Reformation, is discussed with particular focus on Luther; while presented in more sympathetic terms as a long-overdue prophetic reform of Western Christianity based on the priority of the Word of God, it is also criticized for tendencies toward fragmentation into a variety of churches and for periodic reliance on civil authorities.

The final paradigm is that of modernity, originating in the 17th century but fully developed only in later political, philosophical, economic and cultural revolutions. Exemplified theologically by Schleiermacher, this paradigm represents a needed rethinking of Christianity in a new age, but is often weakened by excessive stress on reason, uncritical belief in progress and ominous tendencies toward nationalism. The need thus arises for a sixth paradigm, of a contemporary ecumenical nature, which K[üng] finds foreshadowed by Pope John XXIII and Vatican II but thwarted by subsequent reactionary developments within Catholicism. Sketching the outline of that paradigm—likely, one suspects, to hark back to Jewish Christianity with its relatively low Christology and undeveloped ecclesial structures—is a task for a future volume.

Written in an irenic spirit, K[üng]'s book is intended for a wider public, and persevering readers will enhance their knowledge of church history. In view of the wide range of the work, K[üng]'s reliance on secondary literature and on his earlier publications is inevitable. But the thin description of the essence of Christianity, the general aversion to high Christology (even in John) and to trinitarian theology, the reticence in speaking of soteriology, and the frequent glossing over of complex issues through rhetorical questions and appeal to simplistic alternatives prevent the work from achieving its objective of fostering deeper understanding of the Christian faith. The tone of the book is lowered by its carping at anything associated with Pope John Paul II. That there is more to the essence of Christianity than is claimed here undoubtedly complicates Christian dialogue with Judaism and Islam, but an interreligious consensus in which at least one party is unable to recognize its own faith would be of very limited value.

Bruce Bawer (review date Winter 1998)

SOURCE: A review of *Christianity,* in *Hudson Review,* Vol. L, No. 4, Winter, 1998, pp. 697-98.

[In the following excerpt, Bawer traces the different shifts in Christianity which Küng's Christianity *presents.]*

Godsey, Taylor, and Borg seek to help readers move beyond narrow dogmatism to an understanding that the essence of Christianity is not about dogma but about spiritual experience. This is also a key part of the message of Hans Küng's ***Christianity: Essence, History, and Future.*** Küng, the Swiss architect of Vatican II who may be the greatest theologian of the century but who is currently *persona non grata* at the papal *palazzo,* has produced a magisterial, scholarly 900-page treatise that is at the same time thoroughly accessible to general readers. Though it covers a lot of historical and theological ground, the book's main point is a simple one which recalls Brian Taylor's observation that "religion is just a form"—namely, that while Christianity's predominant form has undergone many radical shifts over the centuries, from the early Christians' apocalyptic paradigm to the early Church's Hellenistic paradigm (which survives in today's Eastern Orthodoxy) to the medieval Roman Catholic paradigm (which led to present-day Catholic authoritarianism) to Reformation Protestantism (which bequeathed us Protestant fundamentalism) to the "Enlightenment modern paradigm" (which is embodied in liberal modernism), the "abiding substance of faith"—namely, the person of Jesus Christ—has remained the same.

These paradigm shifts, Küng argues, have been necessitated by changes in human society; his purpose is to suggest the nature of the shift needed to bring Christianity successfully into the new millennium. Too often, he notes, past paradigm shifts have occasioned acrimony and bloodshed; Küng seeks peaceful transition into a period of global ecumenism when Christians, Jews, and Moslems (he has written substantial books about each of these faiths) live together in mutual respect, understanding, and edification. Drawing on its author's voluminous knowledge of religious history and showcasing his enormous erudition, this book mounts a cogent argument for the proposition that radical theological change, far from representing a betrayal of the Christian past, has been the rule throughout the annals of Christianity and is unavoidable today if the essence and vitality of the faith are to be preserved.

Additional coverage of Küng's life and career is contained in the following sources published by the Gale Group: *Contemporary Authors,* **Vol. 53-56;** *Contemporary Authors New Revision Series,* **Vol. 66; and** *Major 20th-Century Writers,* **Vols. 1, 2.**

Siegfried Sassoon
1886-1967

(Full name Siegfried Lorraine Sassoon) English poet, novelist, autobiographer, diarist, and critic.

The following entry presents an overview of Sassoon's career through 1994. For further information on his life and works, see *CLC*, Volume 36.

INTRODUCTION

One of the most compelling soldier-poets of the First World War, Siegfried Sassoon is best known for his graphic, often shocking portrayal of trench warfare during World War I and the withering psychological distress it imposed upon its combatants. Along with poets Rupert Brooke, Robert Graves, and Wilfred Owen, who also documented their horrific wartime experiences, Sassoon drew attention to the agony and appalling human cost of the "Great War," dismissing at once the popular image of the glorious warrior fighting for a noble cause. His bitterly realistic depictions of cynical soldiers railing against the war effort, particularly the ignorant citizenry, government, and religion that promoted it, contrasted sharply with contemporary literature characterizing battle as a chivalrous national duty.

BIOGRAPHICAL INFORMATION

Born in Brenchley, a county of Kent, England, Sassoon was the second of three sons of Alfred Sassoon, the scion of wealthy Jewish merchants, and Theresa Thornycroft, a member of a prominent landowning family distinguished by its artistic talent. Her grandfather, parents and brother were noted sculptors, another brother a prestigious architect, and Theresa and her sisters were artists. Despite the Thornycrofts' prominence, Alfred Sassoon's mother disowned him for marrying a gentile and refused to have anything to do with his wife and children for the rest of her life. Educated at home as a boy, Sassoon studied at Marlborough College for three years and attended Clare College, Cambridge University, where he first privately published his own poetry. Disinterested in his studies, Sassoon left Cambridge after only two years, returning to his family home in Kent to lead a country gentleman's life of leisure. He continued to write and publish his own poetry, receiving encouragement from his mother's friend, editor Sir Edmund Gosse. Sassoon first gained a measure of literary recognition with the publication of *The Daffodil Murderer* (1913), a parody of John Masefield's narrative poem *The Everlasting Mercy.* Sassoon began to move in literary circles in London where he first met Rupert Brooke, a poet who influenced Sassoon's wartime work. Sassoon joined the army in 1914 and the next year was sent to the trenches as an infantry officer where he met Robert Graves, who became his friend and role model. In 1916 Sassoon was awarded the Military Cross for dragging a wounded man to safety under heavy fire and for single-handedly capturing a German trench during the Battle of the Somme. While convalescing in England after he was wounded in 1917, he encountered British pacifists Robert Ross, Lady Ottoline Morrell, and Bertrand Russell. These political connections combined with his war experience convinced Sassoon that the war was no longer justified and should end. He wrote a public letter of protest in which he refused to fight anymore and accused the British government of unnecessarily prolonging the war. The letter was read aloud in the House of Commons and widely distributed across Britain. Sassoon narrowly avoided court-martial through the intervention of Graves, who convinced military officials that Sassoon was suffering from shell-shock. He was conveyed to a military hospital in Craiglockhart,

Scotland, where he received psychiatric treatment from Dr. William H. R. Rivers and wrote some of his most powerful war poems. However, overcome with guilt at leaving his comrades, Sassoon returned to the war in 1918 but was finally sent home later that year after receiving a serious head wound. After the war, Sassoon briefly worked as the literary editor of the leftist *Daily Herald* and campaigned for the Labour Party. The publication of *Picture Show* (1919) and *The War Poems of Siegfried Sassoon* (1919) brought him critical acclaim and additional public recognition. He was awarded the Hawthornden Prize and the James Tait Black Memorial Prize for *Memoirs of a Fox-Hunting Man* (1928). In 1933 Sassoon married Hester Gatty, with whom he shared a son, George, before separating permanently a decade later. Sassoon converted to Catholicism in 1957 and spent the last decade of his life concerned with religious and spiritual matters.

MAJOR WORKS

Sassoon received the greatest attention for the shocking imagery, graphic language, and bitter satire that permeates his World War I poetry, the core of which is contained in *The Old Huntsman and Other Poems* (1917) and *Counter-Attack and Other Poems* (1918). Much of Sassoon's lyrical, pre-war verse features romantic themes, pastoral imagery, and pagan iconography, linking him with other Georgian poets of the early twentieth century. In "The Daffodil Murderer" and "The Old Huntsman," for example, the poet assumes the personae of English rustics speaking in colloquial blank verse. Characterized as his "Happy Warrior" stage, some of these poems exalt the virtues of patriotism and romanticize the camaraderie of combat soldiers. "To My Brother," written after his younger brother was killed in action, extols death in battle as a grand sacrifice. Likewise, "Absolution" and "The Redeemer," also from this period, celebrate the passion and glory of war. However, the tone and outlook of Sassoon's poetry changed dramatically after he witnessed action in the trenches. As he became well acquainted with the bleak reality of combat, his writing became a vehicle of trenchant protest against the war and its horrors. He used his verse to condemn the hypocrisy of the citizenry on the home front who, oblivious to the real suffering of the soldiers, continued to celebrate the war. "Blighters" satirizes a rousing, pro-war revue he watched while on leave in England, "Glory of Women" angrily mocks the women at home who urged their men to fight, and "They" condemns the patriotic benediction of the Anglican church. These poems are short, satirical, and often sarcastic. In "Stand-To: Good Friday Morning," an exhausted, disillusioned soldier sardonically prays for a wound to deliver him from the peril and squalor of battle. The gruesome imagery of carnage and filth in his poetry underscores the unromantic reality of life in the trenches. Vivid, morbid images such as "sucking mud" and "clotted heads" appear in poems like "Counter-Attack," while "Repression of War Experience" illustrates how war taints the soldier's perception of everything associated with happiness and peace. Sassoon

also employed slang, oaths, and colloquial expressions to talk about serious issues, devices unusual in poetry at that time.

He eventually turned to other subject matter in *Satirical Poems* (1926) and the lyric collection *The Heart's Journey* (1927), but his postwar poetry received little recognition. He returned to his wartime experiences in *Memoirs of a Fox-Hunting Man*, *Memoirs of an Infantry Officer* (1930) and *Sherston's Progress* (1936), a fictional trilogy that chronicles the story of Sassoon alter-ego George Sherston, a country gentleman of leisure whose world is changed by fighting in the war. Sassoon focuses on the contrast between the pastoral estate life of his hero and the psychic journey he takes to a new world created by the war. Sassoon rewrote his story again in memoir form, producing a second trilogy consisting of *The Old Country and Seven More Years* (1938), *The Weald of Youth* (1942), and *Siegfried's Journey, 1916-1920* (1945). Sassoon continued to write poetry in the last decades of his life, focusing on religious and spiritual themes. "Alone" deals with duality of self, particularly the contrast between the social self and the isolated self. His religious poetry, from the earlier "A Last Judgement" and "Earth and Heaven" to later work such as "Lenten Illuminations," features the imagery of angels and ponders creation and the after-life. Sassoon also published *Meredith* (1948), a literary biography of George Meredith.

CRITICAL RECEPTION

Sassoon's war poetry is generally regarded as the highlight of his career. His ability to capture in a few biting lines the nuances of emotion experienced by a whole generation of soldiers earned him admiration. Poems such as "Blighters" and "Counter-Attack" remain among his most famous. While some readers felt that his poetry was too ugly and graphic, and that its interest lay more in its ability to shock and discomfit the reader than in any real artistic merit, most critics regard his war poems as a powerful expression of the savagery and psychic costs of modern, mechanized combat. Though viewed as an antiwar poet, critics clarify that Sassoon's opposition to the First World War was not necessarily motivated by pacifism, but by his belief that the war was unduly protracted by those in power. Commentators frequently praise Sassoon's effective use of irony and potent distillation of fear and despair in his brief, incisive poems. However, his early Georgian verse and later attempts at longer, more sympathetic poems are often characterized as failures which caused him to overreach the bounds of his talents and become sentimental, particularly works that memorialize fallen comrades and family. Sassoon's autobiographical novels and memoirs are considered noteworthy for chronicling the pre-war estate life of the English upper class, a way of life which changed drastically during and after the war, and for the universality of the World War I experience which changed his generation. His later poetry never received the attention or praise accorded to that written during and about the war. For his contribution to the literature of the First World War, Sassoon is considered among the most influential wartime poets.

PRINCIPAL WORKS

The Daffodil Murderer [as Saul Kain] (poetry) 1913
Morning-Glory (poetry) 1916
The Redeemer (poetry) 1916
To Any Dead Officer (poetry) 1917
The Old Huntsman and Other Poems (poetry) 1917
Counter-Attack and Other Poems (poetry) 1918
Picture Show [enlarged and reprinted as *Picture-Show,* 1920] (poetry) 1919
The War Poems of Siegfried Sassoon (poetry) 1919
Satirical Poems (poetry) 1926
The Heart's Journey (poetry) 1927
Memoirs of a Fox-Hunting Man (novel) 1928
Memoirs of an Infantry Officer (novel) 1930
Vigils (poetry) 1934
Sherston's Progress (novel) 1936
The Complete Memoirs of George Sherston [includes *Memoirs of a Fox-Hunting Man, Memoirs of an Infantry Officer,* and *Sherston's Progress*] (novels) 1937
The Old Country and Seven More Years (autobiography) 1938
Rhymed Ruminations (poetry) 1939
The Flower Show Match and Other Pieces (poetry) 1941
The Weald of Youth (autobiography) 1942
Siegfried's Journey, 1916-1920 (autobiography) 1945
Collected Poems (poetry) 1947
Meredith (prose) 1948
Common Chords (poetry) 1950
Sequences (poetry) 1956
The Path to Peace: Selected Poems (poetry) 1960
Siegfried Sassoon Diaries: 1915-1918 (diaries) 1981

CRITICISM

Edmund Gosse (review date October 1917)

SOURCE: "Some Soldier Poets," in *Edinburgh Review,* Vol. 226, No. 4, October, 1917, pp. 296-316.

[*In the following excerpt, Gosse discusses Sassoon's place among the British war poets and offers tempered review of* The Old Huntsman and Other Poems.]

The two years which preceded the outbreak of the war were marked in this country by a revival of public interest in the art of poetry. To this movement coherence was given and organisation introduced by Mr. Edward Marsh's now-famous volume entitled *Georgian Poetry.* The effect of this collection—for it is hardly correct to call it an anthology—of the best poems written by the youngest poets since 1911 was two-fold: it acquainted readers with work few had the 'leisure or the zeal to investigate,' and it brought the writers themselves together in a corporate and selected relation. I do not recollect that this had been done—except prematurely and partially by 'The Germ' of 1850—since the 'England's Parnassus' and 'England's Helicon' of 1600. In point of fact the only real precursor of Mr. Marsh's venture in our whole literature is the 'Songs and Sonnettes' of 1557, commonly known as 'Tottel's Miscellany.' Tottel brought together, for the first time, the lyrics of Wyatt, Surrey, Churchyard Vaux, and Bryan, exactly as Mr. Marsh called public attention to Rupert Brooke, James Elroy Flecker and the rest of the Georgians, and he thereby fixed the names of those poets as Mr. Marsh has fixed those of our youngest fledglings on the roll of English literature.

The general tone of the latest poetry, up to the moment of the outbreak of hostilities, was pensive, instinct with natural piety, given somewhat in excess to description of landscape, tender in feeling, essentially unaggressive except towards the clergy and towards other versifiers of an earlier generation. There was absolutely not a trace in any one of the young poets of that arrogance and vociferous defiance which marked German verse during the same years. These English shepherds might hit at their elders with their staves, but they had turned their swords into pruning-hooks and had no scabbards to rattle. This is a point which might have attracted notice, if we had not all been too drowsy in the lap of our imperial prosperity to observe the signs of the times in Berlin. Why did no one call our attention to the beating of the big drum which was going on so briskly on the Teutonic Parnassus? At all events, there was no echo of such as noise in the 'chambers of imagery' which contained Mr. Gordon Bottomley, or in Mr. W. H. Davies' wandering 'songs of joy,' or on 'the great hills and solemn chanting seas' where Mr. John Drinkwater waited for the advent of beauty. And the guns of August 1914 found Mr. W. W. Gibson encompassed by 'one dim, blue infinity of starry peace.' There is a sort of German 'Georgian Poets' in existence; in time to come a comparison of its pages with those of Mr. Marsh may throw a side-light on the question, Who prepared the War?

The youngest poets were more completely taken by surprise in August 1914 than their elders. The earliest expressions of lyric military feeling came from veteran voices. It was only proper that the earliest of all should be the Poet Laureate's address to England, ending with the prophecy:

> Much suffering shall cleanse thee!
> > But thou through the flood
> Shalt win to Salvation,
> > To Beauty through blood.

As sensation, however, followed sensation in those first terrific and bewildering weeks, much was happening that called forth with the utmost exuberance the primal emotions of mankind; there was full occasion for

exultations, agonies,
And love, and man's unconquerable mind.

By September a full chorus was vocal, led by our national veteran, Mr. Thomas Hardy, with his 'Song of the Soldiers'

What of the faith and fire within us,
   Men who march away
   Ere the barn-cocks say
   Night is growing gray,
To hazards whence no tears can win us;
What of the faith and fire within us,
   Men who march away?

Already, before the close of the autumn of 1914, four or five anthologies of war-poems were in the press, and the desire of the general public to be fed with patriotic and emotional verse was manifested in unmistakable ways. We had been accustomed for some time past to the issue of a multitude of little pamphlets of verse, often very carefully written, and these the critics had treated with an indulgence which would have whitened the hair of the stern reviewer of forty years ago. The youthful poets, almost a trade union in themselves, protected one another by their sedulous generosity. It was very unusual to see anything criticised much less 'slated'; the balms of praise were poured over every rising head, and immortalities were predicted by the dozen. Yet, as a rule, the sale of these little poetic pamphlets had been small, and they had been read only by those who had a definite object in doing so.

The immediate success of the anthologies, however, proved that the war had aroused in a new public an ear for contemporary verse, an attention anxious to be stirred or soothed by the assiduous company of poets who had been ripening their talents in a little clan. These had now an eager world ready to listen to them. The result has been surprising; we may even, without exaggeration, call it unparalleled. There has never before, in the world's history, been an epoch which has tolerated and even welcomed such a flood of verse as has been poured forth over Great Britain during the last three years. These years have seen the publication, as I am credibly informed, of more than five hundred volume of new and original poetry. It would be the silliest compliance to pretend that all of this, or much of it, or any but a very little of it, has been of permanent value. Much of it is windy and superficial, striving in wild vague terms to express great agitations which are obscurely felt by the poet. There was too much of the bathos of rhetoric, especially at first; too much addressing the German as 'thou fell, bloody brute,' and the like, which broke no bones and took no trenches.

When once it was understood that, as a cancelled line in Tennyson's 'Maud' has it,

The long, long canker of peace was over and done,

the sentiments of indignation and horror made themselves felt with considerable vivacity. In this direction, however, none of the youngest poets approached Sir Owen Seaman in the vigour of their invective. Most of them seemed to be overpowered by the political situation, and few could free themselves from their injured pacific habit of speech. Even when they wrote of Belgium, the Muse seemed rather to weep than to curse. Looking back to the winter of 1914, it is almost pathetic to observe how difficult it was for our easy-going British bards to hate the Germans. There was a good deal of ineffective violence, and considerable misuse of technical terms, caused, in many cases, by a too hasty reference to newspaper reports of gallantry under danger, in the course of which the more or less obscure verbiage of military science was picturesquely and inaccurately employed. As the slightly censorious reader looks back upon these poems of the beginning of the war, he cannot resist a certain impatience. In the first place, there is a family likeness which makes it impossible to distinguish one writer from another, and there is a tendency to a smug approval of British prejudice, and to a horrible confidence in England's power of 'muddling through,' which look rather ghastly in the light of the autumn of 1917.

There was, however, a new spirit presently apparent, and a much healthier one. The bards became soldiers, and in crossing over to France and Flanders, each had packed his flute in his kit. They began to send home verses in which they translated into music their actual experiences and their authentic emotions. We found ourselves listening to young men who had something new, and what was better, something noble to say to us, and we returned to the national spirit which inspired the Chansons de Geste in the eleventh century. To the spirit—but not in the least to the form, since it is curious that the war-poetry of 1914-17 is, even in the most skilful hands, poetry on a small scale. The two greatest of the primal species of verse, the Epic and the Ode, have been entirely neglected except, as will later be observed, in one notable instance by Major Maurice Baring. As a rule, the poets have constrained themselves to observe the discipline of a rather confined lyrical analysis in forms of the simplest character. Although particular examples have shown a rare felicity of touch, and although the sincerity of the reflection has in many cases hit upon very happy forms of expression, it is impossible to over look the general monotony. There used to be a story that the Japanese Government sent a committee of its best art-critics to study the relative merits of the modern European painters and that they returned with the bewildered statement that they could make no report, because all European pictures were exactly alike. A student from Patagonia might conceivably argue that he could discover no difference whatever between our various poets of the war.

This would be unjust, but it is perhaps not unfair to suggest that the determined resistance to all restraint, which has marked the latest school, is not really favourable to individuality. There has been a very general, almost a universal tendency to throw off the shackles of poetic form. It has been supposed that by abandoning the normal restraints or artificialities, of metre and rhyme, a greater directness and fidelity would be secured. Of course, if an intensified journalistic impression is all that is desired, 'prose cut up into lengths' is the readiest by-way to effect. But if the poets desire—and they all do desire—to speak to ages yet unborn, they should not forget that all the experience of history goes to prove discipline not unfavourable to poetic sincerity, while, on the other hand, the absence of all restraint is fatal to it. Inspiration does not willingly attend upon flagging metre and discordant rhyme, and never in the whole choral progress from Pindar down to Swinburne has a great master been found who did not exult in the stubbornness of 'dancing words and speaking strings,' or who did not find his joy in reducing them to harmony. The artist who avoids difficulties may be pleased with the rapidity of his effect, but he will have the vexation of finding his success an ephemeral one. The old advice to the poet, in preparing the rich chariot of the Muse, still holds good:

> Let the postillion, Nature, mount, but let
> The coachman, Art, be set.

Too many of our recent rebellious bards fancy that the coach will drive itself, if only the post-boy sticks his heels hard into Pegasus.

It is not, however, the object of this essay to review all the poetry which has been written about the war, not even that part of it which has owed its existence to the strong feeling of non-combatants at home. We rather propose to fix our attention on what has been written by the young soldiers themselves in their beautiful gallantry, verse which comes to us hallowed by the glorious effort of battle, and in too many poignant cases by the ultimate sacrifice of life itself. The poet achieves his highest meed of contemporary glory, if

> some brave young man's untimely fate
> In words worth dying for he celebrate,

and when he is himself a young man striving for the same deathless honour on the same field of blood it is difficult to conceive of circumstances more poignant than those which surround his effort. On many of these poets a death of the highest nobility has set the seal of eternal life. They were simple and passionate, radiant and calm, they fought for their country, and they have entered into glory. This alone might be enough to say in their praise, but star differeth from star in brightness, and from the constellation we propose to select half a dozen of the clearest luminaries. What is said in honest praise of these may be said, with due modification, of many others who miss merely the polish of their accomplishment. It is perhaps worth noticing, in passing, that most of the poets are men of university training, and that certain literary strains are common to the rank and file of them. The influence of Tennyson, Browning, Swinburne, and Rossetti is almost entirely absent. The only one of the great Victorians whom they seem to have read is Matthew Arnold, but it is impossible to help observing that the 'Sharpshire Lad' of Mr. A. E. Housman has been in the tunic-pocket of every one of them. Among the English poets of the past, it is mainly the so-called 'metaphysical' writers in the seventeenth century whom they have studied; Donne seems to have been a favourite with them all, and Vaughan and Treherne are not far behind. . . .

All these poets seem to be drawn into relation to one another. Robert Graves and Siegfried Sassoon are both Fusiliers, and they publish a [stichomythia] 'on Nonsense,' just as Cowley and Crashaw did 'on Hope' two centuries and a half ago. Lieut. Sassoon's own volume is later than those which we have hitherto examined, and bears a somewhat different character. The gallantry of 1915 and the optimism of 1916 have passed away, and in Lieut. Sassoon's poems their place is taken by a sense of intolerable weariness and impatience: **'How long, O Lord, how long?'** The name-piece of the volume, and perhaps its first in execution, is a monologue by an ignorant and shrewd old huntsman, who looks back over his life with philosophy and regret. Like Captain Graves, he is haunted with the idea that there must be fox-hounds in Heaven. All Lieut. Sassoon's poems about horses and hunting and country life generally betray his tastes and habits. This particular poem hardly touches on the war, but those which follow are absorbed by the ugliness, lassitude, and horror of fighting. Lieut. Sassoon's verse has not yet secured the quality of the first work; he is not sufficiently alive to the importance of always hitting upon the best and only word. He is essentially a satirist, and sometimes a very bold one, as in **'The Hero,'** where the death of a soldier is announced home in 'gallant lies,' so that his mother brags to her neighbours of the courage of her dead son. At the close of all this pious make-believe, the Colonel

> thought how "Jack," cold-footed, useless swine,
> Had panicked down the trench that night the mine
> Went up at Wicked Corner; how he'd tried
> To get sent home; and how, at last, he died,
> Blown to small bits;

or, again, as in **'Blighters,'** where the sentimentality of London is contrasted with the reality in Flanders:

> The House is crammed: tier beyond tier they grin
>   And cackle at the Show, while prancing ranks
> Of harlots shrill the chorus, drunk with din;
>   "We're sure the Kaiser loves the dear old Tanks!"
>
> I'd like to see a Tank come down the stalls,
>   Lurching to rag-time tunes, or "Home, sweet Home!"—
> And there'd be no more jokes in Music-halls
>   To mock the riddled corpses round Bapaume.

It is this note of bitter anger, miles away from the serenity of Rupert Brooke, the lion-heart of Julian Grenfell, the mournful passion of Robert Nichols, which differentiates Lieut. Sassoon from his fellows. They accept the war, with gallantry or with resignation; he detests it with wrathful impatience. He has much to learn as an artist, for his diction is often hard, and he does not always remember that Horace, 'when he writ on vulgar subjects, yet writ not vulgarly.' But he has force, sincerity, and a line of his own in thought and fancy. A considerable section of his poetry is occupied with studies of men he has observed at the Front, a subaltern, a private of the Lancashires, conscripts, the dress of a battle-field, the one-legged man ('Thank God, they had to amputate!'), the sniper who goes crazy—savage, disconcerting silhouettes drawn roughly against a lurid background.

The bitterness of Lieut. Sassoon is not cynical, it is the rage of disenchantment, the violence of a young man eager to pursue other aims, who, finding the age out of joint, resents being called upon to help to mend it. His temper is not altogether to be applauded, for such sentiments must tend to relax the effort of the struggle, yet they can hardly be reproved when conducted with so much honesty and courage. Lieut. Sassoon, who, as we learn, has twice been severely wounded and has been in the very furnace of the fighting, has reflected, more perhaps than his fellow-singers, about the causes and conditions of the war. He may not always have thought correctly, nor have recorded his impressions with proper circumspection, but his honesty must be respectfully acknowledged.

We have now called attention to those soldier-writers of verse who, in our judgment, have expressed themselves with most originality during the present war. There is a temptation to continue the inquiry, and to expatiate on others of only less merit and promise. Much could be said of Charles Hamilton Sorley, who gave evidence of precocious literary talent, though less, we think, in verse, since the unmistakable singing faculty is absent in 'Marlborough' (1916), than in prose, a form in which he already excelled. Sorley must have shown military gifts as well as a fine courage, for when he was killed in action in October 1915, although he was but twenty years of age, he had been promoted captain. In the universal sorrow, few figures awaken more regret than his. Something, too, had we space, should be said about the minstrels who have been less concerned with the delicacies of workmanship than with stirring the pulses of their auditors. In this kind the lyric 'A Leaping Wind from England' will long keep fresh the name of W. N. Hodgson, who was killed in the battle of the Somme. His verses were collected in November 1916. The strange, rough drum-taps of Mr. Henry Lawson, published in Sydney at the close of 1915, and those of Mr. Lawrence Rentoul, testify to Australian enthusiasm. Most of the soldier-poets were quite youthful; an exception was R. E. Vernède, whose 'War Poems' (1917) show the vigour of moral experience. He was killed in the attack on Harrincourt, in April 1917, having nearly closed his forty-second year. To pursue the list would only be to make our omissions more invidious.

There can be no healthy criticism where the principle of selection is neglected, and we regret that patriotism or indulgence tempts so many of those who speak of the war poets of the day to plaster them with indiscriminate praise. We have spoken here of a few, in whose honour even a little excess of laudation may not be out of place. But these are the exceptions, in a mass of standardised poetry made to pattern, loosely versified, excellent in sentiment, uniformly meditative, and entirely without individual character. The reviewers who applaud all these ephemeral efforts with a like acclaim, and who say that there are hundreds of poets now writing who equal if they do not excel the great masters of the past, talk nonsense; they talk nonsense, and they know it. They lavish their flatteries in order to widen the circle of their audience. They are like the prophets of Samaria, who declared good unto the King of Israel with one mouth; and we need a Micaiah to clear the scene of all such flatulent Zedekiahs. It is not true that the poets of the youngest generation are a myriad Shelleys and Burnses and Bérangers rolled into one. But it is true that they carry on the great tradition of poetry with enthusiasm, and a few of them with high accomplishment.

Francis Hackett (review date 13 April 1918)

SOURCE: "Absolution," in *New Republic*, April 13, 1918, pp. 330-1.

[*In the following review, Hackett offers qualified praise for* The Old Huntsman and Other Poems.]

When John Masefield returned here some months ago he brought praise of Mr. Sassoon's war-poetry. It was a surprise to him that this poetry, published in London in May, 1917, and dedicated to Thomas Hardy, should not yet have reached Americans. Here is the book now, issued in the handsome war-forgetful style conferred on it by Mr. Heinemann; and only a year late.

It is not all war-poetry. Half of the volume contains verse that Mr. Sassoon must have written in the England that is gone. This part of the volume might by itself have made some reputation if there had never been a long war, and if it had been published with peace-time additions—but it is a thin companion to the verse that its author has added in France. Its anæmia is no evidence that its author is thin-blooded, it is merely a proof that poetry had largely become a function of book-fed human beings in the traditional sphere where Mr. Sassoon resided before the war. It is distinguished verse, some of it quite charming and all of it beyond sentimentality, but it is definitely moon-luminous and pale. *The Old Huntsman* is a boyish attempt to secure a quavering sporting reminiscence. **"Haunted"**, **"Goblin Revel"** and **"Night-Piece"** show the kind of crow's nest of fantasy to which English poets were compelled to climb so long as they had no full community with the life about them and no passionate experiences of their own. **"October"** and **"Morning-Land "** and **"Arcady Unheeding "** exhibit what a man with Mr. Sassoon's gift could do with classic opportunity; and **"Dryads"** is a fair poem to represent what I am taking to be his nostalgic youth:

> When meadows are grey with the morn,
> In the dusk of the woods it is night;

The oak and the ash and the pine
War with the glimmer of light.

Dryads brown as the leaf
Move in the gloom of the glade;
When meadows are gray with the morn,
Dim night in the wood has delayed.

The cocks that crow to the land
Are faint and hollow and shrill:
Dryads as brown as the leaf
Whisper and hide and are still.

                                        "Dryads"

This seems to me lovely, but it is only a forerunner of the true utterance which Mr. Sassoon finds in France. The war that he puts into poetry is not an occasion for pomp or patriotism. The word England is undoubtedly implicit in his singing, but he never gets more political than when he is

Wondering when we'll ever end it,
Back to Hell with Kaiser send it,
Gag the noise, pack up and go.

It is not war the politicality that inspires him, but war the human experience, war the terrific means to a political end. Had he remained in England he might have become a propagandist, a hate-artist. His enlistment carried him at one stroke across the mud-munitions and landed him body and spirit in the zone of death. In that zone he had not felt it necessary to apologize for his thoughts or opinions. He has framed them as they came to him, the bold and natural expression of a citizen-soldier supposedly free. The war has tested him. It has lifted him out of his old associations and lined him up with companions not chosen. It has fed his ears on gunfire and fed his eyes on the monstrosity of slaughter. The landscape of war has imprisoned all his senses, day and night, winter and summer weather. But instead of being stunned, his nature was tautened and his emotional impetus supplied. It is not that war is the supreme impetus, as some men argue. It simply happened to remit this poet's critical difficulties, to give him the spur he needed. Other men have seen and heard these same things and found them incommunicable; but the wounded comrade, the Golgotha of the sentry, the harsh imperative at dawn, the music-hall banality about the tanks, the blunt casualness of death—these incidents took a form for Mr. Sassoon which beauty and truth could arrange on, perhaps not the only form or the deepest form but one with the touch of immortality. And his liveliness, his salty wit, improved his reception of reality without trying to disguise its bitterness.

Most men succumb to the new monotonies of the war routine, the spiritual anodyne of a strangeness beyond their mastery. They surrender personal verdict on their experience. They go dumb. But Mr. Sassoon has really mastered the inwardness and outwardness of what has happened to him. He has breasted the war. And the thrilling effect of this is not to estrange us from old human

nature but to show war, the monstrous parvenu, incapable of perverting or subverting the manhood we have always recognized. That is why Mr. Sassoon's thirty war poems go so deep. Fire and flood invade him only to bring into relief his buoyant and sensitive spirit, his honesty, his normal repugnances, his laughter, his hatred of cant. His spirit has been tempered by the furnace, not contorted or reduced to melted butter. He neither weeps too little not crooks his knee nor inflates his chest nor struts with a proud posterior. He remains a man.

The first war poem is this,

The anguish of the earth absolves our eyes
    Till beauty shines in all that we can see.
War is our scourge; yet war has made us wise,
    And, fighting for our freedom, we are free.

Horror of wounds and anger at the foe,
    And loss of things desired; all these must pass.
We are the happy legion, for we know
    Time's but a golden wind that shakes the grass.

There was an hour when we were loth to part
    From life we longed to share no less than others.
Now, having claimed this heritage of heart,
    What need we more, my comrades and my brothers?

                                        "Absolution"

Only men who have fought can really feel this "absolution," I suppose, but no one has better expressed the purgation of war. There are other moods, however, in which Mr. Sassoon has sung witheringly of this same absolution.

The Bishop tells us: "When the boys come back
"They will not be the same; for they'll have fought
"In a just cause: they lead the last attack
"On Anti-Christ; their comrades' blood has bought
"New right to breed an honorable race.
"They have challenged Death and dared him face to face."
"We're none of us the same!" the boys reply.
"For George lost both his legs; and Bill's stone blind;
"Poor Jim's shot through the lungs and like to die;
"And Bert's gone siphilitic: you'll not find
"A chap who's served that hasn't found *some* change."
And the Bishop said: "The ways of God are strange!"

                                        "They"

Another variant on the theme of absolution is this:

I'd been on duty from two till four.
I went and stared at the dug-out door.
Down in the frowst I heard them snore
"Stand to!" Somebody grunted and swore.
    Dawn was misty; the skies were still;
    Larks were singing, discordant, shrill;
    They seemed happy; but *I* felt ill.
Deep in water I splashed my way
Up the trench to our bogged front line.
Rain had fallen the whole damned night.
O Jesus, send me a wound to-day,

And I'll believe in Your bread and wine,
And get my bloody old sins washed white!

                    "Stand-to: Good Friday Morning"

You may guess from these quotations the happy accent of
**"Conscripts," "Enemies," "The Tombstone-Maker,"
"The One-legged Man," "The Choral Union,"
"Stretcher Case," "The Hero," "In the Pink," "A Subaltern," "The Redeemer."** There is a jolly humor in some
of them, **"Stretcher Case"** being perhaps the cleverest in
the amusing turn it gives to a poignant episode. It is not
forced humor, but a burst of friendly sunshine through the
phantasmagoria of the war. And Mr. Sassoon is no less
willing to express the grave reality, as this fine poem
shows,

> The road is thronged with women; soldiers pass
> And halt, but never see them; yet they're here—
> A patient crowd along the sodden grass,
> Silent, worn out with waiting, sick with fear.
> The road goes crawling up a long hillside,
> All ruts and stones and sludge, and the emptied dregs
> Of battle thrown in heaps. Here where they died
> Are stretched big-bellied horses with stiff legs;
> And dead men, bloody-fingered from the fight,
> Stare up at caverned darkness winking white.
>
> You in the bomb-scorched kilt, poor sprawling Jock,
> You tottered here and fell, and stumbled on,
> Half dazed for want of sleep. No dream could mock
> Your reeling brain with comforts lost and gone.
> You did not feel her arms about your knees,
> Her blind caress, her lips upon your head:
> Too tired for thoughts of home and love and ease,
> The road would serve you well enough for bed.

                                                "The Road"

It is not laid on thick, Mr. Sassoon's version, but his is
one of the true legends of the war, and has the accent of
simpler English poetry. There are phrases and moods
which remind one of ballad, the simplicity is so perfect—
even the supreme imaginative ballad of English, with its
calamities and portents,

> All in a hot and copper sky,
> The bloody Sun, at noon,
> Right up above the mast did stand,
> No bigger than the Moon. . . .

Quotation is often unfair. Sometimes it puts a layer of fine
apples on the top of the barrel, misrepresenting what's
underneath; or else it picks out a random fruit or two that
belie the actual content. But I have striven to take no
advantage in making these quotations from *The Old Huntsman.* They represent the book as a whole. Its tone may not
please every one, it must certainly disappoint the gentlemen who wish to disguise the tiger of war; but it is the
tone of a youth singularly alive to actuality, and you cannot expect the man who is gripping with the actuality to
take the same tone as the war-booster. The soldier is hardly
less patriotic than the booster, and he is just three thousand
miles nearer the fact.

Irwin Edman (review date 24 March 1946)

SOURCE: "Mr. Sassoon Continues His Autobiography,"
in *New York Times Book Review,* March 24, 1946, p. 4.

[*In the following review, Edman offers favorable review of*
Siegfried's Journey.]

The quality of Siegfried Sassoon's prose writing has by
this time become an established and unique mode in
contemporary English letters. Where else is the note of
reminiscence, half-lyric and half-humorous realism, so
delicately sounded? Who else evokes with such combined
detachment and nostalgia the atmosphere of a vanished
quarter-of-a-century ago, or the ardors and endurances of a
poetic and (to use Mr. Sassoon's own phrase about his
own early manhood) chuckle-headed youth? Where else
can one find so precise and yet passionate an evocation of
the very texture of the English sky and the English
landscape, or where find so much good sense and freshen-
ing insight into so many figures, famous and obscure, in
English society, politics and literature?

Mr. Sassoon has exhibited these delicious excellences in a
now considerable series of memoirs with the same subject:
himself. There were semi-fictional personal histories, told
in a thinly-disguised third person, some of them well
known a generation ago on both sides of the Atlantic:
*Memoirs of a Fox-Hunting Man, Memoirs of an Infantry
Officer,* and *Sherston's Progress.* There is the now frankly
first-personal story begun in *The Old Century,* continued
in *The Weald of Youth,* and now in this volume before us.
Siegfried's Journey, the only half-playfully named story
of the author's journey through the war years and their immediate sequel (possibly named, too, for his amused and
amusing and self-deprecatingly reported journey to
America, where he lectured as a then-famous, anti-war
soldier-poet).

One might suppose that to one who had read all these
books, as, for instance, this reviewer has done, the subject-
matter of Siegfried Sassoon's younger years would by this
time have become dull or wearisome. I can only attest that
this third volume of autobiography, from its opening page,
is as beguiling as ever. For Mr. Sassoon in his memoirs
has created a form of his own and achieved a tone in its
combined simplicity, and psychological subtlety unlike
that of any autobiographer I know. The prose itself, never
obtrusive or fancy, remains in itself a peculiar treasure. It
is the prose of a writer—and a man—who has never ceased
to be a poet. And it is not only in the surface of the prose
or in its texture that the poet is felt. Events, even trivial
ones of long ago, become for Mr. Sassoon essences beheld.
They are themes for ruminations, always modest and
always succinct. The passages of *Siegfried's Journey*
become parables of more than his own person. These
memoirs are reflections on the society, the culture of
England, and—in this volume—of the United States, by a
man who, for all his self-deprecations, is a poet with a
mind.

This section of the memoir begins in the midst of the last war. Siegfried, as it will perhaps be simplest to call him (and the title invites the liberty), has just been invalided home from the Western Front. In that earlier World War, the chasm between civilian life and the life of the soldier was more marked in England than it was to be in the later war of robot bombs. To come home was to come to something like pure felicity.

"To be lying in a little white-walled room, looking through the open window on to a college lawn, was for the very first few days very much like Paradise." He is made welcome at the beautiful country house "in the shadow of lofty elms" by a brilliant and eminent titled lady. He visits an old uncle, for whom the war is something remote fought by gallant and proper nephews. After a few weeks of this sort of thing, young Siegfried felt he must write something "that would give comfortable civilians a few shocks." He did—his famous anti-war poems.

On a second invalided leave, this time because of a wound, Siegfried's anti-war opinions crystallized; he felt that the war had become a meaningless slaughter. There are entertaining and touching accounts of what happened when he reduced his opinions to writing, not in verse—which had already attracted both highly favorable and some morally adverse opinion—but in prose. He was declared to have had a nervous breakdown and sent to a hospital. Released, on coming to London he is offered a job by Winston Churchill, then Minister of Munitions, who, in an interview, discussed Siegfried's anti-war views with him. "Our proceeding developed into a monologue. Pacing the room with a big cigar in the corner of his mouth, he gave me an emphatic vindication of militarism as an instrument of policy and stimulation of glorious individual achievement, not only in the mechanism of warfare but in the sphere of social progress."

Winston Churchill is only one of the famous figures who dot these pages, none introduced for the sake of their celebrity but for the part they played in shaping the imagination of the young soldier-poet. There are vignettes of Thomas Hardy at Max Gate, which give a firmer, fresher image of that great writer, whom Sassoon regards above all as a poet, than any I have ever seen. There is the same sort of rememberable account of meetings with T. E. Lawrence, Masefield, the Sitwells, Galsworthy, Robert Bridges, then Poet Laureate. None of these portraits is mere reverence or "official" portraiture. Each is the image, obviously authentic, registered by a poet's eyes and remembered with an artist's fidelity in these pages. Equally good, but more amused, are the American portraits—Amy Lowell among others. Siegfried had come here to lecture, and he is most amused in retrospect at his own apparent incompetence as a speaker, as he was previously amused by his idealistic but fumbling participation in the Labor Movement in England. His notes on his stay in America are proof to an American of his ability to evoke the authentic aspects of things and persons. Robert Frost comes quite as alive as Masefield, and midtown New York

as much as Sussex. Only the rooted affection for the English scene is lacking in these American pages.

Like the previous volumes, this book is a unique record of a personality whom only England could have in one person. A fox-hunting man, a soldier, and a meditative and humorous poet all in one. And few writers today take the care to achieve the exact and musical beauty of Sassoon's simple and noble prose.

Rolfe Humphries (review date 20 April 1946)

SOURCE: "The Happy Warrior," in *Nation*, April 20, 1946, pp. 478-9.

[*In the following review, Humphries offers positive assessment of* Siegfried's Journey, *which he describes as the work of a "dilettante."*]

How pleasant, one is tempted to reflect on reading these memoirs, how pleasant to be born in the leisure class, with a sense of aristocratic tradition, including the medieval, in the blood and bone; to be a welcome guest, for as long as one liked, at great houses with names and ivy and lawns with ilex trees; to have friends, male, like Robbie Ross, who would sympathetically draw out of you every impulse you had toward creativeness; or friends, female, like Lady Ottoline Morrell, a little over-enthusiastic, perhaps, but given to "innumerable acts of generosity and affection." How pleasant to circulate freely, with just the proper amount of diffidence, among the respected writers and artists of one's time; to have the entrée to drawing-rooms where Bach was played for enjoyment; or to go, if one felt in a simpleminded mood, for a jolly canter with the Acting Master of the Southdown Hunt! How pleasant to know the right people, so that after the recovery from wounds the leave could be extended ever so little; so that the pacifism could be diagnosed as shell shock; so that the objector to war could be lectured, benevolently if sincerely, by no less a Dutch uncle than Winston Churchill himself!

These are advantages not to be sneered at: Mr. Sassoon comes closer to taking them for granted, with due appreciation, than to making light of them. It was during these four years, 1916-1920, that his reputation was made, founded on acts of courage. He was brave enough to win the Military Cross for heroism in action; he was also brave enough to write, and have published—the publishers are also entitled to credit—the anti-war poems that have been, are now, and will for some time be, in all the anthologies. Rereading those poems and others in the same volume, one feels that the denunciations of the war, half a dozen items or so, are Sassoon's best work, and that the anthologies are not unfair in representing him by these, as they are unfair in making Rupert Brooke the poet of "If I should die, think only this of me," and so on. Some of Sassoon's war poems, even, tended to degenerate into formula once the ironic method had been established there came to be a bit of trick to it; but on the whole he shows here a tenseness, a humor, plenty grim, and a sense of reality that do not impinge elsewhere on his amiable Georgian melodies. Writing about these years, Mr. Sassoon is rather more candid about his innocence than his luck. He has kindly feelings, and kind words, for almost everyone—Bridges (though the Laureate did manage to make himself a little disagreeable), his devoted friend Owen, Masefield, Hardy, T. E. Lawrence, the Sitwells, and many others.

"Dilettante," like "amateur," is a word which has—as Kenneth Burke might say—pejorative semantic connotations. But the roots mean something else—delighting, loving— and what's the matter with that? Not very important, really—for Mr. Sassoon has lacked either the capacity or the will to live up to his advantages—this memoir of his most important years is nevertheless readable, pleasant, engaging, polite, agreeable. I hope it does not sound too pejorative, or sneering, to dismiss its author as a dilettante who has had moments when he was close to being an artist.

Michael Thorpe (essay date 1966)

SOURCE: "Effective Protest," in *Siegfried Sassoon: A Critical Study,* pp. 15-38. London: Oxford University Press, 1966.

[*In the following essay, Thorpe examines Sassoon's bitter anti-war sentiment, conflicted feelings of betrayal, inglorious depiction of combat experience, and use of brutal satire in his war poetry.*]

> As if the soldier died without a wound;
> As if the fibres of this godlike frame
> Were gored without a pang; as if the wretch,
> Who fell in battle, doing bloody deeds,
> Passed off to Heaven, translated and not killed;
>
> (Coleridge, 'Fears in Solitude' (1.117–121)

> . . . this sudden, stern ecstatic sense of unification, of peace, wrought by the stress of a great call . . . It is like the wakening of a new chivalry.
>
> (*The Athenaeum*, June 19, 1915)

> It must be remembered that in 1914 our conception of war was completely unreal. We had vague childish memories of the Boer War, and from these and from a general diffusion of Kiplingesque sentiments, we managed to infuse into war a decided element of adventurous romance. War still appealed to the imagination.
>
> (Sir Herbert Read, *The Contrary Experience*, 1963)

1 HAPPY WARRIOR

Of the 35 poems in *The Old Huntsman,* about one third were written in the spirit of Happy Warriorism to which Read bears witness. Rupert Brooke gave the lead for such poems as Sassoon's **'Absolution',** with its exultant acclamation of the comradeship of the young—"We are the happy legion"—morally set apart by their sacrifice. With "having claimed this heritage of heart, / What need we

more, my comrades and my brothers?" Sassoon echoes the closing lines of Brooke's 'The Dead': "Nobleness walks in our ways again, / And we have come into our heritage."

Sassoon's poems romanticizing war were, like Brooke's and many others', written before the experience of war had really begun and before the spirit with which it was entered upon had been extinguished by the accumulation of unremitting horrors that took all the sense of "cleanness" out of even the most self-deceived. Thus, it was possible in early 1916 for Sassoon to write of even a brother's death (at Gallipoli, in August 1915) with sombre exaltation. In **'To My Brother',** the dead man is made a symbol and example of selfless courage; bravery and resolution are sufficient in themselves, the exercise of man's highest qualities. In words which recall both the sentiment and situation of Tennyson's disastrous ending to *Maud,* where the sick hero, the prototype of these modern warriors, finds purpose and release in the outbreak of the Crimean War—"We have proved we have hearts in a cause, we are noble still"—he proclaims, "We have made an end of all things base. / We are returning by the road we came."

In this spirit it was possible to obscure the reality with a romantic aura of patriotism and chivalrous sacrifice. In **'The Dragon and the Undying'** the slain are etherealised; we are invited to dwell, not upon the manner of their death, but upon the beauty of the corpse prepared for viewing: "Their faces are the fair unshrouded night, / And planets are their eyes, their ageless dreams." The Dragon War "lusts to break the loveliness of spires"—not the limbs of men. **'France'** tells us that these warriors are fortunate in having a country fit to die in—whether *for* is not yet a problem:

> they are fortunate, who fight
> For gleaming landscapes swept and shafted
> And crowned by cloud pavilions white.

The last line is reminiscent of medieval fields of war. Also reminiscent of the medieval is the conviction, held by many poets at the outset—as also in Germany—that God is on their side. The English are Christian soldiers, cast in the bright and hallowed role cherished by what Professor Pinto calls the Nation at Home. **'The Redeemer'** typifies the crusading spirit of 1915: the modern saviour is the Kiplingesque "English soldier, white and strong, / Who loved his time like any simple chap"; he is "not uncontent to die / That Lancaster on Lune may stand secure." In **'A Subaltern'** and **'A Whispered Tale',** hints of the reality creep in with lines like "squeaking rats scampered across the slime", but they are not allowed to destroy the picture of a rough-and-ready nobility that rises above adversity. The manly answer to "hell" is to light one's pipe and bear it; the bright image of the "good simple soldier" outshines the monstrosity of his slaughter and the horrors are subdued to cliché.

For Sassoon himself, what chiefly sustains is the vision of ideal beauty that animates his youthful writing. In **'Before**

the Battle', written on 25th June, 1916, shortly before the terrible Somme offensive and his first experience of trench warfare, he spurns war's destructiveness and invokes the spirit of nature: "O river of stars and shadows, lead me through the night." Faith in an underlying harmony gives him strength to endure, so that the suffering can be embraced and even glorified as if it will burnish, not scorch, this faith: "But in my torment I was crowned, / And music dawned above despair." It is possible for "beauty" to be "garlanded in hell" (**'Secret Music'**).

The most telling of Sassoon's earliest war poems is **'The Kiss'**—if we accept the satiric interpretation. Graves tells us that it was "originally inspired by Colonel Campbell, V.C.'s bloodthirsty 'spirit of the bayonet' address at an army school. Later, Siegfried offered it as a satire, and it certainly comes off, whichever way you read it." This ambivalence is characteristic. It could, as Graves points out, be taken to represent either of two sides of Sassoon's poetic character—Happy Warrior or Bitter Pacifist. There seems no doubt that its purpose was originally straightforward: the romantic vocabulary applied to the bayonet— "up the nobly marching days / She glitters naked, cold and fair" and "Sweet Sister, grant your soldier this"—is not the kind of language Sassoon was likely to use ironically in early 1916. Included in *Georgian Poetry: 1916-17,* it was doubtless taken at face value: though the phrases "splits a skull" and "sets his heel" have a direct brutality that might have shocked, an intentional irony would have failed, since the *fact* remains vague—there is no face, no clear human victim. A further point in favour of the non-satiric interpretation is that the poem reads like an unconscious echo of the chilling paean to the virtues of "Clear-singing, clean slicing; / Sweet spoken, soft finishing" in 'The Song of the Sword', by W. E. Henley (1892), whose poetry the young Sassoon had read avidly.

With the exceptions of **'The Kiss', 'The Redeemer'** and **'Before the Battle',** three poems fairly representative of Sassoon's part in the first phase of war poetry, all the poems so far mentioned were excluded from his *War Poems.* No similar poem occurs in the volumes following *The Old Huntsman* and none could have been written by an honest and sensitive poet after the terrible massacres of 1916. While there was hope of an early end, the simple motives of pure patriotism, of joining with one's fellows in a righteous cause, reinforced by the sheer physical exaltation felt by youth in positive action, could sustain in the face of reality, even masking the true face of that reality. But the quick and clean satisfaction that chivalry needed never came.

2 BITTER PACIFIST

The ferocious destruction in 1916-17 of what had sustained at first—the death and maiming of comrades and friends, the smothering of chivalry and heroism beneath the mud and the bombardments—aroused in Sassoon, as in others, a revulsion against the War of an intensity far exceeding that with which he had held his original untarnished ide-

als. Bitterness is the keynote of the satires that occupy the central place in *The Old Huntsman* and *Counter-Attack:* bitterness against all who are excluded from the martyrdom and who can be held in some way responsible for its continuance. The counter-attack is directed chiefly against the Nation at Home—the Church, the State, the civilians (whether ignorant or indifferent)—and the 'brass-hats' of the General Staff. Sassoon has suddenly seen 'the truth' and he voices it without concession in a volley of indignant eruptions in which raw emotion, more than any 'art', is the compelling factor.

Almost every poem Sassoon wrote from **'Stand- to'** onwards is a form of protest against the War. The sheer force of feeling, undiluted and unobjectified, carries home a poem like **'Stand-to'.** As Sassoon says, it is "a jaunty scrap of doggerel," but it has the ring of truth—the truth of a moment of sudden realisation. Ten slangy lines unheroically describing his feelings are capped with the prayer:

> O Jesus, send me a wound today,
> And I'll believe in Your bread and wine,
> And get my bloody old sins washed white.

This is Sassoon's distinctive voice—a seemingly cynical, almost inarticulate tossing off of emotion. It is already a far cry from the polished decasyllabics—a vehicle for polished and correct sentiments—of **'The Redeemer'.** In other relatively early poems we see a growing sureness of touch in the use of the colloquial style—for which, in *The Daffodil Murderer,* he had already shown an aptitude— and the feeling of disenchantment that it expresses being turned outwards to voice a fierce sympathy for the now purposelessly suffering soldier. The ignorant "Davies" of **'In the Pink'** is also flatly contrasted with his Christ-like forerunner; he does not know what he is fighting for: "Tonight he's in the pink; but soon he'll die / And still the war goes on—*he* don't know why." In **'A Working Party'** this commonplace hero dies and is "carried back, a jolting lump / Beyond all need of tenderness and care." Both these poems have the beginnings of the qualities of expression and description—the clipped, colloquial style of the first and the vivid trench scene of the second which seems to overmaster and swallow up the casual death of just another "decent chap"—that Sassoon continually refines from now on.

What must have shocked and affronted the reader who had been uplifted by the emotional chivalry of such books as Robert Nichols' *Ardours and Endurances* (which went through three printings between July and October, 1917) is the stark frankness of the description and the hardness of tone, Sassoon is under the compulsion to *show* and his poems burst with the impatience to get the truth out. The truth is simply this (**'Counter-Attack'**):

> The place was rotten with dead: green clumsy legs
> High-booted, sprawled and grovelled along the saps
> And trunks, face downward, in the sucking mud,
> Wallowed like trodden sand-bags loosely filled;
> And naked sodden buttocks, mats of hair,

Bulged, clotted heads slept in the plastering slime.
And then the rain began,—the jolly old rain!

As if, the last line suggests with grotesque irony, that were not the last straw! Nothing, it seems, is to be treated with reverence, not even the weaknesses and misfortunes of one's own comrades. These are seized and thrust brutally in the reader's face: the dying soldier's delirium in **'Died of Wounds'**, "hoarse and low and rapid rose and fell / His troubled voice: he did the business well;" and in **'The Hero'**, "He thought how 'Jack', cold-footed useless swine / Had panicked . . ." It is not merely the truth that shocks, but the fact that this truth is such common fare that it can produce this hard-bitten reaction. Pity, we think, must be in short supply: then the poem has done its work, for it is *our* pity that is needed. In poem after poem, Sassoon deliberately shears off the euphemistic trappings that clutter the notion of the Supreme Sacrifice. There is the hard-bitten joke in **'The Tombstone-Maker'**: "I told him with a sympathetic grin, / That Germans boil dead soldiers down for fat"; the brutal simile of **'The Effect'**: "When Dick was killed last week he looked like that, / Flapping along the fire-step like a fish"; the right words for the actual business of killing: "Our chaps were sticking 'em like pigs" (**'Remorse'**); and the business-like, dismissive line that sets the seal on the earthly careers of "The many men, so beautiful" of **'Twelve Months After'**: "That's where they are today, knocked over to a man." It is not difficult to understand why, as Sassoon tells us in *Siegfried's Journey,* "an old Cambridge man" wrote to *The Cambridge Magazine,* as "'an average Englishman, pained, not to say disgusted, that such a thing as the poem **'The Hero'** should appear in a magazine connected with the University of Cambridge'." It was like finding a corpse left on one's doorstep as a practical joke designed to remind one of the meaning of death. Sassoon includes no scrap of relief in his parcels of truth: the ex-warrior who "[thanks] God they had to amputate" (**'The One-Legged Man'**) and the 'ignoble' one in **'Arms and the Man'**— "though his wound was healed and mended, / He hoped he'd get his leave extended"—can have provided scant consolation for the armchair patriot. The guilt is left firmly in the reader's hands.

The immediate effect of such a poem as **'Does It Matter?'** must often have been to alienate the civilian reader from the poet himself. For Owen, this poem would have been a mere sketch of his primary emotion: whereas, in 'Disabled', Owen focuses attention unwaveringly upon the man, the chill, grey figure alone with his apprehensions of a sadly limited future, Sassoon makes the victim his point of departure and civilian callousness his prime target. Each has its legitimate effect: Sassoon's is a barb that sticks, whilst Owen's shaft goes deeper to a heart that cannot escape involvement with the victim's feelings. Sassoon's rarely avoids this alienation: as the Enemy of Cant he does not seek to. He seldom employs elaborate irony, very much of which would have defeated his purpose. The nearest he comes to this is in **'How to Die'** and **'Lamentations',** where he affects to adopt the romantic

viewpoint. In **'How to Die'** he parodies the heroic manner so successfully that even the closing lines might mislead the insensitive reader. In both, the irony is betrayed by the application of the cheap phrase to the serious theme, so providing a satiric transformation of the equally cheap euphemisms for death. Thus, the one soldier is praised for dying with "due regard for decent taste," and the other castigated for grieving immoderately "all because his brother had gone west." Surely this grief was excessive— had not his brother died in the service of his country? "In my belief / Such men have lost all patriotic feeling." Is this, the reader might have asked, a fair emphasis? Fair or not, it was a picture of the truth.

The truth, as Sassoon presents it in his more characteristic satires, is hard and clean-cut. He had no doubt that he held a number of incontrovertible truths in his hands. He possessed the kind of certainty about this which is probably the satirist's essential attribute. For this reason, his most telling satires are short poems in which he says one thing, with clarity and conciseness. In them a conviction is crystallised once and for all: that the Church is hypocritical, the civilians are callous, that the Staff is cynically incompetent. The outstanding examples are **'Blighters'**, **'The General'**, **'Base Details'** and **'They'.** These are fierce, contemptuous pieces, moments of hate that carry the reader with them at once.

The broad outline of Sassoon's method is well described in his own words: "I merely chanced on the device of composing two or three harsh, peremptory, and colloquial stanzas with a knock-out blow in the last line." **'Blighters'**, inspired by seeing a jingoistic Hippodrome show before he went out to France again in 1917, is the most bitter. The indignation is conveyed in two deft strokes: he first paints the scene in lurid caricature—"they grin and cackle at the show," "prancing ranks of harlots shrill the chorus"—then immediately juxtaposes it with the righteous prophet's vision of the tank lurching down the stalls, bringing the only reality the poet acknowledges into tune with 'Home, sweet Home.' No space is allowed for reflection: the bitterness justifies itself with the last line, "To mock the riddled corpses round Bapaume." In **'The General'** also the truth is made to stand out starkly as the climax of a poem perfect in the equivalence of feeling and tone:

> "Good-morning; good-morning!" the General said
> When we met him last week on our way to the line.
> Now the soldiers he smiled at are most of 'em dead,
> And we're cursing his staff for incompetent swine.
> "He's cheery old card," grunted Harry to Jack
> As they slogged up to Arras with rifle and pack.
>
> . . . .
> But he did for them both by his plan of attack.

The sing-song rhythm of the first two lines conveys the brisk and casual manner of the general and also of the soldiers' death. To change in the next two lines to the heavily accented "we're cursing his staff for incompetent swine" is a grim introduction to the easily moving fifth and sixth lines—the unquestioning willingness to serve and die—and the last line completing a neat triplet with the impression of the tidy dispatch of lives. The scathing ending is put into the words of one wearily accustomed to such events—and the effect is enhanced if we know that in the Battle of Arras British casualties alone totalled 132,000 killed, wounded and missing, in less than a month. In the face of such facts, the fewer words the better.

As Pinto has pointed out, **'The General'**, like its companion-piece **'Base Details'**, **'Blighters'** and many of the other satires, obeys the simplest prescriptions of Georgian rhyming verse in everything but the diction, so that the satiric effect is accentuated by clothing a disreputable body in formal dress. The diction makes all the difference: Sassoon not only hit upon the method of describing the physical reality as it was, he also caught the voice of the reality. Blunden greatly admires **'The General'** for this. Owen, too, noticed it; according to Welland, he was especially impressed by the necessity to use 'the very words', as he set out to do in poems like 'The Dead Beat' and 'The Chances'—in the latter poem excelling anything of this kind achieved by Sassoon: it may be supposed, however, that both poets, consciously or unconsciously, owe something to the example set by Kipling's *Barrack-Room Ballads*.

Sassoon's ear for the very words extends beyond the soldier's cheerful and ignorant blasphemies and bonhomie to the dreadful euphemisms by which the non-combatant comfortably deflated the reality's true meaning: the Scarlet Majors lamenting "we've lost heavily in this last scrap," their "gross, goggle-eyed" counterparts at home assuring themselves that "Arthur's getting all the fun / At Arras with his nine-inch gun" (**'The Fathers'**), the vicariously intrepid journalist of **'Editorial Impressions'**. All the false attitudes to the War are dramatised; their hollowness is exposed simply because Sassoon allows them to speak for themselves. An excellent example of this method is **'They'**, "the one", Sassoon tells us, "most quoted by the reviewers, both adverse and favourable." Its notoriety was to be expected: like **'Stand-to'**, it was calculated to affront one of the most dearly cherished convictions at home—that the War was a contest sanctioned by Heaven and that the British were God's favourite team. The method is closely similar to that of **'Blighters'**: first an ominously inoffensive stanza rehearsing the Bishop's clichés about the ways in which the War will have altered those who "lead the last attack / On Anti-Christ." The second stanza takes up his "They will not be the same" and applies his words to the lowest, most real, level of meaning, as 'they' will see it: "For George lost both his legs; and Bill's stone blind." But the last word, a characteristically impotent ambiguity, is forced upon the Bishop—"The ways of God are strange!" **'They'** is Sassoon's shrewdest thrust at, to use Shelley's phrase, "the priest's delight" in war, and the fact that it could be made so easily with the enemy's own weapons illustrates what sitting ducks many of his targets were. In such circumstances, the hunter's aim is liable to tire: though in **'Choral Union'** and the later **'Joy-Bells'**

Sassoon tackles the theme from differing angles, he does so almost with good humour and fails to achieve full penetration.

'Fight to a Finish', a piece of wish-fulfilment in which the Nation Overseas has the chance to deal with its worst enemy, the Nation at Home, epitomises the strengths and limitations of Sassoon's satires. It is the soldier's emotional reaction against jingoism and involves a brutal inversion of standards. There are no rights in this poem, only the hatred of 'us' for 'them'. 'We', the "grim Fusiliers", make 'them', like pigs, "grunt and squeal"; we are "trusty", they "Junkers". Black and white are flatly opposed: just as the "Yellow-Pressmen" falsify the troops' sufferings, so the troops are distorted into idealized, righteous soldiers of wrath. The poet himself ("with my trusty bombers") is dangerously like the leader of a childish gang. But one only realizes this upon reflection. The sheer force of the language, the vividness of the scene, the basic truth—that the hypocrisy and indifference at home deserve rude exposure—are enough for the initial impact. But the tone of this and such poems as **'Their Frailty'** and **'Glory of Women'** verges upon obsessive hysteria: they inevitably lose force with the passing of time.

The intensity of hatred evinced in Sassoon's satires is, as a revelation of its disintegrating effect upon personality, a salutary indictment of the War and of war itself. It was not his temperament to absorb raw experience, as Owen did, at the time for transmutation into deeper poetry later: "I was a booby-trapped idealist, and 'young men', as Francis Bacon wrote, 'stir more than they can quiet, fly to the end without consideration of the means.'" He passed the hatred on: taking the hands of those spared his direct experience and forcing them to touch the truth—that suffering which Yeats (whose demands of the war poets were far more exacting than those he made upon the work of his friends) thought it "best to forget . . . as we do the discomfort of fever". Satire, if not the highest, is a legitimate form of poetry—and it was Sassoon's distinctive achievement to put it to wholly original ends. In *showing* the dreadfulness of the War, in its surface aspects, he preceded Owen and surpassed him and all English poets who had previously written of war. His satires have, quantitatively, greater 'bite' than those of his fellow war-poets and a sheer brutality of utterance that matches the reality. No English satirist since Byron had had such power of invective—though he lacks even Byron's constructiveness. He relieved the pressure of his emotion by *speaking* the brutality, over and over again.

These poems are the raw stuff of poetry. The reader who would feel their strength should come to them with a mind, not cool and detached, but that can still grow hot with imagining what forced them into being. Such a mind was Virginia Woolf's in 1918, and she acutely justified Sassoon's realistic poems in these words: "There is a stage of suffering, so these poems seem to show us, where any expression save the barest is intolerable; where beauty and art have something too universal about them to meet our particular case." Now, more so after the event, it is natural that some should feel bludgeoned rather than roused, and the effect, as Middleton Murry felt, may be "to [numb], not [terrify], the mind". Yet the response these poems elicit is likely, for many of us, to remain a more active one. It is still possible to say of them, with a reviewer of forty years ago: "Their emotion is still too closely knit into our experience to justify or indeed make desirable a wholly detached criticism." Admittedly, for Owen, who had a more philosophical eye upon cause and effect, mere communication was rarely enough ('Dulce et Decorum Est' and 'The Dead Beat' are the poems most akin to Sassoon's in manner): he sought to create, not force, a change of heart. Several of his poems are like paintings in depth exploring themes upon which Sassoon had earlier sketched a few bold strokes: we could supplement **'Does It Matter?'** with 'Disabled', **'They'** with 'The Chances', **'Suicide in the Trenches'** with 'S. I. W'. (or Herbert Read's 'The Execution of Cornelius Vane'), **'Base Details'** with 'A Terre'. But the effect would be to supplement, not supersede.

3 HIMSELF BEWILDERED

In *Siegfried's Journey,* Sassoon says that, once the War was over and he had some leisure for reflection, "I could now safely admit that army life had persistently interfered with my ruminative and quiet-loving mentality. I may even have been aware that most of my satiric verses were to some extent prompted by internal exasperation." His most subjective poems bear out the truth of this piece of self-analysis. Through them, we can trace the history of his inner self and see how the vacillations of feeling and contradictions of attitude to which, in the *Memoirs,* he freely confesses, are also reflected in the poetry.

A few poems in *The Old Huntsman* show Sassoon striving, during his first months in France, to hold fast the innocent vision that had animated the early nature poems. **'When I'm Among a Blaze of Lights'** well conveys the exasperation he mentions. It is a rather prudish piece, a peevish broadside against the tawdry pleasures of his fellow-officers, which repel the sensitive solitary: "Then someone says 'Another drink?' / And turns my living heart to stone. / A Mystic as Soldier", continues the theme on a more abstract plane, romanticizing the poet who "lived my days apart, / Dreaming fair songs for God", and is now compelled to "walk the secret way / With anger in my brain," his poetry stifled, perhaps forever. Yet the last poem in *The Old Huntsman,* the "jingle" **'A Letter Home',** which was sent to Robert Graves, ends a collection that contains such poems as **'Blighters'** and **'The Hero'** on a note of facile optimism. The mood is a variant of the initial Happy Warriorism and surmounts even the death of his and Graves's courageous mutual friend, David Thomas, who is made into an elegiac pastoral figure, with the assertion:

> I know
> Dreams will triumph, though the dark
> Scowls above me where I go.

But there is a hectic note in the rapid, irregular couplets—a defiant clinging to sanity and hope which can only be called bravado. It is an indication of how insecurely based was the standpoint from which Sassoon wrote his satires.

With *Counter-Attack,* there is no longer the least sense of surety that "dreams" will triumph or even sustain. **'Break of Day'** is a tenuous reverie—"a happy dream to him in hell"—which for a few moments before the attack tranquillises the soldier with peaceful memories of "riding in a dusty Sussex lane / In quiet September." But Sassoon seems unsure whether to intend the dream as a blessing or a mockery sent by "God's blank heart grown blind". Wholly unambiguous is the feverish self-communing of **'Repression of War Experience',** where war infects everything associated with peace and tranquillity: the blundering moths that scorch themselves in the candle flame are patently symbolic, the "breathless air" of the garden and the darkness of the trees form an atmosphere of brooding menace. The memory of the guns shatters the stillness; it is this, not "dreams", that lives in the mind:

> Those whispering guns—Christ, I want to go out
> And screech at them to stop—I'm going crazy;
> I'm going stark, staring mad because of the guns.

The poem is not wholly successful: the hysteria is only conveyed forcibly in these last lines; it does not *rise* to them. At a crucial point, in the petulant castigation of the ghosts of "old men with ugly souls / Who wore their bodies out with nasty sins", Sassoon's language fails him and he overbalances into the ludicrous. As will be shown more fully later, when his attack is not limited to a precisely conceived object of hatred, he is prone to give way to dull imprecations and clichés that dangerously deflate the feeling.

Other poems in *Counter- Attack* reflect the overwrought mental condition that Sassoon later analyses so dispassionately in *Memoirs of an Infantry Officer* and *Sherston's Progress.* 'Sick Leave', 'Banishment' and 'Autumn' all arise from the Craiglockhart period, when he was wrestling with the problem of how to reconcile his pacifist convictions with the feeling that he was betraying his comrades by not returning to the Front. **'Sick Leave',** which Graves identifies as definitely written at that time, is by far the most impressive of the three, with its restrained and unaffected opening, "When I'm asleep, dreaming and lulled and warm,— / They come, the homeless ones, the noiseless dead", and the simple statement, "They whisper to my heart; their thoughts are mine". Commonplace creeps in at the end, with the bond of blood—yet this was doubtless a common feeling and a deep one. It does not, in Sassoon, indicate anything approaching Owen's obsession with the significance of blood-letting. Though **'Sick Leave'** says all that need be said on the theme of the betrayal of comradeship, he returns to it in **'Banishment'** and **'Autumn'** with a disfiguring rhetoric. In **'Banishment',** an apologia for his public protest against the War, he strains after a consciously poetic dignity:

though doubtless the emotion was genuine, it is falsified by phrases like "smote my heart to pity" and "ever in my sight / They went arrayed in honour". A reader of the *Memoirs* will not doubt that the failure is one, not of sincerity, but of poetic tact. In **'Autumn',** he even harks back to the poetic diction of his early style, romanticising war's destruction in conventional images. The melodramatic concluding lines, "O martyred youth and manhood overthrown, / The burden of your wrongs is on my head" come strangely from the poet of **'How to Die'**. They are, however, consistent with the highly emotional nature of his response.

They also betray another weakness to which their author confesses—an inclination for self-dramatisation, which was responsible for an attitude to the War, when he returned to it from Craiglockhart, emotionally akin to that of his Happy Warrior beginnings. **'Dead Musicians'**— "upon my brow / I wear a wreath of banished lives"—and **'The Dream'** are both marred by a high-pitched rhetorical note. Sincere feeling is shown in **'The Dream',** with the sensitive and compassionate observation of the soldiers' petty miseries:

> I'm looking at their blistered feet; young Jones
> Stares up at me, mud-splashed and white and jaded;
> Out of his eyes the morning light has faded.

but as soon as the poet introduces himself and "The secret burden that is always mine" he gropes to express the inexpressible. The wild phrases, "accursed line", "blundering strife", "the foul beast of war that bludgeons life" draw attention to the emotional nature of the poet's sense of helpless responsibility. The poet's emotion is in the centre, not the tragedy to which he bears—or should bear—witness. A poem like Owen's 'The Sentry' works in the reverse way, with no insistence on the feelings the "I" possesses.

4 A LARGER SYMPATHY

The weaknesses of the subjective poems—the rawness of the emotion and the undisciplined expression of it—mar also most of the poems of private grief or of compassion for fellow-soldiers, individually or *en masse*. Seldom is the feeling allowed to work through, or emerge from, the poem itself. More often, feeling outruns expression. The hated phenomena of war—the "cursed wood" that must be stormed, to face death "like a prowling beast"—too readily become stereotypes that evoke no sharp response. The men themselves—"the kind, common ones . . . / What stubborn-hearted virtues they disguised!" (**'Conscripts'**), "Young Fusiliers, strong-legged and bold" (**'In Barracks'**)—are sentimentalised. There is a dangerously high proportion of cliché in the poems of strong feeling, as if he had not the urge for precision or the artistic conscience to vary his expression. While in the poems of protest this roughness serves him well as part of the angry voice almost inarticulate with the urgency of a message whose audience is assured, in a poem intended to evoke a deeper response the deadness of the language dulls the ef-

fect. Phrases like "the wild beast of battle" (**'Prelude: The Troops'**), "dreams that drip with murder" (**'Survivors'**), and the almost perfunctory metaphorical use of "hell", blur the impact of poems in which everything depends on the intensity of description. **'Prelude'** and **'Survivors'** have similar themes, but little of the force of Owen's 'Exposure' and 'Mental Cases'. Sassoon's pen is too liable to slip over the concrete reality which it is his first duty to communicate and which Owen evokes by both word and rhythm: he rushes instead to press upon the reader his own feelings and his view of what the reader's should be. The "seemingly casual, cliché style" that Blunden justly admires is a two-edged weapon. The clichés that in the satire work by contrast with the overwhelming reality have an artistic justification which their counterparts in the poems of compassion, in vainly seeking to match the reality, cannot share.

However genuine his feeling, in expressing it Sassoon is too inclined to adopt the materials nearest to hand. Thus, for the lengthy elegiac poem, **'The Last Meeting',** whose subject was dear to him (it is his friend, David Thomas, who is more buoyantly recalled in **'A Letter Home'**), he chooses a lush romantic style that smothers both the subject and some strong atmospheric description beneath a spurious richness of language. A comparison of a few lines from this poem with a similar passage from Owen's 'Asleep' illustrates how in moments of strong feeling sheer words are liable to get the mastery of Sassoon:

> Ah! but there was no need to call his name.
> He was beside me now, as swift as light.
> I knew him crushed to earth in scentless flowers,
> And lifted in the rapture of dark pines.

Owen's feeling, on the other hand, is not inflated; it makes no romantic leap to the unknowable, but through the concrete is more suggestive of the poignant quality of man's unknowing:

> —Or whether yet his thin and sodden head
> Confuses more and more with the low mould,
> His hair being one with the grey grass
> And finished fields of autumn that are old . . .
> Who knows? Who hopes? Who troubles? Let it pass!

With contrasts such as this (and others previously made) in mind, one is forced to admit the broad justice of D. J. Enright's statement that: "Sassoon's most interesting poetry is composed of what have been called the 'negative emotions'—horror, anger, disgust—and outside that field he inclines to become sentimental in a conventional way." It has become a critical commonplace to set Sassoon down, as B. Ifor Evans does, as "outstandingly the most effective" writer of the 'realist stage' of War poetry, reserving for Owen the prime place of honour as the poet capable of going deeper than emotional and biased outbursts (as **'Blighters'** and **'The Fathers'** are biased) to a quality of pity that is 'not strain'd'. Pinto describes Sassoon's war poetry as "purely destructive", in that it creates nothing with which to rebuild; Johnston, in *English Poetry of the*

First World War, shares this view. While one would not quarrel with the essential justice of these judgments (though Pinto's has an exaggerated negative emphasis), any more than Sassoon does in his generous comments on Owen, it can be shown that his response to the War is not confined to angry satire, sentimentality or a morbid preoccupation with his own predicament. A handful (admittedly) of his poems have a moving directness and simplicity which eschews sentimentality or morbidity; on a humbler scale than Owen's they plead human sympathy and understanding.

As with the satirical epigrams, this is best expressed within a brief compass, when he is not consciously striving for the large statement: the praiseworthy poems are **'Two Hundred Years After'**, **'The Hawthorn Tree'**, **'The Dug-Out'**, and, though it is not a perfect whole, **'Enemies'**; with some reservations, the longer descriptive pieces, **'Concert Party'** and **'Night on the Convoy'**, may be added to these. The range of feeling in these poems is wider than that customarily associated with Sassoon.

In the early sonnet **'Two Hundred Years After'**, he achieves the physical immediacy and simple expression of feeling that are so often absent from the more sensational Front Line poems. It is cleanly and economically constructed. We are first given a vivid picture of one of the most familiar—and least spectacular—sights of the War, a column drawing the rations up to the Line under cover of darkness. There is no intrusive comment; the picture is allowed to do its own work, to serve as a symbol of the futility of the struggle. This done, it is obliterated from the watcher's gaze by "a rainy scud" and the lights of the village—of normality, of peace-time continuity—appear. The few, compassionate words of the old man who has seen this ghostly scene often have a Hardyan simplicity: "Poor silent things, they were the English dead / Who came to fight in France and got their fill." This is indeed all that is likely to be said: it needed distinctive insight to grasp the enduring meaning of the common scene and poetic tact to point its significance without mawkishness.

Another (surprisingly) early poem, **'Enemies'**, is less finished. It begins poorly with the vague "queer sunless place" and the accustomed reference to "Armageddon", but in the crucial part Sassoon avoids the romantic elaboration of **'The Last Meeting'** and allows the one he grieves for to be only suggested. The flat simplicity of statement convinces: "One took his hand / Because his face could make them understand"—wisely, there is no attempt to show why this is so. But what matters most is the idea— the meeting of human beings beyond the hatred and the slaughter—a mere sketch, admittedly, for **'Strange Meeting'** or even Sorley's sonnet 'To Germany': the link between enemies is far from being forged. One is inclined to wish Sassoon had attempted something more ample on this theme: though it is implicit in his war poetry as a whole that he has no strong anti-German feelings, his failure to crystallise this into a positive attitude exemplifies his limitations.

'The Hawthorn Tree' shares the Hardyan simplicity of **'Two Hundred Years After'**. It is a welcome antidote to the bitterly accusing **'Glory of Women'** and **'Their Frailty'**, with their unqualified scorn for the selfishness of woman's love. In **'The Hawthorn Tree'** he allows the woman to speak, to express her love as far as she can. Her perception is limited to this love and partly blinded by it; if she is guilty, it is of ignorance and innocence, not indifference. She knows only that her son has "fearsome things to see", being unable to begin to imagine the extent of his sufferings. In their place she yearns to put a thing of pure and simple beauty which she touchingly believes might cure all—"just one glance / At our white hawthorn tree" (its whiteness is appropriate: he avoids the pitfall of introducing a contrasting red; the voice is strictly the mother's). The rain that cleanses the scene she would have her son see suggests tears, but cannot move her to them; her grief is beyond such things:

> But when there's been a shower of rain
> I think I'll never weep again
>   Until I've heard he's dead.

Without intruding his own, Sassoon has rendered truthfully the quality of another's deepest feelings.

The success of **'The Dug-Out'**, on the other hand, derives from the tension between subjective and compassionate feeling and also from judicious under-statement. In the latter respect it contrasts well with the over-explicit **'Dreamers'**. This is the whole poem:

> Why do you lie with your legs ungainly huddled,
> And one arm bent across your sullen, cold,
> Exhausted face? It hurts my heart to watch you,
> Deep-shadow'd from the candle's guttering gold;
> And you wonder why I shake you by the shoulder;
> Drowsy, you mumble and sigh and turn your head
> . . .
> *You are too young to fall asleep forever;*
> *And when you sleep you remind me of the dead.*

He avoids the sentimental treatment the subject invites (a lament for the doom of the clean, corn-haired youth in the full flower of manhood, etc.): he focuses attention instead upon the symbolic ugliness of the youth's posture, which is reinforced by the body's alienation from the candle. Sleep is a cruel mockery of death: not just the youth's, or of all those that have died, but of the poet's own that may be imminent. When he shakes the youth by the shoulder, it is the instinctive reaction of one who shares his vulnerable humanity. The poem is not obviously (certainly not consciously) self-regarding: there is a subtle tension between the sense of pity—"You are too young"—and the sense of identification with the youth—"you remind me of the dead".

'The Dug-Out' was one of Sassoon's last poems to arise directly from the War—it is dated July 18th, 1918, but according to *Siegfried's Journey* was probably written two months later; it promises a greater refinement of expression which was to be denied the opportunity to mature. In two other poems of this period, also included in *Picture Show,* Sassoon is moving towards the more self-subduing attitude which he had by then come to desire. **'Concert Party'** is the more successful. He relies entirely upon description of the scene and the atmosphere, by which he suggests the pathos of the contrast between the expectations of the deprived troops and the commonplace nature of what moves them. The poet is the compassionate observer, but identified with the men, not superior to them—"*We* hear them, drink them"; at the end he does stand apart, but not to moralise: "Silent, I watch the shadowy mass of soldiers stand. / Silent, they drift away, over the glimmering sand." The scene is made so clear to us that we know what is left unsaid. This is not so in the similarly descriptive **'Night on the Convoy'.** Here, he insists too much upon what could be inferred, risking the commonplace of "lads in sprawling strength" and the obviousness of:

> In the stark
> Danger of life at war, they lie so still,
> All prostrate and defenceless, head by head . . .
> And I remember Arras, and that hill
> Where dumb with pain I stumbled among the dead.

When we turn to the last poems where he is concerned with issues 'above the battle', we find that their most memorable quality is not their expression, but the sentiments they contain. Away from the concrete and visible reality, and dealing with necessary though not moving themes, he relapses disappointingly into dullness and rhetoric. The feeling of **'Reconciliation'** is, as we have seen, nascent in **'Enemies'** and the pitying thought for the "German mother" in **'Glory of Women'.** It is a timely message, expressed directly and unpretentiously, but it is prosaically undistinguished. **'Aftermath'** is more culpable. Something of a postscript, since it was written in March 1919, Sassoon calls it "an effective recitation-poem"—that is, a piece of popular emotion. Its long, measured periods lend themselves readily to declamation, but it will not bear cold-blooded examination, being almost entirely dependent upon cliché and emotive phrasing—"Look up, and swear by the green of the spring that you'll never forget." Doubtless it had its purpose and its effect, though one is grateful to Sassoon for informing us that, on one occasion when he rehearsed it in America, a group of charwomen were far from being carried away.

5 POSTSCRIPTS

Though Sassoon intended **'Aftermath'** to be "my last word on the subject", this word was actually—and more effectively—spoken some years later in two poems included in *The Heart's Journey:* **'To One Who Was With Me in the War'** was first published in 1926, and the sonnet **'On Passing the New Menin Gate'** in 1928.

These poems have the force of accumulated reflection. In **'To One Who Was With Me',** he again employs the heightened conversational tone of such poems as **'To Any**

Dead Officer' and **'Repression of War Experience'** for an imagined return to the war-time past. His purpose is to dispel the treacherous "sense of power / [That] invades us" when we remember war's positive value, the comradeship of "that Company which we served with": treacherous because "Remembering, we forget / Much that was monstrous" and "We forget our fear." He plays the "game of ghosts" with dramatic effect: together they go, stooping and ducking along the trenches—brought concretely to life again, as in **'A Working Party'**—till, "Round the next bay you'll meet / A drenched platoon-commander . . ." This is the other self—the true self that you were, with a face strained and anxious, "Hoping the War will end next week." Fittingly, the poem ends with the ironic question, "What's that you said?" There need be no answer: to resurrect that previous self nostalgically would be to invoke the worst also. This poem might well complement Blunden's 'The Watchers':

> When will the stern fine "Who goes there?"
> Meet me again in midnight air?
> And the gruff sentry's kindness, when
> Will kindness have such power again.

and compared with Martin Armstrong's grotesque nostalgia it shows a fine sense of balance:

> O give us one more day of sun and leaves,
> The laughing soldiers and the laughing stream,
> And when at dawn the loud destruction cleaves
> This silence, and, like men that move in dream,
> (Knowing the awaited trial has begun)
> We climb the trench, and cross the wire, and start,
> We'll stumble through the shell-bursts with good heart
> Like boys who race through meadows in the sun.

It is a relief to turn from this mockery of the dead to **'On Passing the New Menin Gate',** Sassoon's last word on the War and a strong example of the kind of remembrance they would surely have appreciated; again, in comparison with a related poem of Blunden's, 'Return of the Native', resolutely disenchanted. If **'To One Who Was With Me'** warns against forgetfulness of the worst, this poem affirms that the best has been forgotten also, this forgetfulness symbolised by the massive memorial at Ypres. It points the sharp contrast between the plain truth—"The unheroic Dead who fed the guns", "the doomed, conscripted, unvictorious ones"—and the vulgar memorial whose sheer size overwhelms and obliterates the memory: "a pile of peace-complacent stone." By this, the living have paid off their debt. The poem is both anti-heroic, not idealising the dead, and against the cant of the wasters of peace; the taut language exactly conveys barely controlled disgust:

> Was ever an immolation so belied
> As these intolerably nameless names?
> Well might the Dead who struggled in the slime
> Rise and deride this sepulchre of crime.

It is tempting to wish that these forceful and deeply considered poems had been Sassoon's last that one can call war poems. Unhappily, in 1940 he felt impelled to give an elder poet's encouragement—but hardly an old soldier-poet's—to the youth that once more could not choose but fight. His two short patriotic poems, **'The English Spirit'** and **'Silent Service'** do their conventional work (as **'Aftermath'** did) in a martial tone reminiscent of Milton and Wordsworth—and, sadly, of his own early First War poems. England opposes "Apollyon", "daemons in dark", and, more concretely, "The cultural crusade of Teuton tanks". She is the defender of earth's freedom and, it is implied, supported by God himself: "In every separate soul let courage shine— / A kneeling angel holding faith's front-line"—though it remains unclear whether the faith is to be in "ourselves" or in divine sanction. Such poems do have their purpose—they appeared in *The Observer* in 1940—but one cannot avoid a sad comparison between these inflated pieces and Hardy's 'Men Who March Away' (if one must have the martial mood), or, in a mood more in tune with a Second Great War, Herbert Read's 'To a Conscript in 1940':

> But you, my brother and my ghost, if you can go
> Knowing that there is no reward, no certain use
> In all your sacrifice, then Honour is reprieved.

But Sassoon, twenty years before, had already played his part in shaping the response of the new war poet:

> Pity, repulsion, love and anger,
> The vivid allegorical
> Reality of gun and hangar,
> Sense of the planet's imminent fall:

> Our fathers felt these things before
> In another half-forgotten war.

L. Hugh Moore, Jr. (essay date January 1969)

SOURCE: "Siegfried Sassoon and Georgian Realism," in *Twentieth Century Literature,* Vol. 14, No. 4, January, 1969, pp. 199-209.

[*In the following essay, Moore discusses the striking quality of Sassoon's war poetry as a fusion of Georgian poetics and realism.*]

The judgment that Siegfried Sassoon's pre-war poetry is pale, conventional, cloyingly romantic, and weakly derivative—in short, that it epitomizes what is today slightly called "Georgian" verse—has become a critical commonplace. A corollary to this view assumes that the powerful war poetry of *The Old Huntsman* (1917) and *Counter-Attack* (1918) sprang full blown from his head, a result of the trauma of trench warfare. Robert Graves appears to be the first to have foisted this view upon us in his desire to praise the more exciting war verse. He claims in *Goodbye to All That* that Sassoon before the war had published only a few "pastoral pieces of eighteen-ninetyish flavour, and a satire on Masefield which, half-way through, had forgotten to be a satire and turned into rather good Masefield." As

Graves saw it, Edward Marsh, the publisher of *Georgian Poetry,* and Edmund Gosse had retarded Sassoon's poetic development by keeping him to his "moons and nightingales and things." David Daiches, later, agreed with Graves' estimate of the early verse: Sassoon began, he believes, as "a faded romantic," in whom the war developed "a bitter satiric note." The authors of the recent spate of studies of the war poets have picked up and expanded this view. Bernard Bergonzi states colorfully in *Heroes' Twilight* that prior to World War I Sassoon composed "exquisite countrified verses that denoted a poetic talent minor to the point of debility" thus typifying "an *echt*-Georgian state of mind." The radical realism of the war poetry, Bergonzi continues, was forced upon him by the war and was inexplicable in terms of his early life and background. These assumptions need to be reexamined.

While Sassoon's early verse is definitely Georgian, this tradition contained realistic tendencies that culminated in the directness, brutality, and honesty of his best war verses. His mature war poetry, that is, merely extended the realistic revolt that was an important part of the Georgian poetic. And, further, Sassoon did not begin writing his famous war poetry until surprisingly late in World War I. Far from being the result of a shocked mind, his best war verse was the product of a much slower development than critics have assumed, for it was retarded by another, opposed, aspect of Georgianism, the taste for the lushly romantic and the insipidly pastoral.

Realism, the most striking and important phase of the Georgian poetic tradition, provides the best way to understand the Georgian poets and to appreciate the nature of their accomplishment. Georgianism in poetry began, as Robert Ross points out in *The Georgian Revolt,* as a revolutionary attempt to change the nature of poetry, to initiate a renascence. As Edward Marsh said at the beginning of his first anthology: "This volume is issued in the belief that English poetry is once again putting on a new strength and beauty." To these poets Georgianism was synonymous with realism; the new poetic, according to C. K. Stead, was "an attempt to come to terms with immediate experience, sensuous and imaginative, in a language close to common speech." This was the credo of the poets of *Georgian Poetry* I and II like Gordon Bottomley, Lascelles Abercrombie, D. H. Lawrence, and John Masefield. But, unfortunately for the reputations of these poets, Georgianism is frequently identified with the contrived and inept verse of poets like Sir John Squire, Edward Shanks, and W. J. Turner—those who dominated *Georgian Poetry* III and IV when the revolt had lost its drive and freshness. The movement that had begun with revolutionary realism ended with pallid escapism.

Realism, which had already triumphed in the prose of Georgians like Wells, Bennett, Galsworthy, and Shaw, then, was the essence of the new poetic at its inception. From the work of the leaders of the realistic revolt—poets and critics like Harold Monro, Osbert Sitwell, Edward

Marsh, John Middleton Murry, Abercrombie, Bottomley, and Masefield—one can deduce what the term meant to the Georgians. It meant, first, a rejection of the romantic Victorian tradition, as exemplified by the early Tennyson and the fin de siècle poets, and a casting off of genteel reticence. The poet, unhampered by stale conventions and confining poetic traditions, should strive, above all else, for sincerity, vitality, and truth by reproducing honestly and faithfully what he saw and felt. To follow the dictates of poetic realism, then, frequently was to emphasize the commonplace, the trivial, and the ugly and to include details previously regarded as too nasty or coarse for poetry. Realism meant, further, a greater emphasis on physical descriptions and detailed development, a greater concern for the surface facts of the poem and their accuracy. Realism, also, was associated with an attempt to use the accents, rhythms, and diction of common speech, often the speech of the uneducated. And, finally, these poets connected realism with an interest in social justice and a concern for the lowly, the poor, the victimized.

Realism pervaded the work of the early Georgians. Although Rupert Brooke is remembered today chiefly for his World War I heroics and a few set pieces like "The Old Vicarage, Grantchester," he led the realistic revolt with poetic close-ups of subjects like physical decay, senility, and sea-sickness. Out to do violence to the proprieties, Brooke presumably chose these subjects because they possessed the realist's touchstone of poetic excellence, truth to life. In "Menelaus and Helen" the poet imagines the old age of a couple from *The Iliad* and *The Odyssey* with results very different from Tennyson's. Brooke stresses the ugly details of senility: Menelaus "waxed garrulous, and sacked a hundred Troys / Twixt noon and supper" and aging: Helen "weeps, gummy-eyed and impotent," and her "dry shanks twist at Paris' mumbled name." The details of "A Channel Passage" could have been chosen by a black humorist:

> Do I forget you? Retchings twist and tie me,
> Old meat, good meals, brown gobbets, up I throw.
> Do I remember? Acrid return and slimy,
> The sobs and slobber of a last year's woe.
> And still the sick ship rolls. 'Tis hard, I tell ye,
> To choose 'twixt love and nausea, heart and belly.

The reviewers, not attuned to the new poetic, used terms like "sickly animalism" and "swagger and brutality" to describe these lines. Edward Marsh merely objected on the grounds of good taste and a preference for poetry he could read at meals.

Gordon Bottomley, under the aegis of poetic truth and sincerity, expanded Georgian realism to include sex and brutality. "King Lear's Wife," first published in *Georgian Poetry* II and performed, after censorship, by the Birmingham Repertory Company on September 25, 1915, drew a unanimous chorus, consisting of newspaper critics, Edmund Gosse, and even D. H. Lawrence, of outraged and horrified cries of nastiness and obscenity. In its portrayal of passion this verse play does attempt more than was

usual at that time, as this scene in which Lear addresses his wife's maid Gormflaith witnesses: "Enough . . . (kiss) Unless you do . . . (kiss) my will . . . (kiss) I shall . . . (kiss) I'll have you . . . (kiss) sent . . . (kiss) to . . . (kiss)." The play also has a gory stabbing and a grim parody of "A Frog He Would a-Wooing Go" sung by Mrs. Lear's maid as she prepared the body for burial:

> 'A louse crept out of my lady's shift—
> Ahumm, Ahumm, Ahee
> Crying Oi! Oi! We are turned adrift;
> The lady's bosom is cold and stiffed,
> And her arm-pit's cold for me.'

Such was the poetic realism during the period when the young Sassoon at Weirleigh and at Cambridge was writing and publishing his early verse. And, because of his friendship with Edward Marsh, the novice poet was profoundly influenced by the Georgian revolt. That Sassoon was deeply impressed by Georgian realism is evidenced by the fact that his first really successful poem began as a parody of Masefield's "The Everlasting Mercy" (1911), a poem Ross calls "the seminal realistic work of the renascence." Masefield's poem is, indeed, a compendium of the qualities that signified realism to the Georgians. It is direct and open about sex: the plot turns on the seduction of "poor Nell" by Saul Kane who admits "I drunk, I fought, I poached, I whored"; among its characters, drawn from the lower classes, is Doxy Jane, "a bouncing girl" who had a "thirst for men instead of soul." It has racy colloquial diction, that, however, never goes beyond "my closhy put.' / 'You bloody liar'" and several "by damns." It has an abundance of physical detail:

> Then down, past that white-blossomed pond,
> And past the chestnut trees beyond,
> And past the bridge the fishers knew,
> Where yellow flag flowers once grew . . .

Other qualities place "The Everlasting Mercy" squarely in the Georgian realistic revolution. Masefield records, with emphasis, the unpleasant and the ugly, as in the sad fate of a deceived girl who goes from pub to pub "Till health and beauty are departed, / And in a slum the reeking hag / Mumbles a crust with toothy jag." The poet includes violence and brutality in a boxing match and assorted fights. There is social concern behind the denunciation of capitalists, seen by Kane as blood suckers, fawning backstabbers, and cringing hypocrites, and the Church: "The English Church is and was / A subsidy of Caiaphas" because, in league with the greed of the rich, it does nothing for the poor and the working man. Yet basically the poem is more conventional than revolutionary. Saul Kane through his suffering and by means of the love of God and with the help of a lovely Quaker lady is saved from his sinful ways.

Inspired and amused by Masefield's realistic poem, Sassoon wrote **"The Daffodil Murderer,"** The most interesting and accomplished of his pre-war verse, the first of his poems with significant sales, and one of the few of his early poems that gives any indication of the power he exhibited in his war verse. Impressed by Masefield's poem, Sassoon amused himself by composing a parody. But as Graves has pointed out, the poem "half way through had forgotten to be a satire and turned into rather good Masefield." Sassoon seemed to get caught up in his story of a Sussex farmer awaiting trial for the accidental murder of the village tavern keeper. And for the first time he was following Marsh's gentle urgings toward more realistic verse: "It seems a necessity now to write either with one's eye on an object or with one's mind at grips with a more or less definite idea." Although the inspiration for Sassoon's poem was literary, its success derives in large part from the poet's familiarity with the people and places he was writing about. To Masefield, then, belongs part of the credit for turning Sassoon away, at least for a time, from the cloying influence of the pre-Raphaelites, the decadent romantics, and the less robust Georgians. And since the searing realism of Sassoon's war poems stems directly from **"The Daffodil Murderer,"** Masefield deserves some credit for the direction of the younger poet's development.

Like its model, **"The Daffodil Murderer"** exhibits all the tenets of Georgian realism, although some are less well defined than others. The abundance of physical detail impressively documents the world of rural England. Although the "peewits on the fallows, Flapping their wings and sadly calling / Because it's cold and twilight's falling" behave less like birds than literary migrants from "The Everlasting Mercy," elsewhere, Sassoon, as be-fits a fox-hunting man, observes the rural scene closely and accurately. The comic rhyme of Albert Meddle's reminiscence does not totally obscure a real concern for the natural surface of the poem:

> I thought how in the summer weather
> When Bill and me was boys together
> We'd often come this way when trudgin'
> Out by brooks to fish for gudgeon.
> I thought 'when me and Bill are deaders,
> 'There'll still be buttercups in medders,
> 'And boys with penny floats and hooks,
> 'Catchin fish in Laughton brooks.'

Elsewhere he achieves verisimilitude by piling homely detail upon homely detail: "Some chap goes down the street on a bike, / Ringing his bell, he's gone in a jiffey / Down Brighton road; I wonder if'e / Has got his lamp lit; then some motors / Goes by; and a hawker selling bloaters."

Sassoon goes beyond Masefield in the use of colloquial speech and racy diction. The publisher, T. W. H. Crosland, however, perhaps feeling Sassoon had not been bold enough or attempting to forestall criticism, explains, with tongue in cheek, that "in order that the severest taste might not be offended the murderer dictates what he has to say to the Prison Chaplain. By this thoughtful expedient a clear flow of unobjectionable language is secured and the reader will doubtless appreciate the comfortable result." Sassoon approximates common speech with such spellings

as "allus," "oughter," "spittin'," and "picter"; slang like "chaps," "shag," "dotty," "drivel," "gabble," "lout," "toff," and "cosh." And if such curses as "cripes" and "knock-kneed shrimp" seem more characteristic of the public school than the village tavern, others like "blasted skug" and "filthy pimp" are more in character. Even this early in his career Sassoon was as bold in his poetic diction as any of the Georgian realists.

Sassoon could well have been faulted by the critics, had they reviewed his poem, for coarseness in his treatment of sex and violence and for his inclusion of seamy and ugly details. Masefield's Saul does nothing worse than run naked through the village tormented by his betrayal of an innocent maid. Sassoon's Albert awaits the gallows for a senseless murder. And Sassoon gives the reader the truth of the violence in specific terms: "I tripp'd him up and kick'd his face in—/ Bill blinked his eyes and gave a guggle, / And lay there stiff without a struggle." Even in his novels and memoirs of the thirties and forties Sassoon was reticent about sex, but here he brings it in. In prison Albert thinks "It's rotten here to lie and listen / To lovers in the twilight kissin'," a statement that adds sex while violating verisimilitude. Elsewhere he leaves to our imagination what "Talking garbage" and "a dirty yarn" denote. The coarseness of the physical descriptions and emphasis on the unpleasant plainly foreshadow the techniques of the war poems. He has Albert, for example, dwell upon physical decay, a preoccupation of the war poems: "Another month and I'll grow rotten / Like a dead dog. . . ." And he describes the physical results of fear: "And all the guts inside my belly / Were shaking. . . ." Finally, many other words like "sweat-in'," "spittin'," "greasy-drunk," and "stinking" were chosen to suggest the physically repulsive.

Sassoon's social protest seems too sincere, too long and specific to be merely a perfunctory performance to satirize Masefield. These passages leave little doubt that Sassoon was even before the war concerned about the fate of the poor, the lowly, and especially the victimized—the elements of society being sacrificed much as, he would later feel, the young, the brave, and the poor were sacrificed and betrayed in the great war. His increasing sympathy for his peasant hero is probably responsible for the fact that what began as an amusing literary exercise became quite serious for the author. The cruel indifference and selfishness of the officials catch his ire: "The Judge's face will never soften; / The lawyers'll whisper about their fees / And pleecemen go home to their teas." And Albert, like his creator, is aware that he is being punished more for poverty than crime when he says "there's dirtier rogues than me, / Wearing broadcloth, walking free." Near the end of his narrative, Albert has a vision of social injustice so vast, so enormous that even the stars must wonder at it:

> "They watch some beggar breaking stone
> 'For workhouse task, all skin and bone;
> 'They hear 'im bashing till he sickens
> 'Of grinding grit for some one's chickens.
> "They see the King and Queen at Windsor,

'And hear the story that he spins 'er
'Of how he's been to pheasant-shoots
'With Jew-boy lords that lick his boots.

Obviously, then, it was not the war alone that gave the poet an awareness of the injustice and suffering that are not visited upon all classes equally and a compassion for those victimized.

"The Daffodil Murderer" is in itself an interesting poem, but its chief significance lies in its foreshadowing of the more powerful realism of the war poems and in the training for close observation that it provided the young poet. It certainly deserved better treatment than it received in its one review, a two-sentence notice in the anti-Crosland *Athenaeum*: "This is a pointless and weak-kneed imitation of 'The Everlasting Mercy.' The only conclusion we obtain from its perusal is that it is easy to write worse than Mr. Masefield."

In the title poem of another pre-war poem, **"The Old Huntsman,"** Sassoon continues to write in the tradition of Georgian realism, but this time with no hint of satire. Again, he chose for a narrator a plain man from the lower classes who reminisces over his life near its close. In this poem Sassoon has sharpened his eye for physical detail with the result that the poem has greater surface density and accuracy than his earlier poems. He has, moreover, managed to keep the descriptions in character, something he did not always do in **"The Daffodil Murderer."** The old huntsman's regretful sigh over what he will miss becomes poignant because of the dramatized details:

What a grand thing 'twould be if I could go
Back to the kennels now and take my hounds
For summer exercise, be riding out
With forty couple when the quiet skies
Are streaked with sunrise, and the silly birds
Grown hoarse with singing; cobwebs on the furze
Up on the hill, and all the country strange,
With no one stirring; and the horses fresh,
Sniffing the air I'll never breathe again.

And he remembers with pleasure the bloody violence of the hunt. At the end of a successful chase he pulls from the warren "a sharp-nosed cub-face blinking there and snapping, / Then in a moment seen him mobbed and torn / To strips in the baying hurly of the pack."

In **"The Old Huntsman"** Sassoon for the first time exhibits the anti-religious bias of Georgian literary realism, although without the rancor he was to display in such bitter attacks against the church at war as **"They."** Religion lacks any relevance to the old huntsman who is more than content with the physical richness of the world he knows. "Religion beats me. I'm amazed at folk / Drinking the gospels in and never scratching / Their heads for questions." People at prayer seem to him "like children sucking sweets / In school. . . ."

The realism of **"The Old Huntsman,"** however mild it seems today, shocked many reviewers, who, with prissy

sententiousness, guarded public morality. One critic concluded: "The title piece is a racy monologue by an old huntsman, full of grumbles and regrets, in quite good blank verse, with some unnecessary profanity." Yet the nearest thing to profanity in the poem is "I'm but a daft old fool!" Racy, perhaps, but hardly profane.

Several other pre-war poems, especially **"Morning Express,"** reveal Sassoon's early experimentation with some of the techniques of Georgian realism. Virginia Woolf, in a 1917 review of Sassoon's poems, saw how this poem foreshadowed the war poetry. She called it "a solid and in its way beautiful catalogue of facts" that indicated "an early vein of realism" which the war opened up. The poem's solidity of specification, its respect for the accurate detail, its unaffected simplicity of diction distinguish it from such innocuous poems as **"Dryads"** and **"Arcady Unheeding."** In these poems Sassoon was following the less robust aspect of the Georgian poetic practice that would come to stand, in the verse of poets like Turner and Squire, for the Georgian poetry in its entirety. Actually, **"Morning Express"** clearly exemplifies the continuing conflict in Sassoon's poetry between two aspects of Georgianism: romantic escapism versus realistic depiction. On the one hand he writes of "morn's long, slanting arrows" and "resplendent clouds / Of sun-blown vapour." On the other hand he makes the poem memorable with physically realized details:

Boys, indolent eyed, from baskets leaning back,
Question each face; a man with a hammer steals
Stooping from coach to coach; with clang and clack
Touches and tests, and listens to the wheels.

Sassoon, then, even before he had seen the horror of trench warfare had in his poetry a strong vein of realism that denotes a greater strength of mind than he is usually credited with. The theory that the dislocation accompanying his war experiences so profoundly shocked the young poet, given to mooning over rural felicities, that he became a realist to expose the full horror of war to a complacent home front must be abandoned. Such a theory neglects the toughness inherent in the Georgian revolt against Victorianism and fin de siècle romanticism. Rather, Sassoon approached his war experiences with all the poetic techniques that he displayed in the war poetry of *Counter-Attack*. That the shock of war matured him quickly as a man and as a poet cannot be denied. Yet, contrary to expectations, Sassoon's first poetry on the war was a casting back, a rejection of Georgian realism, in order either to forget the war with escapist verse or to hide his real doubts behind noble lines.

At first, even at the front, poetry was for Sassoon an escape into a more pleasant world rather than a means to comprehend and convey the world he was caught up in. In **"The Daffodil Murderer"** and **"The Old Huntsman"** he had tried to come to terms with the real world as he saw it, but that was before reality meant a landscape strewn with mutilated, decaying bodies where instant death fell haphazardly from random shells. He sought picturesqueness rather than honesty. "How I long to be a painter," he wrote to Marsh at the Ministry of Munitions, "everything out here is simply asking to be painted or etched; it is wildly picturesque." As late as 1916 he wrote **"To Victory,"** in which he turned his back on the first tenet of Georgian realism, to depict outward reality honestly and brutally. Here he seems to dislike war on the grounds that it is aesthetically distasteful:

> Return to greet me, colours that were my joy,
> Not in the woeful crimson of men slain,
> But shining as a garden; come with the streaming
> Banners of dawn and sundown after rain.

At this same time, Sassoon when criticizing *Over the Brazier* explained to Robert Graves that the war should not be written about realistically. In *Good-bye to All That* Graves gives his answer: "Siegfried had not yet been in the trenches. I told him, in my old-soldier manner, that he would soon change his style." Graves was right, but, given the poetic techniques which Sassoon brought to the war, the change was a long time coming. Soon the war invalidated lines like:

> I am not sad; only I long for lustre.
> I am tired of the greys and browns and the leafless ash.
> I would have hours that move like a glitter of dancers.
> Far from the angry guns that boom and flash.

The observation here is as false as the sentiment. Sassoon explained to Marsh: "I put 'angry guns that boom and flash' in my poem, but really they flash and thud—the flash comes first, and they only boom when very near and in some valley."

"France" falsifies the emotions of men at war with its idea that the British soldiers are fortunate to die for the lovely landscapes of France.

> And they are fortunate, who fight
> For gleaming landscapes swept and shafted
> And crowned by cloud pavilions white.
> Hearing such harmonies as might
> Only from Heaven be downward wafted—
> Voices of victory and delight.

In a few months Sassoon was to say no in thunder to the idea that God was on the British side. But in **"Absolution"** he communes with the spirit of Rupert Brooke rather than looking closely at the scenes and soldiers around him.

> The anguish of the earth absolves our eyes
> Till beauty shines in all that we see
> War is our scourge; yet war has made us wise.
> And fighting for our freedom, we are free.

After the war Sassoon was not proud of this poem: "The significance of my too nobly worded lines was that they expressed the typical self-glorifying feelings of a young man about to go to the Front for the first time. The poem subsequently found favour with middle-aged reviewers,

but the more I saw of the war, the less noble-minded I felt about it." In 1920 he refused to allow it to be reprinted in an anthology on the grounds that it was completely false in its emotion.

The picturesque and the noble, Sassoon's first reactions in poetry to the war, were not a promising beginning for one who shortly was to become the most powerful voice in poetry to describe and denounce the war. In the war poems that gave him this reputation his poetic technique is merely an extension and development of the techniques of Georgian realism: accurate physical descriptions with an emphasis on the ugly and distasteful; colloquial speech and diction; coarseness, brutality, and directness; an anti-religious bias; and a concern for social justice.

Sassoon became indignant at the exploitation of the young and the poor. The bloated generals, the crafty politicians yelling for German blood, the safe journalists, the indifferent civilians—all cruelly victimize the soldier. The majority of his war poems thus derive from the social concern he had already manifested in **"The Daffodil Murderer"** and **"The Old Huntsman."** Compassion for the lot of the victims alternates with fury at the exploiters. In **"The Redeemer,"** Sassoon, like Owen in "Greater Love," finds the patient, passive suffering of the English foot soldier similar to Christ's agony. "I saw that He was Christ," wearing "a mask / Of mortal pain in Hell's unholy shine." **"A Working Party"** begins with a sketch of the confusion of soldiers repairing the trenches at night under fire. The narrator then poignantly focuses upon one soldier.

> He was a young man with a meagre wife
> And two small children in a Midland town;
> He showed their photographs to all his mates,
> And they considered him a decent chap
> Who did his work and hadn't much to say,
> And always laughed at other people's jokes
> Because he hadn't any of his own.
>
> He pushed another bag along the top,
> Craning his body outward; then a flare
> Gave one white glimpse of No Man's Land and wire;
> And as he dropped his head the instant split
> His startled life with lead, and all went out.

The war, then, strengthened Sassoon's pity for the lowly, and it increased his indignation at those who did not share his concern. In **"Blighters"** he dreams of directing a tank at those to whom the war was a joke: "And there'd be no more jokes in Music halls / To mock the riddled corpses round Bapaume." In **"Base Details,"** a clever parody of Stevenson's children's poetry, he directs his outrage at the comfortable generals:

> If I were fierce, and bald, and short of breath
> I'd live with scarlet Majors at the Base,
> And speed glum heroes up the line to death. . . .
> And when the war is done and youth stone dead
> I'd toddle safely home and die—in bed.

Sassoon's renditions of the landscape of war are unforgettable. In his pre-war verse he had accurately described the

English countryside and, occasionally, even focused on the ugly and distasteful. His main objective now became the destruction of romantic idealizations of war, such as Housman's "I Did Not Lose My Heart," by picking the right detail to bring home the ugly reality of war. Like the Georgian realists he set out to shock received opinions and to rebel against the poetry of the past. **"Counter-Attack"** grimly catalogs physical horrors:

> The place was rotten with dead; green clumsy legs
> High-booted, sprawled and grovelled along the saps
> And trunks, face downward, in the sucking mud,
> Wallowed like trodden sand bogs loosely filled;
> And naked sodden buttocks, mats of hair,
> Bulged, clotted heads slept in the plastering slime.

Winston Churchill so admired this poem that he memorized it, seeing it, not as a protest against war, but as a means of increasing the war effort because it showed what the English soldiers endured. Other poems like **"Break of Day"** stress the destruction of the spirit by the horror of war, "where men are crushed like clods, and crawl to find / Some crater for their wretchedness," by contrast with the remembered scenes of rural England: "Beyond the brambled fences . . . / Are glimmering fields with harvest piled in sheaves, / And treetops dark against the stars grown pale; / Then, clear and shrill, a distant farm-cock crows."

During the war Sassoon used realism to shock the home front out of their easy complacence by making them see the ugly truth. To show the cruel falseness of the romantic glorification of the soldier's attitude, Sassoon in a large number of poems set out to demolish this heroic myth by describing the anti-heroic truth. In **"The Hero"** a brother officer reports to the bereaved mother that Jack died "as he'd have wished." She replies, "We mothers are so proud / Of our dead soldiers!" But the truth is not so comforting:

> He thought how 'Jack,' cold-footed, useless swine,
> Had panicked down the trench that night the mine
> Went up at Wicked Corner; how he'd tried
> To get sent home, and how, at last he died,
> Blown to small bits.

The subject of men at war obviously provided an opportunity for further development of the coarseness Sassoon had somewhat tentatively experimented with in **"The Daffodil Murderer."** His language is now bolder. "Bloody" has become more frequent, and he freely uses curses like "O Christ Almighty" and "O Jesus," expressions not found in his pre-war poetry. The prevailing tone, like the language, is colloquial, as in **"To Any Dead Officer,"** a farewell to a friend recently killed. "Goodbye, old lad! Remember me to God. . . ." He concludes, "Cheero! / I wish they'd killed you in a decent show." But his boldest breach of decorum consists of the use of "syphilitic" in **"They."** Sassoon thought this was his "most publicly effective poem," the one most singled out for attack. In *Siegfried's Journey* Sassoon, still an unrepentant Georgian realist, took pleasure in the fact that he was the first to bring "syphilitic" into "the realms of English verse."

In 1945 Sassoon with characteristic modesty summed up his poetic influence on Wilfred Owen: "My only claimable influence was that I stimulated him towards writing with compassionate and challenging realism." "Compassionate and challenging realism" well describes Sassoon's own poetic technique in his war poetry, but it can also be applied to the best of his pre-war verse. John H. Johnston has pointed out in a recent study that the poems of *Counter-Attack* "constitute the first real attempt to present the truth of the war, and the effect of his break with the conventions and traditions of earlier war poetry can hardly be overestimated." If Sassoon did tell more of the truth of war than did his predecessors, part of the credit must go to the tradition of realism, the most vital part of the Georgian poetic, out of which came some of the most powerful war poetry ever written.

Avrom Fleishman (essay date 1983)

SOURCE: "*The Memoirs of George Sherston:* Sassoon's Perpetual Pilgrimage," in *Figures of Autobiography: The Language of Self-Writing in Victorian and Modern England,* University of California Press, 1983, pp. 337-53.

[*In the following essay, Fleishman examines the recurring motifs of spiritual journey and transformation in Sassoon's autobiographic writings.*]

"I told him that I was a Pilgrim going to the Celestial City." When the reader of the *Complete Memoirs* reaches the epigraph to the final volume, *Sherston's Progress,* the impression is confirmed that he has been accompanying a spiritual wayfarer. All his long, meditative life, Siegfried Sassoon maintained the dual role of action and rumination under the aspect of pilgrim allegory. Throughout his extended autobiographical career—from *The Heart's Journey* poems of 1927 to the final volume of his *propria persona* autobiographical trilogy, *Siegfried's Journey* (1945)—Sassoon was governed by the figure of quest, though his active life diminished and his ruminations increased in inverse proportion. With the benefit of hindsight and with varied degrees of satisfaction in his conversion to Catholicism in 1957, his critics have mapped his religious path in closed or handsome curves, but the view from the road his books report is unencumbered by claims to distance and direction. To apply the phrase with which another long-lived contemporary concluded his autobiography, "the journey not the arrival matters."

The absence of religious conversion and formal completion in Sassoon's self-writings does not, however, bar them from full use of the figures with which spiritual autobiographers have given pattern and meaning to their lives. Sassoon habitually uses the terms *spiritual autobiography* and *private pilgrimage* for his career, and he exhibits a long-standing obligation to Bunyan that goes well beyond the choice of epigraph. Perhaps more significantly, his poetry gives frequent indications of a typological habit of mind in confronting the otherwise unassimilable spectacle of the Great War. **"The Redeemer,"** for one, creates a typological image closely resembling those of other war poets, such as David Jones, that superimpose the sufferings of the human-all-too-human Tommy and the paradigmatic martyrdom:

> He faced me, reeling in his weariness,
> Shouldering his load of planks, so hard to bear.
> I say that He was Christ, who wrought to bless
> All groping things with freedom bright as air,
> And with His mercy washed and made them fair.
> Then the flame sank, and all grew black as pitch,
> While we began to struggle along the ditch;
> And someone flung his burden in the muck,
> Mumbling: "O Christ Almighty, now I'm stuck!"

Other Sassoon war poems take up biblical models for less agonized yet more alarming identifications with their modern instances. Adam becomes "the gaunt wild man whose lovely sons were dead" whereas the modern king sending troops to the slaughter for his selfish purposes stands revealed as another David, quick to exploit the death of Uriah. Some of these identifications are made for their topical, satirical thrust, but the long-standing practice of Sassoon's poetry confirms his autobiographical tendency to apply to the Bible for the figures of life. We may trace the habit to his sense of his Jewish heritage—"as a poetic spirit I have always felt myself—or wanted to be—a kind of minor prophet"—or to his favoring of the devotional and mystical poets of the seventeenth century, especially Herbert and Vaughan.

For all Sassoon's ample provision of biblical analogies with which to piece together the fragments of his war-shattered life, the first volume of the **Complete Memoirs— Memoirs of a Fox-Hunting Man**—is relatively free of figuration. This is the book that made him a venerated relic of the social world he set out to decently bury—the Cranford-Barset—"sceptered isle" world he continued to relish and recall while undertaking to show its limitations and its passing. Sassoon later took his opportunities for mythologizing the idyll of the turn-of-the-century home counties; in the second trilogy, **The Old Century** and **The Weald of Youth** move easily into symbolic ascriptions for childhood scenes, for example, the "half-hour's pilgrimage" to Watercress Well, which becomes a "symbol of life" and the "source of all my journeyings." But in **Memoirs of a Fox-Hunting Man** (**MFM**), the landscape and his activities within it are held to the level of physical density and rich psychological impression: "With a sense of abiding strangeness I see myself looking down from an upper window on a confusion of green branches shaken by the summer breeze. In an endless variety of dream-distorted versions the garden persists as the background of my unconscious existence" (Pt. I, sec. 4).

Sassoon wishes to maintain his native scenes—for all their numinousness in the memory—at the literal level, in preparation for the violent contrast he will draw between them and the war spectacle. Even in these early scenes,

the descriptions are set up for pointed contrast with larger landscapes and other realms of experience. An extended passage on the expanding perceptions of waking follows the boy out beyond his window and garden to the valley, the town, and the historical world behind them: "How little I knew of the enormous world beyond that valley and those low green hills. From over the fields and orchards Butley Church struck five in mellow tones. . . . I inspected the village grocer's calendar which was hanging from a nail. On it there was a picture of 'The Relief of Ladysmith.'. . . Old Kruger and the Boers. I never could make up my mind what it was all about, that Boer War, and it seemed such a long way off' (**MFM,** Pt. II, sec. 1).

The literal prevails in all the prose on his youthful love affair with horses, which takes up the major part of this first volume. But in these detailed accounts as well, a contrast is effected with another level of consciousness that stands outside and judges the vigorous physical activity. At a climactic moment of the young rider's career, his winning of the "Colonel's Cup" at "Dumbridge," the cup is placed next to another treasured object in his room:

> Everything led back to the talisman; while I gazed and gazed on its lustre I said to myself, aloud, "It can't be true that it's really there on the table!" The photograph of Watts's "Love and Death" was there on the wall; but it meant no more to me than the strangeness of the stars which I had seen without question, out in the quiet spring night. I was secure in a cozy little universe of my own, and it had rewarded me with the Colonel's Cup. My last thought before I fell asleep was, "Next season I'll come out in a pink coat." (**MFM,** Pt. VI, sec. 4)

The contrast of the cup and the reproduction seems at first casual, but when the "strangeness of the stars" is brought into the equation, it reveals the young man's lack of curiosity about the truly mysterious and his banal awe at the presence of the apparently numinous and merely fatuous symbol of sporting success. The Watts painting has come up at other summary junctures, we now recall (Pt. I, sec. 4; Pt. II, sec. 1), to suggest the realm of artistic depth and spiritual mystery to which the youth is vaguely sensitive but not as yet committed.

Memoirs of a Fox-Hunting Man does not end with this contrast but with the more primitive one between peace and war. As the part titles indicate, the first volume leaves Sherston "At the Front" whereas **Memoirs of an Infantry Officer** takes up the tale much later, with a 1916 scene, "At the Army School." The form of the opening volume, then, already encompasses the full range of the transition from the idyll of gardens and race courses to the mud of trench life and the clay of death. As the third in a succession of friends troops to the grave, the narrator baldly reports: "A sack was lowered into a hole in the ground. The sack was Dick. I knew Death then" (**MFM,** Pt. X, sec. 5).

The movement downward to this low place begins early, even in the midst of fox-hunting larks. Quick to enlist and proudly mounted, Sherston tries to extend his prewar "picnic in perfect weather" in the mounted infantry: "My notion of acting as ground scout was to go several hundred yards ahead of the troop and look for jumpable fences. But the ground was still hard and the hedges were blind with summer vegetation, and when I put the farrier-sergeant's horse at a lush-looking obstacle I failed to observe that there was a strand of wire in it" (**MFM**, Pt. IX, sec. 1). The resulting fall is figurative as well as literal: its consequence is not merely a broken arm but an alertness to strands of wire impeding movement, freedom, and life. There will be much ado with wire cutters purchased at the army and navy stores and pressed into service at the Battle of Mametz Wood, but already the mortal bonds of the soldier—and with him, man—are laid on.

As Sassoon's commentators observe—and as he himself discloses in one of his frequent chats in the autobiographer's workshop—his creation of a pseudonymous persona to tell an authentic but selective tale allows him to exaggerate the ingenue in his early self-portrait. Yet it is not the young romantic Sherston who is raised as the figure of innocence led to the slaughter but the brother officer who becomes the contents of that sack, "Dick Tiltwood":

> His was the bright countenance of truth; ignorant and undoubting; incapable of concealment but strong in reticence and modesty. . . . he had arrived at manhood in the nick of time to serve his country in what he naturally assumed to be a just and glorious war. Everyone told him so; and when he came to Clitherland Camp he was a shining epitome of his unembittered generation which gladly gave itself to the German shells and machine-guns. . . . (**MFM**, Pt. IX, sec. 4)

The language inclines here not only toward indignation at outraged innocence but also toward universal finality: this "bright countenance of truth" becomes the "shining epitome" not only for his historical generation but for an eternal pattern of human experience. It is this larger burden of the narrator's slowly growing political awareness that begins to emerge in his anticipation of the debacle: "To him, as to me, the War was inevitable and justifiable. Courage remained a virtue. And that exploitation of courage, if I may be allowed to say a thing so obvious, was the essential tragedy of the War, which, as everyone now agrees, was a crime against humanity" (Pt. IX, sec. 2).

The story of Sherston's first years at war is briefly told by comparison with the close attention that will be given the final years in the next volumes. Moving to the Front is to pass a traditional threshold, not merely beyond the familiar world at peace but beyond an insular culture: "For the first time in our lives we had crossed the Channel" (**MFM**, Pt. X, sec. 1). The specific boundary in time and place is marked—and remarked upon—by the line, "We got to Béthune by half-past ten" (Pt. X, sec. 1). From this point, an accretion of baleful events begins to separate the fox-hunting man from his old self: "Everything I had known before the War seemed to be withering away and falling to pieces. . ." (Pt. X, sec. 4). With the loss of his riding friend, "Stephen Colwood," his former groom, "Dixon,"

and then "Dick Tiltwood," a point is reached well known to less naïve but equally spiritual autobiographers: "Somewhere out of sight beyond the splintered tree-tops of Hidden Wood a bird had begun to sing. Without knowing why, I remembered that it was Easter Sunday. Standing in that dismal ditch, I could find no consolation in the thought that Christ was risen" (Pt. X, sec. 6). The pilgrim now embarked on his ways of exile experiences the blankness of despair: "As for me, I had more or less made up my mind to die: the idea made things easier" (Pt. X, sec. 6).

From the point where **Memoirs of an Infantry Officer** (**MIO**) begins, the language of the lower world rises by steady increments to sweeping asseveration: "I remember waiting there in the gloom and watching an unearthly little conflagration caused by some phospherous bombs up the hill on our right" (Pt. IV, sec. 2); "I am staring at a sunlit picture of Hell, and still the breeze shakes the yellow weeds, and the poppies glow under Crawley Ridge where some shells fell a few minutes ago" (Pt. IV, sec. 2); "Our own occupation of Quadrangle Trench was only a prelude to that pandemonium which converted the green thickets of Mametz Wood to a desolation of skeleton trees and blackening bodies" (Pt. IV, sec. 3); "Low in the west, pale orange beams were streaming down on the country that receded with a sort of rich regretful beauty, like the background of a painted masterpiece. For me that evening expressed the indeterminate tragedy which was moving, with agony on agony, toward the autumn. . . . altogether, I concluded, Armageddon was too immense for my solitary understanding" (Pt. IV, sec. 4).

A brief leave at an Oxford college gives him a wary taste of "Paradise"—"Had I earned it? I was too grateful to care" (**MIO**, Pt. X, sec. 1). Here, and on his return to the captured Hindenburg Line, Sherston begins to contrast his knowledge-without-forgiveness with the stolid incomprehension of the "people at home who couldn't understand." The effort to make sense of the inchoate leaves him in spiritual dryness: "But my mind was in a muddle; the War was too big an event for one man to stand alone in. All I knew was that I'd lost my faith in it and there was nothing left to believe in except 'the Battalion spirit'" (Pt. VIII, sec. 2). This last faith proves equally difficult to maintain: "Last summer the First Battalion had been part of my life; by the middle of September it had been almost obliterated." One last hope remains, in the human spirit and the heroic principle:

> I, a single human being with my little stock of earthly experience in my head, was entering once again the veritable gloom and disaster of the thing called Armageddon. And I saw it then, as I see it now—a dreadful place, a place of horror and desolation which no imagination could have invented. Also it was a place where a man of strong spirit might know himself utterly powerless against death and destruction, and yet stand up and defy gross darkness and stupefying shell-fire, discovering in himself the invincible resistance of an animal or an insect, and an endurance which he might, in after days, forget or disbelieve. (Pt. VIII, sec. 4)

These last defiances of the *néant* avail him nothing as he descends into the abyss of the tunnel under the Hindenburg Trench: "The earthy smell of that triumph of Teutonic military engineering was strongly suggestive of appearing in the Roll of Honour and being buried until the Day of Judgment" (Pt. VIII, sec. 4). There is only one further point of exile, the Outpost Trench:

> wherever we looked the mangled effigies of the dead were our *memento mori*. Shell-twisted and dismembered, the Germans maintained the violent attitudes in which they had died. The British had mostly been killed by bullets or bombs, so they looked more resigned. But I can remember a pair of hands (nationality unknown) which protruded from the soaked ashen soil like the roots of a tree turned upside down; one hand seemed to be pointing at the sky with an accusing gesture. Each time I passed that place the protest of those fingers became more expressive of an appeal to God in defiance of those who made the War. Who made the War? . . . the dead were the dead; this was no time to be pitying them or asking silly questions about their outraged lives. Such sights must be taken for granted, I thought, as I gasped and slithered and stumbled with my disconsolate crew. Floating on the surface of the flooded trench was the mask of a human face which had detached itself from the skull. (Pt. VIII, sec. 4)

At this point, Sherston is wounded in the shoulder and is withdrawn to England for convalescence, but his illness is more radical than a tearing of flesh. In company with the other survivors, he feels "estrangement from everyone except the troops in the Front Line": "I couldn't be free from the War; even this hospital ward was full of it, and every day the oppression increased" (*MIO,* Pt. IX, sec. 1). The oppression and bondage express themselves in the characteristic visions of combat neurosis: "Shapes of mutilated soldiers came crawling across the floor; the floor seemed to be littered with fragments of mangled flesh. Faces glared upward; hands clutched at neck and belly; a livid grinning face with bristly moustache peered at me above the edge of my bed; his hands clawed at the sheets" (Pt. IX, sec. 1).

At once, at the point of crisis, a sign is given, though in a medium oddly different from the usual organs of revelation. It is the *"Unconservative Weekly"* (*The Nation*): "The omniscience of this ably written journal had become the basis of my provocative views on world affairs. . . . an article in the *Unconservative Weekly* was for me a sort of divine revelation. It told me what I'd never known but now needed to believe. . ." (*MIO,* Pt. IX, sec. 2). It is true that Sherston goes on to belittle his ability to comprehend and retain the political acumen of the journal, but his comic reduction of his rational response only enhances the power of his faith. This faith is further bolstered by its contention with the traditional beliefs of "Lady Asterisk," who likes having "serious helpful little talks with her officers": "When I had blurted out my opinion that life was preferable to the Roll of Honour she put aside her reticence like a rich cloak. 'But death is nothing,' she said. 'Life, after all, is only the beginning. And those who are killed in the War—they help us from up there. They are helping us to win'" (Pt. IX, sec. 3).

With this travesty of Christian consolation and the news that all but one of the officers of his Second Battalion have become casualties, Sherston writes to consult the editor of his journal of revelation, "Mr. Markington" (H.V. Massingham).

Their first meeting is a luncheon at the editor's club, "the mecca of the Liberal Party," under the visible aegis and spiritual example of Richard Cobden. Markington provides historical perspective on past antiwar campaigns and political insight into one of the chief impediments to a negotiated peace—the Allies' refusal to publish their war aims and secret treaties. He also, almost in passing, provides the idea of moral protest and witnessing resistance to the war: "He told me that I should find the same sort of things described in Tolstoy's *War and Peace,* adding that if once the common soldier became articulate the War couldn't last a month" (*MIO,* Pt. X, sec. 1). Sherston takes the idea home and returns, the following week, to the editorial office: "It was a case of direct inspiration; I had, so to speak, received the call, and the editor of the *Unconservative Weekly* seemed the most likely man to put me on the shortest road to martyrdom" (Pt. X, sec. 1).

Markington spells out the broad lines of a proclamation of protest, and the unpolitical Sherston is led beyond his characteristic diffidence: "His words caused me an uncomfortable feeling that perhaps I was only making a fool of myself; but this was soon mitigated by a glowing sense of martyrdom. I saw myself 'attired with sudden brightness, like a man inspired' . . ." (*MIO,* Pt. X, sec. 1). Literary as well as religious conventions are here put subtly to the test of simultaneous renewal and satire.

To counteract the excessive afflatus of the newly dedicated spirit, Markington also provides contact with the best rational mind—and the most vigorous antiwar protester—of the time, Bertrand Russell ("Thornton Tyrrell"). The philosopher's discourse is clipped and pragmatic, shifting focus quickly from the large political issues to the scale of the man before him and his spiritual crisis: "'It amounts to this, doesn't it—that you have ceased to believe what you are told about the objects for which you supposed yourself to be fighting? . . . Now that you have lost your faith in what you enlisted for, I am certain that you should go on and let the consequences take care of themselves. . . . But I hadn't intended to speak as definitely as this. You must decide by your own feeling and not by what anyone else says'" (Pt. X, sec. 2). The act of protest on which they collaborate takes the form of a traditional religious protest-cum-profession of faith. Sassoon/Sherston's famous declaration begins:

> *I am making this statement as an act of wilful defiance of military authority, because I believe that the War is being deliberately prolonged by those who have the power to end it. . . . I believe that this War, upon which I entered as a war of defence and liberation, has now become a war of aggression and conquest. . . . I have seen and endured the sufferings of the troops, and I can no longer be a party to prolong these sufferings for ends which I believe to be evil and unjust.* (Pt. X, sec. 5)

In difficulty at the unwonted bravado of his position and his prose, Sherston seeks inspiration where he can find it. He goes to Cambridge, drawing mingled sustenance from his alma mater: "Sitting in King's [College] Chapel I tried to recover my conviction of the nobility of my enterprise and to believe that the pen which wrote my statement had 'dropped from an angel's wing.' I also reminded myself that Cambridge had dismissed Tyrrell from his lectureship because he disbelieved in the War" (*MIO*, Pt. X, sec. 3). With these mixed influences, Sherston finds himself in "purgatory" (Pt. X, sec. 4) and returns to his home town to suffer through his condition. There follows one of the classic scenes of autobiographical writing, an ascent of a hill to the point of epiphany, in which a vision of history and of oneself in history enables the divided mind to resolve itself and make its central choice in life:

> Late on a sultry afternoon, when returning from a mutinous-minded walk, I stopped to sit in Butley Churchyard. From Butley Hill one looks across a narrow winding valley, and that afternoon the woods and orchards suddenly made me feel almost as fond of them as I'd been when I was in France. While I was resting on a flat-topped old tombstone I recovered something approximate to peace of mind. Gazing at my immediate surroundings, I felt that "joining the great majority" was a homely—almost a comforting—idea. Here death differed from extinction in modern warfare. I ascertained from the nearest headstone that *Thomas Welfare, of this Parish, had died on October 20th, 1843, aged 72. "Respected by all who knew him." Also Sarah, wife of the above. "Not changed but glorified."* Such facts were resignedly acceptable. They were in harmony with the simple annals of this quiet corner of Kent. . . . And Butley Church, with its big-buttressed square tower, was protectively permanent. One could visualize it there for the last 599 years, measuring out the unambitious local chronology with its bells, while English history unrolled itself along the horizon with coronations and rebellions and stubbornly disputed charters and convenants. Beyond all that, the "foreign parts" of the world widened incredibly toward regions reported by travellers' tales. And so outward to the windy universe of astronomers and theologians. . . .
>
> Meanwhile my meditations had dispelled my heavy heartedness, and as I went home I recovered something of the exultation I'd felt when first forming my resolution. I knew that no right-minded Butley man could take it upon himself to affirm that a European war was being needlessly prolonged by those who had the power to end it. They would tap their foreheads and sympathetically assume that I'd seen more of the fighting than was good for me. But I felt the desire to suffer, and once again I had a glimpse of something beyond and above my present troubles—as though I could, by cutting myself off from my previous existence, gain some new spiritual freedom and live as I had never lived before. (Pt. X, sec. 4)

Coming down from this exalted vision and gritty determination, Sherston's final volume of memoirs might be expected to record a steady progress in pacifist activity and spiritual enlightenment. Indeed, that is what he anticipates; when shunted back to the Front, he suffers pangs of doubt as to his course but accepts them as "an inevitable conjuncture in my progress" (*MIO*, Pt. X, sec. 7). And there is the monitory epigraph to *Sherston's Progress,* indicating movement toward the Celestial City, to lay out the path of the denouement. But the form and content of this last volume are by no means so clear, and Sherston's return to the Front only to suffer a near-fatal wound offers no easy moral or aesthetic resolution—it simply brings his war service to an end and closes the *Memoirs.* It was some such awareness of this inconclusive ending—along with the pressure of other aspects of his life that required telling—that must have led Sassoon to write three further volumes of autobiography in his own name.

Yet running through *Sherston's Progress* there is a figure of life that gives point to his further experiences in battle and hospital. By its very nature, this figure is unlikely to suggest full resolution as it opens the future to possibility rather than resting at a determinate place. Although Sherston's narrative of his treatment by Dr. W. H. R. Rivers is readily reducible to a psychiatric revelation of his fundamental immaturity and new dependence on a father figure, the human figure that emerges is of a less easily grasped kind. The terms of Sassoon's later poem on Rivers cast him in an archetypal form:

> What voice revisits me this night? What face
> To my heart's room returns?
> From that perpetual silence where the grace
> Of human sainthood burns
> Hastes he once more to harmonize and heal?
> . . .
> O fathering friend and scientist of good. . . .

In *Sherston's Progress* (*SP*), this image is scaled down to that of an "alert and earnest" face with the "half-shy look of a middle-aged person intruding on the segregative amusements of the young," steadily regarding one with an "unreprimanding smile" (Pt. 1, sec. 2). Given this dual image of the universal healer and the vividly human friend, suggestions of Christological displacement arise, but Sherston urges no certainty about the good doctor or his cure: "In later years, while muddling on toward maturity, I have made it my business to find out all I can about the mechanism of my spontaneous behaviour; but I cannot be sure how far I had advanced in that art—or science—in 1917. I can only suggest that my definite approach to mental maturity began with my contact with the mind of Rivers" (Pt. 1, sec. 3).

Whether or not Sherston's condition is a rebirth and his activity a progress, the further pages of the volume infuse doses of expansive experience. Sherston even makes a journey to Jerusalem as part of a military force, but the occasion is not one for racial identification or postexilic return; it is instead an encounter with another learned doctor, who provides a running commentary on the flora and fauna of the land. Similarly, Sherston's reading provides no telling insights but a deepening of his response to long-familiar writers like Hardy. Yet he is still trapped inside the war: "And I felt a great longing to be liberated from these few hundred yards of ant-like activity—to travel all the way along the Western Front—to learn through my eyes and with my heart the organism of the monstrous drama which my mind had not the power to envision as a whole. But my mind could see no further than the walls of that dug-out with its one wobbling candle which now burnt low" (*SP,* Pt. IV, sec. 2).

From this antlike limitation he is released with a violence that almost destroys him. He is sent home and decisively begins his lifelong career of trying to make sense of the war and his transformation by it. Back in the hospital, he tries to take stock of his life but is not impressed with the sums; of course, Sherston is prevented from reckoning in the war poetry that Sassoon had published and that was to provide a vocation and a means of establishing his identity. Summing up his faith in his vision and his protest: "I had no conviction about anything except that the War was a dirty trick which had been played on me and my generation" (*SP,* Pt. IV, sec. 3). But at this stage of renewed *accidie,* the good doctor returns:

> And then, unexpected and unannounced, Rivers came in and closed the door behind him. Quiet and alert, purposeful and unhesitating, he seemed to empty the room of everything that had needed exorcising.
>
> My futile demons fled him—for his presence was a refutation of wrong-headedness. . . .
>
> He did not tell me that I had done my best to justify his belief in me. He merely made me feel that he took all that for granted, and now we must go on to something better still. And this was the beginning of the new life toward which he had shown me the way. (Pt. IV, sec. 3)

John Hildebidle (essay date 1983)

SOURCE: "Neither Worthy Nor Capable: The War Memoirs of Graves, Blunden, and Sassoon," in *Modernism Reconsidered,* edited by Robert Kiely, Harvard University Press, 1983, pp. 101- 21.

[*In the following excerpt, Hildebidle discusses the lasting trauma and guilt experienced by World War I veterans. According to Hildebidle, Sassoon's memoirs, as well as those by Robert Graves and Edmund Blunden, reflect his effort to come to terms with the horrors of war and his own survival.*]

Those of the modernist generations who experienced at first hand the apocalypse of the Western Front faced unusual difficulty in achieving that "impersonality" variously prescribed by Eliot and by Stephen Dedalus. By those who had lived through 1914-1918 at some greater distance from Ypres and the Somme, the war could be used as the substance or material of great, if harsh, art—the no-man's-landscape of *The Waste Land,* for instance, or the history that Virginia Woolf borrows for Septimus Smith. One can trace in the war poets an attempt to find or to make a form and language that could control the immediate and shocking experience of the trenches, an effort all too often cut short by death. The survivors of the war

did not necessarily prosper as a result of their apparent good fortune; for it fell to them to devise a way to recall the war both fairly and usefully. To many it seemed, as Erich Maria Remarque insisted in his dedication of *All Quiet on the Western Front,* that even those who had survived physically were nevertheless destroyed by the war.

In an essay written to commemorate the fortieth anniversary of the Armistice, Robert Graves poses what must have been, for those who found themselves still alive after 1918, the supreme question: "Death lurked around every traverse, killing our best friends with monotonous spite. We had been spared, but why? Certainly not because of our virtues." The question is both unanswerable and inescapable. Beneath the question of physical survival there lies another problem, as is made clear by Edmund Blunden's poem "The Welcome," which describes the first moments in the Line of a man just back from leave. No sooner does he sit down in the headquarters pillbox than it is struck by a shell which reduces six men to "a black muck heap." The newcomer, the sole survivor, finds himself "alive and sane"; and the poem, which has up to that point been couched in the plain language of reportage, suddenly rises into near-Scripture: "it shall be spoken / While any of those who were there have tongues." It is not just life, but sanity as well, that is miraculous.

The problem of psychological survival has been extensively studied with reference to survivors of concentration camps and of the Hiroshima bombing, but not, I think, with reference to the veterans of World War I. One need not necessarily equate the experiences of Auschwitz and Ypres to see parallels. R. J. Lifton, writing of the *hibakusha,* the survivors of Hiroshima, mentions, as what he calls "an indirect manifestation of guilt," the *hibakusha's* "stress upon the 'accidents of survival'" ; and it is exactly this element of accident which recurs not only in the Blunden poem, but throughout the memoirs of the First World War.

What I propose to do is to look at three memoirs—those of Robert Graves, Edmund Blunden, and Siegfried Sassoon—and to consider some of the mechanisms of psychological survival which they describe. As artists, these writers faced the problem of lending at least the appearance of coherence to a situation that was, by all accounts, utterly inchoate. They all write, in apparent contradiction to the norm of modernism, about themselves; but only in a curiously abstract way. We will be true to the intention of each work if we see it less as confession or "personality" than as an attempt to generalize from the muddle of the war a description of the peculiar kinds of "heroism" that were effective in the trenches. While description could not provide explanation, it was, at least, a way of at once accepting and deflecting the shame of having lived when so many had died; and such description might allow each writer to rise far enough above the emotions of the war to endeavor to make of those emotions the stuff of art.

I emphasize the psychological rather than the physical aspect of survival, since all three writers agree that the latter was purely a matter of luck. In each book the protagonist, early on, sees graphic representation of exactly how widespread and arbitrary death at the Front is. Blunden, for example, fills the first chapter of his book with reminders that the war is inescapable: ". . . the knowledge that the war had released them [he is referring to the convalescent soldiers he had been in charge of] only for a few moments, that the war would reclaim them, that the war was a jealous war and a long lasting." And that people in its grip are essentially powerless and doomed: "I never saw them [a troop headed from Etaples to the Front] again; they were hurried once more, fast as corks on a mill-stream, without complaint into the bond service of destruction." He provides a chilling instance of the omnipresence of death—and of the fact, as he says, that "experience was nothing but a casual protection." The grenade instructor, having just announced, "I've been down here since 1914, and never had an accident," promptly manages to blow up himself and his students.

One could multiply examples almost indefinitely—the cricket game in *Goodbye to All That* which must be abandoned because of a literal and deadly rain of bullets is an especially striking instance. In contrast to these intrusions of death stand the "lucky" moments when a character who by any kind of logic or reason should be killed, survives. So, for instance, Blunden, about to leave the Front for good, through "ill-luck and stupidity" flashes a signaling lamp at the German lines and, by a "lucky jump," escapes the ensuing hail of machine-gun bullets.

The irony—the word seems unavoidable—which is at the heart of all three books is the persistence, to borrow a phrase from Terence Des Pres, of life in death: human beings manage to play cricket, write poetry, form and maintain friendships, joke, enjoy jam from Selfridges, in the midst of a world that seems absolutely devoted to death. As Blunden puts it, "There was a grace that war never overcast," even though war, like some great beast, was characterized by a "long talon reaching for its victim at its pleasure."

It is of course the pressure of this irony that, psychologically, was one of the greatest obstacles to keeping one's sanity. Graves's admission in *Goodbye to All That* that it took ten years for his blood to recover points to the immensity of the task, and the limited success these memoirists had. The war, like more recent holocausts, was not something to be gotten over. . . .

SASSOON: THE ACCIDENTAL HERO

Siegfried Sassoon's three-volume "memoir" of George Sherston seems to me to be not only the longest but the richest and most complex of the three memoirs, in part at least because it combines the irony and "caricature" of *Goodbye to All That* with elements of pastoral and protective ignorance such as we find in *Undertones of War.*

The texture of the book is apparently so straightforward that it is easy to ignore how carefully arranged it is. For example, Sassoon uses the early pages of the first volume to establish some fundamental paradigms, especially a pattern of what we might call "accidental heroism." Part 2 of the ***Memoirs of a Fox-Hunting Man*** ("The Flower Show Match") is a convenient case in point. The atmosphere of remembrance and rural simplicity is characteristic, as is the gently deflating humor, much of it directed at Sherston himself. What is not so apparent at first reading is the way the narrative shape of the incident parallels many of Sherston's later experiences.

The incident is quite simple: George is involved in the match unexpectedly and by someone else. His initial reaction is disbelief, although he manages a brave front for his Aunt Evelyn; but he seriously doubts his own ability. The match involves Sherston rather little. George spends much of the day watching, not the match but the flower show; and the underlying question of whether he will bat and if so, how well he will do, is present only as a kind of counterpoint. In the end, he does bat; and, almost accidentally, he wins the match: "There was the enormous auctioneer with the ball in his hand. And there I, calmly resolved to look lively and defeat his destructive aim. The ball hit my bat and trickled slowly up the pitch. 'Come on!' I shouted, and Peter came gallantly on. Crump was so taken by surprise that we were safe home before he'd picked up the ball. And that was the end of the Flower Show Match" (***Fox-Hunting***).

The pattern of unwitting involvement, self-doubt, waiting, and abrupt and ironically "heroic" (to everyone but Sherston) activity is repeated almost exactly later in the race for the Colonel's Cup (***Fox-Hunting***, part 6). And it fits rather well many of his experiences in the war, most especially Sherston's part in the Battle of the Somme (***Infantry***). Indeed, it could stand as a kind of outline of the war itself, which was full of orders from above, anxiety and doubt (especially when apparently superior men are killed), long periods of waiting, and sudden and often apparently pointless (to the participants) activity which is quickly (on the Home Front) converted to great deeds and heroic victory.

Even when the entire pattern does not recur, elements of it do. Consider how many figures nearly take over Sherston's life, as Tom Dixon the groom does in the early chapters: Denis Milden later in Sherston's hunting career, Cromlech/Robert Graves and Tyrel/Bertrand Russell during the antiwar crisis, and finally the psychologist Rivers. The power of each of these men over Sherston is based on Sherston's sense of inadequacy and his fear of shame. Sherston, like Graves, feels himself much involved in masquerade; and, even more than Graves, he is morally uncertain about that masquerade. The morning of the flower show match, his great worry is that his pads will not be appropriately white; that is, that he will not look the part (***Fox-Hunting***). And of course at the crucial point, quoted above, he wants to "*look*" lively." Later Sherston again and again will feel himself to be a fraud or imposter. His skills as an actor reach a high point of sorts when, having been seriously wounded, he receives visitors in hospital and carefully tailors his behavior to suit the taste of each (*Infantry*). Running all through his gesture against the war is a persistent note of play-acting; as if Sherston (and Sassoon) can never quite be sure of his own motivation.

Part of that doubt is Sherston's sense of his own lack of knowledge. Waiting to confront the authorities with his statement on the war, Sherston goes home to Butley "resolved to read for dear life—circumstances having made it imperative that I should accumulate as much solid information as I could. But sedulous study only served to open up the limitless prairies of my ignorance" (*Infantry*). Sherston reads, it would appear from this, only under the pressure of circumstance; earlier, he spends most of his time perusing the hunting news and Surtees novels. Sherston feels his ignorance, but not necessarily as a bad thing or an accident. In the present circumstance it chafes a bit, to be sure; but earlier he has made it clear that his parochialism is a matter of choice. For example, he consciously and intentionally ignores lawyer Pennett's advice to go back to Cambridge, even though he admits that "everything [Pennett's] letter said was so true" (*Fox-Hunting*).

Sherston, then, seems able to combine the play-acting which is so important to Graves with something like the protective ignorance of Blunden; but with a crucial element of self-consciousness added to the latter, an element which Blunden (the character) totally lacks. As a result, Sherston's moments of heroism, however real they may be, seem to him to be based on fraud and stupidity. This is one reason he can so easily accept the Medical Board as a way out of his antiwar dilemma; he has throughout the affair been rather doubtful about the whole business. He seems (by his description) to have stumbled into the decision almost by accident of circumstance. A wound, a convalescence, a period in the country, an impulsive letter and lunch with an antiwar editor—all add to the possibility of the ultimate decision, but none seems to have been more than accident or impulse. Finally Sherston makes his decision: "I was conscious of the stream of life going on its way, happy and untroubled, while I had just blurted out something which alienated me from its acceptance of a fine day in the third June of the Great War . . . I saw myself 'attired with sudden brightness, like a man inspired,' and while Markington continued his counsels of prudence my resolve strengthened toward its ultimate obstinacy" (*Infantry*). The language is of great importance: "blurted" and "obstinacy" combined with the self-important literary tag line allow Sassoon to deflate what might otherwise have appeared to the reader to be a moment of heroism; and Sassoon implies that this deflation is not the act of the older man thinking back, but an essential part of Sherston's mind at the time. Linguistically, it is the same as the way in which, at the climax of the flower show match, he deprives young George of any real credit

for his game-winning blow by arranging the syntax so that the ball hits the bat, and not vice versa.

But the language here fits another side of Sherston's character as well. Aside from his moments of rather detached "accidental heroism," Sherston is from time to time seized by fits of irrational or (as Sassoon calls them) "suicidal" activity. Here the motive force is not suggestion but news of a death which strikes Sherston with unusual force—the death of Dick Tiltwood, or of Lance Corporal Kendle during the Somme, or, as a kind of variation on a theme, his own wound: "I began to feel rabidly heroical again, but in a slightly different style, since I was now a wounded hero, with my arm in a superfluous sling . . . I felt that I must make one more onslaught before I turned my back on the War . . . My over-strained nerves had wrought me up to such a pitch of excitement that I was ready for any suicidal exploit" (*Infantry*). Again the language is the key—"rabidly" and "suicidal" are the important words. This is, in a sense, what Sherston has in place of the apparent calculation and logic of Graves; but Sherston at least knows precisely how mad it is, while Graves, explicitly at least, would deny any madness whatever.

In the third volume of the memoir all these characteristics come into play to get Sherston through his last tour in the trenches. His sense of masquerade and fraud underlies his mood as he returns to the Battalion: "In what, for the sake of exposition, I will call my soul (Grand Soul Theatre; performances nightly;) protagonistic performances were keeping the drama alive" (*Progress*). But now the masquerade is not something to feel guilty about, despite the irony of the description; it is a vital part of continuing to live, psychologically: "For my soul had rebelled against the War, and not even Rivers could cure it of that. To feel in some sort of way heroic—that was the only means I could devise for 'carrying on'" (*Progress*).

The previous two volumes make it clear what an immense task it was for Sherston "to feel in some sort of way heroic." He must now intensify his mental limitations into a kind of willed stupidity (he calls it being "as brainless as I could"; *Progress*), and he must learn to play-act without discomfort, to allow "myself to become what they expected me to be" (*Progress*). His sense of irony—which depends on a kind of detachment—must become something greater; he must, as he puts it, get completely outside what is going on, not physically (he has in fact immersed himself intentionally in the war) but psychologically: "Since last year I seem to be getting outside of things a bit better" (*Progress*).

But this detachment founders. Sherston feels a loyalty to the men which at times verges on the Messianic, but which at least provides a purpose for his life and for his presence in the trenches. And his old impulsiveness crops up again: "I was lapsing into my rather feckless 1916 self" (*Progress*). In the end what allows him to survive, really, is luck—the good fortune that makes the shell landing right next to him a dud—and, in the real crisis, his humor. Lying wounded he thinks, "I had been young and exuberant, and now I was just a dying animal, on the verge of oblivion. And then a queer thing happened. My sense of humour stirred in me, and—emerging from that limbo of desolate defeat—I thought, 'I suppose I ought to say something special—last words of a dying soldier'" (*Progress*).

"Emerging from that limbo of desolate defeat"—expanded a bit beyond its immediate context, the phrase can stand rather well as a motto for the survivors. *How* to emerge is the problem; and more, how to emerge *sane*. To Sassoon, it is only possible by means of a complex of devices, such as he recreates in the mind of Sherston.

FORMULATIONS AND MEMOIRS

These three men did survive, physically and (at least to some degree) psychologically; but all of them find it difficult to decide precisely how this came to be. Each writer sees the limitations of the psychological devices he proposes; which points to the greater problem. Granted that they survived at the time; could they survive the remembering?

To put it another way, each of these men had to face the problem of guilt, the sense that their survival was undeserved—the feeling that is the common inheritance of all survivors of twentieth-century holocausts. R. J. Lifton emphasizes the crucial importance of "formulation," the "process by which the [survivor] re-creates himself" as a means of dealing with this guilt:

> Formulation includes efforts to re-establish three essential elements of psychic function: the *sense of connection,* or organic relationship to the people as well as non-human elements in one's life space, whether immediate or distant and imagined; the *sense of symbolic integrity,* of the cohesion and significance of one's life . . . and the *sense of movement,* of development and change, in the continuous struggle between fixed identity and individuation.

These war memoirs represent, I think, a polished and literary form of "formulation," a way of making psychological order out of the experience of the First World War.

But as a literary form, the memoir adds a difficult dimension to this process of formulation. Formulation as Lifton defines it is personal and need have no necessary correspondence to reality. It need not, in other words, be factually correct, because (if for no other reason) few people except its creator will ever hear of it. A memoir, on the other hand, pretends to be a kind of history, however impressionistic; and these memoirists were all aware of their audience. That audience would inevitably test the memoir against its own war experience; these men wrote, quite consciously, to their fellow survivors, and even to those who did not survive. The memoirists could find some protection in an acknowledgment of the distortions of memory, as Blunden does: "I know that memory has her little ways, and by now she has concealed precisely that look, that word, that coincidence of nature without and nature within which I long to remember." And they could indulge, to a degree, in an artistic rearrangement to heighten the consistency of their experience. So Blunden says nothing about his own wounds or gassing, maintaining the picture of the oddly protected "Bunny"; Sassoon, to draw more fully perhaps on the tradition of the dimwitted country gentleman, says nothing of the literary career that was well under way while Sherston was still single-mindedly fox-hunting; and Graves, as Fussell shows, changes the chronology of his own near-fatal wounding for dramatic effect.

But neither the "little ways" of memory nor the usually allowable distortions of fiction would justify straying too far from the nature of the war experience, as these three men had known it and as their fellow-soldiers, like the mysterious Stetson in *The Waste Land,* had also known it. But then, of course, they were brought face to face again with the commonly agreed upon fact that the war was, in almost all important ways, indescribable, even unimaginable. Both segments of their audience—those who had been in the war and those who had not—were potential critics, the one because what was said did not match their own knowledge, the other because the description seemed unreal. The idea that the experience cannot be communicated—"you had to have been there"—is precisely the note that one finds in the accounts of survivors of other holocausts. Here, for example, is Blunden: "I know that the experience to be sketched is very local, limited, incoherent; that it is almost useless, in the sense that no one will read it who is not already aware of all the intimations and discoveries in it, and many more, by reason of having gone the same Journey. No one? Some, I am sure; but not many. *Neither will they understand*—that will not be all my fault" (italics Blunden's). And here is Elie Wiesel, talking about a recent television recreation of the later and always capitalized Holocaust: "The witness feels here duty bound to declare: What you have seen on the screen is not what happened *there.* You may think you know now how the victims lived and died, but you do not. Auschwitz cannot be explained nor can it be visualized . . . The dead are in possession of a secret that we, the living, are neither worthy of nor capable of recovering."

But alongside that sense of the impossibility of the task goes what Terence Des Pres calls "the will to bear witness." Blunden states it as a matter of necessity: "I must go over the ground again." His poem "II Peter ii, 22" amplifies that statement; it is the sense that knowledge of the war is somehow fading away, that people will not remember, that drives him to write.

Although the war in the trenches seems to an outsider neither as catastrophic nor as unimaginable as the death-camps or Hiroshima, in one way at least the psychological problem may have been worse for these memoirists than for later survivors. Instead of being mere victims, these men were volunteers and agents. They enlisted freely and they were officers; and therefore they were inescapably responsible for what happened to themselves and to those around them. Graves, in a typically pseudo-scientific way—Sassoon says "he was always fond of a formula" (*Infantry*)—explains the peculiar difficulties of the officer:

> After a year or fifteen months [in the trenches] he was often worse than useless. Dr. W. H. R. Rivers told me later that the action of one of the ductless glands—I think the thyroid—caused this slow general decline in military usefulness, by failing at a certain point to pump its stimulating chemical into the blood. Without its continued assistance the man went about his tasks in an apathetic and doped condition, cheated into further endurance . . . Officers had a less laborious but a more nervous time than the men.

Of course, as Sassoon realized, even for an officer there was nothing much to be done about the war; and for him, at least, his own agency, his ability to make things a little easier for his men, was a vital part of his ability to carry on. But the burden of that responsibility and guilt was something that Blunden and Sassoon at least seem never quite to have overcome (Graves may have been a bit tougher and therefore more able to go on). In any case the difficulty of psychologically surviving the war and the scars it left on its survivors may be a partial explanation of the fact that the greatest art of that generation was made either by those not involved in the war at all, or by those involved only rather peripherally. The participants could neither escape nor completely accomplish the difficult task of personal, psychological self-preservation.

It is important to remind ourselves that modernist detachment is more than an aesthetic rebellion against the "personality" of Romanticism; it is as well a response to what modernists felt was an increasingly unlivable present: paralyzed Dublin, Mauberly's culturally vapid London, Eliot's yellow fogs and gas works, the monstrous forces of Conversion personified by Woolf's sinister Dr. Bradshaw, Chatterley's sterility—the list is nearly endless. Graves, Blunden, and Sassoon, as memoirists, are modernist in their effort to work out this response under conditions of unusual pain. As works of art their books are unlikely to challenge *Ulysses* or *Mrs. Dalloway,* but they stand, at the very least, at the head of that tragically rich vein of twentieth-century writing which has its roots both in modernism and in atrocity: the literature of survival.

Thomas Mallon (essay date 1983)

SOURCE: "The Great War and Sassoon's Memory," in *Modernism Reconsidered,* edited by Robert Kiely, Harvard University Press, 1983, pp. 81-99.

[*In the following essay, Mallon provides an overview of Sassoon's literary career and examines the lasting impact of his war experiences on his writing.*]

The stage nerves Siegfried Sassoon may have experienced before addressing the Poetry Club at the Harvard Union in

the spring of 1920 were mitigated by the formidable assurances of Miss Amy Lowell, who had recently written to tell him that he "was the one man whom the Harvard undergraduates wanted to hear." Such assurances were more necessary than might be supposed; Sassoon had discovered upon arriving in New York in January that, little more than a year after the Armistice, more than enough British authors were touring America to fill the already slackening desire to hear from and about the soldier-poets. In fact, the war was sufficiently receding in people's minds that Sassoon had to rely on himself, rather than the Pond Lyceum Bureau, to scare up most of his engagements. But at Harvard Sassoon did find a receptive audience for the last of his pleas against militarism, and he finished his tour feeling that his "diminutive attempt to make known to Americans an interpretation of the war as seen by the fighting men" had been "not altogether ineffective."

In some respects the Harvard appearance was the end of a phase in Sassoon's life that began in 1917 with the appearance of *The Old Huntsman* and his public statement against the war, climaxed with the publication of *Counter-Attack* on June 27, 1918, and had its denouement in his post-Armistice lecture tour. In less than four years he went from being a sometime versifier to something of an international literary celebrity, the man who more than any other had brought about the post-Somme poetic rebellion in diction, subject matter, and outlook. Without question these were the most public years of his life, and although he would live for nearly another half century, nothing in his later works would so impress itself on readers' minds and literary history as the angry ironies of **"Base Details," "The General," "To Any Dead Officer,"** and **"Suicide in the Trenches."**

He would continue publishing poetry into the 1960's, including some extremely beautiful and neglected religious verse in the last decades of his life, but after *Counter-Attack* he is best known as a memoirist who twice wrote three volumes about his early years. The "fictional" memoirs, with the non-poet George Sherston as Sassoon's reductive stand-in (*Memoirs of a Fox-Hunting Man,* 1928; *Memoirs of an Infantry Officer,* 1930; *Sherston's Progress,* 1936) were followed by the "real" autobiographies (*The Old Century and Seven More Years,* 1938; *The Weald of Youth,* 1942; and *Siegfried's Journey,* 1945). The Sherston books run from George's childhood until a few months before the Armistice; the autobiographies (as the "real" memoirs will be called hereafter) show Sassoon two years beyond that. The lines marking the refraction and reflection of actual experience are not always clearly drawn in either set. In the Sherston books, for example, the actual Dr. W. H. R. Rivers (who treated Sassoon in Craiglockhart War Hospital, site of conversations between Sassoon and Wilfred Owen) makes more than one appearance, like a "real" character in *Ulysses* or a present-day novel by, say, E. L. Doctorow or Truman Capote. Conversely, Sassoon sometimes admits to a slight bending of material in the autobiographies toward a particular logical or aesthetic effect. Finally, and most important in the case of Sassoon's ordeal on the Western Front, he will occasionally tell the reader of the autobiographies to look to the Sherston memoirs, where the fictional treatment of actual experience is close enough to the way events really happened to make any further discussion in the autobiographies more or less redundant.

In this essay some attention will be drawn to such congruities and discrepancies, but my main purpose is to isolate the—to use a word familiar to soldiers of the Great War—salient features of mind and memory possessed by Sassoon himself, the man who lived between 1886 and 1967, and to determine the extent to which the war did or did not change him.

"Pre-lapsarian" is one of those drearily overused academic adjectives, but is it ever less avoidable than in discussions of the doomed patterns of English country life in the last years before 1914? That those patterns would be extinguished by conflicts originating on the remote continent of Europe was unthinkable to most of the young men who had grown up slowly and securely in English villages. Sassoon's Sherston says that before the war "Europe was nothing but a name to me. I couldn't even bring myself to read about it in the daily paper." Fox hunts and horse races provide the only notable conflicts in Sherston's prewar world: thus the only *agon* he participates in are manufactured and ceremonial ones.

Sassoon's own childhood was spent amidst the considerable comforts assured by an unusual pedigree. Descended from the commercial, but exotic and remotely Oriental, Sassoons and the native Thornycrofts (who included shipbuilders and artists), Siegfried matured in a large Kentish house, was educated mostly by tutors at home, played with by older brothers, cast (once as Mustard Seed) in his mother's *tableaux vivants,* and exposed to such venerable villagers as Miss Horrocks, whom King George IV once kissed. An impractical boy, regarded as delicate, he was often dreamy, and quite unsingleminded about anything. He would later recall the way he was at age eleven: "My undistracted imagination had been decently nourished on poetry, fairy-tales, and fanciful illustrations, and my ideas of how people behaved in real life were mainly derived from *Punch, The Boy's Own Paper,* and F. Anstey's *Voces Populi.*" Sherston is depicted in the same sort of unchallenged and undemanding security as he approaches adolescence. Life seems so calmly and reasonably hospitable as to encourage a natural passivity, even a sort of empirical solipsism: "In this brightly visualized world of simplicities and misapprehensions and mispronounced names everything was accepted without question . . . The quince tree which grew beside the little pond was the only quince tree in the world."

Fox hunting and poetry became the chief imaginative excitements of Sassoon's youth, but if economics gently curbed his pursuit of the first, an admittedly intermittent attraction limited his engagement with the second. Poetry touched in him "a blurred and uncontrolled chord of ecstasy" and became associated with "an undefined heartache." This uncertainty of response (as well as spotty and haphazard reading) caused his own first efforts at composition to be touched by "a fine frenzy of aureate unreality" that he would admit he could still lapse into years later, even after he had achieved the disciplined fury of his antiwar productions. When he at last went away to school, at Marlborough, the verse he entered in a competition came from a "poetic impulse" that he admits had lain "dormant for three years." He collected books as much for the feels and smells of their bindings as the revelations within: "I cannot say that the insides of my antiquated acquisitions made much impression on my mind." The experience of Cambridge remains almost completely unchronicled in the Sherston memoirs and is only hastily recounted in the autobiography. Sassoon says that he left the university convinced of his desire to be a poet, but the enervating split between his comfortable "reynardism" and casual versifying would be part of his life for several more years, until the Great War arrived. In both the early memoirs and the first volumes of autobiography, the announcement that the subject has reached his majority provides the reader with one of the few starts he receives from the tranquilly beautiful narratives. Sherston and Sassoon both seem, at twenty-one, not only far away from adulthood, but even uninterested in it. Sherston recalls: "The word maturity had no meaning for me. I did not anticipate that I should become *different;* I should only become *older.* I cannot pretend that I aspired to growing wiser. I merely *lived,* and in that condition I drifted from day to day." Already more predisposed to remember than anticipate, Sassoon and Sherston impress themselves on the reader as static and ambered; the effect is beautiful in the way that innocence can be, but troubling, too, like a plane that cannot gain altitude.

One experience that imposes narrative movement on the account of any adolescence is sexual exploration. In both the Sherston memoirs and the autobiographies—all three volumes of each, which take both persona and author past the age of thirty—it is almost eerily absent. Allowing for any standard of reticence, literary or social, its want is conspicuous. Sherston and Sassoon are protected from the emotional ravages of love, but their worlds seem deoxygenated, like toys under glass. When women appear they are generally aunts. Men may be models of grace and bearing—like the memoirs' fox-hunter Stephen Colwood, or Mr. Hamilton, the cricketing tutor from Cambridge, or, most important, Denis Milden, Master of the hunt—but their erotic force of attraction is carefully circumscribed. The figure who is Milden in the memoirs and Norman Loder in the autobiographies provides one of the key differences between the two sets of books. The real Loder is considerably endowed with virtues, but of a rather unglamorous kind: "He was kind, decent, and thorough, never aiming at anything beyond plain commonsense and practical ability." Milden, however, even as he behaves with similar strength and simplicity, has a more romantic allure. Sherston meets him when they are both boys: "Already I was weaving Master Milden into my day dreams, and soon he had become my inseparable companion in all my imagined adventures . . . It was the first time that I experienced a feeling of wistfulness for someone I wanted to be with." Years later an invitation from Milden is cause for rapture in Sherston, and the dependable simplicities of the hunt-master's routine are observed with something like awe: "Thought . . . how surprised Stephen [Colwood] would be when I told him all about my visit. Meditated on the difference between Denis hunting the hounds (unapproachable and with 'a face like a boot') and Denis indoors—homely and kind and easy to get on with; would he really want me to come and stay with him again, I wondered." These are the familiar thrills and worries of schoolboy crushes; but Sherston is twenty-five.

If Sassoon gives no indication that romance suddenly galvanized his character, neither does he show London achieving such a result. As an uncertain young poet in the city just before the war, he is encouraged and aided by such professional encouragers as Edmund Gosse and Edward Marsh. But his vocation is not overpowering; he continues to move confusedly between the field and the desk: "I may have wondered why it was so impossible to amalgamate my contrasted worlds of Literature and Sport. Why must I always be adapting my manners—and even my style of speaking—to different sets of people?" His métier was no more defined than his personality. This adaptability, which is after all only a sort of active passivity, is something Sassoon repeatedly admits in himself and ascribes to Sherston. In *The Old Century* he tells us that he has always been "self-adapting to people's estimation of [himself]"; Sherston, in the memoirs, says he has "always been inclined to accept life in the form in which it has imposed itself upon [him]," admitting that "on the whole [he] was psychologically passive," a man whose "terrestrial activities have been either accidental in origin or else part of the 'inevitable sequence of events.'" In his diary from 1922, Sassoon refers to his "mental coma." Of the diary itself he says: "From this jungle of misinterpretations of my ever-changing and never-steadfast selves, some future fool may, perhaps, derive instruction and amusement."

In the summer of 1914, having moved to Gray's Inn at the suggestion of Edward Marsh, Sassoon had a feeling of being "on the verge of some experience which might liberate [him] from [his] blind alley of excessive sport and self-imposed artistic solitude." The war was to make him not only a poet, but one with a mission: all that is certain. But despite Sherston's claim that the war "re-made" him, there is much more evidence that the personality of Sassoon himself (as well as that of his fictional isotope) emerged from the war with most of the protean tentativeness with which it embarked for the Front. His splendid military performance and his brave subsequent protest against the fighting were no more disparate actions that eventually synthesized into a solid character than fox hunting and poetry had been. The evidence of both the memoirs and autobiographies is that far from being remade by the war,

Sassoon had his constitutional capacity to shift and adapt made even more habitual. Wilfred Owen approached him as novice to mentor while they were both in Craiglockhart War Hospital, but in *Siegfried's Journey* Sassoon would admit: "When contrasting the two of us, I find that—highly strung and emotional though he was—his whole personality was far more compact and coherent than mine." The war transformed Owen with almost molecular thoroughness; it seems to have left Sassoon's most fundamental dimensions unpenetrated.

Any clear separation of Sassoon and Sherston will remain forever impossible to achieve. Even when Sassoon attempted it himself, it was with a whimsy that soon became avoidance. In *The Weald of Youth* he decides that to assert Sherston "was 'only me with a lot left out' sounds offhand and uncivil"; after Sherston has made an awkward appearance in the autobiographies, Sassoon must gently dispatch him, apologizing for "a collision between fictionized reality and essayized autobiography." Nevertheless, for purposes of looking at the war, which we now come to, Sherston can indeed be taken as Sassoon with a lot—namely, the poetry—left out: the autobiographies and the memoirs contain essentially the same features of personality that were exposed to killing and inspired to protest.

Both Sassoon and Sherston volunteer for the army with the sort of dutiful inertia that led many of the educated soldier-poets to the Front. Irony and bitterness set in a good deal thereafter. Sherston listens uneasily to the same "Spirit of the Bayonet" lecture that Sassoon did. Echoing Prince Hal's remark about Hotspur and the Scots, Sherston reflects: "Man, it seemed, had been created to jab the life out of Germans. To hear the Major talk, one might have thought that he did it himself every day before breakfast." But a raid can still be as important to the ego as a point-to-point race, and after protesting the war, being hospitalized (instead of court-martialed), and being pronounced fit to return to the Front, he can still have war dreams in which he is "vaguely gratified at 'adding to [his] war experience.'" (Indeed, there is good reason to believe that Sassoon himself conceived the famous lines of **"The Kiss"**—inspired by the bayonet lecture—in a pre-Somme spirit of romance, and only later invited them to be read as satire.) Even after Sherston has learned to be bitter towards the "happy warrior attitudes" imagined back home and recommended by superiors, he can still—a year after the Somme—assume a heroic stance as a kind of prophylactic against danger and death: "I had always found it difficult to believe that these young men had really felt happy with death staring them in the face, and I resented any sentimentalizing of infantry attacks. But here I was, working myself up into a similar mental condition, as though going over the top were a species of religious experience. Was it some suicidal self-deceiving escape from the limitless malevolence of the Front Line?"

It was not so much suicidal as psychologically self-preserving. To act from a sense of purpose, with whatever suspension of disbelief that may involve, is to reduce the possibilities of panic and despair that follow upon a sense of absurdity. So Sherston would "play at being a hero in shining armour" even after he knew better. It was the same with Sassoon himself. On rereading his actual war diary from the end of 1916, he notes in *Siegfried's Journey:* "Some of its entries suggest that I was keeping my courage up by resorting to elevated feelings. My mental behaviour was still unconnected with any self-knowledge, and it was only when I was writing verse that I tried to concentrate and express my somewhat loose ideas."

When Sherston is convalescing from a "blighty" he makes a comic list of the chameleonlike poses he adopts depending on his visitor of the moment: to a hunting friend he is "deprecatory about sufferings endured at the front"; to the sister of a fellow officer he is "jocular, talkative, debonair, and diffidently heroic." When alone except for other patients, he is "mainly disposed toward self-pitying estrangement from everyone except the troops in the Front Line." The reflexes of response here are more psychological than social; they are part of Sherston's (and were of Sassoon's) instinct, in the face of an unusual absence of fixed character, to improvise selves as they are needed.

Although *Siegfried's Journey* gives reasons to form an impression that Sassoon was not quite so dependent on Bertrand Russell and H. W. Massingham as Sherston was on their fictive refractions—"Tyrrell" and "Markington"—the autobiography serves to reinforce many of the features of the memoirs' account of Sassoon's famous written protest against the war in 1917. Both Sherston's and Sassoon's protests are characterized by ambivalence and motives that are at least as personal as political. Just as so many English poets of the 1930's, from Auden to Julian Bell, would have difficulty casting their lot with politics that would, if successfully carried through, do away with the privileged milieux in which they had learned so many humane values, so Sherston, at home on leave, wonders whether his indictment is too inclusive:

> Walking round the garden after tea—Aunt Evelyn drawing [Captain Huxtable's] attention to her delphiniums and he waggishly affirming their inferiority to his own—I wondered whether I had exaggerated the "callous complacency" of those at home. What could elderly people do except try and make the best of their inability to sit in a trench and be bombarded? How could they be blamed for refusing to recognize any ignoble elements in the War except those which they attributed to our enemies?

He concedes that his protest "was an emotional idea based on [his] war experience and stimulated by the acquisition of points of view which [he] accepted uncritically"; he admits that he was as interested in becoming a good golfer in this period as he was in becoming an intellectual.

The real Sassoon, in *Siegfried's Journey,* correspondingly confesses that his protest "developed into a fomentation of confused and inflamed ideas" and that his "disillusionment was combined with determination to employ [his] discon-

tents as a medium for literary expression." The suggestion by the portrait painter Glyn Philpot that the protest is a Byronic gesture helps "to sustain [his] belief that [he is] about to do something spectacular and heroic." He soon realizes that "army life had persistently interfered with my ruminative and quiet-loving mentality. I may even have been aware that most of my satiric verses were to some extent prompted by internal exasperation."

The protest was, like so much else about both Sherston and Sassoon, somewhat impromptu. As its consequences were felt, there were too few certainties of intellect and character on which they could fall back. The protest crumbled; Sassoon accepted a diagnosis of "shell shock" instead of being court-martialed, and after his stay at Craiglockhart he ended up back at the Front—still as inchoate as he was gallant.

The anger Sassoon felt toward the war had an almost boyish sense of right and wrong as its propellant. He endowed Sherston with it, too. Shortly after Dick Tiltwood, another ideal friend—"a young Galahad"—is killed at the Front, Sherston says: "I was angry with the War"—the simplicity of the declaration having an emotional genuineness beyond the usual literary force of the understatement that was employed so often, and with such calculated effect, by First World War poets and memoirists. After observing an unforgivably severe doctor during his convalescence, Sherston says: "I hope that someone gave him a black eye"; in real life Sassoon had an altercation with a photographer who upset the dignity of the grave site of T. E. Lawrence—whose *Seven Pillars of Wisdom,* incidentally, exhibits, like Sassoon's books, heroic behavior proceeding from a personality that remains curiously ad hoc and incipient. Very late in the war, Sherston is at Company H. Q. in a chateau behind the lines at Habarcq. In his diary he locates himself in "this quiet room where I spend my evenings ruminating and trying to tell myself the truth—this room where I become my real self, and feel omnipotent while reading Tolstoy and Walt Whitman." But how can our real selves reside in the fantasies insurgent from our reading? Here again Sherston seems younger than his age. It is a year since his protest, and he records: "'I want to go up to the Line and really do something!' I had boasted thus in a moment of vin rouge elation, catching my mood from those lads who look to me as their leader. How should they know the shallowness of my words? They see me in the daylight of my activities, when I must acquiesce in the evil that is war. But in the darkness where I am alone my soul rebels against what we are doing." He is still "catching" his mood from circumstance instead of imposing his will on it. Surely the horror of his circumstances would make any such imposition heroic, but Sherston's confusion and impotence remain notable.

The memoirs end with Sherston once again in hospital, almost thirty-two and despairingly baffled as to whatever meaning the war may have had for him. Rivers, the mind's physician, appears as a deus ex machina. His smile is a "benediction," and Sherston understands that this is what he has "been waiting for": "He did not tell me that I had done my best to justify his belief in me. He merely made me feel that he took all that for granted, and now we must go on to something better still. And this was the beginning of the new life toward which he had shown me the way." In this biblical language, Sherston delivers his will into Rivers' hands. The final words of the trilogy are these: "It is only from the inmost silences of the heart that we know the world for what it is, and ourselves for what the world has made us." The implication of this line, recognizable from evidence throughout the memoirs and the autobiographies, seems to be that somehow we carry such knowledge in us, but that it remains unspoken to our conscious minds.

The Sherston memoirs, it has already been noted, do not follow Sassoon's fictive self beyond the Armistice, but the autobiographies give evidence that their author reacted to the first circumstances of peacetime with many of the same traits, and much of the same uncertainty, that he displayed in London before the war. Sassoon turned fitfully to reviewing (for the *Daily Herald*) and to Labour Party politics as he made the acquaintance of many of the important writers of the day. *Siegfried's Journey* shows Sassoon in encounters with Hardy, Masefield, Bridges, T. E. Lawrence, Galsworthy, Firbank, Blunt, and Belloc. In most cases he is accompanied or propelled thither by someone like Osbert Sitwell or the indefatigable Ottoline Morrell. His literary celebrity seems as much managed by others as, several years before, his obscurity was by Marsh. He still exhibits the same compelling blankness with which Virginia Woolf endowed Jacob Flanders, destined to move from party to party and house to house and be appreciated for his freshness and potential—but to remain somehow ungraspable, leaving, one suspects, more of an afterglow than an impression. Aware of his still diaphanous personality, Sassoon recalls:

> I am sure that if, for example, my Gosse, Galsworthy, Marsh, and Arnold Bennett selves could have been interchanged, some perplexity would have been present in their acutely observant minds. I resembled the character in a Pirandello play who was told, "Your reality is a mere transitory and fleeting illusion, taking this form today and that tomorrow, according to the conditions, according to your will, your sentiments, which in turn are controlled by an intellect that shows them to you today in one manner and tomorrow . . . who knows how?"

This adaptability would soon serve him well on his American lecture tour; and it would continue to provide temporary bridges between his fox-hunting and poetry-writing worlds. But it also left him with a persistent lack of identity. (Sassoon's diaries from the early twenties show a persisting split between the worlds of the Morrells' Garsington and "Loder-land," with sometimes literature and sometimes sport gaining sway over his ambitions and routine.)

The literary moment was actually receding from Sassoon even as he was attempting to find his place in it. As his wartime subject matter vanished, the poet's boldly col-loquial diction and "knockout" last-line ironies had fewer poems to go into. He was left with his more placid prewar pastoralism and his regular Edwardian metrics. He traveled on a very fast sound wave from being *le dernier cri* to being a respected echo. But the autobiographies show a distinct pride in his place in literary history. Of his prewar encounter with Rupert Brooke, he writes in *The Weald of Youth:* "There is no need to explain that our one brief meeting had a quite unpredictable significance. Nor need I underline the latent irony of the situation." But as the above list of arranged literary pilgrimages shows, Sassoon was really more attuned to the writers of an earlier generation, one soon to be the literary past, than he was to those who would create the great modernist poetry and fiction of the twenties.

His premature eclipse by the literary future complemented Sassoon's constitutional attraction to the past. In *The Weald of Youth* he imagines that "the present is only waiting to become the past and be laid up in lavender for commemorative renewal." During his childhood his Grandmother Thornycroft's senility appeals to his imagination as a kind of magic carpet to the past; when his nurse, Mrs. Mitchell, quits the household, he cannot understand why she doesn't feel the same nostalgia as he does for the past that they shared. Sherston, too, frequently draws attention to his naturally retrospective habits. Inclined "to loiter . . . as long as possible" among the details of the past, he makes fun of himself as a "professional ruminator" and displays an amused awareness of the conventions of memoir writing.

The rovingly retrospective mind that makes the writing of memoirs a generally less intellectual and shape-making task than the practice of autobiography is nevertheless the same mind that gives rise to the "real" books I have been calling autobiographies throughout this essay. Sassoon may refer in *Siegfried's Journey* to his "comparisons between the crude experience and its perspective proportions as they emerge in matured remembering," but even in the autobiographies the past seems more often conjured than interpreted. This would be so in a man who can recall experiencing "the first instance . . . of a detached sense of proportion about [his] doings in relation to life as a whole" at the age of twenty-seven. The autobiographies make frequent use of the present tense ("I see him, chalking the dates of famous battles on the blackboard"), calling the dead and the past to life in the same sort of seance manner Sassoon used in a number of poems about the dead. He romantically describes his way of recollecting in *The Weald of Youth:* "Forgetful of the pen between his fingers, forehead on hand, middle-age looks back across the years, while the clock ticks unheeded on the shelf, and the purring flames of the fire consume the crumbling log." The memoirist Sherston's frequent assertion that the past is apprehended more vividly than it was when it was merely the present would not be contradicted by Sassoon as autobiographer.

The autobiographer's sense that "when you get close up to life, little things are just as important as big ones," and

Sherston's apology that "it is [his] own story that [he is] trying to tell, and as such it must be received; those who expect a universalization of the Great War must look for it elsewhere," display some rare affinities between Sassoon's mind and the modernist sensibility that produced *Ulysses* and *Mrs. Dalloway*—a sensibility that sought, with the logic of paradox, to achieve universality by exploring the particular with more particularity than ever before. But a gentle fastidiousness prevents the reader from seeing almost all of the earthy or unpleasant minutiae of Sassoon's days; indeed, even in the autobiographies the author confesses to enough distortions to make shaky any claim that those books are much more focused into reality than the memoirs: "I prefer to remember my own gladness and good luck, and to forget, whenever I can, those moods and minor events which made me low-spirited and unresponsive. Be at your best, vision enchanting, I cry." One need not recall one's school days with Dotheboys horror, or, to move to the opposite boundary, the detachment of Orwell's "Such, Such Were the Joys," yet all but the most naive reader is likely to be left more quizzical than charmed by the way Sassoon clearly romances schooltime unpleasantness into the picturesque. Nor does Sassoon choose to subject parent-child relations to the realistic but forgiving probings of a Gosse. Conflicts with his mother are only hastily alluded to in the autobiographies; in the Sherston memoirs the deserted and, one suspects, complicated Mrs. Sassoon is woollied and neutered into "Aunt Evelyn." John Lehmann correctly points out the "curious fact that when Sassoon came to write *Memoirs of an Infantry Officer* in 1930 . . . several of the episodes which form the stark subjects of his poems of the time suffer a modification, or rather mollification of effect." In both sets of war recollections the sharp sarcasm of a Graves is avoided in favor of the understatement of an Edmund Blunden, and a periphrasis that is both humorous and self-protecting: "This was a mistake which ought to have put an end to my terrestrial adventures, for no sooner had I popped my silly head out of the sap than I felt a stupendous blow in the back between my shoulders."

Sassoon admits that the "unrevealed processes of memory are mysterious," and he wisely refrains from probing them too strenuously. Throughout the first two volumes of the autobiography he draws attention to the unsystematic nature of his mind, the traits that make it more given to intense apparitions than chains of thought. He says his brain takes in facts one at a time and has trouble relating them to each other, that information best reaches him slowly and visually, that "abstract ideas are uncongenial" to him, and that the study of history made sense to him only in terms of drama or chronology. Chronology is the basic organizing principle of the memoirs and the autobiographies. The continually tentative and experimenting nature of both Sherston's and Sassoon's personalities makes an episodic structure inevitable. The progression of titles in the autobiographies (*The Old Century, The Weald of Youth, Siegfried's Journey*) seems to suggest a steady movement toward personal definition: set beside each other the book spines show first the name of a time, then the

name of a phase, finally the name of the person. But this is misleading, because Sassoon's character really hardens very little; the autobiographer's retrospection must still rely more on the movement of time, rather than on particular traits or any ruling passion, for its narrative trellis. In *The Weald of Youth* Sassoon compares the movement of one of his chapters to the meanderings of the river Teise, and although he remarks elsewhere on his "perspectived" and "matured" rememberings, it is also in that second volume of autobiography that he admits "it seems reasonable to ask how a mind which understood so little of itself at the time can be analysed and explained by its owner thirty years afterwards!"

The episodic recollections of all six volumes are often extremely beautiful. To read of the lonely young Londoner's accidental encounter, at the Regent's Park zoo, with his old, defensive friend Wirgie, or of Sherston sitting in a dugout, "tired and wakeful, and soaked and muddy from [his] patrol, while one candle made unsteady brown shadows in the gloom" is to experience moments of great and quiet power. The opacity of the central figure's personality in each set of recollections is as appealing as it is frustrating. The presentation, like the personality, tantalizes; both excite, entice, and somehow defeat the reader. T. S. Eliot's remark that Henry James "had a mind so fine that no idea could violate it" sounds like a clever dismissal, but it was offered as a kind of awed compliment. One could say the same words, and in something of the same spirit, about all of Sassoon's books of memory.

On his American tour, Sassoon stood and talked with Carl Sandburg on the roof of a large building in Chicago during a sunset. Years later in *Siegfried's Journey* he took exception to Sandburg's definition of poetry as "a series of explanations of life, fading off into horizons too swift for explanations," raising the following Frost-like objections: "I mistrust random improvisings, even when performed by the pioneering genius and bright vocabulary of a Sandburg. 'Explanations of life' should be evolved and stated once and for all, not incontinently ejaculated in blissful immunity from the restrictions of versecraft. For this 'poetry of the immediate present,' invented, of course, by Whitman, is a medium which has deliberately abrogated finality of form." The metrical and logical regularity of Sassoon's poetry is striking to the point of anachronism if it is considered against the production of modernists of the same generation as himself. But his prose recollections certainly exhibit the "deliberately abrogated finality of form" he criticizes above. That they do will impress the reader of all six volumes not simply as a matter of aesthetic decision, but as a case of psychological inevitability as well.

The *Imperator* (a ship once confiscated from the Germans by the allied governments and then allocated to the Cunard Company) brought Sassoon home from New York to Southampton in the summer of 1920. At this point, Sassoon admits, he was remarkably unchanged from the man who, in London at twenty-eight, could be irresolutely "reduced to boarding an omnibus just to see what sort of places it went to." It is unsettling and wondrous that gunfire, celebrity, and the simple accrual of years made so little difference to the uncertain spirit within, but Sassoon shows himself to be by 1920 nearly as baffled and improvisational as he was in 1914 or 1904. There remains something startlingly unformed about the thirty-four-year-old man set before the reader's eyes for one last look. The man in his late fifties who sets him there says that he may, even in these "real" memoirs, be rendering him "stupider than he actually was" in an attempt "at unity of effect," but at the least he assumes his readers are convinced of the great difference between the pliant youth and the matured autobiographer. But was there such a difference? Let us briefly think about the man who wrote and published the autobiographies during his sixth decade.

Sassoon says that the self which stood in a sunny Trafalgar Square one day after his arrival from America "realized that he had come to the end of the journey on which he had set out when he enlisted in the army six years before. And, though he wasn't clearly conscious of it, time has since proved that there was nothing for him to do but begin all over again." But if he did begin again, it was mostly to explore his "impercipient past," first in the Sherston books which were, he admits, in some ways a substitute for the long poem Gosse urged him to write, and then in the actual autobiographies. Certainly nothing to equal the literary impact of *Counter-Attack* was again to come from his pen. He was eventually to become Heytesbury's hermit. In a sense he went home from that Saturday afternoon in Trafalgar Square more to recall life than to live it; his uncertain efforts toward existence were over and a sort of afterlife had begun.

In the final pages of *Siegfried's Journey*, Sassoon speculates:

> Once in his lifetime, perhaps, a man may be the instrument through which something constructive emerges, whether it be genius giving birth to an original idea or the anonymous mortal who makes the most of an opportunity which will never recur. It is for the anonymous ones that I have my special feeling. I like to think of them remembering the one time when they were involved in something unusual or important—when, probably without knowing it at the time, they, as it were, wrote their single masterpiece, never to perform anything comparable again. Then they were fully alive, living above themselves, and discovering powers they hadn't been aware of. For a moment they stood in the transfiguring light of dramatic experience. And nothing ever happened to them afterwards. They were submerged by human uneventfulness. It is only since I got into my late fifties that I have realized these great tracts of insignificance in people's lives. My younger self scornfully rejected the phrase "getting through life" as reprehensible. That I now accept it with an equanimity which amounts almost to affection is my way of indicating the contrast between our states of mind. The idea of oblivion attracts me; I want, after life's fitful fever, to sleep well.

Surely the remarks on "anonymous ones" apply to no one more than himself, however much shielding is given by the third person and the plural; and even the distance between the older and younger selves he contrasts is not as great as he imagines it to be. Sassoon says that the younger one "scornfully rejected the phrase 'getting through life'"; yet the essential passivity of that self is more to be remarked on than anything else. The older autobiographer is just giving final intellectual acceptance to what, for all its fitful rebellions and genuine heroism, was the essential temper and practice of his youth. The later perspective is neither so long, nor the sensibility so different, as the older Sassoon thinks. The narrative lacunae, present-tense reveries, and watercolored judgments found in the autobiographies all spring from the mental and emotional habits of his younger days. Not only is the child father to the man, in this case; the sporadic boy-poet is father to the autobiographer.

Sassoon writes that he is "inclined to compare the living present to a jig-saw puzzle loose in its box. Not until afterwards can we fit the pieces together and make a coherent picture of them. While writing this book I have often been conscious of this process." But that process does not go very far toward coherence. Just when Sassoon wonders if it can be "that the immediacy of our existence amounts to little more than animality, and that our ordered understanding of it is only assembled through afterthought and retrospection," he stops short: "But I am overstraining my limited intelligence and must extricate myself from these abstrusities."

Although both sets of recollections are full of amused self-depreciation, this last line comes not from coyness or false modesty. Sassoon's interpretive intelligence was and remained limited. It could not be otherwise. The dreaming and tentative boy was not meant to become a thinker at thirty-four or even fifty-nine. To say that this is a limitation in his character is to say very little, because it is also the key to that character's unusual beauty. There was something permanently inviolate about it, even in the most exciting and dangerous circumstances. And much of it survived the "old century" well into the miseries of the mid-twentieth. Sassoon remained in large part unreachable to life.

It look a higher power to break the spell. God came to him late, but succeeded in transporting him fully and finally. Religion brought his last volumes of verse new life, and he awaited the next world with far more sustained ambition and interest than he ever really displayed toward this one. But this is another, and better, story.

Elaine Showalter (essay date 1987)

SOURCE: "Rivers and Sassoon: The Inscription of Male Gender Anxieties," in *Behind the Lines: Gender and the Two World Wars,* edited by Margaret Randolph Higonnet, Jane Jenson, Sonya Michel, and Margaret Collins Weitz, Yale University Press, 1987, pp. 61-9.

[In the following essay, Showalter examines the psychological effect of shell shock on male sexual identity and Sassoon's hospitalization under the care of psychiatrist William H. R. Rivers.]

On July 23, 1917, 2d Lt. Siegfried Sassoon arrived at Craiglockhart War Hospital near Edinburgh to be treated for war neurosis by Royal Army Military Corps psychiatrist Capt. William H. R. Rivers. Their three-month-long therapeutic relationship, intensified by the urgency of the war, exerted a powerful influence on each man's life and ideas. The record of this encounter is one of the best sources we have for studying the inscription of male gender anxieties during the war, anxieties that manifested themselves in the body language of neurotic symptoms and in the structures of writing, both memoir and psychiatric text.

"Dottyville," as the hospital was called by Sassoon and his friends Robert Graves and Lt. Wilfred Owen, also a patient, was a former hydropathic hotel for the nervous or alcoholic rich, which boasted extensive facilities for gardening, tennis, swimming, and other games. Yet Sassoon—who had been ordered by a military review board to undergo medical treatment after he published his famous pacifist denunciation of the war, **"A Soldier's Declaration,"** in May 1917—was apprehensive. "After all," he wrote, "a mad-house would be only a few degrees less grim than a prison, and I was still inclined to regard myself in the role of a 'ripe man of martyrdom.'" But he had heard that there was something unusual about Rivers, a professor at Cambridge who had made a distinguished reputation for himself as an anthropologist and clinical psychologist. One of the first in England to support Freud's work, after the war he became a pioneer member of the British Psychoanalytic Society. "Rivers was evidently some kind of great man," Sassoon wrote in his war memoir, **Sherston's Progress.** He looked forward to meeting him, and from the first five minutes of their conversation, he felt reassured: "There was never any doubt about my liking him. He made me feel safe at once and seemed to know all about me."

In order to understand the transactions between Rivers and Sassoon, we must first look at the phenomenon of war neurosis or, to use the term invented by military physicians, shell shock. Although he did not seem to have any unusual physical or behavioral symptoms, the stresses and concerns that motivated Sassoon to publish his open letter of protest against the war could easily be seen as part of the larger syndrome of shell shock to which army doctors and administrators had gradually become accustomed. The Great War was the first large-scale military operation in which mental breakdown played a significant role. This was so, historians have suggested, because of the high degree of impersonality, tension, passivity, and uncertainty trench warfare produced. As Eric Leed explains, "neurosis was a psychic effect not of war in general but of industrialized war in particular . . . the neuroses of war were the direct product of the increasingly alienated relationship of the combatant to the means of destruction." In a study of neurosis in the air corps, Rivers had discovered that the "quantity of neurotic symptoms correlated not with the intensity of battle, the length of an individual's service, or his emotional predisposition, but with the degree of his immobility." Rivers concluded that a man's most rational response to anxiety is some kind of manipulative activity, through which he acquires a sense of himself "as an autonomous actor in a world of instrumentalities." When technological warfare deprived men of their sense of agency, they lost their natural defenses against fear and regressed toward neurosis, magic, or superstition.

The diagnosis of shell shock encompassed a wide range of physical and emotional symptoms, strikingly differentiated by class and rank. In soldiers, symptoms tended overwhelmingly to be physical: paralyses, limps, blindness, deafness, mutism (the most common symptom), contractures of a limb, or vomiting; in officers, symptoms tended toward the emotional: nightmares, insomnia, fatigue, dizziness, disorientation, and anxiety attacks. Sexual impotence was widespread in all ranks, so that the sexual wounds that Sandra Gilbert has noted as a major trope of postwar writing had their source in symbolic disorders of powerlessness.

Shell shock has also developed a unique mythology in the literature of the war. The historian Martin Stone, for example, sees it as the "tragic motif of the death of the Victorian Spirit" and suggests that "the shell-shocked soldier has taken on something of a Romantic guise, like his 19th century counterpart, the tubercular artist." In a psychiatric context, however, shell shock can be seen as the first large-scale epidemic of male hysteria. Doctors had long been aware that hysteria could appear in men, but they were not prepared for the enormous numbers of men who developed hysterical symptoms during the war. By 1916 shell-shock cases accounted for as many as 40 percent of the casualties in the combat zones. By 1918, there were over twenty army hospitals for shell-shock patients in the United Kingdom. And, by the end of the war, eighty thousand cases had passed through army medical facilities. One-seventh of all discharges for disability were for nervous disorders.

This parade of emotionally incapacitated men was in itself a shocking contrast to the heroic visions and masculinist fantasies that had preceded it in the British Victorian imagination. The poetic image of the Great War was one of strong, unreflective masculinity, embodied in the square, solid figure of General Haig, prepared by the poems of Kipling and the male adventure stories of G. R. Henty and Rider Haggard. For officers in particular, the cultural pressures to conform to these British ideals of stoic and plucky masculinity were extreme. As Paul Fussell notes in his glossary of the romantic vocabulary of war literature in which this generation was steeped, "not to complain" is to be "manly." A brochure of *Instructions for the Training of Platoons for Offensive Action* (1917) describes how the platoon commander should gain the confidence of his men.

He must be "well turned out, punctual, and cheery, even in adverse circumstances," look "after his men's comfort before his own and never spare himself," "enforce strict discipline," and be "blood-thirsty and forever thinking how to kill the enemy." Legends circulated of officers who went over the top kicking a football as they charged the enemy trenches. In fact, the rate of war neurosis was four times higher among officers than among enlisted men. Initially, army personnel tried to assimilate the evidence of shell shock into the moral, military, and medical categories they had established before the war. Some tried to excuse it as a physical injury to the central nervous system caused by proximity to an exploding shell. When faced with a hysterical soldier displaying unmanly emotions—such as a private who cried so continuously that he could not handle his rifle—they diagnosed his case as "excessive action of the lachrymal glands" and blamed it on organic causes. Many senior army officers, on the other hand, believed that shell-shock cases were either madmen who should be committed or cowards and malingerers who should be shot.

But gradually most military psychologists and medical personnel came to agree that the real cause of shell shock was the emotional disturbance produced by warfare itself, by chronic conditions of fear, tension, horror, disgust, and grief; and war neurosis was "an escape from an intolerable situation," a compromise negotiated by the psyche between the instinct of self-preservation and the inhibition against deception or flight, which were "rendered impossible by ideals of duty, patriotism, and honor." Placed in intolerable and unprecedented circumstances of fear and stress, deprived of their sense of control, and expected to react with outmoded and unnatural "courage," thousands of men reacted instead with the symptoms of hysteria; soldiers lost their voices and spoke through their bodies. For some, the experience of combat and loss may have brought to the surface powerful and disturbing feelings of love for other men. For most, however, the anguish of shell shock included more general but intense anxieties about masculinity, fears of acting effeminate, even a refusal to continue the bluff of male behavior. If it was the essence of manliness not to complain, then shell shock was the body language of masculine complaint, a disguised male protest, not only against the war, but against the concept of manliness itself. Epidemic female hysteria in late Victorian England had been a form of protest against a patriarchal society that enforced confinement to a narrowly defined femininity; epidemic male hysteria in World War I was a protest against the politicians, generals, and psychiatrists.

"The real source of wonder," wrote Thomas Salmon, was not that neurosis "should play such an important part in military life, but that so many men should find a satisfactory adjustment without its intervention." In *Shell-Shock and Its Lessons* an important book by military doctors G. Elliot Smith and T. H. Pear published toward the end of the war, the authors explained that the long-term repression of feeling that led to shell-shock symptoms in combat was only an exaggeration of male sex-role expectations in civilian life. "The suppression of fear and other strong emotions is not demanded only of men in the trenches," they wrote, "it is constantly expected in ordinary society."

There were two major ways of treating shell shock during the war, both intended to get men back to the trenches as fast as possible. The treatments were differentiated according to rank. Shell-shocked soldiers, on the one hand, were treated with the hostility and contempt that had been accorded hysterical women before the war. Not only in England, but in all European countries, they were subjected to forms of disciplinary treatment, quick cures, shaming, and physical retraining, frequently involving painful electrical shocks to the afflicted parts of their bodies. These were in fact semi-tortures designed to make the hysterical symptom more unpleasant to maintain than the threat of death at the front. Officers, however, were regarded as harder to treat and usually given various kinds of psychotherapy.

Sassoon's therapy raises some interesting specific problems, because he did not think he was suffering from shell shock at all. His assignment to a war hospital rather than a court-martial had been engineered by the desperate efforts of Robert Graves and others to save him from the consequences of his pacifist outburst. Yet there were reasons why Sassoon's late-blooming pacifism could be officially understood and categorized as a form of war neurosis. His letter declaring the war a "deliberately prolonged . . . war of aggression and conquest" seemed like a bizarre aberration from one whose daredevil valor in combat had earned him the nickname Mad Jack and won him the Military Cross. In London, recovering from a war wound in the spring of 1917, he had had hallucinations of corpses on the pavement and fantasies of assassinating General Haig. And some shell-shock experts would have regarded Sassoon as a likely candidate for mental breakdown according to a theory that "strange first names" were symptomatic of latent family degeneracy.

Rivers diagnosed Sassoon's case as a "very strong anti-war complex" and set about curing it through psychoanalytic techniques. In his therapeutic practice, Rivers relied on what he called *autognosis,* or self-understanding, which involved discussion of traumatic experiences; and reeducation, in which the "patient is led to understand how his newly acquired knowledge of himself may be utilized . . . and how to turn energy, morbidly directed, into more healthy channels." In Sassoon's case, this meant Rivers embarked on a delicate and subtle intensification of his fears that pacifism was unmanly and cowardly, a process heightened by Sassoon's strong admiration, respect, and affection for Rivers and by the Craiglockhart regime. In contrast to the passive rest cures favored in this period for hysterical or neurasthenic women of Sassoon's class (such as Virginia Woolf), military doctors felt that intense activity was essential for the restoration of male self-esteem. Sassoon was urged to resume a life of energetic masculine endeavor at Craiglockhart. Unlike the nervous women of the generation, who were forbidden by male psychiatrists to write or work, Sassoon was encouraged to take up a vigorous program of sports, was provided with a room of his own so that he could write undisturbed, and even had a hospital newspaper, *The Hydra,* edited by Wilfred Owen, in which to publish his poems.

In lengthy conversations three times a week, Rivers and Sassoon talked not only about Sassoon's life and war experiences but also about European politics, German military history, and the dangers of a premature peace. This talking cure was intended to make Sassoon feel uneasy about the gaps in his information and to emphasize the contrast between his emotional, and thus feminine, attitude toward the war and Rivers' rational, masculine, Cambridge don's view of it. At the same time, Sassoon found himself in the company of "nurses and nervous wrecks" and men who had "done their bit in France" crying like children. He was anxious to assert his superiority to his fellow officers: "Sometimes I had an uncomfortable notion that none of them respected one another; it was as though there were a tacit understanding that we were all failures, and this made me want to reassure myself that I wasn't the same as the others."

By October, Sassoon was overwhelmed with guilt about his exile from the troops, about betraying the men who had fought with him, and about making a convenient separate peace that served to shorten the war for him. These anxieties were expressed in nightmares about the war, described in such poems of the period as **"Sick Leave":**

> When I'm asleep, dreaming and lulled and warm—
> They come, the homeless ones, the noiseless dead
> . . . .
> Out of the gloom they gather about my bed.
> They whisper to my heart; their thoughts are mine.
> "Why are you here with all your watches ended?
> . . . .
> In bitter safety I awake unfriended;
> And while the dawn begins with slashing rain
> I think of the Battalion in the mud.
> "When are you going out to them again?
> Are they not still your brothers through our blood?"

In November, acceding to Rivers' diagnosis that he had been sick and giving up his antiwar complex, Sassoon was cleared by a medical board, became once more, as he says, an "officer and a gentleman," and went back to the front. Some historians have argued that there was really something neurotic in Sassoon that craved death, loved the war, and derived a drug-like satisfaction from facing danger. But this view seems mistaken to me. Without psychiatric intervention, Sassoon might have stuck to his pacifist principles. Rivers was the agent of a military establishment which had to frame his rebellion as a nervous breakdown and which found it more practical to isolate him in a mental hospital then to let him reach a political and public audience that might have supported his resistance.

Ironically, Rivers was as changed by their discussions as Sassoon was. He began to have antiwar dreams brought on

by what Sassoon had told him. In his posthumous book, *Conflict and Dream* (1922), Rivers explored the psychoanalytic issues of fear, anxiety, and sexual repression which had come out of his work with Sassoon and other patients at Craiglockhart. In a series of brilliant hypotheses, he also began to apply to female hysteria some of the ideas about gender anxiety that he had developed in his study of male hysteria.

Yet the covert intention of Rivers' therapeutic practice had been the reinscription of male gender anxieties in someone who had spoken against the war, and we can see his enormous and lasting success in Sassoon's postwar literary career. As Paul Fussell has pointed out, Sassoon devoted virtually all of his life after the war to an obsessive "revisiting of the war" and his life before the war, "plowing and re-plowing" his experiences in a series of six memoirs. He was one for whom, as Fussell says, "remembering the war became something like a life work." Sassoon described himself as motivated by a "queer craving to revisit the past and give the modern world the slip." He seemed to be continuing the process of autognosis in which he had been trained by Rivers, conducting a kind of self-psychoanalysis the object of which was to justify his life as a man. George Sherston, the autobiographical hero of the war trilogy that comprises **Memoirs of a Fox-Hunting Man, Memoirs of an Infantry Officer,** and **Sherston's Progress,** is a simplified and macho version of what Sassoon called his "outdoor self" not a poet, but rather the manly participant in hunting and combat.

Rivers is installed in the memoirs, in Sassoon's diaries, and in his autobiography **Siegfried's Journey** as a father figure, conscience, or, we might also say, superego. He appears for the first time in **Sherston's Progress.** The first section of the book is named for him, and he is the only character given his real name. As Sassoon declares, "[my] definite approach to mental maturity began with my contact with the mind of Rivers," and in his writings Sassoon continues to use Rivers as the measure of mature masculine wisdom. When, at the end of **Sherston's Progress,** he describes his convalescence from yet another war wound, it is Rivers who comes to see him and to set him straight: "His presence was a refutation of wrongheadedness. I knew then that I had been very lonely while I was at the War; I knew that I had a lot to learn, and that he was the only man who could help me."

The note struck here, of loneliness and dependence, is one of many which hint at the homoerotic element in Sassoon's feeling for Rivers. Fussell suggests that Rivers was the embodiment of the male "dream friend" who had been the companion of Sassoon's boyhood fantasies. Rivers, who was fifty-three when he met Sassoon, was unmarried; he derived his greatest emotional satisfaction from his role as the teacher, mentor, and therapist of troubled young men. His colleague and student Charles Myers was one of many acquaintances who observed that through his psychiatric work in the war Rivers was able to release many of his long-repressed nurturant feelings, and thus "became . . . a far happier man." When Rivers died suddenly in 1922, Sassoon was emotionally devastated. In a poem called **"Revisitation,"** he imagined himself haunted by Rivers' ghost, "selfless and ardent . . . whom I am powerless to repay."

In his diary for March 26, 1921, Sassoon recorded his ambition to write the great English novel about homosexuality, "another *Madame Bovary* dealing with sexual inversion" which would be "free from any propagandistic feeling . . . as natural as life itself." Although he never wrote such a novel, one might argue that the trilogy of war memoirs is Sassoon's disguised epic of homosexual feeling. The romantic homosexual subtext of his memoirs, the chronicle of "a wholly masculine way of life," is one of the indirect forms through which he addresses questions of masculinity, which paradoxically can only *be* indirectly expressed since "to think about masculinity," as Peter Schwenger notes, "is to become less masculine oneself."

However indirectly, the psychiatric discourse of shell shock and the literary discourse of war memoirs opened up a significant discussion of masculinity that had been avoided by previous generations. Feminist interpretations of hysteria in women have helped us decode physical symptoms, psychotherapeutic exchanges, and literary texts as the representations of feminine conflict, conflict over the meaning of femininity within a particular historical context. Yet the meaning and representation of masculinity have been accepted as unproblematic. By applying feminist methods and insights to the symptoms, therapies, and texts of male hysteria, we may begin to understand that issues of gender and sexual difference are as crucial to understanding the history of masculine experience as they have been in shaping the history of women.

Fred D. Crawford (essay date 1988)

SOURCE: "Satire and Protest," in *British Poets of the Great War,* Susquehanna University Press, 1988, pp. 119-38.

[*In the following excerpt, Crawford discusses Sassoon's outspoken antiwar sentiment, realistic evocation of combat conditions, and targets of satire and condemnation in his war poetry.*]

Siegfried Sassoon (1886-1967) was the first soldier poet to achieve public notoriety as an opponent not only of the war, but also of those whose complicity allowed it to continue. His satiric targets included virtually everyone except fighting soldiers of both sides—civilians content to accept the casualties of the war as inevitable, staff officers whose incompetence contributed to the carnage, churchmen who abetted efforts to prolong the war, and profiteers who combined insensibility and greed to become "hard-faced men who did well out of the war." During the war, Sassoon's *The Old Huntsman and Other Poems* (1917), and

"A Soldier's Declaration" (July 1917), and *Counter-Attack and Other Poems* (1918) drew attention to the war's effects.

Nothing in Sassoon's prewar life suggested he would become a public spokesman. Born in Kent, Sassoon was the second of three sons of Alfred Sassoon, who separated from his wife when Sassoon was five, and Theresa Thornycroft, whose family included several distinguished Victorian sculptors. Sassoon's connections were various. Cousins on his father's side intermarried with Rothschilds, and his father's sister Rachel at one point edited two rival London newspapers, the *Observer* and the *Sunday Times* (she owned one, her husband the other). Sassoon attended Clare College, Cambridge, first in law and then in history, but he left without taking a degree. On an income of approximately œ500 per year, he devoted his energies to cricket, fox-hunting, book-collecting (chiefly for the bindings), and poetry. By 1912 Sassoon had published nine volumes of verse, but he did not achieve recognition until 1913, when he published *The Daffodil Murderer,* a parody of Masefield. Both Edmund Gosse and Edward Marsh took an interest in Sassoon's verse, and Marsh convinced Sassoon to move in May 1914 to London, where he met Rupert Brooke and other Georgians.

Sassoon possessed an incredible physical and moral courage that prewar circumstances had not allowed to surface beyond his determination to master fox-hunting. When the war began, however, his response was immediate. By 5 August 1914 the twenty-eight-year-old Sassoon was in uniform as a cavalry trooper. As he recorded in *Memoirs of a Fox-Hunting Man* (1928), he "did not need Hardy's 'Song of the Soldiers' ["Men Who March Away"] to warn me that the Remounts was no place for me," and he transferred to the Royal Welch Fusiliers as an infantry subaltern. Recalling the first weeks of the war, Sassoon commented, "Many of us believed that the Russians would occupy Berlin (and, perhaps, capture the Kaiser) before Christmas. The newspapers informed us that German soldiers crucified Belgian babies. Stories of that kind were taken for granted; to have disbelieved them would have been unpatriotic." He also recalled, "Courage remained a virtue. And that exploitation of courage, if I may be allowed to say a thing so obvious, was the essential tragedy of the War, which, as everyone now agrees, was a crime against humanity."

Sassoon survived the war chiefly through luck. While he was training with the Sussex Yeomanry in January 1915, his horse stumbled over a hidden strand of barbed wire, and Sassoon broke his arm. He did not arrive at the front until November 1915, with his early idealism intact. Little in Sassoon's early poetry distinguished it from Brooke's except for Brooke's superior talent as a poet. Sassoon's **"Absolution"** reveals the extent to which abstractions dominated his verse before Sassoon saw action: "War is our scourge; yet war has made us wise, / And, fighting for our freedom, we are free." **"France"** describes soldiers as "serene" when death is near and argues that "they are fortunate, who fight / For gleaming landscapes swept and shafted / And crowned by cloud pavilions white." When his younger brother Hamo died at Gallipoli in August 1915, Sassoon wrote **"To My Brother,"** an elegy which concludes "But in the gloom I see your laurell'd head / And through your victory I shall win the light."

One early poem, **"The Kiss,"** as Sassoon recalled with chagrin, attempts to satirize "the barbarities of the famous bayonet-fighting lecture. . . . The difficulty is that it doesn't show any sign of satire." The poem, addressing "Brother Lead and Sister Steel," can read as a fire-eating poem because it offers no clue to resolve the ambiguity of the last stanza:

> Sweet Sister, grant your soldier this:
> That in good fury he may feel
> The body where he sets his heel
> Quail from your downward darting kiss.

Still, the poem does reveal Sassoon's early tendency to respond to an outrageous occurrence in verse.

Sassoon's conduct during the war exemplified the highest ideals of courage. He won the Military Cross for bringing back wounded men after a raid, and during the Somme Offensive he singlehandedly occupied a section of German trench. As an officer, his consideration and concern for his men recall the spirit of Read's "My Company." As C. E. Maguire reports, "Ordered to rehearse his men—already much over-rehearsed—for an attack, he led them into a wood and read the *London Marl* to them." Nicknamed "Mad Jack" by his men, Sassoon, like Julian Grenfell, made independent forays into No Man's Land to stalk German snipers. During the Battle of Arras in April 1917, Sassoon received a neck wound and returned to England for convalescence. He had met Ottoline Morrell in 1916, in whose home he spoke with pacifists and conscientious objectors for the first time. With the encouragement of Bertrand Russell, Lady Ottoline, and Middleton Murry, Sassoon wrote **"A Soldier's Declaration"** and mailed it to his commanding officer. Russell had the letter mentioned in the House of Commons. Robert Graves was quick to minimize the consequences of the protest by arranging for a medical board, but Sassoon, whose statement during wartime could have resulted in court martial and even execution for treason, had no reason to expect that he would avoid trial or punishment.

Sassoon's protest differs from today's notions of pacifism. Instead of protesting killing on humanitarian grounds, he opposed the victimization of the fighting soldier:

> I believe that the purposes for which I and my fellow soldiers entered upon this War should have been so clearly stated as to have made it impossible to change them, and that, had this been done, the objects which actuated us would now be attainable by negotiation. I have seen and endured the sufferings of the troops, and I can no longer be a party to prolong these sufferings for ends which I believe to be evil and unjust. I am not protesting against the conduct of the War, but against

the political errors and insincerities for which the fighting men are being sacrificed.

Sassoon did not object to a war that sought and attained specified goals. His major grievance was that only part of the population bore the burden. He ends his declaration by condemning "the callous complacency with which the majority of those at home regard the continuance of agonies which they do not share, and which they have not sufficient imagination to realize." After his medical board, Sassoon became a patient of W. H. R. Rivers at Craiglockhart, where he spent some months convalescing. At Craiglockhart Sassoon met Wilfred Owen, whom he influenced beyond his understanding. Only after the war, according to Sassoon, did he realize the importance of Owen's work. Sassoon could have safely spent the rest of the war at Craiglockhart, but he chose to return to the front.

In **Sherston's Progress** (1936), Sassoon gave as reasons for his return to the front his personal wellbeing, his feeling for his men, and his desire to continue his protest. The effects of the war continued to plague him (he once told Graves of hallucinations of corpses lying on London streets), and he felt that "Army life away from the actual Front is demoralizing." For Sassoon, "The only way to forget about the War was to be on the other side of the Channel," and he felt it was "Better to be in the trenches with those whose experience I had shared and understood than with this medley of civilians who, when one generalized about them intolerantly, seemed either being broken by the War or enriched and made important by it." He justified his return to the front, ironically, in terms of

> exasperation against the people who pitied my "wrong-headedness" and regarded me as "not quite normal." In their opinion it was quite right that I should be safely out of it and "being looked after." How else could I get my own back on them but by returning to the trenches? Killed in action in order to confute the Under-Secretary for War, who had officially stated that I wasn't responsible for my actions. What a truly glorious death for a promising young Pacifist! . . .

Sassoon's return to the front was not immediate. He was stationed in Egypt in February 1918, where he felt almost as uncomfortable among noncombatant officers as he had among civilians. However, his unit transferred to France in May 1918, where he served as a company commander (his second-in-command, a bespectacled subaltern, was Vivian de Sola Pinto). Sassoon resumed his stalking as "Mad Jack." When he returned from a foray into No Man's Land on 13 July 1918, after harassing a German machine-gun nest, his sergeant mistook him for a German and shot him in the head. Sassoon spent the rest of the war convalescing in England.

He had written the poems for **Counter-Attack and Other Poems** during his stay at Craiglockhart and must have viewed at least one effect of the volume with disgust. According to L. Hugh Moore, "Winston Churchill so admired ["**Counter-Attack**"] that he memorized it, seeing it, not as a protest against war, but as a means of increasing the war effort because it showed what the English soldiers endured." Despite later appreciation of Sassoon's pioneering protests, several of his contemporaries dismissed them. Middleton Murry found that the verses of **Counter-Attack** "express nothing, save in so far as a cry expresses pain," and another of Murry's comments anticipates one of Johnston's conclusions by fifty years: "Without the perspective that comes from intellectual remoteness there can be no comprehension, no order and no art." Arnold Bennett had tried to dissuade Sassoon from issuing his declaration of protest. Gosse, respecting Sassoon's sincerity, objected to the verse on similar grounds: "His temper is not altogether to be applauded, for such sentiments must tend to relax the effort of the struggle, yet they can hardly be reproved when conducted with so much honesty and courage." Sassoon's development as a satirist transcended techniques peculiarly Georgian. His rigidly bipolar view of ethical extremes made his poetry effective, although his perception of absolute truths sometimes limited his realism. Sassoon's poems were occasional. When the occasion passed, so did his prominence as a poet.

Before Sassoon's poetry, few civilians could know what the trenches were really like. The soldiers themselves, in their letters and infrequent leaves, kept silent, due partly to a feeling of decency and partly to civilians' incomprehension. In retrospect, Sassoon's satire seems heavy-handed when he dwells on the horrors of the trenches and on the villainy of those responsible, but civilians' prevailing ignorance of modern warfare demanded blunt depiction. The unprecedented carnage and unforeseen suffering were more shocking to Sassoon's audience than any pacifist argument could be. His aim was to force the noncombatant to contemplate the realities of the front. The task required some poetic innovation—Sassoon once commented that he had been the first to use the word *syphilitic* in a poem— but his impact derived chiefly from his new subject matter.

The antichivalric **"A Working Party"** presents a modern "hero" who is commonplace, dull, weary, and unimaginative:

> He was a young man with a meagre wife
> And two small children in a Midland town;
> He showed their photographs to all his mates,
> And they considered him a decent chap
> Who did his work and hadn't much to say,
> And always laughed at other people's jokes
> Because he hadn't any of his own.

Unlike the nondescript of Asquith's "The Volunteer," Sassoon's soldier does not experience an ennobling death: as he fortified his trench with sandbags, "the instant split / His startled life with lead, and all went out." Sassoon's most gruesome depiction occurs in the first stanza of **"Counter-Attack"**:

> The place was rotten with dead; green clumsy legs
> High-booted, sprawled and grovelled along the saps;
> And trunks, face downward, in the sucking mud,

> Wallowed like trodden sand-bags, loosely filled;
> And naked sodden buttocks, mats of hair,
> Bulged, clotted heads slept in the plastering slime.
> And then the rain began,—the jolly old rain!

A war correspondent's bloodlessly abstract report—"The effect of our bombardment was terrific"—inspired **"The Effect,"** which introduces the palpable realities behind the journalist's empty phrase: "When Dick was killed last week he looked like that, / Flapping along the fire-step like a fish, / After the blazing crump had knocked him flat. . . ."

In **"The Rear Guard (Hindenburg Line, April 1917),"** Sassoon describes a lost soldier who angrily kicks a reclining figure for not responding to his request for directions. His flashlight reveals "the lived face / Terribly glaring up, whose eyes yet wore / Agony dying hard ten days before; / And fists of fingers clutched a blackening wound." Sassoon duplicates the surprise and shock of the soldier, who, "with sweat of horror in his hair," emerged from the trench, "Unloading hell behind him step by step." Sassoon also described soldiers' departures from traditional attitudes. In **"Stand-To: Good Friday Morning,"** a sentry ill with fatigue, sick of the rain, offers a prayer that belies civilian expectations of a Happy Warrior: "O Jesus, send me a wound today, / And I'll believe in Your bread and wine, / And get my bloody old sins washed white."

Sassoon was at his best when attacking those who mismanaged the war. **"The General,"** which nearly resulted in the censor's refusal to allow the publication of **Counter-Attack and Other Poems,** satirizes the ineffectiveness of military leadership with masterful economy:

> "Good-morning; good-morning!" the General said
> When we met him last week on our way to the line.
> Now the soldiers he smiled at are most of 'em dead,
> And we're cursing his staff for incompetent swine.
> "He's a cheery old card," grunted Harry to Jack
> As they slogged up to Arras with rifle and pack.
> . . . .
> But he did for them both by his plan of attack.

The poem demonstrates Sassoon's most frequent satiric device, reserving a bitterly ironical twist for the last line. The poem is not pacifistic: Sassoon does not object to the general because he is a military man, but because he does not wage war well enough.

"Base Details" emphasizes the opposition Sassoon frequently exploited between the men doing the fighting and the others (garrison officers wore scarlet tabs to distinguish them from line officers, causing combatants to refer often to the "Red Badge of Funk"):

> If I were fierce, and bald, and short of breath,
> I'd live with scarlet Majors at the Base,
> And speed glum heroes up the line to death.
> You'd see me with my puffy petulant face,
> Guzzling and gulping in the best hotel,
> Reading the Roll of Honour. "Poor young chap."

I'd say—"I used to know his father well;
Yes, we've lost heavily in this last scrap."
And when the war is done and youth stone dead,
I'd toddle safely home and die—in bed.

Whereas **"The General"** is a narrative, **"Base Details"** moves closer to dramatic irony in a monologue, although Sassoon stops short of having an officer condemn himself in his own words.

The opening lines of **"Banishment"** reveal Sassoon's regard for the men of the trenches:

I am banished from the patient men who fight.
They smote my heart to pity, built my pride.
. . . .
Their wrongs were mine; and ever in my sight
They went arrayed in honour.

At the end of the poem, Sassoon justifies his soldier's declaration and his ultimate return to the trenches in terms of his feeling for his men: "Love drove me to rebel. / Love drives me back to grope with them through hell; / And in their tortured eyes I stand forgiven." Sassoon's satire derives force from his conviction that only malice or incompetence could explain others' willingness to allow the fighting to continue.

Had one only the record of Sassoon's verse, one might conclude that the war was fought between soldiers and civilians. As critic Joseph Cohen has observed, Sassoon's "approach was direct and his technique simple: he emphasized and re-emphasized the contrast between the relative comfort and safety of the homefront and the misery and insecurity of the trenches. While the poetic worth of his formula was questionable, its communicative potential was unlimited." Sassoon referred to his "acute antagonism toward anyone whose attitude to the War was what I called 'complacent'—people who just accepted it as inevitable and then proceeded to do well out of it, or who smugly performed the patriotic jobs which enabled them to congratulate themselves on being part of the National Effort."

His contempt for civilians who desired to win the war at all costs appears frequently. In **"Ancient History,"** he has "Adam, a brown old vulture in the rain" recall Cain affectionately and Abel contemptuously: "'Afraid to fight; was murder more disgrace? . . . / *God always hated Cain*' . . . He bowed his head—/ The gaunt wild man whose lovely sons were dead." In **"How to Die"** her ridicules civilian misapprehensions of reality. In the first half of the poem, he presents an idealized version of a soldier's death, complete with "skies / Where holy brightness breaks in flame." Then comes a realistic picture of soldiers who die "with sobs and curses, / And sullen faces white as chalk." Sassoon's ironical conclusion, reserved for the end, is that soldiers die "not with haste / And shuddering groans; but passing through it / With due regard for decent taste." Unlike the early **"The Kiss,"** this poem's consistency enables one to recognize the irony.

"The Hero" makes it almost impossible for a reader to miss the point. Sassoon called the plot of the narrative "Brother officer giving white-haired mother fictitious account of her cold-footed son's death at the front." In the second stanza, the officer reveals that he has lied, and in the third he expresses his contempt for Jack, "cold-footed, useless swine" who panicked in the trenches, tried to effect his transfer home, and died ingloriously, "Blown to small bits" by a shell. The poem inspires conflicting sympathies. One can pity the officer who puts the coward's death in a good light for the mother, one can pity "that lonely woman with white hair," and one can even pity Jack, for the last lines reveal him as a victim for whom no one cares except his mother. The poem almost meets the objection that Sassoon's poetry does not communicate the truth of his conflicting loyalties. Although Sassoon was aware of civilians' ignorance, he invites sympathy with an officer who deliberately ennobles the slain.

"Suicide in the Trenches" is Sassoon's most blatant lapse into overt propaganda. In the first stanza, a soldier maintains an "empty joy" that does not interfere with his peace of mind. In the second, "cowed and glum," after experiencing winter in the trenches, "He put a bullet through his brain." Had Sassoon left the stark biography to speak for itself, the poem might have been more effective, but, after a typographical separation that suggests the impossibility of transition, Sassoon shifts from simple narrative to pointed accusation:

You smug-faced crowds with kindling eye
Who cheer when soldier lads march by,
Sneak home and pray you'll never know
The hell where youth and laughter go.

Sassoon could not resist the opportunity of an easy target.

Sassoon is more sophisticated in **"To Any Dead Officer,"** which presents one side of a telephone conversation between a living officer and his dead comrade. The monologue moves quickly through a description of the officer who had "hated tours of trenches" and desired to live, but who fell, machine-gunned, "in a hopeless dud-attack" and appeared in "the bloody Roll of Honour." After a typographical separation, Sassoon indicates his specific target:

Good-bye, old lad! Remember me to God,
And tell Him that our politicians swear
They won't give in till Prussian Rule's been trod
Under the Heel of England . . . Are you there? . . .
Yes . . . and the War won't end for at least two years;
But we've got stacks of men . . . I'm blind with tears,
Staring into the dark, Cheerio!
I wish they'd killed you in a decent show.

Sassoon's expression of his hatred for excessive patriotism approaches the rabid. In **"Blighters,"** Sassoon attacks the frenzied jingoism of the music hall, using an experience from a convalescent leave that recalls E. A. Mackintosh's "Recruiting." Civilians heartily approve "prancing ranks /

Of harlots" as they sing "We're sure the Kaiser loves our dear old Tanks!" Sassoon imagines a tank coming down the aisle to clear the stage of the performers, to end jokes that "mock the riddled corpses round Bapaume." Similarly, **"Fight to a Finish"** presents soldiers taking revenge on civilians after the war. At a celebration designed to "cheer the soldiers who'd refrained from dying," the "Grim Fusiliers" fix bayonets, charge the civilians, deal "Yellow-Pressmen" their just deserts, and go "To clear those Junkers out of Parliament." The poem neither introduces nor attempts to change any idea but is merely a moment of wishful thinking. **"They"** is also weak, primarily because the target presents no real challenge. The role of the clergy in encouraging the war made a bishop too obvious a target even for civilians, while at the front many churchmen were beneath contempt for the hypocrisy of exhorting others to fight while remaining outside the fighting areas themselves. In **"They,"** a bishop says that returning soldiers "will not be the same; for they'll have fought / In a just cause," will have opposed Anti-Christ, and will have "challenged Death and dared him face to face." To this the soldiers respond "We're none of us the same!", since one has lost his legs and another his sight, a third has received a bullet through the lungs, and a fourth has contracted syphilis. Like the poems of soldiers' revenge on civilians, **"They"** communicates little except the poet's resentment.

Sassoon's poems of brutal reality and vindictive satire, particularly when compared with Owen's verse, have obscured his attempts to convey a sense of pity for the soldier/victim, most of which did, to be sure, appear in combination with satiric thrusts aimed at the insensitive civilian. Sassoon's disgust for the acquiescent obscured his other feelings. He had personal experience of civilians' indifference. According to Robert Wohl, Lady Brassey told Sassoon that "he had nothing to lose in going back to France as he was not the bearer of a great name." Sassoon frequently attacked such attitudes. One of his more successful satires is **"Lamentations,"** which uses a *persona* instead of an authorial intrusion to make its point. The poem reveals the insensitivity of one soldier who sees a second soldier shaken by inconsolable grief at the death of his brother:

> I found him in the guard-room at the Base.
> From the blind darkness I had heard his crying
> And blundered in. With puzzled, patient face
> A sergeant watched him; it was no good trying
> To stop it; for he howled and beat his chest.
> And, all because his brother had gone west,
> Raved at the bleeding war; his rampant grief
> Moaned, shouted, sobbed, and choked, while he was kneeling
> Half-naked on the floor. In my belief
> Such men have lost all patriotic feeling.

Two locutions, "it was no good trying / To stop it" and "all because his brother" has died, establish the narrator's lack of feeling and prepare the reader for the final irony of the poem.

Sassoon uses a similar technique in **"Survivors,"** employing a speaker who discusses shell shock victims with little understanding of their plight. The speaker feels that the soldiers will soon recover, that "they'll be proud / Of glorious war that shatter'd all their pride," but Sassoon assures the reader's sympathy for the patients: they are "boys with old, scared faces, learning to walk," they suffer from "dreams that drip with murder," and they are "Children, with eyes that hate you, broken and mad." The memorable phrases of the poem focus on the suffering of the patients.

Sassoon's response to insensitive civilians was either to lash the target directly or to dramatize an unsympathetic situation. In **"Glory of Women"** Sassoon attacks women who allow their patriotic chauvinism to prevail over pity:

> You love us when we're heroes, home on leave,
> Or wounded in a mentionable place.
> You worship decorations; you believe
> That chivalry redeems the war's disgrace.
> You make us shells. You listen with delight,
> By tales of dirt and danger fondly thrilled.
> You crown our distant ardours while we fight,
> And mourn our laurelled memories when we're killed,
> You can't believe that British troops "retire"
> When hell's last horror breaks them, and they run,
> Trampling the terrible corpses—blind with blood.
>   O German mother dreaming by the fire,
>   While you are knitting socks to send your son
>   His face is trodden deeper in the mud.

Sassoon's anger seems hardly fair since he is condemning attitudes he himself had held before he went to the trenches. However, he explicitly decries support of the war effort by the ignorant who "delight" in "tales of dirt and danger."

More effective as a criticism of insensitivity is **"Does It Matter?"**, which dramatizes the plight of a soldier crippled by the war. The second stanza is particularly fine:

> Does it matter?—losing your sight? . . .
> There's such splendid work for the blind;
> And people will always be kind,
> As you sit on the terrace remembering
> And turning your face to the light.

The effect of combining the clichés of consolation with vivid description is to make the victim pathetic, partly because he is subjected to the "sympathy" of the indifferent. In **"The One-Legged Man,"** whose "Thank God they had to amputate!" deflates civilian expectations of a soldier's unflagging fighting spirit, the poem's effect results from the reader's recognition that, if one prefers amputation to the front, war must indeed be horrible. In **"Does It Matter?"** the reader cannot help feeling that the victim would be better dead than an object of insincere pity.

In **"Dreamers"** and **"Attack,"** Sassoon communicates his pity for soldier/victims. In the sonnet **"Dreamers,"** the octave discusses soldiers in abstract generalizations and, standing alone, would not have been out of place in a

Victorian anthology of romantic war poetry. The sestet, however, offers an officer's concrete observations, conveying his pity for his men:

> I see them in foul dug-outs, gnawed by rats,
>   And in the ruined trenches, lashed with rain,
> Dreaming of things they did with balls and bats,
>   And mocked by hopeless longing to regain
> Bank-holidays, and picture shows, and spats,
>   And going to the office in the train.

By limiting himself to straightforward "reporting," Sassoon conveys more feeling than when his focus shifts to his audience. **"Attack"** describes dawn as the men attack:

> Lines of grey, muttering faces, masked with fear,
> They leave their trenches, going over the top,
> While time ticks blank and busy on their wrists,
> And hope, with furtive eyes and grappling fists,
> Flounders in mud. O Jesus, make it stop!

The technique of expressing pity through the eyes of an officer/narrator worked well in other poems. In **"The Dug-Out,"** written in July 1918, the speaker addresses a soldier sleeping in the trench. Usually poets described the dead as sleeping, but Sassoon inverts this: "You are too young to fall asleep for ever; / And when you sleep you remind me of the dead." **"In the Pink"** describes the thoughts of an officer whose duties include censoring the letters written by his men. He reads between the lines of a soldier's letter to his sweetheart which ends "This leaves me in the pink." In contrast to the soldier's assurances, the officer understands what the soldier is actually thinking: "to-morrow night we trudge / Up to the trenches, and my boots are rotten." The officer summarizes the soldier's situation: "To-night he's in the pink; but soon he'll die. / And still the war goes on—*he* don't know why."

Sassoon's remarkable **"Repression of War Experience"** (which takes its title from a paper read by W. H. R. Rivers to the Royal Society of Medicine on 4 December 1917) delineates the thought processes of a shell shock victim who cannot keep his mind from the war. The soldier's thoughts return to war when other subjects cannot hold his attention:

> Now light the candles; one; two; there's a month;
> What silly beggars they are to blunder in
> And scorch their wings with glory, liquid flame—
> No, no, not that,—it's bad to think of war. . . .

When the soldier lights his pipe, he notes that his hand is steady. When he examines a shelf of books, he sees them "dressed" in the colors of uniforms, a "jolly company" waiting in formation, "quiet and patient." After a typographical separation, Sassoon has the soldier consider his situation:

> You're quiet and peaceful, summering safe at home;
> You'd never think there was a bloody war on! . . .
> O yes, you would . . . why, you can hear the guns.
> Hark! Thud, thud, thud,—quite soft . . . they never

cease—
> Those whispering guns—O Christ, I want to go out
> And screech at them to stop—I'm going crazy;
> I'm going stark, staring mad because of the guns.

This dramatic presentation of the shell shock victim's suffering is among Sassoon's more successful efforts.

Sassoon's achievement as a war poet does not depend on his poetic techniques, which are essentially Georgian, but on the insights that he forced upon the modern consciousness. Chiefly through his poetic protests the public became aware of the brutal reality of trench warfare, the disproportionate burden of suffering borne by the fighting soldier, and the growing disparity between soldiers and civilians. His satires of indifferent civilians, jingoistic patriots, and military incompetents communicated a sense of reality not accessible through the newspapers. His success has obscured his attempt to convey his sense of the pity of war. Sassoon was able to respond to the new world that the war introduced, but, when the Armistice ended the war, it also ended Sassoon's effectiveness as a poet.

During the war Sassoon was not alone in his poetical expressions of dissatisfaction. Several other poets directed satire against civilian and political targets, and some went beyond Sassoon's protest against the conduct of the war. Sassoon was the first, at great risk, to accuse openly those whose complicity was responsible for the prolongation of the war and to reach a large audience with his protests. However, others later attacked the same targets in their verse, and some writers articulated protests comparable to those of the late 1960s and early 1970s.

Sanford Sternlicht (essay date 1993)

SOURCE: "'Golgotha': World War I Poems," in *Siegfried Sassoon*, Twayne, 1993, pp. 30-61.

[*In the following excerpt, Sternlicht examines the dominant themes, subjects, and style of Sassoon's verse in* Counter-Attack, *which Sternlicht identifies as Sassoon's "most memorable and powerful collection of poetry."*]

From a literary critic's viewpoint, one of the outstanding aspects of World War I is the amount of excellent poetry it inspired. What is perhaps the greatest body of war poetry ever written was produced by British poets from 1914 to 1918. Indeed those few bloody years spawned two "generations" of war poets: the first caught up in the awful and blind patriotism of the hour, among them Rupert Brooke, Julian Grenfell, Robert Nichols, Charles Sorley, and the pre-Somme Sassoon, and the second "composed of" antiwar satirists and soldier-poets of pity and disillusionment, among them Sassoon, Wilfred Owen, Isaac Rosenberg, Robert Graves, and Edmund Blunden.

Bernard Bergonzi, in *Heroes' Twilight: A Study of the Literature of the Great War,* notes that the prewar Sassoon "typified an *echt*-Georgian state of mind. Whatever radical-ism he manifested during the war was forced upon him by events." Self-trained by years of writing poetry, Sassoon had developed a good ear and eye for detail. Most of all he knew that

> the writing of poetry was a serious matter to be undertaken carefully, deliberately. It was not to be achieved, as it was with so many of the amateurs, merely by allowing powerful emotions to overflow spontaneously on to a piece of paper in whatever ragged form happened to come most readily to hand. Even in the midst of trench warfare Sassoon labored over his poems, corrected, inserted, emended, to bring them to as near perfection as he was able; he constantly made notes of the scenes he saw and the emotions he experienced so that the poems he would write from them later might have the ring of authenticity; he care-fully stored to overflowing both his memory and his notebooks.

Additionally, Sassoon had absorbed an important lesson in language. From Masefield he had learned to listen care-fully to conversation and to write in everyday language. What his eyes saw and his ears heard, his brain absorbed and his hand wrote. As Bernard Bergonzi explains, "Sas-soon was forced by the need for exactness in registering front-line experience into a degree of colloquial language and a conversational tone that was still a novelty in contemporary verse." The language of modern war thus entered English poetry.

Of course, those who looked back to Victorian poetry for models and standards, and the early modernists like Years, Pound, and Eliot, did not consider verisimilar dialogue to be the workings of "real" poetry. John Middleton Murry, the young advocate of modernism, in reviewing Sassoon's best-selling ***Counter-Attack*** in the 13 July 1918 issue of the *Nation,* decided that Sassoon's work was "not poetry." Sassoon was merely in torment and crying aloud, and by inference "his cry is incoherent." Sassoon's existence, presumably as a fire-eating antiwar activist, is important, "not the poetry." For the objectivist Murry "True art . . . is the evidence of a man's triumph over his experience." Sassoon's language, on the other hand, is "overwrought, dense and turgid." Most damning is the comment that "the unforgettable horror of an inhuman experience can only be rightly rendered by rendering also its relation to the harmony and calm which it shatters. . . . The quality of an experience can only be given by reference to the ideal condition of the human consciousness." In other words Sassoon lacked the philosophy and architectonics against which to measure his experiences and comprehend them. He needed distance and objectivity. Righteous anger is simply too emotional for poetry. How little a noncombatant like Murry understood the nature of conflict and what was happening to those involved. How easy it was to dismiss, superciliously, a "popular" poet, one whose "popularity . . . may end by wrecking the real poetic gift which at rare intervals peeps out." Jealousy, of course, motivated the disdain for and attempted dismissal of the hero-poet. Committed to imagism, symbolism, and black verse, Murry could not appreciate satire, let alone sardonic existential

angst reflecting a desperate search for meaning and convention in the absurdities of war. Sassoon, like other soldier-poets who survived, especially Graves and Blunden, would ever remain outside the canon of modern-ism.

TECHNIQUE

It is obvious that the horror of trench combat, from the Battle of the Somme in 1916 on, matured Sassoon as man and artist, but it must also be recognized that the roots of his craft are Georgian, at least that part of the Georgian tradition which "culminated in the directness, brutality, and honesty of his best war verse." Clearly Sassoon's poetry contains no great technical innovations. Vivian de S. Pinto notes that Sassoon "used the smoothed rhyme de-casyllabics of the Georgians in nearly all the poems and he seem to have learnt from Brooke's realistic poems the trick of producing a humorous effect by the contrast between a stately traditional metre and subject matter very unlike the dignified themes with which such metres are as-sociated." That is the point. The familiarity and control of the Georgian are juxtaposed with the horrors and terrors, the hypocrisy and mendacity, depicted by Sassoon. Without the form the public would have looked at Sassoon's ac-counts as the ravings of a shell-shocked victim. The juxta-positional binaries are the truth about the war and the unruffled life lived at home in Britain. Jon Silkin points out that "Another version of this technique is to juxtapose the language, or even the word, of common speech with the word of a previous, romanticized poetic diction, expos-ing thereby how much this diction and its underlying at-titudes conflicted with the facts of mundane existence in general, but the war in particular."

Whether employing juxtapositional metrics or diction, Sas-soon exploits the variance and discordance between the apathy of the civilian population—his primary audience—and the sufferings of the soldiers. The sharp contrast of black and white served his palette well: the safe life at home and that of the short-lived species, the combat infantryman. Sassoon's motto could have been "Shove it in their faces!" . . .

COUNTER-ATTACK AND OTHER POEMS

Between the publication of ***The Old Huntsman*** and ***Counter-Attack,*** Sassoon's most memorable and powerful collection of poetry, the poet underwent the ordeal of his singular revolt against the continuation of the war. He had become a hero of war and then a hero of peace. This role fit into an existing tradition, for "The poet or artist as hero is obviously a central notion of Romanticism" ([John] Onions). In the West authority is often earned by action. Sometimes, as in the case of Vaclav Havel, for example, it is granted for moral and courageous artistry. In "A Defence of Poetry" Shelley asserts the supreme value of poets, claiming, immortally, that "Poets are the unacknowledged legislators of the world." Sassoon, the poet-warrior, self-seconded as poet-legislator against the war, was under treatment, allegedly for shell shock, in Craiglockhart

Hospital when he wrote most of the poems in *Counter-Attack.* While there he read one of the most significant books written during and about World War I, Henri Barbusse's *Le Feu,* which appeared in 1916 and was translated into English in 1917 by Fitzwater Wray as *Under Fire.* Barbusse, a wounded, hospitalized French combat soldier and Marxist, wrote a starkly realistic novel about how the war and militaristic nations victimized soldiers. For Barbusse, war is the ultimate exploitation of humankind, and its greatest effect is depravity. Sassoon read *Le Feu* in French and then lent his copy to Wilfred Owen. It set both men on fire. They saw how battle impression and reportage could be turned to art. Thus *Le Feu* is a work of great importance to English war poetry. Sassoon recognized his debt to Barbusse by including a long quotation from *Le Feu* as an epigraph to *Counter-Attack.*

In *Counter-Attack,* dedicated to Robert Ross and devoid of Georgian pastorals, Sassoon brings his targets into sharper focus and sustains consistency by continued use of metronomic meters and familiar forms. Directness is paramount. In Sassoon's most significant collection abstraction and allegory are nearly totally banished. *Counter-Attack* rails against the institutions of the establishment: the church, the state, the army, and the general staff. Sassoon's old chief target, the civilian population, is still in his sights. The assault on the military leadership, an extramural government in itself, brought the censor's wrath and nearly caused a refusal of publication. The poems of *Counter-Attack* deeply disturbed the public. The experiences that inspired the collection haunted Sassoon all his life and have haunted readers of poetry ever since.

The opening lines of *Counter-Attack,* in the poem **"Prelude: The Troops,"** reveal a stricken world whose inhabitants have been overwhelmed by some unspeakable disaster"([John H.] Johnston):

> Dim, gradual thinning of the shapeless gloom
> Shudders to drizzling daybreak that reveals
> Disconsolate men who stamp their sodden boots
> And turn dulled, sunken faces to the sky
> Haggard and hopeless.

The troops are survivors of the Deluge; they are men of "The Waste Land." Their lives are a gross nightmare as they "Cling to life with stubborn hands." In the end they are "The unreturning army that was youth." This single, deft phrase strikes the chord of pity architectonic to the collection.

The title poem, **"Counter-Attack,"** is a narrative depicting the chaotic effect of a German counterattack on a section of their own former front line captured by the British "hours before / While dawn broke like a face with blinking eyes." The most gruesome description in the entire Sassoon canon follows the opening report of the seizure of the trench:

> The place was rotten with dead; green clumsy legs
> High booted, sprawled and grovelled along the saps;
> And trunks, face downward, in the sucking mud,
> Wallowed like trodden sand-bags loosely filled;
> And naked sodden buttocks, mats of hair,
> Bulged, clotted heads slept in the plastering slime.
> And then the rain began,—the jolly old rain!

Even rain! The last obscenity and indignity. The anointing of misery. The ensuing counterattack becomes a shambles, and the reader is drawn from a generalized narration into experiencing the poem as an infantryman fighting for his life, which, after a wound and flopping around the trench, he loses from loss of blood. In a mere 39 lines the entire skirmish is presented, like cinema, in unfolding literal images. **"Counter-Attack"** is the storyboard of battle.

In **"The Rear-Guard (Hindenberg Line, April 1917)"** an exhausted British officer is looking for battalion headquarters in a captured tunnel, when, in the dark and wreckage, he stumbles across a soldier seemingly asleep: "Get up and guide me through this stinking place." There is no response. "Savage, he kicked a soft, unanswering heap." The light from his flashlight reveals a 10-day-old corpse still showing the agony of death on its face, and the persona, "with sweat of horror in his hair," staggers out of the hellish tunnel into the twilight. **"The Rear-Guard"** shows Sassoon getting control over his material, just as a soldier must have control over his or her situation. Graphic depiction is a method of controlling that situation and one's own self. Significantly the nationality of the dead soldier is not stated. The officer has spoken English to the corpse, thinking the dead soldier was asleep, but the corpse was part of the sacrificed "rear-guard" and thus a German. Death is an equal opportunity employer. It provides inimical soldiers with an instant initiation into comradeship.

"Wirers" depicts the laying of barbed wire in no-man's-land, an extremely dangerous job, often done at high cost of brave lives. Sassoon, however, does not dwell on individual bravery; he takes it for granted. Cowardice is the exception. In **"Wirers"**

> Young Hughes was badly hit; I heard him carried away,
> Moaning at every lurch; no doubt he'll die to-day.
> But *we* can say the front-line wire's been safely mended.

The important effect, of course, is the irony, not Hughes's courage in no-man's-land. As an antiwar propagandist, Sassoon cannot allow the war any moral significance, even a soldier's personal response to "the imperatives of duty" (Johnston). The experience of war is totally without value, except perhaps for whatever art it engenders. Death in war is routine and matter-of-fact, paradoxically, as life is in peace.

"Attack" again didactically insists on the facts and details of war, just as Sassoon's model, Hardy, had "pessimistically" insisted on a realistic portrayal of life. Here the British assault, the soldiers, grenades, guns, tanks, and even the newfangled wristwatch—"time ticks blank and busy on their wrists"—are presented in detail, until the personification and the prayer of the last two lines, in which "hope, with furtive eyes and grasping fists, / Flounders in mud. O Jesus, make it stop!" The persona, in extremis, cries out, but Jesus does not interfere, perhaps does not care.

"Dreamers," a sonnet, contrasts the reality of life in the trenches, presented in the octave, with the dreams of the soldiers, presented in the sestet. The soldiers dream of "Bank-holidays, and picture shows, and spats, / And going to the office in the train." All they want is the ordinary life from which they were wrenched by the war. **"Dreamers"** contains one of Sassoon's most famous lines, "Soldiers are citizens of death's grey land."

"How to Die?"'s ironic message results from the bitter irony of the poem's two stanzas. The first depicts a soldier's death as it might be presented in a sentimental painting or a poem written by a civilian. He dies radiant and happy, "on his lips a whispered name." In the second stanza the persona mockingly complains that some civilians think soldiers "go West with sobs and curses," when in fact "they've been taught the way to do it," presumably vicariously by staff officers, "like Christian soldiers . . . passing through it / With due regard for decent taste." The poem's last sentence illustrates a technique for a slam closing by incorporating a cliché about dying—"passing through it"—as an indictment of the civilian audience. It thinks in untrue clichés. In mocking the banal conception of death in battle, Sassoon willfully lays a heavy burden of guilt on those who support the war but do not participate in it.

"The Effect" begins with a headnote in which a war correspondent lauds the effect of a British bombardment laid on German troops. "The effect of our bombardment was terrific. One man told me that he had never seen so many dead before." The Germans are dealt with by the press as statistics, but Sassoon insists that humans are humans. He establishes this by shifting from the collective "dead" to the palpable reality behind the headlines and the ignorant journalism, namely that "Dick" was killed last week, "Flapping along the fire-step like a fish." The bitter poem ends with a fishmonger's cry: *Who'll buy my nice fish corpses, two for a penny?* How cheap can death get?

Poems like **"Twelve Months After"** indicate the great loyalty that existed between combat officers and their men in the British army on the western front. Battalion officers were father figures and older brothers to rankers in their outfits, many of whom were considerably older than the platoon and company officers who commanded them. In **"Twelve Months After"** the officer-persona sees or dreams of his old platoon. They muster for him. Then the poem is broken by a line of asterisks, and time or the dream has passed. A marching song is heard: "Old soldiers never die; they simply fide a-why!" The persona tells us that the song is what they used to sing on the road in France "Before the last push began." In typical Sassoon fashion

the last, unexpected line—"That's where they are today, knocked over to a man"—knocks over the reader. Sassoon really was cruelest of all to ordinary civilian readers—mothers, fathers, sisters, wives of soldiers—trying to warn and educate them. Whenever he could, he dumped the bloody corpses on their doorsteps.

"The Fathers," snug in their club, "Gross, goggle-eyed," and wheezing, live their lives through the "adventures" of their soldier-sons, as if the young men were playing sports. They are blissfully unaware of the reality of their sons' precarious lives. The poem is like a satiric cartoon in *Punch.* The persona, like the reader, "watches them toddle through the door—/ These impotent old friends of mine." Sassoon's many middle-aged establishment friends must have chafed under the depiction of their hollowness and insensibility toward the facts of the war and the lengthy casualty lists. Sassoon was unwilling to spare even his patrons and promoters.

"Base Details" is another attack on old men, this time senior officers safe at rear bases, but "fierce, and bald, and short of breath," hardly warrior material. In World War II this type of miles gloriosus was called a Colonel Blimp. The persona pretends he would like to be an old staff officer and "live with scarlet Majors at the Base." They are "scarlet Majors" because they wear red tabs as staff officers and because they are red-faced, blustering, puffed-up male birds. The persona, obviously a serving trench soldier, sardonically says that were he an old staffer, he would "speed glum heroes up the line to death" and when the war was over "toddle safely home and die—in bed." The incompetence, insensitivity, and decadence of senior officers is a major theme in Sassoon's war poems. Sassoon hated the idea that some men had to fight and die, while others in uniform had safe, cushy jobs. It is the eternal grievance of the combat soldier against rear-echelon troops, whom he or she sees as shirkers and parasites.

Sassoon excels as an ironist in **"The Fathers,"** **"Base Details,"** and **"The General."** In the last a kindly, paternal leader greets the men going into the line with "Good-morning; good-morning!" as if they were passing in a street. "Harry" and "Jack" liked him—"He's a cheery old card"—but they are dead now because "he did for them both by his plan of attack." Again Sassoon drives home his attack, this time on the notoriously incompetent British generals, with a shocking last line.

"Lamentations" is the antithesis to **"The Hero"** in *The Old Huntsman.* Now the blooded Sassoon has more sympathy for the "shell-shocked," traumatized soldier suffering the eruption of his grief over the news of his brother's death in battle. He "raved at the bleeding war. . . . Moaned, shouted, sobbed, and choked, while he was kneeling / Half naked on the floor." This time Sassoon keeps an ironist's distance, and the persona is another officer, one who is insensitive to his comrade's suffering. Coldly and precisely he comments, "In my belief / Such men have lost all patriotic feeling." As planned, the reader is shocked by the emotional distance of the persona from the sufferer. Was Sassoon thinking of his own, early war reaction to the death of his younger brother at Gallipoli as perhaps documented in the patriotic **"Brothers"**?

"Does It Matter?" ironically downplays the loss of a leg, "For people will always be kind"; the loss of sight, for "There's such splendid work for the blind"; or even shell shock, for "You can drink and forget." The poem ends in open sarcasm: "And no one will worry a bit." The absurd consolations offered by the civilian establishment for wounds and maiming deserve the mocking scorn they receive.

"Fight to a Finish," an infantryman's fantasy, is a vicious, angry attack on the press and the government. Sassoon's own regiment, the Royal Welch Fusiliers, at the future parade of those "who'd refrained from dying," fix bayonets and charge the "Yellow-Pressmen," those jingoistic, dishonest, and cowardly journalists, and while they are grunting and squeaking like stuck pigs, the persona's "trusty bombers," with their hand grenades, go on "To clear those Junkers out of Parliament." To Sassoon the members of Parliament are no different from the enemy's aristocrats. For the furious soldiers "This moment is their finest," not the welcome-home parade.

"Fight to a Finish" also indicates Sassoon's growing if not fully articulated socialism. The visualized attack on Parliament is a coded call for revolution, a dream of vengeful soldiers, as in Russia in 1917 and Germany, Austria, and Turkey late in 1918, attempting to destroy the institutions that betrayed them.

"Editorial Impressions" is another attack on the jingoistic press, "certain 'all was going well'" and that the troops were in high morale, based on quick visits to the trenches. In the punch line a "severely wounded" soldier sardonically comments, "Ah, yes, but it's the Press that leads the way!"

The depiction in **"Suicide in the Trenches"** of "a simple soldier boy" is derivative of A. E. Housman. The sensitive young soldier is unable to bear conditions in the trenches, and he "put a bullet through his brain." **"Suicide in the Trenches"** is "Sassoon's most blatant lapse into propaganda" ([Fred D.] Crawford), because he does not let the unfortunate story speak for itself as an objective correlative. Instead he editorializes. The last stanza accuses:

> You snug-faced crowds with kindling eye
> Who cheer when soldier lads march by,
> Sneak home and pray you'll never know
> The hell where youth and laughter go.

Sassoon's combat soldiers are seldom fierce and most often depicted as passive victims of circumstances beyond their control. Unheroic, only human, they are no masculine stereotypes of courage, strength, and stoicism. Instead they succumb to depression, stress, hysteria, and suicide, while being driven like khaki sheep to slaughter.

"Glory of Women" and **"Their Frailty"** unfairly attack women as shallow, pliant, manipulated, and narrow of vision. Sassoon apparently disliked women in general and could not see or understand their sufferings over the loss of loved ones, their painful sojourns of waiting, and that they were no more easily controlled by censorship and propaganda than men or indeed even the troops were. Women were the most passive afflicted of the war, but Sassoon fell into the trap of blaming the victim. Clearly false assumptions about heroism in war and "Chocolate Soldiers" are not the special province of women. Not all, and probably very few, are "By tales of dirt and danger fondly thrilled," even though notions of courage and privation are generally valorized in wartime. The endless knitting of socks and comforters that Sassoon derides is a method of suppressing anxiety. At least Sassoon implicitly recognizes the sisterhood of women whose sons are at war:

> O German mother dreaming by the fire,
> While you are knitting socks to send your son
> His face is trodden deeper in the mud.

The woman in the first stanza of **"The Frailty"** is glad her male, whether husband, son, or lover, has "got a Blighty wound." In the second stanza he is back in France, and so now she prays for peace. In the third stanza Sassoon reveals the "truth" about women: they "don't care / So long as He's all right." Woman can merely comprehend the significance of the war in selfish personal terms, in how it affects them through the men of their lives who are in the army. Sassoon's tone in **"Glory of Women"** and **"Their Frailty"** is mean. For a sensitive poet and a gay man, Sassoon's attack on women is surprising, but it is also somewhat in keeping with the traditional paternalistic attitudes of his class and his milieu.

"The Hawthorn Tree" is a pedestrian love lyric with the persona pining for a "lad that's out in France / With fearsome things to see." Nevertheless the poem provides a refreshing break from the suffering and brutality that surrounds it in the collection. It has some of the directness and simplicity of D. H. Lawrence's verse but not the depth or the resonance.

"The Investiture" takes place in Heaven, where "God with a Roll of Honour in His Hand / Sits welcoming the heroes who have died." Then the persona's lover or friend enters, "Wearing a blood-soaked bandage on [his] head." Although Heaven is a grand place, the dead soldier is alone and lonely without the persona, who in his anger at the death of the hero exclaims, "If I were there we'd snowball Death with skulls," a very Jacobean image. The poem's conceits are too extravagant, and the mythical depiction of God, angels, and Heaven detracts from the ghostly, elegiac intent.

"Autumn," a throwback to conventional imagery and Sassoon's prewar, Pre-Raphaelite style, is also a lament for "martyred youth and manhood overthrown," and **"Invoca-**

tion" calls on the dead lover in Heaven to "teach my soul to wake" and bring beauty down from Heaven. **"The Triumph"** seems out of place, reverting to earlier "poetic" language like "the terrible flickering gloom."

Conversational in style but hysterical in intensity, **"Repression of War Experience"** concerns self-communing. The persona is attempting to drive out thoughts of combat, where men, like moths to a candle's flame, "blunder in / And scorch their wings with glory, liquid flame." In his psychotic world there "are crowds of ghosts among the trees," but these are not ghosts of soldiers; they are in France. Instead these are "horrible shapes in shrouds . . . old men with ugly souls, / Who wore their bodies out with nasty sins." In a distracted, melodramatic monologue, the persona, far from the front, hears the sound of guns and the thud of shells: "I'm going stark, staring mad because of the guns." The poem's attack on the war and old civilian men again is unfocused and the effect stagy and unconvincing.

"Survivors," written at Craiglockhart Hospital in October 1917, devises a persona who optimistically discusses shell-shocked patients without understanding their experiences or their plight. The brilliant literal imagery of the poem is in the lines describing the suffering of the victims, who are now "Children, with eyes that hate you, broken and mad." The fatuous persona, perhaps a physician, has only bromides to offer: "No doubt they'll soon get well. . . . Of course they're 'longing to go out again.'"

In **"Joy-Bells"** Sassoon again is sarcastic toward the church and churchmen because their bells, ringing in patriotic fervor, "changed us into soldiers." Now, in the war, the bells are useless and their metal needed for guns. Still, "Fierce-browed prelates" safe at home "proclaim / That if our Lord returned He'd fight for us." Sassoon wants the bishops laboring in the war effort too: "Shoulder to shoulder with the motor bus." For Sassoon and for Owen, Christ was already there in the trenches in the mass martyrdom occurring.

"Remorse" presents the persona in the eternal moral dilemma of soldiery: how can it be right to kill in cold blood? He remembers "how he saw the German run, Screaming for mercy among the stumps of trees. . . . Our chaps were sticking them like pigs." He wonders how he can tell his father of the terrible things he has done: "there's things in war one dare not tell."

"Dead Musicians" and **"The Dream,"** both written at Craiglockhart, evince a mind preoccupied with death. In the former the persona eschews the power of classical musicians, such as Bach, Mozart, and Beethoven, artists who once "built cathedrals in my heart." Now the persona wants "fox-trot tunes" and ragtime, to bring back the ghosts of dead friends. But then "the song breaks off; and I'm alone. / They're dead. . . . For God's sake stop the gramophone." The sad poem deeply pains the reader too. **"The Dream"** once more has Sassoon remembering the enlisted men who served under him. He is filled with "Burning bitterness / That I must take them to the accursed line" and feed them "To the foul beast of war that bludgeons life." **"The Dream"** fully expresses the frustration and helplessness of those with responsibilities to others in a meat-grinder war.

In the Kiplingesque **"In Barracks"** Sassoon sentimentalizes the recruits, bidding them, "Sleep well, you lusty Fusiliers," not willing to admit that later he would put many to bed with a shovel. **"Together,"** the last poem in *Counter-Attack,* is another ghost poem. The persona is remembering his dead friend, who ghostly gallops with him on a spectral ride. And so *Counter-Attack* ends with David Thomas's spirit saying, "at the stable-door . . . good-night." Painful though it was, Sassoon earned dividends from the emotional investment of his deep mourning for Thomas and other lost soldiers whom he loved. The paroxysms of grief were perhaps surrogate for and relief from the submerged, repressed, and encrypted feelings of grief for the death of his youthful, handsome, and disavowed father. Catharsis was at last permissible.

In *Counter-Attack* Sassoon paints war nearly as faithfully as he could. The poems present the ugliness of war without flinching. Sometimes bitter and sardonic, other times elegiac, the poems are those of a haunted man, certainly "a spontaneous overflow of powerful feelings" and emotion recollected not in tranquillity but in a tormented lull between terrors. . . .

Sassoon's war poetry encompasses many modes: satiric, elegiac, comic, horrific, shocking, vengeful, and even pastoral. The poems were extremely therapeutic for himself and his readers, both civilian and military. For Sassoon and his comrades in arms, poetry, both the writing and the reading of it, gave a little dignity to the existential insult of the experiences, and it helped rationalize the bomb bursts of emotion, fear, terror, dehumanization, and horror that, understandably, could lead to insanity. For civilians the poetry permitted guilt and masochistic self-punishment as a way of sharing the suffering and trying to atone for what they had inflicted on their own young.

Sassoon's war poetry is direct and effective, with clear, hard, tough, epigrammatic, literal language and a minimum of metaphor. The poems are minidramas and tableaux. Wisely Sassoon "remained aware of his limitations and did not attempt a profundity that was beyond him: his gifts were pre-eminently those of a satirist, and it was in satire that he excelled" (Bergonzi). Sassoon's syntax marks time, allowing irony its breakthrough. He is at his best when he combines pity for Tommy's ordeal with indignation at the mindlessness and cruelty of the war, the stupidity of the generals and their staffs, and the contemptible vapidity of civilians who closed their eyes to the slaughter in France. The major binaries of Sassoon's world at war are civilians/ soldiers, staff/fighters, and old/young, but not friend/foe of German/English. Sassoon's poetry "performed the great service of debunking the old romantic myth of the glory of war" (Pinto). The war poets in toto related experience to brutal reality as it had never been done before. Sassoon's literary influence as the modern creator of the language of war continues, while his moral authority has guided men and women in the "war over war" ever since. A small body of verse effected this: "It is by virtue of thirty or forty poems that delineate the agony of the fighting in the trenches that he holds an honoured place among English poets" ([John] Press).

Perhaps finally, the appreciation for Sassoon, as with Owen, is in the pity of it all.

Christopher Lane (essay date Summer 1994)

SOURCE: "In Defense of the Realm: Sassoon's Memoirs," in *Raritan,* Vol. XIV, No. 1, Summer, 1994, pp. 89-108.

[*In the following essay, Lane interprets Sassoon's autobiographic writings as an embodiment of his conflicted self-identity and masculinity as a dutiful English soldier, antiwar dissenter, and repressed homosexual.*]

> The war is outside of life, and I'm in the war.
>
> —Siegfried Sassoon

There is a way of referring to the generation of First World War poets that is still popular in Britain today. According to this myth, a group of men set out to chronicle the nation's experience of combat for those back home oblivious of its meaning. By capturing the elegiac testament of a "lost generation," their poetry is presumed to record a nation's suffering.

In line with all myth, an element of truth to this reading cannot be ignored: the task of writing the war was taken up by many soldiers in a spirit of grief and protest. Many of these poets were incensed by the discrepancy between their experience of war and Britain's rhetorical denial of horror and suffering. This was a war in which several million people died, a war that continues to illustrate its historical pointlessness.

Although the large number of killed and maimed in the war cannot be discounted, I propose that the meaning of war is not reducible to a set of political or social determinants. While the conflict came to an end more than seventy years ago, its legacy is still palpable today as an image of global carnage, patriotic fervor, and national shattering that has haunted European—and especially British—memory ever since. The task of separating the "real" from the "mythological" aspects of war may therefore be impossible because it confronts our continued belief that each military event is an empirical and coherent certainty. Britain's First World War poetry illustrates how history is invested with cultural meaning, for its literature is inseparable from the work of national memory and mourning. By framing war as a *literary* event, Britain defines its meaning in terms of a national poetics. The argument that

Sassoon, Owens, Thomas, Graves, and Brooke produced only elegiac accounts of the war generates a single reading of their work by assuming their allegiance to a mythology that is all but indifferent to their ontological resistance.

Rather than argue that Britain has wrongly appropriated this reading, I suggest that there are elements of these writers' work that endorse it, and a resonance to their work that is often ignored. Since Sassoon's writing is emblematic of this link between subjectivity, desire, and loss for British culture, his grief and disorientation appear to mirror the collapse of Britain's imperial power. Similar to an obsessional fantasy, Britain repeats to itself with unfailing fascination the image of its international decline by assuming that its waning power is expressed literarily by Sassoon's dream of a bygone era. In line with all forms of nostalgia, this reading of the war poets signals a commemorative appeal for what was shattered by the war: the pastoral beauty and metropolitan elegance of Edwardian England. Each account of this period helps create a fantasy of national stability that ushers in nostalgia by an alarming "refurbishment of the Empire's tarnished image."

Contrary to the presumption that these poets shared an identical response to the First World War, I will focus on elements of Sassoon's work that question national allegiance and military combat. These elements are central to the war, and to the reflexive and interrogative modernity to which it contributed. I suggest that two aspects of these questions require critical attention: the notion that the iconography of the "war poets" rescinds their ambivalence to Britain's military policies, and the excision of same-sex desire from this ideal to clarify a specific understanding of Britain's wartime allegory.

In terms of the first proposition, Sassoon, Owens, Brooke, and Graves publicly redefined their support for the war, and changed from ardent patriotism at its beginning to prominent criticism by the time of its end. Their trajectory is significant in encouraging a shift in public consciousness that did not jeopardize the alleged integrity of British masculinity, for these poets attempted to end the war by downplaying the idea of surrender as national emasculation. Despite the relative invisibility of homosexual desire in Sassoon's poetry, it is shaped by a tradition of homophilia that encompasses a yearning passion for camaraderie and intimacy. Although many critics have interpreted this yearning as a desire for fraternal bonding, or a generic defense by European allies against the terror of the German enemy, they rely on a select reading of Sassoon's poetry that ignores his memoirs and diaries.

Sassoon's broadly "intermediary" period of protest between unquestioning patriotism and repudiation of violence is related to Britain's wartime allegory of masculinity and the difficulty of encoding same-sex desire, for his anger was directed largely at the cowardice of the British public and the incompetence of its political representatives. The title of one of his collections, *Counter-Attack,* suggests this embittered reversal as a resistance to combat and a suggestion that he might take up arms against an enemy he identified at home. Thus cowardice was reframed as the vindictive aim of a public intent on killing its citizens, not the classic "effeminacy" of those who uphold principles of pacifism.

The authorities' response to Sassoon's "willful defiance" was one of bewildered reproach, followed by silencing strategies, accusations of treachery, and, finally, an order for his detention for the treatment of a psychiatric disorder—"war-shock." Literary criticism of his **Counter-Attack** has paradoxically endorsed this prognosis by suggesting a tone of "adolescent" rage that "bludgeons" the reader into acquiescence by focusing relentlessly on the mutilation and decomposition of men's bodies. In other words, what is unappealing or "unpoetic" about these poems is their refusal to adopt a Romantic esthetic of death as heroic, and their insistently naturalist transposition of the sublime into corporeal abjection.

Sassoon was not the only poet to describe this transposition, but his later writing is significant in representing the war as a constitutive influence on European modernity; his memoirs foreground the impossibility of the sublime as one of their principal effects. I contend that this representation was largely inadvertent, and that Sassoon's resistance to modernism in his early memoirs and poetry sought to reverse a shift toward Cubism, Futurism, and Vorticism, as well as Dada's absurdist response to the war, by reinvoking the Romantic esthetic of the previous century. This may explain why the war poets remain so enduringly popular, and why their esthetic seems central to Britain's disavowal of its imperial dissolution and economic turbulence at the end of the war. While numerous examples attest to a contrary social history, Edwardian Britain is thus *recalled* as a period of untroubled peace and harmony.

One example of this retroactive collation of British culture is the opening volume of Sassoon's 1928 autobiography, **Memoirs of a Fox-Hunting Man.** Sassoon began writing this account after the war had ended as if the danger of forgetting was his principal concern. The task of rewriting the war expanded into a lifelong project, however, as Sassoon devoted his remaining years to revising texts whose sole preoccupation was the anticipated, lived, or protracted experience of combat. While periods overlap in these texts, chronology is oriented toward psychic time, and diaries return to, amend, and rechronicle an experience already detailed by his testimonial poetry—and again by memoir—as if to work through what was clearly the central inspiration of his life.

This reworking of temporality and constant rebinding of the signification of war drew Sassoon closer to the conceptual and stylistic procedures of European modernism. As part of his reminiscence, and contrary to his desire to return to an ideal subjectivity, Sassoon never reached the mythic tranquility of prewar culture, for he could define it only against the turbulence of the present. Thus his project defeated itself because the drive to envisage life

before the war endlessly devolved on a catastrophe he could never forget. The fact that Sassoon never gave up trying means that the actual war recedes in his fiction, and the fantasy that outlasts it hones the event down to an increasingly diffuse recollection.

In addition to his textual accounts of violence, Sassoon's writing is notable because the war configures issues to which it holds no *necessary* relation. The questions of his childhood, choice of career, literary friendships, and homosexual desire seem to cohere around this event because it organizes their meaning. The war encouraged Sassoon to revise the narrative of his childhood, for instance, and to associate the absence of war with domestic and psychic plenitude. Military and personal conflict also coalesce in his **Memoirs** and **Diaries,** for Sassoon seemed unable or unwilling to distinguish between historical and psychic issues. In these terms, war stands in as a metaphor for the breaks and transitions of his childhood by substituting writing for the ontological crisis that precedes it: the conflicts of desire, violence, and symbolization that shatter him into a chaotic order of military symbols.

It would be easy for criticism to adopt a similar procedure, and exchange war for unresolved psychic conflict as if literature were reducible to psychobiography. This is not my suggestion; yet the reverse supposition that war and subjectivity are distinct is also unsatisfactory. The problem with Sassoon's writing is that war repeats *and* interprets moments of immense psychic resonance: while military recollection is not simply fortuitous; it cannot also be consigned in his writing to "incorrect" or idealistic fantasy.

Memoirs of a Fox-Hunting Man supports this association between psychic violence and cultural nostalgia by constituting the past as a time of mythical happiness. Events are isolated and spun into a narrative so overlaid with sentiment that it almost excludes the traumatic events of 1914. Chapters comprise the description of memorable hunts or rounds of golf; adopting the archaisms—now clichés—of Romanticism, Sassoon virtually suspends the influence of the modern by reverting to scenes of pastoral tranquility. His account of his childhood home is so overwritten that the prose seems to balk from the weight of allusion:

> Looking back across the years I listen to the summer afternoon cooing of my aunt's white pigeons, and the soft clatter of their wings as they flutter upward from the lawn at the approach of one of the well-nourished cats. I remember, too, the smell of strawberry jam being made; and Aunt Evelyn with a green bee-veil over her head. . . . The large rambling garden, with its Irish yews and sloping paths and wind-buffeted rose arches, remains to haunt my sleep. . . . In an endless variety of dream-distorted versions the garden persists as the background of my unconscious existence.

Despite his opening caution ("In this brightly visualised world of simplicities and misapprehensions"), Sassoon's prose resists the post-Edenic bathos of war because his irony extends only to childhood fragility, not historical crisis. Sassoon's esthetic is so successful that his frequent digressions into other episodes bolster this ideal instead of puncturing the very drive to recreate it. This counters John Onions's suggestion that Sassoon's memoirs are an "ironic prefiguration" of the war because his narratives strive to displace military conflict, and return to themselves in a strategic hope of forgetting.

Toward the end of this text, the war is absolved of crisis and refigured as an extension of Britain's idyll: "For me, so far, the War had been a mounted infantry picnic in perfect weather. The inaugural excitement had died down, and I was agreeably relieved of all sense of personal responsibility." Sassoon writes, with an irony only modern readers could appreciate, that being in the army is "very much like being back at school" because its structure of discipline encourages heroism and male camaraderie, and—one might add—infantilism. While the emphasis on order and intimacy protects him from violence, the health of outdoor living and "homely smells" recreate lost pleasure: "there was something almost idyllic about those early weeks of the War." As the narrative moves listlessly toward the war, the convolution of figurative language becomes more intense and resists the incipience of conflict by dwelling on each renunciation of pleasure. Yet the struggle for amnesia is impossible because violence surfaces from the place it was formerly denied: "everything I had known before the War seemed to be withering and falling to pieces."

Sassoon often describes "the spellbound serenity" of Edwardian England by metaphorizing a seasonal transition from late summer to bleak winter to emphasize why the "cloudless weather of that August and September [of 1914] need not be dwelt on; it is a hard fact in history." Yet the figurative cannot occlude *the Fall* as a "hard fact" of history because it fetishizes "the peaceful past" as a time of security that is no longer tenable. Analogous to the body of a soldier he confronts whose "whole spurious edifice fell to bits," Sassoon's military experience shatters his illusion of "spellbound serenity" when the figurative fails to supplant the intensity of violence. This metaphor parallels his allusion to English pastoralism, for *Memoirs of a Fox-Hunting Man* struggles to cover the empty space of death and the traumatic *real* of war.

To the extent that he returned to his childhood fourteen years later, Sassoon's first memoir failed to memorialize his past. Sassoon produced two other volumes that chart his youth from the perspective of his literary career, though their remarkable avoidance of death intensifies only the urgency of his lyricism: *The Weald of Youth* (1942) is tinged with such nostalgia that it is closer to Hardy's late-Victorian poetics than the retributive and contemporaneous anger of Osborne, Orton, or Greene: "Some way back I have defined this book as an attempt to compose an outline of my mental history. That sounds safe and comfortable enough, and can be kept modestly plausible while the said history is unfolding itself through actual episodes." The episode in question is not the Second World War, as we might suppose from its historical proximity, or even Sassoon's preoccupation with the First; rather, it is the story of how he came to publish his first book of poetry. Even "this impulsive holocaust" is an exorbitant reference to his destruction of juvenilia in a text that is otherwise obsessed with the "gentle revisitation of the days that are no more." It later transpires that this "revisitation" consists of piecing his childhood together from mnemonic fragments of bicycle rides, games of tennis, and resplendent sunsets:

> Out on the lawn the Eden freshness was like something never breathed before. In a purified ecstasy I inhaled the smell of dew-soaked grass, and all the goodness of being alive now met me in a moment, as I stood on the doorstep outside the drawing-room. . . . In the Arcadian cherry orchard across the road a bird-scaring boy had begun his shouting cries and clattering of pans.

The reference to Arcadia in post-Holocaust Europe is no irony for Sassoon, for it indicates the preoccupation of a man whose present exists with almost no other referent than the legacy of unresolved violence. Thus history and the present converge as Sassoon wistfully meanders from past simple to present continuous—"Meanwhile I am still overhearing . . ."—and from present simple to a future conditional; a tense in which history is reframed by imaginary projection: "revisiting some such house I should go there in summer—preferably on a dozy July morning. I should find myself in an upstairs room. . . . It is an unfrequented room, seeming to contain vibrations of vanished life."

Since he conflates adolescence with middle-aged nostalgia, and psychoanalysis equally insists that "psychic time" is tied to the subject's erratic self-narrativization, it is not surprising that Sassoon's version of the war—at the end of this now supplemental memoir—erases all record of violence and renders the war a vanishing point of his imaginary. Yet despite its *post*-war fantasies of *pre*-war pleasure, *The Weald of Youth* is notable for enumerating much of the war's psychic resonance in Sassoon. Accompanying the rage and bitterness of many of his poems, he remarks: "I should have been quite put out if someone had told me that there might not be a war after all, for the war had become so much my own affair that it was—temporarily and to the exclusion of all other considerations—merely me!" Sassoon's overidentification with the war suggests that the war produced the right conditions for him to bind otherwise disparate elements of his personality. I suggest that it also encouraged him to realize and partially resolve a tension between ambition and desire by bringing each diffuse element of his character to the fore:

> It was possible, I found, to divide myself—as I had existed during the past year [1913]—into three fairly distinct parts: the hunting man; the person who had spent ten weeks in Raymond Buildings [the London esthete]; and the invisible being who shadowed the other two with his lordly ambition to produce original poetry.

If the "hunting man" is restless with inactivity, and the esthete dispirited by the loneliness of city life, "the invisible" third—according to Sassoon—"was mainly responsible for the ineffectiveness of the whole affair." The war seems to dispel this ennui by "tak[ing] the trivial personal problem off his hands," providing a symbol for each component of his personality: the sportsman is transformed into a soldier, the esthete into an officer, the writer into a poet overwhelmed by creative incentive. Yet the personal continues to cut across these symbolic constituents because the war embodies, rationalizes, and finally legitimizes physical intimacy with other men.

Instead of supposing that desire and military ambition are restricted to biographical interest, I interpret Sassoon's *experiential* investment in war as synecdochic to a generic reorientation of sexuality at the time. Although Sassoon gave the "invisible being" that immobilized his existence in London the attributes of a poet, the influence of this persona surfaces at the beginning of **Memoirs of a Fox-Hunting Man** as the missing half of his character.

> As a consequence of my loneliness I created in my childish daydreams an ideal companion who became much more of a reality than such unfriendly boys as I encountered at Christmas parties [when . . .] I was so glad to escape from the horrors of my own hospitality. . . . The "ideal companion" probably originated in my desire for an elder brother.

Since the amount of time Sassoon devotes to childhood is curtailed by this sequel volume, his "ideal companion" is soon displaced by the plenitude of rural life. Sassoon's passion for horses and their caretakers briefly supplants the need for "an elder brother" before memory restores it as a burning demand:

> [He] has cropped up with an odd effect of importance which makes me feel he must be worth a passing mention. The fact is that, as soon as I began to picture in my mind the house and garden where I spent so much of my early life, I caught sight of my small, vanished self with this other non-existent boy standing beside him. And though it sounds silly enough, I felt queerly touched by the recollection of that forgotten companionship.

Sassoon's division of his character into specific interests is arguably related to his *management* of memory, for he later claims that "Sherston"—the fictional protagonist of his memoirs—"is only one-fifth of myself," a figure that is curious for its mathematical precision and the suggestion of a remainder that is excised from his memoirs. The most obvious omission from this fraction is his interest in poetry, though the remainder actually expands in later accounts from "one third" to "one half," to finally "four-fifths" of his missing identity. As Bernard Knox remarks without substantiation: "The persona of Sherston dictated the exclusion of poetry from the trilogy. . . . Poetry, however, was not the only side of Sassoon that was suppressed in Sherston; the war diaries reveal clearly enough that the poet's tenderest feelings were for those of his own sex."

Sassoon's **Diaries** clarify these fractions without rendering him whole. The testimony of his private word explicates,

but never redeems, his artistic disseveration because the fantasy that we can read Sassoon entire rests on a premise that an adequate relation joins language and desire. Instead of searching for this fraction, or paradoxically extolling the critical possibilities of its absence, I suggest that Sassoon's struggle with sexual representation actually surfaces in his preceding narratives. The intrusion of this desire—indeed, the demand that it now be *heard*—suggests more than an assumption that it was formerly denied because Sassoon attributes the entire conflict to the psychological damage of war. Yet the interrogative style of his diary pronounces this conflict a misrecognition by demonstrating that cohesion is an *ontological* impossibility:

> Writing the last words of a book, more than four years ago, I left a man—young for his age, though nearly thirty-four—standing in Trafalgar Square, vaguely conscious that his career had reached a point where he must begin it all over again. That man was, of course, myself. I had conducted him as far as August 1920 with a fair amount of confidence in my ability to get back into his skin and describe his state of mind. He was remote, but *unamenable to the process of reconstruction.* Since leaving him, I have often tried to get in touch with him again. But the distance between us has widened in more than years, and I have found myself complaining that *we are now scarcely on speaking terms*—that he has dropped out of my life, and that if I were to meet him I should not know what to say to him. It seems that *I, his successor, have outlived our former intimacy:* And I am not sure that I want to revive my relationship with one so inexperienced, uninformed, and self-dramatising as he then was. (emphasis mine)

Sassoon adopts many personal pronouns in his diary because each one infers, and immediately questions, the adequacy of self-reference: "I . . . myself . . . I . . . him . . . my . . . he . . . us . . . I . . . myself . . . we . . ." etc. Although the idea of imagining oneself as the other of one's speech is a convention of journal writing, Sassoon also interrogates the adequacy of each possessive pronoun: "myself . . . my . . . *our.*" What does "our" incorporate that "he" cannot, and what does "myself" mean in its radical disseveration from "us"? In their respective ways, poststructuralist and psychoanalytic criticism represent the breach between the "I" and "my" of linguistic utterance as a sign of the insoluble difference between the place from which one speaks and the position from which one is spoken. Sassoon never ceases to probe and confound the fictional unity of the subject as it speaks from the place it has been. To put this another way, Sassoon demonstrates that the desire to solidify the present, and represent oneself *as* "self-present," is possible only by projecting oneself from an imaginary reconstitution of the past. As Lacan recently corroborated, subjectivity can be understood in the future anterior only because this tense collates the "present" from a fantasy of what will have been. Sassoon seemed to imply this when he wrote: "I doubt whether this book is giving anything like a chart of what is really going on inside me. Anyhow it is as near as I can get." The signifier can approximate only the profuse web of fantasy that underlies it.

Beyond this general difficulty of language and expression, Sassoon compounds the drama of self-presence by the meaning he attributes to each register of personality. His "I" confers an authority on a "self" that looks with misgiving and frequent disgust on the parts of a "he" it would rather disown. As his diary testifies, this split occurs whenever Sassoon broaches the question of sexuality, for his desire seems to separate from consciousness and be viewed as a painful incursion on friendship and intimacy: "It was a very lovely and peaceful affair [with the painter, Gabriel Atkin] and made us both feel better . . . because I felt the existence of a bond which is untroubled by animalism." When Sassoon ruminates on Gabriel as a "distraction," however, he comments: "I seem to suffer from a poisoned mind; an unwholesome unhappiness pervades my healthy body. Is it pride—conceited pride—that makes me crave to alienate everyone?" An answer seems to surface the following week as a more extreme self-accusation: "What is wrong with me? Is it this cursed complication of sex that afflicts me?" The question persists throughout the journal, and soon represents the entirety of his discontent.

> Attractive faces in streets. Cursed nuisance of sex . . .
> Rome doesn't disappoint me. *It is myself that fails.*
> Why am I so dreary and unreceptive, incapable of
> imaginative enthusiasm and romantic youthfulness?
> . . . Is it my own fault that I am under this cursed
> obsession of sex-cravings[?] . . . My mind is somehow
> diseased and distorted. I live in myself—seek freedom
> in myself—self-poisoned, self-imprisoned. . . . If I had
> my heart's desire I should be happy; but not for long.
> (emphasis mine)

Although Sassoon's self-loathing and recrimination are poignantly elaborate, they are also contrary to the ongoing *announcement* of homosexual desire in his writing: he oscillates between periods of insanity, "morosity," and "a sort of self-lacerating irritability . . . that . . . is not unconnected with my animal passions." This characterization of desire—and his vigilant wish to control it—exacerbates his self-recrimination by leading him to the brink of suicide at the end of this year (1921). As its etymology (*sui-caedere*) reminds us, suicide is an annihilation of the self that is intimately related to Sassoon's carefully defined, and impossibly proscribed, tasks, values, and behaviors.

It may be reductive and perhaps superfluous to speculate on the relation between Sassoon's homosexual defense and his postwar illness. What is more certain and interesting is the way he enjoined on himself a ferocious command to sublimate, excise, and expel this set of impulses. The command not only failed (the impulses would not go away) but was later attributed to his dearth of creative success. Thus Sassoon associated with such writers as Hardy and Forster, and frantically emulated them in the hope of producing "another *Madame Bovary* dealing with sexual inversion, a book that the world *must* recognise and learn to understand! O, that unwritten book! Its difficulties are overwhelming." Later, stymied by exhaustion and self-censorship, he impulsively dissolved the project altogether: "Now I am no longer in the mood to reveal the workings of my thought-processes for the benefit of unbegotten

generations of psychopathic subjects. I cannot put down more than a fraction of what was in my head."

Recognizing all the dangers of prognosis, I suggest that Sassoon's inability to write had little or nothing to do with his artistic ability (which was clearly considerable). Writing led him to an impasse that seized over the use of acceptable symbols—acceptable, that is, to both its writer and public readers. We risk taking Sassoon at his (frequently unreliable) word if we accept that the residue of the unwritten was little more "than a fraction of what was in my head," for the "cursed" supplement of sexual "obsession" had already emerged, and been displaced, elsewhere. Forster expressed similar discomfort and disingenuous confession when he decided to "burn . . . my indecent writings or as many as the fire will take. Not a moral repentance, but [from] the belief that they clogged me artistically."

I suggest that Sassoon's **Diaries** illustrate a complex literary displacement that represents the compression *and* release of his desire in the trenches. This substitution of "cursed" desires is more successful in a military context because combat, struggle, and tension *already* function as metaphors in his writing. Thus the antagonism of his desire ("and is there anything in life which can be *disconnected* from this curse of sex?" [emphasis mine]) is frequently counterpoised with the threat of it disappearance ("but I must have feelings toward *something!*"), which precipitates a crisis over the very decision to desire: "the question now arises—which of my myselves is the most worthy of survival? Which of myselves is writing this excorium? And, having written it, how can it be responsible for what future selves may reveal?"

Sassoon's questions force us to consider his choice of genre and narrative style: if the **Memoirs** are—by his conscious division—"only one-fifth of myself," the problem remains where (and how) to deposit the remainder. Writing is central to this project for it supports a belief that *internal* war can be exteriorized as a conflict among competing nations. Though the question of self-survival is largely unanswerable to Sassoon, the assumption that it corresponds to political hatred suggests a temporary reprieve from self-accusation. As Sassoon poignantly explained:

> In retrospection we see ourselves as we never existed.
> So I am keeping a journal in order to record my daily
> and essential inconsistency and constitutional silliness.
> From this jungle of misinterpretations of my ever-
> changing and never-steadfast selves, some future fool
> may, perhaps, derive instruction and amusement.

Although this analogy between national and psychic war offers a fleeting resolution, it poses questions about the relation between this "jungle of misinterpretations" and the battlefield on which so many millions of lives were destroyed. As many critics have argued, the war was also fought over questions of meaning and validation, and the point is worth reiterating to question the assumption that military conflict is entirely responsible for mental illness. My suggestion is that it may have *disinhibited* Sassoon's psychic distress before intensifying it later with the prominence of visible devastation.

* * *

> I had done what I could to tidy up the mess in no-man's land.

> —Siegfried Sassoon

By the time Sassoon wrote *Memoirs of an Infantry Officer* (1930), the war it described had receded into popular mythology and another of greater magnitude loomed on the political horizon—the consolidation of National Socialism in Germany was underway. Although Sassoon's perception of the Second World War displaced the terms of its historical truth, he could no longer produce a companion volume that "would lead [him] along pleasant associative lanes connected with the English counties": the creation of "one of those peaceful war pictures" was impossible because they have "vanished for ever and are rarely recovered in imaginative retrospect."

With its emphasis on greater fidelity to historical drama, *Memoirs of an Infantry Officer* describes the substitution of the civilian by its military counterpart. The critic Eric Leed has described the psychic consequence of this transformation by paraphrasing a prominent military strategist: "the purpose of training is to get the soldier to 'pattern himself after his persecutors (his officers)'; if successful, this causes the trainee to undergo a 'psychological regression during which his character is restructured into a combat personality.'"

The "psychological regression" of military training demands nothing less than a return to the place of Law—the moment when the threat of violence is first apprehended, and the infant's imaginary is shattered by the alterity of language, prohibition, and sexual difference. Additionally, the prerequisite unraveling of the civilian into a "combat personality" offers the soldier a fantasy of mastering the "bad object" (the enemy) by submitting to orders that are closer to home. Sassoon's narrative is significant, however, because his defense against this regression *unmakes* each order, and sets up a challenge through irony, illness, and defiance. In other words, the command—and the identification on which it relies—constantly *fails*. By his resistance to full participation, Sassoon empties the command of meaning, assessing its effect on his subjectivity by bringing the personal and the military into profound conflict. Thus he writes of his "spectral presences":

> Such hauntings might be as inadequate as those which now absorb my mental energy. For trench life was an existence saturated by the external senses; and although our actions were domineered over by military discipline, our animal instincts were always uppermost. While I stood there then, I had no desire to diagnose my environment. Freedom from its oppressiveness was what I longed for.

Memoirs of an Infantry Officer juxtaposes Sassoon's precarious loyalty to Britain by his corresponding desire to defy its authority. When Sassoon involuntarily listens to a lecture on "The Spirit of the Bayonet," for instance, he judges the "homicidal eloquence" of the officer with critical disdain. As the officer cites the *Manual of Bayonet Training*—"The bullet and the bayonet are brother and sister"; "if you don't kill him, he'll kill you"; "stick him between the eyes, in the throat, in the chest"—Sassoon responds with understandable revulsion. Yet the officer develops a penetrative fantasy—"Don't waste good steel. Six inches are enough. . . . Three inches will do for him; when he coughs, go and look for another. . . . Remember . . . [the] importance of a 'quick withdrawal'"—in which the bayonet's castrating power encourages the soldier to sexually usurp the enemy. The bayonet is invested with a "spirit" that absolves the soldier of responsibility by conflating his territorial incursion with imaginary insemination: "We will force open the closed door and enter by force into the forbidden land. And for us who have for so long been forced to accumulate in desolate holes of shell holes, the idea of this thrust into the depths holds a compelling fascination."

To the extent that almost all military rhetoric elaborates this "homosexual" fantasy, it is significant that Sassoon's irony inveighs only against the brusque and ruthless manner of the lecturer. This may indicate Sassoon's blindness to what might otherwise have been a sexual critique of both the war and Britain's colonial appropriation of "forbidden land." Instead of this critique, *Memoirs of an Infantry Officer* describes Sassoon's shifting relation to the enemy at home and abroad: his position wavered between a loyalty that subsumed him beneath the camaraderie of his unit and a counter impulse to detach from its contaminating influence. By domesticating the war to the level of a schoolboy "escapade," which develops from an adolescent "prank" into "a form of outdoor sports," the narrative never unifies this oscillation. Yet Sassoon later describes the war with the disdain of an esthete who pursues beauty in order to redeem his surrounding violence.

Sassoon's focus on a love object seems to stabilize this oscillation, however, by encouraging him to grasp the unstable ground between group immolation and solitary detachment. By expanding on the passionate friendships in *Memoirs of a Fox-Hunting Man,* he "betrays" a deep affection for two men—Stephen Colwood and David Cromlech—that releases him from the sexual impediments of London. Thus the war offers a context for same-sex intimacy by representing a generic body to which it can be attributed. Sassoon allows this intimacy to fall under the banner of fraternal or "nonsexual" concern since his "*indefinite* pang of affection" (emphasis mine) for David intercedes between solitude and "the Horde."

If affection is "indefinite" in this memoir, it is largely because Sassoon characterizes it as a diffuse and nonexclusive quality. The love object is not amorphous—but entirely specific—because Sassoon and Cromlech's relationship allows them to anticipate the end of war and speculate on their continued intimacy after it. Since Cromlech occupies in fantasy the place of his missing "half"—the absent brother/lover—he repeats Sassoon's childhood fantasy of an "ideal companion." As Sassoon's memoir fails to distinguish between psychic and military registers, the war is conflated with a psychological drama that compels him to fight and recoil as if from an equivalent scene of violence.

The first half of *Memoirs of an Infantry Officer* anticipates this violence because the enemy is formless and ubiquitous, not recognizable in the narrative. The memoir begins with Sassoon preparing for conflict, though it later elaborates his dread that the unit will stumble on a fantasmatically comparable battle zone. As Sassoon considers the imminence of this attack, he is forced to interpret who and *what* the enemy is, and why he invests it with such a capacity for *psychic* retribution: "then I rushed at the bank, vaguely expecting some sort of scuffle with my imagined enemy." In each projection, the enemy is patterned after a model of internal conflict so that his external encounter with the Germans is *unheimlich* when he discovers them maimed and disfigured: their bodies are sufficiently similar (as men) to endorse his private antagonism, and dissimilar (as enemies in a different uniform) to render the corpse a brutal encounter with the *real*.

Since *Memoirs of an Infantry Officer* struggles to resolve two competing aims, it is split between supporting Britain by converting the "enemy" into a "fiend," and confronting death by associating the German corpses with the military and psychic abject. The liminal border between these aims separates Sassoon's passionate interest in David Cromlech from the German bodies by upholding a precarious distinction between friend and foe on which Sassoon's perception of the war relies. This oscillation is largely inevitable because the line between loyalty and desertion for Sassoon—and the army and nation at large—is particularly fragile.

It would appear that Sassoon experienced difficulty in reconciling this tension, for it haunted him long after the war had receded as historical fact. The difference between national friend and foreign enemy turns on the strength of his identification with the group and his submission to contrary demands. The problem is more urgent when the idea of "brotherhood" is considered, however, because it forces him to recognize what is desirable in and "other" to the brother, and thence to separate the beloved of David Cromlech from the "enemy" that finally kills him. Although this recognition is quite obvious in national and political rhetoric, its psychic distinction is more arbitrary. The difference poses an ontological dilemma for Sassoon that asks him to examine what it means to identify with a nation, the military commands of the "father," and the land that is claimed and violated in the name of his real and imaginary authority.

I suggest that Sassoon failed to resolve these questions because they surface in each memoir as a troubled relation

to national service. Britain's demand that Sassoon identify with, and fight for, its people runs counter to his individualism and desire for a "brother," for instance, because it requires him to renounce these drives in the service of a collective aim. The nation's call up is thus initially received with fervor and later rewarded by a medal for courage: "I wanted to make the World War serve a similar purpose . . . of demonstrating my equality with my contemporaries . . . for if only I could get a Military Cross *I should feel comparatively safe* and confident." (emphasis mine).

As I have earlier described, however, Sassoon reversed this strategy by attacking the home front with a petition he described as "an act of willful defiance." The question of what he needed to be safe from, or to whom his defiance was directed, asks us to consider the terms of his identification because Sassoon repeatedly signified each military representative as an imago of Law: he condemned the surrounding genocide by these "fathers," and continued to fight with a ferocious will to victory. As several members of his unit have commented, it is difficult to reconcile the outraged poet who "had just . . . published . . . a volume full of bitter indignation at the hideous cruelty of modern warfare" with the man who was "also . . . a first-rate soldier and a most aggressive company commander."

During his temporary absence from the war, Sassoon was riven by such guilt that the relief of escape without physical injury seemed to recall memories of an earlier psychological battle:

> It was nice to think that I'd been fighting with them, though exactly what I'd done to help them was difficult to define. An elderly man, cycling along a dusty road in a dark blue suit and a straw hat, removed one hand from the handle-bars to wave comprehensive gratitude. Everything seemed happy and homely. I was delivered from the idea of death, and that other thing which had haunted me, the dread of being blinded.

The guilt of avoiding some of the conflict may have been responsible for Sassoon's precipitous return to it, for the war renewed his desire to fight and reaffiliate: "willfully . . . in 1918 after his protest, . . . [Sassoon] patrolled to the German trenches as exuberantly as Julian Grenfell ever did in 1914-15." Each transition between support and antagonism, submission and defiance, seemed to amalgamate diffuse constituents of his identity that were bound only by the "opaque arenas of War." As he remarked with an inadvertently modernist consciousness: "Our inconsistencies are often what make us most interesting, and it is possible that, in my zeal to construct these memoirs carefully, I have eliminated many of my own self-contradictions."

The zeal of Sassoon's elimination, and the prominence of self-contradiction, ask us to consider the fine line between passionate devotion to the nation and hostile defiance against it. These inconsistencies surface whenever Sassoon interprets heroic commitment, sacrifice to duty, and altruistic virtue on the one hand, and annihilation, grief, and devastation on the other. Though Sassoon never resolved this dilemma, his "indefinite pang of affection" for other men occupied the middle ground—or battle-ground—between these poles of military rhetoric because he was unable to locate desire outside, or beyond, the field of war. In his concern to inhabit this critical terrain, Sassoon identified with neither the sublime nor the abject, but rather the bleak and precarious "No Man's Land" that intercedes between them as their vanishing mediator.

FURTHER READING

Criticism

Barth, R. L. "Sassoon's 'Counter-Attack.'" *Explicator* 49, No. 2 (Winter 1991): 117-8.
    Offers brief critical analysis of the poem "Counter-Attack."

Caesar, Adrian. "Siegfried Sassoon." In his *Taking it Like a Man: Suffering Sexuality, and the War Poets Brooke, Sassoon, Owen, Graves,* pp. 60-114. Manchester: Manchester University Press, 1993.
    Reexamines Sassoon's intellectual development, military experiences, and attitudes concerning warfare and suffering as reflected in his World War I poetry.

Campbell, Patrick. "Sassoon's 'Blighters.'" *Explicator* 53, No. 3 (Spring 1995): 170-1.
    Offers brief critical analysis of the poem "Blighters."

Corrigan, D. Felicitas. "Introduction." In *Siegfried Sassoon: Poet's Pilgrimage,* edited by D. Felicitas Corrigan, pp. 15-42. London: Victor Gollancz, 1973.

Provides an overview of Sassoon's literary career, artistic development, and religious sensibility.

Drinkwater, John. "Two 'New Poets' and Their War Poems as Mr. Drinkwater Sees Them." *New York Times Review of Books* (9 May 1920): 235, 246.
    A positive review of *Picture Show.*

Hibberd, Dominic. "Some Notes on Sassoon's *Counter-Attack and Other Poems.*" *Notes and Queries* 29, No. 4 (August 1982): 341-2.
    Discusses the order of composition, revision, and publication of Sassoon's poetry in *Counter-Attack and Other Poems* as revealed in one of his wartime notebooks.

Johnston, John H. "Realism and Satire: Siegfried Sassoon." In his *English Poetry of the First World War: A Study in the Evolution of Lyric and Narrative Form,* pp. 71-112. Princeton, NJ: Princeton University Press, 1964.
    Provides an overview of the dominant themes, style, and artistic development of Sassoon's war poetry.

Lehmann, John. "Owen and Sassoon." In *The English Poets of the First World War,* pp. 37-62. New York: Thames and Hudson, 1981.
    Discusses the expression of Sassoon's war experiences in his poetry and Sassoon's association with Wilfred Owen.

Shawen, Edgar McD. "Sassoon's 'How to Die.'" *Explicator* 48, No. 3 (Spring 1990): 206-8.
    Offers brief critical analysis of the poem "How to Die."

Wilson, Edmund. "Two Books That Leave You Blank: Carson McCullers, Siegfried Sassoon." *New Yorker* (30 March 1946): 87-8.
    A negative review of *Siegfried's Journey.*

Additional coverage of Sassoon's life and career is contained in the following sources published by the Gale Group: *Contemporary Authors,* **Vols. 25-28R, 104;** *Contemporary Authors New Revision Series,* **Vol. 36;** *Dictionary of Literary Biography,* **Vols. 20, 191;** *DISCovering Authors: British; DISCovering Authors Modules: Most-studied Authors, Novelists,* **and** *Poets; Major 20th-Century Writers;* **and** *Poetry Criticism,* **Vol. 12.**

Léopold Sédar Senghor
1906-

(Also has written under pseudonyms Silmang Diamano and Patrice Maguilene Kaymor) Senegalese poet, essayist, nonfiction writer, and editor.

The following entry presents an overview of Senghor's career through 1996. For further information on Senghor's life and works, see *CLC,* Volume 54.

INTRODUCTION

One of the preeminent African intellectuals of the twentieth century, Senegalese poet and statesman Léopold Sédar Senghor is hailed as a powerful voice of postwar black cultural pride and self-determination. A leading proponent of negritude, a literary movement based on the repudiation of Western imperialism and the reclamation of Pan-African heritage, Senghor was instrumental in the cultivation of postcolonial aesthetics and black racial consciousness. His acclaimed verse in *Chants d'ombre* (1945), *Hosties noires* (1948), *Ethiopiques* (1956), and *Nocturnes* (1962) celebrates the cultural legacy of Africa while attempting to reconcile his affinity for European civilization with the devastating effects of its colonial policies. The recipient of numerous international honors and the first black person to be elected to the prestigious French Academy, Senghor was the first president of modern Senegal, a political position he served with distinction from 1960 to 1980.

BIOGRAPHICAL INFORMATION

Born in Joal, a predominantly Muslim district near the port city of Dakar in French West Africa, Senghor was one of two dozen children belonging to his father, a wealthy peanut farmer and exporter. Senghor was raised Roman Catholic by his mother, one of his father's several wives, and received his early education at mission schools. In 1922 he began studies at a junior seminary in Dakar where he studied Greek and Latin classics for four years. After his rejection as a candidate for the priesthood, he enrolled at the Lycée of Dakar where he won recognition as a brilliant student and graduated in 1928 with high honors and a scholarship to study in France. Though his traditional French education encouraged him to abandon his native roots, Senghor's exposure to the indigenous culture of his Serer ethnic ancestors exerted a lasting impression upon him during his formative years. While in Paris, Senghor came under the literary influence of the French symbolists, poets Paul Claudel and St. John Perse, and surrealist André Breton. He also encountered West Indian students Aimé

Césaire and Léon Damas who introduced him to the works of W. E. B. DuBois and Harlem Renaissance writers Claude McKay, Countee McCullen, and Langston Hughes. In 1933 Senghor became the first African to graduate from the Sorbonne with the *agrégé de grammaire,* the highest distinction of the French educational system. The next year Senghor, along with Césaire and Damas, co-founded *L'étudiant noir,* a journal devoted to black francophone literature and the elaboration of negritude, a term coined by Césaire. Upon the outbreak of World War II Senghor was called into service in the French Colonial Infantry. He was captured the next year during the German occupation of France and spent the next two years in a Nazi prison camp; he was subsequently awarded several military honors. After his release in 1942, he returned to teaching at the Lycée Marcelin Berthelot near Paris, participated in the French Resistance, and became increasingly active in politics.

The publication of *Chants d'ombre* in 1945 established him as a prominent spokesperson of negritude. Two years later he co-founded the literary journal *Présence africaine* with Alioune Diop. In 1946 Senghor married Ginette Eboue, the daughter of a Guyanese administrator; they divorced in 1956 and Senghor married Colette Hubert the next year. Senghor was elected as a delegate to the French National Assembly in 1946, founded the socialist party Bloc Démocratique Sénégalais in 1948, and held a succession of political posts in the French and Senegalese government until 1958. He presided over the legislative body of the Mali Federation, a Senegal-Sudan alliance that declared independence from France in 1959. When Senegal withdrew from the federation the next year, Senghor was elected as the first president of the newly established Republic of Senegal. Despite several attempted coups and civil unrest in Senegal during the late 1960s, Senghor was reelected in 1968 and 1973. During his two decades as president, he worked to stabilize Senegalese national politics, enact economic reforms, and establish a democratic socialist government. He sponsored the First World Festival of Negro Arts in 1966 and headed the formation of the West African Economic Community in 1974. Senghor resigned from office in 1980, becoming the first post-colonial African head of state to peacefully transfer power to a successor. Senghor has received numerous honorary degrees and in 1983 was named one of the forty "immortals" of the Académie Française.

MAJOR WORKS

As the leading theoretician of negritude, Senghor's poetry and prose is in large part an embodiment of the movement's evolving ideology—artistic, political, social, and economic—during the 1930s, 1940s, and 1950s. Rejecting the notion of European supremacy and the forced assimilation of Western culture among colonized Africans, Senghor and other negritude writers, mainly French-speaking African and Caribbean writers, sought to inspire renewed pride in the rich history and cultural tradition of Africa. Senghor's first poetry collection, *Chants d'ombre* (variously translated as "Songs of Shadow," "Shadow Songs," or "Songs of Darkness"), expresses his feelings of exile, cultural estrangement, aversion to the bondage of colonialism, and nostalgia for the African paradise of his childhood and ancestors. Though stylistically influenced by contemporary French poetry and the irrational imagery of surrealism, Senghor's trademark verse merges European forms and allusions with the language and spiritual motifs of African folk song. The controlled, musical rhythms and long, annunciatory lines of his poems, often prefaced with instructions for accompanying instruments, evoke the sounds and atmosphere of his native land and people. *Chants d'ombre* contains several of his best-known poems, including "Nuit de Sine" ("Night of Sine"), "Neige sur Paris" ("Snow Upon Paris"), "Masque négre" ("Black Masks"), and "Femme noir" ("Black Woman"), an exuberant paean to the beauty of African womanhood.

The poems of *Hosties noires* ("Black Sacrifice"), many of which were composed during his wartime captivity, signal Senghor's growing sense of purpose and racial identity.

Several of these, such as "Aux soldats Negro-Americains" ("To the American Negro Soldiers") and "Désespoir d'un volontaire libre" ("Despair of a Free Volunteer") extol the dignity of the African-American, West Indian, and Senegalese soldiers he befriended during the war. These poems also display Senghor's increasingly strident attacks on French colonialism and racial exploitation. In "Prière de paix" ("Prayer for Peace"), for example, he presents a litany of African degradation at the hands of unscrupulous and hypocritical Europeans, thinly tempered with a plea for divine forgiveness. Senghor also served as editor of *Anthologie de la nouvelle poésie nègre et malagache de langue française* (1948), a highly influential anthology of black francophone writers from Africa and the Caribbean. This volume, with its now famous introductory essay "Orphée noir" ("Black Orpheus") by existentialist philosopher Jean-Paul Sartre, became a defining work of the negritude movement. Senghor's third volume of poetry, *Chants pour Naëtt* (1949), contains a series of love lyrics dedicated to his first wife. Here, as in other poems by Senghor, the female subject of the poet's affection serves as a metaphor for Mother Africa.

The poems of *Ethiopiques,* written during his early political involvement, evince Senghor's abiding desire to bridge opposing aspects of European and African culture. In the long poem "Chaka," an adaptation of Thomas Mofolo's 1926 historical novel about a ruthless nineteenth-century Zulu chieftain, Senghor reflects upon the burdens of leadership, the necessity of sacrifice in the name of African unity, and his own persona as a "poet-politician." In "New York" Senghor calls for an end to the city's racial division and acceptance of African-American culture as a regenerative force. Senghor's conciliatory sentiments are also evident in "Epîtres à la Princesse" ("Letters to a Princess"), a sequence of poems describing an African man's romantic attachment to a European princess, representing an allegorical union between North and South that mirrors Senghor's marriage to second wife Colette, a white Frenchwoman. *Nocturnes,* published a year after Senghor was elected president of Senegal, contains a revision of *Chants pour Naëtt,* retitled *Chants pour Signare,* and a series of elegies that explore the nature of poetry and the creative process. Senghor's subsequent volumes of poetry include: *Lettres d'hivernage* (1973); *Elégies majeures* (1979), which contains "Elégie des Alizés" ("Elegy of the Trade Winds") and personal tributes to George Pompidou and Martin Luther King; and *Oeuvres poétique* (1991; *The Collected Poetry*), the definitive edition of Senghor's poetry. Senghor has also produced a large body of commentary on literary, political, and social subjects, including the essay collection *Ce que je crois* (1988) and three volumes under the heading *Liberté—Nation et voie africaine du socialisme* (1961; *On African Socialism*), *Negritude et humanisme* (1964; *Negritude and Humanism*), and *Négritude et civilisation de l'universel* (1977).

CRITICAL RECEPTION

Senghor is widely acclaimed as a poet of remarkable intelligence, versatility, and compassion. Critics consistently praise his ability to synthesize elements of Western and African experience and to evoke universality in the archetypal imagery of his verse, exemplified by "Black Woman," considered one of his finest early poems. His several major works from the 1940s and 1950s—*Chants d'ombre, Hosties noires, Chants pour Naëtt,* and *Ethiopiques*—are generally regarded as his most significant. He is also highly esteemed for his important work as editor of *Anthologie de la nouvelle poésie nègre et malagache de langue française,* which, as K. Anthony Appiah notes, "remains one of the models of African and Afro-Caribbean literary achievement." Critical evaluation of Senghor's poetry is inextricably linked to its basis in negritude, an ideology whose wide-reaching influence waned during the early 1960s, though reemerged in America as a progenitor of the Black Pride movement. While many commentators approve of Senghor's effort to relocate black self-identity and solidarity in traditional African culture, some regard the concept of negritude as a Western intellectual construct that misrepresents black experience and engenders its own harmful racism. In addition, Senghor's assimilation of French language and literature, as well as his Christian piety and remarriage to a white woman, have lead a minority of detractors to view his devotion to Africa with skepticism. However, as Ulli Beier asserts, "Senghor . . . is not merely a Frenchified African who tries to give exotic interest to his French poems; he is an African who uses the French language to express his African soul." Viewed as a prophet of reconciliation—racial, cultural, and political—Senghor is internationally respected for his overriding humanism and important contributions to the literature and politics of modern Africa.

PRINCIPAL WORKS

Chants d'ombre (poetry) 1945

Anthologie de la nouvelle poésie nègre et malagache de langue française [editor] (poetry) 1948

Hosties noires (poetry) 1948

Chants pour Naëtt (poetry) 1949

Ethiopiques (poetry) 1956

Rapport sur la doctrine et le programme du parti [*Report on the Principles and Programme of the Party;* also published as *African Socialism: A Report to the Constitutive Congress of the Party of African Federation*] (prose) 1959

Léopold Sédar Senghor (poetry and prose) 1961

Nation et voie africaine du socialisme [also published as *Liberté II: Nation et voie africaine du socialisme,* 1971; translated as *Nationhood and the African Road to Socialism* and *On African Socialism*] (prose) 1961

Nocturnes (poetry) 1962

Liberté I: Négritude et humanisme [*Freedom I: Negritude and Humanism*] (prose) 1964

Poèmes (poetry) 1964

Selected Poems (poetry) 1964

Prose and Poetry (prose and poetry) 1965

Elégie des Alizés [illustrated by Marc Chagall] (poetry) 1969

Lettres d'hivernage [illustrated by Marc Chagall] (poetry) 1973

Selected Poems/Poesies choises (poetry) 1976

Liberté III: Négritude et civilisation de l'universel (prose) 1977

Selected Poems of Léopold Sédar Senghor (poetry) 1977

Elégies majeures (poetry) 1979

Ce que je crois: Négritude, Francité et la civilisation de l'universel (essays) 1988

Oeuvre poétique [*The Collected Poetry*] (poetry) 1991

CRITICISM

Newsweek (review date 27 July 1964)

SOURCE: "In Praise of Negritude," in *Newsweek,* July 27, 1964, p. 80.

[*In the following review, the critic offers praise for Senghor's* Selected Poems.]

When a head of state so much as writes his own speeches, it is news; but when he writes a distinguished volume of poems, it is epochal. How often has it happened since King David?

Léopold Sédar Senghor is the President of the infant African Republic of Senegal, and a prominent theoretician who has contributed to black nationalism the world over one of its key terms and central concepts—*négritude.* Add to all this the fact that he is Africa's principal poet, and an important contemporary poet by any measure, and it is clear that the 58-year-old Senghor is perhaps the closest figure today to the Platonic ideal of the philosopher-king, the political leader who is also a thinker and artist. He is a figure unique in our time: and the American publication of his ***Selected Poems,*** translated from the original French, is a major event.

Like Walt Whitman, Senghor taps private sources deep within himself to discover in his experience the consciousness of his people and the drama of his continent. Blackness—"Negroness," *négritude*—pervades his poems like ancestral spirits, but it is experienced, not as a stigma or predicament, but as a benefaction and sign of grace. Conquest over despair, acceptance, and pride drive through the poems like a strong river, unifying them by its powerful currents.

Senghor's dialogue with France is a particular version of the black-white encounter. In the earlier poems, the poet feels himself exiled by his blackness, and returns home "seeking to forget Europe in the pastoral heart of Sine." Lonely, despised in Europe, he returns to his native village to "breathe the smell of our Dead, gather and speak out again their living voice, learn to / Live before I go down, deeper than diver, into the high profundities of sleep."

In a series of poems written in the '40s, Senghor conquers his "store of hatred against the diplomats who flash their long teeth / And tomorrow will barter black flesh." In the **"Prayer for Peace"** he finds that he is able to "pray especially for France," though the white oppressor "has stolen my children like a brigand . . . to fatten her cornfields and cottonfields, for the sweat of the Negro is dung."

The victory is achieved most notably in the brilliantly colored, chanting poems from the more recent volumes, *Éthiopiques* (1956) and *Nocturnes* (1961). In **"New York,"** a rhapsodic Whitmanesque poem driven by surging, powerfully cadenced lines, he sings the fusion of black and white—the ultimate fulfillment affected by the reconciliation of opposites: ". . . let the black blood flow into your blood / Cleaning the rust from your steel articulations, like an oil of life / . . . See, the ancient times come again, unity is rediscovered the reconciliation of the Lion the Bull and the Tree . . ." The poem ends on a note of consummation and confidence, the voice of the black poet in a black society deeply in possession of himself: "It is enough to open your eyes to the April rainbow / And the ears, above all the ears to God who with a burst of saxophone laughter created the heavens and the earth in six days. / And on the seventh day, he slept his great Negro sleep."

The final line of the final poem (**"Elegy of the Waters"**) falls from a crescendo of almost Biblical cadences to a calm climax which may stand as the motto-line for all of Senghor's poems: "And life is born again colour of whatever is." We may all refresh ourselves by those life-giving waters.

Gwendolyn Brooks (review date 13 September 1964)

SOURCE: "Singing Love Songs to a Continent," in *New York Herald Tribune Book Week*, September 13, 1964, p. 18.

[*In the following review, Brooks offers positive assessment of Senghor's* Selected Poems.]

Leopold Sedar Senghor, President of the Republic of Senegal, says that he is black. He enjoys the fact. Beyond the simple certainty, he feels, is humanity—to which blackness, brownness, whiteness, yellowness must be secondary.

His I-am-a-black-man, broadcast in a heat-suffused voice, is not a defensive claim. He invites the world to audit his negritude, because the world seems interested. But he does not whine, he does not pant for alms or pity. For what is there, he would ask, in or under his skin that requires these nuisances? He does regret the chasms between man

and man and he does rather believe that creative and public exchange is going to be possible.

As blazing company for this "blackness" urgency, Senghor has an assimilated respect for his art. He was happy to discover that he could sing. He was happy to discover himself in possession of a voice as remarkable for tenor flight as for baritone delve. He did not, however, let it go at that. He worked for technical subtlety. He achieved a language that is virile and beautiful; various, too, in spite of its firm devotion to Whitmanesque, abandon and straddle-stance. (Many of the verses are loved lassoes, managed, however, by a resourceful hand.) "Biblical" lifts and falls Senghor's music must have had in its infancy. But it is chiefly exquisite self-laceration that will produce the deceptive ease of these lines from **"Chaka"**:

> *A cackling farmyard, millet-eaters in a muffled cage.*
> *Yes a hundred glittering regiments, plush velvet silken plumes, gleaming with grease like red copper.*
> *I have set the axe to the dead wood, lit the fire in the sterile bush*
> *Like any careful farmer. When the rains came and the time for sowing, the ashes were ready.*

And these from **"To the American Negro Soldiers"**:

> *. . . their night fills with a sweetness of milk, the blue fields of the sky are covered with flowers, softly the silence sings.*
> *You bring the sun. The air throbs with liquid murmurs and crystalline whistling and the silky beat of wings Aerial cities are warm with nests.*

And the opening lines of **"Congo,"** an authentic and triumphant contrast to that monster of Vachel Lindsay's which purports to be "a study of the Negro race":

> *Oho! Congo oho! I move the voices of the koras of Koyate to make your great name their rhythm*
> *Over the waters and rivers, over all I remember (the ink of the scribe remembers nothing).*
> *Oho! Congo, asleep in your bed of forests, queen over Africa made subject*
> *Phalli of mountains, hold high your pavilion*
> *By my head by my tongue you are woman, you are woman by my belly*
> *Mother of all things in whose nostrils is breath, mother of crocodiles and hippopotami*
> *Manatees and iguanas, fishes and birds, mother of floods that suckle the harvests.*
> *Great woman! Water wide open to the oar and the canoe's stem*
> *My Sao my lover with maddened thighs, with long calm waterlily arms*
> *Precious woman of ouzougou, body of imputrescible oil, skin of diamantine night.*

Selections have been made from five books—*Chants D'Ombre* (1945), *Hosties Noires* (1948), *Chants Pour Naett* (1949), *Éthiopiques* (1956), and *Nocturnes* (1961). *Chants D'Ombre* illumines the frustrations of exiles, the desperate solitudes and languors of an African student in

Paris. Memory returns him to his childhood in the Senegalese village of Joal, where he was born and where he had a sense of belonging. His personal division symbolizes division between Africa and Europe (for the actual electricity of which, incidentally, France had no notion of training her semi-adoptee; Senghor's history includes service to the French government as a deputy to the French Assembly and Secretary of State for Scientific Research). *Hosties Noires* observes the African soldier's isolation, humiliation, fortitude. Here, too, the condition of the American Negro soldier is considered, with candor and in the spirit of wry comradeliness. *Chants Pour Naett,* pieces of which reappeared in *Nocturnes,* features love. A Senghor love poem will often seem as much a cry to the flesh and soul of Africa as to those of a woman. The voice of *Ethiopiques* is not only more dexterous but more self-conscious and more annunciatory than that of its predecessors. In *Nocturnes* Senghor is least public, and if his future route is to derive from this recent speech, the product may be what is currently referred to, with little respect, as "pure poetry." It is, of course, doubtful that life in our day will allow this to happen.

We are told nothing of the translators of this book of poems, his first to appear in America, and this is unfortunate. John Reed and Clive Wake contribute a helpful introduction which should be consulted after the poetry has been read. They assure us that they have adhered to the "detailed meaning" of the French text, and they believe that the result is "readable as English free verse poems." They have furnished a glossary to explain the African words used by the poet.

Senghor is a "literary" poet, in spite of the emotion-rich qualities of his several-faceted heritage, which easily might have induced him to favor more lenient rhythm and diction. His writing roots are French: even Whitman came to him indirectly, *via* his turn-of-the-century influence on the *vers libre* of France.

Able to depart in fury but also able to return, able to hack and heal, able to breathe, Senghor is a curious mosaic of flowers, disquiet, and masculine affirmation.

Robert W. July (review date 25 October 1964)

SOURCE: "Rolling Rhythms," in *New York Times Book Review,* October 25, 1964, p. 54.

[*In the following review, July offers praise for Senghor's Selected Poems.*]

Leopold Senghor, Africa's most celebrated exponent of negritude, has nowhere stated his philosophy more eloquently than in his hundred-odd poems published at intervals since 1945. Yet these major works of the philosopher-statesman of Senegal have been relatively unknown outside the French-speaking world for lack of adequate translation. It is a pleasure, therefore, to welcome

this volume which presents approximately one third of the poet's output in versions which are always careful and frequently as rich in imagery. If not quite as musical, as the originals.

The African quality of Senghor's poetry is easy to trace the rolling rhythms, the vivid evocation of smell, taste, and sound, the romantic dreamy sensuousness, the preoccupation with religion and the supernatural, the insistence on intuitive experience and sympathetic logic, and the ultimate appeal to nature in all its forms.

All this is poised against the materialist, irreligious, rationalist, machine-made West and the lesson is implicit: civilization can only be saved by cleaving to the essential truths of human existence still preserved in Africa. But this does not adequately explain Senghor's poetry which owes at least as much to the West as to Africa. Not only do we have the accomplished craftsman skilled in the tools of a western language and poetic form, but there are artistic and philosophic trends in Europe to be accounted for.

It is after all the music of the French language which sustains Senghor's lyricism. Further, it is through the highly polished French artistic tradition that we experience most clearly the soft scent of the tropical night and the cool rain on the hot land what is more reminiscent of Senghor, for example, than Ravel's three art Songs of Madagascar. Finally disillusionment with material plenty which leads only towards destruction and psychic emptiness is a western not an African, idea.

Ultimately however, the value of Senghor's poetry rests squarely on its own merits which are not parochial but universal. One cannot fail to respond to the quiet beauty of the "Night that dreams Leaning upon this hill of clouds, wrapped in its long milky cloth," to the sensuousness of "My Negress fan with palm oil. Slender as a plume. Thighs of a startled otter, of Kilimanjaro snow. Breasts of mellow rice fields hills of acacias under the East Wind," to the thudding rhythm of "Masks! Masks! Black mask, red mask, you white and black masks," or to the mystery and magic of "the hour of prima, terrors they rise from the bowels of the ancestors. Away inane and shadowy faces evil snout and evil breath." Thus the special pleading of negritude fades before the eloquence of the poet whose humanity represents and refreshes us all. It is the universal artist who speaks.

O. R. Dathorne (essay date 1974)

SOURCE: "Négritude and Black Writers," in *African Literature in the Twentieth Century,* University of Minnesota Press, 1974, pp. 217-48.

[*In the following excerpt, Dathorne discusses Senghor's interpretation of negritude, ancestral archetypes, and the intersection of Western and African influences in his poetry.*]

As has been suggested so far, négritude like Pan-Africanism was a Caribbean sickness. Only people unfamiliar with the norms of tribal life could have diagnosed in such wide conceptual terms a myth of the heart and boldly prescribed such an imaginative recovery. Senghor was Senegalese; he learned his négritude from *deraciné* West Indians, but to it he brought something new—the novelty of the initiated. He alone knew; they could only hazard guesses. Therefore it was in the language of Césaire and Damas that Senghor wrote that "those who colonised us justified our political and economic independence by the theory of *tabula rasa*. We had, they assessed, invented nothing, written nothing. We had neither carved, painted nor sung." Senghor adds that it was impossible to return to what he considered the sources of négritude and that the time of the Songhai Empire and of Chaka had passed. "We were students in Paris and students of the twentieth century," and this conflict is present in Senghor's verse from the very start. His evocations of Africa are in the Césairean manner, though at times perhaps they echo Damas. Later he would arrive at Claude Wauthier's conclusion that négritude could only be understood "in relationship with other people." At first, however, Senghor bluntly admitted that it was to some extent racism. Sartre commented that "because it is the tension between a nostalgic past into which the Black no more completely enters, and a future where it will give way to new values, Négritude fashions itself in tragic beauty and finds expression only in poetry." Earlier in the same essay, which prefaced Senghor's 1948 anthology, Sartre had contended that "we have one hemisphere with three concentric circles. At the periphery stretches the land of exile, colourless Europe. Next comes the dazzling circle of the Indies and of childhood, which dance the round in circling Africa. And then Africa, the last circle, navel of the world, pole of all black poetry . . . Africa beyond reach, imaginary continent." The Pan-Africanist C. L. R. James was to assert at the time that Sartre's "explanation of what he conceives *négritude* to mean is a disaster." But it must be realized that Sartre was mainly describing all the poets represented in Senghor's anthology, only six of whom were Africans. The majority of poets were West Indians who, according to an American writer, "for the most part are more intense in their reaction to the estrangement of the African in the West than the poets of the continent itself are." And, as has been seen, I have not attempted to argue against this contention.

Because of her failure to place négritude in a historical perspective, Lilyan Lagneau disagrees with Sartre. She maintains that Senghor had to make no great effort to retrieve his sources because "elles sont toutes proches et ont nourri sa jeunesse" (they were all near him and had been part of his youth). The imaginary continent was rightly, as she argues, "inventé par les Antillais au sein de leur exil" (invented by the West Indians on account of their exile). Senghor did, however, publish his first two volumes as a Black man in exile, a man who was formless and faceless and who pretended he had to invent a past. Indeed two recent compilers and translators of some of his poems in English believe that although "Senghor feels that his poetry is closer to folk poetry . . . [his] poetry is not folk poetry." The folk-poet takes his sources for granted; Senghor at times seem to flirt with the folk past.

What, then, is his poetry? Most of it is accompanied by an appropriate traditional instrument which sets the rhythm. He makes use of place names from his childhood—Cayor, Futa, Dyilor, Joal—as well as heroes of his tribe—Dyogoy, Sitor, Kumba, Siga. And to all this the belafong, kora, kalam, gorong, kama are supposed to be fitting complements. Senghor had some obvious advantages over his contemporaries because of his nearness to the object of recall and, perhaps more important, to the ancestor-image that frequently dominates his poetry as it does so much African literature. Nevertheless, the poetry is written in a European language, and one has to inquire how right W. E. Abraham was when he dismissed Senghor's poetry as "French verse interlarded with African allusions." This statement could be modified to include French verse written by other Black "Frenchmen" who made use of certain local Senegalese allusions.

His **"Nuit de sine"** from *Poèmes* (1964) portrays the African woman who in the poem archetypically symbolizes the omnipresence of death. Lines such as the following do not distinguish the poem as "Black" or "African."

> It is the time of the stars and the night which dreams
> Lying back on this hill of clouds, dressed in a gown of milk
> Houseroofs are gleaming gently. What are they saying with such confidence to the stars?
> Within, the hearth is put out amidst intimate bitter and sweet scents.

This could have been written by any European poet. The "s" sounds in the French convey the silence and privacy that the poet wishes to intensify, and it possesses none of the harshness of Césaire or the irony of Damas. Perhaps here the tiger does proclaim its tigritude. Were it not for other parts of the poem, however, this would be but a slight piece. The poem builds itself up through spirals of silence until at the apex an unnamed woman and man emerge. References to palm trees, dark blood, forests, children on their mothers' backs, the ancients of Elissa, the smoky hut identify an African (Senegalese) locality. But the high point of the poem is achieved when Senghor switches from the formless to the formed, ditching the descriptive element that has no place in the traditional love for humanizing the abstract.

> Woman, light the lamp of clear oil and let the children, like their parents, talk about their ancestors.
> Listen to the voice of the Ancestors of Elissa. Like us exiled
> They did not wish to die, to lose their seminal flow in dust.
> Let me listen too in the smoky hut for the phantom visit of propitious souls
> My head glistens on your breast like a kuskus ball smoking out of the fire

Let me breathe the smell of our Dead Ones, let me
recall and repeat their living accents, let me learn
To live before I go down, deeper than the diver, into
the deep darkness of sleep.

Here is expressed the theme of exile; the themes of Damas
and Césaire are apparent, but uppermost is the eternal
presence of the ancestors, who, together with the protagonist and the children, form links in the chain of humanity.
This part of the poem succeeds best; in it we see the
African writer who exists with a past that is never past.
The comparison of the dead and the exiled living is a
forced one and indeed does not make sense logically
within the poem or within the framework of the culture
recalled by the poet. To say that the ancestors did not wish
to die just as Senghor and his student-friends did not wish
to be exiled from their cultures is wrong. The importance
of the ancestors is in their immortality, in the fact that they
did die but continue to live. Puny comparisons with the
predicament of Paris students humiliate the ancestor-
archetype.

Clearly the most noteworthy point to emerge here is that
within a French poem Senghor introduces a note that no
European or West Indian poet could have struck. Though
he was westernized and had been taught of the eternal
permanence of matter, his African instincts, in addition,
continuously assured him of the indestructible spirit of
man. What Senghor is therefore attempting is for him the
obvious—the invoking of the ancestor and the presence of
the Vital Force in everything, about which Fr. Placide
Tempels and Alexis Kagamé have also written.

More obviously but no less powerfully, Birago Diop
dramatizes the ancestor-theme in his poem "Souffles."

Those who are dead have never really gone away
They are at the Woman's breast
They are in the Child's weeping
And in the firebrand bursting into life
The Dead are not under the Ground.

Earlier in the same poem Birago Diop asserts, "Les Morts
ne sont pas morts" (the dead are not dead). It is no accident that in the lines just quoted archetypal mother and
child provide a similar link with the apparent dead, as is
true as well in Senghor's poetry. Birago Diop returns to
this theme in "Viatique," another successful poem in *Leu-
rres at Lueurs* (1960), where one learns of the "ancêtres
qui furent des hommes" (the ancestors who were men). It
was a subject that Senghor found lacking in Césaire, as he
says in his **"Lettre à un poète,"** dedicated to Césaire,
"Have you forgotten your nobility, which is to celebrate /
The Ancestors, the Princes and the Gods. . . ." Senghor
failed to realize that Césaire did not have either ancestors,
princes, or gods. All Césaire could do was bemoan their
loss. But it was with this voice that Senghor and Diop
were able—despite their identification—to divorce
themselves from Caribbean writers and to announce their
place in the cosmos of African reality. Sartre admired this
quality in Diop's poetry "because it speaks directly from

the tribal story-tellers and in the same oral tradition."
Though Sartre's contention is not entirely true, it is certain
that the bulk of Diop's work is an attempt, in Senghor's
phrase, to return to the sources. Diop's contribution will
be assessed more fully when we come to consider his
prose.

The ancestor-theme in Senghor as well as in other African
writers often gives way to the emergence of the stereotype.
"Femme noire," which characterizes the eternal woman,
is just this. Written in the form of a praise song, it is
nevertheless a startling departure, for traditional praise
songs never extolled the beauty of women. But like the
praise singer the poet assumes the role of custodian of the
culture.

I sing your beauty which passes and fix your form in
eternity
Before a jealous Fate reduces you to ashes to nourish
the roots of life.

Through the object of praise Senghor comes nearer to an
understanding of himself. The manner in which the woman
experiences her world is meant to show her familiarity
with it. We find therefore that the poem is a very sensuous
one; the sight of the sun and shadow in the first stanza, the
sound of the East wind, the tom-tom, and the lover in the
second bring us closer to the *felt* nature of the experience.

The Black woman in Senghor's poetry is a synthesis of
mother and lover. In this way she is equated with the land,
with harvest and drought; she is both giver and receiver.
Therefore she best appeals to Senghor's poetic demands.
As a mere consumer of French culture, must he be driven
to the despair of Césaire and Damas, or could the African
presence give his poetry more vitality and a source of
positive values?

Some parts in **Chants pour Naëtt** (1949) provide an
answer to this question. The solution was not the total
rejection of the white world and acceptance of the African
world, but the blending of both. This is what Mbella Sonne
Dipoko referred to as the point at which "cultural negotiations are about to open . . . a meeting-place, a compromise, was agreed upon." In the same context, Senghor
wrote that the hero of Peter Abrahams's *Wreath for Udomo*
is "a tissue of contradictions [for he] tyrannically loves his
black Africa, and he loves a white woman." It was to Césaire's "rendez-vous de la conquête" that Senghor had
come in this verse in **Poèmes:**

And we have delighted, my love, in an African pres-
ence
Furniture from Guinea and Congo, heavy and polished,
dark and light.
Masks primitive and pure on walls distant yet so near.
Tabourets of honour for the hereditary hosts, the
princes from the High-Country.
Wild perfumes from the thick tresses of silence
Cushions of darkness and leisure like the source of
quiet wells.
Eternal words; faraway the alternating chant as in

cloths from Sudan.
And then the friendly light of your kindness will soften
the obsession of this presence in
Black, white and red oh red like the soil of Africa.

Here the poet frankly admits that the past was an invented one for the négritude poets. Senghor differed from them in that, though he began with their conclusions, he escaped their bitterness and turned toward the familiar. At the center was always man, the poet-hero himself.

Senghor's method and manner continue in subsequent volumes. The local Africa is used to describe the general, the symbolic, woman. Less of his vituperation is present in *Nocturnes* (1961). He has come a long way from his *Hosties noires* (1948), which is essentially made up of war poems exploring the love-hate relationship with France. He recognizes his "frères noirs" (Black brothers) but adds "ne dites pas que je n'aime pas la France" (do not say I do not love France). Damas described "cousin Hitler" in one poem but Senghor, as both soldier and prisoner of war, could acknowledge France while still retaining an element of "la voix de l'Afrique planant au-dessus de la rage des canons longs" (the voice of Africa sounding near the rage of long cannons). By the time of *Nocturnes* the reconciliation between the spiritual longing for Africa and the physical need for Europe was complete. Senghor is no longer capable of writing purely love poems like those in *Chants pour Naëtt* or poems solely concerned with the backward glance to Africa. In *Nocturnes* he reaches the poetic equivalent of what in his essays he calls humanism and he further develops the idea expressed in **"Chaka"** (*Ethiopiques,* 1956) that poetry must now be sacrificed in the same way that Chaka had to sacrifice No-livé. The **"Elégies"** in *Nocturnes* conclude the poetic quest for pacification. The world is one and man and child are indivisible. Chaka's words could well be Senghor's:

> Here I am re-joined with the earth. How shiny in the Kingdom of childhood
> And it is the end of my passion.

The poetry had completed a circle, coming back to the childhood of a movement, a race, a person for verification. Senghor's conclusion is probably again Chaka's—"Mais je ne suis pas le poème, mais je ne suis pas le tam-tam / Je ne suis pas le rythme . . ." (But I am not the poem, nor am I the drum / I am not the rhythm . . .). Senghor has liberated the Black poet from his dilemma, the imaginative writer has become more than the agent for executing a people's art. Such a writer can no longer dictate to his audience and the debate has ended. There remains, however, the next task, which offers a wide spectrum of possibilities. Senghor not only is exposing the African writer to the dialogue of the whole world but is also asking him to be a witness to private areas of experience.

Lilyan Kesteloot (essay date 1974)

SOURCE: "Léopold Senghor: *Chants d'ombre* and *Hosties noires,*" in *Black Writers in French: A Literary History of Negritude,* translated by Ellen Conroy Kennedy, Temple University Press, 1974, pp. 194-226.

[*In the following excerpt, Kesteloot provides analysis of Senghor's formative influences, African themes, and early poetic style in* Chants d'ombre *and* Hosties noires.]

Léopold Sédar Senghor was attracted to poetry very early. As a lycée student in Dakar, he was composing romantic verse even before he developed an enthusiasm for Corneille and Racine. In Paris, Senghor discovered Péguy, then the modern European and American Negro poets. Later on, while studying for his degree in literature, he read the works of the medieval troubadors and a great deal of Claudel, but experimented with his own talent as a writer mainly by translating into French the poems of his homeland, Senegal.

Much has been made of the profound influence of Saint-John Perse on Senghor. In the part of this chapter devoted to literary analysis, we shall show to what extent the discovery of Saint-John Perse influenced Senghor's style. Senghor did not yet know Perse's work when he composed his own first two books of poems, **Chants d'ombre** and **Hosties noires,** whose major themes we now propose to analyze.

These poems were written between 1936 and 1945, not all at once like Césaire's *Cahier,* but at long intervals. Nor do they follow a psychological progression, like Damas's poems. Only a few of them are dated. Though we can place in time those which were written during World War II and perceive a definite evolution in the thinking, this is possible only occasionally in the other poems. The very first poem, **"A l'appel de la race de Saba,"** which dates from 1936, already reveals the principal themes of Senghor's entire work.

The downbeat of Senghor's negritude is unquestionably his "pilgrimage to the ancestral fountains," his return to Mother Africa, for him not at all "the imaginary continent" invented by West Indians in the depths of their exile. Senghor did not need to make a great effort to rediscover his origins; they were close to him and nourished his youth. He had the privilege of being born in 1906 to a family of very un-Europeanized landowners who lived in an opulent "villa" that sheltered more than sixty persons, including servants. For many years he lived in Djilor and Joal, rural Senegalese villages, and did not attend a "white school" until the age of seven, when he entered the seminary at Ngasobil; he later on went to Dakar for his Latin humanities. During that period, he used to come home to the village for his vacations.

Senghor thus knew his country, his "childhood kingdom," as he called it, extremely well, and was impregnated with its culture.

> J'y ai vécu jadis, avec les bergers et les paysans . . .
> J'ai donc vécu en ce royaume, vu de mes yeux, de mes oreilles entendu les êtres fabuleux par delà les choses:

les Kouss dans les tamariniers, les Crocodiles, gardiens des fontaines, les Lamantins, qui chantaient dans la rivière, les Morts du village et les Ancêtres, qui me parlaient, m'initiant aux vérités alternées de la nuit et du midi. Il m'a donc suffi de nommer les choses, les éléments de mon univers enfantin, pour prophétiser la Cité de demain, qui renaîtra des cendres de l'ancienne, ce qui est la mission du poète.

(I lived there long ago, among the shepherds and the farmers . . . I lived then in this kingdom, saw with my eyes, with my ears heard the fabulous beings beyond things; the ancestral spirits [the *Kouss*] in the tamarind trees; the crocodiles, guardians of the springs; the sea-cows who spoke to me, initiating me in turn to the truths of night and noon. It has therefore been enough for me to name these things, the elements of my childhood universe, to prophesy the City of tomorrow, which shall be born from the ashes of the ancient, which is the poet's mission.)

[Subsequent quotations from Senghor's original French prose and poetry are provided in English translation only; the French text has been omitted, except where the mechanics of the French language are specifically discussed.]

Senghor was rooted in this civilization which had survived the ancient Mali empire, assimilating both Islam and Christianity without losing any of its original traditions. His Africa was living, profuse, completely unlike Césaire's ("Bambara ancestors," his evocation of "the king of Dahomey's amazons") or Damas's ("till now I've kept the conical ancestral faith high among the rafters of my hut"), visions of a mother continent reduced to ethnological reminiscence or disembodied symbols.

Senghor's return to his native land was thus accomplished without any of the pain typical among the West Indians. His were only pleasant memories of a coddled childhood in the bosom of a family which formed a "large household, with its grooms, stablemen, shepherds, servants, and artisans."

At nightfall, the house at Djilor was a veritable painting of biblical opulence.

[Dimly I am on the steps of the deep house
My brothers and sisters press their incubating warmth
against my heart
I rest my head upon the knees of Ngâ my nurse, Ngâ
the poetess
Head throbbing with the warrior gallop of the dyoung-dyoung drums, with the racing of my blood's pure
blood
Head humming with the distant songs of Koumba—
the Orphan Girl
In the center of the court the solitary fig tree
And chatting in its moonlit shade the Man's wives,
voices grave and deep as their eyes and the nighttime
fountains of Fimla.
And my father stretched out on peaceful mats so tall
so strong so handsome a
Man of the Kingdom of Sine, while about him on
their köras, griots with heroic voices make their ardent
fingers dance
While from afar with a sense of warm strong smells
the classic sound of a hundred cattle rises.]

Senghor conserves the memory of a society deeply rooted in its traditions, its values and its history. One can certainly detect the traces of ethnology. It was surely not from the griots that Senghor learned that Pharoah "seated people on his right" or that the glorious Gongo Moussa reigned from 1307 to 1332. But certainly local myths and the genealogies of the dyalis sang the glory of his forbears, who were cousins of Prince Koumba Ndofène, and recounted the sixteen-year struggle against the powerful Almamy of Fouta Djalon.

[They slaughter us, Almamy! We are not dishonored.
Neither could these mountains rule us, nor his horse-men surround us, nor his bright skin seduce us
Nor his prophets corrupt us.]

Two princesses of royal blood and their servants were able to escape the massacre:

[And among them the mother of Sira-Badral, founder
of kingdoms,
Who would be the salt of the Serers, the salt of these
salty people]

This historical past explains the moral values of that warrior and pastoral people—sobriety, a sharp sense of honor, scorn of money but love of the vital riches, children, and cattle:

[. . . sparse were the wants of their bellies.
Their shield of honor never left them nor their loyal
lance
They amassed no silks not even cottons to decorate
their darlings.
Their herds covered their lands, like their dwellings in
the divine shade of fig trees
And their granaries creaked with grain stowed by
children.
Voices of the Blood! Thoughts to ruminate upon!]

A simple and vigorous morality which was developed in an harmonious social order—disparaged by the West for reasons of their own—where the prince was not a tyrant but the defender and guarantor of his subjects:

[You are no parasitic plant on the vegetable abundance
of your people!
They lie; you are no tyrant, you do not feed yourself
upon their fat
You are the rich instrument of savings, granaries swollen for the days of sorrow
. . . .
Behold you are upright, fortress to keep the enemy at
bay
I do not call you silo but chief who gathers up the
strength who strengthens the arm, but head who
receives the blows and bullets
And you do honor to your people . . .]

Religious values give meaning to this universe and animate the cosmic life. The ancients initiate the young to these "forests of symbols" whose poetry Senghor feels extremely deeply. The following poem, perhaps one of the most beautiful he has written, bears witness:

[Toko-Waly, my uncle, do you remember those long
ago nights when my head grew heavy on your patient
back?
Or how you took my hand in yours and guided me
through signs and shadows?
The fields blossom with glow worms; stars alight in
grass and trees.
There is silence all around
The only stirrings are the perfumes of the bush, hives
of russet bees that dominate the crickets
And, muffled tom-tom, the distant breathing of the
night.
You Toko-Waly, you hear what is inaudible
And explain to me the signs our forbears make in the
marine serenity of the constellations
The Bull, the Scorpion, the Leopard, the Elephant and
the familiar Fish
And the Spirits' milky splendor in the infinite celestial
tann.
But here as veils of darkness fall is the Goddess
Moon's intelligence.]

The poet, like every other African, learned nature's
language very early and lived in close relationship to
Ancestors, whom he held in veneration:

[I stretch upon the earth at your feet, in the dust of my
respect
At your feet, Ancestors who are present. . . .]

He knew that the dead were not dead, that he himself was
the "the grandfather of his grandfather . . . his soul and
his ancestry," and he kept preciously secret "in [his] most
intimate vein" the name of his totem, "My ancestor with
the lightning-scarred, the stormy skin," the third name
given at his initiation, which no African dares reveal for
fear of putting himself in the hands of an enemy. Senghor
acquired this knowledge during the long nights of Sine,
nights which he evokes with warm fervor:

[Woman, light the limpid butter lamp, so around it
Ancestors can come to chat like parents when their
children are in bed.
Let us listen to the Ancients of Elissa. Exiled, like us,
They did not wish to die, or lose their fertile torrent in
the sands.
Let me listen in the smoky hut where friendly souls
have come to visit
My head upon your breast, warm as *couscous* newly
steaming from the fire
Let me breathe the odor of our Dead, let me gather
and repeat their living voices, let me learn
To live before I sink, deeper than a diver, into the
lofty depths of sleep.]

The nearness of the dead in no way depreciates life. Senghor tastes its fruits both as poet and artist. **Chants d'ombre**
contains at least eight love poems, of which the most
famous glorifies **"Black woman"**:

[Naked woman, dark woman
Firm fleshed ripe fruit, dark ecstasies of black wine,
mouth that makes mine lyrical;
Savanna with pure horizons, trembling at the ardor of

the East Wind's touch
Sculpted tom-tom, taut tom-tom murmuring beneath
the Conqueror's fingers]

But in addition to love, there were the festivals, high points
of community life, where Christian rites and native
ceremonies mingled:

[I remember funeral feasts steaming with the blood of
slaughtered herds
The noise of quarrels, the griot's rhapsodies.
I remember pagan voices beating out the *Tantum Ergo,*
And the processions and the palms and the triumphal
arches.
I recall the dance of the nubile girls
The battle songs—and oh!—the final dance of the
young men, slender
Chests bent, and the women's pure love cry—*Kor
Siga!*]

Yes, Africa truly lives in Senghor's poems! Yet he left it
"for sixteen years of wandering" through a Europe he
learned to know firsthand "in the narrow shadow of the
Latin Muses," before becoming "a shepherd of blonde
heads" at the lycée in Tours, and later in Paris: "good civil
servant . . . good colleague, elegant, polite . . . Old
France, old university, the works." To all appearances,
Senghor was perfectly assimilated.

Then why his unusual activity with *L'Etudiant Noir?* Why
his defense of Africanism and support of anticolonialism
as early as 1928? For personal reasons, first of all. In
Europe, Senghor felt lonely. There were very few African
students in Paris in those days. Most of the blacks there
were West Indians, and although they succeeded in creating a unity around a New Negro ideology, the various
mentalities differed on many points. Damas regretted that
he had never had a free childhood. Césaire—whose wife
was expecting a second baby when the *Cahier* was
published—was not homesick for his country but wished
to transform it: His memories were painful. As for the
solitary Senghor, "left to the hypocritical silence of this
European night, held prisoner by white, cold, well-
smoothed sheets and all the anguish and qualms which
inextricably encumber me," he turned to the "paradise of
his African childhood," to his friends there, crying out his
immense nostalgia:

[I write to you because my books are white as
boredom, misery and death.
Make room for me around the pot, let me sit once
more in the place still warm for me,
Hands touching as we share the rice that steams with
friendship.
Let the old Serer words pass from mouth to mouth
like a friendly pipe.
May Dargui share his juicy fruits with us—a harvest
of all scented dryness!
You, serve us your good words, as big as the umbilicus
of prodigious Africa.
What singer will call the Ancestors tonight,
Will bring the peaceful jungle beasts about us?
Who will send our dreams to lodge beneath the eyelids
of the stars?]

But these too tangible memories make his exile seem more terrible and intensify his homesickness:

> [I remember, I remember . . .
> My head in motion with
> What weary pace the length of European days where now and then
> An orphan jazz appears sobbing sobbing sobbing.]

Beneath his European clothes, Senghor felt like a foreigner. How far he was from his own clothes, from his own customs! The reproach Senghor puts on the lips of a Senegalese prince in his poem **"Le message"** testifies to his ridiculous appearance as a man "assimilated and uprooted":

> [Children with short memories, what did the kôras sing to you?
> You decline the rose, they tell me, and your ancestors the Gauls.
> You are doctors of the Sorbonne, paunchy with diplomas
> You collect pieces of paper
> Your daughters they tell me paint their faces like whores
> They wear their hair in chignons, go in for free love to elucidate the race!
> Are you happier? Some trumpet goes wa-wa-wa
> And you weep there on the great holiday and family feasts.
> Must the ancient epic story be unfurled for you?
> Go to Mbissel and Fa'oy; say the rosary of the sanctuaries that marked out the Great Way
> Walk upon the royal road again and meditate upon the way of cross and glory.
> Your high priests will answer: Voices of the Blood!]

Yet Senghor's stay in France was far from useless. First, it taught him where his heart was; second, that the suffering of his race was vast. As a child, Senghor had been so happy and docile by nature that he had never criticized his teachers. In Paris, the contact with French intellectuals and West Indians and Americans of his race awakened his conscience. At the Lycée Louis-le-Grand, he was first listed among the "talas," but then he went through a violent crisis and became a socialist. It was then that he met Aimé Césaire, whose rebellion had begun to smoulder while he was still in Martinique. Along with Césaire, Senghor questioned Western values to such a point that for more than a year he lost his religious faith.

All the themes of present-day negritude appear in Senghor's work from this moment on. First, the affirmation of his color! This is clearly shown in the titles of his poems: *Chants d'ombre* ("Shadow songs," or "Songs of darkness")—*Hosties noires* ("Black hosts" or "Black victims")—**"A l'appel de la race de Saba"** (**"At the call of the race of Saba"**)—**"Masque nègre"** (**"Negro mask"**)—**"Femme noire"** (**"Black woman"**), etc. Second, the feeling of solidarity with all oppressed peoples of the world. It has been said that Senghor was moved by the poverty and misery of the proletariat before becoming aware of the passion of his own race. Certainly, however, one encounters his loyalty to his original culture even in his first poem:

> [I do not erase the footsteps of my father nor of the fathers of my fathers in my head open to the winds and plunderers of the North.
> . . . .
> May my guardian spirits not permit my blood to grow insipid like some assimilated, civilized soul.]

His wish for the liberation of Africa can be seen as a proletarian emancipation where there would be

> [Neither masters any more nor slaves nor knights nor griots of griots
> Nothing but the smooth and virile camaraderie of battles
> And may the son of the captive be my equal the Moor and Targui, those congenital enemies, my companions.]

Senghor included in this struggle

> [. . . all white workers in the fraternal struggle
> the miner from Asturia, the Liverpool docker,
> the Jew chased out of Germany, and Dupont and Dupuis
> and all the boys from Saint Denis.]

And hailed it with the classical slogan (printed in capital letters):

> L'AUBE TRANSPARENTE D'UN JOUR NOUVEAU.
>
> [THE TRANSPARENT DAWN OF A NEW DAY.]

Only later was Senghor to realize the particular oppression of which his race had been the victim: slavery, the looting of Africa, the humiliation and servitude of colonization. Gradually, he too accepted these, and to the general indictment against Europe he would add the ancient wounds

> [. . . of a land emptied of its sons
> Sold at public auction cheaper than herring, and with nothing left but its honor.]

He denounced

> [White hands that pulled the trigger on guns that crushed empires
> Hands that whipped slaves, that whipped you
> White powdery hands that slapped you, painted powdery hands that slapped me
> Sure hands that delivered me to solitude and hate
> . . . diplomats who show white teeth
> And tomorrow will barter black flesh.]

Senghor learned all this and would not forget it, even if he did not wish to "bring out his stock of hatred." Too often he has been called the man of conciliation. His words of peace ("Oh! do not say that I do not love France") have been boasted of in contrast to those of his rebellious brothers, particularly Césaire. The indictment against colonization that runs throughout Senghor's poems, however, is not so easily overlooked. His disillusioned contempt of the "mud of civilization" which dehumanizes "the boulevard crowds" of Europe, "sleepwalkers who have rejected their identity as men," as well as Africa, where "on the Sudanese plain, desiccated by the East Wind and the Northern masters of Time," men deprived of freedom are slowly suffocating, are too quickly forgotten.

[. . . nothing but sand taxes forced labor the whip
And spittle the only dew for their inextinguishable thirst in memory of green Atlantic pastures
For barrages of engineers have not satisfied the thirsty souls in polytechnic villages.]

Senghor's bitterness, increased by his personal experience of segregation, has never been sufficiently recognized:

[I no longer recognize my brothers, the white men,
Lost as they were this evening at the films, beyond the emptiness they left about my skin.]

In the crucible of war, Senegalese soldiers were "caught in the toils, delivered to civilized barbarity, exterminated like warthogs" or abandoned at the time of France's downfall in 1940 and deposited in German prison camps:

[Hunger and hatred fermented there in the torpor of one mortal summer.
. . . .
And noble warriors were begging cigarette butts]

And the Negro continued to do K. P. and latrine duty for the "great pink children." "Who else but the high born will do the lowly jobs?" asks Senghor. But his witticism hides only thinly a pain and bitterness he was not always able to contain:

[Europe has crushed me like the flat warrior beneath the pachydermal feet of tanks

We cried out our pain in the night. Not a single voice gave answer.
The Princes of the Church were silent, statesmen claimed the hyenas were magnanimous
"It certainly concerns the Negro! It certainly concerns mankind! Not when Europe is involved!"]

To present Senghor as a tender elegiac, as Aimé Patri has done, is to weaken him. Can he have forgotten Senghor's shouts of virile rebellion?

[. . . I shall tear the banana laughter from all the walls of France

Forward! And may there be no song of praise o Pindare! But shaggy war shout and quick sword thrust!]

To call Senghor a "man of civilization" seems to us ambiguous. The last poem in *Hosties noires,* although entitled **"Prière de paix"** (**"Prayer for peace"**), is the one with the most violent accusations. Reading it, one realizes to what extent the poet's "pardon" is the opposite of "compromise." Senghor forgives while remaining very much aware of his race's suffering and the misdeeds of political and missionary France. His forgiveness is great only because it is offered with complete lucidity:

[At the foot of my Africa, crucified these four hundred years yet breathing still
Lord, let me repeat its prayer of pardon and of peace.

Lord God, forgive white Europe!
It is true, Lord, that for four centuries of enlightenment she threw her yelping, foaming dogs upon my lands
. . . .
Lord, forgive those who made guerrillas of the Askias, who turned my princes into sergeants,
Made houseboys of my servants, and laborers of my country folk, who turned my people into a proletariat.
For you must forgive those who hunted my children like wild elephants
Who trained them to the whip and made them the black hands of those whose hands were white.
You must forget those who stole ten million of my sons in their leprous ships
And who suppressed two hundred million more.
A lonely old age they've made me in the forest of my nights and the savannah of my days.
The glass before my eyes grows misty, Lord.
And the serpent Hatred stirs his head within my heart, the Serpent I'd thought dead . . .

Kill it, Lord, for I must proceed upon my way and strangely, it is for France I want to pray.
Lord, among the white lands, set France upon the Father's right.
Oh, I know she too is Europe, she too like some northern cattle rustler raped my children to swell the cane and cotton fields, for negro sweat is like manure.
. . . .
Yes, Lord, forgive France, who expresses the right way so well and makes her own so deviously
Who invites me to her table, and tells me to bring my own bread, who gives with her right hand while the left takes half back again.
Yes, Lord, forgive France, which hates all occupations and imposes hers so heavily on me
Who throws open her triumphal routes to heroes and treats her Senegalese like hired hands; making them the black dogs of her empire
Who is the Republic and delivers her countries to the concessionary companies
That have made my Mesopotamia, the Congo, a vast cemetery beneath the white sun.]

It was not that Senghor made peace with the West over the dead bodies of his victimized race, but that war had revealed to him all the horror of racism. The spectacle of French people in their turn bruised and ravaged and struggling against oppression enabled him to rise above his resentment and to recognize aspects of France he could love—the faces of its suffering:

[The fiancée who mourns her widowhood
The boy robbed of his youth
And the woman weeping, oh, for her husband's absent eye, and the mother seeking her child's dream among the rubble.]

and that of its freedom:

[Bless these captive people who twice have known how to liberate their lands and dared proclaim the advent of the poor to those of royal lineage

. . . .
. . . .

Bless these people who break their bonds, bless these people reduced to their last extremity who confront the wild greed of the powerful, the torturers.]

This is why Senghor forgives more easily than Damas or Césaire—also, because he benefits from that basic psychological equilibrium due to his happy childhood and, in addition, because he feels strong with the strength of Africa's future.

But if, for the edification of a world henceforth without hate or racism, Senghor asks his Dead, "Oh, black Martyrs, let me say the words of forgiveness," it is not a matter of forgetting blood so abundantly spilled, but rather one of making it bear fruit.

[No, you have not died in vain, O Dead! This blood is no tepid water.
It moistens our thick hope which will blossom at twilight.
It is our thirst, our hunger for honor, those great absolute queens.
No, you did not die in vain. You are the witnesses of Africa immortal.]

Senghor's devotion to his people remains total. It was to the black lands he came in search of "earthy virtues" to arm himself with the qualities of Sudanese heroes, with the "fervent science of Timbuctoo's great doctors" and the "courage of the Guelwars." To dedicate himself, this modern knight spontaneously rediscovered the religious tone appropriate to solemn oaths: "Permit me to die for the cause of my people." What love for the race whose ambassador he aspires to be, what faith in its reserves of life, joy and hope!

[You are the flesh of the primitive couple, the fertile belly, the soft roe

Like the leaven necessary to white flour.
For who shall teach rhythm to a world dead from cannon and machine?
Say who shall revive the memory of life to the man with disemboweled hope?
They call us men of cotton, coffee, oil.
. . . .
We are men of the dance whose feet take on new strength by striking the hard ground.]

When Senghor declares his conviction that "any great civilization, any true culture is the result of cross-breeding," we must not infer from this that he wished to give up any of the African Negro values nor that he was disposed to welcome everything Europe might offer.

The problem we blacks of 1959 now face is to discover how we are going to integrate *African Negro values* into the world of 1959. It is not a question of resuscitating the past, of living in an African Negro museum; it is a question of animating the world, *here and now,* with the values of our past. This, after all, is what the Negro Americans have begun to do.

Senghor does not fail to warn African politicians that "cultural colonialism, in the form of assimilation, is the worst of all." And if today he declares himself in favor of mixed civilizations, this involves—to use his own expression—"confrontation" and "symbiosis." As in Hegelian synthesis, the two contrary assertions—Negro values and Western values—must purify each other, retaining only the best traits of each, in order to achieve the harmonious amalgamation desired by Senghor.

Senghor has a style as different from his confreres as it is possible to imagine. His poems are more elaborated. He knows them by heart and willingly recites them, being somewhat the "man of letters." Like all true poets, however, he composes in response to an inner need. To sing, he must feel deeply moved. He writes his poem in a single outpouring, then reads it, seeks the high points and sometimes the meaning, because when he takes up his pen he does not always know what he will write.

The poems in **Chants d'ombre** and **Hosties noires** quickly attained the breadth of those of his mature period; the well-formed characteristics of Senghor's style are already recognizable.

In the poems one finds a universe where the harmonious background of his Senegalese childhood—the Ancients of Elissa, Joal-the-Shady, the kings of Sine, the griots, the dances, the great house at Djilor, and the black woman with "hands with the scent of balsam"—become corroded by the anxieties of a Prodigal Son torn between two cultures who laments, threatens, or forgives, but who, whether happy or bruised, always returns to drink deep at the fountain of Kam-Dyamé near his "sober-eyed ancestors who understand all things."

We discover a sensuous love of his country's names, names of places and people that have solemn and mysterious sonorities:

[Dyob!—from the Nagabou to the Walo, from Ngalam to the sea the songs of amber virgins will rise
And may the stringed kôras accompany them! . . .

You among all Elephant of Mbissel, who adorn your poet-praise maker with friendship

I recall the splendors of the setting sun
From which Koumba N'Dofene would have cut his royal cloak]

Next his marked taste for transpositions, which lighten biblical-style verses:

[How vast how empty the courtyard with the smell of nothingness

The golden note of the flute of silence leads me, the shepherd, my long ago dream brother leads me

And the warm ashes of the man-with-lightning-eyes, my father, tremble.]

We said that Senghor had read and imitated a good deal. If we recognize from time to time definite analogies with Claudel or Saint-John Perse—it should be remembered that his discovery of the latter occurred considerably after his first poems—we must not forget the influence of Senegalese poets, whose literary methods he assimilated. Senghor's manner of celebrating in song a person he wishes to honor, for example, is the same as that of the Senegalese griots, for whom the repetition of a name is as important as the praise itself and who never fail to call upon the meritorious ancestors:

[Sall! I proclaim your name Sall! from the Fouta-Damga to Cap Vert

Mbaye Dyob! I want to speak your name and tell your worth

And I repeat your name: Dyallo!

Noble must your race be and well-born the woman of Timbo who rocked you in the evenings to the nocturnal rhythm of the earth]

This is true to such an extent that, wishing to honor the heroism of a simple soldier, Mbaye Dyob, the poet almost apologizes for not being able to sing his genealogy or to mention any of his ancestors. The custom of lauding the ancestors of anyone one wishes to praise is so usual in Senegal that suitors for the hand of a maiden always pay a griot to celebrate the great deeds of their ancestors, and the nobility of their beloved's lineage.

Senghor's ambition, moreover, following the example of the griots, was to become the "dyâli" of his people, their "Master of Language" as well as their ambassador.

Yet Senghor's style is distinguished above all by the swing of its rhythm and the length of the verses—the length of a respiration—which gives his poems the monotonous motion of the waves of the sea:

[I summon forth the theory of servants on the dew And great calabashes of milk, calm above the rhythm of their swaying hips.]

This style lends itself to prayers, natural to Senghor's religious spirit:

[O bless this people, Lord, who seek their own face beneath the mask and scarcely recognize it]

as well as to nostalgic songs of regret:

[We shall no longer take part in the sponsorale joy of harvests
. . . .

We shall rehearse for a feast already faded the old-time harvest dance, the light dance of heavy bodies
. . . .
At the hint of dawn, when in the choir the weaker voices of the maids grow tender and tender the smile of the stars!
We shall move forward shoulder to shoulder, bodies fervently quivering
Toward the resonant mouths and the praises and the heavy fruits of the intimate tumult!]

It is also suitable for evoking the mystery that hovers over villages haunted by the ancestors:

[And you pool, of Kam-Dyameacute; at noon I used to drink your mystic water from the hollow of my hands
Surrounded by companions smooth and nude and decked in flowers from the bush
The shepherd's flute would modulate the slow pace of the herds
And in its shadow as it ceased drums would echo in the haunted tanns.]

But Senghor's verse is better than any other at "singing a noble subject":

[Ah! I am sustained by the hope that one day I shall run before you, Princess, bearer of your staff of honor to the assembled populace.
. . . .
And like the white dromedary's, may my lips for nine days at a time be chaste of all terrestrial water, and silent.]

If we had to choose among several adjectives, we might call Senghor's style "processional." The verses spin out, without crests, in groups of about fifteen waves; the words proceed regularly, at a rhythm kept slow by the insertion of deep-toned syllables.

The device is especially noticeable, for example, in the lines repeated below, where the "low note" of the deep-toned French *-an* and *-al* sounds is in contrast to the high-pitched tone of the vowels—*é, i, u*—and to the "occlusive" consonants—*c, d, t, thm, lm, lb:*

Je ressuscite la théorie des serv*an*tes sur la rosée
Et les g*ran*des *c*ale*b*asses de lait, *c*almes, sur le rythme des h*an*ches bal*an*cées.

To give added rhythm to this "processional" style, Senghor often uses alliteration. He either chooses as a dominant note the first consonants, such as the *r, s, t,* of the first line above, or he emphasizes a single consonant or vowel as follows:

Voici que dé*cl*ine *l*a *l*une *l*asse vers son *l*it de mer éta*l*e.

[And now the weary moon sinks into her slack sea bed.]

Sometimes the echoes of two (or three) sounds call and answer one another:

A travers Cayor et Baol de sécheresse où se *tor*dent
les bras les baobabs d'*ango*isse.

[Across Cayor and Baol dryness that twists the arms
of baobabs in pain.]

Sometimes a harmony is begun in an early line and the
poet gets caught in his own trap. In the following verse,
for example, the diphthongs of one line release a series of
further soft diphthongs in the next:

Ses paup*iè*res comme le crépuscule rapide et ses *yeux*
vastes qui s'emplissent de nuit.
Oui c'est b*ien* l'*aïcu*le n*oir*e, la Claire aux *yeux vio*lets
sous ses paup*iè*res de n*w*t.

[Her eyelids like rapid twilight and her vast eyes filling filling up with night.
Yes, it is she, the dark ancestor, Bright with violet
eyes beneath her lids of night.]

Of course, it may be a case of imitative harmony:

Et seize ans de guerre! Seize ans le battement des
tabalas de guerre des tabalas des balles!

Seuls bourdonnent les parfums de brousse, ruches
d'abeilles rousses que domine la vibration grêle des
grillons.

[And sixteen years of war! Sixteen years of war drums
beating, beating out like bullets!

The only humming is the perfumes of the bush,
swarms of russet bees that dominate the crickets' thin
vibrato.]

Most of the time, however, the device has no other aim
but the sensual. The author is attracted by the plastic qualities of certain consonants and repeats them, not in imitation of nature, but because they stimulate or sustain his inner rhythm, even independently of the subject matter
involved.

The rhythm is not always the same. It can rise to the
syncopated beat of the American Negro jazz Senghor is so
fond of:

[But if one must choose at the hour of affliction
I chose the flow of rivers, wind and forests
The assonance of plains and streams, I chose the
pulsebeat of my unclothed body
The vibrations of the balafong, the harmony of strings
and brasses that sound out of tune
I chose swing, swing, yes swing!

More often, the beat quickens to a dance rhythm—
strangely enough, a typically African dance, which doubles
a skipping step, one-two on one foot and one-two on the
other. Senghor re-creates this step by redoubling and
emphasizing the accentuated syllables:

Et quand sur *son om*bre elle se *taisa*it, résonnait le
*tam*tam des tanns ob*sédé*s.

Nous n'avancerons plus dans le frémissem*ent* ferv*ent*
de n*os c*orps *égaux épaul*es *éga*les.

Ma tête bourdonnant au *galop gu*errier des *dyoung-
dyoung*s, au *gr*and *ga*lop de mon *sang* de pur *sang*.

Qui *sera* le *sel* des *Sérè*res, qui *seront* le *sel* des
peuples *sal*és.

[And when at its shadow she grew silent, the drums
of the haunted tanns were echoing.

No more shall we move forward shoulder to shoulder
fervent bodies quivering

My head humming with the warrior gallop of the
dyoung-dyoung drums, with the racing of my blood
pure blood.

Who will be the Serer salt, who will be the salt of the
people who've been soiled.]

He can also re-create this dance step by repetition of the
consonants marking the downbeats. The dentals and
explosive labials play the role of hands beating the tom-
tom:

*Des p*eaux *p*récieu*s*es *des b*arres *d*e sel, *d*e *l'*or *d*u
Bour*e d*e *l'*or *d*u Boun*d*ou.

[Precious skins, bars of salt, of gold from Boure, of
gold from Boundou.]

Senghor's rhythm is processional, but it is often a dancing
procession, like the procession of the Brazilian Negroes in
Marcel Camus's film, who are already vibrating with the
carnival dances as they descend from their hills toward the
Bay of Rio. It is no accident that Senghor took such
pleasure in the movie *Black Orpheus,* whose "incontest-
able negritude" he so much appreciated.

Music is one of the basic elements of Senghor's poetry,
and he is aware of it: "I persist in thinking that a poem is
complete only if it becomes song, with words and music
at the same time." "A poem is like a jazz score where the
execution is as important as the text!"

To understand the crux of a Senghor poem, it is not enough
to have understood the meaning of the words and images,
which seem to us even secondary in importance. Rather
one must communicate with the poet's emotion by
discovering the rhythmic throbs of his work, never forgetting that: "Strangely enough, the Negro belongs to a world
where speech spontaneously becomes rhythm as soon as a
man is moved to emotion, restored to himself and his
authenticity. Yes, speech then becomes a poem."

We have doubtless noticed the assimilation of rhythm and
poetry: "Speech becomes *rhythm*, speech becomes *poem*,"
says Senghor. "Negro poets," he also writes, "are above all
cantors. They are tyrannically obedient to an 'inner
music.'" One final example. The title of Senghor's longest

poem in *Chants d'ombre* is **"Que m'accompagnent köras et balafongs."** In this title, the very names of the instruments give rhythmic resonance to the poetic line: repetition of the hard *c* (Que m'acc . . . ko . . .) and the final "-ong," of which the "g" must be sonorous (. . . agn . . . fong).

This verse must therefore be accented as follows:

> *Que* m'ac*com*pa*gnent* *kô*ras et bala*fongs*

This small example brings out a major difficulty for us Westerners. To "grasp" the rhythm of a Senghor poem, we must first get rid of our French manner of accentuating words. In the above line, we spontaneously place the accent on the syllables *pa, ras,* and *fong,* or on the final syllables. We thus miss the *basic rhythm of the line.*

Senghor himself calls our attention to the importance of this scansion: "Rhythm," he says "does not arise merely from an alternation of short and long syllables. It can also rest upon—and one too easily forgets that this was partly true of Greco-Latin verses—the alternation of accented and unstressed syllables, of downbeats and upbeats. This is the way it is with Negro African rhythm." But he immediately points out that "in a regular poem, each verse has the same number of accents," whereas the basic rhythm of a Negro African poem, the one which gives it its specific character, "is not that of speech, but of the percussion instruments accompanying the human voice, or, to be more exact, those which beat out the basic rhythm."

It is typical of Senghor to indicate, at the head of many of his poems, the instruments which should accompany them: "*Woi* for three kôras and a balafong," "For Khalam," "To a sonorous background of funeral drums," "For three tabalas or war drums."

For these reasons, it is difficult for French-speaking people to recite a Senghor poem. They have to abandon their natural accentuation and avoid emphasizing what seems important to them: "The fashionable diction called expressive, in a theatrical or ordinary style, is anti-poetry." It is because he has not understood this that Mr. Clancier, too French-minded no doubt, has hoped that "Senghor will succeed in creating a language with a more varied rhythm, where a picture, a word, will suddenly raise its crest around which the figure of the poem will take shape; then we shall really penetrate into his poetic universe, which is original and richly human." We hope we have shown with sufficient clarity how right Senghor was to reply: "Don't you see that you are asking me to organize poetry in the French manner, as a *drama,* whereas for us it is a *symphony.*"

With Senghor music and poetry are inseparable. Several attempts have been made in Paris to reproduce the musical rhythm of his poems with the instruments indicated by him. Recently, during a recital of Negro poetry at the Congolese University of Lovanium, the poem **"Chaka"** was chanted by a black student to the accompaniment of a tom-tom. It was an astonishing success, and all Kinshasa was talking about the "Senghor concert," obvious proof that this author's poetry loses its apparent atonality when correctly recited.

We have explained above how to interpret the *poetic phrase,* an expression we use intentionally to suggest the "musical phrase." We have shown how certain sounds give the "tone" and their repetition the "beat" to Senghor's poetry. Also, how this poetry is built on a rhythm whose discovery is essential if one wishes to reach not an external, rationalized understanding of the poem but its creative source, its original impulse.

One realizes then that the screen of "monotony," of which the author is so often accused, has been pierced: that his emotions were not always calm, peaceful, serene, as has so often been said. Senghor can be as intensely affected as Césaire, for example, but he exteriorizes less. The emotion is felt deeply, by a "tightness in the stomach and the throat." Senghor does not have an explosive temperament. "With me, an emergency makes me ill, my face becomes ashen," he has said. In the same way, various emotions are hidden in his poems. Their monotony is not due to incapacity of expression, nor lack of strong feelings; it is an integral part of Senghor's personality. It is the monotony of the savannas, whose rhythm is broader, less hurried than that of the forest, akin to those interminable modulated chants of the Batutsi and close also to the Bantu poems.

> [Fire men see only in the night, on the darkest nights,
> Fire that burns without consuming, that sparkles without burning,
> Fire that flies without body, without wings, knowing neither hearth nor hut,
> Fire, transparent palm-tree fire, a fearless man invokes thee.]

Besides, was not even Césaire considered monotonous? And Edouard Glissant? Western ears that have not learned to listen to the tom-tom and Negro chants, ears that have not yet absorbed their rhythm, will find them monotonous. Yet the monotony of Negro poets, Senghor says, "is the seal of their negritude."

If rhythm is of such importance to the Negro poet, Senghor has often repeated, it is because through his incantations it "permits access to the truth of essential things: the forces of the Cosmos."

These forces, Africans believe, are propagated in the form of *waves.* And Senghor added: "And, since contemporary physics has discovered the energy contained in matter, the waves and radiations, this is no simple metaphor." For modern physicists, too, the "world's substance is made up of rhythmic energy waves." In Sudanese cosmogonies, waves represent water, and water is life: They also represent *technique* (the to-and-fro motion of the weaver's shuttle) and *speech,* which is also propagated in the form of waves. Waves thus represent all the various manifestations of creative energy.

Rhythm enables the artist to participate in the vital cosmic forces thus endowing him with creative power. The object created—be it sculpture, painting, or poem—is a work of art only if this rhythm is apparent. "To respond to and be in harmony with the rhythm of things is the Negro's greatest joy and happiness, his reason for living. In black Africa, a work of art is a masterpiece and fully answers its purpose, only if it is rhythmic."

And this is true not only of works of art, but also of dances, "to dance is to create"; or of work: Negroes weave, sow, reap, always accompanied by voices singing or the sound of the tom-tom. Not only to encourage effort, but to make the work effective. This characteristic is still so deeply rooted today—even when rapport with the cosmogony is lost—that both the West Indian peasant and the African worker still feel the need to sustain their effort with rhythmic songs.

It is also by means of this participation in world forces that rhythm is an instrument of knowledge. Africans only know the Other, only "penetrate" the Other, be it person or object, because they instinctively seize the waves emanating from it. Comparing Descartes to a black African, Senghor would have the latter say: "I feel the Other, I dance the Other, therefore I am." He thus emphasizes the fundamental difference between European logic, "analytic through use," and Negro logic, "intuitive through participation."

Largely inspired by aboriginal cosmogonies, Senghor, one can see, has developed his thoughts on African rhythm to the level of a philosophy. In any case, he has emphasized the importance of rhythm in poetry, and especially in his own work. Not all of his rhythmic poetry, in truth, is successful. Occasionally music that is too facile makes his poems banal:

> *Ry*thmez clochettes, *ry*thmez *lang*ues *ry*thmez *ra*mes
> la danse du Maîtres des *ra*mes.

> [Set the bells in rhythmic motion, the tongues, the oars, the dance of the master oarsmen.]

The difference is palpable in the following line:

> Pais*sez* mes *seins* forts d'homme, l'her*be* de *lait* qui *luit* sur ma poitrine.

> [Feed upon my strong man's breast, the milky grass that gleams upon my chest.]

On the other hand, particularly in recent poems, the image is stronger than the rhythm. It is in this, above all, that one could talk of the influence of writers such as Claudel and Saint-John Perse. We must not forget that Senghor himself admits he is an "intellectual crossbreed," and it is inevitable that he should be marked by Western poetics.

Occasionally he regrets it. For example, in replying to a criticism quoted earlier of Clancier: "I may have yielded to your advice, since repeated by others. I would regret it if I were aware of it." And one must admit that the use of Western images that are almost clichés weakens certain of his poems which have a well-marked rhythm:

> [May twelve thousand stars be lit each night about the Main Square.]

or sometimes destroys their originality:

> [I know the Paradise lost—I have not lost my memory of the childhood garden blossoming with birds.

> The white lilac is mown, and the scent of lilies-of-the-valley has faded.]

On the other hand, Senghor has succeeded in writing admirable verses which he would be wrong to disown, even though they are in a typically French manner:

> [Love is my empire and I have a weakness for thee woman
> Stranger with gladelike eyes, cinnamon apple lips and sex like an ardent thicket.
> . . . You the distant flute that answers in the night
> From the other shore of the inshore sea that joins opposing lands
> Complementary hearts: one the color of flame, the other dark, the color of precious wood.]

Should we confess that we regret Saint-John Perse's influence on Senghor? Certainly his poems have become more polished; he has eliminated the clumsy prosaics that mar certain poems in ***Hosties noires.*** More refined today, Senghor's style cloaks several layers of meaning. On the other hand, the emphatic, occasionally declamatory character of Senghor's poetry has increased. Amid this pomp and ceremony, one sometimes misses certain accents of ***Chants d'ombre,*** so moving in their simplicity.

Frederick Ivor Case (essay date 1975)

SOURCE: "Negritude and Utopianism," in *African Literature Today: A Review,* No. 7, edited by Eldred Durosimi Jones, Heinemann, 1975, pp. 65-75.

[*In the following excerpt, Case discusses elements of intellectual alienation and false idealization in the negritude of Senghor and Aimé Césaire. Negritude, as a product of European acculturation, Case contends, "has nothing to do with the existential reality of the mass of black men."*]

Aimé Césaire and Léopold Sédar Senghor are indisputably the two great leaders of the Négritude movement which was born in France in the late 1930s. It is significant that both men are now politicians of some stature and that Senghor is generally considered as one of the greatest supporters of the concept of Francophonie. He has made use of his position as President of Senegal to promote the recognition of African cultural values throughout the world and is an international figure whose reputation has spread beyond the French-speaking nations. . . .

One of the principal characteristics of any racism is its negative basis. It is, essentially, the negation of the humanity of a racial group and the denial of all the values of that group. Césaire's Négritude, and Senghor's also, is the affirmation of African cultural values. It is a positive expression of human dignity and pride which, of necessity, has to be preceded by a 'purification' of the harmful aspects of the Western European conditioning of the Black which has made him turn against himself. Césaire's repudiation of this conditioning is the recognition that cultural and religious values are not absolute but entirely relative. As Senghor declared in a speech before the Ghanaian Parliament in 1962:

> Négritude is not even attachment to a particular race, our own, although such attachment is legitimate. Négritude is the awareness, defence and development of African cultural values. . . .

However, the struggle for négritude must not be negation but affirmation.

Césaire recognises in his essay, *Discours sur le Colonialisme,* that the principal error of the European lies in the equations:

> Christianity = Civilisation
>
> Paganism = Barbarity

Everything and everyone is judged in relation to these values.

One certainly could not accuse Senghor of racism. Whilst Césaire was once a member of the French Communist Party and is still a Marxist, Senghor has been Catholic for most of his life. Born in 1906, he also left his native land to further his academic education in France and was also a student at the *Ecole Normale Suprieure.*

Senghor's greatest contribution to the Négritude movement appears to have been his personal influence on Caribbean writers, the sons of a people who had for centuries been humiliated, enslaved and alienated from their culture and from themselves in the name of Western European Christianity.

Senghor's poetic work is characterised by a quiet dignity and pride, his richest verse, mostly composed to be set to traditional West African instruments, expresses his desire to return to the native village that he has left so very far behind:

> Toko'Waly my uncle, do you remember those distant nights when my head grew heavy against the patience of your back?
> Or holding me by the hand, your hand led me through the shadows and signs?

> The fields are flowers of glowworms; the stars come to rest on the grass, on the trees.
> All around is silence.
> Only the droning scents of the bush, hives of red bees drowning the stridulation of the crickets
> And the muffled tom-tom, the far-off breathing of the night.

('For Koras and Balafong' in *Chants d'Ombre*)

Then at the end of that very beautiful poem **'Joal'** which is also in the collection *Chants d'Ombre* we read this striking stanza:

> I remember, I remember . . .
> In my head the rhythm of the tramp tramp
> So wearily down the days of Europe where there comes,
> Now and then a little orphaned jazz that goes sobbing, sobbing, sobbing.

It is particularly in this first collection of his poems that the nostalgic note is struck although it is also evident in the later collections of verse.

Senghor also condemns the savagery of the European rape of Africa but acknowledges a great debt to French humanism and to the French language. His speeches and essays are of great importance and interest to the student of Negro-African cultures.

What is very striking indeed in Senghor's writings is the passionate love of Africa and of France which never seem to enter into conflict. Speaking of Africa he says:

> What is forgotten is that this land was abandoned for three centuries to the bloody cupidity of slave traders; that through the murderous actions of the Whites, twenty millions of its children were deported to the West Indies and to the Americas, that two hundred million died in man hunts. What is generally forgotten is that each 'benefit of colonisation' has had its reverse.

(*Négritude et Humanisme*)

In the same article, which appeared in *Présence Africaine* in 1950, he goes on to say that the West's technological contribution to Africa is of value only if the soul of the African is not altogether altered by the new exterior forces that threaten its tranquil homogeneity.

In a very famous article entitled **'French as a Language of Culture'** which appeared in the November 1962 number of *Esprit,* Senghor gives five reasons why the French language is of such great importance to African writers. Firstly, he says, many of the elite think in French and speak it better than their mother tongue. Secondly, there is the richness of the French vocabulary. Thirdly, French, through its syntax, is a concise language:

> To the syntax of juxtaposition of Negro-African languages is opposed the syntax of subordination of French; to the syntax of concrete reality, that of abstract thought: in point of fact, the syntax of reason to that of emotion.

(*Négritude et Humanisme*)

Fourthly, the stylistic demands of the French language open new universal dimensions to the reader. It is the fifth reason that is of particular concern here, and I will quote the entire paragraph that explains it.

> Fifth reason: French Humanism. It is precisely in this elucidation, in this *re-creation,* that French Humanism consists. For man is the object of its activity. Whether it be in the case of Law, of Literature, of Art, even of Science, the distinguishing mark of French genius lies in this concern with Man. French always expresses a *moral.* This gives it its character of *universality* which counterbalances its tendency to individualism.

In the poem **'Prayer for Peace'** dedicated to Georges and Claude Pompidou, Senghor prays for France:

> O Lord, take from my memory the France which is not France, mask of smallness and hatred upon the face of France
> That mask of smallness and hatred for which I have hatred . . . yet I may well hate Evil
> For I have a great weakness for France.
> Bless this people who were tied and twice able to free their hands and proclaim the coming of the poor into the kingdom
> Who turned the slaves of the day into men free equal fraternal
> Bless these people who brought me Thy Good News, Lord, and opened my heavy eyelids to the light of faith.

> **('Prayer for Peace'** in *Hosties Noires*)

This poem was written in 1945 and it hardly seems that Senghor's love of France and his gratitude have altered.

Though Césaire does not insist on his love of France in his work, both he and Senghor, the Marxist and the Catholic, look forward to the day when all peoples will recognise and respect differences in culture and when all the oppressed of the world will join hands in brotherhood.

In his play *Et les Chiens se taisaient,* Césaire's hero illustrates universal tolerance:

> Suppose that the world were a forest. Good!
> There are baobabs, flourishing oaks, black pines and white walnuts;
> I would like them all to grow, firm and strong,
> different in wood, in bearing, in colour,
> but equally full of sap and without one encroaching on the other's space,
> different at the base
> but oh!
> (Ecstatically)
> may their heads join high, very high, in the ether so as to form for all
> a single roof
> I say the only protective roof!

> (*Et les Chiens* . . . Acte II)

It would be superfluous to quote similar sentiments expressed by Senghor since they are easily to be found in his speeches and essays.

What seems to characterise Négritude then is an assertion of African dignity, a desire to return to the cultural values which are deeply rooted in traditional religion, and the future hope of a universal brotherhood in a universal civilisation.

I will now attempt to analyse this black ideology through the application of certain concepts on African ontology discussed by Professor John Mbiti in his book *African Religions and Philosophy.*

John Mbiti defines two dimensions of African reality which he calls the Sasa period and the Zamani. The Sasa is the now, the immediate future, the near period of time in the past, present, and future. Zamani is the period beyond which nothing can go. It is the past incorporating the present. . . .

Mbiti sets out to show that existence is apprehended by the African in traditional society in such a way that the immediate future is the only future perspective that exists. Consequently, in traditional religions there is no prophetism and no future paradise. For time—to use Western terms—recedes rather than progresses and the Golden Age—that era of the black man's greatness—the era of Timbuctoo and Benin, the era of the Yoruba and the Zulu, of Shango and Chaka, lies in the Zamani period. The Sasa is an ever-constant construction of the past and not of the future. Utopia exists in the past.

It is interesting that if one examines the works of Senghor and Césaire it becomes evident that they are characterised by elements peculiar to the Zamani period. The revalorisation of African artistic and humanistic values coincides inevitably with the creation of a myth superimposed on African history. It is difficult to say which comes first since revalorisation and myth are interwoven to the point of identification, one with the other. . . .

Senghor's poems convey an attitude and an atmosphere that are different. But this *normalien* living in Paris and writing of a traditional African society is in fact looking back to what is another age and another place in terms of his evolution within the Western European world. Like so many African and Caribbean writers he is at a great distance in terms of space and time from his subject.

This brings to mind the story of Camara Laye and the composition of *L'Enfant Noir,* translated variously as *The African Child* and *The Black Child.* At the time of writing, Laye was experiencing the solitude and misery of the black worker in France. He would work in the factory during the day and return alone to the Africa he was trying to recreate for himself in his cold, barren room. The result is stunning in its stark simplicity but it is the fruit of a very painful period of parturition.

Senghor, the intellectual, has long left this stage behind him. He does not battle against being an *assimilado* and accepts his cultural *métissage* and is proud of it. In an article entitled **'On the Freedom of the Soul or the Praises of Métissage'** which appeared in the October 1950 issue of *Liberté de l'Esprit,* Senghor reminds us that most great civilisations have depended on the grafting of culture on culture to reach their high stage of development. Africans should therefore take advantage of this opportunity in cultural development being offered by the European colonisation of their native land. The same idea is repeated several times in his essays and speeches. In the 1956 Conference of Black Writers and Artists, held at the Sorbonne, a lively discussion developed between the Afro-Americans and Antilleans on the one hand and the Africans on the other. Here is part of Senghor's contribution to the discussion:

> So we, too, are objectively half-castes. And this is where I would quarrel with Césaire while agreeing with him. Today we are objectively half-castes . . . much of the reasoning of French Africans derives from Descartes. This is why, quite often, you don't follow us, as we don't altogether follow you, because you, like the Anglo-Saxons, are pragmatists.
>
> *(Prose and Poetry)*

However, since Senghor can declare:

> I think in French; I express myself in French better than in my mother tongue.
>
> *(Négritude et Humanisme)*

in that famous essay published in *Esprit,* he has evidently been a victim of the acculturation which appears to have been the aim of the French educational system in Africa. This cultural imperialism serves to make the victim nostalgic and sentimental about a past that still exists in the present reality of the mass of his brothers'.

In terms of space and time the writer is so far removed from the reality of his people that having lived in Western society and having been assimilated by its values, the African has moved out of his traditional ecological milieu, out of the socio-cultural structure of his people and he has begun to move forward in time. . . .

What I am attempting to show is that the concept of Négritude is the direct product of a successful process of acculturation undertaken by the European in Africa. It is an intellectual concept that has nothing to do with the existential reality of the mass of black men. It is the means of integrating alienated man in the security of a myth that he has created for his own benefit and for that of his social class.

The individualism peculiar to the exercise is the antithesis of the authentic cultural values of Africa where art is for the largest possible group but yet not vulgarised. The oral tradition in literature is a community participatory exercise. Dance and sculpture, by their very nature, are community-oriented activities. Aesthetics for its own sake is a nonsense and absurd since man as a collective being is forever at the centre of artistic expression. The esoteric nature of Césaire's writings leaves no doubt about the individualism of his work. His intellectualisation and mythification of the black man's reality further alienate him from his brothers with whom he can feel only an intellectual solidarity.

The black man in the tramway, shunned by Césaire, serves as a catalyst in *Return to my Native Land.* Césaire awakens to the reality of his blackness and to the universality of his Négritude. However, his predilection for the fine French phrase, the obscure word that frequently sends even the educated reader vainly searching in his dictionary, this parade of Western European erudition that Frantz Fanon analyses so well in *Black Skin, White Masks,* serves only to remove him yet further from his people. Indeed he appears to be writing not for them but for a white public. . . .

Both Césaire and Senghor project themselves in another country and at another period which is no longer theirs. For Senghor thinks of a way of life now lost for him among his Serere people. Césaire looks towards a traditional African life that he cannot know and towards periods of the past when Africans governed Africa and when Africans liberated themselves of a foreign yoke in Haiti. Both men are looking towards a utopian state.

I am not trying to say that Senghor and Césaire are completely oblivious to every aspect of the black man's reality. But as a map is an abstraction of a city, province or country, the economic and political awareness of problems is an intellectualisation and institutionalisation of social reality.

Négritude is then a new religion of the middle-class black intellectual and as such it dulls his sense of reality. His eyes are firmly fixed on a utopian period although he can hear the cries of anguish of his brothers struggling through their present reality. But the Western-educated intellectual is also future-oriented and yet another myth is the implication that the Zamani Utopia may return, and the Utopia is the myth that the humanistic values of Négritude will prevail and that eventually, a harmonious universal civilisation will evolve, deeply impregnated with the sap of African cultural and moral values. Western philosophies—Marxist as well as Christian—have led black intellectuals to these conclusions. Angela Davis and Martin Luther King have very much in common.

Western religious philosophy has ensnared the black man into a belief in dialectical or evolutionary processes towards universal harmony where eventually he will be assimilated or integrated. But assimilated and integrated into what? If the black man does become integrated into Western European thought patterns and humanistic values, as Césaire and Senghor have been, then he becomes alienated or a man divided against himself—whichever terminology one prefers.

The concept of Négritude cannot be the answer to any situation pertaining to the reality of the black masses. It is a fine idea, useful and necessary to the cultural development of a Western-educated elite. It is also perhaps a necessary stage in a true renaissance of African culture so long devastated or bastardised by ignorance and prejudice. But at best today Négritude seems no more than yet another of Western Europe's philosophic aberrations.

Janis L. Pallister (essay date April 1980)

SOURCE: "Léopold Sédar Senghor: A Catholic Sensibility?," in *French Review,* Vol. LIII, No. 5, April, 1980, pp. 670-9.

[*In the following essay, Pallister objects to critical interpretations of Senghor's poetry that emphasize the significance of symbolist, surrealist, and Roman Catholic influences in his work.*]

It is arresting to note that many recent trends in Senghorian criticism, relying on a whole new set of critical clichés, should attempt to legitimize this great and fundamentally African poet by seeking to draw him into mainstream literature from France. Perhaps this is partially the product of another earlier critical strain that reproached Senghor the politician, Senghor the poet and Senghor the man for not being sufficiently African, while putting the whole concept of negritude and aggressive assimilation under attack. Now there seems to be a compulsion to make him sufficiently European. Whatever the reason, it is baffling and disconcerting to find Geneviève Lebaud in her 1976 book entitled *Léopold Sédar Senghor, ou la Poésie du royaume d'enfance,* making frequent comparisons of Senghor to Saint-John Perse, Rimbaud, Claudel, and in particular Baudelaire. This latter cue is pursued in a very recent article in *French Review* by Alfred J Guillaume, Jr., who ostensibly authenticates these comparisons between Baudelaire and Senghor by having engaged Senghor himself in a conversation on the subject. A year previous to this, Serge Gavronsky drew parallels between Senghor and the two French poets, Baudelaire and Claudel, while mustering structuralist jargon for his arguments. It is revealing, however, that Lebaud works herself into a corner and is finally forced to conclude correctly that Senghor's universe "n'est pas celui des poètes maudits." (This she must say despite Césaire's assertion that all modern poets are *poètes maudits,* who have taken the train for hell.) It seems to me, also, that Senghor himself refutes the comparison between Baudelaire's poetic vision and his own at many points in Guillaume's reported conversation but especially when he insists upon the African artist's identification with the object; for if the European Symbolist remains separate from the object he evokes and if the non-metaphysical European surrealist embodies simultaneously the signifiant and the *signifié,* they are essentially different from the concrete African poet who names only the *signifié* and leaves it up to the reader to supply the signifiant. Moreover, many passages in Senghor's **Liberté I** make the same basic assertions as we find in Guillaume's

dialogue, which therefore tells us nothing particularly new about Senghor. Furthermore, we must keep in mind that what a poet has to say about his own poetry in a *post hoc* and contrived context such as this is not always fully reliable. Yet, I suppose that many readers of *French Review* would be drawn to a reading of this article because Baudelaire's name is in the title whereas an article devoted exclusively to Senghor might not be so compelling. (Years ago readers were drawn to Senghor's anthology by the fact that Sartre had written an introductory essay for it, and in certain quarters the reading of Senghor is still "justified" in terms of his link with Sartre.)

I would submit, however, that we must regard African literature written in French as a distinct entity, just as we do American and English literature. Senghor's expression "Retour au sources" surely does not suggest that the literary springs from which he has deeply drunk are the *Chanson de Roland* and the French symbolist poets. Nor does it refer to the Catholicism with which Senghor is repeatedly linked. Eager to find ways to stimulate a response in students and readers to so-called Francophone writers, and anxious to offer tags which will ostensibly make Senghor appear appealing and accessible to the Westerner, the writers of French civilization books and manuals sometimes make of Senghor's Catholicism a common denominator. Hence, Denoeu in the 1972 update of his French *Cultural Reader* writes: "Léopold Sédar Senghor, né près de Dakar, Sénégal en 1906, fils d'un riche propriétaire terrien, catholique, alla continuer ses études Paris." One is struck by the strong emphasis given to the "occidental side" of his African "métis culturel."

More damaging still are the serious critics of Senghor, such as Hymans, who in his relatively recent book *Léopold Sédar Senghor, An Intellectual Biography,* repeatedly insists on Senghor's Catholicism as the mainspring of his poetic and political expression. To appreciate Senghor's philosophy, says he, "it is necessary to understand the basic personal characteristics of its author. He is a Catholic intellectual stirred by ardent faith; he is the African political leader most possessed with French culture." Hymans analyzes what he perceives to be the main influences on Senghor, including Claudel and his theory of co-naissance, as well as Maritain and his Neo-Thomism, not to mention the Fathers of the Holy Spirit at Ngasobil and the primacy of the spiritual coming through this order and indeed through the whole *Esprit* movement. He quotes Abacar N'Diaye, for his amusing if peculiar assertion that Senghor is a Christian thinker who has forgotten to close his missal. Then Hymans himself writes, "Senghor's Catholicism sets him apart. His religion is responsible for the catholic (universal) love which characterizes his works. This universal love prevents Senghor from advocating violence and consequently distinguishes his work from that of the majority of other black poets. Catholic love is the basis for both his cultural and political theories."

All this is very troubling. Hymans's attempt to impose *maîtres à penser* on Senghor is one thing. That Senghor has read Claudel, Maritain and Teilhard de Chardin is well known. But he has also read the African literatures and is repeatedly insistent upon the role that the *maîtres griots* and the Dyâli, that Maronyai and Soukeina have played in his formation. "Influence on" is not, after all, synonymous with "explanation for," or "basis of," and Hymans's work disregards the fact that, as Senghor himself says in his response letter, "the elements of symbiosis cannot be reduced to the elements which compose it . . ." Moreover, one would not by the reading of Catholic philosophers and poets thereby be more (or less) Catholic.

The question thus asserts itself. Is Senghor's Catholicism any more "responsible" for his sense of love and fraternity or for his usual gentleness than is his fundamental personality developed in terms of his Serer people and in the pastoral context of his early years spent with such persons as his uncle Tokô'Waly, of whom he writes with considerable lyrical effusion in **"Que m'accompagnent Koras et Balafong"?** Why can it not be an *African* love reinforced by the poet's Catholicism? Is the spiritual content of Senghor's poetry so fundamentally Catholic as Hymans contends? Senghor himself writes: "Catholicism cannot ignore Animism without laying itself open to a serious bankruptcy. In these countries of sandy plains, nothing solid, nothing durable can be built except on the stony foundation of Animism." We must, thus, observe that Senghor himself regards African religion as the foundation, and Catholicism as a type of reinforcement, or superstructure.

I would, then, refute the concept that the essential key to understanding Senghor's poetry is found in the Symbolist and surrealist poets, and, similarly, I would refute the notion that the key to his spirituality or sensibility is summed up in his Catholicism, which, after all, is not a significant aspect of his "royaume d'enfance," that is, of that Serer substratum of his existence he so eloquently recovers in his poetry.

Indeed, if we contemplate the African images and concepts in Senghor's poetry (as so appropriately and meticulously studied by Sylvia Washington Bê and Van Niekerk) we must come away with the overwhelming conviction of their supreme domination over his muse. Animism (or the cult of the *pango*), the cult of the ancestors, the collective peace of the African village, are fundamental themes around which the poems revolve. Rhythm and beat of the tom-tom are the vehicles through which these largely religious but not necessarily Catholic themes are expressed.

Now, can we say that these are mere symbols or poetic poses—that is, forms of exoticism—reflecting the African way of life, whereas the authentic identity of the man lies in his Catholicism? A dangerous hypothesis at best, in view of Senghor's theory of anthropopsychism, or the appropriation by the maskbearer or poet of a psychic form and force wherein the lion does not *represent* strength and courage to the one who invokes the animal, but rather wherein the invoker literally assumes the attributes of the

lion. (Such an idea is not, I suppose, too far from Claudel's concept of *co-naissance,* wherein one simultaneously acquires by mind and comes into being . . . which explains why Claudel, perhaps more than any other Western poet, has revealed in his poems the truly metaphysical character of African art, including its literature.)

I would submit that the identifiably Catholic content of Senghor's poetry happily figures in its intellectual content and metaphor as a superstructure, or, more properly, as a tangential convergence. Let us recall that out of the terrible depths of his artistic frustration, Ezra Pound, reflecting the schizophrenia of the surrealistic and cubistic movements, cried out, "I cannot make it cohere." It is my contention that Senghor the African, with more potential for a fragmented vision than Pound, does indeed make it cohere. How is this done?

If we take as an example Senghor's invocation for the recovery of his *royaume d'enfance,* his Joal, in which he appears to paraphrase the twenty-third (or for the Catholic the twenty-second) Psalm:

> Segneur de la lumière et des ténèbres
> Toi seigneur du Cosmos, fais que je repose sous Joal l'Ombreuse
> Que je renaisse au Royaume d'enfance bruissant de rêves.

> *(Nocturnes)*

One is struck here by the identification of God as the Lord of the Cosmos, the monotheistic primordial creator known to almost all African religions without reference to the Judeo-Christian tradition. One is struck also by the specificity in the replacement of the green valleys by the poet's African cradle: Joal l'Ombreuse. But in particular, one is struck by the fact that the phrases echoing the Psalm have no Eucharistic application, though this is the most common one for most Catholics.

Indeed, reference to the Christocentric Eucharist itself—so fundamental to the Catholic sensibility, so basic, so central to Catholic theology, and everywhere present in the poetry of Claudel—is rare in the poetry of Senghor. The concept of sacrifice is largely restricted to an association with the *hosties noires* or black human sacrifice (especially in times of war). Human sacrifice may be said to be present, too, as it accrues to the fate of the African at Western hands, and to the African cult of the ancestors, anagogically related to the Catholic doctrine of the communion of saints. But the sacrifice of Christ himself remains incidental in the poetry of Senghor, except as it is mystically transposed to the suffering black. In the **"Prière de paix,"** for example, Senghor uses the metaphor of the ciborium for his book, which he thinks of as containing a vision of the blacks as the crucified Jesus, or as crucified Africa, sacrificed for the salvation of the whites, but also representing the scourgers of white consciences. When scrutinized, Senghor's allusions to ritual sacrifice in the Catholic religion seem to be more superficial than those pertaining to *African* ritual sacrifice. For example, reference in **"Masque nègre"** to the "patànes des joues" is merely an image referring to the shape of the host (and the cheeks) rather than a metaphor recalling its Eucharistic and sacrificial meanings.

On the other hand, strong metaphors of African sacrifice, showing the tensions between the peaceful herbivore and the carnivore, between the gallinaceous and the aggressive, abound in Senghor's poetry. Especially noteworthy in this connection is Senghor's recourse to concepts of African sacrifice, found in **"A l'appel de la race de Saba,"** the following lines of which ring with profound lyrical effusion and authenticity:

> J'offre un poulet sans tache, debout près de l'Aîné, bièn que tard venu, afin qu'avant l'eau crémeuse et la bière de mil
> Gicle jusqu'à moi et sur mes lèvres charnelles le sang chaud salé du taureau dans la force de l'âge, dans la plénitude de sa graisse.

The offering and sacrifice of hen and bull are, of course, not consonant with Catholic liturgical worship, but are here conceived as giving greater protection to the African poet's gift than the Eucharist might.

Likewise, though allusions to the Eucharist are, as we have seen, present in Senghor's poetry, there is little to suggest a *Tantum Ergo* (except reference to the song per se, as juxtaposed to the *Kor Siga*), whereas outbursts of joyful praise are to be found for millet beer. "Hê! vive la bière de mil à l'Initié," cries the poet in his ecstasy.

Finally, the rites of circumcision as a bridge between primal innocence and the responsibilities of adulthood within the context of African community have similar profound and lyrical meanings for Senghor that (in his poetry) remain mechanistically unrelated to the Judeo-Christian significances of this rite.

Now, equally basic in the Catholic confession is the doctrine of the Trinity. But the African cosmogony with its notion of the double dialectic of dyad-triad, combining and recombining to create the father-mother-child-cluster—that is, the nucleus of humanity—is more basic to Senghor's world view. Thus, in discussing creativity, he likens the poet to the woman in labor, who must give birth ("Postface"). The poet's triadic references (often linked to fertility) do not evoke the Holy Trinity but rather the earthly trinity, model of the Christian family (Joseph, Mary, and Jesus). Apparent allusions to the Trinity by Senghor must, I think, be regarded as coinciding with what is at least equal if not more basic in Senghor's mind-set: the African concept of the triad. Similarly, dyadic patterns are linked to the African androgynous vision, to the African myths of the primordial couple as much as to any particular Catholic belief. (See "The Elegy of the Trade Winds.") Truly African, for example, is the poet's assertion in **"Kaya Magan"** that he is "les deux battants de la porte, rythme binaire de l'espace, et le troisième temps."

Now, if the Eucharist, the sacrifice of Christ, and the Trinity are concatenate tenets of Catholic dogma, access to the sacraments is through the waters of baptism; and the worship of the Trinity as well as the reception of the sacraments is the preparation for paradise and reunion with God—which is not, surely, the most pressing desire expressed by this poet, as it is by, say, San Juan de la Cruz. In the poetry of Senghor the cleansing waters of Christian baptism—though doubtless the earliest initiation rite the poet ever experienced—seem no more formative of his spirituality than the beneficial Fountains of the Elephants and of Kam-Dyamé, whose mystic water the poet as a child drank in the hollow of his hands, surrounded by his companions—they so smooth and naked, adorned with the flowers of the bush. And after reading the **"Elégie des circoncis,"** can we not say, too, that the African way of circumcision, viewed as an initiation rite, takes precedence in the poet's psychology over Christian baptism, or Holy Communication, or confirmation?

Less importantly, the Virgin Mother, who has for centuries captured the Catholic imagination, is far from uppermost in Senghor's mind, though we all know that in more than one poem he celebrates woman as genetrix, woman mystically bound to Mother Africa. That the *Song of Songs* apparently becomes mixed into the metaphors found in his famous **"Femme noire"** seems merely to add a dimension to the African focus of the poem, rather than to relocate its impetus. Nor can the invocation to the angry, red-eyed Mother in Senghor's **"A l'appel de la race de Saba"** be realigned with the Virgin Mother, despite the repeated Hail Mary-like "Mère, sois bénie" with which the poet begins each strophe.

Similarly, the *Esprit* invoked in the poem **"L'Ouragan"** cannot be readily associated with the Holy Spirit of Christian doctrine, as the poet calls upon his muse, which is the wind or the Spirit, to breathe on the strings of his kora and to let his song rise up. Yet here, as is usually the case, the Christian dimension can be added—like an outer ring to the cortex—without its doing violence to the African thrust of the poem.

I do not wish to belabor the point. We could continue these doctrinal analysis and distinctions *ad infinitum,* but I believe we would only continue to find that while Senghor's Catholicism is not absent from his muse, his missal was definitely closed when he sat down to write his poems, as was also his catechism. The conventional longings of the Catholic spirit seen in such poets as Gerard Manley Hopkins, Thomas Merton, Paul Claudel, even Charles Péguy, do not necessarily surface in this poetry; nor can the presence of gentleness and fraternal love be characterized as more Catholic than African. What some might claim to be most Catholic in Senghor's poetry is the absence of murmuring. Put another way, what for some readers may be most Catholic in Senghor is the frequent presence of conciliation or pardon, that is, of charity, which strongly affects the poetic tone.

Ironically, however, the themes of pardon we are inclined to associate with Senghor's Catholicism are in truth expressed in less than Christian terms. In the **"Prière de paix,"** in which the black race is seen as martyred, Senghor alludes to the petitions for forgiveness in the Our Father. Interestingly enough, he does not ask pardon for Africa's trespasses (perhaps because he feels the Africans have no guilt, no original sin?). The poem is in reality a recital of the white man's crimes and trespasses with a prayer for his pardon tacked on. As Peters says, "The peace prayer proceeds by attack, laying bare the wrongs which must be pardoned." Thus Senghor's notion of pardon is, from a psycho-sociological point of view understandable, but, from a theological point of view, doubtful, to say the very least. In **"Neige sur Paris"** the reader quickly ascertains that the poet expresses no hope that the rewards of heaven will be accorded to the penitent and the erring, but only the desire for an apparently earthly peace. Here again Senghor focuses on the bitter realities of Europe and identifies Africans with the suffering Christ.

Thus, even poems that superficially present the aura of reconciliation and peace, and that would at first blush appear to be the most Catholic or Christian of Senghor's works, must upon close scrutiny be found to emanate from non Christian sources. Towra has thus found **"Neige sur Paris"**—despite its religious fervor—not so much to represent a turning of the cheek as—in view of its period and content—to voice the political platform of peace adopted by the European left and in particular the French Popular Front of the Blum regime. Moreover this poem's long list of the colonists' crimes against the black race, while profoundly moving from a poetic and human point of view, attenuates the plea for pardon expressed in it. The poem—in some ways one of Senghor's greatest and surely one of his most famous—lacks the mysticism of the Joal poems, and on the other hand, fails as a model for even a modern Christian prayer. When set against the Our Father, we have seen that some of the key aspects of the pardon petitions are clearly missing in this poem. It emerges more as a kiss of peace, or the laying down of the sword, prior to communion.

Philosophically speaking, Senghor, like Teilhard de Chardin, has formulated a concept of the universal society or brotherhood of the future, though the concept may be as Serer as it is Catholic. On the one hand we may say that Teilhardian eschatological theories themselves have vied with the traditional doctrine enough to meet with resistance in the Catholic hierarchy (though Pope John XXIII confessed to not understanding them). On the other hand, the concepts as sifted through Senghor's perspectives are necessarily marked with the notion that the black African will have special contributions to make to this future society and to the noosphere—contributions that were doubtless rather remote from the thinking of Teilhard. Furthermore, while the concept of fruitful fraternity is fundamental to Teilhard's teleology and, moreover, is a vital aspect of the Christian ethos, it cannot be said to be exclusively Christian, when also advocated by atheists and agnostics such as Camus and Malraux, as well as by all Marxist thinkers, not to mention many Jewish and Moslem

theologians in the bargain. It is, rather, despite its long heritage, the twentieth-century thinker's highway to the salvation of the world, and—if one happens to still believe in it—of the individual soul.

In a prodigal son who views himself as pure, and whose return is a charitable return to pagan Africa, to his ancestors, to the world of telekinesis and telluric forces, and whose prayer for the fervent knowledge of the doctors of Timbuktu is directed to the Elephant of Mbissel, fraternity is conceived in a dialectical frame. His brothers are sometimes the whites, but are certainly less often the whites of the world (to whom Dadié directs his famous poem) than his *fellow sufferers,* his *fellow blacks.* As Senghor writes, "Je veux revoir le gynécée de droite: j'y jouais avec mes frères les fils du Lion."

Indeed the question of the European white world is in this poetry one of postponement:

> Demain, je reprendrai le chemin de l'Europe, chemin
> de l'ambassade
> Dans le regret du Pays noir.

When dealing with the rubric of fraternity or social interaction, one should recall that religion for Senghor is not to be separated from society or culture. Religion, he writes, represents "l'effort de *socialisation* et de *totalisation.* Un effort pour *comprendre* . . . l'Homme et l'Univers dans une vision de profondeur. Pour les organiser harmonieusement, en intégrant l'Homme dans l'Univers."

If, then, the poetry of Senghor presents a picture that is less than orthodox Catholic, it is because he avoids the particularization of cult in order to achieve *modus vivendi* that offers universal (or total) and serene harmony for man. And the lack of murmur, the picture of serenity that Senghor ultimately presents in his later collections is at once the least Catholic (capital C) and the most catholic (small c) imaginable. Unlike Saint-John Perse, the tension is not between classical calm and romantic storm, and the bridge to be raised is not between the world of gentleness and the hard or epic world. Nor is the bridge to be raised the Claudelian hieratic one between good and evil. The bridge to be erected is, rather, between the dialectical opposites of Africa and the West (or Seine and Sine), between Serer tribal beliefs and Christian values, between plant and phallus, herbivore and carnivore, life and death. And the poetic gospel Senghor preaches in his poetry is not akin to the priestly one of Claudel, who responds to the commandment of Christ to spread His word over the world. Senghor's gospel is that of negritude with everything this implies. Furthermore, the Thomistic *sic et non* which Hyman insists upon as fundamental to Senghor's world view is in reality merely a reinforcement of his own gospel's mission, his own declaration of the values of the black world and the committed living out of those values. And also, unlike Ezra Pound, Léopold Sédar Senghor makes all the forces bearing upon his muse melt together and cohere.

Therefore, while Catholic piety cannot be said to be the grist of his poetic mill, Senghor's verses are the mosaics of a poetic *African Sanctus,* as rich, as diffuse and as varied, but as authentically African in pitch and purpose as the musical one has been. This had to be, if the poet were to express effectively his chosen African way, his toiling black people, his sense of exile. This had to be, too, if he were to celebrate Africa—that night in which he claims all his contradictions are resolved in the primal unity of his negritude. It had to be if he were to declare to us his Empire of Love (**"Le Kaya-Magan"**), his African love, "qui meut les mondes chantants" (**"Que m'accompagnent . . ."**).

These seeming contradictions were necessarily set down in juxtaposition so that Senghor might assert his *africanité,* which, ironically and paradoxically, is his only viaticum. Such dialectical structures are indeed the source of the poet's metaphysical *Angst,* which, while not appeased, is mastered, so that the serene holiness of his poetry is apprehended unequivocally by the reader as the chief manifestation of its emotional depth and of the great-souled quality which obtain, regardless its politico-sociological drift, all too often over-emphasized by the poet's critics. Within his poetry, then, Senghor's sensibility must be judged as African and Catholic, though perhaps more *African* than *Catholic* and it is surely by any standards more eclectic, more ventilated and more catholic (small c) than it is orthodox Roman, doctrinaire or crypt-like. All that is to its credit, or so it seems to me.

Finally, as I asserted at the onset and believe I have demonstrated in this article, if Senghor's is an *AFRICAN Sanctus,* then criticism of his work must not overemphasize the exclusively western features of his poetic expression—such as his debt to surrealism or his Catholicism—to the detriment of his possibly more fundamental African aesthetic, his African super-real and metaphysical vision, and his African religious orientations.

Dorothy S. Blair (essay date 1984)

SOURCE: "The Negritude Generation" and "After Independence, the First Twenty Years: New Themes, New Names," in *Senegalese Literature: A Critical History,* Twayne, 1984, pp. 45-141.

[*In the following excerpt, Blair provides an overview of Senghor's literary and political career, particularly his role as a leading figure of the negritude movement and Senegalese literature.*]

The literary pioneers we discussed in the preceding chapter were, without exception, the docile and grateful products of the French educational system, their "civilizing mission" and assimilation policy as applied to Senegal. Not one of these writers questioned the superiority of Western values; none showed any symptom of disquiet over a possible loss of cultural identity. But neither had any one of them been exposed to the cosmopolitan stimuli and intellectual hurly-burly of Paris student life. At the bottom of the educational ladder was a self-taught herdsman; at the top, a priest formed in the airtight academic chamber of a Catholic seminary.

However, in the 1930s, more and more outstanding young Senegalese were proceeding with scholarships to institutions of higher and professional training in France. They made contact with fellow blacks from Madagascar, the Caribbean, North America, and other parts of Africa. Some American Negro expatriates formed an important element in the intellectual melting pot of the Paris Left Bank: in particular, the writers Countee Cullen, Claude McKay, Langston Hughes, and Jean Toomer, who took refuge in France when their "New Negro" movement seemed to have failed. W. E. B. DuBois and Marcus Garvey, the "Black Moses," had been in the vanguard of this movement. In 1903, DuBois had published his *Souls of the Black Folk,* denouncing the lack of opportunities for Negroes in the United States, invoking the greatness of the African past, and calling upon blacks themselves to refute the idea that they were congenitally inferior. He founded the National Association for the Advancement of Colored People, with a periodical, the *Crisis,* as the organ for their propaganda.

In 1917, Garvey, a Jamaican black nationalist, established a branch of his Universal Negro Improvement Association in Harlem and held rallies and parades to bring Pan-Africanism into the streets. The American exiles brought with them to France DuBois's and Garvey's ideas of a black renaissance, to be discussed wherever black students and prominent personalities met: at the Cité Universitaire, the cafés, or the home of the Martiniquan sisters, Andrée and Paulette Nardal, who kept open house for black intellectuals, poets, novelists, and politicians, as did their compatriot, René Maran, whose novel *Batouala* had won him the Goncourt Prize in 1922.

In 1931, Paulette Nardal, in collaboration with the Liberian Dr. Leo Sajous, founded the bilingual (English-French) *Revue du monde noir/Black World Review,* in which American, Caribbean, and African blacks testified to their powers of independent thought and original personalities. One of the white contributors was the German ethnologist, Leo Frobenius, whose history of African civilization revealed that the so-called Dark Continent had had a medieval culture equal to that of the West, and taught young blacks that they could be as proud of their own history as the one they had learned to adopt with "their ancestors the Gauls." In this period before the outbreak of the Second World War, orthodoxies were being challenged in art, literature, and politics. Earlier in the century, Picasso and Apollinaire had started a vogue for "primitive" sculptures, African masks and statuettes, defying aesthetic canons that had stood unquestioned for five hundred years in Europe. André Breton had published his two manifestos of surrealism (1924 and 1930) and put his theories into practice in the first surrealist novel, *Nadja* (1928), in which he had recourse to primitive myths. Many young intellectuals, including those from the Caribbean, were militant Marxists. All these general factors contributed to a climate favorable for the birth of the Negritude movement.

DuBois and Marcus Garvey, with their call to American Negroes to assume their identity in pride and awareness, can be considered the remoter ancestors of the movement. However, a more direct influence came from a group of students, led by Etienne Léro from Martinique, who frequented the Nardal sisters' "salon." In June 1932 they launched a review called *Légitime défense*. (The title, the legal term for self-defense as an extenuating circumstance in cases of homicide, indicates the aggressivity that informs the contributions and the passionate anger in which the movement, for which the review was to be the organ, was conceived.) *Légitime défense* was the title of a pamphlet by André Breton, published in 1926, in favor of Communism; Léro and his collaborators thus clearly indicated their Marxist-Leninist stance and their adoption of surrealism as the art form of the future. Their foreword spelled this out unambiguously, proclaiming their anticapitalist, antibourgeois, anti-Christian principles. Addressing themselves directly to French-speaking blacks from the West Indies in the first instance, they stated in a verbal splutter of frustration and venom their intention eventually to reach all black intellectuals and students: "Impossible as it is for us to speak to the black proletariat, to whom international capitalism has not given the means to understand us, we speak to the children of the black bourgeoisie, to all those who are not yet killed-off highly-placed done-for turned into successful university academics decorated corrupt rotten well-to-do decorative prudish unequivocal opportunists." (my translation respects the original punctuation!)

Léro and his team launched equally vituperative attacks on poetasters from the Caribbean. Even if they had read any of the works from Senegal we discussed in Chapter 2, they would hardly have thought them worth mentioning. René Ménil indicted "so-called writers" who were producing "this abstract and objectively hypocritical literature" that interested neither the black nor the white man, since it was only a poor imitation of French literature of the past. Léro, in even more blistering terms, arraigned the West Indies writers' pretentiousness, inauthenticity, casuistry, portentousness, impenitent conformism, their cult of the past rooted in their Greco-Latin education. But most of all he berates his compatriots for making it a point of honor to write in such a way that a white man can read their works without being able to guess their pigmentation.

Légitime défense was black writers' first published protest against the process of acculturation to which they had been subjected simultaneously with colonization. The magazine did not survive its first number, but it was to have lasting repercussions. It was the first bugle call, rallying black writers to the banner of what was to be known as the Negritude movement. But where it called for a black renaissance and spurred black writers to a pride in race and color, exhorting them to dig deep down in search of their cultural roots, *primarily* as part of an ideological and political struggle, the apostles of Negritude gave priority to the cultural conflict per se. The latter were not necessarily Communists or even fellow-travelers; they simply insisted on Negro culture and black values as the basis for literary forms and inspirations. The prime movers in this cultural awakening were Aimé Césaire from Martinique, Léon Gontran Damas from Guyana, and Léopold Sédar Senghor from Senegal; associated with them were two other Senegalese, Birago Diop and Ousmane Socé.

Senghor was twenty-two when he came to Paris in 1928 to study for an arts degree at the Sorbonne. In 1935 he became the first African to pass the highly competitive *agrégation* examination, entitling him to teach in French high schools. For the next five years, his academic career took him to various towns within reach of Paris, during which time he was writing the poems he published after the war as **Chants d'ombre**. Birago Diop arrived in France a year after Senghor, to study veterinary medicine at the University of Toulouse and later at the Institute of Tropical Veterinary Studies at Alfort, on the outskirts of Paris. Here he came into contact with the black youth of the Left Bank and, in particular, his compatriots, Socé, who was also studying veterinary medicine, and Senghor.

During his years in France, while he was closely associated with black intellectuals' literary and political ambitions, Socé completed his first novel, *Karim,* begun in Senegal, and started work on *Mirages de Paris*. Birago was recalling the stories his grandmother had told him in his childhood and translating into French the adages of the "Senegalese Socrates," Kotje Barma. He bears witness in his autobiography to the life the three shared in the Latin Quarter and tells how Socé, during visits to the Cuban Cabin, a Montmartre nightclub, "surreptitiously scribbled notes for his next novel, *Mirages de Paris,* which he first called *Panamite,* on the strength of his newly-acquired knowledge," and how all his friends at Alfort lent a hand with correcting the proofs of *Karim* (*La Plume raboutée*).

In 1934 Césaire, Damas, and Senghor founded their *Etudiant noir* as an organ for their theories about Negro-African culture and as an outlet for creative writing by all French-speaking blacks. Donald Herdeck refers to it as a "modest news-sheet" and is probably quoting Lilyan Kesteloot who calls it "un petit journal sans prétentions" (an unpretentious little newspaper). Kesteloot herself admits that none of the original founders had been able to supply her with copies of the paper, nor had they any memory of how many numbers appeared. For information about its aims, we must have recourse to indirect evidence, the most reliable being in subsequent writings by its founders. Kesteloot quotes a letter, written to her by Senghor in February 1960, saying "*L'Etudiant noir* and *Légitime Défense* represented respectively the two tendencies dividing the students. Though the two magazines had been subjected to the same influences, they differed on several points. *L'Etudiant noir* laid down that the cultural aspect was of primary importance. For us politics were only one aspect of culture, whereas *Légitime Défense* maintained that the political revolution should precede the cultural revolution." In the same letter, Senghor explains: "We accepted Surrealism as a means and not as an end, as an ally, not as a master. We were quite prepared to take our inspiration from Surrealism, but only because Surrealist writing discovered the spoken word" ([Kesteloot,] *Les écrivains noirs de langue française*).

Surrealism could offer liberation from the rigorous discipline of formal French syntax: the ellipsis and syntactic license that surrealist poets used could be particularly seductive to those composing in an acquired language, who favored expression and imagery that was intuitive, esoteric, fluid, rather than consciously rational, referential, stable, and semantically significant. However, none of the Senegalese poets, at least those of the first Negritude generation, resorted to basic surrealist techniques: experiments with psychoanalytical inspirations in automatic writing, preference for apparently incongruous elements in the free play of hallucinatory analogies, exploitation of the individual unconscious psyche as a guide to poetic expression. But they did learn from the surrealists that poetry could be used as a revendication of liberty as well as a revolt against traditional modes of literary expression. The aspect of Breton's *Message automatique* that particularly appealed to them was the total equality of all normal human beings when faced by a subliminal message, and the fact that this message constituted a common heritage, of which each can demand his share. They also appreciated the incantatory power that the surrealists ascribed to words, using them as R. Short expresses it, "like talismans with magic power over the world." This is probably what Senghor meant when he said, "Surrealist writing rediscovered the spoken word."

From all the evidence, the word *Négritude* never appeared in *L'Etudiant noir,* nor is it of anything except academic interest to know if it was used in verbal discussions from 1932 to 1935, before Césaire launched it in print in his *Cahier d'un retour au pays natal* (*Notebook of a Return*). But the word soon proved a useful, effective, evocative identification tab for Senghor's, Césaire's, and Damas's theories: a call for black intellectual solidarity, a refutation of assimilation, the assertion of Negro-African cultural heritage, and eventually, the indictment of racism and a rallying cry for anticolonial polemics.

It is not my intention here to give any more general definition or redefinition of Negritude, with its rapidly evolving protean character and the many features that French-African writers subsequently attributed to the term. The reader can refer to the many articles, chapters, and books that have been devoted to the subject, particularly in the last twenty years. What interests us is the motor force it lent in the first place to the three very different and original Senegalese authors, directly associated with *L'Etudiant noir* and the birth of the Negritude movement, and the influence it had on their disciples who published poetry, novels, and dramas in the immediate postwar and preinde-

pendence period. We shall see in their own works the expression of the primary concerns of Negritude: the preservation of oral literature and indigenous folklore; the rediscovery and presentation to Western readers of an African concept of life, with a universe peopled with and governed by invisible, telluric forces; in poetry, the assumption of African symbolism, rhythms, and canons of aesthetics; in novels, the difficulties faced by African society in accommodating an "assimilated," twentieth-century persona to the traditional moral, social, and spiritual values of their ancestors. In a word, to borrow the symbol first popularized by O. Mannoni and discussed at length by Janheinz Jahn, Caliban is still content to use the language of his master, Prospero, not yet to call down the "red plague" upon him, but to break out of the prison of this language and its alien culture and fashion from it a pliant instrument for his own self-expression. . . .

In his preface to the *Nouveaux contes d'Amadou Koumba,* Senghor reminds us that "in olden times prose differed little from poetry. A story was rhythmic, only the rhythm was a little freer than that of the poem." Birago Diop illustrates this blurred frontier between prose and poetry. His contemporaries, the dominant forces behind the Negritude movement—Césaire, Damas, and Senghor—concentrated their literary creativity solely in the field of poetry. Jacques Chévrier suggests that this was a deliberate choice of medium, influenced by their classical studies and contemporary surrealist writing. This would discount the fact that they were all instinctive, gifted poets, such as no amount of deliberate intent could have forged, and all produced poetry as naturally as an apple tree produces apples, irrespective of the influence of their classical education or the artistic climate of the thirties in which they matured.

In the case of Léopold Sédar Senghor, the poetry of his homeland was part of his childhood environment long before he ever came in contact with the languages and literatures of the West. He tells us of the lessons he learned from Marône, the poetess of his village, how, as a child, he listened to the hallucinatory chants of the *griots,* and how he later started on his own road to original composition by transcribing and translating traditional oral poetry. When, as a high school teacher in France, the "black shepherd" explains his own provenance to his white flock, he tells them, "My childhood, my lambs, is old as the world and I am young as the dawn of the world eternally young. / The poetesses of the sanctuary nurtured me / The King's *griots* sang for me the authentic legend of my race, accompanied by the sound of the mighty *kôras*." He returns to this theme of early poetic influences when he relates how he laid his head "throbbing with the warlike gallop of the royal drums, on the lap of Ng the poetess," a head "singing with the distant songs of Koumba-the-orphangirl," while his father, "Man of the Kingdom of Sine, reclines at peace upon his mats and the *griots'* fingers of fire dance to the heroic voice of the *kôra's* strings."

Senghor destroyed all his juvenilia, but we know that at the Lycée Louis-le-Grand in Paris and later at the Sorbonne, he fell under the spell of the Parnassian and symbolist poets and wrote his master's dissertation on Baudelaire, taking these as his models for his first verses. When, with Césaire and Damas, he experienced a spiritual awakening and set out to rediscover his African heritage, to explore again his "Childhood Kingdom," "to be reborn to the land which was (his) mother" (*Chants d'ombre*), he never returned to the regular metrical verse or rhymed stanzas, but proclaimed his Africanness in free verse, with haunting irregular rhythms. In adopting these, Senghor has freely acknowledged the debt he owed to Paul Claudel and Saint-John Perse: "I have read much, from the troubadours to Paul Claudel. And imitated much. . . . I will admit that when I first discovered Saint-John Perse after the Liberation, I was as dazzled as was Paul on the road to Damascus. But what is surprising about this? Such poetry is not entirely that of Europe and it is no accident, as Jean Guéhenno points out, that the texts of the Dogon cosmogony 'are not without analogy with the poems of M. Claudel and M. Alexis Léger' (Saint-John Perse). But I already had in a drawer the material for two volumes of poetry" (*Poèmes*).

These two volumes would be *Chants d'ombre,* poems written from 1930 up to the outbreak of war, and *Hosties noires,* written just before and during the war, including poems from the prison camp, Front-Stalag 230, where he spent two years. On the question of the significance of Claudel and Saint-John Perse to a reading of Senghor's own work, Clive Wake has pointed out that they can be seen as "cognate poets" rather than as models for imitation: "Claudel the professional diplomat, living most of his adult life outside France . . . ; Saint-John Perse, also a career diplomat, also living almost continuously outside France, preoccupied with the theme of exile." Before we leave this question of influences to concentrate on what is specific to Senghor's themes and prosody, we should note the debt he owed to Maurice Barrès's novel *Les Déracinés* (The uprooted), which he read while still a pupil at Louis-le-Grand and which awoke in him a realization of the need to affirm his own roots. J. L. Hymans has drawn attention to the importance of Barrès's influence on Senghor in his "Intellectual Biography" of the poet.

Senghor began his spiritual and literary pilgrimage back to his own roots in the poems he published in the same year he was elected to represent his country in the Constituent Assembly that drew up the constitution for France's Fourth Republic. The first poem in *Chants d'ombre,* "In Memoriam," expresses his nostalgia as an expatriate and affirms his atavistic solidarity with his distant countryfolk, especially their dead. In Africa, the presence of death does not mean the rejection of life, and though death is a key theme of these "Songs of Darkness," they also celebrate the vibrant life of Black Africa. Life is ever-present sound and movement; life is the gamut of human emotions, associated with the traditional themes of lyric poetry, which are all present in these verses: absence, nostalgia, loneliness, love. The latter is best expressed in the celebrated "Femme noire," the black woman who is, in the first

place, the individual loved one and also the archetypal African woman, whose beauty is inventoried in erotic imagery. She is also the "femme obscure," suggesting the dark mysteries of fertility, the fecund symbols of motherhood; so the black woman is also the poet's mother in whose shadow he grew up. Finally, the black woman symbolizes the whole black continent: "And lo! now in the heart of summer and of the noonday, I discover your promised land from the height of a sun-burnt mountaintop / And your beauty strikes me full in the heart like the flash of an eagle. . . ."

Inextricably interwoven with the personal and universal lyric themes is an ever-present reference to the larger issues of Africa's history and Europe's destiny. **"Lettre à un poète"** (a letter addressed to Aimé Césaire) sets out his principles on the black poet's mission and the specific source of his inspirations, and includes praises offered to the "Ancestors, Princes and Gods" of Africa. This poem is important both as a manifesto of Negritude theory and as an example of poetic form. Although we have not space here to analyze Senghor's poetics in detail, it is worth noting that this is one of the few published poems in which he retains a regular rhyme scheme (although not obeying the strict laws of classical prosody, which do not permit feminine and masculine endings rhyming together, for example) in couplets of subtle, irregular rhythmic patterns, marked by assonances, alliterations, and internal half-rhymes, in off-beat, syncopated cadences. Senghor goes on to invite his fellow poet to return to the black poet's themes and preoccupations, the sources of his inspiration and racial identity, and to continue to capture the rhythms and mysterious life of the African night.

In using the subjects of Africa's past in references, imagery, and major thematic treatment, Senghor is as much the *griot's* disciple as Birago Diop. He echoes local tradition, invokes his people's moral and religious values, and recalls the Malinke warrior-emperors' exploits, the wars waged by Samory, and the resistance of the former Serer Kingdom to local conquests. **"Prière aux masques"** (**"Prayer to the masks"**) is an invocation to the ageless ancestral gods to support Africa in her distress after the decline of the former empires, but it also expresses the poet's deep concern for Europe's fate in the years of tension leading up to the Second World War. With the two continents linked by an umbilical cord, he is acutely aware that Europe's downfall must be accompanied by that of Africa, "in the death-throes of a piteous princess." This theme is developed in its full grandeur and solemnity in the long ode **"Que m'accompagnent kôras et balafong"** (To the accompaniment of *kôras* and *balafong,* subtitled *u'oï,* "lament"), a poem that sums up all the themes and preoccupations of *Chants d'ombre,* expressing the poet's full consciousness of his mission, and like **"Prayer to the masks,"** anticipating the war themes of the next volume, *Hosties noires.*

Some of these early poems express Senghor's desire for unity between the two continents, but his **"Neige sur**

Paris" ("**Snow upon Paris**") is a bitter indictment of the ravages the West wrought in Africa. Writing at Christmas 1938, when Christians were celebrating the message of peace and Europe was threatened with imminent war, he contrasts ideals and reality: the theory of universal brotherhood and the facts of a divided world. He draws the parallel between Christ's Calvary and Black Africa's suffering at the hands of the white peoples. Throughout his catalogue of grievances against Europe, he strives to reach a spirit of Christian forgiveness, which he expresses in the last line of the poem, a discreet reference to his white companion whose ". . . mains de rosée, le soir" soothe his burning cheeks. The last poem in *Chants d'ombre,* the important **"Retour de l'enfant prodigue" ("Return of the prodigal son")**, proclaims his allegiance to his origins and solidarity with his fellow Africans. Despite "sixteen years of wandering," his heart is still "pure as the East wind in the month of March," and so he defends himself against the charge of having become merely a black Frenchman.

The next volume, "Black Victims" [*Hosties noires*] is explicit: it opens with homage to the black soldiers, the *tirailleurs sénégalais,* recruited into the French army, and closes with **"Prière de paix" ("Prayer for peace")**. This is his bitterest and most cynical indictment of Europe, home of Christian ideals. He inventories all the injustices white men have meted out to the African continent, from the time of slavery through the whole era of colonization. He specifically arraigns France, because she has set herself up as the upholder of equality and brotherhood, liberty and enlightenment. This poem is the counterpart of the earlier **"Snow upon Paris."**

Whereas most of the poems in this collection belong to the period of the 1939-45 war, the Italian invasion of Ethiopia in 1936 inspired **"A l'appel de la race de Saba" ("To the call from the race of Sheba")** in which Ethiopia, the ancient monarchy which traced its history back to the Queen of Sheba, becomes the symbol for rape of all Africa. When France was defeated and occupied in 1940 and all her allies were fighting for survival, Senghor again found his loyalties divided; from then till 1942, his bitterness is replaced by concern for Europe's ordeal and France's humiliation. In the prisoner-of-war camp, where he, the erudite black *agrégé,* found himself serving as scribe to illiterate *poilus,* he acquired a deep compassion for the common people of France, for whom he felt the same solidarity as for the black conscripts. He paid homage to the former in **"Femmes de France" ("Women of France")**; He celebrated the latter in poems entitled **"Aux Tirailleurs sénégalais morts pour la France" ("To the Senegalese *tirailleurs* who died for France"), "Désespoir d'un volontaire libre" ("Despair of a free volunteer"), "Prière des tirailleurs sénégalais" ("Prayer of the Senegalese *tirailleurs*"), "Camp 1940, au Guélowar" ("To the descendant of the Malinke conqueror"), "Camp 1940, to Abdoulaye Ly."**

In 1942 Senghor was released from captivity on grounds of ill health; he returned to Paris to a teaching post, but lived under surveillance. He missed the warm, spontaneous humanity of the camp; moreover, to the solitude and humiliations a black man had to suffer in occupied France is added his disillusionment with the superficiality, materialism, and insensitivity he saw around him. He again expressed anger and despair in the caustic **"Lettre à un prisonnier" ("Letter to a prisoner")**. As in the poem answering the appeal of the race of Sheba, he turns for consolation and hope to the ancient wisdom of Africa, the spiritual quality of the African, which he opposes to the sophistication, coldness, and alienation of "the crowds on the boulevards, sleepwalkers who have renounced their identity as men."

After the war, Senghor is elected to the French National Assembly; no longer an exile expressing nostalgia for Africa, he is the honored, confident "Ambassador of the black races." He marries Ginette, the daughter of Felix Eboué, a Guyanan who becomes governor-general of French Equatorial Africa, and composed for her *Chants pour Naëtt* (Songs for Naëtt), which were incorporated into *Nocturnes,* after the marriage was dissolved, under the more general title of **"Chants pour Signare."** By removing the personal dedication, he made it possible to interpret the poems as an address to the spirit of Africa in the form of the gracious, noble Senegalese *signare.* These beautiful and moving verses express a lover's deep passion with great discretion and sobriety (there is less sensual, erotic imagery than in many of his other poems), while at the same time suggesting the poet's emotional attachment to his native land.

The unity of theme of Senghor's next volume, *Ethiopiques,* stems from his responsibility as a leader of his people. He evokes the role of the ruler in traditional African societies, as in **"Le Kaya-Magan"** (The emperor of ancient Ghana), with whom he identifies: "Kaya-Magan je suis! la personne première / Roi de la nuit noire de la nuit d'argent, Roi de la nuit de verre" (Kaya-Magan am I! The primordial person / King of the black night of the silver night, King of the night of glass). At the same time he associates his role as voice of his people with his function as diplomat and peacemaker, whose task is the reconciliation of races and healing of differences. In this way he is able to resolve the contradictions and ambiguities arising out of his dual loyalties to Africa and Europe, Senegal and France, to the spiritual essence of Africa—symbolized by the queen of Sheba—and to the white woman who is now his wife. This dichotomy is touched on in **"L'Absente" ("The absent one")**, embodying the poet's muse and expressing his reluctance to abandon his role as a visionary under the pressure of politics; it is then fully resolved in the group of poems **"Epîtres à la princesse" ("Letters to the princess")**, dedicated to his wife's grandmother, the marquise de Betteville. These are, on one level, personal expressions of affection; they are also the affirmation of the spiritual union between the North, symbolized by the princess of Belborg, and the South—the culture of Africa—of which the poet is the embodiment: "Et mon pays de sel et ton pays de neige chantent à l'unison" (And my land of salt and your land of snow sing in unison).

Senghor had long cherished the ideal of universal understanding and brotherhood, an ideal that survived his temporary bouts of bitterness and disillusionment with Europe. In *Chants d'ombre,* he had already declared he had "dreamt of a sunlit world in the fellowship of (his) blue-eyed brothers" (**"Retour de l'enfant prodigue"**). Now, in the dramatic poem **"Chaka"** in *Ethiopiques,* he puts into the dying Zulu king's mouth the retort, "I have wished all men to be my brothers," when challenged by the Voice of the White Man with having a "voice red with hatred." Senghor's Chaka is not the bloodthirsty tyrant of Mofolo's novel, but an astute political leader and military strategist who died trying to ensure African unity. He is also identified with his creator, who presents him as a poet-ruler and poet-prophet.

In giving this dramatic form to his own ambivalence, Senghor attempts the confirmation of his conviction that from contradictions of this kind will stem the reconciliation of the differences between colonized Africa and the European colonizing powers. When his next volume of poems, *Nocturnes,* appears, Senegal has achieved independence and the poet-statesman is elected the first president of the new republic. . . .

In spite of his duties as president of the new Republic of Senegal, his important role in African and international affairs, and his major prose writings on socialism and politics generally, Senghor still continued to find time and inspiration for poetic composition. The first volume of poems published after his election as president was *Nocturnes* (1961). This included the revised version of the love poems, *Chants pour Naëtt,* now entitled **"Chants pour signare,"** five **"Elegies,"** and the **"Song of the Initiate."** Many of the new poems reflect the poet's concept of his personal mission to restore a life of harmony, plenitude, and greater spiritual dimensions to his countrymen and announce his homeland's regeneration. In the **"Song of the Initiate,"** he proclaims himself "the son of Man son of the Lion, roaring in the hollow back of the hills" (the lion being Senghor's ancestral totem and also the symbol of Africa and of a sovereign; it features in the new Senegalese national flag). In his **"Elegy of the Circumcised Boys,"** the circumcision rite, marking the passage of the adolescent boy to manhood, becomes the metaphor both for the poet's personal progress to political maturity and his country's attainment of manhood after having undergone the trial period of pain and mental stress.

The theme of the night, suggested by the title *Nocturnes,* had long been a basic element in Senghor's poetry and is, as Lamine Diakhaté indicates, richer even in symbolic associations in African mythology than in Western writings. Night here suggests a time of serenity and also of disquiet; a time of mystery, linked with the past (and also a nostalgic return to the Kingdom of Childhood) and with the dead;

thus an assertion of the continuity of society. Night is also traditionally in Africa the time for dialogue, communication with one's fellows. So Senghor chooses an apt title for both a statesman's message to his people and the apostle of Negritude's message to his literary disciples, as one chapter in the evolution of the political struggle and the affirmation of black values is closed and the literature of independence is about to be launched. Senghor's next volume of poetry will not appear for nearly ten years, returning then to the inspiration of his earlier intimate love songs. We have already mentioned in Chapter 1 the climatic overtones he gives to this work, *Lettres d'hivernage,* associated with the African equivalent of the European autumn. It includes some of the most moving and certainly the most personal verses that Senghor had yet written, indicating that for the poet-president the moment for committed poetry seemed to have passed, so that he could now devote his gifts to the themes that have universally inspired lyric verse.

Senghor's work did not continue to elicit unqualified praise from a new generation of black intellectuals. To his contemporaries of the interwar years and to the first generation of postwar writers, he had been an inspiration and a trailblazer. In the period of decolonization, some of his younger country folk were beginning to question his literary reputation and contest his political authority, based as it was on a nondogmatic socialism and a desire to conciliate the interests of Africa and France, to arrive at a compromise between capitalism and communism. His literary adversaries criticized his erudition, his pedantry, which made his poetry elitist, inaccessible to the masses. Typical of this attitude is *Vive le président* (Long live the president) by the Cameroonian Daniel Ewande, a satire on "our colonized Africas" whose tone ranges from burlesque to vituperation. However, when political considerations are no longer relevant to judging works of art and the latter are allowed to stand as their own monuments, there seems no doubt that Senghor will be acclaimed by posterity as Africa's greatest French-language poet of the twentieth century, and his postcolonial compositions will be seen to have added considerably to his literary stature.

In his seventies, he shows himself in a deeply contemplative and often melancholy mood in his latest published work, *Elégies majeures* ("Major Elegies"). The first of the six long odes, **"Elégie des alizés"** (**"Elegy of the Trade Winds"**), dedicated to his wife Colette, follows the moods of the changing seasons of his homeland, which in turn echo the poet's emotions and mental states, from disillusion to freshness and renewal, from existential nausea to a sense of deliverance. Finally, at the year's end, the fortified poet is inspired to redefine his relationship to his people and his role as poet, anticipating no doubt his intention to retire from the presidency at the end of 1980.

He also redefines the Negritude that informed his first poetic works thirty years before in a deliberate echo of his friend and contemporary, Aimé Césaire's famous lines in *Cahier d'un retour au pays natal.* "My negritude," writes

Senghor, "is not the slumber of the race but the sunshine of the soul, my negritude is vision and life / My negritude is the trowel in the hand, is the lance in the fist / The Ivory Staff of Office . . . / My task is to rouse my people to their futures aflame . . ." (*Elégies majeures*). He seems to repent of the arcane nature of his verse, proclaiming kinship with all black workers whose approval he calls for so that he can once more be their emissary and Africa's mouthpiece. Yet for all this announcement of solidarity with the common people, he is still unrepentant in his use of excessively abstruse vocabulary. It is useless to search in Littré or Robert for words like *maëstrichtien, gliricidias, l'alhiziazygia,* as unfamiliar to the French reader as to the African, and he supplies no glossary to assist the Europeans' understanding of *combassou* or *moutoumoutous.* But these archaic or recondite terms, together with exotic proper names, imitative harmony of assonances, insistent drumming of alliterations—which do not disdain a quasi-punning interplay of appositions—all invest the verse with the enigmatic mystery of a hieratic incantation, as if we were participating in some arcane rite.

"**Elégies des alizés**" is both the septuagenarian poet's reaffirmation of his role as emissary of his people and an intensely personal pilgrimage into the intimate sensorial experience of his own bicontinental existence: he consciously and constantly attests his African roots while his diapasons vibrate with love for the woman who is not always at his side. The path from the personal to the universal is further affirmed in the "**Elegy for Jean-Marie**," inspired by the premature death of a young friend. Like Victor Hugo in *Contemplations,* drawing from bereavement a strengthening of his resignation to God's will, Senghor too restates in this elegy his religious faith. In the next of the threnodies, the "**Elegy for Martin Luther King**," he takes up the theme of hope for universal brotherhood to be born out of contemporary violence. He echoes Pastor King's own "I had a dream" with "Et je vis une vision" in which black men and white men are gathered at the feet of the "Being who is strength"—townsmen and peasants, those who cut cane and those who chop cotton, the "Just and the Good" from America's past and present who have devoted and often sacrificed their lives for liberty and racial justice. A visit to Tunis in 1975 is the occasion for the "**Elegy of Carthage**," in which Senghor the scholar displays his erudition while Senghor the statesman pays tribute to his host, Habib Bourguiba, reviewing the history, peoples, and heroic figures of North Africa, with a discreet reference to the Algerian war of liberation.

The "**Elegy for Georges Pompidou**," like the "**Elegy of the Trade Winds**," is an intensely personal poem: a lament for a lifelong friend rather than for a public figure. Offering this poem, "like a libation," he recalls his contemporary's long fight with illness, turning naturally then to a preoccupation with dying and the immortality of the soul of which his Catholic faith assures him. He questions his dead friend on the reality of the hereafter and expresses his own fears and weaknesses, asking for the prayers of his "more-than-brother" for strength, courage, and constancy in his task. He finishes again on an ecumenical note of universal love, asking for blessings on his black people, "all people with brown skin, beige skin / Suffering throughout the world . . . who were on their knees, who had too long eaten bitter bread, millet and rice of shame," Negroes, Arabs, Jews, Indochinese, and even, while he is about it, the white superpowers with their superbombs, who also have need of love.

The last of the elegies, "**For the Queen of Sheba**," brings Senghor's poetic composition full circle. Taking as its epigraph "I am black and I am fair" from the *Song of Songs,* it returns to the themes of his youth when he was forging the doctrines of Negritude. It is a more elaborate reworking of his famous "**Femme noire**" from *Chants d'ombre* of thirty years before, celebrating what Sartre had called "the Annunciation of quintessential blackness," clothing in indigenous rhythms the dazzling imagery that seems fostered in African soil and ripened in tropical sunshine. Once more, with "desire suspended in the October of age," the poet returns insistently to the memories of youth, and once more his verses are infused with impassioned eroticism. The poem is a love offering, a song of rapture, a dialogue between poet and muse, an inflammatory courtship dance, culminating in an orgasmic ecstasy.

If this collection of poems should prove to be Senghor's swan song, the best of them, particularly the "**Elegy of the Trade Winds**" and the "**Elegy for the Queen of Sheba**," will prove to have exorcised death more surely than any possible prayers to his friend Georges Pompidou. The verses, which unite word, music, and movement to express the pulsating heart of Africa, will continue to vibrate with life, a testimony to his "Kingdom of Childhood" and his "Ngritude debout."

In the postface to this volume, Senghor elaborates upon that to the earlier *Ethiopiques* to define in detail his poetic theory and practice. He frankly admits both his "biological interbreeding" and his cultural *métissage,* tracing the influences of the great French poets—Hugo, Baudelaire, Rimbaud, Mallarmé, Claudel, Saint-John Perse—combined with the neologisms, wild images, and syncopated rhythms that Negro-African poets have introduced into Francophone verse. Rimbaud's example has been particularly valuable, with his genius for using symbols, rich in analogical imagery, more complex, ambivalent, multivalent than the classical, traditional symbol of the West. The final aim of the poet, he states, is to achieve a "symbiosis of soul and body, grafting the spoken word onto flesh and blood" (*Elégies majeures*).

This essay is more than a poetic manifesto, it is Senghor's profession of faith in which he admits that his poetry has always been the essential aspect of his life. But he makes it clear that he does not consider his poetic creativity distinct from his work as a statesman. The poet-master-of-language is for him the seer, the visionary, exteriorizing his "inspiration- intuition" to create a "total poetry" that is "at one and the same time, idea, vision, spoken word and action." Thus, from his beginnings as a militant exponent of Negritude, he evolves his principle of a humanism of universal dimensions: poetry creating a new cultural world order. "I speak," he says, "of a spoken word as a new vision of the universe and a pan-human creation at one and the same time: of the Fertile word, one last time, because it is the fruit of different civilizations, created by all the nations together, over the whole surface of the planet Earth."

Janet G. Vaillant (essay date 1990)

SOURCE: "Coming of Age," in *Black, French, and African: A Life of Léopold Sédar Senghor,* Harvard University Press, 1990, pp. 117-46.

[*In the following excerpt, Vaillant discusses the significance of Senghor's formative years in France and his early poetry.*]

On the eve of World War II, Tours was a calm little town in the Loire Valley slightly to the south and west of Paris. The people of the region were known as bon vivants, lovers of good food and wine. They were sunny, like their rich and fertile countryside. Tours is, and was when Senghor arrived, a town typical of provincial France and the French heartland. Senghor particularly enjoyed the fact that it had been a Roman settlement, Cesarodunum, and remained rich in signs of its Roman and early Christian history. It encompassed, therefore, all he thought best in French culture.

In the fall of 1935, the forty-four children who arrived for their first day in sixth class met an unexpected sight. They knew they were getting a new teacher, an agrégé from the University of Paris, who was better educated than many of their other teachers. They expected him to be poised and well-prepared. When they entered their groundfloor classroom, the found a man who seemed confident and well-educated but who was black. They had never seen anyone like him before. Senghor sympathized with the awkward situation of the director of the school, who must have wondered how best to present the new teacher to the students' parents. As it turned out, Senghor quickly won the children's confidence as an excellent classics teacher. He set out to teach Latin as a living language and managed to avoid the monotonous declension of nouns and verbs that had characterized his own learning of the classical languages. . . .

The diversity of levels on which Senghor existed is most evident in the poems he wrote during his years in Tours. Most of them were not published until later, but it seems clear that it was during this often lonely period that Senghor first realized his vocation as a poet. His earliest

published poems provide a revealing glimpse of the emotions and concerns that preoccupied him then and would continue to preoccupy him in the future. Senghor has emphasized that in 1935, the same year he moved to Tours, "I discovered myself such as I was."

This coming of age was not an altogether happy one. It was accompanied by moments of doubt and even despair. Looking back, Senghor recalled it as a time of fervor and perpetual tension. He, Césaire, and a few other black friends with whom he met during his trips to Paris resisted taking the easy road of assimilation, becoming the educated black Frenchmen so dear to sentimental colonial bureaucrats. They accepted a call to live life honestly and dangerously, and saw themselves as New Negroes with a mission to spread the word. The struggle to express what they felt led, according to Senghor, to "literary work which was morally, how shall I put it, physically and metaphysically lived right up to the edge of madness." Their inner turmoil was experienced as illness. Césaire actually had a nervous collapse in the fall of 1935. The breakdown was attributable partly to overwork in preparation for the Ecole Normale competition, but it also coincided with Césaire's attempt to absorb the shock of his encounter with Paris and, through Senghor, with Africa.

Senghor has written that Césaire and he suffered through this period together. To a point their anxiety stemmed from the same source. Césaire's attempt at cure mirrored Senghor's, though each was filtered through the prism of a different temperament and personality. There was the further difference that Senghor, unlike Césaire, had a personal memory of a real Africa. Césaire saw Senghor as the more fortunate of the two for this reason. Looking within, Césaire discovered emptiness, whereas Senghor discovered warm memories of another world. Nonetheless, as they came to know each other, each began to see that his individual dilemma was not simply a personal misfortune or the result of undue sensitivity, but the effect of a structure created by a historical relationship between black and white developed over hundreds of years. The Afro-French society of Senegal, the transplanted and mixed culture of the Antilles, as well as the promises and conditions of French education for blacks, had left a difficult legacy. Césaire and Senghor discovered that the educated black man trying to live in France suffered from this situation in the extreme.

The severity of this strain was illustrated dramatically for them by the suicide of a black French-speaking writer, the Malagasy poet Jean-Joseph Rabéarivelo. Rabéarivelo's death received considerable publicity in the Paris press. His last diary, published in the *Mercure de France,* revealed that in taking leave of life he had left "a kiss to the books of Baudelaire," Senghor's favorite poet. This event shook Senghor and his circle, who identified Rabéarivelo's situation with their own. Both Senghor and Damas wrote about it. Damas observed that the suicide was partly the result of "despair brought about by a sense of the uselessness of all effort, by uprooting and exile in the very land of his ancestors [he was in Madagascar at the time of his suicide], . . . but also illustrated the drama of a man who has crossed very quickly, too quickly, the stages of civilization. Rabéarivelo aspired high, not just to be the equal of the white, but to be an intellectual. Yet he became a being apart, neither fish nor fowl, and suffered for it." Senghor reflected on Rabéarivelo's suicide somewhat differently. He saw it as one possible outcome of the failure to make peace within one's own personality. When a man has become French by education, he feels himself an outcast in his own land. This makes Rabéarivelo's suicide understandable. Senghor was determined to integrate in himself the best of both worlds and to be comfortable in both. He understood that this would be impossible without the reevaluation and acceptance of the core values of the Africa of his childhood. This was a part of his basic identity, the remnants of childhood that must be preserved. It would require the creation of a new person with a new voice. The voice would be neither French nor African, for the man was neither French nor African. It would be that of a new historical personage, the French Negro. The whole quest, as Senghor put it, was "nothing but a quest for ourselves." It was no idle or vain goal, but a vital necessity.

The examples provided by Césaire and Rabéarivelo suggest that Senghor was not being overly melodramatic when he spoke of his quest for a new identity as "a question of life and death." The price of failing to achieve equilibrium, he wrote in his reflection on Rabéarivelo, is despair. And, elsewhere, discussing Rabéarivelo and suggesting that he himself was no stranger to this despair, "I would never commit suicide because I think it is giving up. It is the acceptance of defeat. For me, suicide is cowardice. And the fault I scorn the most is cowardice." Despair is also one of the most deadly sins for the Christian, as suicide is considered a crime against God. Senghor's deep Christian belief and his long Christian education helped provide the framework for resisting Rabéarivelo's choice. They promised Senghor that an alternative was possible.

Poetry gave both Césaire and Senghor, and their friend Damas, a language and form in which to express the problem and to reach toward its solution. In Césaire's case, recovery from a psychological breakdown coincided with his sketching out the first draft of a long prose poem, *Cahier d'un retour au pays natal* (Notebook of a Return to the Land of Birth). In Senghor's, it led to the discovery of a vocation for poetry that allowed him to recognize himself "such as he was" and to write the poems that make up his first published collection of poetry, ***Chants d'ombre*** (Songs of, or from, the Shadows). In both cases, it led, as it had for the heroes of Maurice Barrès who had so attracted Senghor in his student days, to a return to the traditions of their homeland.

Césaire's *Cahier* is transparently autobiographical. It presents in poetic form an account of a metaphoric return to his native land, a trip mirrored by Césaire's actual trip to Martinique in the summer of 1936. He looks open-eyed

at his island and accepts the fact that this is his only home. Senghor has emphasized repeatedly how close in their thinking he and Césaire were at this time; thus Césaire's account is valuable for what it suggests about both men. Césaire sets out to assess his native island with an objective eye for the first time. He sees a people who are browbeaten, disease-ridden, and poor. He sees a land that is ugly, with a stench of poverty, "rotting under the sun." He sees hunger and suffering, a place where the river of life has been blocked up and lies, torpid, in its bed. He accepts this as the reality of his home and of his personal past. He sees also that he is connected by virtue of his black skin to the experience of all black men, black men of Africa, Haiti, Virginia, Georgia, and Alabama. He accepts their history as his—the ugliness and ignorance, the poverty and disease, the slavery and cannibalism. This is a real and inescapable part of the black experience. Both the exotic Negro of French invention and the black Frenchman are myths created by white Europeans. To the rest of the world, he now hurls a challenge: "Adapt yourself to me. I do not adapt myself to you." He will cheer for those who are nothing. They at least are not cynical or corrupted by the exploitation of others. This does not mean that he hates other races, only that he will exalt in his own. He accepts unconditionally his membership in a race with a grim and degraded past. In the future he will stand up, as he has not done in the past, and other Negroes will stand up with him. Exoticism and illusion are not fit food for a man. They cannot nourish his growth. Man must stand on what is real. No matter how unpleasant that reality is, only it can provide a steady foundation. For Césaire, in this poem, the progression is simple. First, he will recognize the location of his true homeland; second, he will look objectively at it; and third, he will accept it for what it is. Then, and only then, can he move forward. No more self-deception or seeing himself reflected in the eyes of others.

Senghor saw his task as somewhat different. If Césaire and the black population of Martinique had in fact lost all traces of their distant African heritage and been left only with poverty and slavery, he had not. Senghor argued that blacks had been *taught* for centuries that they had thought nothing, built nothing, painted nothing, sung nothing, and that they and their culture were nothing, the "tabula rasa" of French mythology. This was the stuff of his schooldays, when his French teachers had reminded him over and over again that they had driven barbarism and sickness from his country and had brought him the benefits of civilization. But while he was learning this from his French teachers, he had also known something else, something that he had for a time discounted. He had a direct experience of the African village, of Djilor and Joal. This knowledge contradicted the French doctrine that Africa was a blank page, totally without culture. What Senghor had now to do was to stop pretending either that the French teaching was correct or that it did not exist. He had to acknowledge that most Frenchmen considered blacks inferior men whose best hope was to become discolored Frenchmen. He finally realized that he could never achieve self-respect as long as he continued to pretend that he and the French saw no difference between him and them. Like Césaire, Senghor resolved to confront these attitudes and teachings with another reality. He, too, would make the metaphoric and symbolic trip home.

The poetry Senghor wrote in Tours reflects this resolve. It evokes and examines his childhood heritage and accepts it as an inextricable part of his own personality. The subjects of these poems, their shifting emphases and rich ambivalence, provide a glimpse of Senghor's inner self and the associations that rang through his memory at this time. While it is always dangerous to assume that the voice of a poem and the actual voice of a writer are identical, in Senghor's case the connection seems close indeed in these early poems.

The first theme Senghor takes up is that of exile. Its direct connection to his life as an African student in Paris is clear. He expresses feelings of isolation among strangers, of unease, and of a keen, almost unbearable love for the absent one, Africa. The theme of exile and return, providing opportunity for loving descriptions of home and immersion in memories of childhood, is an understandable one for any student far from home. For Senghor it had a special significance. Immersing himself in memories of childhood, sharing them with sympathetic West Indian friends, and writing about them provided Senghor a source of pleasure and companionship. It lent dignity and wider significance to what otherwise might have been solitary day-dreaming or a grim quest. Csaire and others, hungry to learn about Africa, encouraged him to continue in this direction.

Senghor writes lyrically of his childhood home, Joal, and the nights of Sine:

> Woman, lay on my forehead your perfumed hands, hands softer than fur
> Above, the swaying palms rustle in the high night breeze
> . . . . . .
> Listen to its song, listen to our dark blood beat, listen
> To the deep pulse of Africa beating in the mist of forgotten villages.

Working on these poems in his room, Senghor could travel home in his mind's eye and give outlet to his nostalgia. He could write of his beloved uncle, Waly, his mythic and noble father, the dignity and riches of traditional kings, and the peace and calm of evenings in the still villages. Such was the inspiration for one of his most often quoted poems, a poem written in praise of the beauty of the black woman and of the Africa she embodies:

> Naked woman, dark woman
> Firm-fleshed ripe fruit, sombre raptures of black wine, making lyrical my mouth
> Savannah stretching to clear horizons, savannah shuddering beneath the East Wind's eager caresses.
> Carved tom-tom, taut tom-tom, muttering under the Conqueror's fingers
> Your solemn contralto voice is the spiritual song of the Beloved.

Senghor celebrates the particular texture and physical presence of a concrete place and time, the Africa of his childhood. It is a pure and integrated world that is, to use his own phrase, innocent of Europe.

Into some of Senghor's evocations of Africa, however, creep signs of the European. Even as he remembers Joal with the beautiful women in the cool shade of verandahs, King Koumba Ndofene Diouf, and the rhapsodies of the griots, he also hears with pleasure pagan voices chanting the "tantum ergo," and sees the Catholic religious processions that gather by his grandfather's house in Joal. They, too, are part of his remembered Africa. They appear in the poem as totally compatible with the rest. Both elements are part of a harmonious memory.

These poems are consistent, affectionate, and whole. The merging of Africa, paradise, and childhood is complete. If Baudelaire taught that all great poets are inspired by childhood, Senghor happily bears him out in finding in the kingdom of childhood his chief poetic inspiration. Such an imaginative return also offers the poet an opportunity to relive a period when his experience was integrated, before he felt the impact of the French in Africa or the adult experiences of dislocation and division. With a flash of insight, Senghor acknowledges that childhood and Africa are linked with Eden in his memory, there confused and inseparable. Like Eden, his childhood Africa offered him a place of perfect harmony between man and his surroundings. Perhaps even more important for Senghor, it was the time of emotional peace and internal harmony. In Eden man and God lived in accord. Man did not yet know sin, which cuts him off from an integrated communion with God. In Senghor's imagination Eden and the Africa of his childhood are one and the same, what he calls the kingdom of childhood, to which he can return at will for inspiration.

When Senghor writes of his present situation and feelings, however, the poet's attitude and mood become far more complex and varied. He finds no single consistent stance toward the French world, at least not in his early poems. Even the notion of exile becomes more complex. At times, the poet focuses on the physical exile that leads to solitude and isolation. But he finds that his solitude is deeper than mere physical absence from Africa. He is further isolated by specific qualities of French life. Even this, however, is not the full measure of his separation. He suffers most of all from "that other exile harder on my heart, the tearing of self from self / from the language of my mother, from the thinking of my ancestor, from the beat of my soul." This wrenching of self from self leads to an almost overwhelming sense of being two.

The poet realizes that he has internalized both his African and his French upbringing, and finds the two sets of values and behaviors to be at odds. The colonial administrator and educator Georges Hardy had warned that French schooling could lead Africans to live in two separate worlds and that this could have dire results. For most African children, the French world was but an artificial and temporary existence, while their real world remained securely that of Africa. For Senghor, however, the balance was far more even. He loved France and French culture. He also loved his native Africa. If he was to find a new voice as a French Negro, he had to resolve this problem of twoness. For him, the French Negro could not be the black Frenchman of colonial policy, the Frenchman who happened to be black. That black Frenchman was doomed forever to second-class citizenship. Nor could the French Negro be the African innocent of Europe. Senghor would have to be a black man first, who then acquired French culture and put it to work for his own purposes. It was too late to reject his laboriously acquired French education, nor did he wish to. A linguistic solution of this dilemma, simply by fusing together two words, an adjective and a noun, "Negro" and "French," and announcing oneself a "French Negro" or a "New Negro," was a declaration of intent, but only a first step. What might seem but a small shift in emphasis required in fact a basic redefinition of the nature and possibilities of the black man.

This theme of separation, internal fracture, and the search for wholeness adds a more sombre dimension to the theme of exile. This is the note that dominates Senghor's first published collection of poetry, *Chants d'ombre* (Songs of, or from, the Shadow). So long as he felt these inner divisions, he could not rest. As he explored their nature and consequences, he was comforted by knowing that his painful experience was shared by men like Césaire and Maran, as well as by men who had lived before him and whom he knew only through their writings, such as the black American Dr. W. E. B. DuBois. Senghor was astonished, he later wrote, to discover such kinship in the writings of DuBois, a man living so removed from himself in both time and place. In expressing what he called his constant sense of twoness, DuBois had put the problem of the black man in a white man's world with stark clarity. His writings further convinced Senghor that all black men shared a common experience.

W. E. B. DuBois was born in Massachusetts in 1868, almost forty years before Senghor's birth. The worlds in which the two men grew up bore no resemblance. They did share, however, the experience of moving at a very young age into a world dominated by whites who had certain preconceptions about black people. DuBois grew up in the little New England town of Great Barrington, Massachusetts, and received a Ph.D. from Harvard University, an institution whose relative prestige among Americans rivals that of Louis-le-grand and the Sorbonne among the French. He, like Senghor, was able to excel according to the white man's standards. Yet though DuBois got a degree from Harvard and studied in Europe, when it came time for his adult career, race became the decisive factor. DuBois had to look for employment, as did another black Harvard graduate, Alain Locke, at a black institution such as Fisk, Howard, or Atlanta. Similarly, Senghor was constantly reminded in small ways that, despite his unusual success in the French system, he was not French and never could be. Biology and birth proved decisive in such mat-

ters. When DuBois published *The Souls of Black Folk* in 1903, three years before Senghor was born, he was in his mid-thirties, a gifted and successful young man who appeared to have a promising scholarly career ahead of him. In his book, DuBois describes the position of the black man in America. Living in the American world, he observes,

> yields him [the Negro] no true self-consciousness, but only lets him see himself through the revelation of the other world. It is a peculiar sensation, this double-consciousness, this sense of always looking at oneself through the eyes of others, of measuring one's soul by the tape of a world that looks on in amused contempt and pity. One ever feels his twoness—an American, a Negro; two souls, two thoughts, two unreconciled strivings; two warring ideals in one dark body, whose dogged strength alone keeps it from being torn asunder.

DuBois, like Senghor in his poetry, identifies several dimensions to the problem of "twoness," and of the black man in the white man's culture. On the first and most obvious level, the black self seen through the eyes of whites is an inferior person in every way. He has invented nothing, has done nothing, and is nothing. He can be only an object of contempt, curiosity, or pity. As the dictionary Senghor used at school put it, Negroes are inhabitants of Africa who form a race "inferior in intelligence to the white race called Caucasian." But there is a second part of the problem, both more subtle and more intractable. The educated black American not only is seen by others as inferior but also sees himself as inferior, for he sees with eyes shaped by white values and culture.

DuBois offers a precise description of Senghor's experience. Though African by birth, Senghor had become French by education. He was taught to see Africans as French people saw Africans. No allowance was made for the fact that he himself happened to be African. Nothing in his education encouraged or even allowed him to have a clear sense of himself as an educated black person. According to his French culture, to be black and educated was a contradiction in terms. There was no such person. Hence the sense of twoness. It was not simply a question of being buffeted by the insolence of others. The struggle was between two warring parts of the self. Under these circumstances, to become an integrated, single person with a clear voice was a difficult achievement, and yet to fail was to pay an enormous price. The suicide of Rabéarivelo illustrated just how high that price might be for a sensitive person. Given DuBois's powerful description of an experience Senghor felt to be his own, it is small wonder that Senghor later called DuBois one of the fathers of Negritude and firmly believed that the essential black experience was shared by black men everywhere.

Senghor explored this experience of twoness in his early poetry. The poet discovers first one and than another rift in his personality. At the most obvious there is a division between the outer self he presents to the world, that of the dutiful teacher who "smiles but never laughs," and an inner self, brooding about his African roots. The outer self, carefully constructed to hide emotion, is calm and serene; the inner self is in turmoil. This dichotomy is the subject of Senghor's first extant reliably dated poem, **"Jardin de France"** (**"French Garden"**):

> Calm Garden
> Grave Garden
> Garden with evening eyes
> Lowered for the Night
> . . . .
> White Hands
> Delicate motions
> Soothing gestures
> . . . .
> But the tom-tom's call
> bounding
> over continents
> and mountains
> Who will quiet my heart
> Leaping at the tom-tom's call
> Violently
> Throbbing?

Here the calm, French surface is barely able to contain the African heart that stubbornly leaps to the beat of the drum. The stolid measured rhythms of being in the French world contrast stylistically with the flowing energy of the lines describing the inner African being, reinforcing the explicit content of the poem. It is a contrast parallel to that of the later poem **"Portrait,"** in which the poet expresses the discontinuity between his inner world and that of the French in which he lives, but also acknowledges the appeal of the French world. The spring of Touraine is sweet and makes advances, totally unaware of the poet's "imperious Negritude." The poet makes no attempt at reconciliation of any kind. He is simply descriptive.

At times, the poet wishes only to bury his African side. When he first arrived in Paris, for example, Senghor shared the French view about Africans' lack of contribution to world culture: "Had our black skins allowed it, we would have blushed for our African birth . . . the [African] people made us secretly ashamed." This is the attitude of his schoolboy verse written in imitation of the French romantic poets, an attitude that later made him so ashamed that, as he wrote to Maurice Martin du Gard, he destroyed this early work. It is an attitude he admitted openly only after he had cast it off. In a poem entitled **"Totem,"** he writes of being pursued by a heritage he cannot shake:

> In my inmost vein I must hide him
> My Ancestor with the skin storm-streaked with lightning and thunder
> My guardian animal. I must hide him
> Lest I burst the dam of scandal.

And, elsewhere, "it pursues me, my black blood, right into the solitary heart of the night."

Even as he is trying to hide his ancestor, and so to escape his black blood, Senghor realizes that this is impossible. The advantage may be, as the poet suggests in **"Totem,"**

that the ancestor protects him from his naked pride that might lead him to develop the "arrogance of the lucky races," and from the weakness of civilized man. These arguments are not altogether convincing. The poet seems to be casting about for some consolation for his inescapable blackness. It is a great effort. Senghor had to "hypnotize himself," he said later, to find all that belonged to white Europe, its reason, its art, and its women, ugly and insipid.

The arrangement of the individual poems in the *Chants d'ombre* collection reflects what Senghor calls the order of their general inspiration, if not the actual dates of composition. The progression from poem to poem therefore parallels his own evolution, at least as he later came to see it, and the stages he went through in his growing self-awareness.

The first poem in the collection, **"In Memoriam,"** finds the poet in Paris in his room, alone, apprehensive about the crowd of men "with faces of stone" who await him in the street below. To escape them, and to avoid going down into this world, he dreams of Africa, his race, and the dead ancestors. With images of African power, he builds a protective wall between himself and the world outside. At the end of the poem, he reluctantly gives up this secure fortress and goes out into the world, where he resolves to live with "his brothers with the blue eyes and hard hands." Several short poems that convey similar attitudes are followed by the poems singled out above for their clear, unambivalent evocation of the nights of Sine, Joal, and Djilor, the beauty of the black woman and of Africa, and the comfort and strength of the ancestor. In one poem, however, entitled **"Le message"** (**"The Message"**), the ancestor accuses the poet of ignoring the family songs, of learning new languages, and of memorizing an alien history of other ancestors, the Gauls. The poet is accused of becoming a doctor at the Sorbonne, bedecking himself with diplomas and surrounding himself with piles of papers. The ancestor questions why he has done this, and whether it has led to happiness. Return to me, the voice urges.

At this point in the poetic cycle, the poet finds himself once more in Paris. But now his attitude is somewhat different. In **"Neige sur Paris"** (**"Snow on Paris"**), Senghor evokes the sterility and cold of the city. Whiteness and snow bring death, not purity or innocence. The poet is no longer content with seeking refuge in memory. Rather, he is ready to accuse the white hands "that whipped slaves / . . . that slapped me / . . . that delivered me to solitude and hatred / . . . that cut down the forest of palms which dominated Africa / . . . to build railroads / They pulled down the forests of Africa to save Civilization," because they were weary with their own failures and shortcomings. The expression of anger and bitterness is new. The poet feels these emotions strongly and no longer needs to hide them. Nonetheless, Senghor pulls back from closing even this single poem in anger. He ends with a prayer to the Christian God, and with the resolve not to use up his hatred on "the diplomats who bare their long canine teeth and who, tomorrow, will barter black flesh." He promises that he will achieve reconciliation in the warmth of God's sweetness and embrace his enemies as brothers. Even though he is angry with the Europeans' ravaging of Africa, he still recognizes their God as his God and accepts the Christian goal of reconciliation.

The poet now considers contributions that Africans can make to the European world. If the Africa of the empires has died an agonizing death, Europe, too, is suffering. Like the good Samaritan who gives up his last garment for another, the African will give life to the dying European world. He will provide the leaven for the white flour, the grease for the city's rusty steel, "For who would teach rhythm to a dead world of machines and cannons? / Who would shout the cry of joy to wake the dead and the orphans to the dawn? / . . . / We are the men of the dance, whose feet gain strength by striking the hard earth."

This new stance is not firmly held. Triumph is followed by defeat. At times, as in **"Totem,"** he still wants to hide his ancestry. He writes of false starts, setbacks, frustration, and depression. In two poems that come at this point in the collection, **"Ndéssé ou 'Blues'"** (**"Ndéssé or Blues"**) and **"A la mort"** (**"To Death"**), Senghor records a youthful surge of life and promise that is blighted, confused, left without outlet or direction: "My wings beat and bruise themselves on the bars of a low sky." A child races gaily after a ripe fruit. It rolls under a palm tree, and the child is flattened abruptly to the ground. The poet is pressed down, stopped, smothered. He feels a vivid loss of well-being. Disappointment and the chilling winter rains, too, are the poet's inescapable companions.

In the next long poem, **"Que m'accompagnent kôras et balafong"** (Let Me Be Accompanied by Köras and Balafong), Senghor returns to the theme of Africa the unspoiled, where Africa, Eden, and childhood merge in an eternal present. In this realm, man is always whole. It is a wholeness that encompasses both Christian and African worlds and lies at the center of Senghor's being. In his original plan, this was to be the title poem of the collection. The poem recalls, in loving detail and long, hypnotic rhythms, the Africa of childhood. It states the poet's dilemma: Must he choose? It is no longer a question of rejecting the call of his ancestor for the inviting world of the French, or of forgetting Europe in the warm embrace of his native land. Either choice would diminish the poet. He finds that he is "deliciously torn between these two friendly hands / . . . these two antagonistic worlds / When mournfully—ah! I no longer know which is my sister and which my foster sister." He feels deep love for both. Not to choose but to hold them simultaneously in his desire: "But if I must choose at the hour of the test / I have chosen my distressed people, my peasant people, the whole peasant race throughout the world / . . . To be your trumpet!" And with that choice, the poet heralds a new mission, listening to the new voices and the song of "seven thousand new negroes." And yet it is still not really a

choice, for he takes with him to this Africa a friend from the Breton mist. In Europe he will play the trumpet of Africa for European ears. In Africa he will introduce the good European. Senghor aspires to be like Maran, to whom the poem is dedicated. The poet will combine the strengths of both traditions to serve his people. What makes this poem extraordinarily successful is that it is in itself a tour de force of harmonized styles and symbolic references, an extraordinary blend of classical, French, and African allusions. It resounds with the music of the African instruments that are called for as accompaniment, as well as with classical echoes of Virgil and pious Aeneas, the Roman exemplar of filial piety. It also evokes the Christian Eden and God's promise of redemption to those who are worthy. The effect is a rich harmony, the enhancement of each by the other, for which Senghor yearned in his own life.

The next few poems speak of the difficulty of departure, of giving up the physical and emotional comfort of Africa to return, as he must, to Europe. The poet does not doubt that he must return. The collection closes with a poem that appears from internal evidence to have been written during World War II. It is called **"Le retour de l'enfant prodigue"** (**"The Return of the Prodigal Son"**), and is dedicated to Senghor's nephew, the son of Hélène Senghor, Jacques Maguilen Senghor. Here the theme of deserting the ancestors, of guilt and the need for forgiveness, is explored directly. Tired from years of wandering and exile, the prodigal son has returned home, to the herdsman who shared his childhood dreams, and to his ancestors who have withstood the passage of time unchanged. He seeks from them pure water to wash away the mud of civilization that clings to his feet. He seeks peace, guidance, and strength. In this search, the poet makes a pilgrimage to the ancestral tomb, the Elephant of Mbissel, the tomb Senghor had first visited as a child on his trip from Djilor to mission school and had recently revisited on his trip to Senegal, the tomb where his father now lay buried. Prostrating himself, the poet invokes the African idiom of praise, to the ancestor and his noble lineage, to the greatness and riches of the kings of Sine. He thanks his fathers, who have not allowed him to fall into hatred when faced with "the polite insults and discreet allusions" he has had to endure. To them he confesses his apparent disloyalty and friendship with the princes of form. He has eaten bread that was bought with the hunger of others and has dreamed of a world "in brotherhood with my blue eyed brothers." It is true. Senghor did thirstily drink in French culture, enjoy European friends, and imagine a life of success and general acceptance in the European world. He did neglect his ancestor. He hid him. He pressed on to become an accomplished intellectual, one of the princes of form. For this, the poet now begs forgiveness from his family, the ancestors, and the land. He has recognized that, like the mythic Greek wrestler Antaeus who was invincible as long as his foot touched the earth, his strength depends on contact with his native soil.

Having thus humbled himself and praised his ancestors for their power and endurance, he invokes the most glorious of them and entreats them to hand on to him the knowledge of the great wise men of Timbuktu, the will of the conqueror Soni Ali, the wisdom of the Keita, kings of Mali, the courage of the *guelowar,* conquerors of Sine, and the strength of the *tiedo,* the fierce armed slaves. He offers to give up his life in battle if he must, but in return he asks that the forces of past heroes live on in him, that they make of him their "master of language . . . their ambassador."

This prodigal son, unlike the son of the Biblical parable, does not wish simply to be forgiven by his father. He does want forgiveness, indeed the very title of the poem implies that he will be forgiven, but he also wants something more. He wants his father's blessing on his future life in a different world. Senghor wants to serve his people, not just as the trumpet that blares out his people's virtue and strength, as he had put it in **"Que m'accompagnent kôras et balafong."** He wishes now to be an ambassador, the man who represents and explains his people to alien lands, a trumpet that will play a melody Europeans can understand. In closing the poem, the poet evokes both the emotions that pull him back and the sense of duty that propels him forward. First the familiar evocation of childhood, the security and refuge, "to sleep again in the cool bed of childhood," and then the reluctant departure: "Tomorrow, I will take up again the road to Europe, the road of the ambassador / Longing for my black homeland." This poem, meditative and reflective, calm and measured in tone, expresses a firm determination to take on a mission on behalf of his people. The poet sees his calling as one that requires not simply self-expression, the strident note of the trumpet, but interpretation, the diplomatic skill of the ambassador. He must express his experience and that of his people in a way that can be understood by people of another world and culture. He embraces the duty of becoming a spokesman whose message is intelligible, not simply a poet who allows himself the self-indulgence of beautiful words without regard for his audience.

It is noteworthy that the poet never suggests that his Christianity may be one of his sins against his ancestors. Why should they not be jealous of his worship of an alien God? Instead the poet blends traditional and Christian imagery so that each reinforces the other with grace and fluidity, proof in itself, it might seem, that the choice to serve his ancestor is in harmony with loyalty to his Christian self. Style and meaning are fully adapted to each other. The model for the African Prodigal Son is taken from the Christian Bible. This confident and successful synthesis would seem to reflect the deep level of Senghor's faith and the degree to which he felt it to be compatible with the values of Africa. Of all that he had learned from the French, the Christian belief was most deeply rooted in his personality. The sound of tantum ergos chanted in African rhythms blended with his earliest childhood memories. He found nothing discordant in this. He knew Christian belief to be an essential part of French culture as well, albeit one deserted by most intellectuals of his own generation. Nonetheless in Christianity Senghor

found a system of values he felt to be acceptable in both his worlds. Perhaps this explains why it proved such an effective anchor for him throughout his life. It not only was the first formal intellectual discipline he met in his seminary education but also provided the music, catechism, and values of his earliest schooling. In a phrase to which he returned again and again, Africa-Eden-Childhood, he asserted the identity of Africa, the original Christian paradise, and his childhood self. To be a Christian was a way to be whole, to serve both African and European and to replenish the dogged strength which, to use DuBois's phrase, was necessary to hold warring selves together. Looking forward to the future, Senghor also found in Christianity the promise that reconciliation is not only favored by God but always possible in the world God created.

In the collection taken as a whole, Senghor traces an evolution that bears every mark of being his own. There are many shifts of mood along the way in the poems, as there undoubtedly were in his own life. Admiration for the French, love of their culture, fear of them, and the desire to hide his African ancestor alternate with their opposite, refuge in Africa, the paradise innocent of both Europe and the industrial world. The poet is angry at the French for what they have done to Africa. Elation at finding an apparent solution, the return to his African roots, is followed by despair at finding that it is not truly a solution at all, but only a momentary respite. The poet finally reaches a position he hopes to make his own, that of ambassador of his people to Europe, trumpet of his people to the French world, and a Christian. This persona need not feel the guilt of desertion because he will serve his people. At the same time he will also be free to continue the life of an intellectual in Paris.

This interpretation of ***Chants d'ombre*** is supported by a letter Senghor wrote to René Maran shortly after it was published. Thanking Maran for reading the collection, he continued, "no approval could be more precious than yours . . . By your double culture, French and African, you were more qualified than any other to judge these songs in which I wanted to express myself authentically and integrally, where I wished to express the 'conciliating accord' that I force myself to realize between my two cultures." Elsewhere he wrote: "It is exactly because Eden-Africa-Childhood is absent that I am torn between Europe and Africa, between politics and poetry, between my white brother and myself . . . As for me, I think that to realize myself as a man, it is essential for me to overcome negation, to bridge the chasm." To build these bridges and unite his disparate selves was the task Senghor had to take on in order to become whole. In the most basic way, he had no choice: he was the two. But the difficulty of achieving the integration and perspective from which to begin his adult work required all the strength and self-discipline he could muster. He still felt as if he teetered precariously over the chasm. His chosen self was not yet natural for him. It was a solution to which, as he put it, he "forced myself."

In a letter he wrote during the war to Maurice Martin du Gard, Senghor explained how important language and poetry had been to him during this period. He had begun writing verse in the style of the French romantics while still at lycée. Later, while at the Sorbonne, he had been influenced by the Surrealists and also had begun to learn about Africa through the writings of ethnographers and "above all Negro-American poetry. I even met some Negro-American writers. These discoveries were true revelations for me which led me to seek myself and uncover myself as I was: a Negro [*nègre*], morally and intellectually interwoven with French. I then burned almost all my previous poems to start again at zero. It was about 1935." By the gesture of destroying his previous work, so theatrical and uncharacteristic, Senghor dramatized his determination to break sharply with his past. "Since then, I have wanted to express something. It is this 'New Negro,' this French Negro that I had discovered in myself." Here Senghor used a literal translation of Alain Locke's term, until then not used in French, choosing the pejorative *nègre* rather than *noir*." Furthermore, Senghor continued, in order to express this new departure, he could not use the classic French verse form but had to create a new verse form to convey "the Negro rhythm while respecting the order and harmony of the French language." As a poet, he would use a new style to express his new voice.

The words of the psychologist Erik Erikson, who studied what he called the identity crisis both among his young patients and in some historical figures, express what Senghor experienced during this time: "There is a moment in life when each youth must forge for himself some central perspective and direction, some working unity out of the effective remnants of his childhood and the hopes of his anticipated adulthood; he must detect some meaningful resemblance between what he has come to see in himself and what his sharpened awareness tells him others judge and expect him to be." And historically great men, Erikson continues, "although suffering . . . through what appears to be a prolonged adolescence, eventually come to contribute an original bit to an emerging style of life: the very danger which they have sensed has forced them to mobilize capacities to see and say, to dream and plan, to design and construct in new ways." Such young people then experience a "kind of second birth." Sometimes the creative person will experience more intensely what is shared to a lesser degree by a number of his contemporaries. When this is true, and if he is able to find a solution that makes sense to others, and if he is sufficiently gifted to express this hard-won new perspective in words that resonate in his contemporaries, he may become a leader of his generation.

Senghor wrestled for several years with this question of his identity and his place in the world. He had tried to become what the French admired, a dutiful black Frenchman. Yet in Paris he realized that he was no Frenchman, and that the way French students approached life was, for him, "a perpetual subject of astonishment." He also realized that most Frenchmen considered him first and foremost black, and that for them, to be black was to be inferior. In his first stage of self-discovery, Senghor and his West Indian friends met this French racism with a racism of their own. They accepted the racist premise that black men were basically different from whites, but rejected the way in which Europeans evaluated this difference. Yet even as he was pursuing this discovery of his Negritude, Senghor was confused by his continued attraction to the French, to their culture and their world. He felt at home among his French friends and did not want to give them up. He spent time both with them and in the company of the students of color. Each group welcomed him, but each saw only part of what Senghor felt himself to be. This put him off balance. His intellectual solution remained at odds with his emotional experience, and he suffered from a real depression.

Even his friends seemed not to sense that his surface equilibrium was not the natural expression of a man at ease with himself but rather the hard-won result of enormous self-control. Any doubts, hesitations, or self-revelations that might have allowed his friends to share his intimate experience remained strictly hidden, then and throughout the rest of his life. When he did describe his inner troubles, it was always from a distance, as something that had been felt in the past but since mastered and placed into its proper perspective. Only one of his contemporaries, Marc Sankalé, a Senegalese physician who knew him in Paris in the late 1930s and early 1940s, sensed this other side. Drawing perhaps on his powers as a clinician, Sankalé observed that Senghor domesticated his body with demanding daily exercises and a frugal regime and applied the same discipline to his mental life and his personal life. Every minute of his time was used for some necessary activity. Sankalé was intrigued that such a methodical, orderly person would write a poetry marked by reverie, escapism, and fantasy. He found Senghor contradictory, both eloquent and withdrawn, lively and solemn, and noted what he called a mystical fervor in his exaltation of Negro-African culture, a fervor that had something "pitiful about it." Senghor wished himself to be heart, mouth, and trumpet of his people, Sankalé continued, but his was not a real Africa. Though Senghor, the poet, acknowledged that he had fused Africa-Eden-Child-hood in his imagination, Sankalé implied that this confusion was not simply a poetic convention but a basic and even desperate need. As a result of his strong will, Sankalé concluded with no small admiration, Senghor had become "the complete Man he wanted to be."

The effort Senghor put into this enterprise was no secret to Senghor himself, even it if remained hidden to many of his admirers. Almost twenty years later, in 1950, he published a confident article in which he discussed the future of French Africa. He ended this article on a personal note, choosing one of the most powerful metaphors a Christian has at his command, that of rebirth:

> May I be permitted to end by evoking a personal experience? I think of those years of youth, at that age of division at which I was not yet born, torn as I was

between my Christian conscience and my Serer blood. But was I Serer, I who had a Malinké name—and that of my mother was Peul? Now I am no longer ashamed of my diversity, I find my joy, my assurance in embracing with a catholic eye all these complementary worlds.

Such was the confident integrity of the mature Senghor at his most assured. But the continuing strain of this achievement was a constant companion. A few years later, when he was in his mid-50s, Senghor wrote:

In fact my interior life was, very early, divided between the call of the Ancestors and the call of Europe, between the requirements of Negro-African culture and the requirements of modern life. These conflicts are often expressed in my poems. They are what binds them together.

Meanwhile, I have always forced myself to resolve them in a peaceful accord. Thanks to the confession and direction of my thinking in youth, thanks, later to the intellectual method which my French teacher taught us.

This equilibrium . . . is an unstable equilibrium, difficult to maintain. I must, each day, begin again at zero, when at 6:30 or 7:00 in the morning I get up to do my exercises. In effect, this equilibrium is constantly being broken. I must not only reestablish it but still perfect it. I do not complain about it. It is such divisions and efforts that make you advance by one step each day, and that make for man's greatness.

The achievement, maintenance, and expression of this balance became the task of Senghor's maturity. Above all, he wished to avoid sharp conflict or rupture with France, with Africa, with friends, and, most important, within himself. In his poetry, he often addressed the themes of wholeness and integrity and their connection to the preservation of vitality. In his scholarly life, he worked to analyze and describe African culture in order to increase African self-knowledge and French understanding. Later, in his political life, he took on an additional and enormous task: to persuade his countrymen and the French of the validity of his vision. He then threw his considerable energy into seeking first cooperation and then independence from France without rupture or total separation. And finally, after Senegal's independence, he tried to further the interests of independent Senegal in a close and special relationship with the former colonial power. His public goals represent his determination to create in the outside world a situation congruent with the balance he had had to create within himself.

Roger Shattuck and Samba Ka (review date 20 December 1990)

SOURCE: "Born Again African," in *New York Review of Books,* December 20, 1990, pp. 11-2, 14, 16, 18, 20-1.

[*In the following review, Shattuck and Ka provide an overview of Senghor's political and literary career along with commentary on* Oeuvre poétique, Ce que je crois, *and*

Janet G. Valliant's Black, French, and African: A Life of Leopold Sedar Senghor.]

1.

On July 7, 1928, the graduation ceremonies of the new French lycée in Dakar, Senegal, were dignified by the presence of the governor general of West Africa. Primarily the children of white colonial administrators and businessmen, the school's hundred-odd students included about fifteen Africans, only one in the graduating class. They had been put through their paces for the baccalaureate by examiners sent from Bordeaux to maintain French standards. After the speeches, when the prizes were finally awarded, the same student walked forward time after time to receive the book prize in each academic subject and then one last time to receive the outstanding student award conferred by the governor general himself.

The student who thus swept the field was neither French nor a Creole with French citizenship from one of the four original colonial settlements, but a black Serer from the bush. The triumph of Léopold Sédar Senghor over all his more privileged classmates soon became a legend in West Africa. Ahead of him lay more than ten years of higher education in Paris. His ensuing sixty-year career as Francophone poet, promoter of Negritude, and elected president of Senegal comes close to realizing two different dreams: the Western dream of philosopher-king or poet-legislator, and the African dream of the sage celebrating his people in song and story under the palaver tree. Yet there is an unexpectedly tragic side to this life, a side we shall approach slowly.

Born in 1906, Senghor was nearly the youngest of some two dozen children by several concurrent wives of a successful Serer tradesman and church-going Catholic. Missionaries in West Africa tolerated very latitudinarian forms of Christianity. Senghor was brought up until the age of seven in a small riparian village by his mother and maternal uncle according to local pastoral traditions and without a word of French. Then his father sent him for six years to a French missionary school. He excelled in his studies, grew in piety, and moved on to a Catholic seminary in Dakar. After three years the white Father Director turned Senghor down for the priesthood. This first deep disappointment redirected Senghor's career into secular education without shattering his religious faith.

In 1945, seventeen years after his brilliant lycée graduation, Senghor brought out his first collection of poems, *Chants d'ombre,* with the estimable Seuil publishing house in Paris. At the same time, recently elected a representative from Senegal to the French Constituent Assembly, this Sorbonne-educated black man from Africa was chosen to oversee the grammar and style of the newly drafted Constitution of the Fourth Republic. By 1960 he had become known worldwide as a founding father of Negritude, the Black Consciousness movement of the Francophone world, and as an effective champion of independence for the French colonies. After the failure of the short-lived Mali Federation, the Republic of Senegal elected Senghor its first president. He was regularly and honestly reelected for the following twenty years and helped to establish a remarkably liberal democracy with continuing ties to France. Senghor is the first African head of state in modern times to have turned over power peacefully and voluntarily to his successor. In 1984 the French Academy elected him to membership on the basis of his accomplishments as poet, scholar, and statesman.

Resolute and remarkably gifted as a boy, Senghor benefited enormously from the French presence in his country and then was instrumental in transforming that presence. Every stage of his career throws light on the decline of the French colonial system and on the difficult birth of a postcolonial African polity. As he entered his thirties, this elegiac poet and seasoned veteran of the French university system decided that his skin color carried responsibilities beyond attaining success in the white man's system. The courage of that decision emerges clearly when one understands the itinerary by which a black Frenchman became a born-again African.

In a letter to a white friend he states explicitly that he was "born again" as "a New Negro," a term he borrowed from black Americans he was reading in the Thirties. He had lived through a period of intense assimilation to French culture, to the point of choosing Proust as bedside reading. Then in the years before World War II, a combination of European anthropology about Africa, American authors like W. E. B. DuBois, and discussions with West Indian friends in Paris like the Martinique poet Aimé Césaire and the Guyanan poet Léon Damas reconverted Senghor to his earliest origins and his African culture. Behind his cosmopolitan exterior he remained very much a split identity and never tired of quoting DuBois on "double consciousness." Out of this crisis of conscience came the influential but awkward notion of Negritude, developed with Césaire and Damas.

Senghor's forty years of public life also oblige us to consider anew what he referred to as "the Balkanization of Africa," its self-confinement within frontiers arbitrarily imposed on it by the European colonialist powers at the Berlin Conference in 1885. Those fragile frontiers of national security are also fault lines of weakness and disunity within larger regions. Between 1958 and 1960 black leaders spoke excitedly of the United States of (West) Africa, but one hears little of this idea today.

And finally Senghor sets before us once again an old refrain in history and mythology: the solitude of the chief, the leader alone in his tent or his study. Africa may signify to some people another race, another set of cultures; but situations like that of the revered statesman losing touch with his people are universal and help us to understand that the truly important race is the human race.

The immense journalistic and scholarly attention paid to Africa in the past fifty years has produced no comprehen-sive biography of an important African leader. We may, for example, recognize the names of Nkrumah, Nyerere, Houphouet-Boigny, Skou Touré, and Senghor. But the best studies devoted to them remain partial in one or both senses. Two probing books on Senghor's political career and thinking make little attempt to deal with his poetry.

An Africanist and Sovietologist of long standing, Janet Vaillant has now brought out a biography of Senghor that overlooks no aspect of his life. She has drawn on many new sources in Senegal about his youth and organizes her thirteen chapters firmly around the stages and turning points in his complex international career. Vaillant's evident respect for Senghor sometimes leads her to avoid frank discussion of personal and social matters, even though there are few skeletons to hide in this dedicated life. Her political and intellectual judgments seem generally sound but unevenly documented. Of the several future third world leaders who resided in Paris during the Twenties and Thirties, including Ho Chi Minh and Chou En Lai, Senghor was the least seduced by Communist revolutionary ideology and traveled the furthest toward nonviolent democratic institutions and toward the reconciliation of racial and cultural differences. Today, when the fading of the cold war is forcing us to look at many local and often tribal conflicts, this exceptional life has much to suggest to us about the significance of early personal backgrounds and the depth of ideological conflict among leaders of emerging democracies.

2.

Since antiquity the figure of the black has played far more than a walk-on part in Western culture. A cluster of recent books on the black in Western art has given us a cornucopia of particulars from that history. When did the black as Negro begin to raise his or her voice in the pandemonium of Western thought and literature? Unable to get an education in the United States during the middle of the nineteenth century, the West Indian black Edward W. Blyden moved on to Liberia to write his five remarkable books. This powerful missionary-educated mind occupies the place of Aristotle for African studies and Black Consciousness.

Blyden's isolation, even while he represented Liberia at the Court of St. James, was probably exceeded by that of W. E. B. DuBois, who, after taking a Harvard M. A., was denied a doctoral degree in Germany for not fulfilling the residence requirement. After 1900 DuBois devoted much of his energy to organizing congresses of the Pan-African movement, interracial in principle, pan-Negroist in practice, as the British historian Basil Davidson points out. However, in spite of the congresses, of the intellectual capacities of the leaders, and of the genuine circulation of black elites in the early part of the twentieth century, the voices of Blyden, DuBois, Martin Delaney, James Africanus Horton, and many other blacks were never able to gain the international hearing they deserved.

What happened in Paris in the 1930s and 1940s resembles the rapid forming of a critical mass, composed not only of black intellectuals from the West Indies, the United States, and West Africa but also of white artists, poets, and intellectuals already halfway to Africa because of their responses to primitive art, jazz, blues, and Josephine Baker. Gide, Camus, Emmanuel Mounier, and Sartre joined Senghor, Césaire, Damas, the Senegalese writer Alioune Diop, and Richard Wright as sponsors of the new review *Présence Africaine* (1947). Sartre contributed a lengthy manifesto-like introduction to Senghor's ***Anthologie de la poésie nègre et malagache*** (1948). Through such activities the black voices that represented Negritude laid claim to and were granted a new cultural prominence. The term Negritude represents a set of claims as significant and complex of those of Surrealism and Existentialism.

Senghor, Césaire, and Damas maintained in the 1930s that blacks throughout the world have a different psychological makeup from that of whites. Blacks, they said, have retained profound human values that whites have lost. Black artists share a characteristic style. Africa, the mother continent possesses a rich culture qualitatively different from that of Europe. Senghor and his friends set out to convince black intellectuals to take pride in the fact of being black and to inform the world about black character, black history, and black civilization.

It was a daring and ambitious goal, which soon faced charges of counter-racism. Today, anyone can amass references and quotations to prove that Africa and the Africans have a long history and that prejudice against color is a sign of intellectual backwardness. But in the early years of the twentieth century, blacks had been written out of history both by much evolutionary theory and by writers on culture. There is a debate today over whether ancient Greeks and Romans were racist. But about the eighteenth and nineteenth centuries the evidence is overwhelming. "Enlightened" scholars were shaped by a reverence for science, progress, and the preeminence of European thought. The absence of these values they called "savagery," as many statements of Voltaire, Hume, Hegel, and Darwin attest. The ideology of conquest in the nineteenth century became the next logical step. The American historian and political scientist Robert W. Tucker summarizes that continuity when he describes how Europeans judged colonization to be "both inevitable and just— inevitable because reciprocity could not necessarily be expected from those lacking in civilization, just because the primacy of the European states serves to confer upon the backward the benefits of civilization."

One can imagine the distress of the brilliant black students in European universities sitting quietly and listening to charges brought against the color of their skin and against the African peoples from whom they had sprung. How could they respond? Their equality of opportunity was compromised by theories of race and culture that still went unanswered and by the incontrovertible color of their skin. Even those black students who mastered Greek and Latin were reminded by many true sons of Europe that they were illegitimate children of Western culture.

By the mid-1930s, Senghor and his friends had had enough. In essays and in poems they began to declare their version of "Black is Beautiful." But they were not just writing slogans in public places. Vaillant's book traces their long voyage of cultural self-discovery and discusses several sources of the Negritude movement. A special place is accorded to Senghor's debt to the intellectual vigor of black American poets, writers, and academics such as Countee Cullen, Claude McKay, W. E. B. DuBois, Alain Locke, and Langston Hughes. The Nardals, a black American family established in Paris who held open house, provided the crucial link among black intellectuals of all shores living in or passing through Paris in the 1930s. Vaillant could have provided more information on the two Nardal sisters, particularly on Jane. We are not told that her unpublished article "For a Negro Humanism" launched many of the ideas that Senghor and Césaire would present to the world with such brilliance.

In these pages Vaillant should also have given some attention to Edward W. Blyden, the remarkable Liberian precursor of Negritude mentioned earlier. Between 1857 and 1903 his writings opened up the whole field of "the African personality." A letter Blyden wrote to William Gladstone from Liberia makes "this little Republic, planted here in great weakness" sound like Plymouth Plantation.

The second debt of Negritude traced by Vaillant is not to other blacks but to European anthropologists and artists. Leo Frobenius, Maurice Delafosse, and Robert Delavignette were the first anthropologists to do archaeological work on African cultures. By revealing the antiquity and significance of African precolonial history and civilization, they outlined a new picture of black achievements. In the same period artists who "went native" in their spiritual quest, from Rimbaud to Gauguin to Picasso to Cendrars, left a deep mark on the Western psyche. They also provided a stimulus for Senghor in his rediscovery of Africa. In a few cases, like that of André Gide, Vaillant mentions a highly important name and passes on with no further discussion.

When young black intellectuals in Paris in the 1930s assembled all these resources to reach for a new way of looking at themselves, they did not use the word "Negritude." Borrowing an expression from American blacks, they called themselves "new Negroes" after Alain Locke's anthology, *The New Negro* (1925). Only later did Césaire coin the term "Negritude." It has remained an evolving concept whose definition varies from writer to writer and whose focus shifts, particularly in the case of Senghor.

At the start, Senghor defined Negritude as "the sum total of qualities possessed by all black men everywhere." This definition comes very close to the way in which Blyden, in the previous century, described the "black personality movement": "the sum of values of African civilization, the body of qualities which make up the distinctiveness of the people of Africa."

Later on, during the struggle for independence of African colonies, Senghor presented Negritude as a political ideology designed to promote liberation and self-rule. In a third stage, after independence, Senghor expanded Negritude to emphasize blacks' contribution to a coming civilization of universal values. Themes of cultural exchange were always present in his notion of Negritude, and Vaillant gives a full account of *métissage* in Senghor's thinking.

Negritude or Black Consciousness has at least a 150-year history and has taken many forms, starting well before the name was invented in the 1930s. Senghor's contribution, whose evolution we have traced above in three stages, has lost influence since the late 1950s for a number of reasons. It was difficult for him to put aside "the racial premise," as Vaillant phrases it, of his early declarations, the premise of a genetic distinctiveness. Even Richard Wright, Jacques Stephen Alexis, and many other black intellectuals insisted on the primacy of geographic, cultural, and economic factors—as opposed to genetic ones—in discussing the fate of black people. When generalized into communitarian African socialism for local consumption in Senegal, Negritude lost its edge and its appeal. When later grafted onto the cloudy thinking of Pierre Teilhard de Chardin, it sank into a sea of universal spirituality. All along Senghor clung to a static, idealized notion of precolonial African history as essentially "traditional." Historians can now demonstrate that Africa, including West Africa, has for centuries absorbed cultural and political shocks, including the arrival of Islam in the tenth century.

There will be more to say about Negritude.

3.

After Senghor's retirement as president of Senegal in 1980, the Bibliothèque Nationale in Paris mounted a large exhibition in his honor. Senghor welcomed the event on the condition that the exhibition emphasize his intellectual and literary work rather than his political career. The Senegalese, however, remember Senghor the shrewd politician and charismatic leader better than Senghor the poet and essayist. Other African heads of state sometimes criticized Senghor's ideas but rarely his integrity and his skill. He learned early to navigate in a political system molded by three conflicting forces: precolonial political traditions, the Muslim Brotherhoods, and political institutions inherited from France.

Senegal borders on both the Sahara desert and the Atlantic ocean. Because of the early advent of Islam, most Senegalese are Muslims (83 percent), and Muslim leaders, called Marabouts, play an important role in the political process. Although the Marabouts do not make policy, and attempts to build an Islamic party have failed in Senegal, the support of the Marabouts is essential for the stability and even the viability of any government. The question then becomes how Léopold Senghor, a Catholic, managed to be accepted by the Islamic religious leaders.

Senegal has also had long and continuous contact with Europe by way of the Atlantic. A French colony from 1850 to 1960, Senegal was the only region in Black Africa where France fully implemented its assimilationist policies. As early as 1879, black residents of the major cities along the coast were granted French citizenship and were allowed to elect their own mayors, municipal council, and a representative to the French Chamber of Deputies in Paris.

This disparity in colonial status between citizens and subjects gave rise to two very different styles of political leadership. In the cities, the political leaders were the urban, Western-educated Senegalese beginning with Blaise Diagne. In the countryside leadership came from Islamic and traditional chiefs. In a colony so divided, it was very difficult for political thinking to evolve toward nationhood and unity. After World War II the Senegalese deputy in Paris, Lamine Guèye, obtained passage of a bill extending the vote and rights of free association to all Senegalese citizens, including women. He picked Senghor to seek election as deputy of the newly enfranchised citizens. By accepting, Senghor faced two political challenges. How was a Paris professor and poet born in a rural village to earn recognition as a leader from the black Senegalese political elite of the towns, a turbulent group with habits of unfettered political debate and considerable skills in party organization and campaigning? At the same time, how was a Catholic intellectual educated in Paris to establish a constituency in an essentially feudal system of local Islamic rulers whose power and prestige were determined by the number and the loyalty of their clients? The concept of one-man-one-vote was utterly alien to the rural parts of the country, where the majority of the population lived.

Comparing archival sources and her own interviews with participants, Vaillant traces Senghor's political career from winning that first election in 1945 to his resignation from the presidency in 1980. The story is marked by successes, serious mistakes, and resounding defeats. Against all odds, Senghor and his friends succeeded in dominating the old Senegalese urban elite, and early in his career he was able to win the support of the Muslim leaders by promising them a higher price for peanuts and by including them in the nascent political process. By the mid-1950s, his party, the Senegalese Democratic Bloc (BDS) was able to articulate the political demands of the majority and to represent them vigorously to the French colonial administration.

The growing demand if not for independence at least for greater autonomy pushed the Fourth Republic to issue the "*loi cadre*," of 1956, which established partial self-government in the black African colonies. At the same time, the BDS turned left as it incorporated young radical intellectuals, and its name changed to the Senegalese People's Bloc or BPS. The BPS won again in 1957. Mamadou Dia, an able technocrat and Senghor's political alter ego, became the head of government while Senghor was conducting the battle for autonomy in Paris. A new situation was created by De Gaulle's return to power and the beginning of the Fifth Republic. De Gaulle held out two options to French African colonies: political autonomy within the framework of the French Federation or immediate independence. Senghor, the coalition builder, was obliged to make some tough choices.

Vaillant misses this dramatic juncture, in which a political defeat became one of the two most searing personal crises of Senghor's life. At the Cotonou Congress he convoked in 1958 to consider De Gaulle's offer, he declared in a fifty-page report that the French colonies were not yet ready for independence. The delegates to the congress, including those of Senghor's own party, rejected his report and voted unanimously for independence. Senghor retreated in humiliation to his wife's property in Normandy. His political career was saved by a small change in the constitution allowing an affirmative vote for association with France within the Community to lead eventually to independence.

In 1958 Senegal, like all other French colonies except Guinea, rejected immediate independence and stayed with the French Community. But not for long. Senegal and the former French Sudan became sovereign as the Mali Federation in 1960. The Federation represented an attempt by Senghor to avoid the fragmentation or, as he said, the "Balkanization" of Africa. The Federation, however, collapsed six months later when Senegal seceded from it. This happened because the increasingly radical Sudanese could not work with the conciliatory diplomacy of Senghor. In September 1960 he was proclaimed president of Senegal by the National Assembly and later elected.

Senghor dreamed of being president of a federated country extending from Dakar to Lake Chad, from Nouakchott to Cotonou. Instead, he ended up being president of a country the size of South Dakota with a population of three million in 1960, basically a peasant-dominated society overwhelmed by problems of poverty and illiteracy. Discouraged by the collapse of the Mali Federation but still confident, Senghor and Dia, his prime minister, launched a strategy to overcome economic problems by developing the agricultural sector while building schools and hospitals. But soon another grave political crisis erupted, a power struggle with Dia.

Vaillant describes this conflict carefully and vividly. The two men held diverging concepts of nation-building and of the way in which the peasants should participate in politics and the economy. For Dia, the purpose was to build a modern state without the Muslim Marabouts as middlemen between the government and the peasants. Dia's socialist and nationalist-minded programs also antagonized French interests. Senghor, on the other hand, wanted to maintain and enhance the connection with the Marabouts as intermediaries and to strengthen French interests in Senegal. He believed that a French economic presence was essential for the country's future and adopted a relaxed open-door approach. Dia remained a conscientious technocrat and tried to protect the country's limited resources. Seng-

hor won the struggle with the support of the Marabouts. But he lost a close friend and his most valuable political ally.

Without Dia, Senghor ran a lax economy based on the peanut crop. When successive droughts decimated the harvest, he had to take strong measures to maintain the legitimacy of his government. In the mid-1970s Senghor decentralized the administration, brought young technocrats into the political process (including Abdou Diouf, the current president of Senegal), and made political institutions more democratic by instituting a controlled multiparty system. Among the many one-party governments in Africa since independence, this move by Senghor in 1975 represented the first U-turn from authoritarianism to a relatively open political life.

Scholars are still debating the significance of these developments in Senegalese politics. Vaillant thinks that Senghor, with his long experience of negotiation and compromise, was more at ease with an open political system than with a one-party system. "Senghor's final political wish was to commit Senegal firmly to representative democracy." The trouble with this line of argument is that it reflects a "patrimonial" conception of politics: democracy is a gift from an enlightened leader or powerful elite to a powerless part of society. Vaillant's explanation overlooks the long fight by peasants, trade-union workers, and intellectuals for an open system, and omits Senghor's resistance to that change. As noted by Vaillant herself, beginning in 1962 Senghor advocated a new authoritarianism, whose basis he found in Negritude. When circumstances obliged him to make changes, Senghor helped bring democracy to Senegal. He was not its sole agent.

4.

No published photograph shows Senghor wearing a *boubou,* the flowing costume of his region. His elegant single-breasted suits and tan gloves signified the degree to which he adopted the role of a Frenchman. After three years of special preparation for the Ecole Normale Supérieure, he had failed the oral examination in 1931, and switched to the Sorbonne. Continuing study of Latin and Greek and writing a thesis on Baudelaire did not interrupt his wide reading, including the arch-nationalist Maurice Barès along with Proust and Rimbaud. After obtaining French citizenship in 1933 he became the first African to attain the highly competitive *agrégation.*

But by this time, in 1935, Senghor knew that he was swimming in a river that flowed in two directions. While his formal studies were making him more and more French, or "Hellenic" as he liked to say, a strong countercurrent in French intellectual and artistic life was propelling him back toward "primitive" cultures. Senghor later proposed the name "Revolution of 1889" for the Bergsonian antirational tendencies in philosophy and anthropology that, before and after World War I, accompanied the African influences at work in Apollinaire and Cendrars, in Cubism and Surrealism. These currents received their official apotheosis in the Paris Colonial Exposition of 1931. That was exactly the moment when Senghor met the Nardal family and, through them, the militant group of West Indian poets living in Paris.

Amid these Parisian buffetings Senghor exhibited a double uniqueness compared with Césaire and Damas and the other West Indian writers. His jet-black color left no doubt about the purity of his African origins. He occasionally went so far as to refer impishly to an imaginary drop of Portuguese blood in his veins. At the same time his enduring Catholic faith, though several times profoundly shaken, set him apart from the others, some of whom were lapsed Catholics.

Here then is the turbulent confluence of cultures within which Senghor, entering his thirties, tried to establish a place for himself in France. One current carried him to a high plateau of French education and on to a position teaching Latin at a *lycée* in Tours, and then into the French army as World War II approached. The reverse current, issuing from different forces in French cultural life and from his West Indian friends, pushed him insistently back toward the country he had left behind. In a poem he wrote in 1940 while in a German prison camp, Senghor used a military metaphor to describe his moral turmoil:

> Europe has crushed me like a warrior flattened under
> the elephantine feet of tanks
> My heart is more bruised than my body used to be
> coming back from distant adventures along the
> enchanted shores of Spirits.

> ("**Ndéssé**")

A French reader hears in these lines the long Biblical verses used by Claudel with sidelong glances at Rimbaud.

But Senghor also wrote in a very different mode:

> Mbaye Dyôb! I wish to proclaim your name and your
> honor.
> Dyôb! I wish to run your name up the flagpole of
> homecoming, to ring your name like the victory bell
> I wish to chant your name Dyôbène! You who called
> me your master and
> Warmed me with your fervor on winter evenings
> around the red-hot stove, which made me cold.
> Dyôb!

> ("**Taga for Mbaye Dyôb**")

A Senegalese can hear the dithyrambs of a village singer improvising in formulaic patterns following a wrestling match. Senghor's poetry seems sometimes to combine the European and the African traditions, sometimes to alternate between them. **"Springtime in Touraine,"** an early poem, mixes lyricism echoing Apollinaire with an undercurrent of violence out of Rimbaud. Then it ends abruptly with the jokey, menacing line, "*On ne badine pas avec le Nègre*" ("Don't kid around with a black"), which rides piggyback

on the title of a Musset play, *On ne badine pas avec l'amour.* Some of his best-known and most moving poems, like **"Nuit de Sine"** and **"Femme noire,"** are no more African than European in diction and form. As time went on, Senghor composed increasingly in a strong elegiac mode with a loose sweeping line that hovers among its sources—Lautréamont and the Surrealists, the *guimm* or ode of the Serer people of West Africa, Whitman, the blues. At his weakest, he took refuge in the travelogue style of a self-appointed United Nations poet, a first-person universal that does not reach the power of true incantation.

Like the Surrealist André Breton, Senghor maintained that all great poets write with the ear. He gave clues about how to recite his poems by printing directions on musical accompaniment: "For flutes and balafong," "Ode for kôra." **"Elegy for the Trade Winds,"** a powerful suite illustrated by Marc Chagall in a deluxe edition, cries out for declamation. The language swells through ten pages celebrating childhood, winds and tornadoes, and the alluring place names of West Africa. Out of the night and the rain, the poet performs ritual insistent gestures:

> My negritude has nothing to do with racial lethargy
> but with sunlight in the soul, my negritude is living
> and looking
> My negritude goes trowel in hand, a lance clenched in
> its fist. . . .

> The smell of spring green white gold, smell of albiz-
> zias
> I say lemon smell where one embalms hearts and pas-
> sions have been embalmed.
> And I salute their spurt into the joyous Tradewind
> Let the old nigger die and long live the new Negro.

Senghor's militant affirmation of Negritude turns up in his most expansive poems. He strove neither for epic narrative nor for lyric intensity. His poems celebrate life as directly as songs can.

5.

Senghor, a short, slender, courteous, public man, must sometimes become annoyed at how often he is expected to refine and redefine the notion of Negritude. Yet since the 1930s that term has helped black intellectuals gain confidence in their cultural and racial identity. Unfortunately, Duvalier in Haiti appropriated it to justify his tyranny. But Negritude also helped guide Senegal into independence with a pride and steadiness that blocked many of the evils to which other African countries fell prey.

As Senghor now enters his mid-eighties, two books have appeared in French to complete his career. *Oeuvre poétique* is a compact, four-hundred-page volume, sections of which have already been translated into a dozen languages. The poems express emotions and convictions familiar to readers throughout the third world and are fully accessible in their rolling rhythms and vivid figures to all of us.

In *Ce que je crois* Senghor collects five essays that swing in gradually expanding orbits around the original kernel of Negritude. After drawing ambitious conclusions about the significance of African prehistory and the elements of a native African philosophy, he delivers both subjects into the arms of what he hopes the future will bring: "*La Civilisation de l'Universel.*" This naive and undefined ideal seems to designate a kind of apolitical multiculturalism on a global scale.

Senghor cannot write many pages without evoking the word *métis*. He means primarily cultural intermixture, as in his own career he crossed passionate Negritude with passionate Frenchness. But he also makes much of the special gifts of Maurice Béjart, the dancer-choreographer of mixed white and African birth. And Senghor himself, after observing an early vow to marry a black wife, later married a white Frenchwoman and had a son by her.

One half-hidden suggestion in *Ce que je crois* should interest those concerned with the relation between primitivism and modernism. First implicitly in discussing the syntax of Wolof poetry, and later explicitly in commenting on the influence of Negro arts on Cubism, Dada, and Surrealism, Senghor identifies the common terms, the essential exchange, as the style of "parataxis"—placing words in sequences without explicit connection or transition. Precisely. We have really known it all along. But it takes a grammarian of European and African languages to go to the heart of that great cultural intersection at the opening of the twentieth century and find the precise word.

Behind the beautifully dressed public man, a private individual had disciplined himself all his life, through regular physical exercise and a demanding work schedule, to remarkable habits of concentration and punctuality. How then, considering his many accomplishments, could we have spoken in our opening paragraph of a tragic note in Senghor's life? In her biography Vaillant refers frequently to challenges and difficult decisions, less often to any lasting defeats. To what degree has Vaillant the biographer found her way not only through the swarm of events around Senghor but also into the mind of this dedicated man? What is the tone, the inner sound of his life?

The younger of Senghor's two sons by his first wife and the one son by his second wife both died before their father, one by suicide and the other in an automobile accident. The fate of his sons has brought great sorrow into Senghor's later years. Vaillant tells us virtually nothing about his family life, or about how a good Catholic living in France was able to "dissolve" his first marriage and marry again.

For thirty years, from his early twenties to his early fifties, before he became president, Senghor lived with few interruptions in Paris and, along with the Nardal sisters, served as the great agent of exchange among West Indian, American, and African blacks. Every West African intellectual in Paris accepted his hospitality and sought his friendship. Yet today Senghor, once again living primarily in France, has few close Senegalese friends. After retirement, when he built a house in a suburb of Dakar, he asked the city council to rename the adjoining streets for Aimé Césaire and Léon Damas. His closest friends are still West Indians whom he met early in Paris. When Mamadou Dia broke with him two years after independence, he lost his most valued Senegalese friend. The extroverted African intellectual now finds himself thrown back on his French connections.

In Senghor's early political career even his enemies marveled at his ability to find a way to speak directly to any group, however remote, however destitute, even if he barely knew their language (in a country of six national languages). A Catholic from a trader's family in an Islamic nation intensely aware of noble lineage, Senghor made his way not by violence and military coups but by essentially democratic means of persuasion, compromise, and free elections. What rewards has he reaped?

A few years ago the Senegalese government decided to rename the University of Dakar, the most respected university in French-speaking Africa. Thirty years earlier Senghor had been the moving force behind the university project and its principal fund raiser. The government finally chose the name of Université Cheikh Anta Diop after Senghor's chief political and intellectual rival. In Dakar, where everything in sight carries the name of a colonial administrator or a national hero, people are wondering what is left to name for the country's great leader.

Fifty years after its launching the term Negritude has by no means disappeared. Every black African intellectual and politician has had to find a satisfactory response both to "subjective Negritude"—the way an individual black wears his or her color—and to "objective Negritude"— "patterns of culture" genetically or geographically correlated with the black race and now carried all over the world. Leaders of the Black Consciousness movement in South Africa hold many of Senghor's writings in high regard. Some of the racial tensions that originally provoked subjective Negritude in Europe have surfaced anew in the events leading up to the current military confrontation along the Senegal-Mauritania border between white North Africans, or Moors, and black Africans.

But Negritude has been plagued with ironies and contradictions. Soon after its birth Sartre appropriated many of its advocates (including Césaire) and much of its intellectual capital for revolutionary Marxism. Today one hardly hears any reference to Negritude among ordinary people in Senegal, where it was for twenty years official government doctrine. When Senghor came to draw up policy for Senegalese schools, he modeled the curriculum so closely on the French system that his opponents accused him of forgetting Africa and favoring Europe. Almost no informed and reflective member of either race would today accept a sentence in one of Senghor's earliest writings that has come back often to haunt him: "Emotion is Negro, as reason is Hellenic."

Senghor has spent a long career promoting a Negritude to which he was born again in his late twenties and from whose early racist associations he has had to keep distancing himself. His personal encounter with Nazism as a war prisoner in World War II cured him of any taint of "antiracist racism," as Sartre defensively called it.

Will Senghor's poetry assure him a major place in the world of literature? In the current enthusiasm for African studies his work will undoubtedly receive much attention among scholars. Translators are at work on his poetry in many parts of the world. A complete English version of *Oeuvre poétique* by Melvin Dixon will appear next year in the enterprising CARAF (Caribbean and African literatures translated from the French) series from the University Press of Virginia. As time goes by Senghor's poems will, we are confident, be seen increasingly as an integral part of his political and intellectual career rather than as a free-standing accomplishment demanding separate literary treatment. Not that Senghor's poems are all didactic or discursive. But as he nears the end of his life we can see them more clearly as occasional compositions in the best sense, works attached to the moods of his career rather than creations that leap beyond the vagaries and contingencies of his life. The same might be said of Rimbaud.

6.

A century ago the impatient Liberian voice of Edward Blyden asked in a letter "whether black men, under favorable circumstances, can manage their own affairs." They had been doing so, of course, for ages: Blyden was referring to the special situation being created in Africa by European colonization. Of the many answers to that question now presented by newly independent states, Senegal offers one of the most courageous. This small country beset by the encroaching desert and dependent on a woefully unreliable rainfall, was able to produce a founding father not intent on leaving behind a reigning dynasty or a new capital city bearing his name. In a Muslim country Senghor saw to it that the constitution established complete freedom of religion and that the *Code de la famille* recognized both monogamous and polygamous marriages. For a black people Senghor founded republican *institutions* and an educational system that combine European and African precedents. These are the true creations of *métissage,* the principle of synthesis to which Senghor subscribed with increasing fervor.

One of the great problems for Africa today, at least among the elite, lies in the fact that each of its fifty-odd resolutely independent states wishes to have its own founding parent and its own separate history. For a few years between 1958 and 1960 Senghor came as close as any leader to uniting the splintered factions of French West Africa. But the goal of federation failed everywhere. When Senghor resigned the presidency in 1981, he left a country that had been brought close to economic coma by drought, population increase, rising oil prices, and poor management. But, he never stooped to malfeasance for personal gain of the kind practiced by some other African leaders. The International Monetary Fund and the World Bank had to help the new president to undertake painful measures of economic austerity and reform.

The true monument to Senghor will be found in no economic miracle, in no structure of steel and stone, but in the conviction with which ordinary Senegalese citizens affirm that their country stands for tolerance. That tolerance now faces two serious challenges. A dynamic renewal of a militant Islam, fed by many former Marxist intellectuals, seeks to increase its political power and to reduce the voice of secularism and nonsectarianism. And dealing with a rebellion in the southern breadbasket province of Casamance reinforces the Jacobin, centralist tendencies of the government. But most of the people, encouraged by Senghor's example, continue to believe in tolerance.

Almost on the last page of her summation Vaillant tells us about a dream Senghor described to her in a letter:

> He began as the intellectual who would understand and speak for his toiling black people. Then he became their ambassador to the assembled nations, and finally, their president. This vocation was synonymous with the person Senghor had become. He seemed to sense this, for he once wrote that he had awakened from a dream in panic. He had dreamed that he had become white. The panic derived, he wrote, from the knowledge that if he were white there would be no reason for his suffering. He could no longer be the leader of his black people. Under such circumstances, he would have no choice but suicide. Questioned further why this dream held such terror for him, he answered more prosaically that if he were white, he would have no defense against his pride.

This is the most revealing and moving moment in a biography that elsewhere maintains a respectful distance from its subject. For the first time the word "suffering" appears, and properly. Why did Senghor experience such intense panic over the dream? We understand that waking up white, while lifting from him the black's burden of suffering in a white-dominated world, would also deprive him of his mission as leader of his people. But the second response, if accurately recorded and translated, is more difficult to fathom: "He would have no defense against his pride."

We find these words enigmatic, even Delphic, rather than prosaic. The passage taken as a whole suggests that Negritude has provided Senghor with the source of his primary pride in a mission and also, out in the white world, with an acute awareness of an inescapable condition that protects him from a more dangerous pride of individual achievement and fame. Senghor seems to have glimpsed through his dream a deeper level of DuBois's "double consciousness, this sense of always looking at oneself through the eyes of others." As in some of his early poems,

Senghor acknowledges the suffering that double conscious-ness brings. Here lies the tragic side of an often admirable life.

K. Anthony Appiah (review date 5 July 1992)

SOURCE: "Poet Laureate of Africa," in *Washington Post Book World,* July 5, 1992, p. 2.

[*In the following review, Appiah offers praise for* The Col-lected Poetry.]

Sometime in the late '60s, one summer holiday at home in Ghana, I took down the collected poems that Leopold Se-dar Senghor had sent my parents, and began to translate them from the French. My father was an African politician and diplomat of Senghor's generation, a generation whose leaders knew each other across national and linguistic divides. Senghor had sent him this elegant red volume, "the definitive version," he wrote in his brief introduction, "of my poems." I started at the beginning with **"In Memoriam,"** the opening poem from *Chants d'Ombre* ("Shadow Songs"), published in 1945.

> C'est Dimanche
> J'ai peur de la foule de mes semblables au visage de pierre.
> (Today is Sunday
> I fear the crowd of my fellows with such faces of stone.)

That second rolling line, with what struck my ear as a strong, propulsive beat, is typical of Senghor's poetry. The line is long, the rhythm emphatic, the imagery striking; the language has a rigorous lucidity. And much else about this poem seems exemplary of Senghor's extraordinary oeuvre.

Take the title. Latin, it is a mark of a Sunday reflection on the day after All Saints', the great Catholic feast.

Yet almost immediately—in the third line—we also meet the "impatient Ancestors," who have followed Senghor to Paris from the Sine, a river in Senegal. Senghor in these poems hovers exactly where he always lived, at the crossroads of Africa and Europe. And when we reach the last lines, which speak of going down to the street—"join-ing my brothers / who have blue eyes and hard hands"—we have a final emblematic moment: the outstretched hand of friendship to his French "brothers."

My energy soon ran out. I finished only the first five poems, ending with **"All Day Long,"** whose last line echoed through my own life later, when I returned home to Ghana from university in Europe: "Here I am," the poet writes, "trying to forget Europe in the heartland of the Sine." The line is true only within the poem. In the real world, Western-educated Africans live in Africa without needing to forget Europe and Senghor himself is the ultimate exemplar.

Born in 1906, Senghor began his life fully immersed in the traditions of the Serer, the ethnic group among whom he grew up. At age 7, however, he was dispatched to a Catholic mission school. Thereafter he was educated in French, going on to secondary education in Dakar, and then winning a scholarship to study in Paris, enrolling in the Lycee Louis-le-Grand, opposite the Sorbonne, where his classmates included another future president, Georges Pompidou. In 1935 he took the highly competitive French national exam, the *agregation,* and, in passing, became the first African to qualify to teach in the French school and university system.

In the early '30s in Paris, Senghor met blacks from the French Caribbean and was also introduced to African-American poetry and the literature of the Harlem Renais-sance. It was within this milieu that Senghor and Aime Cesaire, from Martinique, articulated the ideas of Negri-tude, the most important modern literary movement in Africa and its diaspora. Under these influences he developed into a major French—and at the same time a major African—poet.

By now a French citizen, Senghor was drafted into the French army (in a regiment of colonial infantry) and taken prisoner by the Germans. After the war, he became increas-ingly involved in politics; in 1949, he was elected to the European Assembly in Strasbourg. He continued, however, to be deeply committed to literary life, publishing poems, and editing in 1948 the *Anthology of the New Black and Malagasy Poetry in the French Language.* Despite its clumsy title, this book (with a controversial introduction by Jean-Paul Sartre) remains one of the models of African and Afro-Caribbean literary achievement.

But Senghor's political interests increasingly absorbed him, and his involvement in the movement for indepen-dence left him, in 1960, the first president of the new na-tion of Senegal. When he stepped down on New Year's Day 1981, it was after two decades as the respected Catholic leader of a largely Moslem country.

It was an exciting experience struggling, as a youth in the '60s, with these fine poems. But, as I say, the task defeated me. And so I am particularly grateful (as we should all be) to Melvin Dixon, the African-American poet, novelist and literary scholar: Unlike me he persevered, and we now have his graceful translations of Senghor's complete works.

"Poetry," Robert Frost once wrote, "is what gets lost in translation." But where the translator is as skillful and intelligent a poet as Dixon, the resulting work offers us in a new language a point of entry to the original. Wisely, the editors have published the originals along with the transla-tions; those whose French is not quite up to the task should be able, with Dixon's aid, to appreciate much of the flavor of the originals.

By themselves these poems would justify giving Senghor a place in the history of our times. But they were written by the co-founder of the Negritude movement; by the first black member elected to the French Academy, the highest cultural honor in a country that honors culture highly; by a man who was for 20 years the democratically elected president of Senegal, and who retired and handed over power constitutionally at the end of 1980. Each of these three considerable achievements would also warrant him more than a footnote in any history of our century and it should astonish us that these accomplishments are the work of a single man . . . and a splendid poet.

Isaac I. Elimimian (essay date 1994)

SOURCE: "Negritude and African Poetry," in *Critical Theory and African Literature Today: A Review,* edited by Eldred Durosimi Jones, James Currey, 1994, pp. 22-43.

[*In the following excerpt, Elimimian examines Senghor's contribution to the negritude movement, particularly his evocation of deceased African ancestry, black beauty, Western exploitation, and the possibility of reconciliation in his poetry.*]

The word, 'Negritude', which connotes 'blackness', has been employed in literary discourse for decades. Charles Lamb used the word in 1822 in his essay, 'The Praise of Chimney-Sweepers'. Aimé Césaire employed it in 1938 in his poem *Return to my Native Land:* 'my negritude is not a stone / nor deafness flung out against the clamour of the day'. In African literary criticism, Eldred Jones avers that Soyinka has little or no basis for attacking the Negritude writers since 'his work exhibits all that negritude was essentially about, bar the shouting'.

My objective in this article is not only to highlight the use or the emergence of the word Negritude in literary criticism, but to discuss, as much as time and space permit, the theoretical background of the Negritude movement and its impact on African poetry, particularly as it applies to the works of Léopold Sédar Senghor, David Diop, and Birago Diop, Africa's best known Negritude poets.

Negritude, as a literary and cultural movement, was founded in the thirties by three black intellectuals: Léopold Sédar Senghor from Senegal, Aimé Césaire from Martinique, and Leon Damas from French Guyana. The fundamental objective of the movement and its founders was the need to define black aesthetics and black consciousness against a background of racial injustice and discrimination around the world.

Several external and internal factors contributed in various ways to the rise and development of the Negritude movement. With the abolition of the slave trade some individuals felt the need to explore avenues through which the unique contributions of the black man could be better documented or appreciated. For instance, in 1897 Alexander Crummel founded the American Negro Academy whose mission was to promote black cultural values. In

1900, Sylvester Williams, a Trinidadian lawyer, collaborated with Bishop Alexander Walters of the African Episcopal Zion Church to organise in London the first pan-African Congress. And in 1910, W. E. B. DuBois, in response to Booker T. Washington's writings and other activities, founded the National Association for the Advancement of Colored People (NAACP). There were also during this period the 'Back to Africa Movement' led by Marcus Garvey, as well as the surrealist movement inspired by André Breton which accorded pride of place to 'primitive' culture and civilisation. The desire to promote black consciousness and African cultural heritage was fuelled by the spate of discrimination and other injustices unleashed on the black man after the First World War and symbolised, for example, in the Italian invasion of Ethiopia in 1935.

Of the internal factors that inspired the rise of the Negritude movement, one can cite the following: the French policy of assimilation which attempted to propagate French civilisation at the expense of the indigenous culture; the discriminatory policies of French education to which people of African descent, particularly Aimé Césaire, Leon Damas, and Senghor, were subjected in France; and the fact that all three intellectuals were witnesses to the inadequacies of the Western civilisation which not only championed the philosophy that Africa had no history, no culture, but maintained that its people were created to be permanent hewers of wood and drawers of water. Aimé Césaire is credited with having first coined the word 'negritude' among the trio.

In African literature the critical debate regarding the objective and mission of the Negritude movement, as a worthwhile aesthetic endeavour, has raged on for decades. For instance while the francophone writers have generally emphasised the significance of Negritude as a major literary development, the anglophone authors, on the other hand, have generally dismissed it as irrelevant. Of the anglophone authors who have had a negative view of Negritude, one can cite the examples of Ezekiel Mphahlele, Christopher Okigbo, and Wole Soyinka. Mphahlele believed that the Negritude agenda was too romantic; Okigbo not only disliked the Negritude movement, but even turned down the 1966 Dakar Negro Festival of Arts Prize partly because he felt it developed from the Negritude concept which emphasised 'color'; while Soyinka, who coined the phrase 'a tiger does not proclaim its tigritude', thought that Negritude was based on too much noise rather than action.

The francophone African authors who have been Negritude's chief advocates—especially as demonstrated in their works—are Léopold Sédar Senghor, David Diop and Birago Diop, all three being poets and from Senegal. But why were these writers from the same country so deeply affected by the Negritude ethos on the continent? Gerald Moore and Ulli Beier offer the following explanation:

> Senegal is the only part of the African mainland which really witnessed *assimilation* in practice. Elsewhere it

was not even attempted until after 1946 and was abandoned altogether as official policy some ten years later.

Apart from having the same ancestral origin and going through the same assimilationist educational mill, all three men were motivated by their love of the fatherland and the ideals which inspired Negritude's orientation in the first place. It is for these reasons, perhaps more than anything else, that one finds in their work a complete glorification of Africa's cultural values.

Having discussed the genesis of the Negritude movement, the intellectual debate it has stimulated in African literature and the general impact it has had on Senghor, David Diop and Birago Diop, we shall now examine in more detail the way in which these poets have employed the Negritude philosophy to advance their poetry.

Léopold Sédar Senghor is undoubtedly the most prominent of the three. Born in 1906 in Joal, Senegal, of Christian parents, he was educated at the famous Lycée in Dakar and later at the Sorbonne in France. A man of many parts, poet, philosopher, critic, statesman—the first Senegalese indigenous president—he has to his credit several works through which he articulates his philosophy of Negritude. These include *Chants d'ombre* (1945), *Ethiopiques* (1956), *Hosties noires* (1958), and *Nocturnes* (1961).

Senghor defines Negritude as 'the awareness, defence, and development of African cultural values'. It is this principle that underlies much of his poetry. But beyond this general principle, one can easily identify certain specific characteristics which distinguish his verse. For example, Senghor invokes and celebrates the dead ancestors, and he believes in the concept of the unity between the physical and the spiritual, that is, the dead and the living working together for the ultimate good of mankind. He also celebrates black beauty and African womanhood. And he believes that the ideals of both Western civilisation and African culture can and should be promoted for the benefit of the human race.

There are, of course, some critics who attack Senghor's Negritude for what they consider to be the inadequacies of its credo. Others believe that Negritude is patently discriminatory and thus itself falls a victim of racism by celebrating African culture at the expense of other civilisations. And there are those who heavily chide Senghor because they believe he has betrayed the Negritude cause by divorcing his African wife and marrying a white woman.

A theme which features prominently in Senghor's poetry is the celebration of the dead ancestors. In his treatment of this theme he reveals many things about traditional African culture, for example, that the dead ancestors are revered by the living for their ability to ward off evil or offer protection to the living; that in any human endeavour, little or nothing can be achieved without the active support and cooperation of the dead ancestors. Consequently, either in action or mood or feeling the dead are usually

solicited—and sometimes prayers and sacrifices offered to them—especially in situations of need and danger.

In the poem **'In Memoriam'**, Senghor, apparently feeling lonely and insecure in Paris, the poem's setting, makes a fervent supplication to the dead ancestors:

> Ah, dead ones who have always refused to die, who have known how to fight death
> By Seine or Sine, and in my fragile veins pushed the invincible blood,
> Protect my dreams as you have made your sons, wanderers on delicate feet.

Here in the above lines, another important belief is suggested about traditional African culture: that the dead ancestors, in a way, are not really dead, and that their exit from this world really provides them with the opportunity to look after the welfare of the living. In short, the dead constitute part of the universal cosmos.

Senghor similarly acknowledges the dead ancestors in **'Totem'**:

> I must hide him in my innermost veins
> The Ancestors whose stormy hide is shot
> with lightning and thunder
> My animal protector, I must hide him
> That I may not break the barriers of scandal:
> He is my faithful blood that demands fidelity
> Protecting my naked pride against
> Myself and the scorn of luckier races.

The phrase 'luckier races' alludes to the non-blacks, while the word 'scorn' connotes the prejudice and derision in which the coloured peoples are generally held in their encounter with them. Senghor knows that the source of his power and safety derives from the dead ancestors. But he is prudent, as custom demands, to be covert about it. He must not disclose it. Such a disclosure, he warns, borders on 'scandal'.

In **'Visit'**, Senghor salutes the memory of the dead ancestors where through a dream he encounters certain departed souls: 'I dream in the semi-darkness of an afternoon / I am visited by the fatigues of the day / The deceased of the year . . .'; and in **'What Tempestuous Night'** where he reminisces about some rituals which are pertinent in mollifying the dead ancestors: 'And what sacrifice will pacify the white masks of the goddess / Perhaps the blood of chickens or goats, or the worthless blood of veins'.

However, there are poems in which the celebrated dead are not necessarily the benevolent parents, but those who, being victims of disease, or war, or other human machinations, met their untimely death. Senghor also praises their courage and heroism. In **'The Dead'**, for instance, a piece apparently composed during the aftermath of World War Two, Senghor opines that, although the dead soldiers are victims of the evils of this world, they should rest content that they have served humanity well. Besides, he argues, they should feel satisfied that they died for the cause they believed in:

They are lying out there beside the captured roads, all
along the roads of disaster
Elegant poplars, statues of sombre golds draped in
their long cloaks of gold

The great song of your blood will vanquish machines
and cannons
Your throbbing speech evasions and lies
No hate in your soul void of hatred, no cunning in
your soul void of cunning
O Black Martyrs immortal race, let me speak words
of pardon.

Senghor's second most important literary theme is the
celebration of black beauty, which he articulates from
several points of view. Sometimes it involves his praise of
African womanhood. At other times it is one which
acknowledges and celebrates the beauty of the African
continent in its interrelationships with nature. And at still
other times it is one which affords him the opportunity to
reminisce on Western civilisation vis-à-vis the indigenous
culture, but leaving the reader to draw positive conclusions about his affinity for the latter. The basis of Senghor's celebration of black beauty has a historical connection fuelled by the early Western misleading belief that
blackness is symptomatic of evil. Consequently, because
of this widespread belief, the black man was discriminated
against politically, socially and economically by other
races who associated blackness with ill-luck and negative
human traits. Colonialism and the slave trade, which
exploited and dehumanised the black man, only aggravated
matters since he was not only maltreated but conceived of
as sub-human. It is partly to correct this misleading impression of the black man, as well as restore his own dignity,
that Senghor in his poetry continually attributes greatness
and beauty to blackness.

In **'Night of Sine',** Senghor praises the beauty of black
womanhood. The African woman's 'hands' are 'gentler
than fur', her 'breast glowing, like a Kuskus ball smoking
out of the fire'. Her sprightly gait and the dignity with
which she carries herself are suggested by the expression,
'The tall palmtrees swinging in the nightwind / Hardly
rustle'. Perhaps no poem of Senghor's better describes the
physical attributes of the African woman, and the poet's
excitement about it, than **'I Will Pronounce Your Name':**

Naett, your name is mild like cinnamon, it is the
fragrance in which the lemon grove sleeps,
Naett your name is the sugared clarity of blooming
coffee trees
And it resembles the savannah, that blossoms forth
under the masculine ardour of the midday sun.
Name of dew, fresher than the shadows of tamarind,
Fresher even than the short dusk, when the heat of the
day is silenced.
Naett that is the dry tornado, the hard clap of lightning
Naett, coin of gold, shining coal, you my night, my
sun! . . .

But the African woman is more than just physically beautiful. She is equally morally virtuous—faithful, devoted and
loving. As a manifestation of her love, she would, as in
'Be Not Amazed', 'weep in the twilight for the glowing
voice that sang . . . black beauty'. Senghor further
highlights the African woman's moral attributes in **'Night
of Sine':** she can 'light the lamp of clear oil, and let the
children / in bed talk about their ancestors, like their
parents'. In short, the African woman is the embodiment
of hope, one upon whom the suffering youth can depend
for nourishment and growth.

In discussing the beauty of Africa, Senghor praises the
excellent qualities of its animate and inanimate objects,
both living and dead. In **'Night of Sine',** for instance, the
poet speaks of 'cradlesongs', the 'rhythmic silence' which
'rocks us'; he also talks of the 'ancients of Elissa' and the
'shadowy visits of propitious souls'. More than that, the
scenery of the African landscape is celestial:

This is the hour of the stars and of the night that
dreams
And reclines on this hill of clouds, draped in her long
gown of milk
The roofs of the houses gleam gently. What are they
telling so confidently to the stars?
Inside the hearth is extinguished in the intimacy of
bitter and sweet scents.

And where the poet contrasts the beauty of the indigenous
culture with the foreign landscape as in **'New York',** the
reader is left in no doubt that the beauty of the former has
a special place for him:

New York! At first I was confused by your beauty, by
those great golden long-legged girls
So shy at first before your blue metallic eyes, your
frosted smile
So shy.

New York! I say to you: New York let black blood
flow into your blood
That it may rub the rust from your steel joints, like an
oil of life,
That it may give to your bridges the bend of buttocks
and the suppleness of creepers.

In the poems in which he treats the theme of Western
exploitation of Africa, without attacking the Western ways,
he documents his aversion to the ravages of colonialism,
the slave trade, and neo-colonialism in their various
ramifications. The basis of Senghor's abhorrence of
colonial exploitation can be found in his wide educational
background and his sense of justice. As Abiola Irele
observes, 'Senghor rejects the idea that the black man is
inferior in his human quality to the white man.'

True, Senghor believes in a just society, a society in which
everyone can develop his potentialities to the fullest. But
he knows that the black man has not been able to do this
because of the coloniser's conquest of his innate will
through technology. In **'New York'** Senghor remonstrates:
'Listen New York! Oh listen to your male voice of brass /
vibrating with oboes, the anguish choked with tears / fall-

ing in great clots of blood'. In **'Luxembourgh 1939',** he laments: 'Europe is burying the yeast of nations and the hope of / newer races'.

In **'Paris in the Snow',** Senghor highlights the devastating effects of colonialism. He recalls:

> The white hands that loaded the guns that destroyed the kingdoms,
> The hands that whipped the slaves and that whipped you
> The dusty hands that slapped you, the white powdered hands that slapped me
> The sure hands that pushed me into solitude and hatred
> The white hands that felled the high forest that dominated Africa.
>
> That felled the Saras, erect and firm in the heart of Africa, beautiful like the first men that were created by your brown hands.
> They felled the virgin forest to turn into railway sleepers.
> They felled Africa's forest in order to save civilization that was lacking in men.
> Lord, I can still not abandon this last hate,
> I know it, the hatred of diplomats who show their long teeth
> And who will barter with black flesh tomorrow.

The above lines are crucial in appreciating the black man's past and present. They also underscore the colonialist's operative mechanism. For example, while the past for the black man is symbolised by 'Kingdoms' and 'virgin forest', the present is suggested by 'slavery', 'solitude and hatred'. 'Guns' symbolises the colonialist's instrument of dehumanisation suggested by the verbs 'destroyed', 'whipped', 'slapped', 'pushed', and 'fell'. Interestingly Senghor does not employ invective in dealing with the theme of colonialism; rather he is content to be ironical in documenting grave human situations. Thus, events, when viewed carefully and closely, suggest a negative sequence of Western colonialism: exploitation, hypocrisy, stasis.

Coming now to Senghor's final theme, which centres on the spirit of reconciliation, it is important to say that two possible reasons can be adduced for the presence of this theme in Senghor's verse. First, as the foremost African writer who has suffered most severely from the evil effects of colonialism and from World War Two—he was held captive by the German forces between 1940 and 1943—he is in a better position to appreciate the adage which says that two wrongs cannot make a right by practising revenge. Second, having risen to the presidency of his country he not only had the unique opportunity to practise the ideals of statesmanship, which include tolerance and forbearance, but was better exposed to the problems posed by diverse elements from diverse cultural backgrounds and thus would rather encourage the spirit of cooperation and unity among them for the ultimate good of mankind.

Among Senghor's poems which focus on the theme of reconciliation are **'In Memoriam', 'Paris in the Snow'** and **'Prayer to Masks'.** In **'Paris in the Snow',** Senghor draws the reader's attention to the national motto displayed in the capital city and captioned, 'Peace to all men of goodwill', apparently to underscore the hypocrisy of such public displays but more importantly to suggest his own personal belief in such an ideal. At the end of the poem he adds that his life's principle is anchored on being 'kind to my enemies, my brothers with the snowless / white hands'. The interesting thing here is the corresponding equation of 'enemies' with 'brothers'. By implication the colonialists are not to be seen simply as 'enemies', but 'brothers' as well, who deserve kind consideration and forgiveness.

'In Memoriam' also speaks of 'my brothers with stony faces' and of the persona's eagerness 'To join my brothers with blue eyes / With hard hands'. The irony here is predicated on the fact that one would have thought that the poet would be scared by those who misuse others through their own cruelty. On the contrary he prays to understand them as a phenomenon and, apparently, to appreciate their universe. As a poetic metaphor for reconciliation, 'join' indicates the degree to which the poet is ready to spread the gospel of reconciliation and brotherly love among people.

'Prayer to Masks' is a projection of the diverse racial groups which, due to certain ineluctable forces, converge in France: 'Black mask, red mask, you black and white masks, / Rectangular masks through whom the spirit breathes'. The poem's symbolism is clear enough: all human beings come from the same source and will ultimately retire to the grave. Paris is here only the melting pot. The allusion recalls Donne's epithet of 'Nature's Nest of Boxes'.

Appropriately the employment of the plural form 'Masks' vis-à-vis 'Prayer' in the poem's title, suggests the poet's reverence for the past sages of all nationalities who have traversed this earth. Senghor emphasises his belief in the brotherhood of all races: 'Europe' and 'Africa' are 'connected through the navel'. These two continents symbolise the world's diverse racial elements, while 'navel' suggests the link between the complex of life and death through which all human beings must pass. Thus there is the need, the poet seems to say, for all men to be united, to be reconciled to one another even in the face of discord and hate.

What can we now conclude about Senghor's contribution to Negritude and to African poetry in general? Firstly, he pioneered the founding of a socio-cultural and literary movement which championed the promotion of Africa's cultural values. Secondly he was, through his writing and inspiration, a fighter for black rights and human freedom and dignity. And finally, Senghor's poems and the themes they articulate—the dead ancestors, black beauty and African womanhood, colonialism, and of course reconciliation—are not only basic topics of interest in African poetics, but also they offer the reader an opportunity to visualise how Senghor's practical humanity as poet corresponds with his practical humanity as philosopher-statesman. . . .

Two questions arise. The first is, what unique contributions distinguish these poets [Senghor, David Diop, and Birago Diop] as Negritudists? The second is, what impact has Negritude, as a literary movement, had on African literature, particularly poetry?

My answer to the first question is: Whereas Senghor believes strongly in the spirit of reconciliation and the celebration of the dead ancestors, and while David Diop acidly attacks European colonialism for exploiting Africa, Birago Diop can be said to be a *via media* between these extreme positions of his contemporaries, in that while not preaching reconciliation nor openly condemning Western civilisation, at the same time he demonstrates his sensitivity to the evils of European colonialism while glorifying African cultural values.

My response to the second question is: Negritude is important in African aesthetics, for, apart from adding to the African literary vocabulary, it is one of the very few formalised literary movements in African literature. Finally, Negritude has provided Senghor, David Diop, and Birago Diop—the three greatest African Negritude poets—with the literary resource or tool with which to fashion their poetry, and has fostered a healthy critical debate among critics of African literature.

Koffi Anyinefa (essay date Summer 1996)

SOURCE: "Hello and Goodbye to Négritude: Senghor, Dadié, Dongala, and America," translated by Grace E. An, in *Research in African Literatures,* Vol. 27, No. 2, Summer, 1996, pp. 51-69.

[*In the following excerpt, Anyinefa examines Senghor's contribution to negritude ideology and his portrayal of African-Americans in "To the Black American Troops," "Elegy for Martin Luther King," and "To New York."*]

> And I told myself of . . . New York and San Francisco
> not a bit of this earth not smudged by my fingerprint,
> and my calcaneum dug into the backs of the skyscrapers and my dirt
> in the glory of jewels!
> Who can boast of having more than I?
> Virginia, Tennessee, Georgia, Alabama.
> Monstrous putrefaction of ineffective revolts,
> swamps of rotten blood
> trumpets, absurdly stoppered
> red, blood-red lands of one blood.
>
>   Aimé Césaire, *Return to my Native Land*
> Le fait est donc là: il n'y a pas
> de *négritude* de demain. Ce matin, levé avant les coqs,
> Caliban, l'homme des bonnes tempêtes
> de l'espérance, a vu l'Orphée noir de sa jeunesse
> remonter des enfers avec une
> fée sans vie dans ses bras.
>
>   René Depestre, *Bonjour et adieu à la Négritude*
> The facts are there. There will be no
> *négritude* of tomorrow. This morning, having risen

> before the rooster,
> Caliban, man of many stormy hopes,
> saw the Black Orpheus of his youth
> come back up from Hell with a
> lifeless fairy in his arms.

The representations of other countries and their peoples and cultures constitutes undoubtedly not only one of the oldest and most popular literary topics but also one with the most fearsome ideological and socio-political effects. Is there still a need to remind ourselves that the invasion and colonization of Africa were more or less direct consequences of the ways in which she was represented by the West? Western discourse has most often been—and still is—a hegemonic, racial, and racist one. Emerging about half a century ago, one of the primary objectives of African literature in European languages was precisely to correct the rather negative image of Africa provided by Western literatures, to counter the derogatory hetero-image with a positive self-image. This literature thus immediately presented itself as a counterdiscourse against a certain type of Western discourse. Given that all discussion about the Self is simultaneously a discussion about the Other and vice-versa, this literature turns toward the Other as well, which in this case is the West. It is in light of the construction of identity of the Self through the apprehension of the Other that this study addresses the representation of the United States of America (referred to here as "America," according to a well- established custom), by Léopold Sédar Senghor, Bernard B. Dadié, and Emmanuel B. Dongala, three authors from francophone sub-Saharan Africa.

To see or to apprehend the Other always implies a relationship based on real or symbolic power, as Jean-Paul Sartre pointed out in "Black Orpheus," his celebrated introduction to the first anthology of Black francophone poetry edited by L. S. Senghor:

> When you removed the gag that was keeping these black mouths shut, what were you hoping for? That they would sing your praises? Did you think that when they raised themselves up again, you would read adoration in the eyes of these heads that our fathers had forced to bend down to the very ground? Here are black men standing, looking at us, and I hope that you—like me—will feel the shock of being seen. For three thousand years, the white man has enjoyed the privilege of seeing without being seen.

Ever since the works of Michel Foucault—in this particular case I have in mind *Discipline and Punish* and *The Archeology of Knowledge*—we recognize that any discursive formation aims to appropriate for itself a space of power. African discourse on the West does not seek—and cannot seek—to have the same type of hegemonic power as its Western counterpart because of the peripheral position from which it elaborates itself and because of its deeply reflexive character: directed toward the Other, this discourse has no other target than its own source. The point, actually, through the apprehension of the Other, is to constitute one's own identity, to free one's self in face of the Other's discourse on the Self. It is in this idea that the power of the African discourse on the Other resides.

Aside from the perspective that our three authors have on America, it is to be noted that the concept of "race" determines to a great extent its representation, especially since the image of America developed by Senghor, Dadié, and Dongala is based on racial notions. I will attempt to show how the texts discussed in this article reproduce the most common myths of America, and yet illustrate in particular the relationships that Black African intellectuals have maintained with this country. In general, there are two positions that structure these relationships. For Senghor and Dadié, America is the Other, but an Other that is at the same time the Self due to the Black community of African descent. In contrast, for Dongala, any link in identity with America is flatly rejected: she is simply the Other. Essentially, as we will see, emerging beyond this representation of America will be a debate about Négritude between its partisans and its opponents. My discussion will thus embrace this dual aspect of the representation of America. First of all, I address texts that subscribe to the theories of Négritude through their portrayal of America, and then those that do not. To finish off, I will open my discussion to the current debate around the concept of "race": if it is epistemologically problematic, it does not remain any less operational, politically, psychologically, and culturally, and must be, as Paul Gilroy wrote, "retained as an analytical category not because it corresponds to any biological or epistemological absolutes, but because it refers investigation to the power that collective identities acquire by means of their roots in tradition" (*There Ain't No Black*).

Without retracting the genesis of Négritude, a philosophical-literary movement whose kinship is commonly attributed to the troika formed by Aimé Césaire, Léon Gontrand Damas, and Léopold Sédar Senghor—to which many studies have been devoted—let us keep in mind that Négritude seeks to defend and bring recognition to Black civilization. It claims that all Black people, regardless of their historical or geographical situation, would share the same cultural values, defined in opposition to and distinct from those of the West. Furthermore, Négritude would aim at a *civilisation de l'universel* where the divergences between African and Western cultures would be reconciled—in short, it would envision a cultural *métissage*.

Certainly, one of the most characteristic aspects of Négritude is the homage that its writers pay to the great figures of African history. Senghor above all stood out in this kind of panegyric. With regard to America, Senghor composed two poems devoted to African-Americans: **"To the Black American Troops"** and **"Elegy for Martin Luther King."**

On many occasions the Senegalese poet had to stress the theoretical influence exerted on the founders of the Négritude movement by the African-American authors of the Harlem Renaissance (see, e.g., Senghor, *Ce que je crois*). Yet beyond the acknowledgment of this intellectual debt, there also remains the fact that Black America plays a strategic role in the development of the concept of Négri-

tude as suggested by Abiola Irele: without her, the all-inclusive racial project of Négritude would be impossible: "African cultural survivals in the New World have frequently been adduced as evidence of the persistence of an African nature in the New World Negro and this argument served black nationalists on both sides of the Atlantic as the emotional level of their reaction against the West." This observation explains the African-American presence in Senghor's oeuvre, not only in his theoretical essays but also in his poetry. **"To the Black American Troops"** and **"Elegy for Martin Luther King"** eloquently illustrate the racial and historical link between Africans and African-Americans; they celebrate the pride of the race and highlight its contribution to the universal civilization as it is understood by their author.

In **"To the Black American Troops"** (*Black Hosts* [*Hosties noires*]), Senghor addresses the Second World War and the role that African-American soldiers played in this conflict. The poems in this collection are above all dedicated to the famous Senegalese soldiers of the French colonial army, soldiers whom Senghor presents as sacrificial victims, offered in redemption for the sins of the West. This idea is at least suggested by the unexpected and oxymoronic title of the collection. By putting the predicate "Black" next to "Hosts," Senghor uses a reversal technique unique to the Négritude writers, which privileges the color black at the expense of the white, to emphasize the spirit of sacrifice of Black people, their altruism, and humanism, as well as to inscribe their place in History.

"To the Black American Troops" is divided into three narrative sections. At first, the poet fails to recognize the African-Americans because of their "prison of sad-colored uniforms" and because of the "calabash helmet without plumes," the "tremulous whinny of [their] iron horses / That drink but do not eat." For the poet, the war is responsible for this state of non-recognition. It came to distort, so to speak, the image of Blacks in his eyes. But then, through physical contact, he recognizes his brothers and in them the African continent and its essence: "I just touched your warm brown hand and said my name, 'Afrika!' / And I found once again the lost laughter, I greeted the ancient voices / And heard the roar of Congo waterfalls."

By confronting the terms of non-recognition and recognition, the author elaborates upon a series of opposing images. In the first section of the poem (non-recognition), not only are the war and its attributes full of negative connotations, but "I did not recognize you," the formulated expression of unfamiliarity becomes a refrain. The second part (recognition), however, is exempt from all adverbs of negation in the construction of the image of Africa, which presents itself here as an ideal human and natural setting. The second part of the poem is therefore linked as an antithesis to the first. The mode of representation is manichean: the poet establishes a contrast between the sad, violent, and unnatural world of war and the natural and warm world of Africa. The syntagm that sums up this recognition is obviously "Afrika," used in a metonymical manner. Alone by itself, it symbolizes the origin, the ties of blood. In this process of non-recognition/recognition, there is definitely criticism of Western civilization and its war-like, quarrelsome, and violent qualities. Often, the celebration of the Black race and Africa goes hand in hand with a critique of Western values.

Once his Négritude is rediscovered—or rather, "felt"—in the African-Americans, the narrator will be confronted by the harsh reality of war, and thus their factual otherness. It will be necessary for him to resolve the apparent conflict of the identification of the Self in Otherness. First of all, he will question the responsibility of his brothers in the atrocities of the war: "Brothers, I don't know if it was you who bombed the cathedrals, / The pride of Europe, / If you were the lightning of God's hand burning Sodom and Gomorrah." This doubt is purely rhetorical. The poet is conscious of the violence committed by his brothers, but how can he ideologically reconcile this with the nature of the "Black" (warmth, joy of life, the natural)? In the third line, there is already a shift in guilt: African-Americans, actors turning into instruments in the hands of God, a suggestion itself subject to doubt. In the following line, the poet absolves them across the board: "No, you were the messengers of his mercy, / The breath of spring after winter."

The allusion to Sodom and Gomorrah suggests that violence was generated by Europe herself: God would have punished her for her sins. Thus the real violence of the African-American soldiers is ignored in order to focus only on its end: the liberation of the French. If there is in this poem an intention to criticize violence and aggressiveness, it seems to address Europe rather than the African-American soldiers who would not be engaged in the war except in altruism, a spirit of sacrifice and a desire for peace: "To those who have forgotten how to laugh . . . / Who know nothing more than the salt taste of tears / And the irritating stench of blood / You bring the springtime of Peace and hope at the end of waiting . . . / Black brothers, fighters whose mouths are singing flowers, /—O, the delight of life after Winter—I salute you / As messengers of Peace."

At the end, the narrator has a positive image of the African-American soldiers, and commends their contribution to the institution of peace in Europe. Like their Senegalese brothers, they sacrificed their life for world peace: together, they contributed to the redemption of Europe. If this poem celebrates anonymous African-American figures, in another poem Senghor praises the glory of a particular person in his **"Elegy for Martin Luther King"** (*Major Elegies*). This elegy is comprised of five stanzas. In the first, the poet-politician expresses first of all his powerlessness with regard to the international political climate characterized by the antagonism between the Americans and the Soviets, the constant ghostly reminder of the atomic war, and the specter of drought that ravages the Sahel. It is only in the last line that one falls upon King's death:

> Who said I was stable in my mastery . . . / Who said, who said in this century of hate and the atom bomb / When all power is dust and all force a weakness that the Super Powers / Tremble in the night on their deep bomb silos and tombs, / When at the season's horizon, I peer into the fever of sterile / Tornadoes of civil disorder? . . . / . . . but the words like a herd of stumbling buffaloes / Bump against my teeth and my voice opens on the void . . . / I lost my lips, threw up my hands, and trembled harshly. / And you speak of happiness when I am mourning Martin Luther King!

Thus, the death of King comes back at a particularly critical moment in the life of the poet-politician. His happiness and his assurance are only appearances, and the death of King will serve to express his fragility. The death will also recover a symbolic aspect that the poet will let unfold in the rest of the poem.

In the second stanza, the coincidence of the death of King and the national holiday of Senegal gives Senghor an opportunity to develop the theme of seeming happiness and that of personal unrest. We are in the year 1969, and the poet remembers the commemoration of the eighth anniversary of the national holiday in his country. This joyful memory does not fail to evoke the memory of King's death: "I saw laughter stop and teeth become veiled with blue-black lips, / I saw Martin Luther King again, lying with a red rose at his neck." The poet then recalls the deportation, the subjugation into slavery, and the discrimination against his Black brothers. He then sees the death of King as a heavy loss in the struggle for civil rights. Pain is deeply felt by the poet, who has become the confidant of the utter disarray of all African-Americans. His compassion for and identification with the African-Americans is all the more comfortable since the date of April 4 marks a double history: the victory of Senegal over colonialism—hence its death—and the death of King: "And I felt in the marrow of my bones voices and tears come down, / Ha! A blood deposit of four hundred years, four hundred million eyes, / Two hundred million hearts, two hundred million mouths, two hundred million useless deaths / Today, my People, I felt that April fourth, you are vanquished, / Twice dead in Martin Luther King." The poet then crowns King as the king of peace and exhorts his people to mourn him, to pray to God, to double the prayers for King and for the end of the drought.

In the third part, three years after the death of King, the poet describes the scope of the drought and its economic and ecological consequences, then evokes the wars of Vietnam and Biafra, which he interprets as divine punishment. The poet deplores the death of King, the intercessor of God for Man: "Lord, last year you were never so angry as during the great Famine / And Martin Luther King was no longer here to sing of your wrath / And appease it. . . ." At the end of the third part, the poet himself pleads for the mercy of God and wishes that the message of non-violence of King will be heard: "Lord let the voice of Martin Luther King fall on Nigeria and on Negritia."

In these first three sections, it is thus the national and international context, in which the poet marks King's death, that seems important. Yet the punctual return to King himself, especially at the end of these sections, refreshes our memory of him and allows the poet to stress the impact King has had on the history of his time. The poet presents him simultaneously as the apostle of peace, the hope of all African-Americans, and the Christ of modern times. And lastly, the date of King's assassination ties his destiny more than ever to that of the Senegalese.

The fourth part of the poem describes the assassination itself. The Biblical inspiration of the poet is at its paroxysm here. The assassin is compared to the messenger Judas, and King implicitly to Christ. It is the month of April, and the calendar undoubtedly lends itself to this parallel. In a dramatization of the scene, the poet describes in minute detail the gestures of the assassin while he has King dream his famous dream of a non-racist America: "He [King] sees curly, blond heads, dark, / Kinky heads full of dreams like mysterious orchids, and the blue lips / And the roses sing in a chorus like a harmonious organ. / The white man looks hard and precise as steel. James Earl aims / And hits the mark, shoots Martin, who withers like a fragrant flower / And falls."

In the last part of the poem, the poet has a vision. Martin Luther King is resuscitated, and the drought has ended in Africa. In heaven, the chosen whites and blacks, coming from all levels of society, are seated around God the Father to whom the poet pleads: "Mix them so, Lord, / Beneath your eyes and white beard." The poet then draws up a long list of White and Black American heroes, among whom we find, of course, Martin Luther King. For the poet, they are the milestones along the road toward racial peace. America appears to him as a paradise where Whites and Blacks live peacefully side by side. King's dream is confused, though, with the poet's vision, which praises the coming of a harmonious American society: "I sing with my brother, *Rise Up Negritude,* a white hand / In his living hand, I sing of transparent America where light / Is a polyphony of colors, I sing a paradise of peace." The elegy then finishes with a positive vision transcending the drought and the discrimination against African-Americans. As Janice Spleth noted, death is the principal theme of Senghor's elegies. Yet, it is never experienced as an end in itself, but rather as the possibility of regeneration, the possibility of better tomorrows. If Spleth attributes this positive note of the Senghorian elegy to an influence of African values, it is clear that in this case the influence is rather biblical. It is in this sense that King, whose departure is mourned by Senghor, becomes the redeemer of the evils conjured up in the poem.

Senghor often said that his movement was about affirming the values of Negro-African culture, letting the value of Blacks flow into the universal culture, while establishing a fruitful dialogue between the culture of Black people and the cultures of other people in the world. The poems presented here are a poetic illustration of this agenda. The poet puts his art in the service of his ideology in his representation of African-Americans.

Senghor's desire to account for the American Blacks in his elaboration of the concept of Négritude and its illustration is found again in the poem titled **"To New York"** (*Ethiopiques,* 1956). In the beginning of the poem, the poet finds himself in Manhattan. The fascination aroused by the beauty of the city and his confusion in face of the height of the buildings are doubled by feelings of total displacement and spiritual discomfort provoked by the not-so-friendly setting:

> New York! At first I was bewildered by your beauty, / Those huge, long-legged, golden girls. / So shy, at first, before your metallic eyes and icy smile, / . . . And full of despair at the end of skyscraper streets / Raising my own eyes at the eclipse of the sun / Your light is sulfurous against the pale towers / Whose heads strike lightning into the sky, / Skyscrapers defying storms with their steel shoulders / And weathered skin of stone.

Manhattan is a cold place. It can fascinate the visitor but is devoid of any human or spiritual dimension. The poet is exasperated at the end of a couple of weeks: "But two weeks on the naked sidewalks of Manhattan—Two weeks without well water or pasture . . . / No laugh from a growing child . . . / No mother's breast, but nylon legs. Legs and breasts / Without smell or sweat. No tender word, and no lips, / Only artificial hearts paid for in cold cash." What is lacking in Manhattan is Nature and the emotional and natural presence of Mankind, both sacrificed on the altar of materialism. Everything here seems artificial; even love is distorted and impersonal. Manhattan is a dehumanized place, ruled by stress, noise, and a total absence of emotions.

In the second part of the poem, the poet finds himself in Harlem where he discovers a completely different world, full of colors and smells, sensuality and love, and a *joie de vivre.* Harlem is the temple of music and dance, the ruler of the night. Yet the poet finds that Blacks suffer there as well. At the end of the second part of the poem, he calls upon the city of New York to hear the rhythm of its African-American area. The beginning of the third part reiterates this calling but in a much more urgent and imperative manner: "New York! I say New York, let black blood flow into your blood. / Let it wash the rust from your steel joints, like an oil of life / Let it give your bridges the curve of hips and supple vines." In this appeal, the poet not only pleads for a cultural *métissage* and the recognition of the Black culture of Harlem, but also insists on the regenerating role that the latter could play in the highly modern and technical American culture. The image of New York that Senghor presents is rather a kind of face of Janus, a city with two quite distinct features: on one side, the white city, on the other, the black city. The poet faces two contradictory realities that seem to define New York, and he seeks to transcend them in his appeal. He wishes to go beyond the differences in a dialogue, in an interpenetration of different cultures, in a bringing together of the Self and the Other. This poem, apparently inspired by a visit to New York, illustrates better than any other the ideology of Négritude according to Senghor. . . .

The texts of Dadié and Senghor, aside from their critique of American civilization, attempt mainly to underline the importance of African-Americans in global history to forge links between Black Africans and Americans. . . .

The image of America for these three authors [Senghor, Dadié, and Dongala], beyond its content, depends largely on the discussion of Négritude, notably whether Black America should be included and accounted for in the construction of (Black) African identity. The concept of "race" thus remains operational in taking into account certain aspects of cultural expression in Africa. In fact, it comes as no surprise that it seems to determine African-American literary relations—at least from the standpoint of francophone literature. Not only has the latter incurred a debt to the authors of the Harlem Negro-Renaissance, but, in addition, the African imagination, precisely in this case, can neither undo itself nor escape the determinism of the abominable memory of the slave trade, a racial and racist phenomenon *par excellence.*

As such, the near total of the other texts on America, as I have been able to know them, show more or less a particular interest in the condition of African-Americans (slavery, fight for civil rights, discriminations, etc.) in the name of racial solidarity. Interestingly enough, all of these writers are Senegalese. The influence exerted by their elder, Léopold Sédar Senghor, is evident in the archeology of the representation of America. Thus, the racial question counts as one of the most prominent aspects of this representation of America.

Compared to the image of Europe that is offered by Black African francophone literature, and the image of France in particular, I believe that the image of America does not show many great differences: the content of the images and their functions are generally the same, but the criticism of American society definitely stings more: it seems that America is this "super- European monstrosity" that Sartre speaks about in his introduction to *The Wretched of the Earth* by Frantz Fanon. Consequently, one understands the rarity, if not the non-existence, of an image of America as an Eldorado. This is explained not solely by the profoundly tragic nature of the images tied to this country, but also by the fact that the historical bond and the cultural exchange that have contributed to the forging of the image of paradise in the case of France, for instance, are absent in this case. Moreover, the human contact generating this type of image is limited.

Finally, we must note that the texts cited, with very few exceptions, are written prior to 1960. How can one explain the absence of the theme of America in francophone literature in the last three decades? This phenomenon, in my opinion, is not foreign to the history of Négritude. The Pan-Negro discourses having lost their vigor in Africa, the need to identify oneself with the Blacks of the Diaspora and to take interest in their problems becomes less and less felt. The period of Martin Luther King, Malcolm X, and George Jackson seems to have passed. Since their

deaths, would Black America have no longer produced any political and cultural figures of the same caliber of these heroes to raise the recognition, the respect, and the pride of the Black race? The preoccupations of African writers seem simply to be elsewhere.

In effect, since the end of the '60s, they concentrate instead on the socio-political conditions of postcolonial Africa, as Dongala does in *Un fusil dans la main.* Yet if it is true that this novel is critical of the theories of Négritude, it tends at the same time to formulate an "authentic" discourse on Africa, and in this sense aims toward an ideological end similar to that of Négritude. However, the epistemological and philosophical approach underlying this identity project is different.

The writers of Négritude locked (Black) African identity into a racial essentialism, which presents itself in opposition to a Western discourse on Africa, yet partakes of the dualistic structure and the same discourse it seeks to negate. Different critiques of Négritude have insisted on the mimetic character of the movement (see, e.g., Mudimbe and Diawara) and have reproached, from a Marxist perspective (see, e.g., Adotévi and Boukman) its racist and conservative character, its lack of historical perspective. As for Dongala, he places his novel completely in the context of the contemporary history of Africa in a struggle against Western imperialism. It must be emphasized, however, that the discourse in *Un fusil dans la main* does not escape a certain racial determination. . . .

The thematization, the celebration of the race is no longer common practice today in Black African francophone literature, but the problem of difference is not, for all that, over. It is posed in a different way, no longer in essentialist terms, but in cultural terms. The cultural and the racial intersect, as Walter Ben Michaels proved in a study on cultural identity in the United States: "Our sense of culture is characteristically meant to displace race . . . but culture has turned out to be a way of continuing rather than repudiating racial thought. It is only that appeal to race that makes culture an object of affect and that gives notions like losing our culture, preserving it, stealing someone else's culture, restoring people's culture to them, and so on, their pathos." Besides, how would this difference be able to disappear from a literary tradition that is expressed in the language of the former colonizer, this Other in the first place? Even the linguistic frame of this literature betrays this difference forever, as is suggested by Henry Louis Gates, Jr.:

> Black writing . . . served not to obliterate the difference of race; rather, the inscription of the black voice in Western literatures has preserved those very cultural differences to be repeated, imitated, and revised in a separate Western literary tradition, a tradition of black difference.
>
> We black people tried to write ourselves out of slavery, a slavery even more profound than mere physical bondage. Accepting the challenge of the great white Western tradition, black writers wrote as if their lives depended

on it—and, in a curious sense, their lives did, the "life of the race" in Western discourse.

FURTHER READING

Criticism

Grant, Stephen H. "Léopold Sédar Senghor, Former President of Senegal." *Africa Report* 28, No. 6 (November-December 1983): 61-4.
    Senghor discusses his political career, world art and literature, and his advocacy of multicultural "crossbreeding."

Pappageorge, Julia Di Stefano. "Senghor Re-evaluated." In *African Literature Today: A Review,* No. 6, edited by Eldred Durosimi Jones, pp. 54-67. London: Heinemann, 1973.

Provides an overview of Senghor's poetry, discusses his impact on African thought and literature, and English translations of his work.

Peters, Jonathan. "*Chants d'ombre:* Negritude, the Ancestors, the Princes, and the Gods." In *A Dance of Masks: Senghor, Achebe, Soyinka,* pp. 15-39. Washington, DC: Three Continents Press, 1978.
    Provides analysis of Senghor's major themes, poetic style, and artistic development in *Chants d'ombre.*

Skurnik, Walter A. E. "Léopold Sédar Senghor and African Socialism." *Journal of Modern African Studies* 3, No. 3 (1965): 349-69.
    Examines Senghor's interpretation of negritude, his political perspective, and theory of history.

Vaillant, Janet G. "Perspectives on Leopold Senghor and the Changing Face of Negritude." *ASA Review of Books* 2 (1976): 154-62.
    Examines Senghor's contribution to the concept of negritude as presented in critical studies of his work.

Additional coverage of Senghor's life and career is contained in the following sources published by the Gale Group: *Black Literature Criticism; Black Writers,* **Vol. 2;** *Contemporary Authors,* **Vols. 116, 125;** *Contemporary Authors New Revision Series,* **Vol. 47;** *DISCovering Authors Modules: Multicultural* **and** *Poets;* **and** *Major 20th-Century Writers.*

Charles Simic
1938-

Yugoslavian-born American poet, translator, essayist, nonfiction writer, and editor.

The following entry provides an overview of Simic's career through 1997. For further information on his life and works, see *CLC*, Volumes, 6, 9, 22, 49, and 68.

INTRODUCTION

Simic's work blends surrealist and imagist techniques and employs elements of East European folklore and mysticism as well as American jazz and blues music to explore the horrors of war in his homeland and to imbue commonplace objects with philosophical significance. His perception of the subjective and intuitive natures of language is revealed in works that display a variety of influences, including those of German philosopher Martin Heidegger, Yugoslavian poet Vasko Popa, American poets from Walt Whitman to Theodore Roethke, and French surrealists such as André Bréton and Stéphane Mallarmé.

BIOGRAPHICAL INFORMATION

Born in Belgrade, Yugoslavia, just before World War II, Simic experienced as a small child the Nazi occupation of his country and later the brutal tactics of Josef Stalin during the Soviet control of Eastern Europe. In 1954 Simic's family immigrated to the United States, where they lived in New York City before settling in a suburb of Chicago, Illinois. Simic attended the University of Chicago at night while working during the day at the *Chicago Sun-Times* and graduated from New York University in 1967. He has taught English literature at the University of New Hampshire, State University of California, Boston University, and Columbia University. In 1990 Simic won the Pulitzer Prize for poetry for his book of prose poems *The World Doesn't End* (1989).

MAJOR WORKS

Simic's work is strongly informed by his childhood experiences in Yugoslavia and by continuing violence among ethnic groups in the Balkans. In *Dismantling the Silence* (1971), which contains selections from his earlier publications *What the Grass Says* (1967) and *Somewhere among Us a Stone Is Taking Notes* (1969), Simic elevates ordinary objects to the level of horror by associating them with images of political violence. Particularly throughout the

1990s, Simic has evoked the images of war and its devastating effects on the individual. Many of the poems in *Hotel Insomnia* (1992) recall the historical ethnic hatred of the Balkans, continuing into the late-twentieth century with the fighting between Serbs and Croatians. Throughout his work, Simic displays an interest in the deeper meanings in ordinary objects; *Return to a Place Lit by a Glass of Milk* (1974) contains many of these "object poems." Another of Simic's poetic preoccupations is the complex and contradictory atmosphere of large American cities, especially New York and Chicago. Elements of beauty, horror, violence, and alienation all come together for Simic in the poems in *Austerities* (1982), *Weather Forecast for Utopia and Vicinities* (1983), *Unending Blues* (1986), *The World Doesn't End,* and *The Book of Gods and Devils* (1990). In *Dime-Store Alchemy* (1993) Simic temporarily left writing in the genre of poetry to examine in short poetic prose pieces the collage boxes of contemporary American artist Joseph Cornell, finding in Cornell a kindred spirit of surrealistic symbolism. In *A Wedding in*

Hell (1994) and *Walking the Black Cat* (1997) Simic returned to writing poetry, most of it with an even more bleak and ironic outlook than his earlier work.

CRITICAL RECEPTION

Critics have widely praised Simic's deliberately simple structure and diction in his poems and his streamlined presentation of difficult subject matter. Some have detected little development in Simic's continued use of the conversational voice and sinister images, particularly in *Walking the Black Cat*, where many critics found that Simic was relying too much on his reputation and too little on poetic substance. Nevertheless, Simic's ability to explode the details of ordinary life into symbols of philosophical meaning has continued to earn him critical admiration.

PRINCIPAL WORKS

What the Grass Says (poems) 1967
Somewhere among Us a Stone Is Taking Notes (poems) 1969
Dismantling the Silence (poems) 1971
White (poems) 1972; revised edition, 1980
Return to a Place Lit by a Glass of Milk (poems) 1974
Charon's Cosmology (poems) 1977
Classic Ballroom Dances (poems) 1980
Austerities (poems) 1982
Weather Forecast for Utopia and Vicinity (poems) 1983
Selected Poems, 1963-1983 (poems) 1985
The Uncertain Certainty: Interviews, Essays, and Notes on Poetry (nonfiction) 1985
Unending Blues (poems) 1986
The World Doesn't End (poems) 1989
The Book of Gods and Devils (poem) 1990
Wonderful Words, Silent Truth (essays) 1990
Dime-Store Alchemy: The Art of Joseph Cornell (nonfiction) 1992
Hotel Insomnia (poems) 1992
The Unemployed Fortune-Teller: Essays and Memoirs (nonfiction) 1994
A Wedding in Hell (poems) 1994
Walking the Black Cat (poems) 1997

CRITICISM

Hayden Carruth (review date Summer 1971)

SOURCE: "Here Today: A Poetry Chronicle," in *Hudson Review,* Vol. XXIV, No. 2, Summer, 1971, pp. 320-27.

[*In the following review, Carruth uses a poem by Simic to demonstrate what he considers to be wrong with contemporary poetry.*]

Pound once wrote: "No good poetry is ever written in a manner twenty years old, for to write in such a manner shows conclusively that the writer thinks from books, convention and *cliché*, and not from life. . . ."

Again: "Poetry is a centaur. The thinking, word-arranging, clarifying faculty must move and leap with the energizing, sentient, musical faculties. It is precisely the difficulty of this amphibious existence that keeps down the census record of good poets."

Further: "Don't imagine that a thing will 'go' in verse just because it's too dull to go in prose."

Further still: "When you have words of a lament set to the rhythm and tempo of *There'll Be a Hot Time in the Old Town To-night* you have either an intentional burlesque or rotten art."

And then: "Poets who are not interested in music are, or become, bad poets. I would almost say that poets should never be too long out of touch with musicians. . . . I do not mean that they need become virtuosi. . . . It is perhaps their value that they can be a little refractory and heretical, for all arts tend to decline into the stereotype; and at all times the mediocre tend or try, semi-consciously or unconsciously, to obscure the fact that the day's fashion is not the immutable."

Finally, anent the types of verbal clarity: "There is the clarity of the request: Send me four pounds of ten-penny nails. And there is the syntactical simplicity of the request: Buy me the kind of Rembrandt I like. This last is an utter cryptogram. It presupposes a more complex and intimate understanding of the speaker than most of us ever acquire of anyone. It has as many meanings, almost, as there are persons who might speak it. To a stranger it conveys nothing at all."

I am not sorry to quote Ezra Pound at such length. As far as I have served any master during my thirty years' apprenticeship in poetry, he has played the part, and I have never tired of returning to the best of his critical writing, so pointed and spirited, so deeply instinct with formative energy. Wherever I find it I always enjoy it. So do other readers, I know. But at present I have a separate reason for wishing to buttress myself with Pound's authority, for now I feel obliged, actually impelled against my natural desire, to say something that many people will think heretical and stupid, and in doing so to tread on a few toes. My strategy is to disarm these people by quoting to them from texts which they, too, acknowledge as originative, so that they may listen to me without offense. Yet isn't the truth simply that I think these people have paid scant heed to what Pound actually thought and wrote, and that offense is probably inescapable? So much the more reason to have no taste for it, then. The older I get the less I wish to tread on *anyone's* toes, certainly not for poetical reasons—politics being another matter. As Pound also remarked, "Beauty is difficult," damned bloody difficult, and the one aspect of his critical method which I somewhat disparage is his hauteur toward other writers, especially from his own generation, who were working at it as hard as he was. Let me try to do what I must without hauteur.

If what I have suggested is true, namely, that some of Pound's present-day followers accord his teaching more hebetude and neglect than real understanding, this is not the first time. We know what became of Imagism in the years following the first Imagist anthology in 1912: hordes of unfavored vers-librists, mostly Americans, crashed the gate, many under the flowing standard of Amy Lowell, which caused Pound to say that the movement had degenerated into Amygism, and caused both him and his friend Eliot to revert to the corrective traditionalism of *Mauberley* and the Sweeney and Hippopotamus poems. Pound and Eliot are no longer able to apply the corrective; yet I am certain it is coming from someone, somewhere, somehow, because the condition of poetry today resembles closely the condition of poetry in 1915. The common American poetic style, descended lineally if deviously from what Pound proclaimed in his Imagist manifestoes, has become again so common that it is ridiculous; riddled with triteness, sameness, and dullness. It is being turned out virtually by rote at tens of thousands of writing tables all over North America, and given to us, thrown at us, in poems which are interchangeable, in books whose authors, relentless ego-tripping solipsists though they are, remain as indistinguishable as the obit-writers of the *Times*. The tricks, metaphors, cadences, topics, vocabularies: they are standard. "Procedures," as Pound once complained, "are already erected into rules!" We have "syntactical simplicity" by the yard, conveying "nothing at all." I do not mean that there are no good young poets. There are a fair number, and I have praised them, publicly and privately, whenever I could; there would even be enough to sustain this particular "heave," as Pound would say, for years to come. The trouble is that in order for the good poets to sustain themselves, at least in the public or cultural sense, they must be able to offer their work clearly, freely, and with a certain distinctiveness and purity. Today the work of our good young poets is in danger of being swamped by the mass of similar but inferior writing. And the danger is heightened by the fact that many of the inferior writers have worked themselves into positions of power, since a sign of flatulence in any particular poetic movement is its concomitant institutionalization within the structures of academic and literary life.

We are accustomed to think of poetry as sustained by its leaders, because this is the case during periods of innovation when we are all caught up in the sociological dynamism of literary processes. But at other times, just as important in terms of art, when matters of principle are abeyant and each of us turns to the exploitation of his personal capacities, then we are all, leaders and followers alike, sustained by the health of poetry-at-large; or, conversely, let down by its weakness.

But my interest now is poetry itself, the lines that lie on the page and sound in the ear, and I hope my interest agrees with Pound's sense of the perennial needs: for craft, for understanding of technique, for honest serious work, and against carelessness and imprecision. Great poetry is another matter. We know little of its origins, and nothing at all of how to predict it. But poetry that can serve us, as farming and artisanship serve us, poetry that does not smudge its standards, poetry that by the very tension of its striving confutes the recurrent social philosophies of expedience and claptrap: this is what we are looking for. I remember a couple of years ago a good friend of mine, who is also one of our most prominent poets, showed me a new poem in manuscript. I read it, and then read aloud the first seven or eight lines, to show that their language was flat and prosaic. "Ah," was the response, "but you don't understand my prosody." Whereupon the same passage was reread aloud to me, with exaggerated pauses at the end of each line. "Prosody be damned," I said. "Prosody alone doesn't make poetry. And language that is lifeless, syntax that is dead, cannot be vivified merely by typographical division: that's nothing but elocution. If the poetic line means anything, it must mean more than that!"

Here is a paragraph for general inspection:

"Summer Morning"

I love to stretch like this, naked on my bed in the morning; quiet, listening. Outside they are opening their primers in the little school of the cornfield. There is a smell of damp hay, of horses, of summer sky, of laziness, of eternal life. I know all the dark places where the sun hasn't reached yet, where the singing has just ceased in the hidden aviaries of the crickets—anthills where it goes on raining—slumbering spiders dreaming of wedding dresses. I pass over the farmhouses where the little mouths open to suck, barnyards where a man, naked to the waist, washes his face with a hose, where the dishes begin to rattle in the kitchen. The good tree with its voice of a mountain brook knows my steps. It hushes. I stop and listen. Somewhere close by a stone cracks a knuckle, another turns over in its sleep. I hear a butterfly stirring in the tiny soul of the caterpillar. I hear the dust dreaming of eyes and great winds. Further ahead, someone even more silent passes over the grass without bending it. And all of a sudden in the midst of that silence it seems possible to live simply on the earth.

And here is another:

"Moons"

There are moons like continents, diminishing to a white stone softly smoking in a fogbound ocean; equinoctial moons, immense rainbarrels spilling their yellow water; moons like eyes turned inward, hard and bulging on the blue cheek of eternity; and moons half-broken, eaten by eagle shadows. But the moon of the poet is soiled and scratched, its seas are flowing with dust. And other moons are rising, swollen like boils. In their bloodshot depths the warfare of planets silently drips and festers.

I don't know if it is still done—pray heaven it's not—but when I was in public school the poor old maids who taught English would often assign as a class exercise the writing on set themes of what were called "descriptions," or sometimes "word-paintings." Rarely did they turn up anything with the facile imagery of these two paragraphs, though this was what they wanted, what they forlornly strove for among their pubescent charges. Nothing could remind me more forcefully than these two paragraphs, with their complacent suggestiveness, passiveness, inertness, of the chalkdust sentimentality of my early education. It is Proust's madeleine exactly. Yet surely by now everyone recognizes what I have done, and what a sorry old trick it is. I have printed two poems as prose. And their authors are far from being schoolboys, or beginners in any sense; quite the contrary. They are poets who have published a good deal in the past half-decade or longer, and their names are known to everyone who follows contemporary poetry with more than passing attention. They are, respectively, Charles Simic and John Haines.[1]

Now let me restore their poems to the forms they gave them.

"Summer Morning"

I love to stretch
Like this, naked
On my bed in the morning;
Quiet, listening:

Outside they are opening
Their primers
In the little school
Of the cornfield.

There is a smell of damp hay,
Of horses, of summer sky,
Of laziness, of eternal life.

I know all the dark places
Where the sun hasn't reached yet,
Where the singing has just ceased
In the hidden aviaries of the crickets—
Anthills where it goes on raining—
Slumbering spiders dreaming of wedding dresses.

I pass over the farmhouses
Where the little mouths open to suck,
Barnyards where a man, naked to the waist,
Washes his face with a hose,
Where the dishes begin to rattle in the kitchen.

The good tree with its voice
Of a mountain brook
Knows my steps   [*sic*]
It hushes.

I stop and listen:
Somewhere close by
A stone cracks a knuckle,
Another turns over in its sleep.

I hear a butterfly stirring
In the tiny soul of the caterpillar.

I hear the dust dreaming
Of eyes and great winds.

Further ahead, someone
Even more silent
Passes over the grass
Without bending it.

—And all of a sudden
In the midst of that silence
It seems possible
To live simply
On the earth.

. . . . .

"Moons"

There are moons like continents,
diminishing to a white stone
softly smoking
in a fogbound ocean.

Equinoctial moons,
immense rainbarrels spilling
their yellow water.

Moons like eyes turned inward,
hard and bulging
on the blue cheek of eternity.

And moons half-broken,
eaten by eagle shadows . . .

But the moon of the poet
is soiled and scratched, its seas
are flowing with dust.

And other moons are rising,
swollen like boils—

in their bloodshot depths
the warfare of planets
silently drips and festers.

You see? I have changed nothing in my prose versions but typographical arrangement and punctuation (including the possible typographical error in the sixth stanza of Simic's poem). Yet the meaning of my little experiment is so plain that I am willing to risk four contentions upon it.

First, these two poems, taken as formal structures, are perfectly characteristic not only of the work of these two poets but of the great mass of other poems by poets under forty now writing in the U.S. This is crucial, all the rest depends on it. Of course anyone can deny what I say and find plenty of exceptional cases to "prove" the point, but I rely on the good sense and good will of poetry-readers to concede my argument: that in look, tone, movement, imagistic structure, and all other textural qualities, these two poems are fairly and widely representative. For I have no wish to attack Simic and Haines, and would not mention them if it weren't necessary to argue from examples. They are honest, devoted workers. Here I am interested only in what is happening to poetry. What is happening to poets is another—probably far more difficult—question.

Second, both these poems not only lose nothing by being printed as prose, they actually gain from it. This is not because the poems are badly written. I pass over substantial triteness and silliness (dreaming spiders, the caterpillar's tiny soul, moons like rainbarrels, etc.), because I believe that in terms of structural and verbal elements both poems would be passed in any writing seminar in the country. The life endings are reasonable, the diction is simple and expressive, the poets have avoided the amateurish anapestic rhythms of much free verse (caused by excessive dependence on prepositional phrases in standard English speech: to the end, in a nutshell, etc.), and really there seems nothing to criticize: except that the language, taken altogether, is slack, so devoid of formal tension and impetus, that the poems cease to function. What purpose do these lines serve, beyond making us read with unnatural emphasis and in a joggy cadence? It's all very well to say, as we did twenty-five years ago, that the language of prose cast against poetic measures will make good prosody. It wasn't true then and it isn't true now. These poems in free measure are just as flaccid as the limp iambics of the earlier period, and for the same reason. Let me say once and for all: not only must poetry be as well written as prose, it must be better written.[2]

Third, both these poems are part of the main evolution of modern American poetry, descended from Pound and especially from Williams, through Olson-Duncan-Creeley, with a very strong influence from Levertov, a certain influence from the Beats, and a reversionary influence from older poets like H. D., Zukofsky, Oppen, Ignatow, and many others. A few people perhaps even remember the part played by Byron Vazakas. No matter; the point is not to recapitulate a tired history but to recognize that the idea of the poetic line is central to it all. From first to last, whether conceived as a breath unit, an aural device, an inherent function of language, part of a culturally necessary tradition, or whatever—from first to last the line has been our functional key to poetry. I am not speaking of developments outside the main evolution, such as prose poetry, which has not progressed much beyond Fiona Macleod, or poetry based on arbitrary typographical designs, like James Laughlin's little poems that I greatly admire. I reject the feeble conundrum of what is poetry and what is prose, simply say that historically and at present the line is our basic unit of poetry, that for my part I would not have it otherwise, and that ninety-five per cent of the other working poets in America agree with me, whatever their particular allegiances may be.

Fourth, when poems gain in fluency and intelligibility, and hence in meaning, from being printed as prose, it is because the line has ceased to function, as I have already said, and when the line has ceased to function it is because the language has become too dull to sustain the measure. This, incidentally, is the right way to say it: language sustaining measure, not, as many have thought or hoped, the other way round. From this it is not hard to deduce the anterior reason for all language, which is simply the loss of formative energy in the current phase of American poetry. Whatever name we call it, the heave has subsided. If this has happened sooner than we would have expected, I believe the cause lies demonstrably in the proliferation of verse-writing classes at our universities during the past decade; we have been turning out poets by the tens of thousands. These are the poets who give us the evidence of collapse, evidence that smothers us and stultifies our sensibilities as the wave of poetry mounts. The masters, the leaders, are in no danger; in most cases their work continues fresh and strong, though we note that, formally speaking, they are not breaking new ground—not even in the sense that Pound, Williams, and Eliot continued to break new ground as long as they were active. But the followers, not the leaders, are the sufferers now. One needs no great acumen to foresee that a revulsion will come, even if one has no idea of its potential source nor any arguable notion of its form. But unless the vitality has suddenly departed from American poetry, which I do not believe, or unless there are countervailing political and social factors that lie outside the scope of this discussion, which I do not really believe either, it will come soon.

Notes

1. *Dismantling the Silence*, by Charles Simic. Braziller. $3.95. *The Stone Harp*, by John Haines. Wesleyan University Press. $4.00 (cloth); $2.00 (paper).

2. Who wants prose now anyway, if prose is the leaky string of sausage that goes by that name? Barth, Mailer, and Tom Wolfe are welcome to it.

James Atlas (review date February 1975)

SOURCE: "Autobiography of the Present," in *Poetry*, Vol. 125, No. 5, February, 1975, pp. 295-99.

[*In the following review, Atlas praises Simic's ability to condense great meaning into single images in* Return to a Place Lit by a Glass of Milk.]

Charles Simic's second collection [***Return to a Place Lit by a Glass of Milk***] draws on the practices of Surrealism, but his work owes more to East European poetry, with its emphasis on a condensed, sombre, even ballad-like language. Simic is a native of Yugoslavia, and has translated a number of poets from there, most notably Vasko Popa, with whom he has obvious affinities; his poems possess the same incantatory powers, the same cunning and story-telling art. Nor is there any falling-off from his first, much-praised volume, ***Dismantling the Silence***, except for an occasional repetition of images; in some ways, this book seems even subtler in its modulations of the poems' voice, as it dispenses its ironic folk wisdom. Simic has ideas about the phenomenal world, and a marvellous capacity for locating the luminous objects which evoke (and invoke) those ideas; he is so close to everything he writes about that he can recover their most hidden properties. A bird is "shaped / like the insides / of a yawning mouth." the sky "turns cold and lucent / like the water in which / they baptized a small child"; smoke trailing upward resembles "a fisherman, alone / on a quiet autumn lake." These images could serve to illustrate what I. A. Richards called "reconciled impulses"; they are on one level so accurate and on another so strange that their comparison causes us to reflect on the inner congruence of disparate things.

The most impressive quality of these poems resides in their knowledge of what could be named a historical unconscious, the contemplation of a natural world to which eternity has been promised, outlasting those who love and record its features:

> They were talking about the war
> The table still uncleared in front of them.
> Across the way, the first window
> Of the evening was already lit.
> He sat, hunched over, quiet,
> The old fear coming over him . . .
> It grew darker. She got up to take the plate—
> Now unpleasantly white—to the kitchen.
> Outside in the fields, in the woods
> A bird spoke in proverbs,
> A Pope went out to meet Attila,
> The ditch was ready for its squad.

In these poems, men's own history comes back to them through repetition, so that what is known at any given moment is a composite of all that has ever been lived or known, distilled in a single image:

> The fresh snow sobbed under the hoofs of the last
> horse.
> The wagon wheels whined their ancient lineage
> Of country roads, of drunks left lying in the mud—
> A million years of shivering and coughing.

Not all of Simic's poems are so well-wrought; on occasion, he lapses into cadences of exaggerated feeling or a simulated violent rhetoric, especially in the longer poems. All the same, he has a great and original gift, the gift of awakening in us the sensation of being. When he writes of solitude that it "makes another gloomy entry / In its ledger," or that the scent of a woman's body "is the landbirds sighted at sea," he has miraculously provided the material correspondences of our emotions, and so deepened our relation to the world.

Richard Jackson (essay date Winter 1980)

SOURCE: "Charles Simic and Mark Strand: The Presence of Absence," in *Contemporary Literature*, Vol. 21, No. 1, Winter, 1980, pp. 136-45.

[*In the following essay, Jackson discusses Heideggerian meaning in the poetry of Simic and Mark Strand.*]

"If Cleopatra's nose changed the course of the world, it was because it entered the world's discourse, for to change

it in the long or short term, it was enough, indeed it was necessary, for it to be a speaking nose." So writes Jacques Lacan in his essay "The Freudian Thing," incidentally suggesting, for our purposes, something of the surrealistic moods of Charles Simic and Mark Strand, and the absolute priority these two poets give to the ontological function of language. Actually, to headnote a discussion of these two poets by citing a French linguistic psychoanalyst is to follow Simic's advice in a recent essay entitled **"Negative Capability and Its Children"** (*Antaeus*, Spring 1978) in which he talks about the "multiple sources," often conflicting (he uses Hegel and Breton, Nietzsche and Heidegger), that contemporary poets have absorbed: "Their poetics have to do with the nature of perception, with being, with psyche, with time and consciousness. Not to subject oneself to their dialectics and uncertainties is truly not to experience the age we have inherited." And what best characterizes this various age, from the phenomenologists to the structuralists to the deconstructionists, is this relation, even sometimes a lack of it, between language and Being.

"Poetry," says Heidegger, "is the establishing of being by means of the word" ("Hölderlin and the Essence of Poetry"). Thus Mark Strand's "author" says to his future translator in the prose work called *The Monument*, "Only this luminous moment has life, this instant in which we both write, this flash of voice" (# 4). So, too, the characters in his poem "Exiles" (*The Late Hour*) have an existence intimately related to language and "voice," to the "story" they will find themselves in. Now this establishing of being, this passage into language, is for Lacan a passage from what he calls the Imaginary, a preverbal and visually oriented spatial grid of images lacking a phenomenological center of organization, into what he calls the Symbolic, into language as such with its temporal structurings and grammatical orders. For Simic, this is a passage from the simultaneity of experience to the linearity of language: "Form is nothing more than an extension of consciousness in Time" (**"Composition,"** *New Literary History*, 1976). But where does this extension lead? If Being is established, how is it manifested in language? In **"A Day Marked With A Small White Stone,"** Simic describes the dazed stupor of an animal caught in a trap:

> The languorous, lazy chewing
> On the caught leg
> Stripped now to the bone. Pain
> Joining the silence of trees
> And clouds,
>
> In a ring
> Of magnanimous coyotes,
> In a ring of
> Compassionate, melancholy
> Something or other. . . .

The "end" of the poem suggests a "chain of signifiers," as Lacan and Jacques Derrida would say, that "mark," as a gravestone might mark one's absence, a certain set of events in a life whose significance is deferred, as the infinite series implied by the three dots suggests, to further signifiers. The "luminous moment" is expanded, time is extended. In fact, it appears that language has directed us back to the timeless, nonverbal state, that there has been a reinvestment of the Symbolic Order in the Imaginary.

What we encounter here, then, is a dialectic between two orders. For Simic, the paradigmatic poem of this kind of poetic world is **"Charon's Cosmology"** in which the boatsman, "With only his feeble lantern / To tell him where he is," journeys forever between shores: "I'd say by now he must be confused / As to which side is which." What is more, says Simic—rivaling the casualness that ends **"A Day Marked"**—"I'd say it doesn't matter." Strand's tone can be remarkably similar; the "author" of *The Monument* suggests to the translator, "find words for which you yourself have a fondness. . . . If 'nothing' conveys the wrong idea, use 'something'" (# 14). There is a sense with both poets, then, of what Freud and Lacan describe as a "wandering" of meaning into what seemed at first to be irrelevant details, a sense of the emergence of form, the very process of suggesting possible meanings from "antithetical" words and phrases. What we arrive at, finally, is something like what Derrida terms "supplementarity," an excess of both signifiers and signifieds; the dynamism, really, that defines the rich metaphoric quality of these poets.

Yet this excess, or imbalance, leads to what Paul Ricoeur calls the "suspicion" of language that characterizes modern thought. According to Ricoeur, "suspicion" involves the "possibility of signifying another thing than what one believes was signified" ("The Critique of Religion"). For Simic, there is always the possibility that language subverts the preverbal experience—"Suspicion is the voice because language is not mine." Thus there is a consciousness in **"Euclid Avenue"** that is "doubting / the sound of its own footsteps" as they occur in a "Language / as old as rain." But if not the speaker's language, whose? In a sense, it belongs to a collective unconscious. For Lacan, this unconscious is structured like a language and constitutes the "Other." In fact, language itself may be said to constitute this Other; in the passage from Imaginary to Symbolic, language acts as a force which alienates us from ourselves, and in any process of reinvestment in the Imaginary, constitutes suspicion in the form of this alien Other. Thus Simic cites Heidegger to describe the way language lets Being speak: "To let that which shows itself be seen from itself in the very way in which it shows itself from itself" (**"Negative Capability"**). The experience of Otherness can be manifest in a poem like **"Position Without Magnitude"** in which the speaker rises in a theater, "projects his shadow / among the fabulous horsemen / on the screen," and shudders to see his shadow / Other in an alien fiction. In **"The Prisoner"** the speaker imagines the inmate imagining a scene that includes him, "And all along the suspicion / That we do not exist." On a more self-conscious level, the poet who begins by interrogating dispersed images in the Imaginary ("Among all the images / that come to mind, // where to begin?") must

eventually emerge towards the Symbolic by confronting his Other in "a corner where / a part of myself // keeps an appointment / with another part of myself" (**"Description"**).

Strand, too, conceives of the recognition of the Other as an elementary step for the emergence of the self: "consider how often we are given to invent ourselves; maybe once, but even so we say we are another, another entirely similar" (# 4). *The Monument* locates the dialectic between self and Other in the complex relationship between the "author" and his hypothetical translator. If the author recognizes the Other as he constructs the text, so too the verbal text, as it emerges from the Imaginary, is founded, in Lacan's words, upon the "discourse of the Other." The author exclaims: "This word has allowed you to exist, yet this work exists because you are translating it." By extension, of course, we are all "translators" of the text, and the author initiates an endless chain of relationships; moreover, he himself seems to emerge from the diverse texts, sometimes two or three of them together, that act as epigraphs to many of the fifty-two sections, often rivaling the length of the "prime" text. So, for example, a citation from Unamuno seems to prefigure the "author" of *The Monument* by making him an Other projected by a precursor—"the desire to be someone else without ceasing to be myself, and continue being myself at the same time I am someone else." And so by analogy, it is the author of *The Monument* who makes the text of Unamuno or any other writer exist by "translating" it into his own work. *The Monument* thus establishes what Foucault calls the endless referentiality, the infinite contextualism of texts that transcends and subverts the priority of any particular Other, and any particular "author."

What, then, happens to the author? Who *is* the author? He is, first, the speaker who dissolves into the Other's language. He is, then, the author who foresees an apocalyptic "giant of nothingness rising in sleep like the beginning of language" (# 48). But this subversion of the traditional role of the author does not subvert the fundamental structure of desire as a lack which motivates human action. Thus "Nothingness," as Heidegger says in "What is Metaphysics," is "Pure Other," a signifier of openness, of possibility. So, says Strand's author:

> It has been necessary to submit to vacancy in order to begin again, to clear ground, to make space. I can allow nothing to be received. Therein lies my triumph *and* my mediocrity. Nothing is the destiny of everyone, it is our commonness made dumb. I am passing it on. The Monument is a void, artless and everlasting. What I was I am no longer. I speak for nothing, the nothing that I am, the nothing that is this work. And you shall perpetuate me not in the name of what I was, but in the name of what I am. (# 9)

This passage towards "Nothing," towards the absence of the author, must be seen as part of the structure of deferrals in the chain of signifiers. The void opened by Nothingness thus suggests a futural mode of thinking that ratifies events as history or memory once did:

> This poor document does not have to do with a self, it dwells on the absence of a self. I—and this pronoun will have to do—have not permitted anything worthwhile or memorable to be a part of this communication that strains even to exist in a language other than the one in which it was written. So much is excluded that it could not be a document of self-centeredness. If it is a mirror to anything, it is to the gap between the nothing that was and the nothing that will be. It is a thread of longing that binds past and future. (# 22)

This "absence," which eventuates in the self's being spoken of in the third person later on, is thus not so much a self-destruction as an attempt to "grow into the language that calls from the future" (# 46). The desire for what is lacking, the Other, becomes a desire for anonymity. "My greatest hope is his continued anonymity" (# 31), says the author of himself as if he were already an Other. By the end of the book the author/Other no longer speaks in his own words, for the last section consists entirely of three cited epigraphs. It is as if the author had disappeared into the future, or even the past, leaving only these traces, these markings on a page, "the text already written, unwriting itself into the text of promise" (# 38).

For Simic this promise inherent in the absence of the author is established in a way analogous to the pronoun usage Heidegger describes in *Time and Being*, a usage which marks the "presence of absence," a purely ontological perspective. That is, for Simic, "'I' is many. 'I' is an organizing principle, a necessary fiction. Actually, I'd put more emphasis on consciousness: that which witnesses has no need of a pronoun. Of course, consciousness has many degrees, and each degree has a world (or an ontology) appropriate to itself. So, perhaps, the seeming absence of the author is the description of one of its manifestations, in this case an increase of consciousness at the expense of the subject" (**"Domain of the Marvelous Prey,"** *Poetry Miscellany*, 1978). From this perspective a poem can explore the "mythical consciousness that is to be found in language" beyond the rational control of a traditional ego. The result is a poetry constructed of idiomatic expressions and sentence fragments detached from the context of a specific speaker, of indefinite pronouns that seem to refer to several possibilities, of metaphors that are literalized into surrealistic events. When the subject presents himself he seems to be continually shifting his perspective, to be a signifier whose meaning is deferred, to be, that is, a grammatical function: "I find that in my own poems I tend to abandon the original cause and follow wherever the poem leads. that's why my poems seem often to have an impersonal quality to them. It is not clear who the 'I' is. . . . I follow the logic of the algebraic equation of words on the page which is unfolding, moving in some direction" (**"Domain of the Marvelous Prey"**).

Where then does this logic lead us? In **"Nursery Rhyme"** a series of discontinuous propositions leads to the conclusion, "I see a blur, a speck, meagre, receding / Our lives trailing in its wake." It is this recession, this fading of Being, that locates Simic's poetic world. "The poem," he says in very Heideggerian language, "is the place where

origins are allowed to think" (**"Composition"**). This "place" is, as he says in **"Ode,"** a "space between the premonition / and the event // the small lovely realm / of the possible," a realm seen through what Heidegger calls the "forestructure" that exists before language, what Lacan calls the Imaginary. But Simic goes beyond this Heideggerian notion of Being's activity as a kind of spatial "regioning." For him, the region, the place, is what Jacques Derrida in his own criticism of Heidegger calls a "trace," a place that is always already "erased." Thus we can read **"Eraser"** as a deconstruction of the metaphysics of pure presence:

> A summons because the marvelous prey is fleeing
> Something to rub out the woods
> From the blackboard sound of wind and rain
> A device to recover a state of pure expectancy
>
> Only the rubbings only the endless patience
> As the clearing appears the clearing which is there
> Without my even having to look
> The domain of the marvelous prey
>
> This emptiness which gets larger and larger
> As the eraser works and wears out
> As my mother shakes her apron full of little erasers
> For me to peck like breadcrumbs. . . .

The fading thus provides us with a summons, a summons to erase, to clear away our usual conceptions that bind us to a traditional world view, a summons to reinvest the nostalgia of origin as a new beginning, "to recover a state of pure expectancy." Thus the prey itself will always escape, and the language of its hiding places in old "woods" (words) must be replaced by new language, new signifiers, new metaphors as the old "wear out." The summons that the poet hears leads him back towards the origin, the mythical presence revealed by its absence in language, the absent "mother" veiled behind the apron of always more erasers. For Simic, the quest is endless, the region of absence ceaselessly growing "larger and larger," the position of the self becoming like the proverbial fly on the wall he mythologizes—"An eternity / Around that simple event" (**"The Wall"**). His own time belated, searching receding traces, mired in the temporality of his language, the poet knows

> A place
> known as infinity
> toward which that old self
> advances.
>
> The poor son of poor parents
> who aspires to please
> at such a late hour.
>
> (**"Euclid Avenue"**)

For Strand, *The Late Hour* is informed by an absence and otherness which creates the sense of a world and language so large and alien that their "presence" can be enunciated only through an indefinite, intersubjective mood. Somebody seems always to be saying something somewhere that seems to be somewhat significant:

Someone mentioned
a city she had been in before the war, a room with
two candles
against a wall, someone dancing, someone watching.
We began to believe
the night would not end.
Someone was saying the music was over and no one
had noticed.
Then someone said something about the planets, about
the stars,
how small they were, how far away.

("From the Long Sad Party")

In this context, the Other before which the self becomes anonymous can be seen as a principle upon which the self can, to use Heidegger's phrase, "throw itself upon the world" and reside in its possibilities:

In the meantime I thought
of the old stars falling and the ashes of one thing and
another.
I knew that I would be scattered among them,
that the dream of light would continue without me,
for it was never my dream, it was yours.

("Seven Days")

The poet here is located at a point in time where the events described have already begun to occur, and as the past subjunctive implies, continue into the present. This mode of vision constitutes the basis for what Heidegger calls the "retrieve," a movement into the past to recover lost possibilities. Thus in "My Son" Strand reaches back towards a hypothetical son who seems to call "from a place / beyond, // where nothing / everything, / wants to be born." The poet of the retrieve attempts to locate those images from the storehouse of the Imaginary that suggest possible symbolic identifications. That is precisely the motive in "For Jessica, My Daughter"—"I imagine a light / that would not let us stray far apart, / a secret moon or mirror, a sheet of paper."

Whereas Simic's mode is finally to deconstruct presence, to recede back into the growing region of emptiness, Stand's is to expand with that region, to attempt a reconstruction of presence. The result is a transcendental vision that, because it transcends "Nothing" as well as everything, because it does, after all, grasp the problem of the absent Other, avoids the naive solipsism of earlier transcendental visions: "this is another place / what light there is / spreads like a net / over nothing" (**"Another Place"**). The poem **"White"** uses that color to link diverse places, seasons, shades, times, traces, images, events, leading to a final Heideggerian "leap" beyond language and sight:

And out of my waking
the circle of light widens,
it fills with trees, houses,
stretches of ice.
It reaches out. It rings
the eye with white.
All things are one.

All things are joined
even beyond the edge of sight.

And so the poem becomes a means to include even what lies beyond the Heideggerian "horizon of Being," a means to treat absence as presence. In "The Garden" Strand describes a kind of sourceless light of being, "suspended in time" yet resonating with both the past of the poet's parents and the future of the friend, the Other he addresses:

And when my father bends
to whisper in her ear,
when they rise to leave
and the swallows dip and soar
and the moon and stars
have drifted off together, it shines.

Even as you lean over this page,
late and alone, it shines; even now
in the moment before it disappears.

As with the Heideggerian "it" in phrases like "it gives being," the pronoun here suggests a kind of phenomenological naming, an openness towards presence. It attempts to close some of the gaps that a poetry like Simic's, which emphasizes more of the absence in "presence of absence," exposes. The result is not an utter ineffability, but rather, for both poets, a knowledge that poetic language is not simply communication, that it projects, in its relation to absence, to the Other, in its deferral of meanings for its signifiers, a truth that resides in its faithfulness to the multiplicity of the world. The result is, in effect, the creation of a world through language. So, Lacan has said:

I have only to plant my tree in a locution: climb the tree, indeed to project on it the ironic lightning that a descriptive context gives to a word: let it be seen by all, in order not to let myself be imprisoned in some sort of *communication* of facts, however official it may be, and, if I know the truth, make it heard, in spite of all the *between the lines* censures by the only signifier that my acrobatics can constitute in traversing the branches.

Peter Schmidt (essay date Fall 1982)

SOURCE: "*White*: Charles Simic's Thumbnail Epic," in *Contemporary Literature,* Fall, 1982, pp. 528-49.

[*In the following essay, Schmidt analyzes* White, *finding elements that strongly liken the series to the tradition of Walt Whitman and Ralph Waldo Emerson.*]

O how joys, dreads, convolutions, human shapes, and
all shapes, spring as from graves around me!
O phantoms! you cover all the land and all the sea!
O I cannot see in the dimness whether you smile or
frown upon me. . . .

—Whitman, "Out of the Cradle Endlessly Rocking"
(1867 version)

A chaque être, plusieurs *autres* vies me semblaient
dues.

—Rimbaud, *Une Saison en Enfer*

These are examples of Reason's momentary grasp of the scepter; the exertions of a power which exists not in time or space, but an instantaneous instreaming causing power. The difference between the actual and the ideal force of man is happily figured by the schoolmen, in saying, that the knowledge of man is an evening knowledge, *vespertina cognitio*, but that of God is a morning knowledge, *matutina cognitio*.

—Emerson, "Nature"

The number of Charles Simic's readers has been increasing steadily during the last decade, for those who come across his work tend to seek out more and show what they've found to others. His early volumes of poems from George Braziller, *Dismantling the Silence* (1971), *Return to a Place Lit by a Glass of Milk* (1974), and *Charon's Cosmology* (1977), have steadfastly stayed in print, an unusual fate for poetry these days, and his most recent book, *Classic Ballroom Dances* (1980), was reviewed in places ranging from small but important publications like *Field*, a little magazine read by those who write what is in the others, to the *Yale Review*, in which Helen Vendler annexed Simic into her personal pantheon of contemporary poets worth watching.

Much of Simic's early work appeared in George Hitchcock's little magazine *kayak*. With its pages collaging poems and found illustrations, *kayak* was part of the flowering of surrealist experimentation in American verse which began in the 1940s and 1950s in New York and San Francisco but in the 1960s became especially associated with the Midwest—with Robert Bly and James Wright, among many others, and with the Iowa Writers' Workshop and the seminars at the University of Chicago taught by John Logan. Surrealism appealed to many poets coming of age during and after World War II because it gave them a way of rebelling against the allusive, paradoxical, and ironic poetics of high modernism. Its improvised metrics and leaping, associative structures showed such writers how to reground poetic language in simply-stated metaphors rather than in elaborate conceits, synecdoche, and irony, and how to rely on oracular declaratives rather than the distant, ironic use of personae which marked much high modernist work such as that of Pound and Eliot. Instead of requiring that the poet introduce a wide range of historical and contemporary allusion, surrealism taught him how to discover a primitivist poetics, an archetypal voice within him which was too ancient and too visionary to imitate an insider's knowledge of a particular society. By the 1950s, this poetics had created an informal underground network of writers who renounced Eliot and Pound as masters and founded new magazines to compete with the dominant journals of the time which promoted the latest versions of modernist aesthetics, such as the *Kenyon Review* and the *Hudson Review*. By the 1960s, these artists had become numerous enough (and had taught workshops enough) to have disciples of their own. They also had an effect on the canon of writers that young poets were told to study. Bly, Wright, and the new generation of poets coming out of the workshops in the 1960s (including Simic) generally turned away from Donne, Mallarmé, and

LaForgue to the French, Spanish, and Latin American surrealists and the German Symbolists Rilke and Trakl. Simic added to this list Vasko Popa, a surrealist mythographer from his native Yugoslavia.[1] In turning away from Pound and Eliot's tradition, these new American surrealists also returned to Whitman, and discovered that his visionary assertions, associative structures, and plain style could be merged with later Continental and Latin American innovations to become the basis for the new poetics they were searching for. Instead of *Mauberley* and "Gerontion," they would study "The Sleepers" and *Las Alturas de Macchu Picchu*.

If each American generation must make its pact with Whitman, the particulars of that pact tell us much about what makes that generation distinct. Charles Simic is already recognized as one of the most important voices in the generation that came of age in the last decade. As it happens, one poem of his, a sequence of twenty-two lyrics called *White*, is a dramatic example of what sort of pact with Whitman Simic's generation is drawing up. Unfortunately, *White* is not so available or so well known as Simic's other work, for it has been published only by small presses. Simic first issued 1300 copies of it from New Rivers Press back in 1972, and two years ago he finished revising it and reissued it, in an even smaller edition, from Logbridge-Rhodes Press. He now dates the poem 1970-1980. After reading the work, it is easy to see why it has held Simic's imagination for a decade. Its drama, that of learning how to begin again, has always been at the heart of Simic's writing, and the lyrics in *White* provide a behind-the-scenes glimpse of many of Simic's most recognizable characters and settings as they might first emerge in his notebooks, before they are fully portrayed in the lyrics which make up the Braziller collections. It is Simic's private collection of beginnings, of summonings—the daily record of the battles he had confronting the white page. In it, he seeks to recover that ancient yet spontaneous voice which he, like the surrealists (the true last romantics), believes lies beneath the masks and ironies that we adopt in order to survive our history. *White* is also a distinguished attempt to solve a problem which many other poets of Simic's generation are now facing—the creation of a long poem out of a sequence of shorter ones. All poets who do that, particularly American ones, must face comparing their sequences to those by Whitman, and *White* is additionally interesting because, of all the poems Simic has written, it is the one in which he most determinedly confronts his American poetic origins.

White is composed of three parts. The first two are spoken by the poet and consist of ten ten-line lyrics each. The concluding section, two twenty-line poems, contains the reply of "White" to the poet and is entitled **"What The White Had To Say."** The "White" of the poem's title is a particular state of mind that the poet seeks to reach during the writing of each short poem, with the first two ten-part sections of *White* being the sum of these incantations. White is a *tabula rasa et alba*, a realm of pure possibility, new selves, new words, and new names, and may be said to be a modern version of the absolute expectancy of divine grace which was the desired climax of the meditative procedures employed by Catholic and Protestant poets in the Renaissance. "All that is near, / I no longer give it a name," the poet says in the second poem of **White**, and later adds, "There are words I need. / They are not near men."[2] Each poem is thus a summoning of the muse of strangeness and new selfhood; White is the only power who can help him shed his past selves and begin again. Instead of using a Ouija board, as James Merrill, another contemporary poet of meditation, has done, Simic places the "five ears" of his fingertips "Against the white page" (p. 12), listening for signs of the descent of his daemon-muse, the White who speaks at the poem's conclusion. During each ten-poem sequence, Simic uses all the strategies he possesses, from prayer and propitiation to temptation and trickery, to summon her. He puts on many masks, including those of an orphan child, a bridegroom, and a hermit scholar, and envisions White appearing in many forms, from bestial to celestial.

In the first poem, the poet prays that White will descend and teach him how to divest himself of his old identity and its possessions. He also prays that White will give him a new self, a spiritual marriage. He desires to "touch what I can / Of the quick" and be carried across the threshold dividing one life from another:

> Out of poverty
> To begin again:
>
> With the color of the bride
> And that of blindness,
>
> Touch what I can
> Of the quick,
>
> Speak and then wait,
> As if this light
>
> Will continue to linger
> On the threshold.
>
>   (p. 3)

His voice is humble and hushed, and he speaks in infinitives ("to begin") and hypotheses ("as if") as though what he desires and describes has not yet been created. He seems both an aspiring young groom and a hermit scholar determined to marry into spiritual wealth by taking a vow of poverty.

With the second poem, we see the poet beginning in earnest his task of shedding his old self. He starts by taking words which have become as familiar as stones or knives and making them suddenly strange. Habit has become a hardening of the senses, a learned deafness:

> All that is near,
> I no longer give it a name.

> Once a stone hard of hearing,
> Once sharpened into a knife . . .
>
> Now only a chill
> Slipping through.
>
> Enough glow to kneel by and ask
> To be tied to its tail
>
> When it goes marrying
> Its cousins, the stars.
>
>   (p. 4)

This poem has the same mix of humility and resoluteness that the first did. But now there is also an edge of fear: the proposed wedding between the poet and his muse may turn violent. At first, the violence in the lines may be hard to see because of Simic's spare, understated language, so typical of **White**: "To be tied to its tail // When it goes marrying. . . ." Instead of being a human bridge, White appears to have changed into an animal. And what is the poet's role in such a marriage? The lines at first seem festive, perhaps alluding to bows or decorations tied onto the tail of a prize animal. But Simic may in fact be merging a traditional rite of marriage involving tin cans with another, grotesque use for cans: instead of portraying bride and groom in a car with cans rattling behind them in celebration, Simic transforms White (the bride) into an animal running madly and hopelessly from the cans (the groom) tied to its tail. The reference is in fact double-edged; it seems first festive and then turns sinister. The implication is that the proposed marriage between the poet and White is equally risky. Indeed, the darker possibilities of marrying White begin to shadow the poem more and more strongly as the reader glances back at what has come before: "stone," "knife," "a chill / Slipping through."

Later poems in the first section extend these nightmarish premonitions; the poet sees that by summoning White he may be creating a bond which is as torturous as that between an animal and the cans tied to its tail. As the first sequence of poems progresses, the shapes that the poet imagines White to take gradually become more and more frightening. In the fourth poem, for example, she is a "Hard-faced" old woman running a badly aired inner city grocery. She intimidates the poet, who is disguised as a young boy buying a cupcake (p. 6). In the fifth and seventh poems, it is true, she appears in apparently merciful guises, as a "kind nurse" who can show the poet the "place of salves" (p. 7) and as a mother who sings the child-poet an unsettling lullaby about an insomniac shepherd in the Arctic Circle:

> And he can't get any sleep
> Over lost sheep.
>
> And he's got a flute
> Which says Bo-Peep.
>
> Which says Poor boy,
> Take care of your snow-sheep.
>
>   (p. 9)

In the last two poems of the first sequence, however, the sinister animal persona of White returns, and the language suggests that the death of the old self that the poet prays for will be torturous, like an execution or a religious martyr's mortification of the flesh. White also becomes a kind of Our Lady of Pain, a nurse who offers people salves but creates their wounds in the first place:

> Woe, woe, it sings from the bough.
> Our Lady, etc. . .
>
> You had me hoodwinked.
> I see your brand new claws.
>
> Praying, what do I betray
> By desiring your purity?
>
> There are old men and women,
> All bandaged up, waiting
>
> At the spiked, wrought-iron gate
> Of the Great Eye and Ear Infirmary.
>
> (p. 11)

By the next poem, the last one in the first sequence, this female incarnation of White has become even more fiendish; she reopens the poet's wounds indifferently, blindly:

> We hear holy nothing
>
> Blindfolding itself.
> It touched you once, twice,
>
> And tore like a stitch
> Out of a new wound.
>
> (p. 12)

The hushed expectancy and the infinitive verbs of the first poem in the sequence vanish as the poet immerses himself in his various dreams of what White might be like when she answers his summons. Now, at the end of the first sequence, Simic speaks in the past tense, as if his wounding has already happened. (It hasn't; it's just the eloquence of his vision.) In the course of ten poems to White, his dream of a newborn self ("Touch what I can / Of the quick") has turned into a nightmare in which that point of contact with White is far more painful than he ever expected. The situation of the poet waiting for White is precisely that of Whitman in the lines from "Out of the Cradle Endlessly Rocking" which I have used as an epigraph for this essay: "O phantoms! . . . / I cannot see in the dimness whether you smile or frown upon me" (1867 version).

The poet's second sequence of ten poems uses many of the same personae for both himself and White. We see the poet as a young child, aspiring groom, and hermit scholar, and White appears as an old widow, a bride, an animal, a maternal figure comforting orphans, and as a daemonic muse. The second sequence, however, seems to evolve in ways that reverse the pattern of the first. If the first sequence began quietly and evolved into the terrifying vi-

sion of Our Lady of Pain, the second begins violently but gradually modulates its voice to that of a young child praying and singing softly, "Now I lay me down to sleep." The second sequence in *White* thus neatly folds back the unfolding of the first, so that at the end the poet is back to where he began, hushed, prayerful, and alone.

Despite this convergence between the poem's two sequences, there are important distinctions to be made—especially in the matter of tone—between the poems occupying the corresponding positions in each group. If the first poems in the second sequence, for example, do reproduce some of the violence of the final poems in the first sequence, the mirroring is not exact, for the poems about Our Lady of Pain embody the poet's most nightmarish fears of White, whereas the opening poems in the second sequence treat her violence comically. It is as if the poet has survived the worst vision of what White can do and thus has gained the courage to treat his predicament as a dark burlesque. Much of his tone, of course, remains that of a child whistling in the dark. But it also has the snappishness of a street-smart urchin who is proud that he can survive in such a tough neighborhood. In the second sequence's first poem, Simic imagines White's questions, then gives his own wily answers; they parry her thrusts and become comic versions of the tortures imagined with such horror in the last poem of the first sequence:

> What are you up to son of a gun? I roast on my heart's dark side.
>
> What do you use as a skewer sweetheart? I use my own crooked backbone.
>
> What do you salt yourself with loverboy? I grind the words out of my spittle.
>
> And how will you know when you're done chump? When the half-moons on my fingernails set.
>
> With what knife will you carve yourself smartass? The one I hide in my tongue's black boot.
>
> (p. 14)

Here the poet is a sort of spiritual artful dodger, a Huck Finn on New York's lower East Side able to evade any disaster that White may send his way. The next two poems also combine the call-and-response structure of traditional ballads and rope-skipping rhymes with contemporary punk patois. But the poet now can laugh at himself, tempering somewhat the aggressive, boasting tone of the first poem:

> Well, you can't call me a wrestler
> If my own dead weight has me pinned down.
> . . . .
> Well, you can't call me smart,
> When the rain's falling my cup's in the cupboard.
> Nor can you call me a saint,
> If I didn't err, there wouldn't be these smudges.
> . . . .
> The flea I was standing on, jumped.
> One has to manage as best as one can.
> I think my head went out for a walk.
> One has to manage as best as one can.
>
> (pp. 15–16)

As the poems of the second sequence progress, the age of the poet seems to vary greatly, but the modulation in the sequence's overall tone from loud to soft remains clear. The seventh poem in the sequence is another variation on an imagined marriage between the poet and White which neatly merges the language of a child's geometry lesson with that of a marriage ceremony. The implication is that the marriage, if ever consummated, will be difficult to sustain, for the partners are as at odds with each other as a child's fragile body and the eternal purity of geometric truths.

> Do you take this circle
> Bounded by a single curved line?
>
> I take this breath
> That it cannot capture.
>
> Then you may kiss the spot
> Where her bridal train last rustled.
>
> (p. 20)

In other prominent poems in the second half of the sequence, the poet reappears in his familiar guise of the orphan. In the sixth poem, for example, he is confronted yet again by White in the form of an old woman: "She offered him / A tiny sugar cube // In the hand so wizened / All the lines said: fate" (p. 19). In the eighth and tenth poems, the poet seems like a child talking to himself: we are back to the hushed, prayerful persona that opened the first sequence. The eighth poem is a haunting lullaby for an insomniac somewhat like the earlier song about Bo-Peep; clouds and snowflakes form shapes then blow them away, and details from a child's imagination are disconcertingly placed against a vast, indifferent backdrop:

> Winter can come now,
> The earth narrow to a ditch—
>
> And the sky with its castles and stone lions
> Above the empty plains.
>
> The snow can fall . . .
> What other perennials would you plant,
>
> My prodigals, my explorers
> Tossing and turning in the dark
>
> For those remote, finely honed bees,
> The December stars?
>
> (p. 21)

Speaking in the plural, the poet here appears to be addressing not just the child within him but also all his many selves. Each is an explorer, a prodigal returning to where he started from, and each searches for a lost pastoral world where human beings will feel as at home in the universe as bees in a flowering meadow.

The poet's last poem in **White**—his final "summoning," as he calls it (p. 23)—recalls the steadfast, serious tone of his very first poem. There is "Solitude—as in the beginning,"

Simic says, "And fear—that dead letter office. / And doubt—that Chinese shadow play." He still cannot be sure that his prayers will summon White, or that they will give him any hint of what she will be like or how she will treat him if she does arrive. As in the first poem, he speaks and then waits, lingering on the threshold connecting this world and the spirit world. Mixed in with this humble voice, however, is a hint of the urchin who strutted and mocked both White and himself at the beginning of the second sequence of poems. He seems positive that White's presence will be maternal; he imagines her creating him in her own image and then—she is a poet's muse, after all—giving birth through the mouth: "A zero burped by a bigger zero— / it's an awful licking I got." So secure does the poet seem that he jokes about it all. However White may beat me, he puns, her "lickings" will also be maternal, like that of a lioness licking clean her cub after boxing his ears. By the very end of the poem, though, Simic returns to the humble expectancy which is the dominant mood of **White**. The poet is not a tough talker but an orphan in bed, awake, alone, and softly praying for a comforting dream to appear:

> Does anyone still say a prayer
> Before going to bed?
>
> White sleeplessness.
> No one knows its weight.

Simic ends **White** with a masterstroke: after summoning White many times, he evades his own personae and in the two-part section **"What The White Had To Say"** allows White to take over his voice and have the last word. If this is self-effacement, however, it is also victory, for his muse has at last crossed over the threshold from whiteness and has her words appear in black ink on the page. In the two twenty-line monologues which are spoken by White (pp. 26-27), she appears in guises that readers of the earlier sections will readily recognize. At times she is both mother and lover, a force engendering and caring for the poet's many selves:

> Poems are made of our lusty wedding nights . . .
> The joy of words as they are written.
> The ear that got up at four in the morning
> To hear the grass grow inside a word.

Elsewhere in her monologues, she boasts to the poet that she contains all the myriad selves which he will never realize. She forever remains partially undisclosed, the White that got away:

> Cleverly you've invented name after name for me,
> Mixed the riddles, garbled the proverbs,
> Shook your loaded dice in a tin cup,
> But I do not answer back even to your curses,
> For I am nearer to you than your breath.[3]

Just as he'd feared, the poet's muse here rises up in all her daemonic power, ever elusive and always dangerous. She can murder all his earlier selves, all the previous orderings of his life into poems which he fondly calls the "body" of his work, and she can evade all his future figures of speech attempting to figure her forth.

> Because I am the bullet
> That has gone through everyone already,
> I thought of you long before you thought of me.
> Each one of you still keeps a blood-stained handker-
> chief
> In which to swaddle me, but it stays empty. . . .

The previous poems in **White**, those in the poet's ten-poem sequences, were all written using five tidy couplets. But the twin concluding poems by White are a torrential stream of run-on sentences, enjambed lines, mixed metaphors, changing voices, and seemingly formless paragraphs—pure energy vaporizing the poet's well-wrought urns. Moreover, if White in the early lyrics generally was given her personae one by one, in her own section of **White** she shifts her masks much more rapidly, merging and mocking the poet's own descriptions of her. Such simultaneous states of being are appropriate for such a pale muse, even though Simic's mixed voices and metaphors do make it difficult for the reader at first to discern a unified presence in these last two poems. But that is as it should be; accommodating oneself to White's sublime fluidity is one of the demands she makes of us. All her masks of bride, benevolent widow, animal, and Eumenides pass rapidly by us, and, feigning closeness with the poet, she parodies his earlier pretentions to being a hermit-scholar ("Out of poverty / To begin again . . ."):

> One sun shines on us both through a crack in the roof.
> A spoon brings me through the window at dawn.
> A plate shows me off to the four walls
> While with my tail I swing at the flies.
> But there's no tail and the flies are your thoughts.

By the end of White's first poem, she has so taken over the poet's voice that his inhalation of her foreignness—his inspiration—is compared to drowning:

> Steadily, patiently I lift your arms.
> I arrange them in the posture of someone drowning,
> And yet the sea in which you are sinking,
> And even this night above it, is myself.

In the second poem by White, she tempers her invasion of the poet. Her tone becomes tender and elegiac, and she begins sincerely to speak of herself as the poet's equal. Eventually she drops her accusatory use of the second person and adopts the first person plural, speaking of herself as a fellow orphan or as an animal under the poet's care:

> One gaunt shadowy mother wiped our asses,
> The same old orphanage taught us loneliness.
> Street-organ full of blue notes,
> I am the monkey dancing to your grinding . . .

With the introduction of this new tone, the rapidly moving flood of White's masks crests and abates, and White's monologue and **White** itself ends with the poet nestled close to White's side, secure and finally able to stop his tossing and turning. It is as if the poet at the very last moment of the poem has finally earned the right to touch her. Appropriately, the last lines are hushed, as if White's words were a lullaby sung by one orphan to another, and the poet's many incarnations as scholar, husband, and frightened child are at last discarded. His agitated searching gives way to trust, steady breathing, and a dream of children's games. The new self that he prayed for, like a new tooth, seems effortlessly on its way:

> Time slopes. We are falling head over heels
> At the speed of night. That milk tooth
> You left under the pillow, it's grinning.

Helen Vendler has recently argued that Simic is a strong poet plagued by poems with weak endings that merely complete a "known shape."[4] If this assertion may seem odd to a reader familiar with the dramatic accelerations and new twists in the concluding lines of poems such as **"The Forest," "Breasts," "Charon's Cosmology," "Shirt,"** or **"Prodigy,"** it will perplex the reader of **White**, for rarely has a modern sequence of poems ended with such an apocalyptic fusion of tumult and calm—a whirlwind summoning, blending, and erasing the persons, places, and things of the poet's vision. For sheer dramatic power, the two lyrics that make up **"What The White Had To Say"** may stand (or whirl) beside the final sections of Yeats's "1919" and Stevens' "Auroras of Autumn."

The closing passages of **White**, particularly Simic's reference to White as a "gaunt shadowy mother," may remind some readers of the "old crone" swathed in sweet garments who rocks the cradle in Whitman's "Out of the Cradle Endlessly Rocking" (1859). This relation of **White** to Walt Whitman is worth considering more closely. The music of Whitman's poem imitates first the mockingbird's lament for the loss of its mate and then the sinister susurrus of the sea, the "fierce old mother" incessantly moaning the word "death." Together, the songs of bird and sea cause the poet to understand for the first time that he will die. Soon after he overhears the bird pleading for its lost mate to appear against the background of the white breakers ("What is that little black thing I see there in the white?"), he himself is looking out to sea and beholding his own twin, a swimmer, and his "white arms out in the breakers." At first, the boy hopes that this figure's arms are "tirelessly tossing"; his vision is as much a wish-fulfillment as the mockingbird's. But by the poem's end he admits that the secret the sea has shown him is a "drowned" one. Intuitively, he understands that the swimmer could not survive: it was his childhood self struggling against the undertow of his new knowledge that he is not immortal. The adult poet, moreover, understands that the sea has nursed him on this bitter wisdom and given him his voice. It is as if the child's sudden experience of death compelled him to fill the void he felt with song—as if by pouring out words and music he could somehow will into being the vanished sense of wholeness he once knew:

For I, that was a child, my tongue's use sleeping, now
I have heard you,
Now in a moment I know what I am for, I awake,
....
A thousand warbling echoes have started to life within
me . . .
....
My own songs awaked from that hour. . . .

But if the experience of loss destroys the child's illusion that all is permanent (thus rendering him a spiritual orphan from the things of this world), paradoxically such experience also supports the child's new, more mature self. Images which first reminded the poet of his secure childhood (such as "Pour down your warmth, great sun! / While we bask we have two together, // Two together!") are by the end of the poem used to describe the experience of division, not wholeness. The poet's knowledge of death is a kind of grim but benevolent foster-parent, personified as an old crone "swathed in sweet garments" who bends her wrinkled face towards the child's, whispering in his ear, rocking his cradle, "pouring down" upon him her hoarse hissing, her bitter understanding that we are all orphans on this earth.

Simic's muse of Whiteness is also a half-benevolent, half-terrifying foster-mother, and his child-poet an orphan. The first and second parts of **White** have as their epigraph a line from "Out of the Cradle" which implies that the poet's songs, like those of Whitman's mockingbird, are inspired by loss: "What is that little black thing I see there in the white?" To make the connection between his poem and Whitman's even clearer, Simic in 1980 revised a central line in White's monologue from "I am the emptiness that tucks you in like a dove's nest" to "I am the emptiness that tucks you in like a mockingbird's nest."[5] In "Out of the Cradle" this nurturing figure modulated in the middle of the poem from the mockingbird to the sea-mother. Intuitively remembering this transformation, Simic has White in her monologues describe herself as both a mockingbird and an ocean: as a mockingbird she tucks the poet in at night, and as the sea she is the water "in which you are sinking." There are other parallels between "Out of the Cradle" and **White**. Both Whitman and Simic describe the death of the poet's earlier self, and both end their works with an ambiguous moment of rebirth. Whitman is "awaked" and sings of birth yet stares into what passes for a death's-head, the face of the old crone, while Simic "falls" asleep but finds a new self rising within him:

Time slopes. We are falling head over heels
At the speed of night. That milk tooth
You left under the pillow, it's grinning.

Simic's milk tooth seems both sinister and heartening: it grins like a skull, suggesting the self which has died, but it also reminds us that a child's milk teeth are replaced by his adult ones, including his "wisdom" teeth.

Simic's reference to the "milk tooth" may also allude to other famous lines by Whitman about coming of age, the notorious section in "The Sleepers" in which he described a child's passage into adulthood by referring to teething:

[I] am curious to know where my feet stand—and what is this flooding me, childhood or manhood—and the hunber that crosses the bridge between.

The cloth laps a first sweet eating and drinking,
Laps life-swelling yolks—laps ear of rose-corn, milky and just ripened;
The white teeth stay, and the boss tooth advances in darkness. . . .

(1855 version)

The sudden changes of the body during the end of childhood are no less frightening to a child than the advancing stages of the mind's own transformations as one self yields to another. The boss tooth of the boy's manhood—his sexuality, his knowledge of evil and of death—ruthlessly expels his childhood self. This change is a prelude to the continual remaking of the self which is exemplified in "The Sleepers" and which Whitman wants the adult psyche to undergo each night during dreaming. Similarly, in **White** Simic uses references to drowning, falling, and teething to depict not just the passage from childhood to adulthood but also the passage he as an adult wants to make from one self to another.

Simic's **White** is also a meditation on another form of drowning and rebirth—the influence (literally, the inflowing) of a previous writer's voice upon his own. Such a preoccupation with poetic predecessors is appropriate to **White**, for any poem about the poet's urge to be reborn must also be a poem about his origins. Simic seeks a new, "white," unknown voice to inhabit him, yet as his desire for such an event increases, so too does his knowledge of how thoroughly both his new and his old voices resound with those of his predecessors, particularly Whitman's. Indeed, like the child in "Out of the Cradle," he paradoxically comes of age and discovers his own voice only after he loses his illusions of wholeness and admits for the first time the terrifying insurge of an alien, foster-voice whose music is not his own. **White** is Simic's collection of strategies for summoning forth his muse. But when she appears, one of her masks is that of "White-man," Whitman.

Simic alludes most clearly to this necessary inflooding in the penultimate poem of the poet's second sequence (p. 22). With puns on the phrases "getting through" and "going through," he refers both to the process of transformation itself, the new self passing through (or flooding) the old self, and to the poet's stricken understanding of the process as it happens. That is, the spirit which teaches him about death and transformation must "get through" to the poet's obtuse old self, which Simic here portrays as a sort of cantankerous old man indignant at the fact that he can't be around forever. White's forces, however, are irresistible; they have all the power of an army of ants dismantling a body:

Had to get through me elsewhere.
Woe to bone

That stood in their way.
Woe to each morsel of flesh.

White ants
In a white anthill.

The rustle of their many feet
Scurrying—tiptoeing too.

Gravedigger ants.
Village-idiot ants.

White's concluding monologues also tease the defensive poet by playing upon the phrase "getting through." The poet, like the old man, or an innocent child, naïvely believes that his voice and his self are of his own making. But White is disdainful and imperious. "I am the bullet that has gone through everyone," she chants mockingly at the beginning of each of her two speeches, using "everyone" to refer to the poet's menagerie of selves. Then she forces him to locate the source of all of his powers of self-creation *outside* of himself: "I thought of you long before you thought of me." It is a moment of sheer terror; the fragile levees defining the poet's self are inundated and swept away. Like the child in "Out of the Cradle," the poet in *White* loses his illusions of independence and is flooded by a foreign presence; he learns how frail his own voice is, and that it is loaned to him, not his to keep. The poet had prayed for such a gift of a new voice repeatedly throughout his sections of *White*, but even his worst fears of what White might do to him had an arrogance in them, as shown by the involuntary references to himself as heroic martyr in her presence. He still believed that he could "summon" White as if she were a genie and bid her to give him a new self on demand. During White's monologues, however, he learns that even his pretensions to summoning her were under her control: "I thought of you long before you thought of me," she says. She may give him a new self or drown his old self and leave it at that. This is the grim undercurrent of White's monologues, songs whose melodious hissing is kin to that of the old crone who rocks the cradle in Whitman's poem.

By the end of White's poems, however, her tone becomes more benign, even motherly, though an edge of her original anger remains. Her influx lifts or floats a new self to the poet even as it drowns the old one; she seems both a mother in mourning arranging the limbs of her lost child and a mother who rocks a newborn one—Simic's newborn poetic self—in her arms: "Steadily, patiently, I lift your arms . . . / . . . the sea in which you are sinking, / And even this night above it, is myself."

A similar death and transfiguration occurs when Whitman's voice invades Simic's. At first it is Simic's undoing: when in *White* he finds his own voice immersed in the dangerous, powerful rhythms of Whitman's, he can only pray that his fate will not be that of the "white" swimmer in "Out of the Cradle." But after enduring the successive infloodings of White, Simic has earned the right to discover the new voice that he asked for rising slowly but buoyantly within him. This voice is recognizably his own, although the drone of Whitman's sea-mother can still be heard beneath it.

Such an emergence in the last lines of *White*—even as the poet's old self "falls" asleep and is whirled away—shows that Simic, like Whitman, takes up Emerson's oracular challenge to the American poet in "Nature," quoted here as an epigraph. He has confronted "evening knowledge," what Emerson would later call "Fate": the knowledge of powerlessness, limitations, death, an instantaneous instreaming of a force foreign to himself. But he has managed to stay afloat, and thus may have revealed to him what Emerson calls "morning knowledge," the "ideal" force of man—and the poet—which is the right to be broken and reborn again and again. Paradoxically, Simic learns how to free himself from history by immersing himself within a historical tradition that denies history and affirms only "morning knowledge," the poet's inalienable right (as Emerson said in "Nature") to discover an original relation to the universe. Simic assays the dangerous crossing from "evening knowledge" to "morning knowledge" each time he begins a poem in *White*; he seeks to discard his earlier, time-bound selves and return to a place lit by the milk-white light of dawn. But none of the poet's twenty poems in *White* complete that return successfully. White does not appear except hypothetically, and the poet is left in twenty different states of hopefulness, despair, terror, and anger. In **"What The White Had To Say,"** however, the "White" muse representing the American oracular poetic tradition finally descends upon Simic and claims him, and *White* ends with the poet just about to receive the new self and new voice for which he has prayed for so long. Born in Yugoslavia but educated in America, Simic has absorbed many influences during the course of his career, including those of Yugoslavian folklore, Yeats, Rilke, and the surrealists, and I have unavoidably had to slight them in this essay. But *White* shows the central role played by those ambiguous foster-parents Emerson and Whitman.

In 1977, Simic published a short essay—really a collection of paragraphs, a notecard prolegomenon—entitled **"Composition"** which bears on the quest to recover purity in *White*. Simic noted that the poet's search is a search for origins, an epic journey leading backward in time rather than forward in space. He claimed that this desire to discover primordial voices beneath our historical ones is

> the secret strength of poetry and the source of its perpetual renewal. The "difficulty" of modern poetry from Imagism to Surrealism is that it has invested all its energies to permit that ancestral and archetypal thought to become audible in its purity.[6]

Simic's many masks in *White* and in his Braziller volumes accordingly tend to possess the archetypal qualities which Yeats associated with masks. Simic's personae are unlike Browning's, which speak with single, everyday voices, and unlike Pound's and Eliot's, which speak with the many voices of a historical period. They are more kin to the songs sung by the orphans and beggars in Rilke's *Buch der Bilder* or any of Yeat's volumes; they employ the ahistorical, ancestral voices of *the* orphan, *the* vagabond, *the* rogue, *the* stepmother. Simic's use of such generic psychic personae is complemented by his pervasive interest in imitating riddles, incantations, and charms, all primary sources for lyric poetry, and folkloric formulae and notated incident, all kernels of narrative.

Intriguingly, however, the personae in Simic's work in the late 1970s and early 1980s appear to be evolving from the strongly archetypal to a mode that mixes such universal correspondences with much more autobiographical and historical detail. **"Forest,"** for instance, opens Simic's first Braziller volume and strikes its keynote; its hero is somewhat like a blend of Prospero and Whitman, with the former's rough magic ("my roots and streams / Will stitch their chill into the heart of man") and the latter's stentorian confidence ("Ladies and gentlemen, you will hear a star / Dead a million years, in the throat of a bird"). Simic's language stresses the archetypal qualities of all the poem's events—all "man" is involved, time is measured in eons rather than in forty-hour weeks, and the knowledge the poem teaches is ancient, even prehistorical:

> There'll be plenty of time
> When an acorn grows out of your ear
> to accustom yourself to my ways,
> To carve yourself a hermit's toothpick.

In **"Forest,"** identity dependent upon a particular place, time and society gives way to a primordial self, as if the dark forest of man's collective unconscious were reclaiming the collapsing cities of modern personality. In Simic's most recent volume, *Classic Ballroom Dances* (1980), such prehistoric forces remain ever-present, but paradoxically they seem all the more compelling because they are *less* confidently inherited; several of the poems are filled with more personal and historical references than Simic has ever included, and their protagonists' escape from history, when it occurs, is more provisional, more tentative.

In **"Furniture Mover"** for example, the speaker longs to escape from the burden of carrying his possessions, his body, and his self. He wants to arrive at a future destination in his life ahead of time—or, rather, ahead of Time, ahead of his history. The tone of the poem is also much like that of *White*, hushed and prayer-like, but with muted comic asides. For the tragicomic battle of the speaker's soul and his furniture mover is at a standoff. He wants to leave behind his physical, historical self (represented by the furniture mover), but he always arrives in the future just one step too late:

> oh
>   Mr. Furniture Mover
> on my knees
>   let me come
> for once
>   early
> to where it's vacant

> you still
> on the stairs
>   wheezing
> between floors.

The speakers in Simic's earlier poems tended to be archetypal presences, as in **"Forest"**; magicians or fortune-tellers interpreting the mysteries of such presences, as in **"The Needle"** from *Dismantling the Silence*, which begins, "Watch out for the needle, / She's the scent of a plant / The root of which is far and hidden"; or heroic voyagers who escape history entirely, as in **"The Explorers,"** which ends with each of the explorers greeting a newly discovered world: "You are all / that has eluded me. // May this be my country." Such oracular confidence is generally absent in *Classic Ballroom Dances*, where the tone is greyer, the events suggest historical as well as mythic incidents, and the characters tend to be not those who have escaped history but those who have been disfigured by it—orphans, war refugees, beggars, lunatics, widows and widowers, a pair of "ancient lovers" on the "dancefloor of the Union Hall, / where they also hold charity raffles / On rainy Monday nights of an eternal November" (**"Classic Ballroom Dances"**). Such figures have been in Simic's work from the start, but never has their presence loomed so large or been described in such detail. Ironically, part of Simic wants to escape from history, but another part of him knows that he has the responsibility of the furniture mover to remember—to carry—as much as he can bear.[7]

White is indispensable for helping us account for the growing presence of such irony and such historical detail in Simic's work. For in *White* (unlike *Dismantling the Silence*) the poet's desire to transcend history is eventually subverted; the "white" muse of purity and "morning knowledge" is also what I have called Whitman's crone, the muse of eternal tragedy and fallen experience. *White* will become a permanent part of American oracular poetic tradition because it is a well-written poem about a successful quest to leave irony behind and to return to oracular assertion. But it also turns upon itself and becomes simultaneously an ironic *critique* of the oracular poet's belief that he may transcend time and disown the grim absolutes of "evening knowledge." At first glance, perhaps, *White* seems unlike Simic's more recent ironic lyrics, for it appears patently to be a poem in which the poet sheds his old self and ends in free fall, free from space and time and safe in White's embrace. But that moment of free fall cannot last. The last lines of the poem about the milk tooth that the poet has placed under his pillow while his dreams imply that he is poised at the moment of transformation, just about to recross the boundary separating eternity from time to accept the new, time-bound, and necessarily disfigured self that White will give him. Thus, although *White* is a successful quest to return to White's embrace, its ending foretells another beginning when that embrace is broken and the child-poet is exiled and falls into time, selfhood, particular lyric forms, and ink marks on the page. It is apparent that the drama of summoning

White has been enacted again and again, and that Simic's Braziller volumes collect with increasingly ironic detail the various mortal selves that White left the poet each time she descended upon him, passed through him, and then vanished. Guided by his female muse, Simic at the end of *White* is in the same position as the child in "Out of the Cradle Endlessly Rocking"—just on the verge of a tragic awakening. The pain and loss caused by such an orphaning will inspire all his songs: "For I, that was a child, my tongue's use sleeping, now I have heard you, / Now in a moment I know what I am for, I awake. . . ."

If Simic's Braziller volumes contain portraits of the selves that his muse has awakened within him, in *White* he gives us a behind-the-scenes glimpse into what it is like to summon one's psychic forces and then watch them invade, form shapes, and displace each other. In doing so, Simic has created a poem whose intimate immensity gives it a right to be called an epic in scale if not in length. Unlike previous epics, *White* does not incorporate large chunks of narrative; instead, it rewrites narrative in the key of the lyric, with each of its poems compacting its story within the confines of the spot of time, rarely more than a few moments, in which the lyric traditionally takes place. *White* also has the requisite epic subject, the story of the struggle to return home, and it uses the traditional epic mode of characterization, employing larger-than-life archetypal personae for its protagonists. Presenting the struggle between a poet and his predecessors, and between "evening knowledge" and "morning knowledge," the experience of time and the appetite for that power which frees one from time, *White* is a long ur-lyric, a thumbnail or miniature epic about the painful birth of the lyric itself.

Notes

1. Originally published in 1970, the translations were recently reissued as Vasko Popa, *Homage to the Lame Wolf: Selected Poems, 1956-1975* (Oberlin, Ohio: *Field* Translation Series, 1979).

2. Charles Simic, *White* (Durango, Colorado: Logbridge-Rhodes Press, 1980), pp. 4, 8. All other references to this edition will be cited in the text.

3. The present text has "Shook you loaded dice in a tin cup." But since White is addressing the poet in this passage, surely "you" is a misprint for "your."

4. Helen Vendler, *Part of Nature, Part of Us* (Cambridge: Harvard University Press, 1980), p. 358.

5. Simic's revisions also include changing selected lines, transposing a few lyrics, and cutting some others to replace them with new poems. In all cases in this essay except this one, I refer to Simic's 1980 version.

6. *New Literary History*, 9, No. 1 (Autumn 1977), 149-51.

7. For more on the matter of Simic's evolution, see David Young's fine review of *Classic Ballroom Dances* in *Field*, 24 (Spring 1981), 83-88, and David Walker's excellent article "*O What Solitude*: The Recent Poetry of Charles Simic," in *Ironwood*,

4, No. 1-2 (1976), 61-67, which covers Simic's work through *Return to a Place Lit by a Glass of Milk*. That same issue of *Ironwood* also has a brief introduction to Simic's earlier version of *White* by James Carpenter, pp. 72-84, but I do not find useful Carpenter's premise that White convinces the poet that any separation between a poet and his poem or an observer and the object observed is false.

Bruce Bennett (review date 12 March 1983)

SOURCE: "Poems Magical, Poems Mordant," in *Nation*, Vol. 236, No. 10, March 12, 1983, pp. 314-15.

[*In the following excerpted review, Bennett admires the spareness and clarity of poems that make up* Austerities.]

[In *Austerities*] Charles Simic is a story teller, but his tales are mordant. "**Rosalia**" begins typically:

> An especially forlorn human specimen
> Answers a marriage-ad
> On a street of compulsory misfortune,
> One drizzly November afternoon . . .

They are set in landscapes—general cityscapes—despoiled by history ("**From Tooth Crowned With Gold**," "**Punch Minus Judy**"), and in a climate almost unremittingly harsh. Scarcity is the rule and practically everyone practices "austerities" of some sort. Even on those rare occasions of abundance, the results are not precisely satisfying:

> We ate so well after the funeral
> In that shack by the town dump;
> Fingers dripping with barbecue sauce and grease
> Making the quick sign of the cross
> In the cramped, smoke-filled living room . . .

("**Antediluvian Customs**")

In "**Guardian Angel**" the poet refers to "these dark, hell-bent days"; in "**Dear Isaac Newton**" he declares "the maggots romp / In the Sunday roast." A "born doubter," he has been vouch-safed few signs, and like other non-believers has no alternative but to look "both ways at the crossing / At two gusts of nothing and nothing."

Yet, despite the bleakness, the experience of reading *Austerities* is not austere. For one thing, there is abundant humor, albeit of the gallows variety. "**Hurricane Season**" begins: "Just as the world was ending / We fell in love, / Immoderately." In "**Biographical Note**" a rat wanders on stage during the performance of a school Christmas play, creating predictable havoc before it is dispatched moments later in the wings. There is a wonderful sardonic quality in "**The Great Horned Owl**," where "the Grand Seigneur / Is so good as to appear," and the poet makes what he can of this problematic visitation. There is even, in "**Old Mountain Road**," a fleeting glimpse of something, perhaps, beyond the darkness. But most important, there is the pleasure afforded by the poems themselves: precise and pungent, clean and spare, they make Simic's grim vision more than palatable.

Charles Simic with Sherod Santos (interview date 1984)

SOURCE: "An Interview with Charles Simic," in *Missouri Review,* Vol. VII, No. 3, 1984, pp. 59-74.

[*In the following interview, Simic discusses influences on his work, his personal experiences in Eastern Europe and the United States, and the act of writing poetry.*]

[*Santos*]: *Would you mind talking a little about the conditions in Yugoslavia just before you left?*

[Simic]: I had what Jan Kott calls "a typical East European education." He means, Hitler and Stalin taught us the basics. When I was three years old the Germans bombed Belgrade. The house across the street was hit and destroyed. There was plenty more of that, as everybody knows. When the war ended I came in and said: "Now there won't be any more fun!" That gives you an idea what a jerk I was. The truth is, I did enjoy myself. From the summer of 1944 to mid-1945, I ran around the streets of Belgrade with other half-abandoned kids. You can just imagine the things we saw and the adventures we had. You see, my father was already abroad, my mother was working, the Russians were coming, the Germans were leaving. It was a three-ring circus.

I don't want to sound overly psychological, but there is in your work that peculiar element which blends so naturally horror and fun. Do you think it had its origin in those days?

Very probably. I'm the product of chance, the baby of ideologies, the orphan of History. Hitler and Stalin conspired to make me homeless. Well, then, is my situation tragic? No. There's been too much tragedy all around for anyone to feel like a Hamlet. More likely my situation is comic. It's "the amazement of the thinking spirit at itself" and its predicament—or so said Schlegel. One just has to laugh at the extent of our stupidity.

So what happened after 1945?

Well, from 1945 to 1948 it was just poverty. I remember being very, very hungry, and my mother crying because she had nothing to give me. Still later, it became clear to my mother that if I was ever going to become an American poet, we'd better get moving. that's Phil Levine's theory. Actually, my father was already in the U.S.A. working for the same telephone company he had worked for in Yugoslavia before the war. Anyway, we ended up in Chicago, and my father took me out one day to hear Coleman Hawkins. You could say the kid was hooked. Jazz made me both an American and a poet.

What was it about jazz that seemed to you so distinctly American?

I heard in it, experienced in it what it feels like to be sad or happy in America. Or more idiomatically: how to raise hell, or how to break someone's heart and make beautiful music in the process. I mean, it's fine to read the great lyric poets of the past, but one also has to know how the people in the language you're writing in sing.

Is there an identifiable influence jazz has made on your work? I'm wondering, for example, if you see surrealism in any way as a literary equivalent to jazz?

The poet is really not much different from that tenor player who gets up in a half-empty, smoke-filled dive at two in the morning to play the millionth rendition of "Body and Soul." Which is to say that one plays with the weight of all that tradition, but also to entertain the customers and to please oneself. One is both bound and free. One improvises but there are constraints, forms to obey. It's the same old thing which is always significantly different.

As for surrealism, I think there's more of it in the blues. The early stuff, especially. Most people know Bessie Smith and perhaps Robert Johnson, but there are many others. Incredible verbal invention. What one would call "jive," but also eroticism, the tragic sense of life. If the blues was French we'd be studying it at Yale. As it is, hardly anyone knows my heroes, people like Cripple Clarence Lofton; Frankie Jaxon, or Bessie Jackson, who also called herself Lucille Bogan. They are our Villons.

Anyway, blues taught me a number of things. How to tell a story quickly, economically. The value of gaps, ellipses, and most importantly, the virtues of simplicity and accessibility.

That erotic element, since you mention it, is an important part of your work as well; and now that I think about it, you use it in ways that are actually quite similar to the ways it's used in the blues. The last two stanzas of your poem "Breasts" is a good example:

> O my sweet, my wistful bagpipes.
> Look, everyone is asleep on the earth.
> Now, in the absolute immobility
> Of time, drawing the waist
> Of the one I love to mine,
>
> I will tip each breast
> Like a dark heavy grape
> Into the hive
> Of my drowsy mouth.

I don't know if I still care for the ending of that poem. "Wistful bagpipes" is awful. Also, the pace of these stanzas is awkward. The earlier ones are better, I think.

As for eroticism, isn't it synonymous with imagination? Eros as the cause of logos, and that sort of thing. The one lying in the dark and trying to visualize the loved one is at the mercy of both. . . . There's not much more that I can say.

Abstract painting is important to you as well—and, I assume, for many of the same reasons. Does that interest go back as far?

You know, I was in Washington D.C. last fall, and I had a chance to see some paintings I'd known for a long time and to my great surprise I no longer cared for a couple of my old heroes, Pollock and Rothko. Their conceptions struck me as being simple-minded. The work had no depth. The problem with abstract art is that it restricted itself so much. Let's admit, in the end, Mondrian is pretty boring. it's like using only a few keys on the piano. One admires the purity, but that's about it.

Was it because the paintings had finally abandoned representation that made them seem so restricted?

Not necessarily. I mean, I like de Kooning, Guston, Frankenthaler, to speak only of Abstract Expressionists. The two I mentioned just don't have the range of these others. That day in Washington I realized that my early admiration was really an intellectual appreciation of what their work means in the history of modern painting.

Analogies between the arts aren't always accurate, but do you think poetry has ever reached that same level of abstraction?

Hmmm. Perhaps Creeley's *Pieces*, and the work of Bob Grenier. I don't know what to say! Language is much better when it's concrete. "The bride unramples her white dress, the minute-hand of the clock moves slowly," says Whitman, for example. Abstraction is precisely what one should avoid in poetry.

Was that ever an ambition of yours, to be an abstract poet?

Only in the sense that I wanted a poem with just a few elementary verbal gestures.

So there was jazz and painting, but what poets did you start out reading?

The first two poets I truly liked were Vachel Lindsay and Hart Crane. Lindsay is like those primitive painters. He throws everything in, angels and pigs. I mean, you have Salvation Army Generals, Chinese laundrymen, Bible-pounding blacks, factory windows that are always broken, etc. That's how I see the world too. Crane made me go to the dictionary. I realized certain words are very beautiful, very apt. It was a lesson in lyric poetry as well as a lesson in making associations, in using my imagination in a certain way.

Can you say more precisely what that "certain way" is?

Words call to other words and so on. Words know much better what needs to be said than I do. That sort of thing.

Eliot once remarked that a poet's material is his own language as it's actually spoken around him. That would seem to have been a much more complicated issue for a writer like yourself whose first language was not the language actually spoken around him.

I was never at any point capable of writing a poem in Serbian. By the time I started writing poetry in high school all my serious reading had been in English and American literature. So, it was inevitable. I read American poets and wanted to write like them. At that time, I didn't have the slightest idea of Serbian poetry.

What language do you dream in?

The language I dream and know best I speak with an accent.

About 1958 you moved from Chicago to New York. What was your life like there?

I worked during the day and went to school at night. I did just about every kind of work imaginable. I was a shirt salesman, a house painter, a payroll clerk, I had no thought of the future. No plans to be a professor or a poet. I mean, I wrote poetry, even published it, but that was it. That lasted twelve years. New York is, of course, a place that could have been imagined by Hieronymous Bosch. Rome must have been like that at the end of its days when all the barbarians got in. It's a city which either proves that the end of the world is near, or that human beings will survive no matter what. I always get that sense of hope when I watch those guys on street corners peddling stolen umbrellas, or some kind of idiotic wind-up toys. I love to breathe that air.

The more I read your work, the more I think of you as a poet of the city—in that particular way one thinks of poets like Baudelaire or Eliot or Auden or even Lowell—not so much in the landscape itself as in the way the city functions, both internally and externally, as a symbol of modernity.

When I close my eyes I go into cities. Others, I suppose, sail the ocean blue. The rat is my totem animal, the cockroach my wood thrush. My mother is calling my name out of a tenement window. She keeps calling and calling. My entire psychic life is there.

I'm sure you're familiar with The Book of Laughter and Forgetting. *At the end of that book Kundera, who also comes from an East European background, draws a pretty sad picture of the West, sad because it seems to him rather soulless.*

That's a version of the old "suffering ennobles" argument. I suppose the more political repression one experiences, the greater one's chances are for spiritual growth. The guys in the Gulags are overflowing with soul. Stalin was like Buddha. The problem with us is that we don't shoot poets. Meanwhile, millions have been running in our direction. it's one-way traffic. You don't find anyone going the other way to embrace all that soulfullness.

I see your point, but do you really think Kundera was suggesting, even indirectly, that political repression gives rise to a more meaningful life for the individual? In Kundera's book the West is, after all, still clearly "the free world."

Of course. There are many things wrong with the West. I guess I just don't like the way East European intellectuals, at least since Dostoyevsky, have patronized the West and especially this country. One ends by claiming, say, that only Serbians know how to sing and drink, and that the stuffed peppers made by our grandmothers are superior to all French cooking. And then, of course, there's the local wine which is the best in the world, and the women—oh boy! those dark eyes and gypsy black hair . . .

John Bayley has commended Max Hayward for pointing out to us our great debt to Soviet literature: in Bayley's words, "that only a man who has joyfully prostrated himself to embrace an idea, and had a boulder rolled on top of him, has any idea what freedom is. We may all need that awareness and that example in time to come." Is East European and Soviet literature making us more aware of our own freedoms?

It ought to be that way. But I met people in Paris, poets and intellectuals, who assured me that Albania is a wonderful place. For the most part, Western writers have no idea how free they are. You even hear people say that we live in a police state. America is no heaven on earth, but let's not exaggerate. Nadezhda Mandelstam's books ought to be required reading.

Admittedly, you came here at a much younger age, but do you feel any affinity at all with writers like Milosz, Brodsky, Solzhenitsyn?

I admire the people you mention but feel no kinship with the Russians. The Poles I understand better, especially their sense of history. As for Yugoslavia, I feel like a foreigner there. Everything I love and hate with a passion is over here. I'd die of grief if I left this country for long. Still, I'm not so naive as to pretend there aren't certain East European elements in my poetry. They are biographical and temperamental. I am still haunted by images of that war, and then when it comes to history, I'm like one of those late Byzantine intellectuals. I don't believe in History anymore.

Once that belief is gone, what takes its place?

Now you've got me. I don't believe in History as a road to Utopia and the accompanying idea that the present is a kind of fertilizer, in human terms for that future flower garden. Which is to say, I no longer believe in the Marxist

model, which is basically a version of the Christian model, that history ends in some sort of paradise on earth.

At what point did you stop believing in the Marxist model?

When I realized that Marx lacks the most elementary psychology. it's not just classes and economics that make men what they are. Dostoyevsky, Nietzsche, and Freud knew a thing or two about that. Anyway, the world is cruel, humankind is probably insane, but I don't have a solution. Except, I want everybody to disarm. I'm not even asking whether this is possible, but it's the only thing worth yelling about. You could say, I refuse to play the game anymore. Instead of history, we are left now only with the present moment, in which we are all, collectively, like that wild-eyed suicide with the barrel of a shotgun in his mouth. Ergo, first things first. Take the gun away.

In the face of all that, do you ever still feel, as you said more than a decade ago in **"Summer Morning,"** *that "It seems possible / To live simply / On the earth"?*

Not with all these madmen in charge of the world!

To what extent do you think poetry is able to engage those issues?

I never liked the term "political poetry." It implies a cause, partisanship, petitions for this or that, and finally propaganda, regardless of how worthy the reason. On the other hand, the world is mean, stupid, violent, unjust, cruel. I read in the *Times* this morning that 40,000 children die every day in the world from hunger and disease. Well, what do you say to that? And you must say something. A poet who ignores the world is contemptible. I find the narcissism of so much recent poetry obscene. I don't mind people talking about themselves—we all do—but *all* the time! Mao had the right idea. Send the crybabies to dig turnips. I'm kidding, of course. The Chairman wouldn't find my poems so amusing either. Too many tyrants and torture chambers in them. I make sure the executioners are included. Obviously, I'm uncomfortable with poetry which just keeps telling me how wonderful nature is, or how much the author is misunderstood.

Could you name a particular poem which in your mind best exemplifies that commitment to "saying something" without being partisan or propagandistic?

Whitman's "Drum-Taps." Many others since. Quasimodo speaks of "the black howl of the mother gone to meet her son crucified on the telegraph pole." The poet is one of the crowd of witnesses watching her go. Poetry about human suffering requires empathy of course, and humility. It's no place to parade one's ego and make political editorials. That poor woman has been doing that since the beginning of time. One must not presume to understand.

Given all that, do you think it's possible for poetry to be a public force for good?

In the long run, I'm sure. Many souls were ennobled reading Chaucer or Whitman . . . It reminds them of their humanity—poetry does. But the act is private, intimate. Poetry works, one reader at a time.

Okay, then let's talk for a moment about the act itself. Is it for you—as it was apparently for poets like Blake and Whitman—an ecstatic one?

Are you kidding me? My mother almost married a guy who used to compose his symphonies while sitting naked in an empty bathtub. I one've been his son. Anyway, that's not my style. Breton says "poetry is made in bed like love." I too have to be horizontal, and a bit lazy.

*In your essay, "**Some Thoughts About the Line,**" you say, "In the end, I'm always at the beginning. Silence—an endless mythical condition." Obviously you mean by silence something more than just that condition out of which poems grow.*

I call silence what precedes language: the world and the sense of oneself existing. I always thought, if you will, that speaking is a bit like whistling in the dark. The universe, in my humble opinion, doesn't require me saying anything. When I'm attentive and silent I seem to be closer to the way things are. A number of my early poems are attempts to make that predicament into a myth of origins.

What is it then that makes you break that silence?

To speak as the translator of silence rather than its opposer. I think Thoreau said something like that, seeing language as but a minor ripple on the great pool of wordless silence, which, I agree, is our true environment.

In that same essay you say, "To see the word for what it is, one needs the line. . . . For me the sense of the line is the most instinctive aspect of the entire process of writing." One of the noticeable features of your lines is how often they are end-stopped; how often a sentence is a line by itself, or if not a line then a stanza. Is that done to further emphasize the silence?

Yes, the line is the unit of measure, the unit of attention. it's the way one slows down and speeds up the language, the place for the "counterpoint of eye and ear," as Robert Morgan says. I'm still learning how to do it right.

Could you describe the particular way in which an image functions within your poems?

Olga Freidenberg, Pasternak's aunt, says in their correspondence: "A poetic metaphor is an image functioning as a concept." I agree with that. In my poetry images think. My best images are smarter than I am.

Your work has always stood somewhere outside the narrative mode, but do you ever find yourself drifting in that direction?

I hope not. Most of the so-called narrative poems just plod. They have no sense of the line, nor do they imagine well. When poets forget what imagination can do they get into these linear, prosy, redundant, long-winded poems. It's possible to tell a story, the whole story, in twenty lines. The art consists of making a few details and images say everything. They should study Strand's "The Untelling." There's a masterpiece for you.

But don't most poems of any kind just plod? I was really wondering about the exceptional few. Or are you saying that at some point the imagination and the narrative are antithetical?

No. Imagination and narrative go fine together. Consider myths, fairy tales, prose poems, etc. However, most narrative poems I see operate largely in the framework of realism.

I notice in reading reviews of your books that critics at times have a tendency to read your poems as parables. Is that the result of your working beyond the framework of realism?

I don't know. I don't write parables. If I say "rats in diapers" that's to be taken literally.

Then do you think of your poems as having a clearly communicative function, on rational or cognitive levels?

I don't know about "clearly communicative" and "cognitive," but the point of writing a poem, actually the need to do so, is to give, pass on, relate to someone something of value. I don't want to waste people's time. It matters to me (I mean, what goes on in the poem), and I want them to know about it. One can't always make it simple because many things are not simple, but it's worth trying.

You read a good deal of philosophy, and, I'm told, have a particular interest in Heidegger.

I always read philosophy. I suppose I'm a bit envious of that kind of disciplined thinking. Also, I am curious what human beings have been thinking for the last three thousand years about the nature of things. As for Heidegger, I admire the phenomenological impulse to reexamine the simplest, the long-taken-for-granted things. That's what a poet is supposed to do, too.

Is that the most important thing a poet is supposed to do?

No! You must have a pencil handy when the Muse barges in. My father told me that many poems came to him in his lifetime but just in those moments when he couldn't find anything to write with. Otherwise, it's pointless to say what a poem should do. Someone always comes along and does the opposite, and it's perfectly fine. What all good poetry has in common is the use of the imagination. Imagination, on the other hand, is like the universe of which only a small part has been explored.

You've just recently had an incredible piece of news about the MacArthur Foundation Grant. What sort of effect do you think that will have on your work?

I really don't know what to say, and I have no opinion about it yet. I realize it beats breaking a leg, but at the same time the idea that I have five years to just write is frightening. Thank God I still have to finish this busy semester and make the usual ends meet.

We're very happy to have these new poems, particularly **"Birthday Star Atlas,"** *which speaks of an interesting connection between you and Emily Dickinson.*

Yes, Miss Emily is my great love. In fact, I'm the long lost lover to whom she wrote all her poems. I used to play for her all my Billie Holiday records.

Any particular song she was especially fond of?

"I can't believe that you're in love with me," of course. She dug Buck Clayton's muted trumpet and Lester Young's supremely melancholy playing.

Kenneth Funsten (review date 16 March 1986)

SOURCE: A review of *Selected Poems 1963-1983*, in *Los Angeles Time Book Review*, March 16, 1986, p. 9.

[*In the following review, Funsten provides an overview of* Selected Poems 1963-1983, *finding that Simic's later work is neither as startling nor as evocative as his earlier poems.*]

> At night some understand what the grass says.
> The grass knows a word or two.
> It is not much. It repeats the same word
> Again and again, but not too loudly . . .

The best poems by Charles Simic harbor an enigmatic simplicity, contain an evasive weight to them. Influenced by riddles, parables and nursery rhymes, Simic populates the folk world of his poems with simple objects and puzzling omens. His poems have the atmosphere of a Bruegel feast day, without any of the people.

Born in Yugoslavia in 1938, Charles Simic spent his childhood watching Europe turn into rubble. "it's always evening / In an occupied country. / Hour before the curfew. / A small provincial city. / The houses all dark. / The storefronts gutted."

In 1949, he emigrated to America, eventually working as an editorial assistant at *Aperture,* a photography magazine.

The fact is significant. For Simic's best poems share a quality with good photographs, the unceasing attention to objects in an effort to see them anew. At his best, it is the intensity of Simic's imagination as it attempts to animate the objects and renew itself that interests us. For example, in **"Fork"**:

> This strange thing must have crept
> Right out of hell.
> It resembles a bird's foot
> Worn around the cannibal's neck.
> As you hold it in your hand,
> As you stab with it into a piece of meat,
> It is possible to imagine the rest of the bird:
> Its head which like your fist
> Is large, bald, beakless and blind.

Specifics, such as the fork, give the poet's surrealism the focus it needs. His catalogues of imagination improvise the souls of our most everyday objects, bringing them back to life and light as if from the world of our dreams.

His first two books, **What the Grass Says** and **Somewhere Among Us a Stone Is Taking Notes,** were published and championed by George Hitchcock's Kayak Press in the late '60s, and then combined with new poems into Simic's first Braziller volume, **Dismantling the Silence** (1971).

Here, **Selected Poems** gives us some of his best work, including the famous **"Bestiary for the Fingers of My Right Hand."**

When Simic's metaphors are good, the disparate things they yoke together are both contradictory and strangely appropriate. His achievement in these early poems is maintaining that tension of the suspense between known and unknown, object and spirit.

But, of course, a poet cannot perform the same trick *ad infinitum*—even if it is his best. So, in his later books, Simic's task has been to branch out, to grow into the tree his acorn promised.

Simic's third book from Braziller was **Charon's Cosmology**. There is less zip, more speculation on death, more pessimism here. Many poems, like **"The Prisoner,"** seem derivative of an earlier self:

> It's been so long. He has trouble
> Deciding what else is there.
> And all along the suspicion
> That we do not exist.

But **Classic Ballroom Dances** (1980) announced the rebirth of a sort of classic Simic, lean, mystical, authentic again. Many of the poems are about the poet's childhood in war-torn Yugoslavia.

The last 20 or so pieces in this **Selected** volume are from Simic's 1982 book, **Austerities**. Less dark, both literally and figuratively lighter, these are mostly too cute, too pat. Bordering on self-parody, many poems indulge what Auden called "the Dada giggle": "Pascal's own / Prize abyssologist / In marriage. / On her knees / Still scrubbing / The marble stairs / Of a Russian countess."

The tired symbols are recycled again—gravediggers, their spades, mirrors, bones, utensils. But they are no longer unnerving.

So what is the verdict? Has Simic's achievement amounted to automatic, clever writing that must forever sacrifice its future breadth and seriousness to remain its present self? Is this poet finally ensnared in his own cleverness? This collection of *Selected Poems* might make it appear so.

Peter Stitt (review date Spring 1987)

SOURCE: "The Whirlpool of Image and Narrative Flow," in *Georgia Review,* Vol. XLI, No. 1, Spring, 1987, pp. 200-203.

[*In the following review, Stitt traces the evolution of Simic's poetry from dark and terrifying to lighter and gentler in his volume* Unending Blues.]

The voice of Charles Simic is surely one of the most distinct in the world of contemporary poetry. He is known for his terrifying Kafkaesque vision, his propensity for speaking in parables, and his use of pointed and surrealistic images. The title of his newest volume, *Unending Blues,* seems to promise the first two of these characteristics, and the knowing reader assumes the presence of the third. These elements are indeed dominant through most of the book, though subtle forces of change seem to be undermining two of them. Before I talk about the changes I see taking place, I would like to look at an example of the kind of poem we expect from Simic, **"Dark Farmhouses"**:

> Windy evening,
> Chinablue snow
> The old people are shivering
> In their kitchens.
>
> Truck without lights
> Idling on the highway,
> Is it a driver you require?
> Wait a bit.
>
> There's coal to load up,
> A widow's sack of coal.
>
> Is it a shovel you need?
> Idle on,
> A shovel will come by and by
> Over the darkening plain.
> A shovel,
> And a spade.

A threatening world is created in the first stanza and deepened thereafter: something like the State is conspiring against widows and other old folks, taking away their coal and preparing to bury them anonymously. The imagery is suggestive but imprecise, familiar but hauntingly unreal. The shovel and spade suggest the dark knights of chivalric romance; they bring death, seemingly at the behest of a truck that has been personified into the technological overseer of eternal destruction.

In its austerity of both image and narrative, the poem is representative of Simic's work up to now (indeed, one of his earlier books is titled *Austerities*). Almost as though to emphasize this characteristic himself, Simic begins another poem in *Unending Blues*: "I only have a measly ant / To think with today. / Others have pictures of saints, / Others have clouds in the sky." As the volume progresses, however, we begin to see a change (the first of the two that I mentioned above) away from the sparseness of parable towards greater narrative fullness. Consider **"For the Sake of Amelia,"** which begins with the speaker identifying himself and his job:

> Tending a cliff-hanging Grand Hotel
> In a country ravaged by civil war.
> My heart as its only bellhop.
> My brain as its Chinese cook.
>
> It's a run-down seaside place
> With a row of gutted limousines out front,
> Monkeys and fighting cocks in the great ballroom,
> Potted palm trees grown wild to the ceilings.

We meet his heroine, Amelia, "surrounded by her beaus and fortune-tellers, / . . . pleading with me to check the ledgers, / Find out if Lenin stayed here once, / Buster Keaton, Nathaniel Hawthorne, / St. Bernard of Clairvaux, who wrote on love?" She calls the speaker to her at the end of the poem:

> But now a buzz from the suite with mirrors.
> Amelia in the nude, black cotton over her eyes.
> It seems there's a fly
> On the tip of her lover's Roman nose.
>
> Night of distant guns, distant and comfortable.
> I am coming with a flyswatter on a silver tray.
> Ah the Turkish delights!
> And the Mask of Tragedy over her pubic hair.

It is the length of this poem (which in some ways seems a rewriting of Faulkner's "A Rose for Emily"), the fullness of its narrative structure, the wealth of its detail, that make it different from Simic's habitual practice—though the atmosphere is familiarly frightening, the landscape typically devastated.

The other change that I think is taking place in Simic's work involves a subtle undermining of this very sense of Kafkaesque terror. Again there are lines that seem to explain what is going on: "He was writing the History of Optimism / In Time of Madness." Characterizing the twentieth century as a time of madness is entirely in character for Simic; writing a history of optimism certainly is not. And yet that is precisely what he ends up doing in this volume, in an understated way and with some backsliding. The geographical pattern the book falls into is one indication of this: section one is set in the Europeanized City of Dark Intent so familiar to Simic's devoted readers; the poems of section three, however, are set almost entirely in the country, in a place relatively sequestered from the faceless and soulless technological forces of the modern world. The first sign of this change in setting appears in a twisted bucolic image that the reader cannot help but see, on first reading, as ironic, just another twist of the Simic knife: "If Justice and Liberty / Can be raised to pedestals, / Why not History? // It could be that fat woman / In faded overalls / Outside a house trailer / On a muddy road to some place called Pittsfield or Babylon."

That Simic actually might care for this woman becomes a possibility when she makes a second affectionate appearance in another poem, called **"Outside a Dirtroad Trailer,"** which begins: "O exegetes, somber hermeneuts, / Ingenious untanglers of ambiguities, / A bald little man was washing / The dainty feet of a very fat woman." The pattern reaches its climax in the volume's concluding poem, **"Without a Sough of Wind"**:

> Against the backdrop
> Of a twilight world
> In which one has done so little
> For one's soul
>
> She hangs a skirt
> On the doorknob
> She puts a foot on the chair
> To take off a black stocking
>
> And it's good to have eyes
> Just then for the familiar
> Large swinging breasts
> And the cleft of her ass
>
> Before the recital
> Of that long day's
> Woes and forebodings
> In the warm evening
>
> With the drone of insects
> On the window screen
> And the lit dial of a radio
> Providing what light there is
>
> Its sound turned much too low
> To make out the words
> Of what could be
> A silly old love song.

Silly old love song indeed. It seems impossible not to conclude that Simic has arranged the poems in this book so that they will end up contradicting his title. Though blues they may often be, these certainly are not blues unending. A tone of affection enters, lightly sounded midway through the book, and grows in power and range until it drowns out all wailing by the end.

Marci Janas (review date Spring 1991)

SOURCE: "The Secret World of Charles Simic," in *Field*, No. 44, Spring, 1991, pp. 67-76.

[*In the following review, Janas explores the major mythological and philosophical themes in Simic's* The Book of Gods and Devils.]

> What I see is the paradox. What shall I call it? The sacred and the profane? I like that point where the levels meet . . . We know what the Egyptians have said: as above, so below. This is the paradox, and I like to draw them close together. . . .
>
> —Charles Simic, *The Uncertain Certainty*

Charles Simic follows phenomenology all the way back to its hermeneutic roots in his marvelous new collection, *The Book of Gods and Devils*. The Egyptian god alluded to in my epigraph, and identified by Simic in a new book of essays—*Wonderful Words, Silent Truth*—is Hermes Trismegistos, a.k.a. Thoth. He was really the start of it all for the philosopher Heidegger—a major figure in hermeneutical or interpretative phenomenology—and the poet Simic, who has often expressed a deep and abiding interest in Heideggerian philosophy. It is possible to claim Thoth as a sort of unseen—of course!—charismatic presence in the book.

Simic is continuing the saga of the Chaplinesque—he would say Buster Keatonish—seer in a world as inscrutable as a sacred text. He's working again in the verse and stanza forms he virtually abandoned for the compact prose poems of his Pulitzer Prize-winning *The World doesn't End*. And, as his mode of discourse has become increasingly expansive, so too has his cosmology. The dominant theme is still the search for determinate meaning and enlightenment in an indeterminate and secret world—as if in subliminal testament to its mystery, the last word of the book is "secret"—but all the hermeneutic goings-on extend beyond ontology; Simic is playing with the teleological. Who—or what—are these gods and devils? Are they within or without us? These are the questions.

In a sort of nostalgia for the noumenal discoveries of his earlier, truncated "object" poems, where the odd stone, knife or broom—"things as they are"—were conceptualized, Simic reveals his fascination with the implications of concealment and disclosure:

"The White Room"

> The obvious is difficult
> To prove. Many prefer
> The hidden. I did, too.
> I listened to the trees.
>
> They had a secret
> Which they were about to
> Make known to me,
> And then didn't.
>
> Summer came. Each tree
> On my street had its own
> Scheherazade. My nights
> Were a part of their wild

Story-telling. We were
Entering dark houses,
More and more dark houses
Hushed and abandoned.

There was someone with eyes closed
On the upper floors.
The thought of it, and the wonder,
Kept me sleepless.

The truth is bald and cold,
Said the woman
Who always wore white.
She didn't leave her room much.

The sun pointed to one or two
Things that had survived
The long night intact,
The simplest things,

Difficult in their obviousness.
They made no noise.
It was the kind of day
People describe as "perfect."

Gods disguising themselves
As black hairpins? A hand-mirror?
A comb with a tooth missing?
No! That wasn't it.

Just things as they are,
Unblinking, lying mute
In that bright light,
And the trees waiting for the night.

In tight four-line stanzas that are nearly all complete syntactic units—stanzas 3 and 7 are the exceptions—Simic seems to be saying that he's done with hairpins and hand-mirrors; it's not the noumenon but the mysterious force that makes the noumenon so compelling, that makes us all Scheherazades, telling stories for our lives. He focuses here on the revelatory moment when one feels what Keats called "the burden of the Mystery."

What brings us to revelation is often antithesis; Simic's particular concern with opposites is again foregrounded in these new poems; they could be the textual children of Blake's *The Marriage of Heaven and Hell*, sharing its motto: "Without Contraries is no progression." Simic has fun with dialectic, and among the contraries he toys with are mutability and immutability. It may be helpful to think of the way time works in a Simic poem by comparing it to the way Heraclitus and Parmenides viewed reality. For Heraclitus, reality was like a river: "One cannot step into the same river twice, since it is endlessly flowing with fresh waters." In other words, reality is constantly changing, nothing is stable or fixed, and, following that logic, the Truth is elusive (though one can enjoy looking for it, splashing around in all that water). For Parmenides reality was permanence. Extending Heraclitus's metaphor, the river is perpetually frozen, and Truth is therefore attainable.

The one reliable absolute in Simic's cosmology is that time passes:

> Mrs. Digby's watch has no hands.
> But it keeps running.
>
> ("Mrs. Digby's Picture Album")
> You forgot about time
> While you sought its secret
> In the slippery wheels,
> Some of which had teeth.
>
> ("The Pieces of the Clock Lie Scattered")

The other, almost reliable, absolute is that, in the midst of this Heraclitean reality, the philosopher-poet is a presence—sensitive to the tenuousness and fragility of perception, but deeply aware of its Parmenidean value:

> Eternity jealous
> Of the present moment,
> It occurred to me!
> And then the moment was over.
>
> ("The Betrothal")
> Time had stopped at dusk.
> You were shivering at the thought
> Of such great happiness.
>
> ("The Immortal")

The poor speaker in a Simic poem runs out on the ice—having waited so patiently for the river to freeze—and then falls through.

The one who seeks time's secret, who shivers "at the thought / Of such great happiness" is the one susceptible to what can be called divine revelation. A paradigm for the whole collection is the amazing narrative poem "The Initiate," an unusually long work for Simic. Here the revelatory moment occurs at the point of recollection which separates what are actually two surreal pilgrimages: the first is the quest for identity; the second is the acceptance of that identity's burdens and the start of a new quest. Here are the first thirteen stanzas:

"The Initiate"

> St. John of the Cross wore dark glasses
> As he passed me on the street.
> St. Theresa of Avila, beautiful and grave,
> Turned her back on me.
>
> "Soulmate," they shouted. "it's high time."
>
> I was a blind child, a wind-up toy.
> I was one of death's juggling red balls
> On a certain street corner
> Where they peddle things out of suitcases.
>
> The city like a huge cinema
> With lights dimmed.
> The performance already started.
>
> So many blurred faces in a complicated plot.

The great secret which kept eluding me: knowing who
I am . . .

The Redeemer and the Virgin,
Their eyes wide open in the empty church
Where the killer came to hide himself . . .

The new snow on the sidewalk bore footprints
That could have been made by bare feet.
Some unknown penitent guiding me.

In truth, I didn't know where I was going.
My feet were frozen,
My stomach growled.

Four young hoods blocking my way.
Three deadpan, one smiling crazily.

I let them have my black raincoat.

Thinking constantly of the Divine Love and the
Absolute had disfigured me.
People mistook me for someone else.
I heard voices after me calling out unknown names

"I'm searching for someone to sell my soul to,"
The drunk who followed me whispered,
While appraising me from head to foot. . . .

What we have thus far seems more than a compelling
poetics of applied Heidegger, where the essence of what it
is to be human in a world where humans are not autonomous subjects contemplating an objective reality but
somehow inextricably linked with that reality, is sought;
Simic is interpreting the interconnectedness of the
supernatural with the natural world. He has written what
amounts to a teleological riddle: guess the initiate's divine
identity . . . along with him. The initiate finds a nebulous
self-definition through his interaction with or exposure to
others—the mystic Spanish poet-saints, for example, or
the implied other at the other end of a causal relationship—he is a Cartesian "wind-up toy," a "red ball" in the
deft hands of Death. Again, we can turn to Keats. In ***The
Uncertain Certainty***, Simic talks about translating Keats's
notion of "uncertainty" as "Chance," which he says was
made famous and ontological by Dada and the surrealists:
"They turned it into a weapon. Cause and effect as the
archenemies."[1] In **"The Initiate,"** Chance appears to be
the recessive rather than the dominant gene: "I was a blind
child," setting up a dialectic struggle where "cause and effect" appear to have the upper hand.

The question of his identity becomes increasingly
problematic and his situation increasingly threatening as
more characters are met along the way. Do the four young
toughs get the initiate's raincoat out of his own sense of
fear and inevitability or out of benevolence? Simic evokes
multiple visual icons in this brief scene—Christ's robe being divvied up, for example, or St. Martin of Tours and
the beggar. Religious contemplation is cited as the source
of his disfigurement: he is many things to many people.
After the drunk appears on the scene, we begin to wonder:
is he Mephistopheles or Michael? Is it Faustus following

him, or Adam? Is this the point "where the levels meet,"
or is he the Second Coming? This is beginning to feel a
little bit like "What's My Line?" Whoever he is, one
thought resonates: "Without Contraries is no progression
. . .":

At the address I had been given,
The building had large X's over its windows.
I knocked but no one came to open.
By and by a black girl joined me on the steps.
She banged at the door till her fist hurt.

Her name was Alma, a propitious sign.
She knew someone who solved life's riddles
In a voice of an ancient Sumerian queen.
We had a long talk about that
While shivering and stamping our wet feet.

It was necessary to stay calm, I explained,
Even with the earth trembling,
And to continue to watch oneself
As if one were a complete stranger.

Once in a hotel room in Chicago
I caught sight of a man in a shaving mirror
Who had my naked shoulders and face,
But whose eyes terrified me!

Two hard staring, all-knowing eyes!

Alma, the night, the cold, and the endless walking
Brought on a kind of ecstasy.
I went as if pursued, trying to warm myself.

There was the East River; there was the Hudson.
Their waters shone like oil in sanctuary lamps.

Something supreme was occurring
For which there will never be any words.
The sky was full of racing clouds and tall buildings.
Whirling and whirling silently.

In that whole city you could hear a pin drop.
Believe me,
I thought I heard a pin drop and I went looking for it.

The arrival of the enigmatic Alma marks the turning point
in the poem. To see for myself why her name was "a propitious sign," I looked her up in the *OED*; this gave me one
of the joys of discovery which occurs so often when reading a Simic poem. The name comes from the Arabic—
calmah—which means "learned," or "knowing." Alma
also refers to an Egyptian dancing-girl. It is tempting to
link Alma and Thoth, the Egyptian god . . . whom Simic
loves to quote: "as above, so below."

It is after meeting Alma that the initiate reveals he once
glimpsed Truth in a sort of Studs Lonigan milieu:

Once in a hotel room in Chicago
I caught sight of a man in a shaving mirror
Who had my naked shoulders and face,
But whose eyes terrified me!

Two hard staring, all-knowing eyes!

Something about the combination of "Alma, the night, the cold, and the endless walking" operates on the initiate in a kind of alchemy, bringing about a change in his attitude toward himself and his destiny. He now finds comfort in signification: "There was the East River; there was the Hudson. / Their waters shone like oil in sanctuary lamps." Naming is a solace against the abstraction of geography, but there is also an underlying sense that signifiers are illusory; their power is limited: "something supreme was occurring / For which there will never be any words."

Despite the ultimate sense of the ineffable, there is a definite acceptance now of whatever or whoever he is, and what his purpose has been all along:

> In that whole city you could hear a pin drop.
> Believe me,
> I thought I heard a pin drop and I went looking for it.

This is the kind of idiomatic expression Simic has developed before—cliches like "it goes without saying," or "chicken with its head cut off" become profundities in his hands. In this instance, I was reminded of Breton:

> Life, undesirable life, goes on ravishingly. Each one goes at it with the idea of his own freedom that he has managed to frame for himself, and God knows that generally this idea is a timid one. But it is not the man of today who would consent to search in the stars for the head of the pin, the famous pin he can't get out of the game anyhow. He has patiently accepted his lot, poor man, has even been, I do believe, endlessly patient.[2]

The asterisk refers us to the translators' note: "The expression '*tierer l'epingle du jeu*,' literally 'to get the pin out of the game,' figuratively means 'to get out of something without a loss'" (198). It seems to me that this is what We're all trying to do—get out of something without a loss. For the initiate, whoever you decide he ultimately happens to be, the idea may simply be that he must somehow get out with as much of his soul intact as possible. And isn't this the poet's dilemma? Earlier in the same passage, Breton talks about the unhappiness of those who "have done what in all simplicity they believed they had to do . . . they have not taken *the orders of the marvelous*" (197).

In this respect, Charles Simic must be a happy man; he religiously follows "the orders of the marvelous" as he is called to explore—with sly wit and all the melancholy patience of an end-of-the-millennium, urban Job—a compelling, secret world.

Notes

1. Charles Simic. *The Uncertain Certainty, Interviews, Essays, and Notes on Poetry* (Ann Arbor: Univ. of Michigan Press, 1985), p. 84.

2. Andre Breton, "A Letter to the Seers," *Manifestoes of Surrealism*, trans. Richard Seaver and Helen R.

Lane, Ann Arbor: Univ. of Michigan Press, 1989, p. 195, hereafter cited in the text.

Steven Cramer (review date January 1992)

SOURCE: A review of *Selected Poems 1963-1983* and *The Book of Gods and Devils*, in *Poetry*, Vol. CLIX, No. 4, January, 1992, pp. 227-34.

[*In the following review, Cramer examines elements of Simic's poetry throughout his career that effectively distinguish him from other poets of his generation.*]

Though often associated with the "new surrealists" of the 1970s—American poets influenced by "deep imagist" elders like Bly, Wright, Merwin, Kinnell et al.—Charles Simic deserves to be distinguished from this group on at least two counts. First, as a native of Yugoslavia, his attachment to riddles, proverbs, magic formulas, and nursery rhymes has a bona fide regional pedigree, above and beyond the hours he logged studying folklore in the New York Public Library. More important, his memories of growing up in war-torn Belgrade provide an experiential groundwork for the primeval violences in his work. From the earliest poems in his *Selected Poems 1963-1983* to 1990's *The Book of Gods and Devils*, Simic has rarely settled for the Jungian ahistoricity typical of American period surrealism. Instead, Simic's images—pre-industrial and "archetypal" at first, distinctly urban and modern later on—bear the scars of historical witness.

Rereading *Dismantling the Silence* (1971), I'm struck less by its folkloric evocations of "the old country" than by its peripheral hints of political horror. The apron hanging in **"Butcher Shop"** is "smeared into a map / Of the great continents of blood." In **"Marching,"** dressing at dawn invites an image of "boots that have trodden men's faces," while the subsequent morning walk brings "the sound of men marching" and a warning that occupied nationals instinctively heed: "so close your doors and windows and do not look." In the insomniac **"Chorus for One Voice,"** Simic's sleep of reason produces a motley army of night-fears: "A sound of wings doesn't mean there's a bird. / If you've eaten today, no reason to think you'll eat tomorrow. / People can also be processed into soap." The eye of Simic's early poems may be directed inward, but out of its corner we often see men about to be hanged.

Even his famous object poems, though never explicit about Simic's biography, employ complex tonal ironies that belie surrealist anonymity. *Dismantling*'s anthology piece, **"Stone,"** rewards rereading not only as a period anthem to interiority but also as an oblique self-portrait of beleaguered neutrality, caught between the warring claims of pacifism and militance: "Go inside a stone / That would be my way. / Let somebody else become a dove / Or gnash with a tiger's tooth." **"Stone"** also manifests Simic's empirical manner of association, his imagistic turns propelled by skewed extensions of logic: "I have seen sparks fly out / When two stones are rubbed, / So perhaps it is not dark inside after all. . . ."

Much of ***Return to a Place Lit by a Glass of Milk*** (1974) recapitulates Simic's atavistic mutations of common objects, ***Dismantling***'s primitivism beginning to ossify into formula. Still, some poems augur a restlessness with image-driven writing by flirting with self-disclosure—"Charles Simic is a sentence. / A sentence has a beginning and an end"—and one perfect miniature, **"The Place,"** stands out as precursor to the rich tapestries of folklore, autobiography, and history to follow:

> They were talking about the war
> The table still uncleared in front of them.
> Across the way, the first window
> Of the evening was already lit.
> He sat, hunched over, quiet,
> The old fear coming over him . . .
> It grew darker. She got up to take the plate—
> Now unpleasantly white—to the kitchen.
> Outside in the fields, in the woods
> A bird spoke in proverbs,
> A Pope went out to meet Attila,
> The ditch was ready for its squad.

This seems to me one of the lasting poetic responses to the Vietnam war, all the more resonant for its seamlessness of contemporary event, ancient conflict, and timeless dread. Imagine it written during the Gulf war; none of "the old fear" loses relevance. And in a stylistic shift that will bear fruit in later collections, **"The Place"** relies more on psychologically potent detail—"the plate now unpleasantly white"—than decontextualized image.

White (1970-1980) is Simic's anomalous book-length work, a last object poem that, perhaps fittingly, plays a theme and variations on immateriality. The voice sounds valedictory—"All that is near, / I no longer give it a name"—and although some sections are vivid with memory and invention, its total effect is of muted exasperation. Losing interest in his totemic miniatures, Simic may have needed this last gasp of primitivism: "And how will you know when you're done chump? / When the half-moons on my fingernails set."

After three volumes of runic imagery, it's startling to encounter **"The Partial Explanation"** from ***Charon's Cosmology*** (1977), its diction and tone—"Seems like a long time / Since the waiter took my order. / Grimy little luncheonette"—imbued with modernity. **"The Lesson"** follows up on this plunge into the present with an equally bracing immersion into autobiography:

> I lingered more and more
> over the beginnings:
> The haircut of a soldier
> who was urinating
> against our fence;
> shadows of trees on the ceiling,
> the day
> my mother and I
> had nothing to eat. . . .

For Simic, however, a documentary approach insufficiently embodies the nightmares of memory in which he "couldn't get past / that prison train / that kept waking me up." The tonal stance must be riskier, more subversive:

> in this long and terrifying
> apprenticeship,
> I burst out laughing.
> Forgive me, all of you!
> At the memory of my uncle
> charging a barricade
> with a homemade bomb,
> I burst out laughing.

Throughout ***Charon's Cosmology*** and ***Classic Ballroom Dances*** (1980) Simic perfects his agile mature style: straight-faced, outrageously comic, sage and slangy, prankish, always economical. Some poems, more absurdist than surreal in their abutments of history, myth, and metaphysics, create harrowingly funny collages of nostalgia and dread:

> The little pig goes to market.
> Historical necessity. I like to recite
> While you prefer to write on the blackboard.
> Leap frog and marbles.
>
> Their heads are big and their noses are short.
> Lovely afternoon. The firing squad. . . .
>
>   NURSERY RHYME

Others, like **"The Terms,"** approach the mysteries of the moment directly—"A child crying in the night / Across the street / In one of many dark windows. / That, too, to get used to, / Make part of your life"—and still others lend palpable textures to the austerities of abstract thinking. Unlike Simic's earlier totems to concepts, however, poems like **"Euclid Avenue"** pay homage to their personal sources: "The poor son of poor parents / who aspires to please / at such a late hour."

Of the many fine poems in these collections—my very short list includes **"The Variant," "Travelling Slaughterhouse," "Primer," "Prodigy,"** and **"Begotten of the Spleen"**—**"The Prisoner,"** from ***Charon's Cosmology***, is Simic at his most beguiling:

> He is thinking of us.
> These leaves, their lazy rustle
> That made us sleepy after lunch
> So we had to lie down.
>
> He considers my hand on her breast,
> Her closed eyelids, her moist lips
> Against my forehead, and the shadows of trees
> Hovering on the ceiling.
>
> It's been so long. He has trouble
> Deciding what else is there.
> And all along the suspicion
> That we do not exist.

A rendition of the artist's imprisoning self-consciousness, a depiction of erotic love circumscribed by a tyrannical overseer, **"The Prisoner"** shows how the mature Simic entertains paradox and mystery in sharply etched visualizations. We "see" what happens, but does it happen outdoors or indoors? How many characters are involved? Does "thinking" imply an event imagined (i.e., "conjuring") or recalled (i.e., "remembering")? These are a few of the exquisitely unanswerable questions **"The Prisoner"** provokes.

From *Classic Ballroom Dances*, the arrestingly titled **"Baby Pictures of Famous Dictators"** qualifies as one of Simic's great poems. Loosely based on the infamous photograph of Hitler as an infant, it's a poem of grim foreknowledge, first in an aerial view of late-nineteenth-century complacency, then in close up:

> . . . there are always a couple of infants
> Posing for the camera in their sailors' suits,
> Out there in the garden overgrown with shrubs.
> Lovable little mugs smiling faintly toward
> The new century. Innocent. Why not?

Here Simic punctures the poem's billing and cooing with an ingenious triple play on words—"mugs" connoting the babies' faces, the infant thugs themselves, and the "mug shots" these photos will become in retrospect. Had the poem ended here, it might be accused of easy hindsight irony, but Simic obliges the speaker to own up to his outrage at destiny:

> One assumes that they all stayed up late squinting at the stars,
> And were carried off to bed by their mothers and big sisters,
> While the dogs remained behind:
> Pedigreed bitches pregnant with bloodhounds.

The shock of the last line derives in part from its aptness as a displaced image for tyranny in embryonic form. It also unnerves us tonally with harsh consonance and aggressive diction. Yet even as we recoil from its implications—does Hitler's *mother* deserve the appellation "bitch"?—we share the speaker's helpless rage at the dandling of future tyrants.

The poems from *Weather Forecast for Utopia & Vicinity* and *Austerities* (both published in 1982) offer no less capacity for surprise. Both feature poems addressed to Simic's adoptive country, *Weather Forecast* in particular taking stock of the economic victims of America's broken utopian promise: the "rain- / Blurred weedchoked outskirts / Of a dying milltown" in **"A Fall Day"**; the weighted shoulders of Baptist congregationalists in **"Gravity"**; the dirt-poor **"Old Couple,"** who are "waiting to be murdered, / Or evicted." Simic's own impoverished background certifies him as an unsentimental voice of the struggle for survival. As one recurrent detail—the suitcase, often hastily packed—makes plain, Simic recognizes the diaspora in all its incarnations.

Simic published *Unending Blues* in 1986 and the Pulitzer Prize-winning book of prose poems, *The World doesn't*

End, in 1989. These indispensable collections initiated Simic's forays into cagey narrative, experiments he consolidates in *The Book of Gods and Devils*, perhaps his most memory-charged volume so far. **"St. Thomas Aquinas,"** a skewed autobiography of his seedtime in New York City, paints a Boschian portrait of the city as grotesque carnival. Here are two of its ten stanzas, each a discrete chapter in Simic's cockeyed *Bildungsroman*:

> I was already in New York looking for work.
> It was raining as in the days of Noah.
> I stood in many doorways of that great city.
> Once I asked a man in a tuxedo for a cigarette.
> He gave me a frightened look and stepped out into the rain.
>
> Since "man naturally desires happiness,"
> According to St. Thomas Aquinas,
> Who gave irrefutable proof of God's existence and purpose,
> I loaded trucks in the Garment Center.
> Me and a black man stole a woman's red dress.
> It was of silk; it shimmered.

The speaker's naïveté beautifully inheres in the end-stopped lines, the deliberate solecism, and simple declarative sentences, their lack of subordination capturing his childlike, noncausal mode of thinking. When causality does enter the grammar of thought, its logic is disarmingly off-kilter. Later, a reference to "the travels of Melville" suggests that Simic intends this poem, at least in part, as an homage to that master of tall tales and fish stories. In fact, the spirit of Melville's Bartleby presides over a number of the many city poems in *The Book of Gods and Devils*. In **"Factory,"** he makes an invisible cameo in "the chair in the far corner / Where someone once sat facing the brick wall." In **"St. Thomas Aquinas,"** however, this nineteenth-century prophet of urban nihilism serves as Simic's patron saint and doppelganger: "Everyone I met / Wore a part of my destiny like a carnival mask. / 'I'm Bartleby the Scrivener,' I told the Italian waiter. / 'Me, too,' he replied."

In addition to longer poems like **"St. Thomas Aquinas"**—**"Shelley"** and **"The Initiate"** are equally fine—*The Book of Gods and Devils* offers ample views through Simic's miniaturist eye for common oddity. The shorter poems here that touch me most deeply display a new intimacy and emotional directness. **"Heights of Folly"** and **"Cabbage,"** two quirky love poems to his wife, should be read with a pair of equally affecting lyrics in *Unending Blues*. **"The North"** is a sober, even stately, meditation on exile. My favorite among the book's brief lyrics, **"The World,"** hushes all temptation toward analysis. Read it for nourishment:

> As if I were a big old shade tree
> On a side street with a small café.
> Neon beer sign with the word "cold" shining in it.
> Summer dusk.
>
> The solitary customer, who looks like my father,
> Is bent over a book with small print

Oblivious of the young waiter
Who is about to serve him a cup of black coffee.

I have an incalculable number of leaves
Not one of which is moving.
it's because we are enchanted, I think.
We don't have a care in the world.

Rereading Charles Simic's work in bulk reveals a major artist constantly redefining an unmistakable style. You can always identify a Simic poem, even as you can never tell what it will do next with its "incalculable number of leaves." Unlike many in his generation, Simic hasn't run aground on self-imitation. While never losing faith in the expressive possibilities of the image, he consistently widens the contexts for his gnomic figures. I look forward to a more concentrated study of Simic's key motifs—his suitcases, toys, loaves of bread, blackboards, blind people, lampposts, balls, glasses, and geometrical shapes, just to name a few. This fabric of elemental forms suggests the scope of his imaginative project: nothing less than the creation of an individual folklore, one that embraces the privacy of dream without evading the public atrocities of civilization. Future readers will return to Simic's mythic well for enchantment and instruction.

Ileana A. Orlich (essay date Spring 1992)

SOURCE: "The Poet on a Roll: Charles Simic's 'The Tomb of Stéphane Mallarmé,'" in *Centennial Review,* Vol. XXXVI, No. 2, Spring 1992, pp. 413-28.

[*In the following essay, Orlich analyzes Simic's connection to the Surrealists, particularly their respective ideas about chance in their writings.*]

The poet of the future will overcome the depressing idea of an irreparable divorce of action and dream. He will hold the magnificent fruit of the tree whose roots intertwine, and he will be able to persuade all who taste it that there is nothing bitter about it. Carried by the wave of his time, he will assume for the first time without distress the task of reception and transmission of signals pressing towards him from the depths of the ages. He will maintain at all cost the common presence of the two terms of human rapport, by whose destruction the most precious conquest would become instantaneously worthless: the objective awareness of realities, and their internal development in what, by virtue of a sentiment partly individual, partly universal, is magical until proved otherwise. This rapport can pass for magical in the sense that it consists of an unconscious, immediate action of the internal upon the external. . . .

—Andre Breton, "Les vases communicants" in "What is Surrealism?"

. . . There are poems I write where the strategy is directly an offshoot of some traditional mode. There's also no doubt that the manner in which my psyche makes the material available to me is predicated by everything I have absorbed about the tradition of poetry. The act of writing, however, is something else. There I have to forget all that in order to undertake the impos-

sible task of giving these words life. Since all words have a history and the act of composition is presumably ahistorical, the resulting tension can only be overcome if one has faith in the uniqueness of the undertaking.

—Charles Simic, *50 Contemporary Poets: The Creative Process*

With **Classic Ballroom Dances** (1980), Charles Simic consolidated his reputation as a major contemporary American poet, whose popularity has steadily increased since the publication of such earlier volumes as **Dismantling the Silence** (1971), **Return to a Place Lit by a Glass of Milk** (1974), **Charon's Cosmology** (1977) and **White** (1970-80). **Classic Ballroom Dances** was selected as a winner of the Poetry Society of America di Castagnola Award and was reviewed in *The New York Times* and *The Yale Review,* where Helen Vendler included Simic in a "Who's Who" gallery of poets worth watching. Simic's recent books include **Unending Blues** (1986), **The World doesn't End** (1989), and **The Book of Gods and Devils** (1990). In 1990 Simic received the Pulitzer Prize for poetry. In more senses than the casual reader of poetry could possibly imagine, Simic's achievements from 1980 to 1990 constitute his progress toward artistic fulfillment—the poet on a roll, conscious of taking extraordinary chances, "spending for vast returns," as Whitman phrased it.

Simic's early poetry was published in *Kayak,* George Hitchcock's small but interesting magazine, whose surrealist experimentations appealed to many poets who, like Simic, were coming of age during and after World War II. Simic found surrealism particularly attractive because it gave him a way of rebelling against the allusive, highly academic, paradoxical poetics of modernism. Surrealism taught him how to rearrange poetic language on a simple, non-connotative basis, in simply-stated metaphors rather than in elaborate conceits, and how to rely on accessible declaratives rather than the detached, ironic use of personae which marked the work of Pound and Eliot. Simic's acknowledgment of the surrealist tendencies in his work is expressed early in 1972 in "Where the Levels Meet: An Interview with Charles Simic."[1]

My work always had surrealist tendencies. . . . I don't know about my being original. Much of that ["Your poetry is so original, so unique"] comes the way of surrealism. . . . So, in telling about originality, most of that has its roots right there. At the same time I feel to be in that tradition. . . . I don't think of myself as a surrealist. I don't think of myself as anything. But I would say my greatest debt is to surrealism. (53)

Recognized as "a new American surrealist,"[2] Simic turned to Stéphane Mallarmé—one of the Surrealists' most revered precursors—as both a poetic force and an influence he must confront in **"The Tomb of Stéphane Mallarmé,"** one of the poems in *Classic Ballroom Dances.* In spite of the fine review David Young gave the volume in *Field* (Spring 1981), he referred only too briefly to **"The Tomb of Stéphane Mallarmé,"** a poem "only intermittently successful . . . too often so abstract and attenuated that it seems to drift away like smoke." It is my intention to dispel such a notion and to elucidate **"The Tomb of Stéphane Mallarmé"** by discussing the poem in terms of a mobile, fluid relationship to Mallarmé's hermetic last poem, "Un Coup de dés" and the last two sections of the unfinished "Igitur," or "Folie d'Elbehnon," two works that use the same Mallarméan elements and to an extent complement each other.[3] Also necessary in deciphering **"The Tomb of Stéphane Mallarmé"** are André Breton's prose poems entitled "Constellations" (whose structural ellipses and central "constellation" image bear a direct connection to Mallarmé's "Un Coup de dés"), his celebrated work *Nadja*, and some of the tenets of surrealist ideology he so assiduously formulated. Ironically, both Mallarmé's "Un Coup de dés" and "Igitur" and Breton's "Constellations" are culminating poetic works for each of these poets. After having served as spokesman and pathblazer to the symbolists, Mallarmé had proceeded on his own course, outdistancing those tenets, while Breton evolved, developed, and went beyond the stipulations of the First Manifesto of Surrealism, beyond automatic writing to the exploration of the poet as essential observer of energies of language.[4] Acknowledging origins and confronting a precursor, **"The Tomb of Stéphane Mallarmé"** is a pivotal work for Simic, since it recognizes the issue of his surrealism and marks the trajectory to his postmodern poetic craft.

I do not wish to impose Mallarméan models or Breton's surrealist ideology on Simic's poem, but rather to show how their poetic metaphors are resurrected by Simic and to point out the convergence as well as the differences among the three poets' ideas. It is also my purpose to explore Simic's recuperation of Mallarmé as an important influence on Breton, the founder, chief theorist, and charismatic leader of surrealist ideology, and to show the impact surrealism, with its systematic exploration of language, the subconscious mind, and the operations of chance, has had through Mallarmé via Breton on Simic's poetry.

From the start, Simic's poem calls attention not only to the name of Stéphane Mallarmé, but also to the tomb-style poems such as "The Tomb of Edgar Allan Poe" and "The Tomb of Charles Baudelaire," that are among Mallarmé's greatest texts. They are, in their creator's own words, "sumptuous allegories of the void"[5] which emphasize the solitude in which artists must live and create, the submerged reefs upon which they may founder, the guiding stars of their ideals, and the emptiness of their voyages in life. Engaged in a search to attain the absolute, artists become exemplary voyagers, charting a course for mankind and especially for other artists. Simic's title then suggests the author's recognition of the French poet, his intent to emulate Mallarmé, and his knowledge that a similar emulation had taken place earlier, in 1959, when Breton borrowed the title of his last poetic work, "Constellations" from "Un Coup de dés." In Mallarmé's poem, "constellations" is a central word denoting the void of a

poet's sad journey in a cosmos whose rules are outside of his dominion. Breton's "Constellations" is a cosmic venture in which the poet, through his manipulation of language, extends his own sensation in an attempt to decipher the eternal mysteries of the universe. What is important here is the shift in thinking from Mallarmé to Breton in spite of the similar appearance of their works—the cryptographic writing and the common poetic imagery. For that shift and its distinctions held profound implications for Simic's subsequent work.

The opening line of **"The Tomb of Stéphane Mallarmé,"** "Beginning to know" introduces one of the central ideas of Simic's poetry: the poet's need to learn how to begin again, his search to recover that spontaneous voice which he, like Mallarmé and like the Surrealists, believes reenacts "the adventure of the spirit,"[6] as it sails on into the unknown, the subconscious which represents, according to Breton, a possible point of contact with a primordial level of awareness in which will and reason exercise no influence. It is in this region that both sense perceptions and thoughts take form. It is here, in a poetic context, that the creative impulse originates. As the poem, "the die," as Simic calls it, takes over the poet's voice,[7]

> Beginning to know
> how the die
> navigates

(61)

a twist is played on the Mallarméan "tombeau"-style poems: Simic's "tombeau" is not "a sumptuous allegory of the void," but rather a dramatic reenactment, a reassertion of the poetic process, more like Mallarmé's "dice-throw," or Breton's "Constellations."

Simic's "die" in **"The Tomb of Stéphane Mallarmé"** recalls the Mallarméan metaphor of "the dice-throw" to suggest that every time a poem is written the poet is engaged in a throw of the dice, since "toute pensée émet un coup de dés [Every thought emits a dice-throw]." When casting a die, or writing a poem, the poet is involved in a spiritual battle against the mystery of the unknown, in a fashion that recalls the dice player and his game of chance—a sort of chance that, according to Breton in "Surrealist Situations of the Object," "shows man, in a way that is still very mysterious, a necessity that escapes him, even though he experiences it as a vital necessity." The poet thus becomes completely fused with his poem and is expressed completely through it, just as Mallarmé's "dice-throw," or Simic's die

> held tight
> between the thumb
> and the forefinger
> to be hexed
> and prayed over

(61)

is always identifiable with the player experiencing an enjoyment of such intensity and depth that it makes the moment of the throw (or the writing of the poem) eternal, in quality if not in duration. For Simic, then, as well as for Mallarmé, the dice-throw is a metaphor of the poetic process, a concrete formulation of an abstract process which "Un Coup de dés" and **"The Tomb of Stéphane Mallarmé"** try to capture and express, of "the precise instant when a thing outward and objective"—such as the throw of the dice—"transforms itself, or darts into the inward, the subjective"[8] that is the poem.

Since both "Un Coup de dés" and **"The Tomb of Stéphane Mallarmé"** speak preeminently of the sum of poetic energy concentrated on "the throw of the dice," the writing of the poem becomes an exercise always subject to chance, whose operations fascinated Mallarmé and the Surrealists. Consequently, Mallarmé's throw of the dice, i.e. the poet's will, meanders and confronts the absurdities of chance, i.e. the irrational, disorderly will of the universe paralleling Simic's "blindsman's die," which is also an agent of the accidental prone to startling encounters,

> making its fateful decisions
> endlessly changing directions
> and mind
> in a state of blessed uncertainty

(62)

In **"Negative Capability and Its Children,"** Simic equates "uncertainty" with "chance" and goes on to explain that a poet's "project" is to use "Chance to break the spell of our habitual literary expectations and to approach the conditions of what has been called 'free imagination'" (400). For Simic, as for Breton, "Chance remains the great veil to be lifted . . . the form of the manifestation of external necessity as it makes its way into the human unconscious."[9]

Furthermore, Simic defines chance as "a submission to a message from the unconscious, a matter of obedience to inwardness" (402). It is the chance Breton in "Surrealist Situations of the Object" terms, "le hasard objectif," the objective chance encompassing the seemingly inexplicable connections that characterize certain events in everyday life:

> . . . an almost forbidden world of sudden parallels, petrifying coincidences, and reflexes peculiar to each individual, of harmonies struck as though on the piano, flashes of light that would make you see, really *see*, if only they were not so much quicker than all the rest. I am concerned with facts of quite unverifiable intrinsic value . . . facts which may belong to the order of pure observation, but which on each occasion present all the appearances of a signal, without our being able to say precisely which signal, and of what; facts which when I am alone permit me to enjoy unlikely complicities, which convince me of my error in occasionally presuming I stand at the helm alone.[10]

In translation, then, Simic's poem is "the blindsman's die" navigating "in a state of blessed uncertainty" like the Mallarméan throw of dice, which is to abandon itself entirely to chance, to submit to hazard completely and enter without reserve into its intimacy, trusting along with the surrealists in the belief that the events of the outer world were somehow mysteriously aligned with the needs and desires of the unconscious.

Every creative act is a gamble for high stakes. The dice throw proved disastrous for Mallarmé, as his will and the whims of objective chance were pitted in uneven battle culminating in the poet's terrifying awareness of his losing score. The movement of "Un Coup de dés" suggests a rich, slow brooding over the inevitable effort of writing, of casting the die. Poetic inspiration is brought by the "lucid and lordly aigrette"[11]—possibly Mallarmé's equivalent to Poe's raven—with its long, showy plumes shining forth the purity, the quintessential quality of the poetic process. But "the siren twist" of Mallarmé's poetry connotes despair and sterility.

By contrast, Breton sets out to structure the forces of chance in poetic ellipses which, unlike Mallarmé's, do not fall adrift like alien elements but rather successfully combine dexterity and chance ("*adresse et hasard*") in a glorious trajectory. Unlike Mallarmé's egret, the *aigrette* of "Constellations" carries an acorn, which suggests images of love and fertility and all the decomposition and re-composition that the fertilizing process involves in nature. It is almost as if Breton, who in the celebrated early essay "Les Mots sans rides" wrote that "Les mots font l'amour" is making love with words, and words are making love with him: he penetrates language and through language establishes a deep and intimate relationship with the physical world. Far from being melancholic or brooding, poetry becomes a studied and learned activity in which the poet, as molder of language, seizes on the associations of his mind, tests them against the universe, cultivates them by orchestrating harmony around him. The dominant images of the lines relate to "weaving" as the poet moves back and forth in a virtual manual linking of threads which lead toward the secrets of life itself.

A similarly winning course is that followed by Simic's "lucid" and "white" die—an echo of Mallarmé's "lucid" and "white" aigrette, which again closely follows both Mallarmé and Breton. Like Breton's "weaving," Simic's "navigating" involves the poet's movements back and forth as he ventures toward deciphering the underlying harmony which unites external with internal, matter with mind, a system of surrealist correspondences between "the constellations," between the outer world and the human mind. In the parlance of the casino, Simic is the poet "on a roll," as his dice throw, his poetic craft, translates into an exercise of his imagination decoding the apparent incoherence of the natural world. As for Mallarmé in the "Preface" to "Un Coup de dés," poetry is for Simic "the unique source" (106).

For Mallarmé the roll of the dice, the poem, would figure like the shipwreck in the lines: "Un coup de dés jamais n' abolira le hasard quand bien meme lancé dans les circonstances éternelles du fond d'un naufrage [A dice-throw

. . . even when cast in eternal circumstances from the depth of a shipwreck]." For Simic the die would

> navigate
> making its fateful decisions
> in eternal circumstances . . .
> at the heart of the shipwreck

> (61)

The "circonstances éternelles" to which the two poets refer would not be perpetual motion, but the freezing of time for the Parmenidean eternal moment that rebukes the Heraclitean flux. (Simic alludes to "the childhood of Parmenides" in **"The Tomb of Stéphane Mallarmé."**)

With the making of the poem the only enduring value, the poet's only significant ground is the "Abyss" of "dice-throw," the sea of the subconscious, a "whirlpool of hilarity and horror" (117) "from the depth of a shipwreck," or Simic's "heart of the shipwreck." But shipwreck (naufrage) is always the risk of navigation, as Mallarmé warns in "Brise marine":

> Et peut-etre, les mats, invitant les orages
> Sont-ils de ceux qu'un vent penche sur les naufrages
> Perdus, sans mats, sans mats, ni fertile ilots.

> [And perhaps the masts, inviting tempests,
> Are of those which a wind bends over shipwrecks
> Lost, without masts, without masts or fertile isles.]

> (17)

If carried away by the breeze, one tries to go beyond one's limits, one's boundaries, the "borne a l'infini [limit of infinity]" of the "dice-throw." One risks "the memorable crisis" (124), the passage to death, the dream defeated, nothingness. The Master of the "dice-throw," the artist of sovereign mastery, does hold the successful throw of dice in his hand, "the unique Number beyond old time cypherings which does not want to be another" (112), but he fails to throw it outside the world of pure intellect and abstract metaphors and thus renounces a lifetime of illusion that he is to write the Grand Oeuvre. Rejecting the challenge of life, he leaves all attempts to cast the dice to chance and illustrates the meaning of the title. He then dies outside this power, "cadaver pulled away by the arm from the secret he holds" (112), much like Mallarmé himself who allowed chance, or "total submission to a message from the unconscious" in Simic's definition,[12] and his desire for mastery over ideas and purity of the language to drown him in a constellation of the abstract. It is the "Constellation" of "dice-throw" which engulfs the Master or Mallarmé, who wrote the word "Nothing" on the first page of his complete works.[13] "Nothing will have taken place but the place [Rien n' aura en eu lieu que le lieu]" (125). And to substantiate the failed imaginative experience of this chance that is not taken, Mallarmé's dice progress idly on a downward flight:

> before hand fallen back from incapacity to trim the
> flight

> and covering what foams
> cutting back what soars
> most inwardly resumes

> (111)

It is a defeated motion, aiming at misery and self-abandon, paralleled early in **"The Tomb of Stéphane Mallarmé"** by Simic's die, engaged on an aimless course taken

> only to fall
> head over heels
> to be set adrift
> in the middle of
> nowhere

> (61)

and suggesting the inertia of loss in its most devastated form.

But Simic seems to be aware of Mallarmé's "naufrage," of the pitfalls of not loosening the gates of the unconscious so that pure poetry could issue forth, of offering no other certainty but the concentration of chance and its glorification. His die, Simic's will as a poet, would not be lost in the Mallarméan constellation of the abstract; rather, the die would be cast in the realm of the concrete and palpable and brushed against all odds. It would become "the death-defying somersault beating the supreme odds" and allow itself to be "worn clean / by endless conjectures," as the poet transcends the need to decipher old mysteries and makes his die "free of / the divinatory urge," of the Mallarméan "Number," "even if it existed" (62). It is interesting to note that when Mallarmé died pages of mathematical formulae were found on his desk. Breton also refers to mathematics in "Constellations," since numbers are the tools of chance.

Cast upon the world, the die, the poem, is a receptacle of "the poet's inwardness"[14](Simic's other definition of chance) filled with a wide range of choices from a long forgotten past. Clearly, for Simic the making of a poem is both a meditation on the literary influence of his predecessors, and a necessary "rite de passage" since it enables the poet to achieve a new stage of poetic maturity after assimilating tradition. The same idea is expressed by Mallarmé who parallels the stages of a child's transformation to an adult with the incipient poetic self's yielding to ancestral influences for renewed identities on its way to self fulfillment. "Un Coup de dés" speaks of

> his [the Master's] puerile shade
> caressed and polished and rendered and washed
> supplied by the wave and withdrawn
> from the hard bones lost among the timbers

> (114)

while **"The Tomb of Stéphane Mallarmé"** mentions the poet casting his die "among the ghostly salt-cellar bones" (62). In his turn, Breton always acknowledged Mallarmé's influence. The language of "Constellations" is the visionary language to which Mallarmé had accustomed him; the rebus images of Breton's last work, although modeled after the cabala and latter day alchemists, owe much to the graphic combinations of linear and vertical annotations of "Un Coup de dés"; finally, like Mallarmé's "Un Coup de dés," Breton's "Constellations" contains rather than conveys meaning.

But for Simic the experience of tradition adds a new dimension: the rolling of the die is an indication of the poet's flight over the house of the dead, the tomb of Stéphane Mallarmé, where lies his predecessor—an attempt on Simic's part to express his debt to Mallarmé and to supersede Mallarmé and the tradition. Simic crosses the threshold and "the die worn clean" (by brushing not only against the real world, but also against Mallarméan verse) becomes "my die,"

> white
> as a milk tooth
> the perfect die
> rolling
>
> (61)

The old becomes the new poetic self that Simic has waited for, like a new tooth. As in the long poem **"White,"** the milk tooth in **"The Tomb of Stéphane Mallarmé"** is sinister (it grins like a skull, an image summoned by the tomb in the title), suggesting the self which has died, but it is also reminiscent of a child's passage into adulthood in the reference to teething.[15]

The passage from the old self to the new suggested by images of death (the tomb, to be prayed over, to fall) and rebirth (to be set adrift, navigate, rolling) sums up the influence of Mallarmé's voice on Simic's own, but is simultaneously Simic's way of asserting his own renewed identity. For **"The Tomb of Stéphane Mallarmé"** is a poem about writing poetry, about the relationship of the poet to his poem and to tradition. And "the poet," as Simic once remarked,

> is capable of being in uncertainties. [He] is literally in the midst. The poem, too, is in the midst, a kind of magnet for complex literary forces, as well as of maintaining oneself in the face of that multiplicity.[16]

Just as the metaphysical poets made a poetic conceit of "die" in its sexual connotation, its denotation of mortality, and its further connotation of mystical union, Simic might well be fashioning a new conceit on the morphology of the old. The new meaning stresses the old emphasis on chance in the creation of art and in the duration of life; each is a gamble for high stakes. It seems an experience unique to the individual artist, and yet it echoes the experience and expression of precursors. Simic is looking for a new voice to inhabit him, yet as he yearns for it, he realizes how thoroughly his old voice echoes that of Mallarmé[17] (hence the poem's title, the borrowed metaphors of the die and the tomb). However, the new poetic self announced by "the milk tooth" in **"The Tomb of Stéphane Mallarmé"** points out the differences between the two

poets' views and their individual approaches to writing, and marks Simic's determination to treat poetry in the manner prescribed by Breton and the surrealists, i.e. as a liberative experience, released from all critical and academic pressures and habits.

Mallarmé's poet or "Master" in "Un Coup de dés" searches only for himself in the night and, like Igitur, displays self-imposed silence (perhaps to avoid misrepresenting his newly found surreality) and wants to die in the heart of his thoughts. Unlike the "Master" of "Un Coup de dés," Igitur, the poet whose "breath contained chance," rolls his dice in a futile, fruitless attempt for him, or the poetic sensibility he represents and, as Paul Claudel remarks, "awaits for nothing else from the world of science and from art" because he feels, along with Mallarmé, "that the contingent will never be able to touch the absolute or to produce anything other than a combination precarious and as such, useless."[18]

In the fourth section of "Igitur," "The Dice Throw in the Tomb,"

> Igitur simply shakes the dice—a motion before going to rejoin the ashes, the atoms of his ancestors: the moment, which is in him, is absolved. It is understood what its ambiguity means. He closes the books—snuffs out the candle—with his breath which contained chance: and, folding his arms, lies down on the ashes of his ancestors. (100)

There, in the silent night in the tomb where the ashes are and where nothing can be grasped, Igitur attains not the certainty of death, but the eternal torments of Dying. The relevant passage in the text appears with its own marginal commentary:

> *Or the dice chance—*
> *absorbed*
>
> Upon the ashes of stars, the undivided ones of the family, lay the poor character, after having drunk the last drop of nothingness lacking to the sea
>
> (101)

Igitur, whose "dice [are] absorbed by chance," is unable to communicate with the ashes of his ancestors, much like the "Master" of "Un Coup de dés," for whom there is no connecting with the past and who chooses

> to not open the hand
> clenched
> beyond the useless head
> legacy among vanishment
>
> (114)

The dice absorbed by chance, i.e. the poet allowing the unconscious to take over, the world of ashes, dimness, and the despairing darkness, point to the great dangers inherent in Mallarmé's approach to poetry, his excessive dwelling on the "subjects of pure and complex imagination or intellect."[19] As the poetic sensibility loses its élan, Mallarmé turns into an anguished dilettante, trapped in what Simic calls "Death's great amateur / night," while his work, "left unfinished and without inspiration having entered into it"[20] (302), becomes "Cerberus' new toy" (62), subservient to shadows and "chance absorbed."

Perhaps as a response and reaction to Mallarmé's "Un Coup de dés" and "Igitur," which describe only the "state" of the poet's mind as a sort of half revelation of "truths of psychological order"[21] never fully brought up to the light of consciousness, Breton's *Nadja*, which begins with the interrogation "Who am I? [Qui suis-je?]," is an auto-psychoanalysis of the poet's sensibility. Breton becomes two "I"'s: the poetic sensibility is identified with Nadja (from the first syllable of the Russian word that means "hope") and rises to the challenges of ordinary reality, with the rational mind becoming the analyst of the quotidian and its relation to the psyche.

Nadja, whose inability to distinguish between reality and illusion is suggested by the presence of the nonexistent feather on her hat, "cares little but marvelously for life": little in the sense of life's social meaning and duration, marvelously in the intensified sense of the immediacy of experience. It is the same immediacy that surrealist poetry was trying to capture and which draws its essence from Nadja's belief that "all the beyond is in life." Freed from the "cage raisonable," able to break the barrier separating sanity from insanity, and to cross the threshold between the rational and the irrational, Nadja is "une étoile au cœur même du fini" (206), the continuum between the exterior world and the objectification of the subjective Mallarmé had been seeking in "Igitur" or "Folie d'Elbehnon."

For Breton the unconscious was not an adventure in the realm of the unknown, a descent to the *néant* resulting in "déchet" (or nothing, the epitaph Mallarmé added to "Igitur"); rather the unconscious represented for Breton a possible point of contact with a primordial level of awareness where the creative impulse originates. It is in this context that Simic's **"The Tomb of Stéphane Mallarmé"** may be better understood, since the poem is ultimately Simic's attempt to show that the poet, while exploring the dark womb of the unconscious, must rise from the depth of the psychic plunge and break the shell of the solitary spirit. Since "poetry is a concrete living force yearning to humanize the abstract,"[22] the poem, like the poetic sensibility Breton created in Nadja, is at the threshold between the two worlds; "the vague figure in the doorway"[23] is the means to transform the eternal into the temporal and the infinite into the contingent.

In **"The Tomb of Stéphane Mallarmé,"** Simic's ideal poem is

> the perfect die
> rolling
> picking up speed
> how delightful

> this new contingency
> occupancy
> both inside and outside
> the unthinkable

> (62)

The poet's job is that of "gobbling the world"[24] as "the die," the poem, is "cast / on the great improbable table" (62) of life where "the ghostly salt-cellar bones" of the ancestors, of tradition, unlike Igitur's "undivided ashes of the family" in the tomb, mingle with the "breadcrumbs," juxtaposing the sacred and the profane. Simic makes the poet's mission quite clear when he states: "What I see is the paradox. What shall I call it? The sacred and the profane? I like the point where the two levels meet."[25] It is from that point, the threshold between the two realms, that Simic's die is cast.

"The great improbable table" draws attention to Simic's preoccupation with the world of objects which Mallarmé had hoped, as he confesses in a letter to a friend, to destroy by sealing them in hermetic language: "There is no reality left; it has evaporated into language."[26] Recognizing Mallarmé's poetic "naufrage" in annihilating the real world, and in treating "not the object, but the effect which it produces,"[27] Simic, like Breton and the Surrealists, focuses on the partnership between dreams and reality suggested in Breton's metaphor of the two urns connected to each other by what might be termed psychic capillary action. Simic lets "experience choose and then send forth"[28] by focusing his poetry on the essential quality of things, on the objects themselves as well as on the effect which they produce; this is a poetic credo Simic learned from Breton (who placed equal value on both realms of experience and envisioned that one day they might be synthesized into a superior concept of existence) and later developed in poems that speak of knives and spoons, of stubs of red pencils, and of grandmothers with chickens. Fulfilling the requirements stipulated in Breton's, "What is Surrealism?" such poems "display an objective awareness of realities" and trigger "their internal development" forming a magical rapport which "consists of an unconscious, immediate action of the internal upon the external."[29]

As Simic evokes the opening line of **"The Tomb of Stéphane Mallarmé,"** "Beginning to know," he embarks upon a flight over the tomb, and over the project of his predecessor. He then reaches from the imaginary dizzying descent into the tomb to explore the ways in which Breton countered Mallarmé's trajectory. As a result, Simic's rejection of Mallarmé's obscure adventures in the search of an absolute where the physical world and the animate objects lose their natural attributes in pure otherness, coincides with the heralding— through the affirmative "oh yeah"—of Breton's and the Surrealists' objective recording of the external world and their endeavor to make poetic language not an expression of one man's expansion of consciousness but a clarification of the channels of the expansion. In contrast to Mallarmé's despair,[30]Simic's down to earth "oh yeah" is indicative of a kind of relaxed playfulness, a humor so characteristic of Simic who once said: "I never separate humor from the serious. I don't want them separate."[31]

Unlike Mallarmé, who turns his back on life to create a poetry of gloom "located in an indefinable realm," which contemplates "neither an object nor an external world, but rather the very being of the observer—a mirage in which the poet recognizes himself, not by where or how he is, but rather by where he is not and the way he is not,"[32] Simic externalizes his experience of writing poetry and of finding adequate outward symbols for his emotions. Like the Breton of *Nadja*, Simic lives "in a glass house,"[33] resisting any attempt at isolating himself and his work inside the Mallarméan "vitre froide et nue qu'il [Mallarmé] n'a jamais pu rompre."[34] And while in the midst of a web of "uncertainties," subject to the powerful influence of two Masters, Simic maintains himself and his poem, **"The Tomb of Stéphane Mallarmé"**—a document-like poem, a kind of manifesto for Simic's art—in the face of the Mallarméan mirage and of Surrealist dislocation. This act, simultaneously casual and creative, offers a key to his work of the past decade, carries us beyond the frontiers of both verbal and visual imagery, and delivers us to where we recognize the interaction of reason and the unconscious—to "where the levels meet."

Notes

1. Charles Simic, "Where the Levels Meet: An Interview with Charles Simic," *The Ohio Review* (1972).

2. Peter Schmidt "'White': Charles Simic's Thumbnail Epic," *Contemporary Literature* 23:4 (1982): 528, 529. Also, James K. Carpenter in "Charles Simic: White," *Ironwood* 7/8 (1976) 79, refers to Simic's "surrealistic tendencies in poetry."

3. In this sense, see Harold Bloom's review of "Igitur" in *Stéphane Mallarmé: Modern Critical Views*, ed. Harold Bloom (Chelsea House Publishers, 1987) 5-15.

4. According to his second wife, Jacqueline, by the time he wrote "L'Air de l'eau" in 1934 Breton had already abandoned "automatic writing."

5. As quoted by F.C. St. Aubyn in *Stéphane Mallarmé: Updated Edition* (Twayne Publishers, 1989) 94.

6. A phrase from André Breton's surrealist manifesto, quoted by Simic in "Where the Levels Meet," *The Ohio Review* (1972) 54.

7. Simic has called his poem a die before. In *White*, a series of lyrics preceding "The Tomb of Stéphane Mallarmé" and dated 1970-1980, poetry writing is conveyed through the image of the poet who "shook his loaded die in a tin cup."

   All quotations from "The Tomb of Stéphane Mallarmé" are from *Classic Ballroom Dances: Poems by Charles Simic* (Brazilier, 1980).

8. Simic's "Negative Capability and Its Children," *Claims for Poetry*, ed. Donald Hall (U of Michigan P, 1982) 402.

9. André Breton in "Situation of Surrealism Between the Two Wars," in "What is Surrealism?" *Selected Writings*, ed. Franklin Rosemont (New York: Monad P, 1978) 245.

10. André Breton, *Nadja*, 2nd ed. (Gallimard, 1928) 19-20. All subsequent quotations are from this edition.

11. *Stéphane Mallarmé: Selected Poetry and Prose* ed. Mary Ann Caws (New Dictions, 1982). All quotations from "Un Coup de des," "Brise marine" and "Igitur" are from this edition. Mallarmé's admiration for Poe is well-documented. As a very young man, Mallarmé went to London for the acknowledged purpose of studying English to be able to read Poe in original.

12. "Negative Capability" 402.

13. "Nothing, this foam, this virgin verse [Rien, cette écume, vierge vers]."

14. "Negative Capability" 402.

15. The Whitman connection is discussed by Peter Schmidt in "White: Charles Simic's Thumbnail Epic" 542. According to Schmidt, Simic's reference to "the milk tooth" is an allusion to Whitman's use of the "boss tooth" to indicate a child's passage into adulthood in "The Sleeper."

16. "Negative Capability" 399.

17. In "Where the Levels Meet," Simic declared: "I owe the greatest debt to surrealism as an influence rather than a practice," 53.

18. Paul Claudel, "Preface" to "Igitur" in *Stéphane Mallarmé: Selected Poetry and Prose* 101.

19. Mallarmé's "Preface" to "Un Coup de dés" 106.

20. Within the same passage in "Poet and novelist," Marcel Proust, speaks further of Mallarmé "who for ten years had wrestled with a huge work, [and who] clear-sighted in the hour of death like Don Quixote, told his daughter to burn the manuscript." *On Art and Literature: 1896-1919* (New York: Carroll and Gray, 1954).

21. In "Negative Capability" Simic defines the surrealist poet in general as one who "equates the imaginary with a truth of psychological order," 404.

22. "Where the Levels Meet" 50.

23. *50 Contemporary Poets: The Creative Process*, ed. Alberta Turner (New York: Longman, 1977) 280.

24. "Where the Levels Meet" 53.

25. "Where the Levels Meet" 55.

26. Quoted by Sartre in *Mallarmé or the Poet of Nothingness*, trans. and introd. Ernest Sturn (Pennsylvania State UP, 1988) 140.

27. Quoted by Geoffrey Brereton in *An Introduction to The French Poets: Villon to the present day* (Harper and Row, 1973) 217.

28. *50 Contemporary Poets: The Creative Process* 279.

29. Breton, "Les Vases communicants," trans. Stephen Schwartz, in "What is Surrealism?" *Selected Writings*, ed. Franklin Rosemont (New York: Monad P, 1978) 75.

30. As quoted by Brereton, in *An Introduction to the French Poets: Villon to the present day*, Claudel speaks of ". . . ce mot que Mallarmé a dit a l'un de nous: 'Je suis un desespéré,'" 219.

31. "Where the Levels Meet" 53.

32. G. Poulet, *Éspaces et temps Mallarméens* (Lausanne: La Baconniére, Collection "Etre et Penser") 222-25.

33. Anna Balakian in *André Breton: Magus of Surrealims* (Oxford UP, 1971) 111.

34. Brereton in *An Introduction to the French Poets: Villon to the present day*: "cold and empty glass he [Mallarmé] could never break" 218.

Edward Hirsch (review date 21 December 1992)

SOURCE: "Joseph Cornell: Naked in Arcadia," in *The New Yorker,* Vol. LXVIII, No. 44, December 21, 1992, pp. 130-34.

[*In the following excerpted review, Hirsch praises Simic's musings on the artist Joseph Cornell in* Dime-Store Alchemy.]

Charles Simic's new work of prose, **Dime-Store Alchemy: The Art of Joseph Cornell,** is the most sustained literary response thus far to [Joseph] Cornell's boxes, montages, and films. It is a poet's book: incisive, freewheeling, dramatic—a mixture of evocation and observation, as lucid and shadowy as the imagination it celebrates. Simic wears his learning lightly. "I have a dream in which Joseph Cornell and I pass each other on the street," he begins, and that sentence—that dream—sets the tone for what follows: a personal quest to approach Cornell through the urban milieu, to encounter and exalt his spirit. Simic writes, "Somewhere in the city of New York there are four or five still-unknown objects which belong together. Once together they'll make a work of art. That's Cornell's premise, his metaphysics, and his religion, which I wish to understand."

Dime-Store Alchemy tracks Cornell from a unique angle. Simic—an American poet born in Belgrade and weaned on Surrealism; a writer with an antenna for paradox and a penchant for philosophy; an antic, skeptical visionary ("What a mess!" he has written. "I believe in images as vehicles of transcendence, but I don't believe in God!")—is one of Cornell's most unlikely and most genuine literary heirs. For years, the poet tells us, he tried to approximate Cornell's method, to "make poems from found bits of language." He brings to his task a desire to pursue the collagist's ideas and strategies, and a confirmed sense that he is dealing with "an American artist worthy of imitation." The result is a compact book with a large reach, a work that goes on reverberating, like a Duchamp "readymade" or a Mallarmé sonnet.

The book consists of sixty short texts—diverse "illuminations," notebook entries arranged in associative rather than linear fashion, paragraphs put together in tonal blocks that accrue into an homage and a portrait. It is an appreciative assemblage of reveries and meditations, vignettes, memories, lists, and prose poems, quotations from Cornell's copious diaries, and descriptions of the artist's work—his working method—which often read like parables. The pieces range from acute, fairly straightforward mini-essays on Cornell's modernist aims to highly evocative and uncanny responses to the collagist's ideas. Sometimes the two modes are combined, as in **"These Are Poets Who Service Church Clocks,"** which begins with the sociological language "Many people have already speculated about the relationship between play and the sacred" and rises to the ultimate symbolist notion: "Silence is that vast, cosmic church in which we always stand alone. Silence is the only language God speaks."

Simic characteristically proceeds by peering into Cornell's constructions and then describing not only what he sees but where it leads him. "Perhaps the ideal way to observe the boxes is to place them on the floor and lie down beside them," he writes in **"Poetics of Miniature,"** and one pictures him doing precisely that. In this way he becomes a solitary onlooker in a tiny memory theatre, gazing at a floodlit stage where time has been permanently suspended. The curtain goes up on a strange play already in progress—Cornell's boxes, like his films, begin *in medias res*—and the viewer is immediately thrust into a dream world. Simic is so deeply immersed in Cornell's universe that at times he looks right past the actors and into the realm Cornell termed "backstage"—that is, his imagination. In the one-paragraph entry **"Cigars Clamped Between Their Teeth"** Simic writes:

> I've read that Goethe, Hans Christian Andersen, and Lewis Carroll were managers of their own miniature theaters. There must have been many other such playhouses in the world. We study the history and literature of the period, but we know nothing about these plays that were being performed for an audience of one.

He intrudes into Cornell's private sanctum in order to recreate the aura of just such shadow plays.

Simic's response to Cornell is often intuitive and oblique. His meditation may yield an equivalent mood, a kind of light, the look of a place that articulates a parallel reality. Here is **"The Magic Study of Happiness"**:

> In the smallest theater in the world the bread crumbs speak. it's a mystery play on the subject of a lost paradise. Once there was a kitchen with a table on which a few crumbs were left. Through the window you could see your young mother by the fence talking to a neighbor. She was cold and kept hugging her thin dress tighter and tighter. The clouds in the sky sailed on as she threw her head back to laugh.
>
> Where the words can't go any further—there's the hard table. The crumbs are watching you as you in turn watch them. The unknown in you and the unknown in them attract each other. The two unknowns are like illicit lovers when they're exceedingly and unaccountably happy.

This is Simic's own miniature theatre, in which inanimate bread crumbs—the poor leftovers—come to life and speak. it's a fairy-tale kitchen drama that moves offstage to recall a moment of intense domestic happiness, a voyeuristic glimpse of the vulnerable, joyous young mother. This entire scene seems inspired by a constellation of perceptions about the size, scale, and staging of Cornell's work, its deep reverence for the innocence of childhood as well as its Proustian feeling for involuntary memory, for paradise lost and magically recaptured. It illuminates the work's ecstatic, inward nature, how it slips into a range beyond language. What is crucial in Simic's second paragraph is how the solitudes meet and communicate with each other—the secret communion between actor and audience. He dramatizes the way Cornell's boxes activate something immense, lonely, hidden, and almost illicit in the viewer, speaking to him or her with a poignant, blissful intimacy.

As in his poems, Simic's style in **Dime-Store Alchemy** is deceptively offhand and playful, moving fluently between the frontal statement and the indirect suggestion, the ordinary and the metaphysical. In **"Dog Wearing Baby Clothes"** Simic quotes Cornell's description of more than a hundred and fifty working files:

> *a diary journal repository laboratory, picture gallery, museum, sanctuary, observatory, key . . . the core of a labyrinth, a clearinghouse for dreams and visions . . . childhood regained.*

Cornell repeatedly sifted these elaborate dossiers in quest of lost time, seeking to recover, in Simic's words, "our old amazement."

The book has eight useful black-and-white illustrations, an abbreviated but deft chronology, and an epigraph from Gérard de Nerval—"Me? I pursue an image, no more"—which, despite its disclaimer, is like a blinking sign that says "Visionary at Work." Simic includes a poem by the Serbian poet Vasko Popa ("Now in the little box / You have the whole world in miniature") and cites passages by Breton, de Chirico, and Magritte, canonical exemplars of mystery. Cornell was himself an artist who referred continually to his own sources. Nerval was his particular hero, the hallucinatory mystic and precursor of the Surrealists, who was famous, as Simic notes, "for promenading the streets of Paris with a live lobster on a leash." The artist also loved Baudelaire, Rimbaud, and Mallarmé, all alchemists of the word. Like Borges, Cornell was conscious of "inventing" his own precursors, who then served as touchstones and sacred figures. Like Wallace Stevens, he was a stay-at-home who loved the idea of romantic Europe, and especially France—a country he visited often in his mind. "The man who never travelled made up his own Baedeker," Simic writes, and many of the boxes feel like guidebooks in three dimensions, maps to another terrain.

Simic has a humane vision of art as consolation, a certainty that Cornell was trying "to construct a vehicle of reverie,

an object that would enrich the imagination of the viewer and keep him company forever." In this book Simic becomes that ideal viewer and recipient, following the artist into imaginary hotels "frequented by phantoms." He watches as Cornell sets out from the family house on Utopia Parkway, knowing that the surveyor of the commonplace is also an interrogator of the ineffable, who isn't sure exactly where he is going or what he is looking for and so desperately needs to find. Perhaps there is a spiritual point where all contradictions can be resolved: "That point is somewhere in the labyrinth and the labyrinth is the city of New York." Simic presents Cornell as a man who basically "walks and looks." He dreams and watches people. In a piece called **"The Romantic Movement"** Simic summons up the figure of the discharged patient in Poe's story "The Man of the Crowd": "Who among us was not once that pursuer or that stranger?" Simic asks. "Cornell followed shopgirls, waitresses, young students 'who had a look of innocence.' I myself remember a tall man of uncommon handsomeness who walked on Madison Avenue with eyes tightly closed as if he were listening to music." In an entry titled after Wallace Stevens' poem "The Man on the Dump," Simic notes that Cornell "looked the way I imagine Melville's Bartleby to have looked the day he gave up his work to stare at the blank walls outside the office window." For Simic, Cornell resembles no one so much as those familiar-looking strangers in outmoded overcoats who haunt the city like ghosts: "They sit in modest restaurants and side-street cafeterias eating a soft piece of cake. They are deadly pale."

Simic's Cornell is also like Apollinaire ("the poet who loved street performers, musicians with cornets and tambourines, tightrope walkers, jugglers") and Rimbaud ("Arthur, poor boy, you would have walked the length of Fourteenth Street and written many more 'Illuminations'"). For the symbolist poet, eternity has been cut up and scattered into thousands of minuscule pieces. Cornell puts a few of them back together. Simic calls this "the quest for the lost and the beautiful." He writes:

> The disorder of the city is sacred. All things are interrelated. As above, so below. We are fragments of an unutterable whole. Meaning is always in search of itself. Unsuspected revelations await us around the next corner.

Simic believes that, like Whitman, Cornell "saw poetry everywhere." Simic's feeling for this aesthetic imperative and ideal—this way of life, really—is everywhere apparent, since he, too, is a somewhat ironic seeker and witness, an urban lookout. He observes, "On a busy street one quickly becomes a voyeur. An air of danger, eroticism, and crushing solitude plays hide-and-seek in the crowd. The indeterminate, the unforeseeable, the ethereal, and the fleeting rule there."

Once, in a moment of candor, Cornell said, "My work was a natural outcome of my love for the city," and some of Simic's most felicitous passages consider the implications of that basic premise. What he often sees in Cornell's boxes is a freeze-frame of Manhattan in the thirties, forties, or fifties—Cornell's very productive decades. In a particularly affecting piece, the poet peers into a see-through box depicting a window façade and discovers a luminous Hopperesque moment of urban peace:

> Early Sunday morning in June. It had rained after midnight, and the air and the sky have miraculously cleared. The avenues are empty and the stores closed. A glimpse of things before anyone has seen them.

Here Simic stands in Cornell's place and describes a city emptied of people, a world refreshed, renewed, and clarified.

Simic's sense of isolation—his memory of being an immigrant—informs not only his reading of Cornell but also his understanding of the country we inhabit. "America is a place where the Old World shipwrecked. Flea markets and garage sales cover the land," he says in **"Naked in Arcadia,"** and goes on:

> They should have made them undress and throw their possessions into the sea for the sake of an America where everybody goes naked, it occurs to me. My parents would be naked, too, posing for that picture in the Yellowstone Park with my father's much-prized Moroccan red fez.

One of the subtexts of this book is the link between art and loneliness, or, more specifically, the way the wanderer makes what he can out of what he happens upon. The modern artist collects fragments, things that other people throw away. Thus Simic defines an epiphanic instant of poetry: "Three mismatched shoes at the entrance of a dark alley." He recalls the first premise of collage technique—"You don't make art, you find it"—and concludes, "Every art is about the longing of One for the Other. Orphans that we are, we make our sibling kin out of anything we can find."

In **"Medici Slot Machine,"** one of the book's strongest and most charming pieces, and one of the few that take their title from the art, the poet responds to a key work by constructing a separate but analogous universe. The center of Cornell's 1942 construction, his initiating masterwork, is a reproduction of a Renaissance "Portrait of a Young Noble." Black lines crisscross the surface, and the boy stares at us even as we locate him through a telescope lens or a gun sight. He is flanked by fragments of an old map of the Palatine Hill in Rome, which, in turn, are framed by vertical panels of film—strips of Renaissance faces, serial photos of the boy himself. Simic explains:

> The name enchants, and so does the idea—the juxtaposition of the Renaissance boy, the penny arcade, and the Photomat in the subway; what seem at first totally incompatible worlds—but then, of course, we are in Cornell's "magic regions" of Forty-second Street and Times Square.

Simic teases out the implications of the three realms Cornell has radically conjoined, creating a contiguous context

for the imagery, daydreaming about the Renaissance princeling in a seedy urban landscape:

> The boy has the face of one lost in reverie who is about to press his forehead against a windowpane. He has no friends. In the subway there are panhandlers, small-time hustlers, drunks, sailors on leave, teen-aged whores loitering about. The air smells of frying oil, popcorn, and urine. The boy-prince studies the Latin classics and prepares himself for the affairs of the state. He is stubborn and cruel. He already has secret vices. At night he cries himself to sleep.

By projecting outward from the construction, Simic sends the prince—"'He is as beautiful as a girl,' someone says"—into a hustling, shadowy, eroticized world where "blacks shine shoes, a blind man sells newspapers, young boys in tight jeans hold hands." None of these figures exist in the original box—they are Simic's invention. We follow the androgynous figure into the mirrored world of vending machines and then into the underground cityscape, where he represents "an angelic image in the dark of the subway." Simic's summary statement about the heterogeneous but unified character of the "slot machine" is an *ars poetica* that applies to the piece we are reading as well as the one we are looking at:

> Whatever it is, it must be ingenious. Our loving gaze can turn it on. A poetry slot machine offering a jackpot of incommensurable meanings activated by our imagination. Its mystic repertoire has many images.

In essence, ***Dime-Store Alchemy*** rotates on the axis of two perceptions of Cornell as a modernist in the American grain: an updated version of Poe and of Dickinson, one metamorphosing into the other. "Cornell and Dickinson are both in the end unknowable," Simic writes. "They live within the riddle, as Dickinson would say. Their biographies explain nothing. They are without precedent, eccentric, original, and thoroughly American."

To appreciate fully Simic's reading of Cornell, you need to look hard again at Cornell's work, to peer into the looking glass of his objects and dream the boxes back into your hands. Reading this book reminded me time and again of the 1980 Cornell retrospective at the Museum of Modern Art. Emerging from that show, one felt the buoyant Americanness of Cornell's work, its totemic innocence and passionate inwardness, its reverence for the wayward magic of city life. It was like being swept back into the world by a giant revelatory wave. "Like a comic-book Spider-Man," Simic writes, "the solitary voyeur rides the web of occult forces."

Dime-Store Alchemy is a meeting of kindred spirits that is itself a work of art, and a tribute to a precisionist of longings and enigmas, an explorer who used the quotidiana of the past to investigate the secret recesses of the heart.

Lisa Zeidner (review date 21 March 1993)

SOURCE: "Empty Beds, Empty Nests, Empty Cities," in *New York Times,* March 21, 1993, pp. 14-15.

[In the following review, Zeidner finds Insomniac Hotel *occasionally redundant but many of the individual poems "breathtaking."]*

Few contemporary poets have been as influential—or as inimitable—as Charles Simic. For more than 30 years his work has claimed citizenship to its own dreamlike land, an elusive place hard to pinpoint. His poems are like dense medieval towns seen from the air: you get a sharp view, "time only for a glimpse," before the view clouds up and you're not sure where you are or even *when* you are, whether awake or asleep. The dislocation is both spooky and seductive.

Mr. Simic migrated to the United States from Yugoslavia in 1954, and his haunting images have roots in war-torn Europe, where, as a small child, he watched his father being arrested by the Gestapo. In essays, he has described himself as a lonely, frightened boy, sleepless as bombs fell. But there is rarely anything overtly autobiographical in his poems, except the lingering mood of being orphaned by logic and culture: "I spent my childhood on a cross / In a yard full of weeds, / White butterflies, and white chickens."

In his 11th volume, *Hotel Insomnia,* Mr. Simic continues to explore the ghost town he has limned in past collections. It is a world of empty cities filled with empty storefronts, "millions of empty rooms with TV sets turned on." The poet wanders past prisons and convents and theaters in flames, occasionally spying the shadow of someone he knows or used to know, "my mother and her old dog" or, in **"Missing Child"**:

> You of the dusty, sun-yellowed picture
> I saw twenty years ago
> On the window of a dry-cleaning store.
> I thought of you again tonight,
> In this chilly room where I sat by the window
> Watching the street,
> As your mother must've done every night,
> And still does, for all I know.

Hotel Insomnia is not Mr. Simic's most focused or freshest collection. He himself concedes that he's sleepwalking in "the same old city, the same old street." The repetition is intentional, of course. The reader circles images like a sleeping man circling the same hypnagogic thought over and over. Occasionally the insomniac treading the "gloomy corridors" feels more like a tic than a dynamic means of exploring memory and perception. Yet individual poems are breathtaking—like **"The Prodigal,"** in which "Everything is a magic ritual, / A secret cinema," and the poet's trademark tropes seem almost dewy in their immediacy.

Mr. Simic operates like the spiders that frequently creep into his poems. He balances himself on the web of the poem and lies in wait for the reader. The reader is that lone fly on the ceiling—another favorite image. The web's design might be familiar, but more often than not, it still does the trick.

Tam Lin Neville (review date Spring 1993)

SOURCE: "In a Room Where We Are Absent," in *Hungry Mind Review,* Spring, 1993, p. 32.

[In the following review, Neville notes the painful subject matter but eloquent writing in The Horse Has Six Legs, *edited and translated by Simic.]*

I've always thought it eerie the way a voice from another culture can come through in the English of a good translation. it's as though a ghost had passed through a wall. "Poetry is what is retained in translation," not what is lost, poet Charles Simic argues. After reading *The Horse Has Six Legs*, I have to agree with his optimism.

The book begins with "Oral Poetry, Women's Songs," a group of early folk poems collected in the eighteenth and nineteenth centuries. I was drawn to the raw, earthy ones.

> The sky is strewn with stars
> And the wide meadow with sheep.
> The sheep have no shepherd
> Except for crazy Radoye
> And he has fallen asleep.
> His sister Janja wakes him:
> Get up, crazy Radoye,
> Your sheep have wandered off.
> Let them, sister, let them.
> The witches have feasted on me,
> Mother carved my heart out,
> Our aunt held the torch for her.

Another short song ushers out a common, unwanted guest of peasant houses:

> There smoke, sooty smoke,
> There is your door,
> And fried egg.
> And bread and butter,
> And your grandpa's bones
> With which to prick yourself.

The "Women's Songs" show us the ground many of these Serbian poems come from, and they reflect Simic's allegiance to what is plain and down to earth, for what grows out of folk life. The book as a whole represents Simic's own tastes. Simic, who emigrated to the U.S. from Yugoslavia when he was fifteen, is a prolific author, translator, and winner of the Pulitzer Prize for Poetry in 1990 (for *The World doesn't End*, Harcourt Brace Jovanovich). In thirty years of translating, Simic explains in the introduction, he has translated only what he liked; "representing the entire range of Serbian poetry was beyond my ambition and ability."

The other poets in the book are twentieth century: thirteen out of eighteen still alive; two of eighteen women.

Early in the collection there is a lyric and palpable poem, "Snake," by one of these two women, Desanka Maksimović (born 1898).

On the road winding into the distance,
someone's song.
The lonely sound entangles itself
in the grass.
She listens, her head raised
wide-awake into the air.
The sun is shining.

Here's where they killed her mother
with the blade of a scythe.
they'll do the same to her
when she crawls out of the shrubbery.
Her clothes will rot
with their embroideries
and the glow of dew.

One of the pleasures of a good anthology is walking, in the space of a few pages, between two very distinct sensibilities. Unlike the translations of Robert Bly, which manage somehow to make Rilke, Machado, and Kabir all sound alike, in this anthology the individuality of each voice is preserved. Following the strong physical reality of Maksimoviç , it's a long way to the more surreal and metaphysical poems of Vasko Popa (1922-1991), the most widely translated and best-known postwar Yugoslav poet. Soon after the exquisite vulnerability of Maksimoviç's snake, a fantastic, magnified shewolf is painted in bold strokes by Popa: "On the bottom of the sky / the shewolf lies // Body of living sparks / overgrown with grass // . . . They catch the shewolf in steel traps / Sprung from horizon to horizon // Tear out her golden muzzle / And pluck the secret grasses / Between her thighs // With her severed tongue the shewolf / Scoops live water from the jaws of a cloud / And again becomes whole" ("Burning Shewolf").

Popa's "Little Box" poems are also surreal, but unlike his "Burning Shewolf," they are intimate and unassuming in tone. In his essay **"Negative Capability and Its Children,"** Simic says that, unlike imagism, which names what is there, surrealism "endlessly renames what is there, as if by renaming it could get closer to the thing itself." In these eleven short poems we circle around and around the little box, a box which is stubbornly itself and also alive with metaphysical possibilities. Perhaps the little box is pure consciousness or spirit, embodied in affectionate, household terms. "Line the inside of the little box / With your precious skin / And make yourself cozy / Just as you would in your own house" ("The Owners of the Little Box").

There is a notable lack of ego here. In one of the last poems the little box is returned "into the arms / of her inconspicuously honest properties," into her "pure inconspicuousness" ("The Benefactors of the Little Box"). In an interview in *The Uncertain Certainty: Interviews, Essays, and Notes on Poetry* (the source of other prose quotes from Simic in this review) Simic talks movingly about a "profound anonymity" which he feels we all have inside us. Certain texts "are longings to experience that anonymity, the condition where we don't have an 'I' yet. It is as if we were in a room from which, paradoxically,

we were absent." I think "the little box" is a text imbued with this longing.

Several of the poets in this anthology have learned another kind of humility, one taught by history. A friend of mine said today's headlines would make him hesitate before picking up a volume of Serbian poetry. But the current stories of civil strife and fanaticism represent only a fraction of the former Socialist Federal Republic of Yugoslavia's past, a long, hard history that is alive both inside and in the margins of many of these poems.

In "Spring Liturgy for Branko Miljkoviç ," by Ivan V. Laliç (b. 1931), the spirit of a dead friend reappears in the world as a tree, a "tree that stutters with arms full of living rain." The poem continues on in its shattered but majestic certainty, "Beauty endures. It matters not whether it remembers, / The road continues past the broken rails." In the end of the poem beauty returns "like pillage."

In a poem by Jovan Hristiç (b. 1933), "I want you to know, my dear Phaedrus, / We lived in hopeless times." The poet pleads with Phaedrus to remember his people because "The true seriousness, measure, wise exaltation, / And exalted wisdom always eluded us. We were / On no-man's-land, neither being ourselves // Nor being someone else, but always a step or two / Removed from what we are and what we ought to be."

This is a poet overwhelmed by history. Often Hristiç's poems ask forgiveness, from a more noble past, or from "some future morning" whose light the poet will not see. On the whole though, the work in this book does not speak of oppression, fatalism, or defeat, but instead shows poets working to maintain their vulnerable selves in the face of the multiplicity and confusion that surrounds them.

In **"Notes on Poetry and History"** Simic says poets are here to insist on the "unimportant events" of history. He prefers Sappho's insomnia, the small pool of light it throws over the ordinary things around her, to Homer's larger sense of history as sacred myth. Simic's own "thing" poems, **"Fork," "Spoon," "Brooms," "My Shoes,"** come from this impulse and in this anthology he has included others in a similar vein.

Poems about food come to my mind first. I'm thinking of one called "Breakfast," in which the poet Ljubomir Simoviç wakes into a world where "Snow has hatched in every den and lair / putting out every fire. / The snow: our lock and key." But soon he's got three rashers of bacon in his skillet and into this sizzling pan he cracks an egg—"I rejoice because of the egg." The poem too seems like a spoonful of rich yellow swallowed to ward off an obliterating whiteness.

In another poem, "Crucifixion," Simoviç writes about an abandoned country cross, attended only by sparrows, crickets, and snowflakes.

Crucified Jesus on a yellow cross
Washed down by cold rain
Spreads his arms wide
As if playing the accordion.

He bends his ear down to the instrument
Better to hear the sound
Unaware the passing tinker took it
When he went by cold and hungry.

Here is a poet with a strong feeling for the everyday world. At the same time his spirit is working to pull up from the often dull, cheerless weight of the daily. Simic has always been interested in the predicament of a figure like this, caught between the ordinary and the illumined world, oddly, sometimes comically, capable of both. This predicament is what he calls *poverty*, a word to which he brings his own idiosyncratic definition. Uncomfortable with flights of imagination which leave behind the human condition, Simic believes poetry should not try to sustain illumination but should stick close to life—life which is always swinging us between extremes. To me this is a rich sense of *poverty* because of the ambiguity it can absorb and the great delight Simic takes in it.

Others have approached this predicament much more soberly. I think of Dimitri Karamazov, flushed with shame and self-loathing when he has to take off his socks before the police and reveal the flat, coarse nail on his big right toe. I think of Simone Weil, with her severe migraine headaches, laboring in an automobile factory, knowing that grace is possible but pressuring herself, in great pain, to experience with others the cold, leaden gravity of the common world.

I don't think Simic would dismiss this kind of angst, but his own sense of things is lighter, less grave. In Simic's view we are more like sheep, "trying to fly with woolen wings," a line I found toward the end of this anthology in one of three wonderful, comic outhouse poems by Aleksandar Ristoviç (b. 1933). I will quote the first in full:

"Outhouse"

Through a crack on the right
you can see the red rooster,
and through the one on the left,
with a bit of effort,
you can see the table,
the white cover
and a bottle of wine.
Behind your back, if you turn,
you'll make out the sheep
trying to fly with their woolen wings.
And through the heart-shaped
hole in the door,
someone's cheerful face
watching you shit.

In "Spring Liturgy" Ivan Laliç says, "A poem is a poem even when it's made of clay."

The earth can be a comic curse, a reward, or a commemorative marker. In a poem composed by Ljubomir Si-

moviç of "Epitaphs from Karansko Cemetery" little "Stanoje two months old / sleeps in a cradle of soil . . . / his mound cannot be jumped over or avoided." This anthology is like that mound.

Philip Miller (essay date Summer 1993)

SOURCE: "Simic's 'Cabbage'," in *Explicator*, Vol. 51, No. 4, Summer, 1993, pp. 257-58.

[*In the following essay, Miller analyzes similarities between Simic's poem "Cabbage," Andrew Marvell's "To His Coy Mistress," and John Donne's "The Flea."*]

Charles Simic's recent book ***Gods and Devils***, itself a kind of Dantean parody, contains poems that displace a number of other literary myths. One poem, **"Cabbage,"** for example, comes nicely into focus when we see its subtle parody of two well-known seventeenth-century *carpe diem* love poems: Andrew Marvell's "To My Coy Mistress" and John Donne's "The Flea."

The "mistress" of Simic's poem is about to "chop the head" of cabbage "in half," just as the mistress in Donne's poem prepares to kill a flea. The cabbage is Simic's emblem for love, like Donne's conceit, but also brings to mind the "vegetable love" of Marvell's poem. Simic's narrator makes "her reconsider" just as Donne "stays" his mistress's hand, temporarily. Simic's poem reduces the rhetorical seduction, so elaborate in both Donne and Marvell, to only one line: "'Cabbage symbolizes mysterious love.'" Simic's line, however, is still "a line," and appropriately cavalier in its formal and hyperbolic tone and in its allusion to Charles Fourier, not exactly a cavalier lover, but a late-eighteenth-century French socialist. Yet Fourier is a fitting hero for Simic's late-twentieth-century cavalier, who wishes to impress upon a woman the mysteries of love and other "strange and wonderful things" still associated with the "mad" French. Of course, his language would be veiled in "romantic suggestiveness" rather than mock argumentation. In fact, Simic's contemporary lover trusts actions more than words, and his attempted seduction shifts quickly from the rhetorical to a physical attempt to seize the day (although with gentlemanly restraint): "Whereupon I kissed the back of her neck / Ever so gently."

At the end, Simic's narrator cannot suggest (as Marvell's does) rolling "all our strength and all / Our sweetness into one ball. . . ." Nor does Simic's displaced cavalier "win the argument"; he will not have his way. The love emblem—the globe-like cabbage head—(like Donne's flea, with whose "blood of innocence" his mistress "purpled" her nail) is destroyed: ". . . she cut the cabbage in two / With a single stroke of her knife." Again, actions speak louder than words in Simic's poem, and unlike Marvell's "coy" mistress or Donne's, who has the "tables" of the argument turned upon her, Simic's woman succeeds in whimsically cutting the dramatic moment short and exposing the real substance of the narrator's intentions.

Scott Edward Anderson (review date November-December 1993)

SOURCE: A review of *Hotel Insomniac* and *Dime-Store Alchemy,* in *Bloomsbury Review,* Vol. 13, No. 6, November-December, 1993, p. 12.

[*In the following review, Anderson explains how the poems in* Hotel Insomniac *and the prose observations in* Dime-Store Alchemy *compliment each other, noting in particular Simic's interest in the meaning and purpose of art.*]

"The world is beautiful but not sayable. That's why we need art," Charles Simic writes in **Dime-Store Alchemy**. He refers to the artist Joseph Cornell but could have easily been describing his own work and focus. Like Cornell, Simic has been trying to translate the ineffable through his own inimitable language since **Dismantling the Silence** (Braziller, 1971) was published. Critics have often tried, without much success, to define the elusive, beguiling, and seductive quality of his poetry, and have used vague generalizations: "a Central European sensibility," an "accent" laced with "garlic and a readier good will," "the dreamy, unexpected metaphors of a foreigner." His work remains, after a dozen books, provocative, impossible to pigeonhole, and often difficult to decipher.

It is not surprising that Cornell's work and example have had such a profound effect in shaping Simic's own art, for his poetry often resembles a Cornell box: found images and objects, fragments, inscriptions, dolls, birds, balls, bubble pipes—the wispy strains of a tarnished nostalgia, wire cages brought together to make a lyric poem-assemblage. The work of both artists suggests a dream world at once sinister and redolent of a childlike illogic—images are randomly grouped such that their curious juxtaposition might serve to provide a new experience.

"In Cornell's art, the eye and tongue are at cross purposes. Neither one by itself is sufficient. It's the mingling of the two that makes up the third image," Simic writes. In many ways, Cornell is the unwitting godfather of Simic's poetry, supplying the method if not the means for the enigmatic gesture of his writing. Simic's tribute to Joseph Cornell is in the use of his own "language" to translate the beauty that can't be spoken in the artist's creations.

The prose pieces in **Dime-Store Alchemy** occasionally resemble the poems in **The World doesn't End** (Harcourt Brace Jovanovich, 1989), Simic's Pulitzer Prize-winning volume of prose poems:

> The lonely boy must play quietly because his parents are sleeping after lunch. He kneels on the floor between their beds, pushing a matchbox, inside which he imagines himself sitting. The day is hot. In her sleep his mother has uncovered her breasts like the Sphinx.

> The car, for that's what it is, is moving very slowly because its wheels are sinking in the deep sand. Ahead, nothing but wind, sky, and more sand.

> "Shush," says the father sternly to the desert wind.

from **"Postage Stamp with a Pyramid"**

The poems from **Hotel Insomnia** echo the concerns of Cornell:

> Hearing me approach
> He took a rubber toy
> Out of his mouth
> As if to say something,
> But then he didn't.
> It was a head, a doll's head,
> Badly chewed,
> Held high for me to see.
> The two of them grinning at me.

from **"Street Scene"**

For Simic, "Everything is a magic ritual, / A secret cinema," an existence "Which cannot be put into words— / Like a fly on the map of the world / In the travel agent's window." Simic's response to Cornell is so clear, so precise, because they were both insomniacs working the front desk of a "hotel frequented by phantoms." Simic agrees with Magritte's assertion that "people who look for symbolic meaning fail to grasp the inherent poetry and mystery of the images." Perhaps this is how to approach both the poetry of Simic and the constructions of Cornell—each is concerned with constructing "a vehicle of reverie, an object that would enrich the imagination of the viewer and keep him company forever"; both view chance as a means by which "to reveal the self and its obsessions."

This would seem to explain why so many of these two artists' images stay with us for so long. Who can forget, once they've seen it, Cornell's untitled construction ("Bebe Marie"), with its "chubby doll in a forest of twigs. Her eyes are open and her lips and cheeks are red." Or the pig and the angel from **"To Think Clearly"** in **Hotel Insomnia**: "The pig to stick his nose in a slop bucket, / The angel to scratch his back / And say sweet things in his ear."

These two intriguing books seem to be of a piece—the Cornell book serving as a Baedeker to the **Hotel Insomnia**, while the poems further illustrate what Simic calls the "all-inclusive aesthetic" that is the means through which we can "make sense of American reality." The poet, in offering insight into the world of the artist, reveals much more about the poet and his own world in a tantalizing, sometimes beautiful fusion of visions.

Judith Kitchen (review date Winter 1995)

SOURCE: A review of *A Wedding in Hell,* in *Georgia Review,* Vol. XLIX, No. 4, Winter, 1995, pp. 938-41.

[In the following review, Kitchen discusses Simic's political poetry in A Wedding in Hell.*]*

[One] way poets have handled . . . political material is to release it from its historical ties, creating . . . a kind of imaginative transmutation. Charles Simic's latest book, *A Wedding in Hell*, does just this. The poems are vintage "Simic"—cool, surprising, an odd mix of images that disturb as often as they satisfy.

Simic, who was born in Yugoslavia, must, like most of us, respond to the nightly images on the television screen as the people of the former republic wage a multifaceted civil war. But his poems have not been written for this context; instead, they seem to aspire to timelessness by displaying a distanced universality reminiscent of the poetry of Vasco Popa or Jean Follain.

Simic's poems are never locked in the past, but take place in the present tense of the lyric. They transcend chronology, eschewing even imagery that would date them, reaching for eternity. This is true for most of his work, but in *A Wedding in Hell* there is an emphasized dislocation, as though the poems were trying to bridge the gaps between languages—and, in many ways, they are. Simic fuses the multiple connotations of his words by wedding dissimilar images. Things exist in their very particularity even as the landscape they inhabit is nebulous, unknown and unknowable. ("you've no idea what city this is, / What country? It could be a dream.") The first poem, **"Miracle Glass Co.,"** shows us a world seen only in a mirror:

> This street with its pink sky,
> Row of gray tenements,
> A lone dog,
> Children on rollerskates,
> Woman buying flowers,
> Someone looking lost.

But the innocence is short-lived as poem after poem reflects a more sinister world, as in **"Paradise Motel"**:

> I lived well, but life was awful.
> There were so many soldiers that day.
> So many refugees crowding the roads.
> Naturally, they all vanished
> With a touch of the hand.
> History licked the corners of its bloody mouth.

For Simic, History (with a capital *H*) becomes a character playing out its lines on a shabby stage. To a large extent, "No one ever sees the play." The leaves "thrill / and shudder almost individually" in the wind; the wine tastes good; the window is shuttered against late afternoon light. But each innocent image is matched by a threat. A poem that celebrates love is followed by one of loss or fear. More often than not, one line will undercut its predecessor: "here's a city at sunset / Resembling a butcher's fresh carcass." Like paper dolls cut out of a newspaper, the poems make tenuous connections between disparate headlines. The themes of war and destruction brood

throughout the pages. **"Documentary"** and **"The World"** confront the reality head-on, but there are dozens of oblique references as the images slip into the poems, catching the reader unawares. ("There's a war on this morning / And an advertisement for heavenly coffee . . .") Spoken matter-of-factly, the poems enact the persistence of war. The hundred-year-old woman appears in a dream with a dead child in her arms, and she might have lived at any time.

In this indeterminate landscape, it's the poet's job to note the ironies. For example, in **"The Massacre of the Innocents,"** Simic recounts how the poets of the Late Tang Dynasty could do nothing but create poems of beauty. "I couldn't help myself either. I felt joy," says the speaker. The world intrudes with all its worlding—leaf, cloud, evening bird—and the heart responds in spite of itself. The poet's role is to *become* the recording angel. The conclusion of **"Reading History"** emphasizes that point:

> How vast, dark, and impenetrable
> Are the early morning skies
> Of those led to their death
> In a world from which I'm entirely absent,
> Where I can still watch
> Someone's slumped back,
>
> Someone who is walking away from me
> With his hands tied,
> His graying head still on his shoulders,
> Someone who
> In what little remains of his life
> Knows in some vague way about me,
> And thinks of me as God,
> As Devil.

The God of this volume is certainly as silent as any Elie Wiesel could imagine. In fact, for Simic, "he's still trying to make up his mind." Part of the timelessness of this volume is its evocation of an earlier religious rhetoric which is dislocated by a skeptical contemporary mind. God is a given, but not a savior. He spells nothing of hope, but of a monumental indifference—even, at times, a glib and deliberate lack of concern. **"Prayer"** begins by invoking God's ineffectual presence as a clean slate: "You who know only the present moment, / O Lord / You who remember nothing / Of what came before . . ." **"Psalm"** ends in an indictment of a God who has turned away:

> I sought with my eyes, You in whom I do not believe.
> you've been busy making the flowers pretty,
> The lambs run after their mother,
> Or perhaps you haven't been doing even that?
>
> It was spring. The killers were full of sport
> And merriment, and your divines
> Were right at their side, to make sure
> Our final goodbyes were said properly.

These poems have been "liberated" from the specificities of history. They are political without having any particular cause. And yet they feel like little warnings, as though

Simic had unlocked the absurdities of our time and had discovered in them the future as well as the past. It's a sobering thought. And it's equally sobering when Simic does touch on a real, and personal, history, reminding us how poems can connect one life to another. The last stanza of **"The Clocks of the Dead,"** with its restrained simplicity, is unforgettable in any age:

> Just thinking about it, I forgot to wind the clock.
> We woke up in the dark.
> How quiet the city is, I said.
> Like the clocks of the dead, my wife replied.
> Grandmother on the wall,
> I heard the snows of your childhood
> Begin to fall.

Christopher Merrill (review date 19 March 1995)

SOURCE: "Moments Frozen in Time," in *Los Angeles Times Book Review,* March 19, 1995, p. 8.

[*In the following review, Merrill praises Simic's historical sense in* A Wedding in Hell *and* The Unemployed Fortune-Teller.]

Where shall we place our faith, in the individual or in the tribe? For Pulitzer Prize-winning poet Charles Simic the answer is a function of poetry itself: "Lyric poets perpetuate the oldest values on earth," he reminds us. "They assert the individual's experience against that of the tribe." Those values, needless to say, are under attack around the world. Religious fundamentalists, ardent nationalists, tribalists of every color and moral suasion—all seek to diminish the worth of individual experience. Born in solitude, the poem celebrates freedom, the ideologue's enemy; hence the sad history of poets in exile—or worse. As the Russian poet Osip Mandelstam, a victim of Stalin's gulags, wrote of Dante: "To speak means to be forever on the road."

This knowledge is what makes the simultaneous publication of Simic's 12th volume of poetry, *A Wedding in Hell,* and third book of prose, *The Unemployed Fortune-Teller,* such an important literary event. His *ars poetica*—"trying to make your jailers laugh"—is wise as well as funny: his is an essay in liberation. And never has he been more successful at unsettling a reader's certainties. "My aspiration," he admits, "is to create a kind of non-genre made up of fiction, autobiography, the essay, poetry, and of course, the joke!" In these books he fulfills that ambition.

Simic was born in 1938 in Yugoslavia, spent the war years in Belgrade, and in 1954 emigrated to the United States. Unlike many poets of his generation, he served his literary apprenticeship away from the university, forging a unique poetic sensibility out of his encounters with his adopted homeland. The writings of the French Surrealists, Theodore Roethke, Emily Dickinson and Vasko Popa—these were central to his artistic development, inspiring him to use chance operations, myth and folklore in order to say the unsayable. Of equal significance is his interest in translation from Serbian, his native tongue (which, he regrets to tell us, he was never able to use for his own poetry, because when he started to write "all the girls [he] wanted to show [his] poems to were American"). Vasko Popa, Ivan Lalic, Alexander Ristovic and Novica Tadic are just four of the Serbian poets he has translated and promoted in this country; in 1992 he published *The Horse Has Six Legs,* a remarkable anthology of Serbian poetry.

Simic's own poetry has always been informed by his acute historical sense, strange juxtapositions, daring imagery and comic spirit—qualities on full display in *A Wedding in Hell.* **"Paradise Motel"** is one of his best new poems:

> Millions were dead; everybody was innocent.
> I stayed in my room. The President
> Spoke of war as of a magic love potion.
> My eyes were opened in astonishment.
> In a mirror my face appeared to me
> Like a twice canceled postage stamp.
> I lived well, but life was awful.
> There were so many soldiers that day,
> So many refugees crowding the roads.
> Naturally, they all vanished
> With a touch of the hand.
> History licked the corners of its bloody mouth.
> On the pay channel, a man and a woman
> Were trading hungry-kisses and tearing off
> Each other's clothes while I looked on
> With the sound off and the room dark
> Except for the screen where the color
> Had too much red in it, too much pink.

Those refugees may well come from the former Yugoslavia, where day by day History's bloody mouth opens ever wider. Indeed, the Third Balkan War provides the backdrop to much of Simic's recent poetry and prose. And no wonder. What could be worse for the man who has done more to bring Serbian poets to the attention of the English-speaking world than to witness the carnage his former countrymen have committed in Croatia and Bosnia? In a courageous essay first published in the *New Republic* and included in *The Unemployed Fortune-Teller* he makes plain his feelings about Serbia's war machine—and his former countrymen, his tribesmen. "The destruction of Vukovar and Sarajevo," he writes, "will not be forgiven the Serbs."

Whatever moral credit they had as a result of their history they have squandered in these two acts. The suicidal and abysmal idiocy of nationalism is revealed here better than anywhere else. No human being or group has the right to pass a death sentence on a city.

"Defend your own, but respect what others have," my grandfather used to say, and he was a highly decorated officer in the First World War and certainly a Serbian patriot. I imagine he would have agreed with me. There will be no happy future for people who have made the innocent suffer.

"Here is something we can all count on," he adds. "Sooner or later our tribe always comes to ask us to agree to murder." This Simic will not do—to the chagrin of his old friends—perhaps because he witnessed enough carnage in World War II. (In one essay he remembers eating watermelon while Belgrade was bombed in the distance—"The watermelon made a ripe, cracking noise as my mother cut it with a big knife. We also heard what we thought was thunder, but when we looked up, the sky was cloudless and blue.") While epic poets "find excuses for the butcheries of the innocents," he sides with the solitaries, the lyric poets who "deserve to be exiled, put to death, and remembered." And lest we imagine Yugoslavia's tragedy as a local event, Simic warns: "If our own specialists in ethnic pride in the United States ever start shouting that they can't live with each other, we can expect the same bloodshed to follow."

Simic's prose has taken on a new urgency in *The Unemployed Fortune-Teller.* Here are introductions to poets from the former Yugoslavia; meditations on food, music, film and photography; and witty essays on chance, the limitations of nature writing and **"The Necessity of Poetry."** His memoirs about his military service in Luneville, France, and years in New York are lyrical, aphoristic and stunning. As in his previous book of prose, *Wonderful Words, Silent Truth,* Simic has chosen to publish selections from his notebooks, which include some of the most interesting *pensees* on the art of poetry since Wallace Stevens' "Adagia": "A poem is an invitation to a voyage. As in life, we travel to see fresh sights."

And what fresh sights he offers in *A Wedding in Hell.* These lyrics and prose poems are records of marvelous journeys. He addresses mystics; Raskolnikov and a certain Mr. Zoo Keeper; his reading of Pascal, like his depiction of the Miracle Glass Co., is both delightful and terrifying. "I have my excuse, Mr. Death," is how **"The Secret"** begins, "The old note my mother wrote / The day I missed school." And since the poet believes "the secret wish of poetry is to stop time" we are treated to one such moment from Simic's childhood, when he saw his mother:

> In her red bathrobe and slippers
> Talking to a soldier on the street
> While the snow went on falling,
> And she put a finger
> To her lips, and held it there.

The secret? The poetry and presence—the gifts—of Charles Simic.

Helen Vendler (essay date 1995)

SOURCE: "A World of Foreboding: Charles Simic," in *Soul Says: On Recent Poetry,* Belknap Press of Harvard University Press, pp. 102-16.

[*In the following essay, Vendler presents an overview of Simic's major themes and techniques.*]

Charles Simic's riddling poems, for all that they reproduce many things about his century (its wars, its cities, its eccentrics, and so on) in the end chiefly reproduce the Simic sieve—a sorting machine that selects phenomena that suit Simic's totemic desire. There is no escape hatch in a Simic poem: you enter it and are a prisoner within its uncompromising and irremediable world:

> The trembling finger of a woman
> Goes down the list of casualties
> On the evening of the first snow.
>
>
> The house is cold and the list is long.
>
> All our names are included.

This short poem, entitled **"War,"** from the collection *Hotel Insomnia* (1992), exhibits all the hallmarks of the Simic style: an apparently speakerless scene; an indefinite article establishing the vagueness of place and time—"a woman" somewhere, anywhere, on a wintry evening; then a menacing definite article focusing our gaze, in this instance on "the" list; then a late entrance of the personal pronoun engaging the speaker's life and ours. This coercive poem of war excludes everything else that might be going on in "real" wartime (people eating, drinking, going to school, manufacturing guns, and so on) in favor of a single emblem—the domestic Muse enumerating the many war dead—followed (as in emblem books) by a motto underneath: "All our names are included." The motto broadens the emblem from the war dead to all dead.

Thus, Simic's poems, even when they contain a narrative, can almost always be "folded back" into a visual cartoon accompanied by a caption. I say "cartoon" at this point rather than "emblem" because Simic is a master of the mixed style, with vulgarity cheek by jowl with sublimity. Simic's interesting memoir of his youth, **"In the Beginning,"** included in his collection of essays called *Wonderful Words, Silent Truth* (1990), suggests that both the working-class origin of his joking and hard-drinking father and the middle-class origin of his musical mother exerted Oedipal claims on his sensibility. The poems abound in working-class litter, both rustic and urban: pigs, kitchens, newspapers, dishes, gum machines, butchers, sneakers, condoms, grease; but they also exhibit the furniture of the maternally espoused ideal realm—monarchs, clouds, angels, Madonnas, martyrs, palaces, and saints.

Simic's work demands that we cohabit with both classes, with pigs and angels alike. "To think clearly," he says in the poem of that name in *Hotel Insomnia,* "What I need is a pig and an angel." Then the fate of the pig and the task of the angel are sketched in:

> The pig knows what's in store for him.
> Give him hope, angel child,
> With that foreverness stuff.

This is where some will part company with Simic. "I don't mind admitting that I believe in God," he said in an interview almost twenty years ago (reprinted in *The Uncertain Certainty* of 1985), and although the injunction to the "angel child" has a good deal of irony attached, Simic cannot do without the presence of the angel. To describe the world as it is, without the backdrop of the ideal, is to be a collaborator in the world's injustice. As Simic says to his angel, "don't go admiring yourself / In the butcher's knife / As if it were a whore's mirror." The butcher and the pig alone do not a poem make.

Simic's mockery is aimed at the pig, the angel, and himself; the sardonically comic side of his nature alternates with the remorselessly bleak. Life is a vulgar joke; life is tragedy. Perhaps for one who as a child saw World War II in Yugoslavia, life will always be overcast by horror; yet for one who escaped destruction, life will also seem charmed, lucky, privileged. Simic is not unaware of appetite, relish, and gusto. Yet it is in the coercive nature of his writing, as I have described it, that I find the deepest truth about him: "I have you trapped and you can't get out." Think how different from his the lyrics of Wordsworth or Keats are, always leading you from hill to vale, from bower to nook. In them, alternative universes abound, with elbowroom, legroom, headroom; styles meander, migrate, elevate you high and beckon you low. Attention tightens and slackens, lyric solos are followed by choral effects (as in the "Grecian Urn"). All of these fluidities disappear in Simic. An unbearable tension darkens the air. "No one is to be let off," says the punisher. No air. Few windows. No key. Minimal furniture; the bread is stale. The view is circumscribed.

I deduce that this was Simic's fundamental experience of the world for so many years that he was destined to immortalize himself by finding a form that reproduced it exactly, as in this extract from *The Book of Gods and Devils*, (1990):

> Outside, the same dark snowflake
> Seemed to be falling over and over again.
> You studied the cracked walls,
> The maplike water stain on the ceiling,
> Trying to fix in your mind its cities and rivers.

The persistence of the definite article marks this symbolic scene as an iconic one, to be exfoliated into poem after poem. Simic has been annoyed that critics have spoken of his works as "parables," saying, in *The Uncertain Certainty*, "I don't write parables. If I say 'rats in diapers,' that's to be taken literally." Simic's inclination is indeed to present deeply literal details, but they take on parabolic or emblematic significance because so much has been erased in order to isolate those details in a glaring beam of pitiless interrogation. The first poem in *Hotel Insomnia* reads, in its entirety, as follows:

"Evening Chess"

> The Black Queen raised high
> In my father's angry hand.

Like many other Simic poems, this one depends on a verbless sentence fragment, its past participle suspending

forever the father's wrath. Everything else has been suppressed—the chessboard, the table, the mother, the brother, the father's face; we are not told the motive for, or the object of, the father's anger. The largest suppression of all is that of the frightened little boy sitting opposite the angry father. Perhaps we are to understand that the parents are quarreling. Or perhaps the father is angry at his son. In any case, the cowering child, so fully implied and necessary to the scene, is effaced except in his personal pronoun, and the hand grows immense as it occupies the whole world of the poem. The poetics that generates such a poem, dependent on a single detail, is one of ruthless extirpation. What remains on the page is monumentalized, pregnant with signification, a cartoon "hand" that all by itself can be "angry."

The two books of poems under scrutiny here, while preserving Simic's coercive style, vary its content. *The Book of Gods and Devils* is often autobiographical, sometimes covertly (as is Simic's wont) but at other times overtly so. There is, for example, a touching glimpse of Simic's first reading of Shelley in a "dingy coffee shop" in New York: the poem alternates between urban wreckage—drunks, the homeless, broken umbrellas—and the visionary reaches of Shelley's social prophecies:

> How strange it all was . . . The world's raffle
> That dark October night . . .
> The yellowed volume of poetry
> With its Splendors and Glooms
> Which I studied by the light of storefronts:
> Drugstores and barbershops,
> Afraid of my small windowless room
> Cold as a tomb of an infant emperor.

What distinguishes this excerpt, and makes it something more than a reminiscence of adolescent idealization juxtaposed with urban banality, is the presence of two startling phrases—"the world's raffle," and "the tomb of an infant emperor." Neither of these is at all expectable, and one halts in coming to them as before a surrealist effect. Neither is strictly speaking surreal; both can be parsed into sense. But the essentially lawless nature of Simic's imagination, darting against his coercive structures, is continually escaping the very prisons he has himself built.

A comparable poem of adolescence (**"Crepuscule with Nellie"**) chooses as its moment of escape the writer's unearthly sense of joy while listening to jazz at the Five Spot; there follows a jolting comedown at closing time, with "the prospect of the freeze outside," and the disappearance (no doubt because her partner found the jazz more interesting) of the Nellie of the title. But the autobiographical reach of *The Book of Gods and Devils* goes back further than adolescence. There are also reminiscences stemming from Simic's wartime childhood ("We played war during the war, / Margaret. Toy soldiers were in big demand"). One of the best of these, **"The Wail,"** recounts, I believe, the arrest of Simic's father by the Gestapo, recalled in the memoir **"In the Beginning"** (collected in *Wonderful Words, Silent Truth*):

One night the Gestapo came to arrest my father. This time I was asleep and awoke suddenly to the bright lights. They were rummaging everywhere and making a lot of noise. My father was already dressed. He was saying something, probably cracking a joke. That was his style. No matter how bleak the situation, he'd find something funny to say. . . .

I guess I went to sleep after they took him away. In any case, nothing much happened this time. He was released.

Here is **"The Wail,"** complete, in which the atmosphere of that night is recreated. The child Simic, his brother, and their mother wait to see if the father will return:

> As if there were nothing to live for . . .
> As if there were . . . nothing.
> In the fading light, our mother
> Sat sewing with her head bowed.
>
> Did her hand tremble? By the first faint
> Hint of night coming, how all lay
> Still, except for the memory of that voice:
> Him whom the wild life hurried away . . .
>
> Long stretches of silence in between.
> Clock talking to a clock.
> Dogs lying on their paws with ears cocked.
> You and me afraid to breathe.
>
> Finally, she went to peek. Someone covered
> With a newspaper on the sidewalk.
> Otherwise, no one about. The street empty.
> The sky full of gypsy clouds.

Simic here shows us nothing followed by nothing; fading light, coming night; stillness, silence, suspended breath; fear, no one about in an empty street. This is the classic Simic: a landscape or a room full of vague menace, a sinister light hovering above a clustered huddle of victims. The wail as title and caption is the unheard melody of the scene.

Though there are "persons" serving as dramatis personae or addressees in some of these poems—the "Nellie" of the jazz bar, the "Margaret" of the toy soldiers, a "Martha" here, a "Lucille" there, these women, otherwise unidentified, seem to serve only as rhythmic pretexts in a line—"Bite into [the tomatoes], Martha"; "Better grab hold of that tree, Lucille"—and have none of the human power of the mother and her terrified children in **"The Wail."** I'm not clear about Simic's purpose in resorting to these women's names as vocatives of address; they seem inert, pointless, and in some odd way useless to the poem. Their colorful particularity seems an affront to Simic's bleached-out negations; but they may be his way of affirming the verbal color of life even in the absence of situational color.

In *The Book of Gods and Devils*, for all the fascination of the quasirealistic scenes retrieved from Simic's childhood and youth, it is the poems of slightly surrealist malice that still seem to me Simic's best. I can give only one example, for reasons of space; it is his Black Mass parody of the religious quest, called **"With Eyes Veiled"**:

> First they dream about it,
> Then they go looking for it.
>
> The cities are full of figments.
> Some even carry parcels.
>
> Trust me. it's not there.
> Perhaps in the opposite direction,
> On some street you took by chance
> Having grown tired of the search.
>
> A dusty storefront waits for you
> Full of religious paraphernalia
> Made by the blind. The store
> Padlocked. Night falling.
>
> The blue and gold Madonna in the window
> Smiles with her secret knowledge.
> Exotic rings on her fat fingers.
> A black stain where her child used to be.

This poem displays Simic's characteristic anticlimaxes of disappointment falling after line breaks: we see icons "Made by the blind. The store / Padlocked." This is deflationary, but worse is to come. The degradation of the Madonna into fallen woman, "exotic rings on her fat fingers," is followed by the macabre replacement of Innocence by "a black stain." The successive images here—each one worked, significant, memorable—are "locked into" their respective lines by their placement. Simic's alternation of full sentences and sentence fragments mimics the acquisition of knowledge: an original main-clause existential statement ("A dusty storefront waits for you"; "The . . . Madonna smiles") is followed by one or more short "takes" of perceptual noun-phrase noting: a padlock; dusk or exotic rings; a black stain. Once one has felt the point of these placements—both the anticlimactic line-break ones and the "noticing" noun-phrase ones—the poem is by no means exhausted; the semantic freight of its "paraphernalia," the implications of words like "secret," "fat," and "stains," send forth ripples of suggestion in ever-widening circles. The achieved Simic poem is itself often a "black stain" of innocence destroyed, and, like a stain, it spreads and deepens.

Hotel Insomnia, the volume following *The Book of Gods and Devils*, reminds us that Simic (as he tells us in **"In the Beginning"**) suffers from "lifelong insomnia." This book is more an evolving sequence than a collection of separate poems. What makes it a sequence is the inscribing, on every page without exception, of several words from the repeated epistemological master list that forms a backdrop to the whole. The accompanying table shows the words comprising the master list, and the rough categories into which they fall.

Closure	*Menace*	*Home*	*Nature*
evening	black	father	rain
dark	scream(ing)	child	fire
shadow	red	table	cloud
empty	match	mother	moon

sleep(less)	deaf	door	view
insomnia	blood(y)	wall	sky
death	flame	room	flowers
silent(ce)	unhappy	mirror	eternity
shuffle	candle	corner	time
secret	strange	love	light
night	cross	dream	wind
winter	white	happy	morning
end	list	house	sun(light)
snow	blind	book	sea
afternoon	long	window	leaves
late	fallen	bed	woods
storm	broken	coat	bird
fate	chilly	name	quiet
unknown	dumb	roof	beautiful
whisper	pale	watch	truth
	mute	scribble	infinite
	strange(r)	pencil	life
	greasy	memory	world
	knife	wine	golden
	chewing	boy	day
	slaughter	toy	air
	scream	kiss	
	spike	doll	
	funeral		

Body	People	City	Subhuman
hand	old men	hotel	fly
naked	murderer	street	spider
eye	old woman	sidewalk	web
head	prisoner	city	mice
fist	fortune-teller	(dime)-store	crow(ing)
heart	poet	window	pig
mouth	nun	building(ers)	dog
hair	homeless	ceiling	
breasts	preacher	prison(er)	
tongue	glove	school	
	shoe	cage	
		shop	
		shutter	
		glass	

Like Trakl, Simic moves counters such as these into new configurations within each poem. Each poem becomes a new chess game, but the pieces are often invariant. Here is **"Romantic Sonnet,"** played with some twenty of the magic counters, which I have underlined:

> *Evenings* of sovereign clarity—
> *Wine* and *bread* on the *table*,

> *Mother* praying,
> *Father naked* in *bed*.

> Was I that skinny *boy* stretched out
> In the field behind the *house*,
> His *heart* cut out with a *toy knife*?
> Was I the *crow* hovering over him?

> *Happiness*, you are the bright *red* lining
> of the *dark winter coat*
> Grief wears inside out.

> This is about myself when I'm *remembering*,
> And your *long insomniac's* nails,
> O *Time*, I keep *chewing* and *chewing*.

After reading sixty-six pages in which words like these are heard again and again, chiming with and against each other, one has a comprehensive picture of the mind in which they keep tolling. Simic's world has aged. About one poem in three has something old in it—an old dog, a blind old woman, old snow, shoes grown old, a crippled old man, an old cemetery. In Simic's insomniac nights, the world shrivels, wrinkles, dwindles, both physically and metaphysically. The fly on the pale ceiling enlarges its sinister web, the meadows themselves become a theater of cruelty, children and pigs alike are led to slaughter, a nun carries morphine to the dying.

Even the poems recording a moment of happiness or appetite—**"Country Lunch,"** for instance—are shadowed by foreboding: "A feast in the time of plague— / that's the way it feels today." *Hotel Insomnia* celebrates the "funeral of some lofty vision," according to **"Miss Nostradamus,"** one of its many seeresses, Muses, and fortune-tellers. And the lofty visions go by, in cultural history, almost too fast to count. "Gods trying different costumes / . . . emerg[e] one by one / To serve you"; Hellenism, Christianity, and Materialism fuse in "Aphrodite with arms missing dressed as a nun / Waiting to take your order." It is in this sort of philosophical shorthand that Simic sketches the unnerving persistence of the past into the present.

My favorite poem at the moment in *Hotel Insomnia* is a tour de force called **"Tragic Architecture."** With the reverse prophecy of informed hindsight, Simic now knows what his elementary school classmates became when they grew up—madwoman, murderer, executioner. The potential cruelty of all children is laconically remarked: "The janitor brought us mice to play with." The children have "hearts of stone." And though Simic is a grown man on another continent, he is also forever imprisoned in his past, a boy left behind, forgotten by Time. **"Tragic Architecture"** is a circular poem, framed by its past/present trees in the wind:

> School, prison, trees in the wind,
> I climbed your gloomy stairs,
> Stood in your farthest corners
> With my face to the wall.

> The murderer sat in the front row.
> A mad little Ophelia

Wrote today's date on the blackboard.
The executioner was my best friend.
He already wore black.
The janitor brought us mice to play with.

In that room with its red sunsets—
It was eternity's time to speak,
So we listened
As if our hearts were made of stone.

All of that in ruins now.
Cracked, peeling walls
With every window broken.
Not even a naked light bulb left
For the prisoner forgotten in solitary,
And the school boy left behind
Watching the bare winter trees
Lashed by the driving wind.

The achieved musical form of this poem—solitary sentence-quatrain of the "I"; inventory of schoolmates; sentence-quatrain of the "we"; inventory of memory done in the third person—is typical of Simic's studied arrangements. The more extended sentences serve for reverie; the short declarative sentences serve as bricks to build a world. The entire impossibility of jettisoning a wretched past is more starkly exhibited in Simic than in any psychological treatise. Yet he does not treat his past in a "confessional" way; the material, we may say, remains psychologically unanalyzed while being thoroughly poetically analyzed (by image, by placement, by narrative). Simic's stylistic arrangements of experience suggest that tragic memory has found its appropriate architectural form.

It is not surprising, given Simic's gnomic forms, that he found the boxes of Joseph Cornell—mysterious formal arrangements of synecdochic objects—peculiarly congenial. His homage to Cornell's art—*Dime-Store Alchemy* (1992)—could have, as its motto, the closing sentence of one of its prose poems: "The clarity of one's vision is a work of art." Admirers of Cornell's constructions will be drawn to Simic's "versions" of the boxes illustrated here. One Cornell box, for instance, contains a standing doll obscured by a hedge of twigs taller than she is. Needless to say, there could be many "readings" of this silent form, and perhaps only Simic would give this one:

The chubby doll in a forest of twigs. . . .
A spoiled little girl wearing a straw hat
about to be burnt at the stake.

This prose poem might be better without its final line—"All this is vaguely erotic and sinister"—but Simic likes to embroider mottos under his emblems. It seems to me we would have known that the doll-scene, as he has described it, was both erotic and sinister without being told.

Dime-Store Alchemy offers more, though, than poetic versions of Cornell boxes. It is a book of art theory, full of obiter dicta on how to construct an artwork, a vehicle of reverie, an object that would enrich the imagination of the

viewer and keep him company forever. There are reflections on toys, dreams, fetishes, symbolic objects: "Two sticks leaning against each other make a house." Cornell's art of the scavenger is composed out of "the strangest trash imaginable"; it is an invitation to a labyrinth. The successive alternatives offered in the poem **"Matchbox with a Fly in It"** (deriving from Vasko Popa's "The Little Box," reprinted here by Simic) are as applicable to poems as to Cornell's art-boxes:

Shadow box [phenomena]
Music box [the Muses]
Pill box [Apollo as healer]
A box which contains a puzzle [poetry as enigma]
A box with tiny drawers [stanzas; secret contents]
Navigation box [a directive]
Jewelry box [poem as ornamental]
Sailor's box [vital supplies]
Butterfly box [preserved specimens]
Box stuffed with souvenirs of a sea voyage [memory and displacement]
Magic prison [the presentness of the past]
An empty box [art as illusion]

The reader of any Simic poem has to stop—not to "translate," as I've done in shorthand here, but to feel the individual pressure of each modifying phrase, and to construct the sequential interrelations of the whole. Perhaps the order of some of the phrases above could be shuffled, but the restriction and disillusion of the last two namings in **"Matchbox with a Fly in It"** make us see them as unalterable parts of its closure. The fly of the title is mortality itself, found inside all the boxes, no matter what their aspectual surface. Simic's fly, like Stevens' blackbird, inserts itself everywhere.

For Simic as for Cornell, "the city is a huge image machine," and Cornell's daily wanderings through New York, picking up cast-off objects which he would transform into his profoundly meditated arrangements, match Simic's own observant walks through streets full of cinemas, penny arcades, stores, vending machines, newspapers, and mirrors. No other book by Simic transmits so strongly as *Dime-Store Alchemy* what New York must have meant to him when he first arrived from Europe—"A poetry slot machine offering a jackpot of incommensurable meanings activated by our imagination. Its mystic repertoire has many images."

Myself, I draw the line at words like "incommensurable" and "mystic," but that is perhaps my loss. I really do find poetry commensurable with life—not "mystic" (which for me would lessen its wonder) but rather entirely within the realm of human power, however rarely that power appears. Chirico is quoted by Simic a few pages earlier, uttering a sentiment with which Simic explicitly agrees ("He's right"): "Every object has two aspects: one current one, which we see nearly always and which is seen by men in general; and the other, which is spectral and metaphysical and seen only by rare individuals in moments of clairvoyance." I could understand such a statement if it were put in terms of ascribed value. After all, a perfectly bad painting is to its maker a beloved object, as it is to some of its viewers (see, for example, Bishop's "Poem," on the bad painting by her great-uncle); and even an unlovely house is someone's castle. Perhaps the ascription of value to any object is a form of "clairvoyance," because objects look different seen with the eye of love or the eye of poetic scrutiny. But Chirico doesn't seem to be talking about this sort of invisible halo, which we all can confer on many objects. No: some other claim is being made here. The "rare individuals" that Chirico and Simic have in mind are artists. But is there some aspect of objects seeable only by artists? And if so, is the right word for such an aspect "spectral"? Or "metaphysical"? And if so, is a reader or viewer then privileged to see this "spectral" aspect through the eyes of the artist? Artists make us see many aspects of being, but none of them seem to me either spectral or metaphysical, nor do I feel admitted to a form of "clairvoyance," in the usual occult sense of that word. I am wary of vaguely mystical claims made for poetry and the other arts—as wary as I am of ethical and civic claims, and of truth claims. There are better ways of making good citizens, or laying down laws of ethics, or providing a defense of truth claims, than lyric poetry. Poems, like all human fabrications, from straw huts to theology, are made to our measure and by our measure, and are not above or beyond us. We do not need to ascribe more to art than we ascribe to unaided human powers elsewhere. Language and paint are not metaphysical and forms are not spectral. Patterning is a universal human act; and even when it is extended to the most complex and imaginative and individual patterning, it is still ours and of us, no more. The wonder of art, for me, is precisely that it does *not* belong to some rare or spectral realm. As Stevens said of the poet, "As part of nature he is part of us, / His rarities are ours."

Simic is still enough of a surrealist to want to claim some realm that is edgily outside nature—in nonsense, in philosophy, in paintings like Chirico's, or in boxes like Cornell's. It probably seems like reductionism to him if a critic wants to describe, in knowable human terms, that edge of unreason, that irrational element of poetry (as Stevens called it). The weird angles and colors of Chirico, his mute and looming forms, do indeed want to intimate a realm other than the known world, and the same is true for Cornell's tiny environments, which the eye enters into and lives within. Perhaps critics are of two kinds: those who rest in the strangeness of such environments and truly regard them as alternate forms of existence—"spectral and metaphysical"—and more empirical critics who will not rest until they find the link between those environments and the human ones from which they sprang. Like others, I prize Simic for his stanzas of the eerily inexplicable (manifested in his wonderfully varied means of menace and his formally laconic manner), but I would be very unhappy if the stylistic imagination in them were not intimately linked to recognizable human predicaments. The Language Poets have sometimes made common cause with Simic, and he with them; but where they are often

merely clever, he is clever and horrifying and heartrending. He is also down-to-earth and mockingly skeptical, especially with respect to himself; he never forgets the dime store when he is about his stylistic alchemy. He is certainly the best political poet, in a large sense, on the American scene; his wry emblems outclass, in their stylishness, the heavy-handedness of most social poetry, while remaining more terrifying in their human implications than explicit political documentation. In his plainness of speech, he is of the line of Whitman and Williams, but in the cunning strategies of his forms, he has brought the allegorical subversiveness of eastern European poetry into our native practice. The next generation of political poets will need to be on their mettle if they want to surpass him.

Charles Simic with Molly McQuade (interview date 1995)

SOURCE: "Real America: An Interview with Charles Simic," in *Chicago Review,* Vol. 41, Nos. 2-3, 1995, pp. 13-18.

[*In the following interview, Simic discusses his high school and college years in Chicago.*]

Charles Simic was born in Yugoslavia and came to the U.S. in 1954, when he was sixteen. He went to high school in Oak Park, Illinois, and attended the University of Chicago at night while working by day at the Chicago Sun-Times.

His poetry has been collected in **Selected Poems 1963-1983** *(Braziller, 1985),* **The Book of Gods and Devils** *(Harcourt, 1990), and many other books. His translations include* **Homage to the Lame Wolf: Selected Poems** *by Vasko Popa (Field, 1979),* **Roll Call of Mirrors** *by Ivan Lalić; (Wesleyan University Press, 1987), and* **Selected Poems of Tomaz Salamun** *(Ecco Press, 1987). Simic's essays have been published in* **The Uncertain Certainty** *(University of Michigan Press, 1985) and* **Wonderful Words, Silent Truth** *(Michigan, 1990). He won the Pulitzer Prize for poetry in 1990.*

I interviewed Simic about his education in general and about his Chicago experiences in particular. As a recent immigrant, Simic had an experience at the university which was less than typical. That was what he chose to emphasize, modestly but heartily. In what follows, I've edited the transcript of our interview so that it reads as a first-person essay.

My father was an optimist. He always felt like the money would just sort of appear one day, you know? "Here it is!"

But it never did.

He went along with everything I said, as long as I was healthy and did not break the law. In that respect, my parents were very nice. My father wanted me to be an artist of some sort. I studied painting first. He was happy about that.

When I was a senior in high school, my father, who at one time had been accepted at Columbia University—he never actually went—asked me to apply to Columbia, and I did. I also applied to Purdue and to the University of Chicago. I was accepted at all three places, but discovered that my father didn't have the money to put me through those schools. So I went to Chicago at night and worked during the day at the *Chicago Sun-Times*.

I must say, it was a very strange period in my life. I started college in 1957, an émigré from Yugoslavia living in Oak Park. I had been in the United States for only three years.

I never had much confidence. I didn't even raise the question. Everything happened so quickly. For a long time, I couldn't sort things out. I'm saying this only now; I wasn't thinking it in those days. It seems very strange that I should have come from this to that to that.

I just wanted to drift along. It was easy to live, to get a job. But I had no plans. I couldn't imagine what I would be.

We all came to America as if to an ideal. America was Hollywood, an incredible place. All American movies were made in southern California, and if you were in Europe, you were watching those palm trees in the wind, convertibles, Lauren Bacall, Rita Hayworth. There's something about the place that was very attractive, but also troubling. America was too much, too different, enormous compared to what I knew when I came.

There was something wonderfully reassuring, though, in discovering suffering humanity in America. You'd say, "Okay, *this* I understand. This I understand."

Chicago in those days was a scene that Dostoyevsky would have found congenial and familiar. Chicago was like Dostoyevsky's descriptions of the slums of St. Petersburg: there was ugliness, tremendous ugliness. And impoverished Eastern Europeans. Well, not so impoverished, because they did have jobs. A Ukrainian, let's say, would come to Chicago when he was a boy, get on a shift in some factory and then, because overtime was so well paid, stay for the next forty years. He would speak some English, a little bit of Hungarian, a little bit of Italian, and Polish, because he'd worked for years with those people. But these were the kind of people who were not at home in any culture anymore. They had forgotten their own culture, and they were not participating in American culture. Actually, they didn't speak *any* languages.

They became slaves. They liked the idea! They worked four extra hours every day, and they worked weekends. They just worked—all their lives. When you met them,

you couldn't tell what age they were. They were forty, fifty, sixty; they had a gray look.

The Midwest was a tremendously prosperous place. Yet Chicago was odd, provincial in many respects. The Loop would be dark at eight o'clock in winter—nothing going on. If you went on the el, you would see women going off to the factories, wearing babushkas—journeys that would take an hour and fifteen minutes. You know how, in winter, an el door opens with a blast of really cold air? And you shiver, then the door closes, and there's an artificial heat? It was money, it was work; people got along.

Whenever I go to Chicago, I feel at home, as if I could resume my life. It's not as if I would ever do it. But I know how the place works, who the people are.

Chicago gave me a sense of real America, better than if I'd happened to be in a small town in the Midwest, where everybody, the local pastor, neighbors, would have met me, would have been very friendly.

I wrote a six-part poem that describes a scene on Maxwell Street. I like the anarchy in Chicago, the sense of roughness only a few blocks from the lake—where there were gin mills, honky tonks, all the way down the Chicago River. Those were real dives!

In Chicago, you got a sense of all the streams that America could contain. As an education, it was vivid.

A lot of people were educating themselves. I knew many Chicagoans who were not from Chicago originally, or if they were, they came from the lower class. Eventually, they moved out of that; they wanted to educate themselves. There was a tremendous excitement about it. Everybody was sharing it. God, there is so much fun in the world of art and movies and theater and music. You wanted to know everything. I felt annoyed with myself anytime I would hear names dropped. Somebody would say, "Oh, I don't think Pissarro is as good as . . . um . . . Seurat," and I would think, "Oh my God—I've never heard of those guys!" So I'd go and look them up. You didn't want to be left out.

I'd take huge art books out from the library—just take them home and read them. I couldn't believe it. Take *ten* of them! And I did. I wanted to educate myself totally.

Once you get in the habit of discovery, it doesn't end.

As a University of Chicago student, I went to the campus on the South Side. After the first year, I went to a downtown campus in the Loop. I remember endless trips to the campus at night to get to my classes in Hyde Park.

By the time I got to school, I was tired, because I'd gotten up very early for my job at the *Sun-Times*. It was a union job that started at seven o'clock in the morning. Those were long days. But the good deal about the job was that once you had finished, you could leave. I would start fairly early and then kind of goof off for the rest of the day. I was responsible for preparing a section of the paper which consisted of classified and personal ads. It was a prestigious position—you met all these famous Chicago newspaper people. There was a guy called Irv Kupcinet. (Big nose.) Ann Landers worked there. These people were stars; you were almost afraid to approach them.

I expected that the University of Chicago would be a very intellectual place. I was interviewed by a young fellow—I don't know if he was an instructor or a graduate student or simply an admissions officer—and the first question he asked was what did I think of Henry James.

Henry James is one of the few writers I've never cared for much. Like root vegetables—I can take him or leave him. I found him just so slow, and I didn't care about the people he wrote about. In those days, I really hated him. So I remember having a very awkward conversation. I didn't blurt out, "Oh, no, I don't *like* Henry James!" But . . .

I took a course in contemporary poetry that stopped with Pound and Eliot. I remember wanting to write a paper on Hart Crane.

There were very large classes in the evenings. I remember the winter cold, and having to walk through the el and wait on the platform and go to the Loop. Then I had to change els to get to Oak Park.

That was an interesting crew of people in those big evening classes. I was more interested in the girls than in the boys. There was always somebody I'd accompany to the el, you know. . . . They were kind of touching, small-town girls whose parents didn't have the money or the inclination to send them to college. They came to the city and worked somewhere all day, as secretaries. Some were almost too poor for college. There was a heroic element in what they did.

I remember a slight jealousy, more than regret, when my buddies from Oak Park High School all took off to good schools. Before that, their parents had paid for trips to Europe. I was reminded of my poverty, of my immigrant status. I couldn't do what they did, though I found myself in their world.

I was divided. I was ambivalent, you know. I was embarrassed to be around ethnics. I liked to occasionally sneak in by myself to a place like the Drake Hotel. I liked nice places.

Oak Park was a very classy suburb. Mine was the high school where Hemingway had gone to school, as the teachers told us. I had a French teacher, Miss Miller, and she would say almost daily, "Ernest Hemingway sat here, in my class. I taught him French that he later spoke in France."

The most memorable part of my time at the university was a poetry workshop taught by John Logan. I wasn't a member of the workshop, but I sat in on it, because all of my friends were taking it. A number of poets gathered: Dennis Schmitz, Bill Knott, Marvin Bell, Naomi Lazard, William Hunt. A lot of people.

We showed each other what we were writing—constantly. I was writing bad poems, a lot of bad poems. I suspected they were bad when I was writing them. They were derivative. Derivative of all sorts of people. Every couple of months, I would be in love with someone else.

I had all these great friends: poets, would-be writers, painters. And I would see the guys and sit in on the workshop and go out afterwards, stay up late, and talk about poetry.

Working at the *Sun-Times*, I met an aspiring writer named Robert Burling. He was studying for a Ph.D. in philosophy at the university, and had a job as a receptionist for Marshall Field, publisher of the *Sun-Times*. We got to talking. He was writing poetry, and I was writing poetry. So we decided to split from home and live on the North Side. My parents were fighting, and I wanted to be closer to school and work and Chicago.

We got a little basement apartment that doesn't exist anymore on Dearborn between Goethe and Schiller. Though it had a gorgeous address, the house itself was a crummy old tenement, and our place was in the cellar. The Oak Street beach was close; we could go swimming. I met some more writers at a bar called Figaro on Oak Street. I met Nelson Algren then, not at the bar, but at some party, a couple of times.

He was blunt and very nice. The second time I met him, I had *Life Studies*, a volume of Robert Lowell's poetry, with me; I had a friend who was a great fan of Lowell. So Algren said to me, "What do you want to read that for? A kid like you, just off the boat? Read Whitman, read Sandburg, read Vachel Lindsay."

I took him up on it. I was never very happy with Robert Lowell, anyway. His stuff was foreign to me.

Ours was a very small literary scene. We would have a party in a room with the lights lowered, maybe a couple of candles stuck in Chianti bottles, some kind of primitive record player, and records by Thelonius Monk and Charlie Parker. All the women were in black; it was the existentialist period. People would be reading Camus and Sartre. (Existentialism came to Chicago late.) And they'd have their hair in long bangs so you couldn't see their faces. They smoked a lot. Not much to drink, because everyone was broke. The drink would always be pretty odd: a bottle of rum or kirschwasser, something awful.

This was the hip crowd of the Near-North side, people who liked jazz. Among the older crowd were radicals, leftist intellectuals. There were interesting older people, too, at the university. In a course on sociology, old men who had obviously been in the labor movement in the past would ask tough questions of some young teacher: "Hey, wait a minute!" You know, the kinds of questions college students don't ask, ordinarily. Just because it's in the book doesn't mean it's right, you know?

In those days, much more so than today, intellectuals came from a working-class background—Jewish, Irish. They worked all day long at the railroad, the docks, being a boss in the union, or doing manual labor. And there was a tremendous wisdom behind them.

They were very pleasant. And they all had advice for you. They told you what you should do. There was a tremendous suspicion of the Eastern literary establishment.

When you're young, and even more so if you're an immigrant, you're looking for role models; you want to blend in. I was all ready to blend in, and these guys kept saying, "don't read those books! Remember who you are! You come from the Balkans. you're scum of the earth!"

Sure. I agreed.

They were an influence on me. They prevented me from becoming a phony.

One of the temptations for an immigrant is to outdo the natives—to immediately get a three-piece suit and read Henry James. It seemed too genteel. I wanted something gutsy, fast, full of anger.

Even if I don't mention them in every poem, there is an America of hard-working people in the back of my mind. I do not forget them.

I remember once or twice being in WASPy circles of very informed young men and women who were graduate students, Ph.D. candidates. You'd sense that their dream was to be British. If they were ever to become writers, they would like to be reviewed in the London *Times* and be received at Oxford and Cambridge. They were sort of nice people, but . . .

It has always delighted me that I come from an "inferior" race. There we were in Chicago, sitting around, Polacks and Irish and Italians.

I never believe for a minute that I'm inferior or superior.

Those young men in the three-piece suits—they just didn't know!

David Sofield (review date 13 January 1996)

SOURCE: A review of *A Wedding in Hell,* in *America,* Vol. 174, No. 1, January 13, 1996, p. 18.

[*In the following review, Sofield offers a mixed assessment of* A Wedding in Hell.]

In the prose-poem **"Voice from the Cage,"** God seems to appear as "Mr. Zoo Keeper," and we animals know that "sorrow, sickness, and fleabites are our lot. The rabbits still screw but their weakness is optimism. . . . I've dyed my hair green like Baudelaire. . . . Ours is a circus of quick, terrified glances." End of poem. In the penultimate poem of a *A Wedding in Hell,* entitled **"Mystery Writer,"** God figures as a genre author whose apparent interest is to obscure our understanding of urban life. And this poem begins with the deceptively easy "I figured, well, since I can't sleep / I'll go for a walk."

Occasionally a whole short poem will speak in a welcomely guileless voice, the guilelessness in the end serving to make us face How Awful It Is. **"The World,"** in the poem so named, chooses to "torture me / Every day" with its "many cruel instruments," the torture today being two pictures of a woman and a child, first fleeing and then:

> fallen
> With bloodied heads
> On that same winding road
> With its cloudless sky
> Of late summer
> And its trees shivering
> In the first cool breeze
> On days when we put all
> Our trust into the world
> Only to be deceived.

This is one of the two archetypal Simics, lucid as yet another daybreak that brings us nothing but pain, the language plain, the anger huge and entirely implicit. The other voice, relieving dread yet still in touch with it, gives us breathing room. In **"This morning,"** the speaker begins: "Enter without knocking, hard-working ant." The night passed has been troubled, but "Estella" did come to him, only to vanish:

> You visit the same tailors the mourners do,
> Mr. Ant. I like the silence between us,
> The quiet—that holy state even the rain
> Knows about Listen to her begin to fall,
> As if with eyes closed,
> Muting each drop in her wild-beating heart.

With his customary sure touch, Simic states in his prose book: "I'm in the business of translating what cannot be translated: being and its silence." To transmute passion and its evanescence into a suddenly unironic request to a black ant is worthy of the end of Bishop's "Questions of Travel," in which silence and rain are put to rather other excellent purposes.

Often, it must be said, Simic is notably more oblique than here. Sometimes the complicated oppressiveness of Eastern European (and other) governments is a steady undercurrent, but the syntax is frequently a bit skewed; in nearly 80 pages we are offered the consolation of a single and, as it were, accidental full rhyme. The voice can be detached to the point of unintended listlessness, and poem after poem is so ironically titled that on occasion we are unable to engage any other feeling.

A recurrent strategy is to start a poem in such a way as to require a reader to play constant catch-up, to piece together a prehistory—what happened before the first words are spoken—that begins to make sense of puzzlement. It isn't always possible, or at least it's not always worth the effort. Although the poems are more of a piece than in most books, Simic is a less even writer than one might expect. The great successes are only minimally more realized than the flat failures. Still, no other of these poets begins to manage the astringent, attacking wit Simic commands; one may have to go back to Eliot and his mentors Donne and Shakespeare to find the like.

David Bafer (review date April 1996)

SOURCE: "On Restraint," in *Poetry,* Vol. CLXVIII, No. 1, April, 1996, pp. 33-47.

[*In the following review, Bafer compares the works of Ted Kooser to Simic's* A Wedding in Hell, *finding Simic's poetry taut and evocative.*]

I am not concerned here with artistic timidity, moral constraint, or polite decorum—that is, restraint as puritanic virtue—but rather with tactics of restraint which allow us to gauge a poem's opposite pole, its power and passion. Even Walt Whitman is at his most persuasive when his enthusiasms are informed by subdued counter-pressures. In "Crossing Brooklyn Ferry," those ominous, looming "dark patches," which accompany his confessions of secular guilt, temper his later transcendental encouragements to "flow on . . . with the flood-tide." The poem's polar forces—obliteration and regeneration, liability and acceptance—hold themselves in a kind of checks-and-balance. The result is precarious and powerful. Other poets use different methods of restraint: Dickinson with her severe, compact technique ("After great pain, a formal feeling comes—"); Bishop in her very stance, what Jeredith Merrin calls an "enabling humility." Restraint can ironize, enable, even sustain, a poet's great passions and wildness.

Ted Kooser is the most restrained of the five poets I consider here, if restraint also nominates characteristics like compression and control. A critically undervalued poet, Kooser is a joy to read, even if, every now and then, he may be a little *too* restrained. His touch is so light, and his poems generally so compact, that occasionally there doesn't seem to be enough passion or material at hand. But after all, much of the power of Kooser's work is accretive, since for decades he has been constructing out of individual poems a long, sustained, and important life-work in the manner of Robinson's Tilbury Town, Master's Spoon River, or Hugo's Great Northwest. Throughout his splendid new *Weather Central,* Kooser's individual poems are evocative, often perfectly realized, even as they also become part of his larger project, the creation in poetry of a distinctly Midwestern social text, where

> . . . there
> is something beautiful
>
> about a dirty town in rain,
> where tin cans, rails,
> and toppled shopping carts
> are the sutures of silver
> holding the guts in,
>
> keeping the blue wound closed,
> while over a pawnshop, the plain
> wet flag of a yellow window
> holds out the cautious welcome
> of an embassy.

"Lincoln, Nebraska"

Kooser is highly selective in the amount and type of material he includes in a poem. Only seven of the fifty-eight poems in *Weather Central* are longer than a page; the longest, "City Limits," runs to forty lines. He is a devoted chronicler of the Midwest, but so careful, so meticulous, that even his most modest poems ring with pleasing recognitions:

> It is morning. My father
> in shirtsleeves is sweeping
> the sidewalk in front of his store,
> standing up straight in the bow
> of his gondola, paddling
> the endless gray streets of his life
> with an old yellow oar—
> happy there, hailing his friends.

Here in "The Sweeper," and throughout this book, recognition and connection are Kooser's recurrent longings—the connective goodwill of neighbors, families, and of the images themselves. Notice how he activates the poem's only metaphor exactly halfway through this poem, with "in the bow / of his gondola, paddling," where a plain description of the father's movement turns into the stroke of a gondolier—the absolutely familiar touched with wistful exotica. He is uncanny in selecting such right-seeming metaphors; he is also a realist, a nearly haiku-like imagist whose tropes are rarely dramatically transformative but, rather, clarifying. He wants us to see things more sharply. He connects his deliberate images with a kind of restrained, respectful sanity, like "Aunt Mildred" who "picked up a pencil stub and pinched it hard, / straightened her spine, and wrote a small / but generous letter to the world."

Kooser rarely refers to himself in his work, and then hardly ever in the first person. This kind of restraint is particularly striking in a period when so much poetry is, to parrot Hawthorne's Zenobia, so much "Self, self, self!" The closest Kooser comes to self-portraiture may be the image of the blue heron in the book's first poem, "Etude," where the first-person speaker watches "a Great Blue Heron / fish in the cattails, easing ahead / with the stealth of a lover composing a letter." He sees in the bird's actions and its "blue suit" the reflection of a businessman who "holds down an everyday job / in an office" (like Kooser's own occupation as an insurance executive):

Long days swim beneath the glass top
of his desk, each one alike. On the lip
of each morning, a bubble trembles.

No one has seen him there, writing a letter
to a woman he loves. His pencil is poised
in the air like the beak of a bird.
He would spear the whole world if he could,
toss it and swallow it live.

The letter is a figure for the kind of lifelike text Kooser seems to strive for in his poems. The final sentence with its sudden, dramatic feat is even more effective given this love poem's delicate restraint.

Midway into *Weather Central* we encounter the image of the heron again, in "A Poetry Reading," though by now he's "an old blue heron with yellow eyes," a poet opening his "book on its spine, a split fish." These mere hints are among the most directly self-revealing moments in the book. Kooser reserves his more emotional involvements for his characters, as in the tender "Four Secretaries," where all day, like ordinary sirens, they "call back and forth, / singing their troubled marriage ballads, / their day-care, car-park, landlord songs. . . ."

A far more acclaimed and much-awarded poet, Charles Simic plays the Romantic to Kooser's Realist. They were born in 1938, and 1939, respectively, and have published a dozen volumes apiece. Each is masterful at plain-spoken rhetoric and impeccably tight free-verse techniques; each is skilled at creating memorable individual images as well as coherent patterns of metaphor; miniaturists, each exploits the short poem to great advantage (only two of the seventy poems in *A Wedding in Hell* are longer than a page, and the longest is thirty lines). Simic employs many of the same strategies of restraint that distinguish Kooser's poems.

But Simic's metaphors transform where Kooser's clarify:

In the frying pan
On the stove
I found my love
And me naked.

Chopped onions
Fell on our heads
And made us cry.
it's like a parade,
I told her, confetti
When some guy
Reaches the moon.

"Means of transport,"
She replied obscurely
While we fried.
"Means of transport!"

Simic likes to wink at us "obscurely," as here in a poem that opens with the most restrained of rhetorics but the oddest of metaphors. Lovers as potatoes, or cuts of liver? **"Transport"** takes us into the surreal, as many of his

poems ferry us from the familiar to the entirely alien, from the mundane to the holy, or from the dim to the philosophical (or vice versa). As he professes in another poem, "'I'm crazy about her shrimp!' / I shout to the gods above." Simic is a Postmodern Romantic, a mystic grinding his forehead into the stones though he knows that God is dead and buried, a believer who asserts the transcendent moment but who also perceives that transcendence is likely to send us to the kind of place he describes in **"Pascal's Idea"**: "It was terrifying / And I suppose a bit like / What your heaven and hell combined must be." Poem after poem insists on these kinds of metamorphic changes. I like to amass Kooser's poems, letting them gather in a larger social scene, but I prefer Simic's a few at a time. Too much similar magic at once exposes its tricks.

To American audiences part of Simic's charm derives from his Continental-sounding images and cosmopolitan sensibilities. If he has a riddler's sense of humor, he can also don the Romantic's blackest cape. He recalls Kafka's great European absurdist masterpiece "The Hunger Artist" in the prose poem **"Voice from the Cage,"** where caged animals act out their existential agony: "Sorrow, sickness, and fleabites are our lot. . . . Even the lion doesn't believe the fables anymore. 'Pray to the Lord,' the monkeys shriek." Even the freakish speaker has "dyed [his] hair green like Baudelaire." This contorted display of grotesqueries, like a "circus of quick, terrified glances," is repeated in many poems. Toothless monkeys, "chickens living in a rusty old hearse," a gorilla suit with "silly angel wings," a white cat "picking at the bloody head of a fish"—such often feral malformities are the shadow-images of the faceless soldiers and anonymous "refugees crowding the roads" who also populate Simic's poems. Expatriation, the brutal repetitions of history, the chaos of broken walls, of failed faiths, drive the speaker in **"Explaining a Few Things"** underground, like Dostoevsky's "sick man." Once again, armies and animals are Simic's companions:

Every worm is a martyr,
Every sparrow subject to injustice,
I said to my cat,
Since there was no one else around.

It's raining. In spite of their huge armies
What can the ants do?
And the roach on the wall
Like a waiter in an empty restaurant?

I'm going to the cellar
To stroke the rat caught in a trap.
You watch the sky.
If it clears, scratch on the door.

As crisp and plainly spoken as Kooser's documents to the commonplace, still this poem is a world and an age away from "Lincoln, Nebraska."

Charles Simic has been writing like this for a long time, sharply, seriously, with a rhetoric of restraint but with a vision of haunted strangeness. In fact, I think his talent is growing, as his poems continue to deepen, subtly but surely. The poems of *A Wedding in Hell* are more emotionally absorbing than the work of his famous books of the Seventies, such as *Dismantling the Silence* or *Classic Ballroom Dances*. "O dreams like evening shadows on a windy meadow," he sings in **"A Wedding in Hell,"** "And your hands, Mother, like white mice." His plainness makes these surprises, these pointed and surreal mutations, all the more powerful.

Paul Breslin (review date July 1997)

SOURCE: "Four and a Half Books," in *Poetry,* Vol. CLXX, No. 4, July, 1997, pp. 226-39.

[*In the following review, Breslin asserts that Simic relys on his reputation in* Walking the Black Cat *rather than breaking new poetic ground.*]

The dustjacket blurb for Charles Simic's **Walking the Black Cat** invites us to a world in which "a man waits at a bus stop for the love of his life, a woman (Lady Luck?) he's never met. The world's greatest ventriloquist who sits on a street corner uses passersby as dummies and speaks through us all. Hamlet's ghost walks the hallways of a Vegas motel." And more inducements in the same vein. If only they had proved a less accurate harbinger of the poems themselves—which too often have the contrived goofiness, with portentous hints of significance for "us all," that the blurbist promises. The best ones won't submit to their own glibness altogether, but on the whole I have the sense of a style running on automatic pilot, the urgencies that once called it into existence largely forgotten. Strange events do not erupt, but saunter lazily into view, voiced in such inert syntax and blasé affect as to seem oddly comfortable. Instead of a Borgesian dream tiger, Simic offers the leashed housecat of his title, which is, to judge by its gait, fat, sleepy, and a little bit spoiled.

As an instance of this volume's stylistic lassitude, consider the opening of **"Lone Tree,"** not one of the best passages in the book, but not the worst, either:

> A tree spooked
> By its own evening whispers.
> Afraid to rustle,
> Just now
> Bewitched by the distant sunset.
> Making a noise full of deep
> Misgivings,
> Like bloody razor blades
> Being shuffled.

Lines 3-5 repeat the substance of lines 1-2, as if Simic belatedly had realized how weak the word "spooked" is, evoking B horror movies rather than the Abyss, but couldn't be bothered to start the poem over. **"Misgivings,"** ominously perched on a line by itself, fails to deliver the mystery or threat its isolation promises. And just what sort

of noise do "bloody razor blades / Being shuffled" make, anyway? The syntax is as loose as the diction. Although sentence fragments can give an effect of swift associative leaps, or of surging movement (think of the opening of Williams's "Spring and All"), their main effect here is to slow and muffle the language, forcing verbs into participial or passive constructions, lest they startle or disturb. Throughout the book, there's very little interplay between sentence rhythm and line breaks. Sentences extending more than two or three lines are unusual, and as a rule syntactical pauses and line breaks coincide. Even poems that seem relatively intense often dissipate their force in trivializing endings (e.g., **"Talking to Little Birdies," "Against Winter," "The Something"**).

Simic, of course, is not without talent, and flames of imagination occasionally flicker amid the ashes. The best poems in this collection have a trace of urgency in them, some hint of what may have hurt their maker into poetry, to adapt Auden's phrase about Yeats. Urgency needn't mean largeness of theme; the loneliness of the speaker in **"Late Train"** is palpable, even though (or perhaps because) it makes no claim to cosmic profundity:

> In the empty coach, far in the back,
> I thought I could see one shadowy passenger
> Raising his pale hand to wave to me
> Or to put a watch to his ear,
> While I stretched my neck to hear the tick.

The stretch of the sentence, across five lines, signals a modest increase of energy, and the potential cliché, "pale hand," is rescued by the adjective "shadowy" in the previous line: the hand is the one part of the indistinct figure to catch the light. Others among the better poems have some political steel in them, such as **"Cameo Appearance," "The Conquering Hero Is Tired,"** or **"The Emperor."** In **"Cameo Appearance,"** the horrors Simic witnessed as a child in Yugoslavia become a film to be shown to "the kiddies," in which the poet "had a small, nonspeaking part." The numbed affect that elsewhere seems merely an all-purpose varnish for once seems appropriate to the occasion of speaking. But for the most part, this book is long on manner and short on substance, half-imagined and half-formed. It's time to take the black cat off its leash. Given more exercise and freedom, it may actually catch something.

FURTHER READING

Criticism

Ford, Mark. "The Muse as Cook." *Times Literary Supplement,* No. 4814 (7 July 1995): 15.
    Review of *The Unemployed Fortune-Teller* and *Frightening Toys* that examines Simic's ideas about poetry.

Jackson, Richard. "Charles Simic's Mythologies." In *The Dismantling of Time in Contemporary Poetry*, pp. 240-79. Tuscaloosa and London: University of Alabama Press, 1988.

Examines Simic's sense of mythic time.

Nash, Susan Smith. A review of *Walking the Black Cat*. *World Literature Today* 71, No. 4 (Autumn 1997): 793-94.

Praises *Walking the Black Cat* as a coherent and unified presentation of Simic's major themes.

Simic, Charles. "Composition." *New Literary History* IX, No. 1 (Autumn 1977): 149-51.

Brief essay in which Simic describes his poetics of composition.

Additional coverage of Simic's life and career is contained in the following sources published by the Gale Group: *Contemporary Authors*, Vols. 29-32R; *Contemporary Authors Autobiography Series*, Vol. 4; *Contemporary Authors New Revision Series*, Vols. 12, 33, 52, 61; *DISCovering Authors Modules: Poets*; *Dictionary of Literary Biography*, Vol. 105; *Major 20th-Century Writers*, Vol. 2.

How to Use This Index

The main references

> **Calvino, Italo**
>   1923-1985 .... CLC **5, 8, 11, 22, 33, 39,**
>   **73; SSC 3**

list all author entries in the following Gale Literary Criticism series:

> **BLC** = *Black Literature Criticism*
> **CLC** = *Contemporary Literary Criticism*
> **CLR** = *Children's Literature Review*
> **CMLC** = *Classical and Medieval Literature Criticism*
> **DA** = *DISCovering Authors*
> **DAB** = *DISCovering Authors: British*
> **DAC** = *DISCovering Authors: Canadian*
> **DAM** = *DISCovering Authors: Modules*
>   **DRAM:** *Dramatists Module;* **MST:** *Most-Studied Authors Module;*
>   **MULT:** *Multicultural Authors Module;* **NOV:** *Novelists Module;*
> **POET:** *Poets Module;* **POP:** *Popular Fiction and Genre Authors Module*
> **DC** = *Drama Criticism*
> **HLC** = *Hispanic Literature Criticism*
> **LC** = *Literature Criticism from 1400 to 1800*
> **NCLC** = *Nineteenth-Century Literature Criticism*
> **NNAL** = *Native North American Literature*
> **PC** = *Poetry Criticism*
> **SSC** = *Short Story Criticism*
> **TCLC** = *Twentieth-Century Literary Criticism*
> **WLC** = *World Literature Criticism, 1500 to the Present*

The cross-references

> See also CANR 23; CA 85-88;
> obituary CA116

list all author entries in the following Gale biographical and literary sources:

> **AAYA** = *Authors & Artists for Young Adults*
> **AITN** = *Authors in the News*
> **BEST** = *Bestsellers*
> **BW** = *Black Writers*
> **CA** = *Contemporary Authors*
> **CAAS** = *Contemporary Authors Autobiography Series*
> **CABS** = *Contemporary Authors Bibliographical Series*
> **CANR** = *Contemporary Authors New Revision Series*
> **CAP** = *Contemporary Authors Permanent Series*
> **CDALB** = *Concise Dictionary of American Literary Biography*
> **CDBLB** = *Concise Dictionary of British Literary Biography*
> **DLB** = *Dictionary of Literary Biography*
> **DLBD** = *Dictionary of Literary Biography Documentary Series*
> **DLBY** = *Dictionary of Literary Biography Yearbook*
> **HW** = *Hispanic Writers*
> **JRDA** = *Junior DISCovering Authors*
> **MAICYA** = *Major Authors and Illustrators for Children and Young Adults*
> **MTCW** = *Major 20th-Century Writers*
> **SAAS** = *Something about the Author Autobiography Series*
> **SATA** = *Something about the Author*
> **YABC** = *Yesterday's Authors of Books for Children*

Literary Criticism Series
Cumulative Author Index

20/1631
See Upward, Allen

A/C Cross
See Lawrence, T(homas) E(dward)

Abasiyanik, Sait Faik 1906-1954
See Sait Faik
See also CA 123

Abbey, Edward 1927-1989 .... **CLC 36, 59**
See also CA 45-48; 128; CANR 2, 41; DA3;
MTCW 2

Abbott, Lee K(ittredge) 1947- .... **CLC 48**
See also CA 124; CANR 51; DLB 130

Abe, Kobo 1924-1993 ...... **CLC 8, 22, 53, 81;
DAM NOV**
See also CA 65-68; 140; CANR 24, 60;
DLB 182; MTCW 1, 2

Abelard, Peter c. 1079-c. 1142 ...... **CMLC 11**
See also DLB 115, 208

Abell, Kjeld 1901-1961 .... **CLC 15**
See also CA 111

Abish, Walter 1931- .... **CLC 22**
See also CA 101; CANR 37; DLB 130

Abrahams, Peter (Henry) 1919- .... **CLC 4**
See also BW 1; CA 57-60; CANR 26; DLB
117; MTCW 1, 2

Abrams, M(eyer) H(oward) 1912- ... **CLC 24**
See also CA 57-60; CANR 13, 33; DLB 67

Abse, Dannie 1923- . **CLC 7, 29; DAB; DAM
POET**
See also CA 53-56; CAAS 1; CANR 4, 46,
74; DLB 27; MTCW 1

Achebe, (Albert) Chinua(lumogu) 1930-
.... **CLC 1, 3, 5, 7, 11, 26, 51, 75, 127;
BLC 1; DA; DAB; DAC; DAM MST,
MULT, NOV; WLC**
See also AAYA 15; BW 2, 3; CA 1-4R;
CANR 6, 26, 47; CLR 20; DA3; DLB
117; MAICYA; MTCW 1, 2; SATA 38,
40; SATA-Brief 38

Acker, Kathy 1948-1997 .... **CLC 45, 111**
See also CA 117; 122; 162; CANR 55

Ackroyd, Peter 1949- .... **CLC 34, 52**
See also CA 123; 127; CANR 51, 74; DLB
155; INT 127; MTCW 1

Acorn, Milton 1923- .... **CLC 15; DAC**
See also CA 103; DLB 53; INT 103

Adamov, Arthur 1908-1970 .... **CLC 4, 25;
DAM DRAM**
See also CA 17-18; 25-28R; CAP 2; MTCW
1

Adams, Alice (Boyd) 1926-1999 .. **CLC 6, 13,
46; SSC 24**
See also CA 81-84; 179; CANR 26, 53, 75,
88; DLBY 86; INT CANR-26; MTCW 1,
2

Adams, Andy 1859-1935 .... **TCLC 56**
See also YABC 1

Adams, Brooks 1848-1927 .... **TCLC 80**

See also CA 123; DLB 47

Adams, Douglas (Noel) 1952- .... **CLC 27, 60;
DAM POP**
See also AAYA 4; BEST 89:3; CA 106;
CANR 34, 64; DA3; DLBY 83; JRDA;
MTCW 1

Adams, Francis 1862-1893 .... **NCLC 33**

Adams, Henry (Brooks) 1838-1918 . **TCLC 4,
52; DA; DAB; DAC; DAM MST**
See also CA 104; 133; CANR 77; DLB 12,
47, 189; MTCW 1

Adams, Richard (George) 1920- ... **CLC 4, 5,
18; DAM NOV**
See also AAYA 16; AITN 1, 2; CA 49-52;
CANR 3, 35; CLR 20; JRDA; MAICYA;
MTCW 1, 2; SATA 7, 69

Adamson, Joy(-Friederike Victoria)
1910-1980 .... **CLC 17**
See also CA 69-72; 93-96; CANR 22;
MTCW 1; SATA 11; SATA-Obit 22

Adcock, Fleur 1934- .... **CLC 41**
See also CA 25-28R, 182; CAAE 182;
CAAS 23; CANR 11, 34, 69; DLB 40

Addams, Charles (Samuel) 1912-1988
.... **CLC 30**
See also CA 61-64; 126; CANR 12, 79

Addams, Jane 1860-1945 .... **TCLC 76**

Addison, Joseph 1672-1719 .... **LC 18**
See also CDBLB 1660-1789; DLB 101

Adler, Alfred (F.) 1870-1937 .... **TCLC 61**
See also CA 119; 159

Adler, C(arole) S(chwerdtfeger) 1932-
.... **CLC 35**
See also AAYA 4; CA 89-92; CANR 19,
40; JRDA; MAICYA; SAAS 15; SATA
26, 63, 102

Adler, Renata 1938- .... **CLC 8, 31**
See also CA 49-52; CANR 5, 22, 52;
MTCW 1

Ady, Endre 1877-1919 .... **TCLC 11**
See also CA 107

A.E. 1867-1935 .... **TCLC 3, 10**
See also Russell, George William

Aeschylus 525B.C.-456B.C. .. **CMLC 11; DA;
DAB; DAC; DAM DRAM, MST; DC 8;
WLCS**
See also DLB 176

Aesop 620(?)B.C.-564(?)B.C. .... **CMLC 24**
See also CLR 14; MAICYA; SATA 64

Affable Hawk
See MacCarthy, Sir(Charles Otto) Desmond

Africa, Ben
See Bosman, Herman Charles

Afton, Effie
See Harper, Frances Ellen Watkins

Agapida, Fray Antonio
See Irving, Washington

Agee, James (Rufus) 1909-1955 ...... **TCLC 1,
19; DAM NOV**
See also AITN 1; CA 108; 148; CDALB
1941-1968; DLB 2, 26, 152; MTCW 1

Aghill, Gordon
See Silverberg, Robert

Agnon, S(hmuel) Y(osef Halevi) 1888-1970
CLC 4, 8, 14; SSC 30
See also CA 17-18; 25-28R; CANR 60;
CAP 2; MTCW 1, 2

Agrippa von Nettesheim, Henry Cornelius
1486-1535 .... **LC 27**

Aguilera Malta, Demetrio 1909-1981
See also CA 111; 124; CANR 87; DAM
MULT, NOV; DLB 145; HLCS 1; HW 1

Agustini, Delmira 1886-1914
See also CA 166; HLCS 1; HW 1, 2

Aherne, Owen
See Cassill, R(onald) V(erlin)

Ai 1947- .... **CLC 4, 14, 69**
See also CA 85-88; CAAS 13; CANR 70;
DLB 120

Aickman, Robert (Fordyce) 1914-1981
.... **CLC 57**
See also CA 5-8R; CANR 3, 72

Aiken, Conrad (Potter) 1889-1973 .... **CLC 1,
3, 5, 10, 52; DAM NOV, POET; PC 26;
SSC 9**
See also CA 5-8R; 45-48; CANR 4, 60;
CDALB 1929-1941; DLB 9, 45, 102;
MTCW 1, 2; SATA 3, 30

Aiken, Joan (Delano) 1924- .... **CLC 35**
See also AAYA 1, 25; CA 9-12R; 182;
CAAE 182; CANR 4, 23, 34, 64; CLR 1,
19; DLB 161; JRDA; MAICYA; MTCW
1; SAAS 1; SATA 2, 30, 73; SATA-Essay
109

Ainsworth, William Harrison 1805-1882
NCLC 13
See also DLB 21; SATA 24

Aitmatov, Chingiz (Torekulovich) 1928-
.... **CLC 71**
See also CA 103; CANR 38; MTCW 1;
SATA 56

Akers, Floyd
See Baum, L(yman) Frank

Akhmadulina, Bella Akhatovna 1937-
.... **CLC 53; DAM POET**
See also CA 65-68

Akhmatova, Anna 1888-1966 ..... **CLC 11, 25,
64, 126; DAM POET; PC 2**
See also CA 19-20; 25-28R; CANR 35;
CAP 1; DA3; MTCW 1, 2

Aksakov, Sergei Timofeyvich 1791-1859
NCLC 2
See also DLB 198

60127; BLC 1; DA; DAB; DAC; DAM
MST, MULT, NOV, POP; DC 1; SSC
10, 33; WLC
See also AAYA 4; BW 1; CA 1-4R; 124;
CABS 1; CANR 3, 24; CDALB 1941-
1968; DA3; DLB 2, 7, 33; DLBY 87;
MTCW 1, 2; SATA 9; SATA-Obit 54

Ballard, J(ames) G(raham) 1930- . **CLC 3, 6,
14, 36; DAM NOV, POP; SSC 1**
See also AAYA 3; CA 5-8R; CANR 15, 39,
65; DA3; DLB 14, 207; MTCW 1, 2;
SATA 93

Balmont, Konstantin (Dmitriyevich)
1867-1943 .... **TCLC 11**
See also CA 109; 155

Baltausis, Vincas
See Mikszath, Kalman

Balzac, Honore de 1799-1850 ... **NCLC 5, 35,
53; DA; DAB; DAC; DAM MST, NOV;
SSC 5; WLC**
See also DA3; DLB 119

Bambara, Toni Cade 1939-1995 ...... **CLC 19,
88; BLC 1; DA; DAC; DAM MST,
MULT; SSC 35; WLCS**
See also AAYA 5; BW 2, 3; CA 29-32R;
150; CANR 24, 49, 81; CDALBS; DA3;
DLB 38; MTCW 1, 2; SATA 112

Bamdad, A.
See Shamlu, Ahmad

Banat, D. R.
See Bradbury, Ray (Douglas)

Bancroft, Laura
See Baum, L(yman) Frank

Banim, John 1798-1842 .... **NCLC 13**
See also DLB 116, 158, 159

Banim, Michael 1796-1874 .... **NCLC 13**
See also DLB 158, 159

Banjo, The
See Paterson, A(ndrew) B(arton)

Banks, Iain
See Banks, Iain M(enzies)

Banks, Iain M(enzies) 1954- .... **CLC 34**
See also CA 123; 128; CANR 61; DLB 194;
INT 128

Banks, Lynne Reid .... **CLC 23**
See also Reid Banks, Lynne AAYA 6

Banks, Russell 1940- .... **CLC 37, 72**
See also CA 65-68; CAAS 15; CANR 19,
52, 73; DLB 130

Banville, John 1945- .... **CLC 46, 118**
See also CA 117; 128; DLB 14; INT 128

Banville, Theodore (Faullain) de 1832-1891
NCLC 9

Baraka, Amiri 1934- . **CLC 1, 2, 3, 5, 10, 14,
33, 115; BLC 1; DA; DAC; DAM MST,
MULT, POET, POP; DC 6; PC 4;
WLCS**
See also Jones, LeRoi BW 2, 3; CA 21-24R;
CABS 3; CANR 27, 38, 61; CDALB
1941-1968; DA3; DLB 5, 7, 16, 38;
DLBD 8; MTCW 1, 2

Barbauld, Anna Laetitia 1743-1825
.... **NCLC 50**
See also DLB 107, 109, 142, 158

Barbellion, W. N. P. .... **TCLC 24**
See also Cummings, Bruce F(rederick)

Barbera, Jack (Vincent) 1945- .... **CLC 44**
See also CA 110; CANR 45

Barbey d'Aurevilly, Jules Amedee 1808-1889
NCLC 1; SSC 17
See also DLB 119

Barbour, John c. 1316-1395 .... **CMLC 33**
See also DLB 146

Barbusse, Henri 1873-1935 .... **TCLC 5**
See also CA 105; 154; DLB 65

Barclay, Bill
See Moorcock, Michael (John)

Barclay, William Ewert
See Moorcock, Michael (John)

Barea, Arturo 1897-1957 .... **TCLC 14**
See also CA 111

Barfoot, Joan 1946- .... **CLC 18**
See also CA 105

Barham, Richard Harris 1788-1845
.... **NCLC 77**
See also DLB 159

Baring, Maurice 1874-1945 .... **TCLC 8**
See also CA 105; 168; DLB 34

Baring-Gould, Sabine 1834-1924 ... **TCLC 88**
See also DLB 156, 190

Barker, Clive 1952- ...... **CLC 52; DAM POP**
See also AAYA 10; BEST 90:3; CA 121;
129; CANR 71; DA3; INT 129; MTCW
1, 2

Barker, George Granville 1913-1991 . **CLC 8,
48; DAM POET**
See also CA 9-12R; 135; CANR 7, 38; DLB
20; MTCW 1

Barker, Harley Granville
See Granville-Barker, Harley
See also DLB 10

Barker, Howard 1946- .... **CLC 37**
See also CA 102; DLB 13

Barker, Jane 1652-1732 .... **LC 42**

Barker, Pat(ricia) 1943- .... **CLC 32, 94**
See also CA 117; 122; CANR 50; INT 122

Barlach, Ernst (Heinrich) 1870-1938
.... **TCLC 84**
See also CA 178; DLB 56, 118

Barlow, Joel 1754-1812 .... **NCLC 23**
See also DLB 37

Barnard, Mary (Ethel) 1909- .... **CLC 48**
See also CA 21-22; CAP 2

Barnes, Djuna 1892-1982 .... **CLC 3, 4, 8, 11,
29, 127; SSC 3**
See also CA 9-12R; 107; CANR 16, 55;
DLB 4, 9, 45; MTCW 1, 2

Barnes, Julian (Patrick) 1946- .... **CLC 42;
DAB**
See also CA 102; CANR 19, 54; DLB 194;
DLBY 93; MTCW 1

Barnes, Peter 1931- .... **CLC 5, 56**
See also CA 65-68; CAAS 12; CANR 33,
34, 64; DLB 13; MTCW 1

Barnes, William 1801-1886 .... **NCLC 75**
See also DLB 32

Baroja (y Nessi), Pio 1872-1956 ..... **TCLC 8;
HLC 1**
See also CA 104

Baron, David
See Pinter, Harold

Baron Corvo
See Rolfe, Frederick (William Serafino
Austin Lewis Mary)

Barondess, Sue K(aufman) 1926-1977
.... **CLC 8**
See also Kaufman, Sue CA 1-4R; 69-72;
CANR 1

Baron de Teive
See Pessoa, Fernando (Antonio Nogueira)

Baroness Von S.
See Zangwill, Israel

Barres, (Auguste-) Maurice 1862-1923
.... **TCLC 47**
See also CA 164; DLB 123

Barreto, Afonso Henrique de Lima
See Lima Barreto, Afonso Henrique de

Barrett, (Roger) Syd 1946- .... **CLC 35**

Barrett, William (Christopher) 1913-1992
CLC 27
See also CA 13-16R; 139; CANR 11, 67;
INT CANR-11

Barrie, J(ames) M(atthew) 1860-1937
.... **TCLC 2; DAB; DAM DRAM**
See also CA 104; 136; CANR 77; CDBLB
1890-1914; CLR 16; DA3; DLB 10, 141,
156; MAICYA; MTCW 1; SATA 100;
YABC 1

Barrington, Michael
See Moorcock, Michael (John)

Barrol, Grady
See Bograd, Larry

Barry, Mike
See Malzberg, Barry N(athaniel)

Barry, Philip 1896-1949 .... **TCLC 11**
See also CA 109; DLB 7

Bart, Andre Schwarz
See Schwarz-Bart, Andre

Barth, John (Simmons) 1930- ... **CLC 1, 2, 3,
5, 7, 9, 10, 14, 27, 51, 89; DAM NOV;
SSC 10**
See also AITN 1, 2; CA 1-4R; CABS 1;
CANR 5, 23, 49, 64; DLB 2; MTCW 1

Barthelme, Donald 1931-1989 ... **CLC 1, 2, 3,
5, 6, 8, 13, 23, 46, 59, 115; DAM NOV;
SSC 2**
See also CA 21-24R; 129; CANR 20, 58;
DA3; DLB 2; DLBY 80, 89; MTCW 1, 2;
SATA 7; SATA-Obit 62

Barthelme, Frederick 1943- ...... **CLC 36, 117**
See also CA 114; 122; CANR 77; DLBY
85; INT 122

Barthes, Roland (Gerard) 1915-1980
.... **CLC 24, 83**
See also CA 130; 97-100; CANR 66;
MTCW 1, 2

Barzun, Jacques (Martin) 1907- ...... **CLC 51**
See also CA 61-64; CANR 22

Bashevis, Isaac
See Singer, Isaac Bashevis

Bashkirtseff, Marie 1859-1884 .... **NCLC 27**

Basho
See Matsuo Basho

Basil of Caesaria c. 330-379 .... **CMLC 35**

Bass, Kingsley B., Jr.
See Bullins, Ed

Bass, Rick 1958- .... **CLC 79**
See also CA 126; CANR 53; DLB 212

Bassani, Giorgio 1916- .... **CLC 9**
See also CA 65-68; CANR 33; DLB 128,
177; MTCW 1

Bastos, Augusto (Antonio) Roa
See Roa Bastos, Augusto (Antonio)

Bataille, Georges 1897-1962 .... **CLC 29**
See also CA 101; 89-92

Bates, H(erbert) E(rnest) 1905-1974
..... **CLC 46; DAB; DAM POP; SSC 10**
See also CA 93-96; 45-48; CANR 34; DA3;
DLB 162, 191; MTCW 1, 2

Bauchart
See Camus, Albert

Baudelaire, Charles 1821-1867 . **NCLC 6, 29,
55; DA; DAB; DAC; DAM MST,
POET; PC 1; SSC 18; WLC**
See also DA3

Baudrillard, Jean 1929- .... **CLC 60**

Baum, L(yman) Frank 1856-1919 ... **TCLC 7**
See also CA 108; 133; CLR 15; DLB 22;
JRDA; MAICYA; MTCW 1, 2; SATA 18,
100

Baum, Louis F.
See Baum, L(yman) Frank

Baumbach, Jonathan 1933- .... **CLC 6, 23**
See also CA 13-16R; CAAS 5; CANR 12,
66; DLBY 80; INT CANR-12; MTCW 1

Bausch, Richard (Carl) 1945- .... **CLC 51**
See also CA 101; CAAS 14; CANR 43, 61,
87; DLB 130

Baxter, Charles (Morley) 1947- . **CLC 45, 78;
DAM POP**
See also CA 57-60; CANR 40, 64; DLB
130; MTCW 2

See also AAYA 10; CA 69-72; CANR 11, 42, 79; JRDA; SAAS 4; SATA 41, 87; SATA-Brief 27

Bennett, Louise (Simone) 1919- ...... **CLC 28; BLC 1; DAM MULT**
See also BW 2, 3; CA 151; DLB 117

Benson, E(dward) F(rederic) 1867-1940 **TCLC 27**
See also CA 114; 157; DLB 135, 153

Benson, Jackson J. 1930- .... **CLC 34**
See also CA 25-28R; DLB 111

Benson, Sally 1900-1972 .... **CLC 17**
See also CA 19-20; 37-40R; CAP 1; SATA 1, 35; SATA-Obit 27

Benson, Stella 1892-1933 .... **TCLC 17**
See also CA 117; 155; DLB 36, 162

Bentham, Jeremy 1748-1832 .... **NCLC 38**
See also DLB 107, 158

Bentley, E(dmund) C(lerihew) 1875-1956 **TCLC 12**
See also CA 108; DLB 70

Bentley, Eric (Russell) 1916- .... **CLC 24**
See also CA 5-8R; CANR 6, 67; INT CANR-6

Beranger, Pierre Jean de 1780-1857
.... **NCLC 34**

Berdyaev, Nicolas
See Berdyaev, Nikolai (Aleksandrovich)

Berdyaev, Nikolai (Aleksandrovich) 1874-1948 .... **TCLC 67**
See also CA 120; 157

Berdyayev, Nikolai (Aleksandrovich)
See Berdyaev, Nikolai (Aleksandrovich)

Berendt, John (Lawrence) 1939- ...... **CLC 86**
See also CA 146; CANR 75; DA3; MTCW 1

Beresford, J(ohn) D(avys) 1873-1947
.... **TCLC 81**
See also CA 112; 155; DLB 162, 178, 197

Bergelson, David 1884-1952 .... **TCLC 81**

Berger, Colonel
See Malraux, (Georges-)Andre

Berger, John (Peter) 1926- .... **CLC 2, 19**
See also CA 81-84; CANR 51, 78; DLB 14, 207

Berger, Melvin H. 1927- .... **CLC 12**
See also CA 5-8R; CANR 4; CLR 32; SAAS 2; SATA 5, 88

Berger, Thomas (Louis) 1924- .. **CLC 3, 5, 8, 11, 18, 38; DAM NOV**
See also CA 1-4R; CANR 5, 28, 51; DLB 2; DLBY 80; INT CANR-28; MTCW 1, 2

Bergman, (Ernst) Ingmar 1918- . **CLC 16, 72**
See also CA 81-84; CANR 33, 70; MTCW 2

Bergson, Henri(-Louis) 1859-1941 . **TCLC 32**
See also CA 164

Bergstein, Eleanor 1938- .... **CLC 4**
See also CA 53-56; CANR 5

Berkoff, Steven 1937- .... **CLC 56**
See also CA 104; CANR 72

Bermant, Chaim (Icyk) 1929- .... **CLC 40**
See also CA 57-60; CANR 6, 31, 57

Bern, Victoria
See Fisher, M(ary) F(rances) K(ennedy)

Bernanos, (Paul Louis) Georges 1888-1948 **TCLC 3**
See also CA 104; 130; DLB 72

Bernard, April 1956- .... **CLC 59**
See also CA 131

Berne, Victoria
See Fisher, M(ary) F(rances) K(ennedy)

Bernhard, Thomas 1931-1989 ..... **CLC 3, 32, 61**
See also CA 85-88; 127; CANR 32, 57; DLB 85, 124; MTCW 1

Bernhardt, Sarah (Henriette Rosine) 1844-1923 .... **TCLC 75**

See also CA 157

Berriault, Gina 1926-1999 .... **CLC 54, 109; SSC 30**
See also CA 116; 129; 185; CANR 66; DLB 130

Berrigan, Daniel 1921- .... **CLC 4**
See also CA 33-36R; CAAS 1; CANR 11, 43, 78; DLB 5

Berrigan, Edmund Joseph Michael, Jr. 1934-1983
See Berrigan, Ted
See also CA 61-64; 110; CANR 14

Berrigan, Ted .... **CLC 37**
See also Berrigan, Edmund Joseph Michael, Jr. DLB 5, 169

Berry, Charles Edward Anderson 1931-
See Berry, Chuck
See also CA 115

Berry, Chuck .... **CLC 17**
See also Berry, Charles Edward Anderson

Berry, Jonas
See Ashbery, John (Lawrence)

Berry, Wendell (Erdman) 1934- ... **CLC 4, 6, 8, 27, 46; DAM POET; PC 28**
See also AITN 1; CA 73-76; CANR 50, 73; DLB 5, 6; MTCW 1

Berryman, John 1914-1972 ... **CLC 1, 2, 3, 4, 6, 8, 10, 13, 25, 62; DAM POET**
See also CA 13-16; 33-36R; CABS 2; CANR 35; CAP 1; CDALB 1941-1968; DLB 48; MTCW 1, 2

Bertolucci, Bernardo 1940- .... **CLC 16**
See also CA 106

Berton, Pierre (Francis Demarigny) 1920- **CLC 104**
See also CA 1-4R; CANR 2, 56; DLB 68; SATA 99

Bertrand, Aloysius 1807-1841 .... **NCLC 31**

Bertran de Born c. 1140-1215 .... **CMLC 5**

Besant, Annie (Wood) 1847-1933 ..... **TCLC 9**
See also CA 105; 185

Bessie, Alvah 1904-1985 .... **CLC 23**
See also CA 5-8R; 116; CANR 2, 80; DLB 26

Bethlen, T. D.
See Silverberg, Robert

Beti, Mongo . **CLC 27; BLC 1; DAM MULT**
See also Biyidi, Alexandre CANR 79

Betjeman, John 1906-1984 . **CLC 2, 6, 10, 34, 43; DAB; DAM MST, POET**
See also CA 9-12R; 112; CANR 33, 56; CDBLB 1945-1960; DA3; DLB 20; DLBY 84; MTCW 1, 2

Bettelheim, Bruno 1903-1990 .... **CLC 79**
See also CA 81-84; 131; CANR 23, 61; DA3; MTCW 1, 2

Betti, Ugo 1892-1953 .... **TCLC 5**
See also CA 104; 155

Betts, Doris (Waugh) 1932- ...... **CLC 3, 6, 28**
See also CA 13-16R; CANR 9, 66, 77; DLBY 82; INT CANR-9

Bevan, Alistair
See Roberts, Keith (John Kingston)

Bey, Pilaff
See Douglas, (George) Norman

Bialik, Chaim Nachman 1873-1934
.... **TCLC 25**
See also CA 170

Bickerstaff, Isaac
See Swift, Jonathan

Bidart, Frank 1939- .... **CLC 33**
See also CA 140

Bienek, Horst 1930- .... **CLC 7, 11**
See also CA 73-76; DLB 75

Bierce, Ambrose (Gwinett) 1842-1914(?) **TCLC 1, 7, 44; DA; DAC; DAM MST; SSC 9; WLC**

See also CA 104; 139; CANR 78; CDALB 1865-1917; DA3; DLB 11, 12, 23, 71, 74, 186

Biggers, Earl Derr 1884-1933 .... **TCLC 65**
See also CA 108; 153

Billings, Josh
See Shaw, Henry Wheeler

Billington, (Lady) Rachel (Mary) 1942-
.... **CLC 43**
See also AITN 2; CA 33-36R; CANR 44

Binyon, T(imothy) J(ohn) 1936- .... **CLC 34**
See also CA 111; CANR 28

Bion 335B.C.-245B.C. .... **CMLC 39**

Bioy Casares, Adolfo 1914-1999 ... **CLC 4, 8, 13, 88; DAM MULT; HLC 1; SSC 17**
See also CA 29-32R; 177; CANR 19, 43, 66; DLB 113; HW 1, 2; MTCW 1, 2

Bird, Cordwainer
See Ellison, Harlan (Jay)

Bird, Robert Montgomery 1806-1854
.... **NCLC 1**
See also DLB 202

Birkerts, Sven 1951- .... **CLC 116**
See also CA 128; 133; 176; CAAE 176; CAAS 29; INT 133

Birney, (Alfred) Earle 1904-1995 .. **CLC 1, 4, 6, 11; DAC; DAM MST, POET**
See also CA 1-4R; CANR 5, 20; DLB 88; MTCW 1

Biruni, al 973-1048(?) .... **CMLC 28**

Bishop, Elizabeth 1911-1979 ..... **CLC 1, 4, 9, 13, 15, 32; DA; DAC; DAM MST, POET; PC 3**
See also CA 5-8R; 89-92; CABS 2; CANR 26, 61; CDALB 1968-1988; DA3; DLB 5, 169; MTCW 1, 2; SATA-Obit 24

Bishop, John 1935- .... **CLC 10**
See also CA 105

Bissett, Bill 1939- .... **CLC 18; PC 14**
See also CA 69-72; CAAS 19; CANR 15; DLB 53; MTCW 1

Bissoondath, Neil (Devindra) 1955-
.... **CLC 120; DAC**
See also CA 136

Bitov, Andrei (Georgievich) 1937- ... **CLC 57**
See also CA 142

Biyidi, Alexandre 1932-
See Beti, Mongo
See also BW 1, 3; CA 114; 124; CANR 81; DA3; MTCW 1, 2

Bjarme, Brynjolf
See Ibsen, Henrik (Johan)

Bjoernson, Bjoernstjerne (Martinius) 1832-1910 .... **TCLC 7, 37**
See also CA 104

Black, Robert
See Holdstock, Robert P.

Blackburn, Paul 1926-1971 .... **CLC 9, 43**
See also CA 81-84; 33-36R; CANR 34; DLB 16; DLBY 81

Black Elk 1863-1950 .... **TCLC 33; DAM MULT**
See also CA 144; MTCW 1; NNAL

Black Hobart
See Sanders, (James) Ed(ward)

Blacklin, Malcolm
See Chambers, Aidan

Blackmore, R(ichard) D(oddridge) 1825-1900 .... **TCLC 27**
See also CA 120; DLB 18

Blackmur, R(ichard) P(almer) 1904-1965 **CLC 2, 24**
See also CA 11-12; 25-28R; CANR 71; CAP 1; DLB 63

Black Tarantula
See Acker, Kathy

Blackwood, Algernon (Henry) 1869-1951 **TCLC 5**
See also CA 105; 150; DLB 153, 156, 178

Brooks, George
  See Baum, L(yman) Frank
Brooks, Gwendolyn 1917- ..... CLC 1, 2, 4, 5,
    15, 49, 125; BLC 1; DA; DAC; DAM
    MST, MULT, POET; PC 7; WLC
  See also AAYA 20; AITN 1; BW 2, 3; CA
    1-4R; CANR 1, 27, 52, 75; CDALB 1941-
    1968; CLR 27; DA3; DLB 5, 76, 165;
    MTCW 1, 2; SATA 6
Brooks, Mel .... CLC 12
  See also Kaminsky, Melvin AAYA 13; DLB
    26
Brooks, Peter 1938- .... CLC 34
  See also CA 45-48; CANR 1
Brooks, Van Wyck 1886-1963 .... CLC 29
  See also CA 1-4R; CANR 6; DLB 45, 63,
    103
Brophy, Brigid (Antonia) 1929-1995 . CLC 6,
    11, 29, 105
  See also CA 5-8R; 149; CAAS 4; CANR
    25, 53; DA3; DLB 14; MTCW 1, 2
Brosman, Catharine Savage 1934- ..... CLC 9
  See also CA 61-64; CANR 21, 46
Brossard, Nicole 1943- .... CLC 115
  See also CA 122; CAAS 16; DLB 53
Brother Antoninus
  See Everson, William (Oliver)
The Brothers Quay
  See Quay, Stephen; Quay, Timothy
Broughton, T(homas) Alan 1936- ..... CLC 19
  See also CA 45-48; CANR 2, 23, 48
Broumas, Olga 1949- .... CLC 10, 73
  See also CA 85-88; CANR 20, 69
Brown, Alan 1950- .... CLC 99
  See also CA 156
Brown, Charles Brockden 1771-1810
  .... NCLC 22, 74
  See also CDALB 1640-1865; DLB 37, 59,
    73
Brown, Christy 1932-1981 .... CLC 63
  See also CA 105; 104; CANR 72; DLB 14
Brown, Claude 1937- .... CLC 30; BLC 1;
    DAM MULT
  See also AAYA 7; BW 1, 3; CA 73-76;
    CANR 81
Brown, Dee (Alexander) 1908- . CLC 18, 47;
    DAM POP
  See also AAYA 30; CA 13-16R; CAAS 6;
    CANR 11, 45, 60; DA3; DLBY 80;
    MTCW 1, 2; SATA 5, 110
Brown, George
  See Wertmueller, Lina
Brown, George Douglas 1869-1902
  .... TCLC 28
  See also CA 162
Brown, George Mackay 1921-1996 ... CLC 5,
    48, 100
  See also CA 21-24R; 151; CAAS 6; CANR
    12, 37, 67; DLB 14, 27, 139; MTCW 1;
    SATA 35
Brown, (William) Larry 1951- .... CLC 73
  See also CA 130; 134; INT 133
Brown, Moses
  See Barrett, William (Christopher)
Brown, Rita Mae 1944- .... CLC 18, 43, 79;
    DAM NOV, POP
  See also CA 45-48; CANR 2, 11, 35, 62;
    DA3; INT CANR-11; MTCW 1, 2
Brown, Roderick (Langmere) Haig-
  See Haig-Brown, Roderick (Langmere)
Brown, Rosellen 1939- .... CLC 32
  See also CA 77-80; CAAS 10; CANR 14,
    44
Brown, Sterling Allen 1901-1989 . CLC 1, 23,
    59; BLC 1; DAM MULT, POET
  See also BW 1, 3; CA 85-88; 127; CANR
    26; DA3; DLB 48, 51, 63; MTCW 1, 2

Brown, Will
  See Ainsworth, William Harrison
Brown, William Wells 1813-1884 ... NCLC 2;
    BLC 1; DAM MULT; DC 1
  See also DLB 3, 50
Browne, (Clyde) Jackson 1948(?)- ... CLC 21
  See also CA 120
Browning, Elizabeth Barrett 1806-1861
    NCLC 1, 16, 61, 66; DA; DAB; DAC;
    DAM MST, POET; PC 6; WLC
  See also CDBLB 1832-1890; DA3; DLB
    32, 199
Browning, Robert 1812-1889 . NCLC 19, 79;
    DA; DAB; DAC; DAM MST, POET;
    PC 2; WLCS
  See also CDBLB 1832-1890; DA3; DLB
    32, 163; YABC 1
Browning, Tod 1882-1962 .... CLC 16
  See also CA 141; 117
Brownson, Orestes Augustus 1803-1876
    NCLC 50
  See also DLB 1, 59, 73
Bruccoli, Matthew J(oseph) 1931- ... CLC 34
  See also CA 9-12R; CANR 7, 87; DLB 103
Bruce, Lenny .... CLC 21
  See also Schneider, Leonard Alfred
Bruin, John
  See Brutus, Dennis
Brulard, Henri
  See Stendhal
Brulls, Christian
  See Simenon, Georges (Jacques Christian)
Brunner, John (Kilian Houston) 1934-1995
    CLC 8, 10; DAM POP
  See also CA 1-4R; 149; CAAS 8; CANR 2,
    37; MTCW 1, 2
Bruno, Giordano 1548-1600 .... LC 27
Brutus, Dennis 1924- .... CLC 43; BLC 1;
    DAM MULT, POET; PC 24
  See also BW 2, 3; CA 49-52; CAAS 14;
    CANR 2, 27, 42, 81; DLB 117
Bryan, C(ourtlandt) D(ixon) B(arnes) 1936-
    CLC 29
  See also CA 73-76; CANR 13, 68; DLB
    185; INT CANR-13
Bryan, Michael
  See Moore, Brian
Bryan, William Jennings 1860-1925
  .... TCLC 99
Bryant, William Cullen 1794-1878 . NCLC 6,
    46; DA; DAB; DAC; DAM MST,
    POET; PC 20
  See also CDALB 1640-1865; DLB 3, 43,
    59, 189
Bryusov, Valery Yakovlevich 1873-1924
    TCLC 10
  See also CA 107; 155
Buchan, John 1875-1940 .... TCLC 41; DAB;
    DAM POP
  See also CA 108; 145; DLB 34, 70, 156;
    MTCW 1; YABC 2
Buchanan, George 1506-1582 .... LC 4
  See also DLB 152
Buchheim, Lothar-Guenther 1918- .... CLC 6
  See also CA 85-88
Buchner, (Karl) Georg 1813-1837 . NCLC 26
Buchwald, Art(hur) 1925- .... CLC 33
  See also AITN 1; CA 5-8R; CANR 21, 67;
    MTCW 1, 2; SATA 10
Buck, Pearl S(ydenstricker) 1892-1973
    .. CLC 7, 11, 18, 127; DA; DAB; DAC;
    DAM MST, NOV
  See also AITN 1; CA 1-4R; 41-44R; CANR
    1, 34; CDALBS; DA3; DLB 9, 102;
    MTCW 1, 2; SATA 1, 25
Buckler, Ernest 1908-1984 .... CLC 13; DAC;
    DAM MST
  See also CA 11-12; 114; CAP 1; DLB 68;
    SATA 47

Buckley, Vincent (Thomas) 1925-1988
  .... CLC 57
  See also CA 101
Buckley, William F(rank), Jr. 1925- . CLC 7,
    18, 37; DAM POP
  See also AITN 1; CA 1-4R; CANR 1, 24,
    53; DA3; DLB 137; DLBY 80; INT
    CANR-24; MTCW 1, 2
Buechner, (Carl) Frederick 1926- . CLC 2, 4,
    6, 9; DAM NOV
  See also CA 13-16R; CANR 11, 39, 64;
    DLBY 80; INT CANR-11; MTCW 1, 2
Buell, John (Edward) 1927- .... CLC 10
  See also CA 1-4R; CANR 71; DLB 53
Buero Vallejo, Antonio 1916- ..... CLC 15, 46
  See also CA 106; CANR 24, 49, 75; HW 1;
    MTCW 1, 2
Bufalino, Gesualdo 1920(?)- .... CLC 74
  See also DLB 196
Bugayev, Boris Nikolayevich 1880-1934
    TCLC 7; PC 11
  See also Bely, Andrey CA 104; 165; MTCW
    1
Bukowski, Charles 1920-1994 ... CLC 2, 5, 9,
    41, 82, 108; DAM NOV, POET; PC 18
  See also CA 17-20R; 144; CANR 40, 62;
    DA3; DLB 5, 130, 169; MTCW 1, 2
Bulgakov, Mikhail (Afanas'evich) 1891-1940
    TCLC 2, 16; DAM DRAM, NOV; SSC
    18
  See also CA 105; 152
Bulgya, Alexander Alexandrovich 1901-1956
    TCLC 53
  See also Fadeyev, Alexander CA 117; 181
Bullins, Ed 1935- . CLC 1, 5, 7; BLC 1; DAM
    DRAM, MULT; DC 6
  See also BW 2, 3; CA 49-52; CAAS 16;
    CANR 24, 46, 73; DLB 7, 38; MTCW 1,
    2
Bulwer-Lytton, Edward (George Earle
    Lytton) 1803-1873 .... NCLC 1, 45
  See also DLB 21
Bunin, Ivan Alexeyevich 1870-1953
  .... TCLC 6; SSC 5
  See also CA 104
Bunting, Basil 1900-1985 ..... CLC 10, 39, 47;
    DAM POET
  See also CA 53-56; 115; CANR 7; DLB 20
Bunuel, Luis 1900-1983 .. CLC 16, 80; DAM
    MULT; HLC 1
  See also CA 101; 110; CANR 32, 77; HW
    1
Bunyan, John 1628-1688 ... LC 4; DA; DAB;
    DAC; DAM MST; WLC
  See also CDBLB 1660-1789; DLB 39
Burckhardt, Jacob (Christoph) 1818-1897
    NCLC 49
Burford, Eleanor
  See Hibbert, Eleanor Alice Burford
Burgess, Anthony .. CLC 1, 2, 4, 5, 8, 10, 13,
    15, 22, 40, 62, 81, 94; DAB
  See also Wilson, John (Anthony) Burgess
    AAYA 25; AITN 1; CDBLB 1960 to
    Present; DLB 14, 194; DLBY 98; MTCW
    1
Burke, Edmund 1729(?)-1797 . LC 7, 36; DA;
    DAB; DAC; DAM MST; WLC
  See also DA3; DLB 104
Burke, Kenneth (Duva) 1897-1993 ... CLC 2,
    24
  See also CA 5-8R; 143; CANR 39, 74; DLB
    45, 63; MTCW 1, 2
Burke, Leda
  See Garnett, David
Burke, Ralph
  See Silverberg, Robert
Burke, Thomas 1886-1945 .... TCLC 63
  See also CA 113; 155; DLB 197
Burney, Fanny 1752-1840 .. NCLC 12, 54, 81

Collins, Hunt
See Hunter, Evan
Collins, Linda 1931- .... **CLC 44**
See also CA 125
Collins, (William) Wilkie 1824-1889
.... **NCLC 1, 18**
See also CDBLB 1832-1890; DLB 18, 70, 159
Collins, William 1721-1759 . **LC 4, 40; DAM POET**
See also DLB 109
Collodi, Carlo 1826-1890 .... **NCLC 54**
See also Lorenzini, Carlo CLR 5
Colman, George 1732-1794
See Glassco, John
Colt, Winchester Remington
See Hubbard, L(afayette) Ron(ald)
Colter, Cyrus 1910- .... **CLC 58**
See also BW 1; CA 65-68; CANR 10, 66; DLB 33
Colton, James
See Hansen, Joseph
Colum, Padraic 1881-1972 .... **CLC 28**
See also CA 73-76; 33-36R; CANR 35; CLR 36; MAICYA; MTCW 1; SATA 15
Colvin, James
See Moorcock, Michael (John)
Colwin, Laurie (E.) 1944-1992 .... **CLC 5, 13, 23, 84**
See also CA 89-92; 139; CANR 20, 46; DLBY 80; MTCW 1
Comfort, Alex(ander) 1920- .... **CLC 7; DAM POP**
See also CA 1-4R; CANR 1, 45; MTCW 1
Comfort, Montgomery
See Campbell, (John) Ramsey
Compton-Burnett, I(vy) 1884(?)-1969
.... **CLC 1, 3, 10, 15, 34; DAM NOV**
See also CA 1-4R; 25-28R; CANR 4; DLB 36; MTCW 1
Comstock, Anthony 1844-1915 ...... **TCLC 13**
See also CA 110; 169
Comte, Auguste 1798-1857 .... **NCLC 54**
Conan Doyle, Arthur
See Doyle, Arthur Conan
Conde (Abellan), Carmen 1901-
See also CA 177; DLB 108; HLCS 1; HW 2
Conde, Maryse 1937- .... **CLC 52, 92; BLCS; DAM MULT**
See also BW 2, 3; CA 110; CANR 30, 53, 76; MTCW 1
Condillac, Etienne Bonnot de 1714-1780
.... **LC 26**
Condon, Richard (Thomas) 1915-1996
... **CLC 4, 6, 8, 10, 45, 100; DAM NOV**
See also BEST 90:3; CA 1-4R; 151; CAAS 1; CANR 2, 23; INT CANR-23; MTCW 1, 2
Confucius 551B.C.-479B.C. .. **CMLC 19; DA; DAB; DAC; DAM MST; WLCS**
See also DA3
Congreve, William 1670-1729 . **LC 5, 21; DA; DAB; DAC; DAM DRAM, MST, POET; DC 2; WLC**
See also CDBLB 1660-1789; DLB 39, 84
Connell, Evan S(helby), Jr. 1924- . **CLC 4, 6, 45; DAM NOV**
See also AAYA 7; CA 1-4R; CAAS 2; CANR 2, 39, 76; DLB 2; DLBY 81; MTCW 1, 2
Connelly, Marc(us Cook) 1890-1980 . **CLC 7**
See also CA 85-88; 102; CANR 30; DLB 7; DLBY 80; SATA-Obit 25
Connor, Ralph .... **TCLC 31**
See also Gordon, Charles William DLB 92
Conrad, Joseph 1857-1924 .... **TCLC 1, 6, 13, 25, 43, 57; DA; DAB; DAC; DAM MST, NOV; SSC 9; WLC**

See also AAYA 26; CA 104; 131; CANR 60; CDBLB 1890-1914; DA3; DLB 10, 34, 98, 156; MTCW 1, 2; SATA 27
Conrad, Robert Arnold
See Hart, Moss
Conroy, Pat
See Conroy, (Donald) Pat(rick)
See also MTCW 2
Conroy, (Donald) Pat(rick) 1945- ... **CLC 30, 74; DAM NOV, POP**
See also Conroy, Pat AAYA 8; AITN 1; CA 85-88; CANR 24, 53; DA3; DLB 6; MTCW 1
Constant (de Rebecque), (Henri) Benjamin 1767-1830 .... **NCLC 6**
See also DLB 119
Conybeare, Charles Augustus
See Eliot, T(homas) S(tearns)
Cook, Michael 1933- .... **CLC 58**
See also CA 93-96; CANR 68; DLB 53
Cook, Robin 1940- .... **CLC 14; DAM POP**
See also AAYA 32; BEST 90:2; CA 108; 111; CANR 41; DA3; INT 111
Cook, Roy
See Silverberg, Robert
Cooke, Elizabeth 1948- .... **CLC 55**
See also CA 129
Cooke, John Esten 1830-1886 .... **NCLC 5**
See also DLB 3
Cooke, John Estes
See Baum, L(yman) Frank
Cooke, M. E.
See Creasey, John
Cooke, Margaret
See Creasey, John
Cook-Lynn, Elizabeth 1930- . **CLC 93; DAM MULT**
See also CA 133; DLB 175; NNAL
Cooney, Ray .... **CLC 62**
Cooper, Douglas 1960- .... **CLC 86**
Cooper, Henry St. John
See Creasey, John
Cooper, J(oan) California (?)- .... **CLC 56; DAM MULT**
See also AAYA 12; BW 1; CA 125; CANR 55; DLB 212
Cooper, James Fenimore 1789-1851
.... **NCLC 1, 27, 54**
See also AAYA 22; CDALB 1640-1865; DA3; DLB 3; SATA 19
Coover, Robert (Lowell) 1932- ...... **CLC 3, 7, 15, 32, 46, 87; DAM NOV; SSC 15**
See also CA 45-48; CANR 3, 37, 58; DLB 2; DLBY 81; MTCW 1, 2
Copeland, Stewart (Armstrong) 1952-
.... **CLC 26**
Copernicus, Nicolaus 1473-1543 .... **LC 45**
Coppard, A(lfred) E(dgar) 1878-1957
.... **TCLC 5; SSC 21**
See also CA 114; 167; DLB 162; YABC 1
Coppee, Francois 1842-1908 .... **TCLC 25**
See also CA 170
Coppola, Francis Ford 1939- ... **CLC 16, 126**
See also CA 77-80; CANR 40, 78; DLB 44
Corbiere, Tristan 1845-1875 .... **NCLC 43**
Corcoran, Barbara 1911- .... **CLC 17**
See also AAYA 14; CA 21-24R; CAAS 2; CANR 11, 28, 48; CLR 50; DLB 52; JRDA; SAAS 20; SATA 3, 77
Cordelier, Maurice
See Giraudoux, (Hippolyte) Jean
Corelli, Marie 1855-1924 .... **TCLC 51**
See also Mackay, Mary DLB 34, 156
Corman, Cid 1924- .... **CLC 9**
See also Corman, Sidney CAAS 2; DLB 5, 193

Corman, Sidney 1924-
See Corman, Cid
See also CA 85-88; CANR 44; DAM POET
Cormier, Robert (Edmund) 1925- ... **CLC 12, 30; DA; DAB; DAC; DAM MST, NOV**
See also AAYA 3, 19; CA 1-4R; CANR 5, 23, 76; CDALB 1968-1988; CLR 12, 55; DLB 52; INT CANR-23; JRDA; MAICYA; MTCW 1, 2; SATA 10, 45, 83
Corn, Alfred (DeWitt III) 1943- .... **CLC 33**
See also CA 179; CAAE 179; CAAS 25; CANR 44; DLB 120; DLBY 80
Corneille, Pierre 1606-1684 ..... **LC 28; DAB; DAM MST**
Cornwell, David (John Moore) 1931-
.... **CLC 9, 15; DAM POP**
See also le Carre, John CA 5-8R; CANR 13, 33, 59; DA3; MTCW 1, 2
Corso, (Nunzio) Gregory 1930- .... **CLC 1, 11**
See also CA 5-8R; CANR 41, 76; DA3; DLB 5, 16; MTCW 1, 2
Cortazar, Julio 1914-1984 ... **CLC 2, 3, 5, 10, 13, 15, 33, 34, 92; DAM MULT, NOV; HLC 1; SSC 7**
See also CA 21-24R; CANR 12, 32, 81; DA3; DLB 113; HW 1, 2; MTCW 1, 2
CORTES, HERNAN 1484-1547 .... **LC 31**
Corvinus, Jakob
See Raabe, Wilhelm (Karl)
Corwin, Cecil
See Kornbluth, C(yril) M.
Cosic, Dobrica 1921- .... **CLC 14**
See also CA 122; 138; DLB 181
Costain, Thomas B(ertram) 1885-1965
.... **CLC 30**
See also CA 5-8R; 25-28R; DLB 9
Costantini, Humberto 1924(?)-1987 . **CLC 49**
See also CA 131; 122; HW 1
Costello, Elvis 1955- .... **CLC 21**
Costenoble, Philostene
See Ghelderode, Michel de
Cotes, Cecil V.
See Duncan, Sara Jeannette
Cotter, Joseph Seamon Sr. 1861-1949
.... **TCLC 28; BLC 1; DAM MULT**
See also BW 1; CA 124; DLB 50
Couch, Arthur Thomas Quiller
See Quiller-Couch, SirArthur (Thomas)
Coulton, James
See Hansen, Joseph
Couperus, Louis (Marie Anne) 1863-1923
TCLC 15
See also CA 115
Coupland, Douglas 1961- ..... **CLC 85; DAC; DAM POP**
See also CA 142; CANR 57
Court, Wesli
See Turco, Lewis (Putnam)
Courtenay, Bryce 1933- .... **CLC 59**
See also CA 138
Courtney, Robert
See Ellison, Harlan (Jay)
Cousteau, Jacques-Yves 1910-1997 .. **CLC 30**
See also CA 65-68; 159; CANR 15, 67; MTCW 1; SATA 38, 98
Coventry, Francis 1725-1754 .... **LC 46**
Cowan, Peter (Walkinshaw) 1914- .... **SSC 28**
See also CA 21-24R; CANR 9, 25, 50, 83
Coward, Noel (Peirce) 1899-1973 . **CLC 1, 9, 29, 51; DAM DRAM**
See also AITN 1; CA 17-18; 41-44R; CANR 35; CAP 2; CDBLB 1914-1945; DA3; DLB 10; MTCW 1, 2
Cowley, Abraham 1618-1667 .... **LC 43**
See also DLB 131, 151
Cowley, Malcolm 1898-1989 .... **CLC 39**
See also CA 5-8R; 128; CANR 3, 55; DLB 4, 48; DLBY 81, 89; MTCW 1, 2

11, 15, 18, 37, 44, 65, 113; DAM NOV, POP
See also AAYA 22; AITN 2; BEST 89:3; CA 45-48; CANR 2, 33, 51, 76; CDALB 1968-1988; DA3; DLB 2, 28, 173; DLBY 80; MTCW 1, 2

Dodgson, Charles Lutwidge 1832-1898
See Carroll, Lewis
See also CLR 2; DA; DAB; DAC; DAM MST, NOV, POET; DA3; MAICYA; SATA 100; YABC 2

Dodson, Owen (Vincent) 1914-1983 . **CLC 79; BLC 1; DAM MULT**
See also BW 1; CA 65-68; 110; CANR 24; DLB 76

Doeblin, Alfred 1878-1957 .... **TCLC 13**
See also Doblin, Alfred CA 110; 141; DLB 66

Doerr, Harriet 1910- .... **CLC 34**
See also CA 117; 122; CANR 47; INT 122

Domecq, H(onorio Bustos)
See Bioy Casares, Adolfo

Domecq, H(onorio) Bustos
See Bioy Casares, Adolfo; Borges, Jorge Luis

Domini, Rey
See Lorde, Audre (Geraldine)

Dominique
See Proust, (Valentin-Louis-George-Eugene-) Marcel

Don, A
See Stephen, SirLeslie

Donaldson, Stephen R. 1947- . **CLC 46; DAM POP**
See also CA 89-92; CANR 13, 55; INT CANR-13

Donleavy, J(ames) P(atrick) 1926- .... **CLC 1, 4, 6, 10, 45**
See also AITN 2; CA 9-12R; CANR 24, 49, 62, 80; DLB 6, 173; INT CANR-24; MTCW 1, 2

Donne, John 1572-1631 .... **LC 10, 24; DA; DAB; DAC; DAM MST, POET; PC 1; WLC**
See also CDBLB Before 1660; DLB 121, 151

Donnell, David 1939(?)- .... **CLC 34**

Donoghue, P. S.
See Hunt, E(verette) Howard, (Jr.)

Donoso (Yanez), Jose 1924-1996 ... **CLC 4, 8, 11, 32, 99; DAM MULT; HLC 1; SSC 34**
See also CA 81-84; 155; CANR 32, 73; DLB 113; HW 1, 2; MTCW 1, 2

Donovan, John 1928-1992 .... **CLC 35**
See also AAYA 20; CA 97-100; 137; CLR 3; MAICYA; SATA 72; SATA-Brief 29

Don Roberto
See Cunninghame Graham, Robert (Gallnigad) Bontine

Doolittle, Hilda 1886-1961 . **CLC 3, 8, 14, 31, 34, 73; DA; DAC; DAM MST, POET; PC 5; WLC**
See also H. D. CA 97-100; CANR 35; DLB 4, 45; MTCW 1, 2

Dorfman, Ariel 1942- ...... **CLC 48, 77; DAM MULT; HLC 1**
See also CA 124; 130; CANR 67, 70; HW 1, 2; INT 130

Dorn, Edward (Merton) 1929- ... **CLC 10, 18**
See also CA 93-96; CANR 42, 79; DLB 5; INT 93-96

Dorris, Michael (Anthony) 1945-1997
.... **CLC 109; DAM MULT, NOV**
See also AAYA 20; BEST 90:1; CA 102; 157; CANR 19, 46, 75; CLR 58; DA3; DLB 175; MTCW 2; NNAL; SATA 75; SATA-Obit 94

Dorris, Michael A.
See Dorris, Michael (Anthony)

Dorsan, Luc
See Simenon, Georges (Jacques Christian)

Dorsange, Jean
See Simenon, Georges (Jacques Christian)

Dos Passos, John (Roderigo) 1896-1970
..... **CLC 1, 4, 8, 11, 15, 25, 34, 82; DA; DAB; DAC; DAM MST, NOV; WLC**
See also CA 1-4R; 29-32R; CANR 3; CDALB 1929-1941; DA3; DLB 4, 9; DLBD 1, 15; DLBY 96; MTCW 1, 2

Dossage, Jean
See Simenon, Georges (Jacques Christian)

Dostoevsky, Fedor Mikhailovich 1821-1881
NCLC 2, 7, 21, 33, 43; DA; DAB; DAC; DAM MST, NOV; SSC 2, 33; WLC
See also DA3

Doughty, Charles M(ontagu) 1843-1926
TCLC 27
See also CA 115; 178; DLB 19, 57, 174

Douglas, Ellen .... **CLC 73**
See also Haxton, Josephine Ayres; Williamson, Ellen Douglas

Douglas, Gavin 1475(?)-1522 .... **LC 20**
See also DLB 132

Douglas, George
See Brown, George Douglas

Douglas, Keith (Castellain) 1920-1944
.... **TCLC 40**
See also CA 160; DLB 27

Douglas, Leonard
See Bradbury, Ray (Douglas)

Douglas, Michael
See Crichton, (John) Michael

Douglas, (George) Norman 1868-1952
.... **TCLC 68**
See also CA 119; 157; DLB 34, 195

Douglas, William
See Brown, George Douglas

Douglass, Frederick 1817(?)-1895 .. **NCLC 7, 55; BLC 1; DA; DAC; DAM MST, MULT; WLC**
See also CDALB 1640-1865; DA3; DLB 1, 43, 50, 79; SATA 29

Dourado, (Waldomiro Freitas) Autran 1926-
CLC 23, 60
See also CA 25-28R; 179; CANR 34, 81; DLB 145; HW 2

Dourado, Waldomiro Autran 1926-
See Dourado, (Waldomiro Freitas) Autran
See also CA 179

Dove, Rita (Frances) 1952- .... **CLC 50, 81; BLCS; DAM MULT, POET; PC 6**
See also BW 2; CA 109; CAAS 19; CANR 27, 42, 68, 76; CDALBS; DA3; DLB 120; MTCW 1

Doveglion
See Villa, Jose Garcia

Dowell, Coleman 1925-1985 .... **CLC 60**
See also CA 25-28R; 117; CANR 10; DLB 130

Dowson, Ernest (Christopher) 1867-1900
TCLC 4
See also CA 105; 150; DLB 19, 135

Doyle, A. Conan
See Doyle, Arthur Conan

Doyle, Arthur Conan 1859-1930 .... **TCLC 7; DA; DAB; DAC; DAM MST, NOV; SSC 12; WLC**
See also AAYA 14; CA 104; 122; CDBLB 1890-1914; DA3; DLB 18, 70, 156, 178; MTCW 1, 2; SATA 24

Doyle, Conan
See Doyle, Arthur Conan

Doyle, John
See Graves, Robert (von Ranke)

Doyle, Roddy 1958(?)- .... **CLC 81**

See also AAYA 14; CA 143; CANR 73; DA3; DLB 194

Doyle, Sir A. Conan
See Doyle, Arthur Conan

Doyle, Sir Arthur Conan
See Doyle, Arthur Conan

Dr. A
See Asimov, Isaac; Silverstein, Alvin

Drabble, Margaret 1939- . **CLC 2, 3, 5, 8, 10, 22, 53, 129; DAB; DAC; DAM MST, NOV, POP**
See also CA 13-16R; CANR 18, 35, 63; CDBLB 1960 to Present; DA3; DLB 14, 155; MTCW 1, 2; SATA 48

Drapier, M. B.
See Swift, Jonathan

Drayham, James
See Mencken, H(enry) L(ouis)

Drayton, Michael 1563-1631 ..... **LC 8; DAM POET**
See also DLB 121

Dreadstone, Carl
See Campbell, (John) Ramsey

Dreiser, Theodore (Herman Albert)
1871-1945 .... **TCLC 10, 18, 35, 83; DA; DAC; DAM MST, NOV; SSC 30; WLC**
See also CA 106; 132; CDALB 1865-1917; DA3; DLB 9, 12, 102, 137; DLBD 1; MTCW 1, 2

Drexler, Rosalyn 1926- .... **CLC 2, 6**
See also CA 81-84; CANR 68

Dreyer, Carl Theodor 1889-1968 ...... **CLC 16**
See also CA 116

Drieu la Rochelle, Pierre(-Eugene)
1893-1945 .... **TCLC 21**
See also CA 117; DLB 72

Drinkwater, John 1882-1937 .... **TCLC 57**
See also CA 109; 149; DLB 10, 19, 149

Drop Shot
See Cable, George Washington

Droste-Hulshoff, Annette Freiin von
1797-1848 .... **NCLC 3**
See also DLB 133

Drummond, Walter
See Silverberg, Robert

Drummond, William Henry 1854-1907
.... **TCLC 25**
See also CA 160; DLB 92

Drummond de Andrade, Carlos 1902-1987
CLC 18
See also Andrade, Carlos Drummond de CA 132; 123

Drury, Allen (Stuart) 1918-1998 .... **CLC 37**
See also CA 57-60; 170; CANR 18, 52; INT CANR-18

Dryden, John 1631-1700 .... **LC 3, 21; DA; DAB; DAC; DAM DRAM, MST, POET; DC 3; PC 25; WLC**
See also CDBLB 1660-1789; DLB 80, 101, 131

Duberman, Martin (Bauml) 1930- ..... **CLC 8**
See also CA 1-4R; CANR 2, 63

Dubie, Norman (Evans) 1945- .... **CLC 36**
See also CA 69-72; CANR 12; DLB 120

Du Bois, W(illiam) E(dward) B(urghardt)
1868-1963 ... **CLC 1, 2, 13, 64, 96; BLC 1; DA; DAC; DAM MST, MULT, NOV; WLC**
See also BW 1, 3; CA 85-88; CANR 34, 82; CDALB 1865-1917; DA3; DLB 47, 50, 91; MTCW 1, 2; SATA 42

Dubus, Andre 1936-1999 ..... **CLC 13, 36, 97; SSC 15**
See also CA 21-24R; 177; CANR 17; DLB 130; INT CANR-17

Duca Minimo
See D'Annunzio, Gabriele

Ducharme, Rejean 1941- .... **CLC 74**
See also CA 165; DLB 60

See also DLB 192

Feydeau, Georges (Leon Jules Marie) 1862-1921 .... **TCLC 22; DAM DRAM**
See also CA 113; 152; CANR 84; DLB 192

Fichte, Johann Gottlieb 1762-1814 . **NCLC 62**
See also DLB 90

Ficino, Marsilio 1433-1499 .... **LC 12**

Fiedeler, Hans
See Doeblin, Alfred

Fiedler, Leslie A(aron) 1917- .. **CLC 4, 13, 24**
See also CA 9-12R; CANR 7, 63; DLB 28, 67; MTCW 1, 2

Field, Andrew 1938- .... **CLC 44**
See also CA 97-100; CANR 25

Field, Eugene 1850-1895 .... **NCLC 3**
See also DLB 23, 42, 140; DLBD 13; MAICYA; SATA 16

Field, Gans T.
See Wellman, Manly Wade

Field, Michael 1915-1971 .... **TCLC 43**
See also CA 29-32R

Field, Peter
See Hobson, Laura Z(ametkin)

Fielding, Henry 1707-1754 ..... **LC 1, 46; DA; DAB; DAC; DAM DRAM, MST, NOV; WLC**
See also CDBLB 1660-1789; DA3; DLB 39, 84, 101

Fielding, Sarah 1710-1768 .... **LC 1, 44**
See also DLB 39

Fields, W. C. 1880-1946 .... **TCLC 80**
See also DLB 44

Fierstein, Harvey (Forbes) 1954- .... **CLC 33; DAM DRAM, POP**
See also CA 123; 129; DA3

Figes, Eva 1932- .... **CLC 31**
See also CA 53-56; CANR 4, 44, 83; DLB 14

Finch, Anne 1661-1720 .... **LC 3; PC 21**
See also DLB 95

Finch, Robert (Duer Claydon) 1900-
.... **CLC 18**
See also CA 57-60; CANR 9, 24, 49; DLB 88

Findley, Timothy 1930- . **CLC 27, 102; DAC; DAM MST**
See also CA 25-28R; CANR 12, 42, 69; DLB 53

Fink, William
See Mencken, H(enry) L(ouis)

Firbank, Louis 1942-
See Reed, Lou
See also CA 117

Firbank, (Arthur Annesley) Ronald 1886-1926 .... **TCLC 1**
See also CA 104; 177; DLB 36

Fisher, Dorothy (Frances) Canfield 1879-1958 .... **TCLC 87**
See also CA 114; 136; CANR 80; DLB 9, 102; MAICYA; YABC 1

Fisher, M(ary) F(rances) K(ennedy) 1908-1992 .... **CLC 76, 87**
See also CA 77-80; 138; CANR 44; MTCW 1

Fisher, Roy 1930- .... **CLC 25**
See also CA 81-84; CAAS 10; CANR 16; DLB 40

Fisher, Rudolph 1897-1934 .. **TCLC 11; BLC 2; DAM MULT; SSC 25**
See also BW 1, 3; CA 107; 124; CANR 80; DLB 51, 102

Fisher, Vardis (Alvero) 1895-1968 ...... **CLC 7**
See also CA 5-8R; 25-28R; CANR 68; DLB 9, 206

Fiske, Tarleton
See Bloch, Robert (Albert)

Fitch, Clarke
See Sinclair, Upton (Beall)

Fitch, John IV
See Cormier, Robert (Edmund)

Fitzgerald, Captain Hugh
See Baum, L(yman) Frank

FitzGerald, Edward 1809-1883 .... **NCLC 9**
See also DLB 32

Fitzgerald, F(rancis) Scott (Key) 1896-1940 **TCLC 1, 6, 14, 28, 55; DA; DAB; DAC; DAM MST, NOV; SSC 6, 31; WLC**
See also AAYA 24; AITN 1; CA 110; 123; CDALB 1917-1929; DA3; DLB 4, 9, 86; DLBD 1, 15, 16; DLBY 81, 96; MTCW 1, 2

Fitzgerald, Penelope 1916-2000 . **CLC 19, 51, 61**
See also CA 85-88; CAAS 10; CANR 56, 86; DLB 14, 194; MTCW 2

Fitzgerald, Robert (Stuart) 1910-1985
.... **CLC 39**
See also CA 1-4R; 114; CANR 1; DLBY 80

FitzGerald, Robert D(avid) 1902-1987
.... **CLC 19**
See also CA 17-20R

Fitzgerald, Zelda (Sayre) 1900-1948
.... **TCLC 52**
See also CA 117; 126; DLBY 84

Flanagan, Thomas (James Bonner) 1923-
CLC 25, 52
See also CA 108; CANR 55; DLBY 80; INT 108; MTCW 1

Flaubert, Gustave 1821-1880 .... **NCLC 2, 10, 19, 62, 66; DA; DAB; DAC; DAM MST, NOV; SSC 11; WLC**
See also DA3; DLB 119

Flecker, Herman Elroy
See Flecker, (Herman) James Elroy

Flecker, (Herman) James Elroy 1884-1915
TCLC 43
See also CA 109; 150; DLB 10, 19

Fleming, Ian (Lancaster) 1908-1964 . **CLC 3, 30; DAM POP**
See also AAYA 26; CA 5-8R; CANR 59; CDBLB 1945-1960; DA3; DLB 87, 201; MTCW 1, 2; SATA 9

Fleming, Thomas (James) 1927- ...... **CLC 37**
See also CA 5-8R; CANR 10; INT CANR-10; SATA 8

Fletcher, John 1579-1625 .... **LC 33; DC 6**
See also CDBLB Before 1660; DLB 58

Fletcher, John Gould 1886-1950 .... **TCLC 35**
See also CA 107; 167; DLB 4, 45

Fleur, Paul
See Pohl, Frederik

Flooglebuckle, Al
See Spiegelman, Art

Flying Officer X
See Bates, H(erbert) E(rnest)

Fo, Dario 1926- . **CLC 32, 109; DAM DRAM; DC 10**
See also CA 116; 128; CANR 68; DA3; DLBY 97; MTCW 1, 2

Fogarty, Jonathan Titulescu Esq.
See Farrell, James T(homas)

Follett, Ken(neth Martin) 1949- ..... **CLC 18; DAM NOV, POP**
See also AAYA 6; BEST 89:4; CA 81-84; CANR 13, 33, 54; DA3; DLB 87; DLBY 81; INT CANR-33; MTCW 1

Fontane, Theodor 1819-1898 .... **NCLC 26**
See also DLB 129

Foote, Horton 1916- .... **CLC 51, 91; DAM DRAM**
See also CA 73-76; CANR 34, 51; DA3; DLB 26; INT CANR-34

Foote, Shelby 1916- ..... **CLC 75; DAM NOV, POP**
See also CA 5-8R; CANR 3, 45, 74; DA3; DLB 2, 17; MTCW 2

Forbes, Esther 1891-1967 .... **CLC 12**
See also AAYA 17; CA 13-14; 25-28R; CAP 1; CLR 27; DLB 22; JRDA; MAICYA; SATA 2, 100

Forche, Carolyn (Louise) 1950- . **CLC 25, 83, 86; DAM POET; PC 10**
See also CA 109; 117; CANR 50, 74; DA3; DLB 5, 193; INT 117; MTCW 1

Ford, Elbur
See Hibbert, Eleanor Alice Burford

Ford, Ford Madox 1873-1939 ... **TCLC 1, 15, 39, 57; DAM NOV**
See also CA 104; 132; CANR 74; CDBLB 1914-1945; DA3; DLB 162; MTCW 1, 2

Ford, Henry 1863-1947 .... **TCLC 73**
See also CA 115; 148

Ford, John 1586-(?) .... **DC 8**
See also CDBLB Before 1660; DAM DRAM; DA3; DLB 58

Ford, John 1895-1973 .... **CLC 16**
See also CA 45-48

Ford, Richard 1944- .... **CLC 46, 99**
See also CA 69-72; CANR 11, 47, 86; MTCW 1

Ford, Webster
See Masters, Edgar Lee

Foreman, Richard 1937- .... **CLC 50**
See also CA 65-68; CANR 32, 63

Forester, C(ecil) S(cott) 1899-1966 ... **CLC 35**
See also CA 73-76; 25-28R; CANR 83; DLB 191; SATA 13

Forez
See Mauriac, Francois (Charles)

Forman, James Douglas 1932- .... **CLC 21**
See also AAYA 17; CA 9-12R; CANR 4, 19, 42; JRDA; MAICYA; SATA 8, 70

Fornes, Maria Irene 1930- . **CLC 39, 61; DC 10; HLCS 1**
See also CA 25-28R; CANR 28, 81; DLB 7; HW 1, 2; INT CANR-28; MTCW 1

Forrest, Leon (Richard) 1937-1997 .. **CLC 4; BLCS**
See also BW 2; CA 89-92; 162; CAAS 7; CANR 25, 52, 87; DLB 33

Forster, E(dward) M(organ) 1879-1970 ..... **CLC 1, 2, 3, 4, 9, 10, 13, 15, 22, 45, 77; DA; DAB; DAC; DAM MST, NOV; SSC 27; WLC**
See also AAYA 2; CA 13-14; 25-28R; CANR 45; CAP 1; CDBLB 1914-1945; DA3; DLB 34, 98, 162, 178, 195; DLBD 10; MTCW 1, 2; SATA 57

Forster, John 1812-1876 .... **NCLC 11**
See also DLB 144, 184

Forsyth, Frederick 1938- .... **CLC 2, 5, 36; DAM NOV, POP**
See also BEST 89:4; CA 85-88; CANR 38, 62; DLB 87; MTCW 1, 2

Forten, Charlotte L. .... **TCLC 16; BLC 2**
See also Grimke, Charlotte L(ottie) Forten DLB 50

Foscolo, Ugo 1778-1827 .... **NCLC 8**

Fosse, Bob .... **CLC 20**
See also Fosse, Robert Louis

Fosse, Robert Louis 1927-1987
See Fosse, Bob
See also CA 110; 123

Foster, Stephen Collins 1826-1864 . **NCLC 26**

Foucault, Michel 1926-1984 . **CLC 31, 34, 69**
See also CA 105; 113; CANR 34; MTCW 1, 2

Fouque, Friedrich (Heinrich Karl) de la Motte 1777-1843 .... **NCLC 2**
See also DLB 90

Fourier, Charles 1772-1837 .... **NCLC 51**

Fournier, Pierre 1916- .... **CLC 11**
See also Gascar, Pierre CA 89-92; CANR 16, 40

Fowles, John (Philip) 1926- .. **CLC 1, 2, 3, 4,**

Gallant, Mavis 1922- .. CLC 7, 18, 38; DAC;
DAM MST; SSC 5
See also CA 69-72; CANR 29, 69; DLB 53;
MTCW 1, 2
Gallant, Roy A(rthur) 1924- .... CLC 17
See also CA 5-8R; CANR 4, 29, 54; CLR
30; MAICYA; SATA 4, 68, 110
Gallico, Paul (William) 1897-1976 ..... CLC 2
See also AITN 1; CA 5-8R; 69-72; CANR
23; DLB 9, 171; MAICYA; SATA 13
Gallo, Max Louis 1932- .... CLC 95
See also CA 85-88
Gallois, Lucien
See Desnos, Robert
Gallup, Ralph
See Whitemore, Hugh (John)
Galsworthy, John 1867-1933 .... TCLC 1, 45;
DA; DAB; DAC; DAM DRAM, MST,
NOV; SSC 22; WLC
See also CA 104; 141; CANR 75; CDBLB
1890-1914; DA3; DLB 10, 34, 98, 162;
DLBD 16; MTCW 1
Galt, John 1779-1839 .... NCLC 1
See also DLB 99, 116, 159
Galvin, James 1951- .... CLC 38
See also CA 108; CANR 26
Gamboa, Federico 1864-1939 .... TCLC 36
See also CA 167; HW 2
Gandhi, M. K.
See Gandhi, Mohandas Karamchand
Gandhi, Mahatma
See Gandhi, Mohandas Karamchand
Gandhi, Mohandas Karamchand 1869-1948
TCLC 59; DAM MULT
See also CA 121; 132; DA3; MTCW 1, 2
Gann, Ernest Kellogg 1910-1991 ..... CLC 23
See also AITN 1; CA 1-4R; 136; CANR 1,
83
Garber, Eric 1943(?)-
See Holleran, Andrew
See also CANR 89
Garcia, Cristina 1958- .... CLC 76
See also CA 141; CANR 73; HW 2
Garcia Lorca, Federico 1898-1936 . TCLC 1,
7, 49; DA; DAB; DAC; DAM DRAM,
MST, MULT, POET; DC 2; HLC 2; PC
3; WLC
See also CA 104; 131; CANR 81; DA3;
DLB 108; HW 1, 2; MTCW 1, 2
Garcia Marquez, Gabriel (Jose) 1928-
...... CLC 2, 3, 8, 10, 15, 27, 47, 55, 68;
DA; DAB; DAC; DAM MST, MULT,
NOV, POP; HLC 1; SSC 8; WLC
See also AAYA 3; BEST 89:1, 90:4; CA 33-
36R; CANR 10, 28, 50, 75, 82; DA3;
DLB 113; HW 1, 2; MTCW 1, 2
Garcilaso de la Vega, El Inca 1503-1536
See also HLCS 1
Gard, Janice
See Latham, Jean Lee
Gard, Roger Martin du
See Martin du Gard, Roger
Gardam, Jane 1928- .... CLC 43
See also CA 49-52; CANR 2, 18, 33, 54;
CLR 12; DLB 14, 161; MAICYA; MTCW
1; SAAS 9; SATA 39, 76; SATA-Brief 28
Gardner, Herb(ert) 1934- .... CLC 44
See also CA 149
Gardner, John (Champlin), Jr. 1933-1982
CLC 2, 3, 5, 7, 8, 10, 18, 28, 34; DAM
NOV, POP; SSC 7
See also AITN 1; CA 65-68; 107; CANR
33, 73; CDALBS; DA3; DLB 2; DLBY
82; MTCW 1; SATA 40; SATA-Obit 31
Gardner, John (Edmund) 1926- ...... CLC 30;
DAM POP
See also CA 103; CANR 15, 69; MTCW 1
Gardner, Miriam
See Bradley, Marion Zimmer

Gardner, Noel
See Kuttner, Henry
Gardons, S. S.
See Snodgrass, W(illiam) D(e Witt)
Garfield, Leon 1921-1996 .... CLC 12
See also AAYA 8; CA 17-20R; 152; CANR
38, 41, 78; CLR 21; DLB 161; JRDA;
MAICYA; SATA 1, 32, 76; SATA-Obit 90
Garland, (Hannibal) Hamlin 1860-1940
TCLC 3; SSC 18
See also CA 104; DLB 12, 71, 78, 186
Garneau, (Hector de) Saint-Denys 1912-1943
TCLC 13
See also CA 111; DLB 88
Garner, Alan 1934- ..... CLC 17; DAB; DAM
POP
See also AAYA 18; CA 73-76, 178; CAAE
178; CANR 15, 64; CLR 20; DLB 161;
MAICYA; MTCW 1, 2; SATA 18, 69;
SATA-Essay 108
Garner, Hugh 1913-1979 .... CLC 13
See also CA 69-72; CANR 31; DLB 68
Garnett, David 1892-1981 .... CLC 3
See also CA 5-8R; 103; CANR 17, 79; DLB
34; MTCW 2
Garos, Stephanie
See Katz, Steve
Garrett, George (Palmer) 1929- .. CLC 3, 11,
51; SSC 30
See also CA 1-4R; CAAS 5; CANR 1, 42,
67; DLB 2, 5, 130, 152; DLBY 83
Garrick, David 1717-1779 .... LC 15; DAM
DRAM
See also DLB 84
Garrigue, Jean 1914-1972 .... CLC 2, 8
See also CA 5-8R; 37-40R; CANR 20
Garrison, Frederick
See Sinclair, Upton (Beall)
Garro, Elena 1920(?)-1998
See also CA 131; 169; DLB 145; HLCS 1;
HW 1
Garth, Will
See Hamilton, Edmond; Kuttner, Henry
Garvey, Marcus (Moziah, Jr.) 1887-1940
TCLC 41; BLC 2; DAM MULT
See also BW 1; CA 120; 124; CANR 79
Gary, Romain .... CLC 25
See also Kacew, Romain DLB 83
Gascar, Pierre .... CLC 11
See also Fournier, Pierre
Gascoyne, David (Emery) 1916- .... CLC 45
See also CA 65-68; CANR 10, 28, 54; DLB
20; MTCW 1
Gaskell, Elizabeth Cleghorn 1810-1865
NCLC 70; DAB; DAM MST; SSC 25
See also CDBLB 1832-1890; DLB 21, 144,
159
Gass, William H(oward) 1924- . CLC 1, 2, 8,
11, 15, 39; SSC 12
See also CA 17-20R; CANR 30, 71; DLB
2; MTCW 1, 2
Gassendi, Pierre 1592-1655 .... LC 54
Gasset, Jose Ortega y
See Ortega y Gasset, Jose
Gates, Henry Louis, Jr. 1950- .... CLC 65;
BLCS; DAM MULT
See also BW 2, 3; CA 109; CANR 25, 53,
75; DA3; DLB 67; MTCW 1
Gautier, Theophile 1811-1872 .. NCLC 1, 59;
DAM POET; PC 18; SSC 20
See also DLB 119
Gawsworth, John
See Bates, H(erbert) E(rnest)
Gay, John 1685-1732 .. LC 49; DAM DRAM
See also DLB 84, 95
Gay, Oliver
See Gogarty, Oliver St. John
Gaye, Marvin (Penze) 1939-1984 ..... CLC 26
See also CA 112

Gebler, Carlo (Ernest) 1954- .... CLC 39
See also CA 119; 133
Gee, Maggie (Mary) 1948- .... CLC 57
See also CA 130; DLB 207
Gee, Maurice (Gough) 1931- .... CLC 29
See also CA 97-100; CANR 67; CLR 56;
SATA 46, 101
Gelbart, Larry (Simon) 1923- .... CLC 21, 61
See also CA 73-76; CANR 45
Gelber, Jack 1932- .... CLC 1, 6, 14, 79
See also CA 1-4R; CANR 2; DLB 7
Gellhorn, Martha (Ellis) 1908-1998 . CLC 14,
60
See also CA 77-80; 164; CANR 44; DLBY
82, 98
Genet, Jean 1910-1986 .. CLC 1, 2, 5, 10, 14,
44, 46; DAM DRAM
See also CA 13-16R; CANR 18; DA3; DLB
72; DLBY 86; MTCW 1, 2
Gent, Peter 1942- .... CLC 29
See also AITN 1; CA 89-92; DLBY 82
Gentile, Giovanni 1875-1944 .... TCLC 96
See also CA 119
Gentlewoman in New England, A
See Bradstreet, Anne
Gentlewoman in Those Parts, A
See Bradstreet, Anne
George, Jean Craighead 1919- .... CLC 35
See also AAYA 8; CA 5-8R; CANR 25;
CLR 1; DLB 52; JRDA; MAICYA; SATA
2, 68
George, Stefan (Anton) 1868-1933 . TCLC 2,
14
See also CA 104
Georges, Georges Martin
See Simenon, Georges (Jacques Christian)
Gerhardi, William Alexander
See Gerhardie, William Alexander
Gerhardie, William Alexander 1895-1977
CLC 5
See also CA 25-28R; 73-76; CANR 18;
DLB 36
Gerstler, Amy 1956- .... CLC 70
See also CA 146
Gertler, T. .... CLC 34
See also CA 116; 121; INT 121
Ghalib .... NCLC 39, 78
See also Ghalib, Hsadullah Khan
Ghalib, Hsadullah Khan 1797-1869
See Ghalib
See also DAM POET
Ghelderode, Michel de 1898-1962 ..... CLC 6,
11; DAM DRAM
See also CA 85-88; CANR 40, 77
Ghiselin, Brewster 1903- .... CLC 23
See also CA 13-16R; CAAS 10; CANR 13
Ghose, Aurabinda 1872-1950 .... TCLC 63
See also CA 163
Ghose, Zulfikar 1935- .... CLC 42
See also CA 65-68; CANR 67
Ghosh, Amitav 1956- .... CLC 44
See also CA 147; CANR 80
Giacosa, Giuseppe 1847-1906 .... TCLC 7
See also CA 104
Gibb, Lee
See Waterhouse, Keith (Spencer)
Gibbon, Lewis Grassic .... TCLC 4
See also Mitchell, James Leslie
Gibbons, Kaye 1960- .... CLC 50, 88; DAM
POP
See also CA 151; CANR 75; DA3; MTCW
1
Gibran, Kahlil 1883-1931 . TCLC 1, 9; DAM
POET, POP; PC 9
See also CA 104; 150; DA3; MTCW 2
Gibran, Khalil
See Gibran, Kahlil
Gibson, William 1914- .. CLC 23; DA; DAB;

DAC; DAM DRAM, MST
See also CA 9-12R; CANR 9, 42, 75; DLB
7; MTCW 1; SATA 66

Gibson, William (Ford) 1948- ... **CLC 39, 63;**
DAM POP
See also AAYA 12; CA 126; 133; CANR
52; DA3; MTCW 1

Gide, Andre (Paul Guillaume) 1869-1951
TCLC 5, 12, 36; DA; DAB; DAC; DAM
MST, NOV; SSC 13; WLC
See also CA 104; 124; DA3; DLB 65;
MTCW 1, 2

Gifford, Barry (Colby) 1946- .... **CLC 34**
See also CA 65-68; CANR 9, 30, 40

Gilbert, Frank
See De Voto, Bernard (Augustine)

Gilbert, W(illiam) S(chwenck) 1836-1911
TCLC 3; DAM DRAM, POET
See also CA 104; 173; SATA 36

Gilbreth, Frank B., Jr. 1911- .... **CLC 17**
See also CA 9-12R; SATA 2

Gilchrist, Ellen 1935- ...... **CLC 34, 48; DAM**
POP; SSC 14
See also CA 113; 116; CANR 41, 61; DLB
130; MTCW 1, 2

Giles, Molly 1942- .... **CLC 39**
See also CA 126

Gill, Eric 1882-1940 .... **TCLC 85**

Gill, Patrick
See Creasey, John

Gilliam, Terry (Vance) 1940- .... **CLC 21**
See also Monty Python AAYA 19; CA 108;
113; CANR 35; INT 113

Gillian, Jerry
See Gilliam, Terry (Vance)

Gilliatt, Penelope (Ann Douglass) 1932-1993
CLC 2, 10, 13, 53
See also AITN 2; CA 13-16R; 141; CANR
49; DLB 14

Gilman, Charlotte (Anna) Perkins (Stetson)
1860-1935 .... **TCLC 9, 37; SSC 13**
See also CA 106; 150; MTCW 1

Gilmour, David 1949- .... **CLC 35**
See also CA 138, 147

Gilpin, William 1724-1804 .... **NCLC 30**

Gilray, J. D.
See Mencken, H(enry) L(ouis)

Gilroy, Frank D(aniel) 1925- .... **CLC 2**
See also CA 81-84; CANR 32, 64, 86; DLB
7

Gilstrap, John 1957(?)- .... **CLC 99**
See also CA 160

Ginsberg, Allen 1926-1997 . **CLC 1, 2, 3, 4, 6,**
13, 36, 69, 109; DA; DAB; DAC; DAM
MST, POET; PC 4; WLC
See also AITN 1; CA 1-4R; 157; CANR 2,
41, 63; CDALB 1941-1968; DA3; DLB
5, 16, 169; MTCW 1, 2

Ginzburg, Natalia 1916-1991 . **CLC 5, 11, 54,**
70
See also CA 85-88; 135; CANR 33; DLB
177; MTCW 1, 2

Giono, Jean 1895-1970 .... **CLC 4, 11**
See also CA 45-48; 29-32R; CANR 2, 35;
DLB 72; MTCW 1

Giovanni, Nikki 1943- . **CLC 2, 4, 19, 64, 117;**
BLC 2; DA; DAB; DAC; DAM MST,
MULT, POET; PC 19; WLCS
See also AAYA 22; AITN 1; BW 2, 3; CA
29-32R; CAAS 6; CANR 18, 41, 60;
CDALBS; CLR 6; DA3; DLB 5, 41; INT
CANR-18; MAICYA; MTCW 1, 2; SATA
24, 107

Giovene, Andrea 1904- .... **CLC 7**
See also CA 85-88

Gippius, Zinaida (Nikolayevna) 1869-1945
See Hippius, Zinaida
See also CA 106

Giraudoux, (Hippolyte) Jean 1882-1944
TCLC 2, 7; DAM DRAM
See also CA 104; DLB 65

Gironella, Jose Maria 1917- .... **CLC 11**
See also CA 101

Gissing, George (Robert) 1857-1903
.... **TCLC 3, 24, 47; SSC 37**
See also CA 105; 167; DLB 18, 135, 184

Giurlani, Aldo
See Palazzeschi, Aldo

Gladkov, Fyodor (Vasilyevich) 1883-1958
TCLC 27
See also CA 170

Glanville, Brian (Lester) 1931- .... **CLC 6**
See also CA 5-8R; CAAS 9; CANR 3, 70;
DLB 15, 139; SATA 42

Glasgow, Ellen (Anderson Gholson)
1873-1945 .... **TCLC 2, 7; SSC 34**
See also CA 104; 164; DLB 9, 12; MTCW
2

Glaspell, Susan 1882(?)-1948 . **TCLC 55; DC**
10
See also CA 110; 154; DLB 7, 9, 78; YABC
2

Glassco, John 1909-1981 .... **CLC 9**
See also CA 13-16R; 102; CANR 15; DLB
68

Glasscock, Amnesia
See Steinbeck, John (Ernst)

Glasser, Ronald J. 1940(?)- .... **CLC 37**

Glassman, Joyce
See Johnson, Joyce

Glendinning, Victoria 1937- .... **CLC 50**
See also CA 120; 127; CANR 59, 89; DLB
155

Glissant, Edouard 1928- . **CLC 10, 68; DAM**
MULT
See also CA 153

Gloag, Julian 1930- .... **CLC 40**
See also AITN 1; CA 65-68; CANR 10, 70

Glowacki, Aleksander
See Prus, Boleslaw

Gluck, Louise (Elisabeth) 1943- .. **CLC 7, 22,**
44, 81; DAM POET; PC 16
See also CA 33-36R; CANR 40, 69; DA3;
DLB 5; MTCW 2

Glyn, Elinor 1864-1943 .... **TCLC 72**
See also DLB 153

Gobineau, Joseph Arthur (Comte) de
1816-1882 .... **NCLC 17**
See also DLB 123

Godard, Jean-Luc 1930- .... **CLC 20**
See also CA 93-96

Godden, (Margaret) Rumer 1907-1998
.... **CLC 53**
See also AAYA 6; CA 5-8R; 172; CANR 4,
27, 36, 55, 80; CLR 20; DLB 161; MAI-
CYA; SAAS 12; SATA 3, 36; SATA-Obit
109

Godoy Alcayaga, Lucila 1889-1957
See Mistral, Gabriela
See also BW 2; CA 104; 131; CANR 81;
DAM MULT; HW 1, 2; MTCW 1, 2

Godwin, Gail (Kathleen) 1937- ..... **CLC 5, 8,**
22, 31, 69, 125; DAM POP
See also CA 29-32R; CANR 15, 43, 69;
DA3; DLB 6; INT CANR-15; MTCW 1,
2

Godwin, William 1756-1836 .... **NCLC 14**
See also CDBLB 1789-1832; DLB 39, 104,
142, 158, 163

Goebbels, Josef
See Goebbels, (Paul) Joseph

Goebbels, (Paul) Joseph 1897-1945
.... **TCLC 68**
See also CA 115; 148

Goebbels, Joseph Paul
See Goebbels, (Paul) Joseph

Goethe, Johann Wolfgang von 1749-1832
NCLC 4, 22, 34; DA; DAB; DAC; DAM
DRAM, MST, POET; PC 5; SSC 38;
WLC
See also DA3; DLB 94

Gogarty, Oliver St. John 1878-1957
.... **TCLC 15**
See also CA 109; 150; DLB 15, 19

Gogol, Nikolai (Vasilyevich) 1809-1852
NCLC 5, 15, 31; DA; DAB; DAC; DAM
DRAM, MST; DC 1; SSC 4, 29; WLC
See also DLB 198

Goines, Donald 1937(?)-1974 . **CLC 80; BLC**
2; DAM MULT, POP
See also AITN 1; BW 1, 3; CA 124; 114;
CANR 82; DA3; DLB 33

Gold, Herbert 1924- .... **CLC 4, 7, 14, 42**
See also CA 9-12R; CANR 17, 45; DLB 2;
DLBY 81

Goldbarth, Albert 1948- .... **CLC 5, 38**
See also CA 53-56; CANR 6, 40; DLB 120

Goldberg, Anatol 1910-1982 .... **CLC 34**
See also CA 131; 117

Goldemberg, Isaac 1945- .... **CLC 52**
See also CA 69-72; CAAS 12; CANR 11,
32; HW 1

Golding, William (Gerald) 1911-1993
. **CLC 1, 2, 3, 8, 10, 17, 27, 58, 81; DA;**
DAB; DAC; DAM MST, NOV; WLC
See also AAYA 5; CA 5-8R; 141; CANR
13, 33, 54; CDBLB 1945-1960; DA3;
DLB 15, 100; MTCW 1, 2

Goldman, Emma 1869-1940 .... **TCLC 13**
See also CA 110; 150

Goldman, Francisco 1954- .... **CLC 76**
See also CA 162

Goldman, William (W.) 1931- ...... **CLC 1, 48**
See also CA 9-12R; CANR 29, 69; DLB 44

Goldmann, Lucien 1913-1970 .... **CLC 24**
See also CA 25-28; CAP 2

Goldoni, Carlo 1707-1793 .... **LC 4; DAM**
DRAM

Goldsberry, Steven 1949- .... **CLC 34**
See also CA 131

Goldsmith, Oliver 1728-1774 . **LC 2, 48; DA;**
DAB; DAC; DAM DRAM, MST, NOV,
POET; DC 8; WLC
See also CDBLB 1660-1789; DLB 39, 89,
104, 109, 142; SATA 26

Goldsmith, Peter
See Priestley, J(ohn) B(oynton)

Gombrowicz, Witold 1904-1969 .... **CLC 4, 7,**
11, 49; DAM DRAM
See also CA 19-20; 25-28R; CAP 2

Gomez de la Serna, Ramon 1888-1963
.... **CLC 9**
See also CA 153; 116; CANR 79; HW 1, 2

Goncharov, Ivan Alexandrovich 1812-1891
NCLC 1, 63

Goncourt, Edmond (Louis Antoine Huot) de
1822-1896 .... **NCLC 7**
See also DLB 123

Goncourt, Jules (Alfred Huot) de 1830-1870
NCLC 7
See also DLB 123

Gontier, Fernande 19(?)- .... **CLC 50**

Gonzalez Martinez, Enrique 1871-1952
TCLC 72
See also CA 166; CANR 81; HW 1, 2

Goodman, Paul 1911-1972 ..... **CLC 1, 2, 4, 7**
See also CA 19-20; 37-40R; CANR 34;
CAP 2; DLB 130; MTCW 1

Gordimer, Nadine 1923- ...... **CLC 3, 5, 7, 10,**
18, 33, 51, 70; DA; DAB; DAC; DAM
MST, NOV; SSC 17; WLCS
See also CA 5-8R; CANR 3, 28, 56, 88;
DA3; INT CANR-28; MTCW 1, 2

Gordon, Adam Lindsay 1833-1870 . **NCLC 21**

Gordon, Caroline 1895-1981 . **CLC 6, 13, 29, 83; SSC 15**
See also CA 11-12; 103; CANR 36; CAP 1; DLB 4, 9, 102; DLBD 17; DLBY 81; MTCW 1, 2

Gordon, Charles William 1860-1937
See Connor, Ralph
See also CA 109

Gordon, Mary (Catherine) 1949- .... **CLC 13, 22, 128**
See also CA 102; CANR 44; DLB 6; DLBY 81; INT 102; MTCW 1

Gordon, N. J.
See Bosman, Herman Charles

Gordon, Sol 1923- .... **CLC 26**
See also CA 53-56; CANR 4; SATA 11

Gordone, Charles 1925-1995 .... **CLC 1, 4; DAM DRAM; DC 8**
See also BW 1, 3; CA 93-96, 180; 150; CAAE 180; CANR 55; DLB 7; INT 93-96; MTCW 1

Gore, Catherine 1800-1861 .... **NCLC 65**
See also DLB 116

Gorenko, Anna Andreevna
See Akhmatova, Anna

Gorky, Maxim 1868-1936 ..... **TCLC 8; DAB; SSC 28; WLC**
See also Peshkov, Alexei Maximovich MTCW 2

Goryan, Sirak
See Saroyan, William

Gosse, Edmund (William) 1849-1928
.... **TCLC 28**
See also CA 117; DLB 57, 144, 184

Gotlieb, Phyllis Fay (Bloom) 1926- .. **CLC 18**
See also CA 13-16R; CANR 7; DLB 88

Gottesman, S. D.
See Kornbluth, C(yril) M.; Pohl, Frederik

Gottfried von Strassburg fl. c. 1210-
.... **CMLC 10**
See also DLB 138

Gould, Lois .... **CLC 4, 10**
See also CA 77-80; CANR 29; MTCW 1

Gourmont, Remy (-Marie-Charles) de 1858-1915 .... **TCLC 17**
See also CA 109; 150; MTCW 2

Govier, Katherine 1948- .... **CLC 51**
See also CA 101; CANR 18, 40

Goyen, (Charles) William 1915-1983 . **CLC 5, 8, 14, 40**
See also AITN 2; CA 5-8R; 110; CANR 6, 71; DLB 2; DLBY 83; INT CANR-6

Goytisolo, Juan 1931- . **CLC 5, 10, 23; DAM MULT; HLC 1**
See also CA 85-88; CANR 32, 61; HW 1, 2; MTCW 1, 2

Gozzano, Guido 1883-1916 .... **PC 10**
See also CA 154; DLB 114

Gozzi, (Conte) Carlo 1720-1806 .... **NCLC 23**

Grabbe, Christian Dietrich 1801-1836
.... **NCLC 2**
See also DLB 133

Grace, Patricia Frances 1937- .... **CLC 56**
See also CA 176

Gracian y Morales, Baltasar 1601-1658
.... **LC 15**

Gracq, Julien .... **CLC 11, 48**
See also Poirier, Louis DLB 83

Grade, Chaim 1910-1982 .... **CLC 10**
See also CA 93-96; 107

Graduate of Oxford, A
See Ruskin, John

Grafton, Garth
See Duncan, Sara Jeannette

Graham, John
See Phillips, David Graham

Graham, Jorie 1951- .... **CLC 48, 118**
See also CA 111; CANR 63; DLB 120

Graham, R(obert) B(ontine) Cunninghame
See Cunninghame Graham, Robert (Gallnigad) Bontine
See also DLB 98, 135, 174

Graham, Robert
See Haldeman, Joe (William)

Graham, Tom
See Lewis, (Harry) Sinclair

Graham, W(illiam) S(ydney) 1918-1986
.... **CLC 29**
See also CA 73-76; 118; DLB 20

Graham, Winston (Mawdsley) 1910-
.... **CLC 23**
See also CA 49-52; CANR 2, 22, 45, 66; DLB 77

Grahame, Kenneth 1859-1932 ...... **TCLC 64; DAB**
See also CA 108; 136; CANR 80; CLR 5; DA3; DLB 34, 141, 178; MAICYA; MTCW 2; SATA 100; YABC 1

Granovsky, Timofei Nikolaevich 1813-1855
NCLC 75
See also DLB 198

Grant, Skeeter
See Spiegelman, Art

Granville-Barker, Harley 1877-1946
.... **TCLC 2; DAM DRAM**
See also Barker, Harley Granville CA 104

Grass, Guenter (Wilhelm) 1927- ... **CLC 1, 2, 4, 6, 11, 15, 22, 32, 49, 88; DA; DAB; DAC; DAM MST, NOV; WLC**
See also CA 13-16R; CANR 20, 75; DA3; DLB 75, 124; MTCW 1, 2

Gratton, Thomas
See Hulme, T(homas) E(rnest)

Grau, Shirley Ann 1929- . **CLC 4, 9; SSC 15**
See also CA 89-92; CANR 22, 69; DLB 2; INT CANR-22; MTCW 1

Gravel, Fern
See Hall, James Norman

Graver, Elizabeth 1964- .... **CLC 70**
See also CA 135; CANR 71

Graves, Richard Perceval 1945- .... **CLC 44**
See also CA 65-68; CANR 9, 26, 51

Graves, Robert (von Ranke) 1895-1985
.... **CLC 1, 2, 6, 11, 39, 44, 45; DAB; DAC; DAM MST, POET; PC 6**
See also CA 5-8R; 117; CANR 5, 36; CD-BLB 1914-1945; DA3; DLB 20, 100, 191; DLBD 18; DLBY 85; MTCW 1, 2; SATA 45

Graves, Valerie
See Bradley, Marion Zimmer

Gray, Alasdair (James) 1934- .... **CLC 41**
See also CA 126; CANR 47, 69; DLB 194; INT 126; MTCW 1, 2

Gray, Amlin 1946- .... **CLC 29**
See also CA 138

Gray, Francine du Plessix 1930- ..... **CLC 22; DAM NOV**
See also BEST 90:3; CA 61-64; CAAS 2; CANR 11, 33, 75, 81; INT CANR-11; MTCW 1, 2

Gray, John (Henry) 1866-1934 ...... **TCLC 19**
See also CA 119; 162

Gray, Simon (James Holliday) 1936- . **CLC 9, 14, 36**
See also AITN 1; CA 21-24R; CAAS 3; CANR 32, 69; DLB 13; MTCW 1

Gray, Spalding 1941- ..... **CLC 49, 112; DAM POP; DC 7**
See also CA 128; CANR 74; MTCW 2

Gray, Thomas 1716-1771 ..... **LC 4, 40; DA; DAB; DAC; DAM MST; PC 2; WLC**
See also CDBLB 1660-1789; DA3; DLB 109

Grayson, David
See Baker, Ray Stannard

Grayson, Richard (A.) 1951- .... **CLC 38**

Greeley, Andrew M(oran) 1928- ..... **CLC 28; DAM POP**
See also CA 5-8R; CAAS 7; CANR 7, 43, 69; DA3; MTCW 1, 2

Green, Anna Katharine 1846-1935 . **TCLC 63**
See also CA 112; 159; DLB 202

Green, Brian
See Card, Orson Scott

Green, Hannah
See Greenberg, Joanne (Goldenberg)

Green, Hannah 1927(?)-1996 .... **CLC 3**
See also CA 73-76; CANR 59

Green, Henry 1905-1973 .... **CLC 2, 13, 97**
See also Yorke, Henry Vincent CA 175; DLB 15

Green, Julian (Hartridge) 1900-1998
See Green, Julien
See also CA 21-24R; 169; CANR 33, 87; DLB 4, 72; MTCW 1

Green, Julien .... **CLC 3, 11, 77**
See also Green, Julian (Hartridge) MTCW 2

Green, Paul (Eliot) 1894-1981 .... **CLC 25; DAM DRAM**
See also AITN 1; CA 5-8R; 103; CANR 3; DLB 7, 9; DLBY 81

Greenberg, Ivan 1908-1973
See Rahv, Philip
See also CA 85-88

Greenberg, Joanne (Goldenberg) 1932-
.... **CLC 7, 30**
See also AAYA 12; CA 5-8R; CANR 14, 32, 69; SATA 25

Greenberg, Richard 1959(?)- .... **CLC 57**
See also CA 138

Greene, Bette 1934- .... **CLC 30**
See also AAYA 7; CA 53-56; CANR 4; CLR 2; JRDA; MAICYA; SAAS 16; SATA 8, 102

Greene, Gael .... **CLC 8**
See also CA 13-16R; CANR 10

Greene, Graham (Henry) 1904-1991 . **CLC 1, 3, 6, 9, 14, 18, 27, 37, 70, 72, 125; DA; DAB; DAC; DAM MST, NOV; SSC 29; WLC**
See also AITN 2; CA 13-16R; 133; CANR 35, 61; CDBLB 1945-1960; DA3; DLB 13, 15, 77, 100, 162, 201, 204; DLBY 91; MTCW 1, 2; SATA 20

Greene, Robert 1558-1592 .... **LC 41**
See also DLB 62, 167

Greer, Richard
See Silverberg, Robert

Gregor, Arthur 1923- .... **CLC 9**
See also CA 25-28R; CAAS 10; CANR 11; SATA 36

Gregor, Lee
See Pohl, Frederik

Gregory, Isabella Augusta (Persse) 1852-1932 .... **TCLC 1**
See also CA 104; 184; DLB 10

Gregory, J. Dennis
See Williams, John A(lfred)

Grendon, Stephen
See Derleth, August (William)

Grenville, Kate 1950- .... **CLC 61**
See also CA 118; CANR 53

Grenville, Pelham
See Wodehouse, P(elham) G(renville)

Greve, Felix Paul (Berthold Friedrich) 1879-1948
See Grove, Frederick Philip
See also CA 104; 141, 175; CANR 79; DAC; DAM MST

Grey, Zane 1872-1939 . **TCLC 6; DAM POP**
See also CA 104; 132; DA3; DLB 212; MTCW 1, 2

Haley, Alex(ander Murray Palmer)
    1921-1992 . **CLC 8, 12, 76; BLC 2; DA;**
    DAB; DAC; DAM MST, MULT, POP
        See also AAYA 26; BW 2, 3; CA 77-80;
        136; CANR 61; CDALBS; DA3; DLB 38;
        MTCW 1, 2

Haliburton, Thomas Chandler 1796-1865
    NCLC 15
        See also DLB 11, 99

Hall, Donald (Andrew, Jr.) 1928- ...... **CLC 1,**
    13, 37, 59; DAM POET
        See also CA 5-8R; CAAS 7; CANR 2, 44,
        64; DLB 5; MTCW 1; SATA 23, 97

Hall, Frederic Sauser
        See Sauser-Hall, Frederic

Hall, James
        See Kuttner, Henry

Hall, James Norman 1887-1951 ..... **TCLC 23**
        See also CA 123; 173; SATA 21

Hall, Radclyffe
        See Hall, (Marguerite) Radclyffe
        See also MTCW 2

Hall, (Marguerite) Radclyffe 1886-1943
    TCLC 12
        See also CA 110; 150; CANR 83; DLB 191

Hall, Rodney 1935- .... **CLC 51**
        See also CA 109; CANR 69

Halleck, Fitz-Greene 1790-1867 .... **NCLC 47**
        See also DLB 3

Halliday, Michael
        See Creasey, John

Halpern, Daniel 1945- .... **CLC 14**
        See also CA 33-36R

Hamburger, Michael (Peter Leopold) 1924-
    CLC 5, 14
        See also CA 5-8R; CAAS 4; CANR 2, 47;
        DLB 27

Hamill, Pete 1935- .... **CLC 10**
        See also CA 25-28R; CANR 18, 71

Hamilton, Alexander 1755(?)-1804 . **NCLC 49**
        See also DLB 37

Hamilton, Clive
        See Lewis, C(live) S(taples)

Hamilton, Edmond 1904-1977 .... **CLC 1**
        See also CA 1-4R; CANR 3, 84; DLB 8

Hamilton, Eugene (Jacob) Lee
        See Lee-Hamilton, Eugene (Jacob)

Hamilton, Franklin
        See Silverberg, Robert

Hamilton, Gail
        See Corcoran, Barbara

Hamilton, Mollie
        See Kaye, M(ary) M(argaret)

Hamilton, (Anthony Walter) Patrick
    1904-1962 .... **CLC 51**
        See also CA 176; 113; DLB 191

Hamilton, Virginia 1936- ...... **CLC 26; DAM**
    MULT
        See also AAYA 2, 21; BW 2, 3; CA 25-28R;
        CANR 20, 37, 73; CLR 1, 11, 40; DLB
        33, 52; INT CANR-20; JRDA; MAICYA;
        MTCW 1, 2; SATA 4, 56, 79

Hammett, (Samuel) Dashiell 1894-1961
    .... **CLC 3, 5, 10, 19, 47; SSC 17**
        See also AITN 1; CA 81-84; CANR 42;
        CDALB 1929-1941; DA3; DLBD 6;
        DLBY 96; MTCW 1, 2

Hammon, Jupiter 1711(?)-1800(?) . **NCLC 5;**
    BLC 2; DAM MULT, POET; PC 16
        See also DLB 31, 50

Hammond, Keith
        See Kuttner, Henry

Hamner, Earl (Henry), Jr. 1923- ...... **CLC 12**
        See also AITN 2; CA 73-76; DLB 6

Hampton, Christopher (James) 1946-
        .... **CLC 4**
        See also CA 25-28R; DLB 13; MTCW 1

Hamsun, Knut .... **TCLC 2, 14, 49**
        See also Pedersen, Knut

Handke, Peter 1942- ... **CLC 5, 8, 10, 15, 38;**
    DAM DRAM, NOV
        See also CA 77-80; CANR 33, 75; DLB 85,
        124; MTCW 1, 2

Handy, W(illiam) C(hristopher) 1873-1958
    TCLC 97
        See also BW 3; CA 121; 167

Hanley, James 1901-1985 ..... **CLC 3, 5, 8, 13**
        See also CA 73-76; 117; CANR 36; DLB
        191; MTCW 1

Hannah, Barry 1942- .... **CLC 23, 38, 90**
        See also CA 108; 110; CANR 43, 68; DLB
        6; INT 110; MTCW 1

Hannon, Ezra
        See Hunter, Evan

Hansberry, Lorraine (Vivian) 1930-1965
        CLC 17, 62; BLC 2; DA; DAB; DAC;
        DAM DRAM, MST, MULT; DC 2
        See also AAYA 25; BW 1, 3; CA 109; 25-
        28R; CABS 3; CANR 58; CDALB 1941-
        1968; DA3; DLB 7, 38; MTCW 1, 2

Hansen, Joseph 1923- .... **CLC 38**
        See also CA 29-32R; CAAS 17; CANR 16,
        44, 66; INT CANR-16

Hansen, Martin A(lfred) 1909-1955
        .... **TCLC 32**
        See also CA 167

Hanson, Kenneth O(stlin) 1922- .... **CLC 13**
        See also CA 53-56; CANR 7

Hardwick, Elizabeth (Bruce) 1916- . **CLC 13;**
    DAM NOV
        See also CA 5-8R; CANR 3, 32, 70; DA3;
        DLB 6; MTCW 1, 2

Hardy, Thomas 1840-1928 .. **TCLC 4, 10, 18,**
    32, 48, 53, 72; DA; DAB; DAC; DAM
    MST, NOV, POET; PC 8; SSC 2; WLC
        See also CA 104; 123; CDBLB 1890-1914;
        DA3; DLB 18, 19, 135; MTCW 1, 2

Hare, David 1947- .... **CLC 29, 58**
        See also CA 97-100; CANR 39; DLB 13;
        MTCW 1

Harewood, John
        See Van Druten, John (William)

Harford, Henry
        See Hudson, W(illiam) H(enry)

Hargrave, Leonie
        See Disch, Thomas M(ichael)

Harjo, Joy 1951- . **CLC 83; DAM MULT; PC**
    27
        See also CA 114; CANR 35, 67; DLB 120,
        175; MTCW 2; NNAL

Harlan, Louis R(udolph) 1922- .... **CLC 34**
        See also CA 21-24R; CANR 25, 55, 80

Harling, Robert 1951(?)- .... **CLC 53**
        See also CA 147

Harmon, William (Ruth) 1938- .... **CLC 38**
        See also CA 33-36R; CANR 14, 32, 35;
        SATA 65

Harper, F. E. W.
        See Harper, Frances Ellen Watkins

Harper, Frances E. W.
        See Harper, Frances Ellen Watkins

Harper, Frances E. Watkins
        See Harper, Frances Ellen Watkins

Harper, Frances Ellen
        See Harper, Frances Ellen Watkins

Harper, Frances Ellen Watkins 1825-1911
        TCLC 14; BLC 2; DAM MULT, POET;
        PC 21
        See also BW 1, 3; CA 111; 125; CANR 79;
        DLB 50

Harper, Michael S(teven) 1938- ... **CLC 7, 22**
        See also BW 1; CA 33-36R; CANR 24;
        DLB 41

Harper, Mrs. F. E. W.
        See Harper, Frances Ellen Watkins

Harris, Christie (Lucy) Irwin 1907- . **CLC 12**
        See also CA 5-8R; CANR 6, 83; CLR 47;
        DLB 88; JRDA; MAICYA; SAAS 10;
        SATA 6, 74

Harris, Frank 1856-1931 .... **TCLC 24**
        See also CA 109; 150; CANR 80; DLB 156,
        197

Harris, George Washington 1814-1869
        .... **NCLC 23**
        See also DLB 3, 11

Harris, Joel Chandler 1848-1908 ... **TCLC 2;**
    SSC 19
        See also CA 104; 137; CANR 80; CLR 49;
        DLB 11, 23, 42, 78, 91; MAICYA; SATA
        100; YABC 1

Harris, John (Wyndham Parkes Lucas)
    Beynon 1903-1969
        See Wyndham, John
        See also CA 102; 89-92; CANR 84

Harris, MacDonald .... **CLC 9**
        See also Heiney, Donald (William)

Harris, Mark 1922- .... **CLC 19**
        See also CA 5-8R; CAAS 3; CANR 2, 55,
        83; DLB 2; DLBY 80

Harris, (Theodore) Wilson 1921- ..... **CLC 25**
        See also BW 2, 3; CA 65-68; CAAS 16;
        CANR 11, 27, 69; DLB 117; MTCW 1

Harrison, Elizabeth Cavanna 1909-
        See Cavanna, Betty
        See also CA 9-12R; CANR 6, 27, 85

Harrison, Harry (Max) 1925- .... **CLC 42**
        See also CA 1-4R; CANR 5, 21, 84; DLB
        8; SATA 4

Harrison, James (Thomas) 1937- ...... **CLC 6,**
    14, 33, 66; SSC 19
        See also CA 13-16R; CANR 8, 51, 79;
        DLBY 82; INT CANR-8

Harrison, Jim
        See Harrison, James (Thomas)

Harrison, Kathryn 1961- .... **CLC 70**
        See also CA 144; CANR 68

Harrison, Tony 1937- .... **CLC 43, 129**
        See also CA 65-68; CANR 44; DLB 40;
        MTCW 1

Harriss, Will(ard Irvin) 1922- .... **CLC 34**
        See also CA 111

Harson, Sley
        See Ellison, Harlan (Jay)

Hart, Ellis
        See Ellison, Harlan (Jay)

Hart, Josephine 1942(?)- .... **CLC 70; DAM**
    POP
        See also CA 138; CANR 70

Hart, Moss 1904-1961 .... **CLC 66; DAM**
    DRAM
        See also CA 109; 89-92; CANR 84; DLB 7

Harte, (Francis) Bret(t) 1836(?)-1902
    ... **TCLC 1, 25; DA; DAC; DAM MST;**
    SSC 8; WLC
        See also CA 104; 140; CANR 80; CDALB
        1865-1917; DA3; DLB 12, 64, 74, 79,
        186; SATA 26

Hartley, L(eslie) P(oles) 1895-1972 ... **CLC 2,**
    22
        See also CA 45-48; 37-40R; CANR 33;
        DLB 15, 139; MTCW 1, 2

Hartman, Geoffrey H. 1929- .... **CLC 27**
        See also CA 117; 125; CANR 79; DLB 67

Hartmann, Eduard von 1842-1906 . **TCLC 97**

Hartmann, Sadakichi 1867-1944 ... **TCLC 73**
        See also CA 157; DLB 54

Hartmann von Aue c. 1160-c. 1205
        .... **CMLC 15**
        See also DLB 138

Hartmann von Aue 1170-1210 ...... **CMLC 15**

Haruf, Kent 1943- .... **CLC 34**
        See also CA 149

Harwood, Ronald 1934- .... **CLC 32; DAM**
    DRAM, MST
        See also CA 1-4R; CANR 4, 55; DLB 13

Hughes, Colin
See Creasey, John
Hughes, David (John) 1930- .... **CLC 48**
See also CA 116; 129; DLB 14
Hughes, Edward James
See Hughes, Ted
See also DAM MST, POET; DA3
Hughes, (James) Langston 1902-1967
. **CLC 1, 5, 10, 15, 35, 44, 108; BLC 2;
DA; DAB; DAC; DAM DRAM, MST,
MULT, POET; DC 3; PC 1; SSC 6;
WLC**
See also AAYA 12; BW 1, 3; CA 1-4R; 25-
28R; CANR 1, 34, 82; CDALB 1929-
1941; CLR 17; DA3; DLB 4, 7, 48, 51,
86; JRDA; MAICYA; MTCW 1, 2; SATA
4, 33
Hughes, Richard (Arthur Warren)
1900-1976 .... **CLC 1, 11; DAM NOV**
See also CA 5-8R; 65-68; CANR 4; DLB
15, 161; MTCW 1; SATA 8; SATA-Obit
25
Hughes, Ted 1930-1998 . **CLC 2, 4, 9, 14, 37,
119; DAB; DAC; PC 7**
See also Hughes, Edward James CA 1-4R;
171; CANR 1, 33, 66; CLR 3; DLB 40,
161; MAICYA; MTCW 1, 2; SATA 49;
SATA-Brief 27; SATA-Obit 107
Hugo, Richard F(ranklin) 1923-1982 . **CLC 6,
18, 32; DAM POET**
See also CA 49-52; 108; CANR 3; DLB 5,
206
Hugo, Victor (Marie) 1802-1885 .... **NCLC 3,
10, 21; DA; DAB; DAC; DAM DRAM,
MST, NOV, POET; PC 17; WLC**
See also AAYA 28; DA3; DLB 119, 192;
SATA 47
Huidobro, Vicente
See Huidobro Fernandez, Vicente Garcia
Huidobro Fernandez, Vicente Garcia
1893-1948 .... **TCLC 31**
See also CA 131; HW 1
Hulme, Keri 1947- .... **CLC 39, 130**
See also CA 125; CANR 69; INT 125
Hulme, T(homas) E(rnest) 1883-1917
.... **TCLC 21**
See also CA 117; DLB 19
Hume, David 1711-1776 .... **LC 7, 56**
See also DLB 104
Humphrey, William 1924-1997 .... **CLC 45**
See also CA 77-80; 160; CANR 68; DLB
212
Humphreys, Emyr Owen 1919- .... **CLC 47**
See also CA 5-8R; CANR 3, 24; DLB 15
Humphreys, Josephine 1945- ..... **CLC 34, 57**
See also CA 121; 127; INT 127
Huneker, James Gibbons 1857-1921
.... **TCLC 65**
See also DLB 71
Hungerford, Pixie
See Brinsmead, H(esba) F(ay)
Hunt, E(verette) Howard, (Jr.) 1918- . **CLC 3**
See also AITN 1; CA 45-48; CANR 2, 47
Hunt, Francesca
See Holland, Isabelle
Hunt, Kyle
See Creasey, John
Hunt, (James Henry) Leigh 1784-1859
.... **NCLC 1, 70; DAM POET**
See also DLB 96, 110, 144
Hunt, Marsha 1946- .... **CLC 70**
See also BW 2, 3; CA 143; CANR 79
Hunt, Violet 1866(?)-1942 .... **TCLC 53**
See also CA 184; DLB 162, 197
Hunter, E. Waldo
See Sturgeon, Theodore (Hamilton)
Hunter, Evan 1926- . **CLC 11, 31; DAM POP**
See also CA 5-8R; CANR 5, 38, 62; DLBY
82; INT CANR-5; MTCW 1; SATA 25

Hunter, Kristin (Eggleston) 1931- .... **CLC 35**
See also AITN 1; BW 1; CA 13-16R;
CANR 13; CLR 3; DLB 33; INT CANR-
13; MAICYA; SAAS 10; SATA 12
Hunter, Mary
See Austin, Mary (Hunter)
Hunter, Mollie 1922- .... **CLC 21**
See also McIlwraith, Maureen Mollie
Hunter AAYA 13; CANR 37, 78; CLR 25;
DLB 161; JRDA; MAICYA; SAAS 7;
SATA 54, 106
Hunter, Robert (?)-1734 .... **LC 7**
Hurston, Zora Neale 1903-1960 .. **CLC 7, 30,
61; BLC 2; DA; DAC; DAM MST,
MULT, NOV; DC 12; SSC 4; WLCS**
See also AAYA 15; BW 1, 3; CA 85-88;
CANR 61; CDALBS; DA3; DLB 51, 86;
MTCW 1, 2
Husserl, E. G.
See Husserl, Edmund (Gustav Albrecht)
Husserl, Edmund (Gustav Albrecht)
1859-1938 .... **TCLC 100**
See also CA 116; 133
Huston, John (Marcellus) 1906-1987
.... **CLC 20**
See also CA 73-76; 123; CANR 34; DLB
26
Hustvedt, Siri 1955- .... **CLC 76**
See also CA 137
Hutten, Ulrich von 1488-1523 .... **LC 16**
See also DLB 179
Huxley, Aldous (Leonard) 1894-1963 . **CLC 1,
3, 4, 5, 8, 11, 18, 35, 79; DA; DAB;
DAC; DAM MST, NOV; SSC 39; WLC**
See also AAYA 11; CA 85-88; CANR 44;
CDBLB 1914-1945; DA3; DLB 36, 100,
162, 195; MTCW 1, 2; SATA 63
Huxley, T(homas) H(enry) 1825-1895
.... **NCLC 67**
See also DLB 57
Huysmans, Joris-Karl 1848-1907 ... **TCLC 7,
69**
See also CA 104; 165; DLB 123
Hwang, David Henry 1957- .. **CLC 55; DAM
DRAM; DC 4**
See also CA 127; 132; CANR 76; DA3;
DLB 212; INT 132; MTCW 2
Hyde, Anthony 1946- .... **CLC 42**
See also CA 136
Hyde, Margaret O(ldroyd) 1917- ..... **CLC 21**
See also CA 1-4R; CANR 1, 36; CLR 23;
JRDA; MAICYA; SAAS 8; SATA 1, 42,
76
Hynes, James 1956(?)- .... **CLC 65**
See also CA 164
Hypatia c. 370-415 .... **CMLC 35**
Ian, Janis 1951- .... **CLC 21**
See also CA 105
Ibanez, Vicente Blasco
See Blasco Ibanez, Vicente
Ibarbourou, Juana de 1895-1979
See also HLCS 2; HW 1
Ibarguengoitia, Jorge 1928-1983 ...... **CLC 37**
See also CA 124; 113; HW 1
Ibsen, Henrik (Johan) 1828-1906 ... **TCLC 2,
8, 16, 37, 52; DA; DAB; DAC; DAM
DRAM, MST; DC 2; WLC**
See also CA 104; 141; DA3
Ibuse, Masuji 1898-1993 .... **CLC 22**
See also CA 127; 141; DLB 180
Ichikawa, Kon 1915- .... **CLC 20**
See also CA 121
Idle, Eric 1943- .... **CLC 21**
See also Monty Python CA 116; CANR 35
Ignatow, David 1914-1997 .. **CLC 4, 7, 14, 40**
See also CA 9-12R; 162; CAAS 3; CANR
31, 57; DLB 5

Ignotus
See Strachey, (Giles) Lytton
Ihimaera, Witi 1944- .... **CLC 46**
See also CA 77-80
Ilf, Ilya .... **TCLC 21**
See also Fainzilberg, Ilya Arnoldovich
Illyes, Gyula 1902-1983 .... **PC 16**
See also CA 114; 109
Immermann, Karl (Lebrecht) 1796-1840
NCLC 4, 49
See also DLB 133
Ince, Thomas H. 1882-1924 .... **TCLC 89**
Inchbald, Elizabeth 1753-1821 ...... **NCLC 62**
See also DLB 39, 89
Inclan, Ramon (Maria) del Valle
See Valle-Inclan, Ramon (Maria) del
Infante, G(uillermo) Cabrera
See Cabrera Infante, G(uillermo)
Ingalls, Rachel (Holmes) 1940- .... **CLC 42**
See also CA 123; 127
Ingamells, Reginald Charles
See Ingamells, Rex
Ingamells, Rex 1913-1955 .... **TCLC 35**
See also CA 167
Inge, William (Motter) 1913-1973 . **CLC 1, 8,
19; DAM DRAM**
See also CA 9-12R; CDALB 1941-1968;
DA3; DLB 7; MTCW 1, 2
Ingelow, Jean 1820-1897 .... **NCLC 39**
See also DLB 35, 163; SATA 33
Ingram, Willis J.
See Harris, Mark
Innaurato, Albert (F.) 1948(?)- ... **CLC 21, 60**
See also CA 115; 122; CANR 78; INT 122
Innes, Michael
See Stewart, J(ohn) I(nnes) M(ackintosh)
Innis, Harold Adams 1894-1952 .... **TCLC 77**
See also CA 181; DLB 88
Ionesco, Eugene 1909-1994 ... **CLC 1, 4, 6, 9,
11, 15, 41, 86; DA; DAB; DAC; DAM
DRAM, MST; DC 12; WLC**
See also CA 9-12R; 144; CANR 55; DA3;
MTCW 1, 2; SATA 7; SATA-Obit 79
Iqbal, Muhammad 1873-1938 .... **TCLC 28**
Ireland, Patrick
See O'Doherty, Brian
Iron, Ralph
See Schreiner, Olive (Emilie Albertina)
Irving, John (Winslow) 1942- ... **CLC 13, 23,
38, 112; DAM NOV, POP**
See also AAYA 8; BEST 89:3; CA 25-28R;
CANR 28, 73; DA3; DLB 6; DLBY 82;
MTCW 1, 2
Irving, Washington 1783-1859 . **NCLC 2, 19;
DA; DAB; DAC; DAM MST; SSC 2,
37; WLC**
See also CDALB 1640-1865; DA3; DLB 3,
11, 30, 59, 73, 74, 186; YABC 2
Irwin, P. K.
See Page, P(atricia) K(athleen)
Isaacs, Jorge Ricardo 1837-1895 ... **NCLC 70**
Isaacs, Susan 1943- .... **CLC 32; DAM POP**
See also BEST 89:1; CA 89-92; CANR 20,
41, 65; DA3; INT CANR-20; MTCW 1, 2
Isherwood, Christopher (William Bradshaw)
1904-1986 .. **CLC 1, 9, 11, 14, 44; DAM
DRAM, NOV**
See also CA 13-16R; 117; CANR 35; DA3;
DLB 15, 195; DLBY 86; MTCW 1, 2
Ishiguro, Kazuo 1954- . **CLC 27, 56, 59, 110;
DAM NOV**
See also BEST 90:2; CA 120; CANR 49;
DA3; DLB 194; MTCW 1, 2
Ishikawa, Hakuhin
See Ishikawa, Takuboku
Ishikawa, Takuboku 1886(?)-1912
.... **TCLC 15; DAM POET; PC 10**
See also CA 113; 153

Krleza, Miroslav 1893-1981 .... **CLC 8, 114**
    See also CA 97-100; 105; CANR 50; DLB
    147
Kroetsch, Robert 1927- .... **CLC 5, 23, 57;**
    DAC; DAM POET
    See also CA 17-20R; CANR 8, 38; DLB
    53; MTCW 1
Kroetz, Franz
    See Kroetz, Franz Xaver
Kroetz, Franz Xaver 1946- .... **CLC 41**
    See also CA 130
Kroker, Arthur (W.) 1945- .... **CLC 77**
    See also CA 161
Kropotkin, Peter (Aleksieevich) 1842-1921
    TCLC 36
    See also CA 119
Krotkov, Yuri 1917- .... **CLC 19**
    See also CA 102
Krumb
    See Crumb, R(obert)
Krumgold, Joseph (Quincy) 1908-1980
    .... **CLC 12**
    See also CA 9-12R; 101; CANR 7; MAI-
    CYA; SATA 1, 48; SATA-Obit 23
Krumwitz
    See Crumb, R(obert)
Krutch, Joseph Wood 1893-1970 ..... **CLC 24**
    See also CA 1-4R; 25-28R; CANR 4; DLB
    63, 206
Krutzch, Gus
    See Eliot, T(homas) S(tearns)
Krylov, Ivan Andreevich 1768(?)-1844
    .... **NCLC 1**
    See also DLB 150
Kubin, Alfred (Leopold Isidor) 1877-1959
    TCLC 23
    See also CA 112; 149; DLB 81
Kubrick, Stanley 1928-1999 .... **CLC 16**
    See also AAYA 30; CA 81-84; 177; CANR
    33; DLB 26
Kueng, Hans 1928-
    See Kung, Hans
    See also CA 53-56; CANR 66; MTCW 1, 2
Kumin, Maxine (Winokur) 1925- ..... **CLC 5,**
    13, 28; DAM POET; PC 15
    See also AITN 2; CA 1-4R; CAAS 8;
    CANR 1, 21, 69; DA3; DLB 5; MTCW
    1, 2; SATA 12
Kundera, Milan 1929- . **CLC 4, 9, 19, 32, 68,**
    115; DAM NOV; SSC 24
    See also AAYA 2; CA 85-88; CANR 19,
    52, 74; DA3; MTCW 1, 2
Kunene, Mazisi (Raymond) 1930- ... **CLC 85**
    See also BW 1, 3; CA 125; CANR 81; DLB
    117
Kung, Hans 1928- .... **CLC 130**
    See also Kueng, Hans
Kunikida Doppo 1871-1908 .... **TCLC 100**
Kunitz, Stanley (Jasspon) 1905- .. **CLC 6, 11,**
    14; PC 19
    See also CA 41-44R; CANR 26, 57; DA3;
    DLB 48; INT CANR-26; MTCW 1, 2
Kunze, Reiner 1933- .... **CLC 10**
    See also CA 93-96; DLB 75
Kuprin, Aleksander Ivanovich 1870-1938
    TCLC 5
    See also CA 104; 182
Kureishi, Hanif 1954(?)- .... **CLC 64**
    See also CA 139; DLB 194
Kurosawa, Akira 1910-1998 .... **CLC 16, 119;**
    DAM MULT
    See also AAYA 11; CA 101; 170; CANR 46
Kushner, Tony 1957(?)- .... **CLC 81; DAM**
    DRAM; DC 10
    See also CA 144; CANR 74; DA3; MTCW
    2
Kuttner, Henry 1915-1958 .... **TCLC 10**
    See also CA 107; 157; DLB 8
Kuzma, Greg 1944- .... **CLC 7**

See also CA 33-36R; CANR 70
Kuzmin, Mikhail 1872(?)-1936 ...... **TCLC 40**
    See also CA 170
Kyd, Thomas 1558-1594 .... **LC 22; DAM**
    DRAM; DC 3
    See also DLB 62
Kyprianos, Iossif
    See Samarakis, Antonis
La Bruyere, Jean de 1645-1696 .... **LC 17**
Lacan, Jacques (Marie Emile) 1901-1981
    CLC 75
    See also CA 121; 104
Laclos, Pierre Ambroise Francois Choderlos
    de 1741-1803 .... **NCLC 4**
Lacolere, Francois
    See Aragon, Louis
La Colere, Francois
    See Aragon, Louis
La Deshabilleuse
    See Simenon, Georges (Jacques Christian)
Lady Gregory
    See Gregory, Isabella Augusta (Persse)
Lady of Quality, A
    See Bagnold, Enid
La Fayette, Marie (Madelaine Pioche de la
    Vergne Comtes 1634-1693 .... **LC 2**
Lafayette, Rene
    See Hubbard, L(afayette) Ron(ald)
La Fontaine, Jean de 1621-1695 .... **LC 50**
    See also MAICYA; SATA 18
Laforgue, Jules 1860-1887 . **NCLC 5, 53; PC**
    14; SSC 20
Lagerkvist, Paer (Fabian) 1891-1974 . **CLC 7,**
    10, 13, 54; DAM DRAM, NOV
    See also Lagerkvist, Par CA 85-88; 49-52;
    DA3; MTCW 1, 2
Lagerkvist, Par .... **SSC 12**
    See also Lagerkvist, Paer (Fabian) MTCW
    2
Lagerloef, Selma (Ottiliana Lovisa)
    1858-1940 .... **TCLC 4, 36**
    See also Lagerlof, Selma (Ottiliana Lovisa)
    CA 108; MTCW 2; SATA 15
Lagerlof, Selma (Ottiliana Lovisa)
    See Lagerloef, Selma (Ottiliana Lovisa)
    See also CLR 7; SATA 15
La Guma, (Justin) Alex(ander) 1925-1985
    CLC 19; BLCS; DAM MULT
    See also BW 1, 3; CA 49-52; 118; CANR
    25, 81; DLB 117; MTCW 1, 2
Laidlaw, A. K.
    See Grieve, C(hristopher) M(urray)
Lainez, Manuel Mujica
    See Mujica Lainez, Manuel
    See also HW 1
Laing, R(onald) D(avid) 1927-1989 . **CLC 95**
    See also CA 107; 129; CANR 34; MTCW 1
Lamartine, Alphonse (Marie Louis Prat) de
    1790-1869 . **NCLC 11; DAM POET; PC**
    16
Lamb, Charles 1775-1834 ..... **NCLC 10; DA;**
    DAB; DAC; DAM MST; WLC
    See also CDBLB 1789-1832; DLB 93, 107,
    163; SATA 17
Lamb, Lady Caroline 1785-1828 ... **NCLC 38**
    See also DLB 116
Lamming, George (William) 1927- ... **CLC 2,**
    4, 66; BLC 2; DAM MULT
    See also BW 2, 3; CA 85-88; CANR 26,
    76; DLB 125; MTCW 1, 2
L'Amour, Louis (Dearborn) 1908-1988
    .... **CLC 25, 55; DAM NOV, POP**
    See also AAYA 16; AITN 2; BEST 89:2;
    CA 1-4R; 125; CANR 3, 25, 40; DA3;
    DLB 206; DLBY 80; MTCW 1, 2
Lampedusa, Giuseppe (Tomasi) di 1896-1957
    TCLC 13

See also Tomasi di Lampedusa, Giuseppe
    CA 164; DLB 177; MTCW 2
Lampman, Archibald 1861-1899 ... **NCLC 25**
    See also DLB 92
Lancaster, Bruce 1896-1963 .... **CLC 36**
    See also CA 9-10; CANR 70; CAP 1; SATA
    9
Lanchester, John .... **CLC 99**
Landau, Mark Alexandrovich
    See Aldanov, Mark (Alexandrovich)
Landau-Aldanov, Mark Alexandrovich
    See Aldanov, Mark (Alexandrovich)
Landis, Jerry
    See Simon, Paul (Frederick)
Landis, John 1950- .... **CLC 26**
    See also CA 112; 122
Landolfi, Tommaso 1908-1979 .... **CLC 11, 49**
    See also CA 127; 117; DLB 177
Landon, Letitia Elizabeth 1802-1838
    .... **NCLC 15**
    See also DLB 96
Landor, Walter Savage 1775-1864 . **NCLC 14**
    See also DLB 93, 107
Landwirth, Heinz 1927-
    See Lind, Jakov
    See also CA 9-12R; CANR 7
Lane, Patrick 1939- ... **CLC 25; DAM POET**
    See also CA 97-100; CANR 54; DLB 53;
    INT 97-100
Lang, Andrew 1844-1912 .... **TCLC 16**
    See also CA 114; 137; CANR 85; DLB 98,
    141, 184; MAICYA; SATA 16
Lang, Fritz 1890-1976 .... **CLC 20, 103**
    See also CA 77-80; 69-72; CANR 30
Lange, John
    See Crichton, (John) Michael
Langer, Elinor 1939- .... **CLC 34**
    See also CA 121
Langland, William 1330(?)-1400(?) ... **LC 19;**
    DA; DAB; DAC; DAM MST, POET
    See also DLB 146
Langstaff, Launcelot
    See Irving, Washington
Lanier, Sidney 1842-1881 ..... **NCLC 6; DAM**
    POET
    See also DLB 64; DLBD 13; MAICYA;
    SATA 18
Lanyer, Aemilia 1569-1645 .... **LC 10, 30**
    See also DLB 121
Lao-Tzu
    See Lao Tzu
Lao Tzu fl. 6th cent. B.C.- .... **CMLC 7**
Lapine, James (Elliot) 1949- .... **CLC 39**
    See also CA 123; 130; CANR 54; INT 130
Larbaud, Valery (Nicolas) 1881-1957
    .... **TCLC 9**
    See also CA 106; 152
Lardner, Ring
    See Lardner, Ring(gold) W(ilmer)
Lardner, Ring W., Jr.
    See Lardner, Ring(gold) W(ilmer)
Lardner, Ring(gold) W(ilmer) 1885-1933
    TCLC 2, 14; SSC 32
    See also CA 104; 131; CDALB 1917-1929;
    DLB 11, 25, 86; DLBD 16; MTCW 1, 2
Laredo, Betty
    See Codrescu, Andrei
Larkin, Maia
    See Wojciechowska, Maia (Teresa)
Larkin, Philip (Arthur) 1922-1985 ... **CLC 3,**
    5, 8, 9, 13, 18, 33, 39, 64; DAB; DAM
    MST, POET; PC 21
    See also CA 5-8R; 117; CANR 24, 62; CD-
    BLB 1960 to Present; DA3; DLB 27;
    MTCW 1, 2
Larra (y Sanchez de Castro), Mariano Jose
    de 1809-1837 .... **NCLC 17**
Larsen, Eric 1941- .... **CLC 55**

Malcolm, Dan
See Silverberg, Robert

Malcolm X ...... **CLC 82, 117; BLC 2; WLCS**
See also Little, Malcolm

Malherbe, Francois de 1555-1628 .... **LC 5**

Mallarme, Stephane 1842-1898 . **NCLC 4, 41;**
DAM POET; PC 4

Mallet-Joris, Francoise 1930- .... **CLC 11**
See also CA 65-68; CANR 17; DLB 83

Malley, Ern
See McAuley, James Phillip

Mallowan, Agatha Christie
See Christie, Agatha (Mary Clarissa)

Maloff, Saul 1922- .... **CLC 5**
See also CA 33-36R

Malone, Louis
See MacNeice, (Frederick) Louis

Malone, Michael (Christopher) 1942-
.... **CLC 43**
See also CA 77-80; CANR 14, 32, 57

Malory, (Sir) Thomas 1410(?)-1471(?)
.. **LC 11; DA; DAB; DAC; DAM MST;**
WLCS
See also CDBLB Before 1660; DLB 146;
SATA 59; SATA-Brief 33

Malouf, (George Joseph) David 1934-
.... **CLC 28, 86**
See also CA 124; CANR 50, 76; MTCW 2

Malraux, (Georges-)Andre 1901-1976
..... **CLC 1, 4, 9, 13, 15, 57; DAM NOV**
See also CA 21-22; 69-72; CANR 34, 58;
CAP 2; DA3; DLB 72; MTCW 1, 2

Malzberg, Barry N(athaniel) 1939- ... **CLC 7**
See also CA 61-64; CAAS 4; CANR 16;
DLB 8

Mamet, David (Alan) 1947- .. **CLC 9, 15, 34,**
46, 91; DAM DRAM; DC 4
See also AAYA 3; CA 81-84; CABS 3;
CANR 15, 41, 67, 72; DA3; DLB 7;
MTCW 1, 2

Mamoulian, Rouben (Zachary) 1897-1987
CLC 16
See also CA 25-28R; 124; CANR 85

Mandelstam, Osip (Emilievich)
1891(?)-1938(?) .... **TCLC 2, 6; PC 14**
See also CA 104; 150; MTCW 2

Mander, (Mary) Jane 1877-1949 ... **TCLC 31**
See also CA 162

Mandeville, John fl. 1350- .... **CMLC 19**
See also DLB 146

Mandiargues, Andre Pieyre de .... **CLC 41**
See also Pieyre de Mandiargues, Andre
DLB 83

Mandrake, Ethel Belle
See Thurman, Wallace (Henry)

Mangan, James Clarence 1803-1849
.... **NCLC 27**

Maniere, J.-E.
See Giraudoux, (Hippolyte) Jean

Mankiewicz, Herman (Jacob) 1897-1953
TCLC 85
See also CA 120; 169; DLB 26

Manley, (Mary) Delariviere 1672(?)-1724
.... **LC 1, 42**
See also DLB 39, 80

Mann, Abel
See Creasey, John

Mann, Emily 1952- .... **DC 7**
See also CA 130; CANR 55

Mann, (Luiz) Heinrich 1871-1950 ... **TCLC 9**
See also CA 106; 164, 181; DLB 66, 118

Mann, (Paul) Thomas 1875-1955 ... **TCLC 2,**
8, 14, 21, 35, 44, 60; DA; DAB; DAC;
DAM MST, NOV; SSC 5; WLC
See also CA 104; 128; DA3; DLB 66;
MTCW 1, 2

Mannheim, Karl 1893-1947 .... **TCLC 65**

Manning, David
See Faust, Frederick (Schiller)

Manning, Frederic 1887(?)-1935 ... **TCLC 25**
See also CA 124

Manning, Olivia 1915-1980 .... **CLC 5, 19**
See also CA 5-8R; 101; CANR 29; MTCW
1

Mano, D. Keith 1942- .... **CLC 2, 10**
See also CA 25-28R; CAAS 6; CANR 26,
57; DLB 6

Mansfield, Katherine . **TCLC 2, 8, 39; DAB;**
SSC 9, 23, 38; WLC
See also Beauchamp, Kathleen Mansfield
DLB 162

Manso, Peter 1940- .... **CLC 39**
See also CA 29-32R; CANR 44

Mantecon, Juan Jimenez
See Jimenez (Mantecon), Juan Ramon

Manton, Peter
See Creasey, John

Man Without a Spleen, A
See Chekhov, Anton (Pavlovich)

Manzoni, Alessandro 1785-1873 .... **NCLC 29**

Map, Walter 1140-1209 .... **CMLC 32**

Mapu, Abraham (ben Jekutiel) 1808-1867
NCLC 18

Mara, Sally
See Queneau, Raymond

Marat, Jean Paul 1743-1793 .... **LC 10**

Marcel, Gabriel Honore 1889-1973 . **CLC 15**
See also CA 102; 45-48; MTCW 1, 2

March, William 1893-1954 .... **TCLC 96**

Marchbanks, Samuel
See Davies, (William) Robertson

Marchi, Giacomo
See Bassani, Giorgio

Margulies, Donald .... **CLC 76**

Marie de France c. 12th cent. - ..... **CMLC 8;**
PC 22
See also DLB 208

Marie de l'Incarnation 1599-1672 ...... **LC 10**

Marier, Captain Victor
See Griffith, D(avid Lewelyn) W(ark)

Mariner, Scott
See Pohl, Frederik

Marinetti, Filippo Tommaso 1876-1944
TCLC 10
See also CA 107; DLB 114

Marivaux, Pierre Carlet de Chamblain de
1688-1763 .... **LC 4; DC 7**

Markandaya, Kamala .... **CLC 8, 38**
See also Taylor, Kamala (Purnaiya)

Markfield, Wallace 1926- .... **CLC 8**
See also CA 69-72; CAAS 3; DLB 2, 28

Markham, Edwin 1852-1940 .... **TCLC 47**
See also CA 160; DLB 54, 186

Markham, Robert
See Amis, Kingsley (William)

Marks, J
See Highwater, Jamake (Mamake)

Marks-Highwater, J
See Highwater, Jamake (Mamake)

Markson, David M(errill) 1927- .... **CLC 67**
See also CA 49-52; CANR 1

Marley, Bob .... **CLC 17**
See also Marley, Robert Nesta

Marley, Robert Nesta 1945-1981
See Marley, Bob
See also CA 107; 103

Marlowe, Christopher 1564-1593 . **LC 22, 47;**
DA; DAB; DAC; DAM DRAM, MST;
DC 1; WLC
See also CDBLB Before 1660; DA3; DLB
62

Marlowe, Stephen 1928-
See Queen, Ellery
See also CA 13-16R; CANR 6, 55

Marmontel, Jean-Francois 1723-1799 .. **LC 2**

Marquand, John P(hillips) 1893-1960
.... **CLC 2, 10**
See also CA 85-88; CANR 73; DLB 9, 102;
MTCW 2

Marques, Rene 1919-1979 ..... **CLC 96; DAM**
MULT; HLC 2
See also CA 97-100; 85-88; CANR 78;
DLB 113; HW 1, 2

Marquez, Gabriel (Jose) Garcia
See Garcia Marquez, Gabriel (Jose)

Marquis, Don(ald Robert Perry) 1878-1937
TCLC 7
See also CA 104; 166; DLB 11, 25

Marric, J. J.
See Creasey, John

Marryat, Frederick 1792-1848 .... **NCLC 3**
See also DLB 21, 163

Marsden, James
See Creasey, John

Marsh, Edward 1872-1953 .... **TCLC 99**

Marsh, (Edith) Ngaio 1899-1982 . **CLC 7, 53;**
DAM POP
See also CA 9-12R; CANR 6, 58; DLB 77;
MTCW 1, 2

Marshall, Garry 1934- .... **CLC 17**
See also AAYA 3; CA 111; SATA 60

Marshall, Paule 1929- .. **CLC 27, 72; BLC 3;**
DAM MULT; SSC 3
See also BW 2, 3; CA 77-80; CANR 25,
73; DA3; DLB 157; MTCW 1, 2

Marshallik
See Zangwill, Israel

Marsten, Richard
See Hunter, Evan

Marston, John 1576-1634 .... **LC 33; DAM**
DRAM
See also DLB 58, 172

Martha, Henry
See Harris, Mark

Marti (y Perez), Jose (Julian) 1853-1895
NCLC 63; DAM MULT; HLC 2
See also HW 2

Martial c. 40-c. 104 .... **CMLC 35; PC 10**
See also DLB 211

Martin, Ken
See Hubbard, L(afayette) Ron(ald)

Martin, Richard
See Creasey, John

Martin, Steve 1945- .... **CLC 30**
See also CA 97-100; CANR 30; MTCW 1

Martin, Valerie 1948- .... **CLC 89**
See also BEST 90:2; CA 85-88; CANR 49,
89

Martin, Violet Florence 1862-1915 . **TCLC 51**

Martin, Webber
See Silverberg, Robert

Martindale, Patrick Victor
See White, Patrick (Victor Martindale)

Martin du Gard, Roger 1881-1958 . **TCLC 24**
See also CA 118; DLB 65

Martineau, Harriet 1802-1876 .... **NCLC 26**
See also DLB 21, 55, 159, 163, 166, 190;
YABC 2

Martines, Julia
See O'Faolain, Julia

Martinez, Enrique Gonzalez
See Gonzalez Martinez, Enrique

Martinez, Jacinto Benavente y
See Benavente (y Martinez), Jacinto

Martinez Ruiz, Jose 1873-1967
See Azorin; Ruiz, Jose Martinez
See also CA 93-96; HW 1

Martinez Sierra, Gregorio 1881-1947
.... **TCLC 6**
See also CA 115

Martinez Sierra, Maria (de la O'LeJarraga)
1874-1974 .... **TCLC 6**
See also CA 115

McFadden, David 1940- .... **CLC 48**
See also CA 104; DLB 60; INT 104

McFarland, Dennis 1950- .... **CLC 65**
See also CA 165

McGahern, John 1934- ... **CLC 5, 9, 48; SSC 17**
See also CA 17-20R; CANR 29, 68; DLB 14; MTCW 1

McGinley, Patrick (Anthony) 1937- . **CLC 41**
See also CA 120; 127; CANR 56; INT 127

McGinley, Phyllis 1905-1978 .... **CLC 14**
See also CA 9-12R; 77-80; CANR 19; DLB 11, 48; SATA 2, 44; SATA-Obit 24

McGinniss, Joe 1942- .... **CLC 32**
See also AITN 2; BEST 89:2; CA 25-28R; CANR 26, 70; DLB 185; INT CANR-26

McGivern, Maureen Daly
See Daly, Maureen

McGrath, Patrick 1950- .... **CLC 55**
See also CA 136; CANR 65

McGrath, Thomas (Matthew) 1916-1990
CLC 28, 59; DAM POET
See also CA 9-12R; 132; CANR 6, 33; MTCW 1; SATA 41; SATA-Obit 66

McGuane, Thomas (Francis III) 1939-
.... **CLC 3, 7, 18, 45, 127**
See also AITN 2; CA 49-52; CANR 5, 24, 49; DLB 2, 212; DLBY 80; INT CANR-24; MTCW 1

McGuckian, Medbh 1950- .... **CLC 48; DAM POET; PC 27**
See also CA 143; DLB 40

McHale, Tom 1942(?)-1982 .... **CLC 3, 5**
See also AITN 1; CA 77-80; 106

McIlvanney, William 1936- .... **CLC 42**
See also CA 25-28R; CANR 61; DLB 14, 207

McIlwraith, Maureen Mollie Hunter
See Hunter, Mollie
See also SATA 2

McInerney, Jay 1955- .... **CLC 34, 112; DAM POP**
See also AAYA 18; CA 116; 123; CANR 45, 68; DA3; INT 123; MTCW 2

McIntyre, Vonda N(eel) 1948- .... **CLC 18**
See also CA 81-84; CANR 17, 34, 69; MTCW 1

McKay, Claude . **TCLC 7, 41; BLC 3; DAB; PC 2**
See also McKay, Festus Claudius DLB 4, 45, 51, 117

McKay, Festus Claudius 1889-1948
See McKay, Claude
See also BW 1, 3; CA 104; 124; CANR 73; DA; DAC; DAM MST, MULT, NOV, POET; MTCW 1, 2; WLC

McKuen, Rod 1933- .... **CLC 1, 3**
See also AITN 1; CA 41-44R; CANR 40

McLoughlin, R. B.
See Mencken, H(enry) L(ouis)

McLuhan, (Herbert) Marshall 1911-1980
CLC 37, 83
See also CA 9-12R; 102; CANR 12, 34, 61; DLB 88; INT CANR-12; MTCW 1, 2

McMillan, Terry (L.) 1951- .... **CLC 50, 61, 112; BLCS; DAM MULT, NOV, POP**
See also AAYA 21; BW 2, 3; CA 140; CANR 60; DA3; MTCW 2

McMurtry, Larry (Jeff) 1936- .. **CLC 2, 3, 7, 11, 27, 44, 127; DAM NOV, POP**
See also AAYA 15; AITN 2; BEST 89:2; CA 5-8R; CANR 19, 43, 64; CDALB 1968-1988; DA3; DLB 2, 143; DLBY 80, 87; MTCW 1, 2

McNally, T. M. 1961- .... **CLC 82**

McNally, Terrence 1939- ... **CLC 4, 7, 41, 91; DAM DRAM**
See also CA 45-48; CANR 2, 56; DA3; DLB 7; MTCW 2

McNamer, Deirdre 1950- .... **CLC 70**

McNeal, Tom .... **CLC 119**

McNeile, Herman Cyril 1888-1937
See Sapper
See also CA 184; DLB 77

McNickle, (William) D'Arcy 1904-1977
.... **CLC 89; DAM MULT**
See also CA 9-12R; 85-88; CANR 5, 45; DLB 175, 212; NNAL; SATA-Obit 22

McPhee, John (Angus) 1931- .... **CLC 36**
See also BEST 90:1; CA 65-68; CANR 20, 46, 64, 69; DLB 185; MTCW 1, 2

McPherson, James Alan 1943- .. **CLC 19, 77; BLCS**
See also BW 1, 3; CA 25-28R; CAAS 17; CANR 24, 74; DLB 38; MTCW 1, 2

McPherson, William (Alexander) 1933-
.... **CLC 34**
See also CA 69-72; CANR 28; INT CANR-28

Mead, George Herbert 1873-1958 . **TCLC 89**

Mead, Margaret 1901-1978 .... **CLC 37**
See also AITN 1; CA 1-4R; 81-84; CANR 4; DA3; MTCW 1, 2; SATA-Obit 20

Meaker, Marijane (Agnes) 1927-
See Kerr, M. E.
See also CA 107; CANR 37, 63; INT 107; JRDA; MAICYA; MTCW 1; SATA 20, 61, 99; SATA-Essay 111

Medoff, Mark (Howard) 1940- ... **CLC 6, 23; DAM DRAM**
See also AITN 1; CA 53-56; CANR 5; DLB 7; INT CANR-5

Medvedev, P. N.
See Bakhtin, Mikhail Mikhailovich

Meged, Aharon
See Megged, Aharon

Meged, Aron
See Megged, Aharon

Megged, Aharon 1920- .... **CLC 9**
See also CA 49-52; CAAS 13; CANR 1

Mehta, Ved (Parkash) 1934- .... **CLC 37**
See also CA 1-4R; CANR 2, 23, 69; MTCW 1

Melanter
See Blackmore, R(ichard) D(oddridge)

Melies, Georges 1861-1938 .... **TCLC 81**

Melikow, Loris
See Hofmannsthal, Hugo von

Melmoth, Sebastian
See Wilde, Oscar

Meltzer, Milton 1915- .... **CLC 26**
See also AAYA 8; CA 13-16R; CANR 38; CLR 13; DLB 61; JRDA; MAICYA; SAAS 1; SATA 1, 50, 80

Melville, Herman 1819-1891 ..... **NCLC 3, 12, 29, 45, 49; DA; DAB; DAC; DAM MST, NOV; SSC 1, 17; WLC**
See also AAYA 25; CDALB 1640-1865; DA3; DLB 3, 74; SATA 59

Menander c. 342B.C.-c. 292B.C. ... **CMLC 9; DAM DRAM; DC 3**
See also DLB 176

Menchu, Rigoberta 1959-
See also HLCS 2

Menchu, Rigoberta 1959-
See also CA 175; HLCS 2

Mencken, H(enry) L(ouis) 1880-1956
.... **TCLC 13**
See also CA 105; 125; CDALB 1917-1929; DLB 11, 29, 63, 137; MTCW 1, 2

Mendelsohn, Jane 1965(?)- .... **CLC 99**
See also CA 154

Mercer, David 1928-1980 .... **CLC 5; DAM DRAM**
See also CA 9-12R; 102; CANR 23; DLB 13; MTCW 1

Merchant, Paul
See Ellison, Harlan (Jay)

Meredith, George 1828-1909 .. **TCLC 17, 43; DAM POET**
See also CA 117; 153; CANR 80; CDBLB 1832-1890; DLB 18, 35, 57, 159

Meredith, William (Morris) 1919- .... **CLC 4, 13, 22, 55; DAM POET; PC 28**
See also CA 9-12R; CAAS 14; CANR 6, 40; DLB 5

Merezhkovsky, Dmitry Sergeyevich
1865-1941 .... **TCLC 29**
See also CA 169

Merimee, Prosper 1803-1870 ... **NCLC 6, 65; SSC 7**
See also DLB 119, 192

Merkin, Daphne 1954- .... **CLC 44**
See also CA 123

Merlin, Arthur
See Blish, James (Benjamin)

Merrill, James (Ingram) 1926-1995 .. **CLC 2, 3, 6, 8, 13, 18, 34, 91; DAM POET; PC 28**
See also CA 13-16R; 147; CANR 10, 49, 63; DA3; DLB 5, 165; DLBY 85; INT CANR-10; MTCW 1, 2

Merriman, Alex
See Silverberg, Robert

Merriman, Brian 1747-1805 .... **NCLC 70**

Merritt, E. B.
See Waddington, Miriam

Merton, Thomas 1915-1968 ..... **CLC 1, 3, 11, 34, 83; PC 10**
See also CA 5-8R; 25-28R; CANR 22, 53; DA3; DLB 48; DLBY 81; MTCW 1, 2

Merwin, W(illiam) S(tanley) 1927- ... **CLC 1, 2, 3, 5, 8, 13, 18, 45, 88; DAM POET**
See also CA 13-16R; CANR 15, 51; DA3; DLB 5, 169; INT CANR-15; MTCW 1, 2

Metcalf, John 1938- .... **CLC 37**
See also CA 113; DLB 60

Metcalf, Suzanne
See Baum, L(yman) Frank

Mew, Charlotte (Mary) 1870-1928 .. **TCLC 8**
See also CA 105; DLB 19, 135

Mewshaw, Michael 1943- .... **CLC 9**
See also CA 53-56; CANR 7, 47; DLBY 80

Meyer, Conrad Ferdinand 1825-1905
.... **NCLC 81**
See also DLB 129

Meyer, June
See Jordan, June

Meyer, Lynn
See Slavitt, David R(ytman)

Meyer-Meyrink, Gustav 1868-1932
See Meyrink, Gustav
See also CA 117

Meyers, Jeffrey 1939- .... **CLC 39**
See also CA 73-76; CANR 54; DLB 111

Meynell, Alice (Christina Gertrude
Thompson) 1847-1922 .... **TCLC 6**
See also CA 104; 177; DLB 19, 98

Meyrink, Gustav .... **TCLC 21**
See also Meyer-Meyrink, Gustav DLB 81

Michaels, Leonard 1933- .... **CLC 6, 25; SSC 16**
See also CA 61-64; CANR 21, 62; DLB 130; MTCW 1

Michaux, Henri 1899-1984 .... **CLC 8, 19**
See also CA 85-88; 114

Micheaux, Oscar (Devereaux) 1884-1951
TCLC 76
See also BW 3; CA 174; DLB 50

Michelangelo 1475-1564 .... **LC 12**

Michelet, Jules 1798-1874 .... **NCLC 31**

Michels, Robert 1876-1936 .... **TCLC 88**

Monty Python
See Chapman, Graham; Cleese, John (Marwood); Gilliam, Terry (Vance); Idle, Eric; Jones, Terence Graham Parry; Palin, Michael (Edward)
See also AAYA 7

Moodie, Susanna (Strickland) 1803-1885 **NCLC 14**
See also DLB 99

Mooney, Edward 1951-
See Mooney, Ted
See also CA 130

Mooney, Ted .... **CLC 25**
See also Mooney, Edward

Moorcock, Michael (John) 1939- . **CLC 5, 27, 58**
See also Bradbury, Edward P. AAYA 26; CA 45-48; CAAS 5; CANR 2, 17, 38, 64; DLB 14; MTCW 1, 2; SATA 93

Moore, Brian 1921-1999 ... **CLC 1, 3, 5, 7, 8, 19, 32, 90; DAB; DAC; DAM MST**
See also CA 1-4R; 174; CANR 1, 25, 42, 63; MTCW 1, 2

Moore, Edward
See Muir, Edwin

Moore, G. E. 1873-1958 .... **TCLC 89**

Moore, George Augustus 1852-1933 .... **TCLC 7; SSC 19**
See also CA 104; 177; DLB 10, 18, 57, 135

Moore, Lorrie .... **CLC 39, 45, 68**
See also Moore, Marie Lorena

Moore, Marianne (Craig) 1887-1972 . **CLC 1, 2, 4, 8, 10, 13, 19, 47; DA; DAB; DAC; DAM MST, POET; PC 4; WLCS**
See also CA 1-4R; 33-36R; CANR 3, 61; CDALB 1929-1941; DA3; DLB 45; DLBD 7; MTCW 1, 2; SATA 20

Moore, Marie Lorena 1957-
See Moore, Lorrie
See also CA 116; CANR 39, 83

Moore, Thomas 1779-1852 .... **NCLC 6**
See also DLB 96, 144

Mora, Pat(ricia) 1942-
See also CA 129; CANR 57, 81; CLR 58; DAM MULT; DLB 209; HLC 2; HW 1, 2; SATA 92

Moraga, Cherrie 1952- .... **CLC 126; DAM MULT**
See also CA 131; CANR 66; DLB 82; HW 1, 2

Morand, Paul 1888-1976 .... **CLC 41; SSC 22**
See also CA 184; 69-72; DLB 65

Morante, Elsa 1918-1985 .... **CLC 8, 47**
See also CA 85-88; 117; CANR 35; DLB 177; MTCW 1, 2

Moravia, Alberto 1907-1990 .... **CLC 2, 7, 11, 27, 46; SSC 26**
See also Pincherle, Alberto DLB 177; MTCW 2

More, Hannah 1745-1833 .... **NCLC 27**
See also DLB 107, 109, 116, 158

More, Henry 1614-1687 .... **LC 9**
See also DLB 126

More, Sir Thomas 1478-1535 .... **LC 10, 32**

Moreas, Jean .... **TCLC 18**
See also Papadiamantopoulos, Johannes

Morgan, Berry 1919- .... **CLC 6**
See also CA 49-52; DLB 6

Morgan, Claire
See Highsmith, (Mary) Patricia

Morgan, Edwin (George) 1920- .... **CLC 31**
See also CA 5-8R; CANR 3, 43; DLB 27

Morgan, (George) Frederick 1922- .. **CLC 23**
See also CA 17-20R; CANR 21

Morgan, Harriet
See Mencken, H(enry) L(ouis)

Morgan, Jane
See Cooper, James Fenimore

Morgan, Janet 1945- .... **CLC 39**

See also CA 65-68

Morgan, Lady 1776(?)-1859 .... **NCLC 29**
See also DLB 116, 158

Morgan, Robin (Evonne) 1941- .... **CLC 2**
See also CA 69-72; CANR 29, 68; MTCW 1; SATA 80

Morgan, Scott
See Kuttner, Henry

Morgan, Seth 1949(?)-1990 .... **CLC 65**
See also CA 185; 132

Morgenstern, Christian 1871-1914 .. **TCLC 8**
See also CA 105

Morgenstern, S.
See Goldman, William (W.)

Moricz, Zsigmond 1879-1942 .... **TCLC 33**
See also CA 165

Morike, Eduard (Friedrich) 1804-1875 **NCLC 10**
See also DLB 133

Moritz, Karl Philipp 1756-1793 .... **LC 2**
See also DLB 94

Morland, Peter Henry
See Faust, Frederick (Schiller)

Morley, Christopher (Darlington) 1890-1957 **TCLC 87**
See also CA 112; DLB 9

Morren, Theophil
See Hofmannsthal, Hugo von

Morris, Bill 1952- .... **CLC 76**

Morris, Julian
See West, Morris L(anglo)

Morris, Steveland Judkins 1950(?)-
See Wonder, Stevie
See also CA 111

Morris, William 1834-1896 .... **NCLC 4**
See also CDBLB 1832-1890; DLB 18, 35, 57, 156, 178, 184

Morris, Wright 1910-1998 .. **CLC 1, 3, 7, 18, 37**
See also CA 9-12R; 167; CANR 21, 81; DLB 2, 206; DLBY 81; MTCW 1, 2

Morrison, Arthur 1863-1945 .... **TCLC 72**
See also CA 120; 157; DLB 70, 135, 197

Morrison, Chloe Anthony Wofford
See Morrison, Toni

Morrison, James Douglas 1943-1971
See Morrison, Jim
See also CA 73-76; CANR 40

Morrison, Jim .... **CLC 17**
See also Morrison, James Douglas

Morrison, Toni 1931- . **CLC 4, 10, 22, 55, 81, 87; BLC 3; DA; DAB; DAC; DAM MST, MULT, NOV, POP**
See also AAYA 1, 22; BW 2, 3; CA 29-32R; CANR 27, 42, 67; CDALB 1968-1988; DA3; DLB 6, 33, 143; DLBY 81; MTCW 1, 2; SATA 57

Morrison, Van 1945- .... **CLC 21**
See also CA 116; 168

Morrissy, Mary 1958- .... **CLC 99**

Mortimer, John (Clifford) 1923- ..... **CLC 28, 43; DAM DRAM, POP**
See also CA 13-16R; CANR 21, 69; CDBLB 1960 to Present; DA3; DLB 13; INT CANR-21; MTCW 1, 2

Mortimer, Penelope (Ruth) 1918- ...... **CLC 5**
See also CA 57-60; CANR 45, 88

Morton, Anthony
See Creasey, John

Mosca, Gaetano 1858-1941 .... **TCLC 75**

Mosher, Howard Frank 1943- .... **CLC 62**
See also CA 139; CANR 65

Mosley, Nicholas 1923- .... **CLC 43, 70**
See also CA 69-72; CANR 41, 60; DLB 14, 207

Mosley, Walter 1952- . **CLC 97; BLCS; DAM MULT, POP**

See also AAYA 17; BW 2; CA 142; CANR 57; DA3; MTCW 2

Moss, Howard 1922-1987 ...... **CLC 7, 14, 45, 50; DAM POET**
See also CA 1-4R; 123; CANR 1, 44; DLB 5

Mossgiel, Rab
See Burns, Robert

Motion, Andrew (Peter) 1952- .... **CLC 47**
See also CA 146; DLB 40

Motley, Willard (Francis) 1909-1965 .... **CLC 18**
See also BW 1; CA 117; 106; CANR 88; DLB 76, 143

Motoori, Norinaga 1730-1801 .... **NCLC 45**

Mott, Michael (Charles Alston) 1930- .... **CLC 15, 34**
See also CA 5-8R; CAAS 7; CANR 7, 29

Mountain Wolf Woman 1884-1960 .. **CLC 92**
See also CA 144; NNAL

Moure, Erin 1955- .... **CLC 88**
See also CA 113; DLB 60

Mowat, Farley (McGill) 1921- .... **CLC 26; DAC; DAM MST**
See also AAYA 1; CA 1-4R; CANR 4, 24, 42, 68; CLR 20; DLB 68; INT CANR-24; JRDA; MAICYA; MTCW 1, 2; SATA 3, 55

Mowatt, Anna Cora 1819-1870 ..... **NCLC 74**

Moyers, Bill 1934- .... **CLC 74**
See also AITN 2; CA 61-64; CANR 31, 52

Mphahlele, Es'kia
See Mphahlele, Ezekiel
See also DLB 125

Mphahlele, Ezekiel 1919- ... **CLC 25; BLC 3; DAM MULT**
See also Mphahlele, Es'kia BW 2, 3; CA 81-84; CANR 26, 76; DA3; MTCW 2

Mqhayi, S(amuel) E(dward) K(rune Loliwe) 1875-1945 ...... **TCLC 25; BLC 3; DAM MULT**
See also CA 153; CANR 87

Mrozek, Slawomir 1930- .... **CLC 3, 13**
See also CA 13-16R; CAAS 10; CANR 29; MTCW 1

Mrs. Belloc-Lowndes
See Lowndes, Marie Adelaide (Belloc)

Mtwa, Percy (?)- .... **CLC 47**

Mueller, Lisel 1924- .... **CLC 13, 51**
See also CA 93-96; DLB 105

Muir, Edwin 1887-1959 .... **TCLC 2, 87**
See also CA 104; DLB 20, 100, 191

Muir, John 1838-1914 .... **TCLC 28**
See also CA 165; DLB 186

Mujica Lainez, Manuel 1910-1984 ... **CLC 31**
See also Lainez, Manuel Mujica CA 81-84; 112; CANR 32; HW 1

Mukherjee, Bharati 1940- .... **CLC 53, 115; DAM NOV; SSC 38**
See also BEST 89:2; CA 107; CANR 45, 72; DLB 60; MTCW 1, 2

Muldoon, Paul 1951- .... **CLC 32, 72; DAM POET**
See also CA 113; 129; CANR 52; DLB 40; INT 129

Mulisch, Harry 1927- .... **CLC 42**
See also CA 9-12R; CANR 6, 26, 56

Mull, Martin 1943- .... **CLC 17**
See also CA 105

Muller, Wilhelm .... **NCLC 73**

Mulock, Dinah Maria
See Craik, Dinah Maria (Mulock)

Munford, Robert 1737(?)-1783 .... **LC 5**
See also DLB 31

Mungo, Raymond 1946- .... **CLC 72**
See also CA 49-52; CANR 2

Munro, Alice 1931- .... **CLC 6, 10, 19, 50, 95; DAC; DAM MST, NOV; SSC 3; WLCS**

See also AITN 2; CA 33-36R; CANR 33, 53, 75; DA3; DLB 53; MTCW 1, 2; SATA 29

Munro, H(ector) H(ugh) 1870-1916
See Saki
See also CA 104; 130; CDBLB 1890-1914; DA; DAB; DAC; DAM MST, NOV; DA3; DLB 34, 162; MTCW 1, 2; WLC

Murdoch, (Jean) Iris 1919-1999 ... **CLC 1, 2, 3, 4, 6, 8, 11, 15, 22, 31, 51; DAB; DAC; DAM MST, NOV**
See also CA 13-16R; 179; CANR 8, 43, 68; CDBLB 1960 to Present; DA3; DLB 14, 194; INT CANR-8; MTCW 1, 2

Murfree, Mary Noailles 1850-1922 ... **SSC 22**
See also CA 122; 176; DLB 12, 74

Murnau, Friedrich Wilhelm
See Plumpe, Friedrich Wilhelm

Murphy, Richard 1927- .... **CLC 41**
See also CA 29-32R; DLB 40

Murphy, Sylvia 1937- .... **CLC 34**
See also CA 121

Murphy, Thomas (Bernard) 1935- ... **CLC 51**
See also CA 101

Murray, Albert L. 1916- .... **CLC 73**
See also BW 2; CA 49-52; CANR 26, 52, 78; DLB 38

Murray, Judith Sargent 1751-1820
.... **NCLC 63**
See also DLB 37, 200

Murray, Les(lie) A(llan) 1938- .... **CLC 40; DAM POET**
See also CA 21-24R; CANR 11, 27, 56

Murry, J. Middleton
See Murry, John Middleton

Murry, John Middleton 1889-1957 . **TCLC 16**
See also CA 118; DLB 149

Musgrave, Susan 1951- .... **CLC 13, 54**
See also CA 69-72; CANR 45, 84

Musil, Robert (Edler von) 1880-1942
.... **TCLC 12, 68; SSC 18**
See also CA 109; CANR 55, 84; DLB 81, 124; MTCW 2

Muske, Carol 1945- .... **CLC 90**
See also Muske-Dukes, Carol (Anne)

Muske-Dukes, Carol (Anne) 1945-
See Muske, Carol
See also CA 65-68; CANR 32, 70

Musset, (Louis Charles) Alfred de 1810-1857
NCLC 7
See also DLB 192

Mussolini, Benito (Amilcare Andrea) 1883-1945 .... **TCLC 96**
See also CA 116

My Brother's Brother
See Chekhov, Anton (Pavlovich)

Myers, L(eopold) H(amilton) 1881-1944
TCLC 59
See also CA 157; DLB 15

Myers, Walter Dean 1937- . **CLC 35; BLC 3; DAM MULT, NOV**
See also AAYA 4, 23; BW 2; CA 33-36R; CANR 20, 42, 67; CLR 4, 16, 35; DLB 33; INT CANR-20; JRDA; MAICYA; MTCW 2; SAAS 2; SATA 41, 71, 109; SATA-Brief 27

Myers, Walter M.
See Myers, Walter Dean

Myles, Symon
See Follett, Ken(neth Martin)

Nabokov, Vladimir (Vladimirovich) 1899-1977 . **CLC 1, 2, 3, 6, 8, 11, 15, 23, 44, 46, 64; DA; DAB; DAC; DAM MST, NOV; SSC 11; WLC**
See also CA 5-8R; 69-72; CANR 20; CDALB 1941-1968; DA3; DLB 2; DLBD 3; DLBY 80, 91; MTCW 1, 2

Naevius c. 265B.C.-201B.C. .... **CMLC 37**
See also DLB 211

Nagai Kafu 1879-1959 .... **TCLC 51**
See also Nagai Sokichi DLB 180

Nagai Sokichi 1879-1959
See Nagai Kafu
See also CA 117

Nagy, Laszlo 1925-1978 .... **CLC 7**
See also CA 129; 112

Naidu, Sarojini 1879-1943 .... **TCLC 80**

Naipaul, Shiva(dhar Srinivasa) 1945-1985
CLC 32, 39; DAM NOV
See also CA 110; 112; 116; CANR 33; DA3; DLB 157; DLBY 85; MTCW 1, 2

Naipaul, V(idiadhar) S(urajprasad) 1932-
CLC 4, 7, 9, 13, 18, 37, 105; DAB; DAC; DAM MST, NOV; SSC 38
See also CA 1-4R; CANR 1, 33, 51; CD-BLB 1960 to Present; DA3; DLB 125, 204, 206; DLBY 85; MTCW 1, 2

Nakos, Lilika 1899(?)- .... **CLC 29**

Narayan, R(asipuram) K(rishnaswami) 1906- . **CLC 7, 28, 47, 121; DAM NOV; SSC 25**
See also CA 81-84; CANR 33, 61; DA3; MTCW 1, 2; SATA 62

Nash, (Frediric) Ogden 1902-1971 . **CLC 23; DAM POET; PC 21**
See also CA 13-14; 29-32R; CANR 34, 61; CAP 1; DLB 11; MAICYA; MTCW 1, 2; SATA 2, 46

Nashe, Thomas 1567-1601(?) .... **LC 41**
See also DLB 167

Nashe, Thomas 1567-1601 .... **LC 41**

Nathan, Daniel
See Dannay, Frederic

Nathan, George Jean 1882-1958 .... **TCLC 18**
See also Hatteras, Owen CA 114; 169; DLB 137

Natsume, Kinnosuke 1867-1916
See Natsume, Soseki
See also CA 104

Natsume, Soseki 1867-1916 .... **TCLC 2, 10**
See also Natsume, Kinnosuke DLB 180

Natti, (Mary) Lee 1919-
See Kingman, Lee
See also CA 5-8R; CANR 2

Naylor, Gloria 1950- .... **CLC 28, 52; BLC 3; DA; DAC; DAM MST, MULT, NOV, POP; WLCS**
See also AAYA 6; BW 2, 3; CA 107; CANR 27, 51, 74; DA3; DLB 173; MTCW 1, 2

Neihardt, John Gneisenau 1881-1973
.... **CLC 32**
See also CA 13-14; CANR 65; CAP 1; DLB 9, 54

Nekrasov, Nikolai Alekseevich 1821-1878
NCLC 11

Nelligan, Emile 1879-1941 .... **TCLC 14**
See also CA 114; DLB 92

Nelson, Willie 1933- .... **CLC 17**
See also CA 107

Nemerov, Howard (Stanley) 1920-1991
.. **CLC 2, 6, 9, 36; DAM POET; PC 24**
See also CA 1-4R; 134; CABS 2; CANR 1, 27, 53; DLB 5, 6; DLBY 83; INT CANR-27; MTCW 1, 2

Neruda, Pablo 1904-1973 .. **CLC 1, 2, 5, 7, 9, 28, 62; DA; DAB; DAC; DAM MST, MULT, POET; HLC 2; PC 4; WLC**
See also CA 19-20; 45-48; CAP 2; DA3; HW 1; MTCW 1, 2

Nerval, Gerard de 1808-1855 ... **NCLC 1, 67; PC 13; SSC 18**

Nervo, (Jose) Amado (Ruiz de) 1870-1919
TCLC 11; HLCS 2
See also CA 109; 131; HW 1

Nessi, Pio Baroja y
See Baroja (y Nessi), Pio

Nestroy, Johann 1801-1862 .... **NCLC 42**
See also DLB 133

Netterville, Luke
See O'Grady, Standish (James)

Neufeld, John (Arthur) 1938- .... **CLC 17**
See also AAYA 11; CA 25-28R; CANR 11, 37, 56; CLR 52; MAICYA; SAAS 3; SATA 6, 81

Neumann, Alfred 1895-1952 .... **TCLC 100**
See also CA 183; DLB 56

Neville, Emily Cheney 1919- .... **CLC 12**
See also CA 5-8R; CANR 3, 37, 85; JRDA; MAICYA; SAAS 2; SATA 1

Newbound, Bernard Slade 1930-
See Slade, Bernard
See also CA 81-84; CANR 49; DAM DRAM

Newby, P(ercy) H(oward) 1918-1997 . **CLC 2, 13; DAM NOV**
See also CA 5-8R; 161; CANR 32, 67; DLB 15; MTCW 1

Newlove, Donald 1928- .... **CLC 6**
See also CA 29-32R; CANR 25

Newlove, John (Herbert) 1938- .... **CLC 14**
See also CA 21-24R; CANR 9, 25

Newman, Charles 1938- .... **CLC 2, 8**
See also CA 21-24R; CANR 84

Newman, Edwin (Harold) 1919- ...... **CLC 14**
See also AITN 1; CA 69-72; CANR 5

Newman, John Henry 1801-1890 .. **NCLC 38**
See also DLB 18, 32, 55

Newton, (Sir)Isaac 1642-1727 .... **LC 35, 52**

Newton, Suzanne 1936- .... **CLC 35**
See also CA 41-44R; CANR 14; JRDA; SATA 5, 77

Nexo, Martin Andersen 1869-1954 . **TCLC 43**

Nezval, Vitezslav 1900-1958 .... **TCLC 44**
See also CA 123

Ng, Fae Myenne 1957(?)- .... **CLC 81**
See also CA 146

Ngema, Mbongeni 1955- .... **CLC 57**
See also BW 2; CA 143; CANR 84

Ngugi, James T(hiong'o) .... **CLC 3, 7, 13**
See also Ngugi wa Thiong'o

Ngugi wa Thiong'o 1938- .. **CLC 36; BLC 3; DAM MULT, NOV**
See also Ngugi, James T(hiong'o) BW 2; CA 81-84; CANR 27, 58; DLB 125; MTCW 1, 2

Nichol, B(arrie) P(hillip) 1944-1988 . **CLC 18**
See also CA 53-56; DLB 53; SATA 66

Nichols, John (Treadwell) 1940- .... **CLC 38**
See also CA 9-12R; CAAS 2; CANR 6, 70; DLBY 82

Nichols, Leigh
See Koontz, Dean R(ay)

Nichols, Peter (Richard) 1927- .... **CLC 5, 36, 65**
See also CA 104; CANR 33, 86; DLB 13; MTCW 1

Nicolas, F. R. E.
See Freeling, Nicolas

Niedecker, Lorine 1903-1970 ..... **CLC 10, 42; DAM POET**
See also CA 25-28; CAP 2; DLB 48

Nietzsche, Friedrich (Wilhelm) 1844-1900
TCLC 10, 18, 55
See also CA 107; 121; DLB 129

Nievo, Ippolito 1831-1861 .... **NCLC 22**

Nightingale, Anne Redmon 1943-
See Redmon, Anne
See also CA 103

Nightingale, Florence 1820-1910 ... **TCLC 85**
See also DLB 166

Nik. T. O.
See Annensky, Innokenty (Fyodorovich)

Nin, Anais 1903-1977 ..... **CLC 1, 4, 8, 11, 14, 60, 127; DAM NOV, POP; SSC 10**

See also AITN 2; CA 13-16R; 69-72; CANR 22, 53; DLB 2, 4, 152; MTCW 1, 2

Nishida, Kitaro 1870-1945 .... **TCLC 83**

Nishiwaki, Junzaburo 1894-1982 .... **PC 15**
See also CA 107

Nissenson, Hugh 1933- .... **CLC 4, 9**
See also CA 17-20R; CANR 27; DLB 28

Niven, Larry .... **CLC 8**
See also Niven, Laurence Van Cott AAYA 27; DLB 8

Niven, Laurence Van Cott 1938-
See Niven, Larry
See also CA 21-24R; CAAS 12; CANR 14, 44, 66; DAM POP; MTCW 1, 2; SATA 95

Nixon, Agnes Eckhardt 1927- .... **CLC 21**
See also CA 110

Nizan, Paul 1905-1940 .... **TCLC 40**
See also CA 161; DLB 72

Nkosi, Lewis 1936- ... **CLC 45; BLC 3; DAM MULT**
See also BW 1, 3; CA 65-68; CANR 27, 81; DLB 157

Nodier, (Jean) Charles (Emmanuel) 1780-1844 .... **NCLC 19**
See also DLB 119

Noguchi, Yone 1875-1947 .... **TCLC 80**

Nolan, Christopher 1965- .... **CLC 58**
See also CA 111; CANR 88

Noon, Jeff 1957- .... **CLC 91**
See also CA 148; CANR 83

Norden, Charles
See Durrell, Lawrence (George)

Nordhoff, Charles (Bernard) 1887-1947 **TCLC 23**
See also CA 108; DLB 9; SATA 23

Norfolk, Lawrence 1963- .... **CLC 76**
See also CA 144; CANR 85

Norman, Marsha 1947- .... **CLC 28; DAM DRAM; DC 8**
See also CA 105; CABS 3; CANR 41; DLBY 84

Normyx
See Douglas, (George) Norman

Norris, Frank 1870-1902 .... **SSC 28**
See also Norris, (Benjamin) Frank(lin, Jr.) CDALB 1865-1917; DLB 12, 71, 186

Norris, (Benjamin) Frank(lin, Jr.) 1870-1902 **TCLC 24**
See also Norris, Frank CA 110; 160

Norris, Leslie 1921- .... **CLC 14**
See also CA 11-12; CANR 14; CAP 1; DLB 27

North, Andrew
See Norton, Andre

North, Anthony
See Koontz, Dean R(ay)

North, Captain George
See Stevenson, Robert Louis (Balfour)

North, Milou
See Erdrich, Louise

Northrup, B. A.
See Hubbard, L(afayette) Ron(ald)

North Staffs
See Hulme, T(homas) E(rnest)

Norton, Alice Mary
See Norton, Andre
See also MAICYA; SATA 1, 43

Norton, Andre 1912- .... **CLC 12**
See also Norton, Alice Mary AAYA 14; CA 1-4R; CANR 68; CLR 50; DLB 8, 52; JRDA; MTCW 1; SATA 91

Norton, Caroline 1808-1877 .... **NCLC 47**
See also DLB 21, 159, 199

Norway, Nevil Shute 1899-1960
See Shute, Nevil

See also CA 102; 93-96; CANR 85; MTCW 2

Norwid, Cyprian Kamil 1821-1883 .... **NCLC 17**

Nosille, Nabrah
See Ellison, Harlan (Jay)

Nossack, Hans Erich 1901-1978 .... **CLC 6**
See also CA 93-96; 85-88; DLB 69

Nostradamus 1503-1566 .... **LC 27**

Nosu, Chuji
See Ozu, Yasujiro

Notenburg, Eleanora (Genrikhovna) von
See Guro, Elena

Nova, Craig 1945- .... **CLC 7, 31**
See also CA 45-48; CANR 2, 53

Novak, Joseph
See Kosinski, Jerzy (Nikodem)

Novalis 1772-1801 .... **NCLC 13**
See also DLB 90

Novis, Emile
See Weil, Simone (Adolphine)

Nowlan, Alden (Albert) 1933-1983 . **CLC 15; DAC; DAM MST**
See also CA 9-12R; CANR 5; DLB 53

Noyes, Alfred 1880-1958 ...... **TCLC 7; PC 27**
See also CA 104; DLB 20

Nunn, Kem .... **CLC 34**
See also CA 159

Nye, Robert 1939- . **CLC 13, 42; DAM NOV**
See also CA 33-36R; CANR 29, 67; DLB 14; MTCW 1; SATA 6

Nyro, Laura 1947- .... **CLC 17**

Oates, Joyce Carol 1938- .. **CLC 1, 2, 3, 6, 9, 11, 15, 19, 33, 52, 108; DA; DAB; DAC; DAM MST, NOV, POP; SSC 6; WLC**
See also AAYA 15; AITN 1; BEST 89:2; CA 5-8R; CANR 25, 45, 74; CDALB 1968-1988; DA3; DLB 2, 5, 130; DLBY 81; INT CANR-25; MTCW 1, 2

O'Brien, Darcy 1939-1998 .... **CLC 11**
See also CA 21-24R; 167; CANR 8, 59

O'Brien, E. G.
See Clarke, Arthur C(harles)

O'Brien, Edna 1936- ..... **CLC 3, 5, 8, 13, 36, 65, 116; DAM NOV; SSC 10**
See also CA 1-4R; CANR 6, 41, 65; CD-BLB 1960 to Present; DA3; DLB 14; MTCW 1, 2

O'Brien, Fitz-James 1828-1862 ..... **NCLC 21**
See also DLB 74

O'Brien, Flann .... **CLC 1, 4, 5, 7, 10, 47**
See also O Nuallain, Brian

O'Brien, Richard 1942- .... **CLC 17**
See also CA 124

O'Brien, (William) Tim(othy) 1946- . **CLC 7, 19, 40, 103; DAM POP**
See also AAYA 16; CA 85-88; CANR 40, 58; CDALBS; DA3; DLB 152; DLBD 9; DLBY 80; MTCW 2

Obstfelder, Sigbjoern 1866-1900 .... **TCLC 23**
See also CA 123

O'Casey, Sean 1880-1964 .... **CLC 1, 5, 9, 11, 15, 88; DAB; DAC; DAM DRAM, MST; DC 12; WLCS**
See also CA 89-92; CANR 62; CDBLB 1914-1945; DA3; DLB 10; MTCW 1, 2

O'Cathasaigh, Sean
See O'Casey, Sean

Ochs, Phil(ip David) 1940-1976 .... **CLC 17**
See also CA 65-68

O'Connor, Edwin (Greene) 1918-1968 .... **CLC 14**
See also CA 93-96; 25-28R

O'Connor, (Mary) Flannery 1925-1964 . **CLC 1, 2, 3, 6, 10, 13, 15, 21, 66, 104; DA; DAB; DAC; DAM MST, NOV; SSC 1, 23; WLC**

See also AAYA 7; CA 1-4R; CANR 3, 41; CDALB 1941-1968; DA3; DLB 2, 152; DLBD 12; DLBY 80; MTCW 1, 2

O'Connor, Frank .... **CLC 23; SSC 5**
See also O'Donovan, Michael John DLB 162

O'Dell, Scott 1898-1989 .... **CLC 30**
See also AAYA 3; CA 61-64; 129; CANR 12, 30; CLR 1, 16; DLB 52; JRDA; MAICYA; SATA 12, 60

Odets, Clifford 1906-1963 ..... **CLC 2, 28, 98; DAM DRAM; DC 6**
See also CA 85-88; CANR 62; DLB 7, 26; MTCW 1, 2

O'Doherty, Brian 1934- .... **CLC 76**
See also CA 105

O'Donnell, K. M.
See Malzberg, Barry N(athaniel)

O'Donnell, Lawrence
See Kuttner, Henry

O'Donovan, Michael John 1903-1966 .... **CLC 14**
See also O'Connor, Frank CA 93-96; CANR 84

Oe, Kenzaburo 1935- . **CLC 10, 36, 86; DAM NOV; SSC 20**
See also CA 97-100; CANR 36, 50, 74; DA3; DLB 182; DLBY 94; MTCW 1, 2

O'Faolain, Julia 1932- .... **CLC 6, 19, 47, 108**
See also CA 81-84; CAAS 12; CANR 12, 61; DLB 14; MTCW 1

O'Faolain, Sean 1900-1991 ...... **CLC 1, 7, 14, 32, 70; SSC 13**
See also CA 61-64; 134; CANR 12, 66; DLB 15, 162; MTCW 1, 2

O'Flaherty, Liam 1896-1984 .... **CLC 5, 34; SSC 6**
See also CA 101; 113; CANR 35; DLB 36, 162; DLBY 84; MTCW 1, 2

Ogilvy, Gavin
See Barrie, J(ames) M(atthew)

O'Grady, Standish (James) 1846-1928 .... **TCLC 5**
See also CA 104; 157

O'Grady, Timothy 1951- .... **CLC 59**
See also CA 138

O'Hara, Frank 1926-1966 . **CLC 2, 5, 13, 78; DAM POET**
See also CA 9-12R; 25-28R; CANR 33; DA3; DLB 5, 16, 193; MTCW 1, 2

O'Hara, John (Henry) 1905-1970 . **CLC 1, 2, 3, 6, 11, 42; DAM NOV; SSC 15**
See also CA 5-8R; 25-28R; CANR 31, 60; CDALB 1929-1941; DLB 9, 86; DLBD 2; MTCW 1, 2

O Hehir, Diana 1922- .... **CLC 41**
See also CA 93-96

Ohiyesa
See Eastman, Charles A(lexander)

Okigbo, Christopher (Ifenayichukwu) 1932-1967 ... **CLC 25, 84; BLC 3; DAM MULT, POET; PC 7**
See also BW 1, 3; CA 77-80; CANR 74; DLB 125; MTCW 1, 2

Okri, Ben 1959- .... **CLC 87**
See also BW 2, 3; CA 130; 138; CANR 65; DLB 157; INT 138; MTCW 2

Olds, Sharon 1942- ... **CLC 32, 39, 85; DAM POET; PC 22**
See also CA 101; CANR 18, 41, 66; DLB 120; MTCW 2

Oldstyle, Jonathan
See Irving, Washington

Olesha, Yuri (Karlovich) 1899-1960 .. **CLC 8**
See also CA 85-88

Oliphant, Laurence 1829(?)-1888 .. **NCLC 47**
See also DLB 18, 166

Oliphant, Margaret (Oliphant Wilson) 1828-1897 .... **NCLC 11, 61; SSC 25**

Parker, Robert B(rown) 1932- .... **CLC 27; DAM NOV, POP**
See also AAYA 28; BEST 89:4; CA 49-52; CANR 1, 26, 52, 89; INT CANR-26; MTCW 1

Parkin, Frank 1940- .... **CLC 43**
See also CA 147

Parkman, Francis Jr., Jr. 1823-1893
.... **NCLC 12**
See also DLB 1, 30, 186

Parks, Gordon (Alexander Buchanan) 1912- **CLC 1, 16; BLC 3; DAM MULT**
See also AITN 2; BW 2, 3; CA 41-44R; CANR 26, 66; DA3; DLB 33; MTCW 2; SATA 8, 108

Parmenides c. 515B.C.-c. 450B.C. . **CMLC 22**
See also DLB 176

Parnell, Thomas 1679-1718 .... **LC 3**
See also DLB 94

Parra, Nicanor 1914- ...... **CLC 2, 102; DAM MULT; HLC 2**
See also CA 85-88; CANR 32; HW 1; MTCW 1

Parra Sanojo, Ana Teresa de la 1890-1936
See also HLCS 2

Parrish, Mary Frances
See Fisher, M(ary) F(rances) K(ennedy)

Parson
See Coleridge, Samuel Taylor

Parson Lot
See Kingsley, Charles

Parton, Sara Payson Willis 1811-1872
.... **NCLC 85**
See also DLB 43, 74

Partridge, Anthony
See Oppenheim, E(dward) Phillips

Pascal, Blaise 1623-1662 .... **LC 35**

Pascoli, Giovanni 1855-1912 .... **TCLC 45**
See also CA 170

Pasolini, Pier Paolo 1922-1975 .. **CLC 20, 37, 106; PC 17**
See also CA 93-96; 61-64; CANR 63; DLB 128, 177; MTCW 1

Pasquini
See Silone, Ignazio

Pastan, Linda (Olenik) 1932- . **CLC 27; DAM POET**
See also CA 61-64; CANR 18, 40, 61; DLB 5

Pasternak, Boris (Leonidovich) 1890-1960 **CLC 7, 10, 18, 63; DA; DAB; DAC; DAM MST, NOV, POET; PC 6; SSC 31; WLC**
See also CA 127; 116; DA3; MTCW 1, 2

Patchen, Kenneth 1911-1972 .. **CLC 1, 2, 18; DAM POET**
See also CA 1-4R; 33-36R; CANR 3, 35; DLB 16, 48; MTCW 1

Pater, Walter (Horatio) 1839-1894 .. **NCLC 7**
See also CDBLB 1832-1890; DLB 57, 156

Paterson, A(ndrew) B(arton) 1864-1941 **TCLC 32**
See also CA 155; SATA 97

Paterson, Katherine (Womeldorf) 1932-
.... **CLC 12, 30**
See also AAYA 1, 31; CA 21-24R; CANR 28, 59; CLR 7, 50; DLB 52; JRDA; MAICYA; MTCW 1; SATA 13, 53, 92

Patmore, Coventry Kersey Dighton 1823-1896 .... **NCLC 9**
See also DLB 35, 98

Paton, Alan (Stewart) 1903-1988 . **CLC 4, 10, 25, 55, 106; DA; DAB; DAC; DAM MST, NOV; WLC**
See also AAYA 26; CA 13-16; 125; CANR 22; CAP 1; DA3; DLBD 17; MTCW 1, 2; SATA 11; SATA-Obit 56

Paton Walsh, Gillian 1937-
See Walsh, Jill Paton

See also AAYA 11; CANR 38, 83; DLB 161; JRDA; MAICYA; SAAS 3; SATA 4, 72, 109

Patton, George S. 1885-1945 .... **TCLC 79**

Paulding, James Kirke 1778-1860 ... **NCLC 2**
See also DLB 3, 59, 74

Paulin, Thomas Neilson 1949-
See Paulin, Tom
See also CA 123; 128

Paulin, Tom .... **CLC 37**
See also Paulin, Thomas Neilson DLB 40

Pausanias c. 1st cent. - .... **CMLC 36**

Paustovsky, Konstantin (Georgievich) 1892-1968 .... **CLC 40**
See also CA 93-96; 25-28R

Pavese, Cesare 1908-1950 .. **TCLC 3; PC 13; SSC 19**
See also CA 104; 169; DLB 128, 177

Pavic, Milorad 1929- .... **CLC 60**
See also CA 136; DLB 181

Pavlov, Ivan Petrovich 1849-1936 . **TCLC 91**
See also CA 118; 180

Payne, Alan
See Jakes, John (William)

Paz, Gil
See Lugones, Leopoldo

Paz, Octavio 1914-1998 . **CLC 3, 4, 6, 10, 19, 51, 65, 119; DA; DAB; DAC; DAM MST, MULT, POET; HLC 2; PC 1; WLC**
See also CA 73-76; 165; CANR 32, 65; DA3; DLBY 90, 98; HW 1, 2; MTCW 1, 2

p'Bitek, Okot 1931-1982 .... **CLC 96; BLC 3; DAM MULT**
See also BW 2, 3; CA 124; 107; CANR 82; DLB 125; MTCW 1, 2

Peacock, Molly 1947- .... **CLC 60**
See also CA 103; CAAS 21; CANR 52, 84; DLB 120

Peacock, Thomas Love 1785-1866 . **NCLC 22**
See also DLB 96, 116

Peake, Mervyn 1911-1968 .... **CLC 7, 54**
See also CA 5-8R; 25-28R; CANR 3; DLB 15, 160; MTCW 1; SATA 23

Pearce, Philippa .... **CLC 21**
See also Christie, (Ann) Philippa CLR 9; DLB 161; MAICYA; SATA 1, 67

Pearl, Eric
See Elman, Richard (Martin)

Pearson, T(homas) R(eid) 1956- .... **CLC 39**
See also CA 120; 130; INT 130

Peck, Dale 1967- .... **CLC 81**
See also CA 146; CANR 72

Peck, John 1941- .... **CLC 3**
See also CA 49-52; CANR 3

Peck, Richard (Wayne) 1934- .... **CLC 21**
See also AAYA 1, 24; CA 85-88; CANR 19, 38; CLR 15; INT CANR-19; JRDA; MAICYA; SAAS 2; SATA 18, 55, 97; SATA-Essay 110

Peck, Robert Newton 1928- .... **CLC 17; DA; DAC; DAM MST**
See also AAYA 3; CA 81-84, 182; CAAE 182; CANR 31, 63; CLR 45; JRDA; MAICYA; SAAS 1; SATA 21, 62, 111; SATA-Essay 108

Peckinpah, (David) Sam(uel) 1925-1984
.... **CLC 20**
See also CA 109; 114; CANR 82

Pedersen, Knut 1859-1952
See Hamsun, Knut
See also CA 104; 119; CANR 63; MTCW 1, 2

Peeslake, Gaffer
See Durrell, Lawrence (George)

Peguy, Charles Pierre 1873-1914 ... **TCLC 10**
See also CA 107

Peirce, Charles Sanders 1839-1914
.... **TCLC 81**

Pellicer, Carlos 1900(?)-1977
See also CA 153; 69-72; HLCS 2; HW 1

Pena, Ramon del Valle y
See Valle-Inclan, Ramon (Maria) del

Pendennis, Arthur Esquir
See Thackeray, William Makepeace

Penn, William 1644-1718 .... **LC 25**
See also DLB 24

PEPECE
See Prado (Calvo), Pedro

Pepys, Samuel 1633-1703 . **LC 11; DA; DAB; DAC; DAM MST; WLC**
See also CDBLB 1660-1789; DA3; DLB 101

Percy, Walker 1916-1990 . **CLC 2, 3, 6, 8, 14, 18, 47, 65; DAM NOV, POP**
See also CA 1-4R; 131; CANR 1, 23, 64; DA3; DLB 2; DLBY 80, 90; MTCW 1, 2

Percy, William Alexander 1885-1942
.... **TCLC 84**
See also CA 163; MTCW 2

Perec, Georges 1936-1982 .... **CLC 56, 116**
See also CA 141; DLB 83

Pereda (y Sanchez de Porrua), Jose Maria de 1833-1906 .... **TCLC 16**
See also CA 117

Pereda y Porrua, Jose Maria de
See Pereda (y Sanchez de Porrua), Jose Maria de

Peregoy, George Weems
See Mencken, H(enry) L(ouis)

Perelman, S(idney) J(oseph) 1904-1979
.... **CLC 3, 5, 9, 15, 23, 44, 49; DAM DRAM; SSC 32**
See also AITN 1, 2; CA 73-76; 89-92; CANR 18; DLB 11, 44; MTCW 1, 2

Peret, Benjamin 1899-1959 .... **TCLC 20**
See also CA 117

Peretz, Isaac Loeb 1851(?)-1915 ... **TCLC 16; SSC 26**
See also CA 109

Peretz, Yitzhok Leibush
See Peretz, Isaac Loeb

Perez Galdos, Benito 1843-1920 ... **TCLC 27; HLCS 2**
See also CA 125; 153; HW 1

Peri Rossi, Cristina 1941-
See also CA 131; CANR 59, 81; DLB 145; HLCS 2; HW 1, 2

Perrault, Charles 1628-1703 ... **LC 3, 52; DC 12**
See also MAICYA; SATA 25

Perry, Anne 1938- .... **CLC 126**
See also CA 101; CANR 22, 50, 84

Perry, Brighton
See Sherwood, Robert E(mmet)

Perse, St.-John
See Leger, (Marie-Rene Auguste) Alexis Saint-Leger

Perutz, Leo(pold) 1882-1957 .... **TCLC 60**
See also CA 147; DLB 81

Peseenz, Tulio F.
See Lopez y Fuentes, Gregorio

Pesetsky, Bette 1932- .... **CLC 28**
See also CA 133; DLB 130

Peshkov, Alexei Maximovich 1868-1936
See Gorky, Maxim
See also CA 105; 141; CANR 83; DA; DAC; DAM DRAM, MST, NOV; MTCW 2

Pessoa, Fernando (Antonio Nogueira) 1888-1935 .... **TCLC 27; DAM MULT; HLC 2; PC 20**
See also CA 125; 183

Peterkin, Julia Mood 1880-1961 ...... **CLC 31**
See also CA 102; DLB 9

Peters, Joan K(aren) 1945- .... **CLC 39**
See also CA 158
Peters, Robert L(ouis) 1924- .... **CLC 7**
See also CA 13-16R; CAAS 8; DLB 105
Petofi, Sandor 1823-1849 .... **NCLC 21**
Petrakis, Harry Mark 1923- .... **CLC 3**
See also CA 9-12R; CANR 4, 30, 85
Petrarch 1304-1374 .... **CMLC 20; DAM POET; PC 8**
See also DA3
Petronius c. 20-66 .... **CMLC 34**
See also DLB 211
Petrov, Evgeny .... **TCLC 21**
See also Kataev, Evgeny Petrovich
Petry, Ann (Lane) 1908-1997 ... **CLC 1, 7, 18**
See also BW 1, 3; CA 5-8R; 157; CAAS 6;
CANR 4, 46; CLR 12; DLB 76; JRDA;
MAICYA; MTCW 1; SATA 5; SATA-Obit
94
Petursson, Halligrimur 1614-1674 .... **LC 8**
Peychinovich
See Vazov, Ivan (Minchov)
Phaedrus c. 18B.C.-c. 50 .... **CMLC 25**
See also DLB 211
Philips, Katherine 1632-1664 .... **LC 30**
See also DLB 131
Philipson, Morris H. 1926- .... **CLC 53**
See also CA 1-4R; CANR 4
Phillips, Caryl 1958- . **CLC 96; BLCS; DAM MULT**
See also BW 2; CA 141; CANR 63; DA3;
DLB 157; MTCW 2
Phillips, David Graham 1867-1911 . **TCLC 44**
See also CA 108; 176; DLB 9, 12
Phillips, Jack
See Sandburg, Carl (August)
Phillips, Jayne Anne 1952- . **CLC 15, 33; SSC 16**
See also CA 101; CANR 24, 50; DLBY 80;
INT CANR-24; MTCW 1, 2
Phillips, Richard
See Dick, Philip K(indred)
Phillips, Robert (Schaeffer) 1938- .... **CLC 28**
See also CA 17-20R; CAAS 13; CANR 8;
DLB 105
Phillips, Ward
See Lovecraft, H(oward) P(hillips)
Piccolo, Lucio 1901-1969 .... **CLC 13**
See also CA 97-100; DLB 114
Pickthall, Marjorie L(owry) C(hristie)
1883-1922 .... **TCLC 21**
See also CA 107; DLB 92
Pico della Mirandola, Giovanni 1463-1494
LC 15
Piercy, Marge 1936- .... **CLC 3, 6, 14, 18, 27, 62, 128; PC 29**
See also CA 21-24R; CAAS 1; CANR 13,
43, 66; DLB 120; MTCW 1, 2
Piers, Robert
See Anthony, Piers
Pieyre de Mandiargues, Andre 1909-1991
See Mandiargues, Andre Pieyre de
See also CA 103; 136; CANR 22, 82
Pilnyak, Boris .... **TCLC 23**
See also Vogau, Boris Andreyevich
Pincherle, Alberto 1907-1990 .... **CLC 11, 18; DAM NOV**
See also Moravia, Alberto CA 25-28R; 132;
CANR 33, 63; MTCW 1
Pinckney, Darryl 1953- .... **CLC 76**
See also BW 2, 3; CA 143; CANR 79
Pindar 518B.C.-446B.C. .... **CMLC 12; PC 19**
See also DLB 176
Pineda, Cecile 1942- .... **CLC 39**
See also CA 118
Pinero, Arthur Wing 1855-1934 ... **TCLC 32; DAM DRAM**
See also CA 110; 153; DLB 10

Pinero, Miguel (Antonio Gomez) 1946-1988
CLC 4, 55
See also CA 61-64; 125; CANR 29; HW 1
Pinget, Robert 1919-1997 .... **CLC 7, 13, 37**
See also CA 85-88; 160; DLB 83
Pink Floyd
See Barrett, (Roger) Syd; Gilmour, David;
Mason, Nick; Waters, Roger; Wright, Rick
Pinkney, Edward 1802-1828 .... **NCLC 31**
Pinkwater, Daniel Manus 1941- .... **CLC 35**
See also Pinkwater, Manus AAYA 1; CA
29-32R; CANR 12, 38, 89; CLR 4; JRDA;
MAICYA; SAAS 3; SATA 46, 76, 114
Pinkwater, Manus
See Pinkwater, Daniel Manus
See also SATA 8
Pinsky, Robert 1940- . **CLC 9, 19, 38, 94, 121; DAM POET; PC 27**
See also CA 29-32R; CAAS 4; CANR 58;
DA3; DLBY 82, 98; MTCW 2
Pinta, Harold
See Pinter, Harold
Pinter, Harold 1930- .. **CLC 1, 3, 6, 9, 11, 15, 27, 58, 73; DA; DAB; DAC; DAM DRAM, MST; WLC**
See also CA 5-8R; CANR 33, 65; CDBLB
1960 to Present; DA3; DLB 13; MTCW
1, 2
Piozzi, Hester Lynch (Thrale) 1741-1821
NCLC 57
See also DLB 104, 142
Pirandello, Luigi 1867-1936 ...... **TCLC 4, 29; DA; DAB; DAC; DAM DRAM, MST; DC 5; SSC 22; WLC**
See also CA 104; 153; DA3; MTCW 2
Pirsig, Robert M(aynard) 1928- ... **CLC 4, 6, 73; DAM POP**
See also CA 53-56; CANR 42, 74; DA3;
MTCW 1, 2; SATA 39
Pisarev, Dmitry Ivanovich 1840-1868
.... **NCLC 25**
Pix, Mary (Griffith) 1666-1709 .... **LC 8**
See also DLB 80
Pixerecourt, (Rene Charles) Guilbert de
1773-1844 .... **NCLC 39**
See also DLB 192
Plaatje, Sol(omon) T(shekisho) 1876-1932
TCLC 73; BLCS
See also BW 2, 3; CA 141; CANR 79
Plaidy, Jean
See Hibbert, Eleanor Alice Burford
Planche, James Robinson 1796-1880
.... **NCLC 42**
Plant, Robert 1948- .... **CLC 12**
Plante, David (Robert) 1940- ...... **CLC 7, 23, 38; DAM NOV**
See also CA 37-40R; CANR 12, 36, 58, 82;
DLBY 83; INT CANR-12; MTCW 1
Plath, Sylvia 1932-1963 ..... **CLC 1, 2, 3, 5, 9, 11, 14, 17, 50, 51, 62, 111; DA; DAB; DAC; DAM MST, POET; PC 1; WLC**
See also AAYA 13; CA 19-20; CANR 34;
CAP 2; CDALB 1941-1968; DA3; DLB
5, 6, 152; MTCW 1, 2; SATA 96
Plato 428(?)B.C.-348(?)B.C. .... **CMLC 8; DA; DAB; DAC; DAM MST; WLCS**
See also DA3; DLB 176
Platonov, Andrei .... **TCLC 14**
See also Klimentov, Andrei Platonovich
Platt, Kin 1911- .... **CLC 26**
See also AAYA 11; CA 17-20R; CANR 11;
JRDA; SAAS 17; SATA 21, 86
Plautus c. 251B.C.-184B.C. . **CMLC 24; DC 6**
See also DLB 211
Plick et Plock
See Simenon, Georges (Jacques Christian)
Plimpton, George (Ames) 1927- .... **CLC 36**
See also AITN 1; CA 21-24R; CANR 32,
70; DLB 185; MTCW 1, 2; SATA 10

Pliny the Elder c. 23-79 .... **CMLC 23**
See also DLB 211
Plomer, William Charles Franklin 1903-1973
CLC 4, 8
See also CA 21-22; CANR 34; CAP 2; DLB
20, 162, 191; MTCW 1; SATA 24
Plowman, Piers
See Kavanagh, Patrick (Joseph)
Plum, J.
See Wodehouse, P(elham) G(renville)
Plumly, Stanley (Ross) 1939- .... **CLC 33**
See also CA 108; 110; DLB 5, 193; INT
110
Plumpe, Friedrich Wilhelm 1888-1931
.... **TCLC 53**
See also CA 112
Po Chu-i 772-846 .... **CMLC 24**
Poe, Edgar Allan 1809-1849 ..... **NCLC 1, 16, 55, 78; DA; DAB; DAC; DAM MST, POET; PC 1; SSC 34; WLC**
See also AAYA 14; CDALB 1640-1865;
DA3; DLB 3, 59, 73, 74; SATA 23
Poet of Titchfield Street, The
See Pound, Ezra (Weston Loomis)
Pohl, Frederik 1919- .... **CLC 18; SSC 25**
See also AAYA 24; CA 61-64; CAAS 1;
CANR 11, 37, 81; DLB 8; INT CANR-
11; MTCW 1, 2; SATA 24
Poirier, Louis 1910-
See Gracq, Julien
See also CA 122; 126
Poitier, Sidney 1927- .... **CLC 26**
See also BW 1; CA 117
Polanski, Roman 1933- .... **CLC 16**
See also CA 77-80
Poliakoff, Stephen 1952- .... **CLC 38**
See also CA 106; DLB 13
Police, The
See Copeland, Stewart (Armstrong); Sum-
mers, Andrew James; Sumner, Gordon
Matthew
Polidori, John William 1795-1821 . **NCLC 51**
See also DLB 116
Pollitt, Katha 1949- .... **CLC 28, 122**
See also CA 120; 122; CANR 66; MTCW
1, 2
Pollock, (Mary) Sharon 1936- .... **CLC 50; DAC; DAM DRAM, MST**
See also CA 141; DLB 60
Polo, Marco 1254-1324 .... **CMLC 15**
Polonsky, Abraham (Lincoln) 1910- . **CLC 92**
See also CA 104; DLB 26; INT 104
Polybius c. 200B.C.-c. 118B.C. .... **CMLC 17**
See also DLB 176
Pomerance, Bernard 1940- ... **CLC 13; DAM DRAM**
See also CA 101; CANR 49
Ponge, Francis 1899-1988 . **CLC 6, 18; DAM POET**
See also CA 85-88; 126; CANR 40, 86
Poniatowska, Elena 1933-
See also CA 101; CANR 32, 66; DAM
MULT; DLB 113; HLC 2; HW 1, 2
Pontoppidan, Henrik 1857-1943 .... **TCLC 29**
See also CA 170
Poole, Josephine .... **CLC 17**
See also Helyar, Jane Penelope Josephine
SAAS 2; SATA 5
Popa, Vasko 1922-1991 .... **CLC 19**
See also CA 112; 148; DLB 181
Pope, Alexander 1688-1744 .... **LC 3; DA; DAB; DAC; DAM MST, POET; PC 26; WLC**
See also CDBLB 1660-1789; DA3; DLB
95, 101
Porter, Connie (Rose) 1959(?)- .... **CLC 70**
See also BW 2, 3; CA 142; SATA 81

See also Dannay, Frederic; Davidson, Avram (James); Lee, Manfred B(ennington); Marlowe, Stephen; Sturgeon, Theodore (Hamilton); Vance, John Holbrook

Queen, Ellery, Jr.
See Dannay, Frederic; Lee, Manfred B(ennington)

Queneau, Raymond 1903-1976 ..... **CLC 2, 5, 10, 42**
See also CA 77-80; 69-72; CANR 32; DLB 72; MTCW 1, 2

Quevedo, Francisco de 1580-1645 .... **LC 23**

Quiller-Couch, SirArthur (Thomas) 1863-1944 .... **TCLC 53**
See also CA 118; 166; DLB 135, 153, 190

Quin, Ann (Marie) 1936-1973 .... **CLC 6**
See also CA 9-12R; 45-48; DLB 14

Quinn, Martin
See Smith, Martin Cruz

Quinn, Peter 1947- .... **CLC 91**

Quinn, Simon
See Smith, Martin Cruz

Quintana, Leroy V. 1944-
See also CA 131; CANR 65; DAM MULT; DLB 82; HLC 2; HW 1, 2

Quiroga, Horacio (Sylvestre) 1878-1937 **TCLC 20; DAM MULT; HLC 2**
See also CA 117; 131; HW 1; MTCW 1

Quoirez, Francoise 1935- .... **CLC 9**
See also Sagan, Francoise CA 49-52; CANR 6, 39, 73; MTCW 1, 2

Raabe, Wilhelm (Karl) 1831-1910 . **TCLC 45**
See also CA 167; DLB 129

Rabe, David (William) 1940- .. **CLC 4, 8, 33; DAM DRAM**
See also CA 85-88; CABS 3; CANR 59; DLB 7

Rabelais, Francois 1483-1553 ...... **LC 5; DA; DAB; DAC; DAM MST; WLC**

Rabinovitch, Sholem 1859-1916
See Aleichem, Sholom
See also CA 104

Rabinyan, Dorit 1972- .... **CLC 119**
See also CA 170

Rachilde
See Vallette, Marguerite Eymery

Racine, Jean 1639-1699 . **LC 28; DAB; DAM MST**
See also DA3

Radcliffe, Ann (Ward) 1764-1823 ... **NCLC 6, 55**
See also DLB 39, 178

Radiguet, Raymond 1903-1923 ...... **TCLC 29**
See also CA 162; DLB 65

Radnoti, Miklos 1909-1944 .... **TCLC 16**
See also CA 118

Rado, James 1939- .... **CLC 17**
See also CA 105

Radvanyi, Netty 1900-1983
See Seghers, Anna
See also CA 85-88; 110; CANR 82

Rae, Ben
See Griffiths, Trevor

Raeburn, John (Hay) 1941- .... **CLC 34**
See also CA 57-60

Ragni, Gerome 1942-1991 .... **CLC 17**
See also CA 105; 134

Rahv, Philip 1908-1973 .... **CLC 24**
See also Greenberg, Ivan DLB 137

Raimund, Ferdinand Jakob 1790-1836 **NCLC 69**
See also DLB 90

Raine, Craig 1944- .... **CLC 32, 103**
See also CA 108; CANR 29, 51; DLB 40

Raine, Kathleen (Jessie) 1908- ..... **CLC 7, 45**
See also CA 85-88; CANR 46; DLB 20; MTCW 1

Rainis, Janis 1865-1929 .... **TCLC 29**
See also CA 170

Rakosi, Carl 1903- .... **CLC 47**
See also Rawley, Callman CAAS 5; DLB 193

Raleigh, Richard
See Lovecraft, H(oward) P(hillips)

Raleigh, Sir Walter 1554(?)-1618 .. **LC 31, 39**
See also CDBLB Before 1660; DLB 172

Rallentando, H. P.
See Sayers, Dorothy L(eigh)

Ramal, Walter
See de la Mare, Walter (John)

Ramana Maharshi 1879-1950 .... **TCLC 84**

Ramoacn y Cajal, Santiago 1852-1934
.... **TCLC 93**

Ramon, Juan
See Jimenez (Mantecon), Juan Ramon

Ramos, Graciliano 1892-1953 .... **TCLC 32**
See also CA 167; HW 2

Rampersad, Arnold 1941- .... **CLC 44**
See also BW 2, 3; CA 127; 133; CANR 81; DLB 111; INT 133

Rampling, Anne
See Rice, Anne

Ramsay, Allan 1684(?)-1758 .... **LC 29**
See also DLB 95

Ramuz, Charles-Ferdinand 1878-1947
.... **TCLC 33**
See also CA 165

Rand, Ayn 1905-1982 ...... **CLC 3, 30, 44, 79; DA; DAC; DAM MST, NOV, POP; WLC**
See also AAYA 10; CA 13-16R; 105; CANR 27, 73; CDALBS; DA3; MTCW 1, 2

Randall, Dudley (Felker) 1914- .... **CLC 1; BLC 3; DAM MULT**
See also BW 1, 3; CA 25-28R; CANR 23, 82; DLB 41

Randall, Robert
See Silverberg, Robert

Ranger, Ken
See Creasey, John

Ransom, John Crowe 1888-1974 .. **CLC 2, 4, 5, 11, 24; DAM POET**
See also CA 5-8R; 49-52; CANR 6, 34; CDALBS; DA3; DLB 45, 63; MTCW 1, 2

Rao, Raja 1909- ..... **CLC 25, 56; DAM NOV**
See also CA 73-76; CANR 51; MTCW 1, 2

Raphael, Frederic (Michael) 1931- ... **CLC 2, 14**
See also CA 1-4R; CANR 1, 86; DLB 14

Ratcliffe, James P.
See Mencken, H(enry) L(ouis)

Rathbone, Julian 1935- .... **CLC 41**
See also CA 101; CANR 34, 73

Rattigan, Terence (Mervyn) 1911-1977
.... **CLC 7; DAM DRAM**
See also CA 85-88; 73-76; CDBLB 1945-1960; DLB 13; MTCW 1, 2

Ratushinskaya, Irina 1954- .... **CLC 54**
See also CA 129; CANR 68

Raven, Simon (Arthur Noel) 1927- .. **CLC 14**
See also CA 81-84; CANR 86

Ravenna, Michael
See Welty, Eudora

Rawley, Callman 1903-
See Rakosi, Carl
See also CA 21-24R; CANR 12, 32

Rawlings, Marjorie Kinnan 1896-1953
.... **TCLC 4**
See also AAYA 20; CA 104; 137; CANR 74; CLR 63; DLB 9, 22, 102; DLBD 17; JRDA; MAICYA; MTCW 2; SATA 100; YABC 1

Ray, Satyajit 1921-1992 .. **CLC 16, 76; DAM MULT**

See also CA 114; 137

Read, Herbert Edward 1893-1968 ..... **CLC 4**
See also CA 85-88; 25-28R; DLB 20, 149

Read, Piers Paul 1941- .... **CLC 4, 10, 25**
See also CA 21-24R; CANR 38, 86; DLB 14; SATA 21

Reade, Charles 1814-1884 .... **NCLC 2, 74**
See also DLB 21

Reade, Hamish
See Gray, Simon (James Holliday)

Reading, Peter 1946- .... **CLC 47**
See also CA 103; CANR 46; DLB 40

Reaney, James 1926- .. **CLC 13; DAC; DAM MST**
See also CA 41-44R; CAAS 15; CANR 42; DLB 68; SATA 43

Rebreanu, Liviu 1885-1944 .... **TCLC 28**
See also CA 165

Rechy, John (Francisco) 1934- ...... **CLC 1, 7, 14, 18, 107; DAM MULT; HLC 2**
See also CA 5-8R; CAAS 4; CANR 6, 32, 64; DLB 122; DLBY 82; HW 1, 2; INT CANR-6

Redcam, Tom 1870-1933 .... **TCLC 25**

Reddin, Keith .... **CLC 67**

Redgrove, Peter (William) 1932- . **CLC 6, 41**
See also CA 1-4R; CANR 3, 39, 77; DLB 40

Redmon, Anne .... **CLC 22**
See also Nightingale, Anne Redmon DLBY 86

Reed, Eliot
See Ambler, Eric

Reed, Ishmael 1938- .. **CLC 2, 3, 5, 6, 13, 32, 60; BLC 3; DAM MULT**
See also BW 2, 3; CA 21-24R; CANR 25, 48, 74; DA3; DLB 2, 5, 33, 169; DLBD 8; MTCW 1, 2

Reed, John (Silas) 1887-1920 .... **TCLC 9**
See also CA 106

Reed, Lou .... **CLC 21**
See also Firbank, Louis

Reese, Lizette Woodworth 1856-1935 . **PC 29**
See also CA 180; DLB 54

Reeve, Clara 1729-1807 .... **NCLC 19**
See also DLB 39

Reich, Wilhelm 1897-1957 .... **TCLC 57**

Reid, Christopher (John) 1949- .... **CLC 33**
See also CA 140; CANR 89; DLB 40

Reid, Desmond
See Moorcock, Michael (John)

Reid Banks, Lynne 1929-
See Banks, Lynne Reid
See also CA 1-4R; CANR 6, 22, 38, 87; CLR 24; JRDA; MAICYA; SATA 22, 75, 111

Reilly, William K.
See Creasey, John

Reiner, Max
See Caldwell, (Janet Miriam) Taylor (Holland)

Reis, Ricardo
See Pessoa, Fernando (Antonio Nogueira)

Remarque, Erich Maria 1898-1970 . **CLC 21; DA; DAB; DAC; DAM MST, NOV**
See also AAYA 27; CA 77-80; 29-32R; DA3; DLB 56; MTCW 1, 2

Remington, Frederic 1861-1909 ..... **TCLC 89**
See also CA 108; 169; DLB 12, 186, 188; SATA 41

Remizov, A.
See Remizov, Aleksei (Mikhailovich)

Remizov, A. M.
See Remizov, Aleksei (Mikhailovich)

Remizov, Aleksei (Mikhailovich) 1877-1957 **TCLC 27**
See also CA 125; 133

Renan, Joseph Ernest 1823-1892 .. **NCLC 26**

Renard, Jules 1864-1910 .... **TCLC 17**
    See also CA 117
Renault, Mary .... **CLC 3, 11, 17**
    See also Challans, Mary DLBY 83; MTCW
    2
Rendell, Ruth (Barbara) 1930- . **CLC 28, 48;**
    DAM POP
    See also Vine, Barbara CA 109; CANR 32,
    52, 74; DLB 87; INT CANR-32; MTCW
    1, 2
Renoir, Jean 1894-1979 .... **CLC 20**
    See also CA 129; 85-88
Resnais, Alain 1922- .... **CLC 16**
Reverdy, Pierre 1889-1960 .... **CLC 53**
    See also CA 97-100; 89-92
Rexroth, Kenneth 1905-1982 .... **CLC 1, 2, 6,**
    11, 22, 49, 112; DAM POET; PC 20
    See also CA 5-8R; 107; CANR 14, 34, 63;
    CDALB 1941-1968; DLB 16, 48, 165,
    212; DLBY 82; INT CANR-14; MTCW
    1, 2
Reyes, Alfonso 1889-1959 .. **TCLC 33; HLCS**
    2
    See also CA 131; HW 1
Reyes y Basoalto, Ricardo Eliecer Neftali
    See Neruda, Pablo
Reymont, Wladyslaw (Stanislaw)
    1868(?)-1925 .... **TCLC 5**
    See also CA 104
Reynolds, Jonathan 1942- .... **CLC 6, 38**
    See also CA 65-68; CANR 28
Reynolds, Joshua 1723-1792 .... **LC 15**
    See also DLB 104
Reynolds, Michael Shane 1937- .... **CLC 44**
    See also CA 65-68; CANR 9
Reznikoff, Charles 1894-1976 .... **CLC 9**
    See also CA 33-36; 61-64; CAP 2; DLB 28,
    45
Rezzori (d'Arezzo), Gregor von 1914-1998
    CLC 25
    See also CA 122; 136; 167
Rhine, Richard
    See Silverstein, Alvin
Rhodes, Eugene Manlove 1869-1934
    .... **TCLC 53**
Rhodius, Apollonius c. 3rd cent. B.C.-
    .... **CMLC 28**
    See also DLB 176
R'hoone
    See Balzac, Honore de
Rhys, Jean 1890(?)-1979 ...... **CLC 2, 4, 6, 14,**
    19, 51, 124; DAM NOV; SSC 21
    See also CA 25-28R; 85-88; CANR 35, 62;
    CDBLB 1945-1960; DA3; DLB 36, 117,
    162; MTCW 1, 2
Ribeiro, Darcy 1922-1997 .... **CLC 34**
    See also CA 33-36R; 156
Ribeiro, Joao Ubaldo (Osorio Pimentel)
    1941- .... **CLC 10, 67**
    See also CA 81-84
Ribman, Ronald (Burt) 1932- .... **CLC 7**
    See also CA 21-24R; CANR 46, 80
Ricci, Nino 1959- .... **CLC 70**
    See also CA 137
Rice, Anne 1941- .. **CLC 41, 128; DAM POP**
    See also AAYA 9; BEST 89:2; CA 65-68;
    CANR 12, 36, 53, 74; DA3; MTCW 2
Rice, Elmer (Leopold) 1892-1967 ...... **CLC 7,**
    49; DAM DRAM
    See also CA 21-22; 25-28R; CAP 2; DLB
    4, 7; MTCW 1, 2
Rice, Tim(othy Miles Bindon) 1944- . **CLC 21**
    See also CA 103; CANR 46
Rich, Adrienne (Cecile) 1929- ... **CLC 3, 6, 7,**
    11, 18, 36, 73, 76, 125; DAM POET; PC
    5
    See also CA 9-12R; CANR 20, 53, 74;
    CDALBS; DA3; DLB 5, 67; MTCW 1, 2

Rich, Barbara
    See Graves, Robert (von Ranke)
Rich, Robert
    See Trumbo, Dalton
Richard, Keith .... **CLC 17**
    See also Richards, Keith
Richards, David Adams 1950- .... **CLC 59;**
    DAC
    See also CA 93-96; CANR 60; DLB 53
Richards, I(vor) A(rmstrong) 1893-1979
    .... **CLC 14, 24**
    See also CA 41-44R; 89-92; CANR 34, 74;
    DLB 27; MTCW 2
Richards, Keith 1943-
    See Richard, Keith
    See also CA 107; CANR 77
Richardson, Anne
    See Roiphe, Anne (Richardson)
Richardson, Dorothy Miller 1873-1957
    .... **TCLC 3**
    See also CA 104; DLB 36
Richardson, Ethel Florence (Lindesay)
    1870-1946
    See Richardson, Henry Handel
    See also CA 105
Richardson, Henry Handel .... **TCLC 4**
    See also Richardson, Ethel Florence
    (Lindesay) DLB 197
Richardson, John 1796-1852 .... **NCLC 55;**
    DAC
    See also DLB 99
Richardson, Samuel 1689-1761 ...... **LC 1, 44;**
    DA; DAB; DAC; DAM MST, NOV;
    WLC
    See also CDBLB 1660-1789; DLB 39
Richler, Mordecai 1931- . **CLC 3, 5, 9, 13, 18,**
    46, 70; DAC; DAM MST, NOV
    See also AITN 1; CA 65-68; CANR 31, 62;
    CLR 17; DLB 53; MAICYA; MTCW 1,
    2; SATA 44, 98; SATA-Brief 27
Richter, Conrad (Michael) 1890-1968
    .... **CLC 30**
    See also AAYA 21; CA 5-8R; 25-28R;
    CANR 23; DLB 9, 212; MTCW 1, 2;
    SATA 3
Ricostranza, Tom
    See Ellis, Trey
Riddell, Charlotte 1832-1906 .... **TCLC 40**
    See also CA 165; DLB 156
Ridge, John Rollin 1827-1867 ...... **NCLC 82;**
    DAM MULT
    See also CA 144; DLB 175; NNAL
Ridgway, Keith 1965- .... **CLC 119**
    See also CA 172
Riding, Laura .... **CLC 3, 7**
    See also Jackson, Laura (Riding)
Riefenstahl, Berta Helene Amalia 1902-
    See Riefenstahl, Leni
    See also CA 108
Riefenstahl, Leni .... **CLC 16**
    See also Riefenstahl, Berta Helene Amalia
Riffe, Ernest
    See Bergman, (Ernst) Ingmar
Riggs, (Rolla) Lynn 1899-1954 ..... **TCLC 56;**
    DAM MULT
    See also CA 144; DLB 175; NNAL
Riis, Jacob A(ugust) 1849-1914 ..... **TCLC 80**
    See also CA 113; 168; DLB 23
Riley, James Whitcomb 1849-1916
    .... **TCLC 51; DAM POET**
    See also CA 118; 137; MAICYA; SATA 17
Riley, Tex
    See Creasey, John
Rilke, Rainer Maria 1875-1926 .. **TCLC 1, 6,**
    19; DAM POET; PC 2
    See also CA 104; 132; CANR 62; DA3;
    DLB 81; MTCW 1, 2
Rimbaud, (Jean Nicolas) Arthur 1854-1891
    NCLC 4, 35, 82; DA; DAB; DAC; DAM

MST, POET; PC 3; WLC
    See also DA3
Rinehart, Mary Roberts 1876-1958
    .... **TCLC 52**
    See also CA 108; 166
Ringmaster, The
    See Mencken, H(enry) L(ouis)
Ringwood, Gwen(dolyn Margaret) Pharis
    1910-1984 .... **CLC 48**
    See also CA 148; 112; DLB 88
Rio, Michel 19(?)- .... **CLC 43**
Ritsos, Giannes
    See Ritsos, Yannis
Ritsos, Yannis 1909-1990 .... **CLC 6, 13, 31**
    See also CA 77-80; 133; CANR 39, 61;
    MTCW 1
Ritter, Erika 1948(?)- .... **CLC 52**
Rivera, Jose Eustasio 1889-1928 ... **TCLC 35**
    See also CA 162; HW 1, 2
Rivera, Tomas 1935-1984
    See also CA 49-52; CANR 32; DLB 82;
    HLCS 2; HW 1
Rivers, Conrad Kent 1933-1968 .... **CLC 1**
    See also BW 1; CA 85-88; DLB 41
Rivers, Elfrida
    See Bradley, Marion Zimmer
Riverside, John
    See Heinlein, Robert A(nson)
Rizal, Jose 1861-1896 .... **NCLC 27**
Roa Bastos, Augusto (Antonio) 1917-
    .... **CLC 45; DAM MULT; HLC 2**
    See also CA 131; DLB 113; HW 1
Robbe-Grillet, Alain 1922- .... **CLC 1, 2, 4, 6,**
    8, 10, 14, 43, 128
    See also CA 9-12R; CANR 33, 65; DLB
    83; MTCW 1, 2
Robbins, Harold 1916-1997 .... **CLC 5; DAM**
    NOV
    See also CA 73-76; 162; CANR 26, 54;
    DA3; MTCW 1, 2
Robbins, Thomas Eugene 1936-
    See Robbins, Tom
    See also CA 81-84; CANR 29, 59; DAM
    NOV, POP; DA3; MTCW 1, 2
Robbins, Tom .... **CLC 9, 32, 64**
    See also Robbins, Thomas Eugene AAYA
    32; BEST 90:3; DLBY 80; MTCW 2
Robbins, Trina 1938- .... **CLC 21**
    See also CA 128
Roberts, Charles G(eorge) D(ouglas)
    1860-1943 .... **TCLC 8**
    See also CA 105; CLR 33; DLB 92; SATA
    88; SATA-Brief 29
Roberts, Elizabeth Madox 1886-1941
    .... **TCLC 68**
    See also CA 111; 166; DLB 9, 54, 102;
    SATA 33; SATA-Brief 27
Roberts, Kate 1891-1985 .... **CLC 15**
    See also CA 107; 116
Roberts, Keith (John Kingston) 1935-
    .... **CLC 14**
    See also CA 25-28R; CANR 46
Roberts, Kenneth (Lewis) 1885-1957
    .... **TCLC 23**
    See also CA 109; DLB 9
Roberts, Michele (B.) 1949- .... **CLC 48**
    See also CA 115; CANR 58
Robertson, Ellis
    See Ellison, Harlan (Jay); Silverberg, Robert
Robertson, Thomas William 1829-1871
    NCLC 35; DAM DRAM
Robeson, Kenneth
    See Dent, Lester
Robinson, Edwin Arlington 1869-1935
    .... **TCLC 5; DA; DAC; DAM MST,**
    POET; PC 1
    See also CA 104; 133; CDALB 1865-1917;
    DLB 54; MTCW 1, 2

Robinson, Henry Crabb 1775-1867
.... **NCLC 15**
See also DLB 107
Robinson, Jill 1936- .... **CLC 10**
See also CA 102; INT 102
Robinson, Kim Stanley 1952- .... **CLC 34**
See also AAYA 26; CA 126; SATA 109
Robinson, Lloyd
See Silverberg, Robert
Robinson, Marilynne 1944- .... **CLC 25**
See also CA 116; CANR 80; DLB 206
Robinson, Smokey .... **CLC 21**
See also Robinson, William, Jr.
Robinson, William, Jr. 1940-
See Robinson, Smokey
See also CA 116
Robison, Mary 1949- .... **CLC 42, 98**
See also CA 113; 116; CANR 87; DLB 130;
INT 116
Rod, Edouard 1857-1910 .... **TCLC 52**
Roddenberry, Eugene Wesley 1921-1991
See Roddenberry, Gene
See also CA 110; 135; CANR 37; SATA 45;
SATA-Obit 69
Roddenberry, Gene .... **CLC 17**
See also Roddenberry, Eugene Wesley
AAYA 5; SATA-Obit 69
Rodgers, Mary 1931- .... **CLC 12**
See also CA 49-52; CANR 8, 55; CLR 20;
INT CANR-8; JRDA; MAICYA; SATA 8
Rodgers, W(illiam) R(obert) 1909-1969
.... **CLC 7**
See also CA 85-88; DLB 20
Rodman, Eric
See Silverberg, Robert
Rodman, Howard 1920(?)-1985 .... **CLC 65**
See also CA 118
Rodman, Maia
See Wojciechowska, Maia (Teresa)
Rodo, Jose Enrique 1872(?)-1917
See also CA 178; HLCS 2; HW 2
Rodriguez, Claudio 1934- .... **CLC 10**
See also DLB 134
Rodriguez, Richard 1944-
See also CA 110; CANR 66; DAM MULT;
DLB 82; HLC 2; HW 1, 2
Roelvaag, O(le) E(dvart) 1876-1931
.... **TCLC 17**
See also CA 117; 171; DLB 9
Roethke, Theodore (Huebner) 1908-1963
**CLC 1, 3, 8, 11, 19, 46, 101; DAM
POET; PC 15**
See also CA 81-84; CABS 2; CDALB 1941-
1968; DA3; DLB 5, 206; MTCW 1, 2
Rogers, Samuel 1763-1855 .... **NCLC 69**
See also DLB 93
Rogers, Thomas Hunton 1927- .... **CLC 57**
See also CA 89-92; INT 89-92
Rogers, Will(iam Penn Adair) 1879-1935
TCLC 8, 71; DAM MULT
See also CA 105; 144; DA3; DLB 11;
MTCW 2; NNAL
Rogin, Gilbert 1929- .... **CLC 18**
See also CA 65-68; CANR 15
Rohan, Koda
See Koda Shigeyuki
Rohlfs, Anna Katharine Green
See Green, Anna Katharine
Rohmer, Eric .... **CLC 16**
See also Scherer, Jean-Marie Maurice
Rohmer, Sax .... **TCLC 28**
See also Ward, Arthur Henry Sarsfield DLB
70
Roiphe, Anne (Richardson) 1935- .. **CLC 3, 9**
See also CA 89-92; CANR 45, 73; DLBY
80; INT 89-92
Rojas, Fernando de 1465-1541 .... **LC 23;
HLCS 1**

Rojas, Gonzalo 1917-
See also HLCS 2; HW 2
Rojas, Gonzalo 1917-
See also CA 178; HLCS 2
**Rolfe, Frederick (William Serafino Austin
Lewis Mary)** 1860-1913 .... **TCLC 12**
See also CA 107; DLB 34, 156
Rolland, Romain 1866-1944 .... **TCLC 23**
See also CA 118; DLB 65
Rolle, Richard c. 1300-c. 1349 ...... **CMLC 21**
See also DLB 146
Rolvaag, O(le) E(dvart)
See Roelvaag, O(le) E(dvart)
Romain Arnaud, Saint
See Aragon, Louis
Romains, Jules 1885-1972 .... **CLC 7**
See also CA 85-88; CANR 34; DLB 65;
MTCW 1
Romero, Jose Ruben 1890-1952 .... **TCLC 14**
See also CA 114; 131; HW 1
Ronsard, Pierre de 1524-1585 . **LC 6, 54; PC
11**
Rooke, Leon 1934- . **CLC 25, 34; DAM POP**
See also CA 25-28R; CANR 23, 53
Roosevelt, Franklin Delano 1882-1945
.... **TCLC 93**
See also CA 116; 173
Roosevelt, Theodore 1858-1919 ..... **TCLC 69**
See also CA 115; 170; DLB 47, 186
Roper, William 1498-1578 .... **LC 10**
Roquelaure, A. N.
See Rice, Anne
Rosa, Joao Guimaraes 1908-1967 ... **CLC 23;
HLCS 1**
See also CA 89-92; DLB 113
Rose, Wendy 1948- .. **CLC 85; DAM MULT;
PC 13**
See also CA 53-56; CANR 5, 51; DLB 175;
NNAL; SATA 12
Rosen, R. D.
See Rosen, Richard (Dean)
Rosen, Richard (Dean) 1949- .... **CLC 39**
See also CA 77-80; CANR 62; INT
CANR-30
Rosenberg, Isaac 1890-1918 .... **TCLC 12**
See also CA 107; DLB 20
Rosenblatt, Joe .... **CLC 15**
See also Rosenblatt, Joseph
Rosenblatt, Joseph 1933-
See Rosenblatt, Joe
See also CA 89-92; INT 89-92
Rosenfeld, Samuel
See Tzara, Tristan
Rosenstock, Sami
See Tzara, Tristan
Rosenstock, Samuel
See Tzara, Tristan
Rosenthal, M(acha) L(ouis) 1917-1996
.... **CLC 28**
See also CA 1-4R; 152; CAAS 6; CANR 4,
51; DLB 5; SATA 59
Ross, Barnaby
See Dannay, Frederic
Ross, Bernard L.
See Follett, Ken(neth Martin)
Ross, J. H.
See Lawrence, T(homas) E(dward)
Ross, John Hume
See Lawrence, T(homas) E(dward)
Ross, Martin
See Martin, Violet Florence
See also DLB 135
Ross, (James) Sinclair 1908-1996 ... **CLC 13;
DAC; DAM MST; SSC 24**
See also CA 73-76; CANR 81; DLB 88
Rossetti, Christina (Georgina) 1830-1894
**NCLC 2, 50, 66; DA; DAB; DAC; DAM
MST, POET; PC 7; WLC**

See also DA3; DLB 35, 163; MAICYA;
SATA 20
Rossetti, Dante Gabriel 1828-1882 . **NCLC 4,
77; DA; DAB; DAC; DAM MST,
POET; WLC**
See also CDBLB 1832-1890; DLB 35
Rossner, Judith (Perelman) 1935- . **CLC 6, 9,
29**
See also AITN 2; BEST 90:3; CA 17-20R;
CANR 18, 51, 73; DLB 6; INT CANR-
18; MTCW 1, 2
Rostand, Edmond (Eugene Alexis)
1868-1918 .... **TCLC 6, 37; DA; DAB;
DAC; DAM DRAM, MST; DC 10**
See also CA 104; 126; DA3; DLB 192;
MTCW 1
Roth, Henry 1906-1995 ..... **CLC 2, 6, 11, 104**
See also CA 11-12; 149; CANR 38, 63;
CAP 1; DA3; DLB 28; MTCW 1, 2
Roth, Philip (Milton) 1933- ... **CLC 1, 2, 3, 4,
6, 9, 15, 22, 31, 47, 66, 86, 119; DA;
DAB; DAC; DAM MST, NOV, POP;
SSC 26; WLC**
See also BEST 90:3; CA 1-4R; CANR 1,
22, 36, 55, 89; CDALB 1968-1988; DA3;
DLB 2, 28, 173; DLBY 82; MTCW 1, 2
Rothenberg, Jerome 1931- .... **CLC 6, 57**
See also CA 45-48; CANR 1; DLB 5, 193
Roumain, Jacques (Jean Baptiste) 1907-1944
TCLC 19; BLC 3; DAM MULT
See also BW 1; CA 117; 125
Rourke, Constance (Mayfield) 1885-1941
TCLC 12
See also CA 107; YABC 1
Rousseau, Jean-Baptiste 1671-1741 ...... **LC 9**
Rousseau, Jean-Jacques 1712-1778 .... **LC 14,
36; DA; DAB; DAC; DAM MST; WLC**
See also DA3
Roussel, Raymond 1877-1933 .... **TCLC 20**
See also CA 117
Rovit, Earl (Herbert) 1927- .... **CLC 7**
See also CA 5-8R; CANR 12
Rowe, Elizabeth Singer 1674-1737 ..... **LC 44**
See also DLB 39, 95
Rowe, Nicholas 1674-1718 .... **LC 8**
See also DLB 84
Rowley, Ames Dorrance
See Lovecraft, H(oward) P(hillips)
Rowson, Susanna Haswell 1762(?)-1824
NCLC 5, 69
See also DLB 37, 200
Roy, Arundhati 1960(?)- .... **CLC 109**
See also CA 163; DLBY 97
Roy, Gabrielle 1909-1983 . **CLC 10, 14; DAB;
DAC; DAM MST**
See also CA 53-56; 110; CANR 5, 61; DLB
68; MTCW 1; SATA 104
Royko, Mike 1932-1997 .... **CLC 109**
See also CA 89-92; 157; CANR 26
Rozewicz, Tadeusz 1921- .. **CLC 9, 23; DAM
POET**
See also CA 108; CANR 36, 66; DA3;
MTCW 1, 2
Ruark, Gibbons 1941- .... **CLC 3**
See also CA 33-36R; CAAS 23; CANR 14,
31, 57; DLB 120
Rubens, Bernice (Ruth) 1923- .... **CLC 19, 31**
See also CA 25-28R; CANR 33, 65; DLB
14, 207; MTCW 1
Rubin, Harold
See Robbins, Harold
Rudkin, (James) David 1936- .... **CLC 14**
See also CA 89-92; DLB 13
Rudnik, Raphael 1933- .... **CLC 7**
See also CA 29-32R
Ruffian, M.
See Hasek, Jaroslav (Matej Frantisek)
Ruiz, Jose Martinez .... **CLC 11**
See also Martinez Ruiz, Jose

Rukeyser, Muriel 1913-1980 . **CLC 6, 10, 15, 27; DAM POET; PC 12**
See also CA 5-8R; 93-96; CANR 26, 60; DA3; DLB 48; MTCW 1, 2; SATA-Obit 22

Rule, Jane (Vance) 1931- .... **CLC 27**
See also CA 25-28R; CAAS 18; CANR 12, 87; DLB 60

Rulfo, Juan 1918-1986 ...... **CLC 8, 80; DAM MULT; HLC 2; SSC 25**
See also CA 85-88; 118; CANR 26; DLB 113; HW 1, 2; MTCW 1, 2

Rumi, Jalal al-Din 1297-1373 .... **CMLC 20**

Runeberg, Johan 1804-1877 .... **NCLC 41**

Runyon, (Alfred) Damon 1884(?)-1946
.... **TCLC 10**
See also CA 107; 165; DLB 11, 86, 171; MTCW 2

Rush, Norman 1933- .... **CLC 44**
See also CA 121; 126; INT 126

Rushdie, (Ahmed) Salman 1947- .... **CLC 23, 31, 55, 100; DAB; DAC; DAM MST, NOV, POP; WLCS**
See also BEST 89:3; CA 108; 111; CANR 33, 56; DA3; DLB 194; INT 111; MTCW 1, 2

Rushforth, Peter (Scott) 1945- .... **CLC 19**
See also CA 101

Ruskin, John 1819-1900 .... **TCLC 63**
See also CA 114; 129; CDBLB 1832-1890; DLB 55, 163, 190; SATA 24

Russ, Joanna 1937- .... **CLC 15**
See also CANR 11, 31, 65; DLB 8; MTCW 1

Russell, George William 1867-1935
See Baker, Jean H.
See also CA 104; 153; CDBLB 1890-1914; DAM POET

Russell, (Henry) Ken(neth Alfred) 1927-
.... **CLC 16**
See also CA 105

Russell, William Martin 1947- .... **CLC 60**
See also CA 164

Rutherford, Mark .... **TCLC 25**
See also White, William Hale DLB 18

Ruyslinck, Ward 1929- .... **CLC 14**
See also Belser, Reimond Karel Maria de

Ryan, Cornelius (John) 1920-1974 ..... **CLC 7**
See also CA 69-72; 53-56; CANR 38

Ryan, Michael 1946- .... **CLC 65**
See also CA 49-52; DLBY 82

Ryan, Tim
See Dent, Lester

Rybakov, Anatoli (Naumovich) 1911-1998
CLC 23, 53
See also CA 126; 135; 172; SATA 79; SATA-Obit 108

Ryder, Jonathan
See Ludlum, Robert

Ryga, George 1932-1987 .... **CLC 14; DAC; DAM MST**
See also CA 101; 124; CANR 43; DLB 60

S. H.
See Hartmann, Sadakichi

S. S.
See Sassoon, Siegfried (Lorraine)

Saba, Umberto 1883-1957 .... **TCLC 33**
See also CA 144; CANR 79; DLB 114

Sabatini, Rafael 1875-1950 .... **TCLC 47**
See also CA 162

Sabato, Ernesto (R.) 1911- .... **CLC 10, 23; DAM MULT; HLC 2**
See also CA 97-100; CANR 32, 65; DLB 145; HW 1, 2; MTCW 1, 2

Sa-Carniero, Mario de 1890-1916 . **TCLC 83**

Sacastru, Martin
See Bioy Casares, Adolfo

Sacastru, Martin
See Bioy Casares, Adolfo

Sacher-Masoch, Leopold von 1836(?)-1895
NCLC 31

Sachs, Marilyn (Stickle) 1927- .... **CLC 35**
See also AAYA 2; CA 17-20R; CANR 13, 47; CLR 2; JRDA; MAICYA; SAAS 2; SATA 3, 68; SATA-Essay 110

Sachs, Nelly 1891-1970 .... **CLC 14, 98**
See also CA 17-18; 25-28R; CANR 87; CAP 2; MTCW 2

Sackler, Howard (Oliver) 1929-1982 . **CLC 14**
See also CA 61-64; 108; CANR 30; DLB 7

Sacks, Oliver (Wolf) 1933- .... **CLC 67**
See also CA 53-56; CANR 28, 50, 76; DA3; INT CANR-28; MTCW 1, 2

Sadakichi
See Hartmann, Sadakichi

Sade, Donatien Alphonse Francois, Comte de 1740-1814 .... **NCLC 47**

Sadoff, Ira 1945- .... **CLC 9**
See also CA 53-56; CANR 5, 21; DLB 120

Saetone
See Camus, Albert

Safire, William 1929- .... **CLC 10**
See also CA 17-20R; CANR 31, 54

Sagan, Carl (Edward) 1934-1996 .... **CLC 30, 112**
See also AAYA 2; CA 25-28R; 155; CANR 11, 36, 74; DA3; MTCW 1, 2; SATA 58; SATA-Obit 94

Sagan, Francoise .... **CLC 3, 6, 9, 17, 36**
See also Quoirez, Francoise DLB 83; MTCW 2

Sahgal, Nayantara (Pandit) 1927- .... **CLC 41**
See also CA 9-12R; CANR 11, 88

Saint, H(arry) F. 1941- .... **CLC 50**
See also CA 127

St. Aubin de Teran, Lisa 1953-
See Teran, Lisa St. Aubin de
See also CA 118; 126; INT 126

Saint Birgitta of Sweden c. 1303-1373
.... **CMLC 24**

Sainte-Beuve, Charles Augustin 1804-1869
NCLC 5

Saint-Exupery, Antoine (Jean Baptiste Marie Roger) de 1900-1944 .... **TCLC 2, 56; DAM NOV; WLC**
See also CA 108; 132; CLR 10; DA3; DLB 72; MAICYA; MTCW 1, 2; SATA 20

St. John, David
See Hunt, E(verette) Howard, (Jr.)

Saint-John Perse
See Leger, (Marie-Rene Auguste) Alexis Saint-Leger

Saintsbury, George (Edward Bateman) 1845-1933 .... **TCLC 31**
See also CA 160; DLB 57, 149

Sait Faik .... **TCLC 23**
See also Abasiyanik, Sait Faik

Saki .... **TCLC 3; SSC 12**
See also Munro, H(ector) H(ugh) MTCW 2

Sala, George Augustus .... **NCLC 46**

Saladin 1138-1193 .... **CMLC 38**

Salama, Hannu 1936- .... **CLC 18**

Salamanca, J(ack) R(ichard) 1922- .. **CLC 4, 15**
See also CA 25-28R

Salas, Floyd Francis 1931-
See also CA 119; CAAS 27; CANR 44, 75; DAM MULT; DLB 82; HLC 2; HW 1, 2; MTCW 2

Sale, J. Kirkpatrick
See Sale, Kirkpatrick

Sale, Kirkpatrick 1937- .... **CLC 68**
See also CA 13-16R; CANR 10

Salinas, Luis Omar 1937- ..... **CLC 90; DAM MULT; HLC 2**

See also CA 131; CANR 81; DLB 82; HW 1, 2

Salinas (y Serrano), Pedro 1891(?)-1951
TCLC 17
See also CA 117; DLB 134

Salinger, J(erome) D(avid) 1919- .. **CLC 1, 3, 8, 12, 55, 56; DA; DAB; DAC; DAM MST, NOV, POP; SSC 2, 28; WLC**
See also AAYA 2; CA 5-8R; CANR 39; CDALB 1941-1968; CLR 18; DA3; DLB 2, 102, 173; MAICYA; MTCW 1, 2; SATA 67

Salisbury, John
See Caute, (John) David

Salter, James 1925- .... **CLC 7, 52, 59**
See also CA 73-76; DLB 130

Saltus, Edgar (Everton) 1855-1921 . **TCLC 8**
See also CA 105; DLB 202

Saltykov, Mikhail Evgrafovich 1826-1889
NCLC 16

Samarakis, Antonis 1919- .... **CLC 5**
See also CA 25-28R; CAAS 16; CANR 36

Sanchez, Florencio 1875-1910 .... **TCLC 37**
See also CA 153; HW 1

Sanchez, Luis Rafael 1936- .... **CLC 23**
See also CA 128; DLB 145; HW 1

Sanchez, Sonia 1934- .... **CLC 5, 116; BLC 3; DAM MULT; PC 9**
See also BW 2, 3; CA 33-36R; CANR 24, 49, 74; CLR 18; DA3; DLB 41; DLBD 8; MAICYA; MTCW 1, 2; SATA 22

Sand, George 1804-1876 ..... **NCLC 2, 42, 57; DA; DAB; DAC; DAM MST, NOV; WLC**
See also DA3; DLB 119, 192

Sandburg, Carl (August) 1878-1967 . **CLC 1, 4, 10, 15, 35; DA; DAB; DAC; DAM MST, POET; PC 2; WLC**
See also AAYA 24; CA 5-8R; 25-28R; CANR 35; CDALB 1865-1917; DA3; DLB 17, 54; MAICYA; MTCW 1, 2; SATA 8

Sandburg, Charles
See Sandburg, Carl (August)

Sandburg, Charles A.
See Sandburg, Carl (August)

Sanders, (James) Ed(ward) 1939- ... **CLC 53; DAM POET**
See also CA 13-16R; CAAS 21; CANR 13, 44, 78; DLB 16

Sanders, Lawrence 1920-1998 .... **CLC 41; DAM POP**
See also BEST 89:4; CA 81-84; 165; CANR 33, 62; DA3; MTCW 1

Sanders, Noah
See Blount, Roy (Alton), Jr.

Sanders, Winston P.
See Anderson, Poul (William)

Sandoz, Mari(e Susette) 1896-1966 .. **CLC 28**
See also CA 1-4R; 25-28R; CANR 17, 64; DLB 9, 212; MTCW 1, 2; SATA 5

Saner, Reg(inald Anthony) 1931- .... **CLC 9**
See also CA 65-68

Sankara 788-820 .... **CMLC 32**

Sannazaro, Jacopo 1456(?)-1530 .... **LC 8**

Sansom, William 1912-1976 . **CLC 2, 6; DAM NOV; SSC 21**
See also CA 5-8R; 65-68; CANR 42; DLB 139; MTCW 1

Santayana, George 1863-1952 .... **TCLC 40**
See also CA 115; DLB 54, 71; DLBD 13

Santiago, Danny .... **CLC 33**
See also James, Daniel (Lewis) DLB 122

Santmyer, Helen Hoover 1895-1986 . **CLC 33**
See also CA 1-4R; 118; CANR 15, 33; DLBY 84; MTCW 1

Santoka, Taneda 1882-1940 .... **TCLC 72**

Santos, Bienvenido N(uqui) 1911-1996
.... **CLC 22; DAM MULT**

Scumbag, Little Bobby
  See Crumb, R(obert)
Seabrook, John
  See Hubbard, L(afayette) Ron(ald)
Sealy, I. Allan 1951- .... **CLC 55**
Search, Alexander
  See Pessoa, Fernando (Antonio Nogueira)
Sebastian, Lee
  See Silverberg, Robert
Sebastian Owl
  See Thompson, Hunter S(tockton)
Sebestyen, Ouida 1924- .... **CLC 30**
  See also AAYA 8; CA 107; CANR 40; CLR 17; JRDA; MAICYA; SAAS 10; SATA 39
Secundus, H. Scriblerus
  See Fielding, Henry
Sedges, John
  See Buck, Pearl S(ydenstricker)
Sedgwick, Catharine Maria 1789-1867
  .... **NCLC 19**
  See also DLB 1, 74
Seelye, John (Douglas) 1931- .... **CLC 7**
  See also CA 97-100; CANR 70; INT 97-100
Seferiades, Giorgos Stylianou 1900-1971
  See Seferis, George
  See also CA 5-8R; 33-36R; CANR 5, 36; MTCW 1
Seferis, George .... **CLC 5, 11**
  See also Seferiades, Giorgos Stylianou
Segal, Erich (Wolf) 1937- . **CLC 3, 10; DAM POP**
  See also BEST 89:1; CA 25-28R; CANR 20, 36, 65; DLBY 86; INT CANR-20; MTCW 1
Seger, Bob 1945- .... **CLC 35**
Seghers, Anna .... **CLC 7**
  See also Radvanyi, Netty DLB 69
Seidel, Frederick (Lewis) 1936- .... **CLC 18**
  See also CA 13-16R; CANR 8; DLBY 84
Seifert, Jaroslav 1901-1986 .. **CLC 34, 44, 93**
  See also CA 127; MTCW 1, 2
Sei Shonagon c. 966-1017(?) .... **CMLC 6**
Sejour, Victor 1817-1874 .... **DC 10**
  See also DLB 50
Sejour Marcou et Ferrand, Juan Victor
  See S
Selby, Hubert, Jr. 1928- . **CLC 1, 2, 4, 8; SSC 20**
  See also CA 13-16R; CANR 33, 85; DLB 2
Selzer, Richard 1928- .... **CLC 74**
  See also CA 65-68; CANR 14
Sembene, Ousmane
  See Ousmane, Sembene
Senancour, Etienne Pivert de 1770-1846
  NCLC 16
  See also DLB 119
Sender, Ramon (Jose) 1902-1982 ...... **CLC 8; DAM MULT; HLC 2**
  See also CA 5-8R; 105; CANR 8; HW 1; MTCW 1
Seneca, Lucius Annaeus c. 1-c. 65 . **CMLC 6; DAM DRAM; DC 5**
  See also DLB 211
Senghor, Leopold Sedar 1906- . **CLC 54, 130; BLC 3; DAM MULT, POET; PC 25**
  See also BW 2; CA 116; 125; CANR 47, 74; MTCW 1, 2
Senna, Danzy 1970- .... **CLC 119**
  See also CA 169
Serling, (Edward) Rod(man) 1924-1975
  .... **CLC 30**
  See also AAYA 14; AITN 1; CA 162; 57-60; DLB 26
Serna, Ramon Gomez de la
  See Gomez de la Serna, Ramon

Serpieres
  See Guillevic, (Eugene)
Service, Robert
  See Service, Robert W(illiam)
  See also DAB; DLB 92
Service, Robert W(illiam) 1874(?)-1958
  TCLC 15; DA; DAC; DAM MST, POET; WLC
  See also Service, Robert CA 115; 140; CANR 84; SATA 20
Seth, Vikram 1952- .... **CLC 43, 90; DAM MULT**
  See also CA 121; 127; CANR 50, 74; DA3; DLB 120; INT 127; MTCW 2
Seton, Cynthia Propper 1926-1982 .. **CLC 27**
  See also CA 5-8R; 108; CANR 7
Seton, Ernest (Evan) Thompson 1860-1946
  TCLC 31
  See also CA 109; CLR 59; DLB 92; DLBD 13; JRDA; SATA 18
Seton-Thompson, Ernest
  See Seton, Ernest (Evan) Thompson
Settle, Mary Lee 1918- .... **CLC 19, 61**
  See also CA 89-92; CAAS 1; CANR 44, 87; DLB 6; INT 89-92
Seuphor, Michel
  See Arp, Jean
Sevigne, Marie (de Rabutin-Chantal)
  Marquise de 1626-1696 .... **LC 11**
Sewall, Samuel 1652-1730 .... **LC 38**
  See also DLB 24
Sexton, Anne (Harvey) 1928-1974 . **CLC 2, 4, 6, 8, 10, 15, 53; DA; DAB; DAC; DAM MST, POET; PC 2; WLC**
  See also CA 1-4R; 53-56; CABS 2; CANR 3, 36; CDALB 1941-1968; DA3; DLB 5, 169; MTCW 1, 2; SATA 10
Shaara, Jeff 1952- .... **CLC 119**
  See also CA 163
Shaara, Michael (Joseph, Jr.) 1929-1988
  .... **CLC 15; DAM POP**
  See also AITN 1; CA 102; 125; CANR 52, 85; DLBY 83
Shackleton, C. C.
  See Aldiss, Brian W(ilson)
Shacochis, Bob .... **CLC 39**
  See also Shacochis, Robert G.
Shacochis, Robert G. 1951-
  See Shacochis, Bob
  See also CA 119; 124; INT 124
Shaffer, Anthony (Joshua) 1926- ..... **CLC 19; DAM DRAM**
  See also CA 110; 116; DLB 13
Shaffer, Peter (Levin) 1926- .. **CLC 5, 14, 18, 37, 60; DAB; DAM DRAM, MST; DC 7**
  See also CA 25-28R; CANR 25, 47, 74; CDBLB 1960 to Present; DA3; DLB 13; MTCW 1, 2
Shakey, Bernard
  See Young, Neil
Shalamov, Varlam (Tikhonovich)
  1907(?)-1982 .... **CLC 18**
  See also CA 129; 105
Shamlu, Ahmad 1925- .... **CLC 10**
Shammas, Anton 1951- .... **CLC 55**
Shange, Ntozake 1948- .... **CLC 8, 25, 38, 74, 126; BLC 3; DAM DRAM, MULT; DC 3**
  See also AAYA 9; BW 2; CA 85-88; CABS 3; CANR 27, 48, 74; DA3; DLB 38; MTCW 1, 2
Shanley, John Patrick 1950- .... **CLC 75**
  See also CA 128; 133; CANR 83
Shapcott, Thomas W(illiam) 1935- .. **CLC 38**
  See also CA 69-72; CANR 49, 83
Shapiro, Jane .... **CLC 76**
Shapiro, Karl (Jay) 1913- . **CLC 4, 8, 15, 53; PC 25**

See also CA 1-4R; CAAS 6; CANR 1, 36, 66; DLB 48; MTCW 1, 2
Sharp, William 1855-1905 .... **TCLC 39**
  See also CA 160; DLB 156
Sharpe, Thomas Ridley 1928-
  See Sharpe, Tom
  See also CA 114; 122; CANR 85; INT 122
Sharpe, Tom .... **CLC 36**
  See also Sharpe, Thomas Ridley DLB 14
Shaw, Bernard .... **TCLC 45**
  See also Shaw, George Bernard BW 1; MTCW 2
Shaw, G. Bernard
  See Shaw, George Bernard
Shaw, George Bernard 1856-1950 .. **TCLC 3, 9, 21; DA; DAB; DAC; DAM DRAM, MST; WLC**
  See also Shaw, Bernard CA 104; 128; CD-BLB 1914-1945; DA3; DLB 10, 57, 190; MTCW 1, 2
Shaw, Henry Wheeler 1818-1885 .. **NCLC 15**
  See also DLB 11
Shaw, Irwin 1913-1984 . **CLC 7, 23, 34; DAM DRAM, POP**
  See also AITN 1; CA 13-16R; 112; CANR 21; CDALB 1941-1968; DLB 6, 102; DLBY 84; MTCW 1, 21
Shaw, Robert 1927-1978 .... **CLC 5**
  See also AITN 1; CA 1-4R; 81-84; CANR 4; DLB 13, 14
Shaw, T. E.
  See Lawrence, T(homas) E(dward)
Shawn, Wallace 1943- .... **CLC 41**
  See also CA 112
Shea, Lisa 1953- .... **CLC 86**
  See also CA 147
Sheed, Wilfrid (John Joseph) 1930- . **CLC 2, 4, 10, 53**
  See also CA 65-68; CANR 30, 66; DLB 6; MTCW 1, 2
Sheldon, Alice Hastings Bradley
  1915(?)-1987
  See Tiptree, James, Jr.
  See also CA 108; 122; CANR 34; INT 108; MTCW 1
Sheldon, John
  See Bloch, Robert (Albert)
Shelley, Mary Wollstonecraft (Godwin)
  1797-1851 ..... **NCLC 14, 59; DA; DAB; DAC; DAM MST, NOV; WLC**
  See also AAYA 20; CDBLB 1789-1832; DA3; DLB 110, 116, 159, 178; SATA 29
Shelley, Percy Bysshe 1792-1822 .. **NCLC 18; DA; DAB; DAC; DAM MST, POET; PC 14; WLC**
  See also CDBLB 1789-1832; DA3; DLB 96, 110, 158
Shepard, Jim 1956- .... **CLC 36**
  See also CA 137; CANR 59; SATA 90
Shepard, Lucius 1947- .... **CLC 34**
  See also CA 128; 141; CANR 81
Shepard, Sam 1943- .... **CLC 4, 6, 17, 34, 41, 44; DAM DRAM; DC 5**
  See also AAYA 1; CA 69-72; CABS 3; CANR 22; DA3; DLB 7, 212; MTCW 1, 2
Shepherd, Michael
  See Ludlum, Robert
Sherburne, Zoa (Lillian Morin) 1912-1995
  CLC 30
  See also AAYA 13; CA 1-4R; 176; CANR 3, 37; MAICYA; SAAS 18; SATA 3
Sheridan, Frances 1724-1766 .... **LC 7**
  See also DLB 39, 84
Sheridan, Richard Brinsley 1751-1816
  .... **NCLC 5; DA; DAB; DAC; DAM DRAM, MST; DC 1; WLC**
  See also CDBLB 1660-1789; DLB 89
Sherman, Jonathan Marc .... **CLC 55**

Sjowall, Maj
   See Sjoewall, Maj
Skelton, John 1463-1529 .... **PC 25**
Skelton, Robin 1925-1997 .... **CLC 13**
   See also AITN 2; CA 5-8R; 160; CAAS 5;
   CANR 28, 89; DLB 27, 53
Skolimowski, Jerzy 1938- .... **CLC 20**
   See also CA 128
Skram, Amalie (Bertha) 1847-1905
   .... **TCLC 25**
   See also CA 165
Skvorecky, Josef (Vaclav) 1924- ...... **CLC 15,**
   39, 69; DAC; DAM NOV
   See also CA 61-64; CAAS 1; CANR 10,
   34, 63; DA3; MTCW 1, 2
Slade, Bernard .... **CLC 11, 46**
   See also Newbound, Bernard Slade CAAS
   9; DLB 53
Slaughter, Carolyn 1946- .... **CLC 56**
   See also CA 85-88; CANR 85
Slaughter, Frank G(ill) 1908- .... **CLC 29**
   See also AITN 2; CA 5-8R; CANR 5, 85;
   INT CANR-5
Slavitt, David R(ytman) 1935- ..... **CLC 5, 14**
   See also CA 21-24R; CAAS 3; CANR 41,
   83; DLB 5, 6
Slesinger, Tess 1905-1945 .... **TCLC 10**
   See also CA 107; DLB 102
Slessor, Kenneth 1901-1971 .... **CLC 14**
   See also CA 102; 89-92
Slowacki, Juliusz 1809-1849 .... **NCLC 15**
Smart, Christopher 1722-1771 .. **LC 3; DAM**
   POET; PC 13
   See also DLB 109
Smart, Elizabeth 1913-1986 .... **CLC 54**
   See also CA 81-84; 118; DLB 88
Smiley, Jane (Graves) 1949- ...... **CLC 53, 76;**
   DAM POP
   See also CA 104; CANR 30, 50, 74; DA3;
   INT CANR-30
Smith, A(rthur) J(ames) M(arshall)
   1902-1980 .... **CLC 15; DAC**
   See also CA 1-4R; 102; CANR 4; DLB 88
Smith, Adam 1723-1790 .... **LC 36**
   See also DLB 104
Smith, Alexander 1829-1867 .... **NCLC 59**
   See also DLB 32, 55
Smith, Anna Deavere 1950- .... **CLC 86**
   See also CA 133
Smith, Betty (Wehner) 1896-1972 .... **CLC 19**
   See also CA 5-8R; 33-36R; DLBY 82;
   SATA 6
Smith, Charlotte (Turner) 1749-1806
   .... **NCLC 23**
   See also DLB 39, 109
Smith, Clark Ashton 1893-1961 .... **CLC 43**
   See also CA 143; CANR 81; MTCW 2
Smith, Dave .... **CLC 22, 42**
   See also Smith, David (Jeddie) CAAS 7;
   DLB 5
Smith, David (Jeddie) 1942-
   See Smith, Dave
   See also CA 49-52; CANR 1, 59; DAM
   POET
Smith, Florence Margaret 1902-1971
   See Smith, Stevie
   See also CA 17-18; 29-32R; CANR 35;
   CAP 2; DAM POET; MTCW 1, 2
Smith, Iain Crichton 1928-1998 .... **CLC 64**
   See also CA 21-24R; 171; DLB 40, 139
Smith, John 1580(?)-1631 .... **LC 9**
   See also DLB 24, 30
Smith, Johnston
   See Crane, Stephen (Townley)
Smith, Joseph, Jr. 1805-1844 .... **NCLC 53**
Smith, Lee 1944- .... **CLC 25, 73**
   See also CA 114; 119; CANR 46; DLB 143;
   DLBY 83; INT 119

Smith, Martin
   See Smith, Martin Cruz
Smith, Martin Cruz 1942- .... **CLC 25; DAM**
   MULT, POP
   See also BEST 89:4; CA 85-88; CANR 6,
   23, 43, 65; INT CANR-23; MTCW 2;
   NNAL
Smith, Mary-Ann Tirone 1944- .... **CLC 39**
   See also CA 118; 136
Smith, Patti 1946- .... **CLC 12**
   See also CA 93-96; CANR 63
Smith, Pauline (Urmson) 1882-1959
   .... **TCLC 25**
Smith, Rosamond
   See Oates, Joyce Carol
Smith, Sheila Kaye
   See Kaye-Smith, Sheila
Smith, Stevie .... **CLC 3, 8, 25, 44; PC 12**
   See also Smith, Florence Margaret DLB 20;
   MTCW 2
Smith, Wilbur (Addison) 1933- .... **CLC 33**
   See also CA 13-16R; CANR 7, 46, 66;
   MTCW 1, 2
Smith, William Jay 1918- .... **CLC 6**
   See also CA 5-8R; CANR 44; DLB 5; MAI-
   CYA; SAAS 22; SATA 2, 68
Smith, Woodrow Wilson
   See Kuttner, Henry
Smolenskin, Peretz 1842-1885 .... **NCLC 30**
Smollett, Tobias (George) 1721-1771 ... **LC 2,**
   46
   See also CDBLB 1660-1789; DLB 39, 104
Snodgrass, W(illiam) D(e Witt) 1926-
   .... **CLC 2, 6, 10, 18, 68; DAM POET**
   See also CA 1-4R; CANR 6, 36, 65, 85;
   DLB 5; MTCW 1, 2
Snow, C(harles) P(ercy) 1905-1980 ... **CLC 1,**
   4, 6, 9, 13, 19; DAM NOV
   See also CA 5-8R; 101; CANR 28; CDBLB
   1945-1960; DLB 15, 77; DLBD 17;
   MTCW 1, 2
Snow, Frances Compton
   See Adams, Henry (Brooks)
Snyder, Gary (Sherman) 1930- . **CLC 1, 2, 5,**
   9, 32, 120; DAM POET; PC 21
   See also CA 17-20R; CANR 30, 60; DA3;
   DLB 5, 16, 165, 212; MTCW 2
Snyder, Zilpha Keatley 1927- .... **CLC 17**
   See also AAYA 15; CA 9-12R; CANR 38;
   CLR 31; JRDA; MAICYA; SAAS 2;
   SATA 1, 28, 75, 110; SATA-Essay 112
Soares, Bernardo
   See Pessoa, Fernando (Antonio Nogueira)
Sobh, A.
   See Shamlu, Ahmad
Sobol, Joshua .... **CLC 60**
Socrates 469B.C.-399B.C. .... **CMLC 27**
Soderberg, Hjalmar 1869-1941 ...... **TCLC 39**
Sodergran, Edith (Irene)
   See Soedergran, Edith (Irene)
Soedergran, Edith (Irene) 1892-1923
   .... **TCLC 31**
Softly, Edgar
   See Lovecraft, H(oward) P(hillips)
Softly, Edward
   See Lovecraft, H(oward) P(hillips)
Sokolov, Raymond 1941- .... **CLC 7**
   See also CA 85-88
Solo, Jay
   See Ellison, Harlan (Jay)
Sologub, Fyodor .... **TCLC 9**
   See also Teternikov, Fyodor Kuzmich
Solomons, Ikey Esquir
   See Thackeray, William Makepeace
Solomos, Dionysios 1798-1857 .... **NCLC 15**
Solwoska, Mara
   See French, Marilyn

Solzhenitsyn, Aleksandr I(sayevich) 1918-
   CLC 1, 2, 4, 7, 9, 10, 18, 26, 34, 78; DA;
   DAB; DAC; DAM MST, NOV; SSC 32;
   WLC
   See also AITN 1; CA 69-72; CANR 40, 65;
   DA3; MTCW 1, 2
Somers, Jane
   See Lessing, Doris (May)
Somerville, Edith 1858-1949 .... **TCLC 51**
   See also DLB 135
Somerville & Ross
   See Martin, Violet Florence; Somerville,
   Edith
Sommer, Scott 1951- .... **CLC 25**
   See also CA 106
Sondheim, Stephen (Joshua) 1930- . **CLC 30,**
   39; DAM DRAM
   See also AAYA 11; CA 103; CANR 47, 68
Song, Cathy 1955- .... **PC 21**
   See also CA 154; DLB 169
Sontag, Susan 1933- .... **CLC 1, 2, 10, 13, 31,**
   105; DAM POP
   See also CA 17-20R; CANR 25, 51, 74;
   DA3; DLB 2, 67; MTCW 1, 2
Sophocles 496(?)B.C.-406(?)B.C. .... **CMLC 2;**
   DA; DAB; DAC; DAM DRAM, MST;
   DC 1; WLCS
   See also DA3; DLB 176
Sordello 1189-1269 .... **CMLC 15**
Sorel, Georges 1847-1922 .... **TCLC 91**
   See also CA 118
Sorel, Julia
   See Drexler, Rosalyn
Sorrentino, Gilbert 1929- .. **CLC 3, 7, 14, 22,**
   40
   See also CA 77-80; CANR 14, 33; DLB 5,
   173; DLBY 80; INT CANR-14
Soto, Gary 1952- . **CLC 32, 80; DAM MULT;**
   HLC 2; PC 28
   See also AAYA 10; CA 119; 125; CANR
   50, 74; CLR 38; DLB 82; HW 1, 2; INT
   125; JRDA; MTCW 2; SATA 80
Soupault, Philippe 1897-1990 .... **CLC 68**
   See also CA 116; 147; 131
Souster, (Holmes) Raymond 1921- .... **CLC 5,**
   14; DAC; DAM POET
   See also CA 13-16R; CAAS 14; CANR 13,
   29, 53; DA3; DLB 88; SATA 63
Southern, Terry 1924(?)-1995 .... **CLC 7**
   See also CA 1-4R; 150; CANR 1, 55; DLB
   2
Southey, Robert 1774-1843 .... **NCLC 8**
   See also DLB 93, 107, 142; SATA 54
Southworth, Emma Dorothy Eliza Nevitte
   1819-1899 .... **NCLC 26**
Souza, Ernest
   See Scott, Evelyn
Soyinka, Wole 1934- .... **CLC 3, 5, 14, 36, 44;**
   BLC 3; DA; DAB; DAC; DAM DRAM,
   MST, MULT; DC 2; WLC
   See also BW 2, 3; CA 13-16R; CANR 27,
   39, 82; DA3; DLB 125; MTCW 1, 2
Spackman, W(illiam) M(ode) 1905-1990
   .... **CLC 46**
   See also CA 81-84; 132
Spacks, Barry (Bernard) 1931- .... **CLC 14**
   See also CA 154; CANR 33; DLB 105
Spanidou, Irini 1946- .... **CLC 44**
   See also CA 185
Spark, Muriel (Sarah) 1918- . **CLC 2, 3, 5, 8,**
   13, 18, 40, 94; DAB; DAC; DAM MST,
   NOV; SSC 10
   See also CA 5-8R; CANR 12, 36, 76, 89;
   CDBLB 1945-1960; DA3; DLB 15, 139;
   INT CANR-12; MTCW 1, 2
Spaulding, Douglas
   See Bradbury, Ray (Douglas)
Spaulding, Leonard
   See Bradbury, Ray (Douglas)

Stockton, Frank R. .... **TCLC 47**
   See also Stockton, Francis Richard DLB
   42, 74; DLBD 13; SATA-Brief 32
Stoddard, Charles
   See Kuttner, Henry
Stoker, Abraham 1847-1912
   See Stoker, Bram
   See also CA 105; 150; DA; DAC; DAM
   MST, NOV; DA3; SATA 29
Stoker, Bram 1847-1912 .... **TCLC 8; DAB;
   WLC**
   See also Stoker, Abraham AAYA 23; CD-
   BLB 1890-1914; DLB 36, 70, 178
Stolz, Mary (Slattery) 1920- .... **CLC 12**
   See also AAYA 8; AITN 1; CA 5-8R;
   CANR 13, 41; JRDA; MAICYA; SAAS
   3; SATA 10, 71
Stone, Irving 1903-1989 . **CLC 7; DAM POP**
   See also AITN 1; CA 1-4R; 129; CAAS 3;
   CANR 1, 23; DA3; INT CANR-23;
   MTCW 1, 2; SATA 3; SATA-Obit 64
Stone, Oliver (William) 1946- .... **CLC 73**
   See also AAYA 15; CA 110; CANR 55
Stone, Robert (Anthony) 1937- ... **CLC 5, 23,
   42**
   See also CA 85-88; CANR 23, 66; DLB
   152; INT CANR-23; MTCW 1
Stone, Zachary
   See Follett, Ken(neth Martin)
Stoppard, Tom 1937- ... **CLC 1, 3, 4, 5, 8, 15,
   29, 34, 63, 91; DA; DAB; DAC; DAM
   DRAM, MST; DC 6; WLC**
   See also CA 81-84; CANR 39, 67; CDBLB
   1960 to Present; DA3; DLB 13; DLBY
   85; MTCW 1, 2
Storey, David (Malcolm) 1933- . **CLC 2, 4, 5,
   8; DAM DRAM**
   See also CA 81-84; CANR 36; DLB 13, 14,
   207; MTCW 1
Storm, Hyemeyohsts 1935- ..... **CLC 3; DAM
   MULT**
   See also CA 81-84; CANR 45; NNAL
Storm, Theodor 1817-1888 .... **SSC 27**
Storm, (Hans) Theodor (Woldsen) 1817-1888
   NCLC 1; SSC 27
   See also DLB 129
Storni, Alfonsina 1892-1938 . **TCLC 5; DAM
   MULT; HLC 2**
   See also CA 104; 131; HW 1
Stoughton, William 1631-1701 .... **LC 38**
   See also DLB 24
Stout, Rex (Todhunter) 1886-1975 ..... **CLC 3**
   See also AITN 2; CA 61-64; CANR 71
Stow, (Julian) Randolph 1935- ... **CLC 23, 48**
   See also CA 13-16R; CANR 33; MTCW 1
Stowe, Harriet (Elizabeth) Beecher
   1811-1896 .... **NCLC 3, 50; DA; DAB;
   DAC; DAM MST, NOV; WLC**
   See also CDALB 1865-1917; DA3; DLB 1,
   12, 42, 74, 189; JRDA; MAICYA; YABC
   1
Strabo c. 64B.C.-c. 25 .... **CMLC 37**
   See also DLB 176
Strachey, (Giles) Lytton 1880-1932 . **TCLC 12**
   See also CA 110; 178; DLB 149; DLBD
   10; MTCW 2
Strand, Mark 1934- .... **CLC 6, 18, 41, 71;
   DAM POET**
   See also CA 21-24R; CANR 40, 65; DLB
   5; SATA 41
Straub, Peter (Francis) 1943- . **CLC 28, 107;
   DAM POP**
   See also BEST 89:1; CA 85-88; CANR 28,
   65; DLBY 84; MTCW 1, 2
Strauss, Botho 1944- .... **CLC 22**
   See also CA 157; DLB 124
Streatfeild, (Mary) Noel 1895(?)-1986
   .... **CLC 21**

See also CA 81-84; 120; CANR 31; CLR
   17; DLB 160; MAICYA; SATA 20; SATA-
   Obit 48
Stribling, T(homas) S(igismund) 1881-1965
   CLC 23
   See also CA 107; DLB 9
Strindberg, (Johan) August 1849-1912
   ... **TCLC 1, 8, 21, 47; DA; DAB; DAC;
   DAM DRAM, MST; WLC**
   See also CA 104; 135; DA3; MTCW 2
Stringer, Arthur 1874-1950 .... **TCLC 37**
   See also CA 161; DLB 92
Stringer, David
   See Roberts, Keith (John Kingston)
Stroheim, Erich von 1885-1957 ..... **TCLC 71**
Strugatskii, Arkadii (Natanovich) 1925-1991
   CLC 27
   See also CA 106; 135
Strugatskii, Boris (Natanovich) 1933-
   .... **CLC 27**
   See also CA 106
Strummer, Joe 1953(?)- .... **CLC 30**
Strunk, William, Jr. 1869-1946 ...... **TCLC 92**
   See also CA 118; 164
Stryk, Lucien 1924- .... **PC 27**
   See also CA 13-16R; CANR 10, 28, 55
Stuart, Don A.
   See Campbell, John W(ood, Jr.)
Stuart, Ian
   See MacLean, Alistair (Stuart)
Stuart, Jesse (Hilton) 1906-1984 ... **CLC 1, 8,
   11, 14, 34; SSC 31**
   See also CA 5-8R; 112; CANR 31; DLB 9,
   48, 102; DLBY 84; SATA 2; SATA-Obit
   36
Sturgeon, Theodore (Hamilton) 1918-1985
   CLC 22, 39
   See also Queen, Ellery CA 81-84; 116;
   CANR 32; DLB 8; DLBY 85; MTCW 1,
   2
Sturges, Preston 1898-1959 .... **TCLC 48**
   See also CA 114; 149; DLB 26
Styron, William 1925- .... **CLC 1, 3, 5, 11, 15,
   60; DAM NOV, POP; SSC 25**
   See also BEST 90:4; CA 5-8R; CANR 6,
   33, 74; CDALB 1968-1988; DA3; DLB
   2, 143; DLBY 80; INT CANR-6; MTCW
   1, 2
Su, Chien 1884-1918
   See Su Man-shu
   See also CA 123
Suarez Lynch, B.
   See Bioy Casares, Adolfo; Borges, Jorge
   Luis
Suassuna, Ariano Vilar 1927-
   See also CA 178; HLCS 1; HW 2
Suckow, Ruth 1892-1960 .... **SSC 18**
   See also CA 113; DLB 9, 102
Sudermann, Hermann 1857-1928 .. **TCLC 15**
   See also CA 107; DLB 118
Sue, Eugene 1804-1857 .... **NCLC 1**
   See also DLB 119
Sueskind, Patrick 1949- .... **CLC 44**
   See also Suskind, Patrick
Sukenick, Ronald 1932- .... **CLC 3, 4, 6, 48**
   See also CA 25-28R; CAAS 8; CANR 32,
   89; DLB 173; DLBY 81
Suknaski, Andrew 1942- .... **CLC 19**
   See also CA 101; DLB 53
Sullivan, Vernon
   See Vian, Boris
Sully Prudhomme 1839-1907 .... **TCLC 31**
Su Man-shu .... **TCLC 24**
   See also Su, Chien
Summerforest, Ivy B.
   See Kirkup, James
Summers, Andrew James 1942- .... **CLC 26**

Summers, Andy
   See Summers, Andrew James
Summers, Hollis (Spurgeon, Jr.) 1916-
   .... **CLC 10**
   See also CA 5-8R; CANR 3; DLB 6
**Summers, (Alphonsus Joseph-Mary
   Augustus) Montague** 1880-1948
   .... **TCLC 16**
   See also CA 118; 163
Sumner, Gordon Matthew .... **CLC 26**
   See also Sting
Surtees, Robert Smith 1803-1864 .. **NCLC 14**
   See also DLB 21
Susann, Jacqueline 1921-1974 .... **CLC 3**
   See also AITN 1; CA 65-68; 53-56; MTCW
   1, 2
Su Shih 1036-1101 .... **CMLC 15**
Suskind, Patrick
   See Sueskind, Patrick
   See also CA 145
Sutcliff, Rosemary 1920-1992 .... **CLC 26;
   DAB; DAC; DAM MST, POP**
   See also AAYA 10; CA 5-8R; 139; CANR
   37; CLR 1, 37; JRDA; MAICYA; SATA
   6, 44, 78; SATA-Obit 73
Sutro, Alfred 1863-1933 .... **TCLC 6**
   See also CA 105; 185; DLB 10
Sutton, Henry
   See Slavitt, David R(ytman)
Svevo, Italo 1861-1928 . **TCLC 2, 35; SSC 25**
   See also Schmitz, Aron Hector
Swados, Elizabeth (A.) 1951- .... **CLC 12**
   See also CA 97-100; CANR 49; INT 97-
   100
Swados, Harvey 1920-1972 .... **CLC 5**
   See also CA 5-8R; 37-40R; CANR 6; DLB
   2
Swan, Gladys 1934- .... **CLC 69**
   See also CA 101; CANR 17, 39
Swanson, Logan
   See Matheson, Richard Burton
Swarthout, Glendon (Fred) 1918-1992
   .... **CLC 35**
   See also CA 1-4R; 139; CANR 1, 47; SATA
   26
Sweet, Sarah C.
   See Jewett, (Theodora) Sarah Orne
Swenson, May 1919-1989 .... **CLC 4, 14, 61,
   106; DA; DAB; DAC; DAM MST,
   POET; PC 14**
   See also CA 5-8R; 130; CANR 36, 61; DLB
   5; MTCW 1, 2; SATA 15
Swift, Augustus
   See Lovecraft, H(oward) P(hillips)
Swift, Graham (Colin) 1949- ...... **CLC 41, 88**
   See also CA 117; 122; CANR 46, 71; DLB
   194; MTCW 2
Swift, Jonathan 1667-1745 ..... **LC 1, 42; DA;
   DAB; DAC; DAM MST, NOV, POET;
   PC 9; WLC**
   See also CDBLB 1660-1789; CLR 53;
   DA3; DLB 39, 95, 101; SATA 19
Swinburne, Algernon Charles 1837-1909
   **TCLC 8, 36; DA; DAB; DAC; DAM
   MST, POET; PC 24; WLC**
   See also CA 105; 140; CDBLB 1832-1890;
   DA3; DLB 35, 57
Swinfen, Ann .... **CLC 34**
Swinnerton, Frank Arthur 1884-1982
   .... **CLC 31**
   See also CA 108; DLB 34
Swithen, John
   See King, Stephen (Edwin)
Sylvia
   See Ashton-Warner, Sylvia (Constance)
Symmes, Robert Edward
   See Duncan, Robert (Edward)
Symonds, John Addington 1840-1893
   .... **NCLC 34**

See also DLB 57, 144

Symons, Arthur 1865-1945 .... **TCLC 11**
See also CA 107; DLB 19, 57, 149

Symons, Julian (Gustave) 1912-1994 . **CLC 2, 14, 32**
See also CA 49-52; 147; CAAS 3; CANR 3, 33, 59; DLB 87, 155; DLBY 92; MTCW 1

Synge, (Edmund) J(ohn) M(illington) 1871-1909 . **TCLC 6, 37; DAM DRAM; DC 2**
See also CA 104; 141; CDBLB 1890-1914; DLB 10, 19

Syruc, J.
See Milosz, Czeslaw

Szirtes, George 1948- .... **CLC 46**
See also CA 109; CANR 27, 61

Szymborska, Wislawa 1923- .... **CLC 99**
See also CA 154; DA3; DLBY 96; MTCW 2

T. O., Nik
See Annensky, Innokenty (Fyodorovich)

Tabori, George 1914- .... **CLC 19**
See also CA 49-52; CANR 4, 69

Tagore, Rabindranath 1861-1941 ... **TCLC 3, 53; DAM DRAM, POET; PC 8**
See also CA 104; 120; DA3; MTCW 1, 2

Taine, Hippolyte Adolphe 1828-1893
.... **NCLC 15**

Talese, Gay 1932- .... **CLC 37**
See also AITN 1; CA 1-4R; CANR 9, 58; DLB 185; INT CANR-9; MTCW 1, 2

Tallent, Elizabeth (Ann) 1954- .... **CLC 45**
See also CA 117; CANR 72; DLB 130

Tally, Ted 1952- .... **CLC 42**
See also CA 120; 124; INT 124

Talvik, Heiti 1904-1947 .... **TCLC 87**

Tamayo y Baus, Manuel 1829-1898 . **NCLC 1**

Tammsaare, A(nton) H(ansen) 1878-1940
TCLC 27
See also CA 164

Tam'si, Tchicaya U
See Tchicaya, Gerald Felix

Tan, Amy (Ruth) 1952- . **CLC 59, 120; DAM MULT, NOV, POP**
See also AAYA 9; BEST 89:3; CA 136; CANR 54; CDALBS; DA3; DLB 173; MTCW 2; SATA 75

Tandem, Felix
See Spitteler, Carl (Friedrich Georg)

Tanizaki, Jun'ichiro 1886-1965 ... **CLC 8, 14, 28; SSC 21**
See also CA 93-96; 25-28R; DLB 180; MTCW 2

Tanner, William
See Amis, Kingsley (William)

Tao Lao
See Storni, Alfonsina

Tarantino, Quentin (Jerome) 1963- . **CLC 125**
See also CA 171

Tarassoff, Lev
See Troyat, Henri

Tarbell, Ida M(inerva) 1857-1944 . **TCLC 40**
See also CA 122; 181; DLB 47

Tarkington, (Newton) Booth 1869-1946
TCLC 9
See also CA 110; 143; DLB 9, 102; MTCW 2; SATA 17

Tarkovsky, Andrei (Arsenyevich) 1932-1986
CLC 75
See also CA 127

Tartt, Donna 1964(?)- .... **CLC 76**
See also CA 142

Tasso, Torquato 1544-1595 .... **LC 5**

Tate, (John Orley) Allen 1899-1979 .. **CLC 2, 4, 6, 9, 11, 14, 24**
See also CA 5-8R; 85-88; CANR 32; DLB 4, 45, 63; DLBD 17; MTCW 1, 2

Tate, Ellalice
See Hibbert, Eleanor Alice Burford

Tate, James (Vincent) 1943- ..... **CLC 2, 6, 25**
See also CA 21-24R; CANR 29, 57; DLB 5, 169

Tauler, Johannes c. 1300-1361 ...... **CMLC 37**
See also DLB 179

Tavel, Ronald 1940- .... **CLC 6**
See also CA 21-24R; CANR 33

Taylor, C(ecil) P(hilip) 1929-1981 .... **CLC 27**
See also CA 25-28R; 105; CANR 47

Taylor, Edward 1642(?)-1729 ..... **LC 11; DA; DAB; DAC; DAM MST, POET**
See also DLB 24

Taylor, Eleanor Ross 1920- .... **CLC 5**
See also CA 81-84; CANR 70

Taylor, Elizabeth 1912-1975 ..... **CLC 2, 4, 29**
See also CA 13-16R; CANR 9, 70; DLB 139; MTCW 1; SATA 13

Taylor, Frederick Winslow 1856-1915
.... **TCLC 76**

Taylor, Henry (Splawn) 1942- .... **CLC 44**
See also CA 33-36R; CAAS 7; CANR 31; DLB 5

Taylor, Kamala (Purnaiya) 1924-
See Markandaya, Kamala
See also CA 77-80

Taylor, Mildred D. .... **CLC 21**
See also AAYA 10; BW 1; CA 85-88; CANR 25; CLR 9, 59; DLB 52; JRDA; MAICYA; SAAS 5; SATA 15, 70

Taylor, Peter (Hillsman) 1917-1994 .. **CLC 1, 4, 18, 37, 44, 50, 71; SSC 10**
See also CA 13-16R; 147; CANR 9, 50; DLBY 81, 94; INT CANR-9; MTCW 1, 2

Taylor, Robert Lewis 1912-1998 .... **CLC 14**
See also CA 1-4R; 170; CANR 3, 64; SATA 10

Tchekhov, Anton
See Chekhov, Anton (Pavlovich)

Tchicaya, Gerald Felix 1931-1988 .. **CLC 101**
See also CA 129; 125; CANR 81

Tchicaya U Tam'si
See Tchicaya, Gerald Felix

Teasdale, Sara 1884-1933 .... **TCLC 4**
See also CA 104; 163; DLB 45; SATA 32

Tegner, Esaias 1782-1846 .... **NCLC 2**

Teilhard de Chardin, (Marie Joseph) Pierre 1881-1955 .... **TCLC 9**
See also CA 105

Temple, Ann
See Mortimer, Penelope (Ruth)

Tennant, Emma (Christina) 1937- .. **CLC 13, 52**
See also CA 65-68; CAAS 9; CANR 10, 38, 59, 88; DLB 14

Tenneshaw, S. M.
See Silverberg, Robert

Tennyson, Alfred 1809-1892 ... **NCLC 30, 65; DA; DAB; DAC; DAM MST, POET; PC 6; WLC**
See also CDBLB 1832-1890; DA3; DLB 32

Teran, Lisa St. Aubin de .... **CLC 36**
See also St. Aubin de Teran, Lisa

Terence c. 184B.C.-c. 159B.C. ...... **CMLC 14; DC 7**
See also DLB 211

Teresa de Jesus, St. 1515-1582 .... **LC 18**

Terkel, Louis 1912-
See Terkel, Studs
See also CA 57-60; CANR 18, 45, 67; DA3; MTCW 1, 2

Terkel, Studs .... **CLC 38**
See also Terkel, Louis AAYA 32; AITN 1; MTCW 2

Terry, C. V.
See Slaughter, Frank G(ill)

Terry, Megan 1932- .... **CLC 19**
See also CA 77-80; CABS 3; CANR 43; DLB 7

Tertullian c. 155-c. 245 .... **CMLC 29**

Tertz, Abram
See Sinyavsky, Andrei (Donatevich)

Tesich, Steve 1943(?)-1996 .... **CLC 40, 69**
See also CA 105; 152; DLBY 83

Tesla, Nikola 1856-1943 .... **TCLC 88**

Teternikov, Fyodor Kuzmich 1863-1927
See Sologub, Fyodor
See also CA 104

Tevis, Walter 1928-1984 .... **CLC 42**
See also CA 113

Tey, Josephine .... **TCLC 14**
See also Mackintosh, Elizabeth DLB 77

Thackeray, William Makepeace 1811-1863
NCLC 5, 14, 22, 43; DA; DAB; DAC; DAM MST, NOV; WLC
See also CDBLB 1832-1890; DA3; DLB 21, 55, 159, 163; SATA 23

Thakura, Ravindranatha
See Tagore, Rabindranath

Tharoor, Shashi 1956- .... **CLC 70**
See also CA 141

Thelwell, Michael Miles 1939- .... **CLC 22**
See also BW 2; CA 101

Theobald, Lewis, Jr.
See Lovecraft, H(oward) P(hillips)

Theodorescu, Ion N. 1880-1967
See Arghezi, Tudor
See also CA 116

Theriault, Yves 1915-1983 .... **CLC 79; DAC; DAM MST**
See also CA 102; DLB 88

Theroux, Alexander (Louis) 1939- .... **CLC 2, 25**
See also CA 85-88; CANR 20, 63

Theroux, Paul (Edward) 1941- ..... **CLC 5, 8, 11, 15, 28, 46; DAM POP**
See also AAYA 28; BEST 89:4; CA 33-36R; CANR 20, 45, 74; CDALBS; DA3; DLB 2; MTCW 1, 2; SATA 44, 109

Thesen, Sharon 1946- .... **CLC 56**
See also CA 163

Thevenin, Denis
See Duhamel, Georges

Thibault, Jacques Anatole Francois 1844-1924
See France, Anatole
See also CA 106; 127; DAM NOV; DA3; MTCW 1, 2

Thiele, Colin (Milton) 1920- .... **CLC 17**
See also CA 29-32R; CANR 12, 28, 53; CLR 27; MAICYA; SAAS 2; SATA 14, 72

Thomas, Audrey (Callahan) 1935- .... **CLC 7, 13, 37, 107; SSC 20**
See also AITN 2; CA 21-24R; CAAS 19; CANR 36, 58; DLB 60; MTCW 1

Thomas, Augustus 1857-1934 .... **TCLC 97**

Thomas, D(onald) M(ichael) 1935- . **CLC 13, 22, 31**
See also CA 61-64; CAAS 11; CANR 17, 45, 75; CDBLB 1960 to Present; DA3; DLB 40, 207; INT CANR-17; MTCW 1, 2

Thomas, Dylan (Marlais) 1914-1953
.... **TCLC 1, 8, 45; DA; DAB; DAC; DAM DRAM, MST, POET; PC 2; SSC 3; WLC**
See also CA 104; 120; CANR 65; CDBLB 1945-1960; DA3; DLB 13, 20, 139; MTCW 1, 2; SATA 60

Thomas, (Philip) Edward 1878-1917
.... **TCLC 10; DAM POET**
See also CA 106; 153; DLB 98

van der Post, Laurens (Jan) 1906-1996
.... **CLC 5**
See also CA 5-8R; 155; CANR 35; DLB 204
van de Wetering, Janwillem 1931- ... **CLC 47**
See also CA 49-52; CANR 4, 62
Van Dine, S. S. .... **TCLC 23**
See also Wright, Willard Huntington
Van Doren, Carl (Clinton) 1885-1950
.... **TCLC 18**
See also CA 111; 168
Van Doren, Mark 1894-1972 .... **CLC 6, 10**
See also CA 1-4R; 37-40R; CANR 3; DLB 45; MTCW 1, 2
Van Druten, John (William) 1901-1957
TCLC 2
See also CA 104; 161; DLB 10
Van Duyn, Mona (Jane) 1921- . **CLC 3, 7, 63, 116; DAM POET**
See also CA 9-12R; CANR 7, 38, 60; DLB 5
Van Dyne, Edith
See Baum, L(yman) Frank
van Itallie, Jean-Claude 1936- .... **CLC 3**
See also CA 45-48; CAAS 2; CANR 1, 48; DLB 7
van Ostaijen, Paul 1896-1928 .... **TCLC 33**
See also CA 163
Van Peebles, Melvin 1932- . **CLC 2, 20; DAM MULT**
See also BW 2, 3; CA 85-88; CANR 27, 67, 82
Vansittart, Peter 1920- .... **CLC 42**
See also CA 1-4R; CANR 3, 49
Van Vechten, Carl 1880-1964 .... **CLC 33**
See also CA 183; 89-92; DLB 4, 9, 51
Van Vogt, A(lfred) E(lton) 1912- .... **CLC 1**
See also CA 21-24R; CANR 28; DLB 8; SATA 14
Varda, Agnes 1928- .... **CLC 16**
See also CA 116; 122
Vargas Llosa, (Jorge) Mario (Pedro) 1936-
CLC 3, 6, 9, 10, 15, 31, 42, 85; DA; DAB; DAC; DAM MST, MULT, NOV; HLC 2
See also CA 73-76; CANR 18, 32, 42, 67; DA3; DLB 145; HW 1, 2; MTCW 1, 2
Vasiliu, Gheorghe 1881-1957
See Bacovia, George
See also CA 123
Vassa, Gustavus
See Equiano, Olaudah
Vassilikos, Vassilis 1933- .... **CLC 4, 8**
See also CA 81-84; CANR 75
Vaughan, Henry 1621-1695 .... **LC 27**
See also DLB 131
Vaughn, Stephanie .... **CLC 62**
Vazov, Ivan (Minchov) 1850-1921 . **TCLC 25**
See also CA 121; 167; DLB 147
Veblen, Thorstein B(unde) 1857-1929
.... **TCLC 31**
See also CA 115; 165
Vega, Lope de 1562-1635 .... **LC 23; HLCS 2**
Venison, Alfred
See Pound, Ezra (Weston Loomis)
Verdi, Marie de
See Mencken, H(enry) L(ouis)
Verdu, Matilde
See Cela, Camilo Jose
Verga, Giovanni (Carmelo) 1840-1922
.... **TCLC 3; SSC 21**
See also CA 104; 123
Vergil 70B.C.-19B.C. ... **CMLC 9; DA; DAB; DAC; DAM MST, POET; PC 12; WLCS**
See also Virgil DA3
Verhaeren, Emile (Adolphe Gustave)
1855-1916 .... **TCLC 12**

See also CA 109
Verlaine, Paul (Marie) 1844-1896 .. **NCLC 2, 51; DAM POET; PC 2**
Verne, Jules (Gabriel) 1828-1905 ... **TCLC 6, 52**
See also AAYA 16; CA 110; 131; DA3; DLB 123; JRDA; MAICYA; SATA 21
Very, Jones 1813-1880 .... **NCLC 9**
See also DLB 1
Vesaas, Tarjei 1897-1970 .... **CLC 48**
See also CA 29-32R
Vialis, Gaston
See Simenon, Georges (Jacques Christian)
Vian, Boris 1920-1959 .... **TCLC 9**
See also CA 106; 164; DLB 72; MTCW 2
Viaud, (Louis Marie) Julien 1850-1923
See Loti, Pierre
See also CA 107
Vicar, Henry
See Felsen, Henry Gregor
Vicker, Angus
See Felsen, Henry Gregor
Vidal, Gore 1925- . **CLC 2, 4, 6, 8, 10, 22, 33, 72; DAM NOV, POP**
See also AITN 1; BEST 90:2; CA 5-8R; CANR 13, 45, 65; CDALBS; DA3; DLB 6, 152; INT CANR-13; MTCW 1, 2
Viereck, Peter (Robert Edwin) 1916- . **CLC 4; PC 27**
See also CA 1-4R; CANR 1, 47; DLB 5
Vigny, Alfred (Victor) de 1797-1863
.... **NCLC 7; DAM POET; PC 26**
See also DLB 119, 192
Vilakazi, Benedict Wallet 1906-1947
.... **TCLC 37**
See also CA 168
Villa, Jose Garcia 1904-1997 .... **PC 22**
See also CA 25-28R; CANR 12
Villarreal, Jose Antonio 1924-
See also CA 133; DAM MULT; DLB 82; HLC 2; HW 1
Villaurrutia, Xavier 1903-1950 ...... **TCLC 80**
See also HW 1
Villehardouin 1150(?)-1218(?) .... **CMLC 38**
Villiers de l'Isle Adam, Jean Marie Mathias Philippe Auguste, Comte de 1838-1889
NCLC 3; SSC 14
See also DLB 123
Villon, Francois 1431-1463(?) .... **PC 13**
See also DLB 208
Vinci, Leonardo da 1452-1519 .... **LC 12**
Vine, Barbara .... **CLC 50**
See also Rendell, Ruth (Barbara) BEST 90:4
Vinge, Joan (Carol) D(ennison) 1948-
.... **CLC 30; SSC 24**
See also AAYA 32; CA 93-96; CANR 72; SATA 36, 113
Violis, G.
See Simenon, Georges (Jacques Christian)
Viramontes, Helena Maria 1954-
See also CA 159; DLB 122; HLCS 2; HW 2
Virgil 70B.C.-19B.C.
See Vergil
See also DLB 211
Visconti, Luchino 1906-1976 .... **CLC 16**
See also CA 81-84; 65-68; CANR 39
Vittorini, Elio 1908-1966 .... **CLC 6, 9, 14**
See also CA 133; 25-28R
Vivekananda, Swami 1863-1902 .... **TCLC 88**
Vizenor, Gerald Robert 1934- .... **CLC 103; DAM MULT**
See also CA 13-16R; CAAS 22; CANR 5, 21, 44, 67; DLB 175; MTCW 2; NNAL
Vizinczey, Stephen 1933- .... **CLC 40**
See also CA 128; INT 128
Vliet, R(ussell) G(ordon) 1929-1984 . **CLC 22**
See also CA 37-40R; 112; CANR 18

Vogau, Boris Andreyevich 1894-1937(?)
See Pilnyak, Boris
See also CA 123
Vogel, Paula A(nne) 1951- .... **CLC 76**
See also CA 108
Voigt, Cynthia 1942- .... **CLC 30**
See also AAYA 3, 30; CA 106; CANR 18, 37, 40; CLR 13, 48; INT CANR-18; JRDA; MAICYA; SATA 48, 79; SATA-Brief 33
Voigt, Ellen Bryant 1943- .... **CLC 54**
See also CA 69-72; CANR 11, 29, 55; DLB 120
Voinovich, Vladimir (Nikolaevich) 1932-
CLC 10, 49
See also CA 81-84; CAAS 12; CANR 33, 67; MTCW 1
Vollmann, William T. 1959- .. **CLC 89; DAM NOV, POP**
See also CA 134; CANR 67; DA3; MTCW 2
Voloshinov, V. N.
See Bakhtin, Mikhail Mikhailovich
Voltaire 1694-1778 . **LC 14; DA; DAB; DAC; DAM DRAM, MST; SSC 12; WLC**
See also DA3
von Aschendrof, BaronIgnatz
See Ford, Ford Madox
von Daeniken, Erich 1935- .... **CLC 30**
See also AITN 1; CA 37-40R; CANR 17, 44
von Daniken, Erich
See von Daeniken, Erich
von Heidenstam, (Carl Gustaf) Verner
See Heidenstam, (Carl Gustaf) Verner von
von Heyse, Paul (Johann Ludwig)
See Heyse, Paul (Johann Ludwig von)
von Hofmannsthal, Hugo
See Hofmannsthal, Hugo von
von Horvath, Odon
See Horvath, Oedoen von
von Horvath, Oedoen -1938
See Horvath, Oedoen von
See also CA 184
von Liliencron, (Friedrich Adolf Axel) Detlev
See Liliencron, (Friedrich Adolf Axel) Detlev von
Vonnegut, Kurt, Jr. 1922- . **CLC 1, 2, 3, 4, 5, 8, 12, 22, 40, 60, 111; DA; DAB; DAC; DAM MST, NOV, POP; SSC 8; WLC**
See also AAYA 6; AITN 1; BEST 90:4; CA 1-4R; CANR 1, 25, 49, 75; CDALB 1968-1988; DA3; DLB 2, 8, 152; DLBD 3; DLBY 80; MTCW 1, 2
Von Rachen, Kurt
See Hubbard, L(afayette) Ron(ald)
von Rezzori (d'Arezzo), Gregor
See Rezzori (d'Arezzo), Gregor von
von Sternberg, Josef
See Sternberg, Josef von
Vorster, Gordon 1924- .... **CLC 34**
See also CA 133
Vosce, Trudie
See Ozick, Cynthia
Voznesensky, Andrei (Andreievich) 1933-
CLC 1, 15, 57; DAM POET
See also CA 89-92; CANR 37; MTCW 1
Waddington, Miriam 1917- .... **CLC 28**
See also CA 21-24R; CANR 12, 30; DLB 68
Wagman, Fredrica 1937- .... **CLC 7**
See also CA 97-100; INT 97-100
Wagner, Linda W.
See Wagner-Martin, Linda (C.)
Wagner, Linda Welshimer
See Wagner-Martin, Linda (C.)
Wagner, Richard 1813-1883 .... **NCLC 9**
See also DLB 129

See also Lewis, Janet DLBY 87

Winters, (Arthur) Yvor 1900-1968 .... **CLC 4, 8, 32**
See also CA 11-12; 25-28R; CAP 1; DLB 48; MTCW 1

Winterson, Jeanette 1959- .... **CLC 64; DAM POP**
See also CA 136; CANR 58; DA3; DLB 207; MTCW 2

Winthrop, John 1588-1649 .... **LC 31**
See also DLB 24, 30

Wirth, Louis 1897-1952 .... **TCLC 92**

Wiseman, Frederick 1930- .... **CLC 20**
See also CA 159

Wister, Owen 1860-1938 .... **TCLC 21**
See also CA 108; 162; DLB 9, 78, 186; SATA 62

Witkacy
See Witkiewicz, Stanislaw Ignacy

Witkiewicz, Stanislaw Ignacy 1885-1939 **TCLC 8**
See also CA 105; 162

Wittgenstein, Ludwig (Josef Johann) 1889-1951 .... **TCLC 59**
See also CA 113; 164; MTCW 2

Wittig, Monique 1935(?)- .... **CLC 22**
See also CA 116; 135; DLB 83

Wittlin, Jozef 1896-1976 .... **CLC 25**
See also CA 49-52; 65-68; CANR 3

Wodehouse, P(elham) G(renville) 1881-1975 **CLC 1, 2, 5, 10, 22; DAB; DAC; DAM NOV; SSC 2**
See also AITN 2; CA 45-48; 57-60; CANR 3, 33; CDBLB 1914-1945; DA3; DLB 34, 162; MTCW 1, 2; SATA 22

Woiwode, L.
See Woiwode, Larry (Alfred)

Woiwode, Larry (Alfred) 1941- ... **CLC 6, 10**
See also CA 73-76; CANR 16; DLB 6; INT CANR-16

Wojciechowska, Maia (Teresa) 1927-
.... **CLC 26**
See also AAYA 8; CA 9-12R, 183; CAAE 183; CANR 4, 41; CLR 1; JRDA; MAI-CYA; SAAS 1; SATA 1, 28, 83; SATA-Essay 104

Wojtyla, Karol
See John Paul II, Pope

Wolf, Christa 1929- .... **CLC 14, 29, 58**
See also CA 85-88; CANR 45; DLB 75; MTCW 1

Wolfe, Gene (Rodman) 1931- .... **CLC 25; DAM POP**
See also CA 57-60; CAAS 9; CANR 6, 32, 60; DLB 8; MTCW 2

Wolfe, George C. 1954- .... **CLC 49; BLCS**
See also CA 149

Wolfe, Thomas (Clayton) 1900-1938
. **TCLC 4, 13, 29, 61; DA; DAB; DAC; DAM MST, NOV; SSC 33; WLC**
See also CA 104; 132; CDALB 1929-1941; DA3; DLB 9, 102; DLBD 2, 16; DLBY 85, 97; MTCW 1, 2

Wolfe, Thomas Kennerly, Jr. 1930-
See Wolfe, Tom
See also CA 13-16R; CANR 9, 33, 70; DAM POP; DA3; DLB 185; INT CANR-9; MTCW 1, 2

Wolfe, Tom .... **CLC 1, 2, 9, 15, 35, 51**
See also Wolfe, Thomas Kennerly, Jr. AAYA 8; AITN 2; BEST 89:1; DLB 152

Wolff, Geoffrey (Ansell) 1937- .... **CLC 41**
See also CA 29-32R; CANR 29, 43, 78

Wolff, Sonia
See Levitin, Sonia (Wolff)

Wolff, Tobias (Jonathan Ansell) 1945-
.... **CLC 39, 64**

See also AAYA 16; BEST 90:2; CA 114; 117; CAAS 22; CANR 54, 76; DA3; DLB 130; INT 117; MTCW 2

Wolfram von Eschenbach c. 1170-c. 1220 **CMLC 5**
See also DLB 138

Wolitzer, Hilma 1930- .... **CLC 17**
See also CA 65-68; CANR 18, 40; INT CANR-18; SATA 31

Wollstonecraft, Mary 1759-1797 ..... **LC 5, 50**
See also CDBLB 1789-1832; DLB 39, 104, 158

Wonder, Stevie .... **CLC 12**
See also Morris, Steveland Judkins

Wong, Jade Snow 1922- .... **CLC 17**
See also CA 109; SATA 112

Woodberry, George Edward 1855-1930 **TCLC 73**
See also CA 165; DLB 71, 103

Woodcott, Keith
See Brunner, John (Kilian Houston)

Woodruff, Robert W.
See Mencken, H(enry) L(ouis)

Woolf, (Adeline) Virginia 1882-1941
.... **TCLC 1, 5, 20, 43, 56; DA; DAB; DAC; DAM MST, NOV; SSC 7; WLC**
See also Woolf, Virginia Adeline CA 104; 130; CANR 64; CDBLB 1914-1945; DA3; DLB 36, 100, 162; DLBD 10; MTCW 1

Woolf, Virginia Adeline
See Woolf, (Adeline) Virginia
See also MTCW 2

Woollcott, Alexander (Humphreys) 1887-1943 .... **TCLC 5**
See also CA 105; 161; DLB 29

Woolrich, Cornell 1903-1968 .... **CLC 77**
See also Hopley-Woolrich, Cornell George

Woolson, Constance Fenimore 1840-1894 **NCLC 82**
See also DLB 12, 74, 189

Wordsworth, Dorothy 1771-1855 .. **NCLC 25**
See also DLB 107

Wordsworth, William 1770-1850 .. **NCLC 12, 38; DA; DAB; DAC; DAM MST, POET; PC 4; WLC**
See also CDBLB 1789-1832; DA3; DLB 93, 107

Wouk, Herman 1915- ... **CLC 1, 9, 38; DAM NOV, POP**
See also CA 5-8R; CANR 6, 33, 67; CDALBS; DA3; DLBY 82; INT CANR-6; MTCW 1, 2

Wright, Charles (Penzel, Jr.) 1935- .. **CLC 6, 13, 28, 119**
See also CA 29-32R; CAAS 7; CANR 23, 36, 62, 88; DLB 165; DLBY 82; MTCW 1, 2

Wright, Charles Stevenson 1932- ... **CLC 49; BLC 3; DAM MULT, POET**
See also BW 1; CA 9-12R; CANR 26; DLB 33

Wright, Frances 1795-1852 .... **NCLC 74**
See also DLB 73

Wright, Frank Lloyd 1867-1959 .... **TCLC 95**
See also CA 174

Wright, Jack R.
See Harris, Mark

Wright, James (Arlington) 1927-1980
.... **CLC 3, 5, 10, 28; DAM POET**
See also AITN 2; CA 49-52; 97-100; CANR 4, 34, 64; CDALBS; DLB 5, 169; MTCW 1, 2

Wright, Judith (Arandell) 1915- ..... **CLC 11, 53; PC 14**
See also CA 13-16R; CANR 31, 76; MTCW 1, 2; SATA 14

Wright, L(aurali) R. 1939- .... **CLC 44**
See also CA 138

Wright, Richard (Nathaniel) 1908-1960
. **CLC 1, 3, 4, 9, 14, 21, 48, 74; BLC 3; DA; DAB; DAC; DAM MST, MULT, NOV; SSC 2; WLC**
See also AAYA 5; BW 1; CA 108; CANR 64; CDALB 1929-1941; DA3; DLB 76, 102; DLBD 2; MTCW 1, 2

Wright, Richard B(ruce) 1937- .... **CLC 6**
See also CA 85-88; DLB 53

Wright, Rick 1945- .... **CLC 35**

Wright, Rowland
See Wells, Carolyn

Wright, Stephen 1946- .... **CLC 33**

Wright, Willard Huntington 1888-1939
See Van Dine, S. S.
See also CA 115; DLBD 16

Wright, William 1930- .... **CLC 44**
See also CA 53-56; CANR 7, 23

Wroth, LadyMary 1587-1653(?) .... **LC 30**
See also DLB 121

Wu Ch'eng-en 1500(?)-1582(?) .... **LC 7**

Wu Ching-tzu 1701-1754 .... **LC 2**

Wurlitzer, Rudolph 1938(?)- .... **CLC 2, 4, 15**
See also CA 85-88; DLB 173

Wyatt, Thomas c. 1503-1542 .... **PC 27**
See also DLB 132

Wycherley, William 1641-1715 ...... **LC 8, 21; DAM DRAM**
See also CDBLB 1660-1789; DLB 80

Wylie, Elinor (Morton Hoyt) 1885-1928 **TCLC 8; PC 23**
See also CA 105; 162; DLB 9, 45

Wylie, Philip (Gordon) 1902-1971 ... **CLC 43**
See also CA 21-22; 33-36R; CAP 2; DLB 9

Wyndham, John .... **CLC 19**
See also Harris, John (Wyndham Parkes Lucas) Beynon

Wyss, Johann David Von 1743-1818
.... **NCLC 10**
See also JRDA; MAICYA; SATA 29; SATA-Brief 27

Xenophon c. 430B.C.-c. 354B.C. ... **CMLC 17**
See also DLB 176

Yakumo Koizumi
See Hearn, (Patricio) Lafcadio (Tessima Carlos)

Yamamoto, Hisaye 1921- .... **SSC 34; DAM MULT**

Yanez, Jose Donoso
See Donoso (Yanez), Jose

Yanovsky, Basile S.
See Yanovsky, V(assily) S(emenovich)

Yanovsky, V(assily) S(emenovich) 1906-1989 **CLC 2, 18**
See also CA 97-100; 129

Yates, Richard 1926-1992 .... **CLC 7, 8, 23**
See also CA 5-8R; 139; CANR 10, 43; DLB 2; DLBY 81, 92; INT CANR-10

Yeats, W. B.
See Yeats, William Butler

Yeats, William Butler 1865-1939 .... **TCLC 1, 11, 18, 31, 93; DA; DAB; DAC; DAM DRAM, MST, POET; PC 20; WLC**
See also CA 104; 127; CANR 45; CDBLB 1890-1914; DA3; DLB 10, 19, 98, 156; MTCW 1, 2

Yehoshua, A(braham) B. 1936- .. **CLC 13, 31**
See also CA 33-36R; CANR 43

Yellow Bird
See Ridge, John Rollin

Yep, Laurence Michael 1948- .... **CLC 35**
See also AAYA 5, 31; CA 49-52; CANR 1, 46; CLR 3, 17, 54; DLB 52; JRDA; MAI-CYA; SATA 7, 69

Yerby, Frank G(arvin) 1916-1991 . **CLC 1, 7, 22; BLC 3; DAM MULT**

See also BW 1, 3; CA 9-12R; 136; CANR 16, 52; DLB 76; INT CANR-16; MTCW 1

Yesenin, Sergei Alexandrovich
　　See Esenin, Sergei (Alexandrovich)

Yevtushenko, Yevgeny (Alexandrovich) 1933-
CLC 1, 3, 13, 26, 51, 126; DAM POET
　　See also CA 81-84; CANR 33, 54; MTCW 1

Yezierska, Anzia 1885(?)-1970 .... **CLC 46**
　　See also CA 126; 89-92; DLB 28; MTCW 1

Yglesias, Helen 1915- .... **CLC 7, 22**
　　See also CA 37-40R; CAAS 20; CANR 15, 65; INT CANR-15; MTCW 1

Yokomitsu Riichi 1898-1947 .... **TCLC 47**
　　See also CA 170

Yonge, Charlotte (Mary) 1823-1901
　　... **TCLC 48**
　　See also CA 109; 163; DLB 18, 163; SATA 17

York, Jeremy
　　See Creasey, John

York, Simon
　　See Heinlein, Robert A(nson)

Yorke, Henry Vincent 1905-1974 ..... **CLC 13**
　　See also Green, Henry CA 85-88; 49-52

Yosano Akiko 1878-1942 .... **TCLC 59; PC 11**
　　See also CA 161

Yoshimoto, Banana .... **CLC 84**
　　See also Yoshimoto, Mahoko

Yoshimoto, Mahoko 1964-
　　See Yoshimoto, Banana
　　See also CA 144

Young, Al(bert James) 1939- . **CLC 19; BLC 3; DAM MULT**
　　See also BW 2, 3; CA 29-32R; CANR 26, 65; DLB 33

Young, Andrew (John) 1885-1971 ...... **CLC 5**
　　See also CA 5-8R; CANR 7, 29

Young, Collier
　　See Bloch, Robert (Albert)

Young, Edward 1683-1765 .... **LC 3, 40**
　　See also DLB 95

Young, Marguerite (Vivian) 1909-1995
　　.. **CLC 82**

See also CA 13-16; 150; CAP 1

Young, Neil 1945- .... **CLC 17**
　　See also CA 110

Young Bear, Ray A. 1950- ..... **CLC 94; DAM MULT**
　　See also CA 146; DLB 175; NNAL

Yourcenar, Marguerite 1903-1987 ... **CLC 19, 38, 50, 87; DAM NOV**
　　See also CA 69-72; CANR 23, 60; DLB 72; DLBY 88; MTCW 1, 2

Yuan, Chu 340(?)B.C.-278(?)B.C. . **CMLC 36**

Yurick, Sol 1925- .... **CLC 6**
　　See also CA 13-16R; CANR 25

Zabolotsky, Nikolai Alekseevich 1903-1958
TCLC 52
　　See also CA 116; 164

Zagajewski, Adam .... **PC 27**

Zamiatin, Yevgenii
　　See Zamyatin, Evgeny Ivanovich

Zamora, Bernice (B. Ortiz) 1938- .. **CLC 89; DAM MULT; HLC 2**
　　See also CA 151; CANR 80; DLB 82; HW 1, 2

Zamyatin, Evgeny Ivanovich 1884-1937
TCLC 8, 37
　　See also CA 105; 166

Zangwill, Israel 1864-1926 .... **TCLC 16**
　　See also CA 109; 167; DLB 10, 135, 197

Zappa, Francis Vincent, Jr. 1940-1993
　　See Zappa, Frank
　　See also CA 108; 143; CANR 57

Zappa, Frank .... **CLC 17**
　　See also Zappa, Francis Vincent, Jr.

Zaturenska, Marya 1902-1982 ..... **CLC 6, 11**
　　See also CA 13-16R; 105; CANR 22

Zeami 1363-1443 .... **DC 7**

Zelazny, Roger (Joseph) 1937-1995 . **CLC 21**
　　See also AAYA 7; CA 21-24R; 148; CANR 26, 60; DLB 8; MTCW 1, 2; SATA 57; SATA-Brief 39

Zhdanov, Andrei Alexandrovich 1896-1948
TCLC 18
　　See also CA 117; 167

Zhukovsky, Vasily (Andreevich) 1783-1852
NCLC 35
　　See also DLB 205

Ziegenhagen, Eric .... **CLC 55**

Zimmer, Jill Schary
　　See Robinson, Jill

Zimmerman, Robert
　　See Dylan, Bob

Zindel, Paul 1936- ..... **CLC 6, 26; DA; DAB; DAC; DAM DRAM, MST, NOV; DC 5**
　　See also AAYA 2; CA 73-76; CANR 31, 65; CDALBS; CLR 3, 45; DA3; DLB 7, 52; JRDA; MAICYA; MTCW 1, 2; SATA 16, 58, 102

Zinov'Ev, A. A.
　　See Zinoviev, Alexander (Aleksandrovich)

Zinoviev, Alexander (Aleksandrovich) 1922-
CLC 19
　　See also CA 116; 133; CAAS 10

Zoilus
　　See Lovecraft, H(oward) P(hillips)

Zola, Emile (Edouard Charles Antoine) 1840-1902 .... **TCLC 1, 6, 21, 41; DA; DAB; DAC; DAM MST, NOV; WLC**
　　See also CA 104; 138; DA3; DLB 123

Zoline, Pamela 1941- .... **CLC 62**
　　See also CA 161

Zorrilla y Moral, Jose 1817-1893 .... **NCLC 6**

Zoshchenko, Mikhail (Mikhailovich) 1895-1958 .... **TCLC 15; SSC 15**
　　See also CA 115; 160

Zuckmayer, Carl 1896-1977 .... **CLC 18**
　　See also CA 69-72; DLB 56, 124

Zuk, Georges
　　See Skelton, Robin

Zukofsky, Louis 1904-1978 ... **CLC 1, 2, 4, 7, 11, 18; DAM POET; PC 11**
　　See also CA 9-12R; 77-80; CANR 39; DLB 5, 165; MTCW 1

Zweig, Paul 1935-1984 .... **CLC 34, 42**
　　See also CA 85-88; 113

Zweig, Stefan 1881-1942 .... **TCLC 17**
　　See also CA 112; 170; DLB 81, 118

Zwingli, Huldreich 1484-1531 .... **LC 37**
　　See also DLB 179

Literary Criticism Series
Cumulative Topic Index

This index lists all topic entries in Gale's *Classical and Medieval Literature Criticism, Contemporary Literary Criticism, Literature Criticism from 1400 to 1800, Nineteenth-Century Literature Criticism,* and *Twentieth-Century Literary Criticism.*

Topic Index

CLC Cumulative Nationality Index

Nationality Index

CLC-130 Title Index

Title Index

ISBN 0-7876-3205-8